# KOHN ON MUSIC LICENSING

## THIRD EDITION

**AL KOHN**

**BOB KOHN**

*First Published as*
**The Art of Music Licensing**

**ASPEN LAW & BUSINESS**
A Division of Aspen Publishers, Inc.
New York    Gaithersburg

This publication is designed to provide accurate and authoritative information in regard to the subject matter covered. It is sold with the understanding that the publisher is not engaged in rendering legal, accounting, or other professional services. If legal advice or other expert assistance is required, the services of a competent professional person should be sought.

—From a *Declaration of Principles* jointly adopted by a Committee of the American Bar Association and a Committee of Publishers and Associations

Printed in the United States of America

*Library of Congress Cataloging-in-Publication Data*

Kohn, Al.
Kohn on music licensing / Al Kohn, Bob Kohn.—3rd ed.
p. cm.
ISBN 0-7355-1447-X (hardcover)
1. Copyright—Music—United States. 2. Copyright licenses—United States. I. Kohn, Bob. II. Title.
KF3035.K64 2000
346.7304'82—dc21
00-048510

# About Aspen Law & Business

Aspen Law & Business is a leading publisher of authoritative treatises, practice manuals, services, and journals for attorneys, corporate and bank directors, accountants, auditors, environmental compliance professionals, financial and tax advisors, and other business professionals. Our mission is to provide practical solution-based how-to information keyed to the latest original pronouncements, as well as the latest legislative, judicial, and regulatory developments.

We offer publications in the areas of accounting and auditing; antitrust; banking and finance; bankruptcy; business and commercial law; construction law; corporate law; criminal law; environmental compliance; government and administrative law; health law; insurance law; intellectual property; international law; legal practice and litigation; matrimonial and family law; pensions, benefits, and labor; real estate law; securities; and taxation.

Other Aspen Law & Business products treating intellectual property and communications law issues include:

**Drafting License Agreements**
**Epstein on Intellectual Property**
**Scott on Multimedia Law**
**Scott on Computer Law**
**Perle and Williams on Publishing Law**
**Libel & Privacy**
**The Computer Lawyer**
**The Journal of Proprietary Rights**

**ASPEN LAW & BUSINESS**
**A Division of Aspen Publishers, Inc.**
**A Wolters Kluwer Company**
*www.aspenpublishers.com*

## SUBSCRIPTION NOTICE

This Aspen Law & Business product is updated on a periodic basis with supplements to reflect important changes in the subject matter. If you purchased this product directly from Aspen Law & Business, we have already recorded your subscription for the update service.

If, however, you purchased this product from a bookstore and wish to receive future updates and revised or related volumes billed separately with a 30-day examination review, please contact our Customer Service Department at 1-800-901-9074 or send your name, company name (if applicable), address, and the title of the product to:

**Aspen Law & Business**
**A Division of Aspen Publishers, Inc.**
**7201 McKinney Circle**
**Frederick, MD 21704**

What neat repast shall feast us, light and choice,
Of Attic taste, with wine, whence we may rise
To hear the lute well touched, or artful voice
Warble immortal notes and Tuscan air?
He who of those delights can judge, and spare
To interpose them oft, is not unwise.

*—from a sonnet by John Milton (1608-1674)*

*To Edna*

# FOREWORD

Like a father talking to his son or daughter, in telling of *The Art of Music Licensing*, Al unfolds an encyclopedia of experience and information, gently and gracefully sharing the wisdom and joy of an art and expertise of which, with all humility, he reveals himself to be a master.

The fascination, affection, and almost reverential respect that Al holds for the songwriters and artists that he represents is an essential guidepost for the reader. I would venture to say that Al's whole being, as it permeates *The Art of Music Licensing*, is as much a model and resource as the technical information and good advice that he shares. Like Al, there is a gentleness to the word of caution about pitfalls and shortsightedness, and because it is Al who advises, there is the implicit instruction that the pursuit of success in the practice of licensing need never be a cutthroat game.

To Al, successful negotiation and guidance of licensing comes from an understanding and respect for the real value of the creative work, the diligent study of the extremely complex issues, precedents and processes surrounding the field of licensing, and a sympathetic view of some of the fears and confusions of those who want to do the best for their clients work (but are unsure as to how to proceed in the volatile and ever changing world of technology and labyrinthine law); but above all, one gets the message, imbedded in each sentence of the book, that fairness and understanding of both sides of the issues is the only road to ultimate success in the practice of the art of music licensing.

Al has spent a lifetime living his art, and what he shares in this prodigious work is much more than an encyclopedic textbook. Because Al has lived the golden ages of music, has been part of its creation and has represented the titans of music history, he is able to reveal, through loving anecdotes that illustrate the themes and premises of business practice, the real fun and energy, the behind-the-scenes personality, and understandable artistic compulsivity that is the world of music we inherit.

Al, as much as he is a teacher, is a bard weaving the history of the music business into a work that might well become a model for future attempts to communicate such complexity of information of any field or art form.

This book is a remarkable gift. It's much more than facts and figures. It's even much more than sound advice and a lifetime of wisdom.

It's Al, whom we all admire and love and who has managed, with the extraordinary partnership of a loving and gifted son, to help us remember who we are and might be, as we try to meet the challenges, and share the rewards and joys, of the music business.

Peter Yarrow
September 1992

Peter Yarrow is a member of Peter, Paul & Mary and has been represented through Warner Bros. Publishing by Al Kohn for over 30 years as the writer and co-writer of such songs as *Puff The Magic Dragon*, *Weave Me The Sunshine*, *Light One Candle*, *Torn Between Two Lovers*, and *Day Is Done*.

# ABOUT THE AUTHORS

## Al Kohn

Al Kohn, a 50-year veteran of the music industry, was Vice President, Licensing for Warner/Chappell Music, Inc., when he retired in 1993. Prior to his 23-year association with Warner Bros., he served for over 11 years as the U.S. representative for the London-based Francis, Day & Hunter music publishing organization, developing acquisition patterns that moved them into the global pop music market.

Prior to that, Al was a member of the creative team at Hummert Radio Features and was the key arranger for some of the syndicate's major network radio programs including *Waltz Time* and *Manhattan Merry-Go-Round*. During World War II, Irving Berlin tapped Al to orchestrate his all-soldier show, *This Is the Army*.

He also served as an arranger for orchestras, including those of Paul Whiteman, Abe Lyman, Ted Dale, Orrin Tucker and others, and arranged nightclub revues at Lou Walter's Latin Quarter, Billy Rose's Diamond Horseshoe, and the Steel Pier Music Hall. Later, he served as a television arranger for the Milton Berle, Katherine Murray, George Jessel, Martha Raye, and Jane Pickens shows. He also arranged or conducted for Bob Hope, Billy Rose, Jerry Vale, and many others.

Al lives in Tarzana, California and serves as a consultant and expert witness in copyright and music publishing matters.

## Bob Kohn

Bob Kohn is an attorney and seasoned executive with experience in both the entertainment and high-tech industries. He was founder of EMusic.com, Inc., the pioneering music download subscription service, where he served as Chairman until the company was sold to Vivendi/Universal in June 2001. He is currently Chairman & CEO of Laugh.com, the world's leading comedy record company, which he founded with comedian George Carlin, as well as legendary comedians Milton Berle, Shelley Berman, Red Buttons, Norm Crosby, Bill Dana, Phyllis Diller, Rich Little, Gary Owens, Jonathan Winters, and others. He also currently serves as Vice Chairman of the Board of Borland Software Corporation (NASDAQ: BORL), one of the world's largest developers and marketers of computer software.

He was previously Vice President, Business Development of Pretty Good Privacy, Inc., a leading developer and marketer of encryption software, and Senior Vice President, Corporate Affairs, Secretary, and General Counsel of Borland International, Inc. Bob also served as Associate General Counsel for Candle Corporation, a developer of software for IBM mainframe computers, and Corporate Counsel for Ashton-Tate, a microcomputer software company.

Prior to Ashton-Tate, he was an associate attorney at the law offices of Milton A. "Mickey" Rudin in Beverly Hills, California, an entertainment law firm whose clients included Frank Sinatra, Liza Minnelli, Cher, and Warner Bros. Music. He also worked as Associate Editor of the *Entertainment Law Reporter*, for which he continues to serve as a member of the Advisory Board. He is currently Adjunct Professor of Law at Monterey College of Law, Monterey, California.

In 1994, Bob won the prize offered by the Encyclopaedia Britannica for the best solution to a philosophical problem posed by the editors, and his winning essay, *Mind and Brain: The Genius of Fortune*, was published in the 1994 edition of the Britannica's *The Great Ideas Today*.

Bob became a member of the California Bar in 1981 after graduating from Loyola Law School, Los Angeles. He lives with his family in Pebble Beach, California.

# THE REASONS FOR THIS BOOK

One need go no further to seek the reasons for this book than to the many friends and colleagues of mine who have urged me over the years to memorialize my thoughts on its subject in writing. Since many of these same people are lawyers, I can only assume they are more interested in the expression of my practical experience as a licensor of music than my knowledge of the law.

It should be no surprise, therefore, that, though this book is thoroughly intertwined with, and dependent upon, the law of copyright, the primary emphasis of this book is not on the law, but on experience and practice. A book on copyright law would have been easier to write, because, in writing such a book, one can rely on the large body of statutes and legal decisions with which to adorn the pages. In the pages which follow, citations are given for few legal decisions. Presented, instead, is how music publishers and other copyright owners think or, more accurately, should think, in connection with licensing the music in their repertoire.

In contrast to the acquisition side of music publishing, which involves acquiring the publishing rights to new music and established songs, music licensing, the subject of this book, concerns the revenue side of the music publishing business — what you do after you own the song. Of course, what is revenue to the music copyright owner, is cost to the music user. Consequently, this book also addresses the other side of the coin — what you need to do if you want to use the song for commercial purposes.

Music licensing can thus be viewed from two perspectives: (1) the considerations used by music publishers and songwriters in earning a living from their music copyrights, and (2) the clearance of music rights by those who desire to use copyrighted music for commercial purposes.

Because my business career in the music industry has been spent largely in the employ of music publishers, this book will more naturally reflect the perspectives of the copyright owner and songwriter. Yet, my sympathy for those whose job it is to obtain music clearances has concretely found its way into this book. The reader should find no contradiction in the expression of a music publisher's sympathies for the task of rights clearance. If the music publisher is doing its job correctly, the licensing of music rights by those who desire to use music commercially should be a simple, straightforward, and often rewarding effort. The music publisher's reward for facilitating the licensing effort is better representation of the songwriters whose livelihood may often depend on proper representation.

The reader is forewarned that some controversy may attend some of the opinions expressed in this book. Some will resent being shown that their language is confused, inconsistent, and often used unwittingly against their own best interest. At first, I hesitated to speak frankly, but, with a lifetime in this business behind me, I feel I have earned a license to finally declare, *Anything Goes*. Though some will inevitably disagree with the positions taken in this book, it is hoped that they will be viewed, if nothing more, as a call for a common understanding of the terms upon which we do business.

There's no business like show business. That issue was well settled by Ethel Merman. Yet, as Irving Berlin might have agreed, there would be no show business without music. For this reason, I could not begin without first thanking the many songwriters on behalf of whom I've had the great pleasure of working with over the years as a publisher representative and as an arranger and producer of successful radio and television productions.

AL KOHN
October 1992

# ACKNOWLEDGMENTS
# TO THE THIRD EDITION

The only people we really have to thank in connection with the preparation of this Third Edition are the thousands of lawyers, law students, law librarians, music industry professionals, and others who so often have expressed their desire for us to continually rekindle the flame of this work with the fuel of new material. "The only end in writing," said Dr. Samuel Johnson, "is to enable the reader better to enjoy life, or better to endure it." We had this very sentiment in mind as we wrote much of the new material on the Internet, and we hope it will be of some guidance to those who find the current challenges faced by the music industry something both to enjoy and to endure.

Of course, Dr. Johnson was also known to have said, "Sir, no man but a blockhead ever wrote except for money," which reminds us that, without those who have faithfully purchased the prior editions, and continue to purchase our annual supplements, this new edition would not have been possible.

We must also gratefully acknowledge the assistance we have received over the years from our friends at Aspen Law & Business, particularly our editor Matt Gallaway, for his tireless efforts in keeping this book up to date, and to Rick Kravitz, for his tireless support of everyone involved in its publication.

Finally, we again thank the entire Kohn family, for, without their spending, this book would not have been necessary. Above all, we thank that special person to whom we have thrice lovingly dedicated this book.

AL KOHN
BOB KOHN
November 2001

# ACKNOWLEDGMENTS
# TO THE SECOND EDITION

W e have several people to thank for their assistance in the development of the new materials we prepared for this edition. We wish to especially express our gratitude to Don Biederman, Esq. and Gary Ford for their review of selected chapters added to this work and to Lionel S. Sobel, Esq. for permission to include his materials on live musical performances. We also wish to thank the following individuals who furnished some of the forms or other information furnished in the new materials: Vincent S. Castellucci, Don Biederman, Esq., Michael Sandoval, Ronald H. Gertz, Esq., Bennett M. Lincoff, Esq., Vic DeMona, Don Williams, and Roy Kohn.

We also gratefully acknowledge the assistance of Noah J. Gordon, Esq., our editor, and the dedication, encouragement and cooperation we have received from Aspen Publishers, especially Dan Mangan and Richard Kravitz. Special thanks again to Joan Kanady for her tireless assistance in optically scanning, typing and editing the forms and other information that went into this volume and printing and copying numerous drafts of the manuscript. We also thank Joanne Butler, Esq. for her legal research.

We again thank the entire Kohn family, including Ted and Joanne Kohn, and their children Beth and Todd, for their continuous encouragement and, most especially, Lori, Katie and Joey for their patience and unwavering love and support during this intensive effort. We also thank Matthew D. Kohn, Esq. for his insight and experience in representing contemporary artists and firms in the entertainment field, and we welcome his wife Sharon, and her family, to the Kohn family. Above all, we wish to acknowledge the encouragement, support, and wisdom of the person to whom this book we lovingly dedicate.

AL KOHN
BOB KOHN
November 1995

# ACKNOWLEDGMENTS
# TO THE FIRST EDITION

We have many people to thank for their assistance in the preparation of this work. We wish to especially express our gratitude to Prof. Lionel S. Sobel, Esq., Ronald H. Gertz, Esq., and Vincent S. Castellucci who made critical readings of parts of the work and provided very helpful suggestions for its improvement. We also wish to thank the following individuals who furnished some of the forms or other information included in this volume: M. William Krasilovsky, Esq., Bernard Korman, Esq., Gary Ford, Marvin L. Berenson, Esq., Ira B. Selsky, Esq., Martin Cohen, Esq., Don Biederman, Esq., Naomi Saltzman, Sid Luft, and Roy Kohn. We give special acknowledgment to Matthew D. Kohn, Esq. for his insight and experience in representing contemporary artists and firms in the entertainment field.

Our sincerest thanks and gratitude are due to those who have contributed to the cumulative experiences that have found their way into this book, including Abe Lyman, Ben Yost, Irving Caesar, Patty Andrews, Wally Weschler, Danny Gould, Arthur Hamilton, John Clark, Esq., Edward Slattery, Mrs. Frank Hummert, David Day, Bernard Sorkin, Esq., Louise Dembeck, Esq., Milton A. Rudin, Esq., Ed Perlstein, Esq., Walter Evans, Ed Silvers, Mel Blye, James Cornelius, Chuck Kaye, Les Bider, Jay Morgenstern, Michael Sandoval, Joe Guardino, and Max Berkovitz. It is painful for us to think that while we were carrying on this work, several of those to whom it would have been most interesting have passed away. We therefore wish to add to our acknowledgement the friendship and encouragement of the late Ira Gershwin, Leonore Gershwin, Harry Warren, Jerry Livingston, Herb Magidson, Milton Ager, Ben Oakland, Sammy Fain, and Howard and Lucinda Dietz.

We thank Philippe Kahn, Chairman and Chief Executive Officer of Borland International, Inc. for having the foresight to provide the company's long-term employees with the sabbatical time required to complete works such as this. We also thank Spencer Leyton, John

Hensen, Linda Wallraff, John Smart, Allen Dixon, and other members of the the law and corporate affairs department of Borland International, and its outside counsel Peter Astiz, Esq., Gary Reback, Esq., Martin Greenstein, Esq., Steven Brower, Esq., Stan Sokoloff, Esq., Peter Gelhaar, Esq., Allen Grogan, Esq., and Samuel Farb, Esq., without whom there would have been no opportunity to take advantage of that sabbatical time. Special thanks to Joan Kanady for her tireless assistance in optically scanning, typing and editing the forms that went into this volume and printing and copying numerous drafts of the manuscript. We also gratefully acknowledge the assistance of Noah J. Gordon, Esq., our editor, and the creative staff at Prentice Hall Law and Business, and Lisa Nielsen of Borland International for a beautiful jacket design.

We also must thank the entire Kohn family, including Ted and Joanne Kohn, and their children Beth and Todd, for their continuous encouragement and, most especially, Lori, Katie and Joey for their patience and unwavering love and support during this prolonged endeavor. Above all, we wish to acknowledge the encouragement, support, and wisdom of the person to whom this book we lovingly dedicate.

Now, let's get on with the show. . . .

AL KOHN
BOB KOHN
October 1992

# Summary of Contents

# TABLE OF CONTENTS

## CHAPTER 2
### THE ART OF MUSIC PUBLISHING

#### SUMMARY

## CHAPTER 5
### INTERNATIONAL SUBPUBLISHING

### SUMMARY

## CHAPTER 6
## THE SPLIT COPYRIGHT SYNDROME

### SUMMARY

## CHAPTER 7
## THE LANGUAGE OF MUSIC LICENSING

### SUMMARY

CHAPTER 8
FORMALITIES OF MUSIC LICENSING

SUMMARY

CHAPTER 9

DURATION OF COPYRIGHT, ASSIGNMENTS
OF COPYRIGHT, AND LICENSES

SUMMARY

## CHAPTER 10
### BASIC CONSIDERATIONS IN
### MUSIC LICENSING

#### SUMMARY

## CHAPTER 11
## PRINT LICENSES

### SUMMARY

## CHAPTER 12
## MECHANICAL LICENSES

### SUMMARY

CHAPTER 13
ELECTRICAL TRANSCRIPTION LICENSES

SUMMARY

CHAPTER 14
SYNCHRONIZATION LICENSES

SUMMARY

**CHAPTER 15**
**VIDEOGRAM LICENSES**

**SUMMARY**

CHAPTER 16
OLD LICENSES, NEW USES

SUMMARY

CHAPTER 17
PERFORMANCE LICENSES

SUMMARY

## CHAPTER 18
## THE GRAND RIGHTS CONTROVERSY

### SUMMARY

**CHAPTER 19**
**THEME PARKS AND ATTRACTIONS**

**SUMMARY**

**CHAPTER 20**
**TELEVISION, RADIO, AND PRINT ADVERTISING**

**SUMMARY**

**CHAPTER 21**

**LICENSES FOR MUSIC BOXES AND
CONSUMER MUSICAL PRODUCTS**

**SUMMARY**

CHAPTER 22
LICENSES FOR COMPUTER SOFTWARE,
MULTIMEDIA, AND NEW MEDIA
PRODUCTS

SUMMARY

**CHAPTER 23**

**LICENSING MUSICAL WORKS AND SOUND RECORDINGS
ON THE INTERNET**

**SUMMARY**

CHAPTER 24
THE DIGITAL SAMPLING CONTROVERSY

SUMMARY

**CHAPTER 25**
**THE FAIR USE CONTROVERSY**

**SUMMARY**

## CHAPTER 26
### LIVE MUSICAL PERFORMANCES

#### SUMMARY

## CHAPTER 27
### TYPICAL LICENSE FEES

#### SUMMARY

# THE ART OF MUSIC LICENSING

## SUMMARY

### I. THE ART OF GRANTING LICENSES

A. Share in the Economic Success of the Work in Which the Music Is Going to Be Used

B. Maximize the Long-Term Value of the Work

C. Maintain an Active Relationship Between the Song and the Listening Public

### II. THE ART OF CLEARING LICENSES

A. Understanding the Nature of Rights Involved

B. Know What Music You Wish to License

C. Develop a Licensing Strategy

    1. Approaching the Simple Project

        a. Find Out Who Owns the Song

        b. Getting Help from the Harry Fox Agency, ASCAP, BMI, the Copyright Office, or Professional Search Agencies

        c. A Last Resort

        d. Contacting the Music Publisher

    2. Approaching the Complex Project

        a. Popular Music-Driven Motion Picture Soundtracks, New Media Works

        b. Music Clearing Houses and Other Professional Assistance

        c. Finding the Recording or Orchestration

    3. Maybe You Just Need a Needledrop

    4. Maybe You Don't Need a License

        a. Using Music in the Public Domain

        b. Originating Your Own Music

        c. Purchasing All Rights in the Work You Desire to Use

        d. Making a Fair Use of Another's Copyrighted Work

# THE ART OF MUSIC LICENSING

This book on music licensing is really about two distinct, yet related, arts: (1) the art of *granting* licenses for the purpose of earning a living from one's music copyrights, and (2) the art of obtaining licenses, or *clearing* permission, to commercially use music owned by another.

The ancient Greeks used the term "art" to refer to the technique, skill, or know-how for making things, such as a chair, a statue, or a house. They also recognized that art refers to the accomplishment of anything that requires human skill or know-how to render well, such as the art of cultivating crops, the art of making wine, and the art of singing a song.

We are living in a world today in which an increasing number of things which individuals desire to consume are not really *things* at all, in a material sense. In the pursuit of the good life, people are desiring the *intangible* — that which they cannot touch, but can feel or experience in an intellectual or emotional sense, such as reading a good story, identifying with a virtuous character, listening to good music, and receiving information (and, with the last-mentioned, one would hope, gaining some knowledge, understanding, and, ultimately, some wisdom).

What we are grappling with in this book may best be illustrated by a gag Victor Borge had used to tease his audience. The comedian asks, "Would you like a bit of music now?" Upon hearing the audience applauding their assent, he reaches into his piano bench, grabs a handful of sheet music, and passes it out. The joke invariably earns a good laugh. The point is that if the music the audience came to enjoy were really those bits of paper, few would have laughed. Clearly, what we are talking about is that which the audience has come to *hear* — something diffuse, something intangible.

The practice of an art is particularly complex when the product of the activity is diffuse or intangible. This is because the building blocks used to create intangible goods, such as a play or a movie, comprise a vast variety of other intangibles that are easily transportable and combinable. For example, consider a video clip and the intangible nature of the intellectual property of which it can be composed: a few bars of a melody, a few seconds of a sound recording, a short clip from a movie or a television program, a few steps from a choreographed dance routine or ballet, the plot of a novel or short story, the virtue or vice of a lead character, a biographical sketch, a scene from an opera, an animated character, a line of poetry, a still photograph, the cadence of a well-known distinctive voice, the likeness of a rock star. One simple work of art may comprise one or all of these intangible ingredients in some form or to some degree.

The complexity of the law governing transactions in intangible works of authorship seems to have inherited the complexity involved in creating these works, and the complexity of the questions concerning their ownership, transfer, use, and distribution are compounded by the fact that any one intangible work may be comprised of a multitude of other works. This makes the distillation, disposition, and exploitation of the ownership rights in intangible products an extremely complex activity. Fortunately, the skill or art of performing this activity may be acquired with cooperative effort and some practical experience.

When an art is performed well, it is the result of something the ancient Greeks called *arete*, which translated into English means having a quality that is something between *virtuous* and *excellent*. To have virtue or excellence in performing an art is to have practical wisdom about the art. The goal of this book, in these noblest of terms, is to impart to the reader some practical wisdom about granting licenses and obtaining clearances for the use of music. We hope this book, together with some practical experience of your own, will help you acquire the art of music licensing.

## I. THE ART OF GRANTING LICENSES

Music has been defined as the art of organizing sounds and silences into meaningful patterns. Music publishing can be similarly defined: the art of organizing sounds and silences into meaningful revenue. Certainly, the goal of the music copyright owner is to maximize the revenues generated by the musical composition. Maximizing revenue, however, involves more than merely how much money you can negotiate in exchange for granting licenses. It involves appraising the value of the song and recognizing that a variety of subtle factors dynamically affect the value of the song over time, including the types of uses, the number of uses, and the scope of uses that you permit over time. Maximizing revenue generated by a musical composition depends more on how you approach the exploitation of your music in the long run than how much money you demand in exchange for each license in the short run.

*Arete* in granting licenses to use music, accordingly, is achieved by putting the *long term* interests of the song and the songwriter first. Recognizing that maximizing a song's revenue is a dynamic process — with the earnings potential of the music changing depending upon licensing decisions made over a period of time — is the first step in acquiring excellence in music licensing. With that in mind, we suggest that anyone who is responsible for maximizing the revenues of a song or a song catalog acquire the following three key habits:

A. Share in the economic success of the work in which the music is going to be used;

B. Maximize the long-term value of the work and avoid short-sightedness; and,

C. Maintain an active relationship between the song and the listening public.

We will explore each of these in turn.

## A. Share in the Economic Success of the Work in Which the Music Is Going to Be Used

The compensation one can collect in exchange for granting permission to use copyrighted music in another's work can be structured in a variety of ways. For example, one can receive a one-time flat fee (e.g., $1000 payable upon signing the license) for perpetual use, a flat fee for a limited period of use (e.g., $100 for a 3 year license), or a flat fee for a limited period of use with options to renew the term of use (e.g., $100 for a 3 year license and options to renew for additional one year periods at a rate of $100 per year). However, flat fee arrangements, even if payable over a period of time, do not take into consideration the economic success of the work in which the music is used. Under a flat fee arrangement, whether a record album in which the music is used sells 100 copies or 1 million copies, the fee for the use of the music is the same.

Music copyright owners prefer to share the risk of success or failure of works that embody their music in exchange for receiving the potential rewards of having their music associated with *hit* records, motion pictures and other works. Producers and other users of music will assert that music copyright owners do not deserve to participate in the success of the user's work, because the copyright owner does not bear any of the financial risks associated with the production of the work. In other words, how can the music licensor fail? What does he have at risk that justifies the reward from the success of the work he seeks?

Music copyright owners respond that the producers are undervaluing the importance of their music to the producer's work. For example, a major motion picture may cost $20 million to make and perhaps an equal amount to market. Music is often an extremely important element in these movies, yet the music owners only receive a few thousand dollars at most for the use of the music. An artist performing a song in the movie might command a fee of $1 million for his work in the picture, but only a tiny fraction of that amount is paid to the songwriter who wrote the very song the artist may be performing in the film. From the music copyright owner's perspective, he is taking a risk by accepting a low fee up front in the hope that he can make up for the value the music is adding to the film by sharing in additional revenues from television performances and videocassette sales should the motion picture become successful. Music copyright owners can also point to the profit participation percentages paid to actors, writers, and directors, who are taking no more "risk" in making their contributions than the music copyright owners.

Whatever its justification, this sharing in the economic success (and failure) of works is important and is accomplished by structuring the compensation payable for music licenses in the form of a *royalty*.

Royalties are generally calculated on the basis of the number of copies of the work distributed or the revenues received from the sale or performance of the work. For example, one can receive a royalty of 5 cents for each copy of the work distributed or a royalty of 5% of the net revenues derived from the sale or licensing of the work.

Few music licenses do not provide some form of royalty or other compensation based on the economic success of the work in which the music is included. Where the license does not explicitly provide for royalty payments, some other mechanism usually exists that implicitly provides the music copyright owner with the upside earnings potential that a successful work may provide.

For example, when music licensed for use in a television program is broadcast on television, the music copyright owner will receive payments derived from the collection of performance royalties from the television stations that broadcast the program, through separate fees charged to the stations. The mechanisms involved in the collection of performance royalties are explained in some detail in Chapter 17, on *Performance Licenses.* Suffice it to say here, that the license granted to the producer of the television program to include the music in the program is, as a matter of practice, granted in exchange for a flat fee. However, the music copyright owner knows that his share in the economic success of the television program is assured from the separate license fees charged for the performance of the television program in which his music is included. If the television program becomes popular and enjoys years of broadcast in syndication, the music copyright owner will similarly enjoy continuing performance royalty credit as long as the television program remains on the air in reruns and exploitation in other markets.

For this reason, music copyright owners should not lose sight of the performance royalty earnings when considering what license fee to charge for the initial inclusion of the song in works such as television programs. If, for example, a television producer is only willing to pay a certain flat fee for permission to use your song and you insist on a fee that is double what the producer is willing to pay, the producer will often find and use a substitute for your song. Ironically, more often than not, the performance royalties earned from the broadcast of the television program would have more than compensated for the difference between the flat fee you were quoting and the fee last offered by the producer. If the television program becomes a hit and enjoys lengthy rerun exhibitions, the music copyright owner will have lost substantial performance revenues. The potential upside from having the song associated with a hit program is substantial, while the downside for accepting a lower up front fee is slight.

Of course, where there is no potential for receiving performance royalties, the music copyright owner should find alternative means of sharing in the economic success in the work. This, for example, is the case with respect to the sale of videocassettes containing copyrighted music; the types of royalty structures used in licenses for videocassette use is discussed at length in Chapter 15.

## B. Maximize the Long-Term Value of the Work

We have just seen in the preceding section an example of the folly of placing too much emphasis on the short term in negotiating the compensation of a license fee. In failing to resolve the difference between what the music copyright owner is willing to accept and what the music user is willing to pay in exchange for a license, the music copyright owner often overlooks the additional flow of revenue that could be earned from performance royalties.

The causes of such shortsightedness can be generally identified. It is difficult or perhaps impossible to measure the marginal performance royalties earned in connection with any one license, because performance rights societies do not calculate performance royalties on the basis of every single performance. Further, the increase in performance royalties occurs over time, and usually not in the same quarter in which the license was granted. Thus, it is usually difficult to tie the issuance of one specific license to a specific dollar increase in performance royalties.

Sometimes the shortsightedness is due to inexperience or misunderstanding of the dynamics of music publishing revenues. A songwriter or small music publisher might be represented by a personal manager or attorney who, because he or she may only physically see the checks for the flat fee licenses he negotiates and not the performance royalty statements, only appreciates the short term maximization of the size of these flat fee payments. Such representatives often fail to appreciate the dynamic effect that entering into licenses have on performance royalties. In other cases, representatives get mired in the details of the specific language of the license, agonizing over, for example, the inadequacies of a "warranties and representation" clause, losing sight of what's really important to the publishing company or songwriter he or she is representing.

Whatever the reason for this short-term thinking, though the marginal performance royalties earned in connection with any one license may not be measurable, they are real and this additional revenue from the collection of performance royalties is a tangible benefit not to be ignored while negotiating many flat fee licenses. More subtle benefits, such as those discussed in the section that immediately follows, should also encourage the copyright owner to come to resolution on negotiating license fees, even if it means taking less than the going rate on some up front fees.

## C. Maintain an Active Relationship Between the Song and the Listening Public

As we have pointed out, maximizing a song's revenue is a dynamic process: the earnings potential of the music changes depending upon licensing decisions made over a period of time. One of the most important, but often ignored, factors that affects the value of the song over the life of the copyright is the *quantity* of licenses issued and the number of uses made of the song. The more often a song is used in other works, the greater the value of the copyright.

The essence of what you are doing when you license the use of the song is helping to maintain the relationship between the song and the listening public. Entering into licenses provides the song with a means of continual exposure to the listening public, including those who select music for use in television programs, motion pictures, commercial advertising and other works that offer alternative licensing revenues. By encouraging use, you therefore increase the likelihood that future requests for licenses of the song will continue. The listening public is surprisingly fickle and will easily forget a tune. You should never let a song fall into a state of such disuse that no one will remember it. Accordingly, the first principal of *arete* in granting music licenses is this: *Encourage as much activity in the song as possible.*

For this reason, a music copyright owner should not allow short term thinking, fear, or uncertainty to creep into the negotiating of fees and get in the way of concluding a license. A music copyright owner should not be afraid to make a decision. Life is decision making, and if you remember that the goal is to encourage as much use of the song as possible, you will inevitably make decisions that are in the long term interest of the song and its songwriter, and *arete* in granting licenses will be achieved.

## II. THE ART OF CLEARING LICENSES

The counterpart to the art of granting licenses is the art of obtaining permission, or "clearing the rights," to commercially use music owned by another. *Arete* in obtaining clearance, or permission, to use music may best be achieved by establishing a good relationship with the music copyright owners from whom you seek to obtain permission. We suggest that the best way to accomplish that is to acquire the following habits:

A.  Understand the rights involved;

B.  Know what music you wish to license;

C.  Develop a licensing strategy;

D.  Understand the needs and fears of the copyright owner;

E.  Devote some time and effort to educate the copyright owner about your intended use of the music; and,

F.  Allow enough time to complete the process.

We will explore each of these in turn.

## A.  Understanding the Nature of Rights Involved

The importance of understanding the rights involved is best illustrated by a common mistake made by many who are new to the music clearance process: thinking first of a popular recording of the desired song, a person seeking to clear a license to use the recording might overlook the fact that getting permission to do so involves not one, but two copyrights: (1) the copyright in the sound recording and (2) the copyright in the underlying song. While you may properly obtain permission to use the recording, clearance to use the underlying song is sometimes entirely overlooked. (Just as often, persons obtaining clearance to use the music will overlook the need to clear permission to use the recording.)

The copyright in a sound recording is completely separate from the copyright in the underlying song featured in the sound recording. For example, there exists a valid copyright in the song *I've Got You Under My Skin* by Cole Porter and the copyright is owned by Warner/Chappell Music, Inc., a music publishing company. At the same time, several records of *I've Got You Under My Skin* have been recorded by numerous recording artists over the years. A completely separate copyright exists for each particular recording — the sequence of sounds that make up the performance of the song by a singer and orchestra. These recordings are owned by the respective record companies that commissioned their creation. For example, Frank Sinatra's recording of *I've Got You Under My Skin*, arranged by Nelson Riddle, is owned by Reprise Records.

Thus, if you wished to obtain permission to use Sinatra's recording of *I've Got You Under My Skin*, you would require the permission of Reprise to use the recording *and* the permission of Warner/Chappell to use the underlying song. You could not use the recording without permission from both companies.

Most record companies have special divisions, often called *special products* departments, dedicated to granting licenses to use sound recordings in their catalog. Licenses for the use of such recordings are sometimes effected by what is called a *master use license,* derived from the term record "master" — a final, mixed recording used in the manufacture of other copies, such as albums, cassette tapes, or compact discs. If you have trouble obtaining approval to use a particular artist's recording of the song, the record company, or other record companies, may have substitute recordings that may meet your needs. You can, of course, always create your own original recording, in which event permission from a record company would not be necessary — the only permission required would be that sought from the copyright owner of the underlying song.

If all you want to do is make and distribute compact discs of a single audio-only recording of a song, the rights that you need to understand are relatively straightforward. The same is true if all you intend to do is quote a song lyric in a book or use a song in a television commercial. In each case, you are dealing with one copyright — the copyright in the song you are seeking permission to use.

Imagine, however, that you wanted to use a short clip from a particular dance scene in the motion picture, *West Side Story*. Not only would you require a license from the studio who owned the film, you would require a license from the record company who owned the soundtrack recording, a license from the music publisher of the song performed in the scene, a license from the authors who owned the "grand rights" to the Broadway play of the same name. You may also require permission from the representatives of Jerome Robbins, who reserved by his contract with the producers of the movie the right to approve uses of the film's choreography that were not performed in conjunction with the exhibition of the entire motion picture.

Of course, not all clearances will be so complicated. However, it is good practice to first carefully analyze the work you wish to license and break it down into its component parts. In complex works — i.e., works that contain multiple copyrights and other rights — the break down may result in one or more of the following separate rights: a copyright in the underlying song, a copyright in the recording of the song, a copyright in the video aspects of the work (motion picture, television program, etc.), a copyright in any choreography appearing in the work, a copyright in a literary work (where the work is based upon a novel, non-fiction book, newspaper article, biography, autobiography, etc.), a copyright in a theatrical production (such as a musical play, opera, or ballet), a copyright in an animated character, a copyright in a still photograph appearing in the work, a copyright of a translation or arrangement of a work in the public domain, the right of privacy (i.e., the right one has "to be left alone") of one or more individuals, or the right of publicity (i.e., the right an individual has to exclude others from using his or her name, voice, photograph, and likeness) of one or more individuals.

The above list is not exhaustive, and this book does not cover all of the potential rights that must be cleared in connection with the variety of potential uses. It is hoped, however, that the balance of this book will give you a better understanding of each of the music-related rights underlying many of the uses likely to be made of musical compositions, as well as some of the general principles of licensing that may be useful in clearing permission to use some of these other kinds of works.

## B.  Know What Music You Wish to License

Before approaching a music publisher, it would be helpful if you knew the name of the song for which you are seeking a license. Humming a few bars over the phone might not be adequate or helpful, especially in recent years, as many popular tunes, such as heavy metal and rap songs, are not particularly recognizable when you hum them. Even old standards, many of which have melodies that are quite hummable, might not be recognized by younger staff members of major music publishers who were raised exclusively on popular music of the past ten to twenty years.

It might help to know a few important lines of lyrics, particularly with very old tunes, such as those published by Robbins Music Corp. early in this century. To the great consternation of many a lyrical artist, Jack Robbins insisted that the title of virtually all songs published by his company comprise the first few words of the lyrics. Examples include, *I'm in the Mood for Love*, *Blue Moon*, *Don't Blame Me*, *Sweet and Lovely*, and *You'll Never Know*. As opprobrious as the practice might seem to many songwriters, Jack Robbins knew his business and his idea is one which should be seriously considered today. Many contemporary songwriters attach bizarre titles to their songs which often have no resemblance to any of the lyrics contained in the song. Where the song's title is not readily apparent from reading the lyrics, the clearance of a license for the use of the song can become very difficult. Accordingly, the use of such titles may adversely impact a songwriter's earnings.

If the music was originally featured in a well known motion picture, then knowing the name of the film might help. For example, if you asked for the music in the movie starring Humphrey Bogart, *Casablanca*, or the Woody Allen film, *Play it Again, Sam*, the publisher is likely to know that you are referring to the song, *As Time Goes By*. You might ask for the love theme from the movie, *Superman*, without knowing the title, *Can You Read My Mind*.

If you don't know the name of the song, but somehow know the name of the songwriter, the publisher may be able to look up the name of the song in a biographical index.

If you have heard a recording of the song, and you can locate a copy of an LP or CD album containing the recording, you should have no trouble determining the name of the song, as it should be written on the album cover or in the CD booklet.

If you don't even have a particular song in mind, but are looking for music from a particular era, major publishing firms that have vast music catalogs should be of service in helping you identify songs that meet your requirements. For example, if you were looking for music that was popular during the 1920's, a publisher might recommend, *Baby Face*, *Ain't She Sweet*, and *Ain't We Got Fun.*

Note, however, that many of today's publishing firms are staffed by younger people who are not familiar with many of the older popular tunes. To address this problem, several years ago I helped compile a list of standard songs controlled by Warner Bros. Music, arranged in categories, such as 1920's music, 1930's music, 1940's music, western music, popular music, etc.[1] Warner/Chappell, for example, has prepared a compact disk containing hundreds of short recordings of many of the songs they have available for license.

The bottom line, however, is that unless you know the name of a specific song you are interested in, you might run into some serious problems finding what you are looking for.

## C.  Develop a Licensing Strategy

Before making your first phone call, develop a licensing strategy. The basic decision to make at this point is whether you *do it yourself* or whether you *hire a specialist.* The answer will often depend on the complexity of the project involved. Thus, you should, at the outset, get a feel for the complexity of the project.

Music clearance projects can be categorized into the simple and the complex. A simple project would be, for example, obtaining clearance to use one or two songs in a traditional kind of work, such as a novel, record album, or motion picture. A complex project would be obtaining clearance to use many songs for use in a traditional work or in a new form of media, such as a multimedia optical disk program. The approach you might use in obtaining music licenses for a simple project is likely to be significantly different from that of a complex project.

---

[1] Throughout this book, references to "I" means co-author, Al Kohn, unless otherwise indicated.

Whether a clearance project is simple or complex will often be a factor of the kind of music you require. If you can get by with what is commonly called, *canned music*, your licensing strategy can be greatly simplified. In some cases, you may find that you don't require a license at all, as when the song you want to use is in the *public domain* or your use of the song is a *fair use* under the copyright law. But, even in these instances, some licensing strategy is still required, as determining whether a song is public domain or whether your use would be considered a fair use, may require the assistance of an attorney.

## 1.  Approaching the Simple Project

You can probably clear licenses for simple projects yourself. If you know you are facing a complex project, or if, after a few attempts, your simple project turns out to be more complex than you originally anticipated, consider hiring a specialist.

### a.  Find Out Who Owns the Song

If you know the name of the song, or you managed to discover it without too much trouble, the next thing you need to know is who controls the rights to the song. In other words, with whom do you need to deal to obtain a license? This is not as easy a question to answer as you might expect. If you already know the answer, you are way ahead of the game. If you don't, you may be in for a rude awakening.

Even if you have a copy of another work in which the music originally appeared, such as a record album or a videocassette of a motion picture, it is not likely that it will contain any useful information about where to find the person who controls the rights to the music. This is because credit in these works is rarely given to the music publishers or even to the songwriters on record albums, motion pictures, and television programs. Few recording artists follow the fine tradition of performers like Frank Sinatra. Mr. Sinatra not only endeavors to give credit to songwriters but to the arrangers of the particular orchestrations he uses on records and in public performances.

I often receive calls directly from film companies, television producers, advertising agencies and others who seek permission to use a particular song. When I'm forced to regretfully inform the caller that the song is not among those in the catalog I represent, I am usually asked the next logical question: "Who *does* own the rights?" Quite often, I happen to be familiar with the song in question and would know off the top of my head the name of the music publisher who controlled the rights. Sad to say, the days of music publishers who have staffs familiar with the songs in their catalogs is nearing an end. Yet, even if licensing staffs were to become familiar with the songs contained in the major catalogs, it is becoming more difficult for any-one to know who owns or controls what song, as publishing interests of an increasing number of songs are being retained by songwriters and an increasing number of songs are becoming the subject of *split copyrights*, a problem discussed at length in Chapter 6.

### b.  Getting Help from the Harry Fox Agency, ASCAP, BMI, the Copyright Office, or Professional Search Agencies

*Harry Fox.* One of the best places to begin your search for a license is the Harry Fox Agency in New York City.[2] The Harry Fox Agency represents over 27,000 music publishers, or over 60% of all music publishers in the United States. The Harry Fox Agency is best known for its service of issuing licenses for the use of copyrighted music in commercial records, tapes, and CDs, but the Agency also issues licenses for the use of music in audiovisual works, such as motion pictures and television programs, and in other works, such as computer chips, MIDI, karaoke, and multi-media programs. Before issuing a license, however, the Agency will require certain basic in-formation about the music you wish to use, including the title and the names of the writers of the composition, and the name of the pub-lisher(s), if known.

To assist potential licensees in assembling this information, the Agency offers the "Song Information Request" system, or SIR-Net, an online service making the Agency's song information database ac-cessible via personal computer and phone line. The Agency plans to upgrade the service to allow online transmission of license requests,

---

[2] Harry Fox Agency, Inc. 711 Third Avenue, New York, New York 10017. Phone: 212-370-5330, Fax 212-953-2384, *www.nmpa.org*.

which will eventually allow the Agency to fully automate the issuance of requested licenses. Access to SIR-Net requires permission from the Harry Fox Agency. Before contacting the Harry Fox Agency, you might try their affiliated web site, *www.songfile.com*, which contains a database of over 2,000,000 songs. The Agency also offers POLI-PLUS, an online service which allows its music publisher members to access the Agency's information database. This service will soon be updated to permit publishers to provide electronically to the Agency any authorizations necessary for the Agency to issue licenses on behalf of the publishers. Additional information about the services of the Harry Fox Agency is set forth in Chapter 12.

*ASCAP and BMI.* If you do not know who the copyright owner is, the next best place to inquire is with the appropriate performance rights society. If you know the particular performance rights society (such as ASCAP[3] or BMI[4]) with which the writer of the song is affiliated, call the society and ask for the "index" department. The index department maintains a large database that can be accessed by computer and the staff can usually give you over the telephone the names of one or more of the music publishers who own the song.

If you don't know the society with which the writer is affiliated, or if you don't know the name of any of the writers of the song, you might take a look at the liner notes on your audiocassette or the little booklet that comes with your CD; nearly all records will list the name of the songs on the album and many records will also list the performance rights society (i.e., ASCAP or BMI) with which the song is registered. If you can't determine which performance rights society to call, you're in luck — the performance rights societies that control performance rights for nearly all the music performed in the United States are only two in number. Flip a coin. (If the coin should land

---

[3] ASCAP (American Society of Composers, Authors & Publishers), 1 Lincoln Plaza, New York, New York 10023, Phone: 212-621-6000, Fax: 212-787-1381, *www.ascap.com*.

[4] BMI (Broadcast Music, Inc.), 320 West 57th Street, New York, New York 10019, Phone: 212-586-2000, Fax 212-489-2368, *www.bmi.com*.

on its edge, you might try calling SESAC,[5] the third, albeit the smallest of the performance rights societies in the United States.)[6]

If you have a personal computer equipped with a modem and you have access to the Internet through a World Wide Web browser, you're in luck. Both ASCAP and BMI maintain "World Wide Web" pages that allow you to perform your own search to determine the name of the publisher of any song in their respective repertoires. The ASCAP address on the Internet Web is *http://www.ascap.com.* The BMI address on the Internet Web is *http://www.bmi.com.*

*U.S. Copyright Office.* If the performing rights societies are unable to help you, consider commissioning a search of the records of the Copyright Office[7] of the U.S. Library of Congress to find the copyright registration of the song in order to obtain the name and address of the copyright owner appearing on the registration. Yes, the Copyright Office has web site at *http://lcweb.loc.gov/copyright/.*[8]

*Thomson & Thomson.* Thomson & Thomson is an outstanding provider of copyright research reports for the music industry.[9] The firm routinely conducts research for major music publishers, record companies and many independent music publishers, musicians, and songwriters. They also provide extensive research services for the motion picture, television, publishing and computer industries. Research reports include information from the Library of Congress and Copy-

---

[5] SESAC, Inc., 421 West 54th Street, New York, New York 10019, Phone: 212-586-3450, Fax: 212-489-5699. Also, 55 Music Square East, Nashville, TN 37203, Phone: 615-320-0055, Fax: 615-329-9627, *www.sesac.com.*

[6] For a discussion of performance rights societies, see Chapter 17.

[7] For information about commissioning a search of the records of the Copyright Office, see the Copyright Office Circular R22 ("How to Investigate the Copyright Status of a Work"), which is set forth in the appendix of this Chapter 1. Further information regarding searches may be obtained by conferring directly with the Copyright Office, Register of Copyrights, Library of Congress, Washington D.C., Phone: 202-287-8239.

[8] Further intellectual property information may be found at the page maintained by the U.S. Patent & Trademark Office: *http://www.uspto.gov* and the U.S. Congress's THOMAS Legislative Information: *http://thomas.loc.gov/.* Links to these and other Internet resources may be found at *Kohn On Music Licensing* located on the Web at *http://www.kohnmusic.com.*

[9] Thomson & Thomson, 1750 K Street, N.W. Suite 200, Washington, D.C. 20006-2305. Telephone: 800-356-8630, 202-835-0240; Fax: 202-728-0744, 800-822-8823.

right Office records, from 1870 to the present, as well as information from online sources, Thomson & Thomson's own private databases, library and files. An example of a Thomson & Thomson research report of a copyright search is included in the appendix to this chapter. They, too, have a web site at *www.thomson.com/thomthom.html/*.

### c.  A Last Resort

If you cannot find the music publisher, copyright owner, songwriter, heirs of the songwriter, or someone authorized to grant licenses for use of a song, there is one last resort, if you still want to use the song and are prepared to take some risk. You can attempt to document the fact that you made good faith efforts to locate the licensing source. Perhaps the best way of doing so is to send a registered letter containing your request to clear a license to the name and address found in the Copyright Office files relating to the song you desire to use. If the letter is returned undelivered, you can use it as evidence some later time to show, perhaps to a federal judge if you must, that you used good faith to locate and obtain permission from the copyright owner.

Before relying on this procedure, however, you should be certain that you have used every commercially reasonable effort to discover the identity and location of the copyright owner. This may entail engaging a specialist to make sure that you have exhausted all possibilities.

### d.  Contacting the Music Publisher

When, and if, you finally obtain the name of the music publisher who controls the rights to the song, you must speak to the appropriate person at the publisher. When calling a music publisher, ask for the "director of licensing" or "licensing department." Most large music publishing houses have large staffs to handle licensing of their copyrights, and are able to assign individuals who specialize in granting licenses for the various kinds of uses, such as record albums, motion pictures, and television advertising. Knowing the standard terminology employed for these uses (e.g., mechanical, synchronization) can help you get to the right person more quickly. So, if you successfully learn the jargon, you should feel free to use it.

### 2. Approaching the Complex Project

As you can see from the preceding section, even a project that looks simple can turn out to be complex if the search for the music copyright owner becomes problematic. But some projects are complex from the start.

#### a. Popular Music-Driven Motion Picture Soundtracks, New Media Works

Many years ago, most music used in motion pictures was acquired by commissioning a composer to write an original score for the film's soundtrack. Obtaining the appropriate license to use the music in the motion picture was merely a matter of entering a standard composer's agreement with the composer.[10] That all changed in the mid-1970's with the release of the movie, *Saturday Night Fever*, the music soundtrack of which was comprised of a series of disco tunes that were popular hits at that time. That event spawned a series of song driven motion pictures, such as *Fast Times at Ridgemont High, Footloose, Top Gun*, and others. The process of obtaining clearance to use several popular music songs in a motion picture will always be complex. This is because the producer should be thinking that he needs permission to use the songs not only in the motion picture, but on the soundtrack album for the picture. Once you begin thinking about soundtrack albums, you need to think about resolving any conflicts with exclusive record contracts and songwriter agreements to which the performing artists are likely to be bound. Further, the music publishing interests of songs composed by members of rock groups are often divided among the members of the group and you may find the need to obtain permission from more than one publishing source for each song in the picture.

Clearing music for use in a new media work, such as an electronic multimedia encyclopedia for distribution on optical compact discs, will also be complex. These new media works may contain recordings of hundreds of songs each of which will require separate clearance.

---

[10] An example of a standard Composer's Agreement is set forth as Form 3.8 at the end of Chapter 3, *on Songwriter Agreements.*

The clearance of a few songs for use in a motion picture might look like child's play to one who might wish, for example, to clear several thousand songs for use in an electronic encyclopedia or discography.

Accordingly, for any work that involves the clearance of several songs, particularly recent recordings, you should consider getting professional assistance to clear your licenses.

### b.  Music Clearing Houses and Other Professional Assistance

A number of organizations specialize in providing professional assistance for the clearance of music licenses, including EMG Music Clearance,[11] the Winogradsky Company,[12] BZ Rights and Permissions, Inc.,[13] Music Rightz,[14] and Total Clearance.[15] These organizations typically charge a flat fee which varies by project. These organizations cannot promise to actually obtain clearances for all the music you want to license, but because of their long-established relationships with most of the major music publishers and substantial experience in dealing with the problem of split copyrights, they will have a significantly better chance of succeeding than someone approaching the problem of clearance for the first time. You might consider hiring an attorney to clear your rights, but you will find the use of clearance companies less expensive, generally more effective, and often staffed or operated by trained attorneys experienced in the field.

The consulting fees charged by these companies is in addition to the cost of the licenses they may obtain for you. Accordingly, if you're responsible for a budget, don't just budget for the license fee. Be sure

---

[11] EMG Music Clearance, 11846 Ventura Boulevard, Suite 140, Studio City, California 91604, Phone: 818-762-9656, Fax: 818-762-2624, *www.clearance.com.*

[12] The Winogradsky Company, 11240 Magnolia Blvd., Suite 104, North Hollywood, California 91601-3604, Phone: 818-761-6906, Fax: 818-761-5719.

[13] BZ Rights and Permissions, Inc., 121 W. 27th Street, Suite 901, New York, New York 10001, Phone: 212-924-3000, Fax: 212-924-2525, *www.bzrights.com.*

[14] Music Rightz, 1968 Palmerston Place, 2nd Fl., Los Angeles, CA 90027, Phone: 323-663-0070, Fax: 323-663-0071.

[15] Total Clearance, P.O. Box 836, Mill Valley, California 94942, Phone: 415-389-1531; Fax: 415-380-9542. Stock footage agencies may also be of assistance. Try, Second Line Search, 1926 Broadway, New York, New York 10023, Phone: (212) 787-7500, Fax: (212) 787-7636.

to budget for consulting fees for clearing rights and any additional research fees that may be required to obtain copies of the music you need.

### c.  Finding the Recording or Orchestration

The rights to use all this wonderful music is not worth anything if you can't find the music. Often, your particular use might call for having a copy of a recording of the song, a lead sheet, or a full orchestration. You should be prepared to do your own researching for any tangible copies of the music you seek. Don't expect a music publisher to help you find a recording. Many publishers, especially older and larger firms, might not have files with complete listings of recordings of particular copyrights, such as very old standard songs. The publisher might be able to get you a lead sheet, but don't count on it. The new copyright law that took effect in 1978 allows a publisher or composer to register their song with a tape recording in lieu of creating and filing lead sheets; therefore, if a lead sheet is required for the use intended, the user might have to be satisfied with a lyric sheet and an audio tape of the song.

If the music you require originally appeared in a motion picture, and you are seeking a copy of the complete score, you may need to get in touch with the appropriate film music library. A listing of public libraries, motion picture studios, university libraries, libraries of historical societies, art museums, and private collections that contain original film score manuscripts can be obtained by writing for the *Directory of Film Music Collections in the United States* published by the Society for the Preservation of Film Music.[16] You might also try the *Film Composer's Guide,* published by The Lone Eagle Publishing Company.[17]

Even if you find the original orchestrations, you may find the studios who own them highly reluctant to license them. Scores for some film music, however, are available from Warner Bros. through special archive services provided by a major university.[18] Silent film

---

[16] Society for the Preservation of Film Music, P.O. Box 93536, Hollywood, California 90093-0536.

[17] Lone Eagle Publishing Co., 2337 Roscomare Rd., Suite Nine, Los Angeles, California 90077-1815, Phone: 213-471-8066, Fax: 213-471-4969.

[18] Warner Bros. Archive, USC School of Cinema Television, University of Southern California, Los Angeles, California 90089.

soundtracks were compiled from many separately published pieces (rather than commissioned from one composer). Scores from silent films were compiled in so-called, "conductor books." Even if you are able to find the conductor book you are looking for, the studio that possesses it may not have the right to license it. A studio might issue a quitclaim license for the use of the score (a license from them without any warranty or representation that they own the proper rights), but you would still need to obtain licenses from the copyright owners of the underlying music.

### 3. Maybe You Just Need a Needledrop

If you don't know what specific song you wish to license, but you know the kind of music you require, or if you do know the song you want, but you either can't find the copyright owner, or if you found him, you wish you hadn't, because he refuses to budge from the exorbitant fee he quoted you for the license you need, perhaps you should consider turning to what is known as a *production music library*.

A *production music library* is a special kind of music publishing company that licenses what is commonly referred to by any of the following names: *production music, library music, canned music,* and *needledrop music* — i.e., music that has been pre-recorded over the years for various production purposes and is now available as part of a vast library of music, organized by genre (e.g., pop, swing, jazz, classical, electronic), mood (e.g., blues, dixie, comedy), and even by instrument (e.g., piano, violin, saxophone, symphony orchestra) from which a producer may select. The great advantage of using production music is that the music library typically owns both the sound recording and the underlying musical composition. Accordingly, often for one flat fee, you can get a license to use both a song and a production quality sound recording of the song, on tape, ready for incorporation into your project, without the need to account for royalties.

Although a production music library will not contain the latest Michael Jackson hits or Frank Sinatra standards, producers of television programs rely quite heavily on these libraries for many music needs. For example, a particular scene of a television program or motion picture may depict a juke box, radio, or phonograph in the background. When a director or producer requires music to be added to the motion picture soundtrack so that it appears to be playing from one of these sources, the music is called *source music*. Often, in these circumstances, any music will suffice, and the producer will turn to a music library for the appropriate canned music to add to the sound-track. Sometimes a band will be depicted performing on camera. In these circumstances, a producer on a low budget can save considerably by using canned music rather than renting a recording studio and hiring a small band to make the necessary recording.

If the project calls for classical music, even a producer with a substantial production budget will consider saving the cost of engaging a large symphony orchestra by instead using production music from a music library. Producers will often prefer newly composed and recorded music for important foreground purposes, but turn to production music licensed from a music library to fulfill the incidental or source music needs of the film. When a producer is looking for that standard song sound, he might consider choosing among the many sound-a-like songs — e.g., songs that sound like *As Time Goes By* or *Over the Rainbow* also available from music libraries. When only the original standard song will do, the producer can clear the music license from the music publisher and license the appropriate sound recording desired from a music library. Finally, many production music libraries also carry a large variety of sound effects, such as glass breaking or a toilet flushing, and these may be licensed on a basis similar to canned music (i.e., a canned flush for the can scene).

One disadvantage of using music libraries is that a producer may have to sift through much of the music library's catalog to find precisely the music for which he is seeking. For this purpose, many music libraries are beginning to offer their catalogs on compact discs, but this still requires the producer to spend hours listening to alternatives, often without a natural ear for the task before him.

A good music library will have a staff that knows its catalog and can help you find and compile the appropriate source music. Roy Kohn, the manager and marketing director of one of the largest production music libraries, the Southern Library of Recorded Music,[19]

---

[19] Southern Library of Recorded Music, 4621 Cahuenga Blvd., Toluca Lake, CA 91602; Phone: 818-752-1530, Fax: 213-656-3298. Ralph Peer II, President; Roy Kohn, Manager.

provides substantial assistance to producers, often using his library's music to score an entire show or film, complete with an open and close, main title theme and incidental music of every type called for by the production. This service can save the producer thousands of dollars, and also offers the producer the advantage of hearing the melodies before paying for the music, unlike where a composer is contracted to deliver a score.

Producers of multimedia programs who run into difficulties getting incidental or bumper music for their CD-ROM productions, or software publishers looking for music to include in product demonstrations, often turn to production music libraries for these purposes. Getting a license for both the song and the recording, royalty and hassle free, is a major advantage to a producer with a low budget and little time or patience to seek complex music clearances.

Production music is licensed either by *cue* or on a *blanket* basis. A cue is a single cut of music, often referred to as a *needledrop*. This term was derived from the vinyl record era when recordings were played by dropping a diamond stylus needle onto the grooves of a record revolving on a turntable (groovy, man). Production music was traditionally licensed for each cue or segment of music which began when the needle was dropped onto the record and ended when the needle was lifted. Production music is also licensed on a blanket basis, with the producer paying a yearly fee to the music library for a license to use an unlimited number of cues from the library, but typically the music used must still be reported to the production library and separate licenses will be issued for each use.

A form license agreement used by one production music library is set forth as Form 22.10 at the end of Chapter 22, on *Licenses for Computer Software, Multimedia and New Media Products*. The fees typically charged by production music libraries are set forth in Chapter 27, on *Typical Fees*.

### 4.  Maybe You Don't Need a License

You may not always require a license to use a particular musical work. Besides getting a license (i.e., getting permission to use the music owned by another in your work), you may acquire the necessary legal privilege to use a copyrighted work by any of the following means: (a) using a work that is in the *public domain* (i.e., taking steps to assure the music is not subject to any legal rights of another); (b) *originating* the work (i.e., creating the music yourself); (c) *purchasing* the work (i.e., buying from another all the rights in the music); and (d) making a *fair use* of another's copyrighted work.

### a.  Using Music in the Public Domain

No permission is required to use a musical composition if it is in the public domain. A work in the *public domain* is a work (1) for which copyright protection was never available; (2) for which copyright protection was never properly secured; or (3) for which copyright protection, though it may have once existed, has expired or otherwise has been lost. Determining whether a particular work is in the public domain, or "PD," is discussed more fully in Chapter 7, *The Language of Music Licensing*, and the appendix to Chapter 9 contains a list of compositions in the public domain in the United States.

### b.  Originating Your Own Music

Of course, to the extent you create your own work, and you own the work, free and clear of any obligation to pay royalties to anyone, you won't require a license to use it in another work. Creating your own work is known as, *originating* the work. You may originate a work by either creating a completely original work, by making an original adaptation of a work in the public domain, or by combining a completely original work with content taken from the public domain. Examples of origination include composing a new musical composition yourself or writing an original arrangement of the *Star Spangled Banner.*

Under certain circumstances, you do not have to take any special action to secure the privileges required to use content that you originate yourself. As noted later in Chapters 7 and 9, ownership of copyright subsists in the author the moment the work is fixed in a tangible medium of expression — e.g., the moment a song is written down or recorded. Under the law, an author has, at that moment, all the rights and privileges he requires to use his own work.

In practice, however, the circumstances under which no action is required to secure the appropriate privilege to use originated content are limited to those situations in which you are doing the origination, either personally or in direct collaboration with another. If, for example, you are a member of a partnership or corporation, or you are obtaining contributions from others to create the work, some formality may be required to properly evidence your procurement of the necessary privilege to use the work created, such as the execution of a written copyright assignment or work for hire agreement.

While the process of acquiring the privileges necessary to use content which you or your firm originates is considerably less complex than that of acquiring what you need to use content owned by another, some diligence is still required to secure the necessary privileges you will require. The necessary formalities are discussed in Chapter 8, on the *Formalities of Music Licensing*.

### c. Purchasing All Rights in the Work You Desire to Use

The preceding section sketched one basic way of acquiring permission to use music: originating it yourself. Of course, it is not always possible or practical for you to originate a work, and in some cases you may be unable to use the "work for hire" status in dealing with your contractors. More likely, the music you wish to use already exists, in which event you may clear your use either by obtaining permission or purchasing ownership rights in the content. The formalities necessary to effect a purchase or sale of a copyrighted composition are discussed in Chapter 8, on the *Formalities of Music Licensing*.

### d. Making a Fair Use of Another's Copyrighted Work

No permission is required to use a musical composition if the use is considered a *fair use*. However, the determination of whether a particular use falls within the fair use doctrine is often not an easy one, and should not be made lightly, and certainly not without the advice of competent legal counsel. The consequences of being wrong may be a costly lawsuit for copyright infringement. Determining whether a particular use would be considered a fair use is discussed in Chapter 25, on *The Fair Use Controversy*.

## D. Understand the Needs and Fears of the Music Copyright Owner

Having gained some understanding of the rights involved, having developed some strategy for obtaining the license you need, and hav-

ing learned where to contact the music copyright owner, you should
be mindful of the basic needs and fears of music copyright owners at
the time you approach them for the licenses you require.

Music copyright owners have three basic fears:

1. Fear of piracy

2. Fear of making a bad deal

3. Fear of getting sued

Each of these fears is discussed in turn.

### 1.  Fear of Piracy

Copyright means what the word implies — the right to copy. It
is the right to exclude others from copying unless they have the right
holder's permission to do so. But this right is violated as often as it
is respected. Copyright owners lose billions of dollars a year to copyright *piracy*, the unauthorized use of copyrighted works. Ironically,
the problem of copyright piracy stems from the very intangibility that
gives music its value to mankind: The intangible nature of music renders copying easy to perform and unauthorized copying difficult to
discover. Piracy has always been an insidious backdrop to the daily
exercise of a music copyright owner's rights. However, recent developments have hurled a new challenge to those who rely on the exercise
of copyrights to earn a living: The advent of the new technologies —
such as the digital technology that forms the basis of computers, digital tape and laser discs — has made the process of copying faster,
cheaper, easier, and more accurate than ever before. At the same time,
few strides have been made to render unauthorized copying less difficult to discover. The recent emergence of these new capabilities has
caused music copyright owners to have a heightened perspective on
some old fears.

It should therefore be no surprise when you approach a music
publisher for a license to use music, especially in new media works,
to discover in the copyright owner an immediate resistance to license.
The resistance will generally stem from the copyright owner's unwillingness to enter into any arrangement that might have unknown
consequences on the value of his work. As far as the copyright owner

is concerned, anything that he does not understand may, in fact, result in unforeseen adverse consequences.

The antidote to this fear, of course, is some combination of education and trust. The importance of educating the copyright owner is discussed later in this chapter. Establishing trust is often a function of the relationship between the copyright owner and the licensee or, quite often, the licensee's representative. The use of a reputable music clearing house that has had prior dealings with the music publisher may prove the decisive factor in closing a license to new or esoteric uses.

### 2. Fear of Making a Bad Deal

One of a copyright owner's worst fears is entering into a deal he will later regret having made. For example, a music copyright owner may regret having quoted too low a fee for the use of his music in a low-budget movie that unexpectedly became a *blockbuster*. Also, if the copyright owner is dealing with a studio, a clearing house, or other person with whom he deals often, the copyright owner will be concerned about setting a precedent of which he will no doubt be reminded in future deals.

More important, because of the nature of copyright (i.e., intangible) and the means by which they may be exploited (i.e., granting permission to use), a bad deal may involve significantly more than failing to obtain a sufficiently high fee. If the copyright owner is not careful, he may find himself on the wrong end of a deal that has serious adverse consequences on the value of his copyright.

For example, a copyright owner may be persuaded to provide a license to use his music in computer software for a flat fee using a written license that grants permission to use the music "in digital form." Notwithstanding the copyright owner's rudimentary understanding of the phrase "in digital form" at the time the license was granted, the license may well have the affect of reducing the value of the copyright to virtually nothing if later virtually all distribution and performance of music is made "in digital form."

The fear of making a bad deal is more pronounced in owners of copyright than in owners of other kinds of assets. The owner of an asset, such as a car, can fairly predict the limited consequences of leasing the asset at an unprofitable rate; the risk of leasing the asset to one who would negligently destroy it may be covered by insurance and, in any event, the loss may be measured precisely and in advance. The value of a copyright, however, may vary over time and is directly affected by the nature and scope of the licenses granted by its owner. The copyright owner will be very concerned about limiting the scope of the license and to do so, he will be required to understand exactly what the nature of the use is.

Thus, the copyright owner's unwillingness to enter into any arrangement that might have unknown consequences on the value of his work — stemming from a lack of understanding of the use and its consequences — manifests itself in the fear of making a bad deal. Again, the best remedy is education and establishing a relationship with the copyright owner. In the end, you should find that copyright owners are actually quite eager to benefit from the opportunities afforded by the new technologies and most do not wish to be left behind.

### 3.  Fear of Getting Sued

This is of the same genre as making a deal that the copyright owner may regret, but the remorse has another cause. Getting sued is high on the list of a copyright owner's fears. The uncertainty of damage awards, the high costs of litigation, and the immeasurable damage to important long-term contractual relationships and business reputation all tend to make a copyright owner extremely conservative in making decisions that involve any risk that he may become embroiled in a lawsuit.

The latitude a copyright owner has in granting licenses is often limited by the terms of the contracts he may have with the songwriters and co-owners of the copyright. For example, as noted in Chapter 3 on *Songwriter Agreements,* a common provision of many songwriter contracts requires the music publisher to obtain the permission of the songwriter before authorizing anyone to alter or make any changes to the copyrighted work. Thus, if your use involves changing the lyrics of a song, the music publisher may require the written consent of the songwriter before issuing the license. Songwriter contracts may also restrict the music publisher's authority to grant licenses for the use of music in radio, television, and print advertising. Some artists are very sensitive about this and will deny consent for all kinds of uses, except recordings which are subject to the compulsory license provisions of the copyright law, discussed in Chapter 12, on *Mechanical Licenses.*

You should not expect that a publisher will be able to give you a definitive answer right away. The publisher may wish to first review a contract to determine whether any consents are required for the use. The publisher might seek a legal opinion on the scope of his ability to grant to you the license you require. All of this will take time, and, where there is a possibility that an ambiguity could be decided against the publisher, there is no assurance that he will want to take any risk to help you.

The fear a publisher has of taking any action that may result in a legal dispute is coupled with a certain amount of frustration; the publisher often desires to issue a license, but may be forced to acquiesce to the shortsightedness of the artist or the artist's representative who insists on arbitrarily invoking a contractual right of approval. Thus, when faced with a situation where the publisher's hands are tied, you should be aware that inability, not unwillingness, is at the root of the matter and you should keep communication with the publisher open in the hope that together you can find an alternative solution to your music clearance problem.

### E. Spend Time Educating the Copyright Owner About Your Intended Use of the Music

After you find the person authorized to grant the license you require, you should be prepared to educate that person about precisely how you intend to use the music. Ideally, the person calling a music publisher for a license will know the language of music licensing as described in this book. Understanding the language will go a long way to facilitate the communication between the parties and the result should be a fruitful and efficient experience for all concerned.

In any negotiation, however, there are often hidden assumptions that can be the cause of some misunderstanding. Publishers are likely to test those assumptions, because of the precision they strive to achieve in fashioning the scope of the licenses they grant. You should therefore expect the music publisher to ferret out the precise scope of the permission you need in an effort to limit the scope of the permission to be granted solely to the uses that you intend, and no more. Further, the publisher will also attempt to determine the importance of the song in relation to its intended use or any other information that would be helpful in establishing the appropriate licensee fee structure and license fee. In this regard, you should be prepared to answer some or all of the following questions:

- What is the nature of the work in which the music will appear?

- How will the music be rendered in the work?

- Will the music be featured prominently or used only in the background?

- Will the music comprise all or any part of the work?

- Do you intend to use other songs in the work?

- Will you use non-music components, such as motion pictures, animation, text, photographs, dialogue, or other visual or audio elements?

- Will the music or lyrics be changed or edited?

- Will the title of the song be used in a special way?

- Will the work be a dramatic adaptation of the song's lyrics?

- Will the song be performed dramatically?

- In what markets will the work be distributed?

- Will the song be used to promote a product?

- Will the song be made part of a product?

In inquiring about the use of a song, be prepared to specify the type of use you seek. If the use is in a recording, you should specify whether the recording will be audio-only, or combined with motion pictures or other audiovisual materials. If the use is for television, you should distinguish between *free* television and *pay/cable* television. If the use is in a motion picture, you should specify if it will be in a film for normal theatrical release or whether it will be in a non-theatrical motion picture, such as a corporate training film or student documentary. Presenting this information correctly will assist the publisher in quoting the proper fees.

Some works may defy description. Perhaps the producer of the work can describe the work using the special jargon of a particular field, such as computers, but he should not assume that music publishers are even remotely familiar with the latest developments in technology. For example, if you require a license to use a song in "an MPC-formatted CD-ROM running under on Intel-based machines using the MS-DOS operating system with multimedia extensions," you might need to spend a little time explaining just what that means.

Even if the music copyright owner begins to understand the work in which you intend to use the song, he may be entirely unprepared to determine just what kind of license would be appropriate for the use. The fear of making a bad deal suddenly takes center stage, and your project gets delayed while the publisher takes the matter to his lawyers, who are likely to know little more than the publisher about the media for which a license is sought.

Upon the advent of the home videocassette tape market for motion pictures, it took years for standard business practices to evolve that addressed how music copyright owners would be compensated for the use of their music in these tapes. It may not take as long for practices to emerge that resolve issues in licensing music for use in multimedia software and internet transmission services, but producers of these new programs and services will find that they will not be able to ignore the established business practices of the music publishing business when negotiating the appropriate licenses for these uses.

If you have a work that is unusual or complex, such as a multimedia product, you might be asked to send copies of similar products that you developed or copies of any marketing materials that would help the publisher understand how the music will be used in the context of the work.

Many songwriter contracts restrict the publisher's ability to permit others to make changes to lyrics of a song or make fundamental changes to the character of the music. For example, while Ira Gershwin was alive, he would never permit the rendition of his brother George's composition *Rhapsody in Blue*, unless it was performed in its entirety. (He made the first exception when I persuaded him to allow Woody Allen to use a substantial excerpt in the film, *Manhattan*). A user should never consider making any substantial changes to lyrics or the music without first obtaining a license with special provisions permitting such changes.

## F.  Allow Enough Time to Complete the Process

Licensing music may sound as simple as knowing the name of the song you want, calling the performance rights society to find out who controls the rights, and obtaining the proper license. It sounds easy, but it's rarely that simple in practice.

Any number of things may come up that will delay the completion of a project that contains copyrighted music. For example, music publishers are well aware of the frustrations that producers experience when trying to track down copyright owners. A music publisher on the other side of a phone call will hear a producer express a long sigh of relief when, after nine or ten phone calls, he learns that he finally located the publisher. That's the good news. Then the producer learns the bad news, that the song is also controlled by three other publishers. When he finally finds all the publishers, he discovers that he also requires a print license to clear his particular use and then gets hit with the news that none of them control the print rights!

Allow yourself enough time to do the research and complete the negotiations necessary to obtain a license. You should always attempt to obtain your clearance *before* you begin integrating the music into your work. If you use the music before you receive a license and the copyright owner discovers it, you do two things: (i) you create a bad impression that may anger the publisher, who thinks you are trying to pressure him into giving you a license, and, perhaps more important, (ii) you greatly increase the publisher's leverage in the negotiation for the license.

After you've already spent the time and money recording the song or taping the performance, the publisher knows that it will cost you a fortune to find another song and re-record or retape the performance. While most professional publishers would not unreasonably "hold you up," you could find that any persuasive reason you may have had to support a lower fee will fall on deaf ears. Further, remember that these rights are often split up and you just don't know whether you can even obtain the license you require *at all*. If you can't obtain clearance, and you've recorded the song, you are a copyright infringer, subject to civil action and possible criminal penalties. In this situation, impatience can cost you, as the song goes, *More Than You Know.*

## III. SUMMARY

Excellence in the art of granting licenses for the purpose of earning a living from one's copyrighted music involves:

A. Sharing in the economic success of the work in which the music is going to be used;

B. Maximizing the long-term value of the work; and,

C. Maintaining an active relationship between the song and the listening public.

Excellence in obtaining licenses to use copyrighted music of others for commercial purposes involves:

A. Understanding the nature of the rights involved;

B. Knowing what music you wish to license;

C. Developing a licensing strategy;

D. Understanding the needs and fears of the copyright owner;

E. Spending time educating the copyright owner, particularly when licensing for high tech use; and

F. Allowing enough time (and budget) to complete the process.

# APPENDIX TO CHAPTER 1
# THE ART OF MUSIC LICENSING

## CIRCULAR 1.1

### U.S. COPYRIGHT OFFICE CIRCULAR R22—"HOW TO INVESTIGATE THE COPYRIGHT STATUS OF A WORK"

# How to Investigate the Copyright Status of a Work

## IN GENERAL

### Methods of Approaching a Copyright Investigation

There are several ways to investigate whether a work is under copyright protection and, if so, the facts of the copyright. These are the main ones:

1.  Examine a copy of the work for such elements as a copyright notice, place and date of publication, author and publisher. If the work is a sound recording, examine the disk, tape cartridge, or cassette in which the recorded sound is fixed, or the album cover, sleeve, or container in which the recording is sold.

2.  Make a search of the Copyright Office catalogs and other records; or

3.  Have the Copyright Office make a search for you.

### A Few Words of Caution About Copyright Investigations

Copyright investigations often involve more than one of these methods. Even if you follow all three approaches, the results may not be conclusive. Moreover, as explained in this circular, the changes brought about under the Copyright Act of 1976, the Berne Convention Implementation Act of 1988, the Copyright Renewal Act of 1992, and the Sonny Bono Copyright Term Extension Act of 1998 must be considered when investigating the copyright status of a work.

This circular offers some practical guidance on what to look for if you are making a copyright investigation. It is important to realize, however, that this circular contains only general information and that there are a number of exceptions to the principles outlined here. In many cases it is important to consult with a copyright attorney before reaching any conclusions regarding the copyright status of a work.

## HOW TO SEARCH COPYRIGHT OFFICE CATALOGS AND RECORDS

### Catalog of Copyright Entries

The Copyright Office published the *Catalog of Copyright Entries (CCE)* in printed format from 1891 through 1978. From 1979 through 1982 the CCE was issued in microfiche format. The catalog was divided into parts according to the classes of works registered. Each CCE segment covered all registrations made during a particular period of time. Renewal registrations made from 1979 through 1982 are found in Section 8 of the catalog. Renewals prior to that time were generally listed at the end of the volume containing the class of work to which they pertained.

A number of libraries throughout the United States maintain copies of the *Catalog,* and this may provide a good starting point if you wish to make a search yourself. There are some cases, however, in which a search of the *Catalog* alone will not be sufficient to provide the needed information. For example:

- Because the *Catalog* does not include entries for assignments or other recorded documents, it cannot be used for searches involving the ownership of rights.

- The *Catalog* entry contains the essential facts concerning a registration, but it is not a verbatim transcript of the registration record. It does not contain the address of the copyright claimant.

Effective with registrations made since 1982 when the CCE was discontinued, the only method of searching outside the Library of Congress is by using the Internet to access the automated catalog. The automated catalog contains entries from 1978 to the present. Information for accessing the catalog via the Internet is provided below.

### Individual Searches of Copyright Records

The Copyright Office is located in the Library of Congress James Madison Memorial Building, 101 Independence Avenue, S.E., Washington, D.C. 20559-6000.

Most Copyright Office records are open to public inspection and searching from 8:30 a.m. to 5 p.m., eastern time, Monday through Friday, except federal holidays. The various records freely available to the public include an extensive card catalog, an automated catalog containing records from 1978 forward, record books, and microfilm records of assignments and related documents. Other records, including correspondence files and deposit copies, are not open to the public for searching. However, they may be inspected upon request and payment of a $65 per hour search fee.*

If you wish to do your own searching in the Copyright Office files open to the public, you will be given assistance in locating the records you need and in learning procedures for searching. If the Copyright Office staff actually makes the search for you, a search fee must be charged. The search will not be done while you wait.

In addition, the following files dating from 1978 forward are now available over the Internet: COHM, which includes all material except serials and documents; COHD, which includes documents; and COHS, which includes serials.

The Internet site addresses for the Copyright Office files are:
World Wide Web: **www.loc.gov/copyright**
Telnet: **locis.loc.gov**

*NOTE: Registration filing fees and search fees are effective through June 30, 2002. For information on the fee changes, please write the Copyright Office, check the Copyright Office Website at www.loc.gov/copyright, or call (202) 707-3000.

Access to LOCIS requires Telnet support. If your online service provider supports Telnet, you can connect to LOCIS through the World Wide Web or directly by using Telnet.

The Copyright Office does **not** offer search assistance to users on the Internet.

## SEARCHING BY THE COPYRIGHT OFFICE

### In General

Upon request, the Copyright Office staff will search its records at the statutory rate of $65* for each hour or fraction of an hour consumed. Based on the information you furnish, we will provide an estimate of the total search fee. If you decide to have the Office staff conduct the search, you should send the estimated amount with your request. The Office will then proceed with the search and send you a typewritten report or, if you prefer, an oral report by telephone. If you request an oral report, please provide a telephone number where you can be reached from 8:30 a.m. to 5 p.m., eastern time.

Search reports can be certified on request for an extra fee of $65 per hour.* Certified searches are most frequently requested to meet the evidentiary requirements of litigation.

Your request and any other correspondence should be addressed to:

Library of Congress
Copyright Office
Reference and Bibliography Section, LM-451
101 Independence Avenue, S.E.
Washington, D.C. 20559-6000

Tel:  (202) 707-6850
Fax: (202) 707-6859
TTY: (202) 707-6737

See NOTE, page 2.

### What the Fee Does Not Cover

The search fee does not include the cost of additional certificates, photocopies of deposits, or copies of other Office records. For information concerning these services, request Circular 6, "Obtaining Access to and Copies of Copyright Office Records and Deposits."

### Information Needed

The more detailed information you can furnish with your request, the less expensive the search will be. Please provide as much of the following information as possible:

- The title of the work, with any possible variants

- The names of the authors, including possible pseudonyms

- The name of the probable copyright owner, which may be the publisher or producer

- The approximate year when the work was published or registered

- The type of work involved (book, play, musical composition, sound recording, photograph, etc.)

- For a work originally published as a part of a periodical or collection, the title of that publication and any other information, such as the volume or issue number, to help identify it

- The registration number or any other copyright data

Motion pictures are often based on other works such as books or serialized contributions to periodicals or other composite works. **If you desire a search for an underlying work or for music from a motion picture, you must specifically request such a search. You must also identify the underlying works and music and furnish the specific titles, authors, and approximate dates of these works.**

### Searches Involving Assignments and Other Documents Affecting Copyright Ownership

For the standard hourly search fee, the Copyright Office staff will search its indexes covering the records of assignments and other recorded documents concerning ownership of copyrights. The reports of searches in these cases will state the facts shown in the Office's indexes of the recorded documents but will offer no interpretation of the content of the documents or their legal effect.

## LIMITATIONS ON SEARCHES

In determining whether or not to have a search made, you should keep the following points in mind:

*No Special Lists.* The Copyright Office does not maintain any listings of works by subject or any lists of works that are in the public domain.

*Contributions Not Listed Separately in Copyright Office Records.* Individual works such as stories, poems, articles, or musical compositions that were published as contributions to a copyrighted periodical or collection are usually not listed separately by title in our records.

*No Comparisons.* The Copyright Office does not search or compare copies of works to determine questions of possible infringement or to determine how much two or more versions of a work have in common.

*Titles and Names Not Copyrightable.* Copyright does not protect names and titles, and our records list many different works identified by the same or similar titles. Some brand names, trade names, slogans, and phrases may be entitled to protection under the general rules of law relating to unfair competition. They may also be entitled to registration under the provisions of the trademark laws. Questions about the trademark laws should be addressed to the Commissioner of Patents and Trademarks, Washington, D.C. 20231. Possible protection of names and titles under common law principles of unfair competition is a question of state law.

*No Legal Advice.* The Copyright Office cannot express any opinion as to the legal significance or effect of the facts included in a search report.

## SOME WORDS OF CAUTION

### Searches Not Always Conclusive

Searches of the Copyright Office catalogs and records are useful in helping to determine the copyright status of a work, but they cannot be regarded as conclusive in all cases. The complete absence of any information about a work in the Office records does not mean that the work is unprotected. The following are examples of cases in which information about a particular work may be incomplete or lacking entirely in the Copyright Office:

- Before 1978, unpublished works were entitled to protection under common law without the need of registration.

- Works published with notice prior to 1978 may be registered at **any** time within the first 28-year term.

- Works copyrighted between January 1,1964, and December 31, 1977, are affected by the Copyright Renewal Act of 1992, which automatically extends the copyright term and makes renewal registrations optional.

- For works under copyright protection on or after January 1, 1978, registration may be made at any time during the term of protection. Although registration is not required as a condition of copyright protection, there are certain definite advantages to registration. For further information, request Circular 1, "Copyright Basics."

- Since searches are ordinarily limited to registrations that have already been cataloged, a search report may not cover recent registrations for which catalog records are not yet available.

- The information in the search request may not have been complete or specific enough to identify the work.

- The work may have been registered under a different title or as part of a larger work.

### Protection in Foreign Countries

Even if you conclude that a work is in the public domain in the United States, this does not necessarily mean that you are free to use it in other countries. Every nation has its own laws governing the length and scope of copyright protection, and these are applicable to uses of the work within that nation's borders. Thus, the expiration or loss of copyright protection in the United States may still leave the work fully protected against unauthorized use in other countries.

## OTHER CIRCULARS

For further information, request Circular 6, "Obtaining Access to and Copies of Copyright Office Records and Deposits"; Circular 15, "Renewal of Copyright"; Circular 15a, "Duration of Copyright"; and Circular 15t, "Extension of Copyright Terms," from:

Library of Congress
Copyright Office
Publications Section, LM-455
101 Independence Avenue, S.E.
Washington, D.C. 20559-6000

You may call the Forms and Publications Hotline (202) 707-9100 at any time, day or night, to leave a recorded request for forms or circulars. Requests are filled and mailed promptly.

## IMPACT OF COPYRIGHT ACT ON COPYRIGHT INVESTIGATIONS

On October 19, 1976, the President signed into law a complete revision of the copyright law of the United States (title 17 of the United States Code). Most provisions of this statute came into force on January 1,1978, superseding the copyright act of 1909. These provisions made significant changes in the copyright law. Further important changes resulted from the Berne Convention Implementation Act of 1988, which took effect March 1, 1989; the Copyright Renewal Act of 1992 (P.L. 102-307) enacted June 26,1992, which amended the renewal provisions of the copyright law; and the

Sonny Bono Copyright Term Extension Act of 1998 (P.L. 105-298) enacted October 27, 1998, which extended the term of copyrights for an additional 20 years.

If you need more information about the provisions of either the 1909 or the 1976 law, write or call the Copyright Office. For information about the Berne Convention Implementation Act, request Circular 93, "Highlights of U.S. Adherence to the Berne Convention." For information about renewals, request Circular 15, "Renewal of Copyright." For information about the Sonny Bono Copyright Term Extension Act, request SL-15, "New Terms for Copyright Protection." For copies of the law ($8.50 each), request "Copyright Law, Circular 92," stock number 030-002-00187-0 from:

> Superintendent of Documents
> P.O. Box 371954
> Pittsburgh, PA 15250-7954

> Tel: (202) 512-1800
> Fax: (202) 512-2250

For copyright investigations, the following points about the impact of the Copyright Act of 1976, the Berne Convention Implementation Act of 1988, and the Copyright Renewal Act of 1992 should be considered:

**A Changed System of Copyright Formalities**

Some of the most sweeping changes under the 1976 Copyright Act involve copyright formalities, that is, the procedural requirements for securing and maintaining full copyright protection. The old system of formalities involved copyright notice, deposit and registration, recordation of transfers and licenses of copyright ownership, and United States manufacture, among other things. In general, while retaining formalities, the 1976 law reduced the chances of mistakes, softened the consequences of errors and omissions, and allowed for the correction of errors.

The Berne Convention Implementation Act of 1988 reduced formalities, most notably making the addition of the previously mandatory copyright notice optional. It should be noted that the amended notice requirements are not retroactive.

The Copyright Renewal Act of 1992, enacted June 26, 1992, automatically extends the term of copyrights secured between January 1, 1964, and December 31, 1977, making renewal registration optional. Consult Circular 15, "Renewal of Copyright," for details. For additional information, you may contact the Renewals Section.

> Tel:  (202) 707-8180
> Fax: (202) 707-3849

**Automatic Copyright**

Under the present copyright law, copyright exists in original works of authorship created and fixed in any tangible medium of expression, now known or later developed, from which they can be perceived, reproduced, or otherwise communicated, either directly, or indirectly with the aid of a machine or device. In other words, copyright is an incident of creative authorship not dependent on statutory formalities. Thus, registration with the Copyright Office generally is not required, but there are certain advantages that 'arise from a timely registration. For further information on the advantages of registration, write or call the Copyright Office and request Circular 1, "Copyright Basics."

### Copyright Notice

The 1909 Copyright Act and the 1976 Copyright Act as originally enacted required a notice of copyright on published works. For most works, a copyright notice consisted of the symbol ©, the word "Copyright," or the abbreviation "Copr.," together with the name of the owner of copyright and the year of first publication. For example: "© Joan Crane 1994" or "Copyright 1994 by Abraham Adams."

For sound recordings published on or after February 15,1972, a copyright notice might read "Ⓟ1994 XYZ Records, Inc." See below for more information about sound recordings.

For mask works, a copyright notice might read "ⓂSDR Industries." Request Circular 100, "Federal Statutory Protection for Mask Works," for more information.

As originally enacted, the 1976 law prescribed that all visually perceptible published copies of a work, or published phonorecords of a sound recording, should bear a proper copyright notice. This applies to such works published before March 1,1989. After March 1,1989, notice of copyright on these works is optional. Adding the notice, however, is strongly encouraged and, if litigation involving the copyright occurs, certain advantages exist for publishing a work with notice.

Prior to March 1, 1989, the requirement for the notice applied equally whether the work was published in the United States or elsewhere by authority of the copyright owner. Compliance with the statutory notice requirements was the responsibility of the copyright owner. Unauthorized publication without the copyright notice, or with a defective notice, does not affect the validity of the copyright in the work.

Advance permission from, or registration with, the Copyright Office is not required before placing a copyright notice on copies of the work or on phonorecords of a sound recording. Moreover, for works first published on or after January 1, 1978, through February 28, 1989, omission of the required notice, or use of a defective notice, did not result in forfeiture or outright loss of copyright protection. Certain omissions of, or defects in, the notice of copyright, however, could have led to loss of copyright protection if steps were not taken to correct or cure the omissions or defects. The Copyright Office has issued a final regulation (37 CFR 201.20) that suggests various acceptable positions for the notice of copyright. For further information, write to the Copyright Office and request Circular 3, "Copyright Notice," and Circular 96, Section 201.20, "Methods of Affixation and Positions of the Copyright Notice on Various Types of Works."

### Works Already in the Public Domain

Neither the 1976 Copyright Act, the Berne Convention Implementation Act of 1988, the Copyright Renewal Act of 1992, nor the Sonny Bono Copyright Term Extension Act of 1998 will restore protection to works that fell into the public domain before the passage of the laws. However, the North American Free Trade Agreement Implementation Act (NAFTA) and the Uruguay Round Agreements Act (URAA) may restore copyright in certain works of foreign origin that were in the public domain in the United States.

Under the copyright law in effect prior to January 1, 1978, copyright could be lost in several situations. The most common were publication without the required notice of copyright, expiration of the first 28-year term without renewal, or final expiration of the second copyright term. The Copyright Renewal Act of 1992 automatically renews first term copyrights secured between January 1,1964, and December 31,1977.

### Scope of Exclusive Rights Under Copyright

The present law has changed and enlarged in some cases the scope of the copyright owner's rights. The new rights apply to all uses of a work subject to protection by copyright after January 1, 1978, regardless of when the work was created.

---

## DURATION OF COPYRIGHT PROTECTION

---

### Works Originally Copyrighted On or After January 1, 1978

A work that is created and fixed in tangible form for the first time on or after January 1, 1978, is automatically protected from the moment of its creation and is ordinarily given a term enduring for the author's life plus an additional 70 years after the author's death. In the case of "a joint work prepared by two or more authors who did not work for hire," the term lasts for 70 years after the last surviving author's death. For works made for hire and for anonymous and pseudonymous works (unless the author's identity is revealed in the Copyright Office records), the duration of copyright will be 95 years from publication or 120 years from creation, whichever is less.

Works created before the 1976 law came into effect but neither published nor registered for copyright before January 1,1978, have been automatically brought under the statute and are now given federal copyright protection. The duration of copyright in these works will generally be computed in the same way as for new works: the life-plus-70 or 95/120-year terms will apply. However, all works in this category are guaranteed at least 25 years of statutory protection.

### Works Copyrighted Before January 1, 1978

Under the law in effect before 1978, copyright was secured either on the date a work was published with notice of copyright or on the date of registration if the work was registered in unpublished form. In either case, copyright endured for a first term of 28 years from the date on which it was secured. During the last (28th) year of the first term, the copyright was eligible for renewal. The copyright law extends the renewal term from 28 to 67 years for copyrights in existence on January 1, 1978.

However, for works copyrighted prior to January 1, 1964, the copyright still must have been renewed in the 28th calendar year to receive the 67-year period of added protection. The amending legislation enacted June 26, 1992, automatically extends this second term for works first copyrighted between January 1,1964, and December 31, 1977. For more detailed information on the copyright term, write or call the Copyright Office and request Circular 15a, "Duration of Copyright," and Circular 15t, "Extension of Copyright Terms."

## WORKS FIRST PUBLISHED BEFORE 1978: THE COPYRIGHT NOTICE

### General Information About the Copyright Notice

In investigating the copyright status of works first published before January 1, 1978, the most important thing to look for is the notice of copyright. As a general rule under the previous law, copyright protection was lost permanently if the notice was omitted from the first authorized published edition of a work or if it appeared in the wrong form or position. The form and position of the copyright notice for various types of works were specified in the copyright statute. Some courts were liberal in overlooking relatively minor departures from the statutory requirements, but a basic failure to comply with the notice provisions forfeited copyright protection and put the work into the public domain in this country.

### Absence of Copyright Notice

For works first published before 1978, the complete absence of a copyright notice from a published copy generally indicates that the work is not protected by copyright. For works first published before March 1,1989, the copyright notice is mandatory, but omission could have been cured by registration before or within 5 years of publication and by adding the notice to copies published in the United States after discovery of the omission. Some works may contain a notice, others may not. The absence of a notice in works published on or after March 1,1989, does not necessarily indicate that the work is in the public domain.

*Unpublished Works.* No notice of copyright was required on the copies of any unpublished work. The concept of "publication" is very technical, and it was possible for a number of copies lacking a copyright notice to be reproduced and distributed without affecting copyright protection.

*Foreign Editions.* In the case of works seeking *ad interim* copyright,* copies of a copyrighted work were exempted from the notice requirements if they were first published outside the United States. Some copies of these foreign editions could find their way into the United States without impairing the copyright.

*Accidental Omission.* The 1909 statute preserved copyright protection if the notice was omitted by accident or mistake from a "particular copy or copies."

*Unauthorized Pubilcation.* A valid copyright was not secured if someone deleted the notice and/or published the work without authorization from the copyright owner.

*Sound Recordings.* Reproductions of sound recordings usually contain two different types of creative works: the underlying musical, dramatic, or literary work that is being performed or read and the fixation of the actual sounds embodying the performance or reading. For protection of the underlying musical or literary work embodied in a record-

---

* *"Ad interim copyright"* refers to a special short term of copyright available to certain pre-1978 books and periodicals. For further information on *ad interim* copyright, see page 10.

ing, it is not necessary that a copyright notice covering this material appear on the phonograph records or tapes on which the recording is reproduced. As noted above, a special notice is required for protection of the recording of a series of musical, spoken, or other sounds that were fixed on or after February 15, 1972. Sound recordings fixed before February 15,1972, are not eligible for federal copyright protection. The Sound Recording Act of 1971, the present copyright law, and the Berne Convention Implementation Act of 1988 cannot be applied or be construed to provide any retroactive protection for sound recordings fixed before February 15, 1972. Such works, however, may be protected by various state laws or doctrines of common law.

### The Date in the Copyright Notice

If you find a copyright notice, the date it contains may be important in determining the copyright status of the work. In general, the notice on works published before 1978 must include the year in which copyright was secured by publication or, if the work was first registered for copyright in unpublished form, the year in which registration was made. There are two main exceptions to this rule.

1.  For pictorial, graphic, or sculptural works (Classes F through K under the 1909 law), the law permitted omission of the year date in the notice.

2.  For "new versions" of previously published or copyrighted works, the notice was not usually required to include more than the year of first publication of the new version itself. This is explained further under "Derivative Works" below.

The year in the notice usually (though not always) indicated when the copyright began. It is, therefore, significant in determining whether a copyright is still in effect; or, if the copyright has not yet run its course, the year date will help in deciding when the copyright is scheduled to expire. For further information about the duration of copyright, request Circular 15a, "Duration of Copyright."

In evaluating the meaning of the date in a notice, you should keep the following points in mind:

WORKS PUBLISHED AND COPYRIGHTED BEFORE JANUARY 1, 1978: A work published before January 1, 1978, and copyrighted within the past 75 years may still be protected by copyright in the United States if a valid renewal registration was made during the 28th year of the first term of the copyright. If renewed by registration or under the Copyright Renewal Act of 1992 and if still valid under the other provisions of the law, the copyright will expire 95 years from the end of the year in which it was first secured.

Therefore, the U.S. copyright in any work published or copyrighted prior to January 1, 1923, has expired by operation of law, and the work has permanently fallen into the public domain in the United States. For example, on January 1,1997, copyrights in works first published or copyrighted before January 1, 1922, have expired; on January 1,1998, copyrights in works first published or copyrighted before January 1, 1923, have expired. Unless the copyright law is changed again, no works under protection on January 1, 1999 will fall into the public domain in the United States until January 1, 2019.

WORKS FIRST PUBLISHED OR COPYRIGHTED BETWEEN JANUARY 1,1923, AND DECEMBER 31, 1949, BUT NOT RENEWED: If a work was first published or copyrighted between January 1, 1923, and December 31, 1949, it is important to determine whether the copyright was renewed during the last (28th) year of the first term of the copyright. This can be done by searching the Copyright Office records or catalogs as explained previously. If no renewal registration was made, copyright protection expired permanently at the end of the 28th year of the year date it was first secured.

WORKS FIRST PUBLISHED OR COPYRIGHTED BETWEEN JANUARY 1, 1923, AND DECEMBER 31, 1949, AND REGISTERED FOR RENEWAL: When a valid renewal registration was made and copyright in the work was in its second term on December 31, 1977, the renewal copyright term was extended under the latest act to 67 years. In these cases, copyright will last for a total of 95 years from the end of the year in which copyright was originally secured. Example: Copyright in a work first published in 1925 and renewed in 1953 will expire on December 31, 2020.

WORKS FIRST PUBLISHED OR COPYRIGHTED BETWEEN JANUARY 1, 1950, AND DECEMBER 31, 1963: If a work was in its first 28-year term of copyright protection on January 1, 1978, it must have been renewed in a timely fashion to have secured the maximum term of copyright protection. If renewal registration was made during the 28th calendar year of its first term, copyright would endure for 95 years from the end of the year copyright was originally secured. If not renewed, the copyright expired at the end of its 28th calendar year.

WORKS FIRST PUBLISHED OR COPYRIGHTED BETWEEN JANUARY 1, 1964, AND DECEMBER 31, 1977: If a work was in its first 28-year term of copyright protection on June 26,1992, renewal registration is now optional. The term of copyright for works published or copyrighted during this time period has been extended to 95 years by the Copyright Renewal Act of 1992 and the Sonny Bono Term Extension Act of 1998. There is no need to make the renewal filing to extend the original 28-year copyright term to the full 95 years.

However, there are several advantages to making a renewal registration during the 28th year of the original term of copyright. If renewal registration is made during the 28th year of the original term of copyright, the renewal copyright vests in the name of the renewal claimant on the effective date of the renewal registration; the renewal certificate constitutes *prima facie* evidence as to the validity of the copyright during the renewed and extended term and of the facts stated in the certificate; and, the right to use the derivative work in the extended term may be affected. Request Circular 15, "Renewal of Copyright," for further information.

UNPUBLISHED, UNREGISTERED WORKS: Before 1978, if a work had been neither "published" in the legal sense nor registered in the Copyright Office, it was subject to perpetual protection under the common law. On January 1,1978, all works of this kind, subject to protection by copyright, were automatically brought under the federal copyright statute. The duration of copyright for these works can vary, but none of them will expire before December 31, 2002.

**Derivative Works**

In examining a copy (or a record, disk, or tape) for copyright information, it is important to determine whether that particular version of the work is an original edition of the work or a "new version." New versions include musical arrangements, adaptations, revised or newly edited editions, translations, dramatizations, abridgments, compilations, and works republished with new matter added. The law provides that derivative works, published or unpublished, are independently copyrightable and that the copyright in such a work does not affect or extend the protection, if any, in the underlying work. Under the 1909 law, courts have also held that the notice of copyright on a derivative work ordinarily need not include the dates or other information pertaining to the earlier works incorporated in it. This principle is specifically preserved in the present copyright law. Thus, if the copy (or the record, disk, or tape) constitutes a derivative version of the work, these points should be kept in mind:

- The date in the copyright notice is not necessarily an indication of when copyright in all the material in the work will expire. Some of the material may already be in the public domain, and some parts of the work may expire sooner than others.

- Even if some of the material in the derivative work is in the public domain and free for use, this does not mean that the "new" material added to it can be used without permission from the owner of copyright in the derivative work. It may be necessary to compare editions to determine what is free to use and what is not.

- Ownership of rights in the material included in a derivative work and in the preexisting work upon which it may be based may differ, and permission obtained from the owners of certain parts of the work may not authorize the use of other parts.

**The Name in the Copyright Notice**

Under the copyright statute in effect before 1978, the notice was required to include "the name of the copyright proprietor." The present act requires that the notice include "the name of the owner of copyright in the work, or an abbreviation by which the name can be recognized, or a generally known alternative designation of the owner." The name in the notice (sometimes in combination with the other statements on the copy, records, disk, tape, container, or label) often gives persons wishing to use the work the information needed to identify the owner from whom licenses or permission can be sought. In other cases, the name provides a starting point for a search in the Copyright Office records or catalogs, as explained at the beginning of this circular.

In the case of works published before 1978, copyright registration is made in the name of the individual person or the entity identified as the copyright owner in the notice. For works published on or after January 1, 1978, registration is made in the name of the person or entity owning all the rights on the date the registration is made. This may or may not be the name appearing in the notice. In addition to its records of copyright registration, the Copyright Office maintains extensive records of assignments, exclusive licenses, and other documents dealing with copyright ownership.

**Ad Interim**

*Ad interim* copyright was a special short-term copyright that applied to certain books and periodicals in the English language that were first manufactured and published outside the United States. It was a partial exception to the manufacturing requirements of the previous U.S. copyright law. Its purpose was to secure temporary

U.S. protection for a work, pending the manufacture of an edition in the United States. The *ad interim* requirements changed several times over the years and were subject to a number of exceptions and qualifications.

The manufacturing provisions of the copyright act expired on July 1,1986, and are no longer a part of the copyright law. The transitional and supplementary provisions of the act provide that for any work in which *ad interim* copyright was subsisting or capable of being secured on December 31, 1977, copyright protection would be extended for a term compatible with the other works in which copyright was subsisting on the effective date of the new act. Consequently, if the work was first published on or after July 1, 1977, and was eligible for *ad interim* copyright protection, the provisions of the present copyright act will be applicable to the protection of these works. Anyone investigating the copyright status of an English-language book or periodical first published outside the United States before July 1,1977, should check carefully to determine:

- Whether the manufacturing requirements were applicable to the work; and

- If so, whether the *ad interim* requirements were met.

---

## FOR FURTHER INFORMATION

---

**Information via the Internet:** Frequently requested circulars, announcements, regulations, other related materials, and all copyright application forms are available via the Internet. You may access these via the Copyright Office homepage at www.loc.gov/copyright.

**Information by fax:** Circulars and other information (but not application forms) are available by Fax-on-Demand at (202)707-2600.

**Information by telephone:** For general information about copyright, call the Copyright Public Information Office at (202)707-3000. The TTY number is (202)707-6737. Information specialists are on duty from 8:30 a.m. to 5:00 p.m., eastern time, Monday through Friday, except federal holidays. Recorded information is available 24 hours a day. Or, if you know which application forms and circulars you want, request them from the Forms and Publications Hotline at (202)707-9100 24 hours a day. Leave a recorded message.

**Information by regular mail:** Write to:

Library of Congress
Copyright Office
Publications Section, LM-455
101 Independence Avenue, S.E.
Washington, D.C. 20559-6000

**search request form**

Library of Congress
Copyright Office
101 Independence Avenue, S.E.
Washington, D.C.
20559-6000

Reference & Bibliography
Section
(202) 707-6850
8:30 a.m. to 5 p.m., Monday
through Friday, eastern time

**Type of work:**

☐ Book   ☐ Music   ☐ Motion Picture   ☐ Drama   ☐ Sound Recording   ☐ Computer Program
☐ Photograph/Artwork   ☐ Map   ☐ Periodical   ☐ Contribution   ☐ Architectural Work   ☐ Mask Work

**Search information you require:**

☐ Registration   ☐ Renewal   ☐ Assignment   ☐ Address

**Specifics of work to be searched:**

TITLE:

AUTHOR:

COPYRIGHT CLAIMANT:
(name in © notice)

APPROXIMATE YEAR DATE OF PUBLICATION/CREATION:

REGISTRATION NUMBER (if known):

OTHER IDENTIFYING INFORMATION:

If you need more space please attach additional pages.

*Estimates are based on the Copyright Office fee of $65* an **hour or fraction of an hour** consumed. The more information you furnish as a basis for the search, the better service we can provide. The time between the date of receipt of your fee for the search and your receiving a report will vary from 8 to 12 weeks depending on workload.*

**Names, titles, and short phrases are not copyrightable.**

Please read Circular 22 for more information on copyright searches.

YOUR NAME:                                                                        DATE:

ADDRESS:

DAYTIME TELEPHONE NO. (     )

Convey results of estimate/search by telephone                Fee enclosed? ☐ yes   Amount $
☐ yes   ☐ no                                                                 ☐ no

**\* NOTE: Registration filing fees and search fees are effective through June 30, 2002. For information on the fee changes, please write the Copyright Office, check the Copyright Office Website at www.loc.gov/copyright, or call (202) 707-3000.**

**Library of Congress • Copyright Office • 101 Independence Avenue, S.E. • Washington, D.C. 20559-6000**
**http://www.loc.gov/copyright**

June 1999—20,000
WEB REV: June 1999        PRINTED ON RECYCLED PAPER                        ☼ U.S. GOVERNMENT PRINTING OFFICE: 1999 454-879/21

# REPORT 1.1

## THOMSON & THOMSON'S SEARCH OF THE COPYRIGHT OFFICE ON THE NAME, "ALBERT JOSEPH KOHN."

SAMPLE REPORT
July 20, 1995

### Author/Claimant Search - ALBERT JOSEPH KOHN

A search of the records of the Copyright Office reveals the following copyright registrations and subsequent renewal information in connection with **ALBERT JOSEPH KOHN, ALBERT KOHN, AL KOHN** and/or **AL KOHN MUSIC** as the author and/or copyright claimant.

Our search reveals the following copyright registrations and subsequent renewals identifying **ALBERT JOSEPH KOHN** as the author and/or copyright claimant:

ONE LONELY NIGHT
Alternate Title:
Description:  Unpublished musical composition
Author:  Music by Albert Joseph Kohn
Application Author:
Copyright Claimant:  Albert Joseph Kohn
Date of Publication:
Date of Registration (if unpublished): May 16, 1934
Registration Number:  EU: 87617
New Matter:
Notes:  With Pf. acc.
Renewal Claimant:  No record of renewal is found

Our search reveals the following copyright registrations and subsequent renewals identifying **ALBERT KOHN** as the author and/or copyright claimant:

ACCIDENTS
Alternate Title:
Description:  Musical composition
Author:  Words and music by John Keen, arrangement by Albert Kohn
Application Author:  Track Music, Inc., employer for hire of Albert Kohn
Copyright Claimant:  Fabulous Music, Ltd.
Date of Publication:  January 25, 1971
Date of Registration (if unpublished):
Registration Number:  EP: 282175
New Matter:  Arrangement for piano
Notes:  Application states previously registered July 30, 1970, under entry No. EU: 197941.  In Tunderclap Newman-- Hollywood Dream.
Renewal Claimant: N/A

HOLLYWOOD DREAM
Alternate Title:
Description:  Musical composition
Author:  Music by Jimmy McCulloch, arrangement by Albert Kohn
Application Author:  Track Music, Inc., employer for hire of
Albert Kohn
Copyright Claimant:  Fabulous Music, Ltd.
Date of Publication:  January 25, 1971
Date of Registration (if unpublished):
Registration Number:  EP: 282176
New Matter:  Arrangement for piano
Notes:  Application states previously registered July 30,
1970, under entry No. EU: 197943.  In Tunderclap Newman--
Hollywood Dream.
Renewal Claimant: N/A

HOLLYWOOD 1
Alternate Title:
Description:  Musical composition
Author:  Words and music by John Keen, arrangement by Albert
Kohn
Application Author:  Track Music, Inc., employer for hire of
Albert Kohn
Copyright Claimant:  Fabulous Music, Ltd.
Date of Publication:  January 25, 1971
Date of Registration (if unpublished):
Registration Number:  EP: 282180
New Matter:  Arrangement for piano
Notes:  Application states previously registered July 30,
1970, under entry No. EU: 197946.  In Tunderclap Newman--
Hollywood Dream.
Renewal Claimant: N/A

HOLLYWOOD 2
Alternate Title:
Description:  Musical composition
Author:  Words and music by John Keen, arrangement by Albert
Kohn
Application Author:  Track Music, Inc., employer for hire of
Albert Kohn
Copyright Claimant:  Fabulous Music, Ltd.
Date of Publication:  January 25, 1971
Date of Registration (if unpublished):
Registration Number:  EP: 282181
New Matter:  Arrangement for piano
Notes:  Application states previously registered July 30,
1970, under entry No. EU: 197947.  In Tunderclap Newman--
Hollywood Dream.
Renewal Claimant: N/A

I DON'T KNOW
Alternate Title:
Description:  Musical composition
Author:  Words and music by John Keen, arrangement by Albert
Kohn

Author/Claimant Search - ALBERT JOSEPH KOHN

Application Author:  Track Music, Inc., employer for hire of
Albert Kohn
Copyright Claimant:  Fabulous Music, Ltd.
Date of Publication:  January 25, 1971
Date of Registration (if unpublished):
Registration Number:  EP: 282182
New Matter:  Arrangement for piano
Notes:  Application states previously registered July 30,
1970, under entry No. EU: 197940.  In Tunderclap Newman--
Hollywood Dream.
Renewal Claimant: N/A

IT'S TIME FOR A CHANGE
Alternate Title:
Description:  Unpublished musical composition
Author:  Kevin Beverly and Albert Kohn
Application Author:  Lyrics and music arranged by Kevin A.
Beverly, lyrics by Albert Kohn
Copyright Claimant:  Kevin A. Beverly and Albert Kohn
Date of Creation:  1980
Date of Publication:
Date of Registration (if unpublished):  November 17, 1980
Registration Number:  PAU: 248-662
New Matter:
Notes:
Renewal Claimant:  N/A

KOLAN KOLOZALZ
Alternate Title:
Description:  Unpublished musical composition
Author:  Al Kohn and Mike Lanni
Application Author:  Music and words to 1 song by Albert Kohn,
words by Michael Lanni
Copyright Claimant:  Albert Kohn and Michael Lanni
Date of Creation:  1984
Date of Publication:
Date of Registration (if unpublished):  March 13, 1984
Registration Number:  PAU: 596-861
New Matter:
Notes:  Collection of songs
Renewal Claimant:  N/A

LOOK AROUND
Alternate Title:
Description:  Musical composition
Author:  Words and music by John Keen, arrangement by Albert
Kohn
Application Author:  Track Music, Inc., employer for hire of
Albert Kohn
Copyright Claimant:  Fabulous Music, Ltd.

**Author/Claimant Search - ALBERT JOSEPH KOHN**

Date of Publication:  January 25, 1971
Date of Registration (if unpublished):
Registration Number:  EP: 282178
New Matter:  Arrangement for piano
Notes:  Application states previously registered July 30,
1970, under entry No. EU: 197949.  In Tunderclap Newman--
Hollywood Dream.
Renewal Claimant: N/A

OLD CORNMILL
Alternate Title:
Description:  Musical composition
Author:  Words and music by John Keen, arrangement by Albert
Kohn
Application Author:  Track Music, Inc., employer for hire of
Albert Kohn
Copyright Claimant:  Fabulous Music, Ltd.
Date of Publication:  January 25, 1971
Date of Registration (if unpublished):
Registration Number:  EP: 282184
New Matter:  Arrangement for piano
Notes:  Application states previously registered July 30,
1970, under entry No. EU: 197945.  In Tunderclap Newman--
Hollywood Dream.
Renewal Claimant: N/A

REASON
Alternate Title:
Description:  Musical composition
Author:  Words and music by John Keen, arrangement by Albert
Kohn
Application Author:  Track Music, Inc., employer for hire of
Albert Kohn
Copyright Claimant:  Fabulous Music, Ltd.
Date of Publication:  January 25, 1971
Date of Registration (if unpublished):
Registration Number:  EP: 282183
New Matter:  Arrangement for piano
Notes:  Application states previously registered July 30,
1970, under entry No. EU: 197948.  In Tunderclap Newman--
Hollywood Dream.
Renewal Claimant: N/A

THESE DAYS
Alternate Title:  Application title:  I'VE BEEN OUT WALKING
Description:  Musical composition
Author:  Words and music by Jackson Browne, arrangement by
Albert Kohn
Application Author:  Warner Tamerland Publishing Corporation,
employer for hire of Albert Kohn

Author/Claimant Search - ALBERT JOSEPH KOHN

Copyright Claimant:  Warner Tamerlane Publishing Corporation
Date of Publication:  May 17, 1971
Date of Registration (if unpublished):
Registration Number:  EP: 314354
New Matter:  Piano accompaniment with guitar chords
Notes:  In Tom Rush/Wrong End of the Tainbow.  Previously
registered Jnauary 12, 1967, under entry No. EU: 974715.
Renewal Claimant: N/A

WEDDING WALTZ
Alternate Title:
Description:  Musical composition
Author:  Music by Nick D'Amico, Gil Mills and Billy Faber,
arrangement by Albert Kohn
Application Author:
Copyright Claimant:  Leeds Music Corp.
Date of Publication:  June 16, 1947
Date of Registration (if unpublished):
Registration Number:  EP: 15091
New Matter:
Notes:  Piano-conductor score (orchestra) and parts
Renewal Claimant:  No record of renewal is found

WHEN I THINK
Alternate Title:
Description:  Musical composition
Author:  Words and music by John Keen, arrangement by Albert
Kohn
Application Author:  Track Music, Inc., employer for hire of
Albert Kohn
Copyright Claimant:  Fabulous Music, Ltd.
Date of Publication:  January 25, 1971
Date of Registration (if unpublished):
Registration Number:  EP: 282177
New Matter:  Arrangement for piano
Notes:  Application states previously registered July 30,
1970, under entry No. EU: 197944.  In Tunderclap Newman--
Hollywood Dream.
Renewal Claimant: N/A

WHEN THE SAINTS GO MARCHING ON
Alternate Title:
Description:  Musical composition
Author:  Traditional arrangement by Albert Kohn
Application Author:
Copyright Claimant:  Kohn Music Corp.
Date of Publication:  October 1, 1964
Date of Registration (if unpublished):
Registration Number:  EP: 192778
New Matter:  Piano arrangement

Author/Claimant Search - ALBERT JOSEPH KOHN

Notes:  With words
Renewal Claimant:  MCA Music, a division of MCA, Inc.
Capacity:  Proprietor of copyright in a work made for hire
Date of Renewal:  March 6, 1975
Renewal No.:  R: 599676

WILD COUNTRY
Alternate Title:
Description:  Musical composition
Author:  Words and music by John Keen, arrangement by Albert
Kohn
Application Author:  Track Music, Inc., employer for hire of
Albert Kohn
Copyright Claimant:  Fabulous Music, Ltd.
Date of Publication:  January 25, 1971
Date of Registration (if unpublished):
Registration Number:  EP: 282179
New Matter:  Arrangement for piano
Notes:  Application states previously registered July 30,
1970, under entry No. EU: 197950.  In Tunderclap Newman--
Hollywood Dream.
Renewal Claimant: N/A

      In addition, we also find the following books listing
ALBERT KOHN as the author and/or claimant:

CREATION LITTERAIRE ER CONNAISSANCE ESSAIS EDITION ET
INTRODUCTION (DICHTEN UND ERKENNEN)
Alternate Title:
Description:  Book
Author:  Hannah Arendt, translated from German by Albert Kohn
Application Author:
Copyright Claimant:  Editions Gallimard
Date of Publication:  November 25, 1966
Date of Registration (if unpublished):
Registration Number:  AFO: 50214
New Matter:
Notes:  Copyright is claimed on translation
Renewal Claimant:  No record of renewal is found

GRANDEUR INCONNUE; BOOK BY JEUNESSE, LETTRES A WILLA MUIR (DIE
UNBEKANNTE GROSSE), LA
Alternate Title:
Description:  Book, Du monde entier
Author:  Edition er introd. by Ernst Schonwiese, translated
from German by Albert Kohn
Application Author:
Copyright Claimant:  Editions Gallimard
Date of Publication:  March 20, 1968
Date of Registration (if unpublished):

Author/Claimant Search · ALBERT JOSEPH KOHN

Registration Number:  AFO: 54333
New Matter:
Notes:  Copyright is claimed on translation
Renewal Claimant:  N/A

MONTE DE VIRGILE (DER TOD DES VERGIL), LA
Alternate Title:
Description:  Musical composition
Author:  Translated from German by Albert Kohn
Application Author:
Copyright Claimant:  Librairie Gallimard
Date of Publication:  February 25, 1955
Date of Registration (if unpublished):
Registration Number:  AFO: 17201
New Matter:
Notes:
Renewal Claimant: No record of renewal is found

ROMAN D'NEHRI IV (LA GUERRIER PACIFIQUE), LE
Alternate Title:  Original title:  DIE VOLLENDUNG DES KOENIGS
HENRI QUATRE
Description:  Book
Author:  Translated from German by Albert Kohn
Application Author:
Copyright Claimant:  Editions Gallimard
Date of Publication:  May 20, 1972
Date of Registration (if unpublished):
Registration Number:  AFO: 69664
New Matter:
Notes:  Copyright is claimed on translation
Renewal Claimant: N/A

ROMAN D'NEHRI IV (LA JEUNESSE DU ROI), LE
Alternate Title:  Original title:  DIE JUGEND DES KOENIGS
HENRI QUATRE
Description:  Book
Author:  Translated from German by Albert Kohn
Application Author:
Copyright Claimant:  Editions Gallimard
Date of Publication:  January 1, 1972
Date of Registration (if unpublished):
Registration Number:  AFO: 67821
New Matter:
Notes:  Copyright is claimed on translation
Renewal Claimant: N/A

ROMAN D'NEHRI IV (LE METIER DE ROI), LE
Alternate Title:  Original title:  DIE VOLLENDUNG DES KOENIGS
HENRI QUATRE
Description:  Book

Author/Claimant Search - ALBERT JOSEPH KOHN

Author:   Translated from German by Albert Kohn
Application Author:
Copyright Claimant:   Editions Gallimard
Date of Publication:   March 30, 1972
Date of Registration (if unpublished):
Registration Number:   AFO: 69253
New Matter:
Notes:   Copyright is claimed on translation
Renewal Claimant: N/A

SOMNAMBULES (DIE SCHLAFWANDLER) 3: HUGUENAU ON LE REALISME,
LES
Alternate Title:
Description:   Book
Author:   Translated from German by Albert Kohn
Application Author:
Copyright Claimant:   Librairie Gallimard
Date of Publication:   January 15, 1957
Date of Registration (if unpublished):
Registration Number:   AFO: 22145
New Matter:
Notes:
Renewal Claimant:   No record of renewal is found

VIE COMBATIVE (STREITBAUS LEBER), UNE
Alternate Title:
Description:   Book, Connaissance de soi
Author:   Translated from German by Albert Kohn
Application Author:
Copyright Claimant:   Editions Gallimard
Date of Publication:   March 30, 1964
Date of Registration (if unpublished):
Registration Number:   AFO: 41993
New Matter:
Notes:
Renewal Claimant:   No record of renewal is found

VIES POLIQUESTI
Alternate Title:   Original title:   MEN IN DARK TIMES
Description:   Book
Author:   Hanna Arendt, translated from German by Eric Adda,
Jacques Bontemps, Barbara Cassin, Didier Don, Albert Kohn,
Patrick Levy and Agnes Oppenheimer-Faure
Application Author:
Copyright Claimant:   Editions Gallimard
Date of Publication:   October 30, 1974
Date of Registration (if unpublished):
Registration Number:   AFO: 79399

Author/Claimant Search - ALBERT JOSEPH KOHN

New Matter:
Notes:  Copyright is claimed on translation.
Renewal Claimant: N/A

     Our search reveals the following copyright registrations
and subsequent renewals identifying AL KOHN as the author
and/or copyright claimant:

ART OF MUSIC
Alternate Title:
Description:  Textual work
Author:  Al Kohn and Bob Kohn
Application Author:
Copyright Claimant:  Al Kohn and Bob Kohn
Date of Creation:  1992
Date of Publication:  October 27, 1992
Date of Registration (if unpublished):  March 23, 1993
Registration Number:  TX: 3-507-365
New Matter:  Additions, compilation
Notes:
Renewal Claimant:  N/A

AT THE ZOO
Alternate Title:
Description:  Unpublished musical composition
Author:  Words and music by Paul Simon, piano-vocal
arrangement by Al Kohn
Application Author:  Paul Simon, employer for hire
Copyright Claimant:  Paul Simon
Date of Publication:  May 31, 1967
Date of Registration (if unpublished):
Registration Number:  EP: 232807
New Matter:  Arrangement
Notes:  Application states previously registered February 28,
1967, under entry No. EU: 983206.  In "Songs by Paul Simon."
Renewal Claimant:  This registration is up for renewal this
year, however, no application has been filed as yet

AUCTION FROLIC
Alternate Title:
Description:  Musical composition
Author:  Al Kohn
Application Author:
Copyright Claimant:  Al Kohn Music
Date of Publication:  February 14, 1953
Date of Registration (if unpublished):
Registration Number:  EP: 69786
New Matter:
Notes:  For piano
Renewal Claimant:  No record of renewal is found

Author/Claimant Search  - ALBERT JOSEPH KOHN

AWAKEN LOVE
Alternate Title:
Description:  Unpublished musical composition
Author:  Words and music by Bob Jaxon and Al Kohn
Application Author:
Copyright Claimant:  Leo Feist, Inc.
Date of Publication:
Date of Registration (if unpublished):  August 5, 1957
Registration Number:  EU: 488382
New Matter:
Notes:
Renewal Claimant:  Bob Jaxon
Capacity:  Author
Date of Renewal:  January 3, 1985
Renewal No.:  RE: 248-147

BIG, BRIGHT GREEN PLEASURE MACHINE
Alternate Title:
Description:  Musical composition
Author:  Words and music by Paul Simon, piano-vocal
arrangement by Al Kohn
Application Author:  Paul Simon, employer for hire
Copyright Claimant:  Paul Simon
Date of Publication:  May 31, 1967
Date of Registration (if unpublished):
Registration Number:  EP: 232817
New Matter:
Notes:  Copyright is claimed on arrangement.  Application
states previously registered October 4, 1966, under entry No.
EU: 961603.  In "Songs by Paul Simon."
Renewal Claimant:  This registration is up for renewal this
year, however, no application has been filed as yet

BIG YELLOW TAXI
Alternate Title:
Description:  Musical composition
Author:  Words and music by Joni Mitchell, arrangement by Al
Kohn
Application Author:  WB Music Corp., employer for hire of Al
Kohn
Copyright Claimant:  Siquomb Pub. Corp.
Date of Publication:  May 5, 1970
Date of Registration (if unpublished):
Registration Number:  EP: 296797
New Matter:  Piano accompaniment and guitar chords
Notes:  Application states previously registered January 7,
1970, under entry No. EU: 155770
Renewal Claimant:  N/A

Author/Claimant Search · ALBERT JOSEPH KOHN

CLASS OF '63
Alternate Title:
Description:  Musical composition
Author:  Words and music by mark Charron, arrangement by Al
Kohn
Application Author:  Viva Music, Inc., employer for hire of Al
Kohn
Copyright Claimant:  Viva Music, Inc.
Date of Publication:  April 21, 1969
Date of Registration (if unpublished):
Registration Number:  EP: 354672
New Matter:  Piano/vocal arrangement with guitar chords
Notes:  Previously registered January 14, 1969, under entry
No. EU: 93342
Renewal Claimant: N/A

CLOUDY
Alternate Title:
Description:  Musical composition
Author:  Words and music by Paul Simon, piano-vocal
arrangement by Al Kohn
Application Author:  Paul Simon, employer for hire
Copyright Claimant:  Paul Simon
Date of Publication:  May 31, 1967
Date of Registration (if unpublished):
Registration Number:  EP: 232808
New Matter:
Notes:  Copyright is claimed on arrangement.  Application
states previously registered October 4, 1966, under entry No.
EU: 961604.  In "Songs by Paul Simon."
Renewal Claimant:  This registration is up for renewal this
year, however, no application has been filed as yet

DAY GIG
Alternate Title:
Description:  Musical composition
Author:  Words and music by Sonny Curtis and Jerry Allison,
arrangement by Al Kohn
Application Author:  Viva Music, Inc., employer for hire of Al
Kohn
Copyright Claimant:  Viva Music, Inc.
Date of Publication:  April 21, 1969
Date of Registration (if unpublished):
Registration Number:  EP: 354674
New Matter:  Piano/vocal arrangement with guitar chords
Notes:  in "Songs for all Seasons."  Previously registered
January 14, 1969, under entry No. EU: 93341
Renewal Claimant: N/A

Author/Claimant Search - ALBERT JOSEPH KOHN

DAYS
Alternate Title:
Description:  Musical composition
Author:  Words and music by Anthony Paul Byrne, arrangement by
Al Kohn
Application Author:  Viva Music, Inc., employer for hire of Al
Kohn
Copyright Claimant:  Viva Music, Inc.
Date of Publication:  April 21, 1969
Date of Registration (if unpublished):
Registration Number:  EP: 354673
New Matter:  Piano/vocal arrangement with guitar chords
Notes:  Previously registered November 21, 1968, under entry
No. EU: 86264.  In "Songs for all Seasons, Book No. 01."
Renewal Claimant: N/A

FAKIN' IT
Alternate Title:
Description: Musical composition
Author:  Words and music by Paul Simon, arrangement by Al Kohn
Application Author:  Paul Simon, employer for hire
Copyright Claimant:  Paul Simon
Date of Publication:  August 14, 1967
Date of Registration (if unpublished):
Registration Number:  EP: 237967
New Matter:  Complete piano part
Notes:  Application states previously registered July 7, 1967,
under entry No. EU: 3352.
Renewal Claimant:  This registration is up for renewal this
year, however, no application has been filed as yet

59TH STREET BRIDGE SONG (FEELIN' GROOVY)
Alternate Title:
Description:  Musical composition
Author:  Words and music by Paul Simon, arrangement by Al Kohn
Application Author:  Paul Simon, employer for hire
Copyright Claimant:  Paul Simon
Date of Publication:  March 17, 1967
Date of Registration (if unpublished):
Registration Number:  EP: 229687
New Matter:
Notes:  Copyright is claimed on arrangement.  Application
states previously registered October 4, 1966, under entry No.
EU: 961605
Renewal Claimant:  This registration is up for renewal this
year, however, no application has been filed as yet

FOR EMILY, WHENEVER I MAY FIND HER
Alternate Title:
Description:  Musical composition

Author/Claimant Search - ALBERT JOSEPH KOHN

Author:  Words and music by Paul Simon, piano-vocal
arrangement by Al Kohn
Application Author:  Paul Simon, employer for hire
Copyright Claimant:  Paul Simon
Date of Publication:  May 31, 1967
Date of Registration (if unpublished):
Registration Number:  EP: 232812
New Matter:
Notes:  Copyright is claimed on arrangement.  Application
states previously registered October 4, 1966, under entry No.
EU: 961606.  In "Songs by Paul Simon."
Renewal Claimant:  This registration is up for renewal this
year, however, no application has been filed as yet

FOR TOMORROW
Alternate Title:
Description:  Musical composition
Author:  Al Kohn
Application Author:
Copyright Claimant:  Al Kohn Music
Date of Publication:  May 20, 1952
Date of Registration (if unpublished):
Registration Number:  EP: 62781
New Matter:
Notes:  For piano
Renewal Claimant:  Al Kohn
Capacity:  Author
Date of Renewal:  December 29, 1980
Renewal No.:  RE: 85-151

GIVE IN
Alternate Title:
Description:  Musical composition
Author:  Words and music by Jerry Puller, arrangement by Al
Kohn
Application Author:  Viva Music, Inc., employer for hire of Al
Kohn
Copyright Claimant:  Viva Music, Inc.
Date of Publication:  April 21, 1969
Date of Registration (if unpublished):
Registration Number:  EP: 354665
New Matter:  Piano/vocal arrangement with guitar chords
Notes:  Previously registered October 30, 1968, under entry
No. EU: 81992.  In "Songs for all Seasons, Book 01."
Renewal Claimant: N/A

HAZY SHADE OF WINTER
Alternate Title:
Description:  Musical composition

Author/Claimant Search - ALBERT JOSEPH KOHN

Author:  Words and music by Paul Simon, piano-vocal
arrangement by Al Kohn
Application Author:  Paul Simon, employer for hire
Copyright Claimant:  Paul Simon
Date of Publication:  November 25, 1966
Date of Registration (if unpublished):
Registration Number:  EP: 225928
New Matter:  Arrangement, new musical notations
Notes:  Application states previously registered October 10,
1966, under entry No. EU: 961602
Renewal Claimant: Paul Simon
Capacity:  Claiming as author
Date of Renewal:  January 21, 1994
Renewal No.:  RE: 681-213

HEAVEN BELOW
Alternate Title:
Description:  Musical composition
Author:  Words and music by Jerry Fuller, arrangement by Al
Kohn
Application Author:  Viva Music, Inc., employer for hire of Al
Kohn
Copyright Claimant:  Viva Music, Inc.
Date of Publication:  April 21, 1969
Date of Registration (if unpublished):
Registration Number:  EP: 354666
New Matter:  Piano/vocal arrangement with guitar chords
Notes:  Previously registered April 10, 1969, under entry No.
EU: 109697
Renewal Claimant: N/A

HOT FUN IN THE SUMMERTIME
Alternate Title:
Description:  Musical composition
Author:  Words and music by Sylvester Stewart, arranged by Al
Kohn
Application Author:  Stone Flower Music, employer for hire of
Al Kohn
Copyright Claimant:  Stone Flower Music
Date of Publication:  October 14, 1969
Date of Registration (if unpublished):
Registration Number:  EP: 300215
New Matter:
Notes:  Copyright is claimed on arrangement.  Application
states previously registered August 21, 1969, under entry No.
EU: 146667
Renewal Claimant: N/A

HOW LITTLE MEN CARE
Alternate Title:

Author/Claimant Search - ALBERT JOSEPH KOHN

Description: Musical composition
Author: Words and music by Sonny Curtis, arrangement by Al
Kohn
Application Author: Viva Music, Inc., employer for hire of Al
Kohn
Copyright Claimant: Viva Music, Inc.
Date of Publication: April 21, 1969
Date of Registration (if unpublished):
Registration Number: EP: 354667
New Matter: Piano/vocal arrangement with guitar chords
Notes: Previously registered January 15, 1968, under entry
No. EU: 32678. In "Song for all Seasons, Book 01."
Renewal Claimant: N/A

I NEED YOU
Alternate Title:
Description: Musical composition
Author: Words and music by Gerry Beckley, arrangement by Al
Kohn
Application Author: WB Music Corp., employer for hire of Al
Kohn
Copyright Claimant: Kinney Music, Ltd.
Date of Publication: May 9, 1972
Date of Registration (if unpublished):
Registration Number: EP: 300216
New Matter: Piano accompaniment
Notes: Application states previously registered February 4,
1972, under entry No. EU: 314658.
Renewal Claimant: N/A

I WISH YOU COULD BE HERE
Alternate Title:
Description: Musical composition
Author: Words and music by Paul Simon and Bruce Woodley,
piano-vocal arrangement by Al Kohn
Application Author: Lorna Music Co., Ltd., employer for hire
of Al Kohn
Copyright Claimant: Lorna Music Co., Ltd.
Date of Publication: May 31, 1967
Date of Registration (if unpublished):
Registration Number: EP: 232810
New Matter: Arrangement
Notes: Application states previously registered January 18,
1967, under entry No. EU: 978970. In "Songs by Paul Simon."
Renewal Claimant: This registration is up for renewal this
year, however, no application has been filed as yet

LITTLE TEA ROOM
Alternate Title:
Description: Musical composition

Author/Claimant Search - ALBERT JOSEPH KOHN

Author:  Music by Al Kohn
Application Author:
Copyright Claimant:  Al Kohn Music
Date of Publication:  May 20, 1952
Date of Registration (if unpublished):
Registration Number:  EP: 62780
New Matter:
Notes:  For piano
Renewal Claimant:  Al Kohn
Capacity:  Author
Date of Renewal:  December 29, 1980
Renewal No.:  RE: 85-152

MAIN STREET
Alternate Title:
Description:  Musical composition
Author:  Words and music by Jimmy Griffin and Mike Gordon,
arrangement by Al Kohn
Application Author:  Stone Canyon Music, Inc., employer for
hire of Al Kohn
Copyright Claimant:  Stone Canyon Music, Inc.
Date of Publication:  April 21, 1969
Date of Registration (if unpublished):
Registration Number:  EP: 354668
New Matter:  Piano/vocal arrangement with guitar chords
Notes:  Previously published November 15, 1968, under entry
No. EP: 324567.  In "Songs for all Seasons, Book 01."
Renewal Claimant: N/A

MAIN STREET
Alternate Title:
Description:  Musical composition
Author:  Words and music by Jimmy Griffith and Mark Gordon,
arrangement by Al Kohn
Application Author:  Stone Canyon Music, Inc., employer for
hire of Al Kohn
Copyright Claimant:  Stone Canyon Music, Inc.
Date of Publication:  November 15, 1968 (in notice 1966 and
1968)
Date of Registration (if unpublished):
Registration Number:  EP: 324567
New Matter:  Piano with guitar chords, easy piano easy organ
arrangements
Notes:  Previously registered July 11, 1966, under entry No.
EU: 947514
Renewal Claimant: N/A

MARRAKESH EXPRESS
Alternate Title:
Description:  Musical composition

Author/Claimant Search - ALBERT JOSEPH KOHN

Author:  Words and music by Graham Nash, arrangement by Al
Kohn
Application Author:  WB Music Corp., employer for hire of Al
Kohn
Copyright Claimant:  Siquomb Pub. Corp.
Date of Publication:  September 10, 1969
Date of Registration (if unpublished):
Registration Number:  EP: 300214
New Matter:  Piano accompaniment
Notes:  Application states previously registered June 5, 1969,
under entry No. EU: 119528
Renewal Claimant: N/A

MELODEE
Alternate Title:
Description:  Musical composition
Author:  Words and music by Jerry Fuller, arrangement by Al
Kohn
Application Author:  Viva Music, Inc., employer for hire of Al
Kohn
Copyright Claimant:  Viva Music, Inc.
Date of Publication:  April 21, 1969
Date of Registration (if unpublished):
Registration Number:  EP: 354675
New Matter:  Piano/vocal arrangement with guitar chords
Notes:  Previously registered February 19, 1969, under entry
No. EU: 100634.  In "Songs for all Seasons, Book 01."
Renewal Claimant: N/A

MEMPHIS
Alternate Title:
Description:  Musical composition
Author:  Music by Chuck Berry, arrangement by Al Kohn
Application Author:
Copyright Claimant:  Arc Music Corp.
Date of Publication:  July 12, 1963
Date of Registration (if unpublished):
Registration Number:  EP: 177732
New Matter:  New arrangement with chords and harmony added
Notes:  Guitar and piano solo.  Application states previously
registered as MEMPHIS, TENN.
Renewal Claimant:  No record of renewal is found

MISTER MEMORY
Alternate Title:
Description:  Musical composition
Author:  Words and music by Christopher Quinn and Michael
Laurence, arrangement by Al Kohn
Application Author:
Copyright Claimant:  Gringo Music Company

Author/Claimant Search - **ALBERT JOSEPH KOHN**

Date of Publication:  April 21, 1969
Date of Registration (if unpublished):
Registration Number:  EP: 354676
New Matter:  Piano/vocal arrangement with guitar chords
Notes:  Previously registered December 2, 1969, under entry
No. 87646.  In "Songs for all Seasons, Book 01."
Renewal Claimant: N/A

MORE THAN I CAN SAY
Alternate Title:
Description:  Musical composition
Author:  Words and music by Sonny Curtis and Jerry Allison,
arrangement by Al Kohn
Application Author:  Viva Music, Inc., employer for hire of Al
Kohn
Copyright Claimant:  Viva Music, Inc.
Date of Publication:  April 21, 1969
Date of Registration (if unpublished):
Registration Number:  EP: 354669
New Matter:  Piano/vocal arrangement with guitar chords
Notes:  Previously registered March 22, 1960, under entry No.
EU: 617637, previously published March 23, 1961, under entry
No. EP: 327863.  In "Songs for all Seasons, Book 01."
Renewal Claimant: N/A

PATTERNS
Alternate Title:
Description:  Musical composition
Author:  Words and music by Paul Simon, piano-vocal
arrangement by Al Kohn
Application Author:  Charing Cross Music, employer for hire of
Al Kohn
Copyright Claimant:  Charing Cross Music
Date of Publication:  May 31, 1967
Date of Registration (if unpublished):
Registration Number:  EP: 232814
New Matter:
Notes:  Copyright is claimed on arrangement.  Application
states previously registered September 24, 1965, under entry
No. EP: 210630.  In "Songs by Paul Simon."
Renewal Claimant:  This registration is up for renewal this
year, however, no application has been filed as yet

POEM ON THE UNDERGROUND WALL
Alternate Title:
Description:  Musical composition
Author:  Words and music by Paul Simon, piano-vocal
arrangement by Al Kohn
Application Author:  Paul Simon, employer for hire
Copyright Claimant:  Paul Simon

Author/Claimant Search - ALBERT JOSEPH KOHN

Date of Publication:  May 31, 1967
Date of Registration (if unpublished):
Registration Number:  EP: 232813
New Matter:
Notes:  Copyright is claimed on arrangement.  Application
states previously registered October 4, 1966, under entry No.
EU: 961607.  In "Songs by Paul Simon."
Renewal Claimant:  This registration is up for renewal this
year, however, no application has been filed as yet

SCARBOROUGH FAIR/CANTICLE
Alternate Title:
Description:  Musical composition
Author:  Words and music by Paul Simon and Art Garfunkel,
piano-vocal arrangement by Al Kohn
Application Author:
Copyright Claimant:  Paul Simon
Date of Publication:  May 31, 1967
Date of Registration (if unpublished):
Registration Number:  EP: 232809
New Matter:
Notes:  Copyright is claimed on arrangement.  Application
states previously registered October 4, 1966, under entry No.
EU: 961608.  In "Songs by Paul Simon."
Renewal Claimant:  This registration is up for renewal this
year, however, no application has been filed as yet

7 O'CLOCK NEWS/SILENT NIGHT
Alternate Title:
Description:  Musical composition
Author:  Narration by Paul Simon, piano-vocal arrangement by
Al Kohn
Application Author:  Paul Simon, employer for hire
Copyright Claimant:  Paul Simon
Date of Publication:  November 25, 1966
Date of Registration (if unpublished):
Registration Number:  EP: 227325
New Matter:  Arrangement, new musical notations and narration
Notes:
Renewal Claimant: Paul Simon
Capacity:  Claiming as author
Date of Renewal:  January 21, 1994
Renewal No.:  RE: 660-893

SOMEDAY, ONE DAY
Alternate Title:
Description:  Musical composition
Author:  Words and music by Paul Simon, piano-vocal
arrangement by Al Kohn

Author/Claimant Search - ALBERT JOSEPH KOHN

Application Author:  Charing Cross Music, employer for hire of
Al Kohn
Copyright Claimant:  Charing Cross Music
Date of Publication:  May 31, 1967
Date of Registration (if unpublished):
Registration Number:   EP: 232816
New Matter:
Notes:  Copyright is claimed on the arrangement.  Application
states previously registered March 11, 1966, under entry No.
EP: 215473.  In "Songs by Paul Simon."
Renewal Claimant:  This registration is up for renewal this
year, however, no application has been filed as yet

TEACH YOUR CHILDREN
Alternate Title:
Description:  Musical composition
Author:  Words and music by Graham Nash, arrangement of piano
accompaniment and guitar chords by Al Kohn
Application Author:  Giving Room Music, Inc., employer for
hire of Al Kohn
Copyright Claimant:  Giving Room Music, Inc.
Date of Publication:  June 11, 1970
Date of Registration (if unpublished):
Registration Number:  EP: 296799
New Matter:  Piano accompaniment with guitar chords
Notes:  Application states previously registered 1970, under
entry No. EU: 162978.
Renewal Claimant: N/A

THREE TEARS FOR THE SAD, HURT AND BLUE
Alternate Title:
Description:  Musical composition
Author:  Words and music by Jerry Fuller, arrangement by Al
Kohn
Application Author:  Viva Music, Inc., employer for hire of Al
Kohn
Copyright Claimant:  Viva Music, Inc.
Date of Publication:  April 21, 1969
Date of Registration (if unpublished):
Registration Number:  EP: 354670
New Matter:  Piano/vocal arrangement with guitar chords
Notes:  Previously registered November 21, 1968, under entry
No. EU: 86263.  In "Songs for all Seasons, Book 01."
Renewal Claimant: N/A

TRAIN OF THOUGHT
Alternate Title:
Description:  Musical composition
Author:  Words and music by Jerry Fuller, arrangement by Al
Kohn

Author/Claimant Search - ALBERT JOSEPH KOHN

Application Author: Viva Music, Inc., employer for hire of Al Kohn
Copyright Claimant: Viva Music, Inc.
Date of Publication: April 21, 1969
Date of Registration (if unpublished):
Registration Number: EP: 354677
New Matter: Piano/vocal arrangement with guitar chords
Notes: Previously registered June 25, 1968, under entry No. EU: 60176. In "Songs for all Seasons, Book 01."
Renewal Claimant: N/A

WALK RIGHT BACK
Alternate Title:
Description: Musical composition
Author: Words and music by Sonny Curtisarrangement by Al Kohn
Application Author: Viva Music, Inc., employer for hire of Al Kohn
Copyright Claimant: Viva Music, Inc.
Date of Publication: April 21, 1969
Date of Registration (if unpublished):
Registration Number: EP: 354678
New Matter: Piano/vocal arrangement with guitar chords
Notes: Previously registered 1960, under entry No. EU: 652642. In "Songs for all Seasons, Book 01."
Renewal Claimant: N/A

WEDNESDAY MORNING, 3 A.M.
Alternate Title:
Description: Musical composition
Author: Words and music by Paul Simon, piano-vocal arrangement by Al Kohn
Application Author: Charing Cross Music, employer for hire of Al Kohn
Copyright Claimant: Charing Cross Music
Date of Publication: May 31, 1967
Date of Registration (if unpublished):
Registration Number: EP: 232811
New Matter:
Notes: Copyright is claimed on arrangement. Application states previously registered November 7, 1966, under entry No. EU: 966034. In "Songs by Paul Simon."
Renewal Claimant: This registration is up for renewal this year, however, no application has been filed as yet

Author/Claimant Search - ALBERT JOSEPH KOHN

WOMAN HELPING MAN
Alternate Title:
Description:  Musical composition
Author:  Words and music by Mark Charron, arrangement by Al Kohn
Application Author:  Viva Music, Inc., employer for hire of Al Kohn
Copyright Claimant:  Viva Music, Inc.
Date of Publication:  April 21, 1969
Date of Registration (if unpublished):
Registration Number:  EP: 354671
New Matter:  Piano/vocal arrangement with guitar chords
Notes:  Previously registered October 28, 1968, under entry No. EU: 81668.  In "Songs for all Seasons, Book 01."
Renewal Claimant: N/A

WOODSTOCK
Alternate Title:
Description:  Musical composition
Author:  Words and music by Joni Mitchell, arrangement by Al Kohn
Application Author:  WB Music Corp., employer for hire of Al Kohn
Copyright Claimant:  Siquomb Pub. Corp.
Date of Publication:  May 9, 1970 (in notice: 1969)
Date of Registration (if unpublished):
Registration Number:  EP: 296798
New Matter:  Piano accompaniment and guitar chords
Notes:  Application states previously registered October 22, 1969, under entry No. EU: 144626.
Renewal Claimant: N/A

YOU DON'T KNOW WHERE YOUR INTEREST LIES
Alternate Title:
Description:  Musical composition
Author:  Words and music by Paul Simon, piano-vocal arrangement by Al Kohn
Application Author:  Paul Simon, employer for hire
Copyright Claimant:  Paul Simon
Date of Publication:  May 31, 1967
Date of Registration (if unpublished):
Registration Number:  EP: 232815
New Matter:  Arrangement
Notes:  Application states previously registered January 18, 1967, under entry No. EU: 978969.  In "Songs by Paul Simon."
Renewal Claimant:  This registration is up for renewal this year, however, no application has been filed as yet

Author/Claimant Search - ALBERT JOSEPH KOHN

A search of the assignment files of the Copyright Office reveals the following documents identifying the above as a party thereto:

DOCUMENT DESCRIPTION: Instrument executed June 30, 1971
ASSIGNOR: Kohn Music Corp.
ASSIGNEE: Creston Music Co.
DATE OF RECORDATION: July 14, 1971
VOLUME/PAGE: Vol. 1422, pages 33-35
WORK(S): A GLISS TO REMEMBER and 39 others. A photocopy of the pertinent pages listing additional titles is attached for your reference.

DOCUMENT DESCRIPTION: Instrument executed July 1, 1979
ASSIGNOR: Danny O'Keffe by Al Kohn (Atty)
ASSIGNEE: Warner-Tamerlane Publishing Corporation and Road Cannon Music, Inc.
DATE OF RECORDATION: September 11, 1979
VOLUME/PAGE: Vol. 1748, pages 321-322
WORK(S): FLYING; GIVE ME THE MEDICINE; HAIR OF THE DOG; IT'S AN OLD SONG; RIDE, RIDE, RIDE; SEX AND MONEY; and YOU DON'T HAVE TO BE RIGHT

DOCUMENT DESCRIPTION: Assignment executed October 10, 1979
ASSIGNOR: Warner-Tamerlane Publishing Corporation by Al Kohn
ASSIGNEE: W B Music Corporation
DATE OF RECORDATION: October 22, 1979
VOLUME/PAGE: Vol. 1752, page 186
WORK(S): No titles given

The in-process records of the Copyright Office failed to reveal any pending applications or documents in connection with the above.

If we may be of any further assistance, or if you have any questions regarding this report, please do not hesitate to call me at 1-800-356-8630.

Sincerely yours,

Debra A. Paeth

DAP
Enclosures

## CHAPTER 2

# THE ART OF MUSIC PUBLISHING

## SUMMARY

# THE ART OF MUSIC PUBLISHING

**M** *usic publishing* is the activity of (1) promoting and licensing the performance and publication of musical compositions, (2) administering the legal protection of the compositions and the collection of income arising from such promotion and licensing, and (3) paying the songwriters their share of the collected income. During the heyday of Tin Pan Alley, beginning around the turn of the century through the 1940's, the hallmark of music publishing was the creative aspects of commercial song promotion: discovering songwriting talent, teaming up one songwriter with another, and getting a song performed or recorded by popular performing artists. Today, the music publisher more closely resembles an accountancy or law firm, with emphasis primarily on the administrative aspects of publishing. The future of music publishing hangs on the course of recent technological developments and the emergence of electronic commerce in intellectual property.

This chapter sketches the historical and legal background of music publishing, describes the major sources of music publishing income, and provides an overview of the division of music publishing income among music publishers and songwriters.

## I. HISTORICAL BACKGROUND

### A. Music Publishing in Early America

When John Smith and his fellow settlers established the first permanent English settlement at Jamestown, Virginia in 1607, they undoubtedly raised their spirits by singing verses from psalm books they brought with them from Europe. Though the first printing press in the colonies was installed at Harvard College in 1640, it was not until nearly the end of the 17th century that the colonies were enriched by their first printed music book. Published in 1698, the ninth edition of *The Bay Psalm Book,* derived from earlier English editions published by John Playford, was the first book printed in the United States that contained musical notation.

In 1712, the first of a series of musical instruction books appeared — written by Reverend John Tufts of Newburyport, Massachusetts, *An Introduction to the Singing of Psalm Tunes in a Plain and Easy Method with a Collection of Tunes in Three Parts*, which provided a musical notation that the author thought would be easier to read than what was available at the time. In 1764, Paul Revere and Joseph Flagg claimed that their new publication of a compilation of popular and religious music, engraved by Revere himself, was printed on the first paper made in America.

## B.  The First Professional Music Publishers in America

In 1793, Benjamin Carr moved his family from England and established the first music publishing firm in the United States, printing chiefly music that had become popular in England. Other music publishers were established in many of the major cities on the eastern seaboard.

During the year of 1814, following the burning of our nation's capitol, the Library of Congress, and the White House by the British, a young lawyer named Francis Scott Key made history by writing the *Star Spangled Banner*, which became our national anthem in 1931 by an act of the 71st Congress. The years spanning 1850 through 1860 were the most productive years of one of the greatest melodists America has ever produced: Stephen Collins Foster, who wrote *Oh! Susanna, Old Folks at Home, My Old Kentucky Home, Old Black Joe, Jeannie with the Light Brown Hair,* and *Come Where My Love Lies Dreaming.*

In 1866, Gustav Schirmer, the son of a German immigrant, after working various jobs in music importing and merchandising businesses, acquired control of Kerksieg and Breusing and opened up shop as G. Schirmer, Inc. His first interest was the day's most famous and controversial composer, Wagner, which set the tone for the firm's successful importation and printing of classical music.

With the development and increasing popularity of the piano, singing became a popular form of entertainment, and sales of printed sheet music of popular songs began to flourish. Music publishers of sheet music, sometimes no more than a printer with an interest in music, would hire traveling salesmen, some of whom could actually perform the music they promoted, to sell sheet music on a commission basis to the "general stores" located within the salesman's territory. It is estimated that, during the first 25 years of the 19th century, over 10,000 popular songs were published in the United States. By the end of the century, *After the Ball*, written and published by Charles K. Harris in 1893, became the first song to sell a million copies.

## C. Tin Pan Alley

As we approached this section of our history, we stopped to consider a passage by Cicero — "To remain ignorant of things that happened before you were born is to remain a child." The music business, more so than others, is a business that weaves relationships with deals. We could think of no better way to convey the texture of the music publishing industry as it existed in the early part of the 20th century than to provide the following chronicle of the place and time they called, *Tin Pan Alley*.

In 1880, after winning a toy printing press from school, Isidore, Julius and Jay Witmark, aged seventeen, thirteen, and eleven, opened a printing business in their home on West 40th Street in New York City. They earned a modest living printing Christmas cards. To augment his earnings, "Julie" became a performer of ballads in minstrel and variety shows. After achieving some success, Julie thought that if it were possible for him to establish hit songs for others, why couldn't he publish his own music? After all, Isidore could write songs, and they had a printing press on which to print the music. Since the brothers were still minors, they had their father, Marcus become director of the company, and thus, M. Witmark & Sons was established in 1886 as a publisher and printer of sheet music. After hearing a rumor that President Grover Cleveland was about to announce his engagement, Isidore went quick to work on a wedding march for the President and, upon the announcement, the Witmarks were the first to capitalize on the event.

Within a year after their establishment, the Witmarks purchased the song catalog of the New York Variety Publishing Company; a few years later, they acquired the Dobson Banjo Music catalog, and in 1892, with the acquisition of the Prophetic Catalogue, the Witmarks became the representatives for a number of important composers, among them Gussie L. Davis. They later acquired the song catalogs of Dave Marion, the Fred J. Hamill Company, B.D. Nice, Weber & Field, the Roger Brothers, including the songs of Maurice Levi. They also acquired the Gus Edwards catalog, including *Tammany* and *In My Merry Oldsmobile*, and the Sol Bloom catalog, including Hutchinson's *Sammy* and Arthur Penn's *Carrissma*. In 1903, Witmark hired a young pianist, Ernest R. Ball who wrote, with Irish musical star Chauncy Olcott, *Mother Machree* and *When Irish Eyes Are Smiling*, and with future mayor of New York City, James J. "Jimmy" Walker, *Will You Love Me In December As You Do In May?* Perhaps one of the Witmarks' most memorable hits at that time was *Sweet Adeline*, an *echo song* (i.e., one in which the title is echoed in every line of the lyric), which caught the attention of barbershop quartets.

In the late 1880's, Jerome H. Remick, a milkman, acquired a music publishing firm in Detroit known as Whitney-Warner Publishing Company and met success with hits such as *Creole Bells* and *Hiawatha*. In 1894, Remick moved his offices to New York City. Remick's offices were located near the corner of Fourteenth Street and Fourth Avenue, but Remick was soon drawn, along with other music publishers, to where the action was — the theaters and restaurants that were opening further uptown, around Twenty Eighth Street between Fifth Avenue and Broadway.

In 1886, Joseph Stern, a necktie salesman, and Edward B. Marks, a button salesman, formed a partnership called the Joseph W. Stern Company. Both, however, had a strong desire to write songs. Their first song, *The Little Lost Child*, relates the story of a lost little girl who meets a policeman. Upon returning the child to her mother, the policemen discovers that the girl's mother was his long lost wife. One day in 1894 the songwriters came across a new device invented by a Brooklyn electrician which could flash a series of photographs or drawings onto a wall. Hiring professional actors to produce slides dramatizing the story of *The Little Lost Child* and engaging professional singers to perform the song while the slides were being projected on a background screen, the writers produced a sensation that resulted in the sales of over a million copies of sheet music.

Other publishers soon copied this popular new way to plug their songs, and new publishers were opening up shop nearly every month. In 1896, Maurice Shapiro and Louis Bernstein, both from retailing businesses, formed Shapiro-Bernstein Publishing, and at about the same time, Leo Feist, a corset salesman and amateur songwriter, opened his doors with his famous slogan, "You can't go wrong with a Feist song." Harry Von Tilzer, born Harry Gumm in Detroit, Michigan, ran away from home at fourteen years of age to join the circus. Working for an itinerant theatrical company, Von Tilzer began a prolific songwriting career, writing his first hit, *My Old New Hampshire Home* which he sold to a printer named William C. Dunn. Dunn later sold out to Shapiro-Bernstein, who made Von Tilzer a staff writer and later a partner in the firm. Von Tilzer went on to write several million-copy selling songs, including *A Bird in a Gilded Cage.* In 1902, he formed his own publishing company.

The offices of nearly all of the major music publishing houses of that time began to congregate on that single street: Twenty Eighth Street between Fifth Avenue and Broadway, the street that became known, beginning around 1900, as "Tin Pan Alley." The appellation is believed to have been coined by Monroe Rosenfeld, a reporter for the *New York Herald*, who after meeting with Von Tilzer wrote a column about his experience in the 28th Street "alley" that reverberated the "tin pan" sounding cacophony of pianos blaring from the windows of the music publishing houses lined along the street.

In 1902, together with Maurice Shapiro, Remick established Shapiro-Remick & Company. In 1905, they sold several million copies of *In the Shade of the Old Apple Tree* (Harry Williams and Egbert van Alstyne), but by 1906, Shapiro split with Remick and Remick formed his own publishing company, Jerome H. Remick & Co., which went on to publish a string of hit songs, including *Pretty Baby* and *Your Eyes Have Told Me So.* In 1909, Remick published three ballads that sold more than a million copies, one being *Put On Your Old Grey Bonnet.* These were followed by other successes, including *Moonlight Bay* in 1912 and *When You Wore a Tulip* in 1914.

It was about this time that a young man by the name of George Gershwin came to Tin Pan Alley. In 1914, Remick hired Gershwin as a song plugger — his job was to perform the songs in the Remick catalog for theater managers, dance bands, and stores selling sheet music. He would sometimes play inside the stores for customers passing by. Sheet music was one of the prime sources of income for music publishers at the time and song plugging was an integral part of the Tin Pan Alley music publishing operation.

While working for Remick, Gershwin composed many songs hoping they would be published, but shortly after they finally published one, *Rialto Ripples* written in 1917 with lyricist Will Donaldson, he left Remick and Tin Pan Alley. He did not have much luck until he teamed up with Irving Caesar in 1919 to write *Swanee*,[1] which sold over two million records and one million copies of sheet music within a year after it was performed by Al Jolson. Although both Gershwin and Caesar signed up with Harms, Inc., Remick met the competition by signing such young talents as Harry Warren, Al Dubin, Gus Kahn, Richard Whiting and others.

A composer by the name of Harry Dacre came to the United States in 1891 with a bicycle for which he had to pay duty. William Jerome, a lyricist friend, met him at the pier and jokingly remarked that if Dacre came over with a bicycle built for two he would have to pay double duty. The phrase stuck in Dacre's mind and he used it for the first song he wrote in America. The song, *Bicycle Built for Two*, became an instant hit was published by Tom B. Harms in 1892.

Tom Harms became the first publisher to discover the profitability in printing the sheet music of successful Broadway shows. He published *The Bowery*, *Reuben, Reuben*, and *Push Them Clouds Away*, from the show, *A Trip to Chinatown*, in 1892. This was the first time a stage production in the United States proved an instant source of revenue for a music publisher.

Max Dreyfus joined the Tom B. Harms Company in 1901 as an arranger. He had a talent for lifting songs out of Broadway musicals and making them hits, but he also demonstrated a talent for placing many of the firm's songs in Broadway shows. This talent did not go unnoticed and he was soon promoted to an executive position with the firm. In 1904, Alex and Tom Harms left the company and Dreyfus, who by that time had acquired a 25% interest in the firm, not only

---

[1] For the rest of the story, see Chapter 11, *Print Licenses*.

became its head, but his creativity as a publisher made him one of the most influential figures in the music publishing business.

In 1905, Francis, Day & Hunter, Ltd., one of the larger British music publishing firms, opened an office in New York City. The firm soon discovered, however, that American writers and performers were too busy promoting their own material and English songs were never favored despite all of the efforts they made to promote them. As a result, Francis, Day & Hunter agreed to merge their American branch with the T.B. Harms firm, lead at the time by both Max and Louis Dreyfus. T.B. Harms and Francis Day & Hunter, Inc., was incorporated in 1908, with Fred Day, Max Dreyfus and Louis Dreyfus as equal shareholders, and the firm became the largest music publishing house in America at the time.

In 1920, William Boosey of Chappell & Co., Ltd. Approached Max and Louis Dreyfus to take over the business of Chappell & Co. Inc. in New York under a long term contract. In return, Chappell & Co., Ltd. would become the subpublisher of the catalog of T.B. Harms for the territory of Great Britain.

Max Dreyfus was a master at signing up successful talented song pluggers, hiring, for example, a nineteen year old Jerome Kern. Kern's job was to play the piano and sell songs at department stores such as R.H. Macy's in New York City. He also served as a rehearsal pianist for Broadway musicals. Kern's talent as a composer soon made music critics take notice. Kern became such a top contributor to the T.B. Harms catalog that Max Dreyfus gave him a partnership interest in the firm.

In 1917, Kern wrote some special material for a Victor Herbert show, *Miss 1917*. Kern was so impressed with its rehearsal pianist that he insisted that Max Dreyfus meet him. Dreyfus, therefore, arranged a time to meet this young pianist who turned out to be George Gershwin. Dreyfus hired Gershwin on the spot just to write songs and gave him a salary of $35 per week.

Like Jerome Kern and George Gershwin, Vincent Youmans became another Max Dreyfus discovery, and was also employed as a staff pianist and song plugger. As M. Witmark & Sons had the big three operetta composers, Victor Herbert, Sigmund Romberg and Rudolf Friml, so Max Dreyfus had the new popular Broadway musical writers, Jerome Kern, George Gershwin, and Vincent Youmans.

In 1925, the young members of the Theater Guild put on an intimate revue to raise money for draperies and curtains for a new Broadway theater. Richard Rodgers and Lorenz Hart contributed several songs to the successful performance. Max Dreyfus called Rodgers and Hart into his office to sign exclusive songwriter agreements with Harm, Inc. In 1924, Cole Porter contributed five songs to the Greenwich Village Follies, but it wasn't until 1928 when Irene Bordoni's rendition of *Let's Do It* in her provocative French accent caused Max Dreyfus to add another composer to his already well stocked staff of writers.

By the end of the 1920's the Harms, Inc. office at 62 West 45th Street became a "club" were composers made it a habit to meet at noon for "shoptalk" and listen to George Gershwin play the piano. Harms, Inc. had become the top Broadway music publisher, whose songwriting staff also included Arthur Schwartz, Bert Kalmer, E.Y. Harburg, Irving Caesar, Harry Ruby, Herman Hupfeld, Howard Dietz, Vernon Duke and Ira Gershwin.

On October 6, 1927, a startled audience at New York's Warner Theater watched and heard Al Jolson utter his famous, "Wait a minute, wait a minute, you ain't heard nothin' yet. Wait a minute, I tell ya, you ain't heard nothin'." Within months after his release of the first "talking picture," *The Jazz Singer*, film producer Jack Warner foresaw the great importance that music would play in the making of talkies. By the end of 1929, Warner Bros. had purchased the entire catalogs of M. Witmark & Sons, Remick Music Corporation, and Max Dreyfus's Harms, Inc. Tin Pan Alley would never be the same.

## II. MUSIC PUBLISHING TODAY

Today, music publishers can be classified into three main categories delineated primarily by size: (1) the major worldwide publisher, (2) the independent music publisher, and (3) the self-publishing songwriter.

The largest publishers in the first of the above categories would include Warner/Chappell Music (owned by AOL Time Warner), EMI Music (owned by Thorn/EMI), each with catalogs in excess of 500,000 songs. Other major worldwide publishing companies include

MCA Music (owned by Universal Music Group.), Sony Music (formerly CBS Music), and BMG Music (owned by Bertelsmann Music Group). A small group of major publishers are those such as Polygram Music, Virgin Music, and Chrysalis Music who are affiliated with major record companies.

There are a large group of publishers who would fall in the category of independent music publisher, who publish music written by others, but leave the mechanical aspects of publishing administration to others. These independent publishers engage in some creative activities, but many of them, at their core, perform the function of administering the administrators — that is, they may contract with one of the major worldwide publishers to perform their administration functions on a worldwide basis or they may engage one of the majors to administer their rights in the U.S. and separately contract with music publishers around the world for local overseas administration. Examples of independent music publishers include Peermusic Publishing, Zomba Music, Irving/Almo Music, and Jobette Music. Many motion picture studios and production companies have their own music publishing companies which are used to administer the compositions written for their motion pictures and television programs.

The third category is the writer who maintains his own publishing rights and sets up his own publishing company. These may include popular recording artists who write their own material and don't require the creative services of a major or independent publisher. Examples include Bob Dylan, Bruce Springsteen, and Neil Diamond. Often, the objective of these composer/publishers is to get the best administration at the lowest possible price, and, to that end, enter into administration deals directly with the majors and overseas music publishers. The terms of administration agreements are discussed in Chapter 4. The vast majority of music publishers existing today are in this third category.

## III. SOURCES OF MUSIC PUBLISHING INCOME

The sources of a music publisher's income can be divided into three categories: (1) major sources of income (i.e., where the largest share is derived), (2) secondary sources of income, (3) and emerging sources of income (i.e., other sources that may be minor today, but could play an important role in the future of music publishing).

The *major* sources of music publishing income include the following kinds of uses:

- Sound recordings

- Public performances

- Theatrical motion pictures

- Television programs

- Videocassettes and video laserdiscs

- Advertising

The *secondary* sources of music publishing income include:

- Printed music

- Foreign subpublishing

- Radio programs (broadcast and closed circuit)

- Music boxes and other consumer musical products

- Non-theatrical motion pictures

- Non-theatrical videocassettes and laserdiscs

- Dramatic performances

- Dramatic adaptations

The *emerging* sources of income include:

- Computer software, multimedia, and new media products

- Digital transmission (e.g., Internet)

The business and legal aspects of each of these sources of music publishing income are discussed in the chapters which follow, organized by the type of license agreement used as the basis of the underlying transaction. These sources of income and their related licenses are summarized below:

## A.  Major Sources of Income

Music used in sound recordings, and distributed in compact discs and audiocassettes, is permitted by the grant of what is known, for historical reasons, as a *mechanical license*,[2] and these generate *mechanical royalties*. Music that is publicly performed on, for example, radio and television, is generally permitted under a *performance license* issued to the user on a *blanket* basis by a *performance rights society*,[3] which pays *performance royalties* to songwriters and music publishers. Music that is embodied in copies of motion pictures for theatrical distribution generate *synchronization royalties*, the licensing for which is granted in a *theatrical synchronization license*.[4] Music that is embodied in copies of television programs for television broadcast also generate *synchronization royalties*, the licensing for which is granted in a *television synchronization license*.[5] When a previously produced theatrical motion picture or television program, or newly produced video program (e.g., nature film or music video), is embodied in videocassettes or laserdiscs for home distribution, a separate license, commonly called a *videogram license*, is required.[6] When music is used as part of a commercial advertising campaign a *special commercial advertising synchronization license* is required.[7]

## B.  Secondary Sources of Income

Music used in *sheet music, music folios*, and other printed copies of music is permitted by the grant of a *print license*,[8] and these generate *print royalties*. Income from sources outside of the United States

---

[2] For a full discussion of mechanical licensing, see Chapter 12.

[3] For performance licensing, see Chapter 17.

[4] For theatrical synchronization licensing, see Chapter 14.

[5] For television synchronization licensing, see Chapter 14.

[6] For videogram licensing, see Chapter 15.

[7] For advertising in television, radio, and print, see Chapter 20.

[8] For print licensing, see Chapter 11.

is generally derived from agreements with international music *sub-publishers*, who engage, in their local countries, in many of the same licensing activities as the music publishers they represent. Music used in sound recordings that are intended to be used solely for public radio or closed-circuit broadcast (e.g., the music you hear in elevators and on airplanes) is permitted by the grant of what is known as an *electrical transcription license*,[9] and these generate *electrical transcription royalties*.

When music is embodied in a music box or similar musical product, such as a talking doll or singing greeting card, a *music box license* or *consumer musical product license* is required.[10] Music used in promotional or training videos produced by corporations is licensed under a *non-theatrical synchronization license*[11] and when these videos are distributed in videocassette or laserdisc form, a *non-theatrical videogram license* is required.[12]

Though rarely a significant source of publishing income, a *dramatic performance license* is required by anyone who wishes to render a dramatic performance of a song — that is, when the song is used to carry forward the plot or story of a dramatic work, such as a motion picture, television program, or theatrical play. A dramatic performance license should not be confused with a *grand performance license*, the latter of which is not a license strictly for music — it is a license to perform a grand opera or grand musical play, or portion thereof.[13] Finally, if you desire to produce a dramatization of a musical composition, or more accurately, its lyrics (i.e., much like one would produce a motion picture adaptation of a novel or short story), you would require a *dramatic adaptation license*.

## C.  Emerging Sources of Income

In the emerging sources of music publishing income may be found the very beginnings of the future of the music publishing business.

---

[9] For electrical transcription licensing, see Chapter 13.

[10] For videogram licensing, see Chapter 15.

[11] For non-theatrical synchronization licensing, see Chapter 14.

[12] For non-theatrical videogram licensing, see Chapter 15.

[13] For dramatic performance licensing, grand performance licensing, and dramatic adaptation licensing, see Chapter 18.

While standards of licensing in these areas are only now being developed, licensors and licensees of music for these new uses are laying an important foundation which should be studied carefully, particularly by owners of copyrighted music. A variety of licenses are being drafted on a case by case basis for the use of music in computer software, multimedia products, and new media products, including the electronic distribution of software on commercial on-line services, electronic bulletin boards and Web sites. These new sources of income will be discussed in detail in Chapters 22 and 23.

## IV. DISTRIBUTION OF MUSIC PUBLISHING INCOME

When the promotion, publication and performance of music results in the collection of royalty income by the music publisher, it's time to pay the songwriter his share. The share of the music publishing income which the songwriter is entitled to receive is known as, the *writer's share*. The share the publisher is entitled to keep is called, the *publisher's share*. Under a standard music publishing arrangement, the writer's share and the publisher's share, for the most part,[14] are equal (i.e., the publisher and writer split most of the publishing income on a 50-50 basis). The terms and conditions of this sharing of income is set forth in the agreement between the publisher and writer, discussed in Chapter 3, on *Songwriter Agreements*.

### A. Writer's Share

If there are two or more writers, the writer's share will be shared among them, usually, but not always, in equal shares. Agreements among songwriting collaborators is discussed in Chapter 3, on *Songwriter Agreements*. With one exception, the writer's share of music publishing income is paid to the writer *by the music publisher*. The one exception is *performance royalties* (i.e., royalties generated from the public performance of the songwriter's music), which are paid directly to the writer *by his performance rights society* (e.g., ASCAP or BMI).[15]

---

[14] Royalties on revenues arising from print licensing comprise a notable exception.

[15] See Chapter 3, on *Songwriter Agreements*, and Chapter 17, on *Performance Licenses*.

## B. Publisher's Share

The publisher's share may be shared among several co-publishers, in accordance with their respective percentage interests in the publisher's share of income. Before distribution to co-publishers, the publisher's share may also be subject to the payment of an administration fee in exchange for the services of an administrator, a service one of the co-publishers often provides to the others. Arrangements among co-publishers and music publishing administrators is discussed further in Chapter 4, on *Co-Publishing and Administration Agreements*.

## V. ORGANIZATION OF THE MUSIC PUBLISHER

Though the organization of a music publisher will vary considerably depending upon its size, the typical professional music publisher will be organized along functional lines. As we have noted, music publishing can be divided between two functional aspects: *creative* and *administrative*, with the latter increasingly becoming the dominant of the two functions.

## A. Creative

The creative activities of a music publisher are generally lead by the creative staff, more commonly called, the *professional department*, but sometimes referred to as the *creative department*. The domain of the *professional manager* includes: signing up songwriting talent, developing that talent, and getting songs recorded by popular performing artists. In short, the job of the professional manager involves discovering, nurturing, and plugging.

The days of a publisher hiring the likes of a young George Gershwin or Jerome Kern to perform a publisher's repertoire for theater managers, dance bands, and stores selling sheet music are long gone. Today's professional manager is more likely to be found hanging out in night clubs, listening for that new sound, in hope of discovering a hit act just at the dawning of their career. Professional managers have played an increasing role in discovering new talent, signing them up to music publishing contracts, and then helping the act secure a recording contract.

On occasion, by bringing the right song to the right performer, the professional manager becomes the catalyst for propelling good talent to stardom. Michael Sandoval, former head of the professional management department of Warner/Chappell Music, received a movie script from Warner Bros. Pictures together with a request to have a love song written. He asked Jon Lind and John Bettis, both staff writers at the time for Warner/Chappell, to come up with something. When Joel Sill of Warner Bros. Pictures received delivery of the song, *Crazy for You*, for the motion picture, *Vision Quest*, he replied "Great, any ideas who should record it?" Sandoval suggested an unknown, but up and coming singer named Madonna.

Opportunities such as these generally arise only after many years of building the necessary professional contacts with the people who can "make it happen." A good professional manager therefore works tirelessly to build long-term personal relationships with key band members, record producers, personal managers of successful performing groups and producers, executives in the A&R (i.e., artist and repertoire) departments of major record companies, and producers of motion pictures and television programs. By "doing" that lunch or dinner, keeping in touch, commissioning demo recordings and getting them to the right people, the professional manager increases his chances of leveraging his relationships into *covers* (i.e., recordings) of songs in the publisher's catalog or songs written by the publisher's exclusive staff writers.

Keeping in touch also means listening closely to trends and seeing beyond, what Sandoval calls, "the flavor of the month." The professional manager must learn to anticipate new trends and seek or nurture the talent to fill it. For this reason, it is critical for songwriters to change as the music does. To that end, the professional manager can play an invaluable role in providing guidance to songwriters, critiquing their work, and helping them develop their talent to meet the changing tastes of the listening public. Often, that development stems from a professional manager's efforts to match the talents of one songwriter with that of another. Many of today's hits are the result of collaborations suggested by professional managers.

During the first half of the 20th century, the creative activities of the music publisher was the source of the publisher's power. Today, the center of power at a music publisher often resides in the computer they use for computing songwriter royalties. This may all change, however, with the advent of electronic commerce. Professional managers of the future may find themselves more and more involved in discovering talent that appears on the electronic landscape and figuring out how to capitalize upon that talent through both traditional and non-traditional music publishing channels.

## B.  Administrative

The administrative aspects of music publishing are traditionally distributed among the following publishing departments: Copyright Administration, Licensing, Legal Affairs, Royalty Accounting, International, and Print.

### 1.  Copyright Department

The Copyright Administration department is responsible for completing and filing of applications for copyright registration and copyright renewal (see Chapter 9), and the recording of copyright assignments (see Chapter 8), for the musical compositions in its catalog with the U.S. Copyright Office and other applicable copyright authorities.

This department also apprises performing rights societies (e.g., ASCAP and BMI) when new songs are added to the publisher's catalog of compositions, and notifies its royalty accounting department of any changes of ownership in any of the compositions in its catalog. Such changes may occur as a result of the sale of portions of the catalog, the exercise by songwriters of termination rights (see Chapter 9), or by the terms of any applicable agreements with songwriters (see Chapter 3).

### 2.  Licensing Department

Often combined with the copyright administration department, the Licensing department negotiates and issues licenses to those seeking to use any of the musical compositions in the publisher's catalog, including many of the kinds of licenses discussed in this book.

Licensing departments tend to be passive, generating synchronization and other license revenue simply by *taking orders* (i.e., waiting for the phone to ring), but the better Licensing departments aggressively pursue new licensing opportunities by offering special services to producers of works that require music. When the music coordinator of a television or film production calls a licensing department not only to negotiate fees, but to seek a particular type of music needed, the licensing department should be able to provide a list of sample tunes from its catalog. In just this way, I was able to assist Harvey Becal, the music producer for the hit television game show, *Name That Tune*, where the contestants would bet they could name a given tune by hearing just a few bars or notes of the music. I would suggest songs from the Warner/Chappell catalog, by song genre, that were appropriate for use in the game. When a representative from Woody Allen's office expressed interest in using some of George Gershwin's music in Woody Allen's film, *Manhattan,* I was instrumental in persuading them to use strictly all Gershwin music, which they did.

Sometimes, a particular use will require the consent of the songwriter under the terms of the songwriter's agreement with the publisher. For example, Ira Gershwin had a policy of never allowing the licensing of an edited version of his brother's *Rhapsody In Blue*. When Woody Allen wanted to use an edited version of *Rhapsody In Blue* in the opening of *Manhattan*, I personally went to Ira's house, helped him understand who Woody Allen was, described the nature of the project, and ultimately persuaded him to consent to the use. When we later rendered a special screening of the movie in Ira's living room, he was delighted with the result.[16] I mention this to illustrate how far a Licensing department can go to strike a deal which benefits the publisher, the writer, and the customer.

As a result of the Split Copyright Syndrome, discussed in Chapter 6, producers have been finding it increasingly difficult to clear licenses for songs they desired to use. Often, the catalog of Warner/Chappell contained close substitutes for the songs requested and the advantage to the producer of using one of these substitutes is that they could quickly get a license from a single source, without having to track down and negotiate with the multiple owners of songs tainted by the

---

[16] When I asked Ira if he had any further comments, he remarked, in jest, "They didn't give credit to the lyric writer." From that point on, I made it a point in negotiating motion picture synchronization licenses to attempt to require producers to provide screen credit to songwriters and music publishers of the licensed music.

split copyright problem. One day, it occurred to me that if I could compile and publish a list of standard songs in the Warner/Chappell catalog which we could offer quickly and easily (i.e., with no need to get permission from co-publishers or consent of the songwriters), producers would more likely turn to the songs on such a list than to songs in the catalogs of other publishers. This is, in fact, just what I did: I made just such a list and organized the songs by genre, such as the Roaring 20's, Country & Western, 50's Rock & Roll, and chronologically by year of publication.

Finally, perhaps the best service a licensing manager can provide is a thorough knowledge of his catalog. Having been in music publishing for most of my professional career, and having a musician's ear and memory for good melodies, it was not difficult for me to provide a high level of service. Often, a producer need only hum a few bars and I could not only "name that tune," but "name that publisher" — that is, not only could I tell a producer if a song was in my catalog, I could often direct a caller to the publisher who owned the music — like Macy's sending a customer to Gimbel's. Today, with aging catalogs and (seemingly) younger licensing managers, it may be more difficult for a publisher to provide this level of service.

Technology is making a difference, however. Both ASCAP and BMI offer on the Internet the ability to electronically search their catalogs so that you can now easily determine the publisher of a particular composition.[17] Perhaps, someone will next develop a computer software application that will combine a song database with "song recognition" — a form of voice recognition for standard melodies.

The responsibilities of the licensing department may seem to overlap with those of the professional department, but licensing managers tend to focus on issuing synchronization licenses for older, and generally *standard* songs (i.e., classics, oldies, or popular theme songs), and the professional managers tend to focus on increasing mechanical and performance license revenue by obtaining *covers* (i.e., new recordings) of the songs in the catalog, especially songs written by its *staff* songwriters (i.e., songwriters with whom the publisher has contracted on an exclusive basis for a period of years).

---

[17] ASCAP can be found on the Internet at *http://www.ascap.com,* and BMI is located at *http://www.bmi.com.*

### 3. Legal Affairs Department

The Legal Affairs department of a music publisher performs many of the same functions of a typical corporate in house legal department. These include the drafting of the form agreements commonly used by the publisher, including the publisher's standard songwriter agreements, co-publishing agreements, and license agreements. The Legal Affairs department will often participate in the negotiation of particular agreements, and will at least be consulted when any changes are made to any of the legal language used in a standard form.

A most important service a Legal Affairs department can provide is something that my son emphasizes in his role as general counsel to a major publisher of computer software: that is, in any transaction, *preserve your ability to change your mind*. This may be as simple as including an *out* clause (e.g., termination for convenience) or preferring nonexclusive over exclusive arrangements. If in each transaction a lawyer would ask, "What happens if you change your mind?," a solution will come to mind that will allow the publisher to negotiate, in advance, a satisfactory way out should circumstances change later on.

Finally, a responsible Legal Affairs department will assume a law enforcement role, making sure the publisher's activities are conducted within the dictates of the law. The management of a music publisher should look to its Legal Affairs department as its *corporate conscience* and should respect not only the legal, but the ethical aspects of the advice given. Smaller publishers, as with smaller businesses, not large enough to support this function in house, will rely primarily on the services of a law firm specializing in entertainment and copyright, for its legal affairs function. Of course, songwriters who manage their own music publishing often rely on, "I have this lawyer friend . . ."

### 4. Royalty Accounting Department

If the check is in the mail, it was probably prepared and sent by the Royalty Accounting department. The Royalty Accounting department manages royalties that come in to the publisher, such as revenues from the issuance of mechanical, synchronization and videogram licenses, and royalties that go out, primarily to co-publishers and songwriters with whom the publisher has entered songwriter, co-publishing, and administration agreements.

The Royalty Accounting department has, over the years, become the heart of the modern music publisher, and the heart of the Royalty Accounting department has become the mainframe computer (and, increasingly, mini- and micro-computers). Information from royalty income statements are entered into the computer, the computer is programmed with the appropriate royalty splits, and the computer churns out royalty statements and corresponding checks for payment to the publishers and writers. An increasing share of a publisher's expenses is being devoted to improving its management information systems. The bulk of these resources are used to improve the speed and accuracy of royalty accounting, but an increasing emphasis is being placed on the storage and retrieval of copyright ownership and other information. In the future, computers will be used to enhance the licensing process itself, with storage and retrieval capabilities for sheet music, MIDI files, and other sound processing applications.

### 5. International Department

The International department[18] is responsible for managing the administration of the publisher's catalog outside of the United States. Major music publishing firms have publishing subsidiaries located in each of the major markets around the world. Independent music publishers have either arrangements with a major music publisher for the administration of overseas music publishing revenue or arrangements directly with subpublishing companies located around the world. When a U.S. publisher is acting as a subpublisher for an overseas music publisher, the International department is generally responsible for managing the relationship.

### 6. Print Department

In a modern era of radio, television, motion pictures, compact disc recordings, and electronic distribution, the Print department in most music publisher's today has become little more than a file of contracts.

---

[18] We prefer to use the word, "international" in place of the commonly used "foreign," because of the pejorative, and often xenophobic, connotation which the latter word tends to carry. In a global economy, it is important to avoid language that may be considered offensive in international business transactions.

These contracts authorize third party print publishing specialists to reproduce the music publisher's catalog of musical compositions in sheet music and songbook form. Since the 1930's, income from licensing the mechanical reproduction and broadcast performance of music has replaced printed music sales as the primary source of music publishing revenue to the point that, today, printed music represents only a small portion of a music publisher's income. Basic considerations in negotiating licenses for the reproduction and distribution of printed music are discussed in detail in Chapter 11, on *Print Licenses*.

## VI. How to Establish a Music Publishing Company

Establishing a music publishing company is much the same as setting up any small business. For example, you must consider the best legal form for your business — that is, whether you will operate as a sole proprietorship, partnership, corporation, or limited liability company.[19] Before choosing the legal form for your business, however, you should first consult your legal or tax advisor.

But even before you consult the accountants and lawyers, you should first consult one of the two major performance rights societies, ASCAP or BMI. Which society you choose is often a metaphysical question, one we can't answer.[20] Nevertheless, if you are already a member of one of these societies as a songwriter, the decision is easy: you *must* join that society as a publisher as well. Ask the society for an application for publisher membership.[21]

When you apply for affiliation in the society, you must offer the society three choices for the name you wish to use for your publishing company, ranked in your order of preference. The society will tell you

---

[19] A *limited liability company* (or "LLP") is the newest form of business enterprise and just might be the most attractive legal form for someone just starting out — an LLP provides its owners with *limited liability* (i.e., the owners liability is limited to the amount he or she invests in the business), a benefit normally available only to shareholders of a corporation, but, for tax purposes, the LLP is treated as a sole proprietorship, which may be very important, particularly if you expect to operate at a loss for some period of time.

[20] But see Chapter 17, on *Performance Licenses*.

[21] Information on where you may contact these societies is in Chapter 17.

which of these names they will accept, if any — their objective is to avoid misdirection of performance royalty payments resulting from two publishing companies having confusingly similar names. By first gaining the society's approval of your publishing company's name, you will avoid the expense and headache of reprinting stationery, re-opening bank accounts, changing your corporate name, and the like.

At the time you affiliate with your performance rights society, or shortly thereafter, you should register all of your songs with the so-ciety, which lets them know the titles of your songs and who to pay when it comes time to give royalty credit for their public perform-ances. Note, that unless you have at least one song that is either about to be recorded or used commercially in a film or television program, the society may not let you become a member.

Once you have become affiliated with a performance rights soci-ety, with a name of which they approve, then you establish your legal form (i.e., sole proprietorship, partnership, corporation, limited liabil-ity company). If you choose to remain a sole proprietorship, you must, in most states, publish in a newspaper, and file with the county in which your business resides, what is known in California as a *fictitious name statement* (also known as, a "DBA," or "doing business as" statement). You should first contact your local newspaper, as most newspapers will offer the service of both publishing the statement, and filing with the county, for a modest fee. You will find that, in many states, a duly filed and published fictitious business name state-ment will be a prerequisite to opening up a bank account under a fictitious business name.

Finally, you should register the copyrights in your songs with the U.S. Copyright Office[22] and record any assignments of copyrights[23] in the songs created by your writers from them to your publishing com-pany.

## VII. THE FUTURE OF MUSIC PUBLISHING

During the 18th and early 19th centuries, the music publisher was someone with a printing press, an interest in music, and either a store

---

[22] Copies of Form PA, together with straightforward instructions on how to complete the application, may be obtained by calling the Copyright Office at 202-707-9100.

[23] For a sample short form copyright assignment, see Chapter 8.

front or a network of traveling salesmen. By 1900, music publishing became a serious, but more creative, business, with most of it concentrated in a Manhattan city block known as Tin Pan Alley. From that time on, until about the 1950's, music publishing was largely a creative endeavor. It meant discovering songwriting talent, teaming up one songwriter with another, and getting a song performed or recorded. Today, the major music publisher would seem to rely more on the talents of its Chief Information Officer than its creative staff.

But what about the future? As will be suggested in Chapter 23, on *Licensing Musical Works and Sound Recordings on the Internet*, recent technological developments herald another change in the orchestration of music publishing. The emergence of electronic commerce, and the ability for virtually anyone to inexpensively become their own publisher and distributor of musical compositions, will have by the end of this century an impact on music publishing no less profound as the impact Tin Pan Alley had at the beginning of this century.

CHAPTER 3

# SONGWRITER AGREEMENTS

## SUMMARY

## I. SELECTING A MUSIC PUBLISHER

## II. NEGOTIATING THE SONGWRITER/PUBLISHER RELATIONSHIP

A. Negotiating for All or a Portion of the Publisher's Share
B. Negotiating the Writer's Share (i.e., the Songwriter Agreement)

## III. NEGOTIATING THE SINGLE SONG MUSIC PUBLISHING AGREEMENT

A. Grant of Rights
B. Territory
C. Term
D. Reversion of Rights
E. Advances
F. Cross-Collateralization
G. Royalties
    1. Sheet Music
    2. Printed Folios
    3. Other Printed Editions
    4. Print Sublicensing
    5. Mechanical, Synchronization, and Other Royalties
    6. Performance Royalties
    7. International Royalties
    8. Promotional Copies
    9. Collaborative Royalties
    10. Demo Recordings
    11. Other Publishing Expenses
    12. No Other Royalties
    13. Advances from Licenses

## V. Collaborators

A. Who Gets the Publishing?

B. How Are Royalties Shared Among Collaborators?

C. What Happens When Collaborators Sign-Up with the Same Publisher?

D. Should Co-Authors Enter into a Collaboration Agreement?

## VI. Summary

## Appendix to Chapter 3

| | |
|---|---|
| **Form 3.1** | Songwriter Agreement for Single Song I |
| **Form 3.2** | Songwriter Agreement of Single Song II |
| **Form 3.3** | Exclusive Term Songwriter Agreement |
| **Form 3.4** | 1939 Songwriters Protective Association Uniform Popular Songwriters Contract |
| **Form 3.5** | 1969 American Guild of Authors & Composers Uniform Popular Songwriters Contract |
| **Form 3.6** | 1978 American Guild of Authors & Composers Popular Songwriters Renewal Contract |
| **Form 3.7** | 1978 Songwriters Guild of America Popular Songwriters Contract |
| **Form 3.8** | Standard Studio Film Music Composer/ Arranger-Conductor Employment Agreement; Exhibit A, Exhibit B |

# CHAPTER 3

# SONGWRITER AGREEMENTS

A s noted in the previous chapter, income arising from the licensing of a musical composition is shared among the music publishers and songwriters who have an interest in the composition. The share of the music publishing income which the songwriter is entitled to receive is called, the *writer's share*, and the share the publisher is entitled to keep is called, the *publisher's share*. The process by which this sharing of income occurs is defined and governed by an agreement between the music publisher and the songwriter, called a *songwriter agreement*.

This chapter sketches the common terms and conditions contained in the typical songwriter agreement and suggests many of the common variations negotiated on behalf of songwriters.

## I. SELECTING A MUSIC PUBLISHER

The considerations that a songwriter uses in selecting a particular music publisher vary depending upon the circumstances. Obviously, a new songwriter seeking to "break into" the business will have fewer alternatives from which to choose than a successful recording artist. Moreover, each is likely to have a different goal: the new songwriter will seek a publisher willing to commit sufficient time to effectively promote the writer's songs in the hope of obtaining a commercial recording that will launch the writer's career; by contrast, the objective of a popular recording artist, who has his own means of promoting his songs, may be to gain the largest share of music publishing income as possible while incurring the lowest possible transaction costs.

In either case, the music publisher selected may ultimately fail to achieve the writer's goal. This may not always be the fault of the music publisher, as the writer's goals may change over time. For example, the amateur songwriter may become a star, in which case his or her music publishing objectives will change accordingly; similarly, a fickle public may quickly reverse the fortunes of a successful artist, whose music publishing goals consequently shift to securing a lesser percentage of a bigger pie, with the music publisher playing a greater role in promoting the writer's published catalog.

In any case, the songwriter can reduce his risk of choosing the wrong publisher, realign his music publishing relationship to fit changing objectives — in short, preserve his ability to "change his mind" — by carefully negotiating the terms and conditions of his or her songwriter agreement in advance.

## II. NEGOTIATING THE SONGWRITER/PUBLISHER RELATIONSHIP

When a songwriter signs a typical songwriter agreement with a music publisher, he is granting to the publisher full ownership in the copyright in his musical compositions in exchange for the publisher's services and payment of the *writer's share*. The music publisher earns his *publisher's share* by providing creative, promotional, and administrative services intended to enhance the income upon which the writer's and publisher's shares are based. Though the songwriter who is negotiating his songwriter agreement will want to maximize the potential size of his writer's share, relative to the publisher's share, he should consider the possibility of participating in (i.e., receiving a portion of) the publisher's share itself.

Arrangements under which a songwriter receives a portion of the publisher's share of music publishing income is known as a *participation deal*. Whether the songwriter will be able to negotiate a participation deal, and take share of the publisher's share, will depend entirely on the writer's circumstances and bargaining leverage.

### A. Negotiating for All or a Portion of the Publisher's Share

As noted, the songwriter agreement defines how the total publishing income is divided into the *writer's share* and the *publisher's share*. Negotiating the standard songwriter agreement traditionally involves reviewing and discussing solely that fundamental division. However, in the larger context of the relationship between the publisher and writer, the question of how the *publisher's share* of total publishing income is allocated often becomes the subject of additional negotiation.

A songwriter who has some bargaining power may be in a position to negotiate for all or a portion of the *publisher's share* of the total music publishing income, which, as we have said, is called a participation deal. His participation in the publisher's share would be in addition to his writer's share as defined by the songwriter agreement. For example, if the writer's share and publisher's share each amount to 50% of the total publishing income, then a writer who negotiates 50% of the publisher's share, would be entitled to receive 75% of the total publishing income (i.e., his writer's share, which equals 50% of the total publishing income, plus one-half of the publisher's share).

When the songwriter is able to retain a portion of the publisher's share, he typically enters into a *co-publishing agreement* with the music publisher, which will govern the co-ownership of the compositions and how the publisher and writer will split in the proceeds of the *publisher's share*. When the songwriter is able to retain all of the publisher's share, retaining full ownership in his compositions, he may enter into an *administration agreement*, under which the publisher agrees to perform certain administrative duties in return for an administration fee. The negotiation of co-publishing and administration agreements are discussed in detail in Chapter 4.

Most participation deals are effected by the entry of a co-publishing agreement, with administration agreements reserved for those songwriters who have a very high degree of bargaining leverage. Whether a writer retains all or a portion of the publisher's share of income under a co-publishing or administration arrangement, he will often enter into a *songwriter agreement* with a music publisher (or co-publishers), which sets forth the terms and conditions under which the writer is entitled to receive his *writer's share* of the music publishing income. Sometimes the songwriter agreement, governing the writer's share, and the copublishing agreement, governing the writer's participation in the publisher's share, are combined into a single agreement, an example of which is set forth as Form 4.1 at the end of Chapter 4 on *Co-Publishing and Administration*. Because interests in the publisher's share are often bought and sold, even a writer who self-publishes his compositions should carefully consider the terms and conditions of the songwriter agreement he enters into with his own publishing company.

## B. Negotiating the Writer's Share (i.e., the Songwriter Agreement)

Standard songwriter publishing agreements are of two types: the *single song* agreement and the *exclusive term* agreement. Under the *single song* agreement, the songwriter grants to the publisher full ownership in the copyright in the particular musical composition or compositions involved. Though a misnomer in this context, the *single song* agreement may actually cover several songs, which would be listed in an exhibit or schedule attached to the agreement. Under an *exclusive term* agreement, the writer agrees to grant to the publisher any songs he writes during the term of the agreement.

Exclusive term agreements tend to be used with writers who have demonstrated a consistent ability to create successful songs or writers who are also recording artists who, by having recording contracts with record companies, have a natural opportunity to consistently effect the recording and publication of songs he or she has written. The exclusive term agreement, in this context, reduces the transaction costs of having to continually prepare and execute single song agreements for each song or group of songs written by the songwriter.

A songwriter may also enter into an exclusive term agreement to take advantage of the steady, periodic advances that are often associated with them, to gain access to a publisher's recording facilities to create high quality demonstration recordings, and to join a small circle of other talented staff writers through which successful collaborations may be generated. Some attorneys, however, advise songwriters against entering into exclusive term agreements unless they need the cash or unless the publisher is really in a special position to assist the writer's career through means just mentioned. They assert that any additional transaction costs associated with entering into a series of single song agreements is outweighed by the flexibility afforded by avoiding the confines of exclusivity. This flexibility, however, comes not without its costs. The songwriter should consider the additional transaction costs, such as attorneys fees, associated with spreading his compositions among a number of different music publishers.

Many of the provisions of the *single song* and *exclusive term* agreements are the same, though the exclusive term agreement contains certain additional provisions relating to the engagement of the writer's services over a period of time. Accordingly, we will first review each material provision of a standard single song agreement and then discuss only the relevant additional provisions of the exclusive term deal.

## III. NEGOTIATING THE SINGLE SONG MUSIC PUBLISHING AGREEMENT

It seems there are as many songwriter agreements as there are music publishers who use them. The appendix to this chapter includes several different forms that have typically been used by songwriters and music publishers over the years, and we have selected one of those forms as the starting point for the analysis which we present in the following pages.[1]

Our review here will focus only on the major business points of the transaction. Many of the legal boilerplate provisions are discussed in Chapter 10, on *Basic Considerations in Music Licensing*. Additional issues, and the way they may be resolved from the songwriter's point of view, may be found by a close review of the provisions of the AGAC and Songwriter's Guild agreements, set forth at the end of this chapter as Forms 3.4 to 3.7. Although few major music publishers today are willing to sign them, the AGAC and Songwriter's Guild agreements are still useful mainly for the ideas they may contribute to the negotiation of form agreements used by music publishers.

### A. Grant of Rights

The following is a typical grant of rights provision from a standard songwriter agreement:

1. Composer hereby sells, assigns and delivers to Publisher, its successors and assigns, the original musical composition written and composed by Composer (words of which were written by _____ and music by _____ and), presently entitled "_____" (the "Composition"), including the title, words and music thereof, all worldwide rights therein, all cop-

---

[1] Form 3.2, Standard Single Song Songwriter Agreement II.

yrights therein and thereto, all registrations with respect thereto, and
the exclusive right to secure copyrights and any extensions of copyrights in the same and in any arrangements and adaptations thereof,
all throughout the world, and any and all other rights, claims and
demands that Composer now has or to which he might be entitled
or that he hereafter could or might secure throughout the world with
respect thereto if these presents had not been made, and to have and
to hold the same absolutely and forever unto Publisher, its successors
and assigns, subject only to any existing agreements between Composer and Publisher and the Performing Rights Society (with which
they are affiliated).

The grant of rights provision effects the transfer of the copyright
in the composition from the songwriter to the publisher.[2] It is the entire
*undivided* copyright that is being transferred or granted to the publisher, not just one or several of the exclusive rights of the author
under the copyright. Note that the provision recognizes, in the last
clause of its last sentence, the songwriter's prior grant to his performance rights society (e.g., ASCAP or BMI) of a license to authorize
public performances of the composition, and accordingly, the songwriter's grant of copyright is specifically made subject to that license
grant.[3]

The above provision also includes a grant of the *title* of the composition. (The title referred to here is not the legal title, as in ownership, but the song title, as in *Melancholy Baby*). Though titles are
not copyrightable, they may be subject to other forms of legal protection, such as the law of *unfair competition*, which, among other things,
may prevent one songwriter from "palming off" or "passing off" his
song as that of another. Titles can become important in certain licensing contexts.[4]

Finally, note that the above grant of rights provision does not
impose any obligation upon the publisher to file appropriate applications for copyright registration. A songwriter might reasonably request
that the publisher be obliged to file such registrations, and record any
assignments concerning the transfer of copyright,[5] but the publisher

---

[2] See Chapter 7, *The Language of Music Licensing.*
[3] See Chapter 17, *Performance Licenses.*
[4] See Chapter 20, *Licensing Music in Television, Radio, and Print Advertising.*
[5] See Chapter 8, *The Formalities of Music Licensing.*

might reasonably insist that this obligation be limited to filings with the U.S. Copyright Office.

## B. Territory

The *grant of rights* provision set forth above grants to the publisher the entire copyright, including all worldwide rights. Certainly, if the writer had previously granted exclusive publishing rights for one or more territories outside of the United States, the grant should specifically carve out the rights previously granted.

If international rights have not been previously granted, the writer should still consider whether a worldwide deal makes sense under the circumstances. If the writer is dealing with a large publisher which has its own publishing subsidiaries in the major international markets, the writer will benefit from having to deal with only one point of contact to manage all of his worldwide publishing. If, however, the publisher is only active in the United States, and would only turn over the writer's international publishing administration to a large publisher or several overseas subpublishers, the writer may desire to restrict the publisher's territory to the United States and make his own deals for subpublishing in international markets. Worldwide music publishing administration through the use of international subpublishers is discussed at length in Chapter 5, on *International Subpublishing*.

## C. Term

Similarly, because the transfer involves the entire copyright, the term of the agreement is implicitly for the life of the copyright, subject, of course, to any statutory rights of termination under the copyright law (i.e., the right of an author or his heirs to terminate, at a later date, the grant of rights the author is making under the songwriter agreement).[6] Leaving aside any statutory termination rights, the term of the agreement will be for the life of the copyright (e.g., life of the author, plus 70 years), unless (1) the agreement specifies a fixed term (e.g., 10 years) at which point the agreement will automatically terminate and the copyrights will automatically revert to the writer, or (2) the agreement includes a *right of reversion*, in which event the

---

[6] See Chapter 9, *Duration of Copyright, Assignments and Licenses*.

agreement would terminate, and the copyrights revert, upon the writer's proper exercise of the reversion.

## D.  Reversion of Rights

Songwriters with some degree of bargaining leverage may be able to negotiate a provision under which the writer will obtain, upon certain conditions, what is known as a *reversion* of the rights granted.

Typically, the writer will request that if the song is not commercially released within a specified period of time, he will have the right to terminate the agreement and demand that the copyright revert (i.e., be transferred) back to him.[7] A publisher might counterpropose that the condition could be satisfied by either the recording, synchronization, or public performance of the composition. Ideally, a writer would insist that his right of reversion could be exercised if the publisher does not effect a commercial recording of the composition within six months after the agreement is signed *and* the recording is commercially released within six months thereafter.[8] The publisher may insist upon a one to two year time frame and that the termination and reversion be conditioned upon the writer returning any unrecouped advances he received for the compositions, as well as reimbursing the publisher the cost of any demo recordings made by the publisher.

The precise terms will vary considerably with the bargaining leverage of the writer. The Popular Songwriter's Contract recommended by the Songwriter's Guild of America, set forth in the appendix to this chapter, contains several provisions resulting in the reversion of rights to the songwriter upon the publisher's failure to comply with specified conditions.

## E.  Advances

An *advance*[9] is a lump-sum payment to the writer that is *recoupable* (i.e., deductible), by the publisher from future royalties that

---

[7] Reversion clauses have become common in songwriter agreements entered into in the U.K. as a result of *Schroeder v. Macaulay* (1974) 3 All E.R. 616 (HL), discussed below.

[8] Note, the condition should be the *commercial release* of a sound or synchronized recording, not merely the *recording*, of the composition, the latter of which could be effected by the recording of a demonstration record.

[9] See Chapter 10, *Basic Considerations in Music Licensing*.

would otherwise be payable to writer (except performance royalties the writer receives directly from his performance rights society). The following is an example of an advance provision:

> Upon execution hereof, Publisher shall pay to Composer the amount of five hundred dollars ($500.00) as an advance, receipt of which is hereby acknowledged, which sum shall remain the property of Composer, and shall be recoupable from payments hereafter becoming due Composer under this or any other agreement with Publisher or any of its affiliated music companies.

Though the advance is recoupable, it is not *returnable* (i.e., if the advances turn out to be greater than the amount of royalties ever earned from sales, the writer will not have to pay the unearned balance of the advance back to the person who paid it, unless of course he is otherwise in breach of the agreement; in other words, an advance is not a *loan*. However, the advance may be *returnable* in certain circumstances at the option of the writer, such as when the writer exercises a reversion of rights provision). Thus, an advance is more accurately referred to as a "non-returnable, recoupable advance."

As suggested by its name, an advance is generally paid *up front*, such as upon signing of the agreement, but also may be paid on a periodic basis, regardless of whether sufficient royalties have been earned during the period in which the advance is paid. The amount of an advance in any particular deal is highly negotiable and depends entirely upon the circumstances. For example, an advance offered in a single song agreement for an unpublished composition written by an average songwriter may run anywhere from nothing to $500 or more, per song. A publisher would be willing, however, to pay higher advances if a popular recording artist has committed to recording the song or if there are other immediate prospects for licensing the work. By the same token, a publisher would tend to offer a lower advance where a reversion clause (see above) allows him only a short period of time within which to effect a commercial release of the composition. An advance for an established song could be based upon the present value of a revenue forecast; projections are usually based upon the composition's historical income and the publisher's prospects for improving upon the song's track record.

A songwriter should insist upon receiving at least some minimum advance to give the publisher some incentive, however small, to promote the song. Of course, the writer's best protection against an unpromoted song is the *reversion of rights* provision, discussed above.

## F.  Cross-Collateralization

Whenever an agreement provides for an advance, a cross-collateralization[10] provision is likely to be nearby. Contracts that are *cross-collateralized* are those under which royalties earned under one contract are used to recoup advances earned under another contract. You can spot cross-collateralization by looking for the following *Three Little Words*: "or any other." For example, the last clause of the advance provision set forth above states that the advance

> "shall be deductible from payments hereafter becoming due Composer *under this or any other agreement* with Publisher or any of its affiliated music companies."

Under certain circumstances, cross-collateralization will defeat one of the primary reasons artists seek advances. If the purpose of the advance is to give the person paying the advance the proper incentive to promote a particular song, allowing the cross-collateralization of that advance against royalties payable under a contract for another song, which by reason of its popularity might sell itself, will defeat the purpose of the original advance. Accordingly, a writer might reasonably insist that the cross-collateralization provision be stricken from the agreement.

## G.  Royalties

A typical royalty provision from a standard songwriter agreement would begin in this way:

> 3. In consideration of this agreement and of the rights and interests hereby conveyed and granted, Publisher agrees to pay to Composer the following royalties in respect of the Composition:

---

[10] Id.

and then proceed to list the writer's royalty for a variety of sources of income.

## 1. Sheet Music

The first source listed is typically the royalty for *sheet music*:

> (a) Seven cents ($.07) per copy for each copy of sheet music in standard piano-vocal notation of the Composition printed, published and sold in the United States and Canada by Publisher or its affiliates, for which payment has been received by Publisher, or been finally credited to Publisher's account in reduction of an advance after deduction of reasonable returns. (Wherever the terms "paid," "received," or the equivalent appear in this agreement, they shall be deemed to include such final credit.)

Earlier, we suggested that the *writer's share* derived from the exploitation of his musical compositions is, for the most part, 50% of the total music publishing income. Well, this is where the "for the most part" enters the picture. When a music publisher grants to a print publisher the exclusive rights to publish a composition in sheet music form,[11] the publisher typically receives a royalty of 20% of the retail price of the sheet music. If, for example, the retail price of the sheet music is $4.00, then the publisher would be entitled to receive a royalty of 80 cents.

With the writer's share of most other music publishing income being 50% (see below), then why would the writer receive only 7 cents (i.e., less than 10%) of that 80 cents received by the publisher? Very simply because the provision is considered a long standing music publishing *sacred cow* (i.e., in reference to the inviolability of the cow among the Hindus; hence, something which is considered to be exempt from criticism or questioning). Only writers with a high degree of bargaining leverage should expect to negotiate more than 10 or 12 cents per copy, but not much more. Because sheet music sales are such a small percentage of music publishing income, heated arguments about the sacrosanctity of the provision is generally not worth the writer's time or emotional resources.

---

[11] See Chapter 11, *Print Licenses.*

## 2.   *Printed Folios*

Closely related to sheet music royalties is income from *folios* and *songbooks* containing the compositions:

> (b) (i) If the Composition is included in any folio, songbook or similar publication ("mixed folio"), a proportionate share of a royalty of twelve and one-half percent (12 1/2%) of the net whole-sale selling price of such publication for all copies sold by Publisher or its affiliates and paid for in the United States and Canada. Said proportionate share shall be equal to the percentage computed by dividing the number "one" by the total number of all copyrighted musical compositions contained therein.

The above provision assumes the publisher is engaging in reproducing and distributing the printed editions on its own, rather than merely sublicensing the activity to a third party print publisher. Typically, the songwriter will receive a royalty of 10%, which, with some leverage, may be negotiated up to 12 1/2% or even 15% in some cases. The royalty percentage should be based upon the *wholesale* selling price; if the agreement states *retail* selling price, the writer should attempt to change it.

Note that the last sentence of the above section makes it clear that the pro ration will be computed on the basis of the number of *copyrighted* compositions contained in the folio. This is to prevent the publisher from including public domain songs, like the *Star Spangled Banner*, in the calculation, which would otherwise have the effect of reducing the revenue due the songwriter. A careful songwriter might add, "but not including copyrighted arrangements of musical compositions in the public domain." Alternatively, the pro ration could be computed on the basis of the number of *copyrighted, royalty-bearing* songs in the songbook.

However, this still leaves open the possibility that the publisher will promote the sale of a folio by including one or two of the writer's biggest hit songs, and adding a number of lesser known songs from the catalog of the publisher or of other publishers. Under those circumstances, pro rating the songs on an equal basis would not fairly reflect the role the writer's songs play in generating sales of the folio. To address this problem, a writer might seek to limit the proportion of compositions written by other composers that are allowed to be included in a folio that contains the writer's compositions. However, because of the popularity of mixed folios, such as "Hits of the '70s," such a limitation could severely discourage the use of the writer's songs in printed editions, which already represents a decreasing portion of total music publishing income. Of course, if the folio were comprised primarily of the writer's own songs, then the problem would not arise.

If the writer's name and likeness is used in a *personality folio* (i.e., a songbook consisting of songs written, recorded, or performed by the same artist or recording group, or written by the same songwriter),[12] the writer may insist upon an additional royalty (e.g., up to an additional 5%).

### 3. Other Printed Editions

Royalties for other printed editions, including editions for educational use, generally carry a lower royalty:

> (ii) If the Composition is included in a "fake book", "educational edition" or an instrumental, orchestral, choral or band arrangement or other arrangement intended for pedagogical purposes, a royalty of ten percent (10%), or a proportionate share thereof (calculated in the manner prescribed above in the case of a mixed folio) of the net wholesale selling price for all copies of such work sold by Publisher or its affiliates and paid for in the United States and Canada.

### 4. Print Sublicensing

Where the music publisher sublicenses the printed edition activity to an unaffiliated print publisher, then the writer should receive 50% of the publisher's revenues:

> (iii) If, pursuant to a license granted by Publisher to a licensee not controlled by or affiliated with it, the Composition is included in any mixed folio in the United States and/or Canada, a pro rata share of fifty percent (50%) of the gross amount received by Publisher from the licensee as the number of uses of the Com-

---

[12] Id.

position under the license and during the license period bears to the total number of uses of Publisher's copyrighted musical compositions (including the Composition) under the license and during the license period.

### 5. Mechanical, Synchronization, and Other Royalties

The following provision sets forth the writer's share of *mechanical, electrical transcription, synchronization,*[13] and other royalties on revenue received by the publisher in the United States and Canada:

> (c) Fifty percent (50%) of any and all net sums actually received (less any cost for collection) by Publisher or credited to Publisher's account in the United States from the exploitation in the United States and Canada by licensees of Publisher of mechanical rights, electrical transcription and reproducing rights, motion picture and television synchronization rights, and all other rights in the Composition (except print rights which are covered in paragraphs 3(a) and 3(b) above and public performance rights which are covered in (d) below), whether or not such licensees are affiliated with, owned in whole or in part by, or controlled by Publisher.

A writer may seek to impose certain restrictions, discussed later in this chapter, on the publisher's ability to grant mechanical, synchronization and other music licenses.

It is important to note that the above provision includes the all important *catch all* phrase (i.e., "and all other rights in the Composition"), which assures that the writer will receive 50% of income from uses not specifically listed. Many standard songwriter agreements limit the writer's royalties only to those derived from uses specifically listed in the agreement.

### 6. Performance Royalties

The last clause of the above provision, together with the provision which follows, makes it clear that the writer does *not* receive any portion of the *publisher's share* of performance royalties.[14] As noted,

---

[13] See Chapters 12, 13, and 14 on *Mechanical Licenses, Electrical Transcription Licenses,* and *Synchronization Licenses,* respectively.

[14] See Chapter 17, on *Performance Licenses.*

the writer will receive *the writer's share* of performance royalties directly from his performance rights society:

> (d) (i) Composer shall receive his public performance royalties throughout the world directly from his own affiliated performing rights society and shall have no claim whatsoever against Publisher for any royalties received by Publisher from any performing rights society which makes payment directly (or indirectly other than through Publisher) to writers, authors and composers.

Because of changes in the way performance royalties are collected, it would be wise to include a provision, such as the following, which anticipates the possibility that the publisher may some day collect all of the writer's share of performance fees directly from licensees. In fact, the publisher already directly collects performance royalties when granting theatrical synchronization licenses (see, Chapter 14, on *Synchronization Licenses*) and the writer should be entitled to 50% of that income:

> (ii) If, however, (and to the extent that) Publisher shall collect both the Composer's and Publisher's share of performance income directly and such income shall not be collected by Composer's public performance society, Publisher shall pay to Composer fifty percent (50%) of all such net sums which are received by Publisher in the United States from the exploitation of such rights in the Composition, throughout the world.

## 7. *International Royalties*

The following provision sets forth the writer's share of income from publishing sources outside the United States and Canada:

> (e) Fifty percent (50%) of any and all net sums, after deduction of foreign taxes, actually received (less any reasonable costs for collection) by Publisher in the United States from sales, licenses and other uses of the Composition in countries outside of the United States and Canada (other than public performance royalties described in subparagraph 3(d)(i)) from collection agents, licensees, subpublishers or others, whether or not same are affiliated with, owned in whole or in part by, or controlled by Publisher. This provision shall not apply to copies of printed music shipped from the

United States to such countries, to which the rates set forth in paragraphs 3(a) and 3(b) above shall apply.

In Chapter 5, on *International Subpublishing*, we discuss the concept of the music publisher's income from its international subpublishers being computed "at the source." Such a provision is intended to prevent the practice of using multiple layers of subpublishing companies, owned or closely affiliated with the music publisher, solely for the purpose of reducing the writer's royalties from international publishing income.[15]

In some circumstances, it may be difficult for a songwriter to require that the publisher have all of its subpublishing deals include an *at the source* provision, but a writer may reasonably insist upon a provision in the songwriter agreement specifying the maximum percentage that may be retained by the publisher's international subpublishers for the purpose of determining the writer's share of subpublishing income. Recognizing that the publisher may have a subsidiary in some countries and may independently contract with unaffiliated subpublishers in other countries, such percentage may vary according to territory. For example, with respect to income derived in territories in which the publisher has a subsidiary, the writer will receive 75% of publishing income, and with respect to all other territories a minimum of 50%. The percentages may also vary depending upon whether the subpublisher successfully creates language translations and *cover records* (i.e., commercially released recordings of the songwriter's composition by local artists in the territory) of the compositions.

### 8.  *Promotional Copies*

A publisher should not be expected to pay royalties on copies made for the purpose of promoting the compositions or on copies distributed on a consignment basis:

> (f) Publisher shall not be required to pay any royalties on reasonable numbers of professional or complimentary printed copies

---

[15] Such practices have been successful challenged in court. See, *Elton John v. Dick James Music* [1982 J. No. 15026, High Court of Justice, Chancery Division].

of the Composition or copies of mechanical derivatives of the Composition which are distributed gratuitously to performing artists, orchestra leaders and disc jockeys or for advertising, promotional or exploitation purposes for which Publisher receives no payment. Furthermore, no royalties shall be payable to Composer on consigned copies of the Composition unless paid for, and not until the accounting statement for the accounting period within which such payment is received.

The distribution of copies of the songs, in printed or recorded form, for the purpose of promoting them is an essential part of the publisher's business and should not only be permitted on a royalty free basis, but expected and encouraged by the songwriter. Distribution of copies on a consignment basis should be royalty free unless and until the consigned copies are paid for. However, the practice is subject to abuse, as when it is used solely for the purpose of delaying the payment of royalties to writers. The writer may have a cause to claim that consignment sales, under certain circumstances, are really sales upon which royalties, subject to a reasonable reserve for returns, should be paid.

### 9.   Collaborative Royalties

In Chapter 7, on *The Language of Music Licensing*, we discuss the standard for determining whether a work is considered a *joint work*. Briefly, when the music and lyrics of a composition are originally composed and written with the knowledge and intention that they would be merged as "an inseparable or interdependent part of a unitary whole," the resulting combination is considered a *joint work*. The authors of a joint work are co-owners of copyright in the work,[16] and each author automatically acquires an *undivided* ownership interest in the entire work.

This means that, unless otherwise agreed among the co-authors, the authors will share equally in the revenues generated by *all or any portion of* the work. For example, royalties generated by the sale or performance of any instrumental version of the composition will go to both the composer and the lyricist — equally, or according to per-

---

[16] 17 U.S.C. Sec. 201(a).

centages otherwise agreed upon — not just to the composer of the
music. Likewise, royalties from the licensing of any printed edition
containing only the lyrics will go to both authors, not just the lyricist.

The following provision is intended to make it clear that if lyrics
are later added to an instrumental composition, the composer will only
be entitled to one-half of the writer's share of publishing income and
that the revenues will be split as though the work were a joint work.

> (g) If the Composition does not now have lyrics, and lyrics
> shall hereafter be added by Publisher, the above royalties shall be
> divided equally between Composer on the one hand and the writer
> or writers of the lyrics on the other hand.

A writer may well insist upon the right to approve any added lyrics
and may, in fact, have that right, notwithstanding the terms of the
agreement, by virtue of the author's *moral rights* in certain countries
outside the United States.[17] Moreover, the above provision leaves unanswered the question of how royalties are to be shared among the
original songwriter and writers preparing changes or additions to the
melodic or instrumental aspects of the composition. Some standard
songwriter agreements are more specific about the division of royalties
in such cases, and tend, naturally, to resolve the question in favor of
the publisher. For example,

> Royalties as hereinabove specified shall be payable solely to
> Writer in instances where Writer is the sole author of the entire
> composition, including the words and music thereof. However, in
> the event that one or more other songwriters are authors together

---

[17] *Moral rights* include the right of an author to be named as the author of a work
(the right of paternity) and the right for an author to object to uses of the work which
could bring dishonor or discredit on the author's reputation (the right of integrity).
The nature and scope of moral rights varies considerably from country to country,
but regardless of their scope and extent, moral rights are typically not transferable
and sometimes, may not be waived. In some countries, moral rights are protected by
a combination of statutory provisions and common law. In the United States, for
instance, this protection is found in Federal legislation, such as the Lanham Act and
the Copyright Act, various state legislative provisions and the common law of privacy,
defamation and the like. *See Final Report of the Ad Hoc Working Group on U.S.
Adherence to the Berne Convention,* 10 COLUM. VLA J.L. & ARTS 513, 548-57
(1986); 2 NIMMER ON COPYRIGHT § 8D.02[A] (1995).

with Writer on any composition (including songwriters employed by Publisher to add, change or translate the words or to revise or change the music), then the foregoing royalties shall be divided equally between Writer and the other songwriters of such composition unless another division of royalties is agreed upon in writing between the parties concerned.

As discussed in more detail below in the section on *Creative Controls*, most songwriter agreements provide the publisher with a great deal of flexibility in making additions to, and modifications and translations of, the compositions covered by the agreement. That flexibility, combined with a collaborative royalties provision such as set forth above, could result in a significant and unfair reduction in the writer's royalty with the writer having little power to do anything about it.

For example, if the publisher engages another writer to rewrite the lyrics, the original songwriter's royalties would be reduced to 50%. If publisher engages two other writers to write new lyrics, the original songwriter's royalties would be reduced to 33⅓%. Further, a formula for splitting the royalties into equal shares based on the number of writers involved does not take into account the percentage each party contributed to the composition. Thus, the original songwriter's royalty share could be reduced to 33⅓%, if two other writers are used, even though it is clear the original songwriter's contribution exceeded 50% or more.

Some songwriter agreements give the publisher the sole right to determine how royalties are to be shared among collaborators. A provision which provides for equal sharing of royalties among collaborators will probably provide better protection to the original songwriter than one which leaves the matter entirely within the control of the publisher. At a minimum, the collaborators should always be given the flexibility to reach an agreement among themselves on a split acceptable to them, such as a split that is other than on an equal basis.

Finally, under the collaborative royalty provision set forth above, a writer engaged to prepare a foreign language translation of lyrics could receive a share of royalties equal to that of the original songwriter, though only with respect to income derived from the exploitation of the translation (but including instrumental versions of the translation). On the one hand, it could be argued that a mere translation of lyrics does not justify a 50% share of royalties; on the other, a case can be made that the translation of lyrics, like the translation of poetry, is an art which, done well, deserves an equal share with the original writer (especially if substantial modifications or additions are required to make the translation successful). If the composition was written by a composer and lyricist in collaboration, then, under the provision set forth above, the translator would receive 33⅓% share and each of the original writers would each receive 33⅓% share of the translated composition.

It is difficult, if not impossible, to determine in advance precisely what division of royalties would be fair and appropriate under all potential circumstances. However, a songwriter may negotiate a provision that provides him with some greater control over these situations when they arise. The best solution, for the writer with a significant amount of bargaining leverage, is to obtain the complete right of approval over the engagement of other writers to make additions, changes or translations. Alternatively, a writer could negotiate a specific percentage (e.g., 50%) below which his share of royalties may not be reduced without his consent. This would give the publisher the flexibility to make changes and additions while assuring the writer of an acceptable level of royalty participation.

### 10.  Demo Recordings

The following provision allows the publisher to recoup from the writer's future royalties one-half the cost the publisher incurs in making *demo recordings* (i.e., recordings used for demonstrating or promoting the compositions):

> (h) To the extent approved by Publisher in writing in advance, Publisher shall pay the cost of making demonstration records of the Composition. One-half (1/2) of a pro rata share corresponding to Composer's percentage of the Composition as set forth in paragraph 1 above, of such total costs shall be deemed additional advances to Composer hereunder.

A songwriter with a high degree of bargaining power may be able to negotiate the percentage of demo costs that will be charged to him down to 25% or to 0%. Whatever the percentage charged to the writer, it should be charged against the writer's account as an *advance*; that is, the writer should not be required to pay for these costs out of his pocket, unless he records or reproduces copies of demos on his own without the approval of the publisher.

## 11. Other Publishing Expenses

Some publishers also charge to the writers, as advances against royalties, the costs of copyright registration, advertising, the creation of lead sheets, and similar charges. A songwriter with a substantial amount of bargaining leverage might be able to negotiate these charges out of the contract on the basis that these are some of the very services the publisher is expected to provide in exchange for his publisher's share of the publishing income.

## 12. No Other Royalties

The first sentence of the following section should be acceptable to the songwriter, because section (c) above contains a *catch all* provision, entitling the writer to 50% of all income from sources not specifically referred to in the agreement:

> (i) Except as herein expressly provided, no other royalties or moneys shall be paid to Composer.

Without a *catch all* provision, discussed above, the first sentence of the above provision would effectively limit the writer's royalties to a percentage of only those sources of publishing income specifically set forth in the royalty section of the agreement. The writer, therefore, would not be entitled to royalties based upon publishing revenues from new uses, not set forth in the agreement, because they were only conceived or devised years after the signing of the agreement.

## 13. Advances from Licenses

Many standard songwriter agreements do not afford the writer a share in any advances received by the music publisher from its licensees. The writer would only receive these moneys when the advances are actually *earned* according to royalty statements eventually received from the licensees. But some provisions allow a writer to share in such advances under certain circumstances.

In no event shall Composer be entitled to share in any advance
payments, guarantee payments or minimum royalty payments which
Publisher may receive in connection with any subpublishing agreement, collection agreement, licensing agreement or other agreement
covering the Composition, unless such payment shall be solely related to the Composition; in which event Publisher shall credit Composer's royalty account with fifty percent (50%) of all such sums
received by Publisher.

This refusal to share advances with the songwriter is justified in
certain circumstances. For example, when a publisher receives an advance for the licensing of an entire catalog of compositions composed
by several (or several hundred) writers, it would be difficult or impractical to fairly allocate the advance among the respective songs in
the catalog prior to the time royalties on the catalog deal are actually
earned by the respective songs. However, such proration is not necessary when the advance relates only to one song. Thus, the second
clause in the above provision — affording the writer 50% of the advances received by the publisher if the advance was solely related to
the composition covered by the agreement — renders the limitation
on the payment of advances reasonable.

## H. Accounting

Music publishing agreements will contain a series of provisions
governing the way in which royalties will be accounted and paid to
the writer.

### 1. Accounting Statements

Most music publishers will account and pay royalties to writers
every six months under terms similar to the following:

> 4. (a) (i) Publisher shall compute the royalties earned by
> Composer pursuant to this agreement within sixty (60) days follow-
> ing the end of each semiannual calendar period during which mon-
> eys are received (or finally credited) with respect to the Composition,
> and shall thereupon submit to Composer the royalty statement for
> each such period together with the net amount of royalties, if any,
> which shall be payable after deducting any and all unrecouped ad-

vances and chargeable costs under this agreement. However, if a particular statement indicates a balance due of less than Fifty Dollars ($50.), Publisher shall not be required to make payment, and the balance due shall be carried forward until the end of the next subsequent accounting period during which the balance due exceeds Fifty Dollars ($50.), at which time such balance due shall be paid. Upon the submission of each statement, Publisher shall have the right to retain, as a reserve against subsequent charges, credits or returns, such portion of payable moneys hereunder (not exceeding 25%) with respect solely to print sales by Publisher or its affiliates as shall be necessary and appropriate in its best business judgment, but each such reserve shall be liquidated within two (2) quarter annual calendar periods following the period in respect of which such reserve is established. The payments to Composer provided for under this agreement shall be computed as of the date each such statement is due and shall be paid for in United States currency by Publisher to Composer. The rate(s) of exchange utilized by third parties in accounting to Publisher shall also apply as between Publisher and Participant in accounting for the same moneys.

Note that, unlike similar provisions in many songwriter agreements, the above provision does *not* provide for the cross-collateralization of royalties with sums related to "any other agreement between Writer and Publisher or companies related to or affiliated with Publisher."

Most publishers provide accountings to writers on a semi-annual basis. Though it would be more advantageous for a writer to receive accounting statements and royalty payments on a quarterly basis, it would be virtually impossible for many publishers to agree to change their entire royalty accounting practices to provide statements to single songwriters more frequently than their usual practices. However, a writer with high bargaining leverage may be able to negotiate that at least an advance be paid on a quarterly, monthly, or even bi-weekly basis, the amount to be determined on the basis of some percentage (e.g., in the case of quarterly advances, 25 to 50%) of the royalties earned during the most recent semi-annual accounting period.

The provision set forth above allows the publisher to dispense with sending an accounting statement when royalties earned fall under a minimum level. A publisher might be willing, albeit reluctantly, to remove this provision for writers having a moderate amount of bargaining leverage.

## 2. Reserves Against Returns

It is customary for a publisher to maintain a *reserve against returns* by withholding a portion of the royalties due the writer. This generally only applies to royalties derived from print licensing, but some songwriter agreements do not limit the type of royalties upon which reserves may be taken. When a publisher makes sales of printed editions of a writer's compositions, the publisher may expect that some of the copies sold to distributors and retailers during one quarter will be returned to the publisher during a subsequent quarter. These returns may be the result of less than expected consumer demand or product defects or misprints. Of course, the writer is only entitled to royalties on the basis of *net revenues* (i.e., the gross revenues earned by the publisher minus the returns). If the publisher previously paid royalties based upon the gross revenues and returns were subsequently made, then the publisher will have overpaid the writer by the amount of royalties that were based upon the returned sales. Thus, when a publisher holds a reserve against returns, he deducts a certain percentage (e.g., 25%) from the royalties he would otherwise be required to pay for sales of the work in a particular quarter, and holds on to that deduction in anticipation that there might later be a return of 25% of the copies previously sold.

The actual percentage used in calculating the reserve is intended to approximate the percentage of copies shipped that are expected, in the worst case, to be subsequently returned. Many songwriter agreements leave the determination of this percentage, and the length of time the publisher may retain the reserve, within the sole discretion of the publisher, as in the following reserve provision:

> Upon the submission of each statement, Publisher shall have the right to retain, as a reserve against subsequent charges, credits or returns, such portion of payable royalties as shall be necessary and appropriate in its best business judgment.

The *reserve* provision set forth in the section labeled 4(a)(i) above, however, reflects a compromise and limits the publisher's ability to retain a reserve in three ways: (1) by limiting the withholding of reserves solely with respect to the sales of printed editions (on the basis that returns of copies sold in the music publishing business is only applicable with respect to sales of printed editions), (2) by providing for a specific percentage limitation (i.e., 25%) on the amount that may be reserved in any one period, and (3) providing that the publisher liquidate the reserve within a specified period (i.e., two quarters).

### 3. Objections

Many songwriter agreements provide that accounting statements will be deemed binding unless specific objections are submitted to the publisher within one year after the date on which the statement is rendered, as in the following example:

> (b) Each statement submitted by Publisher to Composer shall be binding upon Composer and not subject to any objection by Composer for any reason unless specific written objection, stating the basis thereof, is sent by Composer to Publisher within one (1) year after the date said statement is received (or deemed received as provided below).

The provision arises from the publisher's desire to achieve some level of "closure" on statements provided in the past. However, a writer is not likely to conduct an audit within one year after receiving each statement and such an audit may be necessary to provide the requisite "specific written objection, stating the basis thereof." A writer should be able to increase the one year limitation to at least two years, or perhaps as long as the typical statute of limitations period for breach of contract (e.g., four years).

### 4. Audit Privileges

The typical songwriter agreement will also provide the writer with the privilege to *audit* (i.e., inspect) the books and records of the publisher as follows:

> Composer or a certified public accountant in Composer's behalf may, at Composer's expense, at reasonable intervals (but not more frequently than once each year), examine Publisher's books insofar as same contain data of concern to Composer, during Publisher's usual business hours and upon thirty (30) days' notice, for the purpose of verifying the accuracy of any statement submitted to Composer hereunder. Publisher's books relating to activities during any accounting period may only be examined as aforesaid during

the one (1) year period following receipt by Composer of the statement for said accounting period.

Again, a songwriter should be able to have the one year limitation in the last sentence of the previous paragraph increased to two or more years. Songwriters with some bargaining leverage should be able to negotiate the addition of a provision to the effect that, if the audit reveals that the publisher underpaid the royalties due by more than 5 or 10%, then the publisher will pay for the costs of the audit. Further, an audit provision should also contain a requirement that obligates the publisher to maintain accurate books and records in the first place. A number of accounting firms specialize in performing audits of such records, and a writer should consider having its publisher audited on a periodic basis to, as the saying goes, "keep 'em honest."

To avoid any misunderstandings regarding the calculation of the time limitations discussed above (often arising from the misdirection of accounting statements by virtue of the writer's failure to report a change of address), a publisher might include the following provision:

> (e) For the purpose of calculating the time period for audits and legal action by Composer, a statement shall be deemed to have been received thirty (30) days after the same is due unless, within such period, Publisher shall receive notice of nonreceipt of such statement from Composer. However, Composer's failure to give such notice shall not affect Composer's right to receive such statement (and any accompanying payment) thereafter.

### 5. *International Payments*

The following is a typical provision setting forth the procedures under which the writer would receive royalties in the event the publisher is unable to receive payments from sources overseas due to currency control laws or other restrictions.

> (ii) If Publisher shall be unable to receive payment in United States dollars in the United States in respect of any exploitation of the Composition due to currency control laws or regulations, royalties in respect thereof shall not be credited to Composer's royalty account hereunder. Publisher shall, however, use its best efforts to accept such payments in foreign currency and deposit in a

foreign bank or other depository, at Composer's expense, in such foreign currency such portion thereof, if any, as shall equal the royalties which would have actually been payable to Composer hereunder in respect of such exploitation had such payments been made to Publisher in United States dollars in the United States, and Publisher shall notify Composer thereof promptly. Deposit as aforesaid shall fulfill Publisher's royalty obligations hereunder as to such exploitation.

Because the publisher is in a better position to deal with the intricacies of foreign exchange matters, the writer should attempt to negotiate a provision to the effect that, if the Publisher is unable to receive payment in United States dollars in the United States, the Publisher shall pay to the writer an *advance* against royalties in an amount equal to the royalties that would have been payable had such payments been made to the publisher in United States dollars in the United States.

## I.   Name and Likeness

A publisher will often require a license to use the name, likeness, and biography of the writer in connection with the exploitation of the composition:

> 5. Composer hereby grants to Publisher, its associates, affiliates, subsidiaries and licensees the perpetual, nonexclusive right to use and publish and to permit others to use and publish Composer's name (including any professional name heretofore or hereafter adopted by Composer), likeness and biographical material, or any reproduction or simulation thereof and the title of the Composition in connection with the exploitation of the Composition.

Writers, who are also recording artists, have been known to become film stars (e.g., Sting) or otherwise famous celebrities (e.g., Madonna), and being such, their name, likeness and biography often becomes a valuable intellectual property (e.g., referred to as the artist's *right of publicity*), which may form the basis of a significant source of licensing revenue.

Some standard songwriter agreements include a very broad grant of these rights to the publisher. For example, an agreement may permit the publisher to use the writer's name, likeness, and biographical information in connection with the exploitation of the compositions and for any purpose related to the business of the publisher, or its affiliated companies, which may, of course, include, a film production company and a merchandising company (e.g., fan clubs, photographs, t-shirts, etc.). The writer should therefore carefully consider limiting the scope of the grant to uses that are directly in connection with the commercial exploitation of the compositions covered by the agreement and require the writer's consent for all other uses. A writer with stronger bargaining leverage might insist upon the right to approve any use of his name, likeness, or biographical materials by the publisher. A publisher may insist that any use the writer permits his record company, should automatically be deemed approved for use by the music publisher.

Note also, as discussed above, a writer might insist upon an additional royalty, and related advance, for the use of his name and likeness in connection with the publication of a *personality folio*. Unless the agreement specifically provides for such additional royalty, by granting to the Publisher an unrestricted right to use the writer's name and likeness, the writer would be relinquishing his ability to collect additional royalties for the use of his name and likeness on personality folios and other materials.

## J.   Creative Controls

A typical songwriter agreement will contain a provision which affords the publisher the privilege to make changes to the compositions covered by the agreement:

> 6. Composer hereby acknowledges that Publisher has the right hereunder, in its sole discretion, to substitute a new title or titles for the Composition, to make changes, arrangements, adaptations, translations, dramatizations and transpositions of the Composition, in whole or in part, and in connection with any other musical, literary or dramatic material, and to add new lyrics to the music of the Composition or new music to the lyrics of the Composition. Composer hereby waives any and all claims which he has or may have against Publisher, its associates, affiliates and subsidiaries and licensees by reason of the fact that the title of the Composition may be the same as or similar to that of any other musical compositions heretofore acquired by Publisher.

Many songwriters are quite sensitive to other's making changes to their compositions and will insist that some limitations, or creative controls, be imposed upon the kinds of modification privileges set forth in the above section. In general, publishers will allow some creative controls to the writer, but only to the extent the publisher believes their ability to recoup advances paid to the writer would not be impeded by the writer's unreasonable exercise of the control.

In the days when music publishers played a substantial role in the creative aspects of publishing, publishers would insist upon complete flexibility to make changes in the title, lyrics and other aspects of the musical compositions submitted to them by songwriters. For example, Jack Robbins of Robbins Music Corp. insisted that the *title* of virtually all songs published by his company be composed of the initial few words of the lyric — e.g., *I'm in the Mood for Love, Blue Moon, Don't Blame Me, Sweet and Lovely,* and *You'll Never Know.* Today, by contrast, a publisher is not likely to resist a restriction on its right to change the title of the composition.

Nevertheless, there are circumstances under which publishers are justified in maintaining some flexibility to make changes without having to obtain the writer's consent. For example, if the title of a composition is confusingly similar to that of another song, potential errors in royalty accounting and the crediting of valuable performance fees may be avoided by a slight change in the title. Perhaps a recording artist who is in the middle of a recording session may wish to record a writer's composition, but only if the artist is permitted to make several minor changes to the lyrics; the ability of the publisher to quickly approve the change may mean the difference between the commercial release of a major cover recording, with lucrative performance royalties to follow, and no release.

The publisher's professional staff may also play a valuable role in suggesting changes that may make the composition more popular. As song lyrics become increasingly violent and indecent, and radio stations and record distributors are becoming more sensitive to the objections of their listeners and the record buying public, publishers may come under increasing pressure — particularly if they find themselves potentially liable under obscenity laws — to tone down the lyrics of songs they publish. By making changes to the lyrics for the purpose of increasing record sales and public performances of the song, the publisher may infringe upon the artistic integrity of the writer's work, but he is legitimately and justifiably intending to enhance the total music publishing income from the song.

Of course, songwriters particularly sensitive to changes to their compositions will insist on specific limitations. For example, a songwriter might insist that any changes in the music or lyrics be limited to those reasonably necessary to conform to the style of a performing or recording artist or that the writer have the opportunity to make the desired changes himself before the changes are made by anyone else. More than an issue of mere artistic integrity or vanity, such a limitation would prevent a publisher from arbitrarily or unnecessarily using third parties to alter the writer's compositions, resulting in a reduction in the writer's economic participation in the composition. Worse yet, such a limitation would prevent an unscrupulous publisher from making changes sufficient to justify a publishing executive's adding his name as co-author of the composition.

A publisher, however, may justifiably resist the requirement to obtain the songwriter's consent for the creation of foreign language translations of the lyrics, but the writer might reasonably ask to be consulted with respect to such translations.

## K.  Other Restrictions

### 1.  *Restrictions on Mechanical Licensing*

#### a.  *Statutory Rate*

A songwriter with some bargaining leverage might try to limit the publisher's right to issue mechanical licenses for a fee below the *statutory rate*,[18] but a publisher is likely to agree only to the requirement that it issue mechanical licenses at no less than the statutory rate when the licensee is a company affiliated with the publisher, such as a record or motion picture company who is a parent, subsidiary or sister company of the publisher. As noted in Chapter 10, on *Basic Considerations in Music Licensing*, regarding the Affiliated Company Problem, a music publisher who is affiliated with a record company or motion picture studio should always be issuing licenses to their affiliates on

---

[18] See Chapter 12, on *Mechanical Licenses*.

an *arms length* basis (i.e., on the same rates, terms and conditions as though they were dealing with licensees who are not affiliated with the publisher). A writer may wish to add a general provision to this effect.

### b. First Use Licensing

A songwriter who is also a recording artist may request that neither the publisher, nor its subpublishers, issue a mechanical license for a *cover record* (i.e., a commercially released recording of the songwriter's composition by an artist other than the songwriter) for a specified period after the artist's own recording of the composition has been released. The publisher may wish to limit this restriction to a specified number of songs at any one time and to a specified period of time, such as nine months to one year.

As a practical matter, the publisher's ability to deny the issuance of a mechanical license may be limited in the United States by the compulsory license provision of the U.S. copyright law. After the first recording of a song is made and distributed to the public in the United States, others may acquire compulsory mechanical licenses for other recordings under Section 115 of the Copyright Act.[19]

### c. Controlled Compositions

Further, a writer may require the publisher to issue licenses in accordance with any *controlled composition* clauses[20] in any recording agreement into which the writer/artist may enter. The publisher may insist in return that, if some minimum mechanical license fee cannot be collected due to the writer's controlled composition clauses, the publisher may recover the shortfall out of the writer's royalties.

### 2. Restrictions on Synchronization Licensing

A songwriter with a high degree of bargaining power might retain the right to approve television or motion picture synchronization licenses,[21] but any approval rights over synchronization licenses the

---

[19] Id.

[20] Id.

[21] See Chapter 14, *Synchronization Licenses.*

writer receives is more likely to be limited to approving the use of his compositions in (1) *X-rated films*, (2) *commercial advertisements*,[22] or at least advertisements for those specified products the writer finds distasteful (e.g., cigarettes, nuclear power plants, condoms, and the like), and (3) *political advertisements.*

### 3.  Restrictions on the Use of the Song's Title and on Dramatic Uses

A writer might also obtain the right of approval over any use of the song's title as the title of a motion picture or television program or series, any dramatic adaptation of the lyrics, or any licenses for the dramatic performance of the song.[23]

### 4.  Restrictions on Print Licensing

A songwriter may ask that he have the right to consent to, or alternatively, the right to be consulted on, the content and appearance of any printed editions of the compositions.

## IV.  NEGOTIATING THE EXCLUSIVE TERM SONGWRITER AGREEMENT

The second type of songwriter agreement is known as the *exclusive term* agreement. The exclusive term agreement is sometimes referred to as a *staff writer* agreement, and the writers signed up by publishers under these agreements are called, not surprisingly, *staff writers.*

Unlike the *single song* agreement, under which the songwriter grants to the publisher the copyrights in one or more specific musical compositions, the *exclusive term* or *staff writer* agreement is used when the publisher wishes to sign up the writer on an exclusive basis for a specified period of time during which the writer is obliged to turn over to the publisher all songs he writes during that period. Note, there have evolved hybrid forms of the exclusive term songwriter

---

[22] See Chapter 20, *Licensing Music in Radio, Television and Print Advertising.*

[23] See Chapter 18, *The Grand Rights Controversy.*

agreements, such as an agreement that only covers songs written and recorded by a writer in connection with his services as a recording artist, but the discussion is essentially the same.

Because both forms of agreement define how the publisher and writer share in the income generated by the compositions covered, many of the provisions of the exclusive term agreement are the same as those in the single song agreement discussed above. Accordingly, in the following discussion, we focus primarily on those provisions that pertain to exclusive term agreements.

## A. Exclusive Employment

Many exclusive term songwriter agreements attempt to create an employment relationship between the songwriter and publisher. Such an agreement may begin as follows:

> 1. *Employment.* Publisher hereby employs Writer to render his services as a songwriter and composer and otherwise as may be hereinafter set forth. Writer hereby accepts such employment and agrees to render such services exclusively for Publisher during the term hereof, upon the terms and conditions set forth herein.

### 1. Works Made for Hire

Whether the relationship is deemed one of employment, rather than contractual, could affect the length of time the publisher will control the copyrights in the compositions. If the songwriter is considered an *employee* for hire of the publisher under the terms of the copyright law, then the songwriter would be unable to exercise the statutory rights he would otherwise have had to terminate the grant of rights and reacquire his copyrights after the statutory period of time.[24] The *author,* for purpose of determining an author's rights under the copyright law, is considered the employer, or the person for whom the work was made, not the actual creator of the work. In other words, given the existence of an employment relationship, the *publisher* is considered the author of the songs, not the songwriter.

---

[24] See Chapter 9, *Duration of Copyrights, Assignments, and Licenses.*

However, not all work relationships are automatically deemed employment relationships. In 1989, the U.S. Supreme Court ruled that whether one is an "employee" for hire under the copyright law is determined by applying the general rules of agency law.[25] For the relationship between the publisher and the writer to be legally deemed one between an employee and employer, the publisher would have to show the publisher exercised a sufficient degree of control over the manner and means by which the work of the writer was accomplished. Factors to be considered may include, the skill required, the source of the work tools, the location of the work, the duration of the relationship, the method of payment, and other factors.

Although the relationship between staff songwriter and music publisher would not typically meet this test, it may under certain circumstances. For example, arrangers employed to create lead sheets or demonstration recordings, or writers hired to create international language translations of compositions in the publisher's catalog may be deemed employees for hire. But unless circumstances show sufficient control exercised by the publisher, it is not likely that the popular musical works composed by a songwriter will be deemed a work made for hire by a mere statement in the songwriter agreement the songwriter is the employee of the publisher.

Nevertheless, a publisher may wish to include the following provision to improve the chances that the compositions created under the agreement will be considered a work made for hire of the publisher,

> 11. *Writer's Services.* Writer agrees to perform the services required hereunder conscientiously and solely and exclusively for and as requested by Publisher. Writer is deemed to be a "writer for hire" hereunder, and the works created hereunder shall be considered "works made for hire," with full rights of copyright vested in Publisher. Writer further agrees to promptly and faithfully comply with all requirements and requests made by Publisher in connection with its business as set forth herein.

There is a second way a work may be considered a work made for hire. The definition of *work for hire*, under the copyright law, is as follows:

---

[25] *Community for Creative Non-Violence v. Reid*, 490 U.S. 730 (1989).

A "work made for hire" is

(1) a work prepared by an employee within the scope of his or her employment; or

(2) a work specially ordered or commissioned for use as a contribution to a collective work, as a part of a motion picture or other audiovisual work, as a translation, as a supplementary work, as a compilation, as an instructional text, as a test, as answer material for a test, or as an atlas, if the parties expressly agree in a written instrument signed by them that the work shall be considered a work made for hire. For the purpose of the foregoing sentence, a "supplementary work" is a work prepared for publication as a secondary adjunct to a work by another author for the purpose of introducing, concluding, illustrating, explaining, revising, commenting upon, or assisting in the use of the other work, such as forewords, afterwords, pictorial illustrations, maps, charts, tables, editorial notes, musical arrangements, answer material for tests, bibliographies, appendixes, and indexes, and an "instructional text" is a literary, pictorial, or graphic work prepared for publication and with the purpose of use in systematic instructional activities.

Thus, if a publisher engages a songwriter to write a song under a written agreement that states the work is a work made for hire, *and* it is commissioned for use in one of the works listed in subsection (2) of the above definition, then the work will be considered a work made for hire and the publisher will be considered the author of the work. Note that general songwriting does not appear to fall within any of the categories of works set forth in section (2) of the definition. However, *audiovisual work* is listed in section (2) and, accordingly, songs written for motion pictures, television programs, music videos, and similar works, will qualify as a work that may clearly be a work for hire if the publisher or other person commissioning the work enters into a written agreement with the songwriter stating that the work shall be a work made for hire. Some would assert that such an agreement must be entered into before the songwriter commences his work for hire.

### 2. Demos

Demonstration recordings made at the music publisher's facilities could, under many circumstances, be considered the works made for hire of the publisher. In fact, many exclusive term songwriter agreements now specifically provide that demonstration recordings made by the writer during the term of the agreement are owned by the publisher. As the technology to create commercial quality demonstration has decreased, the question of who controls these demo recordings has become an increasingly important issue.

If the music publisher is to own the copyright in these demo recordings, songwriters should be certain they will be paid a fair portion of any revenues associated with their license, such as for synchronization with motion pictures, television commercials, and music videos. Though the publisher will receive a synchronization fee for the use of the underlying musical composition, half of which will be distributed as part of the writer's share of publishing income, the publisher may also receive a fee for the use of the sound recording master. At a minimum, the songwriter agreement should provide for the writer to be paid a share of these "master use" fees.

More important, however, a songwriter who is also a recording artist would want to restrict the publisher from licensing these demo recordings, by either requiring the artist's prior consent or by placing specific restrictions on the kinds of uses that may be licensed. This may be particularly important where the demo contains the performance of the songwriter and the songwriter has entered into a recording contract. Under such circumstances, the promotion of the demo may pose a conflict with the artist's recording activities.

### 3.  *Withholding*

By virtue of the purported employment relationship, a publisher may wish to make it clear it has the right to withhold from amounts payable to the writer any amounts required to be withheld under applicable taxation laws.

> Writer agrees and acknowledges that Publisher shall have the right to withhold from the royalties payable hereunder such amount, if any, as may be required under the applicable provisions of the California Revenue and Taxation Code, and Writer agrees to execute such forms and other documents as may be required in connection therewith.

Under California law, an employer engaging another to create a work made for hire must comply with applicable wage withholding provisions.[26]

### 4. Consideration

Some legal commentators have suggested that the typical exclusive term songwriter agreement is not a valid agreement because it lacks the legal requirement of sufficient *legal consideration.*

The basic legal rule is that, for a promise (i.e., agreement) to be enforceable, the promise must be supported by legal consideration. Legal consideration is the return given by one in exchange for the act or promise of another — that return may be in the form of an act, a detriment, or a return promise. It has been said that a songwriter's promise to render his services exclusively for a period of time, and to assign any compositions he writes during that time to the publisher, lacks sufficient legal consideration, because all the songwriter is getting in return is a promise to pay royalties, *if any,* to the writer, with no more than a vague and implied promise that the publisher will do something to generate income upon which such royalties could be based. Thus, the argument continues, if the publisher does not assume any express obligation under the songwriter agreement to exert any effort to generate the income upon which royalties would be based, would not his promise to pay royalties be illusory?

Under U.S. law, any detriment, such as the payment of $1.00, will constitute sufficient consideration. Most songwriter agreements don't even provide that. Instead, consideration is based upon the publisher's payment of an *advance* against future royalties or, if no advance is paid, consideration may be based upon the publisher's *implied promise* to ex-ploit the song, together with the publisher's promise to pay royalties if and when the song generates income.[27] Though this has been the established law in the United States, a different result was reached in several cases brought by songwriters in the United Kingdom.

---

[26] See California Labor Code Sec. 3351.5(c).

[27] See, *Wood v. Lucy, Lady Duff Gordon,* 222 N.Y. 88, 118 N.E. 214 (1917).

A U.K. court, in the seminal case of *A. Schroeder Music Publishing Company Limited v. Macaulay,*[28] ruled that an exclusive songwriter agreement was unenforceable, even though the publisher agreed to pay to the writer advances against royalties, because, under the songwriter's agreement, the publisher was not bound with a positive undertaking to exploit the composer's works.[29] The court in *Macualay* suggested, however, that had the songwriter been granted the right to recover ownership of the copyrights after a reasonable time of inactivity by the publisher, the agreement probably would have been declared enforceable. As a result, reversion of rights clauses, discussed above in connection with single song agreements, have become common in songwriter agreements entered into in the U.K.

### 5. *Exclusivity*

The extent of *exclusivity* may be set forth in a separate provision, such as the following:

> 4. *Exclusivity.* From the date hereof and during the term of this agreement, Writer will not write or compose, or furnish or dispose of, any musical compositions, titles, lyrics or music, or any rights or interests therein whatsoever, nor participate in any manner with regard to the same for any person, firm or corporation other than Publisher, nor permit the use of his name and likeness as the writer or co-writer of any musical compositions by any person, firm or corporation other than Publisher.

A writer with some bargaining leverage might negotiate exceptions depending upon the circumstances. For example, motion picture

---

[28] (1974) 3 All E.R. 616 (HL); See also, *W. Witmark & Sons v. Peters*, 149 N.Y.S. 642, (1914) and *Mellencamp v. Riva Music Ltd.*, 698 F.Supp. 1154 (S.D.N.Y. 1988).

[29] See also, *Clifford Davis Management Ltd. v. WEA Records, Ltd.*, (1975) 1 All E.R. 237 (refusing to allow the manager/publisher to enforce a publishing agreement against the rock group Fleetwood Mac, citing the *Macaulay* case with approval); *O'Sullivan v. Management Agency*, (1985) 3 All E.R. 351 (setting aside the songwriter agreement between Gilbert O'Sullivan and his publishing company, citing *Macaulay* with approval). However, in *Elton John v. Dick James Music* [1982 J. No. 15026, High Court of Justice, Chancery Division], the court refused to set aside the agreement between Elton John and his publisher, because of the long span of time that had elapsed between his first questioning the validity of the agreement and his bringing the lawsuit.

producers typically require copyright ownership when they engage writers to compose theatrical film scores and corporations or advertising agencies typically require copyright ownership when they engage writers to compose commercial jingles. Accordingly, a writer who is likely to engage in such composing would want an exception allowing the songwriter to do so. This is typically effected by excluding compositions *written on assignment*. The publisher may wish to limit the number of such compositions to a specified number per year, require the writer to use best efforts to retain a portion of the copyright for the music publisher, and require the writer to pay to the music publisher, to the extent of the writer's outstanding unrecouped advances, all or a portion of the composer fee earned by the writer on assignment. The exclusivity may be further circumscribed by a provision limiting the agreement to songs written and recorded by the writer in connection with his services as a recording artist. Exclusivity should certainly not apply to the artist's *recording* activities.

The exclusivity, however, will often extend not only to the writer's songwriting activity, but to the writer's name and likeness:

> Writer grants to Publisher, without any compensation other than as specified herein, the perpetual right to use and publish and to permit others to use and publish Writer's name (including any professional name heretofore or hereafter adopted by Writer), likeness and biographical material, or any reproduction or simulation thereof and titles of all compositions hereunder in connection with the printing, sale, advertising, distribution and exploitation of music, folios, recordings, performances, player rolls and otherwise concerning any of the compositions hereunder, and for any other purpose related to the business of Publisher, its affiliated and related companies, or to refrain therefrom. *This right shall be exclusive during the term hereof and nonexclusive thereafter.* Writer shall not authorize or permit the use of his name or likeness or biographical material concerning him, or other identification, or any reproduction or simulation thereof, for or in connection with any musical composition covered by this agreement, other than by or for Publisher. Writer grants Publisher the right to refer to Writer as Publisher's "Exclusive Songwriter and Composer" or other similar appropriate appellation.

As discussed in connection with single song agreements, a writer should try to limit the scope of the publisher's right to use his name, likeness and biography to conform to the writer's career circumstances. Remember, however, unlike under single song agreements, in the context of exclusive term agreements, these rights of publicity are granted to the publisher on an *exclusive* basis, making it all the more important for the writer to carefully consider the scope of the rights granted. For example, many of the same rights of publicity granted in the above provision to the music publisher on an exclusive basis will also be required by the artist's record company. The above provision, unless modified, could be used by the music publisher as a means to affect or restrict the artist's freedom to negotiate and close his record deal.

### 6. Specific Enforcement

The 13th Amendment to the United States Constitution outlawed slavery for good, so even a publisher can not force a writer to compose music if the latter refuses to work. Nevertheless, the exclusive term agreement will allow the publisher to enforce the exclusive nature of the relationship by legally preventing the writer from submitting compositions covered by the agreement to other publishers. The following provision clarifies the publisher's right to seek the appropriate equitable remedies necessary to enforce the publisher's exclusive rights:

> 12. *Unique Services.* Writer acknowledges that the services rendered hereunder are of a special, unique, unusual, extraordinary and intellectual character which gives them a peculiar value, the loss of which cannot be reasonably or adequately compensated in damages in an action at law, and that a breach by writer of any of the provisions of this agreement will cause Publisher great and irreparable injury and damage. Writer expressly agrees that Publisher shall be entitled to the remedies of injunction and other equitable relief to prevent a breach of this agreement or any provision thereof, which relief shall be in addition to any other remedies, for damages or otherwise, which may be available to Publisher.

### B. Term

When considering the *term*, or duration, of the exclusive term songwriter agreement, keep in mind the important distinction between the two separate contexts in which the word *term* is used. When we refer to the phrase, *exclusive term*, we are referring to the period of time, specified in the agreement, during which any songs created by the writer must be delivered and assigned to the publisher. This is sometimes referred to as the *administration period*. This should not be confused with the term, or period of time, during which the publisher will have the exclusive right to exploit any of the compositions delivered and assigned during the exclusive term — usually, the *life of copyright*, subject to any statutory termination rights or contractual rights of reversion (see above).

The exclusive term of an exclusive term songwriter agreement is typically one year with the publisher having a series of options to extend the term, usually up to an additional three years, but sometimes an additional four to six years. The exclusive term provision might be stated as follows:

> 2. *Term*. The term of this Agreement shall commence with the date hereof and shall continue in force for a period of one (1) year from said date. Writer hereby grants to Publisher four (4) separate and irrevocable options each to extend this agreement for a one (1) year term, such extension terms to run consecutively beginning at the expiration of the original term hereof, all upon the same terms and conditions as are applicable to the original term. Each option shall be automatically exercised unless written notice to the contrary is sent by Publisher to Writer at least ten (10) days prior to the expiration of the then current term. Such notice to the contrary may, at Publisher's election, be effective as to individual members of Writer or as to all members of Writer.

Publishers will seek to extend the exclusive term as long as possible. Some exclusive term agreements permit the publisher to extend the term if the advances received by the writer are unrecouped as of the date the agreement would otherwise expire. Others allow the publisher to extend the term in the event the writer does not meet certain delivery requirements. For example, the term may last for the longer of one year or until the date the writer completes the delivery to the publisher of ten acceptable songs, but these ten songs must be composed *solely* by the writer (i.e., if the writer delivers ten songs co-written with another writer, five songs remain to be delivered — to meet the delivery requirement, he must deliver either five additional songs written entirely by him or the equivalent number of songs partially written by him (e.g., two entirely written by him plus six partially written by him)). Further, the songs must be *acceptable*, or reasonably acceptable, to the publisher, which is intended to prevent the writer from, for example, composing several arrangements of songs in the public domain solely for the purpose of meeting the delivery requirement.

Songwriters might try to establish a minimum royalty level that must be achieved within any year as a condition to the publisher's exercise of the option for the following year. Alternatively, the songwriter could try to condition each option exercise with the publisher's ability to effect the commercial release of a minimum number of recordings each year. Again, the terms will vary with the bargaining leverage of the writer. A writer with a high degree of leverage may be able to require a minimum number of recordings released by artists who have been on the *charts* during the year (e.g., have had hit records listed on charts published by industry trade magazines, such as *Billboard*). Of course, if the writer possessed that degree of leverage, he would probably resist entering into an exclusive term agreement at the outset and, instead, insist upon entering a series of single song agreements having well negotiated reversion provisions (see above). Alternatively, a songwriter with a high degree of bargaining leverage would be able to command substantial advances, including advances upon the publisher's exercise of each of its options to extend the agreement. Where a music publisher has agreed to pay substantial advances, it is extremely unlikely the publisher would also agree to condition its option exercises upon either the achievement of minimum royalty levels or a minimum level of recordings released.

When a songwriter who is also a recording artist signs an exclusive term songwriter agreement with a music publishing company that is affiliated with his record company, the exclusive terms of the songwriter agreement and the recording agreement may be tied together. It should be to the writer's advantage for his exclusive term agreement to automatically terminate upon any termination of his recording contract. The following provision is an example of how the term of an exclusive term agreement may be tied with the term of a recording contract with an affiliated company:

> 8. *Other Agreements.* Simultaneously herewith Writer is entering into a recording contract with Publisher's record company

affiliate. Notwithstanding any provision to the contrary herein contained, it is the intent of the parties hereto that the term of this agreement be coterminous with the term of said recording contract. Accordingly, in the event said record company affiliate fails to exercise any renewal option with respect to the recording contract, Publisher shall not have the right to exercise any extension option hereunder; further, any extension, renewal, suspension or termination of the recording contract by said record company affiliate shall automatically and without further notice extend, renew, suspend or terminate this agreement in like manner.

The parties to an exclusive term agreement should also be aware of any state laws that may limit the length of time a music publisher can enforce a personal services contract. For example, in California, a personal services contract cannot be enforced against the writer for more than seven years.[30] In New York, there is precedent for the enforcement of a ten year personal services contract.[31]

## C. Advances

In the previous discussion of *single song agreements*, we mentioned that sometimes the songwriter receives, upon signing, a "nonreturnable, recoupable advance" against future royalties (except performance royalties the writer receives directly from his performance rights society). The advance tends to be higher if the songwriter has a track record, if the publisher believes the song's prospects for an early recording are good, or if the song had been previously published and has its own earnings track record.

Advances paid in the context of an exclusive term agreement are a little different in that the advance is often paid on a periodic (e.g., weekly) basis, and is paid for the purpose of providing the songwriter with a small living. These advances may range from $250 per week for a new writer to several thousands of dollars per week for established writers or writers who are also recording artists. Alternatively, advances may be paid upon the delivery of songs, but this often raises

---

[30] California Labor Code Section 2855; see, *Foxx v. Williams*, 244 Cal.App.2d 223, 52 Cal.Rptr. 896 (1966).

[31] *Ketcham v. Hall Syndicate, Inc.*, 37 M.2d 693, 236 N.Y.S.2d 206, aff'd 242 N.Y.S.2d 182.

the practical difficulty of determining what really constitutes a song for purpose of meeting the delivery requirement. For example, the writer may compose an arrangement of a song in the public domain solely for the purpose of meeting the delivery requirement.

A songwriter with some bargaining leverage may be able to negotiate an *escalation* clause, under which the amount of the minimum advance increases each year as a condition to the publisher's exercise of each its options to extend by one year the term of the agreement. For example, each such advance may be calculated on the basis of some percentage of the songwriter's previous year's music publishing earnings, with a minimum and a maximum dollar figure set for each option year. A songwriter who is also a recording artist may have his advances tied to the commercial release of recordings containing the compositions covered, providing him with an extra incentive to use the songs covered by the exclusive term agreement, early and often.

Some attorneys suggest that songwriters should avoid entering exclusive term agreements unless they need the cash or unless the publisher is in a special position to assist the writer's career though an exclusive relationship.

## D. Cross-Collateralization

When a songwriter who is also a recording artist signs an exclusive term songwriter agreement with a music publishing company that is affiliated with his record company, the publisher may try to cross-collateralize the writer's publishing and recording agreements. In other words, the writer's songwriter agreement will permit his music publisher (1) to recoup advances the writer received from the publisher from payments due writer under the writer's recording agreement with the publisher's affiliated record company *and* (2) to recoup advances received from the affiliated record company from payments due writer under the writer's songwriter agreement. The provision might take the following form:

> 21. *Recoupments.* It is understood and acknowledged that any and all charges against royalties under this agreement which are not recouped by Publisher may be recouped by Publisher's record company affiliate from any and all royalties earned by Writer as a recording group under their recording contract of even date with said record company, and that any and all charges against royalties under

said recording contract which are not recouped by said record company may be recouped by Publisher from any and all royalties earned by Writer hereunder.

Experienced writer/artists know that, because of the way their recording contracts are structured, their only true and reliable cash flow arises from their songwriter agreements. Artists who do not have the bargaining leverage to have the cross-collateral provision stricken in its entirety should at least insist that cross-collateralization be limited to payments due under other agreements with the music publisher (such as other single song publishing agreements or a co-publishing agreement), and never with his recording agreement.

## E. Compositions Covered

The compositions covered by the agreement are normally intended to include only those compositions written by the songwriter during the exclusive term of the agreement. Nevertheless, some exclusive term songwriting agreements provide that even songs composed prior to the signing of the agreement are granted to the publisher, sometimes referred to as the writer's *back catalog*. Such provisions may be found in the grant of rights clause, as illustrated by italicized language below:

> 3. *Grant of Rights.* Writer hereby irrevocably and absolutely assigns, transfers, sets over and grants to Publisher its successors and assigns each and every and all rights and interests of every kind, nature and description in and to the results and proceeds of Writer's services hereunder, including but not limited to the titles, words and music of any and all original musical compositions in any and all forms and original arrangements of musical compositions in the public domain in any and all forms, and/or all rights and interests existing under all agreements and licenses relating thereto, together with all worldwide copyrights and renewals and extensions thereof, *which musical works have been written, composed, created or conceived, in whole or in part, by Writer* alone or in collaboration with another or others, *and which hereafter, during the term hereof, be written, composed, created or conceived by Writer, in whole or in part*, alone or in collaboration with another or others, *and which are now owned or controlled and which may, during the term hereof,*

*be owned or controlled, directly or indirectly, by Writer,* alone or
with others, . . ."

A writer should independently review any of the compositions in
his back catalog to determine whether the copyrights in such compositions have already been granted to another publisher. In the event
the writer had previously composed some songs that are now controlled by another publisher, the back catalog provision should be limited to those compositions "owned or controlled" by the songwriter.
To avoid any misunderstandings as to which songs were intended to
be included, the parties would be advised to attach to the agreement
a schedule listing those back catalog compositions to be covered. If
the writer still controls the compositions and they are already earning
publishing income, then the writer might consider either withholding
the rights or offering them to the publisher for additional compensation.

Note that the foregoing grant of rights clause includes a grant of
compositions composed *in whole or in part* by the writer during the
term of the agreement, which means that if the writer begins the writing of a song during the exclusive term and completes it after the term
expires, the composition is owned by the publisher, not the writer or
the writer's new publisher. To protect themselves from writers who
withhold material created until after the exclusive term expires, some
publishers add a provision that grants them the publishing rights to
any song written by the writer and recorded or released within six
months after the exclusive term expires. This would eliminate the need
to prove whether the writing of a song recorded shortly after the expiration of the exclusive term did in fact commence prior to such
expiration.

The songwriter may insist, however, that only songs commercially
recorded during the exclusive term should be subject to the grant and
ownership in any songs previously granted that were not commercially
recorded by the expiration of the exclusive term (or within six months
of delivery to the publisher, whichever is later) should revert to the
writer.

## F.  Other Provisions

Provisions in exclusive term songwriter agreements relating to
grant of rights, territory, reversion of rights, royalties, accounting, au-

dit privileges, international payments, creative controls, and other restrictions, are generally the same as those contained in single song songwriter agreements, and the discussion regarding them in the previous section is applicable here.

## V. COLLABORATORS

It has been said that "two heads are better than one." That maxim can certainly find support in the long list of successful songwriting teams this century, including George and Ira Gershwin, Rodgers and Hart, Lennon and McCartney, and Elton John and Bernie Taupin. Several important questions arise when two or more writers work together to create musical works. Who gets the publishing rights? How are royalties shared among the collaborators? What happens when both writers sign up with the same publisher? Should the writing partners enter into a collaboration agreement? We will discuss each of these questions in turn.

### A. Who Gets the Publishing?

Where each collaborator is signed up to an exclusive term agreement with the same music publisher or each typically assigns his or her songs to the same publisher as a matter of course, the question of who gets the publishing is straightforward. But what happens when each writer is engaged to work with a different publisher? The following provision, used by some publishers to address this problem, may be found in many exclusive term agreements:

> 10. *Collaboration with other Writers.* Whenever Writer shall collaborate with any other person in the creation of any musical composition, any such musical composition shall be subject to the terms and conditions of this agreement and Writer warrants and represents that prior to the collaboration with any other person, such other person shall be advised of this exclusive agreement and that all such compositions must be published by Publisher. In the event of such collaboration with any other person, Writer shall notify Publisher of the extent of interest that such other person may have in any such musical composition and Writer shall cause such other person to execute a separate songwriter's agreement with respect

thereto, which agreement shall set forth the division of the song-writer's share of income between Writer and such other person, and Publisher shall make payment accordingly. If Publisher so desires, Publisher may request Writer to execute a separate agreement in Publisher's customary form with respect to each musical composition hereunder. Upon such request, Writer will promptly execute such agreement. Publisher shall have the right, pursuant to the terms and conditions hereof, to execute such agreement in behalf of Writer hereunder. Such agreement shall supplement and not supersede this agreement. In the event of any conflict between the provisions of such agreement and this agreement, the provisions of this agreement shall govern. The failure of either of the parties hereto to execute such agreement, whether requested by Publisher or not, shall not affect the rights of each of the parties hereunder, including but limited to the rights of Publisher to all of the musical compositions written and composed by Writer.

Thus, under above provision, the writer agrees to cause the copyright in the entire song, including the publishing rights of both his share and that of his collaborator, to be assigned to the writer's publisher. But how is the writer going to cause this to happen? Perhaps, before the song is written, the writer and his partner have entered into a collaboration agreement under which the partners agreed in advance that all songs they write together will be assigned to the writer's publisher. Nevertheless, unless the two writers are a standing team, that solution may not always be practical. Moreover, the writer's partner is likely to have his own ideas about who gets the right to publish his compositions. In any event, if the writer's partner had already been bound to an exclusive term agreement with another publisher at the time the composition was created, the partner may already be obligated to assign his copyright in the composition (including perhaps his partner's share) to that other publisher.

In practice, the onerous provision set forth above is rarely enforced. The typical solution is that the two publishers involved enter into a co-publishing or co-administration agreement that determines the respective rights of the parties in the composition. The several alternative forms these co-publishing and co-administration deals may take are described in the next chapter. If a songwriting team regularly collaborates on the writing of compositions, they and their publishers might agree to an arrangement under which the publishing or administration rights to the first song go to one publisher and the rights to the next song go to another publisher — in effect, alternating the allocation of rights among the parties involved. At a minimum, the songwriter should seek to limit his obligation to using *reasonable efforts* to secure the publishing of the other writer's share.

## B. How Are Royalties Shared Among Collaborators?

As discussed in the *collaborative royalties* section of our discussion of single song music publishing agreements, when the music and lyrics of a composition are originally composed and written with the knowledge and intention that they would be merged as "an inseparable or interdependent part of a unitary whole," the resulting combination is considered a *joint work.* The authors of a joint work are co-owners of copyright in the work,[32] and each author automatically acquires an *undivided* ownership interest in the entire work. This means that, unless otherwise agreed among the co-authors, the authors of the work will share equally in the revenues generated by *all or any portion of* the work.

For example, royalties generated by the sale or performance of any instrumental version of the composition will go to both the composer and the lyricist — equally, or according to percentages otherwise agreed upon — not just to the composer of the music. Likewise, royalties from the licensing of any printed edition containing only the lyrics will go to both authors, not just the lyricist.

However, this does not prevent co-authors from agreeing among themselves to another division of the copyright and the publishing royalties. For example, where one author contributed words and music and the other authored only the words, the two may agree to a 75/25% division. Composer George Gershwin always insisted upon receiving a full 50% interest in a composition, even when two lyric writers contributed to the song, each lyric writer in such an instance sharing the other 50% interest equally.

If the writers desire to agree upon a division other than in equal shares, they should notify their publisher. Many songwriter agreements

---

[32] 17 U.S.C. Sec. 201(a); See also the discussion of *joint works* in Chapter 7, on *The Language of Music Licensing.*

specify that royalties will be paid in equal shares unless the contract specifies otherwise:

> 10. The term "Composer" shall be understood to include all the writers and composers of the Composition. If there be more than one, the covenants herein contained shall be deemed to be both joint and several on the part of the writers and composers and the royalties hereinabove specified to be paid to Composer shall, unless a different division of royalties be specified herein, be due to all the writers and composers collectively, to be paid by Publisher in equal shares to each.

As noted above, some songwriter agreements give the publisher the sole right to determine how royalties are to be shared among collaborators. At a minimum, collaborators should always be given the flexibility to reach an agreement among themselves on a split acceptable to them.

## C.  What Happens When Collaborators Sign-up with the Same Publisher?

When two or more co-authors grant to a publisher (or group of co-publishers) the copyright and publishing rights in their jointly created work, each writer would be advised to enter into a separate songwriter agreement with the publisher. This is to assure that if one writer breaches his songwriter agreement, the other writer's rights and obligations will not be affected.

However, if the writers are truly an inseparable team, and each has entered into an exclusive term agreement with the same publisher, each agreement should be made co-terminous with the other. In other words, if the publisher terminates, or fails to exercise an option to renew the term of one of the writer's exclusive term agreement, the other writer's exclusive term agreement is automatically terminated.

Finally, a writer should try to eliminate any cross-collateralization between his songwriter agreement and that of his co-author. This will prevent any unfair distribution of royalties, and recoupment of advances, in the event that one of the writers collaborates in the writing of a song with a third writer or if the collaborators stop writing songs together.

## D. Should Co-Authors Enter into a Collaboration Agreement?

In the absence of a written agreement, the co-authors of a composition will be deemed to have equal shares in the copyright. This is because a transfer of copyright, or any exclusive rights under copyright, is not valid unless it is effected by a writing signed by the owner of the rights.[33]

Accordingly, where the co-authors agree to a division of copyright or royalties that is other than that of equal shares, they should enter into a written agreement to reflect their understanding. Alternatively, the co-authors may rely on a written communication to their music publisher evidencing their agreement, but the writer having the greater share would be advised to have his partner sign a short agreement to avoid any misunderstanding.

Members of performing groups are often advised to enter into a collaboration agreement, partnership agreement, or shareholder agreement, depending upon the circumstances, to deal with a broad range of issues concerning their respective rights to the musical works, recordings, group name, merchandising rights, and other business and legal matters arising from what is likely to be a dynamic relationship among the members over time.

### VI. Summary

Whether you work for a major music publisher or are just starting your own music publishing business, you should understand the basic terms and conditions of the standard songwriter agreement. If you are a songwriter, or songwriter's representative, you should be aware of the typical variations to the terms and conditions in these agreements that may be negotiated with music publishers.

---

[33] 17 U.S.C. Sec. 204(a)

# APPENDIX TO CHAPTER 3
# SONGWRITER AGREEMENTS

# FORM 3.1

## SONGWRITER AGREEMENT
## FOR SINGLE SONG I

### SONGWRITER'S AGREEMENT

AGREEMENT entered into this _____ day of _____ 20__, by and between _____ ("Publisher") and _____ ("Composer").

1. Composer hereby sells, assigns, conveys, grants and transfers irrevocably and exclusively to Publisher, its successors and assigns, the original musical composition written and composed by Composer presently entitled _____ ("the Composition"), including, without limitation, the title, words, and music thereof, all copyrights therein and thereto throughout the universe for the full term of copyright and for any renewals or extensions thereof under any present or future laws throughout the universe, the right to secure copyright registration and protection in the Composition, in any arrangements, adaptations or other versions thereof, and in any works derived therefrom, and any and all other rights relating to the Composition (including, without limitation, public performance rights, printing and publication rights, mechanical and electrical reproduction rights, dramatization rights and synchronization rights) which Composer now has or could have had if this agreement had not been entered into.

2. Composer hereby grants irrevocably to Publisher, its successors and assigns, the right in perpetuity to use and to permit others to use throughout the universe Composer's name (both legal and professional, and whether presently or hereafter used by Composer), likeness, other identification, and biographical material concerning Composer, for purposes of trade, and otherwise without restriction, in connection with the Com-

position and any uses thereof, and in connection with Publisher's music business, or to refrain therefrom.

3. Publisher shall pay Composer the following royalties in respect of the Composition:

(a) Six cents ($.06) per copy for each copy of sheet music in standard piano/vocal notation printed, published and sold in the United States and Canada by Publisher or its licensees, for which payment shall have been received by Publisher, after deduction of returns.

(b) Ten percent (10%) of the wholesale selling price of each printed copy of each other arrangement and edition printed, published and sold in the United States and Canada by Publisher or its licensees, for which payment shall have been received by Publisher, after deduction of returns, except that if the Composition shall be used or caused to be used, in whole or in part, in conjunction with one or more other musical compositions in a folio, compilation, song book or other publication, Composer shall be entitled to receive that proportion of the foregoing royalty which the number one (1) shall bear to the total number of musical compositions contained therein.

(c) Fifty percent (50%) of any and all net sums actually received (less any costs for collection) by Publisher in the United States from the exploitation in the United States and Canada by licensees of mechanical rights, grand rights, electrical transcription and reproduction rights, motion picture and television synchronization rights, dramatization rights and all other rights therein (except print rights, which are covered in (a) and (b) above, and public performance rights, which are covered in (d) below), whether or not such licensees are affiliated with, owned in whole or in part by, or controlled by Publisher.

(d) Composer shall receive Composer's public performance royalties throughout the world directly from the performing rights society with which Composer is affiliated, and shall have no claim whatsoever against Publisher for any royalties received by Publisher from any performing rights society which makes payment directly (or indirectly other than through Publisher) to writers, authors and composers.

(e)  Fifty percent (50%) of any and all net sums actually received by Publisher in the United States as damages awarded to Publisher in any infringement action instituted by Publisher with respect to the Composition after the deduction therefrom of all costs or expenses incurred by Publisher in connection therewith, including, without limitation, attorneys' and accountants' fees, court costs, and expert fees.

(f)  Fifty percent (50%) of any and all net sums, after deduction of foreign taxes, actually received (less any costs for collection) by Publisher in the United States from the exploitation of the Composition in countries outside of the United States and Canada (other than public performance royalties, which are covered in (d) above), whether from collection agents, licensees, subpublishers or others, and whether or not same are affiliated with, owned in whole or in part by, or controlled by Publisher.

(g)  Publisher shall not be required to pay any royalties on professional or complimentary printed copies or records or on printed copies or records which are distributed gratuitously to performing artists, orchestra leaders and disc jockeys or for advertising, promotional or exploitation purposes. Furthermore, no royalties shall be payable to Composer on consigned copies unless paid for, and not until such time as an accounting therefor can properly be made.

(h)  If any additions, modifications or substitutions (including translations) to or in the Composition are hereafter made by any party who shall be entitled to royalties with respect thereto, Composer's royalties hereunder shall be reduced by the royalties payable to such party.

(i)  Except as herein expressly provided, no other royalties or moneys shall be payable to Composer hereunder.

(j)   Publisher shall have the right to withhold from the royalties payable to Composer hereunder such amount, if any, as may be required under the provisions of all applicable Federal, State and other tax laws and regulations, and Composer shall execute such forms and other documents as may be required in connection therewith.

(k)   Composer shall not be entitled to share in any advance payments, guarantee payments, or minimum royalty payments which Publisher may receive in connection with any subpublishing agreement, collection agreement, licensing agreement or other agreement relating to the Composition.

4.   Statements as to royalties payable hereunder shall be sent by Publisher to Composer on or before the thirtieth day of September for the semiannual period ending the preceding June 30th and on or before the 31st day of March for the semiannual period ending the preceding December 31st, together with payment of accrued royalties, if any, earned by Composer hereunder during such semiannual period, less all advances and charges under this agreement or under any other agreement between Composer and Publisher or its affiliates. Publisher shall have the right to retain, as a reserve against charges, credits, or returns, such portion of royalties payable on print sales by Publisher or its affiliates as shall be reasonable in Publisher's best business judgment. Composer shall be deemed to have consented to all royalty statements rendered by Publisher hereunder, and each such royalty statement shall be conclusive, final, and binding, shall constitute an account stated, and shall not be subject to any objection for any reason whatsoever, unless specific objection in writing, stating the basis thereof, is given by Composer to Publisher within two (2) years after the date rendered.

Publisher shall maintain books of account concerning income derived from the exploitation of the Composition. Composer or a certified public accountant in Composer's behalf may, at Composer's sole expense, examine Publisher's said books solely for the purpose of verifying the accuracy of royalty statements rendered hereunder, only during Publisher's normal business hours and upon reasonable written notice, not more frequently than once each year. Publisher's said books relating to any particular royalty statement may be examined as aforesaid only within two (2) years after the date rendered, and Publisher shall have no obligation to permit Composer to examine Publisher's said books relating to any particular royalty statement more than once. The rights hereinabove granted to Composer shall constitute Composer's sole and exclusive rights to examine Publisher's books and records.

5. Composer hereby warrants, represents, covenants and agrees that: Composer has the full right, power, and authority to enter into and perform this agreement and to sell, assign, convey, grant and transfer the Composition to Publisher and to vest in Publisher all the rights herein set forth, free and clear of any and all claims, rights, encumbrances and obligations whatsoever; the Composition was written solely by Composer, is new and original, and is capable of copyright protection throughout the universe; neither the Composition nor any part thereof is an imitation or copy of, or infringes upon, any other material, or violates or infringes upon any common law, statutory, or other rights of any party, including, without limitation, contractual rights, copyrights and rights of privacy; Composer has not sold, assigned, leased, licensed or in any other way disposed of or encumbered the Composition or any of the rights herein granted to publisher: Composer shall not take or authorize or permit to be taken any action in derogation of Publisher's rights hereunder.

6. Composer hereby indemnifies, saves and holds Publisher, its successors and assigns, harmless from any and all liability, claims, demands, loss and damage (including counsel fees and court costs) arising out of or connected with any claim or action by a third party which is inconsistent with any of the warranties, representations or agreements made by Composer in this agreement, and Composer shall reimburse Publisher, on

demand, for any loss, cost, expense or damage to which said indemnity applies. Publisher shall give Composer prompt written notice of any claim or action covered by said indemnity, and Composer shall have the right, at Composer's expense, to participate in the defense of any such claim or action with counsel of Composer's choice. Pending the disposition of any such claim or action, Publisher shall have the right to withhold payment of such portion of any moneys which may be payable by Publisher to Composer under this agreement or under any other agreement between Composer and Publisher or its affiliates as shall be reasonably related to the amount of the claim and estimated counsel fees and costs.

7.   Publisher may, in its best business judgment, substitute a new title or titles for the Composition, make changes, arrangements, adaptations, translations, dramatizations, and transpositions of the Composition, in whole or in part, and in connection with any other musical, literary, dramatic, or other material, and add new lyrics to the music of the Composition or new music to the lyrics of the Composition. Composer hereby waives any "droit moral" or other right comparable thereto. Composer hereby waives any and all claims which Composer has or may have against Publisher, its affiliates and subsidiaries, by reason of the fact that the title of the Composition may be the same as or similar to that of any other musical compositions heretofore or hereafter acquired by Publisher.

8.   The term "Composer" shall include all the writers and composers of the Composition. If there be more than one, the warranties, representations and covenants herein contained shall be deemed to be both joint and several on the part of such writers and composers, and the royalties payable hereunder shall be paid by Publisher to each of them in the percentages set forth below:

COMPOSER                          PERCENTAGE

_____           _____

_____           _____

9.   Publisher shall have the right to assign this agreement and any of its rights hereunder and to delegate any of its obligations hereunder, in whole or in part, to any party. Without limiting the generality of the foregoing, Publisher shall have the right to enter into subpublishing, collection, print or other agreements with respect to the Composition with any parties. Composer shall not have the right to assign any of Composer's rights hereunder without Publisher's prior written consent.

10.   Composer shall, at Publisher's request, cooperate fully with Publisher with respect to any claim, action, or proceeding relating to the Composition. Publisher shall have the right to institute, defend, compromise and settle any such claim, action or proceeding in such manner as publisher shall determine in its best business judgment.

11.   Composer hereby irrevocably constitutes, authorizes, empowers and appoints Publisher or any of its officers Composer's true and lawful attorney (with full power of substitution and delegation), in Composer's name, and in Composer's place and stead, or in Publisher's name, to take and do such action, and to make, sign, execute, acknowledge and deliver any and all instruments or documents, which Publisher from time to time may deem desirable or necessary to vest in Publisher, its successors and assigns, all of the rights or interests granted by Composer hereunder, including, without limitation, such documents as Publisher shall deem desirable or necessary to secure to Publisher, its successors and assigns, the copyright for the Composition throughout the universe for the entire term of copyright and for any and all renewals and extensions under any present or future laws throughout the universe. The foregoing is acknowledged to be a power coupled with an interest and therefore irrevocable.

12.   All notices to be given to Composer hereunder and all statements and payments to be sent to Composer hereunder shall be addressed to Composer at the address set forth below or at such other address as Composer shall designate in writing

from time to time. All notices to be given to Publisher hereunder shall be addressed to Publisher at the address set forth below or at such other address as Publisher shall designate in writing from time to time. All notices shall be in writing and shall be served by certified or registered mail, or telegraph, all charges prepaid. Except as otherwise provided herein, such notices shall be deemed given when mailed or delivered to a telegraph office, all charges prepaid, except that notices of change of address shall be effective only upon the actual receipt thereof.

13.　If Publisher shall produce any demonstration recordings of the Composition, Publisher shall pay the costs of such production, and one-half (1/2) of such costs shall be deemed advances to Composer which shall be recoupable by Publisher from royalties payable to Composer under this agreement or under any other agreement between Composer and Publisher or its affiliates. All demonstration recordings shall be the sole and exclusive property of Publisher.

14.　This agreement sets forth the entire understanding of the parties hereto relating to the subject matter hereof. No modification, amendment, waiver, termination or discharge of this agreement or of any provision hereof shall be effective unless confirmed by a written instrument signed by the party sought to be bound. No waiver of any provision of this agreement or of any default hereunder shall affect the waiving party's right thereafter to enforce such provision or to exercise any right or remedy in the event of any other default, whether or not similar. If any provision of this agreement shall be held void, voidable, invalid or inoperative, no other provision of this agreement shall be affected as a result thereof, and, accordingly, the remaining provisions of this agreement shall remain in full force and effect as though such void, voidable, invalid or inoperative provision had not been contained herein. This agreement shall not be deemed to give any right or remedy to any third party unless said right or remedy is specifically granted by Publisher in writing to such third party. This agreement shall not be binding upon Publisher until signed by Composer and countersigned by

Publisher. This agreement shall be deemed to have been made in the State of California, and its validity, construction and legal effect shall be governed by the laws of the State of California applicable to contracts entered into and performed therein. The use of the singular in this agreement shall include the plural where appropriate.

15. Composer hereby acknowledges receipt from Publisher of the sum of _____, as an advance recoupable by Publisher from royalties payable to Composer under this agreement or under any other agreement between Composer and Publisher or its affiliates.

IN WITNESS WHEREOF, the parties hereto have executed this agreement on the date hereinabove set forth.

By _____

Address:

Birth Date: _____

Soc. Sec. No.: _____

# FORM 3.2

## SONGWRITER AGREEMENT
## FOR SINGLE SONG II

### SINGLE SONG MUSIC PUBLISHING AGREEMENT

AGREEMENT entered into this _____nd day of
_____, 20___, by and between _____ (here-
inafter referred to as "Composer") and BIG MUSIC PUBLISH-
ING CORP. (ASCAP) (hereinafter referred to as "Publisher").

1.     Composer hereby sells, assigns and delivers to
Publisher, its successors and assigns, the original musical compositions written and composed by Composer (words of which
were written by _____ and music by _____),
presently entitled "_____" (the "Composition"), including
the title, words and music thereof, all worldwide rights therein,
all copyrights therein and thereto, all registrations with respect
thereto, and the exclusive right to secure copyrights and any
extensions of copyrights in the same and in any arrangements
and adaptations thereof, all throughout the world, and any and
all other rights, claims and demands that Composer now has
or to which he might be entitled or that he hereafter could or
might secure throughout the world with respect thereto if these
presents had not been made, and to have and to hold the same
absolutely and forever unto Publisher, its successors and assigns, subject only to any existing agreements between Composer and Publisher and the Performing Rights Society (with
which they are affiliated).

2.     Composer hereby warrants and represents that the
Composition is an original work, that neither the Composition
nor any part thereof infringes upon the title, literary or musical
property or copyright of any other work nor the statutory, common law or other rights (including rights of privacy or publicity)
of any person, firm or corporation or violates any applicable

criminal statute, that he is the sole writer and composer and the sole owner of the Composition and of all the rights therein, that he has not sold, assigned, transferred, hypothecated or mortgaged any right, title or interest in or to the Composition or any part thereof or any of the rights herein conveyed, that he has not made or entered into any agreement with any other person, firm or corporation affecting the Composition or any right, title or interest therein or in the copyright thereof, that no person, firm or corporation other than Composer has or has had claims or has claimed any right, title or interest in or to the Composition or any part thereof, any use thereof or any copyright therein, that the Composition has never been published, and that Composer has full right, power and authority to make this present instrument of sale and transfer.

3.     In consideration of this agreement and of the rights and interests hereby conveyed and granted, Publisher agrees to pay to Composer the following royalties in respect of the Composition:

(a)     Seven cents ($.07) per copy for each copy of sheet music in standard piano-vocal notation of the Composition printed, published and sold in the United States and Canada by Publisher or its affiliates, for which payment has been received by Publisher, or been finally credited to Publisher's account in reduction of an advance after deduction of reasonable returns. (Wherever the terms "paid," "received," or the equivalent appear in this agreement, they shall be deemed to include such final credit.)

(b)     (i)     If the Composition is included in any folio, songbook or similar publication ("mixed folio"), a proportionate share of a royalty of twelve and one-half percent (12 1/2%) of the net wholesale selling price of such publication for all copies sold by Publisher or its affiliates and paid for in the United States and Canada. Said proportionate share shall be equal to the percentage computed by dividing the number "one" by the total number of all copyrighted musical compositions contained therein.

(ii)    If the Composition is included in a "fake book", "educational edition" or an instrumental, orchestral, choral or band arrangement or other arrangement intended for pedagogical purposes, a royalty of ten percent (10%), or a proportionate share thereof (calculated in the manner prescribed above in the case of a mixed folio) of the net wholesale selling price for all copies of such work sold by Publisher or its affiliates and paid for in the United States and Canada.

(iii)    If, pursuant to a license granted by Publisher to a licensee not controlled by or affiliated with it, the Composition is included in any mixed folio in the United States and/or Canada, a pro rata share of fifty percent (50%) of the gross amount received by Publisher from the licensee as the number of uses of the Composition under the license and during the license period bears to the total number of uses of Publisher's copyrighted musical compositions (including the Composition) under the license and during the license period.

(c)    Fifty percent (50%) of any and all net sums actually received (less any cost for collection) by Publisher or credited to Publisher's account in the United States from the exploitation in the United States and Canada by licensees of Publisher of mechanical rights, electrical transcription and reproducing rights, motion picture and television synchronization rights, and all other rights in the Composition (except print rights which are covered in paragraphs 3(a) and 3(b) above and public performance rights which are covered in (d) below), whether or not such licensees are affiliated with, owned in whole or in part by, or controlled by Publisher.

(d)    (i)    Composer shall receive his public performance royalties throughout the world directly from his own affiliated performing rights society and shall have no claim whatsoever against Publisher for any royalties received by Publisher from any performing rights society which makes payment directly (or indirectly other than through Publisher) to writers, authors and composers.

(ii) If, however, (and to the extent that) Publisher shall collect both the Composer's and Publisher's share of performance income directly and such income shall not be collected by Composer's public performance society, Publisher shall pay to Composer fifty percent (50%) of all such net sums which are received by Publisher in the United States from the exploitation of such rights in the Composition, throughout the world.

(e) Fifty percent (50%) of any and all net sums, after deduction of foreign taxes, actually received (less any reasonable costs for collection) by Publisher in the United States from sales, licenses and other uses of the Composition in countries outside of the United States and Canada (other than public performance royalties described in subparagraph 3(d)(i)) from collection agents, licensees, subpublishers or others, whether or not same are affiliated with, owned in whole or in part by, or controlled by Publisher. This provision shall not apply to copies of printed music shipped from the United States to such countries, to which the rates set forth in paragraphs 3(a) and 3(b) above shall apply.

(f) Publisher shall not be required to pay any royalties on reasonable numbers of professional or complimentary printed copies of the Composition or copies of mechanical derivatives of the Composition which are distributed gratuitously to performing artists, orchestra leaders and disc jockeys or for advertising, promotional or exploitation purposes for which Publisher receives no payment. Furthermore, no royalties shall be payable to Composer on consigned copies of the Composition unless paid for, and not until the accounting statement for the accounting period within which such payment is received.

(g) If the Composition does not now have lyrics, and lyrics shall hereafter be added by Publisher, the above royalties shall be divided equally between Composer on the one hand and the writer or writers of the lyrics on the other hand.

(h)     To the extent approved by Publisher in writing in advance, Publisher shall pay the cost of making demonstration records of the Composition. One-half (1/2) of a pro rata share corresponding to Composer's percentage of the Composition as set forth in paragraph 1 above, of such total costs shall be deemed additional advances to Composer hereunder.

(i)     Except as herein expressly provided, no other royalties or moneys shall be paid to Composer. In no event shall Composer be entitled to share in any advance payments, guarantee payments or minimum royalty payments which Publisher may receive in connection with any subpublishing agreement, collection agreement, licensing agreement or other agreement covering the Composition, unless such payment shall be solely related to the Composition; in which event Publisher shall credit Composer's royalty account with fifty percent (50%) of all such sums received by Publisher.

4.     (a)     (i)     Publisher shall compute the royalties earned by Composer pursuant to this agreement within sixty (60) days following the end of each semiannual calendar period during which moneys are received (or finally credited) with respect to the Composition, and shall thereupon submit to Composer the royalty statement for each such period together with the net amount of royalties, if any, which shall be payable after deducting any and all unrecouped advances and chargeable costs under this agreement. However, if a particular statement indicates a balance due of less than Fifty Dollars ($50.), Publisher shall not be required to make payment, and the balance due shall be carried forward until the end of the next subsequent accounting period during which the balance due exceeds Fifty Dollars ($50.), at which time such balance due shall be paid. Upon the submission of each statement, Publisher shall have the right to retain, as a reserve against subsequent charges, credits or returns, such portion of payable moneys hereunder (not exceeding 25%) with respect solely to print sales by Publisher or its affiliates as shall be necessary and appro-

priate in its best business judgment, but each such reserve shall be liquidated within two (2) quarter annual calendar periods following the period in respect of which such reserve is established. The payments to Composer provided for under this agreement shall be computed as of the date each such statement is due and shall be paid for in United States currency by Publisher to Composer. The rate(s) of exchange utilized by third parties in accounting to Publisher shall also apply as between Publisher and Participant in accounting for the same moneys.

(ii)    If Publisher shall be unable to receive payment in United States dollars in the United States in respect of any exploitation of the Composition due to currency control laws or regulations, royalties in respect thereof shall not be credited to Composer's royalty account hereunder. Publisher shall, however, use its best efforts to accept such payments in foreign currency and deposit in a foreign bank or other depository, at Composer's expense, in such foreign currency such portion thereof, if any, as shall equal the royalties which would have actually been payable to Composer hereunder in respect of such exploitation had such payments been made to Publisher in United States dollars in the United States, and Publisher shall notify Composer thereof promptly. Deposit as aforesaid shall fulfill Publisher's royalty obligations hereunder as to such exploitation.

(b)    Each statement submitted by Publisher to Composer shall be binding upon Composer and not subject to any objection by Composer for any reason unless specific written objection, stating the basis thereof, is sent by Composer to Publisher within two (2) years after the date said statement is received (or deemed received as provided below). Composer or a certified public accountant in Composer's behalf may, at Composer's expense, at reasonable intervals (but not more frequently than once each year), examine Publisher's books insofar as same contain data of concern to Composer, during Publisher's usual business hours and upon thirty (30) days' notice, for the purpose of verifying the accuracy of any statement submitted to Composer hereunder. Publisher's books relating to activities during any accounting period may only be examined as aforesaid during the two (2) year period following receipt by Composer of the statement for said accounting period.

(c)    Notwithstanding any provision to the contrary herein contained, moneys hereunder shall only be payable by Publisher to Composer with respect to moneys actually received by Publisher in the United States or amounts finally credited to Publisher's account in reduction of a previous advance.

(d)    Legal action by Composer with respect to a specific accounting statement or the accounting statement to which the same relates shall be forever barred if not commenced in a court of competent jurisdiction within three (3) years after such statement is received (or deemed received as provided below).

(e)    For the purpose of calculating the time period for audits and legal action by Composer, a statement shall be deemed to have been received thirty (30) days after the same is due unless, within such period, Publisher shall receive notice of nonreceipt of such statement from Composer. However, Composer's failure to give such notice shall not affect Composer's right to receive such statement (and any accompanying payment) thereafter.

5.    Composer hereby grants to Publisher, its associates, affiliates, subsidiaries and licensees the perpetual, nonexclusive right to use and publish and to permit others to use and publish Composer's name (including any professional name heretofore or hereafter adopted by Composer), likeness and biographical material, or any reproduction or simulation thereof and the title of the Composition in connection with the exploitation of the Composition.

6.    Composer hereby acknowledges that Publisher has the right hereunder, in its sole discretion, to substitute a new title or titles for the Composition, to make changes,

arrangements, adaptations, translations, dramatizations and transpositions of the Composition, in whole or in part, and in connection with any other musical, literary or dramatic material, and to add new lyrics to the music of the Composition or new music to the lyrics of the Composition. Composer hereby waives any and all claims which he has or may have against Publisher, its associates, affiliates and subsidiaries and licensees by reason of the fact that the title of the Composition may be the same as or similar to that of any other musical compositions heretofore acquired by Publisher.

7.    Composer agrees to execute and deliver to Publisher all documents which may be required to effectuate the intent of this agreement, including, without limitation, a short-form copyright assignment in the form attached hereto as Exhibit "A," and, in the event that Composer fails to do so within ten (10) days following Composer's receipt of notice requesting same, Composer does hereby irrevocably empower and appoint Publisher, or any of its officers, Composer's true and lawful attorney (with full power of substitution and delegation) in Composer's name, and in Composer's place and stead, or in Publisher's name, to take and do such action, and to make, sign, execute, acknowledge, deliver, and record any and all instruments or documents which Publisher, from time to time, may deem desirable or necessary to vest in Publisher, its successors, assigns and licensees, any of the rights granted by Composer hereunder, including, without limitation, such instruments or documents required to secure to Publisher copyright registration and protection for the Composition for the full term of copyright and for any extensions thereof.

8.    Composer shall not transfer nor assign this agreement nor any interest therein nor any sums that may be or become due hereunder without the prior written consent of Publisher, which shall not be unreasonably withheld. Publisher shall not be deemed unreasonable for withholding its consent to a proposed assignment of Composer's right to receive royalties hereunder to more than one person. No purported as-

signment or transfer in violation of this restriction shall be valid to pass any interest to the assignee or transferee.

9. (a) Publisher may take such action as it deems necessary, either in Composer's name or in its own name, against any person to protect the rights and interest acquired by Publisher hereunder. Publisher will promptly notify Composer of any claims, action, demand or proceeding which may affect Publisher or Composer's interest in the Composition and Composer shall have the right to participate therein by counsel of Composer's choice, at Composer's sole cost and expense. Composer will, at Publisher's request, cooperate fully with Publisher (but at no material expense to Composer), in any controversy which may arise or litigation which may be brought concerning Publisher's rights and interests acquired hereunder.

(b) Publisher shall have the right, in its absolute discretion, to employ attorneys and to institute or defend any action or proceeding and to take any other proper steps to protect the right, title and interest of Publisher in and to the Composition and every portion thereof and in that connection, to settle, compromise or in any other manner dispose of any matter, claim, action or proceeding and to satisfy any judgment that may be rendered, in any manner as Publisher in its sole discretion may determine, provided that Composer's written consent shall be required to settle any claims and such consent shall not be unreasonably withheld. If Composer shall not give written consent to a proposed settlement of a claim which Publisher believes is reasonable within five (5) days after Composer's receipt of notice of such settlement offer, then on Publisher's request Composer shall promptly undertake any further action in regard to the claim at Composers sole cost and expense, and Composer shall thereafter be fully and totally responsible and liable for any damages or costs in excess of the amount set forth in the proposed settlement offer.

(c) Any legal action brought by Publisher against any alleged infringer of the Composition shall be initiated and prosecuted by Publisher, and if there is any recovery made by Publisher as a result Thereof, the expenses of litigation, including but not limited to attorney's fees and court costs, shall be deducted therefrom and Composer shall be paid one-half (1/2) of a pro rata share of the net proceeds corresponding to Composer's percentage of The Composition as set forth in paragraph 1 above.

(d) Composer hereby indemnifies, saves and holds Publisher, its assigns, licensees and its and their directors, officers, shareholders, agents and employees harmless from any and all liability, claims, demands, loss and damage (including reasonable counsel fees and court costs) arising out of or connected with or resulting from any breach of any of the warranties, representations or agreements made by Composer in this agreement which results in an adverse judgment or a settlement entered into with Composer's prior written consent. Notwithstanding the foregoing, such indemnity shall also extend to the deductible under Publisher's errors-and-omissions policy without regard to judgment or settlement. In the event that Composer refuses to consent to a proposed settlement which Publisher considers reasonable, Composer shall assume the defense of the subject claim, action or proceeding, at Composer's expense. Such indemnity shall also extend to reasonable counsel fees and court costs incurred in connection with any claim, action or proceeding brought at Composer's written request. Publisher shall give Composer prompt written notice of any claim, action or proceeding covered by said indemnity, and the notified party shall have the right to participate by counsel of Composer's choice, at Composer's sole cost and expense. Pending the disposition of any adverse claim or action, Publisher shall have the right to withhold payment of such portion of moneys hereunder as shall be reasonably related to the amount of the claim and estimated legal expenses; provided, that any amount so withheld shall be released if (and to the extent that) legal action shall not have been commenced with respect thereto in a court of competent jurisdiction within one (1) year following such withholding; and provided, further, that

Publisher shall not withhold moneys otherwise due to Composer if Composer shall deliver to Publisher an indemnity or surety bond, in form satisfactory to Publisher, which shall cover the amount of the claim and estimated legal costs.

10.    The term "Composer" shall be understood to include all the writers and composers of the Composition. If there be more than one, the covenants herein contained shall be deemed to be both joint and several, subject to the terms of paragraph 2, above, on the part of the writers and composers and the royalties hereinabove specified to be paid to Composer shall, unless a different division of royalties be specified in paragraph 16 below, be due to all the writers and composers collectively, to be paid by Publisher in equal shares to each.

11.    (a)    Publisher shall have the right to assign this agreement and any of its rights hereunder to any parent, subsidiary or affiliated person, firm or corporation, any entity into which or with which Publisher may merge or consolidate, or any purchaser of substantially all of Publisher's stock or assets.

(b)    Publisher shall also have the right to enter into sub-publishing, collection, print or other agreements with respect to the Composition with any person, firm or corporation for any one or more countries of the world.

12.    This agreement contains the entire understanding between the parties, and all of its terms, conditions and covenants shall be binding upon and shall inure to the benefit of the respective parties and their heirs, successors and assigns. No modification or waiver hereunder shall be valid unless the same is in writing and is signed by The party sought to be bound.

13.    This agreement has been entered into in, and is to be interpreted in accordance with the Laws of, the State of California. All actions or proceedings seeking the interpretation and/or enforcement of this agreement shall be brought only in the State or Federal Courts located in Los Angeles County, both

parties hereby submitting themselves to the jurisdiction of such courts for such purpose.

14.    (a)    All notices, statements and payments required or desired to be given hereunder shall be given by addressing same to the addresses of the respective parties hereinbelow set forth, or to such other address as either party may hereafter designate, by writing and shall be delivered by the United States mails, certified or registered, postage prepaid, or in a telegraph or cable office (except for royalty statements and payments which shall be sent by regular mail). If the party's consent is required, it shall not be unreasonably withheld (unless expressly provided otherwise herein) and shall be deemed denied unless the notified party gives notice of consent within 15 days after receipt of notice requesting consent. All notices to Publisher shall be sent to the attention of Publisher's Legal Department.

(b)    Publisher shall not be deemed to be in default hereunder unless Composer shall notify Publisher thereof and Publisher shall fail to remedy the same within thirty (30) days thereafter (or, if the alleged default is of such a nature that it cannot be completely remedied within such thirty-day period, Publisher shall fail to commence the remedying of such alleged default within such thirty-day period and to proceed to complete the same within a reasonable time thereafter).

15.    The use of the singular in this agreement shall apply to and mean the plural where appropriate.

16.    Composer hereby acknowledges that presently he is not affiliated as a writer with any Performing Rights Society and will do so as soon as he qualifies as a member. Composer agrees that he will promptly advise Publisher of such affiliation and Publisher shall, if necessary, have the right to assign this Agreement and all of Publisher's interest in The Composition to an affiliated publishing company which is a member of the Society which Composer joins.

IN WITNESS WHEREOF, the parties hereto have executed this agreement as of the date hereinabove set forth.

IMPORTANT

This is a legal document,
and you should review it with
an experienced attorney
before you sign it.

BIG MUSIC PUBLISHING CORP.

By: _____
Vice President
1000 Sunset Boulevard
Hollywood, CA 90069

_____
MR. JOHN DOE (MUSIC)
Address:
S.S.#:
Date of Birth:

_____
MS. JANE DOE (LYRICS)
Address:
S.S.#:
Date of Birth:

# FORM 3.3

## EXCLUSIVE TERM SONGWRITER AGREEMENT

### SONGWRITER'S AND COMPOSER'S AGREEMENT

THIS AGREEMENT made and entered into this _____ day of January 1, 20__ by and between _____ (hereinafter referred to as "Publisher") and _____ (hereinafter collectively referred to as "Writer").

1.    Employment. Publisher hereby employs Writer to render his services as a songwriter and composer and otherwise as may be hereinafter set forth. Writer hereby accepts such employment and agrees to render such services exclusively for Publisher during the term hereof, upon the terms and conditions set forth herein.

2.    Term. The term of this agreement shall commence with the date hereof and shall continue in force for a period of _____ from said date. Writer hereby grants to Publisher _____ separate and irrevocable option each to extend this agreement for a one (1) year term, such extension terms to run consecutively beginning at the expiration of the original term hereof, all upon the same terms and conditions as are applicable to the original term. Each option shall be automatically exercised unless written notice to the contrary is sent by Publisher to Writer at least ten (10) days prior to the expiration of the then current term. Such notice to the contrary may, at Publisher's election, be effective as to individual members of Writer or as to all members of Writer.

3.    Grant of Rights. Writer hereby irrevocably and absolutely assigns, transfers, sets over and grants to Publisher its successors and assigns each and every and all rights and interests of every kind, nature and description in and to the results and proceeds of Writer's services hereunder, including but not

limited to the titles, words and music of any and all original musical compositions in any and all forms and original arrangements of musical compositions in the public domain in any and all forms, and/or all rights and interests existing under all agreements and licenses relating thereto, together with all worldwide copyrights and renewals and extensions thereof, which musical works have been written, composed, created or conceived, in whole or part, by Writer alone or in collaboration with another or others, and which may hereafter, during the term hereof, be written, composed, created or conceived by Writer, in whole or in part, alone or in collaboration with another or others, and which are now owned or controlled and which may, during the term hereof, be owned or controlled, directly or indirectly, by Writer, alone or with others, or as the employer of transferee, directly or indirectly, of the writers or composers thereof, including the title, words and music of each such composition, and all worldwide copyrights and renewals and extensions thereof, all of which Writer does hereby represent are and shall at all times be Publisher's sole and exclusive property as the sole owner thereof, free from any adverse claims or rights therein by any other person, firm or corporation.

Writer acknowledges that, included within the rights and interests hereinabove referred to, but without limiting the generality of the foregoing, is Writer's irrevocable grant to Publisher, its successors, licensees, sublicensees and assigns, of the sole and exclusive right, license, privilege and authority throughout the entire world with respect to the said original musical compositions and original arrangements of compositions in the public domain, whether now in existence or hereafter created during the term hereof, as follows:

(a)     To perform said musical compositions publicly for profit by means of public and private performance, radio broadcasting, television, or any and all other means, whether now known or which may hereafter come into existence.

(b)     To substitute a new title or titles for said compositions and to make any arrangement, adaptation, translation, dramatization and transposition of said composition, in whole or in part, and in connection with any other musical, literary or dramatic material, and to add new lyrics to the music of said compositions or new music to the lyrics of said compositions, all as Publisher may deem expedient or desirable.

(c)   To secure copyright registration and protection of said compositions in Publisher's name or otherwise as Publisher may desire at Publisher's own cost and expense and at Publisher's election, including any and all renewals and extensions of copyrights, and to have and to hold said copyrights, renewals, extensions and all rights of whatsoever nature thereunder existing, for and during the full term of all said copyrights and all renewals and extensions thereof.

(d)   To make or cause to be made, master records, transcriptions, sound tracks, pressings, and any other mechanical, electrical or other reproductions of said compositions, in whole or in part, in such form or manner and as frequently as Publisher's sole and uncontrolled discretion shall determine, including the right to synchronize the same with sound motion pictures and the right to manufacture, advertise, license or sell such reproductions for any and all purposes, including but not limited to private performances and public performances, by broadcasting, television, sound motion pictures, wired radio and any and all other means or devices whether now known or which may hereafter come into existence.

(e)   To print, publish and sell sheet music, orchestrations, arrangements and other editions of the said compositions in all forms, including the right to include any or all of said compositions in song folios or lyric magazines with or without music, and the right to license others to include any or all of said compositions in song folios or lyric magazines with or without music.

(f)   Any and all other rights of every and any nature now or hereafter existing under and by virtue of any common law rights and any copyrights and renewals and extensions thereof in any and all of such compositions. Writer grants to Publisher, without any compensation other than as specified herein, the perpetual right to use and publish and to permit others to use and publish Writer's name (including any professional name heretofore or hereafter adopted by Writer), likeness and biographical material, or any reproduction or simulation thereof and title of all compositions hereunder in connection with the printing, sale, advertising, distribution and exploitation of music, folios, recordings, performances, player rolls and otherwise concerning any of the compositions hereunder, and for any other purpose related to the business of Publisher, its affiliated and related companies, or to refrain therefrom. This right shall be exclusive during the term hereof and nonexclusive thereafter. Writer shall not authorize or permit the use of his name or likeness or biographical material concerning him, or other identification, or any reproduction or simulation thereof, for or in connection with any musical composition covered by this agreement, other than by or for Publisher. Writer grants Publisher the right to refer to Writer as Publisher's "Exclusive Songwriter and Composer" or other similar appropriate appellation.

4.    Exclusivity. From the date hereof and during the term of this agreement, Writer will not write or compose or furnish or dispose of, any musical compositions, titles, lyrics or music, or any rights or interests therein whatsoever, nor participate in any manner with regard to the same for any person, firm or corporation other than Publisher, nor permit the use of his name or likeness as the writer or co-writer of any musical composition by any person, firm or corporation other than Publisher.

5.    Warranties, Representations, Covenants and Agreements. Writer hereby warrants, represents, covenants and agrees as follows: Writer has the full right, power and authority to enter into and perform this agreement and to grant to and vest in Publisher all the rights herein set forth, free and clear of any and all claims, rights and obligations whatsoever; all the

results and proceeds of the services of Writer hereunder, including all of the titles, lyrics, music and musical compositions, and each and every part thereof, delivered and to be delivered by Writer hereunder are and shall be new and original and capable of copyright protection throughout the entire world, and that no musical composition hereunder or any part hereof shall be an imitation or copy of, or shall infringe upon, any other material, or shall violate or infringe upon any common law or statutory rights of any party including, without limitation, contractual rights, copyrights and rights of privacy, and that Writer has not sold, assigned, leased, licensed or in any other way disposed of or encumbered the rights herein granted to Publisher, nor shall Writer sell, assign, lease, license or in any other way dispose of or encumber said rights.

6. <u>Power of Attorney</u>. Writer does hereby irrevocably constitute, authorize, empower and appoint Publisher, or any of its officers, Writer's true and lawful attorney (with full power of substitution and delegation) in Writer's name, and in Writer's place and stead, or in Publisher's name, to take and do such action, and to make, sign, execute, acknowledge and deliver any and all instruments or documents which Publisher, from time to time, may deem desirable or necessary to vest in Publisher, its successors, assigns and licensees, any of the rights or interests granted by Writer hereunder, including but not limited to such documents required to secure to Publisher the renewals and extensions of copyrights throughout the world of musical compositions written or composed by Writer and owned by Publisher, and also such documents necessary to assign to Publisher, its successors and assigns, such renewal copyrights, and all rights therein for the terms of such renewals and extensions for the use and benefit of Publisher, its successors and assigns.

7. <u>Compensation</u>. Provided that Writer shall faithfully and completely perform the terms, covenants and conditions of this agreement, Publisher hereby agrees to pay Writer for the services to be rendered by Writer under this agreement and for

the rights acquired and to be acquired hereunder, the following compensation based on the musical compositions which are the subject hereof.

(a)    ($.) per copy for each piano copy and dance orchestration printed, published and sold in the United States and Canada by Publisher or its licensees, for which payment has been received by Publisher, after deduction or returns.

(b)    (  ) of the wholesale selling price upon each printed copy of each other arrangement and edition printed, published and sold in the United States and Canada by Publisher, for which payment has been received by Publisher, after deduction of returns, except that in the event that any composition shall be used or caused to be used, in whole or in part, in conjunction with one or more other musical compositions in a folio, album or other publication, Writer shall be entitled to receive that proportion of said ten percent (10%) which the subject composition shall bear to the total number of musical compositions contained in such folio, album or other publication.

(c)    Fifty percent (50%) of any and all net sums actually received (less any costs for collection) by Publisher in the United States from the exploitation in the United States and Canada by licensees of Publisher of mechanical rights, electrical transcription and reproducing rights, motion picture and television synchronization rights, printing rights (except as provided in (a) above), and all other rights (excepting public performing rights) therein, whether or not such licensees are affiliated with, owned in whole or in part by, or controlled by Publisher.

(d)    Writer shall receive his public performance royalties throughout the world directly from his own affiliated performing rights society and shall have no claim whatsoever against Publisher for any royalties received by Publisher from any performing rights society which makes payment directly (or indirectly other than through Publisher) to writers, authors and composers.

(e)    (  ) of any and all net sums, after deduction of foreign taxes, actually received (less any costs for collection) by Publisher in the United States from sales, licenses and other uses of the subject musical compositions in countries outside of the United States and Canada (other than public performance royalties as hereinabove mentioned in (d) above) from collection agents, licensees, subpublishers or others, whether or not same are affiliated with, owned in whole or in part by, or controlled by Publisher.

(f)    Publisher shall not be required to pay any royalties on professional or complimentary copies or any copies or mechanical derivative which are distributed gratuitously to performing artists, orchestra leaders and disc jockeys or for advertising, promotional or exploitation purposes. Furthermore, no royalties shall be payable to Writer on consigned copies unless paid for, and not until such time as an accounting therefor can properly be made.

(g)    Royalties as hereinabove specified shall be payable to Writer in instances where Writer is the sole author of the entire composition, including the words and music thereof. However, in the event that one or more other songwriters are authors together with Writer on any composition (including songwriters employed by Publisher to add, change or translate the words or to revise or change the music), then the foregoing royalties shall be divided equally between Writer and the other songwriters of such composition unless another division of royalties is agreed upon in writing between the parties concerned.

(h)    Except as herein expressly provided, no other royalties or moneys shall be paid to Writer.

(i)    Writer agrees and acknowledges that Publisher shall have the right to withhold from the royalties payable to Writer hereunder such amount if any, as may be required under the applicable provisions of the California Revenue and Taxation Code, and Writer agrees to execute such forms and other documents as may be required in connection therewith.

(j)    In no event shall Writer be entitled to share in any advance payments, guarantee payments or minimum royalty payments which Publisher shall receive in connection with any subpublishing agreement, collection agreement, licensing agreement or other agreement covering the subject musical compositions.

8.    Other Agreements. Simultaneously herewith Writer is entering into a recording contract with Publisher's record company affiliate. Notwithstanding any provision to the contrary herein contained, it is the intent of the parties hereto that the term of this agreement be coterminous with the term of said recording contract. Accordingly, in the event said record company affiliate fails to exercise any renewal option with respect to the recording contract, Publisher shall not have the right to exercise any extension option hereunder; further, any extension, renewal, suspension or termination of the recording contract by said record company affiliate shall automatically and without further notice extend, renew, suspend or terminate this agreement in like manner.

9.    Accounting. Publisher will compute the total composite royalties earned by Writer pursuant to this agreement and pursuant to any other agreement between Writer and Publisher, whether now in existence or entered into at any time subsequent hereto, on or before March 31 for the semiannual period ending the preceding December 31st and on or before September 30 for the semiannual period ending the preceding June 30th, and will submit to Writer the royalty statement for each such period together with the net amount of such royalties, if any, which shall be payable after deducting any and all unrecouped advances and chargeable costs under this agreement or any other agreement between Writer and Publisher. Upon the submission of each statement, Publisher shall have the right to retain, as a reserve against subsequent charges, credits or returns, such portion of payable royalties as shall be necessary and appropriate in its best business judgment. All royalty statements rendered by Publisher to Writer shall be

binding upon Writer and not subject to any objection by Writer for any reason unless specific written objection, stating the basis thereof, is submitted by Writer to Publisher within one (1) year from the date rendered. Writer or a certified public accountant in his behalf may, at Writer's expense, at reasonable intervals, examine Publisher's books insofar as same concern Writer, during Publisher's usual business hours and upon reasonable notice, for the purpose of verifying the accuracy of any royalty statement rendered to writer hereunder. Publisher's books relating to activities during any accounting period may only be examined as aforesaid during the one (1) year period following service by the Publisher of the royalty statement for said accounting period.

10.    Collaboration with other Writers. Whenever Writer shall collaborate with any other person in the creation of any musical composition, any such musical composition shall be subject to the terms and conditions of this agreement and Writer warrants and represents that prior to the collaboration with any other person, such other person shall be advised of this exclusive agreement and that all such compositions must be published by Publisher. In the event of such collaboration with any other person, Writer shall notify Publisher of the extent of interest that such other person may have in any such musical composition and Writer shall cause such other person to execute a separate songwriter's agreement with respect thereto, which agreement shall set forth the division of the songwriter's share of income between Writer and such other person, and Publisher shall make payment accordingly. If Publisher so desires, Publisher may request Writer to execute a separate agreement in Publisher's customary form with respect to each musical composition hereunder. Upon such request, Writer will promptly execute such agreement. Publisher shall have the right, pursuant to the terms and conditions hereof, to execute such agreement in behalf of Writer hereunder. Such agreement shall supplement and not supersede this agreement. In the event of any conflict between the provisions of such agreement and this agreement, the provisions of this agreement shall gov-

ern. The failure of either of the parties hereto to execute such agreement, whether requested by Publisher or not, shall not affect the rights of each of the parties hereunder, including but not limited to the rights of Publisher to all of the musical compositions written and composed by Writer.

11.    Writer's Services. Writer agrees to perform the services required hereunder conscientiously and solely and exclusively for and as requested by Publisher. Writer is deemed to be a "writer for hire" hereunder with full rights of copyright renewal vested in Publisher. Writer further agrees to promptly and faithfully comply with all requirements and requests made by Publisher in connection with its business as set forth herein. Writer will deliver a manuscript copy of each musical composition hereunder immediately upon the completion or acquisition of such musical composition. Nothing contained in this agreement shall obligate Publisher to exploit in any manner any of the rights granted to Publisher hereunder. Publisher at its sole discretion shall reasonably make studio facilities available for writer so that Writer, subject to the supervision and control of Publisher, may make demonstration records of the musical compositions hereunder and also for Writer to perform at such recording sessions. Writer shall not incur any liability for which Publisher may be responsible in connection with any demonstration record session without having first obtained Publisher's written approval as to the nature, extent and limit of such liability. In no event shall Writer incur any expense whatsoever in behalf of Publisher without first having received written authorization from Publisher. Writer shall not be entitled to any compensation (in addition to such compensation as may be otherwise provided for herein) with respect to services rendered in connection with such demonstration record recording sessions. Publisher shall advance the costs for the production of demonstration records, and one-half (1/2) of such costs shall be deemed additional nonreturnable advances to Writer and shall be deducted from royalties payable to Writer by Publisher under this or any other agreement between the parties. All recordings and reproductions made at demonstration recording

session hereunder shall become the sole and exclusive property of Publisher, free of any claims whatsoever by Writer or any person deriving any rights from Writer.

Writer shall, from time to time, at Publisher's reasonable request, whenever the same will not unreasonably interfere with other professional engagements of Writer, appear for photography, artwork and other similar reasons under the direction of Publisher or its duly authorized agent, appear for interviews and other promotional purposes, and confer and consult with Publisher regarding Writer's services hereunder. Writer shall not be entitled to any compensation (other than applicable union scale if appropriate) for rendering such services, but shall be entitled to reasonable transportation and living expenses if such expenses must be incurred in order to render such services.

12.   Unique Services. Writer acknowledges that the services rendered hereunder are of a special, unique, unusual, extraordinary and intellectual character which gives them a peculiar value, the loss of which cannot be reasonably or adequately compensated in damages in an action at law, and that a breach by Writer of any of the provisions of this agreement will cause Publisher great and irreparable injury and damage. Writer expressly agrees that Publisher shall be entitled to the remedies of injunction and other equitable relief to prevent a breach of this agreement or any provision hereof, which relief shall be in addition to any other remedies, for damages or otherwise, which may be available to Publisher.

13.   Actions. Publisher may take such action as it deems necessary, either in Writer's name or in its own name, against any person to protect all rights and interests acquired by Publisher hereunder. Writer will at Publisher's request, cooperate fully with Publisher in any controversy which may arise or litigation which may be brought concerning Publisher's rights and interests obtained hereunder. Publisher shall have the right, in its absolute discretion, to employ attorneys and to institute or defend any action or proceeding and to take any other proper

steps to protect the right, title and interest of Publisher in and to each musical composition hereunder and every portion thereof and in that connection, to settle, compromise or in any other manner dispose of any matter, claim, action or proceeding and to satisfy any judgment that may be rendered, in any manner as Publisher in its sole discretion may determine. Any legal action brought by Publisher against an alleged infringer of any musical composition hereunder shall be initiated and prosecuted by Publisher, and if there is any recovery made by Publisher as a result thereof, after deduction of the expense of litigation, including but not limited to attorneys' fees and court costs, a sum equal to fifty percent (50%) of such net proceeds shall be paid to Writer. Writer agrees to and does hereby indemnify, save and hold Publisher harmless from any and all loss and damages (including reasonable attorneys' fees) arising out of or connected with any claim by a third party which is inconsistent with any of the warranties, representations, covenants or agreements made by Writer in this agreement, and Writer agrees to reimburse Publisher, on demand, for any payment made by Publisher at any time after the date hereof with respect to any liability or claim to which the foregoing indemnity applies. Pending the determination of any such claim, Publisher may withhold payment of Royalties or other monies hereunder.

14.    Notices. Any written notices which Publisher shall desire to give to Writer hereunder and all statements, royalties and other payments which shall be due to Writer hereunder shall be addressed to Writer at the address set forth on page 1 hereof until Writer shall give Publisher written notice of a new address. All notices which Writer shall desire to give to Publisher hereunder shall be addressed to Publisher at the address set forth on page 1 hereof until Publisher shall give Writer written notice of a new address. All notices shall be delivered by hand (to any member of Writer if Writer shall be the addresses or to an officer of Publisher if Publisher shall be the addressee) or served by mail, postage prepaid, or telegraph, charges prepaid, addressed as aforesaid. The date of making personal service or of mailing or of depositing in a telegraph office, whichever shall be first, shall be deemed the date of service.

15.     Entire Agreement. This agreement supersedes any and all prior negotiations, understandings, and agreements between the parties hereto with respect to the subject matter hereof. Each of the parties acknowledges and agrees that neither party has made any representations or promises in connection with this agreement or the subject matter hereof not contained herein.

16.     Modification, Waiver, Illegality. This agreement may not be canceled, altered, modified, amended or waived, in whole or in part, in any way, except by an instrument in writing signed by both Publisher and Writer. The waiver by Publisher of any breach of this agreement in any one or more instances, shall in no way be construed as a waiver of any subsequent breach (whether or not of a similar nature) of this agreement by Writer. If any part of this agreement shall be held to be void, invalid or unenforceable, it shall not affect the validity of the balance of this agreement. The agreement shall be governed by and construed under the laws and judicial decisions of the State of California.

17.     Termination. Publisher shall have the right to terminate this agreement upon thirty (30) days prior written notice.

18.     Assignment. Publisher shall have the right to assign this agreement or any of its rights hereunder to any party. This agreement shall inure to the benefit of and be binding upon each of the parties hereto and their respective successors, assigns, heirs, executors, administrators and legal and personal representatives.

19.     Definitions. For purposes of this agreement, the word "person" means and refers to any individual, corporation, partnership, association or any other organized group of persons or legal successors or representatives of the foregoing. Whenever the expressions "the term of this agreement" or "period hereof" or words of similar connotations are included herein, they shall be deemed to mean and refer to the original period of this agreement and the period of all renewals, exten-

sions, substitutions or replacements of this agreement whether expressly indicated or otherwise.

20.    Attorneys' Fees. In the event of any action suit or proceeding by Publisher against Writer under this agreement, in which Publisher shall prevail, Publisher shall be entitled to recover reasonable attorneys' fees and costs of said action, suit or proceeding.

21.    Recoupments. It is understood and acknowledged that any and all charges against royalties under this agreement which are not recouped by Publisher may be recouped by Publisher's record company affiliate from any and all royalties earned by Writer as a recording group under their recording contract of even date with said record company, and that any and all charges against royalties under said recording contract which are not recouped by said record company may be recouped by Publisher from any and all royalties earned by Writer hereunder.

22.    Division of Royalties. As has hereinabove been provided, the word "Writer" as used throughout this agreement, refers collectively to all of the undersigned, all of whom are members of the group known as _____, provided however, that all restrictive and exclusive provisions herein contained apply individually to each of the undersigned. Notwithstanding any provision to the contrary contained in this agreement, it is understood and acknowledged that Writer's royalties for any musical composition hereunder shall be payable only to the undersigned individual or individuals whose name or names are submitted in writing to Publisher as the actual composer or composers of said composition and shall not be payable to any others of the undersigned unless Publisher is advised in writing to the contrary at the time such composition is submitted to Publisher hereunder. In the event this agreement is terminated for any reason whatsoever as to any of the undersigned who comprise Writer, this agreement shall nevertheless remain in full force and effect as to each of the

undersigned comprising Writer with whom this agreement is not so terminated.

23. <u>Inducement</u>. Writer acknowledges that this agreement with Publisher is further consideration for Publisher's record company affiliate to enter in this recording contract referred to in Paragraph 8 hereof and that Writer is entering in to this agreement to induce said record company affiliate to enter into said recording contract.

IN WITNESS WHEREOF the parties hereto have executed this agreement as of the day and year first above written.

By:

_____          _____

# FORM 3.4

## 1939 SONGWRITERS PROTECTIVE ASSOCIATION UNIFORM POPULAR SONGWRITERS CONTRACT

Form No. 2

Approved by

1939

For use by _____

Publisher

## UNIFORM POPULAR SONGWRITERS CONTRACT

AGREEMENT made this       day of       , 19   , between

(hereinafter called "Publisher") and

jointly and/or severally, (hereinafter called (Writer(s)");

WITNESSETH:

1. The Writer(s) hereby sells, assigns, transfers and delivers to the Publisher, its successors and assigns, a certain heretofore unpublished original musical composition written and/or composed by the above named Writer(s) now entitled

including the title, words and music thereof, and the right to secure copyright therein throughout the entire world, and to have and to hold the said copyright and all rights of whatsoever nature thereunder existing (herein referred to as "said composition"), upon the terms and conditions hereinafter set forth.

2. In all respects this contract shall be subject to any existing agreements between all of the parties hereto and the American Society of Composers, Authors and Publishers.

3. The Writer(s) hereby warrants that the said composition is his sole, exclusive and original work, and that he has full right and power to make the within agreement, and that there exists no adverse claim to or in the said composition, and that there is no outstanding claim to any moneys to accrue to the Writer(s) therefrom, except as aforesaid in Clause 2 hereof, and except such rights as are specifically set forth in Paragraph 17 hereof.

4. In consideration of this agreement, the Publisher agrees to pay the Writer(s) jointly, in respect of said composition the following:

    (a) An advance of $      in hand paid, receipt of which is hereby acknowledged, which sums shall be deductible from any payments hereafter becoming due the Writer(s) under this agreement.

    (b) In respect of regular piano copies sold and paid for at wholesale in the United States of America, royalties per copy as follows:

| | | | | |
|---|---|---|---|---|
| Wholesale price | cents — — — | royalty | cents per copy. | |
| Wholesale price | cents — — — | royalty | cents per copy. | |
| Wholesale price | cents — — — | royalty | cents per copy. | |
| Wholesale price | cents (or less) — | royalty | cents per copy. | |

    (c) A royalty of      % (in no case however less than 50% jointly) of all net sums received by the Publisher in respect of regular piano copies and/or orchestrations thereof and in respect of the use of said composition in any folio or composite work, sold and paid for in any foreign country.

(d) A royalty of        cents per copy of orchestrations thereof in any form sold and paid for in the United States of America.

(e) Said composition shall not be published in any folio or composite work until after publication thereof in regular piano copies. Subsequent to said date said composition may be published in the United States and Canada in such form, only upon such terms and conditions as may hereafter be agreed to in writing by the parties hereto.

(f) Folios and/or composite works as referred to in the next preceding paragraph shall be deemed to include any publication of ten or more compositions within the same volume and/or binding.

(g) For purposes of royalty statements, if a composition is printed and published in the United States of America, as to copies and rights sold in the Dominion of Canada, revenue herefrom shall be considered as of domestic origin.

If, however, the composition is printed by a party other than the Publisher in the Dominion of Canada, revenue from sales of copies and rights in Canada shall be considered as originated in a foreign country.

(h) As to "professional material"—not sold or resold, no royalty shall be payable.

(i) An amount equal to        % (in no case, however, less than 50% jointly) of:

All receipts of the Publisher in respect of any licenses issued authorizing the manufacture of parts of instruments serving to mechanically reproduce said composition, or to use said composition in synchronization with sound motion pictures, or to reproduce it upon so-called electrical transcription for broadcasting purposes; and of any and all receipts of the Publisher from any other source or right now known or which may hereafter come into existence (except for which specific royalty provision is otherwise made or which are specifically excepted under this agreement), all such sums to be divided amongst the Writer(s) of said composition as provided in Paragraph 5 hereof; provided, however, that if the Publisher administers the said licenses, or any of them, through the agent, trustee or other administrator acting for a substantial part of the industry and not in the exclusive employ of the Publisher, the Publisher, in determining his receipts, shall be entitled to deduct from gross license fees paid by the licensees a sum equal to the charges paid by the said Publisher to said agent, trustee or administrator, said deduction in no event, however, to exceed 10% of the license fee.

The percentage of the Writer(s) on moneys received from foreign sources shall be computed on the Publisher's net receipts.

The Writer(s) shall not be entitled to any share of the moneys distributed to the Publisher by the American Society of Composers, Authors and Publishers, or by or through any other performing rights society or agency throughout the world if writers receive through the same source an amount which, in the aggregate, is at least equal to the aggregate amount distributed to publishers.

(j) Upon the use of said composition in synchronization with motion pictures under any bulk or block license made before June 1, 1939, the Writer(s) shall be entitled to receive an amount equal to      % (in no case less than 50% jointly) of the license fee for each synchronization by the licensee, but in no event less than the following:

FOR WORLD-WIDE USE

For Entire Uses

In Shorts

$25 for each background instrumental or background vocal use.

$37.50 for each visual instrumental use.

$50 for each visual vocal use.

In Features

$25 for each background instrumental or background vocal use.

$50 for each visual instrumental use.

$75 for each visual vocal use.

For Partial Uses—One-half of foregoing rates.

(k) The Publisher agrees that the use of said composition will not be included in any bulk or block license and that it will not grant any bulk or block license to include the same, without the written consent of Song Writers' Protective Association on behalf of the Writer(s) in each instance, except: (1) That the Publisher may permit the use of the said composition in accordance with and subject to the provisions of Subdivision (j) hereof; (2) In connection with the making of records for electrical transcription for broadcasting purposes, the Publisher may grant licenses for specific medleys or selections.

A license or transaction in bulk or block shall be deemed to mean the licensing of two or more compositions where the currently prevailing license fees are not charged specifically for each separate use of each composition.

(l) Except to the extent that the Publisher and Writer(s) may hereafter assign to or vest in the American Society of Composers, Authors and Publishers the said rights or the right to grant licenses therefor, it is agreed that no licenses shall be granted without the written consent of Song Writers' Protective Association on behalf of the Writer(s) in each instance, for the use of the said composition by means of television, or by any means or for any purpose not commercially established, or for which licenses were not granted by the Publisher on musical compositions prior to June 1, 1937.

(m) The Publisher shall not, without the written consent of the Writer(s) in each case, give or grant any right or license (a) to use the title of the musical composition, or (b) for the exclusive use of said composition in any form or for any purpose, or for any period of time, or for any territory, or (c) to give a dramatic representation of the said musical composition or to dramatize the plot or story thereof, or (d) for a vocal visual rendition of said composition in synchronization with a motion picture. If, however, the Publisher shall give to the Writer(s) written notice, by registered mail or telegram, specifying the right or license to be given or granted, the name of the licensee and the terms and conditions thereof, including the price or other compensation to be received therefor, then, unless the Writer(s) (or any one or more of them, or anyone acting on their behalf) shall, within seventy-two hours (exclusive of Saturdays, Sundays and holidays) after the sending of such notice, if sent by telegram, or within one hundred and forty-four hours (exclusive of Saturdays, Sundays and holidays) after the sending of such notice by registered mail, notify the Publisher of his or its objection thereto, either by registered mail or telegram, the Publisher may grant such right or license, in accordance with such notice without first obtaining the consent of the Writer(s). Such notice shall be deemed sufficient notice to the Writer(s) (whether one or more) if sent to

at

(or at the address of such party last furnished to the Publisher in writing by the Writer(s), or any of them).

(a) Any portion of the receipts which may become due to the Writer(s) from license fees (in excess of offsets), whether received directly from the licensee or from the agent, administrator and trustee, shall, if not paid immediately on the receipt thereof by the Publisher, belong to the Writer(s) and shall be held in trust for such Writer(s) until payment is made; the ownership of said trust fund by the Writer(s) shall not be questioned whether the moneys are physically segregated or not.

(o) The Publisher shall not, without the written consent of Song Writers' Protective Association on behalf of the Writer(s) in each instance, authorize the use of said composition upon the parts of instruments serving to reproduce said composition on commercial phonograph records for a royalty of less than the statutory fee on each such part manufactured.

5. It is understood and agreed by and between all of the parties hereto that all sums hereunder payable jointly to the Writer(s) shall be divided amongst them respectively as follows:

Name                                                 Share

_____     _____

_____     _____

_____     _____

_____     _____

6. The Publisher shall render the Writer(s), as above, on or before each May 15th covering the three months ending March 31st; each August 15th covering the three months ending June 30th; each November 15th covering the three months ending September 30th; each February 15th covering the three months ending December 31st; hereafter, so long as it shall continue publication or the licensing of any rights in the said composition, royalty statements accompanied by remittance of the amount due, provided, however, that if it shall have heretofore been the custom of the Publisher to render royalty statements accompanied by remittance semi-annually, such custom may be continued.

7. The Publisher agrees to publish in salable form the said musical composition within from the date hereof. Should he fail so to do the Writer(s) shall have the right in writing to demand the return of said composition, whereupon the Publisher must within one (1) month after receipt of such notice either publish the said composition, in which event this agreement remains in full force and effect, or upon failure so to publish, all rights of any and every nature, and the right to secure copyright and/or any copyright secured by the Publisher before publication, in and to the said composition, shall revert to and become the property of the Writer(s) and shall be reassigned to him.

8. Anything to the contrary notwithstanding, nothing in this agreement contained shall prevent the Publisher from authorizing publishers, agents and representatives in countries outside of the United States and Canada (and in Canada if said composition is printed by a party other than the publisher in Canada) from exercising exclusive publication and all other rights in said foreign countries in said composition on the customary royalty basis. If foreign publication or other rights in said composition are separately conveyed, otherwise than as a part of the Publisher's current and/or future catalog, then, but not otherwise, any advance received in respect thereof shall be divided in accordance with paragraph 4, subdivision (i) hereof, and credited to the accounts of the respective Writer(s).

9. The Writer(s) or his representative may appoint a certified public accountant who shall at any time during usual business hours have access to all records of the Publisher relating to said composition for the purpose of verifying royalty statements rendered or which are delinquent under the terms hereof.

10. (a) The Publisher shall, upon written demand of the Writer(s) or his (their) representative, cause the agent, trustee or administrator referred to above, to furnish to the Writer(s) or his (their) representative, statements showing in detail all licenses granted, uses had and payments made in connection with said composition, which licenses or permits were granted, or payments were received, by or through said agent, trustee or administrator, and to permit the Writer(s), or his (their) representative to inspect at the place of business of such agent, trustee or administrator all books, records and documents of the agent, trustee or administrator relating thereto.

(b) The Publisher shall from time to time, upon written demand of the Writer(s) or his (their) representative, furnish to the Writer(s) or his (their) representative, statements showing in detail all licenses granted, uses had and payments made therefor in connection with said composition (other than licenses, uses and payments for commercial phonograph records and music rolls) for which licenses or permits were granted or payments received by the Publisher without the intervention of said agent, trustee or administrator, and to permit the Writer(s) or his (their) representative to inspect at the place of business of the Publisher, all books, records and documents relating to said composition and all licenses granted, uses had and payments made therefor, such right of inspection to include, but not by way of limitation, the right to examine all original accountings and records relating to uses and payments by manufacturers of commercial phonograph records and music rolls. Nothing in this paragraph contained, furthermore, shall be deemed or construed to relieve the Publisher of its obligation to pay royalties on the use of said composition on commercial phonograph records and music rolls or the obligation to include a statement of such royalties in the periodical royalty statements to be rendered to the Writer(s) in accordance with Paragraph 6 of this agreement.

(c) Any and all agreements made by the Publisher with the said agent, trustee or administrator shall provide that said agent, trustee or administrator will comply with the terms and provisions hereof. In the event that the Publisher shall instruct the said agent, trustee or administrator referred to above, to furnish to the Writer or his representative the statements as provided for in paragraph 10 (a) hereof, and to permit the inspection of the books, records and documents as therein provided, and if the said agent, trustee or administrator should refuse to comply with the said instructions, or any of them, then the Publisher agrees to institute and prosecute diligently and in good faith such action or proceedings as may be necessary to compel compliance with the said instructions.

11. In the event that the Publisher shall fail or refuse, within sixty days after written demand, to furnish said statements, or cause the same to be furnished, or to make available or cause to be made available to the Writer(s) or his (their) representative all of such books, records or documents as provided in subdivision (b) of paragraph 10, or to cause the agent or trustee to furnish the same as provided in subdivision (a) of paragraph 10 and the agent or trustee shall refuse to comply with the instructions of the Publisher, then to take such steps as provided in subdivision (c) of paragraph 10, or in the event that the Publisher shall fail to make the payment of any royalties due within thirty days after written demand therefor, then the Writer(s) shall have the option, to be exercised upon ten days' written notice to cancel this agreement.

Upon such cancellation, all rights of the Publisher, of any and every nature, in and to said compositions, shall cease and come to an end and the same rights, including but not limited to the right to secure copyright and/or any copyright theretofore secured by the Publisher, shall revert to and become the property of the Writer(s) and shall be assigned to him (them). The Publisher agrees that it will thereupon execute any and all assignment or other documents which may be necessary or proper to vest the said rights in the Writer(s).

12. Written demands and notices provided for in Paragraphs 10 and 11 hereof shall be sent to the Publisher by registered mail.

13. Any legal action brought by the Publisher against any alleged infringer of said composition shall be initiated and prosecuted at his sole expense, and of any recovery made by him as a result thereof, after deduction of the expense of the litigation, a sum equal to fifty per cent shall be divided as agreed among the Writer(s) of the said composition.

(a) If a claim is presented against the Publisher alleging that the said composition is an infringement upon some other, and because thereof the Publisher is jeopardized, he shall thereupon serve written notice upon the Writer(s), containing the full details of such claim and thereafter until the claim has been adjudicated or settled shall pay any moneys coming due the Writer(s) hereunder in escrow to any bank or trust company to be held pending the outcome of such claim; provided however, if no suit be filed within twelve months, after written notice to the Writer(s) by the Publisher of the adverse claim, the said bank or trust company shall release and pay to the Writer(s) all sums held in escrow, plus any interest which may have been earned thereupon. Such payment shall be without prejudice to the rights of the Publisher in event of a subsequent adverse adjudication.

(b) From and after the service of summons in a suit for infringement filed against the Publisher in respect of the said composition, any and all payments hereunder thereafter coming due the Writer(s) shall be paid by the Publisher in trust to any bank or trust company until the suit has been finally adjudicated and then be disbursed accordingly, unless the Writer(s) shall elect to file an acceptable bond in the sum of such payments, in which event the sums due shall be paid to him.

14. The parties hereto hereby agree to submit to arbitration under the rules of the American Arbitration Association, and pursuant to the New York Arbitration Law any differences arising under this agreement, and hereby agree individually and jointly to abide by and perform any award rendered by the Arbitration and that a judgment of the Supreme Court of the State of New York may be entered upon such award.

15. This agreement is binding upon the parties hereto and their respective successors in interest.

16. Three identical copies hereof are executed by the parties, the original copy of which shall remain in the possession of the Publisher, the duplicate in possession of the Writer(s), and the triplicate thereof be forwarded by mail by the Publisher to the Song Writers' Protective Association.

17. The rights specifically excepted, as provided in Paragraph 3 hereof, are as follows:

Witness:

_____

Witness:

_____

Witness:

_____

Witness:

_____

Publisher:

By _____ (L.S.)

Address _____ LS

Writer _____ (L.S.)

Address _____ LS

Writer _____ (L.S.)

Address _____ LS

Writer _____ (L.S.)

Address:

# FORM 3.5

## 1969 AMERICAN GUILD OF AUTHORS AND COMPOSER UNIFORM POPULAR SONGWRITERS CONTRACT

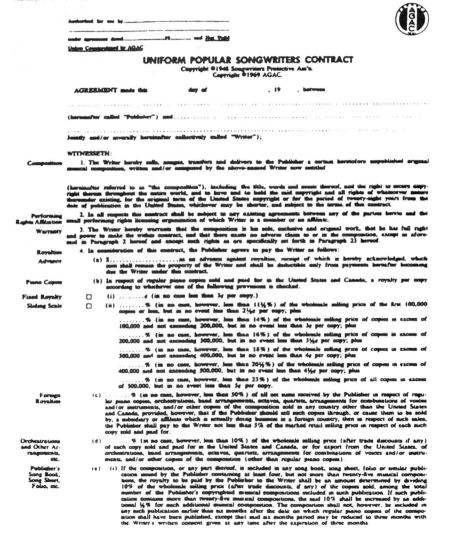

(ii) If, pursuant to a license granted by the Publisher to a licensee not controlled by or affiliated with it, the composition, or any part thereof, is included in any song book, song sheet, folio or similar publication, containing at least four musical compositions, the royalty to be paid by the Publisher to the Writer shall be that proportion of 50% of the gross amount received by it from the licensee, as the number of uses of the composition under the license and during the license period, bears to the total number of uses of the Publisher's copyrighted musical compositions under the license and during the license period. The lyrics alone of the composition may be included in such a publication at any time, but the lyrics and music thereof, in combination, shall not be included earlier than two years after the date on which regular piano copies of the composition shall have been published. Such royalties shall be computed and paid within 30 days after the expiration of the term of each license, but if any such license term is in excess of one year, such royalties shall be computed and paid annually.

(iii) In computing the number of the Publisher's copyrighted musical compositions under subdivisions (i) and (ii) hereof, there shall be excluded musical compositions in the public domain and arrangements thereof and those with respect to which the Publisher does not currently publish and offer for sale regular piano copies.

(iv) Royalties on publications containing less than four musical compositions shall be payable at regular piano copy rates.

*Professional Material and Free Copies*

(f) As to "professional material" not sold or resold, no royalty shall be payable. Free copies of the lyrics of the composition shall not be distributed except under the following conditions: (i) with the Writer's written consent; or (ii) when printed without music in limited numbers for charitable, religious or governmental purposes, or for similar public purposes, if no profit is derived, directly or indirectly; or (iii) when authorized for printing in a book, magazine or periodical, where such use is incidental to a novel or story (as distinguished from use in a book of lyrics or a lyric magazine or folio), provided that any such use shall bear the Writer's name and the proper copyright notice; or (iv) when distributed solely for the purpose of exploiting the composition, provided, that such exploitation is restricted to the distribution of limited numbers of such copies for the purpose of influencing the sale of the composition, that the distribution is independent of the sale of any other musical compositions, services, goods, wares or merchandise, and that no profit is made, directly or indirectly, in connection therewith.

*Mechanicals, Electrical Transcription, Synchronization, All Other Rights*

(g)     % (in no case, however, less than 50%) of:

All gross receipts of the Publisher in respect of any licenses (including statutory royalties) authorizing the manufacture of parts of instruments serving to mechanically reproduce the composition, or to use the composition in synchronization with sound motion pictures, or to reproduce it upon electrical transcription for broadcasting purposes; and of any and all gross receipts of the Publisher from any other source or right now known or which may hereafter come into existence, except as provided in subdivision (1) of this paragraph 4

*Licensing Agent's Charges*

(h) If the Publisher administers licenses authorizing the manufacture of parts of instruments serving to mechanically reproduce said composition, or the use of said composition in synchronization or in timed relation with sound motion pictures or its reproduction upon electrical transcriptions, or any of them, through an agent, trustee or other administrator acting for a substantial part of the industry and not under the exclusive control of the Publisher (hereinafter sometimes referred to as licensing agent), the Publisher, in determining his receipts, shall be entitled to deduct from gross license fees paid by the Licensees, a sum equal to the charges paid by the Publisher to said licensing agent, provided, however, that in respect to synchronization or timed relation with sound motion pictures, said deduction shall in no event exceed $150.00 or 10% of said gross license fee, whichever is less; in connection with the manufacture of parts of instruments serving to mechanically reproduce said composition, said deductions shall not exceed 2½% of said gross license fee; and in connection with electrical transcriptions, said deductions shall not exceed 10% of said gross license fee.

*Small Performing Royalties*

(i) Nothing contained in this agreement shall alter, vary or modify the rights of Writer and Publisher to share in, receive and retain the proceeds distributed to them by the small performing rights licensing organization (i.e.,
of which both Writer and Publisher are members or affiliated pursuant to their respective agreements with such small performing rights licensing organization.

*Block Licenses*

(j) The Publisher agrees that the use of the composition will not be included in any bulk or block license heretofore or hereafter granted, and that it will not grant any bulk or block license to include the same, without the written consent of American Guild of Authors and Composers on behalf of the Writer in each instance, except (i) that the Publisher may grant such licenses with respect to electrical transcription for broadcasting purposes, but in such event, the Publisher shall pay to the Writer that proportion of 50% of the gross amount received by it under each such license as the number of uses of the composition under each such license during each such license period bears to the total number of uses of the Publisher's copyrighted musical compositions under each such license during each such license period; in computing the number of the Publisher's copyrighted musical compositions for this purpose, there shall be excluded musical compositions in the public domain and arrangements thereof and those with respect to which the Publisher does not currently publish and offer for sale regular piano copies; and with respect to such licenses, the Publisher shall account to the Writer annually; (ii) that the Publisher may appoint agents or representatives in countries outside of the United States and Canada to use and to grant licenses for the use of the composition on the customary royalty fee basis under which the Publisher shall receive not less than 10% of the marked retail selling price in respect of regular piano copies, and 50% of all other revenues; if, in connection with any such bulk or block license, the Publisher shall have received any advance, the Writer shall not be entitled to share therein, but no part of said advance shall be deducted in computing the composition's earnings under said bulk or block license. A bulk or block license shall be deemed to mean any license or agreement, domestic or foreign, whereby rights are granted in respect of two or more musical compositions.

*Television and New Uses*

(k) Except to the extent that the Publisher and Writer have heretofore or may hereafter assign to or vest in the small performing rights licensing organization of which Writer is a member or an affiliate, the said rights or the right to grant licenses therefor, it is agreed that no licenses shall be granted without the written consent, in each instance, of the Writer for the use of the composition by means of television, or by any means, or for any purpose not commercially established, or for which licenses were not granted by the Publisher on musical compositions prior to June 1, 1937.

*Writer's Consent to Licenses*

(l) The Publisher shall not, without the written consent of the Writer in each case, give or grant any right or license (i) to use the title of the composition, or (ii) for the exclusive use of the composition in any form or for any purpose, or for any period of time, or for any territory, other than its customary arrangements with foreign publishers, or (iii) to give a dramatic representation of the composition or to dramatize the plot or story thereof, or (iv) for a vocal rendition of the composition in synchronization with sound motion pictures, or (v) for any synchronization use thereof after the expiration of two years from the date on which regular piano copies of the composition shall have been first published, or (vi) for the use of the composition or a quotation or excerpt therefrom in any article, book, periodical, advertisement or other similar publication. If, however, the Publisher shall give to the Writer written notice, by registered mail or telegram, specifying the right or license to be given or granted, the name of the licensee and the terms and conditions thereof, including the price or other compensation to be received therefor, then, unless the Writer (or any one or more of them) shall, within seventy-two hours (exclusive of Saturdays, Sundays and holidays) after the delivery of such notice to the address of the Writer hereinafter designated, object thereto, the Publisher may grant such right or license in accordance with the said notice without first obtaining the consent of the Writer. Such notice shall be deemed sufficient if sent to the Writer at the address or addresses hereinafter designated or at the address or addresses last furnished to the Publisher in writing by the Writer.

**Trust for Writer** (m) Any portion of the receipts which may become due to the Writer from license fees (in excess of offsets), whether received directly from the licensee or from any licensing agent of the Publisher, shall, if not paid immediately on the receipt thereof by the Publisher, belong to the Writer and shall be held in trust for the Writer until payment is made; the ownership of said trust fund by the Writer shall not be questioned whether the monies are physically segregated or not.

**Writer Participation** (n) The Publisher agrees that it will not issue any license as a result of which it will receive any financial benefit in which the Writer does not participate.

**Writer Credit** (o) Every license or authorization issued by the Publisher authorizing the publication of the composition or any part thereof shall contain a provision requiring the user thereof to print, in addition to the copyright notice, the name of the Writer as the author thereof.

**Change in Piano Copy Royalty** (p) If a fixed royalty is designated to be payable with respect to regular piano copies of the composition (as provided in paragraph 4 (b) (1), then, if at any time, the Publisher shall increase or decrease the wholesale selling price which it charged on January 1, 1947 to regular music jobbers for regular piano copies of musical compositions of the same class or category as the composition, then the said fixed royalty shall be increased or decreased in proportion to the change in said wholesale selling price.

**Writers' Respective Shares** 5. Whenever the term "Writer" is used herein, it shall be deemed to mean all of the persons named herein below, and any and all royalties herein provided to be paid to the Writer shall be paid jointly to the following persons if there be more than one, and shall be divided among them as follows:

| Name | Share |
|---|---|
| | |
| | |
| | |

**Publication** 6. (a) The Publisher shall, within one year from the date hereof, make, publish and offer for sale regular piano copies of the composition in the form and through the channels customarily employed by it for that purpose, and in addition, either (i) cause a commercial phonograph recording to be made and distributed in the customary form and through the customary commercial channels, or (ii) make, publish and offer for sale a dance orchestra arrangement. As an alternative to compliance with (i) or (ii), the Publisher shall pay to the Writer the sum of $250.00 less the aggregate of any advances paid, as stated in Paragraph 4 (a) hereof, and any royalties paid to the Writer within said one-year period. If in the statement of "Special Exceptions" hereinafter set forth, the composition shall have been designated as one which is not intended for publication in regular piano copies, the Publisher shall be deemed to have complied with this paragraph by the making and distribution of a commercial phonograph recording and either the publication of a dance orchestra arrangement or the payment of $250.00, all as aforesaid.

**Failure to Publish** (b) Should the Publisher fail to comply with the provisions of subdivision (a) hereof, the Writer shall be entitled to demand in writing the return of the composition at any time after the expiration of said year, whereupon the Publisher must, within one month after the receipt of such notice, either comply with the provisions of subdivision (a) hereof, in which event this contract will remain in full force and effect, or upon its failure so to comply, this contract shall terminate and all rights of any and every nature in and to the composition and in and to any and all copyrights secured thereon in the United States and throughout the world, shall re-vest in and become the property of the Writer and shall be reassigned to him by the Publisher; the Writer shall not be obligated to return or pay to the Publisher any advance or indebtedness as a condition of such re-assignment; the said re-assignment shall be in accordance with and subject to the provisions of Paragraph 13 hereof, and in addition, the Publisher shall pay to the Writer all gross sums which it has theretofore or may thereafter receive in respect of the composition.

**Writer's Copies** (c) The Publisher shall furnish the Writer copies of the composition which it publishes and shall use its best efforts to furnish or cause to be furnished to the Writer copies published by others.

**Foreign Copyright** 7. (a) Each copyright on the composition in countries other than the United States shall be secured only in the name of the Publisher, and the Publisher shall not at any time divest itself of said foreign copyright directly or indirectly, except to the extent that it may be obligated to do so by virtue of an agreement entered into by the Publisher with a foreign publisher prior to January 1, 1947, and then only for the term of said agreement.

**Foreign Publication** (b) Except to the extent that the Publisher is obligated to a foreign publisher or licensee by written agreement made prior to January 1, 1947, and then only for the term of said agreement, no rights shall be granted by the Publisher in the composition to any foreign publisher or licensee inconsistent with the terms hereof, nor shall any foreign publication rights in the composition be given to a foreign publisher or licensee unless and until the Publisher shall have complied with the provisions of Paragraph 6 hereof.

**Foreign Advance** (c) If foreign rights in the composition are separately conveyed, otherwise than as a part of the Publisher's current and/or future catalog, not less than 50% of any advance received in respect thereof shall be credited to the account of and paid to the Writer.

**Foreign Percentage** (d) The percentage of the Writer on monies received from foreign sources shall be computed on the Publisher's net receipts, provided, however, that no deductions shall be made for offsets of monies due from the Publisher to said foreign sources; or for advances made by such foreign sources to the Publisher, unless the Writer shall have received at least 50% of said advances.

**No Foreign Allocations** (e) In computing the receipts of the Publisher from licenses granted in respect of synchronization with sound motion pictures, or in respect of any world-wide licenses, or in respect of licenses granted by the Publisher for use of the composition in countries other than the United States, no amount shall be deducted for payments or allocations to publishers or licensees in such countries.

**Terms of Contract** 8. All rights in and to the composition and any copyrights secured thereon throughout the world, shall revest in the Writer upon expiration of the original term of the United States copyright or at the end of twenty-eight (28) years from the date of publication in the United States, whichever period shall be shorter. The Publisher shall, at the expiration of said period, execute any and all documents which may be necessary or proper to re-vest in the Writer any and all rights in and to the composition and in and to any copyright in the United States or any other country throughout the world, provided, however, that if the Writer shall sell or assign to some person other than the Publisher, his rights in the United States renewal copyright in the composition, or any of his rights in the composition in the United States or elsewhere, for the period beyond said original term or twenty-eight years, as the case may be, then, unless there shall have been given to the Publisher at least six months' written notice of an intention to offer said rights for sale, the Publisher shall not be obligated to assign to the Writer any rights in countries other than the United States and Canada, and this contract, and the assignment under Paragraph 1 hereof, shall all continue in respect of such rights in countries other than the United States and Canada.

**Negotiations for New or Unspecified Uses**

9. If the Publisher desires to exercise a right in and to the composition now known or which may hereafter become known, but for which no specific provision has been made herein, the Publisher shall give written notice to the Writer thereof. Negotiations respecting all the terms and conditions of any such disposition shall thereupon be entered into between the Publisher (and/or the National Music Publishers' Association, Inc.) and the American Guild of Authors & Composers; and no such right shall be exercised until specific agreement has been reached.

**Royalty Statements and Payments**

10. The Publisher shall render to the Writer, hereafter, royalty statements accompanied by remittance of the amount due on or before, each May 15th covering the 3 months ending March 31st; each August 15th covering the 3 months ending June 30th; each November 15th covering the 3 months ending September 30th; each February 15th covering the 3 months ending December 31st; provided, however, that if it shall have heretofore been the custom of the Publisher to render royalty statements accompanied by remittance of the amount due semi-annually, or quarterly at the end of different quarterly periods, such custom may be continued. The Writer may at any time, or from time to time, make written request for a detailed royalty statement, and the Publisher shall, within sixty days, comply therewith. Such royalty statements shall set forth in detail the various items, foreign and domestic, for which royalties are payable thereunder and the amounts thereof, including, but not limited to, the number of copies sold and the number of uses made in each royalty category. If a use is made in a publication of the character provided in Paragraph 8, subdivision (e) hereof, there shall be included in said royalty statement the title of said publication, the publisher or issuer thereof, the date of and number of uses, the gross license fee received in connection with such publication, the share thereto of all the writers under contract with the Publisher, and the Writer's share thereof. There shall likewise be included in said statement a description of every other use of the composition, and if by a licensee or licensees their name or names, and if said use is upon a part of an instrument serving to reproduce the composition mechanically, the type of mechanical reproduction, the title of the label thereon, the name or names of the artists performing the same, together with the gross license fees received, and the Writer's share thereof.

**Examination of Books**

11. (a) The Publisher shall from time to time, upon written demand of the Writer or his representative, permit the Writer or his representative to inspect at the place of business of the Publisher, all books, records and documents relating to the composition and all licenses granted, uses had and payments made therefor, such right of inspection to include, but not by way of limitation, the right to examine all original accountings and records relating to uses and payments by manufacturers of commercial phonograph records and music rolls; and the Writer or his representative may appoint a certified public accountant who shall at any time during usual business hours have access to all records of the Publisher relating to the composition for the purpose of verifying royalty statements rendered or which are delinquent under the terms hereof.

(b) The Publisher shall, upon written demand of the Writer or his representative, cause any licensing agent in the United States and Canada to furnish to the Writer or his representative, statements showing in detail all licenses granted, uses had and payments made in connection with the composition, which licenses or permits were granted, or payments were received, by or through said licensing agent, and to permit the Writer or his representative to inspect at the place of business of such licensing agent, all books, records and documents of such licensing agent, relating thereto. Any and all agreements made by the Publisher with any such licensing agent shall provide that any such licensing agent will comply with the terms and provisions hereof. In the event that the Publisher shall instruct such licensing agent to furnish to the Writer or his representative statements as provided for herein, and to permit the inspection of the books, records and documents as herein provided, then if such licensing agent should refuse to comply with the said instructions, or any of them, the Publisher agrees to institute and prosecute diligently and in good faith such action or proceedings as may be necessary to compel compliance with the said instructions.

(c) With respect to foreign licensing agents, the Publisher shall make available the books or records of said licensing agents in countries outside of the United States and Canada to the extent such books or records are available to the Publisher, except that the Publisher may in lieu thereof make available any accountants' reports and audits which the Publisher is able to obtain.

**Default in Payment or Prevention of Examination**

12. If the Publisher shall fail or refuse, within sixty days after written demand, to furnish or cause to be furnished, such statements, books, records or documents, or to permit inspection thereof, as provided for in Paragraphs 10 and 11 hereof, or within thirty days after written demand, to make the payment of any royalties due under this contract, then the Writer shall have the option, to be exercised upon ten days' written notice, to terminate this contract. However, if the Publisher shall:

(a) Within the said ten-day period:

  (i) serve upon the Writer a written notice demanding arbitration; and

  (ii) if the demand be for statements, books, records or documents, or to permit inspection thereof, deposit with National Music Publishers' Association, Inc. a re-assignment to the Writer of the copyright and all other rights in and to the composition, to be held in escrow pending the determination of the arbitration, or if the demand be for royalties, then deposit in escrow with National Music Publishers' Association, Inc., the amount shown by its books to be due the Writer under the provisions of this contract; and,

(b) Submit to arbitration its claim that it has complied with its obligation to furnish statements, books, records or documents, or permitted inspection thereof, or to pay royalties, as the case may be, or both, and thereafter comply with any award of the arbitrators within ten days after such award or within such time as the arbitrators may specify;

then this contract shall continue in full force and effect as if the Writer's option had not been exercised. But if the Publisher shall fail to comply with the foregoing provisions, then this contract shall be deemed to have been terminated as of the date of the Writer's exercise of his option to terminate this contract.

**Termination of Contract**

13. Upon the termination of this contract, all rights of any and every nature in and to the composition and in and to any and all copyrights secured thereon in the United States and throughout the world, shall re-vest in and become the property of the Writer, and shall be re-assigned to the Writer by the Publisher free of any and all encumbrances of any nature whatsoever, provided that:

(a) The said re-assignment by the Publisher may, however, be subject to such rights, if any, as may have been vested in a foreign publisher respecting the use of the composition in countries other than the United States and Canada under any agreement made prior to January 1, 1947.

(b) If the Publisher, prior to such termination, shall have granted a domestic license for the use of the composition, not inconsistent with the terms and provisions of this contract, the re-assignment may be subject to the terms of such license.

(c) In either of the events mentioned in subdivisions (a) and (b) of this paragraph, however, the Publisher shall assign to the Writer all rights which it may have under any such agreement or license in respect of the composition, including, but not limited to, the right to receive all royalties or other monies earned by the composition thereunder after the date of termination of this contract. Should the Publisher thereafter receive or be credited with any royalties or other monies so earned, it shall pay the same to the Writer.

(d) The Writer shall not be obligated to return or pay to the Publisher any advance or indebtedness as a condition of the re-assignment provided for in this Paragraph 13, and shall be entitled to receive the plates and copies of the composition in the possession of the Publisher.

(e) The termination of this contract shall not relieve the Publisher of his obligation to pay any and all royalties which may have accrued to the Writer prior to such termination.

(f) The Publisher shall execute any and all documents and do any and all acts or things necessary to effect any and all re-assignments to the Writer herein provided for.

14. All written demands and notices provided for herein shall be sent by registered mail.

**Suits for Infringement**
15. Any legal action brought by the Publisher against any alleged infringer of the composition shall be instituted and prosecuted at its sole cost and expense, but if the Publisher should fail, within thirty days after written demand, to institute such action, the Writer shall be entitled to institute such not at his cost and expense. All sums recovered as a result of any such action shall, after the deduction of the reasonable expenses thereof, be divided equally between the Publisher and the Writer. No settlement of any such action may be made by either party without first notifying the other; in the event that either party should object to such settlement, then such settlement shall not be made if the party objecting assumes the prosecution of the action and all expenses thereof, except that any sums thereafter recovered shall be divided equally between the Publisher and the Writer after the deduction of the reasonable expenses thereof.

**Infringement Claims**
16. (a) If a claim is presented against the Publisher alleging that the composition is an infringement upon some other work or a violation of any other right of another, and because thereof the Publisher is jeopardized, it shall forthwith serve a written notice upon the Writer setting forth the full details of such claim. The pendency of said claim shall not relieve the Publisher of the obligation to make payment of the royalties to the Writer hereunder, unless the Publisher shall deposit said royalties as and when they would otherwise be payable, in an account in a bank or trust company in the City of New York in the joint names of the Publisher and the Writer. If no suit be filed within nine months after said written notice from the Publisher to the Writer, all moneys deposited in said joint account shall be paid over to the Writer plus any interest which may have been earned thereon.

(b) Should an action be instituted against the Publisher claiming that the composition is an infringement upon some other work or a violation of any other right of another, the Publisher shall forthwith serve written notice upon the Writer containing the full details of such claim. Notwithstanding the commencement of such action, the Publisher shall continue to pay the royalties hereunder to the Writer unless it shall, from and after the date of the service of the summons, deposit said royalties as and when they would otherwise be payable, in an account in a bank or trust company in the City of New York in the joint names of the Publisher and the Writer. If the said suit shall be finally adjudicated in favor of the Publisher or shall be settled, there shall be released and paid to the Writer all of such sums held in escrow less any amount paid out of the Writer's share with the Writer's written consent in settlement of said action. Should the said suit finally result adversely to the Publisher, the said amount on deposit shall be released to the Publisher to the extent of any expense or damage it incurs and the balance shall be paid over to the Writer.

(c) In any of the foregoing events, however, the Writer shall be entitled to payment of royalties or the moneys so deposited at and after such time as he files with the Publisher a surety company bond, or a bond in other form acceptable to the Publisher, in the sum of such payments to secure the return thereof to the extent that the Publisher may be entitled to such return. The foregoing payments or deposits or the filing of a bond shall be without prejudice to the rights of the Publisher or Writer in the premises.

**Arbitration**
17. Any and all differences, disputes or controversies arising out of this contract shall be submitted to arbitration under the laws of the State of New York, and the parties hereby individually and jointly agree to abide by and perform any award rendered in such arbitration, and agree that a judgment of the Supreme Court of the State of New York may be entered upon such award. Together with the demand for arbitration, the party making said demand shall designate an arbitrator and the adverse party shall, within ten days thereafter, likewise designate an arbitrator. The two arbitrators so chosen shall promptly appoint a third arbitrator who shall act as Chairman and any award concurred in by a majority of the arbitrators shall be binding upon the parties. Should the party against whom arbitration is demanded fail to select an arbitrator, or should the arbitrators selected by the parties be unable to agree upon a third arbitrator, then said arbitrator or arbitrators, as the case may be, shall be designated and appointed in the manner provided by the Arbitration Law of the State of New York.

**Assignment**
18. Except to the extent herein otherwise expressly provided, the Publisher shall not sell, transfer, assign, convey, encumber or otherwise dispose of the composition or the copyright or copyrights secured thereon without the prior written consent of the Writer. The Writer has been induced to enter into this contract in reliance upon the value to him of the personal service and ability of the Publisher in the exploitation of the composition, and by reason thereof it is the intention of the parties and the essence of the relationship between them that the rights herein granted to the Publisher shall remain with the Publisher and that the same shall not pass to any other person, including, without limitation, successors or to receivers or trustees of the property of the Publisher, either by act or deed of the Publisher or by operation of law, and in the event of the voluntary or involuntary bankruptcy of the Publisher, this contract shall terminate, provided, however, that the composition may be included by the Publisher in a bona fide voluntary sale of its music business or its entire catalog of musical compositions, or in a merger or consolidation of the Publisher with another corporation; and provided further that the composition and the copyright therein may be assigned by the Publisher to a subsidiary or affiliated company generally engaged in the music publishing business. If the Publisher is an individual, the composition may pass to a legatee or distributee as part of the inheritance of the Publisher's music business and entire catalog of musical compositions. Any such transfer or assignment shall, however, be conditioned upon the execution and delivery by the transferee or assignee to the Writer of an agreement to be bound by and to perform all of the terms and conditions of this contract to be performed on the part of the Publisher.

**Subsidiary Defined**
19. A subsidiary, affiliate, or any person, firm or corporation controlled by the Publisher or by such subsidiary or affiliate, as used in this contract, shall be deemed to include any person, firm or corporation, under common control with, or the majority of whose stock or capital contribution is owned or controlled by the Publisher or by any of its officers, directors, partners or associates, or whose policies and actions are subject to domination or control by the Publisher or any of its officers, directors, partners or associates.

**Minimums**
20. The minimum amounts and percentages specified in this contract shall be deemed to be the amounts and percentages agreed upon by the parties hereto, unless greater amounts or percentages are inserted in the blank spaces provided therefor.

**Countersignature and Modifications**
21. This contract is binding upon and shall enure to the benefit of the parties hereto and their respective successors in interest (as hereinbefore limited), but shall be effective only when countersigned by the American Guild of Authors & Composers. If the Writer (or one or more of them) shall not be living, any notices may be given to, or consents given by, his or their successors in interest. No change or modification of this contract shall be effective unless reduced to writing, signed by the parties hereto, and countersigned by the American Guild of Authors & Composers.

**Marginal Notes**
22. The marginal notes are inserted only as a matter of convenience and for reference, and in no way define, limit or describe the scope or intent of this contract nor in any way affect this contract.

**Exceptions to Warranties**
23. The rights specifically excepted, as provided in Paragraph 3 hereof are as follows:

# FORM 3.6

## 1978 AMERICAN GUILD OF AUTHORS & COMPOSERS POPULAR SONGWRITERS RENEWAL CONTRACT

**AMERICAN GUILD OF AUTHORS & COMPOSERS**

NOTE TO SONGWRITERS (A) DO NOT SIGN THIS CONTRACT IF IT HAS ANY CHANGES UNLESS YOU HAVE FIRST DISCUSSED SUCH CHANGES WITH AGAC. (B) FOR YOUR PROTECTION PLEASE SEND A FULLY EXECUTED COPY OF THIS CONTRACT TO AGAC

### POPULAR SONGWRITERS RENEWAL CONTRACT
Copyright 1978 AGAC

AGREEMENT made this _____ day of _____ 19 ___ between

_____
(hereinafter called "Publisher") and _____

_____
jointly and/or severally hereinafter collectively called "Writer".

**WITNESSETH**

**Composition**  1  The Writer hereby sells, assigns, transfers and delivers to the Publisher any and all rights and interests whatsoever now or at any time or times hereafter known or in existence which he now possesses or which he may at any time or times hereafter acquire or possess in or to the following described musical compositions

| Title | Original Publisher | Date of Copyright Registration | Copyright Registration Number |
|---|---|---|---|
| | | | |

(hereinafter referred to as "the composition"), including the title, words and music thereof and any and all adaptations, arrangements and versions thereof respecting which he is entitled to obtain renewal copyright, for and during the second or renewal period of the United States copyright or for the period of twenty-eight years from the date of expiration of the first original term of the United States copyright, whichever may be shorter, and subject to the terms of this contract

**Performing Rights Affiliation**  2  In all respects this contract shall be subject to any existing agreements between the parties hereto and the following small performing rights licensing organization with which Writer and Publisher are affiliated

**(Delete Two)** ⟶ (ASCAP, BMI, SESAC) Nothing contained herein shall, or shall be deemed to, alter, vary or modify the rights of Writer and Publisher to share in, receive and retain the proceeds distributed to them by such small performing rights licensing organization pursuant to their respective agreement with it

**Warranty**  3  The Writer, individually and not jointly, warrants and represents that the following are the only co-owners and composers of said composition

that he has the right to renew and extend the copyright of the said composition; that he has not bargained, sold, assigned, transferred, hypothecated, pledged or encumbered any of his right, title or interest in or to the renewal copyright in said composition, except as aforesaid in paragraph 2 hereof, but nothing herein contained shall be construed as a warranty or representation by any individual Writer-signatory hereof, as to the rights of any other Writer or composer of said composition, it being understood that the warranties by the Writer are individual and not joint

| | | |
|---|---|---|
| Royalties | 4 | In consideration of this contract, the Publisher agrees to pay the Writer as follows: |
| (Insert amount of Payment and Advance here) | (a) | (i) $_____ receipt of which is hereby acknowledged, said sum shall constitute an outright payment, shall remain the property of the Writer and shall not be deductible from any payment heretofore or hereafter due the Writer |
| | | (ii) $_____ as an advance against royalties, receipt of which is hereby acknowledged, which sum shall remain the property of the Writer and shall be deductible only from payments hereafter becoming due the Writer under this Contract |

**Piano Copies**
**Sliding Scale**
(Insert percentage here)

(b) In respect of regular piano copies sold and paid for in the United States and Canada, the following royalties per copy:

......% (in no case, however, less than 10%) of the wholesale selling price of the first 200,000 copies or less; plus

......% (in no case, however, less than 12%) of the wholesale selling price of copies in excess of 200,000 and not exceeding 500,000; plus

......% (in no case, however, less than 15%) of the wholesale selling price of copies in excess of 500,000

**Foreign Royalties**

(c) ......% (in no case, however, less than 50%) of all net sums received by the Publisher in respect of regular piano copies, orchestrations, band arrangements, octavos, quartets, arrangements for combinations of voices and/or instruments, and/or other copies of the composition sold in any other country other than the United States and Canada, provided, however, that if the Publisher should sell such copies through, or cause them to be sold by, a subsidiary or affiliate which is actually doing business in a foreign country, then in respect of such sales, the Publisher shall pay to the Writer not less than 5% of the marked retail selling price in respect of each such copy sold and paid for

**Orchestrations and Other Arrangements, etc.**

(d) In respect of each copy sold and paid for in the United States and Canada, or for export from the United States, of orchestrations, band arrangements, octavos, quartets, arrangements for combinations of voices and/or instruments, and/or other copies of the composition (other than regular piano copies) the following royalties on the wholesale selling price (after trade discounts, if any):

(Insert percentage here)

......% (in no case, however, less than 10%) on the first 200,000 copies or less; plus

......% (in no case, however, less than 12%) on all copies in excess of 200,000 and not exceeding 500,000; plus

......% (in no case, however, less than 15%) on all copies in excess of 500,000

**Publisher's Song Book, Folio, etc.**

(e) (i) If the composition, or any part thereof, is included in any song book, folio or similar publication issued by the Publisher containing at least four, but not more than twenty-five musical compositions, the royalty to be paid by the Publisher to the Writer shall be an amount determined by dividing 10% of the wholesale selling price (after trade discounts, if any) of the copies sold, among the total number of the Publisher's copyrighted musical compositions included in such publication. If such publication contains more than twenty-five musical compositions, the said 10% shall be increased by an additional ½% for each additional musical composition

**Licensee's Song Book, Folio, etc.**

(ii) If, pursuant to a license granted by the Publisher to a licensee not controlled by or affiliated with it, the composition, or any part thereof, is included in any song book, folio or similar publication, containing at least four musical compositions, the royalty to be paid by the Publisher to the Writer shall be that proportion of 50% of the gross amount received by it from the licensee, as the number of uses of the composition under the license and during the license period, bears to the total number of uses of the Publisher's copyrighted musical compositions under the license and during the license period.

(iii) In computing the number of the Publisher's copyrighted musical compositions under subdivisions (i) and (ii) hereof, there shall be excluded musical compositions in the public domain and arrangements thereof and those with respect to which the Publisher does not currently publish and offer for sale regular piano copies.

(iv) Royalties on publications containing less than four musical compositions shall be payable at regular piano copy rates

**Professional Material and Free Copies**

(f) As to "professional material" not sold or resold, no royalty shall be payable. Free copies of the lyrics of the composition shall not be distributed except under the following conditions: (i) with the Writer's written consent, or (ii) when printed without music in limited numbers for charitable, religious or governmental purposes, or for similar public purposes, if no profit is derived, directly or indirectly, or (iii) when authorized for printing in a book, magazine or periodical, where such use is incidental to a novel or story (as distinguished from use in a book of lyrics or a lyric magazine or folio), provided that any such use shall bear the Writer's name and the proper copyright notice, or (iv) when distributed solely for the purpose of exploiting the composition, provided, that such exploitation is restricted to the distribution of limited numbers of such copies for the purpose of influencing the sale of the composition, that the distribution is independent of the sale of any other musical compositions, services, goods, wares or merchandise, and that no profit is made, directly or indirectly, in connection therewith

**Mechanicals, Electrical Transcription, Synchronization, All Other Rights**   (Insert percentage here)

(g) ......% (in no case, however, less than 50%) of:

All gross receipts of the Publisher in respect of any licenses (including statutory royalties) authorizing the manufacture of parts of instruments serving to mechanically reproduce the composition, or to use the composition in synchronization with sound motion pictures, or to reproduce it upon electrical transcription for broadcasting purposes, and of any and all gross receipts of the Publisher from any other source or right now known or which may hereafter come into existence, except as provided in paragraph 2.

**Licensing Agent's Charges**

(h) If the Publisher administers licenses authorizing the manufacture of parts of instruments serving to mechanically reproduce said composition, or the use of said composition in synchronization or in timed relation with sound motion pictures or its reproduction upon electrical transcriptions, or any of them, through an agent, trustee or other administrator acting for a substantial part of the industry and not under the exclusive control of the Publisher (hereinafter sometimes referred to as licensing agent), the Publisher, in determining his receipts, shall be entitled to deduct from gross license fees paid by the Licensees, a sum equal to the charges paid by the Publisher to said licensing agent, provided, however, that in respect to synchronization or timed relation with sound motion pictures said deduction shall in no event exceed $150.00 or 10% of said gross license fee, whichever is less, in connection with the manufacture of parts of instruments serving to mechanically reproduce said composition, said deductions shall not exceed 5% of said gross license fee, and in connection with electrical transcriptions, said deduction shall not exceed 10% of said gross license fee

**Block Licenses**

(i) The Publisher agrees that the use of the composition will not be included in any bulk or block license heretofore or hereafter granted, and that it will not grant any bulk or block license to include the same, without the written consent of the Writer in each instance, except (i) that the Publisher may grant such licenses with respect to electrical transcription for broadcasting purposes, but in such event, the Publisher shall pay to the Writer that proportion of 50% of the gross amount received by it under each such license as the number of uses of the composition under each such license during each such license period bears to the total number of uses of the Publisher's copyrighted musical compositions under each such license during each such license period, in computing the number of the Publisher's copyrighted musical compositions for this purpose, there shall be excluded musical compositions in the public domain and arrangements thereof and those with respect to which the Publisher does not currently publish and offer for sale regular piano copies. If, that the Publisher may appoint agents or representatives in countries outside of the United States and Canada to use and to grant licenses for the use of the composition on the customary royalty fee basis under which the Publisher shall receive not less than 10% of the marked retail selling price in respect of regular piano copies, and 50% of all other revenue; if, in connection with any such bulk or block license, the Publisher shall have received any advance, the Writer shall not be entitled to share therein, but no part of said advance shall be deducted in computing the composition's earnings under said bulk or block license. A bulk or block license shall be deemed to mean any license or agreement, domestic or foreign, whereby rights are granted in respect of two or more musical compositions.

**Television and New Uses** (j) Except to the extent that the Publisher and Writer have heretofore or may hereafter assign to or vest in the small performing rights licensing organization with which Writer and Publisher are affiliated, the said rights or the right to grant licenses therefor, it is agreed that no licenses shall be granted without the written consent, in each instance, of the Writer for the use of the composition by means of television, or by any means, or for any purposes not commercially established, or for which licenses were not granted by the Publisher on musical compositions prior to June 1, 1937.

**Writer's Consent to Licenses** (k) The Publisher shall not, without the written consent of the Writer in each case, give or grant any right or license (i) to use the title of the composition, or (ii) for the exclusive use of the composition in any form or for any purpose, or for any period of time, or for any territory, other than its customary arrangements with foreign publishers, or (iii) to give a dramatic representation of the composition or to dramatize the plot or story thereof, or (iv) for a vocal rendition of the composition in synchronization with sound motion pictures, or (v) for any synchronization use thereof, or (vi) for the use of the composition or a quotation or excerpt therefrom in any article, book, periodical, advertisement or other similar publication. If, however, the Publisher shall give to the Writer written notice by certified mail, return receipt requested, or telegram, specifying the right or license to be given or granted, the name of the licensee and the terms and conditions thereof, including the price or other compensation to be received therefor, then, unless the Writer (or any one or more of them) shall, within five business days after the delivery of such notice to the address of the Writer hereinafter designated, object thereto, the Publisher may grant such right or license in accordance with the said notice without first obtaining the consent of the Writer. Such notice shall be deemed sufficient if sent to the Writer at the address or addresses hereinafter designated or at the address or addresses last furnished to the Publisher in writing by the Writer.

**Trust for Writer** (l) Any portion of the receipts which may become due to the Writer from license fees (in excess of offsets), whether received directly from the licensee or from any licensing agent of the Publisher, shall, if not paid immediately on the receipt thereof by the Publisher, belong to the Writer and shall be held in trust for the Writer until payment is made the ownership of said trust fund by the Writer shall not be questioned whether the monies are physically segregated or not.

**Writer Participation** (m) The Publisher agrees that it will not issue any license as a result of which it will receive any financial benefit in which the Writer does not participate.

**Writer Credit** (n) On all regular piano copies, orchestrations, band or other arrangements, octavos, quartets, commercial sound recordings and other reproductions of the composition or parts thereof, in whatever form and however produced, Publisher shall include or cause to be included, in addition to the copyright notice, the name of the Writer, and Publisher shall include a similar requirement in every license or authorization issued by it with respect to the composition.

**Power of Attorney** 5       The Writer covenants and agrees to make, execute and deliver any and all further instruments, documents and writings that may be requested by the Publisher for the purpose of perfecting and confirming in the Publisher the rights and interests in the renewal(s) of the copyright(s) in the composition herein granted, and the Writer hereby nominates and appoints the Publisher his true and lawful attorney to make, execute and deliver any and all such instruments, documents and writings in the name of the Writer and to renew and extend the copyright in the composition and to make applications therefor in the name of the Writer, subject to the terms of this contract.

**Exploitation** 6 (a) The Publisher agrees that it shall (i) at all times maintain a stock of regular piano copies of the composition in the form customarily published by it, (ii) include and (iii) use every reasonable effort and means to exploit and promote the sale of the various uses of the composition. Unless the aggregate amount of any advances (as provided in paragraph 4 (a) (ii) ) and the royalties paid to the Writer within two years from the date hereof, shall equal or exceed the sum of $250.00, the Publisher shall pay to the Writer the difference between said aggregate amount and said sum of $250.00

**Failure to Exploit** (b) Should the Publisher fail to comply with the provisions of subdivision (a) hereof, the Writer shall be entitled to demand in writing the return of the composition at any time after the expiration of said two-year period, whereupon the Publisher must within one month after the receipt of such notice either comply with the provisions of subdivision (a) hereof, in which event this contract will remain in full force and effect, or upon its failure so to comply, this contract shall terminate and all rights of any and every nature in and to the composition and in and to any and all copyrights and renewal copyrights secured thereon in the United States and throughout the world (subject, however, to the terms of paragraph 7 hereof), shall re-vest in and become the property of the Writer and shall be reassigned to him by the Publisher. the Writer shall not be obligated to return or pay to the Publisher any outright payment, advance or indebtedness as a condition of such reassignment. the said reassignment shall be in accordance with and subject to the provisions of paragraph 8 hereof, and in addition, the Publisher shall pay to the Writer all gross sums which it has theretofore or may thereafter receive in respect of the composition.

**Foreign Copyright** (a) Each copyright on the composition in countries other than the United States shall be secured only in the name of the Publisher, and the Publisher shall not at any time divest itself of said foreign copyright directly or indirectly.

**Foreign Publication** (b) No rights shall be granted by the Publisher in the composition to any foreign publisher or licensee inconsistent with the terms hereof.

**Foreign Advance** (c) If foreign rights in the composition are separately conveyed, otherwise than as a part of the Publisher's current and/or future catalog, not less than 50% of any advance received in respect thereof shall be credited to the account of and paid to the Writer.

**Foreign Percentage** (d) The percentage of the Writer on monies received from foreign sources shall be computed on the Publisher's net receipts, provided, however, that no deductions shall be made for offsets of monies due from the Publisher to said foreign sources, or for advances made by such foreign sources to the Publisher, unless the Writer shall have received at least 50% of said advances

**No Foreign Allocations** (e) In computing the receipts of the Publisher from licenses granted in respect of synchronization with sound motion pictures, or in respect of any world-wide licenses, or in respect of licenses granted by the Publisher for use of the composition in countries other than the United States, no amount shall be deducted for payments or allocations to publishers or licensees in such countries

**Termination or Expiration of Contract** 8 Upon the termination or expiration of this contract, all rights of any and every nature in and to the composition and in and to any and all copyrights secured thereon in the United States and throughout the world, shall re-vest in and become the property of the Writer, and shall be re-assigned to the Writer by the Publisher free of any and all encumbrances of any nature whatsoever provided that

(a) If the Publisher, prior to such termination or expiration, shall have granted a domestic license for the use of the composition, not inconsistent with the terms and provisions of this contract, the re-assignment may be subject to the terms of such license

(b) Publisher shall assign to the Writer all rights which it may have under any such agreement or license referred to in subdivision (a) in respect of the composition, including, but not limited to, the right to receive all royalties or other monies earned by the composition thereunder after the date of termination or expiration of this contract Should the Publisher thereafter receive or be credited with any royalties or other monies so earned, it shall pay the same to the Writer

(c) The Writer shall not be obligated to return or pay to the Publisher any advance or indebtedness as a condition of the re-assignment provided for in this Paragraph 8, and shall be entitled to receive the plates and copies of the composition in the possession of the Publisher

(d) Publisher shall pay any and all royalties which may have accrued to the Writer prior to such termination or expiration.

(e) The Publisher shall execute any and all documents and do any and all acts or things necessary to effect any and all re-assignments to the Writer herein provided for

**Negotiations for New or Unspecified Uses** 9. If the Publisher desires to exercise a right in and to the composition now known or which may hereafter become known, but for which no specific provision has been made herein, the Publisher shall give written notice to the Writer thereof Negotiations respecting all the terms and conditions of any such disposition shall thereupon be entered into between the Publisher and the Writer and no such right shall be exercised until specific agreement has been made

**Royalty Statements and Payments** 10. The Publisher shall render to the Writer, hereafter, royalty statements accompanied by remittance of the amount due at the times such statements and remittances are customarily rendered by the Publisher, provided, however, that such statements and remittances shall be rendered either semi-annually or quarterly and not more than forty-five days after the end of each such semi-annual or quarterly period, as the case may be. The Writer may at any time, or from time to time, make written request for a detailed royalty statement, and the Publisher shall, within sixty days, comply therewith. Such royalty statements shall set forth in detail the various items, foreign and domestic, for which royalties are payable thereunder and the amounts thereof, including, but not limited to, the number of copies sold and the number of uses made in each royalty category. If a use is made in a publication of the character provided in Paragraph 4, subdivision (e) hereof, there shall be included in said royalty statement the title of said publication, the publisher or issuer thereof, the date of and number of uses, the gross license fee received in connection with each publication, the share thereto of all the writers under contract with the Publisher, and the Writer's share thereof. There shall likewise be included in said statement a description of every other use of the composition, and if by a licensee or licensees their name or names, and if said use is upon a part of an instrument serving to reproduce the composition mechanically, the type of mechanical reproduction, the title of the label thereon, the name or names of the artists performing the same, together with the gross license fees received, and the Writer's share thereof.

**Examination of Books** 11. (a) The Publisher shall from time to time, upon written demand of the Writer or his representative, permit the Writer or his representative to inspect at the place of business of the Publisher, all books, records and documents relating to the composition and all licenses granted, uses had and payments made therefor, such right of inspection to include, but not by way of limitation, the right to examine all original accountings and records relating to uses and payments by manufacturers of commercial sound recordings and music rolls, and the Writer or his representative may appoint an accountant who shall at any time during usual business hours have access to all records of the Publisher relating to the composition for the purpose of verifying royalty statements rendered or which are delinquent under the terms hereof

(b) The Publisher shall, upon written demand of the Writer or his representative, cause any licensing agent in the United States and Canada to furnish to the Writer or his representative, statements showing in detail all licenses granted, uses had and payments made in connection with the composition, which licenses or permits were granted, or payments were received, by or through said licensing agent, and to permit the Writer or his representative to inspect at the place of business of such licensing agent, all books, records and documents of such licensing agent, relating thereto Any and all agreements made by the Publisher with any licensing agent shall provide that any such licensing agent will comply with the terms and provisions hereof. In the event that the Publisher shall instruct such licensing agent to furnish to the Writer or his representative statements as provided for herein, and to permit the inspection of the books, records and documents as herein provided, then if such licensing agent should refuse to comply with the said instructions, or any of them, the Publisher agrees to institute and prosecute diligently and in good faith such action or proceedings as may be necessary to compel compliance with the said instructions

(c) With respect to foreign licensing agents, the Publisher shall make available the books or records of said licensing agents in countries outside of the United States and Canada to the extent such books or records are available to the Publisher, except that the Publisher may in lieu thereof make available any accountants' reports and audits which the Publisher is able to obtain

(d) If as a result of any examination of books, records or documents pursuant to Paragraphs 11(a), 11(b) or 11(c) hereof, it is determined that, with respect to any royalty statement rendered by or on behalf of the Publisher to the Writer, the Writer is owed a sum equal to or greater than five percent of the sum shown on that royalty statement as being due to the Writer, then the Publisher shall pay to the Writer the entire cost of such examination, not to exceed 50% of the amount shown to be due the Writer

(e) (i) In the event the Publisher administers its own licenses for the manufacture of parts of instruments serving to mechanically reproduce the composition rather than employing a licensing agent for that purpose, the Publisher shall include in each license agreement a provision permitting the Publisher, the Writer or their respective representatives to inspect, at the place of business of such licensee, all books, records and documents of such licensee relating to such license. Within 30 days after written demand by the Writer, the Publisher shall commence to inspect such licensee's books, records and documents and shall furnish a written report of such inspection to the Writer within 90 days following such demand. If the Publisher fails, after written demand by the Writer, to so inspect the licensee's books, records and documents, or fails to furnish such report, the Writer or his representative may inspect such licensee's books, records and documents at his own expense.

(ii) In the further event that the Publisher and the licensee referred to in subdivision (i) above are subsidiaries or affiliates of the same entity or one is a subsidiary or affiliate of the other, then, unless the Publisher employs a licensing agent to administer the licenses referred to in subdivision (i) above, the Writer shall have the right to make the inspection referred to in subdivision (i) above without the necessity of making written demand on the Publisher as provided in subdivision (i) above.

(iii) If as a result of any inspection by the Writer pursuant to subdivisions (i) and (ii) of this subparagraph (c) the Writer recovers additional monies from the licensee, the Publisher and the Writer shall share equally in the cost of such inspection.

**Default in Payment or Prevention of Examination**

12. If the Publisher shall fail or refuse, within sixty days after written demand, to furnish or cause to be furnished, such statements, books, records or documents, or to permit inspection thereof, as provided for in Paragraphs 10 and 11 hereof, or within thirty days after written demand, to make the payment of any royalties due under this contract, then the Writer shall be entitled, upon ten days' written notice, to terminate this contract. However if the Publisher shall

(a) Within the said ten-day period serve upon the Writer a written notice demanding arbitration, and

(b) Submit to arbitration its claim that it has complied with its obligation to furnish statements, books, records or documents, or permitted inspection thereof or to pay royalties, as the case may be, or both, and thereafter comply with any award of the arbitrator within ten days after such award or within such time as the arbitrator may specify;

then this contract shall continue in full force and effect as if the Writer had not sent such notice of termination. If the Publisher shall fail to comply with the foregoing provisions, then this contract shall be deemed to have been terminated as of the date of the Writer's written notice of termination.

**Derivative Works**

13. No derivative work prepared under authority of Publisher during the term of this contract may be utilized by Publisher or any other party after termination or expiration of this contract.

**Notices**

14. All written demands and notices provided for herein shall be sent by certified mail, return receipt requested.

**Suits for Infringement**

15. Any legal action brought by the Publisher against any alleged infringer of the composition shall be initiated and prosecuted at its sole cost and expense, but if the Publisher should fail, within thirty days after written demand, to institute such action, the Writer shall be entitled to institute such suit as his cost and expense. All sums recovered as a result of any such action shall, after the deduction of the reasonable expense thereof, be divided equally between the Publisher and the Writer. No settlement of any such action may be made by either party without first notifying the other; in the event that either party should object to such settlement, then such settlement shall not be made if the party objecting assumes the prosecution of the action and all expenses thereof, except that any sums thereafter recovered shall be divided equally between the Publisher and the Writer after the deduction of the reasonable expenses thereof.

**Infringement Claims**

16. (a) If a claim is presented against the Publisher alleging that the composition is an infringement upon some other work or a violation of any other right of another, and because thereof the Publisher is jeopardized, it shall forthwith serve a written notice upon the Writer setting forth the full details of such claim. The pendency of said claim shall not relieve the Publisher of the obligation to make payment of the royalties to the Writer hereunder, unless the Publisher shall deposit said royalties as and when they would otherwise be payable, in an account in the joint names of the Publisher and the Writer in a bank or trust company in New York, New York, if the Writer on the date of execution of this contract resides East of the Mississippi River, or in Los Angeles, California, if the Writer on the date of execution of this contract resides West of the Mississippi River. If no suit be filed within nine months after said written notice from the Publisher to the Writer, all monies deposited in said joint account shall be paid over to the Writer plus any interest which may have been earned thereon.

(b) Should an action be instituted against the Publisher claiming that the composition is an infringement upon some other work or a violation of any other right of another, the Publisher shall forthwith serve written notice upon the Writer containing the full details of such claim. Notwithstanding the commencement of such action, the Publisher shall continue to pay the royalties hereunder to the Writer unless it shall, from and after the date of the service of the summons, deposit said royalties as and when they would otherwise be payable, in an account in the joint names of the Publisher and the Writer in a bank or trust company in New York, New York, if the Writer on the date of execution of this contract resides East of the Mississippi River, or in Los Angeles, California, if the Writer on the date of execution of this contract resides West of the Mississippi River. If the said suit shall be finally adjudicated in favor of the Publisher or shall be settled, there shall be released and paid to the Writer all of such sums held in escrow less any amount paid out of the Writer's share with the Writer's written consent in settlement of said action. Should the said suit finally result adversely to the Publisher, the said amount on deposit shall be released to the Publisher to the extent of any expense or damage it incurs and the balance shall be paid over to the Writer.

(c) In any of the foregoing events, however, the Writer shall be entitled to payment of said royalties or the money so deposited at and after such time as he files with the Publisher a surety company bond, or a bond in other form acceptable to the Publisher, in the sum of such payments to secure the return thereof to the extent that the Publisher may be entitled to such return. The foregoing payments or deposits or the filing of a bond shall be without prejudice to the rights of the Publisher or Writer in the premises.

**Arbitration**

17. Any and all differences, disputes or controversies arising out of or in connection with this contract shall be submitted to arbitration before a sole arbitrator under the then prevailing rules of the American Arbitration Association. The location of the arbitration shall be New York, New York, if the Writer on the date of execution of this contract resides East of the Mississippi River, or Los Angeles, California, if the Writer on the date of execution of this contract resides West of the Mississippi River. The parties hereby individually and jointly agree to abide by and perform any award rendered in such arbitration. Judgment upon any such award rendered may be entered in any court having jurisdiction thereof.

**Assignment**

18. Except to the extent herein otherwise expressly provided, the Publisher shall not sell, transfer, assign, convey, encumber or otherwise dispose of the composition or the copyright or copyrights secured thereon without the prior written consent of the Writer. The Writer has been induced to enter into this contract in reliance upon the value to him of the personal service and ability of the Publisher in the exploitation of the composition, and by reason thereof it is the intention of the parties and the essence of the relationship between them that the rights herein granted to the Publisher shall remain with the Publisher and that the same shall

not pass to any other person, including, without limitations, successors to or receivers or trustees of the property of the Publisher, either by act or deed of the Publisher by operation of law, and in the event of the voluntary or involuntary bankruptcy of the Publisher, this contract shall terminate, provided, however, that the composition may be included by the Publisher in a bona fide voluntary sale of its music business or its entire catalog of musical compositions, or in a merger or consolidation of the Publisher with another corporation, in which event the Publisher shall immediately give written notice thereof to the Writer, and provided further that the composition and the copyright therein may be assigned by the Publisher to a subsidiary or affiliated company generally engaged in the music publishing business. If the Publisher is an individual, the composition may pass to a legatee or distributee as part of the inheritance of the Publisher's music business and entire catalog of musical compositions. Any such transfer or assignment shall, however, be conditioned upon the execution and delivery by the transferee or assignee to the Writer of an agreement to be bound by and to perform all of the terms and conditions of this contract to be performed on the part of the Publisher.

**Subsidiary Defined**    19   A subsidiary, affiliate, or any person, firm or corporation controlled by the Publisher or by such subsidiary or affiliate, as used in this contract, shall be deemed to include any person, firm or corporation, under common control with, or the majority of whose stock or capital contribution is owned or controlled by the Publisher or by any of its officers, directors, partners or associates, or whose policies and actions are subject to domination or control by the Publisher or any of its officers, directors, partners or associates.

**Amounts**    20   The amounts and percentages specified in this contract shall be deemed to be the amounts and percentages agreed upon by the parties hereto, unless other amounts or percentages are inserted in the blank spaces provided therefor.

**Modifications**    21   This contract is binding upon and shall enure to the benefit of the parties hereto and their respective successors in interest (as hereinbefore limited). If the Writer (or one or more of them) shall not be living, any notices may be given to, or consents given by, his or their successors in interest. No change or modification of this contract shall be effective unless reduced to writing and signed by the parties hereto.

The words in this contract shall be so construed that the singular shall include the plural and the plural shall include the singular where the context so requires and the masculine shall include the feminine and the feminine shall include the masculine where the context so requires.

**Paragraph Headings**    22   The paragraph headings are inserted only as a matter of convenience and for reference, and in no way define, limit or describe the scope or intent of this contract nor in any way affect this contract.

**Special Provisions**    23

**Writers Respective Shares**    24   Whenever the term "Writer" is used herein (except as provided in Paragraph 3 hereof), it shall be deemed to mean all of the persons executing this agreement below, (the same being the authors and composers of said compositions or their respective lawful successors), and any and all royalties herein provided to be paid to the Writer shall be paid jointly to the following persons executing this agreement if there be more than one, and shall be divided among them as follows:

| Name and Soc Sec # | Address | Share | Signature |
|---|---|---|---|
|  |  |  |  |
|  |  |  |  |
|  |  |  |  |
|  |  |  |  |
|  |  |  |  |
|  |  |  |  |
|  |  |  |  |
|  |  |  |  |

Witness _____    Publisher _____

_____    By _____

Address _____

**FOR YOUR PROTECTION,
SEND A COPY OF THE FULLY SIGNED CONTRACT TO AGAC.**

# FORM 3.7

## 1978 SONGWRITERS GUILD OF AMERICA POPULAR SONGWRITERS CONTRACT

### The Songwriters Guild of America

Note to songwriters: (A) Do not sign this contract if it has any changes unless you have first discussed such changes with the Guild; (B) For your protection please send a fully executed copy of this contract to the Guild.

### POPULAR SONGWRITERS CONTRACT
© Copyright 1978 AGAC

AGREEMENT made this _____ day of _____, 20__, between _____ (hereinafter called "Publisher") and _____

(Jointly and/or hereinafter collectively called "Writer");

WITNESSETH:

1.    The Writer hereby assigns, transfers and delivers to the Publisher a certain heretofore unpublished original musical composition, written and/or composed by the above-named Writer now entitled _____ (hereinafter referred to as "the composition"), including the title, words and music thereof, and the right to secure copyright therein throughout the entire world, and to have and to hold the said copyright and all rights of whatsoever nature thereunder existing, for _____ years from the date of this contract or 35 years from the date of the first release of a commercial sound recording of the composition, whichever term ends earlier, unless this contract is sooner terminated in accordance with the provisions hereof.

2.     In all respects this contract shall be subject to any existing agreements between the parties hereto and the following small performing rights licensing organization with which Writer and Publisher are affiliated:

(ASCAP, BMI, SESAC). Nothing contained herein shall, or shall be deemed to, alter, vary or modify the rights of Writer and Publisher to share in, receive and retain the proceeds distributed to them by such small performing rights licensing organization pursuant to their respective agreement with it.

3.     The Writer hereby warrants that the composition is his sole, exclusive and original work, that he has full right and power to make this contract, and that there exists no adverse claim to or in the composition, except as aforesaid in Paragraph 2 hereof and except such rights as are specifically set forth in paragraph 23 hereof.

4.     In consideration of this contract, the Publisher agrees to pay the Writer as follows:

(a)     $_____ as an advance against royalties, receipt of which is hereby acknowledged, which sum shall remain the property of the Writer and shall be deductible only from payments hereafter becoming due the Writer under this contract.

(b)     In respect of regular piano copies sold and paid for in the United States and Canada, the following royalties per copy:

_____% (in no case, however, less than 10%) of the wholesale selling price of the first 200,000 copies or less; plus

_____% (in no case, however, less than 12%) of the wholesale selling price of copies in excess of 200,000 and not exceeding 500,000; plus

_____% (in no case, however, less than 15%) of the wholesale selling price of copies in excess of 500,000.

(c) \_\_\_% (in no case, however, less than 50%) of all net sums received by the Publisher in respect of regular piano copies, orchestrations, band arrangements, octavos, quartets, arrangements for combinations of voices and/or instruments, and/or other copies of the composition sold in any country other than the United States and Canada, provided, however, that if the Publisher should sell such copies through, or cause them to be sold by, a subsidiary or affiliate which is actually doing business in a foreign country, then in respect of such sales, the Publisher shall pay to the Writer not less than 5% of the marketed retail selling price in respect of each such copy sold and paid for.

(d) In respect of each copy sold and paid for in the United States and Canada, or for export from the United States, of orchestrations, band arrangements, octavos, quartets, arrangements for combinations of voices and/or instruments, and/or other copies of the composition (other than regular piano copies) the following royalties on the wholesale selling price (after trade discounts, if any):

\_\_\_% (in no case, however, less than 10%) on the first 200,000 copies or less; plus

\_\_\_% (in no case, however, less than 12%) on all copies in excess of 200,000 and not exceeding 500,000; plus

\_\_\_% (in no case, however, less than 15%) on all copies in excess of 500,000.

(e) (i) If the composition, or any part thereof, is included in any song book, folio or similar publication issued by the Publisher containing at least four, but not more than twenty-five musical compositions, the royalty to be paid by the Publisher to the Writer shall be an amount determined by dividing 10% of the wholesale selling price (after trade discounts, if any) of the copies sold, among the total number of the Publisher's copyrighted musical compositions included in such publication. If such publication contains more than twenty-five musical compositions, the said 10% shall be increased by an additional .50% for each additional musical composition.

(ii)    If, pursuant to a license granted by the Publisher to a license not controlled by or affiliated with it, the composition, or any part thereof, is included in any song book, folio or similar publication, containing at least four musical compositions, the royalty to be paid by the Publisher to the Writer shall be that proportion of 50% of the gross amount received by it from the licensee, as the number of uses of the composition under the license and during the license period, bears to the total number of uses of the Publisher's copyrighted musical compositions under the license and during the license period.

(iii)    In computing the number of the Publisher's copyrighted musical compositions under subdivisions (i) and (ii) hereof, there shall be excluded musical compositions in the public domain and arrangements thereof and those with respect to which the Publisher does not currently publish and offer for sale regular piano copies.

(iv)    Royalties on publications containing less than four musical compositions shall be payable at regular piano copy rates.

(f)    As to "professional material" not sold or resold, no royalty shall be payable. Free copies of the lyrics of the composition shall not be distributed except under the following conditions: (i) with the Writer's written consent; or (ii) when printed without music in limited numbers for charitable, religious or governmental purposes, or for similar public purposes, if no profit is derived, directly or indirectly; or (iii) when authorized for printing in a book, magazine or periodical, where such use is incidental to a novel or story (as distinguished from use in a book of lyrics or a lyric magazine or folio), provided that any such use shall bear the Writer's name and the proper copyright notice; or (iv) when distributed solely for the purpose of exploiting the composition, provided, that such exploitation is restricted to the distribution of limited numbers of such copies for the purpose of influencing the sale of the composition, that the distribution is independent of the sale of any other musical compositions, services, goods, wares or merchandise, and that no profit is made, directly or indirectly, in connection therewith.

(g)      ____% (in no case, however, less than 50%) of:

All gross receipts of the Publisher in respect of any licenses (including statutory royalties) authorizing the manufacture of parts of instruments serving to mechanically reproduce the composition, or to use the composition in synchronization with sound motion pictures, or to reproduce it upon electrical transcription for broadcasting purposes; and of any and all gross receipts of the Publisher from any other source or right now known or which may hereafter come into existence, except as provided in Paragraph 2.

(h)      If the Publisher administers licenses authorizing the manufacture of parts of instruments serving to mechanically reproduce said composition, or the use of said composition in synchronization or in timed relation with sound motion pictures or its reproduction upon electrical transcriptions, or any of them, through an agent, trustee or other administrator acting for a substantial part of the industry and not under the exclusive control of the Publisher (hereinafter sometimes referred to as licensing agent), the Publisher, in determining his receipts, shall be entitled to deduct from gross license fees paid by the Licensees, a sum equal to the charges paid by the Publisher to said licensing agent, provided, however, that in respect to synchronization or timed relation with sound motion pictures, said deduction shall in no event exceed $150.00 or 10% of said gross license fee, whichever is less; in connection with the manufacture of parts of instruments serving to mechanically reproduce said composition, said deduction shall not exceed 10% of said gross license fee.

(i)      The Publisher agrees that the use of the composition will not be included in any bulk or block license heretofore or hereafter granted, and that it will not grant any bulk license to include the same, without the written consent of the Writer in each instance, except (i) that the Publisher may grant such licenses with respect to electrical transcription for broadcasting purposes, but in such event, the Publisher shall pay to the Writer that proportion of 50% of the gross amount received by it under each such license as the number of uses of the composition under each such license during each such license period bears to the total number of uses of the Publisher's copyrighted musical compositions under each such license during each such license period; in computing the number of the Publisher's copyrighted musical compositions for this purpose, there shall be excluded musical compositions in the public domain and arrangements thereof and those with respect to which the Publisher does not currently publish and offer for sale regular piano copies; (ii) that the Publisher may appoint agents or representatives in countries outside the United States and Canada to use and to grant licenses for the use of the composition on the customary royalty fee basis under which the Publisher shall receive not less than 10% of the marked retail selling price in respect of regular piano copies, and 50% of all other revenue; if, in connection with any such bulk of block license, the Publisher shall have received any advance, the Writer shall not be entitled to share therein, but no part of said advance shall be deducted in computing composition's earnings under said bulk or block license. A bulk or block license shall be deemed to mean any license or agreement, domestic or foreign, whereby rights are granted in respect of two or more musical compositions.

(j)     Except to the extent that the Publisher and Writer have heretofore or may hereafter assign to or vest in the small performing rights licensing organization with which the Writer and Publisher are affiliated, the said rights or the right to grant licenses therefor, it is agreed that no licenses shall be granted without the written consent, in each instance, of the Writer for the use of the composition by means of television, or by any means, or for any purposes not commercially established, or for which licenses were not granted by the Publisher on musical compositions prior to June 1, 1937.

(k)     The Publisher shall not, without the written consent of the Writer in each case, give or grant any right or license (i) to use the title of the composition, or (ii) for the exclusive use of the composition in any form or for any purpose, or for any period of time, or for any territory, other than its customary arrangements with foreign publishers, or (iii) to give a dramatic representation of the composition or to dramatize the plot or story thereof, or (iv) for a vocal rendition of the composition in synchronization with sound motion pictures, or (v) for any synchronization use thereof, or (vi) for the use of the composition or a quotation or excerpt therefrom in any article, book, periodical, advertisement or other similar publication. If, however, the Publisher shall give to the Writer written notice by certified mail, return receipt requested, or telegram, specifying the right or license to be given or granted, the name of the licensee and the terms and conditions thereof, including the price or other compensation to be received therefor, then, unless the Writer (or any one or more of them) shall, within five business days after the delivery of such notice to the address of the Writer hereinafter designated, object thereto, the Publisher may grant such right or license in accordance with the said notice without first obtaining the consent of the Writer. Such notice shall be deemed sufficient if sent to the Writer at the address or addresses hereinafter designated or at the address or addresses last furnished to the Publisher in writing by the Writer.

(l)     Any portion of the receipts which may become due to the Writer from license fees (in excess of offsets), whether received directly from the licensee or from any licensing agent of the Publisher, shall, if not paid immediately on the receipt thereof by the Publisher, belong to the Writer and shall be held in trust for the Writer until payment is made; the ownership of said trust fund by the Writer shall not be questioned whether the monies are physically segregated or not.

(m)     The Publisher agrees that it will not issue any license as a result of which it will receive any financial benefit in which the Writer does not participate.

(n)    On all regular piano copies, orchestrations, band or other arrangements, octavos, quartets, commercial sound recordings and other reproductions of the composition or parts thereof, in whatever form and however produced, Publisher shall include or cause to be included, in addition to the copyright notice, the name of the Writer, and Publisher shall include a similar requirement in every license or authorization issued by it with respect to the composition.

5.    Whenever the term "Writer" is used herein, it shall be deemed to mean all of the persons herein defined as "Writer" and any and all royalties herein provided to be paid to the Writer shall be paid equally to such persons if there be more than one, unless otherwise provided in Paragraph 23.

6.    (a)    (i)    The Publisher shall, within ____ months from the date of this contract (the "initial period"), cause a commercial sound recording of the composition to be made and released in the customary form and through the customary commercial channels. If at the end of such initial period a sound recording has not been made and released, as above provided, then, subject to the provisions of the next succeeding subdivision, this contract shall terminate.

(ii)    If, prior to the expiration of the initial period, Publisher pays the Writer the sum of $_____ (which shall not be charged against or recoupable out of any advances, royalties or other monies theretofore paid, then due, or which thereafter may become due the Writer from the Publisher pursuant to this contract or otherwise), Publisher shall have an additional ____ months (the "additional period") commencing with the end of the initial period, within which to cause such commercial sound recording to be made and released as provided in subdivision (i) above. If at the end of the additional period a commercial recording has not been made and released, as above provided, then this contract shall terminate.

(iii)    Upon termination pursuant to this Paragraph 6(a), all rights of any and every nature in and to the composition and in and to any and all copyrights secured thereon in the United States and throughout the world shall automatically re-vest in and become the property of the Writer and shall be reas-signed to him by the Publisher. The Writer shall not be obligated to return or pay to the Publisher any advance or indebtedness as a condition of such re-assignment; the said re-assignment shall be in accordance with and subject to the provisions of Paragraph 8 hereof, and, in addition, the Publisher shall pay to the Writer all gross sums which it has theretofore or there-after receive of the composition.

(b)     The Publisher shall furnish, or cause to be furnished, to the Writer six copies of the commercial sound recording re-ferred to in Paragraph 6(a).

(c)     The Publisher shall [Select (i) or (ii)] _____ (i) within 30 days after the initial release of a commercial recording of the composition, make, publish and offer for sale regular piano cop-ies of the composition in the form and through the channels customarily employed by it for that purpose; _____ (ii) within 30 days after execution of this contract make a piano arrangement or lead sheet of the composition and furnish six copies thereof to the Writer.

In the event neither subdivision (i) nor (ii) of this paragraph (c) is selected, the provisions of subdivision (ii) shall be auto-matically deemed to have been selected by the parties.

7.     (a)     Each copyright on the composition in countries other than the United States shall be secured only in the name of the Publisher, and the Publisher shall not at any time divest itself of said foreign copyright directly or indirectly.

(b)     No rights shall be granted by the Publisher in the composition to any foreign publisher or licensee inconsistent with the terms hereof, nor shall any foreign publication rights in the composition be given to a foreign publisher or licensee un-less and until the Publisher shall have complied with the pro-visions of Paragraph 6 hereof.

(c)     If foreign rights in the composition are separately con-veyed, otherwise than as a part of the Publisher's current and/or future catalog, not less than 50% of any advance received in respect thereof shall be credited to the account of and paid to the Writer.

(d)     The percentage of the Writer on monies received from foreign sources shall be computed on the Publisher's net re-ceipts, provided, however, that no deductions shall be made for offsets of monies due from the Publisher to said foreign sources; or for advances made by such foreign sources to the Publisher, unless the Writer shall have received at least 50% of said advances.

(e)     In computing the receipts of the Publisher from li-censes granted in respect of synchronization with sound motion pictures, or in respect of any world-wide licenses, or in respect of licenses granted by the Publisher for use of the composition in countries other than the United States, no amount shall be deducted for payments or allocations to publishers or licenses in such countries.

8.     Upon the termination or expiration of this contract, all rights of any and every nature in and to the composition and in and to any and all copyrights secured thereon in the United States and throughout the world, shall re-vest in and become the property of the Writer, and shall be re-assigned to the Writer by the Publisher free of any and all encumbrances of any nature whatsoever, provided that:

(a)     If the Publisher, prior to such termination or expiration, shall have granted a domestic license for the use of the com-position, not inconsistent with the terms and provisions of this contract, the re-assignment may be subject to the terms of such license.

(b)     Publisher shall assign to the Writer all rights which it may have under any such agreement or license referred to in subdivision (a) in respect of the composition, including, but not limited to, the right to receive all royalties or other monies earned by the composition thereunder after the date of termination or expiration of this contract. Should the Publisher thereafter receive or be credited with any royalties or other monies so earned, it shall pay the same to the Writer.

(c)    The Writer shall not be obligated to return or pay to the Publisher any advance or indebtedness as a condition of the re-assignment provided for in this Paragraph 8, and shall be entitled to receive the plates and copies of the composition in the possession of the Publisher.

(d)    Publisher shall pay any and all royalties which may have accrued to the Writer prior to such termination or expiration.

(e)    The Publisher shall execute any and all documents and do any and all acts or things necessary to effect any and all re-assignments to the Writer herein provided for.

9.    If the Publisher desires to exercise a right in and to the composition now known or which may hereafter become known, but for which no specific provision has been made herein, the Publisher shall give written notice to the Writer thereof. Negotiations respecting all the terms and conditions of any such disposition shall thereupon be entered into between the Publisher and the Writer and no such right shall be exercised until specific agreement has been made.

10.    The Publisher shall render to the Writer, hereafter, royalty statements accompanied by remittance of the amount due at the times such statements and remittances shall be rendered either semi-annually or quarterly and not more than forty-five days after the end of such semi-annual or quarterly period, as the case may be. The Writer may at any time, or from time to time, make written request for a detailed royalty statement, and the Publisher shall, within sixty days, comply therewith. Such royalty statements shall set forth in detail various items, foreign and domestic, for which royalties are payable thereunder and

the amounts thereof, including, but not limited to, the number of copies sold and the number of uses made in each royalty category. If a use is made in a publication of the character provided in Paragraph 4, subdivision (e) hereof, there shall be included in said royalty statement the title of said publication, the publisher or issuer thereof, the date of and number of uses, the gross license fee received in connection with each publication, the share thereto of all the writers under contract with the Publisher, and the Writer's share thereof. There shall likewise be included in said statement a description of every other use of the composition, and if by a licensee or licensees their names, and if said use is upon a part of an instrument serving to reproduce the composition mechanically, the type of mechanical reproduction, the title of the label thereon, the name or names of the artists performing the same, together with the gross license fees received, and the Writer's share thereof.

11. (a) The Publisher shall from time to time, upon written demand of the Writer or his representative, permit the Writer or his representative to inspect at the place of business of the Publisher, all books, records and documents relating to the composition and all licenses granted, uses had and payments made therefor, such right of inspection to include, but not by way of limitation, the right to examine all original accountings and records relating to uses and payments by manufacturers of commercial sound recordings and music rolls; and the Writer or his representative may appoint an accountant who shall at any time during usual business hours have access to all records of the Publisher relating to the composition for the purpose of verifying royalty statements rendered or which are delinquent under the terms hereof.

(b) The Publisher shall, upon written demand of the Writer or his representative, cause any licensing agent in the United States and Canada to furnish to the Writer or his representative, statements showing in detail all licenses granted, uses had and payments made in connection with the composition, which licenses or permits were granted, or payments were received, by or through said licensing agent, and to permit the Writer or his representative to inspect at the place of business of such licensing agent, all books, records and documents of such licensing agent, relating thereto. Any and all agreements made by the Publisher with any such licensing agent shall provide that any such licensing agent will comply with the terms and provisions hereof. In the event that the Publisher shall instruct such licensing agent to furnish to the Writer or his representative statements as provided for herein, and to permit the inspection of the books, records and documents as herein provided, then if such licensing agent should refuse to comply with the said instructions, or any of them, the Publisher agrees to institute and prosecute diligently and in good faith such action or proceedings as may be necessary to compel compliance with the said instructions.

(c)     With respect to foreign licensing agents, the Publisher shall make available the books or records of said licensing agents in countries outside of the United States and Canada to the extent such books or records are available to the Publisher, except that the Publisher may in lieu thereof make available any accountants' reports and audits which the Publisher is able to obtain.

(d)     If as a result of any examination of books, records or documents pursuant to Paragraphs 11(a), 11(b) or 11(c) hereof, it is determined that, with respect to any royalty statement rendered by or on behalf of the Publisher to the Writer, the Writer is owed a sum equal to or greater than five percent of the sum shown on that royalty statement as being due to the Writer, then the Publisher shall pay to the Writer the entire cost of such examination, not to exceed 50% of the amount shown to be due the Writer.

(e)     (i)     In the event the Publisher administers its own licenses for the manufacture of parts of instruments serving to mechanically reproduce the composition rather than employing a licensing agent for that purpose, the Publisher shall include in each license agreement a provision permitting the Publisher, the Writer or their respective representatives to inspect, at the place of business of such licensee, all books, records and documents of such licensee relating to such license. Within 30 days after written demand by the Writer, the Publisher shall commence to inspect such licensee's books, records and documents and shall furnish a written report of such inspection to the Writer within 90 days following such demand. If the Publisher fails, after written demand by the Writer, to so inspect the licensee's books, records and documents, or fails to furnish such report, the Writer or his representative may inspect such licensee's books, records and documents at his own expense.

(ii)    In the further event that the Publisher and the licensee referred to in subdivision (i) above are subsidiaries or affiliates of the same entity or one is a subsidiary or affiliate of the other, then, unless the Publisher employs a licensing agent to administer the licenses referred to in subdivision (i) above, the Writer shall have the right to make the inspection referred to in subdivision (i) above without the necessity of making written demand on the Publisher as provided in subdivision (i) above.

(iii)    If as a result of any inspection by the Writer pursuant to subdivisions (i) and (ii) of this subparagraph (e) the Writer recovers additional monies from the licensee, the Publisher and the Writer shall share equally in the cost of such inspection.

12.    If the Publisher shall fail or refuse, within sixty days after written demand, to furnish or cause to be furnished, such statements, books, records or documents, or to permit inspection thereof, as provided for in Paragraphs 10 and 11 hereof, or within thirty days after written demand, to make the payment of any royalties due under this contract, then the Writer shall be entitled, upon ten days written notice, to terminate this contract. However if the Publisher shall:

(a)     Within the said ten-day period serve upon the Writer a written notice demanding arbitration; and

(b)     Submit to arbitration its claim that it has complied with its obligation to furnish statements, books, records or documents, or permitted inspection thereof or to pay royalties, as the case may be, or both, and thereafter comply with any award of the arbitrator within ten days after such award or within such time as the arbitrator may specify; then this contract shall continue in full force and effect as if the Writer had not sent such notice of termination. If the Publisher shall fail to comply with the foregoing provisions, then this contract shall be deemed to have been terminated as of the date of the Writer's written notice of termination.

13.     No derivative work prepared under authority of Publisher during the term of this contract may be utilized by Publisher or any other party after termination or expiration of this contract.

14.     All written demands and notices provided for herein shall be sent by certified mail, return receipt requested.

15.     Any legal action brought by the Publisher against any alleged infringer of the composition shall be initiated and prosecuted at its sole cost and expense, but if the Publisher should fail, within thirty days after written demand, to institute such action, the Writer shall be entitled to institute such suit at his cost and expense. All sums recovered as a result of any such action shall, after the deduction of the reasonable expense thereof, be divided equally between the Publisher and the Writer. No settlement of any such action may be made by either party without first notifying the other; in the event that either party should object to such settlement, then such settlement shall not be made if the party objecting assumes the prosecution of the action and all expenses thereof, except that any sums thereafter recovered shall be divided equally between the Publisher and the Writer after the deduction of the reasonable expenses thereof.

16.     (a)     If a claim is presented against the Publisher alleging that the composition is an infringement upon some other work or a violation of any other right of another, and because thereof the Publisher is jeopardized, it shall forthwith serve a written notice upon the Writer setting forth the full details of such claim. The pendency of said claim shall not relieve the Publisher of the obligation to make payment of the royalties to the Writer hereunder, unless the Publisher shall deposit said royalties as and when they would otherwise be payable, in an account in the joint names of the Publisher and the Writer in a bank or trust company in New York, New York, if the Writer on the date of execution of this contract resides East of the Mississippi River, or in Los Angeles, California, if the Writer on the date of execution of this contract resides West of the Mississippi River. If no suit be filed within nine months after said written notice from the Publisher to the Writer, all monies deposited in said joint account shall be paid over to the Writer plus any interest which may have been earned thereon.

(b)     Should an action be instituted against the Publisher claiming that the composition is an infringement upon some other work or a violation of any right of another, the Publisher shall forthwith serve written notice upon the Writer containing the full details of such claim. Notwithstanding the commencement of such action, the Publisher shall continue to pay the royalties hereunder to the Writer unless it shall, from and after the date of the service of the summons, deposit said royalties as and when they would otherwise be payable, in an account in the joint names of the Publisher and the Writer in a bank or trust company in New York, New York, if the Writer on the date of execution of this contract resides East of the Mississippi River, or in Los Angeles, California, if the Writer on the date of execution of this contract resides West of the Mississippi River. If the said suit shall be finally adjudicated in favor of the Publisher or shall be settled, there shall be released and paid to the Writer all of such sums held in escrow less any amount paid out of the Writer's share with the Writer's written consent in settlement of said action. Should the said suit finally result adversely to the Publisher, the said amount on the deposit shall be released to the Publisher to the extent or damage it incurs and the balance shall be paid over to the Writer.

(c)     In any of the foregoing events, however, the Writer shall be entitled to payment of said royalties or the money so deposited at and after such time as he files with the Publisher a surety company bond, or a bond in other form acceptable to the Publisher, in the sum of such payments to secure the return thereof to the extent that the Publisher may be entitled to such return. The foregoing payments or deposits or the filing of a bond shall be without prejudice to the rights of the Publisher or Writer in the premises.

17.     Any and all differences, disputes or controversies arising out of or in connection with this contract shall be submitted to arbitration before a sole arbitrator under the then prevailing rules of the American Arbitration Association. The location of the arbitration shall be New York, New York, if the Writer on the date of execution of this contract resides East of the Mississippi River, or in Los Angeles, California, if the Writer on the date of execution of this contract resides West of the Mississippi River. The parties hereby individually and jointly agree to abide by and perform any award rendered in such arbitration. Judgment upon any such award rendered may be entered in any court having jurisdiction thereof.

18.     Except to the extent herein otherwise expressly provided, the Publisher shall not sell, transfer, assign, convey, encumber or otherwise dispose of the composition or the copyright or copyrights secured thereon without the prior written consent of the Writer. The Writer has been induced to enter into this contract in reliance upon the value to him of the personal service and ability of the Publisher in the exploitation of the composition, and by reason thereof it is the intention of the parties and the essence of the relationship between them that the rights herein granted to the Publisher shall remain with the

Publisher and that the same shall not pass to any other person, including, without limitations, successors to or receivers or trustees of the property of the Publisher, either by act or deed of the Publisher or by operation of law, and in the event of the voluntary or involuntary bankruptcy of the Publisher, this contract shall terminate, provided, however, that the composition may be included by the Publisher in a bona fide voluntary sale of its music business or its entire catalog of musical compositions, or in a merger or consolidation of the Publisher with a another corporation, in which event the Publisher shall immediately give written notice thereof to the Writer; and provided further that the composition and the copyright therein may be assigned by the Publisher to a subsidiary or affiliated company generally engaged in the music publishing business. Any such transfer or assignment shall, however, be conditioned upon the execution and delivery by the transferee or assignee to the Writer of an agreement to be bound by and to perform all of the terms and conditions of this contract to be performed on the part of the Publisher.

19.    A subsidiary, affiliate, or any person, firm or corporation controlled by the Publisher or by such subsidiary or affiliate, as used in this contract, shall be deemed to include any person, firm or corporation, under common control with, or the majority of whose stock or capital contribution is owned or controlled by the Publisher or by any of its officers, directors, partners or associates, or whose policies and actions are subject to domination or control by the Publisher or any of its officers, directors, partners or associates.

20.    The amounts and percentages specified in this contract shall be deemed to be the amounts and percentages agreed upon by the parties hereto, unless other amounts or percentages are inserted in the blank spaces provided therefor.

21.    This contract is binding upon and shall enure to the benefit of the parties hereto and their respective successors in interest (as hereinbefore limited). If the Writer (or one or more of

them) shall not be living, any notices may be given to, or con-sents given by, his or their successors in interest. No change or modification of this contract shall be effective unless reduced to writing and signed by the parties hereto.

The words in this contract shall be so construed that the singular shall include the plural and the plural shall include the singular where the context so requires and the masculine shall include the feminine and the feminine shall include the mas-culine where the context so requires.

22.     The paragraph headings are inserted only as a matter of convenience and for reference, and in no way define, limit or describe the scope or intent of this contract nor in any way affect this contract.

23. *

Witness: Publisher: *_____

*_____ By: *_____

Address: *_____

Writer: *_____ (L.S.)

Witness: Address: *_____

*_____ Soc. Sec.#: *_____

# FORM 3.8

## STANDARD STUDIO FILM MUSIC
## COMPOSER/ARRANGER/CONDUCTOR
## EMPLOYMENT AGREEMENT

January 1, 2000


Mr. Cameron Composer
c/o John Lawyer, Esq.
1880 Century Park East, Suite 100
Los Angeles, California 90067

Dear Mr. Composer:

The following, when signed by you ("Artist") and by us ("Producer"), will constitute our agreement.

1.    EMPLOYMENT OF ARTIST: Producer hereby employs Artist to compose original music and to arrange and conduct all of the music Producer may require for a sixty minute videotaped television program intended primarily for pay television exhibition (the "Program") entitled _____.

2.    TERM: Artist's services shall start on January 1, 2000 and shall be completed in sufficient time to permit Producer to score the music to meet delivery requirements.

3.    DELIVERY: Artist will deliver the score and the arrangements to Producer for all the music for the Program in sufficient time to permit Producer to make the preparations necessary to score the music in the Program.

4.    PAYMENT: In full consideration for this Agreement, Producer will pay Artist:

(a)      Upon completion of all services referred to in Paragraph 1. and compliance with Paragraph 3., the sum of

_____

(b)      Royalties for any publication and other use of music composed by Artist, in accordance with Exhibit "B" (Schedule of Music Royalties) attached hereto.

(c)      Upon initial theatrical exhibition of the Motion Pictures, 50% of the sum set forth in subparagraph (a) hereof.

5.      SCREEN CREDIT: Provided that Artist is not in default, Artist shall be accorded substantially the following screen credit on the Motion Picture:

            MUSIC BY

6.      ASCAP, BMI OR OTHER: Artist represents that Artist is a member of:

        ASCAP (X)              BMI ( )              _____ ( )

7.      STANDARD TERMS: The Standard Terms for Employment of Services and the Schedule of Music Royalties, attached hereto as Exhibit "A" and "B" respectively, are hereby incorporated in and made a part of this Agreement.

If the foregoing correctly sets forth the agreement between Producer and Artist please sign in the place indicated below.

            Very truly yours,

            THEATRICAL FILM CORPORATION

            By _____

AGREED:

_____

# EXHIBIT "A"

## STANDARD TERMS FOR EMPLOYMENT OF SERVICES

## COMPOSER/ARRANGER/CONDUCTOR

Exhibit to Agreement ("Main Agreement") dated January 1, 2000 between THEATRICAL FILM CORPORATION ("Producer") and _____ ("Artist").

1. STANDARD TERMS FOR EMPLOYMENT OF SERVICES: These Standard Terms for Employment of Services are hereby incorporated in and made a part of the Main Agreement. The Main Agreement and these Standard Terms for Employment of Services are together referred to as "this Agreement."

2. ACCEPTANCE: Artist hereby accepts employment hereunder and will comply with Producer's directions, requests, rules and regulations and perform services to the full limit of Artist's capabilities as, when and where, in the United States or any other place, designated by Producer. The judgment of Producer shall be final in all matters, including, but not limited to, matters of artistic taste and the importance and manner of performance of Artist's services.

3. EXCLUSIVITY: During the Term, Artist will not render any services which would interfere with the services to be rendered by Artist hereunder.

4. PAYMENT: As full compensation for all services rendered hereunder, the rights granted and warranties, representations and agreements made, and provided that Artist is not in default Producer shall pay Artist, less applicable withholdings, the applicable sums set forth in this Agreement. Producer shall have the right to apply any portion of Artist's salary as a musician which is in excess of the minimum salary rate to any of the minimum payments, premiums, allowances, doubling, penal-

ties, overtime or any other minimum requirements of the A.F. of M. Agreement.

5.      START DATE: Unless a start date for Artist's services is set forth in the Main Agreement, Producer will give Artist reasonable notice of such start date, and Artist agrees to be available for services hereunder during schedules established by Producer.

6.      RESULTS AND PRODUCT: Producer shall be the sole owner of all of the results and product ("Work") of all services rendered by Artist hereunder. As the employer for whom the Work is being prepared as a work made for hire by Artist as an employee of Producer within the scope of Artist's employment, Producer shall be the author and copyright owner of the Work.

7.      NAME AND LIKENESS: Producer and its licensees shall have the exclusive and perpetual right, but not the obligation, to use and license the use of Artist's name, photograph, likeness and biographical data ("Name and Likeness") for the following: (a) in billing and credits with respect to the motion pictures produced hereunder, (b) in publicizing Artist's services hereunder and/or the results and proceeds of all Artist's services hereunder, any motion pictures produced hereunder, any television series of which the motion pictures may be a part and in connection therewith and any distributor, network, sponsor, advertising agency or licensee of exhibition rights in the motion pictures produced hereunder or other parties and its or their products and services, (c) in connection with the publication and exploitation of books based on the motion pictures produced hereunder and music and sound recordings of music written for or performed in the motion pictures produced hereunder. Any breach by Artist of the exclusivity provisions of this Paragraph shall be deemed a Default and Producer shall have the right to terminate this Agreement by notice to Artist and/or to withhold any screen and advertising credit provided for hereunder. Producer may not use or license use of Artist's Name and Likeness as a direct endorsement of any sponsor's product or service.

8.     PAY OR PLAY: Nothing in this Agreement shall obligate Producer actually to utilize Artist's services or to exploit the results and proceeds of Artist's services hereunder. If Producer elects not to utilize Artist's services, payment to Artist of the applicable sums set forth in this Agreement constitutes discharge in full of all of Producer's obligations to Artist hereunder.

9.     FEDERAL COMMUNICATIONS ACT: Artist warrants and represents that Artist will neither pay nor agree to pay any money, service or other valuable consideration as defined in Section 508 of the Federal Communications Act of 1934 as amended, for the inclusion of any matter in any motion picture, and that Artist has not accepted nor will accept nor agree to accept any money, service or other valuable consideration (other than payment to Artist hereunder) for the inclusion of any matter in any motion picture. Artist will, during or after the Term, promptly on request, complete Producer's standard Section 508 report forms.

10.     DEFAULT; INCAPACITY; FORCE MAJEURE: In the event of default, incapacity of Artist, or event of force majeure any interference with or suspension or postponement of production by reason of any cause or occurrence beyond the control of Producer, including labor dispute, strikes, any acts of God, war, riot, governmental action, regulations or decrees, casualties, accidents, illness or incapacity of the director or of a member of the cast or other person in connection with any motion pictures produced hereunder, or similar or dissimilar causes which prevent rendition of services), Producer may, at its election, terminate this Agreement by notice to Artist without payment after termination or suspend services without payment during suspension for such period of time, or any part thereof, as such default, incapacity of Artist or event of force majeure shall continue. Producer may, at its election, add to the Term a period of time equal to the period of any such suspension.

11.     ORIGINALITY; INDEMNIFICATION: Artist warrants and represents that all material, if any, written by Artist for Producer

will be wholly original with Artist, or in the public domain, and was not and will not be copied in whole or in part from any other work except for material furnished by Producer for use by Artist hereunder, and does not and will not knowingly invade the right of privacy of any person. Artist further warrants and represents that any material furnished or written by Artist does not and will not constitute a defamation of any person, firm or corporation, or violate or infringe upon any copyright, common law or statutory, or any other right of any person, firm or corporation. Artist hereby agrees to indemnify and hold Producer and its successors, licensees and assigns harmless from and against any claim, loss, damage, liability, judgment, cost or expense of any kind and character, including attorneys' fees, suffered or incurred by Producer resulting from or arising out of any breach or alleged breach of any of the foregoing warranties by Artist, and Producer similarly indemnifies and holds Artist harmless as to material furnished by Producer for use by Artist hereunder.

12.     UNIQUE SERVICES: Artist acknowledges that Artist's services hereunder are of a special, unique, unusual, extraordinary and intellectual character, giving them a peculiar value, the loss of which cannot be reasonably or adequately compensated in damages in an action at law, and in the event of the breach or threatened breach of this Agreement by Artist, and without limiting any other rights or remedies, Producer shall be entitled to equitable relief by way of injunction or otherwise.

13.     SERVICES AS MUSICIAN: Artist's services if any as a musician shall be subject to the applicable collective bargaining agreement between Producer and the American Federation of Musicians.

14.     CREDIT: No casual or inadvertent failure to accord Artist any credits that may be required under this Agreement, or under any applicable collective bargaining agreement, shall constitute a breach of this Agreement. The failure to accord Artist any required credits shall not entitle Artist to injunctive relief or to terminate this Agreement.

15. MOTION PICTURE RELIEF FUND: Artist hereby authorizes Producer on Artist's behalf to pay to Motion Picture Relief Fund of America, Inc. one percent (1%) of all compensation accruing under this Agreement.

16. DISTANT LOCATION: If, at Producer's request, Artist is required to remain at a distant location overnight, Artist will be furnished first class round trip transportation (if available and if used), meals and, for each such day, first class accommodations (if available).

17. ASSIGNMENT; LOANOUT: Producer may assign this Agreement and any of Producer's rights hereunder or lend Artist's services to any third party and this Agreement shall inure to the benefit of Producer, its successors and assigns. No assignment shall relieve Producer of its obligations. Artist may not assign this Agreement.

18. NOTICES: A notice to Artist may be given orally to Artist or to Artist's agent, if any, set forth on the first page of the Main Agreement, or to any substitute agent designated in writing by Artist or by mailing or telegraphing the notice to Artist at Artist's address set forth on the first page of the Main Agreement. A notice to Producer shall be given by mailing or telegraphing it to Producer addressed to Box 1, Beverly Hills, California 90210, marked Attention: Studio Legal Affairs Department. Producer or Artist may designate a substitute address by written notice to the other. A notice given by mail, postage prepaid, or telegram thereof shall be deemed received on the date mailed or telegraphed. Any notice from Artist to Producer must be in writing.

19. ARTIST'S WARRANTIES AND REPRESENTATIONS: Artist warrants and represents that Artist has no commitments which will or might conflict or interfere with Artist's ability fully to comply with this Agreement, and that Artist has no outstanding agreement or arrangement for use of Artist's Name and Likeness to advertise any product or service, whether by way of endorsements, testimonials, merchandising, commercial tie-ups, television or radio commercials, or otherwise. No warran-

ties have been made other than those expressly set forth in this Agreement.

20.    COMPLETE UNDERSTANDING; GOVERNING LAW: This Agreement sets forth the complete understanding between Artist and Producer with respect to the subject matter, and all prior agreements have been merged herein, whether written or oral, and may not be modified except by a written instrument signed by the party to be charged. Artist acknowledges that no representation or promise not expressly contained in this Agreement has been made by Producer or any of its agents, employees or representatives. The laws of the State of California applicable to contracts signed and to be fully performed within the State of California shall apply to this Agreement.

# Exhibit "B"

## Schedule of Music Royalties

## Employment Agreement

Exhibit to Agreement ("Main Agreement") dated January 1, 2000 between THEATRICAL FILM CORPORATION ("Producer") and _____ ("Artist").

All music, including lyrics, arrangements and orchestrations composed and created by Artist under the Main Agreement are hereinafter referred to as "Musical Compositions". Pursuant to 114 (b) of the Main Agreement, Producer will pay Artist or cause Artist to be paid, semi-annually, within ninety (90) days after June 30 and December 31 of each year after the signing of the Main Agreement, the applicable royalties listed below. Producer makes no warranty or representation that the Musical Compositions will be utilized or that any royalties will become payable to Artist.

1.  Eight cents (8 cents) per copy for each regular piano copy of the Musical Compositions, if any, sold and paid for, to Producer or to the publisher designated by Producer ("Publisher") in the United States and Canada.

2.  Ten percent (10%) of the wholesale selling price (after trade discounts, if any) of each copy sold, if any, and paid for, to Publisher in the United States and Canada of orchestrations, band arrangements, octavos, quartets, arrangements for combinations of voices and instruments, and other copies of the Musical Compositions (other than regular piano copies).

3.  Fifty percent (50%) of all Net Receipts, if any, received by Publisher for regular piano copies, orchestrations, band arrangements, octaves, quartets, arrangements for

combinations of voices and instruments, and other copies of the Musical Compositions sold in any country, other than the United States and Canada.

4.     With respect to mechanical reproduction (other than in synchronization with motion pictures including television programs) of the Musical Compositions, a royalty equal to fifty percent (50%) of Net Receipts, if any, attributable to such uses of the Musical Compositions, received by Publisher from licenses, if any, authorizing the manufacture of parts of instruments serving to mechanically reproduce the Musical Compositions.

5.     With respect to synchronization in motion pictures including television programs of the Musical Compositions, a royalty of fifty percent (50%) of all Net Receipts, if any, received by Publisher from said uses of the Musical Compositions except as excluded in the next sentence. Artist shall not be entitled to receive from Producer or Publisher any royalties or payments for the use by Producer, its parent, subsidiaries, successors or assigns, or by third parties producing motion pictures or television programs for or in association with Producer, of the Musical Compositions in synchronization with motion pictures or television programs produced by or for Producer.

6.     Publisher's "Net Receipts" means gross moneys actually received by Publisher in the United States less: (i) taxes other than income taxes thereon, (ii) fifteen percent (15%) of said gross and (iii) Publisher's actual direct costs and expenses, if any.

The above royalties shall cover entire Musical Compositions, including lyrics, if any. If, in addition to the material or any part thereof written by Artist, any such Musical Compositions shall, with Producer's prior written consent, contain the work of other composers, such royalties shall be paid jointly to Artist and to such other composers; and if any such Musical Compositions contain both music and lyrics, such royalties shall be paid one-half jointly to all composers of the music and one-half jointly to all authors of the lyrics.

Notwithstanding anything to the contrary herein contained, if Producer provides for payment to Artist of the aforesaid royalties in a contract with any third party covering publication of the Musical Compositions, which third parties assume Producer's obligations hereunder, Artist will look solely to such third party for payment, and will release Producer from any and all liability or obligation in connection with payment if Producer gives Artist notice of Producer's contract with such third party.

Artist will not be entitled to share in any sum received by Publisher from any performing rights society and Artist will look solely to the performing rights society of which Artist is or becomes a member for any share of performance royalties paid by such societies to composers and authors. Publisher will not be entitled to share in any sum received by Artist from any performing rights society and Publisher will look solely to the performing rights society of which Publisher is or becomes a member for any share of performance royalties paid by such societies to publishers.

Payments to Artist hereunder shall be accompanied by statements in reasonable detail reflecting all receipts from use of the Musical Compositions for each period for which there are receipts. Publisher shall maintain accurate books and records with respect to receipts hereunder and sums payable to Artist. Artist shall have the right, at Artist's expense, to have Artist's representative examine said books and records during reasonable business hours and to make copes and extracts therefrom. Such inspections and audits may not be made more than once each calendar year, and may not be made with respect to any period of time occurring prior to two (2) years before the date of such audit or with respect to any period of time covered by a previous audit, and provided further that each such audit shall be completed within a reasonable period of time after it is commenced.

Any objection to any statement of accounting is to be made to Publisher within eighteen (18) months after the submission of such statement and, failing any such objection, such statement shall be deemed accepted and shall be final and binding upon Artist. Except for any books and records relating to any such objection, Publisher shall not be required to retain any records for more than four (4) years after the date of the incorporation of the information in such records into a statement.

## CHAPTER 4

# CO-PUBLISHING AND ADMINISTRATION

## SUMMARY

### I. CO-PUBLISHING AGREEMENTS

A. As Distinguished from Administration and Collection Agreements

B. When Used

C. Negotiating the Co-Publishing Agreement

   1. Copyright Ownership

   2. Administration Rights

      a. Appoint an Exclusive Administrator

      b. Appoint an Exclusive Administrator Subject to Restrictions

      c. Allow Each Owner to Administer His Own Share—Co-Administration

   3. Revenue Sharing

      a. Writer's Share

      b. Direct Publishing Expenses

D. Administration Fee

### II. ADMINISTRATION AGREEMENTS

A. When Used

B. Negotiating the Administration Agreement

   1. Administration Fee

   2. Term

   3. Restrictions on the Exercise of Administration Rights

### III. COLLECTION AGREEMENT

### APPENDIX TO CHAPTER 4

FORM 4.1     Combination Songwriter Agreement/ Co-Publishing Agreement

FORM 4.2     Co-Publishing Agreement with Exclusive Administration Rights Granted on One Co-Owner

# CO-PUBLISHING AND ADMINISTRATION

A s noted in the previous chapter, a songwriter with some bargaining leverage can often negotiate with a publisher a variation to the standard music publishing deal, one which affords him not only the *writer's share*, but a portion of the *publisher's share* of publishing income. This is often referred to as a *participation deal*, and there are two basic ways these deals are typically done. The first is for the writer to maintain a portion of the copyright in the compositions and enter into a *co-publishing agreement*, under which the publisher's share is split between the writer (or his own music publishing firm) and the music publisher. The second is for the writer to retain all interest in the copyrights and merely grant to the music publisher the right to administer the publishing of the compositions under what is known as an *administration agreement*. The effect of each of these deals is the same: it reduces the publisher's share by the amount of the share retained by the songwriter.

The *co-publishing* agreement, *administration* agreement, and a third form, the *collection* agreement, arise not only in the context of songwriter/publisher relationships, but as a result of a variety of music publishing circumstances. This chapter sketches the common terms and conditions contained in the typical co-publishing, administration, and collection agreements.

## I. CO-PUBLISHING AGREEMENTS

A *co-publishing agreement* is an agreement between two or more parties, generally co-owners of one or more copyrights, that defines the rights of the parties over division of ownership of copyrights, the administration of publishing activities, and the sharing of revenue relating to the musical compositions covered by the agreement.

## A.  As Distinguished from Administration and Collection Agreements

An *administration agreement* is an agreement between an owner, or co-owner, of copyright and another, called the *administrator*, who is provided the right and obligation to administer the musical compositions covered by the agreement, in exchange for the payment of an administration fee. A *co-publishing* agreement is similar to an *administration* agreement, but under a co-publishing agreement each of the parties typically has some co-ownership interest in each of the copyrights covered by the agreement; under an administration agreement, the administrator acquires a license for a term of years, but does not acquire an interest in any of the copyrights.

Every co-publishing agreement will contain a provision dealing with the question of who among them will have the right to *administer* the exploitation of the compositions covered by the agreement. Although these *administration rights* may be allocated among the parties to a co-publishing agreement, such rights should not be confused with what is properly called an *administration agreement.*

Another difference between a *co-publishing* and an *administration* agreement is that a co-publishing agreement typically has a term that lasts the entire life of the copyrights in the compositions; by contrast, the typical administration agreement has a stated term extending for a limited period of time. However, many co-publishing agreements also carry a limited term, so the distinction between these agreements cannot generally be made on the basis of their length of term.

A *collection* agreement is virtually the same as an administration agreement, except that the administrator is generally not obliged or given the incentive to undertake any affirmative actions to exploit the songs.

## B.  When Used

A co-publishing agreement may arise from a variety of circumstances. As stated at the outset of this chapter, a co-publishing agreement typically arises as a result of a participation deal — i.e., when a writer negotiates to maintain a portion of, or "participate in," the *publisher's share* of music publishing income. But there are other circumstances that give rise to the negotiation and entry into co-publishing agreements.

For example, where two songwriters who collaborate in the writing of a single composition have previously signed up with separate music publishing firms, the publishing firms will generally enter into a co-publishing agreement with each other to govern their respective rights in the composition. If each of these songwriters had previously negotiated for a piece of the publisher's share of income from their compositions, there will have already existed a co-publishing or administration agreement between each songwriter and his or her respective music publisher. Thus, if they should collaborate in the writing of a song, a new co-publishing agreement would be negotiated among the four publishing firms involved — the first songwriter's "self-publishing" company and the major or independent music publisher with whom he has a publishing deal, and the second songwriter's "self-publishing" company and the major or independent music publisher with whom he has a publishing deal.

Where several members of a rock band each have contributed to the writing of a single song, the complexities arising from multiple publishing companies can be daunting. Depending upon the terms of the co-publishing or partnership agreement among the members, should someone have had the presence of mind to create one for them, the resulting "split of copyright" could raise the problems that often stem from what we call the Split Copyright Syndrome, lamented in more detail in Chapter 6.

Other circumstances out of which a co-publishing agreement may arise include the situation where a writer receives control over his copyright as a result of a termination of a prior grant of rights (under statutory termination rights under the copyright law[1]) or a reversion of rights under an existing songwriter agreement, and, now, when his bargaining position is improved, wishes to gain a share in the publishing income. An emerging area that has called for the co-publishing solution is where a recording artist illegally takes a digital sample from a recording of another and the owner of the underlying musical composition and the sampling artist settle the matter by entering into a co-publishing agreement that calls for the sharing of income from the publication of (and, often, the sharing of the copyright in) the new

---

[1] See Chapter 9, *Duration of Copyrights, Assignments and Licenses.*

work. This negotiation is covered in more detail in Chapter 24, *The Digital Sampling Controversy.*

## C. Negotiating the Co-Publishing Agreement

The primary business points on which to focus in negotiating a co-publishing agreement include: (1) copyright ownership, (2) administration rights, and (3) revenue sharing.

### *1. Copyright Ownership*

Ordinarily, when a songwriter writes a song, he assigns his entire interest in the copyright to a music publisher, which, as we have pointed out, is the arrangement set forth in the typical songwriter agreement. As a result of that transaction, the copyright is owned by a single person or entity. As discussed in the previous chapter, and later in Chapter 7, on *The Language of Music Licensing*, a copyright can also be *co-owned.* Co-ownership of a musical composition often arises from collaboration of two or more songwriters in the creation of the song — commonly, a composer and a lyricist. Traditionally, when a composer and lyricist collaborated in the writing of a song, they each assigned their respective ownership interest in the copyright to a single music publisher, resulting in the control of the composition by a single copyright owner. In recent years, however, the trend has been for songwriters to retain all or a portion of the copyright in their compositions,[2] resulting in the co-ownership of copyright among each of the songwriters and their respective publishers.

In the case of co-authorship, each co-author of a musical composition acquires an ownership interest in the song's copyright, and unless otherwise agreed between or among the several co-authors, each co-author receives an *equal share* in that copyright ownership interest. For example, where two authors collaborate in the writing of a song, each would have a 50% interest in the entire work; where there are three authors, each would have a 33⅓% undivided interest in the entire work, etc.

---

[2] See Chapter 3, *Songwriter Agreements,* and Chapter 6, *The Split Copyright Syndrome.*

Co-authors may, however, agree to another division, and that division is entirely subject to negotiation. For example, where one author contributed words and music and the other worked only on the words, the two may agree to a 75/25% division. Non-equal divisions of copyright ownership and co-publisher revenue sharing frequently arises in the context of a multiple member rock band, where the band is comprised of both songwriter and non-songwriter members. A non-songwriter member, perhaps a well known lead singer, may assert that the band as a whole should benefit from the band's recording and performance of the songs written by its members. As a result, the band itself, or each of the non-songwriter members, may receive a portion of the copyright, or a portion of the publisher's share of revenues from such songs. Such negotiations, a potential source of some heated discussions, will often pose a challenging conflict of interest problem for the attorney representing the band as a whole.

The percentage ownership of copyright usually determines the percentage that each co-author will share in the publisher's share of income, but not always — in other words, the revenue sharing percentages may not always follow the copyright ownership percentages. Copyright ownership may be split 50/50, or transferred entirely to one party (i.e., 100/0), with the revenue split under completely different terms (e.g., 75/25, 60/40). For example, if the songwriter members of a rock band are unwilling to assign a copyright ownership interest to the non-songwriter members, or to the band as a whole, they might retain the copyright, but, recognizing the band's contribution to the success of the compositions, they may be willing to share a portion of the publishing income with the other members of the band. This compromise is typically effected by the entry of a *rate participation* agreement in a form similar to Form 4.4 set forth in the appendix to this chapter.

*Term.* Because the co-publishing agreement generally involves the co-ownership of copyright, the term of the agreement generally lasts the life of the copyrights. Some co-publishing agreements, however, will have a term, sometimes called the *administration term*, that is limited in much the same way as the term of an administration agreement. Of course, the term of co-ownership as between co-authors who each retain at least a portion of his undivided interest in his copyrights will always last the life of the copyrights. Where, however, co-authors

with a high degree of bargaining leverage assign a co-ownership interest in their copyrights to a major music publisher, they might negotiate a limited administration term, such as three to five years, upon
the expiration of which all rights will revert back to the writers. Other
variations in *term* provisions are discussed below with respect to the
duration of *administration agreements*.

## 2.  Administration Rights

It may be recalled that *administration rights* is the term used to
define who among the copyright owners, or co-publishers, has the
authority to grant licenses for the use of the music. Because of the
problems that arise when ownership of copyright is split among several parties,[3] how administration rights are allocated among the parties
may be one of the most important factors affecting the long term value
of the copyright. Accordingly, the parties should very carefully consider how they are going to address the question of how administration
rights are allocated in their co-publishing agreement.

There are three basic ways administration rights can be allocated
among the parties: (a) appoint an exclusive administrator, (b) appoint
an exclusive administrator, but subject his authority to certain restrictions, or (c) allow each owner to administer his own share of the
copyright.

### a.  Appoint an Exclusive Administrator

The parties to a co-publishing agreement may appoint one of the
parties as the *exclusive administrator*, who would have the exclusive
right to administer all publishing matters with respect to the musical
compositions covered by the agreement. This means that anyone desiring a license to use the music covered by the agreement need only
locate, negotiate with, and acquire a license from a single person, the
exclusive administrator, who would have the right to issue a license
on behalf of all the copyright owners. The exclusive administrator
collects all the income and is responsible for distributing the appropriate shares of the income, less agreed upon expenses, to the respective co-publishers. The only rights the other co-publishers have is

---

[3] See Chapter 6, *The Split Copyright Syndrome.*

the right to receive the share of publishing income to which they are entitled under the agreement.

Where an exclusive administrator is appointed, a copyright which is split (i.e., co-owned by several persons), — and which would otherwise be plagued by the *split copyright syndrome*[4] — can be efficiently administered, provided, of course, the exclusive administrator competently represents the co-publishing group. Which leads to the question of, who among the co-publishers should be appointed the exclusive administrator. This may prove to be most difficult to answer.

One commentator has suggested that the administration rights be granted to the co-publisher having the greatest percentage in the copyright. Another idea, which the present authors recommend, is what might be called, *alternating administration rights* — that is, allow each co-publisher to control the administration rights for alternating terms of two, three, or five years. The acting administrator could waive the collection of an administration fee or he could be awarded a fee for achieving a minimum level of publishing income established in advance by the parties.

Co-publishers indisposed to grant exclusive administration rights to a co-publisher for financial reasons might be satisfied with a provision requiring the exclusive administrator to waive any administration fee and by requiring that shares of certain income be paid directly to each co-publisher from the source of the income, as many co-publishing agreements typically require. For example, the parties may instruct the Harry Fox Agency, and the applicable performance rights society (e.g., ASCAP or BMI), to pay any income generated by them directly to each co-publisher according to his or her share, in effect bypassing the administrator. This will reduce any unnecessary transaction costs associated with flowing these payments through to the co-publishers and reduce the amount of time it takes for these payments to reach their pockets.

Should the parties be unable to immediately agree upon a single administrator, or alternating administration program, it may do them well to list their particular concerns, use that list to craft contractual provisions addressing their concerns, and appoint an exclusive administrator who would be subject to those restrictions.

---

[4] *Id.*

### b. Appoint an Exclusive Administrator Subject to Restrictions

The parties to a co-publishing agreement may appoint an *exclusive administrator*, but impose certain restrictions that affect either the administrator's authority to issue licenses or his authority to collect money on behalf of the other parties.

Just as a songwriter may wish to retain a right of consent over the licensing of certain kinds of uses by his publisher, a co-publisher granting administration rights to another may wish to retain similar rights of consent. For example, the agreement may specify that the consent of each co-publisher is required before the administrator issues a license (a) allowing another to make changes to the music or lyrics (b) allowing creation and distribution of mechanical reproductions for less than the statutory rate, (c) allowing the use of the title of the song as the title of a play, film, or television program, (d) allowing the use of the song in a political or commercial advertisement, (e) allowing the synchronization of the song in a motion picture, television program, or videogram bearing a rating of "X" or its equivalent, or (f) allowing the production of a dramatic adaptation of the song. Any of these restrictions may vary depending upon the tastes of the particular co-publishers and nature of the relationship they have with the exclusive administrator. Restrictions such as these are becoming increasingly common.

Again, parties otherwise reluctant to appoint a single administrator, might agree to do so where the administration fee is waived, much of the income is paid directly to the co-publishers from the source, and the administrator's licensing activities are subject to adequate restrictions.

### c. Allow Each Owner to Administer His Own Share — Co-Administration

The third alternative, and probably the least attractive of the three, is where the parties agree to *co-administer* the compositions covered by the agreement — that is, each of the parties maintains the right to administer his or her respective share.

The effect of this arrangement is to require anyone who desires a license to use a composition covered by the agreement to locate, negotiate with, and acquire a separate license from each of the co-publisher parties to the agreement. While this may not appear burdensome to the co-publishers, it generally has the effect of significantly increasing the transaction costs (which often include expensive attorneys fees) of using the compositions covered by the agreement and will, in the long term, tend to have an adverse affect on the potential income from these compositions.

For this reason, some co-administration provisions permit any of the co-publisher parties to issue mechanical licenses, provided the rate charged is at the full statutory rate. Nevertheless, this does little to ameliorate the split copyright problem, illustrated in Chapter 6, created by the co-administration of copyrights. We therefore strongly recommend that the parties attempt to work out some compromise using the suggestions set forth above.

### 3.   Revenue Sharing

As noted in Chapter 2, on *The Art of Music Publishing*, the publisher's share of music publishing income may be shared among several co-publishers in accordance with their respective percentage interests in that income. As noted above, that percentage is usually, but not always, the same as the percentage ownership interest which that co-publisher has in the copyright — which itself, as we have said, is entirely subject to negotiation.

Note that each co-owner's interest in the copyright is normally a co-ownership interest in the *entire* composition (i.e., the *undivided* copyright in the entire composition), including both the music *and* the lyrics.[5] Accordingly, any royalties generated by the sale or performance of either the music or the lyrics will normally become part of the publisher's share (and, for that matter, the writer's share) and will be divided among all of the co-owners (and writers) regardless of the nature the co-owner's (or writer's) contribution to the composition. For example, income from licensing the use of solely an instrumental version of the composition will normally be shared by all of the co-publishers and writers (even the writer of only the lyrics), and income from licensing the use of a printed edition of only the lyrics will

---

[5] See, generally, the subject of *joint works* in Chapter 7, *The Language of Music Licensing.*

normally be shared by all of the co-publishers and writers (even the composer of the music). Exceptions may exist where the parties otherwise agree or where the contributions to a composition are deemed not to be joint works.[6]

Before splitting the publisher's share among the co-publishers in accordance with their respective interests in the income, you must first determine what constitutes the publisher's share. The publisher's share is equal to the *gross receipts*, or *gross publishing income,* less (1) the amount of the *writer's share*, (2) any *direct expenses* incurred in connection with the publishing of the music, and, (3) if one of the parties has administration rights, the *administration fee,* if any. The result is referred to in most co-publishing agreements as the *net income* or *net publishing income.*

### a.  Writer's Share

The writer's share of music publishing income is determined in accordance with the provisions of the songwriter's agreement, discussed in Chapter 3. As we have said, with a couple of exceptions, the writer's share amounts to 50% of the income the publisher receives in connection with the publishing of the music. The first exception is that most songwriter's agreements provide for less than 50% of income generated in connection with the sale or licensing of printed editions of the music. The other exception concerns performance royalties: the writer receives his writer's share, and the publisher receives its publisher's share, of performance royalties directly from their performance rights society — because the performance rights society has already split the performance royalties between writer and publisher, the *writer's share* of music publishing income includes no portion of the *publisher's share* of performance royalties.

### b.  Direct Publishing Expenses

In the co-publishing agreement set forth as Form 4.1 in the appendix to this chapter, the following publishing expenses are listed as among those the administrator may deduct from *gross receipts:*

---

[6] *Id.*

(c)  Collection or other fees customarily charged by The Harry Fox Agency or any other collection agent which may be used by Company;

(d)  Actual out-of-pocket administrative and exploitation expenses of Company with respect to the Composition for registration fees, advertising and promotion expenses directly related to the Composition, the costs of transcribing lead sheets, and the costs of producing demonstration records.

(e)  Attorneys fees directly related to the defense of claims respecting the Composition, if any, actually paid by the Company;

The deduction of commissions charged by agencies like the Harry Fox Agency, and costs associated with the preparation of lead sheets, demonstration recordings, copyright office registration fees, subpublisher fees, and legal fees incurred in the collection of income or the defense of claims directly related to the compositions, is generally considered fair and acceptable. However, advertising and promotion expenses, legal fees incurred to draft license agreements, and specific overhead expenses such as word processing and secretarial expenses are typically negotiated off of the list of expenses which an administrator is entitled to deduct. A party might also negotiate a specific dollar limit to the amount of such fees which may be deducted during each payment period.

## D.  Administration Fee

The *administration fee* is the fee charged by the person responsible for administering the music publishing of the compositions covered by a co-publishing agreement. Of course, if the parties have agreed upon a co-administration arrangement, under which each party maintains the right to administer his or her own respective share, each collecting income directly from licensees, no administration fee is applied. The fee is calculated as a percentage of the gross publishing income, including *both* the writer's share and the publisher's share. Administration fees vary, but usually amount anywhere from 10% to 25%. In the typical co-publishing agreement between a songwriter and a major music publisher, the publisher rarely charges an administration fee. For further details about negotiating administration fees, please refer to the discussion of administration fees in the following section regarding administration agreements.

*Revenue Sharing Example.* Assume that two parties of a co-publishing agreement, having equal shares in the publishing income, appoints one of the parties as the exclusive administrator and allows that party to deduct customary publishing expenses and a 10% administration fee. Assuming further that the gross publishing income is $100, the writer's share is $45, and direct expenses amount to $10, then the *net publishing income* is $35 (i.e., $100, less the 10% administration fee of $10, less the writer's share of $45, less the direct expenses of $10). These deductions first having been made, each publisher would then split $35 equally, or $17.50 each.

## II. ADMINISTRATION AGREEMENTS

An *administration agreement* is an agreement between two or more people that provides one of the parties, called the *administrator*, the right to administer the music publishing activities (i.e., copyright administration, use licensing, and distribution of net publishing income among the parties) relating to the musical compositions covered by the agreement, in exchange for the payment of an administration fee. Unlike an exclusive administrator under a co-publishing agreement, the administrator under an administration agreement generally does not acquire any ownership interest in the compositions covered by the agreement.

### A. When Used

As noted in the previous section, there are a variety of circumstances which may lead the owner or owners of the copyright in a musical composition to enter into a *co-publishing agreement*. Many of these circumstances may also lead to the entry of an *administration agreement*, particularly when the writer or publisher desiring to retain the entire publisher's share of income has a high degree of bargaining leverage.

A common example is where a songwriter is also a successful recording artist, circumstances which afford him the leverage to retain *all* interest in the copyrights to his compositions; but rather than devoting his personal time and resources to a self-publishing business, he finds it more attractive to grant to a music publisher the right to administer the publishing of the compositions. This is accomplished by the writer's entering into an *administration agreement* with the publisher, under which the publisher does not receive ownership of the copyrights, but only, in effect, *administration rights* and the right to receive an *administration fee* in exchange for the administration services it provides the writer.

In addition, just about any situation that may call for the grant of co-publishing rights to a music publisher could instead involve the mere grant of administration rights under an administration agreement.

## B. Negotiating the Administration Agreement

Because a grant of copyrights is usually not a part of a straight administration arrangement, the primary areas on which to focus in negotiating an administration agreement only include: (1) the administration fee, (2) the term of the agreement, and (3) restrictions on the exercise of administration rights.

### 1. Administration Fee

As noted above with respect to co-publishing agreements, the *administration fee* is the fee charged by the person responsible for administering the music publishing of the compositions. Even though the administrator under an administration agreement does not own a portion of any of the copyrights covered by the agreement, the administration fee is calculated in the same way as in the co-publishing agreement: as a percentage of the gross publishing income, including *both* the writer's share and the publisher's share.

Administration fees vary, but usually amount to 10% or 25%. If the agreement calls for the administrator to pay advances, the size of administration fee will often be a function of the size of the advances; in other words, the higher the advance, the higher the administration fee.

Before payment is made to the publishers, the administrator is also entitled to deduct his direct expenses incurred in connection with administering the publication of the compositions. Provisions concerning what direct expenses the administrator is entitled to deduct are generally the same as that found in co-publishing agreements; please refer to the previous section for a discussion of negotiating the direct expense provision.

Because the administration fee is calculated on the basis of both the writer's share (50%) and publisher's share (50%), the administrator who receives an administration fee of 20%, will end up with an amount equal to 40% of the publisher's share. Thus, the administrator actually has some inherent incentive to promote publication and performance of the song.

*Cover Records.* Co-publishers may wish to enhance that incentive by giving the administrator additional consideration when cover records are made during the term of the agreement. A *cover record* is a commercially released recording of the songwriter's composition by an artist other than the songwriter. The structure of the incentives given to administrators to effect cover records varies widely. For example, the term of the agreement with respect to the covered song may be extended or an interest in its copyright may be transferred to the administrator. More commonly, the administration fee with respect to mechanical royalties generated by the cover recording is increased by an additional 10% or 15%. Because of the difficulty of identifying what performance royalties were associated with performances of the cover, as opposed to those generated from performances of existing recordings, the administrator might either receive no additional percentage of performance royalties or an increased percentage (i.e., the additional 10 or 15%) of that portion of performance royalties determined by the amount the mechanical royalties generated by the cover recording bears in relation to mechanical royalties generated by existing recordings.

## 2.  Term

Unlike the typical co-publishing agreement, which commonly has a term lasting the life of the copyright, the term of the typical administration agreement is limited to a term of three to five years, or two or three years with several successive year options to renew. The exercise of such options may be conditioned upon the payment of advances. Other variations are entirely subject to negotiation.

For example, as noted in the previous section, should the administrator succeed in obtaining a cover record for a particular composition, the term of the administration agreement, at least with respect to that composition, may be extended for an additional period of years. However, this means of providing the administrator with the incentive to effect cover recordings is not favored, because it may result in some of the copyright owner's compositions being administered by one administrator and some being administered by another.

Thus, should the administrator insist upon extending the term of the agreement as an incentive for successful performance, that incentive should be made on the basis of achieving minimum net publishing income performance levels generated by the entire catalog. Such a provision might contain a condition that if the net publishing income for all or a selected portion of the compositions covered by the agreement fails to meet certain minimum performance levels in any year, the copyright owner may terminate the administration on ninety days notice or any subsequent option for renewal may not be exercised.

### 3.  *Restrictions on the Exercise of Administration Rights*

Just as a co-publisher may wish to restrict the exercise of administration rights by its co-publisher(s), a publisher may wish to impose similar controls on its appointed administrator. Recording artists with a significant amount of bargaining leverage, who maintain their own publishing, and who either have sufficient time to devote to their publishing business or sufficient publishing income to pay attorneys or others to act on their behalf, will sometimes require consent for any licensing activity proposed to be taken by the administrator, with the possible exception of issuing mechanical licenses for no less than the statutory rate.

More typically, however, the administrator will be given some greater latitude, being allowed to issue straightforward synchronization and other conventional licenses, but requiring the publisher's consent for one or more of the following kinds of uses: (a) allowing another to make changes to the music or lyrics (b) allowing creation and distribution of mechanical reproductions for less than the statutory rate, (c) allowing the use of the title of the song as the title of a play, film, or television program, (d) allowing the use of the song in a political or commercial advertisement, (e) allowing the synchronization of the song in a motion picture, television program, or videogram bearing a rating of "X" or its equivalent, or (f) allowing the production of a dramatic adaptation of the song. Any of these restrictions may vary depending upon the tastes of the particular publishers and nature of the relationship they have with the administrator.

## III. COLLECTION AGREEMENT

A *collection agreement* is virtually the same as an administration agreement, except the fee for administering the publishing, called the *collection fee*, is generally only about 5% to 10% of the gross receipts. Because the fee is very low compared to that of administration and co-publishing deals, the music publisher has little or no incentive to promote the publication or performance of the songs covered by the agreement, and the services provided will be limited to collecting publishing income, applying for copyright registrations, and registering songs with the performance rights societies and mechanical rights agencies.

Many publishers believe that a collection fee barely covers the publisher's overhead for royalty collection and disbursement, and collection fees of less than 10% may be uneconomical for anything but catalogs that generate considerable performance royalties. However, where a catalog produces a large amount of publishing income, a publisher can earn a profit on an administration fee of less than 10%, after taking into account the "float," or interest income, it will receive between the time it receives publishing income and the time the publisher is required to pay out the publisher's and writer's share of that income, typically on a semi-annual basis.

# APPENDIX TO CHAPTER 4
## CO-PUBLISHING AND
## ADMINISTRATION AGREEMENTS

# FORM 4.1

## COMBINATION SONGWRITER AGREEMENT/ CO-PUBLISHING AGREEMENT

Dated: As of January 1, 2000

_____

_____

_____

Dear _____

The following, when signed by you and by us, will constitute the terms and conditions of the exclusive co-publishing agreement between you and us.

1. <u>Term:</u>

    1.1.    The Term of this Agreement shall consist of an

initial period of _____ (_____) **"Contract Years"** (as defined below) commencing as of the above date. In addition, we shall have two consecutive and successive options to renew such Term for periods of one contract year in each instance. our failure to exercise the first of such options shall cause the second option to lapse as well.

    1.2.    Options are exercisable in each instance by notice (all references to "notice" in this agreement are notice in the manner prescribed in ¶ 9 below) within thirty (30) days following the completion of delivery of your **"Delivery Commitment"** (as defined below) for the then-current contract year, **provided,** that we shall in no event be required to exercise an option prior to the end of the eleventh month of the then-current contract year.

1.3.     Contract Year/Delivery Commitment:

1.3.1.     A **"Contract Year"** shall continue for the later of twelve months or, until 30 days following completion of your **"Delivery Commitment"** for such contract year.

1.3.2.     Your **"Delivery Commitment"** for each contract year shall consist of _____ (____) 100% newly-written compositions (or the equivalent in compositions only partly written by you) but without counting any **"Reduced Share SCs"** (as defined below), together with notice to us of the completion of delivery of the requisite number of compositions (with titles, names of co-writers and percentages subject to this Agreement, as well as the name(s) of any co-writer(s) and/or co-publisher(s) and the respective share(s) of each such third party).

2.     Territory: The World

3.     Scope of Agreement:

3.1.     Subject Compositions:

3.1.1.     Subject to those requirements and/or restrictions set forth in ¶ 3.2., below, your music publishing designee and we will each own an undivided 50% share of your interest in all songs included on the attached Schedule "A" **("Existing Compositions")** and all songs written or co-written during the Term by you, subject to the provisions of ¶ 3.1.2., below, in the case of co-written compositions, or otherwise now or hereafter owned or controlled directly or indirectly by you or your music publishing designee or any other person or entity directly or indirectly controlled by you (collectively referred to below as **"Subject Compositions" or "SCs"),** and we will have exclusive worldwide life-of-copyright administration of the SCs. A composition first recorded and/or released during the Term or within three months following the expiration of the Term shall be deemed to have been written and composed during the Term.

3.1.2.    In the case of co-written compositions, such co-ownership and administration shall only extend to your fractional interest which shall be calculated by multiplying 100% by a fraction, the numerator of which is 1 and the denominator of which is the total number of contributing writers, unless we have received notice prior to the initial U.S. release of the specific composition indicating different ownership shares (accompanied by a fully executed writer acknowledgment of such shares utilizing the form on the attached Schedule "C"); however, in the event that our ownership share in a specific composition derived through you would be reduced below 25% by reason of the number of writers collaborating with you with respect to that composition, such composition shall be subject to this agreement but shall be deemed a "Reduced Share SC" and shall not be counted toward your Delivery commitment.

3.2.    Administrative Requirements and Restrictions:

Although it is intended that we and our foreign subsidiaries, affiliates and licensees have the fullest possible rights to administer and exploit SCs, to utilize your name and likeness in connection therewith and to execute PA forms (and other routine copyright documents) in your name and on your behalf as your attorney-in-fact (which appointment is coupled with an interest and is therefore irrevocable), neither we nor they shall do any of the following without your prior written consent in each instance (which consent, unless expressly provided otherwise, shall not be unreasonably withheld by you):

3.2.1.    Authorize any change in the English-language title and/or lyric of any SC, alter the harmonic structure of any SC, or alter the melody of any SC (except insubstantial changes necessary to accommodate the syllabic requirements of foreign languages);

3.2.2.    Issue a mechanical license for the use of any SC at less than the prevailing statutory or society rate, except in connection with those types of uses for which reduced-rate licenses are customarily granted in the country in question;

3.2.3.    Authorize the use of the title of any SC as the title of a play, film or TV program, or authorize the dramatization of any SC;

3.2.4.    Authorize the synchronization of any SC in (1) a film or TV program bearing a rating of "NC-17", or (2) any political advertisement.

4.    Collection and Division of Income:

4.1.    We will be entitled to collect (and shall employ best efforts consistent with our reasonable business judgment to collect) all writer/publisher income (except the writer's share of public performances collected by societies and any other amount normally paid directly to songwriters by a disbursing agent) generated by each SC (including pre-Term earnings on Existing Compositions not subject to collection by third parties under presently-existing agreements listed on Schedule "A").

4.2.    Royalties/Net Income Share:

4.2.1.    We shall pay you songwriter royalties with respect to monies received by us from our exploitation of SCs in accordance with the annexed Schedule "A" all such royalties (except for royalties with respect to printed editions) to be based upon **"Gross Receipts"** (as defined below).

4.2.2.    In addition to your songwriter royalties, we shall pay you 50% of the **"Net Income"** (as defined below) from SCs.

4.2.3.    As used herein, **"Gross Receipts"** shall include the following:

(A)    Except with respect to printed editions, amounts received by us in the United States (or credited to our account in reduction of an advance previously received by us in the United States) in respect of the use or exploitation of SCs, it being understood and agreed that our share of amounts collected by our foreign music publishing subpublishers (which shall be calculated by them **"at the source"**, i.e., as received by them from performing and mechanical rights societies and other licensees, and shall not be reduced by intermediate distribution between various units of our music publishing group) shall be deemed to be 85% of such amounts (other than the publisher's share of public performance income and mechanical income from **"Local Cover Recordings,"** as defined below) 70% of the publisher's share of public performance income, and 60% of mechanical income from **"Local Cover Recordings"** (i.e., recordings of SCs not performed and/or produced by you in whole or in part, which are recorded and released outside of the United States).

(B)    With respect to printed editions manufactured and sold by us or by our subsidiaries or affiliates in the United States and/or Canada, the following percentages of the marked or suggested retail list price **("List")** on copies sold and not returned for which payment is received **("Net Paid Sales"),** prorated where less than 100% of a composition is an SC and also prorated where any edition does not consist solely of SCs (such proration to be based upon the number of copyrighted, royalty bearing compositions in-cluded therein):

(1)    20%, in the case of piano/vocal sheet music;

(2)    12.5% in the case of conventional folios (with an extra 5% in the case of a so-called "personality" folio featuring SCs written or co-written by you together with your name and likeness as a recording artist) or a "matching" folio (i.e., compositions from a specific album on which you are a featured recording artist, together with a replica of the album cover artwork therefrom). Such royalty shall be reduced prorata in any case in which a "personality" or "matching" folio features you together with another recording artist. For example: the royalty in respect of an "A, B & C" personality folio would be 1/3 of 5%, or 1.667%, while the royalty in respect of an "A,B,C & D" matching folio would be 1/4 of 5%, or 1.25%;

(3)     10% in the case of so-called "educational" editions (including, but not limited to, band and vocal group arrangements) and "fake books".

(C)     In the case of printed editions manufactured and sold by us or by our subsidiaries or affiliates outside of the United States and Canada, 12.5% of List on Net Paid Sales (subject to the prorations set forth above).

(D)     50% of all sums received from third party print licensees.

4.2.4.     **"Net Income"** is hereby defined as Gross Receipts less:

(A)     Your songwriter royalties as prescribed in Schedule "A";

(B)     Copyright registration fees, the costs of preparing lead sheets, and other direct, out-of-pocket administration expenses (excluding general overhead);

(C)     Actual and reasonable out-of-pocket audit and litigation collection expenses; and

(D)     "Demo costs" (approved by both parties in writing) to the extent not recouped from your songwriter's royalties with respect to SCs.

5.     Advances: We shall make the following nonrefundable payments, which shall be recoupable from your writer royalties and your publishing company's share of Net Income hereunder:

5.1.     Upon receipt of duly countersigned copies of this letter and completed Schedules "A" and "B", $;

5.2.     In the event that we exercise a renewal option, an amount (payable in equal installments on the first day of each calendar quarter) equal to ____% of your combined writer/publisher royalties and Net Income share hereunder (as reported on your royalty statements for the first four quarters of the immediately preceding contract year), but not less than nor more than the following:

Renewal Period Minimum Maximum

5.3.    In the event that you request an advance **("extra-contractual advance")** at a time when such advance is not due hereunder, such extracontractual advance shall constitute a pre-payment (in whole or in part, as applicable) of the next advance(s) becoming due and payable hereunder.

6.    Accounting and Payment:

6.1.    We will account to you (and make payment where appropriate) within 60 days following the end of each semi-annual calendar period. However, if the amount due for a specific statement is less than $50, payment may be deferred until the aggregate amount due to you exceeds $50. The exchange rates used by third parties in accounting to us shall be used by us in accountings hereunder.

6.2.    We will only be required to account and pay with respect to amounts actually received by us in the U.S. (or credited to our account in reduction of a previous advance received by us in the U.S.).

6.3.    Audit and Suit:

6.3.1.    You (or a certified public accountant on your behalf) shall have the right to audit our books and records as to each statement for a period of 2 years after such statement is received (or deemed received as provided below). Legal action with respect to a specific accounting statement or the accounting period to which such statement relates shall be barred if not commenced in a court of competent jurisdiction within 3 years after such statement is received (or deemed received as provided below).

6.3.2.    For the purposes of calculating such time periods, you shall be deemed to have received a statement when due unless we receive notice of nonreceipt from you (in the manner prescribed in ¶ 9, below) within 30 days thereafter. However, your failure to give such notice shall not affect your right to receive such statement (and, if applicable, your royalty and/or net income payment) after such thirty-day period.

6.4.    In "blocked currency" situations, we shall not be required to pay you until the blockage shall have been removed, but if requested to do so, we shall deposit blocked currency royalties in the local currency in a depository of our choice.

6.5.    All payments hereunder shall be subject to all applicable taxation statutes, regulations and treaties.

7.    Warranties and Representations:

7.1.    By your signature below, and in each instance in which SCs are delivered to us (**"delivery"** to include a DAT and/or cassette copy and lyric sheet, together with complete writer and publisher splits and society affiliations and satisfactory written clearance of any and all so-called "samples" embodied in any SC), you warrant and represent (1) that you have the right to do so, (2) that such SC does not infringe any third party's rights or violate any applicable criminal statute, including but not limited to such third party's copyright, trademark, servicemark, or right of privacy or publicity, (3) that the SC is not defamatory and (4) that you and your music publishing designee are and will remain affiliated with ASCAP, BMI or another recognized performing rights society (and in the event of your failure to so affiliate and for the purpose of preventing loss of income due to such failure, we shall be entitled to claim 100% of the publisher's share with the performing rights society and account to you for income derived therefrom per ¶ 4.2.2. until such time as you formally affiliate and notify us of such affiliation).

7.2.    Additional Warranties and Representations:

7.2.1.    Except as set forth in the annexed Schedule "B," neither you nor your music publishing designee, nor anyone acting on your and/or your music publishing designee's behalf or deriving rights from or through you or your music publishing designee (A) has received or will receive an advance, loan or other payment from a performing rights society, record company or other third party which is or may be recoupable from (or otherwise subject to offset against) monies which would otherwise be collectible by us hereunder, (B) is presently subject to any so-called "controlled compositions" clause under a recording agreement or (C) is presently subject to any provision of a recording agreement which would allow a record company to charge any amount against mechanical royalties.

7.2.2.    Notwithstanding the foregoing, in the event that any record company to whom you (or an entity furnishing your services) are or may hereafter be under contract charges any advance(s) or other amount(s) against mechanical royalties earned by the SCs from recordings made under such recording agreement or reduces the amount of mechanical royalties otherwise due to you because the mechanical royalties payable with respect to "outside material" embodied in your recordings causes aggregate mechanical royalties to exceed the per-record maximum rate(s) prescribed in the controlled compositions clause of your recording agreement or fails to pay mechanical royalties in respect of all records for which record royalties are payable, then, in addition to any other rights and remedies available to us, we shall be entitled to (A) send a letter of direction in your name advising your record company of the terms of this ¶ 7 and instructing such record company (upon recoupment from record and/or video royalties of any portion(s) of the advance(s) or other amount(s) so charged) to re-credit us directly to the same extent (not to exceed the total amount originally recouped from or charged against mechanical royalties) and (B) reimburse ourselves from any and all monies (including your writer/publisher royalties) earned or due hereunder, for any amount charged against mechanical royalties, except to the extent later recovered through the re-crediting process.

7.2.3.    In the event of a breach of this ¶ 7.2., we shall (in addition to any other remedies available to us) be entitled to reimburse ourselves from monies otherwise becoming due to you or your music publishing designee hereunder to the extent that monies are not collectible by us by reason thereof.

## 8. Indemnities; Cure of Breaches; Waiver:

8.1.    Each party will indemnify the other against any loss or damage (including court costs and reasonable attorneys' fees) due to a breach of this agreement by that party which results in a judgment against the other party or which is settled with the other party's prior written consent (not to be unreasonably withheld). In addition, your indemnity shall extend to the "deductible" under our errors-and-omissions policy without regard to judgment or settlement. You shall give us prompt notice of any third party claim which you receive in respect of any SC and we shall consult with you prior to responding to such claim. Each party is entitled to be notified of any action against the other brought with respect to any SC, and to participate in the defense thereof by counsel of its choice, at its sole cost and expense and, otherwise, the defense of such action shall be controlled in our sole discretion. In the event that one of us refuses to approve a settlement which the other party considers reasonable, the party refusing its consent shall assume the further defense of the subject claim, action or proceeding.

8.2.    If a claim is made against us, we may withhold a reasonable amount from monies due or to become due to you, but we will refund it (together with interest on the amount released at the regular savings and loan passbook interest rate prevailing in Los Angeles from time to time during the period of withholding) if (and to the extent that) suit is not brought with respect to that sum within 1 year thereafter, and we won't withhold monies hereunder if (and to the extent that) you provide us with a satisfactory commercial surety bond.

8.3.    Neither party will be deemed in breach unless the other party gives notice and the notified party fails to cure within

30 days after receiving notice; <u>provided</u>, that if the alleged breach is of such a nature that it cannot be completely cured within 30 days, the notified party will not be deemed to be in breach if the notified party commences the curing of the alleged breach within such thirty-day period and proceeds to complete the curing thereof with due diligence within a reasonable time thereafter. However, either party shall have the right to seek injunctive relief to prevent a threatened breach of this agreement by the other party. All payments required to be made by us hereunder shall be subject to any rights and/or remedies which may otherwise be available to us in the event of a breach of this agreement on your part not cured in the manner prescribed above, and to any withholding which may be required by the rules and regulations of any taxing jurisdiction having authority.

8.4. The waiver of the applicability of any provision of this Agreement or of any default hereunder in a specific instance shall not affect the waiving party's rights thereafter to enforce such provision or to exercise any right or remedy in the event of any other default, whether or not similar.

9. <u>Notices/Statements/Consents:</u>

9.1. Notices shall be sent by certified (return receipt requested), registered mail or Federal Express to you and to us at the following addresses, or to such other addresses as the parties may designate from time to time by notice in like manner:

**To You:**

**To Us:**

       c/o Big Music Publishing Corp.
       Attn: Executive VP, Business Affairs

A courtesy copy of each notice to you shall be sent by ordinary mail or fax to:

Attn:

9.2.     Statements (and payments, if applicable) shall be sent by ordinary mail.

9.3.     Where the consent or approval of a party is required, it shall not be unreasonably withheld (unless expressly provided otherwise herein) and shall be deemed given unless the party whose consent or approval has been requested delivers notice of nonconsent or disapproval to the other party within 15 days after receipt of notice requesting such consent or disapproval.

## 10.    Law and Forum:

10.1.     This Agreement has been entered into in, and is to be interpreted in accordance with the laws of, the State of California. All actions or proceedings seeking the interpretation and/or enforcement of this Agreement shall be brought only in the State or Federal Courts located in Los Angeles County, all parties hereby submitting themselves to the jurisdiction of such courts for such purpose.

10.2.     Service of Process:

10.2.1.     Service of process in any action between the parties may be made by registered or certified mail addressed to the parties' then-current addresses for notice as prescribed in ¶9, above.

10.2.2.     Service shall become effective 30 days following the date of receipt by the party served (unless delivery is refused, in which event service shall become effective 30 days following the date of such refusal).

Very truly yours,

By: _____

Executive Vice President
Business Affairs

AGREED AND ACCEPTED:

By: _____

Fed. ID or

Soc Sec.#: _____

## SCHEDULE "A"

## WRITER ROYALTIES

### U.S. and Canada

(1)    Print: (all on net paid sales):

Piano/vocal sheet: 7 cents

Folios (other than "fake books" or "educational editions"): 10% of wholesale (prorated in the case of "mixed" folios to reflect number of royalty-bearing compositions);

"Fake books" and "educational editions": 10% of wholesale (subject to same pro-ration);

(2)    Mechanical Royalties: 50% of Gross Receipts

(3)    Performance Royalties: if collected directly by us and not through a society: 50% of Gross Receipts

(4)    Foreign Income: 50% of Gross Receipts

(5)    Other Income: 50% of Gross Receipts; *provided*, that Writer shall not be entitled to receive any portion of any amount received by us from a source which pays Writer an equivalent amount directly (including but not limited to distributions from a performing rights society and direct payments of portions of any blank tape tax or charge which may be enacted by Congress if writers and publishers are paid separately).

Above royalties to be prorated where only part of a composition is subject to this agreement.

(6)    Demo Costs: To the extent approved by both parties in writing in advance, we shall pay for the cost of making dem-

onstration records of the SCs. One-half (1/2) of a pro rata share corresponding to Writer's percentage of the SCs of such total costs shall be deemed additional advances to Writer hereunder.

## EXISTING COMPOSITIONS

| Title | Co-Authors (Co-Publishers) | % Controlled |
|---|---|---|

## EXISTING THIRD-PARTY AGREEMENTS

None

## SCHEDULE "B"

(Pursuant to subparagraph 7.2.1.)

## SCHEDULE "C"

(Pursuant to subparagraph 3.1.2.)

TO WHOM IT MAY CONCERN:

I am the writer of the compositions entitled:

My respective ownership interests in the compositions, and my share of the royalties payable with respect to the compositions are stated below.

My publishing designee: _____

My publishing administrator:

Very truly yours,

_____

(Writer)

Date:

Publisher Relations Department
Broadcast Music, Inc.
10 Music Square East
Nashville, TN 37203

Gentlemen:

This is to advise BMI that we have entered into a copublishing agreement with another BMI publisher for the administration of our catalog, and that BMI's records should be marked to reflect the agreement as follows:

1.    Name of BMI publisher acting as our administrator:


2.    Effective date of agreement:

Immediately, including all royalties now payable or which hereafter become payable, regardless of when performances took place.

CHECK ONE

Effective with the performances on and after _____, 20__. (Must be as of the beginning of a calendar quarter; i.e., January 1, April 1, July 1 or October 1.)

3.    Checks for all our BMI royalties, both domestic and foreign, should be made payable to the administrator and should be sent together with statements and all other correspondence to the administrator at its address on BMI's records.

We understand that BMI cannot mark its records at this time so as to indicate the termination date of the administration agreement and that, therefore, the above information will continue to be reflected on BMI's records until such time as we or the administrator notifies BMI that the administration agreement is about to terminate.

Very truly yours,


_____

(Publisher)

By: _____

_____

      Title

Date:

American Society of Composers,
Authors & Publishers
One Lincoln Plaza
New York, NY 10023

Gentlemen:

You are hereby authorized and directed to pay to our administrator, Big Music Publishing Corp., and we hereby assign to Administrator, all monies payable from and after the date hereof (regardless of when earned) as the publisher's share of performance royalties with respect to the compositions described below:

Each and every musical composition co-owned by the undersigned and Administrator.

Copies of all statements shall be sent to Administrator and to US.

The foregoing authorization and direction shall remain in full force and effect until modified or terminated by both the undersigned and Administrator.

Very truly yours,

---

By:

## ASSIGNMENT

ASSIGNOR(S): _____

_____

_____

ASSIGNEE(S) _____

_____

_____

PORTION CONVEYED: _____

_____

_____

For valuable consideration, ASSIGNOR hereby assigns, transfers, sets over and conveys to ASSIGNEE that portion of all right, title and interest set forth above in and to the following musical composition(s):

including the copyrights and proprietary rights therein and in any and all versions of said musical composition(s), and any renewals and extensions thereof (whether presently available or subsequently available as the result of intervening legislation) in the United States of America and elsewhere throughout the world, and further including any and all causes of action for infringement of the same, past, present and future, and all proceeds from the foregoing accrued and unpaid and hereafter accruing.

IN WITNESS WHEREOF, the undersigned has (have) executed the foregoing Assignment as of this _____ day of _____ 20__.

_____

(ASSIGNOR)

By _____

Assignment by Publisher

## ASSIGNMENT

ASSIGNOR(S): _____

_____

_____

ASSIGNEE(S): _____

_____

_____

PORTION CONVEYED: _____

_____

_____

For valuable consideration, ASSIGNOR hereby assigns, transfers, sets over and conveys to ASSIGNEE and its successors and assigns that portion of all right, title and interest set forth above in and to the following musical composition(s):

including the copyrights and proprietary rights therein and in any and all versions of said musical composition(s), and any renewals and extensions thereof (whether presently available or subsequently available as the result of intervening legislation) in the United States of America and elsewhere throughout the world, and further including any and all causes of action for infringement of the same, past, present and future, and all proceeds from the foregoing accrued and unpaid and hereafter accruing.

This Assignment includes the exclusive, worldwide right to administer and exploit 100% of said compositions (or fractional interests) in accordance with the terms and conditions of the Co-Publishing Agreement between the parties of even date herewith.

ASSIGNOR agrees to sign any and all other papers which may be required to effectuate the purpose and intent of this Assignment, and hereby irrevocably authorizes and appoints ASSIGNEE his attorney and representative in its name or in his name as his true and lawful attorney-in-fact to take such actions and make, sign, execute, acknowledge and deliver all such documents as may from time to time be necessary to convey to ASSIGNEE, its successors and assigns, all rights granted herein.

IN WITNESS WHEREOF, the undersigned has (have) executed the foregoing Assignment as of this _____ day of _____ 20\_\_.

_____

_____

Assignment by Writer

(INSERT NAME OF UNDERSIGNED AND ADDRESS)

Dated:

TO WHOM IT MAY CONCERN:

This is to advise that we have entered into a co-publishing agreement dated _____ with _____ ("Administrator") for the co-ownership and administration of our catalog for the territory of the world.

You are hereby authorized and directed to address all correspondence, inquiries, royalty statements and royalty payments (regardless of when earned) to Administrator at the following address or otherwise as it directs you in writing:

Any such payments made by you pursuant to this authorization shall discharge you of any obligation to make any such payments to the undersigned.

The foregoing authorization shall remain in full force and effect until modified or terminated by both the undersigned and Administrator.

Very truly yours,

By: _____

# FORM 4.2

## CO-PUBLISHING AGREEMENT WITH EXCLUSIVE ADMINISTRATION RIGHTS GRANTED TO ONE CO-OWNER

### CO-PUBLISHING AGREEMENT

THIS AGREEMENT made this _____ day of _____ 2000, by and between _____ (hereinafter referred to as "Company") and _____ (hereinafter referred to as "Participant")

### W I T N E S S E T H:

WHEREAS, it is the intention of Company and Participant that they shall jointly own, in equal shares, the musical compositions (hereinafter collectively referred to as the "Composition") listed or described below, so that fifty percent (50%) of the entire worldwide right, title and interest, including the copyright, the right to copyright and the renewal right, in and to the Composition shall be owned by Company and fifty percent (50%) thereof shall be owned by Participant:

WHEREAS, the Composition has been or shall be registered for copyright in the names of Company and Participant in the Copyright Office of the United States of America;

NOW, THEREFORE, for good and valuable consideration the receipt of which is hereby acknowledged by each party hereto, it is agreed as follows:

1.     Company and Participant shall jointly own the Composition, in equal shares, including all of the worldwide right, title and interest, including the copyrights, the right to copyright and the renewal rights, therein and thereto.

2.     The Composition shall be registered for copyright by Company in the names of Company and Participant in the office of the Register of Copyrights of the United States of America and Company shall take all reasonable measures to protect the copyright in the Composition in those territories which are signatories to the Universal Copyright Convention. If the Composition has heretofore been registered for copyright in the name of Participant, Participant shall simultaneously herewith deliver to Company an assignment of a one-half interest therein, in form acceptable to Company.

3.     Company shall have the sole and exclusive right to administer and exploit the Composition, to print, publish, sell, use and license the use of the Composition throughout the world, and to execute in its own name any and all licenses and agreements affecting or respecting the Composition, including but not limited to licenses for mechanical reproduction, public performance, synchronization uses, subpublication, merchandising, and advertising and to assign or license such rights to others. This statement of exclusive rights is only in clarification and amplification of the rights of Company hereunder and not in limitation thereof.

4.     Company shall be entitled to receive and collect and shall receive and collect all gross receipts derived from the Composition. "Gross receipts," as used herein, shall mean any and all revenue, income and sums derived from the Composition from any and all sources whatsoever.

5.     Company shall pay to Participant fifty percent (50%) of the net income actually received and derived by Company from the Composition. "Net income," as used herein, shall mean the gross receipts derived by Company from the Composition, less the following:

(a)     A sum equal to ten percent (10%) of the Gross Receipts as an administration charge for overhead;

(b)    Royalties and other sums which are paid by Company to the composers and writers of the Composition pursuant to the provisions of the songwriter's agreements between Participant and such composers and writers (a copy of which is attached hereto as Exhibit "A") or which, at Company's election, are paid by Company to Participant, in trust, for payment over by Participant to such composers and writers pursuant to the provisions of said songwriter's agreements;

(c)    Collection or other fees customarily and actually charged by

or any other collection agent which may be used by Company;

(d)    Actual, out-of-pocket administrative and exploitation expenses of company with respect to the Composition for registration fees, advertising and promotion expenses directly related to the Composition, the costs of transcribing for lead sheets, and the costs of producing demonstration records;

(e)    Attorneys' fees directly related to the defense of claims respecting the Composition, if any, actually paid by Company;

(f)    The costs of printing, engraving, arranging and editing printed editions of the Composition incurred by Company.

6.    The performing rights in the Composition, to the extent permitted by law, shall be assigned to and licensed by The American Society of Composers, Authors and Publishers (ASCAP). ASCAP shall be and hereby is authorized to collect and receive all moneys earned from the public performance of the Composition and to pay directly to Company one hundred percent (100%) of the amount allocated by ASCAP as the publisher's share of public performance fees.

7. Mechanical royalties for the Composition for the United States and Canada shall be collectible by or any other collection agent which may be designated by Company, provided however, that Company shall, in the case of any record company affiliated with Company, issue the mechanical licenses directly to said record company at the then current statutory rate and collect mechanical royalties directly therefrom in which case there shall be no collection fee as referred to in paragraph 5(c).

8. Statements as to moneys payable hereunder shall be sent by Company to Participant semiannually within ninety (90) days after the end of each semiannual calendar period. Statements shall be accompanied by appropriate payments. Participant shall be deemed to have consented to all royalty statements and other accounts rendered by Company to Participant, and said statements and other accounts shall be binding upon Participant and not subject to any objection for any reason, unless specific objection in writing, setting forth the basis thereof, is given by Participant to Company within two (2) years from the date rendered. Participant or a certified public accountant in its behalf may, at reasonable intervals, examine the books of Company pertaining to the Composition during Company's usual business hours and upon reasonable notice. Said books relating to activities and receipts during any accounting period may only be examined as aforesaid during the two (2) year period following service by Company of the statement for said accounting period only during Company's normal business hours and upon ten days written notice.

9. Each party hereto shall give the other the equal benefits of any warranties or representations which it obtained or shall obtain under any agreements affecting the Composition.

10. Company shall have the sole right to prosecute, defend, settle and compromise all suits, claims, and actions respecting the composition, and generally to do and perform all things necessary concerning the same and the copyrights

therein, to prevent and restrain the infringement of copyrights or other rights with respect to the Composition. In the event of the recovery by Company of any moneys as a result of a judgment or settlement, such moneys, less an amount equal to the expense of obtaining said moneys, including counsel fees, shall be deemed additional gross receipts hereunder. Participant shall have the right to provide counsel for itself, but at its own expense, to assist in any such manner. Company will not settle any claim respecting the Composition without Participant's consent, which consent shall not be unreasonably withheld.

11.    The rights of the parties hereto in and to the Composition shall extend for the term of the copyright of the Composition and of any derivative copyrights therein in the United States of America and throughout the rest of the world and for the terms of any renewals or extensions thereof in the United States of America and throughout the rest of the world.

12.    This agreement sets forth the entire understanding between the parties, and cannot be changed, modified or canceled except by an instrument signed by the party sought to be bound. This agreement shall be governed by and construed under the laws of the State of California applicable to agreements wholly performed therein.

13.    Participant hereby warrants and represents that it has the right to enter into this agreement and to grant to Company all of the rights granted herein, and that the exercise by Company of any and all of the rights granted to Company in this agreement will not violate or infringe upon any common law or statutory rights of any person, firm or corporation, including, without limitation, contractual rights, copyrights and rights of privacy. The rights granted herein are free and clear of any claims, demands, liens or encumbrances. Participant agrees to and does hereby indemnify, save and hold Company, its assigns, licensees, and its and their directors, officers, shareholders, agents and employees harmless from any and all liabilities, claims, demands, loss and damage (including attorneys fees

and court costs) arising out of or connected with any claim by a third party which is inconsistent with any of the Warranties, representations, covenants, or agreements made by Participant herein and Participant agrees to reimburse Company, on demand, for any payment made by Company at any time after the date hereof with respect to any liability or claim to which the foregoing indemnity applies. Pending the determination of any such claim, Company may withhold payment of royalties or other moneys hereunder, provided that all amounts so withheld are reasonably related to the amount of said claim and the estimated attorneys' fees in connection therewith, and provided further that Participant shall have the right to post a bond in an amount reasonably satisfactory to Company by a bonding company reasonably satisfactory to Company, in which events Company shall not withhold payments as aforesaid.

14. All notices, statements or other documents which either party shall be required or shall desire to give to the other hereunder must be in writing and shall be given by the parties hereto only in one of the following ways: (1) by personal delivery; or (2) by addressing them as indicated below, and by depositing them postage prepaid, in the United States mail, airmail if the address is outside of the state in which such notice is deposited; or (3) by delivering them toll prepaid to a telegraph or cable company. If so delivered, mailed, telegraphed or cabled, each such notice, statement or other document shall, except as herein expressly provided, be conclusively deemed to have been given when personally delivered or on the date of delivery to the telegraph or cable company or 24 hours after the date of mailing, as the case may be. The addresses of the parties shall be those of which the other party actually receives written notice and until further notice are:

"Company"        "Participant"

A copy of all notices to Participant hereunder shall be sent to:

15. This agreement shall not be deemed to give any right or remedy to any third party whatsoever unless said right or

remedy is specifically granted to such third party by the terms hereof.

16.    The parties hereto shall execute any further documents including, without limitation, assignments of copyrights, and do all acts necessary to fully effectuate the terms and provisions of this agreement.

17.    Company may enter into subpublishing agreements with, or assign, or license any of its rights hereunder to, one or more other person, firms, or corporations for any one or more countries of the world. In the event Company enters into a subpublishing or administration agreement for any country of the world with a company affiliated with or otherwise related to Company, such agreement shall be deemed to have been made with an independent third party provided, that no foreign subpublishing agreement respecting the Composition shall be on terms less favorable to Company than what is commonly referred to in the music publishing industry and a 75/25/10 division of royalties and a 50/50/10 division with respect to so-called foreign cover records. Participant acknowledges that Company has the right to administer and publish compositions other than the Composition.

IN WITNESS WHEREOF, the parties have executed this agreement the day and year above set forth.


By _____    By _____

# FORM 4.3

## CO-PUBLISHING AGREEMENT
## WITH EXCLUSIVE ADMINISTRATION RIGHTS
## GRANTED TO ONE CO-OWNER
## SUBJECT TO CERTAIN RESTRICTIONS

Dated:

INDEPENDENT MUSIC PUBLISHING COMPANY
Attn:
1234 Main Street
San Jose, California 95000

Re: Co-Publishing and Exclusive Administration Agreement

Gentlemen:

The following, when signed by you and by us, will constitute the terms and conditions of the exclusive co-publishing (i.e., "participation") agreement between you and us.

1.   Scope of Agreement:

    1.1.   Subject to those requirements and/or restrictions set forth in subparagraph 1.2., below, you and we will each own an undivided 50% share of the copyright in, and we will have exclusive worldwide life-of-copyright administration of, your interest in the songs (and all derivative works based thereon) listed on the attached Schedule "A" (referred to below as the "Subject Compositions").

    1.2.   Although it is intended that we and our foreign subsidiaries, affiliates and licensees have the fullest possible rights to administer and exploit the Subject Compositions, to utilize your name and likeness in connection therewith and to execute PA forms (and other routine copyright documents) in your name and on your behalf as your attorney-in-fact (which appointment is coupled with an interest and is therefore irrevocable), neither we nor they shall do any of the following without your prior written consent in each instance (which consent, unless expressly provided otherwise, shall not be unreasonably withheld by you):

1.2.1.     Authorize any change in the English-language title and/or lyric of any Subject Composition, alter the harmonic structure of any Subject Composition, or alter the melody of any Subject Composition (except insubstantial changes necessary to accommodate the syllabic requirements of foreign languages);

1.2.2.     Issue a mechanical license for the use of any Subject Composition at less than the prevailing statutory or society rate, except in connection with those types of uses for which reduced-rate licenses are customarily granted in the country in question;

1.2.3.     Authorize the use of the title of any Subject Composition as the title of a play, film or TV program, or authorize the dramatization of any Subject Composition;

1.2.4.     Authorize the synchronization of any Subject Composition in (A) a film or TV program bearing a rating of "X" or the equivalent, or (B) any political advertisement.

2.     <u>Collection and Division of Income</u>:

2.1.     Subject to any rights and/or remedies which may be available to us in the event of a material breach of this agreement on your part not cured as provided in par. 6.3., below, we will be entitled to collect (and shall employ our best efforts consistent with our reasonable business judgment to collect) all writer/publisher income (except the writer's share of public performances collected by societies and any other amount normally paid directly to songwriters by a disbursing agent) generated by the Subject Compositions (including pre-Term earnings).

2.1.1. (A) Net Income from Subject Compositions shall be divided 50% to us, 50% to you.

(B) As used herein, "Net Income" shall mean all amounts received by us, or credited to our account in reduction of an advance, from licensees and performing and mechanical rights societies ("Gross Receipts") after deduction of writer royalties as per the annexed Schedule "B" and (1) actual and reasonable out-of-pocket collection costs (including local subpublisher fees or income shares) (2) out-of-pocket copyright registration costs, (3) costs of lead sheets, and (4) demo costs (approved by both parties in writing) to the extent not recouped from writer royalties.

2.1.2. For the purposes of this paragraph, Gross Receipts on printed materials sold (and paid for) shall be deemed to be:

2.1.3. (A) Outside of the U.S. and Canada 12.5% of the marked or suggested retail list price (or the price deemed to be the local equivalent, in any country in which there are no marked or suggested retail list prices) ("list") (prorated in the case of mixed folios and other editions not consisting entirely of Subject Compositions);

(B) In the U.S. and Canada, 20% of list on piano/vocal sheet music, 12 1/2% of list on folios other than "fake books" or "educational editions", 10% of list on "fake books" and "educational editions" (prorated in either event in the case of mixed folios and other mixed editions), on copies sold and paid for;

(C) In the case of amounts received from third-party print licensees your co-publisher's share shall be 25% while the writer's share shall be 50%; and

(D)   Print royalties are subject to proration where only part of the composition is a Subject Composition.

2.1.4.   Gross Receipts received from our affiliates and licensees outside of the U.S. and Canada shall be deemed to be 80% of mechanical income from original records, 60% of mechanical income from Cover Records, 60% of the publisher's share of public performance income, and 80% of other categories of income (other than print).

3.   Accounting and Payment:

3.1.   We will account to you (and make payment where appropriate) within 60 days following the end of each semi-annual calendar period. However, if the amount due for a specific statement is less than $50., payment may be deferred until the aggregate amount due to you exceeds $50.

3.2.   We will only be required to account and pay with respect to amounts actually received by us in the U.S. (or credited to our account in reduction of a previous advance received by us in the U.S.).

3.2.1.   You (or a certified public accountant on your behalf) shall have the right to audit our books and records as to each statement for a period of 2 years after such statement is received (or deemed received as provided below). Legal action with respect to a specific accounting statement or the accounting period to which such statement relates shall be barred if not commenced in a court of competent jurisdiction within 3 years after such statement is received (or deemed received as provided below).

3.2.2.   For the purposes of calculating such time periods, you shall be deemed to have received a statement when due unless we receive notice of nonreceipt from you (in the manner prescribed in paragraph 7, below) within 30 days thereafter. However, your failure to give such notice shall not affect your right to receive such statement (and, if applicable, your royalty and/or net income payment) after such thirty-day period.

3.3.    In "blocked currency" situations, we shall not be required to pay you until the blockage shall have been removed, but if requested to do so, we shall deposit blocked currency royalties in the local currency in a depository of your choice. The exchange rates used by third parties in accounting to us shall be used by us in accountings hereunder.

3.4.    All payments hereunder shall be subject to all applicable taxation statutes, regulations and treaties.

4.    Warranties and Representations:

4.1.    By your signature below, you warrant and represent (1) that you have the right to grant the rights granted to us hereunder, (2) that the Subject Composition does not infringe any third party's rights or violate any applicable criminal statute, including but not limited to such third party's copyright, trademark, service mark, or right of privacy or publicity, (3) that the Subject Composition is not defamatory and (4) that your music publishing designee will affiliate with ASCAP, BMI or another recognized performing rights society to which the writers of the Subject Compositions are affiliated, and you will immediately advise us of said affiliation.

4.1.1.    Except as set forth in the annexed Schedule "C", neither you nor your music publishing designee, nor anyone acting on your and/or your music publishing designee's behalf or deriving rights from or through you or your music publishing designee (A) has received or will receive an advance, loan or other payment from a performing rights society, record company or other third party which is or may be recoupable from (or otherwise subject to offset against) moneys which would otherwise be collectible by us hereunder, (B) is presently subject to any so-called "controlled compositions" clause under a recording agreement or (C) is presently subject to any provision of a recording agreement which would allow a record company to charge any amount against mechanical royalties.

4.1.2.    Notwithstanding the foregoing, in the event that any record company to whom you (or an entity furnishing your services) are or may hereafter be under contract charges any advance(s) or other amount(s) against mechanical royalties earned by the Subject Compositions from recordings made under such recording agreement or reduces the amount of mechanical royalties otherwise due to you because the mechanical royalties payable with respect to "outside material" embodied in your recordings causes aggregate mechanical royalties to exceed the per-record maximum rate(s) prescribed in the controlled compositions clause of your recording agreement, then, in addition to any other rights and remedies available to us, we shall be entitled to (A) send a letter of direction in your name advising your record company of the terms of this paragraph 5 and instructing such record company (upon recoupment from record and/or video royalties of any portion(s) of the advance(s) or other amount(s) so charged) to re-credit us directly to the same extent (not to exceed the total amount originally recouped from or charged against mechanical royalties) and (B) reimburse ourselves from any and all moneys (including your writer/publisher royalties) earned hereunder, for any amount charged against mechanical royalties, except to the extent later recovered through the re-crediting process.

4.1.3.    In the event of a breach of this paragraph 5.2., we shall (in addition to any other remedies available to us) be entitled to reimburse ourselves from moneys otherwise becoming due to you or your music publishing designee hereunder to the extent that moneys are not collectible by us by reason thereof.

5.    Indemnities; Cure of Breaches:

5.1.    Each party will indemnify the other against any loss or damage (including court costs and reasonable attorneys' fees) due to a breach of this agreement by that party which results in a judgment against the other party or which is settled with the other party's prior written consent (not to be unreasonably withheld). In addition, your indemnity shall extend to the "deductible" under our errors-and-omissions policy without regard to judgment or settlement. Each party is entitled to be notified of any action against the other brought with respect to any Subject Composition, and to participate in the defense thereof by counsel of its choice, at its sole cost and expense. In the event that one of us refuses to approve a settlement which the other party considers reasonable, the party refusing its consent shall assume the further defense of the subject claim, action or proceeding.

5.2. If a claim is made against us, we may withhold a reasonable amount from moneys due or to become due to you, but we will refund it (together with interest on the amount released at the regular savings and loan passbook interest rate prevailing in Los Angeles from time to time during the period of withholding) if (and to the extent that) suit is not brought with respect to that sum within 1 year thereafter, and we won't withhold moneys hereunder if (and to the extent that) you provide us with a satisfactory commercial surety bond.

5.3. Neither party will be deemed in breach unless the other party gives notice and the notified party fails to cure within 30 days after receiving notice; provided, that if the alleged breach is of such a nature that it cannot be completely cured within 30 days, the notified party will not be deemed to be in breach if the notified party commences the curing of the alleged breach within such thirty-day period and proceeds to complete the curing thereof with due diligence within a reasonable time thereafter. However, either party shall have the right to seek injunctive relief to prevent a threatened breach of this agreement by the other party. All payments required to be made by us hereunder shall be subject to any rights and/or remedies which may otherwise be available to us in the event of a breach of this agreement on your part not cured in the manner prescribed above, and to any withholding which may be required by the rules and regulations of any taxing jurisdiction having authority.

6.    Notices: Notices shall be sent by certified (return receipt requested) or registered mail or telex to you and us (to the attention of our Senior Vice President of Legal and Business Affairs) at the above addresses or any other addresses the parties designate by notice in like manner. Statements (and payments, if applicable) shall be sent by ordinary mail. If the party's consent is required, it shall not be unreasonably withheld (unless expressly provided otherwise herein) and shall be deemed given unless the notified party gives notice of nonconsent within 15 days after receipt of notice requesting consent.

7.    Law and Forum: This Agreement has been entered into in, and is to be interpreted in accordance with the laws of, the State of California. All actions or proceedings seeking the interpretation and/or enforcement of this Agreement shall be brought only in the State or Federal Courts located in Los Angeles County, all parties hereby submitting themselves to the jurisdiction of such courts for such purpose.

Very truly yours,

BIG MUSIC PUBLISHING CORP.


By: _____

AGREED AND ACCEPTED:

INDEPENDENT MUSIC PUBLISHING COMPANY


By: _____
      Fed. I.D.#:
      Soc. Sec. #:

## SCHEDULE "A"

| Titles | Composers/% | % Controlled |
|---|---|---|
| I LOVE YOU | Cameron Composer (1/2) | 100% |
| | Larry Lyrics (1/2) | |

## SCHEDULE "B"

### WRITER ROYALTIES

(1)  U.S. and Canada:
Print: (all on net paid sales):

Piano/vocal sheet: 7 cents

Folios (other than "fake books" or "educational editions"): 12 1/2% of wholesale (prorated in the case of "mixed" folios to reflect number of royalty-bearing compositions);

"Fake books" and "educational editions": 10% of wholesale (subject to same pro-ration);

(2)  Mechanical Royalties: 50% of gross receipts

(3)  Performance Royalties: if collected directly by us and not through a society: 50% of gross receipts

(4)  Foreign Income: 50% of gross receipts

(5)  Other Income: 50% of gross receipts; provided, that Writer shall not be entitled to receive any portion of any amount received by us from a source which pays writer an equivalent amount directly (including but not limited to distributions from

a performing rights society and direct payments of portions of any blank tape tax or charge which may be enacted by Congress if writers and publishers are paid separately).

(6)    Demo Costs: To the extent approved by both parties in writing in advance, we shall pay for the cost of making demonstration records of the Subject Compositions. One-half (1/2) of a pro rata share corresponding to Writer's percentage of the Subject Compositions of such total costs shall be deemed additional advances to Writer hereunder.

Above royalties to be prorated where only part of the subject composition is subject to this agreement.

---

## SCHEDULE "C"

(Pursuant to subparagraph 5.2.1., if applicable.)

## EXHIBIT "D"

Date: January 1, 2000

American Society of Composers,
Authors & Publishers
One Lincoln Plaza
New York, N.Y. 10023

Gentlemen:

You are hereby authorized and directed to pay to our administrator, Big Music Publishing Corp. ("Administrator"), at 1000 Sunset Boulevard, Hollywood, California 90069, and we hereby assign to Administrator, all moneys payable from and after the date hereof (regardless of when earned) as our share of the publisher's public performance royalties with respect to the compositions described below:

<u>COMPOSITION</u>                    <u>COMPOSERS</u>

Copies of all statements shall be sent to Administrator and to us.

The foregoing authorization and direction shall remain in full force and effect until modified or terminated by both the undersigned and Administrator.

Very truly yours,

INDEPENDENT MUSIC
PUBLISHING COMPANY

By: _____

# FORM 4.4

## ADMINISTRATION AGREEMENT

MUSIC PUBLISHING ADMINISTRATION AGREEMENT

AGREEMENT made as of the _____ day of _____, 20__, between _____, a New York corporation (hereinafter referred to as "Publisher", whose address is _____ and _____, a New York corporation (hereinafter referred to as "Administrator"), whose address is

IN CONSIDERATION of the mutual covenants and promises hereinafter set forth, it is hereby agreed by the parties hereto as follows;

1.    Publisher hereby designates Administrator and Administrator hereby accepts such designation and undertakes to act as the sole selling agent and business supervisor of Publisher throughout the world.

2.    Administrator shall provide all necessary administrative management services and supervisory facilities for Publisher and agrees to take all necessary and proper steps to protect the copyrights owned by Publisher. Such services, facilities and protective measures shall be comparable, at least to the best facilities, services and protective measures provided by Administrator to any other company for which Administrator shall also be acting during the term hereof in the same capacity as it agrees herein to act for Publisher. Such services and facilities shall include rent, procurement of supplies, selling, invoicing dispatching, shipping, bookkeeping, and collection of accounts, local telephone service and all other services not hereinafter specifically excepted. For all such services and personnel, Administrator shall be authorized to retain _____ percent (__%) of the gross income received by or on behalf of

Publisher from all sources during the term of this agreement (the "Administration Fee").

3.    Publisher will pay the salaries of any employees (subject to written approval by Publisher) employed by and for Publisher exclusively for the exploitation of its catalogue. Administrator agrees, nevertheless, to advance for the account of Publisher all sums required for the defraying of the costs and expenses with respect thereto.

4.    With respect to all compositions owned or controlled by Publisher, Publisher will pay the following:

(a)    All expenses for the purchase of music paper and other inventory, printing engraving, autographing, orchestrating, authors' royalties, advertising in trade periodicals, disc jockey records and other trade publicity;

(b)    Costs of any authorized special arrangements required by Publisher for the exploitation of its catalogue;

(c)    All accounting and legal fees incurred solely with respect to the compositions;

(d)    Any fees required to be paid to _____ for the collection of mechanical and synchronization fees due to Publisher by reason of licenses issued by but in no event shall such fees exceed five percent (5%) of mechanical license fees and ten percent (10%) of synchronization license fees without first having obtained the consent of Publisher. No expenses other than those referred to above shall be charged to Publisher without the consent of Publisher. Administrator agrees to advance for the account of Publisher all sums required for the defraying of the costs and expenses with respect thereto.

5.    Advances made by Administrator pursuant to paragraphs 3 and 4 of this agreement, and any additional advances made by Administrator which Administrator agrees to advance to or for the account of Publisher when and if necessary, for the

purpose of conducting the music business of Publisher, will be repaid to Administrator from the gross income received by or on behalf of Publisher from all sources, after first deducting the Administration Fee.

6.    After deduction of its administration fee and all costs and expenses which it is permitted to charge against gross income pursuant to the terms of this agreement (including all advances properly made), Administrator shall pay or cause the payment to Publisher of the entire net income earned by or with respect to each musical composition presently in the Publisher's catalogue or which may during the term of this agreement be acquired by Publisher.

7.    Administrator agrees to render semi-annual financial statements prepared by a Certified Public Accountant to the stockholders of Publisher, no later than ninety (90) days following the termination of each semi-annual accounting period.

8.    This agreement shall commence on the date hereof and shall continue for _____ (___) years. Thereafter, this agreement shall continue from year to year unless terminated upon ninety (90) days written notice delivered by either party to the other.

9.    This agreement shall be construed in accordance with the laws of the State of New York applicable to agreements wholly to be performed therein. The invalidity or unenforceability of any provision hereof shall in no way affect the validity or enforceability of any other provisions of this agreement.

10.    This agreement contains the entire understanding between the parties hereto and all of its terms and conditions shall be binding upon and shall inure to the benefit of the respective parties hereto and their respective successors and assigns. No subsequent modification or waiver shall be valid or binding unless reduced to written form and signed by the party or parties sought to be charged.

Publisher

By: _____

Administrator

By: _____

# FORM 4.5

## RATE PARTICIPATION AGREEMENT

January ___, 2000

RE:    RATE PARTICIPATION AGREEMENT

Gentlemen:

This will confirm our understanding and agreement as follows:

1.    You represent and warrant that you are free to enter into this agreement and to grant all the rights and make all the representations, promises and undertakings granted and made by you hereunder.

2.    You have submitted a song entitled "_____" (herein "Composition") written by _____ for consideration as a recording master to be made by the group known as ABC (herein "Group"). We agree to consider whether or not to record a master of said song.

3.    If we shall decide to cause said Group to record said song, you agree to forthwith issue a mechanical license to XYZ Records, Inc. in the then form established by The Harry Fox Agency, Inc., at not more than _____ cents (__) per record manufactured and sold, for any recording of the composition with a playing time of less than five (5) minutes and at the rate established by The Harry Fox Agency, Inc. for any such recording with a playing time in excess of five (5) minutes.

4.    If said recording shall be made by the Group and released in the United States (and there shall be no obligation to so record and/or release any such recording) you agree to pay

us _____ per record manufactured and sold throughout the world, computed, payable and accountable to us on the same basis and upon the same terms and conditions as XYZ Records, Inc. would be required to compute, account and pay same to you pursuant to the license to be issued by you to XYZ Records, Inc. as aforesaid. If the license is issued at a higher rate than two cents due to the duration of the recording, or an increase in the statutory rate for mechanical licenses under the then existing Copyright Act, the aforesaid payment to us shall be increased on a pro rata basis so that we shall receive _____ of the license rate.

5.    Upon our request, you shall furnish us with an irrevocable assignment to XYZ Records, Inc. of the right to receive said sums payable to us directly from XYZ Records, Inc. Notwithstanding the foregoing, however if we do not request such an assignment you agree to advise The Harry Fox Agency of this agreement and instruct and authorize them to account and pay to ABC Music sums payable under this agreement.

6.    You agree to indemnify and hold harmless the undersigned and all members of the Group against any and all loss, damage, liability and expense (including reasonable attorney's fees and costs) arising out of any breach by you of any of your representations and agreements hereunder or arising out of any plagiarism or infringement claims in connection with said song.

7.    This agreement shall inure to the benefit of and be binding upon you and the undersigned and your and our respective heirs, executors, administrators, personal representatives, successors, assigns and licenses.

If the foregoing correctly reflects our understanding and agreement, please signify your agreement thereto by signing at the place provided below.

Very truly yours,

By _____

AGREED:

By _____

# INTERNATIONAL SUBPUBLISHING

## SUMMARY

### I. BUSINESS BACKGROUND

A. The International Market for Music

B. International Performing Rights Administration

C. International Mechanical Rights Administration

### II. SELECTING A SUBPUBLISHER

A. Worldwide or Territory-By-Territory Representation

B. Promotion or Administration

C. Entire Catalog or Individual Songs

D. Reciprocal Relationships

E. Doing Without a Subpublisher

### III. NEGOTIATING THE SUBPUBLISHING AGREEMENT

A. Introduction

B. Compositions Covered

C. Territory

D. Rights Granted

   1. Print Rights

   2. Performance Rights

   3. Mechanical and Electrical Transcription Rights

   4. Synchronization Rights

   5. Videogram and Other Audiovisual Rights

   6. Commercial Advertising Rights

   7. Reserved Rights

E. Subpublisher Fees and Publishing Income

   1. Print Income

   2. Mechanical and Electrical Transcription Income

   3. Performance Income

   4. Other Income

   5. Payment "At Source"

CHAPTER **5**

# INTERNATIONAL SUBPUBLISHING

T he activity of music publishing — licensing the use of musical compositions, administering their legal protection, and collecting income arising from their use — is a worldwide effort. As the world increasingly resembles the global village projected decades ago by futurists, with cultural boundaries coming down as fast as satellites are going up, music publishers can expect an increasing portion of their income generated by the publication and performance of their compositions overseas. How a music publisher located in one country performs his responsibilities on a worldwide basis is through a process called *subpublishing* — that is, by entering into an agreement with a music publishing firm located in each overseas market, called a *subpublisher*, to represent the publisher, called the *original publisher*, in promoting the use of the original publisher's compositions, and collecting the publishing income, in the subpublisher's market.

This chapter sketches the business background of international subpublishing, describes certain aspects of music publishing that are unique to international subpublishing, analyzes the considerations used in selecting an international subpublishing strategy, and provides some guidelines for negotiating some of the more common terms and conditions contained in a typical *subpublishing agreement*.

## I. BUSINESS BACKGROUND

### A. The International Market for Music

Although the United States is the largest source of music publishing royalties in the world, it represents only about 23% of total worldwide music publishing revenues.[1] Clearly, given that 77% of music publishing revenue is derived from sources outside of the United States, the international aspects of music publishing international revenues cannot be ignored by today's music copyright owner.

Total worldwide music publishing royalties for the year 1997 are estimated to have been about $6.3 billion, with the United States representing about $1.5 billion of that. Germany was a close second with about $858 million, or 14% of worldwide revenue. The United Kingdom was next at 13%, or $790 million, followed by Japan at 11%, or $704 million, and France at 9% and $542 million. Other major countries included Italy, the Netherlands, Spain, the Nordic countries, and Austria. The top ten markets accounted for over 85% of music publishing revenues.

## B.  International Performing Rights Administration

As mentioned in Chapter 2, royalties arising from the licensing of public performances of music is one of the major sources of music publishing income. It is estimated that 45% of all worldwide music publishing revenues are derived from the licensing of public performances. In 1997, this amounted to $2.65 billion, about $572 million of which derived from radio performances, about $941 million from various forms of television broadcast, and $1.1 billion from live and recorded performances (i.e., nightclubs, restaurants, elevators, etc.). Less than a fourth of the total worldwide performance income was generated in the United States.

In Chapter 17, on *Performance Licenses*, we provide an overview of the operation of performance rights societies operating in the United States (i.e., ASCAP, BMI, and SESAC), but these societies were modeled after performing rights societies established long before in Europe. The first European performance rights society, *Societe des Auteurs, Compositeurs et Editeurs de Musique* (SACEM), was formed in France in 1851. The first German society, *Genosenschaft Deutscher Tonsetzer* (GDT), the predecessor to today's GEMA, was founded in

---

[1] The music publishing revenue data provided in this chapter is from a report entitled, *International Survey of 1997 Music Publishing Revenues*, provided to the authors courtesy of the National Music Publisher's Association, 711 Third Avenue, New York New York 10017, 212-370-5330, www.nmpa.org.

Berlin in 1903. The English *Performance Right Society* (PRS) was established in 1914.

Every major market for music in the world has a performance rights society collecting income on behalf of authors and publishers of music, and several of the major societies administer the collection of performance royalties in countries where no local society exists. Though each society is governed by its own unique rules, all use some form of blanket license for the collection of income, sampling surveys for the distribution of income, and all distribute income to writers and publishers. Many, like the U.S. societies, distribute income to writers and publishers on a 50/50 basis, but this varies from society to society. For example, the division of publisher and writer shares for Dutch works is approximately 2/3 to writers and 1/3 to publishers. Distributions by ASCAP and BMI arising from performance royalties collected on Dutch works performed in the U.S. would follow the local rule, remitting the writer's share (2/3) to the Dutch society, BUMA, and the publisher's share (1/3) to the U.S. subpublisher representing the Dutch original publisher.

## C. International Mechanical Rights Administration

Another major source of publishing income are mechanical royalties, derived from the grant by music publishers of *mechanical licenses*—the form of permission that authorizes another to make mechanical reproductions of a musical composition, such as recordings on compact discs and audiocassettes. Income derived from mechanical reproductions represent about 41% of all worldwide music publishing income. Mechanical royalties are as significant a source of income in international markets as they are in the United States, but the means of collection are significantly different.

As discussed in Chapter 12, on *Mechanical Licenses*, once a copyright owner licenses a song for mechanical reproduction for the first time, he could thereafter be compelled to license it for mechanical reproduction in the United States to anyone else for the fee set by the copyright law. The provision of the copyright statute compelling copyright owners to issue mechanical licenses is known as the *compulsory license* provision,[2] and the prescribed per unit fee set forth in the law

---

[2] 17 U.S.C. Sec. 115, which is set forth in the appendix to Chapter 12.

is referred to as the *statutory rate.* Because the statutory rate is prescribed in terms of *cents per copy,* mechanical licenses in the United
States are generally issued on a cents per copy rate for each song
recorded. Moreover, the license is issued either directly by the music
publisher or, at the publisher's election, by an agent, such as the Harry
Fox Agency. This is *not* the way mechanical licenses are generally
issued overseas.

To begin with, the collection of mechanical royalties is conducted
by a single mechanical rights collection society in each territory.
Moreover, licensing from that society is *mandatory.* This means that
all mechanical licenses in the territory are issued by the collection
society, not by the individual music publishers; in other words, all
record companies in the territory are required to pay mechanical royalties to the collection society, not to the individual publishers.

Further, rather than being set by statute, mechanical rates overseas
are generally set by some form of collective bargaining agreement
between the mandatory mechanical rights organizations and the record
companies, or an organization representing them. These agreements
are often negotiated with the participation of a copyright tribunal, min-
istry of culture, or other government agency. At one time, the record
companies in a country would collectively negotiate with the single
mandatory mechanical rights society in that country to set the rates
and other terms of the local mechanical licenses. Consistent with the
evolution of the European Community, which by stages required the
free flow of goods, services, and people among its member countries,
record companies began negotiating, not with the mechanical license
societies of each nation, but on a multinational basis with a coalition
of mechanical licensing societies from different countries. Thus, today,
IFPI, *the International Federation of Phonogram Industries*, representing the record companies, negotiates a collective bargaining agreement for mechanical licensing with a confederation of mechanical
rights organizations from 30 countries called, BIEM, the *Bureau International des Societes Gerant les Droits d'Enregistrement et de Reproduction Mecanique.* The terms of the agreement negotiated by IFPI
and BIEM are then administered by the member mechanical rights
societies on a country by country basis. The mechanical fees in some
territories, however, are set by the local government, which is the case
in Japan and India.

Mechanical royalties overseas, whether established by a mechanical licensing society, the local government, or collective bargaining arrangement, are usually expressed as a *percentage* of either the retail selling price (RSP) or the published price to the dealer (PPD) of the compact disc or audiocassette recordings in which the composition is embodied. Further, the license is not issued on a per song basis, but this license is issued and the fee is collected on the entire album, regardless of the number of songs it contains. The percentage fees vary from about 6% to over 10% of PPD for the entire album. These rates are generally higher than those charged for mechanical reproduction in the United States and Canada.

The means by which the publishers get paid the mechanical royalties to which they are entitled is through a *claims* process — each local publisher registers with the collection society its claim to mechanical royalties with respect to each of its compositions, indicating its interest in the entire song or, in the case of split copyright ownership, its percentage interest in the composition. Subpublishers are often required to prove their claim by filing a copy of their subpublishing agreement with the collection society.

What happens when mechanical (or performance royalties) collected for a particular song are not claimed by any music publisher? Under the "Warsaw Rule," adopted by societies who are members of the Paris-based, *International Confederation of Societies of Authors and Composers* (CISAC), performance rights organizations will pay the entire share of performance fees to the appropriate society if they can identify at least one writer or publisher as a member of that society. Otherwise, unclaimed mechanical and performance moneys may go into what is referred to metaphorically as, a *black box*. In many countries, royalties that have not been claimed are maintained by the rights society for a specified period of time. Upon the expiration of that period, the black box moneys are paid to local publishing companies, which they may keep without any obligation to remit funds to the original publishers of the unclaimed songs. In some of these countries, the share of black box moneys paid to a local publisher is determined by dividing the amount of revenues received by the subpublisher from the society by the total revenues of the society. In other countries, the subpublisher's share is based upon seniority. Contractual terms and conditions relating to the disposition of black box moneys are discussed further below.

## II. SELECTING A SUBPUBLISHER

The selection of an individual subpublisher will depend upon the nature of the overall subpublishing administration you are seeking worldwide. Determining the kind of international publishing regime that is appropriate for you is a function of five basic factors:

A. Whether you are seeking worldwide representation by the minimum number of publishers possible or by several publishers on a territory by territory basis,

B. Whether you are seeking to augment the publishing revenue potential of the compositions through the promotional activities of local professional staffs or you are seeking the most efficient administration of international royalty collection,

C. Whether you are seeking representation of an entire catalog of songs or the representation of your catalog on a song by song basis,

D. Whether you are seeking a reciprocal relationship with a subpublisher, and

E. Whether you want to engage a subpublisher at all.

### A. Worldwide or Territory-By-Territory Representation

The first factor to consider in establishing proper representation of your compositions overseas is whether you wish to be represented by the minimum number of publishers possible or by several publishers on a territory by territory basis.

Spreading your publishing rights among subpublishers on a territory by territory basis may put you in a better position to maximize worldwide publishing income. The territory by territory approach allows you to select the best publisher in each region for your particular song or catalog. If one of your objectives is to receive a substantial advance against royalties, the territory by territory approach allows you to pit a greater number of bidders against each other, increasing your chances of obtaining the maximum advance which the circumstances and your bargaining leverage would allow.

In addition, by entering into subpublishing deals on a territory by territory basis, an original publisher can avoid putting all of its "eggs in one basket," avoiding the risk of choosing one publisher who fails to meet your objectives. Similarly, if a worldwide publisher is performing poorly in one or two territories, but doing well in all others, it may be difficult to extricate the poorly performing territories from the worldwide subpublishing deal. By contrast, when deals are done on a territory by territory basis, if an original publisher is disappointed with the performance of a particular subpublisher, he can more easily make the necessary adjustment when the term of the agreement for that territory expires.

The territory by territory approach, however, carries with it significantly greater transaction costs. Obviously, this approach requires that a separate subpublishing agreement be negotiated with each and every subpublisher. The attorneys fees alone could be a significant deterrent to this approach, especially if the original publisher has little experience in negotiating international publishing contracts. The original publisher must also consider the long distance telephone and overseas courier charges that will necessarily be incurred in conferring with the subpublishers, in not only negotiating the agreements, but in communicating to them from time to time the information they will need to properly represent its interests. Though electronic mail and facsimile transmissions are replacing the need for many face-to-face meetings, language and cultural differences still require telephone conversations to maintain good communications. Nevertheless, telephone conversations require that each correspondent be available at the same time. In this regard, an original publisher should not underestimate the inconvenience caused by the significant differences in time zones, between both the U.S. and Europe, and the U.S. and the Far East.

By contrast with territory by territory representation, which has significantly high transaction costs associated with it, using a single music publisher for all territories worldwide, or all territories outside of the United States, has the benefit of a single point of contact. Should any problems arise in a particular country, you can discuss it with your major publisher's international department located in the United States.

An original publisher should also consider the advantages of a single multi-national subpublisher in the area of song promotion. A multi-national subpublisher is often in a better position to conduct song promotion on a coordinated worldwide basis. For example, if a song becomes popular in one territory, the professional department of the multi-national subpublisher in that territory will often call the song to the attention of its professional departments located in other territories. It may be that the original publisher's catalog will only be a small portion of the hundreds of thousands of compositions represented by the major publisher, but an original publisher using a major worldwide publisher can improve the visibility of his catalog overseas by developing relationships, and communicate directly, with the major publisher's subsidiaries and affiliated subpublishers.

An original publisher should also consider the significantly lower cost of adjudicating a dispute with a single major U.S. publisher representing its worldwide interests. If an irreconcilable dispute should arise anywhere in the world, the original publisher can file suit in the United States, even with respect to disputes relating to the U.S. publisher's overseas affiliate. As expensive as that may be, filing suit in the U.S. will be considerably less expensive than suing a subpublisher in his own local territory.

Often, the choice between a single subpublisher or multiple subpublishers will depend upon the circumstances of the original publisher. If the original publisher is a busy recording artist, he may not have the time necessary to properly manage the territory by territory approach. He can allow his attorney to manage his subpublishing affairs, but the costs of using someone at high hourly rates may prove to be more expensive than it's worth. Alternatively, an artist who is at the height of his recording career might consider granting rights to a single subpublisher, and when the artist reaches a point at which he has more time to devote to his international publishing affairs, he can revise his worldwide subpublishing structure at that time.

Finally, anyone who chooses to manage his own international publishing by granting rights on a territory by territory basis should consider what has been said about market size: The top ten markets account for nearly 90% of music publishing revenues. This would suggest that a publisher considering territory-by-territory deals, should focus most of his time and resources on those ten countries. These include: the United States, Germany, France, Japan, the United Kingdom, Italy, the Netherlands, Spain, the Nordic countries (including

Denmark, Sweden, Norway, and Finland), and Belgium, with Austria, Argentina, and Canada, close behind. Accordingly, the original publisher might license these countries on a territory by territory basis and use a single major publisher for all other countries.

## B. Promotion or Administration

The reputations of international subpublishers vary with their respective talents for promoting the use of musical compositions and administering the collection of income in their local territories. If an original publisher is seeking to augment the publishing revenue potential of its catalog, it should seek those subpublishers who have local professional staffs with good working relationships with local record companies, motion picture and television producers, and advertising agencies. If an original publisher is seeking the most efficient collection of local royalties, it should seek those subpublishers with reputations for good administrative abilities.

Ideally, a subpublisher will have a talent for both promotion and administration, but the likelihood of finding a subpublisher ideally suited to promoting and administering your catalog in each territory around the world is remote. Compromises will inevitably be made and the best an original publisher can do is build good working relationships with both the creative and administrative personnel of his subpublishers and keep himself informed of developments.

## C. Entire Catalog or Individual Songs

In addition, the nature of your worldwide subpublishing administration, and your choice of a particular subpublisher, will be affected by whether you are seeking representation of an entire catalog of songs or merely representation on a song by song basis. Because of the high transaction costs of having numerous subpublishers in various territories each representing different songs in an original publisher's catalog, a strategy of splitting international subpublishing rights on a per song basis is rarely advisable.

Nevertheless, circumstances can arise that may allure the inexperienced into establishing just such a structure. For example, a song which has topped the charts in the United States may quickly attract a number of international subpublishers seeking to represent the original publisher for the subpublishing of that one song. These deals will

often involve offers of substantial advances, which may be hard for
an original publisher to resist. If the original publisher already has
relationships with satisfactory subpublishers covering various territories, one practical solution is for the original publisher to offer the
song to his existing subpublishers, giving each of them a chance to
match the advances being offered by the subpublisher's competitors.
If, under these circumstances, the original publisher is only just beginning to establish its worldwide subpublishing program, he should
carefully consider all the factors set forth above and in the pages
which follow before adopting a song by song disposition of his subpublishing rights.

Occasionally, however, a small publisher will be fortunate enough
to come up with that one successful song that would only have the
potential of being acceptable in one particular country overseas. Such
a situation did arise in my career when the manager of the German
branch of European music publisher, Francis, Day & Hunter, Mr. Johann Michel (presently owner/general manager of Melodie der Welt
GmbH, Frankfurt/Main, Germany) sent me a cable conveying to me
his interest in the theme song from John Wayne's film, *The Green
Berets*. The song, *The Ballad of the Green Berets* by Sergeant Barry
Sadler, had that "om-pa, om-pa" feeling that Mr. Michel believed
would make it a successful hit in Germany. On his behalf, I negotiated
a subpublishing agreement with the American publisher of the song
through its attorney, William Krasilovsky. The song did stay in the
number one position in Germany for many weeks.

## D.  Reciprocal Relationships

A fourth, albeit uncommon, factor, in determining the structure of
your international music publishing administration is whether you are
seeking reciprocal relationships with subpublishers. In other words, an
original publisher may seek to serve as the U.S. subpublishing representative for overseas catalogs that might be appropriate for the U.S.
market. Under certain circumstances, the original publisher may find
it advantageous to enter into subpublishing agreements with those international publishers willing to assign their U.S. subpublishing rights
to the original publisher.

For London-based publishing firm Francis, Day & Hunter, Ltd.,
Mr. Fred Day effected very satisfactory long term subpublishing ar-

rangements with many American publishing firms, including Leo Feist Company and Robbins Music Corp. During the 1960's, I served as U.S. representative for Francis, Day & Hunter and their affiliates throughout the world. With an office in New York provided by the Robbins-Feist-Miller music publishing companies, I not only acquired U.S. copyrights for Francis, Day & Hunter, but I was in a position to place overseas copyrights with the Robbins-Feist-Miller companies. In this regard, in my travels abroad, I was successful in placing with The Big Three (as Robbins-Feist-Miller were called) such copyrights as *Volare, You Don't Have to Say You Love Me, The Last Waltz,* and countless others.

Though reciprocal subpublishing arrangements are not always practical, it should always remain an option for those original publishers seeking material that has hit potential in the United States.

## E. Doing Without a Subpublisher

An original publisher is not required to have a subpublisher in a territory in order to collect music publishing income generated from its catalog in that territory. If the original publisher has not appointed a subpublisher in a territory to collect its share of performance income from the local performance rights society, the performance rights society will pay the publisher's share over to the publisher's U.S. performance rights society (e.g., ASCAP or BMI), which will then pay it over to the publisher. Further, if there is no subpublisher in a territory to collect mechanical royalty income from the local mechanical rights collection society, the collection society will, if instructed, pay the publisher's mechanical royalty income from the territory over to the Harry Fox Agency in the United States, which will then remit it to the original publisher. The Harry Fox Agency has established relationships with over twenty three mechanical collection societies operating in about 100 countries throughout the world for this purpose.

If this is the case, then why does one need a subpublisher? An original publisher may rely on its performance rights society to collect overseas performance income and, if it is affiliated with the Harry Fox Agency, the publisher can rely on the Agency's international relationships for the collection of its international mechanical licensing income, but the original publisher should consider that by doing so it may be foregoing many of the benefits of having a subpublisher. For

some, a key benefit is simply having someone in the territory watching
out for your interests. For others, having a subpublisher means having
an opportunity to obtain advances against royalties and to having a
local representative promote the generation of new income through
local cover recordings, local performances, and local translated printed
editions. If the original publisher's songwriters are also recording artists, it can be a nice touch to have a local subpublisher take the songwriters out to dinner when they are on tour overseas.

While performance rights societies claim to do a good job of collecting overseas income, some publishers claim to have experienced
substantial delays in the collection of overseas income when relying
solely on their performance rights society. Whether these delays are
myth or reality, an original publisher will not get its fair share of
international publishing income if its compositions are not being properly registered with the local performance rights and collections societies. Accordingly, to avoid any potential for delay, and to assure
that it is getting its proper share of overseas income, an original publisher should appoint a subpublisher to register its compositions with
the local societies and collect the performance income on behalf of
the original publisher.

### III. NEGOTIATING THE SUBPUBLISHING AGREEMENT

## A. Introduction

As discussed above, the choice of an international subpublisher
will depend upon whether you desire worldwide representation by one
publisher for all your international publishing needs, or several publishers on a territory by territory basis, whether you are placing a
higher value on effective promotion or efficient administration, and
whether you have a single song or an entire catalog to offer. To those
factors you must add the specific deal points you are likely to be
offered for the subpublishing rights, including the potential advances
obtainable, the term or duration of the agreement, and the subpublisher
fee charged for the international representation, among others.

These latter provisions are all subject to negotiation and will be
discussed in this section. It may be well to remember that music pub-

lishing is a business of personal relationships, and perhaps the best way to assure that your subpublishing objectives are met is to actually arrange to meet face-to-face those with whom you expect to sign an agreement. If this is impractical for you, then it may serve you well to rely on long-standing relationships established by others, including those of a multi-national major music publisher.

The appendix to this chapter includes three different subpublishing agreement forms that are typical of those used by original publishers and subpublishers. Form 5.1 is a form that might commonly be used for the subpublishing of an original publisher's catalog in a single territory or group of related territories. Forms 5.2 and 5.3 each might be used by a major multi-national publisher to represent a U.S. original publisher in all territories outside of the United States and Canada. The analysis in the following pages includes a review of only the business provisions of the first form, which is broad enough to illustrate nearly all of the salient terms of standard subpublishing agreements.

Subpublishing agreements are very similar in nature to administration agreements. For this reason, concepts covered at length in the previous chapter, as well as those covered in Chapter 3 on *Songwriter Agreements* and Chapter 10 on *Basic Considerations in Music Licensing*, will be repeated here only where the context requires.

## B. Compositions Covered

The following is the first paragraph of a typical grant of rights provision from a typical subpublishing agreement:

> 1. (a) Owner hereby assigns to Publisher, only for the countries set forth in Schedule A annexed hereto (hereinafter collectively referred to as "the Territory"), the following rights in and to each musical composition owned or controlled by Owner and presently uncommitted for the Territory and in and to each musical composition the ownership or control of which shall be acquired by Owner during the term of this agreement in the ordinary course of business (excluding any so-called "catalog acquisitions") and which shall be uncommitted for the Territory at the time of acquisition (all such musical compositions hereinafter being referred to as "Compositions"):

The above provision is used for a *catalog deal*, a subpublishing agreement under which the subpublisher will be representing in the territory the entire catalog of the original publisher — that is, (a) each song owned or controlled by the original publisher as of the effective date of the subpublishing agreement, and (b) each song which is later acquired by the original publisher during the term of the agreement, except "catalog acquisitions." The exclusion of catalog acquisitions is intended to limit the songs automatically added to the subpublishing agreement to those songs acquired in the normal course of the business of the original publisher, and to exclude songs acquired by the original publisher as part of a catalog (e.g., such as when the original publisher acquires another publisher). Of course, the original publisher may always add acquired catalogs without otherwise changing the terms of the subpublishing agreement, but the benefit of that addition to the subpublisher may be significant enough to warrant the original publisher's attempt to negotiate an additional advance, or other improved terms, in exchange for adding the acquired catalog to the existing subpublishing agreement.

The territory covered by the agreement will be those countries listed in a schedule to be attached to the agreement. Considerations of granting subpublishing rights on a territory by territory basis, as opposed to granting to a single publisher worldwide rights, is discussed above in section II.A. entitled, *Worldwide or Territory-By-Territory Representation.*

## C. Territory

The territory covered by the agreement will either be set forth in the body of the contract or in a schedule attached to the agreement. This will generally be a list of countries. But, an original publisher considering the territory by territory approach must ask, "Which countries?" Is each country unique, requiring a separate subpublisher, or are some countries related in a way that would suggest that certain subpublishers be granted rights for more than one territory?

Though the subpublishing rights for many territories, such as Japan, are granted separately, many other countries are licensed as part of a related group. For example, if you are seeking to grant your subpublishing rights to a subpublisher in the *United Kingdom*, the subpublisher will also try to represent you in *the Republic of Ireland*

*and South Africa.* The countries of *Germany, Austria, and Switzerland* are typically licensed together, as are *Belgium, the Netherlands, and Luxembourg* (or *Benelux*). Often *all member countries of the European Community* are licensed together. The countries of *Central America* (*including Panama*) are often licensed as a group, and the countries of *South America* (*excluding Brazil*) are also typically licensed together. The same is true for *Australia and New Zealand.* Because of the ambiguity of the terms, "English speaking territories" or "French speaking territories" (ex., is Switzerland a French speaking country?), these terms should be avoided. However, it is not unusual for the territory to be defined as, *the country of France, its colonies, dominions and possessions, Monaco and all territories under the perception of SACEM.* Finally, it is always preferable to use the names of specific countries, rather than continents (e.g., the term, *Asia*, may or may not include the country of Russia).

It has been traditional to recognize that, from a creative perspective, Europe has been divided into two parts: The *English block*, consisting of the United Kingdom, the Nordic countries, and Holland; and the *Continental block*, consisting of Germany, Austria, France, Belgium, Switzerland, Italy, Spain, and Portugal. English-language recordings made in the United States were more likely to be successful in the English block countries, and local translations or adaptations were more likely to be necessary to extend the life of a song in the Continental countries. Nevertheless, as American entertainment has become more and more integrated with international culture, particularly as a result of satellite transmissions of U.S. television productions, the cultural and language boundaries between countries are becoming less important in the international marketing of music.

In addition, digital transmission by streaming and download over the Internet portend to make territorial boundaries irrelevant. Careful consideration should be given to these emerging issues before granting exclusive territorial rights.

## D. Rights Granted

The grant of rights provision enumerates the subpublishing rights granted. This section will sketch the basic considerations in negotiating the subpublishing of print rights, performance rights, mechanical and transcription rights, synchronization rights, videogram and other audiovisual rights, and those rights reserved to the original publisher.

## 1. Print Rights

The following is typical of a grant of *print rights* in a standard subpublishing agreement:

> (i) The exclusive right to print, publish, vend, and cause to be printed, published and vended printed copies of the Compositions in the Territory.

In a world where an increasing amount of manufacturing and distribution is being conducted on a centralized basis, with many companies moving local reproduction facilities to centralized manufacturing and worldwide distribution operations in countries such as Ireland or Singapore, the exclusivity granted to the subpublisher in the above provision may cause significant problems for the original publisher. It would, in effect, allow the subpublisher, in many countries, to legally stop the importation of printed copies for sale within the territory. This may unnecessarily involve the original publisher in disputes arising from the normal activities of its distributors, and perhaps expose the original publisher to a claim of breach of contract. Accordingly, the original publisher should consider adding the following limitation on the subpublisher's exclusivity:

> provided, however, that Owner reserves to itself the right to ship or license the shipment into the Territory of printed music embodying Compositions manufactured by Owner or by its subsidiaries, affiliates or licensees outside of the Territory, and Publisher shall have no right to receive any portion of any sums received by Owner on account of such importation or licensing;

Thus, though the print rights provision is exclusive, the exclusivity is limited to copies made in the territory — that is, the original publisher is, in effect, merely agreeing not to grant to anyone other than the subpublisher the right to reproduce printed copies in the territory. Copies of printed music reproduced outside of the territory under the authority of the original publisher may be shipped into and sold within the subpublisher's territory without compensation to the subpublisher. In response, a subpublisher concerned about the bad faith circumvention of its exclusivity by the original publisher or its licensees, may insist that the limitation only be applied to copies made *in the United States* by the original publisher or its licensees.

### 2. Performance Rights

The following is typical of a grant of *public performance rights* in a standard subpublishing agreement:

> (ii) The exclusive right of public performance of the Compositions, for profit or otherwise (including broadcasting and television), and of licensing such rights in and for the Territory;

*Writer's Share.* Recall from Chapter 3, on *Songwriter Agreements*, that the performance rights society pays the *writer's share* of performance royalties collected by the society directly to the songwriter. Where performance royalties are collected by performance rights societies overseas, such as PRS in England and SACEM in France, these societies pay the writer's share over to the writer's U.S. performance rights society, (i.e., ASCAP, BMI or SESAC), which in turn remits that share directly to the writer. Neither the subpublisher nor the original publisher receive any portion of the writer's share.

*Publisher's Share.* Unless the original publisher appoints a subpublisher to collect the *publisher's share* from the local performance rights society in the subpublisher's territory, the performance rights society will pay the publisher's share over to the publisher's U.S. performance rights society, which will then pay it over to the publisher. As mentioned above, however, an original publisher may consider the benefits of appointing a subpublisher to register its compositions with the local performance rights society and collect the performance income on its behalf.

### 3. Mechanical and Electrical Transcription Rights

The following is typical of a grant of *mechanical and electrical transcription rights* in a standard subpublishing agreement:

> (iii) The exclusive right, for sale within the Territory only, to grant non-exclusive licenses for the manufacture of parts serving to reproduce the Compositions and the making of mechanical, elec-

trical and similar reproductions for phonograph records, audiotapes of any configuration or type, piano rolls, transcriptions or any other method of audio reproduction as yet known or unknown, in and for the Territory.

Recall from our discussion above, regarding *International Mechanical Rights Administration*, that in most countries outside of the United States, all mechanical licenses are issued by a mechanical rights collection society, not by the individual music publishers, and that mechanical rates overseas are generally set by the terms of a collective bargaining agreement between the mandatory mechanical rights organizations and the record companies, or an association representing them.

Unless the original publisher appoints a subpublisher to collect the publisher's share from the local mechanical rights collection society, the collection society will, if instructed, pay the publisher's mechanical royalty income from the territory over to the Harry Fox Agency in the United States, which will then remit it to the original publisher. An original publisher who is affiliated with the Harry Fox Agency can rely on the Agency's relationships with twenty three mechanical collection societies operating in about 100 countries throughout the world for the collection of its international mechanical licensing income, but the original publisher should consider that by doing so it may be foregoing the opportunity to obtain advances against royalties and to have a local representative promote the generation of new income through local cover recordings, local performances, and local translated printed editions.

### 4.   Synchronization Rights

The grant of right provision will typically go on to specify the subpublisher's authority to issue licenses for the synchronization of the compositions with motion pictures and television programs:

> (iv) Upon securing the prior written consent of Owner, the non-exclusive right to grant non-exclusive synchronization licenses for the recording of the Compositions in and with motion pictures and television productions produced in the Territory, and of making copies of recordings thereof, and exporting such copies to all countries of the world.

Note that the above section provides that the original publisher's consent must be obtained before the subpublisher issues any synchronization licenses. Note also, the inclusion of the language, "and of making copies of recordings thereof, and exporting such copies to all countries of the world," would allow the distribution of copies of the licensed motion pictures and television productions, not only for theatrical exhibition and broadcast, but for distribution in videocassettes, laserdiscs, and other home video devices.[3] However, this appears to be limited to the reproduction of copies of "motion pictures and television productions" produced in the territory, and there does not appear to be a separate provision for licensing the reproduction of other kinds of audiovisual works, such as multi-media programs. In any event, under this form of agreement, all forms of licensing for audiovisual reproductions would require the consent of the original publisher.

The subpublisher's authority to issue synchronization licenses is nearly always granted on a *non-exclusive* basis and limited to motion pictures and television programs *produced in the subpublisher's territory*. By the following language, the original publisher may clarify that the subpublisher's share of performance income, even when generated by the issuance of a local synchronization license, is limited to that income generated by performances occurring within the territory:

> It is specifically understood and agreed that Publisher shall not share in any fees derived from the public performance outside of the Territory of any Compositions contained in a motion picture or television production produced in the Territory, and that all such fees shall be payable to and collected by Owner or its designees.

The original publisher's intent with respect to non-exclusivity may be clarified with the following language:

> Owner hereby reserves for itself the exclusive right to grant licenses for the entire world (including the Territory) for the synchronization and public performance of the Compositions with motion pictures or television productions produced outside the Territory, and Pub-

---

[3] See Chapter 15, *Videogram Licensing*.

lisher shall not be entitled to share in any fees received by Owner in respect to such worldwide use.

## 5. Videogram and Other Audiovisual Rights

That the subpublisher's right to issue synchronization and video-gram licenses is *non-exclusive* is important. When negotiating a synchronization license for the use of music in a motion picture produced in the United States, U.S. film producers typically require that the music publisher also grant a *worldwide* license to make and distribute videocassettes and other home video devices containing the compositions licensed. For this reason, royalties for the distribution and sale of videograms overseas are paid to the original publisher in the United States. The same is true for other audiovisual works produced in the United States, such as music videos of recording artist performances, multimedia programs distributed on CD-ROM, and similar audiovisual works.

## 6. Commercial Advertising Rights

The original publisher will typically reserve the right to license the compositions as part of any commercial advertisements. The original publisher may be required to reserve these rights to comply with any restrictions contained in its agreements with songwriters, who are increasingly demanding the right to approve the use of their songs in advertisements. At a minimum, the subpublishing agreement should contain restrictions on the grant of commercial advertising licenses that mirror any restrictions contained in the songwriter agreement with respect to the composition. Because the terms of songwriter agreements vary, and many subpublishing agreements are catalog deals (e.g., covering numerous compositions written by different songwriters), the original publisher is advised to grant the right to issue licenses for commercial advertisements, but condition the subpublisher's exercise of that right upon its obtaining the original publisher's prior written consent with respect to each proposed license.

It should be noted that performance rights societies in some countries, such as Italy, Argentina, and Mexico, do not pay performance royalties for the use of music in commercial advertising, and in Canada only commercials with musical content of 60 seconds or more are credited for payment of performance royalties. This should be considered in connection with setting synchronization license fees for the use of music in commercial advertising in these countries.

### 7.  Reserved Rights

Unless the subpublishing agreement contains a broad grant of subpublishing rights, such as the grant contained in Section 3 of the Subpublishing Agreement set forth as Form 5.2 in the appendix to this chapter, the scope of the subpublisher's right to issue licenses will be limited to the specific rights listed in the subpublishing agreement. Among the rights an original publisher might typically reserve are:

(a) All rights in the Compositions and the copyrights therein for the world outside the Territory, and all rights within the Territory other than as are specifically herein granted to Publisher;

(b) The exclusive right to dramatize, worldwide, the Compositions, and to license the use and performance of such dramatic versions throughout the world;

(c) The exclusive right to license worldwide uses of the titles of the Compositions; and

(d) The exclusive right to make literary versions of the Compositions throughout the world, and to print, publish and vend such literary versions (as well as the dramatic versions aforementioned) throughout the world.

## E.  Subpublisher Fees and Publishing Income

In exchange for its publishing services, the subpublisher will retain a fee similar to the administration fee charged under an administration agreement. Subpublisher fees range anywhere from 10% to 50% of publishing income, with the typical fees falling between 15% to 25%. Hybrid deals that look more like a U.S. *collection agreement* (described in the previous chapter), with the subpublisher retaining as little as 5%, but providing merely those minimum services necessary to collect and remit local publishing income, are not uncommon for catalogs owned by popular recording artists who have a great degree of bargaining leverage.

The subpublishing fee is generally reflected in the percentage of publishing income that the subpublisher pays over to the original publisher. For example, if the subpublishing fee is 25%, the agreement will provide that the subpublisher will pay to the original publisher "75% of the publisher's share . . . earned in the Territory."

Provisions in a subpublishing agreement concerning the fees a subpublisher is permitted to retain from the publishing income collected may begin as follows:

> 4. All monies payable to Publisher with respect to the exploitation of rights granted hereunder shall be referred to herein as "Publishing Income." Publisher agrees that it shall have the duty to collect and to be responsible for the collection of all Publishing Income payable within the Territory. Publisher shall pay to Owner the following royalties in respect of the Compositions upon the following terms and provisions:

## 1. *Print Income*

With respect to royalties for printed editions, the subpublisher will typically pay to the original publisher,

> (a) Twelve and one-half percent (12.5%) of the marked or suggested retail selling price of each copy of each Composition in any and every printed edition sold by Publisher or its permitted subpublishers, on all gross sales (after deduction of actual returns), and that proportion of twelve and one-half percent (12.5%) of the marked or suggested retail selling price of each songbook, folio or similar compilation edition sold by Publisher or its permitted subpublishers, on all gross sales (after deduction of returns), which the number of Compositions included in each edition shall bear to the total number of copyrighted compositions (including the Compositions) contained therein for which a royalty is payable.

The percentage royalty may vary from 10% to 15%, with the typical being 121/2%. Where the subpublisher permits local print publishers to manufacture and sell printed editions, the publishing income arising from such arrangements will be paid over to the original publisher, less the subpublisher's fee. Thus, assuming subpublisher fee rate is 25%, the subpublisher shall pay to the original publisher,

> (b) seventy-five percent (75%) of any and all gross receipts paid by printing licensees of Publisher or of its permitted

subpublishers for the use of each Composition in any piano copies, songbooks, folios, books, newspapers, magazines or other printed editions.

## 2. Mechanical and Electrical Transcription Income

The following provision is typical of one governing income from the licensing of mechanical and electrical transcription reproductions in the territory. Again, assuming the subpublisher fee is 25%, the subpublisher shall pay to the original publisher,

> (c) seventy-five percent (75%) of all monies paid by licensees of Publisher as royalties for the sale in the Territory of phonograph records or other such devices embodying mechanical, electrical or other audio reproductions of the Compositions (as described in paragraph 1(c) above), with respect to audio master recordings originally produced outside of the Territory;

*Cover Records.* Except in the case of a collection deal, where the original publisher has no expectation of the subpublisher's exerting efforts to promote the compositions covered by the agreement, the original publisher will often provide the subpublisher with an incentive to effect the recording and release of *cover records* (i.e., a recording of a composition, often translated into the local language, by an artist popular in the territory). That incentive is provided by increasing the subpublisher fee rate, with respect to income generated by cover recordings, by an amount ranging between 5% to 15%. For example, if the subpublisher fee rate is 25%, the rate may be increased to 40% with respect to cover recordings made and released in the territory.

The provision providing the incentive for the subpublisher to effect cover records might look like the following addition to paragraph (c) set forth above:

> provided, however, that if Publisher secures the release in the Territory during the term hereof of a master audio recording of a Composition originally produced within the Territory (hereinafter referred to as a "Territory-originated cover recording"), Publisher shall pay to Owner only sixty percent (60%) of all monies paid by licensees of Publisher as royalties with respect to such Territory-originated cover recording.

The above language makes it clear that the subpublisher is only entitled to an increased percentage of income with respect to the *particular* cover recording originated in the territory, and does not apply to *all* recordings released in the territory (i.e., including any original hit recording released in the United States), as some subpublishing agreements provide.

However, the above language appears to leave an ambiguity as to whether the increased subpublisher fee applies merely to *mechanical* income generated by the cover recording or whether it also includes *performance* income generated from public performances of the cover recording. Clearly, if the subpublisher is to be entitled to an increased fee on performance royalties generated by cover recordings, it seems reasonable that such increase should only apply to those performance fees associated with performances of the cover recording. However, because performance rights societies do not distinguish between particular recordings when reporting public performance royalties, it is difficult to determine what portion of performance fees generated in a particular country is associated with a particular cover recording.

One solution to the problem is to limit the application of the rate increase solely to royalties generated from *mechanical* licensing of the cover recording. This is because it is fairly easy to distinguish mechanical fees generated from the cover recording from those generated by all other recordings, as collection societies receive and report mechanical collection information on the basis of particular albums and recording artists. Though the subpublisher won't benefit by the amount of the *increased rate* on performance royalties, it will benefit from the overall increase in performance royalties caused by the cover recording, as the subpublisher will be entitled to retain its normal percentage on performance royalties generated by public performances in the territory, which, of course, will include broadcasts of the cover recording.

Another solution, one which is more favorable to the subpublisher, is to compute the portion of performance royalties to which the increased rate shall be applied using a ratio of the mechanical income associated with the cover recording to mechanical income associated with all recordings sold in the territory. In other words, if 30% of the total mechanical royalties generated in the territory were derived from sales of the cover recording, then the subpublisher's increased fee rate (e.g., 40%) would apply to 30% of the performance royalties and, of course, the subpublisher's normal fee rate (e.g., 25%) would apply to the balance, or 70% of the performance royalties.

*Related Restrictions.* The original publisher will typically impose the following restrictions upon the subpublisher with respect to the issuance of mechanical and transcription licenses in the territory:

> (h) Publisher shall not license the mechanical, electrical or other reproduction of any Composition for phonorecords or other such devices at a rate less than the highest prevailing rate in the Territory. Publisher shall not refuse to grant a mechanical license for a Composition at the prevailing rate in the Territory to any authorized manufacturer in the Territory of a recording of said Composition made by Owner or its parent, affiliate or subsidiary.

> (i) Notwithstanding any provision to the contrary herein contained, Publisher shall collect royalties under subparagraph (c) above only with respect to phonograph records and other devices sold in the Territory, irrespective of whether such phonorecords or devices are manufactured within the Territory or outside of the Territory. Accordingly, Publisher shall not collect royalties hereunder with respect to phonograph records and other such devices manufactured within the Territory but sold outside of the Territory.

### 3. Performance Income

As mentioned in our discussion above, regarding *International Performance Rights Administration*, unless the original publisher appoints a subpublisher to collect the *publisher's share* of performance income from the local performance rights society, the performance rights society will pay the publisher's share over to the publisher's U.S. performance rights society, which in turn will remit the amount over to the publisher. But to rely on this process is to risk substantial delays and even errors in the collection of overseas performance income. A U.S. publisher is therefore advised to appoint a subpublisher to register its compositions with the local performance rights society and collect the performance income on behalf of the original publisher. To that end, the typical subpublishing agreement contains the following provision; assuming the subpublishing fee is 25% of publishing income, the subpublisher will pay to the original publisher,

        (d) seventy-five percent (75%) of the publisher's share
of all public performance fees earned in the Territory with respect
to the Compositions, it being understood and agreed that the Publisher shall authorize and direct the appropriate performance rights
society in the Territory to pay to Publisher one hundred percent
(100%) of said publisher's share and that Publisher shall remit to
Owner its aforesaid share thereof, together with a statement signed
by said performance rights society indicating in detail the titles of
the Compositions and the amounts paid to Publisher on account of
the public performance in the Territory of such Compositions.

Some subpublisher's insist that they should receive a greater percentage for collecting performance royalties on the basis that if they
apply the subpublisher fee percentage to the amount of performance
income collected, the subpublisher is really only receiving one-half of
the amount to which they feel entitled. Recall that the subpublisher
only collects the *publisher's share* of performance income, the writer's
share being paid directly to the writer through the performance rights
societies. Thus, for example, if a subpublisher fee of 25% is applied
to only the publisher's share, then the subpublisher is really only getting 12.5% of total performance income, yet the work the subpublisher
does to maximize performance income, including the prompt and accurate registration of compositions with the local performance rights
society, benefits *all* performance income, not just the publisher's share.
Thus, a subpublisher may assert, that if the subpublisher fee rate is
25% for all publishing income, the rate should be 50% for performance income. Few knowledgeable original publishers, however, concede the point.

### 4.  Other Income

The following provision confirms that all other publishing income
arising from the exercise of rights granted under the agreement shall
be remitted to the publisher, less the subpublisher fee:

        (e) seventy-five percent (75%) of all gross monies paid
by licensees of Publisher with respect to any other rights to the
Compositions which are expressly assigned to Publisher hereunder.

The following provision makes it clear that any moneys collected
by the subpublisher arising from rights not specifically granted under

the agreement, including income from unauthorized licenses issued by the subpublisher, shall be paid over to the original publisher without deduction of the subpublisher's fee.

(f) One hundred percent (100%) of all Publishing Income received by Publisher from any exploitation of rights in and to the Compositions other than those rights expressly set forth in paragraph 1 above. Nothing herein shall in any way increase or enlarge the rights granted to Publisher hereunder, which are solely as set forth in paragraph 1.

## 5. *Payment "At Source"*

Nearly all modern subpublishing agreements will contain a provision making certain that publishing income be computed "at the source." The provision may look like this:

(j) Notwithstanding anything to the contrary herein contained, all royalties or other monies payable to Owner hereunder are to be computed at the source from which the payments giving rise to such royalties or other monies are originally made, less only the actual commissions or collection fees (if any) retained by the performing rights society or agency and the mechanical royalty collection society or agency in the Territory.

Such a provision is intended to prevent the unscrupulous practice of using multiple layers of subpublishing companies, owned or closely affiliated with the subpublisher, solely for the purpose of reducing the original publisher's royalties from international publishing income.[4] For example, where a subpublisher, who is entitled to retain as its fee 50% of the publishing income it collects, sublicenses its subpublishing rights for the territory to an affiliated company, allowing the affiliate to retain 50% of publishing income collected by the affiliate, then the subpublisher's income will only be those receipts from its affiliate, or 50% of the true publishing income derived from the territory. Thus, if the subpublisher remits to the original publisher 50% (retaining its 50% subpublisher fee) of the 50% received from its affiliate, then the

---

[4] Such practices have been successfully challenged in court. See *Elton John v. Dick James Music* [1982 J. No. 15026, High Court of Justice, Chancery Division].

amount ultimately remitted to the original publisher will only be 25% of the true publishing income derived from the territory. If the affiliate adds another subpublishing layer under the same terms, the original publisher will only receive 12.5% of the true publishing income from the territory, and so on.

Though this practice of layering subpublishing deals to reduce royalties remitted to original publishers is no longer common, including the *at source* provision in a subpublishing agreement with a major U.S. publisher (i.e., acting as a worldwide subpublisher) will assure that intercompany agreements between the U.S. publisher and its international subsidiaries and affiliates may not be used to reduce the royalties of the original publisher. This is not to suggest that major U.S. publishers engage in this practice, but intercompany agreements among subsidiaries and affiliated companies of a multinational firm are often modified for international income tax reasons, and the at source provision will assure that such changes will not adversely affect the original publisher.

### 6.   *Frozen Funds*

From time to time, in certain countries, government regulations may restrict the ability of the local subpublisher to remit funds to the original publisher in the United States and in United States dollars. To address these circumstances, the following provision is commonly included in subpublishing agreements:

> (1) In the event Publisher is prevented from paying any monies hereunder due to currency restrictions, Publisher shall so advise Owner by written notice accompanied by a copy of the applicable law, regulation or order (with an accurate English translation), and Owner shall have the right to elect to accept payment of such monies in foreign currency in a depository selected by Owner, and if Owner shall so elect, by written notice to Publisher, Publisher shall promptly deposit or cause to be deposited all such payable monies to the credit of Owner in such foreign currency and shall promptly give Owner written notice of said deposit. Payment so made to the depository so elected by Owner shall fulfill Publisher's obligations hereunder as to the monies so payable to Owner.

By virtue of such a provision, the original publisher gains control over the money, removing the funds from the risks of subpublisher insolvency, and enabling the original publisher to preserve the value of the funds by making interest bearing investments. The original publisher may either wait until circumstances allow the remittance of funds to the United States or use the money for defraying local expenses, as when the original publisher pays a visit to review his subpublishing affairs, or when a record or motion picture company affiliated with the original publisher produces a record, motion picture, or other work in the territory.

As noted in Chapter 3, on *Songwriter Agreements*, some songwriters are successful in negotiating a provision which requires, under circumstance where funds are frozen, that the music publisher pay to the songwriter an *advance* against royalties in an amount equal to the royalties that would have been earned had the publisher received the funds in the United States. In requesting such a provision, the songwriter would argue that the publisher is simply in a better position than the songwriter to deal with the intricacies of foreign exchange matters and therefore the publisher should bear the risks of being unable to remit frozen funds. Further, as mentioned above, even though the funds have not been paid in U.S. currency, the publisher often does have control over the funds and may actually put the funds to practical use.

For the same reasons, an original publisher signing a subpublishing agreement with a major U.S. publisher should be in the same position to request a similar provision: in circumstances where the subpublisher is prevented from paying publishing income due to currency restrictions, the subpublisher should pay to the original publisher an *advance* against publishing income in an amount equal to the publishing income that would have been earned had the major U.S. subpublisher received the funds in the United States.

### 7.   Black Box Moneys

Earlier in this chapter, under the discussion of *International Mechanical Rights Administration*, we explained the concept of the *black box* — in many countries, mechanical royalties that have not been claimed are, after a certain period of time has elapsed, paid to local publishing companies, which they may keep without any obligation to remit funds to the original publishers of the unclaimed songs. In some of these countries, the share of black box moneys entitled to be received by a local publisher is calculated by dividing the amount of mechanical revenues received by the subpublisher from the society by the total mechanical revenues of the society; in other countries, disbursement is based upon seniority and other factors.

In many cases, a major original publisher, who has placed a large catalog with a local subpublisher, may have the leverage to require the subpublisher to pay over to the original publisher a share of the black box money received by the subpublisher. This share would be calculated, roughly, by dividing the revenues the subpublisher derived from the original publisher's catalog by the total earnings of the subpublisher. The following provision, which again assumes a 25% subpublisher fee, is intended to effect such terms in favor of the original publisher:

> (m) To the extent that authorization from Owner is necessary or desirable, Owner hereby grants to Publisher the right and authority within the Territory to collect from performing rights societies or agencies, mechanical rights licensing and/or mechanical royalty collection societies or agencies or any other persons, firms or corporations, unclaimed, unregistered or unallocated receipts, bonuses or other sums distributable to Publisher by reason of seniority or membership in or affiliation with any such society or agency, or otherwise, not calculated on the basis of actual uses of the Compositions, to which the Publisher is or shall be entitled (hereinafter referred to as "accruals"). Publisher shall pay to Owner, with the accounting statements hereinafter provided for, seventy-five percent (75%) of that portion of such accruals which shall be calculated by multiplying the total amount of each such distribution of accruals to Publisher by a fraction, the numerator of which shall be the total public performance fee or mechanical royalty distribution, as the case may be, from such society, agency or other party, to Publisher which is allocable to identified uses of the Compositions during the relevant accounting period and the denominator of which shall be the total public performance fee or mechanical royalty distribution, as the case may be, from such society, agency or other party, to Publisher which is allocable to identified uses of any and all musical compositions controlled by Publisher, including the Compositions, during the relevant accounting period.

## F. Translations

Many subpublishing agreements drafted from the perspective of the subpublisher will include the following grant, entitling the subpublisher to make translations and adaptations:

> (v) The exclusive right to make orchestral and other arrangements and adaptations of the Compositions, to procure any new or translated lyrics or titles thereof, and to publish, sell or use the compositions and to authorize others to do so in the Territory, either with or without any such arrangement, adaptation, new lyric or translations thereof.

Good local adaptations are not literal translations, but are ones which capture the spirit and idea of the song. The creation of localized lyrics and adaptations may be necessary for a subpublisher to fully exploit a composition in its territory. In the past, this was true for a number of the continental countries of Europe, including Germany, Austria, France, Belgium, Switzerland, Italy, Spain, and Portugal. Today, however, the original English versions tend to predominate. In certain countries where English is not widely spoken, such as Japan, a localized lyric will breathe life into a song where it would not otherwise become popular. Thus, the right to create local language translations and adaptations is commonly granted to the subpublisher.

Nevertheless, when the subpublisher exercises the foregoing right by engaging a writer to create new, local language lyrics, there arises the question of royalties for the local writer and who is responsible for them. Under the rules of many performance rights societies, the local lyricist will get a portion of the original *writer's share* (i.e., the total writer's share, even if there were two original writers, one being a lyricist and the other a composer) of *all* versions of the work, including the original English-language version. However, under the "Amalfi" resolution adopted by CISAC member societies, local performance rights societies are only supposed to allocate fees to local lyricists for the translated versions. In addition, a local lyric writer may receive a portion of the subpublisher's receipts arising from mechanical, synchronization and print licenses. Of course, the subpublisher would want to deduct these obligations from the original publisher's share, but it is customary for the subpublisher to bear these costs.

Recall, in Chapter 3, on *Songwriter Agreements*, that songwriters who have significant amount of bargaining leverage are generally able to obtain in their songwriter agreements the complete right of approval over the engagement of other writers to make additions, changes or trans-lations. Under these circumstances, the original publisher would have no choice but to require its consent before the subpublisher were able to engage a lyricist to create a local language translation. It would also be advisable to make it clear that any costs incurred by the sub-publisher in connection with the creation of new lyrics or local ad-aptations, permitted by the original publisher, will be borne by the subpublisher:

> (b) Publisher shall have the right to make and publish new adaptations and arrangements of any Composition and to trans-late the lyrics thereof into any language of the Territory, but only with Owner's prior written approval thereof. Publisher shall be re-sponsible for and shall pay to local adapters, arrangers, translators and lyricists any royalties or fees for such services, solely out of Publisher's share of Publishing Income. All new matter shall be the property of Owner and shall be copyrighted solely in the name of Owner or Owner's designee.

When the original publisher provides its written consent to the creation of translations or adaptations, it should take such measures necessary to assure that publishing income is properly accounted for. For example, as noted above, the subpublisher may be entitled to retain a greater portion of publishing income with respect to cover recordings. The original publisher will want to take special care that the cover recordings of translated versions are accounted for as such, and are not confused with royalties stemming from the sale or per-formance of the original U.S. version. One measure is to make certain the local translation is given a different title than the original U.S. version, and that the local translation is registered separately with the local performance rights society. Another is to make sure that no more than one lyric version is released in the same language. This frequently happens with Spanish lyrics created in both Spain and Latin America, French lyrics created in both France and French Quebec, and Portu-guese lyrics created in both Portugal and Brazil.

In addition, an experienced original publisher will always require that ownership in any local lyrics, modifications, or other new matter created with respect to the compositions shall remain with the original publisher. For example, Spanish lyrics created by a subpublisher in Latin America can become quite popular among the Hispanic population in the United States and the original publisher will want to collect mechanical and performance royalties in the U.S. without payment to the subpublisher. Further, ownership of the translation will assure the original publisher complete flexibility to exploit the song in the territory upon termination of the subpublishing agreement. Without full rights to the translation, the original publisher may find it difficult to develop new lyrics without infringing upon the translation owned by the subpublisher.

Finally, if the original songwriter has approval rights over the creation of translations, the original publisher should obtain a copy of the proposed new lyrics, together with an English translation of them, for purposes of obtaining the original writer's approval.

## G. Term

Historically, subpublishing agreements endured for the life of the copyrights in the compositions they covered. In recent years, however, the trend has been to shorten the term of these agreements to the point that, today, the term of the typical subpublishing agreement is from *three* to *five* years. Most international performance rights societies, however, require a minimum three year term.

The variations in structuring the durations of subpublishing agreements are as numerous as those found in co-publishing, administration and other music publishing agreements. For example, fixed terms may be extended by exercise of options to renew, and such extensions may be conditioned upon the payment of advances or achieving minimum amounts of publishing income. These variations are entirely subject to negotiation.

When the subpublisher pays a large advance against royalties, the term is typically at the high end of the range, perhaps with the subpublisher having certain rights to extend the term beyond its originally anticipated date of expiration.

*1. Cover Records.* For example, the subpublisher may have the right to extend the term of the agreement (e.g., typically for one to three years) with respect to compositions for which it effected cover recordings during the term. The following provision is an example of such a right:

> Notwithstanding any provision to the contrary herein contained, in the event Publisher shall secure the release during the term hereof of a Territory-originated cover recording of a Composition and said cover recording shall during the term hereof reach 20 or better on the popular single records chart of one of the two most popular record industry publications in the Territory, Publisher's rights hereunder with respect to said Composition shall continue for two (2) years after the date of release in the Territory of the first such qualifying Territory-originated cover recording.

An original publisher should be mindful, however, that such a provision may result in some of the original publisher's compositions being published in the territory by this subpublisher and some being administered by another. Splitting one's catalog in this way will, at best, be an inconvenience, and, at worst, could lead to increased transaction costs or costly errors in collection accounting.

*2. Unrecouped Advances.* The subpublisher may also have the right to extend the term of the agreement if advances paid to the original publisher have not been fully recouped. The original publisher would seek to restrict this right by (a) limiting the exercise of such right only *to the extent* the subpublisher has not recouped a specified percentage (e.g., 75%) of the advances, and (b) providing that in no event shall such extension continue for a specified period of time (e.g., one or two years from the stated expiration of the agreement).

*3. Pipeline Revenues.* Another variation that affects the negotiated term of the agreement concerns publishing income earned during the term but not collected as of the time of its stated expiration date. A subpublisher will typically be provided the right to collect and disburse (after retaining its subpublisher's fee) these revenues, called *pipeline* revenues. The provision may look like the second sentence of the following *term* paragraph:

> 10. The term of this agreement shall commence as of the date hereof and shall continue for a period of three (3) years. At the expiration or termination of this agreement, all rights of any kind or nature granted to Publisher hereunder shall automatically revert and

be the sole and exclusive property of Owner without formality or execution of any documents. Notwithstanding the foregoing, upon the expiration of this agreement (but not upon any termination of this agreement by Owner for good cause), Publisher shall have the right for six (6) months thereafter to continue to collect and disburse, in accordance with the provisions hereof, the Publishing Income which shall have been earned during the term of this agreement but which shall not have become payable until after the expiration of this agreement.

An original publisher may insist that (a) the subpublisher's right to collect pipeline revenues should cease upon the subpublisher's recoupment of most or all of the advances paid to the original publisher, (b) a time limit, such as the *six* month limit set forth in the above illustration, be placed on such rights, and (c) during the extension period, the subpublisher's rights be limited to collection and disbursement, it being understood the subpublisher shall have no right to exercise administration rights over the compositions.

*4. Reciprocal Relationships.* A further consideration is whether the original publisher has an important reciprocal relationship with the subpublisher. In other words, if the original publisher serves as the U.S. subpublisher to the international subpublisher's overseas catalog, the international subpublisher may insist upon identical provisions with regard to the term of that agreement, and may, in fact, insist upon *co-termination* — that is, upon the termination of the overseas subpublishing agreement, the U.S. subpublishing agreement shall automatically terminate as well.

## H.  Advances

Original publishers can usually expect to receive some form of advance against royalties in exchange for signing up with a subpublisher. The structure of the advance, however, varies considerably from deal to deal, and is often related to the exercise of options to renew the term of the agreement.

If the subpublisher has experience with the catalog to be represented, or access to reliable information furnished by the original publisher, the size of the advance may be determined on the basis of historical data with respect to publishing income previously generated by the compositions in the territory. Often, however, the advance is

more a function of the sheer bargaining power that a popular artist
with a hit album brings to the original publisher's catalog.

A typical structure for advances may look like this:

> 22. Publisher shall pay to Owner (in United States Dollars) the
> following amounts, at the commencement of each one (1) year pe-
> riod of the term hereof, as nonreturnable advances recoupable by
> Publisher from Owner's share of the Publishing Income earned dur-
> ing the applicable one (1) year period:
>
> (a) _____ Dollars ($_____), upon the
> execution hereof, for the first one (1) year period.
>
> (b) _____ Dollars ($_____), at the com-
> mencement of the second one (1) year period, for said one (1) year
> period.
>
> (c) _____ Dollars ($_____), at the com-
> mencement of the third one (1) year period, for said one (1) year
> period.

Note, in the above example, the advance paid at the beginning of
each year is recoupable only from the publishing income generated
during the one year period immediately following the date the advance
is due.

An original publisher should bear in mind that the subpublisher's
risk/reward ratio will vary with every demand made during negotiations. The size and structure of the advance is likely to affect how the
subpublisher negotiates other provisions in the agreement, particularly
the subpublisher fee and the term of the agreement.

Though a higher advance may reduce certain risks of the original
publisher, if the increase comes at the expense of an increase in the
subpublisher's fee, it may well not be worth insisting upon. The original publisher should be considering factors other than the advance,
such as the reduction of risk through a shorter agreement term.

Finally, a most important consideration is to remember that music
publishing is a business built upon relationships. An original publisher
should not advance his short term interests by watching an outstanding
subpublisher consistently lose money on the original publisher's catalog. Because of the high costs and risks associated with adjudication
of disputes overseas, good relationships are nowhere more important
than in the setting of international business transactions.

## I.  Disputes

In Chapter 10, on *Basic Considerations in Music Licensing*, we discuss the important distinction between a *choice of law* provision and a *choice of forum* provision. It is important that your international subpublishing agreement contain *both* provisions, such as in the following example:

> 17. . . . This agreement shall be deemed to have been made in the State of California, and its validity, construction and effect shall be governed by the laws of the State of California applicable to agreements wholly performed therein. . . . The venue for any action, suit or proceeding brought by either party against the other with respect to this agreement shall be in the County of Los Angeles, State of California, and both parties hereby consent to the personal jurisdiction of the courts of the State of California. Service of process may be made by registered or certified mail addressed to the defendant in accordance with the notice provisions hereof, and the time to respond to such process shall be thirty (30) days after the date of mailing thereof.

## IV.  WORKING WITH YOUR SUBPUBLISHER

The working relationship between you and your subpublisher will have administrative aspects, such as providing in a timely fashion the information the subpublisher requires to effectively administer the collection of your royalties, and creative aspects, including the promotion of the musical compositions in your catalog.

A subpublisher will require a significant amount of information from the original publisher to properly represent the administration of royalty collection. For example, the subpublisher will require information about the release of any popular recordings of the compositions worldwide, copies of music cue sheets of motion pictures or television programs in which any of the compositions are featured, lead sheets or lyric sheets available for the compositions, the names of the songwriters and the amount of their percentage interests in the compositions, the performance rights affiliations of the songwriters, and if there are co-owners of any of the copyrights, their relative percentage interests in the compositions. The subpublisher registers much of this information with its local mechanical license collection agency and performance rights society to improve the chances that collections by those entities with respect to the original publisher's compositions can be properly allocated and claimed as publishing income by the sub-publisher. The effectiveness of the subpublisher will be as much de-pendent upon its diligence in using this information as upon the original publisher's diligence in supplying it.

The art of personal relationships is one of the precious keys to successful music publishing. This is why a successful working rela-tionship with your subpublisher will often begin with a personal meet-ing. I will leave the reader with one example:

Murry Wilson, not to be outdone by his sons Brian, Carl, and Dennis's success as *The Beach Boys*, embarked on his own career as a songwriter and conductor of a studio size orchestra in his own al-bum, released by Capitol Records in 1967. The album was entitled, "The Many Moods of Murry Wilson." Aiming at a global play, I set in motion on behalf of Francis, Day & Hunter, the publishing orga-nization which handled Wilson's music interests and subpublishing for The Beach Boys' *Sea of Tunes* catalog, a campaign to help promote his music and album in Europe. Prior to a three week visit to each of the subpublisher's offices in London and on the European continent, I arranged for a roundtable promotional meeting, at the George V Hotel in Paris, of all the subpublisher's European branch managers, together with 90-year old Mr. Fred Day, his son Eddie Day, Director, and his son, David Day. The meeting afforded Wilson the opportunity to meet the heart and soul of Francis, Day & Hunter, as well as each branch manager prior to the promotional campaign to Copenhagen, Stockholm, London, Hamburg, Berlin, Rome, and Milan. Now, even-tually, Wilson's album didn't top the charts, but the meeting had the affect of satisfying Wilson that his subpublisher had the talent and enthusiasm to effectively represent his new compositions, as well as those in the *Sea of Tunes* catalog. Meanwhile, Francis, Day, knowing the importance of the Beach Boys catalog to their business, seized the opportunity to show Murry Wilson who they were and what they could do. There is simply no substitute for a face-to-face meeting to establish the *Good Vibrations* necessary for a successful subpublishing rela-tionship.

# APPENDIX TO CHAPTER 5
## SUBPUBLISHING AGREEMENTS

# FORM 5.1

## SUBPUBLISHING AGREEMENT I

### SUBPUBLISHING AGREEMENT

This Agreement made this ___ day of 2000, by and between _____ (hereinafter referred to as "Owner") and _____ (hereinafter referred to as "Publisher").

In consideration of the mutual promises herein contained, and other good and valuable consideration, the receipt of which is hereby acknowledged, the parties agree as follows:

1.    (a)    Owner hereby assigns to Publisher, only for the countries set forth in Schedule A annexed hereto (hereinafter collectively referred to as "the Territory"), the following rights in and to each musical composition owned or controlled by Owner and presently uncommitted for the Territory and in and to each musical composition the ownership or control of which shall be acquired by Owner during the term of this agreement in the ordinary course of business (excluding any so-called "catalog acquisitions") and which shall be uncommitted for the Territory at the time of acquisition (all such musical compositions hereinafter being referred to as "Compositions"):

(i)    The exclusive right to print, publish, vend, and cause to be printed, published and vended copies of the Compositions in the Territory, provided, however, that Owner reserves to itself the right to ship or license the shipment into the Territory of printed music embodying Compositions manufactured by Owner or by its subsidiaries, affiliates or licensees outside of the Territory, and Publisher shall have no right to receive any portion of any sums received by Owner on account of such importation or licensing;

(ii)     The exclusive right of public performance of the Compositions, for profit or otherwise (including broadcasting and television), and of licensing such rights in and for the Territory;

(iii)     The exclusive right, for sale within the Territory only, to grant non-exclusive licenses for the manufacture of parts serving to reproduce the Compositions and the making of mechanical, electrical and similar reproductions for phonograph records, audiotapes of any configuration or type, piano rolls, transcriptions or any other method of audio reproduction as yet known or unknown, in and for the Territory; and

(iv)     Upon securing the prior written consent of Owner, the non-exclusive right to grant non-exclusive synchronization licenses for the recording of the Compositions in and with motion pictures and television productions produced in the Territory, and of making copies of recordings thereof, and exporting such copies to all countries of the world. It is specifically understood and agreed that Publisher shall not share in any fees derived from the public performance outside of the Territory of any Compositions contained in a motion picture or television production produced in the Territory, and that all such fees shall be payable to and collected by Owner or its designees. Owner hereby reserves for itself the exclusive right to grant licenses for the entire world (including the Territory) for the synchronization and public performance of the Compositions with motion pictures or television productions produced outside the Territory, and Publisher shall not be entitled to share in any fees received by Owner in respect to such worldwide use.

(b)     Owner does not warrant or represent that it has or will have the right to assign to Publisher any or all of the rights above set forth in the case of each and every musical composition which it owns or controls or the ownership or control of which it shall acquire during the term hereof, but Owner undertakes to assign to Publisher for the Territory all of the aforesaid rights which it has or shall have the legal right to grant, subject, however, to any restrictions which may have been or which may be imposed upon Owner, and subject to the terms and conditions of this agreement.

2.   Owner hereby reserves unto itself:

(a)   All rights in the Compositions and the copyrights therein for the world outside the Territory, and all rights within the Territory other than as are specifically herein granted to Publisher;

(b)   The exclusive right to dramatize, worldwide, the Compositions, and to license the use and performance of such dramatic versions throughout the world;

(c)   The exclusive right to license worldwide uses of the titles of the Compositions; and

(d)   The exclusive right to make literary versions of the Compositions throughout the world, and to print, publish and vend such literary versions (as well as the dramatic versions aforementioned) throughout the world.

3.   Owner shall dispatch to Publisher, promptly after copies of each Composition shall have been printed or acquired by Owner, two (2) copies of any piano edition of any Composition, and two (2) copies of any other arrangement of any Composition printed or acquired by Owner.

4.   All monies payable to Publisher with respect to the exploitation of rights granted hereunder shall be referred to herein as "Publishing Income." Publisher agrees that it shall have the duty to collect and to be responsible for the collection of all Publishing Income payable within the Territory. Publisher shall pay to Owner the following royalties in respect of the Compositions upon the following terms and provisions:

(a)   Twelve and one-half percent (12.5%) of the marked or suggested retail selling price of each copy of each

Composition in any and every printed edition sold by Publisher
or its permitted subpublishers, on all gross sales (after deduction of actual returns), and that proportion of twelve and one-
half percent (12.5%) of the marked or suggested retail selling
price of each songbook, folio or similar compilation edition sold
by Publisher or its permitted subpublishers, on all gross sales
(after deduction of returns), which the number of Compositions
included in each edition shall bear to the total number of copyrighted compositions (including the Compositions) contained
therein for which a royalty is payable.

(b)      _____ percent (___%) of any and all gross receipts paid by printing licensees of Publisher or of its permitted
subpublishers for the use of each Composition in any piano
copies, songbooks, folios, books, newspapers, magazines or
other printed editions.

(c)      _____ percent (___%) of all monies paid by licensees of Publisher as royalties for the sale in the Territory of
phonograph records or other such devices embodying mechanical, electrical or other audio reproductions of the Compositions (as described in paragraph 1(c) above), with respect
to master audio recordings originally produced outside of the
Territory; provided, however, that if Publisher secures the release in the Territory during the term hereof of a master audio
recording of a Composition originally produced within the Territory (hereinafter referred to as a "Territory-originated cover
recording"), Publisher shall pay to Owner only _____ percent
(___%) of all monies paid by licensees of Publisher as royalties
with respect to such Territory-originated cover recording.

(d)      _____ percent (___%) of the publisher's share of
all public performance fees earned in the Territory with respect
to the Compositions, it being understood and agreed that the
Publisher shall authorize and direct the appropriate performance rights society in the Territory to pay to Publisher one hundred percent (100%) of said publisher's share and that Publisher
shall remit to Owner its aforesaid share thereof, together with a

statement signed by said performance rights society indicating in detail the titles of the Compositions and the amounts paid to Publisher on account of the public performance in the Territory of such Compositions.

(e) _____ percent (___%) of all gross monies paid by licensees of Publisher with respect to any other rights to the Compositions which are expressly assigned to Publisher hereunder.

(f) One hundred percent (100%) of all Publishing Income received by Publisher from any exploitation of rights in and to the Compositions other than those rights expressly set forth in paragraph 1 above. Nothing herein shall in any way increase or enlarge the rights granted to Publisher hereunder, which are solely as set forth in paragraph 1.

(g) Provided that Publisher performs each and all of its covenants, warranties and agreements hereunder, it shall be entitled to deduct and retain for its own benefit the balance of Publishing Income not payable hereunder to Owner.

(h) Publisher shall not license the mechanical, electrical or other reproduction of any Composition for phono-records or other such devices at a rate less than the highest prevailing rate in the Territory. Publisher shall not refuse to grant a mechanical license for a Composition at the prevailing rate in the Territory to any authorized manufacturer in the Territory of a recording of said Composition made by Owner or its parent, affiliate or subsidiary.

(i) Notwithstanding any provision to the contrary herein contained, Publisher shall collect royalties under sub-paragraph (c) above only with respect to phonograph records and other devices sold in the Territory, irrespective of whether such phonorecords or devices are manufactured within the Territory or outside of the Territory. Accordingly, Publisher shall not collect royalties hereunder with respect to phonograph records and other such devices manufactured within the Territory but sold outside of the Territory.

(j)    Notwithstanding anything to the contrary herein contained, all royalties or other monies payable to Owner hereunder are to be computed at the source from which the payments giving rise to such royalties or other monies are originally made, less only the actual commissions or collection fees (if any) retained by the performing rights society or agency and the mechanical royalty collection society or agency in the Territory.

(k)    In the event that Owner shall obtain the collection or administration rights for the Territory or any part thereof to any catalog or any specific musical compositions, under the terms providing for the retention by or the payment to Owner of a collection fee based upon collections at the source (excluding the deduction of any subpublisher's collection fees), under such terms as would make the inclusion hereunder of said catalog or musical compositions economically unfeasible for Owner, Publisher shall only be entitled under this agreement to one-half (1/2) of Owner's flat collection fee for the Territory, in lieu of any of the royalties or fees hereinabove provided for and shall remit the entire balance of such royalties or fees to Owner. Owner shall notify Publisher by written notice if any Compositions are covered by this subparagraph (k) and of the collection fee to which Owner is entitled.

(l)    In the event Publisher is prevented from paying any monies hereunder due to currency restrictions, Publisher shall so advise Owner by written notice accompanied by a copy of the applicable law, regulation or order (with an accurate English translation), and Owner shall have the right to elect to accept payment of such monies in foreign currency in a depository selected by Owner, and if Owner shall so elect, by written notice to Publisher, Publisher shall promptly deposit or cause to be deposited all such payable monies to the credit of Owner in such foreign currency and shall promptly give Owner written notice of said deposit. Payment so made to the depository so elected by Owner shall fulfill Publisher's obligations hereunder as to the monies so payable to Owner.

(m)    To the extent that authorization from Owner is necessary or desirable, Owner hereby grants to Publisher the right and authority within the Territory to collect from performing rights societies or agencies, mechanical rights licensing and/or mechanical royalty collection societies or agencies or any other persons, firms or corporations, unclaimed, unregistered or un-allocated receipts, bonuses or other sums distributable to Publisher by reason of seniority or membership in or affiliation with any such society or agency, or otherwise, not calculated on the basis of actual uses of the Compositions, to which the Publisher is or shall be entitled (hereinafter referred to as "accruals"). Publisher shall pay to Owner, with the accounting statements hereinafter provided for, seventy-five percent (75%) of that portion of such accruals which shall be calculated by multiplying the total amount of each such distribution of accruals to Publisher by a fraction, the numerator of which shall be the total public performance fee or mechanical royalty distribution, as the case may be, from such society, agency or other party, to Publisher which is allocable to identified uses of the Compositions during the relevant accounting period and the denominator of which shall be the total public performance fee or mechanical royalty distribution, as the case may be, from such society, agency or other party, to Publisher which is allocable to identified uses of any and all musical compositions controlled by Publisher, including the Compositions, during the relevant accounting period.

5.    (a)    Publisher shall forward to Owner two (2) copies of each printed edition of each Composition published in the Territory and two (2) copies of each phonograph record or other such device embodying a Territory-originated cover recording, all within one (1) month after publication of the printed edition or release of the phonograph record or other device.

(b)     Publisher shall have the right to make and publish new adaptations and arrangements of any Composition and to translate the lyrics thereof into any language of the Territory, but only with Owner's prior written approval thereof. Publisher shall be responsible for and shall pay to local adapters, arrangers, translators and lyricists any royalties or fees for such services, solely out of Publisher's share of Publishing Income. All new matter shall be the property of Owner and shall be copyrighted solely in the name of Owner or Owner's designee.

6.     True and correct accounts shall be kept by Publisher, and a statement of such accounts shall be delivered to Owner as of June 30th and December 31st of each year, within sixty (60) days after each of said dates, and all monies shown to be due thereunder shall be paid by Publisher to Owner, in United States currency, together with each statement. Each statement shall include the following information for each Composition: its title, the number of copies of each printed edition sold, the number of copies of each phonograph record or other such device sold embodying the Composition, the nature and amount of the Publishing Income received with respect thereto, and Owner's share thereof. Without limiting the generality of the foregoing, each statement shall account for and be accompanied by payment to Owner of all Owner's share of all Publishing Income received by Publisher and/or Publisher's affiliated or subsidiary companies during the preceding semiannual period. Prompt and accurate accountings and payments shall be the essence of this agreement, and failure to submit accurate and timely statements and payments shall entitle Owner to terminate this agreement by written notice to Publisher.

Publisher, in submitting accountings and payments to Owner, shall account and pay separately on each Composition, in accordance with the provisions of this agreement.

Publisher shall permit Owner and its representatives to visit Publisher's place of business, upon reasonable notice, during Publisher's usual business hours, for the purpose of inspecting and making copies or excerpts of all books, records and other documents relating to the Compositions, for the purpose of verifying royalty statements rendered by Publisher or which are delinquent under the terms hereof. Such inspections shall be at the expense of Owner unless a discrepancy of Five Hundred Dollars ($500.00) or more is discovered, in which event such expense shall be borne by Publisher.

7.    As a condition precedent to the grant of rights herein contained, all printed editions of the Compositions published in the Territory shall bear appropriate copyright notice in the name of the appropriate American publisher, as Owner shall designate, and same shall be printed at the bottom of the title page or first page of music of each such edition. Such edition shall be published in accordance with all applicable copyright laws, including the Berne Convention and the Universal Copyright Convention. Any printed edition embodying any Composition published in the Territory which does not conform to the aforesaid requirements shall be deemed to have been published without the authority of Owner, and shall constitute a breach by Publisher of this agreement. In addition, all printed editions shall bear the following legend at the bottom of the title page in easily readable type: "Authorized for sale only in [appropriate country(ies) of the Territory]."

8.    Owner hereby grants to Publisher the non-exclusive right to enforce and protect its rights in the Compositions in the Territory and, in Publisher's sole judgment, to join others as it deems advisable, as parties plaintiff or defendant, in any suits or proceedings in the name of Owner or Publisher, all at the expense of Publisher. Publisher further undertakes not only to protect and enforce the copyrights of the Compositions and any subsequent or derivative copyright produced therefrom, but also to undertake all necessary proceedings to prevent and restrain infringement of copyright in the Territory. In the event of any recovery, Publisher shall pay to Owner, after deducting

reasonable expenses of litigation, _____ percent (____%) of the resulting net proceeds. If, however, Publisher has not instituted suit within thirty (30) days after Owner's written request therefor, Owner shall have the right, exercisable any time thereafter, to institute suit in its own name and at its expense, in which case one hundred percent (100%) of the recovery shall be retained by Owner.

9.     This agreement shall be binding upon and shall inure to the benefit of the parties hereto and their respective successors and assigns, provided, however, that Publisher shall not have the right to assign any of its rights hereunder to any person, firm or corporation without Owner's prior written consent, except for its grant of subpublishing rights for portions of the Territory to its affiliates or subsidiaries. No assignment by Publisher shall relieve Publisher of its obligations hereunder.

10.     The term of this agreement shall commence as of _____ and shall continue through _____. At the expiration or termination of this agreement, all rights of any kind or nature granted to Publisher hereunder shall automatically revert and be the sole and exclusive property of Owner without formality or execution of any documents. Notwithstanding the foregoing, upon the expiration of this agreement (but not upon any termination of this agreement by Owner for good cause), Publisher shall have the right for six (6) months thereafter to continue to collect and disburse, in accordance with the provisions hereof, the Publishing Income which shall have been earned during the term of this agreement but which shall not have become payable until after the expiration of this agreement.

11.     All notices to be given to Owner hereunder and all statements and payments to be submitted to Owner hereunder shall be addressed to it at the address set forth below or at such other address as Owner shall designate to Publisher in writing from time to time. All notices to be given to Publisher hereunder shall be addressed to it at the address set forth below or at such other address as Publisher shall designate to Owner in writing from time to time.

*Owner* *Publisher*

All notices shall be in writing and shall either be served by registered airmail or by cable or telex, all charges prepaid. The date of service shall be deemed to be the date of deposit in the post office or the date of deposit in a cable office, all charges prepaid. A courtesy copy of each notice to Owner shall be sent to Flywheel, Shyster, & Flywheel, 100 Beverly Drive, Beverly Hills, California 91210, U. S. A., Attention _____.

12.    Each party hereto warrants and represents that it has the right to enter into this agreement, to grant the rights herein granted by it, and to perform all of its obligations herein set forth, and covenants and agrees that it will perform all of its obligations hereunder.

13.    The parties hereto shall execute any further documents and do all acts necessary to fully effectuate the terms and provisions of this agreement.

14.    If either party hereto institutes any action or proceeding against the other under or in connection with this agreement, the prevailing party in such action or proceeding shall be entitled to reasonable attorneys' fees and court costs.

15.    Publisher shall indemnify, defend and hold Owner harmless from and against any liability, loss, damage, costs or expenses, including reasonable attorneys' fees, paid or incurred by Owner by reason of any breach or alleged breach by Publisher of any warranties, representations, covenants or agreements by Publisher hereunder. Any amount due pursuant to this paragraph 15 shall be paid within ten (10) days following Publisher's receipt of notice demanding such payment, and failure to make such payment within such ten-day period shall constitute a material default by Publisher and Owner shall have the right to terminate this agreement for cause pursuant to paragraph 19, below.

16.    This agreement sets forth the entire agreement between the parties hereto with respect to the subject matter

hereof. No modification, amendment, waiver, termination or discharge of this agreement or of any provisions hereof shall be effective unless confirmed by a written instrument signed by a duly authorized officer of the party sought to be bound. No waiver of any provision of this agreement or of any default hereunder shall affect the waiving party's rights thereafter to enforce such provision or to exercise any right or remedy in the event of any other default, whether or not similar.

17.     This agreement shall not be binding upon Owner until signed by a duly authorized officer of Publisher and countersigned by a duly authorized officer of Owner. This agreement shall be deemed to have been made in the State of California, and its validity, construction and effect shall be governed by the laws of the State of California applicable to agreements wholly performed therein. If any provision of this agreement shall be declared invalid (other than any provision with respect to the payment of monies hereunder to Owner), same shall not affect the validity of the remaining provisions hereof. The venue for any action, suit or proceeding brought by either party against the other with respect to this agreement shall be in the County of Los Angeles, State of California, and both parties hereby consent to the personal jurisdiction of the courts of the State of California. Service of process may be made by registered or certified mail addressed to the defendant in accordance with the notice provisions hereof, and the time to respond to such process shall be thirty (30) days after the date of mailing thereof.

18.     No third party shall be deemed to be or is intended by the parties hereto to be a third party beneficiary of this agreement.

19.     In the event Publisher becomes insolvent, or any insolvency, bankruptcy or composition proceeding is commenced by or against Publisher and is not dismissed within thirty (30) days, or in the event Publisher makes or attempts to make an assignment for the benefit of creditors or the equivalent thereof, this agreement shall automatically be deemed terminated by

Owner for good cause. In the event Publisher shall fail to account and make payments hereunder in accordance with the terms and provisions hereof, Owner shall have the right, in addition to its other rights and remedies at law or otherwise, to terminate this agreement for good cause, as provided in paragraph 6 above. In the event Publisher shall fail to perform or comply with any other material obligation hereunder and Owner shall have given written notice to Publisher thereof and such failure shall not have been cured within thirty (30) days after such notification, Owner shall have the right, in addition to its other rights and remedies at law or otherwise, to terminate this agreement for good cause by giving Publisher written notice of its election to do so. Upon any such termination as above described, all rights of any kind or nature granted to Publisher hereunder shall revert to and be the sole and exclusive property of Owner, free and clear of any rights, claims or demands on the part of Publisher, its successors or assigns, without in any way affecting the rights of Owner.

20. In the event Publisher shall be obligated by the laws of the Territory to declare and withhold income, corporate or other similar taxes from royalties or other monies payable to Owner hereunder, Publisher shall furnish to Owner, with each accounting statement, a certificate in the form of an affidavit, setting forth the amount of tax which shall have been withheld, the rate of tax and any other necessary information which shall enable Owner, upon presentation of such certificate, to obtain income tax credit from the United States Internal Revenue Service for the tax so withheld.

# FORM 5.2

## SUBPUBLISHING AGREEMENT II

(Form For Use by Major U.S. Publisher
Acquiring International Publishing Rights)

Dated: As of _____, 20__

Gentlemen:

The following, when signed by you and by us, will constitute the terms and conditions of the subpublishing agreement between you and us concerning the subject matter.

1.   *Term:* _____ (___) years, from _____, 20__ to _____, 20__

2.   *Territory:* The world excluding the United States of America and Canada.

3.   *Scope of Agreement:*

(a)   (i)   We will have exclusive subpublishing within the Territory during the Term of your interest (including the right to collect all income earned but not yet collected, i.e., "pipeline" earnings) in the subject compositions listed on the annexed Schedule "A" (the "Existing SCs") as well as all songs written or co-written during the Term by _____ (but in the case of co-written compositions, our administration shall only extend to your fractional interest, calculated [at a minimum] by multiplying 100% by a fraction, the numerator of which is 1 and the denominator of which is the total numbers of contributing writers) or otherwise now or hereafter owned or controlled directly or indirectly by you or your music publishing designee or any other persons or entity directly or indirectly controlled by you (collectively referred to below as "Subject Compositions" or "SCs").

(ii)    The Term as to each SC embodied on a recording produced, recorded and released commercially within the Territory ("Local Cover Recording") will continue as to such SC until the end of the accounting period during which occurs the second anniversary of the expiration of the Term.

(b)    Although it is intended that we and our subsidiaries, affiliates and licensees have the fullest possible rights to administer and exploit the SCs, we shall not do any of the following without your prior written consent in each instance (which consent, unless expressly provided otherwise, may be withheld by you for any reason):

(i)    Authorize any change in the English-language title and/or lyric of any SC, alter the harmonic structure of any SC, or alter the melody of any SC (except insubstantial changes necessary to accommodate the syllabic requirements of foreign languages);

(ii)    Issue a mechanical license for the use of any SC at less than the prevailing statutory or society rate, except in connection with those types of uses for which reduced-rate licenses are customarily granted in the country in question (consent not to be unreasonably withheld);

(iii)    Authorize the use of the title of any SC as the title of a play, film or TV program, or authorize the dramatization of any SC (consent not to be unreasonably withheld).

4.    *Collection and Division of Income*:

(a)    We will be entitled to collect (and we shall employ best efforts consistent with our reasonable business judgment to collect) pre-Term earnings in respect of SCs, as well as all writer/publisher income (except the writer's share of public performances collected by societies) generated by SCs within the

Territory during the Term and during the Local Cover Recording period, which is collected during the Term (and, if applicable, the Local Cover Recording retention period) or within _____ years thereafter; *provided*, that in the event you receive any writer/publisher income to which we are entitled hereunder, you agree in each instance to remit such income to us, together with an accounting, within 10 days of your receipt thereof.

(b)    (i)    Net Income (as defined below) from SCs shall be divided 25% to us, 75% to you (as writer/publisher royalties, in each instance), except with respect to the publisher's share of public performance income as to which the split will be 50% to us, 50% to you, and with respect to mechanicals from Local Cover Recordings, as to which the split will be 40% to us, 60% to you.

(ii)    "Net Income" shall mean all amounts received by us (or credited to our account in reduction of an advance) all calculations to be "at source," country-by-country, from licensees and performing and mechanical rights societies ("gross receipts") after deduction of local society fees and reasonable out-of-pocket collection costs and litigation expenses incurred in the collection of sums due for the uses of the SCs but without deduction therefrom of any portion of said sums or fees paid to, received or retained by our foreign affiliates, subpublishers, licensees or agents and without reduction by intermediate distribution.

(iii)    With respect to printed materials sold in the Territory, we shall pay to you 12.5% of the marked or suggested retail list price (or the price deemed to be the local equivalent, in any country in which there are no marked or suggested retail list prices) ("List") on all copies sold, paid for, and not returned (prorated, where less than 100% of a specific composition is a SC). Where an edition does not consist exclusively of SCs, the above royalty shall be prorated in the same ratio as the number of SCs bears to the total number of royalty-bearing compositions included in such edition. Our sell-off period with respect to printed materials embodying a specific SC shall be one (1) year following the expiration of our subpublishing rights hereunder in respect of such SC, as to sheet music, "matching folios" and "personality folios," and until stocks are exhausted (including copies sold to customers and subsequently returned) as to other editions.

(iv) In the case of amounts received by our subpublishers and licensees from third-party print licensees, your share shall be 50%.

5. As advances recoupable from your share of Net Income hereunder we shall make the following advances/payments (as the same may be reduced by any withholding which may be required by the rules and regulations of any taxing authority having jurisdiction):

(a) Upon receipt of duly countersigned copies of this letter, $_____.

(b) If the foregoing advances have been recouped (including a reasonable estimate of "pipeline" monies collected by our foreign music publishing subsidiaries but not yet reported to us by them) as of _____, 20__, a further $ _____.

6. (a) We will account to you (and make payment where appropriate) within 60 days following the end of each semi-annual period. However, if the amount due for a specific statement is less than $50., payment may be deferred until the aggregate amount due to you exceeds $50.

(b) We will only be required to account and pay with respect to amounts actually received by us in the U.S. (or credited to our account in reduction of a previous advance received by us in the U.S.).

(c) (i) You (or a certified public accountant on your behalf) shall have the right to audit our books and records as to each statement for a period of 2 years after such statement is received (or deemed received as provided below). Legal action with respect to a specific accounting statement or the accounting period to which such statement relates shall be barred if not commenced in a court of competent jurisdiction within 3 years after such statement is received (or deemed received as provided below).

(ii)    For the purposes of calculating the time periods for audit and suit, a statement shall be deemed to have been rendered when due, unless we receive notice of nonreceipt within 30 days following the due date. However, failure to give us such notice shall not affect your right thereafter to receive such statement (as well as any related payment).

(d)    In "blocked currency" situations, we shall not be required to pay you until the blockage shall have been removed, but if requested to do so, we shall deposit blocked currency royalties in the local currency in a depository of your choice. The exchange rates used by third parties in accounting to us shall be used by us in accountings hereunder.

(e)    All payments hereunder shall be subject to all applicable taxation statutes, regulations and treaties.

7.    (a)    By your signature below, and in each instance in which SCs are delivered to us, you warrant and represent (i) that you have the right to do so and that we have thereby acquired all rights necessary to administer each SC under the terms and conditions of this agreement and to collect all income generated thereby (without reduction due to third-party rights), (ii) that such SC does not infringe any third party's rights, including but not limited to such third party's copyright, trademark, servicemark, or right of privacy or publicity, and (iii) that the SC is not defamatory.

(b)    By his assent hereto, _____ warrants and represents that there is presently in effect an agreement between you and _____ granting to you all rights necessary for you to license to us all rights referred to in paragraphs 3(a) and 4(a) above. You will account to _____ for his writer's share of any monies paid to you by us hereunder, and _____ will look solely to you for such payment.

8. (a) Each party will indemnify the other party against any loss or damage (including court costs and reasonable attorneys' fees) due to a breach of this agreement by that party which results in a judgment against the other party or which is settled with the other party's prior written consent (not to be unreasonably withheld). In addition, you will indemnify us without regard to judgment or settlement to the extent of the deductible under our errors-and-omissions policy (which, in our case, is presently $50,000. per claim). Each party is entitled to be notified of any action against the other brought with respect to any SC, and to participate in the defense thereof by counsel of its choice, at its sole cost and expense. In the event that one of us refuses to approve a settlement which the other party considers reasonable, the party refusing its consent shall assume the further defense of the subject claim, action or proceeding.

(b) If a claim is made against us, we may withhold a reasonable amount from monies due to or to become due to you, but we will refund it (together with interest on the amount released at the regular savings and loan passbook interest rate prevailing in Los Angeles from time to time during the period of withholding) if (and to the extent that) suit is not brought with respect to that sum within 1 year thereafter, and we won't withhold if you provide us with a satisfactory commercial surety bond.

(c) Neither party will be deemed in breach unless the other party gives notice and the notified party fails to cure within 30 days after receiving notice.

9. Notices shall be by certified (return receipt requested) or registered mail or telex to you and us (to the attention of our Senior Vice President of Legal and Business Affairs) at the above addresses or any other addresses the parties designate

by notice in like manner. Statements (and payments, if applicable) shall be sent by ordinary mail. If the party's consent is required, it shall not be unreasonably withheld (unless expressly provided otherwise herein) and shall be deemed given unless the notified party gives notice of nonconsent within 15 days after receipt of notice requesting consent. A courtesy copy of each notice to you shall be sent to _____.

10.    *Law and Forum*: This Agreement has been entered into in, and is to be interpreted in accordance with the laws of, the State of California. All actions or proceedings seeking the interpretation and/or enforcement of this Agreement shall be brought only in the State or Federal Courts located in Los Angeles County, all parties hereby submitting themselves to the jurisdiction of such courts for such purpose. You shall at all times maintain a California agent for service of process, which agent, until further notice (in the manner prescribed in paragraph 9) will be _____.

Very truly yours,

_____

By: _____

_____

Senior Vice President
Legal and Business Affairs

*Agreed and Accepted:*

_____

By: _____

Fed. ID #: _____

The undersigned hereby assents to the execution of the foregoing agreement and agrees to be bound by the provisions of paragraphs 3(a)(i), 4(a) and 7(b) thereof.

Agreement dated as of _____, 20\_\_

_____        Re: _____

_____

# Form 5.3

## SUBPUBLSIHING AGREEMENT III

(Alternative Form For Use by Major U.S. Publisher
Acquiring International Publishing Rights)

SUBPUBLISHING AGREEMENT

Effective _____, this agreement is made and entered into by and between:

(hereinafter referred to as "OWNER")

-and-

(hereinafter referred to as "SUBPUBLISHER")

NOW, THEREFORE, in consideration of the mutual terms and conditions herein contained, the parties hereto agree as follows:

1. <u>DEFINITIONS</u>

(a)    The term "Licensed Territory", as that term is used herein, is defined and set forth in the attached Schedule "A", which is made a part of this agreement.

(b)    The term "Compositions", as that term is used herein, is defined and set forth in the attached Schedule "B", which is made a part of this agreement.

(c)     The term "Printed Music", as that term is used herein, is defined as and includes copies of each or any of the Compositions whether copied, printed, lithographed, photo-offset, reproduced by xerography, by thermal processing, or by any other means of reproduction now known or hereafter devised.

(d)     The term "Mechanical Rights", as that term is used herein, is defined as the right to manufacture parts serving to produce and reproduce the Compositions and to make mechanical, electrical, magnetic or optical reproductions thereof on records, prerecorded tapes, tape cassettes and piano rolls, or to make reproductions by any other method or on any other media now known or hereafter devised. Subpublisher shall have the right to collect all mechanical income derived from Sales and Uses of the Compositions on all records sold within the Licensed Territory, regardless of where such records are manufactured.

(e)     The term "Performing Rights", as that term is used herein, is defined as and includes the right to perform the Compositions in and for the general public, whether in live performance, by radio or television broadcasting, or otherwise.

(f)     The term "Limited Synchronization Rights", as that term is used herein, is defined as the right to record, reproduce, perform, represent and exhibit the Compositions in, or in connection with, radio and television productions produced in the Licensed Territory, and upon securing the prior written consent of Owner, the right to record, reproduce, perform, represent and exhibit the Compositions in, or in connection with theatrical motion pictures produced in the Licensed Territory, and of making copies of the recordings thereof, and exporting such copies to all countries of the world.

(g)     The term "Sales and Uses", as that term is used herein, is defined as any and all means of use or exploitation of the Compositions and any and all rights pertaining thereto, and includes, but is not limited to, the sale or lease of Printed Music, the sale, use or license of Mechanical Rights, the sale, use or license of Performing Rights, and the sale, use or license of Limited Synchronization Rights.

(h)    The term "Income", as that term is used herein, is defined as and includes any and all gross payments, royalties, fees, income, receipts, revenue, collections, monies and other considerations of any and every kind derived or payable by reason of any and all Sales and Uses of any of the Compositions.

(i)    The term "All Income Received", as used in Schedule "C", attached hereto, is defined as and includes Income received, less taxes, if any, after deducting customary service charges, if any, of the respective Mechanical Rights societies or Performing Rights societies; such deduction shall be made only in the event similar charges are made with respect to Subpublisher's own catalog or other catalogs administered by Subpublisher.

## 2.    APPOINTMENT OF SUBPUBLISHER:

(a)    (i)    Owner hereby appoints Subpublisher as its sole and exclusive sub-publisher throughout the "Licensed Territory", for the purpose of collecting all Income from Sales and Uses of the Compositions.

(ii)    Owner grants to Subpublisher the right to collect, on owner's behalf, all Income heretofore unpaid, and now payable and all Income which becomes payable during the term of this agreement, from the date of the original copyrights of the Compositions to the effective date hereof and from all Sales and Uses of the Compositions, subject to accounting hereunder.

(b)    Notwithstanding the above, Owner shall have the right, at any time during the term of this agreement or during any extensions thereof, whether under Section 10 hereof or otherwise, to elect to collect its share of income directly from Performing Rights societies and Mechanical Rights societies or indirectly through any other agency appointed by Owner.

(c)     Subpublisher agrees that it shall have the duty to collect and to be responsible for the collection of all Income due owner from all Sales and Uses whatsoever of the Compositions throughout the Licensed Territory; that it shall use its best efforts and due diligence in promoting and procuring such Sales and Uses; and that it will obtain therefor the maximum payment consistent with good business judgment.

(d)     Subject to any contractual restrictions which have or may hereafter be imposed upon owner by Owner's contracting parties (notice of which shall be given by owner to Subpublisher) ("Contractual Restrictions"), Subpublisher shall have the following rights with respect to the Compositions:

(i)     Except for the reservation to owner set forth in 7(h) hereof, the exclusive right to print, publish and sell or lease Printed Music and to authorize others to print, publish and sell or lease Printed Music in any and all parts of the Licensed Territory in the form of sheet music, arrangements, song books, albums, folios or educational works as those terms are known and understood in the music publishing business.

(ii)     The exclusive right to license Performing Rights within and for the Licensed Territory.

(iii)     The exclusive right to license Mechanical Rights within and for the Licensed Territory.

(iv)     The non-exclusive right to grant non-exclusive licenses for the use of Limited Synchronization Rights within and for the Licensed Territory.

(v)     The right to make or have made, translations of the lyrics or new lyric versions of the Compositions into the languages of the Licensed Territory other than English, and the right to make or have made, band, choral, orchestral, or other arrangements of the Compositions.

3.   TERM:

The initial period of the term of this agreement shall commence as of _____ and shall continue through
_____.

4.   ADDITIONAL OBLIGATIONS OF OWNER:

Upon request, Owner will furnish Subpublisher with copyright information on each of the Compositions, including:

(a)   Full title of work;

(b)   Date of first publication;

(c)   Full name of composer;

(d)   Full name of author;

(e)   Full name of arranger, if work in its original form is in the Public Domain.

If, after request, owner does not furnish copyright information as to any of the Compositions, or should a deficiency appear in owner's title or right to grant rights to Subpublisher with respect to any of the Compositions, Subpublisher will be relieved of all responsibility for collection of Income with respect to such Composition(s) as its sole remedy hereunder, notwithstanding Section 5(a) hereof.

5.   WARRANTIES:

(a)   By Owner: Owner represents and warrants that it owns or controls such rights in the Compositions as are granted hereunder to Subpublisher, and that it will obtain those rights with respect to all future works, which are required by Subpublisher to exercise its rights and perform its duties hereunder.

(b)     By Subpublisher:

(i)     Subpublisher represents and warrants that it has not made and does not contemplate making any assignment for the benefit of creditors, that no bankruptcy or other proceeding based upon insolvency is pending or threatened against it, and that there are no impediments, agreements or litigation, actual or threatened, which would prevent or impair Subpublisher from performing its duties hereunder.

(ii)     Subpublisher represents and warrants that it now is and that it will remain, during the term hereof and extensions thereto, a member in good standing of all necessary Performing Rights societies and Mechanical Rights societies and that it knows of no impediments or charges, actual or threatened, against it with respect to said societies which might prevent or impair Subpublisher from performing its duties hereunder.

## 6.     PAYMENTS:

(a)     Subpublisher shall pay to Owner the percentages of Income specified in Schedule "C", which is attached hereto and made a part of this agreement. With respect to those Compositions, if any, for which Owner has administration or collection rights for the Licensed Territory under terms providing for a "Flat Collection Fee" then, in lieu of the royalties set forth in Schedule "C", Subpublisher shall pay to Owner one hundred percent (100%) of the gross monies or other considerations received by Subpublisher in respect to such Compositions, less an amount equal to one-half (1/2) of the collection fee to which Owner is entitled. owner shall give Subpublisher written notice of which Compositions, if any, are covered by this subparagraph and of the collection fee to which Owner is entitled.

(b)     Subpublisher shall pay to Owner an amount equal to One Hundred Percent (100%) of All Income Received by Subpublisher from all Sales and Uses of the Compositions other than those Sales and Uses with respect to which Subpublisher is commissioned herein. The above is not intended to enlarge or increase the rights granted to Subpublisher hereunder, which rights are set forth in detail in ¶ 2 of this agreement.

(c)     All payments to Publisher by Subpublisher hereunder shall be subject to all applicable taxation statutes, regulations and treaties.

## 7.     RESERVATIONS BY OWNER:

Owner reserves to itself and its successors and assigns, and Subpublisher shall not be entitled to, nor have any right whatever in any fees, payments or other compensation received by Owner with respect to:

(a)     All rights not expressly granted to Subpublisher hereunder, and all income derived from sales or exploitation of such rights.

(b)     Any and all copyrights in the Compositions and in any adaptations, arrangements, translations and new lyric versions thereof, throughout the world, and in "Similar Rights", as that term is defined hereinafter, together with all rights existing under such copyrights throughout the Licensed Territory, other than those which are expressly granted herein to Subpublisher.

(c)     The exclusive right to dramatize the Compositions in live performance or in any recorded medium and to license the use and performance of such dramatic versions throughout the world.

(d)     The exclusive right to license the use of the titles of the Compositions separate and apart from the Compositions throughout the world.

(e)     The exclusive right to make literary versions of the Compositions and to print, publish and sell such literary versions thereof throughout the world.

(f)     The exclusive right to grant licenses throughout the world for any form of use (whether now known or hereafter devised) of the Compositions or any part thereof for or in connection with purposes of trade, advertisements, commercials, or merchandising of any goods, products, wares or services of any and every kind, except that Subpublisher may advertise or grant licenses for the purpose of advertising sales of printed music, sound recordings or other Sales or Uses of Compositions, with respect to which Subpublisher is commissioned herein.

(g)     Except for the Limited Synchronization Rights set forth in ¶ 2 (d) (iv) above, the sole and exclusive right to grant licenses for the entire world (including the Licensed Territory) for the synchronization and public performance of the Compositions with theatrical motion pictures or television productions produced outside of the Licensed Territory, and Subpublisher shall not be entitled to share in any fees received by Owner in respect to such worldwide uses, except that Subpublisher shall have the right to collect and receive from the Performing Rights society in the Licensed Territory all performing fees earned by the Compositions during the term hereof from public performances in the Licensed Territory of theatrical motion pictures with sound accompaniment, subject to Subpublisher's payment to owner of the royalties specified in ¶ 6 and Schedule "C" hereof.

(h)     The licensing of Performing Rights in United States-based ships and airplanes and the right to import or license the importation into the Licensed Territory, of sound recordings and/or Printed Music manufactured by Owner or its subsidiaries or affiliates in the United States.

8.     ADDITIONAL RIGHTS, RESTRICTIONS AND OBLIGATIONS OF SUBPUBLISHER:

(a)   (i)   All payments due Owner hereunder shall be based upon all Sales and Uses of the Compositions throughout the Licensed Territory and except as provided herein, in ¶ i (i) hereof, shall not be reduced or diminished by reason of any charges whatsoever.

(ii)   Without limiting the generality of ¶ (a) above, Subpublisher shall be responsible for, and shall pay to, all local adaptors, composers, arrangers, translators and lyricists, any royalties, fees or any other compensation due, out of Subpublisher's share of income hereunder, however, Subpublisher shall, upon the request of owner, furnish copies of any and all contracts or other arrangements requiring the payment of compensation to said local adaptors, composers, arrangers, translators and lyricists.

(iii)   Should the obligations to pay royalties, fees or other compensation to local adaptors, composers, arrangers, translators or lyricists extend beyond the term of this agreement, such obligation may only be incurred with the written consent of Owner.

(b)   It is expressly understood that Subpublisher may publish, sell and use the Compositions acquired hereunder in the Licensed Territory only and, to the extent permitted by law, will not export nor authorize others to export any copies or material therefrom.

(c)   To the extent permitted by law, upon all Printed Music published and distributed in the Licensed Territory, there will be printed at the bottom of the first page of music an inscription (in addition to the proper copyright notice of the copyright owner) the words:

> "It shall be unlawful to publish, sell or distribute this copy outside of (the Licensed Territory)."

or some comparable inscription which shall have been approved by Owner in writing.

(d)     Subpublisher agrees, not later than thirty (30) days after each and every publication by Subpublisher under this agreement, to notify Owner in writing of such publication and to send six (6) copies of each published edition to owner.

(e)     Subpublisher agrees, not later than thirty (30) days after the release of a local cover recording of any of the Compositions, to notify Owner in writing of such release and distribution and to send six (6) copies of each recording released to Owner.

(f)     Subpublisher agrees that it will promptly register or cause to be registered each and all of the Compositions with each of the local Mechanical Rights societies and Performing Rights societies in all parts of the Licensed Territory, and Subpublisher shall be responsible for collection with respect thereto of uncollected income accruing to Owner both prior to and during the term of this agreement.

(g)     To the full extent required to protect Owner's rights in the Compositions and Owner's copyrights therein, and all similar or equivalent rights and protection in those parts of the Licensed Territory or any other countries or areas to which any printed publications of any of the Compositions may be imported pursuant to the terms hereof which do not have copyright as such (hereinafter referred to as "Similar Rights"), Subpublisher shall imprint or cause to be imprinted on each copy of every printed publication of any of the Compositions hereunder, proper copyright and like notices and do all other acts necessary to obtain, preserve and protect Owner's copyrights and Similar Rights in the Compositions in full compliance with all formalities of all applicable laws, treaties, conventions and the like in the name of Owner or such other name or names as Owner may direct by notice to Subpublisher from time to time; and in all countries and areas where Subpublisher or any of its agents sells or publishes any copies of the Compositions, Subpublisher shall obtain copyrights and Similar Rights therein in the name of Owner, or such other name or names as owner may direct by notice to Subpublisher from time to time, by doing all necessary acts and complying with all formalities under all applicable laws, treaties, conventions and the like, including without limitation, simultaneous first publication whenever and wherever necessary to obtain, preserve and protect Owner's rights in the Compositions and Owner's copyrights and Similar Rights thereto. Subpublisher understands and agrees that all of its rights and licenses hereunder are conditioned upon its compliance with all of said notice provisions and other formalities of all applicable laws, treaties, conventions and the like, and that any publication of any of the Compositions (in any form, including without limitation, arrangements or versions of the same) without such copyright or like notice, or without compliance with all such notice provisions and other formalities shall be without the authority of the copyright proprietor, author or owner thereof.

(h)    Subpublisher agrees that all new arrangements and new or translated lyrics of Owner's Compositions published by Subpublisher shall be copyrighted in the name of Owner, and shall be the sole and exclusive property of Owner, free from royalty obligation or other restriction, except as may be approved in writing by Owner.

(i)    Owner hereby grants to Subpublisher the non-exclusive right to enforce and protect its rights in the Compositions in the Licensed Territory and to join others as it deems advisable, as parties plaintiff or defendant, in any suits or proceedings in the name of Owner or Subpublisher, all at the expense of Subpublisher, and the right to enter into settlements and compromises in connection therewith; provided, however, that Subpublisher shall first obtain owner's written approval and consent with respect to any such settlement or compromise. Subpublisher further undertakes not only to protect and enforce the copyrights of the Compositions and any subsequent or derivative copyrights produced therefrom, but also to undertake all necessary proceedings to prevent and restrain infringement of copyright in the Licensed Territory. In the event of any recovery, Subpublisher shall pay to Owner, after deducting reasonable expenses of litigation _____ of the resulting net proceeds. If, however, Subpublisher has not instituted suit within thirty (30) days after owner's written request therefor, owner shall have the right, exercisable any time thereafter, to institute suit in its own name and at its expense, in which case one hundred percent (100%) of the recovery shall be retained by Owner.

## 9.   TERMINATION:

If Subpublisher shall make any assignment for the benefit of creditors, or if a bankruptcy proceeding under any provision of any bankruptcy act or any insolvency statute shall be filed by or against Subpublisher, or in the event of any breach or default hereunder by Subpublisher, Owner shall have, in addition to any and all other available rights and remedies, which rights and remedies shall be cumulative, the right to terminate this agreement, and upon such termination all rights hereunder shall revert to Owner; provided, however, that subsequent to any such termination Subpublisher shall continue to account and pay to owner as provided herein owner's share of all Income then due owner or in the possession or control of Subpublisher or thereafter coming into the possession or control of Subpublisher in respect to Subpublisher's activities in connection with the Compositions prior to such termination, but Subpublisher shall not continue to collect any further Income after such termination unless expressly authorized by Owner to do so in writing, in which event Subpublisher shall so continue and all such Income shall be set aside by Subpublisher in an express trust account clearly segregated and designated as being for the benefit of owner and shall not be commingled with any other funds. Upon expir-ation or termination of this agreement, Owner shall have the right immediately to constitute and appoint any other agent(s) and/or publisher(s) in or for the Licensed Territory. This agreement shall forthwith cease and terminate in the event that Subpublisher shall go into liquidation, either voluntary or involuntary.

## 10.    RIGHTS ON TERMINATION:

Provided Subpublisher has performed in accordance with all of the terms and conditions required to be performed by Subpublisher hereunder (and subject to any Contractual Restrictions):

(a)    (i)    As to Printed Music distributed commercially by Subpublisher during the term hereof in adaptations, arrangements or translations thereof in the Licensed Territory, Subpublisher shall have the non-exclusive right to continue to sell off (subject to accountings hereunder) copies on hand at the expiration of the term hereof for a period up to six (6) months thereafter ("Sell-Off Period").

(ii)    Subpublisher shall not print, reprint or otherwise reproduce copies of said Printed Music after the date of expiration of the term hereof or after the termination of this agreement under Section 9, above.

(iii)    Within forty-five (45) days after the end of said Sell-Off Period, Subpublisher shall render separate final accounting statements to Owner computing payments of all monies, as hereinabove provided, in respect to the sell-off; and such statements shall be accompanied by payment to Owner of all monies due Owner in respect to the sell-off.

(b)    As to Income from rights granted herein not covered by sub-paragraph (a) of this ¶ 10, Subpublisher shall have the right to collect (subject to accountings hereunder) such Income accrued up to the expiration of the term hereof, and actually collected by Subpublisher for a period up to six (6) months from the date of expiration of the term hereof.

(c)    It is further agreed that in the event of the termination of Subpublisher's rights under this agreement pursuant to ¶ 9 hereof, Subpublisher shall collect (subject to accountings hereunder) only Income for which payment to Owner is specified herein as shall have been actually received by Subpublisher pursuant to this agreement up to and including the date of such termination and Owner shall have the right to collect and receive One Hundred Percent (100%) of all Income not received by Subpublisher up to the date of such termination under ¶ 9 hereof.

(d) (i) In any event, at the termination of the rights granted Subpublisher herein, whether by reason of expiration of term under ¶ 3 hereof or by reason of prior termination under ¶ 9 hereof, all of said rights shall revert to Owner free from any and all encumbrances, automatically and without formality and without any requirements to execute any documents or assignments. Further, Subpublisher shall send to Owner all copyright data, correspondence, statistical and financial data relative to each and all of the Compositions.

(ii) In addition, but without prejudice to any other rights owner may have under this or any other agreement, Subpublisher agrees that upon the termination of the right to produce printed editions hereunder, all or any of the plates, negatives and any and all materials pertaining to publication shall, at Owner's option; either

(aa) be destroyed in the presence of one of Owner's duly authorized representatives; or

(bb) be delivered to Owner or its designees in the Licensed Territory at Owner's cost and upon the payment to Subpublisher of (1) actual cost in case of plates, negatives and other such production materials (2) fifteen percent (15%) of MRSP (which Owner shall retain for its own account) of unsold copies without obligation by Subpublisher for royalties in connection with such sale, or for royalties in respect of editions subsequently printed or reproduced from such materials (which shall be Owner's sole responsibility).

In connection with such option, Subpublisher agrees to furnish to owner or to its designees an accurate inventory of materials on hand and actual costs thereof within thirty (30) days after such termination.

(iii)    Subpublisher further agrees that upon the termination of the Sell-Off Period set forth in ¶ 10(a) (i) above, any and all copies of music published hereunder shall, at owner's option; either

(aa)    be destroyed in the presence of one of Owner's duly authorized representatives; or

(bb)    be delivered to owner or its designees in the Licensed Territory at owner's cost and upon the payment to Subpublisher or actual cost in case of plates, negatives and other such production materials (2) fifteen percent (15%) of MRSP (which Owner shall retain for its own account) of unsold copies without obligation by Subpublisher for royalties in connection with such sale, or for royalties in respect of editions subsequently printed or reproduced from such materials (which shall be Owner's sole responsibility).

In connection with such option, Subpublisher agrees to furnish to Owner or its designees an accurate inventory of copies of music on hand and actual costs thereof within thirty (30) days after such termination.

## 11.    STATEMENTS AND ACCOUNTING

(a)    (i)    (aa)    Subpublisher agrees to furnish to Owner statements of income in the form set forth below, together with payment in accordance therewith, for the periods ending June 30th and December 31st of each year, within sixty (60) days after such dates, all subject to deductions for income tax, if any, required to be paid for owner's account.

(bb)    Notwithstanding the foregoing, however, in any instance in which Owner notifies Subpublisher that a specific agreement requires earlier payment (e.g., where, under a specific agreement, monies collected by Subpublisher are deemed received by owner in the accounting period during which such monies are collected by Subpublisher), Subpublisher shall employ best efforts to remit Owner's share of the subject monies as promptly as possible after the close of the applicable accounting period.

(ii)     It is expressly agreed that any tax required to be withheld or paid upon earned income shall not be deducted unless a Certificate of Deduction and Withholding shall accompany the statement rendered to Owner and unless, upon payment of such tax, there is sent to Owner a photostatic copy of the governmental receipt establishing the payment thereof. In the event Subpublisher is prevented from paying any monies hereunder due to currency restrictions, Subpublisher shall so advise owner by written notice, and owner shall have the right to elect to accept payment of such monies in foreign currency in a depository selected by Owner, and if owner shall so elect, by written notice to Subpublisher, Subpublisher shall promptly deposit or cause to be deposited all such payable monies to the credit of owner in such foreign currency and shall promptly give owner written notice of said deposit. Payment so made to the depository so elected by owner shall fulfill Subpublisher's obligations hereunder as to the monies so payable to Owner.

(b)     The payments to owner provided for under this agreement shall be computed, accounted for and paid by Subpublisher to Owner separately for each country of the Licensed Territory, as if separate contracts had been made between Owner and Subpublisher for each country of the Licensed Territory with each such contract granting to Subpublisher for one country the rights herein granted, upon the payment terms herein contained. Statements and payments shall be rendered separately to Owner. Such statements shall include the following for each of the Compositions in detail:

(i)     Title and author(s) and composer(s) of the Composition;

(ii)    Number of copies of Printed Music and recorded copies of each of the Compositions sold;

(iii)    Source of Income (i.e., mechanical, performance sheet music, synchronization);

(iv)    Gross amount of Income, including the percentage of Income received by SubPublisher;

(v)    owner's percentage and share of Income;

(vi)    Period during which Income was earned;

(vii)    An itemization and explanation, in the English
language, of any deductions made;

(viii)    Rate of Exchange.

Without limiting the generality of the foregoing, each statement shall account for and be accompanied by payment to
Owner of all Owner's share of all Income received by Subpublisher and/or Subpublisher's affiliated or subsidiary music publishing companies during the preceding semiannual period.

(c)    Prompt and accurate accountings and payments shall
be the essence of this agreement. Notwithstanding anything to
the contrary contained herein, in the event that any of the
amounts payable pursuant to Schedule "C" are inaccurate, or
disapproved of or disallowed by any governmental authority of
the Licensed Territory, owner shall have the right to terminate
this agreement by giving Subpublisher written notice thereof, in
which event all rights of any kind or nature herein granted to
Subpublisher shall immediately revert to and be the sole and
exclusive property of owner and Subpublisher shall retain no
interest whatsoever in and to any of the Compositions.

(d)    In addition, and whether or not owner elects to terminate the term of this agreement in accordance with the pre-

ceding ¶ 11(c) , in the event that any payment is not made when due, Owner shall have the right to select any rate of exchange prevailing between the date such payment is due and the date upon which such payment is actually received (both dates inclusive).

(e)    Subpublisher agrees that all financial books and records shall, at all times, be kept by or under the active supervision of a chartered accountant.

(f)    (i)    It is further agreed that Owner shall have the right at all reasonable times during the term of this agreement to have owner's duly authorized representative or chartered accountant examine Subpublisher's records and accounts pertaining to transactions in connection with each and all of the Compositions covered by this agreement, and all statements rendered by any Mechanical Rights society, Performing Rights society, recording company, broadcasting company, or any other person, firm or corporation, for any and all Sales and Uses.

(ii)    All costs of any audit of Subpublisher's books and records shall be paid by owner; provided, however, that if it shall be determined that an underpayment greater than ten percent (10%) of the total royalties paid by Subpublisher to Owner for the period audited has occurred, all reasonable costs of such audit (excluding the cost of travel and/or subsistence) shall be paid by Subpublisher.

## 12.    ASSIGNMENT

None of the rights or obligations of Subpublisher hereunder shall be transferred, assigned, licensed, delegated or otherwise conveyed to any person, firm or corporation, directly, indirectly, voluntarily, involuntarily, or by operation of law, including without limitation, any successor to, receiver of, or trustee of the property or assets of Subpublisher, without the prior written consent of Owner. Notwithstanding the foregoing, in the event that the

Licensed Territory includes more than one country, Subpublisher may license all of its rights under this agreement for each country of the Licensed Territory.

## 13.    SPECIAL PROVISIONS

Musical compositions or the rights in musical compositions which Owner acquires for the Licensed Territory as a result of purchasing a catalog of musical compositions are deemed to have been acquired by Owner not in the ordinary course of business, are not compositions, and are thus excluded from this agreement ("Excluded Compositions"). Owner agrees, however, that Subpublisher shall have the right of first negotiation to acquire the rights in the Excluded Compositions for the Licensed Territory. If no agreement is reached between Subpublisher and Owner within sixty (60) days after Owner notifies Subpublisher in writing of the acquisition of a catalog of Excluded Compositions or if, due to contract restrictions, owner is unable to grant Subpublisher a right of first negotiation regarding the Excluded Compositions, Owner shall be entitled to subpublish or license the Excluded Compositions to any party of Owner's choice, free of the terms hereof.

## 14.    MISCELLANEOUS:

(a)    In any suit or proceeding arising out of or in connection with this agreement, the prevailing party shall be entitled to recover reasonable attorney's fees.

(b)    All notices, royalty statements, payments, delivery of materials and other communications required or desired to be given to owner or Subpublisher shall be given by addressing the same to the addresses of the respective parties as set forth above, or to such other address as either party may hereafter designate to the other in writing, or shall be sent by cablegram (or similar means of communication).

(c)    (i)    This agreement has been entered into in, and is to be interpreted in accordance with the laws of, the State of

California. All actions or proceedings seeking the interpretation and/or enforcement of this agreement shall be brought only in the State or Federal Courts located in Los Angeles County, all parties hereby submitting themselves to the jurisdiction of such courts for such purpose.

(ii)　Service of process in any action between the parties may be made by registered or certified mail addressed to the parties' then-current addresses for notice as set forth above.

(iii)　Service shall become effective 30 days following the date of receipt by the party served (unless delivery is refused, in which event service shall become effective 30 days following the date of such refusal).

(d)　This agreement contains the entire understanding of the parties and supersedes all prior and collateral agreements, discussions and negotiations between the parties as to the subject matter hereof. Each party acknowledges that no representations, inducements, promises or agreements, oral or written, with reference to the subject matter hereof have been made other than as expressly set forth herein. No modification, alteration, amendment or waiver of any of the provisions of this agreement shall be valid unless in writing and signed by each of the parties.

Owner's failure to terminate this agreement upon any default or defaults shall not be deemed to constitute a waiver of owner's right to terminate the same upon any subsequent default.

IN WITNESS WHEREOF, the parties hereto have caused this agreement to be executed the date and year hereinabove set forth.

OWNER: _____

a division of _____

By _____

SUBPUBLISHER:

By _____

## SCHEDULE "A"

Annexed to and made part of the following agreement:

Date:

Owner:

Subpublisher:

For the purposes of this agreement, the Licensed Territory shall be

## SCHEDULE "B"

Annexed to and made part of the following agreement:

Date:

Owner:

Subpublisher:

Territory:

For the purposes of this agreement, the Compositions shall include each and every musical composition with respect to which owner presently owns or controls rights for the Licensed Territory at the time of execution of this agreement, including but not limited to those included in the catalogs set forth below, together with those musical compositions the ownership or control of which shall be acquired by Owner for the Licensed Territory during the term of this agreement, and shall exclude musical compositions acquired by Owner pursuant to so-called catalog acquisitions as described in ¶ 13 of this agreement.

Notwithstanding the foregoing, to the extent that Owner acquires ownership or control of any of the Compositions for the Licensed Territory pursuant to agreements which provide for terms and conditions which conflict with this agreement (as defined in ¶ 2(d) as "Contractual Restrictions"), or which provide for a Flat Collection Fee (as defined in ¶ 6(a)), Owner agrees to advise Subpublisher in writing of such Contractual Restrictions and/or Flat Collection Fee and such Contractual Restrictions and/or Flat Collection Fee are hereby incorporated into this agreement.

## SCHEDULE "C"

Annexed to and made part of the following agreement:

Date:

Owner:

Subpublisher:

Territory:

Set forth below is a schedule of the respective percentages of Income and other payments to be made by Subpublisher to Owner in accordance with ¶ 6 of this agreement.

## 1. PRINTED MUSIC:

(a)    Subpublisher shall pay to Owner an amount equal to Twelve and One-Half Percent (12 1/2%) of the marked retail selling price of each copy of Printed Music in any and every form sold or otherwise distributed by Subpublisher, except that no payment shall be made by Subpublisher on professional copies distributed without charge for promotional or professional exploitation.

(b)    Subpublisher shall pay to Owner an amount equal to that portion of Twelve and One-Half Percent (12 1/2%) of the marked retail selling price of each and every album, song book or folio sold by Subpublisher, determined by the proportion of the number of Compositions to the total number of copyrighted original compositions contained in said album, song book or folio.

## 2. MECHANICAL RIGHTS:

(a)    Subpublisher shall pay to Owner an amount equal to _____ Percent (_____%) of All Income Received from Sales and Uses of Mechanical Rights received from any Mechanical

Rights society, recording company, or other person, firm or corporation. Notwithstanding any provision to the contrary herein contained, Subpublisher shall collect Income under this subparagraph (a) only with respect to phonograph records and other such devices sold in the Licensed Territory, irrespective of whether such phonograph records or devices are manufactured within the Licensed Territory or outside of the Licensed Territory. Accordingly, Subpublisher shall not collect royalties hereunder with respect to phonograph records and other such devices manufactured within the Licensed Territory but sold outside of the Licensed Territory.

(b)    Should Subpublisher obtain release and commercial distribution to the general public in the Licensed Territory of a recording of any of the Compositions derived from a new master originated in the Licensed Territory during the term hereof, with a vocal, if any, in any of the languages of the Licensed Territory (hereinafter referred to as a "Local Cover Recording"), Subpublisher shall pay to Owner an amount equal to Percent (____%) of All Income Received from Sales and Uses of Mechanical Rights arising from the manufacture, sale or distribution of said Local Cover Recording of each of the Compositions.

(c)    (i)    In the event of any form of payment or distribution of funds, special or regular, including without limitation, increased royalty rates or bonus payments based on the amount of income derived from catalogs controlled or administered by Subpublisher, from any Mechanical Rights society, recording company, or any other person, firm or corporation to Subpublisher based upon or related to the sale or use of Mechanical Rights pertaining to any of the Compositions, Subpublisher shall pay to Owner an amount equal to _____ Percent of such payment or distribution of funds.

(ii)    In the event of any form of payment or distribution of funds to Subpublisher, special or regular, including, without limitation, increased royalty rates or bonus payments based on the amount of income derived from catalogs controlled or administered by Subpublisher, by any Mechanical Rights society, recording company or any other person, firm or corporation to Subpublisher, based upon unidentified or general funds, Subpublisher shall pay to Owner an amount equal to _____ Percent (\_\_\_\_%) of that portion of the total amount of such payment or distribution determined by the ratio of identified Income received by Subpublisher from the same source attributable to the Compositions to the total identified income received by Subpublisher for all musical compositions owned or controlled by Subpublisher, including the Compositions, derived during the same period for which the unidentified or general funds are distributed.

3.    PERFORMING RIGHTS:

(a)    In each instance herein wherein reference is made to "Publisher's share of performing fees", it shall mean not less than 6/12 of the total performing fees.

(b)    Subpublisher shall pay to Owner an amount equal to _____ Percent (\_\_\_\_%) of All Income Received from Sales and Uses of Performing Rights received from any Performing Rights society, recording company, or any other person, firm or corporation, as Owner's share of Publisher's share of performing fees, on each of the Compositions.

(c)    In the event of any form of payment or distribution of funds, special or regular, including, without limitation, increased royalty rates or bonus payments based on the amount of income derived from catalogs controlled or administered by Subpublisher, from any Performing Rights society, recording company or any other person, firm or corporation to Subpublisher, based upon or related to the sale or use of Performing Rights pertaining to any of the Compositions, Subpublisher shall pay to Owner an amount equal to _____ Percent of such payment or distribution of funds.

In the event of any form of payment or distribution of funds, special or regular, including, without limitation, increased royalty

rates or bonus payments based on the amount of income derived from catalogs controlled or administered by Subpublisher,
from any Performing Rights society, recording company or any
other person, firm or corporation to Subpublisher, based upon
unidentified or general funds, Subpublisher shall pay to Owner
an amount equal to Percent (____%) of that portion of the total
amount of such payment or distribution determined by the ratio
of identified Income received by Subpublisher from the same
source attributable to the Compositions to the total identified
income received by Subpublisher for all musical compositions,
derived during the same period for which the unidentified or
general funds are distributed.

In the event of any form of payment or distribution of funds,
special or regular, including, without limitation, increased royalty
rates or bonus payments based on the amount of income derived from catalogs controlled or administered by Subpublisher,
to Subpublisher of any writers' share of performing fees, including but not limited to fees attributable to writers who are
unaffiliated with any Performing Rights society, Subpublisher
shall pay to Owner One Hundred Percent (100%) of such payment or distribution.

4.    SYNCHRONIZATION RIGHTS:

Subpublisher shall pay to owner an amount equal to _____
(____%) of All Income Received from Sales and Uses of Limited
Synchronization Rights received from any Performing Rights society, Mechanical Rights society, radio or television production
company or broadcasting station, or any other person, firm or
corporation.

5.    RENTED MUSIC:

Subpublisher shall pay to Owner an amount equal to _____
Percent (____%) of All Income Received by Subpublisher from
the rental or leasing of band, choral or orchestral arrangements.

## 6.    OTHER INCOME:

Subpublisher shall pay to Owner an amount equal to _____ Percent (____%) of All Income Received by Subpublisher with respect to any other rights to the Compositions which are expressly assigned to Subpublisher hereunder.

## 7.    ADVANCES AND/OR GUARANTEES:

Upon execution hereof, Subpublisher shall pay to Owner the sum of _____ U.S. Dollars (U.S. $____), as a non-returnable advance, fully recoupable from royalties payable to owner hereunder with respect to Sales and Uses of the Compositions set forth in Schedule "B-1". It is understood and agreed that Subpublisher shall not have the right to recoup said advance from royalties payable to owner or to Owner's subsidiaries from Sales and Uses of the Compositions set forth in Schedule "B-2".

CHAPTER 6

# THE SPLIT COPYRIGHT SYNDROME

SUMMARY

# THE SPLIT COPYRIGHT
# SYNDROME

A *split copyright* is a copyright owned by two or more people (i.e., one in which two or more persons own an undivided interest). As noted in Chapter 1, control of a copyright by more than one person may pose one of the most frustrating barriers to clearing licenses — locating and obtaining permission from each of the several owners of the copyright. This chapter sketches the chaos that can result from co-ownership of copyright and suggests to copyright co-owners a solution that should enhance the value of their copyright and simplify the task of persons seeking to clear permission for the use of copyrighted compositions.

## I. LEGAL BACKGROUND

### A. Undivided Co-Ownership of Copyright

As discussed at length in Chapter 7, on *The Language of Music Licensing*, when a composer and lyricist collaborate in the writing of a song, a copyright is said to *subsist* in the composer and lyricist the moment they fix the song on paper or recording tape. From that moment, the composer and lyricist co-own the *undivided* interest in the entire copyright of the song. The co-owners of a copyright are much like tenants in common of real property. Each author automatically acquires an undivided ownership interest in the *entire* work.

Unless they agree otherwise, the composer and lyricist each acquire a 50% undivided interest in the entire work and they will share equally in the revenues generated by the song. Where there are three writers, each will have a 33⅓% undivided interest in the entire work, and so forth. The writers may, however, agree to another division. For example, where one writer's contribution involved words and music and the other's involved only the words, the two may agree to a 75/25% division.

A concept discussed in Chapter 8, on the *Formalities of Music Licensing*, is the *assignment* (i.e., transfer or sale) of copyrights. In other words, copyrights, and exclusive rights under copyright, may be transferred from one person to another, much like other forms of property. The composer, in the above example, may sell to another his 50% undivided interest in the copyright. If he does so, he will then own no part of the copyright and the person to whom the assignment is made, the "assignee," will become the owner of that 50% undivided interest in the copyright. This is typically the effect of the standard songwriter agreement between a composer and a music publisher, discussed in Chapter 3, on *Songwriter Agreements* — in exchange for granting his 50% undivided interest in the copyright to the music publisher, the composer is given contractual rights under which he receives the benefits of the publisher's administration services, including the administration of the copyright, the promotion of the song, the collection of revenues from licensing use of the song, and payment of royalties to the composer, representing the composer's share of such revenues.

In short, when a writer signs a standard songwriter agreement, he is generally agreeing to assign to the music publisher all of his undivided interest in his song. In some cases, however, the composer assigns only one-half of his undivided interest in the song to the music publisher, with the composer retaining the other half personally or in a separate sole proprietorship music publishing company established for the purpose of holding that interest. This is typically the effect of the standard co-publishing agreement between a composer's publishing company and a major music publisher, discussed in Chapter 4, on *Co-Publishing and Administration*. In the example of our composer, who started out only owning 50% of the song (his lyricist collaborator owning the other 50%), if the composer should assign half of his 50% undivided interest to a music publisher, then the composer and his music publisher would each own a 25% undivided interest in the copyright, leaving the lyricist, or course, with his 50% undivided interest, which he may retain or assign to the same or another music publisher.

Thus, in the above example, concerning one song written by two collaborators, as many as four music publishing companies may claim

to have an undivided interest in the whole copyright in the song —
i.e., the two respective major music publishers normally used by the
composer and lyricist and the two respective sole proprietorship music
publishing companies operated by the composer and lyricist or their
respective attorneys, agents, or business managers.

Co-ownership of copyright can also result from a variety of other
circumstances. Copyright ownership may be split by a statutory termination of a prior grant of copyright. When a grant of copyright is
terminated under the 35 year termination rule[1] or the 19 year termination rule[2] (discussed in Chapter 9, on *Duration of Copyright, Assignments and Licenses*), the copyright reverts to the author or authors
of the work, or to other persons owning the termination interests, such
as a deceased author's surviving spouse or children. Each author or
other person to which an undivided interest in the copyright reverts
under a statutory termination is in a position to make a further grant
of his or her interest to another, such as a music publisher of that
person's choosing. Each may choose to grant the reverted rights to a
different music publisher or choose to administer those rights himself.
A similar split may occur where the *renewal* rights of a co-writer,
discussed in Chapter 9, are assigned to a different publisher than the
publisher of the rights of another co-writer.

The provisions of U.S. copyright law concerning termination of
grants and renewal rights in no way affects rights arising under any
foreign laws. Laws of certain countries provide similar statutory mechanisms that may cause a split copyright. For example, under the British
copyright law, all rights under copyright reverts to an author's heirs
upon the twenty-fifth anniversary of the author's death. Thus, a split
copyright results when the British reversionary rights of a co-writer
are assigned to a different publisher than the publisher of the rights
of another co-writer.

Finally, a division by percentage of ownership between writers is
not the only way a copyright may be split. As we have seen in Chapter
5, on *International Subpublishing*, a copyright also may be split by
territory. For example, one publisher may own exclusive rights to a

---

[1] 17 U.S.C. Sec. 203.
[2] 17 U.S.C. Sec. 304(c).

composition for exploitation in the United States and several others may own rights for the rest of the world.

## B.  Licensing Rights of Co-Owners

The general rule governing the right of a co-owner to grant non-exclusive licenses for use of the work is this: Unless co-owners have a contract among them which states otherwise, a co-owner can grant a license for the use of the song without the consent of the co-owners, as long as the licensing co-owner accounts and pays to the others their share of the license fee collected.[3]

However, this rule is not entirely settled law. Courts have held that one co-owner may not unilaterally grant a license that will effectively destroy the value of the copyright. Just what kinds of licenses would be construed as having destroyed the value of the copyright is not clear. Further, and perhaps more important, the above rule is not followed in many countries around the world. In the United Kingdom, France, and many other countries, the rule is: a license is not valid unless all co-owners consent to it.

Relying solely on the U.S. rule, persons seeking to clear permission should feel comfortable in accepting a license offered by only one of several co-owners, provided that the territory of the license is limited to the United States and that the licensee has no reason to believe that there exists an agreement among the co-owners restricting the granting of licenses by the other co-owners. The licensee might also rely on a written warranty from the licensing co-owner that the latter has the right to grant the license without the consent of any of the co-owners.

The practical problem faced by producers of works that include music licensed from one co-owner is the risk that another co-owner will later make an objection. The consequences of having an ineffectual license are great: the producer risks having the distribution of his entire work enjoined by a court. A more important practical problem stems from the fact that advances in worldwide telecommunications are making the economies of countries increasingly interdependent. As a result, licensees are increasingly demanding that the territories

---

[3] See generally, 1 Nimmer *On Copyright*, Sec. 6.10.

of music licenses be made worldwide. If the territory of the license is worldwide, the producer must insist upon receiving the written permission from *all* of the co-owners of the song.

## II. THE PROBLEM — AN ILLUSTRATIVE EXAMPLE

Let us consider an example in which the five members of a rock band collaborated in the writing of a song. Suppose that, upon formation of the band, they had agreed that each contributor would own an equal share of the copyright in any songs composed in collaboration. Thus, in this example, each writer owns a 20% interest in the undivided copyright in the composition.

The first member had previously established his own publishing company, to which he promptly assigned his entire 20% undivided interest.

The second member had previously signed an exclusive songwriter's contract with a major music publisher, and, under that contract, was obligated to assign his entire 20% undivided interest to the publisher. Since this member had no contractual control over his colleague's music publishing rights, he was unable to assist his major publisher in obtaining the remaining undivided interest in the copyright.

The third member had also signed an exclusive songwriter's agreement, but with a publisher affiliated with the record company with which the band had signed, and his deal was a "Co-Publishing" deal, under which he agreed to assign only half of any undivided interest in any songs he wrote during the term of the contract; this resulted in his assigning a 10% undivided interest in the copyright to his music publisher, but still retaining the other 10%, which he assigned to his own publishing company.

The fourth member also had previously signed an exclusive songwriter's agreement, but his deal was an administration agreement, under which he maintained his entire 20% undivided interest in the copyright, but granted to a major music publisher exclusive administration rights for the United States and Canada who will be issuing licenses in and for that territory and collecting income in exchange for retaining a 15% administration fee. This member's own music publishing company is run by his attorney. In exchange for a large advance against royalties, this fourth member promptly assigned his subpublishing rights, with respect to his 20% undivided interest, to a major European music publishing company for exploitation in member countries of the European Community. He received additional advances for parceling out his remaining subpublishing rights for all other territories on a territory-by-territory, song-by-song basis.

The fifth member didn't know anything about copyright, but was satisfied that the other members placed his name on the copyright registration form and took no further action, except to send a letter to ASCAP requesting a membership application form.

After several years, the song was becoming recognized as a standard hit and motion picture producers began to seek worldwide synchronization licenses and advertisers began offering large sums for permission to use the song in national television commercials. The band, of course, has long since broken up. One member died of a drug overdose, leaving a widow and two children, and another committed suicide over the frustration of determining his music rights, leaving no heirs but the Chase Manhattan Bank as the executor of his estate.

## III. THE MUSIC CLEARANCE INDUSTRY — A PARTIAL SOLUTION

The foregoing is an example of what might be called the "Split Copyright Syndrome," and it is not as far-fetched as it might initially appear. The Split Copyright Syndrome has spawned a new industry: music clearance companies. As noted and discussed in Chapter 1, music *clearance* is the process of (1) ascertaining whether a musical composition is protected by copyright, (2) if it is protected, determining who owns the copyright, or, more important, who has the right to administer its licensing, and (3) obtaining permission for the proposed use. Responding to the complexities posed by an increasing number of split copyrights, several entrepreneurs have established companies that specialize in performing the task of music clearance on behalf of motion picture producers, television producers, advertising agencies, and virtually anyone seeking to clear a license for the use of music.

For any clearance projects involving multiple music compositions or new technologies, such as multi-media works, the services of a professional clearance firm is highly recommended.

The Clearing House, Ltd. is one such firm that specializes in representing producers of television programs and motion pictures and others in clearing the use of copyrighted music by its clients. Ronald H. Gertz, Esq., a lawyer and the chief executive officer of Clearing House, Ltd. makes his living on the chaos resulting from the split copyright problem. In his commentary entitled, *Hung Up on Splintered Rights*, which appeared in a January, 1984 issue of *Billboard* magazine Mr. Gertz artfully describes the problem of split copyrights. The article is so instructive that we have obtained his permission to reprint it here in its entirety:

> Everyone has heard variations of the oft recycled joke about the three biggest lies in Hollywood. The first two usually are, "The Mercedes is paid for" and "The check is in the mail." The third always seems to be rooted in social comment, like "It's only a cold sore."

> My vote for lie number three is, "Don't worry, I control the rights." Accordingly, I am treating all publishers who say that as though they have some bizarre social disease, until proven otherwise.

> Behind lie number three are the issues of terminated rights, reversionary rights, split copyrights and separate administration. These concepts and practices have a tendency to fragment the bundle of rights we call a song into a number of separately controlled pieces, creating havoc for anyone wishing to license its use.

> The problems engendered apply in any licensing situation, whether the song is to be performed on a television show or the lyrics are to be reprinted on T-shirts.

> Terminations and reversions aren't the only way that compositions get split up into little pieces. It happens as a result of legitimate collaboration. It happens when six members of a musical group co-write a song with each member keeping his own publishing and administration.

It also happens when an artist, as an inducement to record a song, takes a percentage of the copyright and administers his or her own share. I've seen situations like the latter with shares as small as 6¼%. At that rate, the income generated doesn't even pay the fees of the attorney handling the administration.

When a song is divided into several parts, whether by percentages, territories or both, the result is invariably chaos. How does one locate all the owners? Which owner has the right to give a license to a potential user? What happens when all the owners can't agree on a price for their respective shares?

At what point will an owner, relying on joint ownership rules, tire of the game and license the whole song without regard to the feelings of his co-owners? Will that owner ever account to the other parties? Will he first deduct the cost of traveling to Hollywood to complete the negotiation?

Can the potential music user trust the publisher who says, "Don't worry, I control the rights?"

I have always believed that the basic rule in the music publishing business is to get songs performed. Performances mean royalties and royalties make people happy. But a split copyright, for whatever reason, frequently means fewer performances and less royalties.

While most publishers approach the administration of their catalogs in a professional manner, a growing number fail to grasp the practical and business issues presented. The inability to contact these publishers by phone or letter, and their own lack of knowledge about what causes royalties to be generated, will frequently result in a composition being deleted from a program.

Perhaps a recent experience in attempting to license a song in a two-hour television variety special will serve to illustrate the problem. I squared off against a composition which was to be used as a vocal bridge for about 30 seconds during the course of a 10-song production number. The rights to the song were divided into four separate interests. One publisher controlled the rights in all territories of the world, excluding the United States. The other three publishers each owned 33 1/3% of the U.S. rights.

Publisher number one demanded a laughably high license fee. Number two referred us to his agent, who wouldn't do anything until all the others agreed. Number three, an obvious disciple of Newton Minnow, didn't want his part of the song to contribute to television's vast wasteland, and wouldn't grant permission. Number four was on vacation and could not be reached.

When I told the producer that we could not obtain the rights he needed within his time frame, his musical director came up with a substitute song that, as fate would have it, was divided into only three parts. The owners were willing to grant a license, but each wanted a full license fee for his fractional interest.

When I told the producer that his second choice was going to be the most expensive song in the show, he decided to find a new clearance company. I'm sure that in his mind, with production costs mounting and the minutes ticking by, the most logical thing to do in the face of the message was to kill the messenger.

Since Old Testament prophets frequently suffered the same fate, I didn't feel so bad. But I lost a client, and the publishers lost their respective share of about $5,000 income over the network and syndicated runs. Although the mutuality of loss also softened the blow, I have the hollow feeling that the publishers I dealt with didn't care, and that is what I find so disturbing.

It is clear to me that fragmentation of rights will make it harder and harder for television and film producers to use certain songs. When that occurs, the royalties generated by those songs will begin to decrease. The widows and the publishers will wake up one morning to the startling revelation that "the checks are no longer in the mail."

The solution might be as simple as letting the party with the greatest percentage have the administration rights. That way each party would take his share of the total fee rather than require a user to negotiate a separate dollar amount for each share.

In conclusion, all is again well in Hollywood, the Mercedes is on a lease, and my producer friend is back in the fold. He read the first draft of this commentary and now realizes what the problem really was. His next project is going to be a star-studded musical salute to Stephen "Public Domain" Foster.

## IV. TIP ON CLEARING LICENSES
### FROM MULTIPLE CO-OWNERS

When you are seeking to clear a license requiring permission from more than one owner, you should condition any obligation to pay license fees to any one co-owner upon your obtaining the necessary license from all the other co-owners. Thus, if you can not obtain the consent of all other co-owners of the composition, it would then be clear that you have no obligation to pay the negotiated fee to the co-owners from whom you were able to obtain a license, provided, of course, that you make no use of the song.

Alternatively, you may negotiate all the necessary licenses from the various co-owners and then sign them all at once. The problem is that you may find, as co-owners have an opportunity to confer with each other, one or more may have a change of mind and you may find yourself in an endless circle of negotiation. It would be better to get each co-owner to sign an agreement when the fire is hot, and condition your obligations to pay upon your obtaining the consent of the other co-owners.

## V. COMMENT ON
### PRUDENT COPYRIGHT ADMINISTRATION

It is ironic that the most common cause of lost licensing opportunities is the inexperienced co-owner, or the co-owner's attorney, manager or publisher representative, who, in insisting upon a fee that is far higher than any reasonable fee that should be charged for the license, loses the licensing opportunity entirely, not just for him or his client, but for all co-owners — indeed, for the song itself.

It has been the experience of both music clearance firms and professional publishers that too many songwriters who own their own publishing companies turn over absolute control of their publishing activities to an inexperienced or inappropriate representative, often an attorney. Many of these writers do not keep track of what their own attorney is doing. In some cases, the writer fails to realize that, as much as an attorney can be valued for providing legal advice and drafting contracts, the basic business skills of managing the copyright of a song is an entirely different matter. How many times have we seen, where a copyright is split, a poor co-writer is losing thousands of dollars of revenue due to one co-writer's stubborn lawyer? And when years after a song was a hit, when the songwriter is old and gray and wonders why the licensing revenue for that song has been reduced to a trickle in his retirement years, it may never have occurred to him that the reason for his circumstances is that his attorneys and managers have over the years either asked for exorbitant fees for synchronization licenses or withheld licenses under the assumption that his client didn't want the song used.

It is therefore strongly recommended that the administration of copyright should either be exercised directly by the writer, given to one of several co-owners, or turned over to a professional music publisher who can make the delicate judgments required to keep their copyrights returning revenues well into the writer's retirement. The risks of turning over administration of rights to a single co-owner or the wrong publisher may be reduced by many of the means suggested in the next section.

## VI. CURING THE SPLIT COPYRIGHT SYNDROME

An economist would view the problem of split copyright as one which unnecessarily increases the transaction costs of deriving income from the copyright. Clearly, transaction costs would be reduced if only one person owned or controlled the administration of the copyright.[4] Where only one person controls the administration of a copyright, the person seeking to clear a license for use of the copyrighted material would need only locate and negotiate with that one person — the sole copyright owner or administrator could make the appropriate decisions without requiring the consent of the co-owners. The risk that one of the co-owners, or their representatives or heirs, will impede the income potential of the copyright will be significantly reduced.

The most obvious way to effect the administration of publishing rights by one party is one which provides the exclusive right to ad-

---

[4] Landes and Posner, *An Economic Analysis of Copyright Law*, 18 Journal of Legal Studies 325 (1989).

minister the copyright to just one of the co-owners of the copyright or to an independent third party who has an incentive and the appropriate resources to maximize the value of the copyright for all concerned.

## A. Co-Publishing Agreement

Control over the administration of the copyright by one co-owner or an independent third party does not require the other co-owners to transfer their ownership interest in the copyright. As noted above, co-owners of copyright can always enter into an agreement that specifically governs their respective rights to grant licenses. This may be effected by the signing of a Co-Publishing Agreement, discussed at length in Chapter 4, which would define and govern the respective administration rights of co-owners of copyright. An example of a co-publishing agreement that vests in one of the parties the exclusive right to issue non-exclusive licenses for the use of the music they co-own is set forth as Form 4.1 at the end of Chapter 4.

## B. Restrictions

If a co-owner has certain sensitivities about the licensing of his or her music, then appropriate safeguards can be built into the copublishing agreement. To that end, the agreement could provide that the writer's consent be obtained where the permission being requested broaches that area of sensitivity. For example, a co-owner may grant exclusive administration rights to another co-owner, but still require that his consent be obtained to permit any change in the lyrics or harmonic structure of the music, to issue any mechanical license at less than the prevailing statutory rate, to authorize the use of the title of the song as the title of a play, film or TV program, to authorize the production of a dramatic adaptation of the song, to authorize the synchronization of the song in a motion picture, television program, or videogram bearing a rating of "X" or its equivalent, or authorize the use of the song in any political advertisement. Any of these restrictions may vary depending upon the tastes of the particular co-owners and nature of the relationship they have with the administrative co-owner.

## C. Who Controls?

After a decision is made among the co-owners to grant exclusive administration rights to one of the parties, what still remains is the question of who among the co-owners should be given administrative control. As noted in Chapter 4 on *Co-Publishing and Administration*, there are several alternatives.

Of course, prudent co-owners should each grant their respective administration rights to the one co-owner who has shown the greatest amount of business acumen and interest in spending the time required to properly manage the copyright. Needless to say, this is easier said than done. If it is not readily apparent who among the co-owners would be best for this job, perhaps, as Ron Gertz has suggested, the solution is as simple as letting the party with the greatest percentage have the administration rights.

Another idea, which the present authors recommend, is what might be called, *alternating administration rights* — that is, allow each co-publisher to control the administration rights for alternating terms of two, three, or five years. The acting administrator could waive the collection of an administration fee or he could be awarded a fee for achieving a minimum level of publishing income established in advance by the parties. The co-owners may also impose restrictions that affect the administrator's authority to issue licenses, including many of the restrictions set forth in the preceding section.

To improve the efficiency of distributing publishing income among the co-owners, or if a co-owner doesn't completely trust the efficiency of the administrative co-owner, the co-owners may require that shares of certain income be paid directly to each co-publisher from the source of the income. For example, the parties may instruct the Harry Fox Agency, and the applicable performance rights society (e.g., ASCAP or BMI), to pay any income generated by them directly to each co-publisher according to his or her share, in effect bypassing the administrator. This will reduce any unnecessary transaction costs associated with flowing these payments through to the co-publishers and reduce the amount of time it takes for these payments to reach their pockets.

Should the parties be unable to immediately agree upon a single administrator, or alternating administration program, it may do them well to list their particular concerns, use that list to craft contractual provisions addressing their concerns, and appoint an exclusive administrator who would be subject to those restrictions.

## D. Major Music Publisher

Should the co-owners fail to reach an agreement on an effective co-publishing arrangement, they could still effect exclusive control of administration rights in one party by turning to one independent, professional music publisher to administer the copyright on their behalf. Under this arrangement, each writer can maintain his own publishing company and his share of the publishing revenues, but each would agree to grant to a professional music publisher the exclusive right to administer those rights, without restriction, or subject only to restrictions on licensing uses over which one or more of the co-owners may be particularly sensitive. As noted in Chapter 4, many music publishers will agree to administer the copyrights owned by others for an administration fee — usually 10-15% of net revenues — without taking an ownership interest in the copyright of the song. An example of a music publishing *administration agreement* is set forth as Form 4.4 at the end of Chapter 4.

Granting administration rights to an independent music publisher may be the only solution that assures each of the co-owners that the copyright will be administered with each of their interests in mind. The only key decision that would remain is choosing the right music publisher. The risks of that decision can be alleviated in part by limiting the term of the administration agreement to three to five years.

Granting administration rights to a professional music publisher may, in fact, be the best solution for the co-owners under many circumstances. Because of its access to vast amounts of information regarding the standard terms and conditions and going rates and practices in licensing music, the professional music publisher is in a better position than most others in maximizing the value of the musical composition.

What has been said about administering copyrights in the United States applies equally to international subpublishing administration. As noted in the previous chapter, because of the high transaction costs of having numerous subpublishers in various territories each representing different songs in an original publisher's catalog, a strategy of splitting international subpublishing rights on a per song basis is rarely advisable. Where a U.S. publisher is being offered substantial advances overseas under deals that would split up the international exclusive rights under the copyright, the U.S. publisher should first consider offering the song to its existing subpublishers, preferably a single major publisher handling all rights outside of the U.S. and Canada. If, under these circumstances, a U.S. publisher is only just beginning to establish its worldwide subpublishing program, he should carefully consider all the factors set forth in the previous chapter before adopting a song by song, or territory by territory disposition of his subpublishing rights. Such a splitting of rights would only compound the split copyright problems that have such a detrimental affect on the long term value of copyrights.

## VII. THE FINAL SOLUTION — COMPULSORY LICENSE?

As discussed in Chapter 12, owners of copyright in music may be compelled to issue licenses for the use of their works in audio recordings provided they pay the copyright owners the rate set forth in the law. One of the benefits of this compulsory license provision is that it appears to be an effective solution to the split copyright syndrome insofar as it facilitates the clearing of licenses to use music in sound recordings that are not accompanied by audiovisual works. Split copyright does not become an issue when all the co-owners are required to accept no more than the statutory rate. Further, when the person seeking to clear a mechanical license cannot identify or locate the owner of the copyright, the compulsory license provision provides a safe harbor: if the public records of the Copyright Office do not identify the copyright owner and include an address at which notice under the provision can be served, it is sufficient to file the required notice with the Copyright Office.[5] By properly following the procedure and paying the statutory rate set forth in the compulsory license provision, a person seeking to clear permission will be assured a license without taking any risk of liability for copyright infringement.

---

[5] 17 U.S.C. Sec. 115(b)(1).

It has been suggested that a compulsory license provision may be an effective solution to the split copyright problem with respect to the use of music in certain recordings that are accompanied by audiovisual works, multi-media works, and transmissions of musical works occurring in cyberspace. It remains to be seen whether this solution will result in the fair compensation to owners of copyrighted works or will ever receive legislative attention.[6]

## VIII. CONCLUSION

Each of the foregoing alternatives will almost always be superior to a copyright which is excessively split up. The reduced transaction costs of having only one person control the administration rights will surely increase the net income to the copyright owners. More important, however, is the direct affect on the long-term value of the copyright. The more co-owners of a song there are, the more difficult it is to obtain the consent of all of the owners, and the result will be fewer licenses granted. Fewer licenses will lead to fewer performances; with fewer performances, the song will begin to lose its share of mind of the listening public, resulting in even fewer performances and fewer requests for licenses. The ultimate result will be a lower income stream for the copyright owners, equating to a reduced copyright value. In cases of three or more co-owners, the solution of a single administrator of all rights should always be superior than each co-owner maintaining control over his or her share of a split copyright.

In the absence of a single administrator solution, it is hoped that co-owners of copyright who insist upon full control of the administration of his or her co-ownership interest will at least recognize the benefits of maintaining a long-term outlook when considering what fees to charge for permission to use his or her music.

---

[6] Licensing practices in certain countries appear to be making a move in this direction. Consider, for example, "extended collective license" used in the Nordic countries, more information about which may be found on the Internet at, *http://www.oslonett. no/home/kopinor/KOPINOR.html.*

## CHAPTER 7

# THE LANGUAGE OF MUSIC LICENSING

## SUMMARY

**I. MUSIC AS PROPERTY**

**II. COPYRIGHT**

**III. RIGHT VERSUS LICENSE**

**IV. OWNERSHIP OF MUSIC**

**V. WORKS MADE FOR HIRE**

**VI. JOINT OWNERSHIP OF MUSIC**

**VII. NON-OWNERSHIP OF MUSIC—THE PUBLIC DOMAIN**

A. Where No Copyright Protection Was Ever Available
B. Where Proper Copyright Protection Was Never Secured
C. Copyright Protection Has Expired or Has Been Lost
D. Hidden Problems

**VIII. DERIVING INCOME FROM MUSIC**

A. Sale of Copyright
B. Divisibility of Copyright and Sale of Exclusive Rights Under Copyright
C. Deriving Income by Licensing Use on a Non-Exclusive Basis

**IX. TYPES OF LICENSES FOR MUSIC**

A. Print Licenses
B. Mechanical Licenses
C. Electrical Transcription Licenses
D. Synchronization Licenses
E. Videogram Licenses
F. Commercial Synchronization Licenses

# THE LANGUAGE OF MUSIC LICENSING

T he rules and symbols of musical notation is the language with which composers and arrangers communicate with musicians and singers. The language is precise and the better the writer and the reader understand the common rules of the language the better the performance is likely to be. The same is true with music licensing. The better the owners of music and users of music each understand the basic language of music licensing, the better the chances that they will each get what they expected out of a licensing arrangement. Though this chapter is technical, a better understanding of the language of music licensing will form the basis of successful music licensing.

## I. Music as Property

The term *property* should not be confused with the term *property right*. A *property right* represents a relationship among people, recognized and defined by law, with respect to a certain thing or *object*. *Property* is the object over which the *right of property* is exercised. An acre of land, a diamond ring, or a song about a diamond ring lost on an acre of land are all objects which may be the subject of property rights. The property right with respect to a particular diamond ring is a relationship among people, enforceable by law, that dictates that a particular person, for example, has the privilege of possessing, using, and disposing of the diamond ring as that person sees fit and, more important, the right to exclude all others from possessing, using, or even looking at it.

Though there are some obvious differences between them, it should be clear that a song is just as much an object as a diamond ring. Like a diamond ring, a song is an object of perception, the former

425

perceivable by the sense of sight and touch and the latter perceivable by the sense of hearing. As one music industry professional observed, a piece of sheet music is not a song; it only becomes a song when the music is sung.[1] Unlike a diamond ring, however, music is more than an object of perception. It is also an object of conceptual, or intellectual thought — a song's organized patterns of sounds and silences, whether written in musical notation or performed live, can only be understood by man. While many animals have the sensory perceptions necessary to hear the sounds of music, only man has the intellect necessary to understand and appreciate its beauty. It is, perhaps, for this reason, that music is often referred to as a subject of *intellectual* property.

The property right — or relationship among people — established by law to which an acre of land is the object is called the law of *real property*. The property right to which a diamond ring is the object is called the law of *personal property*. Although a right in music is a form of personal property right, the specific form of personal property right to which music is the object is called *copyright*. The set of laws defining property rights in music is known as the *copyright law*, or *law of copyright*. When used in this book, the term *copyright law* shall refer to the law of copyright as enacted by the Congress of the United States and which took effect in 1978, with all subsequent amendments,[2] and the term *law of copyright* shall refer to general principals of copyright as agreed upon by international treaty.

## II. COPYRIGHT

Copyright has been defined as, quite simply, *the exclusive right to copy.* More specifically, the law of copyright provides the owner of copyright in a musical work with the exclusive right to make and

---

[1] Leonard Feist, *An Introduction to Popular Music Publishing in America,* (National Music Publisher's Association, Inc., N.Y., New York 1980).

[2] 17 U.S.C. Sec. 101, et seq. Act of Oct. 19, 1976, Pub. L. 94-553, 90 Stat. 2541 (the "1976 Act"). An extensive treatment of the law of copyright is beyond the scope of this book. For comprehensive coverage, the reader is referred to the following legal treatises: Nimmer on Copyright (Matthew Bender 2000); Goldstein, *Copyright,* 2nd Edition (Aspen 2000).

publish copies of the musical work, to make other versions of the work, to make recordings of the work, and to perform the work in public.[3] The concept of *exclusivity* signifies that it is illegal for anyone other than the copyright owner of the work to perform any of the foregoing activities. It is this power to *exclude* others from using the music that forms the basis of one's *claim* to ownership in the music.

When someone makes a copy of or performs a song without the copyright owner's permission, he is said to *infringe upon* the copyright in the song.[4] The copyright owner may file a lawsuit against an infringer to collect damages arising from the infringement and to stop the further infringement of the copyright owner's rights.

This ability to take legal action to exclude others from doing the things that the copyright owner has the exclusive right to do empowers the copyright owner with the ability to grant others the privilege to make copies or render performances of a copyrighted musical composition and to require the payment of compensation in exchange for that privilege. The income that the copyright owner can collect in exchange for granting permission to do such acts is precisely the reward the law of copyright seeks to provide to creators of copyrightable works. Without such a reward, anyone would be free to use an author's works without payment. If authors were not compensated for the use by others of the works they create, few authors could afford to devote sufficient efforts to fully exercise their talents. By providing a means by which talented authors can earn a living by creating works of authorship, more works of authorship by a greater number of people, regardless of their economic background, will be created. The assumption is that society benefits when more original works of authorship are created by a greater number of talented individuals from a wide variety of backgrounds. Few would argue with that assumption.

## III. Right Versus License

The terms *right* and *license* are often used interchangeably, but they refer to two entirely different concepts and much confusion can

---

[3] 17 U.S.C. Sec. 106.
[4] 17 U.S.C. Sec. 501.

be avoided by using these terms with all the precision the law demands.

As we have said, although music is property, the property right in music properly refers to the *legal relation* that the law recognizes between one person and all other persons. The legal relation of one who has a property right in an object is an ownership *claim* to the object. It is a claim to a certain object in relation to all other persons. That claim allows him to exclude all others from making copies of the work. A *right*, properly defined, is a claim in the sense just used. When one is said to have a *right*, one has the ability, enforceable by law, to exclude others from exercising the *privilege* of possessing, using or disposing of the object. And therein lies a most important point: The term *right* should not be used to describe what is really a *privilege*.

A *right*, as we have said, is a claim to property that enables the owner of the right to exclude others from doing some act. A *license* is a permission to exercise a privilege. A *privilege* is a freedom from the claim of another, allowing you to do an act regardless of someone else's claim. A license, therefore, is not a right (i.e., claim of ownership), but merely a *permission* to do something you would not otherwise have the *privilege* to do. For example, if you have a right, or claim of ownership, in a song, it means that you have the right to exclude, or prevent, all others from publicly performing the song. While your *right* affords you the *privilege* to perform the song yourself, others have a duty not to perform the song, unless you give them permission to do so. When you grant to me a license, or permission, to perform a song publicly, I do not acquire any right in, or claim to, the song; I acquire only a limited privilege to perform it. My privilege, or license, is limited by the scope of the permission, or license, which you gave to me.

It should thus be apparent that the term *right* and *license* refer to two completely different concepts — the former a claim to ownership and the latter a permission or privilege to act. Unfortunately, the term *right* is too often confounded with the term *license*.[5] Some examples

---

[5] This imprecision in language extends even to many of the major treatises on copyright law. In the social sphere, it leads to some pretty astounding errors in thinking

of these errors, as well as their consequences, will be called to the reader's attention at later points in this book. Although we have no expectation that these errors will be rectified by practitioners overnight, we do hope that a recognition of the issue will aid the reader in understanding and finding solutions to practical problems in the licensing and administration of copyrights.

## IV. OWNERSHIP OF MUSIC

When a composer writes a song, a copyright is said to *subsist* in the composer the moment he fixes the song in tangible form (for example, on paper or recording tape). Because the copyright automatically "subsists" at that moment, the composer does not need to do anything else to "secure" protection;[6] copyright protection is automatically secured at the moment the work is fixed in some tangible medium of expression.[7] From that moment, the composer is the copyright owner and is considered to *own* a 100% "undivided" interest in the copyright of the song.

## V. WORKS MADE FOR HIRE

The one exception to this principal — that the copyright in the work subsists initially in the person who created it — is where the work was *made for hire*. In the case of a work made for hire, the employer or other person for whom the work was prepared, not the actual creator of the work, is considered to be the *author* of the work and becomes the owner of the 100% undivided interest in the copyright the moment the work is fixed in tangible form.

A *work made for hire* is (i) a work prepared by an employee within the scope of his employment or (ii) a work which is specially

---

about such fundamental concepts as "property rights," "civil rights," "human rights," and "individual liberty."

[6] Prior to 1978, copyright under the U.S. copyright law was *secured* by publication of the work with a proper copyright notice. 17 U.S.C. Sec. 10 (1909 Act).

[7] 17 U.S.C. Sec. 102(a).

ordered or commissioned in a writing that says the work is made for hire and which falls within one of several categories enumerated in the copyright law, such as a language translation, a musical arrangement, a contribution to a collective work, a compilation, or a work created for use as part of a motion picture or other audiovisual work.[8]

In 1989, the U.S. Supreme Court ruled that whether a creator of a work is an "employee" under the "scope of employment" clause (i.e., clause (i) above) is to be determined by applying the general rules of agency.[9] Among the criteria to be considered in making such a determination are the hiring party's right to control the manner and means by which the work is accomplished, the skill required, the source of the work tools, the location of the work, the duration of the relationship between the parties, the method of payment, and similar factors. If the creator of the work is not found to be "an employee acting within the scope of employment," then the work product can be considered a work for hire only if the specific criteria set forth in the "specially ordered or commissioned" works clause of the work for hire definition are met — namely, that the work falls within one of the categories specified in clause (ii) and the parties expressly agree in a written instrument signed by them that the work shall be considered a work made for hire.

## VI. JOINT OWNERSHIP OF MUSIC

Like any other piece of property, a copyright can be *co-owned*. In other words, a copyright may be owned by more than one person, each of whom is called a *co-owner* of the copyright. In the music business, co-ownership most likely arises from the fact that two or more authors collaborated in the creation of the musical composition — commonly, a composer and a lyricist. Such a work is known as a *joint work*. In the case of a joint work, the co-authors of the work are likewise co-owners of the copyright.

A work is joint if the authors collaborated with each other in the creation of the work, or if each of the authors prepared his or her

---

[8] 17 U.S.C. Sec. 101.

[9] *Community for Creative Non-Violence v. Reid*, 490 U.S. 730 (1989).

contribution with the knowledge and intention that it would be merged with the contributions of other authors as "inseparable or interdependent parts of a unitary whole."[10] The key fact is the intention of the collaborators. The parts themselves may be either "inseparable" (as in the case of a novel or painting) or "interdependent" (as in the case of a motion picture, opera, or the words and music of a song). If it were the authors' intention at the time the writing was done that the parts be absorbed or combined into an integrated unit, then the work is considered a "joint work."

The contributions of words and music are usually intended by their authors to be merged to form a joint work. The authors of a joint work are co-owners of copyright in the work,[11] and each author automatically acquires an *undivided* ownership interest in the entire work. Unless otherwise agreed among the co-authors, the authors of a joint work usually share equally in the revenues generated by the work. Thus, where two authors collaborate in the creation of a work, each will have a 50% undivided interest in the entire work; where there are three authors, each will have a 33⅓% undivided interest in the entire work, etc. The authors may, however, agree to another division. For example, where one author contributed words and music and the other worked only on the words, the two may agree to a 75/25% division. Composer George Gershwin always insisted upon receiving a full 50% interest in a composition, even when two lyric writers contributed to the song, each lyric writer in such an instance sharing the other 50% interest equally.

Because each has an interest in the "entire work," each author will benefit to the extent of his or her percentage share in the licensing or exploitation of all or any portion of the joint work. For example, where two authors collaborate in the writing of a song, one writing the words and the other the music, royalties generated by the sale or performance of any instrumental version of the composition will go to both of the authors — equally, or according to percentages otherwise agreed upon — not just the composer of the music. Likewise, royalties from the licensing of any printed edition containing only the lyrics will go to both authors, not just the writer of the words.

---

[10] 17 U.S.C. Sec. 101.
[11] 17 U.S.C. Sec. 201(a).

Co-owners of copyright are generally treated as *tenants-in-common,* with each co-owner having, unless otherwise agreed, an independent right to use, or issue non-exclusive licenses for use of the work, subject to the duty of accounting to the other co-owners for any profits. Co-owners may not issue exclusive licenses without the consent of the other co-owners, and a co-owner may transfer or assign only that portion of the copyright which he or she owns.

## VII. NON-OWNERSHIP OF MUSIC — THE PUBLIC DOMAIN

If a musical composition is in the *public domain*, then no one owns it. Obviously, if no one has a legal claim to the work, then no one else has a legal duty to refrain from using it. Accordingly, no permission is required to use a work that is in the public domain.

A work in the *public domain* (also referred to as, "PD") is a work (1) for which copyright protection was never available, (2) for which copyright protection was never properly secured, or (3) for which copyright protection, though it may have once existed, has expired or otherwise has been lost. For this last reason, public domain has been called the place where copyrights go to die.

In the remainder of this section, we will review some of the considerations used in determining whether a work is in the public domain. The reader should be aware, however, such a determination can be extremely complex. Moreover, recent changes in the copyright law[12] have actually brought within U.S. copyright protection certain works that had previously fallen into the public domain in the U.S.— an action which has no precedent.

## A. Where No Copyright Protection Was Ever Available

Determining whether copyright protection is, or was ever, available for a particular musical composition depends upon the characteristics of the work and whether they, taken together, amount to an *original work of authorship*. Thus, to be a subject of copyright pro-

---

[12] 17 U.S.C. Sec. 104A.

tection, a composition must meet two tests: It must be (1) original, and (2) a work of authorship.

The requirement of *originality* does not mean the work must be novel, unique, or meet any particular standard of esthetic merit. A work is *original* if it is merely original with the author — that is, it was created by the author and not copied from another source. The merest level of creativity is enough. A copyrighted work may be based upon or derived from another work which is not copyrightable, but the test is applied to the *new matter* the author created. For example, a view of the Eiffel Tower from a street in Paris is not copyrightable subject matter, but a photograph of that view is copyrightable by virtue of the photographer's selecting the position from which the photograph was taken, the time of day and year at which it was taken, the type of film used, and other elements that contribute to the resulting work. If what the author added comprises the requisite minimal level of creativity and was not merely copied from another source, then it is *original* for purposes of determining whether it is subject to copyright protection.

Nevertheless, that a work is original with its creator is not enough; to be the subject of a copyright, the work must also be a *work of authorship*. It would seem we would have no trouble considering most musical compositions, no matter how bizarre, as works of authorship, but there is more than some doubt about whether simple drum beats, rhythms, or lyrics comprised merely of common short phrases, such as "I love you, I love you," would be considered a musical work. Justice Oliver Wendell Holmes once defined a musical composition as "a rational collocation of sounds apart from concepts, reduced to a tangible expression from which the collocation can be reproduced either with or without continuous human intervention."[13] Yet that definition may provide little help in drawing the line in particular cases, which are generally decided by the "I know it when I see it" standard. For example, a single taped track of a long repetitive drum beat is not likely to constitute a musical work (though it clearly would be a copyrightable sound recording), but that track, creatively combined with others similar to it, could very well constitute a copyrightable *techno* song.

---

[13] *White-Smith Music Pub. Co. v. Apollo Co.*, 209 U.S. 1, 18 (1908).

Whether a work is a *work of authorship* is often easier defined in negative terms. Section 102(b) of the copyright act states,

> In no case does copyright protection for an original work of authorship extend to any idea, procedure, process, system, method of operation, concept, principle, or discovery, regardless of the form in which it is described, explained, illustrated, or embodied in such work.[14]

A well known axiom of copyright law is that copyright will not protect an *idea*, only an *expression of an idea*. Distinguishing between ideas and expressions of ideas is not always easy. A clear example is the protectability of a particular composition, but not the idea, concept or genre of the composition (e.g., *disco*, or *rap*), or the protectability of the lyrics of *I Want to Hold Your Hand*, but not lyrics about hand holding. A more difficult case might be posed when the story line of one lyric is substantially similar to the story line of another.

In a recent decision concerning Section 102(b), one federal court ruled that the words "idea," "system," "method of operation," "discovery," etc. were synonymous (e.g., suggesting that, just as there are "ideas" and "expressions of ideas," there are "discoveries" and "expressions of discoveries"). Subsequently, a court of appeals reversed that decision, recognizing that "systems," "procedures," "methods of operation," "processes," "discoveries," etc. may be more than mere abstractions.[15] Thus, a new system of musical notation used to record, publish, perform or display a composition (such as the command structure of MIDI, the Musical Instrument Digital Interface) is not copyrightable, though a musical composition written using those commands would be protectable by copyright.[16] Similarly, a new lyric

---

[14] 17 U.S.C. 102(b).

[15] *Lotus v. Borland*, 49 F.3d 807 (1st Cir. 1995) (holding that the commands constituting the method by which a user operated a computer program constituted an uncopyrightable method of operation). The co-author of the present work was General Counsel to defendant.

[16] Inventors of command languages with which people use to instruct computers, or to write computer programs that instruct computers, should look to the patent law for protection of their languages.

form would be no more copyrightable than an original variation of the Miltonian or Shakespearean form of sonnet.

## B. Where Proper Copyright Protection Was Never Secured

Under the copyright act in effect in the U.S. prior to 1978,[17] a copyright in a work was *secured* by publication of the work with a proper copyright notice. If you published the work without affixing to copies of the work a proper copyright notice, the work failed to acquire federal copyright protection and, because publication of the work meant the automatic loss of common law copyright protection (under state law), the work fell into the public domain. Such works, being in the public domain, may be freely used.

Under the new copyright act, and under most copyright laws around the world, copyright is not *secured*; rather, it automatically *subsists* in original works of authorship the moment the work is fixed in a tangible medium of expression, such as on paper or audiotape. Thus, as of January 1, 1978, the concept of common law copyright, governed by the laws of the individual states, ended, and a work immediately acquired copyright protection upon its creation.

## C. Copyright Protection Has Expired or Has Been Lost

When the duration of protection for copyright expires, the work falls into the public domain. The duration of copyright protection must be determined with respect to each country in which you expect to reproduce or distribute the work. As discussed in Chapter 9, on the *Duration of Copyright, Assignments of Copyright and Licenses*, the duration of copyright protection in the U.S. depends upon when the work was created. The reader is referred to that chapter for further details.

Generally, beginning January 1, 2001, works first published in the United States before January 1, 1925 will have fallen into the public domain. Great songs such as, *Rock-A-Bye-Your Baby With a Dixie Melody, Oh! How I Hate to Get Up in the Morning*, and *K-K-K-Katy*, all originally published in 1918, have already passed into the public

---

[17] 17 U.S.C. Sec. 10 (1909 Act).

domain in the United States. In addition, works created before January 1, 1964, the copyrights in which expired after its initial 28 year term because of a failure to properly effect the copyright's renewal term, are in the public domain.[18] And as mentioned above, a work that had been protected by common law copyright under state law, lost that protection upon publication, and, if such publication occurred without copies of the work bearing a valid copyright notice, copyright protection under the federal copyright act was never secured. In addition, before March 1, 1989, the effective date of the Berne Convention Implementation Act, a work for which copyright had been secured by proper publication with notice could lose its copyright protection in the United States if copies of the work were subsequently published in the United States without bearing a valid copyright notice.[19] However, the law provided some exceptions, including the right of the copyright owner to cure the defect within a certain period of time. Subsequent to March 1, 1989, failure to affix a copyright notice on a copy of a work no longer jeopardized the U.S. copyright status of the work. Note, because a work falls in the public domain in the U.S. does not mean that it loses copyright protection overseas.

Determining the copyright status of works overseas is more problematic. For many years, the duration of copyright in most countries has been 50 years after the composer's death, which is now the law in the United States. Further, as noted above, many foreign works which had previously passed into the public domain in the United States have been miraculously revived by the United States's adherence to the terms of the North American Free Trade Agreement (NAFTA) and, more recently, the Uruguay Round of multilateral trade negotiations.[20] As it stands now, by virtue of the Uruguay Round Agreements Act of 1994, copyright protection now subsists in the United States for all works published within the last 75 years, as long as the original work was of foreign origin.

---

[18] See Chapter 9, *Duration of Copyright, Assignments of Copyright and Licenses.*
[19] 17 U.S.C. Sec. 405.
[20] 17 U.S.C. Sec. 104A.

## D. Hidden Problems

Though the above considerations may be useful in ascertaining whether a work is in the public domain,[21] you should take care to exercise the appropriate diligence to be certain there are no hidden rights by virtue of which a license may still be required. The following are areas that may be traps for the unwary:

*1. Territory.* As noted above, while you may be certain that a particular work has fallen into the public domain in the United States, such may not be the case outside of the United States, where durations of copyright have been based upon when the author passed away, as opposed to a specified number of years. There are many works that have fallen into the public domain in the United States, for one reason or another (e.g., failure to renew, publication without copyright notice, expiration of copyright), but whose copyright remains in force throughout the world. In that case, if your plans encompass distributing the work overseas, you must separately ascertain the copyright status in each relevant country.

*2. Arrangements.* Though many popular songs are clearly in the public domain, certain arrangements and orchestrations of those songs, created years after the original authorship of the song, may have been separately copyrighted as "derivative works," and to the extent the copyrights in the arrangements and orchestrations remain in effect, a license will be required to use them. If you plan to use a song in the public domain, and you want to avoid having to license the use of a copyrighted arrangement, it is therefore advisable to obtain a copy of the sheet music dated over 75 years ago. This will assure that the particular arrangement is also in the public domain. Another approach is to gather as many arrangements and orchestrations as possible and copy only those portions which each version has in common with one or more of the others.

---

[21] The reader should consult a copyright treatise, such as Nimmer *On Copyright*, for further rules concerning the copyright status of works around the world.

*3. Translations.* Similarly, copyright in translations of works in the public domain may have been secured separately from the underlying public domain work. If you are going to use a public domain song, and you wish to use translations, you must separately ascertain the status of the copyrights in the translations.

*4. Underlying Works.* Care must be taken to carefully analyze the public domain work to be sure that no copyright in any work underlying the work being examined still subsists. For example, when the copyright in a motion picture expires at the end of a normal full term of copyright, the copyright on any underlying literary property on which the picture was based (e.g., novel, short story, play, screenplay) will normally have expired as well. However, should the copyright in the picture terminate before its full potential term of copyright (e.g., for failure to file a copyright renewal application), the underlying literary property may still be subject to copyright protection. In such event, if you wished to reproduce or distribute the public domain film, a license would still be required from the owner of the copyright in the underlying work. Though rarely is this applicable in the music field, one could well imagine a song's lyric having been derived from a copyrighted short story. If the song fell into the public domain early, permission from the owner of copyright in the underlying short story would be required for continued use of the lyric.

## VIII. DERIVING INCOME FROM MUSIC

The law provides three basic ways for you to derive income from your musical copyright:

A. You may *sell* your copyright or portions of it (i.e., assign all or a portion of your interest in the "undivided copyright");

B. You may carve up your copyright and sell to others one or more *exclusive rights under the copyright*; and

C. You may *license* (i.e., permit) others to use your music on a *non-exclusive* basis.

The remainder of this book primarily concerns this third and most common means of exploiting music copyrights: giving others permission to use the music on a non-exclusive basis, commonly known as *licensing*. Nevertheless, it is essential to understand the meaning of the first and second means of deriving income from music copyrights before delving into the concept of licensing.

## A. Sale of Copyright

Copyright, like other property rights, may be bought and sold, given away, taken away, bequeathed, or otherwise transferred. The transfer of copyright may occur in three basic ways: (1) upon the copyright owner's death by his will or, where no will is left, by the operation of state law (i.e., intestate succession), (2) by voluntary transfer, or assignment, and (3) by involuntary transfer, as in the course of a bankruptcy proceeding. By far the most important of these means of copyright transfer is by *assignment*. As has been noted above, assignment is the first basic means an owner of a copyright can exploit his property — he can sell it.

A copyright may be assigned, or sold, in exchange for legal *consideration*, meaning something of value — for example, money or a promise to pay money or to perform certain obligations. An unusual story of consideration paid for an undivided interest in a song involved the famous big band orchestra leader, Abe Lyman, who collaborated as a writer of such famous songs as, *Mary Lou* and *After I Say I'm Sorry*. The story goes that Abe was waving his baton on the bandstand of the Cocoanut Grove nightclub in Los Angeles in his usual fashion — with his back to the band and his face grinning at the couples on the dance floor — when suddenly he motioned to his pianist to carry on while he stepped off the platform. With typical Lyman brashness, he tapped one of the dancing patrons on the shoulder and explained he had a problem: he had recently purchased a luxury car and needed a few quick bucks to make his payment the next day or lose the car. "If you give me the necessary three C-notes and fifty," he said, "I'll give you a piece of my share of the profits on a song I just wrote with Arthur Freed." The stranger took the proposition in stride and asked to hear the song. Lyman jumped back on the bandstand, played the song, and a few minutes later completed the deal. The impromptu investor was later to be astounded with his first royalty check in the amount of $7,000. The song turned out to be *I Cried For You*, one of the great torch songs[22] of all time.

Money is not the only thing of value that may be given in exchange for a copyright. Copyrights have been known to be assigned in exchange for physical objects of either economic or sentimental value. For example, Judy Garland's Transcona Company, producers of the Warner Bros. Pictures release, A *Star is Born*, employed Roger Edens and Leonard Gersh to write the *Born in a Trunk* sequence used in the film. Gersh admired a certain chest of drawers that had been moved from Judy Garland's bedroom to her hallway. He asked for the chest in exchange for the copyright and in lieu of any future royalties, and Judy gave it to him.

If money or furniture will not do, then promises to pay or do something will be sufficient. When a songwriter signs a songwriter agreement with a music publisher, the publisher is promising to pay to the songwriter the royalties set forth in the contract based upon the publishing revenues from the song. The publisher's obligations under the agreement, together with an implied obligation to use good faith efforts to promote the song, is considered sufficient legal consideration.

Where a copyright is assigned in exchange for a promise, the assignment is said to be made *by contract*, which is the most common way copyrights are assigned or transferred. An assignment of copyright, however, does not require that legal consideration be given in exchange for it; a copyright may be given away as a gift.

As mentioned above, when a composer writes a song, a single copyright is said to *subsist* in the composer the moment he fixes the song in tangible form, such as on paper or recording tape. From that moment, the composer is the copyright owner and is considered to own a 100% *undivided* interest in the copyright of the song. The composer may transfer to another his 100% undivided interest in the copyright. If he does, he will then retain no part of the copyright and his *assignee* (i.e., the recipient in the assignment) will become the owner of the entire 100% interest in the copyright.

---

[22] The term *torch song,* adapted from the colloquial expression, "to carry a torch for" a loved one, became the phrase for a slow, sad, melancholy ballad.

The composer is not limited to assigning 100% of his undivided interest in the copyright; he may assign a lesser percentage, such as 50%, or 33⅓% of his undivided interest. Upon assigning his 50% interest, for example, the composer, and the assignee, will then both own a 50% undivided interest in the copyright.

When a songwriter signs a standard songwriter contract, he is generally assigning to the music publisher all of his 100% undivided interest in his songs. Where a songwriter signs a *co-publishing* agreement or *participation* deal, he is generally agreeing to assign only 75% or 50% of his undivided interest in the songs, reserving the remaining percentage to himself, which in turn the publisher may agree to *administer* on his or her behalf for a standard or negotiated administration fee. Examples of co-publishing and adminstration agreements are set forth at the end of Chapter 4, on *Co-Publishing and Administration.*

## B. Divisibility of Copyright and Sale of Exclusive Rights Under Copyright

Any or all of the exclusive rights under copyright, or any subdivision of those rights, may be assigned. This concept is known as the *divisibility* of copyright, and is one of the more important, but frequently misunderstood features of the copyright law.

Because copyright is "divisible," a copyright owner is not limited to assigning just some percentage of his undivided interest in his copyright. He may also transfer any of an endless number of exclusive rights which comprise the copyright. Under section 106 of the copyright law,[23] the owner of copyright has the exclusive rights to do and to authorize any of the following:

1. to reproduce the copyrighted work in copies or phonorecords;

2. to prepare derivative works based upon the copyrighted work;

3. to distribute copies or phonorecords of the copyrighted work to the public by sale or other transfer of ownership, or by rental, lease, or lending;

---

[23] 17 U.S.C Sec. 106.

4. in the case of literary, musical, dramatic, and choreographic works, pantomimes, and motion pictures and other audiovisual works, to perform the copyrighted work publicly; and

5. in the case of literary, musical, dramatic, and choreographic works, pantomimes, and pictorial, graphic, or sculptural works, including the individual images of a motion picture or other audiovisual work, to display the copyrighted work publicly.

Thus, for example, a copyright owner may assign to another the exclusive right to perform the work publicly, reserving all other exclusive rights, such as the right to reproduce the copyrighted work in copies or phonorecords and the right to prepare derivative works. This was at one time what songwriters and music publishers did when they became members of performing rights societies, such as ASCAP or BMI. In exchange for the copyright owner's assignment of performing rights from the songwriters and publishers, the performing rights society agreed to perform certain tasks, such as surveying performances, collecting performance fees, and distributing royalties to the songwriter and publisher members.[24]

The type of exclusive right which may be assigned, however, is not limited to the several listed in the copyright law. The copyright law provides that any subdivision of any of the rights specified in Section 106, may be transferred and owned separately.[25] Thus, a work may be exclusively licensed in particular markets, in particular forms, in particular territories, and over particular periods of time.

For example, the owner of a copyright in a song may assign any or all of the following exclusive rights: the exclusive right to print sheet music throughout the world; the exclusive right to publish the song in songbooks in the United States and Canada; the exclusive right to publish the song in songbooks in all countries except the United States and Canada; the exclusive right to record the song and distribute

---

[24] Under certain consent decrees negotiated with the U.S. government, the performing rights societies were required to convert the agreements with their writer and publisher members from an exclusive to a non-exclusive basis, but as a practical matter the societies today exercise their licenses to sublicense music performances virtually on an exclusive basis.

[25] 17 U.S.C. Sec. 201(d)(2).

phonorecords throughout the world for a period of five years; the exclusive right to record the song and distribute phonorecords in the United States only beginning in five years; the exclusive right to perform the song throughout the world; the exclusive right to record the song in synchronization with audiovisual images for theatrical distribution in the European Common Market countries for three years, and in all other countries for ten years, etc. As the foregoing may suggest, the potential number of exclusive rights comprised in copyright would appear to be, if not unlimited, then limited only by the business practices and imaginations of the buyers and sellers of exclusive rights under copyright.

When a copyright owner assigns any of the many possible exclusive rights under the copyright, he reserves to himself all other rights that comprise and remain with the copyright. Using any or all of the examples mentioned above, the owner of the full *undivided* copyright, after having assigned the several exclusive rights mentioned, would still remain the owner of the undivided copyright, which would, of course, become subject to the rights of the new owners of the exclusive rights. That is, the copyright owner would be able to exercise all of his rights and privileges as owner of the copyright in the song except that he cannot do or authorize any of the things in which he has assigned to others the exclusive rights to do or authorize others to do.

It is important to note that the interest in the copyright remaining with the owner would still be considered "undivided," even though certain exclusive rights have been carved or "divided" out and separately assigned to others, because the interest in all of the unassigned exclusive rights remaining under the copyright (infinite in number) is still undivided.

As we have seen, the copyright owner may then transfer 100%, or any lesser percentage, of that "undivided" copyright interest in what remains of the copyright. His assignee would become the owner of all or a lesser percentage of the "undivided" copyright, subject, of course, to the rights of the owners of any exclusive rights previously assigned to others.

A songwriter signing a standard music publishing agreement should be aware that he is promising (i.e., look for the words, "warranting and representing") to the publisher that he has not previously assigned to anyone else any of the exclusive rights under the copyrights he is transferring to the music publisher (with the exception of the writer's share in performance rights, which are routinely licensed to the writer's performing rights society, such as ASCAP or BMI). Publishers may sometimes refuse to take anything less than full rights, particularly in the case of new, previously unpublished material, for which the publisher may be taking a measure of financial risk to promote. Songwriters should therefore consider carefully any decision to transfer any of the exclusive rights under copyrights, giving particular attention to the potential effect such a decision may have on the value of the copyright. The value of the whole copyright may be greater than the value of the sum of its parts.

## C. Deriving Income by Licensing Use on a Non-Exclusive Basis

The most common means of deriving income from music copyrights arises from granting to others permission to use the music on a non-exclusive basis. This is commonly known as *issuing* or *granting* licenses, or merely, *licensing*. Nearly all licenses for the use of music involve the exercise of one of the four following exclusive rights under copyright:

1. the exclusive right to make copies: the *reproduction right*,

2. the exclusive right to perform: the *performance right*,

3. the exclusive right to prepare derivative works: the *adaptation right*, and

4. the exclusive right to distribute copies: the *distribution* right.

## IX. TYPES OF LICENSES FOR MUSIC

The copyright law gives the owner of copyright the exclusive rights to make and publish copies of the copyrighted work, to make other versions of the work, to make recordings of the work, and to perform the work in public.[26] As we have said, these exclusive rights involve, by definition, the rights to exclude others, through the power

---

[26] 17 U.S.C. Sec. 106.

of the legal system, from performing those acts. It is this *right to exclude* that forms the basis of the *right to license*, or, in other words, *right to give permission*. The various types of licenses that a copyright owner may grant are defined by *the use* for which permission is sought.

The following are the primary forms of licenses customarily used in the music industry:

## A.  Print Licenses

A *print license* is a permission that authorizes one to make printed copies of music, such as sheet music and printed music folios, and reprints of lyrics in books, magazines, and print advertising. Print licenses are discussed in Chapter 11.

## B.  Mechanical Licenses

A *mechanical license* is the form of permission that authorizes one to make mechanical reproductions of a musical composition, that are not accompanied by a motion picture or other audiovisual work, and which are made for the purpose of distributing them to the public for private use. Examples of such mechanical reproductions include music embodied in piano rolls, record albums, audiocassettes, digital audio tapes, compact optical discs, and computer chips. Motion picture films, videotapes, and audiovisual laser discs that contain music accompanied by motion pictures or other audiovisual works are never the subject of mechanical licenses. Mechanical licenses are discussed at length in Chapter 12.

## C.  Electrical Transcription Licenses

An *electrical transcription license* is the form of permission that authorizes one to make mechanical reproductions of a musical composition, that are not accompanied by a motion picture or other audiovisual work, and which are made for radio broadcast or for purposes other than distribution to the public for private use. Mechanical reproductions of music for radio broadcast are called, "electrical transcriptions," or simply, "transcriptions," the term "electrical" being a holdover from the days before magnetic tape. Examples of transcriptions include recordings of radio theme music, musical introductions, and background music for commercial advertising made specifically for radio broadcast, as well as recordings compiled for use in syndicated radio programs. Electrical Transcription licenses are discussed at length in Chapter 13.

## D. Synchronization Licenses

A *synchronization license* is the form of permission that authorizes one to make mechanical reproductions of a musical composition, that are accompanied by a motion picture or other audiovisual work, for use in connection with motion picture theatrical performance and television broadcast. Examples of such reproductions include, motion pictures, television programs, and music videos, embodied in any form, such as film, tape, and optical laser disc. Technically, the music is not always "synchronized" or recorded, as some licenses say, "in timed-relation with" the motion picture, but these terms convey the notion that the permission to make reproductions of the music is strictly limited to copies embodying the specified motion picture together with the music. Most synchronization licenses contain a further restriction relating to how the copies of a motion picture which embodies a recording of the licensed music may be distributed: these licenses limit the distribution of the motion picture to only those copies that are directly related to effecting the performance of the picture in motion picture theaters and on television. These licenses may impliedly or explicitly restrict any other form of distribution, including distribution on videocassette laser discs for the home video market. Synchronization licenses are discussed at length in Chapter 14.

## E. Videogram Licenses

A *videogram license* is the form of permission that authorizes one to make mechanical reproductions of a musical composition, that are accompanied by a motion picture or other audiovisual work, and which may be distributed on videocassette, optical laser disc, or other home video device for distribution into the home video market. Videogram licenses are discussed at length in Chapter 15.

## F. Commercial Synchronization Licenses

A *commercial synchronization license* is the form of synchronization license, that authorizes one to make reproductions of and broadcast performances of a musical composition in connection with the promotion or advertising of a commercial product. See Chapter 20 for a more detailed discussion of licenses for the use of music in commercial advertising.

## G. Musical Product Licenses

A *musical product license* is the form of permission that authorizes one to make mechanical reproductions of a musical composition in connection with the distribution of a commercial product, such as wind-up music boxes, singing dolls, and musical greeting cards.

This form of license may resemble either a mechanical license or a videogram license, depending on whether the use of music in the product is accompanied by audiovisual images. See Chapter 21 for a more detailed discussion of musical product licenses.

## H. Multimedia License

A *multimedia license* is a "catch-all" term for the form of permission that authorizes one to make reproductions of a musical composition in connection with the distribution of multimedia compact discs, computer software, karaoke, and other new media devices. See Chapter 22 for a more detailed discussion of these emerging forms of licenses.

## I. Digital Transmission Licenses and Digital Reproduction Licenses

The forms of licenses that authorize one to digitally transmit musical works and to reproduce them by means of digital transmissions do not have generally accepted names yet, but they are discussed in Chapter 23 on *Licensing Musical Works and Sound Recordings on the Internet*.

## J. Performance Licenses

A *performance license* is a permission that authorizes one to perform a work publicly. Performance licenses are discussed in Chapter 17.

## K. Dramatic Performance Licenses and Grand Performance Licenses

A *dramatic performance license* is a permission that authorizes the performance of a song dramatically — that is, when the song is used to carry forward the plot or story of a dramatic work, such as a motion picture, television program, or theatrical play. A *grand performance license* is a not a license in music at all — it is a license to perform a grand opera or grand musical play, or portion thereof. The rights that form the basis of these types of licenses are discussed at length in Chapter 18.

## L. Dramatic Adaptation Licenses

A *dramatic adaptation license* is a permission that authorizes one to make a dramatization of a musical composition, or more accurately, its lyrics. Just as a motion picture can be a dramatic adaptation of a novel, a motion picture or television program may be a dramatic adaptation of the lyrics of a song. Although a motion picture adaptation of a song may include a performance of the song, a dramatic adaptation license does not authorize one to render a dramatic performance of the song, a license for which must be acquired separately. This type of license is discussed in Chapter 18.

## X. DIFFERENCES IN THE RIGHTS AND PRIVILEGES OF HOLDERS OF EXCLUSIVE RIGHTS AND NON-EXCLUSIVE LICENSES

The copyright law entitles the owner of any exclusive right, to the extent of that right, "all of the protection and remedies accorded to the copyright owner."[27] This means, for example, that a person holding an exclusive right to do something, such as perform a particular composition on television may sue in his own name anyone who infringes that particular right, even though the undivided copyright remains in the hands of someone else. By contrast, a non-exclusive

---

[27] 17 U.S.C. Sec. 201(d)(2).

licensee of a similar right of performance would not be able to sue in his own name to stop others who perform the song without permission.

Similarly, an owner of exclusive rights under copyright, unlike a licensee, may file an application for copyright registration for his exclusive claim. (Though the exclusive rights owner may file the application, he must still identify the owner of the "undivided" copyright as the "claimant" on the copyright application.)

As will be noted in Chapter 8, the formalities required to effectuate an assignment of exclusive rights and a grant of non-exclusive licenses differ significantly. An assignment of exclusive rights must be in writing; a non-exclusive license may be effected orally.

Thus, the owner of an exclusive right, to the extent of his exclusive right, is treated much the same as the owner of the "undivided" copyright. By contrast, the non-exclusive licensee of a right under the copyright is not treated at all like an "owner" — he merely has permission to do an act which without such permission would constitute copyright infringement.

As we have pointed out, the potential number and variety of exclusive rights comprised in copyright, and the potential number and variety of non-exclusive licenses, would appear to be limited only by the imaginations of the owners and users of music. Interestingly enough, as the precision with which exclusive rights are defined increases, the distinction between exclusive rights and non-exclusive rights becomes rather nebulous.

Consider, for example, the "exclusive right to perform a song on a certain television program to be broadcast in the United States next Tuesday evening between the hours of 7:00 and 9:00 PM EST." Would the owner of such an exclusive right have fewer privileges if the equivalent grant were made instead on a non-exclusive basis? The exclusivity being rather ephemeral, it becomes difficult to distinguish such an exclusive right from a non-exclusive license covering the same use.

We have listed above several differences between the rights of owners of exclusive rights and the privileges of non-exclusive licensees. An owner of an exclusive right under copyright, unlike a non-exclusive licensee, may sue in his own name anyone who infringes his exclusive right; an owner of exclusive rights under copyright, unlike a licensee, may file an application for copyright registration; and an assignment of exclusive rights must be in writing, while a non-exclusive license may be effected orally.

Though the foregoing suggests that there are some legal differences between transferring a narrowly defined exclusive license and granting an equivalent license on a non-exclusive basis, it is likely that the differences will have little or no practical significance, if for no other reason than virtually all narrowly defined licenses are formulated on a non-exclusive basis.

## XI. AVOIDING CONFUSION
## — EXCLUSIVE RIGHT VERSUS NON-EXCLUSIVE LICENSE

At the outset of this chapter, we explained the difference between a right and a license, saying that a right is a *claim* — the ability, enforceable by law, to exclude others from exercising the privilege of possessing, using or disposing of an object — and a license is a *permission* to do something with the object which, by reason of another's claim in it, one would not otherwise have the privilege to do.

Because the terms *right* and *license* refer to two completely different concepts, they should not be used interchangeably. For example, you should never see the term, "exclusive license," a term which at best contradicts itself. The proper term is "exclusive right." If the "right" is not exclusive (i.e., no intent is present to give the licensee the legal author-ity to exclude others from doing the same thing), then it probably is a license (i.e., merely permission). If a license purports to be exclusive, then it is actually a right.

A phrase that is commonly used in contracts regarding intellectual property is "exclusive right and license." The use of this phrase may be proper depending upon the context. The only context in which such a use would be proper is if you consider the terms "exclusive right" and "license" separately. When you grant a license, you are granting a permission to another to exercise a privilege to do something. In addition to granting to another a license to do something, you may grant an exclusive right — that is, the right to exclude others from doing the same thing. Correctly construed, the phrase "A hereby grants to B the exclusive right and license to" do something means that (i) A grants to B the privilege to do something that otherwise B would not be able to do, and (ii) A grants to B the right to exclude others from doing the same thing.

It might therefore be helpful if practitioners replaced the phrase, "exclusive right and license" (which may be improperly construed as, "exclusive right and exclusive license") with "license and exclusive right."

As will be noted in greater detail in Chapters 8 and 9, the distinction between a grant of an "exclusive right" and a grant of a "non-exclusive license" is significant in at least two respects: (1) the formalities necessary to effectuate assignments and licenses, and (2) the duration of assignments and licenses.

## XII. AVOIDING CONFUSION
## — UNDERSTANDING OWNERSHIP OF THE "UNDIVIDED" COPYRIGHT

The understanding of the foregoing definitions and principals, and the solving of many day-to-day copyright problems, can be facilitated by considering one point: there is always just one copyright for each work — we call this the *undivided* copyright.

The undivided copyright may be owned by one or more individuals each with equal or varying shares of a 100% total. Even though the copyright may be "divided" into numerous exclusive rights, and even though some of those rights may be transferred away and owned by others, remember that each separately assigned exclusive right always relates back to that "undivided" copyright.

When this is understood, common legal questions relating to copyright, such as determining the proper copyright "claimant" in an application for copyright registration or the proper name to include in the "copyright notice" becomes simple: in each case it is always the owner or owners of the "undivided" copyright.

## XIII. AVOIDING CONFUSION
## — SELLING, ASSIGNING, GRANTING, AND LICENSING

Many of the formal terms used in copyright transfers and licenses are also misunderstood and may become the source of some confusion.

When you transfer (e.g., sell or give away) an interest in your undivided copyright, or in any exclusive rights under the copyright, the document effecting the transfer will typically state that you *grant*, *transfer*, *sell*, or *assign* such interest to the person receiving the interest. Any one of these words, alone or in combination, will be sufficient. If you are the buyer or assignee of a copyright or exclusive right, you would be advised to use the words, "sells and assigns," which should make it absolutely certain that you are receiving an ownership claim, rather than merely a license.

If the instrument is intended to effect a non-exclusive license, then it would be improper for the instrument to use the words "assign," "transfer," or "sell." Non-exclusive licenses, unlike interests in the undivided copyright or exclusive rights under it, are not "rights." As we have pointed out, a right is a *claim* to ownership. A license is not a claim to ownership; it is merely a *permission* to do something which you would not otherwise have the privilege to do. People *grant* permission; they do not *transfer* or *assign* permission. Likewise, you do not transfer or assign a license, you *grant* a license. (Arguably, you can "sell" your permission, and, accordingly, sell a license, but it is recommended that the word sell be used solely in the context of an actual transfer of rights).

By the same token, to say "Publisher grants a non-exclusive right to . . ." is incorrect, because only a permission is being conferred, not a claim to ownership, or *right*, in any portion of either the undivided copyright or in any of the exclusive rights under the copyright. It is better, therefore, to say "Publisher grants a non-exclusive license to . . . ," in the sense that a permission or privilege to do something (i.e., to use the music in a certain way) is being allowed or granted, but not a claim of ownership (i.e., the legal ability to exclude others from doing the same thing).

Finally, the phrase, "Publisher grants the right and license to . . ."is redundant in the context of a non-exclusive license, because only a permission is being conferred, not a claim to ownership, or *right*, and, in that context, the word "right" can only have meant to be synonymous with "license."

## XIV. THE LANGUAGE OF THE ART

The language of music licensing is the lifeblood of the music business. The business of music, more than any other, is inextricably intertwined with the laws and contracts that define the legal relationships among owners and the users of the "objects" produced. These laws and contracts are comprised of words that express important concepts relating to the structure of legal relationships — but merely words, nothing more.

An art that is so reliant upon the use of words requires precision in the use of those words to perform the art well. For this reason, words that refer to completely different concepts should not be confounded or used indiscriminately. On the contrary, terms of art should be treated as such. When so much rests upon how and when these words are used, it behooves those who wish to succeed to use them well.

We mean no pedantry. On the contrary, it is fervently hoped that this be genuinely viewed as an aid to understanding. Clarity of thought about an art should increase one's understanding and appreciation of it and should make one's reaction to it more certain. If the precision suggested in this book aids the reader in understanding and finding solutions to practical problems in the business of music licensing, then its has served its purpose.

CHAPTER 8

# FORMALITIES OF MUSIC LICENSING

## SUMMARY

### I. FORMALITIES OF ASSIGNMENT

A. Assignment Must Be in Writing

B. Recordation of Assignments

C. Short Form Assignment Document

### II. FORMALITIES OF LICENSING

A. Written Licenses

B. Oral Licenses

C. Implied Licenses

D. Operation of Law

### III. GET IT IN WRITING

### IV. LETTER FORM VERSUS CONTRACT FORM

### V. REFERENCE TO THE PARTIES

### VI. STANDARD TERMS AND CONDITIONS

### VII. FORMS USED IN THIS BOOK

### APPENDIX TO CHAPTER 8

# FORMALITIES OF
# MUSIC LICENSING

T his chapter reviews the formalities necessary to effectuate grants of copyright, exclusive rights under copyright, and licenses.

As noted in the preceding chapter, only interests in undivided *copyrights* and *exclusive rights under copyright* may be *assigned* (i.e., sold, or otherwise transferred from one person to another). Permission to use music on a non-exclusive basis is the subject of a *license*, and licenses are not proper subjects for "assignments," "transfers," or "sales" of rights.[1] A grant of license, or permission, does not require that any particular formalities be followed, but there are good reasons to comply with certain formalities when granting or clearing licenses, and these are discussed later in this chapter.

Certain formalities, however, are necessary conditions for effecting assignments of copyright, and exclusive rights under copyright, and these will be discussed in the following section.

## I. FORMALITIES OF ASSIGNMENT

To *assign* a copyright means to transfer ownership of that copyright from one person to another. The ownership of copyright may be transferred in whole or in part by any means of conveyance or by operation of law, and may be bequeathed by will or pass as personal property by the applicable laws of intestate succession.[2] In recognition

---

[1] "A 'transfer of copyright ownership' is an assignment, mortgage, exclusive license, or any other conveyance, alienation, or hypothecation of a copyright or any of the exclusive rights under copyright, whether or not it is limited in time or in place of effect, *but not including a nonexclusive license*." 17 U.S.C. Sec. 101 (emphasis added).

[2] 17 U.S.C. Sec. 201(d)(1)

of the divisibility of copyright, the law provides that any of the exclusive rights comprised in a copyright maybe transferred and owned separately.[3]

## A. Assignment Must Be in Writing

A transfer of copyright, or any exclusive rights under copyright, other than by operation of law, is not valid unless an instrument of conveyance, or a note or memorandum of the transfer, is in writing and signed by the owner of the rights or such owner's duly authorized agent.[4]

Legal *consideration* is not required for an assignment to be valid. This means the *assignee* (i.e., person receiving the assignment of rights) does not need to give something of value (e.g., money, promise to pay royalties, etc.) in return for the rights, unless, of course, the assignment was conditioned upon the receipt of such consideration. Thus, an assignment of rights may be a gift.

An assignment of copyright in a composition may be executed even when the song is not yet in existence; in such cases, the assignment will be deemed effective upon the song's creation. An example of such an assignment appears in any exclusive term songwriter agreement under which the songwriter promises to the music publisher the copyrights in all of the songs which the songwriter creates during the term of the contract.

The assignment form need not be notarized or witnessed to be valid. Nevertheless, a procedural advantage, though slight, in possible future court actions may be gained by a notarial acknowledgment.[5]

It is important to note that ownership of copyright in a work, or any of the exclusive rights under the copyright, is distinct from ownership of any material object in which the work may be embodied.[6] Accordingly, transfer of ownership of any material object, including the copy or phonorecord in which the work is first fixed (e.g., the

---

[3] 17 U.S.C. Sec. 201(d)(2)

[4] 17 U.S.C. Sec. 204(a)

[5] A properly executed certificate of acknowledgment is prima facie evidence of the execution of the transfer. 17 U.S.C. Sec. 204(b)

[6] 17 U.S.C. Sec. 202

original lead sheet or audiocassette recording), does not of itself convey any rights in the copyrighted work embodied in the object.[7] Nor, for that matter, does an assignment of the copyright convey property rights in any material object, even if that object contains the only existing copy or recording of the work. Further, the physical transfer of a certificate of copyright registration will not constitute an assignment of copyright. Transfer of ownership in copyrights and exclusive rights under copyright may be effected only by the express terms of written legal instruments, such as contracts, assignment forms, and the like.

## B. Recordation of Assignments

Although the Copyright Office does not supply any forms for transfers of copyright, the law does provide for the recordation in the Copyright Office of transfers of copyright.[8] Although recordation is not required to make a valid transfer as between parties, it does provide certain legal advantages and may be required to validate the transfer against third parties. For example, as between two conflicting transfers of the same copyright, the one executed first will be recognized and given legal effect if it is recorded in the Copyright Office within one month after its execution or at any time before the recordation of the later transfer. (Otherwise the later transfer prevails if it is recorded and was received in good faith, for consideration, and without notice of the earlier transfer). It is therefore good practice for assignees to record all assignments within thirty days after the execution of the assignment.

In addition to resolving conflicting assignments, another good practical reason for promptly recording all assignments is to maintain a complete and independent record of the copyright's *chain of title*. Maintaining a record of the important documents pertaining to a copyright in a safe, central location, such as the Copyright Office of the Library of Congress, will enable the copyright owner to reconstruct his copyright records in the event of a natural disaster or fire.

---

[7] *Id.*
[8] 17 U.S.C. Sec. 205

## C. Short Form Assignment Document

Most assignments of copyrights in musical compositions are effected by contract, usually a music publishing contract. Several forms of agreements containing assignments of copyright, portions of copyright, and exclusive rights under copyright are included in this book. For example, a standard form single song music publishing agreement assigning the entire undivided copyright in an individual composition is set forth at the end of Chapter 3 on *Songwriter Agreements*. Examples of co-publishing agreements that assign an undivided 50% interest in a copyright is set forth at the end of Chapter 4, on *Co-Publishing and Administration*. An exclusive print agreement, assigning certain exclusive rights under copyright, is set forth as Form 11.1 at the end of Chapter 11 on *Print Licenses*.

Each of these agreements involve an assignment of copyright, portion of copyright, or exclusive right under copyright, and each may be recorded in the Copyright Office. As previously discussed, there are a number of good reasons for recording assignments of copyrights. Nevertheless, there is good reason not to record these or any other kind of detailed music publishing agreement: it may be undesirable for the parties to allow the terms of their contract to become a matter of public knowledge. The problem is that a publishing agreement may contain (i) the detailed terms of the relationship which the parties desire to maintain in confidence, but, at the same time, (ii) a clear assignment of rights, the existence of which the parties desire to disclose to the world.

The industry, however, has provided a solution that apprises the public of the existence of the assignment without disclosing the terms of the contract. When a songwriter, or other assignor of copyright, signs a contract setting forth the full terms of the assignment of copyright (e.g., royalty rates, advances), he will usually be asked to simultaneously sign a second, often one page, document, which describes the rights assigned, but omits all other information about what the assignee may have paid for, or agreed to perform, in exchange for the rights assigned. This document is known as a *short-form copyright assignment*.

The assignee records with the Copyright Office only the short-form, and the parties maintain in confidence the details of the agreement contained in their *long-form* contract. The short form assignment should not refer by its terms to any long-form contract covering the relationship between the parties, because the Copyright Office has been known to require that a copy of any document referred to in the assignment form also be recorded, which would defeat the purpose of using the short form. If the assignee is uncomfortable having a document that does not state the consideration being given in exchange for the assignment, he can include a provision in the short-form that the assignment was made "for good and valuable consideration" or "for and in consideration of One Dollar ($1)." A sample "short-form" copyright assignment is set forth as Form 8.1 at the end of this chapter.

## II. FORMALITIES OF LICENSING

In contrast to what is required to effect an assignment of copyright, or exclusive rights under copyright, the grant of a license on a non-exclusive basis is not required to be in writing. Licenses can be conferred in a number of ways: (1) in writing, (2) orally, (3) implied from the acts of the parties, or (4) created by operation of law.

### A. Written Licenses

The most common form of license is a formal written document setting forth precisely the scope of the permission. A *written license* may be in the form of a contract signed by the licensor and the licensee, or merely by a letter granting permission signed by the licensor.

### B. Oral Licenses

*Oral licenses* are licenses spoken in person or over the telephone. Oral licenses are sometimes referred to as *verbal licenses*, even though such use of the word verbal is poor diction — the word "verbal" refers to that which contains or concerns words, and certainly both oral and written licenses fit comfortably within that definition.

Oral licenses are uncommon for a variety of reasons which are discussed below. An apt observation that has been ascribed to movie producer, Samuel Goldwyn, is that "Oral agreements are not worth the paper they're written on."

## C. Implied Licenses

An *implied license* is a license that is not expressed in verbal (i.e., oral or written) form. A license may be *implied* where a person could reasonably infer from the conduct of the copyright owner that permission was granted.[9]

For example, a record company could be deemed to have an implied license to distribute an album containing a song written by the album's recording artist who, by recording the song under the terms of a separate agreement for purposes of putting on the album, lead the record company to reasonably believe it had permission to distribute copies of the song on that album, notwithstanding the absence of a written mechanical license to do so. The scope of the permission would be determined by the conduct of the parties. In the above example, the record company's license would probably be limited to distribution of the song on the album, but would not include a synchronization license in the absence of evidence showing the uses implied from the circumstances would go beyond that of use in the form of mechanical reproductions of the album (e.g., circumstances may also imply that the song was also to be used by the record company in connection with some audiovisual work, such as a music video, but not in a motion picture unrelated to the artist's obligations or performance under his recording agreement).

Licenses that are implied may be revoked at any time, but in certain instances the copyright owner's right to revoke may be limited or *estopped*, particularly where the licensee can show he acted in justifiable reliance upon the owner's conduct and would be damaged by an unreasonable or untimely revocation of the license.

---

[9] See, *Effects Associates, Inc. v. Cohen*, 908 F.2d 555 (9th Cir. 1990) (Expressing its dismay at the parties' failing to memorialize a license in writing — "Movie-makers do lunch, not contracts" — the court nevertheless found a license was implied by the conduct of the parties); *Johnson v. Jones,* 885 F. Supp 1008, 1014 (E.D. Mich. 1995) ("[A]ll of the circumstances surrounding the negotiations made between the parties must be considered to determine if and to what extent an implied license was granted."). See also *McLean v. Wm. M. Mercer-Meidinger-Hanson,* 952 F.2d 769, 779 (3rd Cir. 1991)) ("Since a non-exclusive license does not transfer ownership of the copyright from the licensor to the licensee, the licensor can still bring suit for copyright infringement if the licensee's use goes beyond the scope of the nonexclusive license." [Citing *Effects Association,* 908 F.2d at 558 n.5]).

## D. Operation of Law

Licenses can also be created by *operation of law*. For example, licenses may be bequeathed by will or pass as personal property by the applicable laws of intestate succession. Licenses may also be conferred by operation of the compulsory license provision of the copyright law.[10]

## III. GET IT IN WRITING

All transactions discussed in this book should be reduced to writing. It is not a matter of having or showing a trust or distrust in another, or even trust in an otherwise honest person's memory.

Having a license in writing may protect you from a conflicting license or transfer of the copyright. A non-exclusive license, whether recorded with the Copyright Office or not, will be effective even if there exists a transfer of copyright ownership in conflict with it, as long as the license was *in writing* and was either granted before the transfer of copyright was executed or was received in good faith before the recordation of the transfer of copyright and taken without notice of the transfer.

A producer of a work that contains copyrighted works of others would be prudent to maintain a written record showing the contractual basis demonstrating that the producer has all the rights and licenses necessary to effect the intended use of the work. Having a good record of rights and licenses will become useful, and often essential, at the time the producer considers signing an important agreement for the distribution of the work or selling the work to another. Upon a sale of copyright, or important exclusive rights under copyright, the buyer is likely to perform an extensive *due diligence* investigation to confirm whether the seller, indeed, has all of the rights and licenses necessary to support the warranties and representations he is making in the sale contract. Keeping good files of contracts with, and licenses from, all the contributors of intellectual property to the final work will avoid

---

[10] 17 U.S.C. Sec. 115

unnecessary delay and unanticipated costs when it comes time to exploit or dispose of the work.

Even licensors are advised to memorialize all licenses in writing. If a copyright owner takes action leading a producer to believe he had a license to synchronize music in a motion picture, a license may be *implied* from the circumstances. In any dispute with the producer regarding the scope of the license, the terms of the implied license would become a matter for the courts to decide. Because of the high costs of litigation, it may be uneconomical to file a lawsuit to have the courts circumscribe the scope of the license, thereby making it difficult to assert the right to collect additional fees for other uses, such as, for example, a royalty on the distribution of videogram copies of the work.

## IV. LETTER FORM VERSUS CONTRACT FORM

A common question in music licensing is what's the difference between a license in *letter* form and a license in standard *contract* form, or long-form, and under what circumstances should one form be used over the other? An example of a "letter agreement" is set forth as Form 11.4 and an example of a "long-form contract" is set forth as Form 11.2 at the end of Chapter 11, on *Print Licenses*.

Letter agreements are generally shorter, omitting much of the usual boilerplate contained in longer form contracts. Used for simpler licenses, such as letters permitting the reprint of a song lyric, the letter form is clearly a more informal way of reducing an agreement to writing. Letter agreements are also used, however, to memorialize longer, more sophisticated agreements. Sometimes it is felt that, because of the long standing relationship and previous dealings between the parties, the informality of the letter agreement is more appropriate. Some feel that letter forms should always be used in lieu of long-form contracts, because, if the agreement ever became the subject of litigation, the letter form would be more approachable[11] by the courts and juries.

---

[11] In computer parlance, more "user-friendly."

In answer to the question when to use a letter agreement or long-form contract, we offer the following suggestion: all licenses should be issued using an informal letter agreement; all grant of copyrights, or exclusive rights under copyright, should be effected by the more formal standard contract form. Following this procedure would properly reflect the fundamental difference between granting permission to exercise a privilege, which is the subject of a *license*, and granting a property right, which is the subject of an *assignment* of copyright or exclusive rights under copyright. Granting permission, or license, is a less formal event than assigning a property right, and the form used to effect each should reflect their relative formality. Accordingly, the license form that is most appropriate to the circumstances of the deal will always be used.

A common observation about contracts in the entertainment industry is that the more money that is involved in a transaction, the longer the contract. Motion picture distribution contracts, often involving hundreds of millions of dollars tend to be longer and more complex than contracts used in the music recording industry which usually involve only millions of dollars, which in turn tend to be longer and more complex than contracts used in the relatively smaller music publishing industry. Mere licenses for the use of music should be placed at the appro-priate point along the scale of complexity. In today's world of word processing machines, it is a wonder how even the simplest permission letters have not become the subject of multiple page tomes that can now be generated at the touch of a button. It is hoped that people responsible for drafting or generating licenses from word processing software will continue to use the license form that is most appropriate to the circumstances of the deal.

## V. REFERENCE TO THE PARTIES

Sometimes the letter form goes one step further to become informal, more readable, or user-friendly: discarding terms such as "licensor" and "publisher," and "licensee," and "producer," the letter refers to the parties as "we" and "us," and "you" and "your." Though this approach can be confusing when used in longer agreements, it is often quite appropriate and welcome in short letter agreements of one or two pages. An example of a letter agreement that uses this approach is set forth as Form 11.6 at the end of Chapter 11, on *Print Licenses*.

By contrast, the use of the formal terms, "Licensor" and "Licensee," "Grantor" and "Grantee," or "Assignee" and "Assignor," in longer contracts, each of which pair differ only by two letters, can make longer agreements quite tedious to read, and can even create some confusion in shorter contracts or letter agreements. It is therefore recommended that when selecting terms with which to refer to the parties, the draftor should choose a pair of words that are dissimilar and less likely to cause confusion. For example, the music copyright owner, the party granting the license or transferring the rights, may be referred to as, the "Owner." The licensee may be referred to as "Licensee," "Producer," or some other term that best describes the party requiring the clearance.

If, in addition to the privilege to do something with respect to the music, the contract grants an assignment of exclusive rights (i.e., the right to exclude others from doing the same thing), then neither "Licensor" nor "Licensee" may be the most appropriate means of referring to a party. The "Licensor" is doing more than granting a license and, therefore, should be called something else, such as "Owner." Because the grantee is receiving more than a mere permission to do something, he should be called something other than "Licensee," such as "Producer."

## VI. STANDARD TERMS AND CONDITIONS

An increasingly popular compromise between the informality of the letter agreement and the benefits of long-form license agreements is the use of a letter agreement that incorporates by reference a standard set of terms and conditions that is often applicable to several kinds of licenses. An example of such an agreement is set forth as Form 3.8 at the end of Chapter 3, on *Songwriter Agreements*.

## VII. FORMS USED IN THIS BOOK

The forms used in this book do not consistently reflect the principals discussed above. They certainly do not always reflect the best principals of drafting and their inclusion here should *not* be construed as their representing some form of ideal. On the contrary, the forms selected are representative of those customarily used in the music publishing industry today and are included primarily for the purpose of illustrating the practical guidance outlined in this book for both copyright owners and persons seeking to clear licenses. Accordingly, the forms should be used primarily to improve the reader's understanding and appreciation of that guidance. They should not be used without further consideration about how they should be applied to the transaction at hand, and should not be used by laymen without seeking the advice of an attorney experienced in the field of licensing or music publishing.

# APPENDIX TO CHAPTER 8
# FORMALITIES OF MUSIC LICENSING

# FORM 8.1

## SHORT FORM COPYRIGHT ASSIGNMENT

### ASSIGNMENT

DATED:                          January 1, 2000

ASSIGNOR (S):                   Cameron Composer
                                Lawrence Lyrics

ASSIGNEE(S):                    BIG MUSIC PUBLISHING CORP.

PORTION CONVEYED:    One Hundred Percent (100%)

For valuable consideration, ASSIGNOR hereby assigns, transfers, sets over and conveys to ASSIGNEE that proportion of all rights, title and interest set forth in and to the musical composition(s):

### I LOVE YOU, BABY

including the copyrights and proprietary rights therein and in any and all versions of said musical composition(s), and any renewals and extensions thereof (whether presently available or subsequently available as a result of intervening legislation) in the United States of America and elsewhere throughout the world, and further including any and all causes of action for infringement of the same, past, present and future, all of the proceeds from the foregoing accrued and unpaid hereafter accruing.

ASSIGNOR agrees to sign any and all other papers which may be required to effectuate the purpose and intent of this Assignment, and hereby irrevocably authorizes and appoints ASSIGNEE his attorney and representative in its name or in his name as his true and lawful attorney-in-fact to take such action and make, sign, execute, acknowledge and deliver all such documents as may from time to time be necessary to convey to ASSIGNEE, its successors and assigns, all rights herein granted.

IN WITNESS WHEREOF, the undersigned has executed this Assignment as of the date above written.


Signed: _____

Signed: _____

# FORM 8.2

## MULTI-PURPOSE WORK FOR HIRE AGREEMENT

### WORK FOR HIRE

THIS AGREEMENT MADE THIS _____ day of _____, 20____, by and between _____ "Employee") and _____ hereinafter referred to as "Employer")

This agreement is made with reference to the following facts:

    A.   Definition:   A "work made for hire" is:

       1.   A work prepared by an employee within the scope of his or her employment; or

       2.   A work specially ordered or commissioned for use by employer or other person for whom the work was prepared where the parties expressly agree in a written instrument signed by them that the work shall be considered a work made for hire. For purposes of this agreement, employer is synonymous with any such person for whom the work was prepared.

       3.   Any other work that is within the definition of work made for hire within 17 U.S.C. Sec. 101.

    B.   Employer is engaged in the business of _____. Employer desires to acquire the exclusive services of employee for the purpose of _____.

    C.   Employee desires to make his services available exclusively for Employer in accordance with the terms and conditions hereinafter stated.

The parties agree as follows:

1.    Employee acknowledges and expressly agrees that each _____ work prepared hereunder embodying the results and proceeds of employee's services

    (a)    is prepared within the scope of employer's engagement of employee's personal services and is a work made for hire, or

    (b)    as part of a work specially ordered by employer or commissioned for use by employer as a contribution to a collective work shall be considered a work made for hire, or

    (c)    as part of a motion picture or other audiovisual work, as a translation, as a supplementary work, as a compilation, or as an instructional text shall be considered a work made for hire.

2.    Employee further acknowledges that employer is considered the author of the work and employer is the exclusive owner of copyright in each work made for hire, and of all rights comprised in copyright, and that employer shall have the right to exercise all rights of copyright owner with respect thereto, including but not limited to: all exclusive rights specified in 17 U.S.C Sec. 106.

Employer shall register for copyright in the name of Employer.

EMPLOYEE

By _____

EMPLOYER

By _____

# FORM 8.3

## MUSICAL ARRANGEMENT WORK FOR HIRE AGREEMENT

### MUSICAL ARRANGER AGREEMENT

WHEREAS, the undersigned, _____
an employee for hire of _____
("Employer") will at Employer's request and at direction will make an arrangement of the music of a composition ("composition") entitled _____

_____

_____

NOW, THEREFORE, in consideration of the sum of _____
_____ and other good and valuable considerations, the receipt of which is hereby duly acknowledged, the undersigned hereby confirms said employment and agrees that such arrangement shall be a work made for hire of Employer. In the event such arrangement shall be deemed not to be a work made for hire, then the undersigned hereby sells, assigns, and transfers over to Employer, and releases and quitclaims unto Employer, its successors and assigns, all right, title and interest in and to the Composition and all rights therein and thereto, for the United States and throughout the world, forever, including any and all copyright terms, and all extension terms of copyright, for all uses and purposes whether now known or hereafter created, free from payment of any royalty or further compensation. Credit may be given for said arrangement to the undersigned or not at all. The undersigned warrants and represents that he has not sold, transferred, assigned or otherwise disposed of any right, title or interest in or to any of the rights, referred to in this agreement; and that except insofar as the work is based on material hereinabove described the same is original with him.

IN WITNESS WHEREOF, the undersigned has hereunto set his hand and seal this _____ day of _____, 20__.

                                    _____

# FORM 8.4

## LYRIC TRANSLATION WORK FOR HIRE AGREEMENT

### LYRIC TRANSLATION

I, _____, hereby certify that as an employee-for-hire of _____, I have been engaged to create a [French/Spanish/Italian/German/Other] lyric, per copy attached ("Translation"), under the title _____ for the musical composition _____ by _____, with the consent and permission of _____, the copyright owner of said musical composition, and that the Translation shall be a work made for hire of _____, who, as proprietor of copyright in a work made for hire is the author and owner of the copyright in all renewals and extensions thereof and all other rights of every kind and character in and to said Translation free from the payment of any royalty, or further compensation whatsoever and without participation in any earnings or credits therefrom including public performances credits and fees. It is understood that on all uses of and references to said lyric, including record labels and record album liners, I am not to receive writer credit.

Dated: _____

By _____

# DURATION OF COPYRIGHT, ASSIGNMENTS OF COPYRIGHT, AND LICENSES

## SUMMARY

## V. DURATION OF AN ASSIGNMENT OF RENEWAL COPYRIGHT

A. Limited Relevancy

B. Renewal Copyright Versus Renewal Expectancy

C. Transfer of Renewal Expectancy

D. Operation of the Rule of Renewal Expectancy

E. Formalities of Assigning Renewal Expectancies

F. Renewal Copyright Vesting

G. Renewal Vesting Under Copyright Renewal Act of 1992

H. Affect of 1992 Act on Assignments of Role of Renewal Expectancies

I. Persons Entitled to Submit Renewal Applications

J. Advice for Music Publishers

K. Advice for Songwriters

## VI. DURATION OF LICENSES

A. By Terms of the License

B. By Terms of the Copyright Law

   1. Termination of Licenses Granted by Authors After January 1, 1978

   2. Licenses Covering the Initial Term of Copyright

   3. Licensing Purporting to Cover the Renewal Term of Copyright

   4. Effects of Rear Window on Music Licensing

      a. Effect on Which Songs Will Be Used in New Derivative Works

      b. Effect on the Terms, If Any, upon Which Previously Produced Derivative Works May Continue to Be Exploited

         (1) Licenses Granted to Music Publishers

         (2) Mechanical Licenses Granted to Record Companies

         (3) Synchronization Licenses Granted to Producers

    (4)   Master Licenses Granted to Producers to Use Sound Recordings

    (5)   Owners of Copies or Phonorecords Containing Affected Works

5. Effect of 1992 Act

6. Advice for Derivative Licensees

7. Advice for Music Publishers

8. Advice for Songwriters

9. Licenses Covering the Extended (19-Year) Term of Copyright

## VII. After Life

## Appendix to Chapter 9

# DURATION OF COPYRIGHT ASSIGNMENTS OF COPYRIGHT, AND LICENSES

T his chapter is about the life of copyrights, including their creation, their expiration, and their renewal. This chapter will also outline the duration of transfers of copyright, transfers of renewal copyrights, and grants of licenses under copyright, and their termination.

Each of these subjects will be discussed in the sections which follow. The reader should be forewarned, however, that topics such as the *duration of copyright, renewal of copyright*, and *termination of grants* are among the most complex provisions of the copyright law. Although a great deal of thought has been devoted to organizing these materials in a way that should be understandable to anyone willing to invest in them a thoughtful reading, intricate materials such as these, like good poetry, should not be expected to blossom forth enlightenment in the reader's mind upon a first reading.

A thorough understanding of these subjects is *not*, however, a requisite to understanding the practical licensing guidance and other advice offered in this book. Nevertheless, certain licensing problems cannot be resolved without some understanding of one or more of the topics covered in this chapter.

## I. INTRODUCTION

The duration of copyright protection is prescribed by law. The duration of assignments and licenses are governed by the applicable *term* provisions of agreements that effect assignments and licenses, but may also be subject to certain provisions of the copyright law that allow previously granted assignments and licenses to be terminated.

The discussion which follows is divided into five primary sections:

1. Duration of Copyright;

2. Renewal of Copyright;

3. Duration of Assignments of Copyright, and Exclusive Rights Under Copyright;

4. Duration of Assignments of Interests in Renewal Copyrights; and

5. Duration of Licenses

It should be noted that readers using the following materials to help analyze a particular duration of copyright, assignment of copyright, or termination of grant problem should bear in mind that there is a significant difference in the way the problem is approached depending upon whether the work was created before or after January 1, 1978. Accordingly, the reader should try to determine the applicable category in which the work falls before attempting to analyze the impact of any circumstances that may affect ownership questions.

## II. DURATION OF COPYRIGHT

### A. Life

Like life itself, copyright protection does not last forever. In fact, the limitation on the duration of copyright protection is a restriction that is prescribed by *the people* under the U.S. Constitution, which states:

> Congress shall have the power . . . To promote the progress of science and useful arts, by securing *for limited times* to authors and inventors the exclusive right to their respective writings and discoveries.[1]

The *duration* of copyright (i.e., how long the copyright protection lasts) is often referred to as the *life of the copyright*. When the life of

---

[1] U.S. Const. Art. I, Sec. 8.

a copyright expires, the work is said to fall into the public domain. Works in the *public domain* are works for which copyright protection was never secured or works that were protected by a copyright which has expired.[2]

## B.  Creation

And, as in life, according to certain philosophers, the duration of copyright begins upon *creation*. Copyright is secured automatically when the work is created, and a work is *created* when it is fixed in a tangible medium of expression for the first time.

The copyright law recognizes two types of *tangible media of expression*: copies and phonorecords. A *copy* is a material object from which a work can be read or visually perceived either directly or with the aid of a machine or device, such as a book, manuscript, piece of sheet music, film, videotape, or microfilm. A *phonorecord* is a material object that embodies fixations of sounds (other than those sounds that are accompanied by a motion picture or other audiovisual work), such as audio tapes, phonograph records, and compact audio disks. Thus, for example, a song (i.e., a *work*) can be fixed in sheet music (i.e., a *copy*) or a compact audio disk (i.e., a *phonorecord*), or both.[3]

A work is *fixed* in a tangible medium of expression when its embodiment in a copy or a phonorecord is "sufficiently permanent or stable to permit it to be perceived, reproduced, or otherwise communicated for a period of more than transitory duration."[4] A work consisting of sounds, images, or both, that are bring transmitted, is fixed if a fixation of the work is being made simultaneously with its transmission.[5] If a work is prepared over a period of time, the part of the work existing in fixed form on a particular date constitutes the created work as of that date.

While a work may be fixed in a copy or a phonorecord, the ownership of copyright in the work, or any of the exclusive rights under

---

[2] For a further discussion of *public domain,* see Chapter 7, on the *Language of Music Licensing.*

[3] 17 U.S.C. Sec. 101.

[4] Id.

[5] Id.

the copyright, is distinct from ownership of any material object in which the work is embodied.[6]

## C. History

Anglo-American copyright legislation began in England with the Statute of Anne, enacted in 1709. The Statute gave authors the protection of copyright for 14 years from publication, and at the expiration of the 14 years, if the author was living, the copyright could be renewed for another 14 years. The statute stated in part:

> Whereas *printers, booksellers, and other persons have of late frequently taken the liberty of printing, reprinting and publishing, or causing to be printed, reprinted, and published, books and other writings, without the consent of the authors or proprietors of such books and writings, to their very great detriment, and too often to the ruin of them and their families*: for preventing therefor such practices for the future and for the encouragement of learned men to compose and write useful books; may it please your Majesty, that it may be enacted, and be it enacted by the Queen's most excellent majesty, by and with the advice and consent of the lords spiritual and temporal, and commons, in this present parliament assembled, and by the authority of the same, . . . that the author of any book or books already composed, and not printed and published, or that shall hereafter be composed, and his assignee or assigns, shall have the sole liberty of printing and reprinting such book and books for the term of fourteen years, to commence from the day of the first publishing the same, and no longer;
>
> . . . Provided, always, That after the expiration of the said term of fourteen years, the sole right of printing or disposing of copies shall return to the authors thereof, if they are then living, for another term of fourteen years.

In this country, the copyright laws governing the original thirteen states were based largely upon the Statute of Anne. On May 31, 1790, the Congress of the United States enacted this nation's first copyright statute, which reflected its historical antecedents. Under the Copyright

---

[6] 17 U.S.C. Sec. 202.

Act of 1790, the author was afforded copyright protection for 14 years and "if, at the expiration of said term, the author or authors, or any of them, be living, and a citizen or citizens of these United States, or resident therein, the same exclusive right shall be continued to him or them, his or their executors, administrators or assigns, for the further term of fourteen years."

The copyright law has undergone three major changes since 1790. The Copyright Act of 1831 amended the 1790 Act in two respects: the original term was increased to 28 years, and the renewal term, though still only 14 years long, could pass to the author's widow or children if he did not survive the original term. The Copyright Act of 1909 maintained the original term of 28 years, but extended the length of the renewal term from 14 years to 28 years, and provided additional changes as to who may apply for renewal.[7] Finally, the copyright law underwent a complete overhaul with the Copyright Act of 1976, which took effect on January 1, 1978. Provisions of the law regarding the duration of certain copyrights created prior to January 1, 1978, was amended in 1992 and 1998. The provisions of the 1976 Act and its recent changes are discussed below.

## D. The Appropriate Duration of Copyright Protection

Before moving on to answering the question of how long *do* copyrights last under the law, it may be interesting to first take a moment to ask the question: how long *should* copyright protection last? While the question is interesting to ask, it is not one that can easily be answered, if it can be answered at all.

The purpose of copyright is to secure the general benefits derived by the public from the labors of authors. To this end, the copyright law seeks "to motivate the creative activity of authors . . . by the provision of a special reward."[8] That special reward is the recognition of the exclusive right of copyright — a limited *monopoly* on the exercise of privileges that others would otherwise have but for the author's exclusive rights.

---

[7] Act of March 4, 1909, chap. 320, 35 Stat. 1075 (the "1909 Act").

[8] *Sony Corp. v. Universal City Studios, Inc.,* 464 U.S. 417 (1984).

It is generally agreed that, for the most part, monopolies are bad. The owner of a monopoly has the ability to charge monopoly pricing, and economists call the resulting loss to society a loss of economic welfare. If the market economy were a *static* place, there could be no justification for the monopoly of copyright. But the market economy is not static — it is quite, to the contrary, *dynamic*. The special incentive provided to authors serves to motivate the creative activity of authors *over time*. Thus, in contrast to the negative effects of monopolies under a static analysis, the monopoly of copyright in a dynamic world provides positive benefits to society.

The question, then, is whether and to what extent do the *dynamic benefits* to society of copyright outweigh the *static losses* to society resulting from the exercise of that monopoly by authors. Only to the extent that such benefits outweigh such losses should copyright be enforced. This principal of modern economic analysis was recognized over a century and a half ago by Lord Macaulay in a speech delivered to the British House of Commons:

> It is good that authors should be remunerated; and the least exceptionable way of remunerating them is by a monopoly. Yet monopoly is evil. For the sake of good we must submit to evil; but the evil ought not to last a day longer than is necessary for the purpose of securing the good.[9]

If the net effect of copyright protection is good for society, then why shouldn't copyright protection last forever? In 1908, Justice Oliver Wendell Holmes suggested one reason:

> The notion of property starts, I suppose, from confirmed possession of a tangible object and consists in the right to exclude others from interference with the more or less free doing with it as one wills. But in copyright property has reached a more abstract expression. The right to exclude is not directed to an object in possession or owned, but is *in vacuo*, so to speak. It restrains the spontaneity of men where but for it there would be nothing of any kind to hinder

---

[9] Speech by Lord Macaulay in the British House of Commons, *The Works of Lord Macaulay* (1866).

their doing as they saw fit. It is a prohibition of conduct remote from the persons or tangibles of the party having the right. It may be infringed a thousand miles from the owner and without his ever becoming aware of the wrong. It is a right which could not be recognized or endured for more than a limited time.[10]

Modern scholars have pointed to more specific grounds. As Professor Nimmer instructs:

It may be questioned why literary property should be treated differently from other forms of property? If I may own Blackacre in perpetuity, why not also *Black Beauty*? The answer lies in the First Amendment. There is no countervailing speech interest which must be balanced against perpetual ownership of tangible real and personal property. There is such a speech interest with respect to literary property, or copyright.[11]

The issues regarding the appropriate duration of copyright protection were framed long ago by legal jurists, well before they were even taken up in the United States. For example, in 1785, Lord Mansfield said,

[W]e must take care to guard against two extremes equally prejudicial; the one, that men of ability, who have employed their time for the service of the community, may not be deprived of their just merits, and the reward of their ingenuity, and labour; the other, that the world may not be deprived of improvements, nor the progress of the arts be retarded.[12]

No doubt Lord Mansfield was familiar with the works of Aristotle.[13]

With that, and without answering the question precisely how long is enough protection, we shall proceed by answering the question we began with: how long *do* copyrights last under the law.

---

[10] *White-Smith Music Publishing Co. v. Apollo Co.,* 209 U.S. 1, 19 (1907).

[11] 1 Nimmer *On Copyright,* Sec. 1.10[C][1] (1991).

[12] *Sayre v. Moore,* 1 East 361, 362, 102 Eng. Rep. 139, 140 (K.B. 1785).

[13] *See, generally,* Aristotle, *The Nicomachean Ethics,* on "the rule of the mean."

## E. Duration of Copyright in Works Created After January 1, 1978

Under the new copyright law, the term of copyright protection of works created (i.e., fixed in tangible form for the first time) after January 1, 1978 starts at the moment of creation and lasts for the author's life, plus an additional fifty years after the author's death.[14] In the case of a *joint work* prepared by two or more authors, the term of protection lasts for 50 years after the last surviving author's death.

On October 27, 1998, President Clinton signed into law the "Sonny Bono Copyright Term Extension Act." The legislation extended the term of ownership of a copyrighted work by twenty years. Thus the term of copyright protection for works created after January 1, 1978, starts at the moment of creation and lasts for the author's life, plus an additional seventy years after the author's death. In the case of joint works prepared by two or more authors, the term of protection lasts for seventy years after the last surviving author's death.

The above terms will not apply if the work was a work for hire, an anonymous work, or a pseudonymous work. A *work for hire* is (i) a work prepared by an employee within the scope of his employment or (ii) a work which is specially ordered or commissioned in a writing that says the work is made for hire and which falls within one of several categories enumerated in the copyright law.[15] (See Chapters 3 and 7). An *anonymous work* is a work on the copies or phonorecords of which no natural person is identified as author. A *pseudonymous work* is a work on copies or phonorecords of which the author is

---

[14] In 1995, legislation was introduced in the U.S. Congress which would extend the term of ownership of a copyrighted work from the life of the author plus 50 years to the life of the author plus 70 years. This change is intended to bring U.S. law into conformity with that of the European Union, which, in October 1993, adopted a directive mandating that each of its members extend, by no later than the July 1, 1995, the copyright term of protection to the life of the author plus 70 years for all works originating in the EU. Without so conforming U.S. law to EU legislation, works of U.S. authors would fall subject to the Berne Convention's "rule of the shorter term," a policy of reciprocity under which a Berne member state with a longer copyright term can limit copyright protection for foreign nationals to the foreign country's shorter term.

[15] 17 U.S.C. Sec. 101.

identified under a fictitious name. The term of protection for works made for hire, and for anonymous and pseudonymous works (unless the author's identity is revealed in Copyright Office records), the duration of copyright is 75 years from publication or 100 years from creation, whichever is shorter.

In the case of anonymous, pseudonymous works and works made for hire, the Sonny Bono Copyright Term Extension Act extended the copyright term of protection to 95 years from publication, or 120 years from creation, whichever expires first. *See* 17 U.S.C. § 302(c).

## F. Duration of Copyright in Works Created Before January 1, 1978

Under the copyright law in effect before 1978, copyright was secured either on the date a work was published, or on the date of registration if the work was registered in unpublished form.

Works that had been created before the new law came into effect but had neither been published nor registered for copyright before January 1, 1978, have been automatically brought under the new law and are now given federal copyright protection. The duration of copyright in these works is generally computed in the same way as for new works: the life-plus-50 or 75/100-year terms. However, all works in this category are guaranteed at least 25 years of statutory protection; the law specifies that in no case will copyright in a work of this sort expire before December 31, 2002, and if the work is published before that date the term may be extended by another 25 years, through the end of 2027. Under the terms of the Sonny Bono Copyright Term Extension Act of 1998, the copyright for unpublished works created before January 1, 1978 that were not copyrighted exists from January 1, 1978 and endures for the same term as for new works, the life of the author plus seventy years. However, if the work is published on or before December 31, 2002, the term of copyright shall not expire before December 31, 2047. 17 U.S.C. § 303.

For works in which statutory copyright protection had been secured before January 1, 1978, the new law retains the old system for computing the duration of protection, but with some changes. The law provides for a first term of 28 years, measured from the date protection was originally secured by publication or registration, with a right to a renewal term of 47 years. Renewal of copyright is discussed at length in the next section. The Copyright Term Extension Act of 1998 extended the renewal term from 47 to 67 years.

Copyrights that were in their renewal terms (i.e., second 28 year term) during the time spanning December 31, 1965 to December 31, 1977 were automatically extended an additional 19 years (thereby extending the total copyright duration for such works up to a maximum of 75 years), without the need for further renewal. This is referred to as the *19-year extended term*.[16] The Copyright Term Extension Act of 1998 states that any copyright still in its renewal term at the end of the time that the Sonny Bono Copyright Term Extension Act becomes effective shall have a copyright term of 95 years from the date copyright was originally secured.

Until 1992, copyrights that were in their first term during the time spanning December 31, 1965 to December 31, 1977 were still required to be renewed to receive the full new maximum term of 75 years. After the Copyright Renewal Act of 1992 was signed into law, copyrights first published in 1964 or later are considered automatically renewed. The 1992 Act only applies to copyrights which still had to be renewed in the calendar year 1992 or later. Copyrights that have previously fallen into the public domain as a result of failure to file a renewal registration are not affected (i.e., they remain in the public domain).

The copyright law also provides that all terms of copyright will run through the end of the calendar year in which they would otherwise expire. This not only affects the duration of copyrights, but also the time limits for renewal registrations, discussed below.

## III. RENEWAL OF COPYRIGHT

As may be evident from the historical background noted above, the concept of renewal dates back to the earliest legislative enactments on copyright law. Under a renewal system, the duration of copyright is divided into two consecutive terms. The second term is normally conditioned upon the copyright owner filing a registration, within strict

---

[16] 17 U.S.C. Sec. 304(b).

time limits, to secure copyright protection for the second term. However, under a subsequent amendment to the U.S. copyright law, registration is no longer a condition for renewal of copyright under the copyright law. The Copyright Term Extension Act of 1998 extended the renewal term from 47 to 67 years.

## A. Permissive Registration

As noted, registration of renewal is no longer a condition for extending copyright protection through the renewal term (i.e., an additional 67 years beyond the original 28 year term) under U.S. copyright law. By the amendment to the copyright law signed into law on June 26, 1992, renewal is now automatic. Nevertheless, the law retains a permissive procedure of renewal registration which (i) provides a slight procedural incentive for claimants who file a renewal registration and (ii) has a potential impact upon determining who primarily benefits from the renewal.

If the application for renewal is filed within one year of expiration of the original term of copyright, the registration certificate would constitute *prima facie* evidence of validity of the copyright during its renewed and extended term and of the facts stated in the certificate of renewal registration.[17] It has always been the case that an original copyright registration, if filed within certain time limits, would constitute *prima facie* evidence of validity of the copyright and of the facts stated in the certificate of registration,[18] but, until the Copyright Renewal Act of 1992, renewal certificates never enjoyed the same recognition. The advantage is a slight one, but it does afford some convenience to copyright owners seeking to enforce their copyrights; in lawsuits for copyright infringement, the copyright owner with a certificate that constitutes evidence of validity of the copyright and of the facts stated in the certificate may avoid having to call to the stand witnesses to prove all of the facts in the certificate. This is a useful convenience in copyright piracy cases filed in jurisdictions that are a great distance away from the witnesses who could testify as to these facts.

---

[17] 17 U.S.C. Sec. 304(a)(4)(A).
[18] 17 U.S.C. Sec. 410(c).

Renewal registration may have an enormous, though hidden, impact on the determination of who primarily benefits from the renewal term. If the author of the work had previously granted his expectancy interest in the renewal copyright to his music publisher, then under certain circumstances, renewal registration may affect whether the renewal copyright will vest in the author's music publisher or the heirs to the author's estate. This important subject will be discussed further below with respect to assignments of renewal interests.

## B. When May Renewal Registration Be Submitted

In accordance with the Copyright Renewal Act of 1992, an application to register a claim to the renewed and extended term of copyright in a work created during the time spanning the calendar years 1964 through 1977, inclusive, may be made to the Copyright Office (i) within 1 year before the expiration of the original term of copyright and (ii) at any time during the renewed and extended term.[19] For all works created prior to 1964, the renewal application and fee must have been received in the Copyright Office within one year prior to the expiration of the original term; otherwise, the duration of the copyright expired at the end of the 28th year, and the work fell into the public domain.

Note, all terms of copyright run through the end of the year in which they would otherwise expire. Thus, all copyright terms will expire on December 31st of their year of expiration. Accordingly, all periods for renewal registration will run from January 1st of the 28th year of the original term of the copyright and will end on December 31st of the 28th year.

To determine the proper year in which to file a renewal application, follow these steps:

1. Find out the date of original copyright for the work.

    In the case of works originally registered in unpublished form prior to publication, the date of copyright is the date of its registration in the Copyright Office. Otherwise, the date of

---

[19] 17 U.S.C. Sec. 304(a)(3)(A).

copyright is the date of first publication of a copy or phonorecord of a work bearing a valid copyright notice. *Publication*
is the distribution of copies or phonorecords of a work to the
public by sale or other transfer of ownership, or by rental, lease
or lending.[20] In one limited exception, the date of copyright
may be other than above: In any case where the year date in
the copyright notice on copies distributed by authority of the
copyright owner is earlier than the year of first publication, the
date of copyright is considered to be the year contained in the
notice.

2. Add 28 years to the date of copyright.

The answer will be in the calendar year during which the copyright will be eligible for renewal registration, and December
31st of that year will be the renewal deadline.

The following table may be used to determine the time limits for
filing a renewal application:

Mandatory
Renewal

| | | | |
|---|---|---|---|
| 1950 | 1-1-78 | 12-31-78 | 12-31-2045 |
| 1951 | 1-1-79 | 12-31-79 | 12-31-2046 |
| 1952 | 1-1-80 | 12-31-80 | 12-31-2047 |
| 1953 | 1-1-81 | 12-31-81 | 12-31-2048 |
| 1954 | 1-1-82 | 12-31-82 | 12-31-2049 |
| 1955 | 1-1-83 | 12-31-83 | 12-31-2050 |
| 1956 | 1-1-84 | 12-31-84 | 12-31-2051 |
| 1957 | 1-1-85 | 12-31-85 | 12-31-2052 |
| 1958 | 1-1-86 | 12-31-86 | 12-31-2053 |
| 1959 | 1-1-87 | 12-31-87 | 12-31-2054 |
| 1960 | 1-1-88 | 12-31-88 | 12-31-2055 |
| 1961 | 1-1-89 | 12-31-89 | 12-31-2056 |
| 1962 | 1-1-90 | 12-31-90 | 12-31-2057 |
| 1963 | 1-1-91 | 12-31-91 | 12-31-2058 |

[20] 17 U.S.C. Sec. 101.

Permissive
Renewal

| | | | |
|---|---|---|---|
| 1964 | 1-1-92 | 12-31-92 | 12-31-2059 |
| 1965 | 1-1-93 | 12-31-93 | 12-31-2060 |
| 1966 | 1-1-94 | 12-31-94 | 12-31-2061 |
| 1967 | 1-1-95 | 12-31-95 | 12-31-2062 |
| 1968 | 1-1-96 | 12-31-96 | 12-31-2063 |
| 1969 | 1-1-97 | 12-31-97 | 12-31-2064 |
| 1970 | 1-1-98 | 12-31-98 | 12-31-2065 |
| 1971 | 1-1-99 | 12-31-99 | 12-31-2066 |
| 1972 | 1-1-00 | 12-31-00 | 12-31-2067 |
| 1973 | 1-1-01 | 12-31-01 | 12-31-2068 |
| 1974 | 1-1-02 | 12-31-02 | 12-31-2069 |
| 1975 | 1-1-03 | 12-31-03 | 12-31-2070 |
| 1976 | 1-1-04 | 12-31-04 | 12-31-2071 |
| 1977 | 1-1-05 | 12-31-05 | 12-31-2072 |

---

* If the application for renewal for a work created prior to January 1, 1964 was not filed by the deadline, then the work fell into the public domain. This would not be the result for works created on or after January 1, 1964; renewal for such works is now automatic and the only consequence of failing to file a renewal application during the 28th year is the loss of certain procedural advantages in litigation and possibly an affect on who will own the renewal copyright upon its vesting.

Renewal registration is effective upon the Copyright Office's receipt of a completed application and the appropriate fee. Being unable to supply all of the information requested in the form should not deter the applicant from submitting the application, even if it is incomplete. The Copyright Office will consider a renewal application to be "acceptable" if it identifies the work by title and contains a correct statement of either the claimant or basis of claim. All other information supplied in the form will be considered minor and may by supplied later, even after the deadline for renewal, by a supplementary registration on Form CA. Whenever an applicant has cause to believe a formal application for renewal (Form RE), if sent by mail, might not be received in the Copyright Office before the renewal deadline, the application for renewal may be made by telephone, telegram or other method of communication. However, the renewal fee was also required to be received by the Copyright Office by the deadline. Fortunately, as a result of the Copyright Renewal Act of 1992, the practice of getting a friend who lives in the vicinity of Washington, D.C. to brave the cold on New Year's Eve to run down to the Copyright Office with your check or money order is now history.

Note, in the event the last day for filing the renewal falls on a Saturday, Sunday, holiday or other non-business day within the District of Columbia or the Federal Government, the application may be filed on the next succeeding business day, and is effective as of the date when the period expired. Further, in any case in which the Register of Copyrights determines the application, fee or any other material to be delivered to the Copyright Office by the renewal deadline, would have been received in the Copyright Office in due time except for a general disruption or suspension of postal or other transportation or communications services, the actual receipt of such material in the Copyright Office within one month after the date on which the Register makes such determination, shall be considered timely.

The Copyright Office has no discretion to extend the renewal time limits. If an acceptable application and fee for works created prior to 1964 were not received within the strict time limits, copyright protection is lost permanently and the work fell into the public domain. Should that have happened, the copyright cannot be revived.

## C. Renewal Copyright Claimants

This section will summarize who under the law is entitled to claim a renewal copyright. Crucial to the understanding of renewal registration is the understanding of the difference between who may *claim* a renewal, who may *submit* an application for renewal, and who ultimately gets to *own* the renewal copyright. The answer is not necessarily the same for each, depending upon the circumstances.

Renewal copyright may be *claimed* only by those persons specified in the copyright law. (The statutory provisions on this point are essentially the same in the 1992 Act as those contained in the 1976 Act and 1909 Act.) Under the Copyright Renewal Act of 1992, an application to register a claim for renewal of copyright may be made (i) within one year before the expiration of the original term by any person entitled to claim the renewal (see below) or (ii) at any time after expiration of the original term by any person in whom such further term vested, or by any successor or assign of such person, if the application is made in the name of such person.

In general, the law gives the right to *claim* renewal to the individual author of the work, regardless of who owned the copyright during the original term. If the author is deceased at the time for renewal, the statute gives the right to claim renewal to certain of the author's heirs in a particular order of preference, listed below.

In the case of the following three types of works, however, the person or entity entitled to claim renewal is not necessarily the individual creator of the work (or his heirs), but the copyright proprietor (i.e., owner of the copyright at the time application is made for renewal):

1. *Posthumous Works.* The owner of a posthumous work may claim renewal in such work. A *posthumous* work is a work as to which no copyright assignment or other contract for exploitation has occurred during the author's lifetime.

2. *Collective Work.* The owner of a collective work (e.g., periodical, encyclopedia, anthology, etc.) may claim renewal in all material in which he originally secured copyright, including the collective work as a whole, as well as any contributions to the collective work in which the owner originally claimed copyright. The author of any contribution to a collective work may claim renewal in his own name with respect to his contribution, if he originally secured a separate copyright in the contribution (i.e., he separately registered the contribution in unpublished form, or, upon publication, copies of the work contained a separate copyright notice in the name of the author).

3. *Works Made For Hire.* The owner of a work-made-for-hire may claim renewal in such work. Renewal rights may not be claimed by an employee-for-hire. To determine whether the relationship between the individual who actually created the work and the person for whom the work was created was a work-for-hire, see Chapter 7.

The persons in the following order of preference may claim renewal in all types of works except those three enumerated above:

1. The author, if living.

2. The widow (or widower) and children of the author.

   If the author is not living, the author's widow (or widower) and children are entitled to claim renewal. All members of this class share the renewal interest equally. For example, if the deceased author leaves a widow and two children, the widow and each child shall receive a one-third interest in the right to claim renewal copyright.

   An author's "children" are his or her immediate offspring, whether legitimate or not, and any children legally adopted by the author. The author's widow (or widower) is the author's surviving spouse, as determined under the law of the author's domicile at the time of his or her death, whether or not the spouse has later remarried. Where the author and spouse were divorced, the former spouse does not constitute a "widow" upon the author's death.

3. The executor(s) named in the author's will.

   If there is no surviving widow (or widower) or children, then the executor(s) named in the author's will are entitled to claim the renewal copyright. This will be the case even if the author leaves surviving grandchildren.

   An *executor* is one who has been designated in a will as the person to carry out the directions and provisions designated in the will by the deceased author. When the renewal rights are claimed by the executors, they are not claimed for their personal benefit, but rather in trust for the benefit of those named in the will to receive the renewals or the residuary assets of the estate of the author. When the author dies leaving a will, but an executor is not named in the will, the courts will appoint an "administrator" to perform the duties of an executor. For renewal purposes, an administrator is the equivalent of an executor.

4. The next of kin of the deceased author.

   If there is no surviving widow (or widower) or children, and the author left no will, then the next of kin of the deceased author are entitled to claim the renewal copyright. Who comprises *next of kin* is determined by the intestate succession laws of the state of the author's domicile at the time of his or her death.

In summary, a person may not be a renewal *claimant* unless he is a member of the appropriate class set forth in the copyright law: a proprietor of the copyright (in the case of a posthumous work, collective work, or work made for hire); the author of the work; the widow (or widower) of the author; a child of the deceased author; or, where none of the foregoing are living, the executor under the author's will; or then, in the event no will is left, the next of kin of the deceased author.

One need not, however, be a member of one of the above classes to be entitled to submit an application for renewal on behalf of a proper renewal claimant. A discussion of who is entitled to submit an application for renewal is the subject of a section set forth below.

## D. Proper Claimants for Renewal of Arrangements, Translations, Compilations and Other Collective Works, and Derivative Works

In the case of the renewal of copyright in a new version of a previous work, such as an arrangement, translation, dramatization, compilation or work published with new material, a further consideration must be made in determining the proper claimant.

Generally, the copyright secured in a new version of a work is independent of any protection in the material published earlier. In other words, the copyright in the new version covers only the additions, changes or other new material appearing for the first time in that version, and not to the underlying preexisting material. Thus, for renewal purposes, the "authors" of the new version are only those persons who contributed the new copyrightable matter to it; the person who wrote the original version on which the new work is based cannot be regarded as an "author" of the new version, unless that person also contributed to the new matter.

In the context of music publishing, arrangements, translations, and compilations are usually prepared by employees-for-hire of the publishing company. Therefore, the proper renewal claimant for such works will usually be the music publishing company, claiming as "proprietor of the copyright," not the composer of the song (or his statutory heirs).

Music publishers may ask whether it is desirable to file renewal registrations for their copyrighted arrangements, particularly where a renewal copyright has already been claimed in the underlying composition. The best policy is to file renewal registrations for all copyrighted arrangements of musical compositions. Some arrangements may continue to have sale and performance value well after the copyright in the underlying song has expired. In many instances, arrangements originally prepared for publication in the form of sheet music that was once discontinued were later reprinted, either as part of a folio, or when a decision is made to reprint the song and no replacement for the discontinued arrangement was readily available. Renewal should certainly be claimed if the arrangement was of a work in the public domain to begin with or where the arranger is entitled to a royalty on sales of the arrangement.

## E. Renewal Copyright Owners

Determining who is the proper *claimant* of the renewal copyright does not definitively lead to the determination of who will become the *owner* of the renewal copyright upon the expiration of the initial term of copyright. If the author never assigned to another his or her rights in his renewal copyright during the original term, then the claimant(s) will become the owner(s) of the renewal copyright upon the expiration of the initial term.

If the author did assign to another his or her rights in his renewal copyright during the original term, then the claimant(s) will not necessarily become the owner(s) of the renewal copyright. The effect of an assignment of a renewal prior to the expiration of the original copyright term on the claimant's potential right to own the renewal copyright is discussed below.

## IV. DURATION OF ASSIGNMENTS OF COPYRIGHT

An assignment of copyright, or assignment of any of the exclusive rights under copyright, may be limited in duration. The duration of an assignment may be limited (1) by the assignment itself, or (2) by the terms of the copyright law.

## A. Duration Limited By the Terms of the Assignment

The duration of an assignment may be limited by the terms of the assignment or contract relating to the assignment. For example, a songwriter may assign to a music publisher his copyright in a song for a period of 10 years; at the expiration of the 10 years, the copyright reverts to the songwriter. Such reversion may or may not be automatic, depending on the terms of the assignment. For example, the copyright may revert only if the publisher fails to have a commercial recording of the song distributed or if certain income levels are not achieved.

Sometimes, some specific action is required on the part of the songwriter to effect reversion. For example, under the terms of the AGAC Uniform Popular Songwriter's Contract of 1948 (Paragraph 8), the writer is entitled to be re-vested with all rights and copyrights outside of the United States and Canada. To cause such re-vesting of foreign rights, the writer must send a notice to the publisher within 6 months of the writer's grant of such rights to another music publisher.

## B. Duration Limited By the Terms of the Copyright Law

In the event the assignment document does not expressly indicate the term of its duration, it will be deemed effective for the remainder of the copyright term existing at that time. However, certain provisions of the new copyright law, which went into affect on January 1, 1978, affect the duration of certain assignments.

### 1.  Grants Executed by the Author After January 1, 1978

The congressional purpose, in enacting the 1909 Act, in granting an author two consecutive 28-year terms was to guarantee him the enjoyment of the fruits of his creation after the initial 28-year term during which his work was exploited by his assignee. Under the 1909 Act, after the first term of 28 years, the renewal copyright was suppose to revert to the author or other specified beneficiaries. In the words of the Register of Copyrights, the renewal term was intended to remedy the situation "where the author actually turns out to have sold his birthright for a mess of pottage."[21] To a certain extent, however, this remedy was thwarted by a ruling of the Supreme Court in 1943, discussed below.[22] In enacting the 1976 Act, Congress dropped the renewal feature, except for works already in their first term of statutory protection when the new law took effect, but included several new provisions clearly intended to reinstate the right of the author to enjoy the fruits of his authorship years after his initial assignment of the copyright.

An assignment of copyright subject to the 1976 Act, or exclusive rights under such copyright, which is silent about its *term* (i.e., how long it will remain in effect) or *reversion* (i.e., circumstances under which rights will revert to the assignor), will endure for the life of the copyright. Under the 1976 Act, however, any assignment by an author after January 1, 1978, regardless of the term stated in the agreement effecting the transfer, is subject to being terminated 35 years after the date of the grant.[23] This power to terminate a transfer of copyright or exclusive rights under copyright (and, for that matter, non-exclusive licenses, discussed below) is sometimes referred to as the *35-year termination rule.*

Specifically, for transfers of rights made by an author on or after January 1, 1978, the copyright law permits the author or certain heirs of the author (of a work other than a work made for hire) to terminate a transfer during a 5 year period beginning at the end of 35 years from the date of the grant, or if the grant covers the right of publication, 35 years from the date of publication or 40 years from the date of the grant, whichever is shorter. To terminate a grant, a written notice must be served on the transferee within the time limits specified by the copyright law.[24]

To effect the congressional purpose of the rule, certain key provisions were included to prevent the author from prematurely waiving

---

[21] Register of Copyrights, *Copyright Law Revision Pt. 3, Preliminary Draft for Revised U.S. Copyright Law and Discussions and Comments on the Draft,* 88th Cong., 2d Sess. (Comm. Print 1964).

[22] See discussion below concerning *Fred Fisher Co. v. M. Witmark & Sons,* 318 U.S. 643 (1943).

[23] 17 U.S.C. Sec. 203.

[24] 17 U.S.C. Sec. 203 (a)(3),(4).

or contracting away his right of termination. For example, termination of the grant may be effected notwithstanding any agreement to the contrary, including an agreement to make a will or to make any further grant.[25] Also, the rule provides that a re-grant of rights that revert after termination is valid only if it is executed after the effective date of termination.[26] An exception, however, was provided in favor of the current grantee: A further grant of a reverted right may be made to the original grantee or his successor in title, after the service of notice has been made.[27] Thus, for example, an author who serves notice of termination on his current music publisher may enter into a contract granting rights covering the remainder of the life of the copyright with that music publisher beginning the date the publisher is served with the notice. This in effect gives the current publisher a right of first refusal, affording him a two to ten year lead time over other publishers in dealing for the reverted rights.

An author may overcome the competitive advantage of his current publisher by merely waiting until the termination actually takes effect before accepting any offer from the publisher. Some clever publishers have conceived interesting ways of increasing their leverage in the negotiation for these reverted rights. The following is a rather innovative provision that may be found in some music publishing contracts drafted since the passage of the 1976 Act:

> Writer and Publisher hereby acknowledge that the copyrights and certain other rights in the Compositions granted to Publisher hereunder may be terminated by Writer or his successors (hereinafter, individually and collectively, "Writer") in accordance with the provisions of the Copyright Act. Writer and Publisher further acknowledge that it is their intention that, in the event that any such grants of copyright or other rights are terminated by Writer, Publisher shall have the exclusive right of first refusal with respect thereto, which right of first refusal shall be exercised as follows:

> Until the expiration of a period of sixty (60) days following the Publisher's receipt of a valid notice of termination with respect to

---

[25] 17 U.S.C. Sec. 203 (a)(5).

[26] 17 U.S.C. Sec. 203 (b)(4).

[27] Id.

any such copyrights and other rights, Writer shall not negotiate with any third party with respect to the grant, sale, assignment, license, or other transfer thereof. During said sixty (60) day period, Writer agrees to negotiate in good faith and to exert best efforts to reach an agreement with Publisher for Publisher's acquisition of such copyrights and other rights. In the event that Publisher and Writer fail to reach agreement by the end of said sixty (60) day period, Writer shall be free to negotiate with third parties for the grant, sale, assignment license or other transfer of such copyrights and other rights, only for terms and conditions more favorable to Writer than those last offered by Publisher. If Writer receives such an offer from a bona fide third party, which offer Writer wishes to accept, Writer shall notify Publisher of the terms thereof in writing and Publisher shall have ten (10) days from its receipt thereof to notify Writer in writing that it desires to acquire the copyrights and other rights subject to the terms of such offer on the terms and conditions contained therein. In the event that Publisher so notifies Writer, said copyrights and other rights shall automatically vest in Publisher, and Writer shall enter into a written agreement with Publisher reflecting such terms and conditions promptly after Writer's receipt of such notice. In the event that Publisher does not so notify Writer and Writer does not accept such third party offer, the foregoing procedures shall apply to any future offers which Writer receives and wishes to accept, including any offer containing identical terms and conditions previously rejected by Writer, whether received by Writer from the same or from a different third party.

It is not clear whether such a provision will be enforceable. Arguably, it may be enforceable because it does not preclude the grant from being terminated. On the other hand, although the clause will not directly affect the right of termination, it does interfere with the free exploitation or re-sale of the copyright after termination becomes effective, and, on that ground, may be held unenforceable. Because the rights of termination for songs created under the 1976 Act will not begin to be exercised until 35 years has passed after the execution of the applicable grants, it will be a long time before the enforceability of such a provision is tested in court.

### 2. Grants Covering the Initial Term of Copyright

An assignment of a copyright in a song created before January 1, 1978 in its original (i.e., first 28-year) term of copyright, which does not provide for any term or reversion, and *did not* provide for an assignment of renewal rights, will endure until the expiration of the original term of copyright only.

### 3. Grants Covering the Renewal Term of Copyright

The duration of assignment of a copyright in a song created before January 1, 1978 in its original (i.e., first 28-year) term of copyright, which does not provide for any term or reversion, but *did* provide for an assignment of the author's interest in renewal rights will depend upon the circumstances discussed in the section below on Duration of Assignment of Renewal Copyright.

### 4. Grants Covering the Extended (19-Year) Term of Copyright

For works created before January 1, 1978 and in their first term of copyright as of December 31, 1977, a similar right of termination is provided with respect to transfers covering the newly added years extending the maximum term of copyright by 19 years, from 56 to 75 years.[28]

The assignment of a copyright in a song created before January 1, 1978 in its original term or its renewal term of copyright will endure until the expiration of the copyright (i.e., the 75th, and final year of the life of the copyright), unless otherwise provided by the terms of the assignment agreement or unless the author (or certain statutory beneficiaries) exercises a statutory right of termination which may be effective as early as 19 years prior to the final year of the copyright. Within certain time limits, an author or specified heirs of the author, are generally entitled to file a notice terminating the author's transfers covering any part of the 19 year period that has now been added to the end of the second term of copyright in a work.

The same procedures provided for regarding the 35-year termination rule discussed above are applicable to terminations of grants covering the 19-year extended term. A termination of the grant may be effected notwithstanding any agreement to the contrary, including an agreement to make a will or to make any further grant.[29] Further,

---

[28] 17 U.S.C. Sec. 304 (c).
[29] 17 U.S.C. Sec. 304 (c)(5).

a re-grant of rights that revert after termination is valid only if it is executed after the effective date of termination, and an exception was provided in favor of the current grantee.[30] While the procedures for such termination resemble those for termination under the 35-year termination rule, there are important differences. For example, while the 35-year termination rule provides for the recapture of only those rights that the *author* has transferred after January 1, 1978, grants by *either the author or his statutory successors* covering the 19-year extended term may be terminated, which effectively allows successors to terminate transfers of renewal expectancies, discussed below, and benefit fully from the 19-year extended term of copyright.

## V. DURATION OF AN ASSIGNMENT OF RENEWAL COPYRIGHT

As noted above, an author's assignment of his renewal interest to another prior to the expiration of the original copyright term may affect a renewal claimant's potential right to own the renewal copyright. The person to whom the author assigned his renewal interest (or that person's successors or assigns) may become the owner of the renewal copyright under certain circumstances. Those circumstances — which involve the unfortunate subject of death — are discussed in this section.

### A. Limited Relevancy

Before proceeding into this gravely important topic, it will be useful to note what this discussion does and does not concern. This discussion only concerns those works that were created before January 1, 1978 *and* that were in their original term of copyright as of January 1, 1978. Thus, this discussion concerns primarily the generation of musical compositions written and published during the mid-1950s to the end of 1977. Further, this discussion only concerns those compositions in which the author assigned to another during the original term of copyright his or her interest in the renewal copyright. If the author never assigned his or her rights in his renewal copyright or

---

[30] 17 U.S.C. Sec. 304 (c)(6)(D)

assigned such interest during the renewal term, then this discussion is not relevant to the ownership interests in the copyright.

If the author did assign to another his or her rights in his interest in the renewal copyright during the original term, then, under certain circumstances, the claimant(s) will not become the owner(s) of the renewal copyright.

## B. Renewal Copyright Versus Renewal Expectancy

Under the 1909 Act, a copyright was secured by publication of the work with the proper copyright notice. The initial 28-year term was said to have *vested* immediately upon such securing. Though the law provided that the author of the work had the right, upon the expiration of the initial term, to *renew* the copyright for an additional 28-year term, the author's right to renew was not considered *vested* until the renewal period. Until then, the author had a mere *expectancy* in the renewal copyright.

In other words, upon the securing of copyright protection in a work created before January 1, 1978, a copyright owner possesses two things: (1) a right in the initial 28-year term of copyright, and (2) an expectancy interest in the 28-year (now, 67-year) renewal. A *right* is not the same as an *expectancy interest*, and the difference may have an impact upon who is entitled to *own* the renewal copyright.

## C. Transfer of Renewal Expectancy

The assignment of the *right* in the initial 28-year term of copyright operates the same as the assignment of any other type of property right: the assignee becomes the owner of the right, and may immediately exercise any or all of the incidents of ownership. The assignment of the *expectancy* in the renewal term before the actual commencement of the renewal term (i.e., before the renewal *vests*), does not operate to convey any legal *right* (over which the assignee may exercise as an owner), only the mere *expectancy* in the renewal copyright.

The distinction between *rights* and *expectancies* formed the basis of the following fundamental rule of copyright law concerning claims in renewal copyright announced by the U.S. Supreme Court:

An assignment of a renewal expectancy will, upon its vesting, be binding upon the author so that if the author is living at the time of renewal, the assignee, not the author, will be entitled to own such renewal; if the author is not living at the time of renewal, then those persons who, as specified in the copyright law, are entitled to claim the renewal copyright (i.e., the statutory renewal claimants) are not bound by any assignment executed by the author, so that the assignee of the renewal expectancy takes nothing and the statutory renewal claimants take legal title to the renewal.[31]

## D. Operation of the Rule of Renewal Expectancy

In other words, an assignment by an author of his or her interest in the renewal copyright before the initial copyright term expires is valid against the world, if the author lives until the commencement of the renewal period. For convenience, this rule will be called the *rule of renewal expectancy.*

Suppose, for example, a songwriter composed a song and assigned his copyright, including the renewal copyright, to his music publisher in 1967 and the original 28-year term of copyright in the song is expected to expire on December 31, 1995. Even though the music publishing contract may have included an assignment of "any and all renewal copyrights," the law only recognizes an assignment of the author's renewal "expectancy," which will not *vest* (i.e., become a renewal "right") until the renewal period. Accordingly, the rule of renewal expectancy will operate as follows: If the songwriter is living at the time the renewal copyright vests, then the legal title in the renewal right will automatically become the property of the music publisher. If the songwriter is not living when the renewal copyright vests, then the legal title will become the property of the author's beneficiaries (in a particular order of preference as specified in the copyright law).

The result in the foregoing example may differ if the author's statutory beneficiaries have previously transferred their own renewal expectancies. Suppose, for example, at the time the songwriter as-

---

[31] *Fred Fisher Co. v. M. Witmark & Sons,* 318 U.S. 643 (1943); *Miller Music Corp. v. Charles N. Daniels, Inc.,* 362 U.S. 373 (1960); *Stewart v. Abend,* 495 U.S. 207 (1990), hereinafter called, the *Rear Window* decision. The subject of the case was the 1954 film, "Rear Window," starring Grace Kelly and James Stewart, and directed by Alfred Hitchcock.

signed his copyright and renewal expectancy in 1967, the songwriter's wife and children (as statutory beneficiaries) also signed documents assigning to the music publisher their own renewal expectancies in the song. In that event, even where the author is not living at the time the renewal vests, the music publisher would still take legal title to the renewal copyright. This, of course, assumes the author's wife and children or other statutory beneficiaries were living at the time the renewal copyright vested, because the renewal expectancies assigned by them to the music publisher are also subject to the rule of renewal expectancies. Thus, if the wife and children were not living when the renewal copyright vested, then the legal title in the renewal copyrights would become the property of the next order of beneficiaries under the statute, not the music publisher.

A music publisher's attempt to secure renewal rights by obtaining assignments of expectancies from as many potential beneficiaries as possible is not foolproof. The effort may be defeated by the songwriter's divorce and subsequent remarriage before death. In that case, his second wife, and widow, assuming she did not subsequently assign to the publisher her expectancy, will take title to her share of the renewal copyright at the commencement of the renewal term. A similar result would occur in the event the songwriter, subsequent to his wife's and childrens' assignment of their renewal expectancies, has additional children, by either birth or adoption; in that case, the children who did not join in the assignment of renewal expectancies will share in the renewal copyright upon its vesting if the songwriter is not living at the time the renewal copyright vests.

It appears a music publisher may never be absolutely certain about whether it will acquire the entire renewal copyright at the time it receives an assignment of copyright and renewal expectancies. The publisher can only attempt to obtain as many assignments of renewal expectancies as possible from every known member of the class of possible successors to the renewal copyright. For example, the songwriter, his spouse, all of his children, and all known next of kin of the songwriter. The music publisher may also seek agreement from the songwriter to write a will bequeathing to the publisher renewal rights. These attempts are often impractical and not worth the expense, but remain standard in the contracts of some music publishers.

The rule of renewal expectancy will only apply to works created before January 1, 1978 currently in their initial 28-year term of copyright. Works created before that date, but which are already in their renewal term are, of course, not subject to the rule, as the renewal copyrights in those works have vested in their owners. Works created after January 1, 1978 are also not subject to the rule, because under the new copyright law there will never be a renewal term of copyright (or renewal expectancies) in these works.

## E.  Formalities of Assigning Renewal Expectancies

Virtually all of the normal formalities and other aspects of assigning copyrights discussed earlier in Chapter 8 apply equally to the assignment of renewal expectancies. Note, however, that it appears assignments of renewal expectancies will be binding against their assignors only if the assignment was supported by sufficient legal consideration (e.g., something of value).[32] Note, further, that renewal expectancies may not pass as personal property under a will or by the operation of state law in the absence of a will, because the federal copyright law, by specifying the particular classes of individuals entitled to claim renewal upon the author's death, preempts any state law regarding wills and inheritances.

The courts have ruled on the contractual language necessary to effect an assignment of a renewal expectancy. Briefly, an assignment of "renewal copyright" or just "renewals" will be sufficient to effect an assignment of renewal expectancies. Also, "extensions of copyright" will suffice. In the absence of such relatively express language, the courts are hesitant to construe an assignment of "copyright" to include renewal copyright, without some other evidence the parties intended an assignment of renewal. A transfer of "all, right, title and interest" has been held not sufficient to cover renewals, but an assignment of rights "forever" has.

## F.  Renewal Copyright Vesting

As indicated above, the copyright law gives the author the right to claim renewal if he is living at the time the renewal copyright vests. Gone unanswered throughout the discussion has been the question, at what time must one be living for a renewal claimed in his name to

---

[32] *Fisher v. Morris & Co.*, 113 U.S.P.Q. 251 (S.D.N.Y. 1957).

be effective? In other words, when do rights in the renewal copyright *vest*?

Prior to the Copyright Renewal Act of 1992, there were two possibilities: (1) the date on which the renewal application was filed or duly registered with the Copyright Office, or (2) the commencement of the renewal term. Until as recently as 1991, the question was the subject of a split of authority, with a court in the Southern District of New York holding that rights in a renewal copyright vested on the date on which the renewal application was filed with the Copyright Office[33] and the 9th Circuit Court of Appeals in California holding that rights in a renewal copyright do not vest until the actual commencement of the renewal term.[34]

The consequence of the rule suggested by the 9th Circuit is that it may become impossible to determine with any degree of certainty who will be the proper copyright claimant until it becomes too late to file the claim. For example, the author is alive at the beginning of the 28th year of the original term and shortly thereafter files an application for renewal naming himself as renewal claimant. Shortly before the end of the same year, before the actual commencement of the renewal term, the author dies. Upon the author's death, the proper renewal claimants would be those in the appropriate successor class as listed above. Unless one of the members of the successor class is able to file a timely application for renewal, the renewal claim would fail, resulting in the work's falling into the public domain. Requiring members of the successor renewal class to file renewal claims in their name as an act of insurance against the possibility of the author's dying before the year is up would often result in redundant applications, and it is not clear whether the Copyright Office will even accept this practice.

Further, if you were an assignee of a renewal expectancy, you will want to know upon the commencement of the renewal term of copyright whether the copyright is vested in you or in the author or his heirs. The best way to determine this would be to perform a search of the records of the copyright office (see Circular R22 set forth at the end of Chapter 1) to discover whether the author was alive at the

---

[33] *Frederick Music Company v. Sickler,* 708 F.Supp. 587 (S.D.N.Y. 1989).
[34] *Marascalco v. Fantasy, Inc.,* 953 F.2d 469 (9th Cir. 1991).

time of renewal. If the rule announced by the 9th Circuit were followed, then an author could file a renewal application during the 28th year, die subsequent to the filing, but before the end of the year, and the records of the copyright office would not reflect the true ownership status of the renewal copyright. Unless the holder of the renewal expectancy had some separate way of confirming whether the author survived the expiration of the original term of copyright, it might take some investigation to determine, in fact, whether the holder is actually the owner of the copyright, or whether, if he continues to exploit the work, he is liable for copyright infringement. Similarly, as will be discussed at length later in this chapter, if you are a *derivative work licensee* (i.e., owner of a derivative work based upon an underlying work of another under license from the author of the underlying work), you will want to know if, under the ruling in the *Rear Window* decision, you have the right to continue distributing your derivative work without further license from the author or his heirs.

## G. Renewal Vesting Under Copyright Renewal Act of 1992

It is the better view that, as long as the author survives until the date the renewal application is registered in the Copyright Office, a renewal claimed in the name of an author will be effective, even if he should die subsequent to the registration but before the end of the 28th year. This is in fact the rule adopted by Congress in the 1992 Act.

(B) At the expiration of the original copyright term of copyright in a work specified in paragraph (1)(C) of this subsection, the copyright shall endure for a renewed and extended further term of 67 years, which —

(i) if an application to register a claim to such further term has been made to the Copyright Office within 1 year before the expiration of the original term of copyright and the claim is registered, shall vest, upon the beginning of such further term, in any person who is entitled under paragraph (1)(C) [i.e., the statutory beneficiaries, such as author, widow, widower, children, etc.] to the renewal and extension of the copyright at the time the application is made; or

(ii) if no such application is made or the claim pursuant to such application is not registered, shall vest, upon the beginning of such further term, in any person entitled under paragraph (1)(C), as of the last day of the original term of copyright, to the renewal and extension of the copyright.

The new law clearly indicates that the renewal copyright always *vests* upon the commencement date of the renewal term (i.e., "the copyright shall endure for a renewed and extended further term . . . which . . . shall vest . . . upon the beginning of such further term . . ."). However, it is also clear that the person or persons in whom the renewal copyright will actually vest may directly depend upon whether a permissive renewal application is filed with the Copyright Office and when during the 28th year of the original term that application was filed.

If an application to register the renewal is filed within 1 year before the expiration of the original term of copyright, then the renewal copyright will vest in the person(s) entitled to claim the renewal *living at the time the application is made*. If, however, an application to register the renewal was not filed within 1 year before the expiration of the original term, then the renewal copyright will vest in the person(s) entitled to claim the renewal *living as of the last day of the original term of the copyright*.

## H.  Effect of 1992 Act on Assignments of Rule of Renewal Expectancies

The 1992 Act has no effect on the rule of renewal expectancies itself, which remains the law of the land. Depending upon the circumstances, however, the new law may have important consequences on the application of the rule in particular cases.

Taking a previous example, suppose a songwriter composed a song and assigned his copyright, including the renewal copyright, to his music publisher in 1967 and the original 28-year term of copyright in the song is expected to expire on December 31, 1995. Suppose further that the publisher did not receive any assignments of renewal expectancies from the songwriter's family, other than the songwriter's own renewal expectancy granted in 1967 under the terms of the music publishing agreement with the songwriter.

If an application to register the renewal is filed on December 1, 1995 (i.e., within 1 year before the expiration of the original term of copyright), then the renewal copyright will vest in the person entitled to claim the renewal living on December 1, 1995 (i.e., living at the time the application is made). If the songwriter is alive as of December 1, 1995, and the renewal application was filed in the name of the songwriter, then the songwriter's assignee (i.e., music publisher) will own the renewal copyright when it vests on January 1, 1996. If the songwriter died before December 1, 1995, and the renewal application was filed in the name of the songwriter's widow, then the widow will own the renewal copyright when it vests on January 1, 1996.

If no application to register the renewal is made during the calendar year 1995, then the renewal copyright will vest in the person entitled to claim the renewal living on December 31, 1995 (i.e., living as of the last day of the original term of copyright). If the songwriter is alive as of December 31, 1995, then the songwriter's assignee (i.e., music publisher) will own the renewal copyright when it vests on January 1, 1996. If the songwriter had died in a car accident driving home from a Christmas party on December 26, 1995, then the songwriter's widow will own the renewal copyright when it vests on January 1, 1996.

Accordingly, it appears that the determination of who will *own* the renewal copyright may depend on whether a renewal application has been filed and the timing of the author's death in relation to the time the renewal application is filed. This suggests that, even though registration is no longer a condition to claiming renewal copyrights, music publishers and songwriters should give serious consideration as to whether and when to file applications for renewal registration. Some of the issues to be considered by songwriters and publishers in this regard will be discussed below in the context of advice for music publishers and songwriters.

## I.   Persons Entitled to Submit Renewal Applications

As noted, a registration for renewal of copyright will be valid only if it is claimed in the name of the person or persons who are among the statutory class of individuals entitled to such renewal. This does not mean, however, the person entitled to *claim* renewal must himself *submit* the application for renewal registration.

Generally, as long as the renewal application is filed in the name of the persons entitled to claim renewal the application may be filed by any person authorized by the proper claimant to do so. A person is considered authorized to file a renewal claim when (1) he is expressly authorized by a proper renewal claimant to do so, or (2) he has an express power of attorney to act generally, or with respect to copyright and renewal copyright matters, on behalf of the renewal claimant.

Of course, anyone who is specifically requested by a claimant to file a renewal application may do so. To remove any doubt about his agent's authority to file renewal applications on his behalf, the claimant should execute a power of attorney. A *power of attorney* is simply a written instrument authorizing another to act as one's agent or "attorney-in-fact." An attorney-in-fact, under a written power of attorney, need only have general powers to act on a person's behalf to be authorized to file renewal applications. Usually, however, copyright owners grant powers of attorney that are limited to the specific actions required by the attorney-in-fact to handle the copyright affairs of the copyright owner. For example, a copyright owner may grant a power of attorney to another for the purpose of filing renewal applications and notices of termination with respect to the 19-year extended term. An example of a power of attorney relating to an assignment of copyrights, including any renewals and extensions, is set forth as part of Form 8.1 at the end of Chapter 8. An attorney licensed to practice law ("attorney-at-law") will always be considered authorized to file renewal applications on behalf of his clients whether or not expressed in writing.

It has also been commonly understood that a person is authorized to file a renewal claim when (1) he himself has a beneficial interest in the renewal copyright; or (2) by virtue of special circumstances, he is considered to have an implied power of attorney to file the renewal application on behalf of the claimant.

Because the failure to file a timely application for renewal registration for pre-1964 works had such drastic consequences, wide latitude was given to allowing persons filing renewal applications in the names of others. For example, it has been thought that, even in the absence of a specific request, anyone who is generally entrusted to conduct the music or copyright affairs of the renewal claimant may probably file an application on the claimant's behalf. Similarly, one who has a beneficial interest in the renewal copyright may file an application for renewal on behalf of the renewal claimants. For example, in the case of a deceased author and no living widow or children, a person who is named in the will to receive the renewal rights will have a beneficial interest in the renewal copyright. (Recall, however, that under these circumstances, the renewal must be claimed in the name of the executor of the will, who will hold legal title in the renewal in trust for the beneficiaries named in the will. Though the renewal must be filed *in the name of* the executor, a beneficiary may nevertheless *submit* the renewal application, by virtue of his beneficial interest in the renewal copyright.)

One who has been granted a renewal expectancy interest (i.e., one who will be entitled to own the renewal once it vests) has also been entitled to submit applications for renewal on behalf of claimants. As previously noted, if the author has interest in the renewal copyright to a music publisher, then, depending on the circumstances, the ownership of the renewal copyright may vest in the music publisher, not in the author or his heirs, in accordance with the rule of expectancies. Though the renewal application must still be filed in the name of the author, not the publisher, the publisher may nevertheless file the application for renewal. He does so either by virtue of a power of attorney granted to him in the original music publishing contract with the author, or, in the absence of such a power, by virtue of the publisher's beneficial interest in the renewal (obtaining ownership upon its vesting).

However, because of the 1992 Act, the publisher's privilege to submit a renewal application may be subject to challenge if the publisher does not have a written power of attorney authorizing him to submit the application. This will be discussed further below.

## J. Advice for Music Publishers

As noted above, the determination of who will *own* the renewal copyright may depend on whether a renewal application has been filed and the timing of the author's death in relation to the time the renewal application is filed. This suggests that, to the extent music publishers have a right to file renewal applications in the name of songwriters, a strategy may be available for increasing the likelihood that a publisher's renewal expectancy will mature into a renewal copyright vested in the music publisher, rather than in the songwriter or the songwriter's heirs.

The strategy would be as follows: Music publishers who hold assignments of renewal expectancies should attempt to file renewal claims (on behalf of and in the name of each of the authors, as soon into the beginning of the final (i.e., 28th) year of the original term of copyright as possible. The following should illuminate the benefits of this strategy.

Using the previous example, should a music publisher file a renewal application on January 2, 1995 (i.e., the first business day of the 28th and final year of the original term of copyright of a song created in 1967), then the renewal copyright will vest in the person entitled to claim the renewal living on January 2, 1995 (i.e., living at the time the application is made). If the songwriter dies any time during the year 1995 after January 2, then the music publisher (i.e., the assignee of the songwriter's renewal expectancy) will own the renewal copyright when it vests on January 1, 1996. If the publisher waits until December 1, 1995 to file the renewal application, and the songwriter dies prior to that date, then the songwriter's statutory beneficiaries at the time the application was filed will own the renewal copyright when it vests on January 1, 1996. If the music publisher and the songwriter's statutory beneficiaries fail to file the renewal application at all during the calendar year 1995, and the songwriter dies at any time during the year prior to December 31, 1995, then the songwriter's statutory beneficiaries as of December 31, 1995 will own the renewal copyright when it vests on January 1, 1996.

If the music publisher did not have a power of attorney from the songwriter to file renewal applications, can the music publisher nevertheless file the application in connection with implementing the strategy above suggested? As noted, even in the absence of a specific request, anyone who has been generally entrusted to conduct the music or copyright affairs of the renewal claimant has been allowed to file an application on the claimant's behalf. The Copyright Office has liberally allowed persons other than the claimant to file renewal applications, because failing to file had such drastic consequences (i.e., the work falling into the public domain). However, a question arises as to the effect of the Copyright Renewal Act of 1992, which has made renewal automatic, on the scope of the class of persons permitted to *submit* a renewal application to the Copyright Office.

The Act clearly does not affect the ability of the claimant's agent or one with a valid power of attorney to file renewal applications in the name of renewal claimants. Thus, if a music publisher had a power of attorney covering the filing of renewal applications, it could probably implement such a strategy without serious challenge. Suppose, however, the music publisher does not have a power of attorney or some other express authorization by the claimants to file the renewal application. Absent a power of attorney or some agency relationship between the claimant and the person submitting the application, may a music publisher who desires to submit the application do so solely on the basis of his beneficial interest in the renewal expectancy?

Under the law prior to 1992, the answer would clearly have been yes, because it was in both the claimant's interest and the claimant's music publisher's interest that the renewal application be filed (otherwise the term of copyright would expire at the end of the 28th year). Under the 1992 Act, however, the interests of the music publisher and those of the claimants may be in conflict and such a conflict may suggest another conclusion. In fact, the music publisher's authority to file an application on the claimant's behalf may be subject to some doubt if the claimant specifically asked the publisher not to file a renewal application.

## K. Advice for Songwriters

Just as there is a strategy for music publishers, there is a strategy for songwriters and their heirs for increasing the likelihood that ownership in the renewal copyright will vest in them over a publisher's renewal expectancy.

The songwriter's strategy might be as follows: If you previously assigned your interest in the renewal copyright and there is a chance you might not live through the end of the original term, don't file an application for renewal registration. If you file and you should then die before the expiration of the original term of copyright, then, while you will be entitled to *claim* the renewal, the person who will be entitled to *own* the renewal is the person to whom you previously assigned your expectancy interest (e.g., the music publisher).

If you have retained (e.g., never assigned to another) your renewal expectancy interest, then your decision whether to file a renewal registration will depend on the chances of your not surviving the expiration of the original term of copyright, and whether you wish your renewal copyright to pass to your beneficiaries either (i) as defined under the copyright law or (ii) as specified in your will. Assuming you wish the copyright to be bequeathed in accordance with your will, then you should file the renewal registration as soon into the final year of the original copyright term as possible. Remember, too, the slight legal advantages of filing a renewal application within 1 year prior to the expiration of the original term of copyright (i.e., renewal certificate becomes prima facie evidence of validity of the renewal copyright in infringement actions).

Each person who is entitled to claim renewal may file or cause to be filed a renewal application in his or her own name. This may be the case, for example, where a song was written by the collaboration of a composer and a lyricist. Though several persons may be entitled to file a renewal application, the filing of only one application, even if it is submitted in the name of only one of several proper renewal claimants, is required to effect renewal registration. The filing co-claimant and any non-filing co-claimants are considered to be in precisely the same position as though they had all properly filed applications. It would therefore appear that as long as one co-claimant files an application for renewal, it is not necessary for the other co-claimants to file separate, additional renewal applications. Though more than one renewal claimant may wish to file claims, it may be more economical for them to do so on the same form, rather than in separate applications. A renewal application contains room for three claimants, yet the same renewal registration fee will cover all three claims. In the event a question arises as to who will prove to be the proper claimant(s), the registration of competing renewal applications should be made. The Copyright Office will issue competing renewal certificates if, for example, it is not known whether an author, who has been missing for some time, is living or deceased, or there is a question as to the status of an illegitimate child. However, before filing an application for renewal registration, the songwriters or their survivors should carefully consider the potential affects on the vesting of the ultimate ownership interest in the renewal copyright.

Should the author specifically decide not to file an application for renewal registration, and it is thought that a music publisher who was previously assigned a renewal expectancy might file an application as a precaution against the author dying during the 28th year of the initial term of copyright, the author should send a letter to the publisher advising that he does not wish the publisher to file the application. If the author should die during the 28th year, this action may provide his heirs with some grounds for claiming the renewal copyright should vest in their name and not in the name of the music publisher.

## VI. DURATION OF LICENSES

### A. By Terms of the License

A license normally lasts for as long as it says it lasts, usually in a provision called the *term* of license. For example, a license having a term of "five (5) years" will last five years. If the license does not state any limit on its term and if there is no evidence the parties intended the term to be limited, it will normally be deemed to continue effective for the life of the copyright. Non-exclusive licenses for which there is no stated term and for which there was no legal consideration (e.g., payment in exchange for the license) are revocable by the licensor at any time, unless circumstances are present that would make it unreasonable to allow the licensor to revoke permission.

A music copyright owner may grant licenses only for a term covering the time during which it has a right to grant licenses. For example, if a music publisher were only granted rights with respect to the original term of copyright, he could not grant licenses that purport to extend beyond the original term. An example of contracts containing such a songwriter provision are those that were entered using the form Uniform Popular Songwriter's Contract published in 1947 by the American Guild of Authors & Composers (now known as The Songwriter's Guild). Paragraph 8 of that form provides in part:

> 8. Terms of Contract. All rights in and to the composition and any copyrights thereon throughout the world, shall revert to the Writer upon the expiration of the original term of the United States copyright or at the end of twenty-eight (28) years from the date of publication in the United States, which ever period shall be shorter.

The AGAC contract provided, however, that if the songwriter failed to give to the publisher at least six months notice of any sale of the writer's United States renewal copyright to anyone other than the publisher, then the publisher shall be entitled to retain its rights under the contract for the renewal term in all countries outside the United States and Canada.

Further, paragraph 13 of the AGAC contract provided:

> 13. Termination of Contract. Upon the termination of this contract, all rights of any and every nature in and to the composition and in and to any and all copyrights secured thereon in the United States and throughout the world, shall re-vest in and become the property of the Writer, and shall be re-assigned to the Writer by the Publisher free of any and all encumbrances of any nature whatsoever, provided that: . . . (b) If the Publisher, prior to such termination, shall have granted a domestic license for the use of the composition, not inconsistent with the terms and provisions of this contract, the re-assignment may be subject to the terms of such license.

Accordingly, licenses issued by publishers during the original term of copyright and providing for a term that extended into the renewal term remain effective into the renewal term to the extent their territory is limited to the United States. As a practical matter, many licenses typically granted by music publishers have been made on a worldwide basis. Accordingly, if producers and other users of music cannot acquire from the music publisher a license of sufficient duration to meet his requirements, at least options to extend the term for additional periods of time, then producers will choose to use substitute songs for which such terms are available. Accordingly, the parties to an AGAC form contract have an incentive to alleviate any impediments to producers' licensing songs that revert to writers under the AGAC form.

Music publisher and songwriters can alleviate the problem by entering into an agreement allowing the music publisher to continue actively issuing licenses that go beyond the original term of copyright, such as will be required for the issuance of synchronization licenses to exploit the songwriter's compositions in motion pictures, television productions, commercials and videograms. An example of such an agreement is set forth as Form 14.6 at the end of Chapter 14 on *Synchronization Licenses*. Arrangements such as these should improve the licensing prospects of songs covered by these agreements.

However, the problem is only partially alleviated with respect to certain songs. It was once thought that licenses granted during the original term of copyright purporting to cover the renewal term would continue in effect through the renewal term even though the renewal copyright reverted to a deceased author's survivors.[35] However, under the *Rear Window* decision, discussed below, it is now the law that such licenses may expire at the end of the original term if the renewal copyright reverted to the author's beneficiaries.

## B. By Terms of the Copyright Law

Certain provisions of the copyright law affect the duration of certain licenses.

### 1. Termination of Licenses Granted by Authors After January 1, 1978

Any license that is silent about its *term* (i.e., how long it will remain in effect) will endure for the life of the copyright. However, any license granted by an author after January 1, 1978, regardless of the term stated in the license agreement, is subject to being terminated 35 years after the date of the grant of license.[36] This power to terminate a license is sometimes referred to as the *35-year termination rule* (which is also applicable to the termination of assignment of copyright or exclusive right under copyright made by an author after January 1, 1978).

Specifically, licenses made by an author (of a work other than a work made for hire) on or after January 1, 1978 may be terminated by the author or certain heirs during a 5-year period beginning at the end of 35 years from the date of the grant, or if the grant covers the right of publication, 35 years from the date of publication or 40 years from the date of the grant, whichever is shorter. To terminate a grant, a written notice must be served on the transferee within the time limits specified by the copyright law.[37]

If termination is not effected under the terms of the rule, then the grant of license will continue in effect for the life of the copyright or

---

[35] *Rohauer v. Killiam Shows, Inc.,* 551 F.2d 484 (2d Cir. 1977); overturned by the U.S. Supreme Court in *Steward v. Abend,* 495 U.S. 207 (1990) (the *Rear Window* decision).

[36] 17 U.S.C. Sec. 203.

[37] 17 U.S.C. Sec. 203 (a)(3),(4).

will expire sooner in accordance with any applicable provisions of the agreement effecting the grant. If the termination is properly effected under the rule, then the grant of license terminates, provided that:

> A derivative work prepared under the authority of the grant before its termination may continue to be utilized under the terms of the grant after its termination, but this privilege does not extend to the preparation after the termination of other derivative works based upon the copyrighted work covered by the terminated grant.[38]

This is an important limitation on the rights of a copyright owner of a terminated grant. For example, a synchronization license to use music in a motion picture granted before termination would continue in effect for as long as provided in the license, but the licensee would not be able to use the music in other derivative works without a new license from the terminated rights owner. In other words, a motion picture producer could continue to distribute the motion picture without requiring a further license from the owner of the terminated rights, but, unless the terms of the original license permitted it, he could not use the music in a "remake" of the motion picture (i.e., "preparation after termination of other derivative works") without a new license.

Where a music publisher created derivative works under the terms of its music publishing agreement with a songwriter who has terminated the grant of rights under that agreement, the terminated rights will be subject to the music publisher's right to continue to exploit any derivative works. Such derivative works may include arrangements, translations, compilations, and sound recordings created during the term of agreement.

### 2. Licenses Covering the Initial Term of Copyright

A license to use a work created before January 1, 1978 in its original (i.e., first 28-year) term of copyright, which does not purport to cover the renewal term of copyright, will endure until the expiration of the original term of copyright only. As a practical matter, very few licenses, other than those that contain a fixed limitation on its term (e.g., five years), would fall into this category. A license "under the

---

[38] 17 U.S.C. Sec. 203 (b)(1).

copyright" would probably expire at the end of the first term. A license granted during the first term of copyright, however, whose term is "in perpetuity" would be construed as covering the renewal term.

### 3. Licensing Purporting to Cover the Renewal Term of Copyright

Under a decision handed down by the U.S. Supreme Court in 1990 that has been described as "macabre," the duration of license, for the use of a song created before January 1, 1978 in its original (i.e., first 28-year) term of copyright, purporting to cover the renewal term would remain effective during the renewal term only if the author was living at the time at commencement of the renewal term.[39] Thus, it is an infringement of copyright to distribute a derivative work that is based on or incorporates a pre-1978 underlying work to which a license was obtained during its initial term if the author dies before the commencement of the renewal term, even though the author granted the producer of the derivative work a license to use the underlying work for its full term of copyright "including renewals and extensions."

The *Rear Window* decision does not affect (1) derivative works that were based on underlying works that were created or published for the first time since January 1, 1978, (2) derivative works that were based on underlying works that were in their renewal terms of copyright when the license to use the underlying work was granted, (3) derivative works that were based on underlying works that were works-made-for-hire of the owner of the derivative work, (4) derivative works that were based on underlying works that were in their initial term of copyright when the license to use the underlying work was granted, provided that the author of the underlying work lives until the time the renewal copyright may be claimed (i.e., 28th year of the original term of copyright) and an application to register the renewal copyright is actually filed while the author was alive,[40] and (5) deriv-

---

[39] *Stewart v. Abend,* 110 S. Ct. 1750 (1990); *see, generally,* Lionel S. Sobel, *View from the "Rear Window": A Practical Look at the Consequences of the Supreme Court's Decision in Stewart vs. Abend,* 12/1 Entertainment Law Reporter 3 (June, 1990).

[40] Except in the 9th Circuit: Under *Marascalco v. Fantasy, Inc.,* 953 F.2d 469 (9th Cir. 1991), the rule as stated in this clause should read, "provided that the author of the underlying work lives until the commencement of the renewal term."

ative works that were based on underlying works created prior to 1964 that fell into the public domain because a claim for renewal was not filed by the applicable deadline.

The rule only affects derivative works created before January 1, 1978 that were based on underlying works of others that were in their initial terms of copyright when the license to use the underlying work was granted, provided that the author of the underlying work died prior to the renewal copyright could be claimed in his name [or the renewal otherwise vested in the author by contract] and the derivative licensee did not receive licenses from the author's statutory beneficiaries under their renewal expectancy interests. Nevertheless, because of the number of works that it does affect, the *Rear Window* decision has had far reaching consequences.

### 4. Effects of Rear Window on Music Licensing

#### a. Effect on Which Songs Will Be Used in New Derivative Works

As noted in Chapters 10 and 14, producers of derivative works, such as motion pictures, television programs, and other audiovisual works, generally desire to obtain licenses that last as long as possible. Because of the possibility that a license subject to the *Rear Window* rule may have its term prematurely terminated by the untimely death of the songwriter, *derivative works licensees* (i.e., producers of derivative works obtaining licenses to use underlying works, such as music, in their productions) might wish to avoid using music that may be subject to a *Rear Window* termination.

Producers desiring to obtain licenses for the use of songs should ask the music copyright owner whether the song sought to be licensed is *safe* from the Rear Window decision or *tainted* by it. For example, works created or first published since 1978 are "safe" from the affects of the *Rear Window* decision. Also safe are works in their renewal terms (e.g., songs first published prior to 1964 are in their renewal term as of 1992). Works potentially "tainted" by the *Rear Window* decision, as of 2000, are works published between 1972 and 1977. The initial year of the tainted period will become 1973 in 2001, 1974 in 2002, 1975 in 2003, and 1977 will always be the final year of this period.

A song that would otherwise be tainted because it falls inside of the tainted period may have become safe if the songwriters have already died before an application for renewal registration could be filed, because a license for the renewal term can then be obtained directly from the surviving spouses and children. However, there remain many unanswered legal questions that may affect whether or not a particular song is safe from the affects of the *Rear Window* decision. If the work falls within the tainted period, the producer may wish to consider a substitute song that is safe, such as songs falling in the safe periods or songs commissioned on a works for hire basis.

Music publishers and songwriters controlling rights in songs affected by the *Rear Window* decision may actually begin to find their licensing revenue from these songs decrease as expiration of the original term of copyright approaches. With respect to songs still in their original term, where it is clear the publisher will not have the right to issue licenses covering the renewal term, music publishers find themselves unable to issue licenses that have terms that go beyond the expiration of the original copyright term. As discussed in Chapter 9, many producers are now requiring licenses that have a term of perpetuity, or at least include options to extend the term by providing notice and additional payment. If the publisher is unable to provide these terms, producers will choose to use substitutes for which such terms are available. Accordingly, music publishers and songwriters have an incentive to alleviate any impediments to producers' licensing their songs affected by the Rear Window decision.

As noted above, where renewal copyrights revert to songwriters under the provisions of a music publishing agreement, such as under the AGAC form contract, unless the writer and the publisher enter into an arrangement allowing the publisher to issue licenses during the original term whose term may extend into the renewal term, publishing income for songs whose protection is nearing the end of the original term may decline, because producers will avoid licensing compositions for which long term licenses are not available. It is interesting to note that, under *Rear Window*, songwriters and music publishers have no similar ability to avoid a similar decline in their publishing income arising from producers' choosing to avoid licensing songs tainted by the *Rear Window* problem, because, under *Rear Window*, any such agreement would be unenforceable against the beneficiaries of the renewal copyright in the event the author should die prior to the commencement of the renewal term. Accordingly, there is some reason to doubt whether the intent of the ruling in *Rear Window* actually serves to further its purported purpose.

    *b.   Effect on the Terms, If Any, Upon Which Previously*
        *Produced Derivative Works May Continue to Be Exploited*

    Not all is doom and gloom for producers and other owners of derivative works containing songs whose licenses are affected by the *Rear Window* decision. It appears that the distribution of such derivative works during the renewal term will probably not be subject to court injunction. The 9th Circuit in deciding the *Rear Window* case specifically refused to grant an injunction and the Supreme Court did not upset the lower court's ruling in that regard.[41] The issue, then, will probably be limited to how much of the proceeds from the exploitation of the derivative work will have to be paid to the author's heirs during the term of the renewal copyright.

    Discussion of the variety of works affected by the *Rear Window* decision is beyond the scope of this book. Indeed, some of the most dramatic effects caused by the *Rear Window* decision have been on agreements between producers of motion pictures and television programs and the authors of the literary works that underlie them and perhaps mainframe and minicomputer computer software not created on a work-for-hire basis that has become contributions to other computer programs. The following section sketches some of the affects of the *Rear Window* decision on existing music licenses.

### (1)   Licenses Granted to Music Publishers

    Music publishers create a variety of derivative works during the term of music publishing contracts. Such derivative works may include arrangements, translations, compilations, and sound recordings. Under the *Rear Window* decision, the use of music in all such derivative works will require new licenses from the renewal copyright owner.

---

[41] See, 110 S.Ct. at 1757, 1768.

### (2)    Mechanical Licenses Granted to
###        Record Companies

Rights reverting to renewal copyright claimants under *Rear Window* also have the effect of terminating all mechanical licenses issued during the original term of copyright. This should have no practical effect, however, to the extent the original mechanical license provided that mechanical fees were payable at the statutory rate in effect at the time phonorecords were made and distributed. If the renewal copyright owner decided to terminate the mechanical license, the derivative licensee would simply enter into a new one under the same statutory terms, or if the copyright owner refused, the derivative licensee could compel the renewal owner to issue a mechanical license at the statutory rate. However, if the mechanical license was originally issued at a *rate* (see Chapter 12) or otherwise provided that the fee be set at the statutory rate in effect at the time the license was entered (i.e., without the benefit of subsequent increases), then the renewal owner could obtain more favorable terms by terminating the license and renegotiating the new license at the more favorable statutory rate.

### (3)    Synchronization Licenses Granted to Producers

To the extent producers of motion pictures and television programs have used in the soundtracks of their derivative works music that is tainted by the *Rear Window* decision, new licenses for the use of such music will be required from the renewal copyright owners. To the extent the music is replaceable (e.g., recorded on a separate track or not materially featured in the picture), the producer has increased leverage in the negotiations over obtaining the license required.

### (4)    Master Licenses Granted to Producers to Use
###        Sound Recordings

Producers of motion pictures and television programs who have licensed sound recordings from record companies for use in their derivative works, probably do not have much to be concerned about with respect to the continued use of those recordings. This is because virtually all sound recordings are produced under work for hire contracts. Because the recording company is considered the *author* of works it commissioned on a work for hire basis, the recording company's license to the producer for the full term of copyright "including any renewals and extensions" will remain in full force and effect.

### (5)   Owners of Copies or Phonorecords Containing Affected Works

If a licensee whose license has been terminated upon the expiration of the original term of copyright is the lawful owner of copies (or phonorecords) of works affected by *Rear Window*, then he may still distribute or otherwise dispose of such copies. Of course, he may not produce any new copies without a license covering the renewal term.

### 5.   *Effect of 1992 Act*

For works created on or after January 1, 1964, the rule of the *Rear Window* case will not apply if a renewal application is not made within 1 year before the expiration of the original term of copyright in such works. The Copyright Renewal Act of 1992 states:

> If an application to register a claim to the renewed and extended term of copyright in a work is not made within 1 year before the expiration of the original term of copyright in a work, or if the claim pursuant to such application is not registered, then a derivative work prepared under the authority of a grant of a transfer or license of the copyright that is made before the expiration of the original term of copyright may continue to be used under the terms of the grant during the renewed and extended term of copyright without infringing the copyright, except that such use does not extend to the preparation during such renewed and extended term of other derivative works based upon the copyrighted work covered by such grant.[42]

Thus, if the songwriter or his survivors fail to file within 1 year before the expiration of the original term of copyright for a work created between January 1, 1964 and December 31, 1977, then a producer's previous license covering the term of copyright "including any

---

[42] 17 U.S.C. Sec. 304 (a)(4)(B).

renewals or extensions thereof" will be effective during the renewal term.

### 6. Advice for Derivative Licensees

The cost of identifying the thousands of songs tainted with the *Rear Window* problem that may be contained in previously produced motion pictures and television programs may be exorbitant. Accordingly, the producer's only practical alternative may be to simply continue distributing the pictures until a demand letter is received from a songwriter or his estate.

Leaving that alternative aside, a producer who has identified a song affected by *Rear Window* has to choose another path, such as developing a strategy for negotiating with the songwriters, or their applicable statutory beneficiaries or survivors. If the song's copyright is already in its renewal term, the producer can withdraw the picture from distribution and begin negotiating with the songwriter's survivors or executor. If the author died before his statutory beneficiaries are entitled to file a claim for renewal (i.e., before the beginning of the 28th year of the original copyright term), the producer may continue distributing the motion picture under his license for the original term while commencing negotiations with the writer's survivors or executor for a license covering the renewal term. If the author has not died yet, the producer may seek to obtain licenses covering the renewal term from the songwriter's current spouse, children, or other beneficiaries; this strategy will only be effective if the author does not subsequently remarry or have any more children before dying.

The problem with the strategies in the foregoing paragraph is that they alert the author's beneficiaries of their rights concerning renewal. As noted above, under the 1992 Act, if a renewal application is not timely made (i.e., within 1 year before the expiration of the original term of copyright) for a work created between January 1, 1964 and December 31, 1977, then a derivative work prepared under the authority of a grant of a license made before the expiration of the original term of copyright may continue to be used under the terms of the grant during the renewed and extended term of copyright without infringing the copyright. If the songwriter or his survivors fail to file a renewal application, then a producer's previous license covering the term of copyright "including any renewals or extensions thereof" will be effective during the renewal term.

However, if the author has not died yet, and the original license agreement gives the producer the authority to renew the author's underlying copyright, the producer should file a renewal application as soon as possible after January 1st of the 28th year of the initial term. If the author is alive when the renewal application is registered, the renewal application is effective (under the 1992 Act), even if the author dies before the 29th year copyright protection begins.

### 7. Advice for Music Publishers

Because licensing music is the life blood of a music publisher's business, music publishers should take whatever measures available to facilitate the licensing of music in their catalogs. Music publishers should try to identify those songs in its catalog that have been affected by the *Rear Window* decision and that were previously licensed in derivative works, such as motion pictures and television programs. If it appears that the song may revert to the author or his survivors, the publisher should attempt to attain the renewal copyright from the estate of the author, entering into contracts giving the publisher renewal expectancy interests if necessary, or obtaining exclusive administration rights to the music for the renewal term. With control of the renewal rights, the publisher can then issue the necessary licenses for the use of music in derivative works that cover the renewal term.

Barring the ability to control the renewal copyright, there is not much else the music publisher can do to alleviate the problems caused by *Rear Window*.

### 8. Advice for Songwriters

Nor is there much songwriters can do to alleviate the adverse affect *Rear Window* may have on pre-renewal licensing revenue for songs tainted by the decision.

With respect to filing renewal applications, it has been noted that under the Renewal Copyright Act of 1992, if a renewal application is not made within 1 year before the expiration of the original term of copyright, then "a derivative work prepared under the authority of a grant of a transfer or license of the copyright that is made before the expiration of the original term of copyright may continue to be used under the terms of the grant during the renewed and extended term of copyright without infringing the copyright, except that such use does not extend to the preparation during such renewed and extended term of other derivative works based upon the copyrighted work covered by such grant."[43] This might lead a songwriter to file a registration within the prescribed time period. However, as noted above, if filing the renewal application could cause the renewal copyright to vest in the music publisher, rather than the heirs of the songwriter, it might be best not to file the application within one year before the expiration of the original term. However, should the songwriter die during the 28th year, then his beneficiaries should strongly consider filing a renewal application subsequent to his death in order to avoid the effect of Section 304(a)(4)(B) and preserve the ability to renegotiate licenses for the use of the song in derivative works during the renewal term.

When the songwriter or his beneficiaries are in a position to renegotiate licenses for use of music in derivative works during the renewal term, they should not overlook the importance of coming to an agreement to license the song in derivative works. Remember that it is unlikely that you will be able to obtain an injunction stopping the exploitation of the derivative work during the renewal term and any litigation will boil down to just determining what a reasonable license fee ought to be. Under these circumstances, litigation will rarely be worth the costs. Further, regardless of how unreasonably low the fee being offered may seem to be in relation to what the producer may stand to gain by exploiting the derivative work (or stand to cost him if you proceed to litigation), in the long run, you will tend to make up more than the difference between what is being offered and what you think you deserve by collecting important performance royalties from exhibition on television or otherwise from maintaining an active relationship between the song and the listening public.

### 9.  Licenses Covering the Extended (19-Year) Term of Copyright

For works created before January 1, 1978 and in their first term of copyright as of December 31, 1977, a right of termination, similar

---

[43] 17 U.S.C. Sec. 304 (a)(4)(B).

to that provided to authors of works created after January 1, 1978 (discussed above), is provided with respect to transfers covering the newly added years extending the maximum term of copyright by 19 years, from 56 to 75 years.[44]

The assignment of a copyright in a song created before January 1, 1978 in its original term or its renewal term of copyright, will endure until the expiration of the copyright (i.e., the 75th, and final year of the life of the copyright), unless otherwise provided by the terms of the assignment agreement or unless the author (or certain statutory beneficiaries) exercises a statutory right of termination which may be effective as early as 19 years prior to the final year of the copyright. Within certain time limits, an author or specified heirs of the author are generally entitled to file a notice terminating the author's transfers covering any part of the 19 year period that has now been added to the end of the second term of copyright in a work.

If termination is not effected under the terms of the rule, then the grant of license will continue in effect for the life of the copyright or will expire sooner in accordance with any applicable provisions of the agreement effecting the grant. If the termination is properly effected, then the grant of license terminates, provided that:

> A derivative work prepared under the authority of the grant before its termination may continue to be utilized under the terms of the grant after its termination, but this privilege does not extend to the preparation after the termination of other derivative works based upon the copyrighted work covered by the terminated grant.[45]

This provision is worded identically to the similar provision concerning termination of terminated grants by authors made after January 1, 1978, and has the same legal and practical effects.

## VII. AFTER LIFE

The Sonny Bono Copyright Term Extension Act of 1998 effectively pushed back by 20 years the date on which songs were sched-

---

[44] 17 U.S.C. Sec. 304 (c).
[45] 17 U.S.C. Sec. 304 (c)(6)(A).

uled to fall into the public domain in the United States.[46] For example, songs initially published in the year 1923 that were scheduled to fall into the public domain on January 1, 1999, will now retain their copyright until January 1, 2019. To give the reader some idea of what is happening, the appendix to this chapter includes a short list of songs that are now in the public domain in the United States, followed by a list of songs that will enter the public domain in the United States beginning in 2019. Persons involved in music licensing, whether granting licenses or clearing them, should take note that an ever increasing number of songs will be available free of charge as substitutes to be used for those purposes for which music is used.

Yes, there is life after copyright. The continuing popularity of songs that will soon enter the public domain will demonstrate that musical works are destined to maintain an active relationship with the listening public, long after the life of their copyright has expired.

---

[46] Note, the fact that a work has fallen into the public domain in the United States does not necessarily mean that it has fallen into the public domain in other countries. Each country has its own laws regarding the duration of copyright. For example, many countries follow the "rule of the shorter term." In such a country, the duration of copyright protection will last the shorter of (i) the term of protection accorded to nationals of that country or (ii) the term of protection accorded to the work in the home country of the work's author. Thus, if the copyright in a work has expired in the United States, it will not be protected in a country which follows the rule of the shorter term, even if that country provides a longer term of protection for its own citizens. However, because several significant countries (including the United Kingdom and Canada) do not follow the rule of the shorter term, an independent analysis must be made of the status of copyright for each country in which a user desires to exploit the work.

# APPENDIX TO CHAPTER 9
## DURATION OF COPYRIGHT, ASSIGNMENTS OF COPYRIGHT, AND LICENSES

# LIST 9.1

## SOME POPULAR SONGS IN THE PUBLIC DOMAIN IN THE UNITED STATES

**1814**
STAR SPANGLED BANNER, THE
*Francis Scott Key*
*John Stafford Smith*

**1823**
HOME SWEET HOME
*John Howard Payne*

**1832**
AMERICA (My Country 'tis of Thee)
*Samuel Francis Smith*

**1837**
WOODMAN, SPARE THAT TREE
*Henry Russell*
*George P. Morris*

**1843**
OPEN THY LATTICE, LOVE
*Stephen Collins Foster*

**1848**
OH! SUSANNAH
*Stephen Collins Foster*

**1851**
OLD FOLKS AT HOME
*Stephen Collins Foster*

**1852**
MASSA'S IN DE COLD, COLD GROUND
*Stephen Collins Foster*

**1853**
MY OLD KENTUCKY HOME
*Stephen Collins Foster*

**1854**
JEANNIE WITH THE LIGHT BROWN HAIR
*Stephen Collins Foster*

**1855**
COME WHERE MY LOVE LIES DREAMING
*Stephen Collins Foster*

**1860**
DIXIE
*Daniel Emmett*
OLD BLACK JOE
*Stephen Collins Foster*

**1861**
MARYLAND, MY MARYLAND
*James Ryder Randall*

**1862**
BATTLE HYMN OF THE
REPUBLIC, THE
*Julia Ward Howe*
*William Steffe*

**1864**
BEAUTIFUL DREAMER
*Stephen Collins Foster*

**1869**
SWEET GENEVIEVE
*George Cooper*
*Henry Tucker*

**1876**
I'LL TAKE YOU HOME
AGAIN KATHLEEN
*Thomas P. Westendorf*

**1878**
CARRY ME BACK TO OL'
VIRGINNY
*James A. Bland*
IN THE EVENING BY THE
MOONLIGHT
*James A. Bland*

**1879**
OH, DEM GOLDEN SLIPPERS
*James A. Bland*

**1880**
HAND ME DOWN MY
WALKING CANE
*James A. Bland*

**1885**
AMERICAN PATROL
*F. W. Meacham*

**1888**
SEMPER FIDELIS
*John Philip Sousa*

**1889**
WASHINGTON POST MARCH
*John Philip Sousa*

**1890**
OH PROMISE ME
*Reginald DeKoven*

**1891**
PICTURE THAT'S TURNED
TOWARDS THE WALL, THE
*Charles Graham*
TA-RA-RA BOOM-DER-E'
*Henry J. Sayers*

**1892**
AFTER THE BALL
*Charles K. Harris*
DAISY BELL
*Harry Dacre*
BOWERY, THE
*Charles H. Hoyt*
*Percy Gaunt*

**1894**
FORGOTTEN
*Flora Wulschner*
*Eugene Cowles*

I DON'T WANT TO PLAY IN
YOUR YARD
*Philip Wingate*
*H. W. Petrie*
SHE IS MORE TO BE PITIED
THAN CENSURED
*William B. Gray*
SHE MAY HAVE SEEN
BETTER DAYS
*James Thornton*
SIDEWALKS OF NEW YORK
*James W. Blake & Charles B.
Lawlor*

**1895**
AMERICA THE BEAUTIFUL
*Catherine Lee Bates*
*Samuel A. Ward*
BAND PLAYED ON, THE
*John F. Palmer*
*Charles B. Ward*
EL CAPITAN
*John Philip Sousa*
KING COTTON
*John Philip Sousa*

**1896**
MOTHER WAS A LADY
*Edward B. Marks*
*Joseph W. Stern*
SWEET ROSIE O'GRADY
*Maude Nugent Jerome*
THERE'LL BE A HOT TIME
IN THE OLD TOWN
TONIGHT
*Theodore Metz*
*Joe Hayden*

**1897**
BREAK THE NEWS TO
MOTHER
*Charles K. Harris*
ON THE BANKS OF THE
WABASH
*Paul Dresser*
STARS AND STRIPES
FOREVER
*John Philip Sousa*

**1898**
GYPSY LOVE SONG
*Victor Herbert & Harry B.
Smith*
MY OLD NEW HAMPSHIRE
HOME
*Andrew B. Sterling*
*Harry Von Tilzer*
ROSARY, THE
*Ethelbert Nevin & Robert
Cameron Rodgers*
WHEN GOOD FELLOWS GET
TOGETHER
*Richard Hovey*
*Frederick Field Bullard*

**1899**
HEARTS AND FLOWERS
*T. M. Tobani*
*Mary D. Brine*
HELLO MA BABY
*Joe E. Howard*
*Ida Emerson*
MAPLE LEAF RAG
*Scott Joplin*

MY WILD IRISH ROSE
*Chauncey Olcott*
YOU TELL ME YOUR
DREAMS
*Seymour Rice*
*Albert H. Brown*
*Charles N. Daniels*

**1900**
BIRD IN A GILDED CAGE, A
*Arthur J. Lamb & Harry Von Tilzer*

**1901**
I LOVE YOU TRULY
*Carrie Jacobs Bond*
JUST A-WEARYIN' FOR YOU
*Carrie Jacobs Bond & Frank Stanton*
MIGHTY LAK' A ROSE
*Ethelbert Nevin & Frank Stanton*

**1902**
BECAUSE
*GuyD'Hardelot*
*Edward Teschemacher*
BILL BAILEY WON'T YOU
PLEASE COME HOME
*Hughie Cannon*
DOWN WHERE THE
WURZBURGER FLOWS
*Vincent P. Bryan*
*Harry Von Tilzer*
GLOW WORM, THE
*Paul Lincke*
*Lilla C. Robinson*

IN THE GOOD OLD
SUMMER TIME
*Ren Shields*
*George Evans*
ON A SUNDAY AFTERNOON
*Harry Von Tilzer*
*Andrew B. Sterling*
OH! DIDN'T HE RAMBLE
*Bob Cole*
*Billy Johnson*
*J. Rosimond Johnson*

**1903**
BEDELIA
*William Jerome & Jean Schwartz*
DEAR OLD GIRL
*Theodore Morse*
*Richard Henry Buck*
ENTERTAINER, THE
*Scott Joplin*
IDA, SWEET AS APPLE
CIDER
*Eddie Leonard*
*Eddie Munson*
KASHMIRI LOVE SONG
*Lawrence Hope & Amy Woodforde-Finden*
MARCH OF THE TOYS
*Victor Herbert*
TOYLAND
*Victor Herbert & Glen MacDonough*
YOU'RE THE FLOWER OF
MY HEART, SWEET
ADELINE
*Harry Armstrong & Richard H. Gerard*

## 1904

FASCINATION (Valse Tzigane)
*F. D. Marchetti*
GIVE MY REGARDS TO
BROADWAY
*George M. Cohan*
MEET ME IN ST. LOUIS,
LOUIS
*Kerry Mills & Andrew B.
Sterling*
PLEASE COME AND PLAY IN
MY YARD
*Edward Madden
Theodore F. Morse*
YANKEE DOODLE BOY
*George M. Cohan*

## 1905

I DON'T CARE
*Jean Lenox
Harry O. Sutton*
IN MY MERRY OLDSMOBILE
*Vincent Bryan & Gus
Edwards*
IN THE SHADE OF THE OLD
APPLE TREE
*Egbert Van Alstyne & Harry
Williams*
KISS ME AGAIN
*Henry Blossom & Victor
Herbert*
MARY'S A GRAND OLD
NAME
*George M. Cohan*
MY GAL SAL
*Paul Dresser*

PARADE OF THE WOODEN
SOLDIERS
*Ballard MacDonald
Leon Jessel*
SO LONG MARY
*George M. Cohan*
TAMMANY
*Vincent P. Bryan
Gus Edwards*
WAIT TILL THE SUN SHINES
NELLIE
*Andrew B. Sterling & Harry
Von Tilzer*
WHERE THE RIVER
SHANNON FLOWS
*James I. Russell*
WHISTLER AND HIS DOG,
THE
*Arthur Pryor*
WILL YOU LOVE ME IN
DECEMBER (AS YOU DO IN
MAY)
*James J. Walker
Ernest R. Ball*
WON'T YOU COME OVER
TO MY HOUSE
*Harry Williams
Egbert Van Alstyne*

## 1906

BECAUSE YOU'RE YOU
*Victor Herbert
Henry Blossom*
DILL PICKLES
*Charles L. Johnson*
EVERY DAY IS LADIES' DAY
WITH ME
*Henry Blossom & Victor
Herbert*

I LOVE YOU TRULY
*Carrie Jacobs Bond*
LOVE ME AND THE WORLD
IS MINE
*Ernest R. Ball &*
*David Reed, Jr.*
MOONBEAMS
*Henry Blossom & Victor*
*Herbert*
NATIONAL EMBLEM
*E. E. Bagley*
SCHOOL DAYS
*Will D. Cobb & Gus Edwards*
WAITING AT THE CHURCH
*F. W. Leigh & Henry E.*
*Pether*
YOU'RE A GRAND OLD
FLAG
*George M. Cohan*

**1907**
ANCHORS AWEIGH
*George D. Lottman, A. H.*
*Milies, Domenico Savino &*
*Charles A. Zimmerman*
HARRIGAN
*George M. Cohan*
ON THE ROAD TO
MANDALAY
*Rudyard Kipling & Oley*
*Speaks*
RED WING
*Thurland Chattaway & Kerry*
*Mills*

**1908**
CUDDLE UP A LITTLE
CLOSER, LOVEY MINE

*Otto Harbach & Karl*
*Hoschna*
DEAR LITTLE BOY OF MINE
*J. Keirn Brennan*
*Ernest R. Ball*
DOWN IN JUNGLE TOWN
*Edward Madden*
*Theodore Morse*
I WISH I HAD A GIRL
*Grace LeBoy Kahn & Gus*
*Kahn*
SHINE ON HARVEST MOON
*Nora Bayes & Jack Norworth*
SUNBONNET SUE
*Will D. Cobb & Gus Edwards*
SWEET VIOLETS
*W. C.Powell*
TAKE ME OUT TO THE
BALL GAME
*Jack Norworth & Albert Von*
*Tilzer*

**1909**
BY THE LIGHT OF THE
SILVERY MOON
*Gus Edwards & Edward*
*Madden*
CASEY JONES
*Eddie Newton*
*T. Lawrence Seibert*
FROM THE LAND OF THE
SKY BLUE WATER
*Charles Wakefield Cadman &*
*Nelle Richmond Eberhart*
HAS ANYBODY HERE SEEN
KELLY?
*C. W. Murphy*
*Will Letters*

*William J. McKenna*
I WONDER WHO'S KISSING
HER NOW
  *Frank R. Adams, Will M.*
  *Hough & Joseph E. Howard*
I'VE GOT RINGS ON MY
FINGERS
  *F. P. Barnes, Maurice Scott &*
  *R. P. Weston*
MEET ME TONIGHT IN
DREAMLAND
  *Leo Friedman & Beth Slater*
  *Whitson*
MY HERO
  *Stanislaus Stange & Oscar*
  *Straus*
ON WISCONSIN
  *Carl Beck & W. T. Purdy*
PUT ON YOUR OLD GREY
BONNET
  *Stanley Murphy & Percy*
  *Wenrich*
THAT'S A PLENTY
  *Henry Creamer*
  *Bert A. Williams*
WHEN YOU AND I WERE
YOUNG, MAGGIE
  *George W. Johnson*
  *J. A. Butterfield*


**1910**
AH! SWEET MYSTERY OF
LIFE
  *Victor Herbert & Rida*
  *Johnson Young*
ALL ABOARD FOR
BLANKET BAY
  *Andrew B. Sterling*

*Harry Von Tilzer*
BIRTH OF PASSION
  *Otto Harbach*
  *Karl Hoschna*
CAPRICE VIENNOIS
  *Fritz Kreisler*
CHINATOWN MY
CHINATOWN
  *William Jerome & Jean*
  *Schwartz*
COME JOSEPHINE IN MY
FLYING MACHINE
  *Fred Fisher*
  *Alfred Bryan*
DOWN BY THE OLD MILL
STREAM
  *Tell Taylor*
EVERY LITTLE MOVEMENT
  *Otto Harbach & Karl*
  *Hoschna*
I'D LOVE TO LIVE IN
LOVELAND (WITH A GIRL
LIKE YOU)
  *W. R. Williams*
I'M FALLING IN LOVE WITH
SOMEONE
  *Victor Herbert & Rida*
  *Johnson Young*
ITALIAN STREET SONG
  *Victor Herbert & Rida*
  *Johnson Young*
LET ME CALL YOU
SWEETHEART
  *Leo Friedman & Beth Slater*
  *Whitson*
LIEBESFREUD
  *Fritz Kreisler*
LIEBESLIED

*Fritz Kreisler*
MOTHER MACHREE
*Ernest R. Ball, Chauncey
Olcott & Rida Johnson Young*
PERFECT DAY, A
*Carrie Jacobs Bond*
PUT YOUR ARMS AROUND
ME, HONEY
*Junie McCree & Albert Von
Tilzer*
SOME OF THESE DAYS
*Shelton Brooks*
STEIN SONG
*Lincoln Colcord & E. A.
Fenstad*

**1911**
ALEXANDER'S RAGTIME
BAND
*Irving Berlin*
EVERYBODY'S DOIN' IT
NOW
*Irving Berlin*
GOODNIGHT LADIES
*Harry Williams
Egbert Van Alstyne*
I WANT A GIRL (JUST LIKE
THE GIRL THAT MARRIED
DEAR OLD DAD)
*William Dilton & Harry Von
Tilzer*
LITTLE GREY HOME IN THE
WEST
*Hermann Lohr & D. Eardley
Wilmot*
LITTLE LOVE, A LITTLE
KISS, A
*A. Nilson Fysher, Adrian Ross
& Lao Silesu*

OH YOU BEAUTIFUL DOLL
*Nat D. Ayer & A. Seymour
Brown*
ROAMIN' IN THE GLOAMIN'
*Sir Harry Lauder*
SOMEWHERE A VOICE IS
CALLING
*Eileen Newton & Arthur P.
Tate*

**1912**
BE MY LITTLE BABY
BUMBLE BEE
*Henry Marshall & Stanley
Murphy*
GIANNINA MIA
*Rudolf Friml & Otto Harbach*
IT'S A LONG, LONG WAY TO
TIPPERARY
*Jack Judge & Harry Williams*
MOONLIGHT BAY
*Edward Madden & Percy
Wenrich*
MY MELANCHOLY BABY
*Ernie Burnett & George A.
Norton*
RAGTIME COWBOY JOE
*Maurice Abrahams. Grant
Clarke & Lewis F. Muir*
ROW, ROW, ROW
*William Jerome & James V.
Monaco*
SWEETHEART OF SIGMA
CHI
*Byron D. Stokes & F.
Dudleigh Vernor*
SYMPATHY
*Rudolf Friml & Otto Harbach*

WAITING FOR THE ROBERT E. LEE
*L. Wolfe Gilbert & Lewis F. Muir*
WHEN I GET YOU ALONE TONIGHT
*Fred Fisher*
*Joe McCarthy*
*Joe Goodwin*
WHEN I LOST YOU
*Irving Berlin*
WHEN IRISH EYES ARE SMILING
*Ernest R. Ball, George Graff, Jr. & Chauncey Olcott*
WHEN THE MIDNIGHT CHOO CHOO LEAVES FOR ALABAM'
*Irving Berlin*

*Alfred Bryan & Fred Fisher*
SWEETHEARTS
*Victor Herbert & Robert B. Smith*
TOO-RA-LOO-RA-LOO-RAL, THAT'S AN IRISH LULLABY
*James Royce Shannon*
TRAIL OF THE LONESOME PINE, THE
*Harry Carroll & Ballard MacDonald*
YOU MADE ME LOVE YOU, I DIDN'T WANT TO DO IT
*Joseph McCarthy & James V. Monaco*
WHERE DID YOU GET THAT GIRL?
*Bert Kalmar*
*Harry Puck*

**1913**
CURSE OF AN ACHING HEART, THE
*Al Piantadosi*
DANNY BOY
*Fred E. Weatherly (old Irish Air)*
GET OUT AND GET UNDER
*Grant Clarke, Edgar Leslie & Maurice Abrahams*
IF I HAD MY WAY
*James Kendis & Lou Klein*
MARCHETA
*Victor Schertzinger*
MY WIFE'S GONE TO THE COUNTRY
*Irving Berlin*
PEG O' MY HEART

**1914**
ABA DABA HONEYMOON, THE
*Walter Donovan & Arthur Fields*
BALLIN' THE JACK
*Chris Smith & James H. Burris*
BY THE BEAUTIFUL SEA
*Harold Atteridge & Harry Carroll*
BY THE WATERS OF MINNETONKA
*Thurlow Lieurance*
CAN'T YOU HEAR ME CALLIN' CAROLINE
*William H. Gardner & Caro Roma*

DOWN AMONG THE
SHELTERING PALMS
  *James Brockman & Abe
  Olman*
GOOD-BYE, GIRLS, I'M
THROUGH
  *Ivan Caryll &
  John Golden*
HE'S A DEVIL IN HIS OWN
HOME TOWN
  *Irving Berlin & Grant Clarke*
I WANT TO GO BACK TO
MICHIGAN, DOWN ON THE
FARM
  *Irving Berlin*
IF YOU DON'T WANT MY
PEACHES, YOU'D BETTER
STOP SHAKING MY TREE
  *Irving Berlin*
KEEP THE HOME-FIRES
BURNING, TILL THE BOYS
COME HOME
  *Lena G. Ford & Ivor Novello*
LITTLE BIT OF HEAVEN,
SHURE THEY CALL IT
IRELAND, A
  *Ernest R. Ball & J. Keirn
  Brennan*
MISSOURI WALTZ
  *Frederick Knight Logan &
  James R. Shannon*
ON THE 5:15
  *Henry I. Marshall & Stanley
  Murphy*
ST. LOUIS BLUES
  *W. C. Handy*
SIMPLE MELODY
  *Irving Berlin*

SISTER SUSIE'S SEWING
SHIRTS FOR SOLDIERS
  *Hermann E. Darewski & R. P.
  Weston*
SYLVIA
  *Clinton Scollard & Oley
  Speaks*
THAT'S A PLENTY
  *Lew Pollack*
THERE'S A LONG, LONG
TRAIL
  *Zo Elliott & Stoddard King*
THEY DIDN'T BELIEVE ME
  *Jerome Kern & M. E. Rourke*
TWELFTH STREET RAG
  *Euday L. Bowman*
WHEN YOU WORE A TULIP
AND I WORE A BIG RED
ROSE
  *Jack Mahoney & Percy
  Wenrich*
WHEN YOU'RE AWAY
  *Henry Blossom & Victor
  Herbert*
WHEN YOU'RE A LONG,
LONG WAY FROM HOME
  *Sam M. Lewis & George W.
  Meyer*
YOU PLANTED A ROSE IN
THE GARDEN OF LOVE
  *Ernest R. Ball & J. Will
  Callahan*

**1915**
ALABAMA JUBILEE
  *George L. Cobb & Jack Yellen*
ALONG THE ROCKY ROAD
TO DUBLIN

*Bert Grant & Joe Young*
ARE YOU FROM DIXIE
*Jack Yellen*
*George L. Cobb*
AUF WIEDERSEHN
*Herbert Reynolds & Sigmund*
*Romberg*
BABES IN THE WOOD
*Schuyler Greene & Jerome*
*Kern*
BEATRICE FAIRFAX, TELL
ME WHAT TO DO
*Grant Clarke, Joe McCarthy*
*& James V. Monaco*
BY HECK
*S. R. Henry*
CANADIAN CAPERS
*Earl Burtnett, Gus Chandler,*
*Henry Cohen & Bert White*
FASCINATION
*Harold Atteridge & Sigmund*
*Romberg*
GIRL ON THE MAGAZINE
COVER
*Irving Berlin*
HELLO, FRISCO!
*Gene Buck & Louis A. Hirsch*
HELLO, HAWAII, HOW ARE
YOU
*Bert Kalmar, Edgar Leslie &*
*Jean Schwartz*
I DIDN'T RAISE MY BOY TO
BE A SOLDIER
*Alfred Bryan & Al Piantadosi*
IF WE CAN'T BE THE SAME
OLD SWEETHEARTS, WE'LL
JUST BE THE SAME OLD
FRIENDS

*Joe McCarthy & James V.*
*Monaco*
I LOVE A PIANO
*Irving Berlin*
IN A MONASTERY GARDEN
*Albert W. Ketelbey*
IRELAND IS IRELAND TO
ME
*Ernest R. Ball, J. Keirn*
*Brennan & Fiske O'Hara*
IT'S TULIP TIME IN
HOLLAND
*Dave Redford & Richard A.*
*Whiting*
JELLY ROLL BLUES
*Ferd (Jelly Roll) Morton*
JUST TRY TO PICTURE ME
DOWN HOME IN
TENNESSEE
*Walter Donaldson & William*
*Jerome*
LOVE IS THE BEST OF ALL
*Henry Blossom & Victor*
*Herbert*
MEMORIES
*Egbert Van Alstyne & Gus*
*Kahn*
M-O-T-H-E-R, A WORD THAT
MEANS THE WORLD TO ME
*Howard Johnson & Theodore*
*Morse*
MY LITTLE GIRL
*Will Dillon, Sam M. Lewis &*
*Albert Von Tilzer*
MY MOTHER'S ROSARY
*Sam M. Lewis & George W.*
*Meyer*
NEAPOLITAN LOVE SONG

*Henry Blossom & Victor
Herbert*
PACK UP YOUR TROUBLES
IN YOUR OLD KIT-BAG
  *George Asaf & Felix Powell*
PUT ME TO SLEEP WITH AN
OLD-FASHIONED MELODY
  *Dick Howard, Harry Jentes &
  Sam M. Lewis*
RAGGING THE SCALE
  *Edward B. Claypoole*
SIAM
  *Fred Fisher & Howard
  Johnson*
SO LONG LETTY
  *Earl Carroll*
SOME LITLE BUG IS GOING
TO FIND YOU
  *Burt & Roy Atwell, Benjamin
  Hapgood, & Silvio Hein*
SUNSHINE OF YOUR SMILE,
THE
  *Leonard Cooke & Lillian Ray*
THERE'S A BROKEN HEART
FOR EVERY LIGHT ON
BROADWAY
  *Fred Fisher & Howard
  Johnson*
THERE'S A LITTLE LANE
WITHOUT A TURNING ON
THE WAY TO HOME SWEET
HOME
  *Sam M. Lewis & George W.
  Meyer*
UNDERNEATH THE STARS
  *Fleta Jan Brown & Herbert
  Spencer*
WE'LL HAVE A JUBILEE IN
MY OLD KENTUCKY HOME

*Walter Donaldson & Coleman
Goetz*
WHEN THE BOYS COME
HOME
  *John Hays & Oley Speaks*
WHEN I LEAVE THE WORLD
BEHIND
  *Irving Berlin*
WHEN YOU'RE IN LOVE
WITH SOMEONE WHO IS
NOT IN LOVE WITH YOU
  *Grant Clarke & Al Piantadosi*
YOU KNOW AND I KNOW
AND WE BOTH
UNDERSTAND
  *Schuyler Greene & Jerome
  Kern*
YOU'LL ALWAYS BE THE
SAME SWEET GIRL
  *Andrew B. Sterling & Harry
  Von Tilzer*


**1916**
ALLAH'S HOLIDAY
  *Rudolf Friml & Otto Harbach*
ARRAH GO ON, I'M GONNA
GO BACK TO OREGON
  *Bert Grant, Sam M. Lewis &
  Joe Young*
BABY SHOES
  *Joe Goodwin, Al Piantadosi
  & Ed Rose*
BEALE STREET BLUES
  *W. C. Handy*
BOY SCOUTS OF AMERICA
  *John Philip Sousa*
DOWN IN HONKY TONKY
TOWN

Charles McCarran & Chris
Smith
GIVE A LITTLE CREDIT TO
YOUR DAD
William Tracey & Nat Vincent
GOOD-BYE, GOOD LUCK,
GOD BLESS YOU
Ernest R. Ball & J. Keirn
Brennan
HAVE A HEART
Jerome Kern & P. G.
Wodehouse
HOW'S EVERY LITTLE
THING IN DIXIE
Albert Gumble & Jack Yellen
I AIN'T GOT NOBODY
Rogert Graham & Spencer
Williams
I CAN DANCE WITH
EVERYBODY BUT MY WIFE
Joseph Cawthorn & John L.
Golden
IF I KNOCK THE "L" OUT
OF KELLY
Bert Grant, Sam M. Lewis &
Joe Young
IF YOU HAD ALL THE
WORLD AND ITS GOLD
Bartley Costello, Harry
Edelheit & Al Piantadosi
IF YOU WERE THE ONLY
GIRL IN THE WORLD
Nat D. Ayer & Clifford Grey
I'M SORRY I MADE YOU
CRY
N. J. Clesi
IRELAND MUST BE
HEAVEN, FOR MY MOTHER
CAME FROM THERE

Fred Fisher, Howard Johnson
& Joe McCarthy
KATINKA
Rudolf Friml & Otto Harbach
LI'L LIZA JANE
Ada De Lachau
MAMMY'S LITTLE COAL
BLACK ROSE
Raymond Egan & Richard A.
Whiting
M-I-S-S-I-S-S-I-P-P-I
Bert Hanlon, Benny Ryan &
Harry Tierney
NAT'AN, NAT'AN, NAT'AN,
TELL ME FOR WHAT ARE
YOU WAITIN', NAT' AN
James Kendis
NOLA
Felix Arndt
OH! HOW SHE COULD
YACKI, HACKI, WICKI,
WACKI, WOO
Charlene McCarron, Stanley
Murphy & Albert Von Tilzer
POOR BUTTERFLY
Raymond Hubbell & John L.
Golden
PRETTY BABY
Egbert Van Alstyne, Tony
Jackson & Gus Kahn
ROSES OF PICARDY
Frederick E. Weatherly &
Haydn Wood
SINCE MAGGIE DOOLEY
LEARNED THE HOOLEY
HOOLEY
Bert Kalmar, Edgar Leslie &
George W. Meyer

THERE'S A LITTLE BIT OF
BAD IN EVERY GOOD
LITTLE GIRL
  *Grant Clarke & Fred Fisher*
THERE'S A QUAKER DOWN
IN QUAKER TOWN
  *David Berg & Alfred Solman*
THEY MADE IT TWICE AS
NICE AS PARADISE (AND
THEY CALLED IT
DIXIELAND)
  *Raymond Egan & Richard A.
  Whiting*
THEY'RE WEARING 'EM
HIGHER IN HAWAII
  *Joe Goodwin & Halsey K.
  Mohr*
THROW ME A ROSE
  *Emmerich Kalman, Herbert
  Reynolds & P. G. Wodehouse*
TURN BACK THE UNIVERSE
AND GIVE ME YESTERDAY
  *Ernest R. Ball & J. Keirn
  Brennan*
WAY DOWN IN IOWA I'M
GOING TO HIDE AWAY
  *Sam M. Lewis, George W.
  Meyers & Joe Young*
WHAT DO YOU WANT TO
MAKE THOSE EYES AT ME
FOR
  *Howard Johnson, Joe
  McCarthy & James V.
  Monaco*
YAAKA HULA HICKEY
DULA
  *E. Ray Goetz, Joe Young &
  Pete Wendling*

YOU CAN'T GET ALONG
WITH 'EM OR WITHOUT
'EM
  *Grant Clarke & Fred Fisher*

**1917**
ALL THE WORLD WILL BE
JEALOUS OF ME
  *Ernest R. Ball & Al Dubin*
BEALE STREET BLUES
  *W. C. Handy*
BELLS OF ST. MARY'S, THE
  *Emmett Adams & Douglas
  Furber*
BRING BACK MY DADDY TO
ME
  *Howard Johnson, George
  Meyer &William Tracey*
DARKTOWN STRUTTER'S
BALL
  *Shelton Brooks*
EILEEN (ALLANINA
ASTHORE)
  *Henry Blossom & Victor
  Herbert*
EVERYBODY OUGHT TO
KNOW HOW TO DO THE
TICKLE TOE
  *Otto Harbach & Louis A.
  Hirsch*
FOR ME AND MY GAL
  *E. Ray Goetz, Edgar Leslie &
  George W. Meyer*
GIVE A MAN A HORSE HE
CAN RIDE
  *Geoffrey O'Hara & James
  Thomson*
GIVE ME THE MOONLIGHT,
GIVE ME THE GIRL

*Lew Brown & Albert Von Tilzer*

GOING UP
*Otto Harbach & Louis A. Hirsch*

GOOD-BYE BROADWAY, HELLO FRANCE
*Billy Baskette, Benny Davis & C. Francis Riesner*

HAIL, HAIL, THE GANGS ALL HERE
*Theodore Morse*
*Sir Arthur Sullivan*

HOMING
*Teresa Del Riego & Arthur L. Salmon*

I'D LOVE TO BE A MONKEY IN THE ZOO
*Bert Hanlon & Willie White*

I DON'T KNOW WHERE I'M GOING BUT I'M ON MY WAY
*George Fairman*

I DON'T WANT TO GET WELL
*Harry Jentes, Howard Johnson & Harry Pease*

I'M ALL BOUND 'ROUND WITH THE MASON DIXON LINE
*Sam M. Lewis, Jean Schwartz & Joe Young*

INDIANA
*James F. Hanely & Ballard MacDonald*

IRISH HAVE A GREAT DAY TONIGHT, THE
*Henry Blossom & Victor Herbert*

JOAN OF ARC, THEY ARE CALLING YOU
*Alfred Bryan, Willie Weston & Jack Wells*

JOHNSON RAG
*Henry Kleinkauf & Guy Hall*

JUMP JIM CROW
*Sigmund Romberg & Rida Johnson Young*

LEAVE IT TO JANE
*Jerome Kern & P. G. Wodehouse*

LITTLE MOTHER OF MINE
*Walter H. Brown & Harry T. Burleigh*

LORRAINE, MY BEAUTIFUL ALSACE LORRAINE
*Alfred Bryan & Fred Fisher*

LOVE WILL FIND A WAY
*Harry Graham & Harold Fraser-Simson*

NEAPOLITAN NIGHTS
*Harry D. Kerr & J. S. Zamecnik*

OH JOHNNY, OH JOHNNY, OH!
*Abe Olman & Ed Rose*

OUT WHERE THE WEST BEGINS
*Arthur Chapman & Estelle Philleo*

OVER THERE
*George M. Cohan*

RIALTO RIPPLES
*George Gershwin*

SAILIN' AWAY ON THE HENRY CLAY
*Egbert Van Alstyne & Gus Kahn*

SEND ME AWAY WITH A
SMILE
　Al Piantadosi & Louis Weslyn
SMILES
　J. Will Callahan & Lee S.
　Roberts
SOME SUNDAY MORNING
　Raymond Egan, Gus Kahn &
　Richard A. Whiting
THEY GO WILD, SIMPLY
WILD OVER ME
　Fred Fisher & Joe McCarthy
THINE ALONE
　Henry Blossom & Victor
　Herbert
TIGER RAG
　Harry DeCosta & The
　Original Dixieland Jazz Band
TILL THE CLOUDS ROLL BY
　Jerome Kern & P. G.
　Wodehouse
WAIT TILL THE COWS
COME HOME
　Anne Caldwell &
　Ivan Caryll
WHEN YANKEE DOODLE
LEARNS TO PARLEZ VOUS
FRANCAIS
　William Hart & Ed Nelson
WHERE DO WE GO FROM
HERE?
　Howard Johnson & Percy
　Wenrich
WHERE THE BLACK-EYED
SUSANS GROW
　Dave Radford & Richard A.
　Whiting
WHERE THE MORNING
GLORIES GROW

Raymond Egan, Gus Kahn &
　Richard A. Whiting
WILL YOU REMEMBER
　Sigmund Romberg & Rida
　Johnson Young


**1918**
AFTER YOU'VE GONE
　Henry Creamer & Turner
　Layton
BEAUTIFUL OHIO
　Mary Earl & Ballard
　MacDonald
CHONG
　Harold Weeks
CLARINET MARMALADE
　H. W. Ragas
　Larry Shields
DAUGHTER OF ROSIE
O'GRADY, THE
　Monty C. Brice & Walter
　Donaldson
DEAR LITTLE BOY OF MINE
　Ernest R. Ball & J. Keirn
　Brennan
DEAR OLD PAL OF MINE
　Gitz Rice & Harold Robe
EVERYTHING IS PEACHES
DOWN IN GEORGIA
　Milton Ager, Grant Clarke, &
　George W. Meyer
GARDEN OF MY DREAMS
　Gene Buck & Dave Stamper
GOOD MAN IS HARD TO
FIND, A
　Eddie Green
GOOD-MORNING, MR. ZIP-
ZIP-ZIP

*Robert Lloyd*
HAVE A SMILE (FOR
EVERYONE YOU MEET)
*J. Keirn Brennan, Paul
Cunningham & Bert Rule*
HELLO, CENTRAL, GIVE ME
NO MAN'S LAND
*Sam M. Levin, Jean Schwartz
& Joe Young*
HINDUSTAN
*Oliver G. Wallace & Harold
Weeks*
I FOUND THE END OF THE
RAINBOW
*Joseph McCarthy, John
Mears, & Harry Tierney*
I HATE TO LOSE YOU
*Grant Clarke & Archie
Gottler*
I'M ALWAYS CHASING
RAINBOWS
*Harry Carroll & Joseph
McCarthy*
JA-DA
*Bob Carleton*
JUST A BABY'S PRAYER AT
TWILIGHT
*M. K. Jerome, Sam Lewis &
Joe Young*
K-K-K-KATY
*Geoffrey O'Hara*
LONESOME - THAT'S ALL
*Lee S. Roberts & Ben J.
Bradley*
MADELON
*L. Bousquet, Alfred Bryan &
Camille Robert*
MICKEY

*Neil Moret & Harry Williams*
OH! FRENCHY
*Con Conrad & Sam Ehrlich*
OH! HOW I HATE TO GET UP
IN THE MORNING
*Irving Berlin*
OUI, OUI, MARIE
*Alfred Bryan, Fred Fisher &
Joe McCarthy*
ROCK-A-BYE YOUR BABY
WITH A DIXIE MELODY
*Sam M. Lewis, Jean Schwartz
& Joe Young*
ROSE OF NO MAN'S LAND
*James A. Brennan & Jack
Caddigan*
ROSE ROOM
*Art Hickman
Harry H. Williams*
SMILIN' THROUGH
*Arthur Penn*
SOMEBODY STOLE MY GAL
*Leo Wood*
SOMETIMES I FEEL LIKE A
MOTHERLESS CHILD
*H. T. Burleigh*
SUNRISE AND YOU
*Arthur Penn*
THAT TUMBLE-DOWN
SHACK IN ATHLONE
*Monte Carlo, Richard W.
Pascoe & Alma Sanders*
THAT WONDERFUL
MOTHER OF MINE
*Walter Goodwin & Clyde
Hager*
THEY WERE ALL OUT OF
STEP BUT JIM

*Irving Berlin*
TILL WE MEET AGAIN
  *Raymond B. Egan & Richard*
  *A. Whiting*
WHEN YOU LOOK IN THE
HEART OF A ROSE
  *Marian Gillespie & Florence*
  *Methven*
WOULD YOU RATHER BE A
COLONEL WITH AN EAGLE
ON YOUR SHOULDER, OR A
PRIVATE WITH A CHICKEN
ON YOUR KNEE?
  *Archie Gottler & Sidney D.*
  *Mitchell*

**1919**
ALICE BLUE GOWN
  *Joseph McCarthy & Harry*
  *Tierney*
ALL THE QUAKERS ARE
SHOULDER SHAKERS,
DOWN IN QUAKER TOWN
  *Bert Kalmar, Edgar Leslie &*
  *Pete Wendling*
AND HE'D SAY OO-LA LA!
WEE WEE
  *George Jessel & Harry Ruby*
BABY WON'T YOU PLEASE
COME HOME
  *Charles Warfield & Clarence*
  *Williams*
CHINESE LULLABY
  *Robert Hood Bowers*
DADDY LONG LEGS
  *Sam M. Lewis, Harry Ruby &*
  *Joe Young*

DARDANELLA
  *Felix Bernard, Johnny S.*
  *Black & Fred Fisher*
HOW YA GONNA KEEP 'EM
DOWN ON THE FARM
AFTER THEY'VE SEEN
PAREE?
  *Walter Donaldson, Sam M.*
  *Lewis & Joe Young*
I MIGHT BE YOUR "ONCE-
IN-A-WHILE"
  *Victor Herbert & Robert B.*
  *Smith*
I WISH I COULD SHIMMY
LIKE MY SISTER KATE
  *Armand J. Piron*
I'M FOREVER BLOWING
BUBBLES
  *John W. Kellette & Jean*
  *Kenbrovin*
INDIAN SUMMER
  *Al Dubin & Victor Herbert*
IRENE
  *Harry Tierney*
  *Joseph McCarthy*
JUST LIKE A GYPSY
  *Nora Bayes & Seymour B.*
  *Simons*
LET THE REST OF THE
WORLD GO BY
  *Ernest R. Ball & J. Keirn*
  *Brennan*
LOVE SENDS A LITTLE GIFT
OF ROSES
  *Leslie Cooke & John*
  *Openshaw*
MAMMY O'MINE

*Maceo Pinkard & William*
*Tracey*
MANDY
  *Irving Berlin*
MY HOME TOWN IS A ONE
HORSE TOWN, BUT IT'S BIG
ENOUGH FOR ME
  *Alex Gerber & Abner Silver*
MY ISLE OF GOLDEN
DREAMS
  *Walter Blaufuss & Gus Kahn*
NOBODY KNOWS AND
NOBODY SEEMS TO CARE
  *Irving Berlin*
OH BY JINGO, OH BY GEE,
YOU'RE THE ONLY GIRL|
FOR ME
  *Lew Brown & Albert Von*
  *Tilzer*
OH HOW I LAUGH WHEN I
THINK HOW I CRIED ABOUT
YOU
  *George Jessel, Roy Turk &*
  *Willy White*
OH! WHAT A PAL WAS
MARY
  *Bert Kalmar, Edgar Leslie &*
  *Pete Wendling*
OLD FASHION GARDEN
  *Cole Porter*
ON MIAMI SHORE
  *Victor Jacobi & William*
  *LeBaron*
PEGGY
  *Neil Moret & Harry Williams*
PRETTY GIRL IS LIKE A
MELODY, A

*Irving Berlin*
ROSE OF WASHINGTON
SQUARE
  *James F. Hanley & Ballard*
  *MacDonald*
ROYAL GARDEN BLUES
  *Clarence & Spencer Williams*
SUGAR BLUES
  *Lucy Fletcher & Clarence*
  *Williams*
SWANEE
  *Irving Caesar & George*
  *Gershwin*
TAKE YOUR GIRLIE TO THE
MOVIES IF YOU CAN'T
MAKE LOVE AT HOME
  *Bert Kalmar, Edgar Leslie &*
  *Peter Wendling*
TELL ME
  *J. Will Callahan & Max*
  *Kortlander*
THAT NAUGHTY WALTZ
  *Sol P. Levy & Edwin Stanley*
TULIP TIME
  *Gene Buck & Dave Stamper*
WAIT TILL YOU GET THEM
UP IN THE AIR, BOYS
  *Lew Brown & Albert Von*
  *Tilzer*
WHAT'LL WE DO ON A
SATURDAY NIGHT, WHEN
THE TOWN GOES DRY
  *Harry Ruby*
WHIP-POOR-WILL
  *Bud DeSylva & Jerome Kern*
WORLD IS WAITING FOR
THE SUNRISE, THE

*Eugene Lockhart & Ernest Seitz*

YOU ARE FREE
*Victor Jacobi & William LeBaron*

YOUR EYES HAVE TOLD ME SO
*Egbert Van Alstyne, Walter Blaufuss & Gus Kahn*

YOU'RE A MILLION MILES FROM NOWHERE WHEN YOU'RE ONE LITTLE MILE FROM HOME
*Walter Donaldson, Sam M. Lewis & Joe Young*


**1920 (Public Domain in the United States on January 1, 1996)**

ALL SHE'D SAY WAS UMH HUM
*Mac Emery, Van & Schenck, King Zany*

ALT-WEIN
*Leopold Godowsky*

AVALON
*B. G. DeSylva, Al Jolson & Vincent Rose*

BEAUTIFUL ANNA BELL LEE
*Alfred Bryan, Artie Mehlinger & George W. Meyer*

BRIGHT EYES
*M. K. Jerome, Otto Motzan & Harry B. Smith*

BROADWAY ROSE
*Martin Fried, Otis Spencer &*

*Eugene West*

CHILE BEAN
*Lew Brown & Albert Von Tilzer*

DADDY, YOU'VE BEEN A MOTHER TO ME
*Fred Fisher*

DO YOU EVER THINK OF ME
*Earl Burtnett*

DOWN BY THE O-HI-O
*Abe Olman & Jack Yellen*

FEATHER YOUR NEST
*James Brockman, James Kendis & Howard Johnson*

I LOST THE BEST PAL THAT I HAD
*Dick Thomas*

I NEVER KNEW I COULD LOVE ANYBODY LIKE I'M LOVING YOU
*Ray Egan, Roy K. Marsh & Tom Pitts*

I USED TO LOVE YOU BUT IT'S ALL OVER NOW
*Lew Brown & Albert Von Tilzer*

I'D LOVE TO FALL ASLEEP AND WAKE UP IN MY MAMMY'S ARMS
*Fred E. Ahlert, Sam M. Lewis & Joe Young*

IF YOU COULD CARE
*Herman Darewski & Arthur Wimperis*

I'LL BE WITH YOU IN APPLE BLOSSOM TIME

*Neville Fleeson & Albert Von Tilzer*
JAPANESE SANDMAN, THE
   *Raymond B. Egan & Richard A. Whiting*
LEFT ALL ALONE AGAIN BLUES
   *Anne Caldwell & Jerome Kern*
LILAC TREE (Perspicacity)
   *George H. Gartlan*
LITTLE TOWN IN THE OULD COUNTY DOWN
   *Monte Carlo, Richard W. Pascoe & Alma Sanders*
LOOK FOR THE SILVER LINING
   *Bud DeSylva & Jerome Kern*
LOVE NEST
   *Otto Harbach & Louis A. Hirsch*
MAH LINDY LOU
   *Lily Strickland*
MARGIE
   *Con Conrad, Benny Davis & J. Russel Robinson*
MY MAMMY
   *Walter Donaldson, Sam Lewis & Joe Young*
OLD PAL WHY DON'T YOU ANSWER ME
   *M. K. Jerome, Sam M. Lewis & Joe Young*
PALE MOON
   *Jesse G. M. Glick & Frederick Knight Logan*
PRETTY KITTY KELLY

*Edward G. Nelson & Harry Pease*
SAN
   *Lindsay McPhail & Walter Michels*
SO LONG OO-LONG, HOW LONG YOU GONNA BE GONE
   *Bert Kalmar & Harry Ruby*
TELL ME LITTLE GYPSY
   *Irving Berlin*
THAT OLD IRISH MOTHER OF MINE
   *William Jerome & Harry Von Tilzer*
TRIPOLI (On the Shores of Tripoli)
   *Paul Cunningham, Al Dubin & Irving Weill*
WHEN BIG PROFUNDO SANG LOW C
   *Marion T. Bohannon & George Botsford*
WHEN MY BABY SMILES AT ME
   *Ted Lewis, Billy Munro, Andrew B. Sterling & Harry Von Tilzer*
WHISPERING
   *Richard Coburn, John Schonberger & Vincent Rose*
WHOSE BABY ARE YOU
   *Anne Caldwell & Jerome Kern*
WILD ROSE
   *Clifford Grey & Jerome Kern*
YOUNG MAN'S FANCY, A
   *Milton Ager, John Murray Anderson & Jack Yellen*

**1921**

AIN'T WE GOT FUN
*Raymond B. Egan, Gus
Kahn& Richard A. Whiting*

ALL BY MYSELF
*Irving Berlin*

APRIL SHOWERS
*B. G. DeSylva & Louis Silvers*

BANDANA DAYS
*Eubie Blake & Noble Sissle*

BIMINI BAY
*Raymond B. Egan, Gus Kahn
& Richard Whiting*

DAPPER DAN
*Lew Brown & Albert Von
Tilzer*

DEAR OLD SOUTHLAND
*Henry Creamer & Turner
Layton*

I AIN'T NOBODY'S DARLING
*Elmer Hughes & Robert A.
King*

I FOUND A ROSE IN THE
DEVIL'S GARDEN
*Fred Fisher & Willie Raskin*

I'LL FORGET YOU
*Ernest R. Ball & Annelu
Burns*

I'M JUST WILD ABOUT
HARRY
*Eubie Blake & Noble Sissle*

I'M NOBODY'S BABY
*Benny Davis
Milton Ager
Lester Santley*

KA-LU-A
*Anne Caldwell & Jerome
Kern*

KITTEN ON THE KEYS
*Zez Confrey & Sam Coslow*

LEARN TO SMILE
*Otto Harbach & Louis A.
Hirsch*

LEAVE ME WITH A SMILE
*Earl Burtnett & Charles
Koehler*

LOVE WILL FIND A WAY
*Eubie Blake & Noble Sissle*

MA, HE'S MAKING EYES AT
ME
*Sidney Clare & Con Conrad*

MAKE BELIEVE
*Bennie Davis & Jack Shilkret*

MY MAN
*Jacques Charles, Channing
Pollack, Albert Willemetz &
Maurice Yvain*

PEGGY O'NEIL
*Gilbert Dodge, Ed G. Nelson
& Harry Pease*

SALLY
*Clifford Grey & Jerome Kern*

SAY IT WITH MUSIC
*Irving Berlin*

SECOND HAND ROSE
*Grant Clarke & James F.
Hanley*

SHEIK OF ARABY, THE
*Harry B. Smith, Ted Snyder &
Francis Wheeler*

SHE'S MINE, ALL MINE
*Bert Kalmar & Harry Ruby*

SHUFFLE ALONG
*Eubie Blake & Noble Sissle*

SONG OF LOVE
*Dorothy Donnelly, adapted
from melodies of H. Berte &*

F. Schubert by Sigmund
Romberg
SWANEE RIVER MOON
H. Pitman Clarke
SWEET LADY
Frank Crumit, Howard
Johnson & Dave Zoob
TEN LITTLE FINGERS AND
TEN LITTLE TOES, DOWN IN
TENNESSEE
Ed. G. Nelson, Harry Pease,
Ira Schuster & Johnny White
THERE'LL BE SOME
CHANGES MADE
W. Benton Overstreet & Bill
Higgins
THREE O'CLOCK IN THE
MORNING
Julian Robledo & Dorothy
Terriss
TUCK ME TO SLEEP IN MY
OLD 'TUCKY HOME
Sam Lewis, George W. Meyer
& Joe Young
WABASH BLUES
Fred Meinken & Dave Ringle
WANG-WANG BLUES
Henry Busse, Buster Johnson,
Gus Mueller & Leo Wood
WHEN BUDDHA SMILES
Nacio Herb Brown, Arthur
Freed & King Zany
WHEN FRANCIS DANCES
WITH ME
Benny Ryan & Violinsky
WYOMING
Gene Williams
YOO-HOO

B. G. DeSylva & Al Jolson

**1922**
AGGRAVATIN' PAPA DON'T
YOU TRY TO TWO-TIME ME
Addy Britt, J. Russel Robinson
& Roy Turk
ALL OVER NOTHING AT
ALL
J. Keirn Brennan, Paul
Cunningham & James S. Rule
ANGEL CHILD
Benny Davis, George E. Price
& Abner Silver
BLUE (AND BROKEN
HEARTED)
Lou Handman
CAROLINA IN THE
MORNING
Walter Donaldson & Gus
Kahn
CHICAGO, THAT TODDLING
TOWN
Fred Fisher
CHINA BOY
Phil Boutelje & Dick Winfree
CRINOLINE DAYS
Irving Berlin
DANCING FOOL
Harry B. Smith, Ted Snyder &
Francis Wheeler
DO IT AGAIN
B. G. DeSylva & George
Gershwin
DREAMY MELODY
Ted Koehler
Frank Magine
Charlest Nast

GEORGIA
  *Walter Donaldson & Howard
  Johnson*
HOT LIPS
  *Henry Busse, Lou Davis &
  Henry Lange*
I'LL BUILD A STAIRWAY TO
PARADISE
  *B. G. DeSylva, George
  Gershwin & Ira Gershwin*
KISS IN THE DARK, A
  *B. G. DeSylva & Victor
  Herbert*
LADY OF THE EVENING
  *Irving Berlin*
L'AMOUR TOUJOUR
L'AMOUR
  *Catherine C. Cushing &
  Rudolf Friml*
LIMEHOUSE BLUES
  *Philip Braham & Doulgas
  Furber*
LOVESICK BLUES
  *Cliff Friend & Irving Mills*
LOVIN' SAM, THE SHEIK OF
ALABAM'
  *Milton Ager & Jack Yellen*
MARY, DEAR, SOME DAY
WE WILL MEET AGAIN
  *Harry De Costa & M. J.
  Jerome*
MY BUDDY
  *Walter Donaldson & Gus
  Kahn*
MY HONEY'S LOVIN' ARMS
  *Joseph Meyer & Herman
  Ruby*
'NEATH THE SOUTH SEA
MOON

  *Gene Buck, Louis A. Hirsch,
  & Dave Stamper*
NOBODY LIED (When They
Said That I Cried Over You)
  *Hyatt Berry, Karyl Norman &
  Edwin J. Weber*
ON THE ALAMO
  *Isham Jones, Gilbert Keyes &
  Joe Lyons*
O-OO ERNEST, ARE YOU
EARNEST WITH ME
  *Sidney Clare, Cliff Friend &
  Harry Tobias*
ROSE OF THE RIO GRANDE
  *Ross Gorman, Edgar Leslie &
  Harry Warren*
RUNNIN' WILD
  *A. Harrington Gibbs, Joe
  Grey & Leo Wood*
SAY IT WHILE DANCING
  *Benny Davis & Abner Silver*
STUMBLING
  *Zez Confrey*
TOOT, TOOT, TOOTSIE
(Goo'Bye)
  *Ernie Erdman, Ted Fiorito,
  Gus Kahn & Robert A. King*
TREES
  *Joyce Kilmer & Oscar
  Rasbach*
'WAY DOWN YONDER IN
NEW ORLEANS
  *Henry Creamer & J. Turner
  Layton*
WHEN HEARTS ARE YOUNG
  *Alfred Goodman, Sigmund
  Romberg & Cyrus Wood*
WHY SHOULD I CRY OVER

YOU
*Ned Miller*
*Chester Conn*
WONDERFUL ONE

*Ferde Grofe, Dorothy Terriss*
*& Paul Whiteman*
YOU TELL HER I STUTTER
*Cliff Friend & Billy Rose*

# LIST 9.2

## SOME POPULAR SONGS TO FALL INTO THE PUBLIC DOMAIN IN THE UNITED STATES BEGINNING IN THE YEAR 2019

**1923**

ANNABELLE
*Lew Brown & Ray Henderson*

ANNABEL LEE
*John Murray Anderson, Irving Caesar & Louis A. Hirsch*

BAMBALINA
*Oscar Hammerstein, 2nd, Otto Harbach, Herbert Stothart & Vincent Youmans*

BARNEY GOOGLE
*Con Conrad & Billy Rose*

BESIDE A BABBLING BROOK
*Walter Donaldson & Gus Kahn*

BUGLE CALL RAG
*Bill Meyers, Jack Pettis & Elmer Schoebel*

CHANSONETTE
*Irving Caesar, Rudolf Friml, Dailey Paskman & Sigmund Spaeth*

CHARLESTON
*Jimmy Johnson & Cecil Mack*

COME ON, SPARK PLUG!
*Con Conrad & Billy Rose*

DEAREST YOU'RE THE NEAREST TO MY HEART
*Harry Akst & Benny Davis*

DIZZY FINGERS
*Zez Confrey*

FAREWELL BLUES
*Elmer Schoebel*
*Paul Mares & Leon Rappolo*

I CRIED FOR YOU (Now It's Your Turn To Cry Over Me)
*Gus Arnheim, Arthur Freed & Abe Lyman*

I LOVE LIFE
*Irwin M. Cassel & Mana-Zucca*

I LOVE YOU (from "Little Jessie James")
*Harry Archer & Harlan Thompson*

I'M SITTING PRETTY IN A PRETTY LITTLE CITY
*Abel Baer, Lou Davis & Henry Santly*

I WON'T SAY I WILL, BUT I WON'T SAY I WON'T
*Buddy DeSylva, George Gershwin & Arthur Francis*

I'M GOIN' SOUTH
*Abner Silver & Harry Woods*

IT AIN'T GONNA RAIN NO MO'
*Wendell Hall*

JUST A GIRL THAT MEN FORGET
*Al Dubin, Joe Garren & Fred Rath*

LAST NIGHT ON THE BACK
PORCH, I LOVED HER BEST
OF ALL
  *Lew Brown & Carl
  Schraubstader*
LINGER AWHILE
  *Harry Owens & Vincent Rose*
MAMMA LOVES PAPA -
PAPA LOVES MAMMA
  *Cliff Friend & Abel Baer*
MEXICALI ROSE
  *Helen Stone & Jack B. Tenny*
MY SWEETIE WENT AWAY,
SHE DIDN'T SAY WHERE,
WHEN OR WHY
  *Lou Handman & Roy Turk*
NO, NO, NORA
  *Ernie Erdman, Ted Fiorito, &
  Gus Kahn*
O, GEE, OH GOSH, OH
GOLLY I'M IN LOVE
  *Ernest Breuer, Olson &
  Johnson*
ON THE MALL
  *Edwin Franko Goldman*
RAGGEDY MAN
  *Anne Caldwell & Jerome
  Kern*
REMEMB'RING
  *Vivian & Rosetta Duncan*
SITTIN' IN A CORNER
  *Gus Kahn & George W.
  Meyer*
SLEEP (based on "Visions of
Sleep")
  *Earl Lebier*
SMILE WILL GO A LONG,
LONG WAY, A

  *Harry Akst & Benny Davis*
SUGAR BLUES
  *Lucy Fletcher
  Clarence Williams*
SUPPOSE I HAD NEVER MET
YOU
  *Harry Archer
  Harlan Thompson*
SWINGIN' DOWN THE LANE
  *Gus Kahn & Isham Jones*
THAT OLD GANG OF MINE
  *Mort Dixon, Ray Henderson
  & Billy Rose*
WESTWARD HO! (The
Covered Wagon March)
  *R. A. Barnet & Hugo
  Riesenfeld*
WHEN IT'S NIGHT-TIME IN
ITALY, IT'S WEDNESDAY
OVER HERE
  *Lew Brown & James Kendis*
WHEN YOU WALKED OUT
SOMEONE ELSE WALKED
RIGHT IN
  *Irving Berlin*
WHO'LL BUY MY VIOLETS
  *E. Ray Goetz & Jose Padilla*
WHO'S SORRY NOW
  *Bert Kalmar, Harry Ruby &
  Ted Snyder*
WILD FLOWER
  *Otto Harbach. Oscar
  Hammerstein,2nd, Herbert
  Stothart & Vincent Youmans*
YES! WE HAVE NO
BANANAS
  *Irving Cohn & Frank Silver*
YOU'VE GOTTA SEE
MAMMA EV'RY NIGHT OR

YOU CAN'T SEE MAMMA
AT ALL
  *Con Conrad & Billy Rose*


**1924**
ALL ALONE
  *Irving Berlin*
CALIFORNIA, HERE I COME
  *Bud DeSylva, Al Jolson &
  Joseph Meyer*
CHARLEY, MY BOY
  *Ted Fiorito & Gus Kahn*
COPENHAGEN
  *Charlie Davis & Walter
  Melrose*
DEEP IN MY HEART, DEAR
  *Dorothy Donnelly & Sigmund
  Romberg*
DOES THE SPEARMINT
LOSE ITS FLAVOR ON THE
BEDPOST OVER NIGHT
  *Marty Bloom, Ernest Breuer
  & Billy Rose*
EVERYBODY LOVES MY
BABY, BUT MY BABY
DON'T LOVE NOBODY BUT
ME
  *Jack Palmer & Spencer
  Williams*
FASCINATING RHYTHM
  *George Gershwin & Ira
  Gershwin*
FOLLOW THE SWALLOW
  *Mort Dixon, Ray Henderson
  & Billy Rose*
GOLDEN DAYS
  *Dorothy Donnelly & Sigmund
  Romberg*

HARD HEARTED HANNAH
  *Milton Ager, Charles Bates,
  Bob Bigelow & Jack Yellen*
HOW COME YOU DO ME
LIKE YOU DO
  *Gene Austin & Roy Bergere*
I WANT TO BE HAPPY
  *Irving Caesar & Vincent
  Youmans*
I WONDER WHAT'S
BECOME OF SALLY
  *Milton Ager & Jack Yellen*
I'LL SEE YOU IN MY
DREAMS
  *Isham Jones & Gus Kahn*
INDIAN LOVE CALL
  *Rudolf Friml, Otto Harbach &
  Oscar Hammerstein, 2nd*
IT HAD TO BE YOU
  *Isham Jones & Gus Kahn*
JEALOUS
  *Dick Finch, Jack Little &
  Tommie Malie*
JUNE NIGHT
  *Abel Baer & Cliff Friend*
KING PORTER STOMP
  *Ferd (Jelly Roll) Morton*
MAN I LOVE, THE
  *George Gershwin & Ira
  Gershwin*
MEMORY LANE
  *Con Conrad, B. G. DeSylva &
  Larry Spier*
MOUNTIES, THE
  *Rudolf Friml, Otto Harbach,
  Oscar Hammerstein, 2nd &
  Herbert Stothart*
MY DREAM GIRL, I LOVED
YOU LONG AGO

*Victor Herbert & Rida
Johnson Young*
MY TIME IS YOUR TIME
*Leo Dance & Eric Little*
NO, NO, NANETTE
*Irving Caesar
Otto Harbach
Vincent Youmans*
NOBODY'S SWEETHEART
*Ernie Erdman, Gus Kahn,
Billy Meyers & Elmer
Schoebel*
OH KATHERINA!
*Richard Fall & L. Wolfe
Gilbert*
OH, LADY BE GOOD
*George Gershwin & Ira
Gershwin*
ONE I LOVE BELONGS TO
SOMEBODY ELSE, THE
*Isham Jones & Gus Kahn*
PRISONER'S SONG, THE
*Gus Massey*
RHAPSODY IN BLUE
*George Gershwin*
ROSE MARIE
*Rudolf Friml, Otto Harbach,
Oscar Hammerstein, 2nd &
Herbert Stothart*
SERENADE
*Dorothy Donnelly & Sigmund
Romberg*
S-H-I-N-E
*Lew Brown, Ford Dabney &
Cecil Mack*
SOMEBODY LOVES ME
*B. G. DeSylva, George
Gershwin & Ballard
MacDonald*

TEA FOR TWO
*Irving Caesar & Vincent
Youmans*
THERE'S YES, YES, IN YOUR
EYES
*Cliff Friend & Joseph H.
Santly*
TOO MANY RINGS AROUND
ROSIE
*Irving Caesar
Vincent Youmans*
TOTEM-TOM-TOM
*Rudolf Friml, Otto Harbach,
Oscar Hammerstein, 2nd &
Herbert Stothart*
WEST OF THE GREAT
DIVIDE
*Ernest R. Ball & George
Whiting*
WHAT'LL I DO
*Irving Berlin*
WHEN MY SUGAR WALKS
DOWN THE STREET, ALL
THE BIRDIES GO TWEET-
TWEET-TWEET
*Gene Austin, Jimmy McHugh
& Irving Mills*
WHY DID I KISS THAT
GIRL?
*Lew Brown, Robert King &
Ray Henderson*

**1925**
ALABAMY BOUND
*Bud DeSylva, Bud Green &
Ray Henderson*
ALWAYS
*Irving Berlin*

BAM, BAM, BAMY SHORE
  *Mort Dixon & Ray Henderson*
BROWN EYES-WHY ARE
YOU BLUE?
  *Alfred Bryan & George W.*
  *Meyer*
BYE AND BYE
  *Lorenz Hart & Richard*
  *Rodgers*
CECILIA (Does Your Mother
Know You're Out, Cecilia?)
  *Dave Dreyer & Herman Ruby*
CHEATIN' ON ME
  *Lew Pollack & Jack Yellen*
CLAP HANDS, HERE COMES
CHARLEY
  *Ballard MacDonald*
  *Billy Rose & Joseph Meyer*
COLLEGIATE
  *Moe Jaffe, Nat Bonx & Lew*
  *Brown*
CUP OF COFFEE, A
SANDWICH AND YOU, A
  *Al Dubin, Joseph Meyer &*
  *Billy Rose*
DINAH
  *Harry Akst, Sam M. Lewis &*
  *Joe Young*
DON'T BRING LULU
  *Lew Brown, Ray Henderson &*
  *Billy Rose*
DON'T WAKE ME UP, LET
ME DREAM
  *Abel Baer, L. Wolfe Gilbert &*
  *Mabel Wayne*
DOWN BY THE WINEGAR
WOIKS
  *Don Bester, Walter Donovan*
  *& Roger Lewis*

DRIFTING AND DREAMING
  *Egbert Van Alstyne, Loyal*
  *Curtis, Haven Gillespie &*
  *Erwin R. Schmidt*
DRINKING SONG
  *Dorothy Donnelly & Sigmund*
  *Romberg*
D'YE LOVE ME?
  *Jerome Kern, Otto Harbach &*
  *Oscar Hammerstein, 2nd*
FIVE FOOT TWO, EYES OF
BLUE
  *Ray Henderson, Sam M.*
  *Lewis & Joe Young*
HERE IN MY ARMS
  *Lorenz Hart & Richard*
  *Rodgers*
HILLS OF HOME, THE
  *Floride Calhoun & Oscar J.*
  *Fox*
I LOVE MY BABY, MY BABY
LOVES ME
  *Bud Green & Harry Warren*
I MISS MY SWISS, MY
SWISS MISS MISSES ME
  *Abel Baer & L. Wolfe Gilbert*
I NEVER KNEW
  *Ted Fiorito & Gus Kahn*
I WANNA GO WHERE YOU
GO, DO WHAT YOU DO,
THEN I'LL BE HAPPY
  *Lew Brown, Sidney Clare &*
  *Cliff Friend*
IF YOU KNEW SUSIE, LIKE I
KNOW SUSIE
  *Bud DeSylva & Joseph Meyer*
I'M IN LOVE AGAIN
  *Cole Porter*

I'M SITTING ON TOP OF
THE WORLD
  *Ray Henderson, Sam M.*
  *Lewis & Joe Young*
IN THE LUXEMBOURG
GARDENS
  *Kathleen Lockhart Manning*
JALOUSIE
  *Vera Bloom & Jacob Gade*
JUST A COTTAGE
  SMALL-BY A WATERFALL
  *B. G. DeSylva & James F.*
  *Hanley*
LOOKING FOR A BOY
  *Ira Gershwin*
  *George Gershwin*
MANHATTAN
  *Lorenz Hart*
  *Richard Rodgers*
MILENBERG JOYS
  *Paul Mares, Walter Melrose,*
  *Ferd (Jelly Roll) Morton &*
  *Leon Roppolo*
MOONLIGHT & ROSES
  *Ben Black, Edwin H Lemare*
  *& Neil Moret*
MY YIDDISHE MOMME
  *Lew Pollack & Jack Yellen*
OH, HOW I MISS YOU
TONIGHT
  *Benny Davis, Joe Burke &*
  *Mark Fisher*
ONLY A ROSE
  *Rudolf Friml & Brian Hooker*
PADDLIN' MADELIN' HOME
  *Harry Woods*
PAL OF MY CRADLE DAYS
  *Marshall Montgomery & Al*
  *Piantadosi*

REMEMBER
  *Irving Berlin*
RIVERBOAT SHUFFLE
  *Hoagy Carmichael, Irving*
  *Mills, Dick Volynow &*
  *additional material: Mitchell*
  *Parish*
SAVE YOUR SORROW FOR
TOMORROW
  *B. G. DeSylva & Al Sherman*
SHOW ME THE WAY TO GO
HOME
  *Irving King*
SLEEPY TIME GAL
  *Joseph R. Alden, Raymond B.*
  *Egan, Ange Lorenzo &*
  *Richard A. Whiting*
SOME DAY
  *Rudolf Friml & Brian Hooker*
SOMETIMES I'M HAPPY
  *Irving Caesar, Clifford Grey*
  *& Vincent Youmans*
SONG OF THE VAGABONDS
  *Rudolf Friml & Brian Hooker*
SUNNY
  *Jerome Kern, Otto Harbach &*
  *Oscar Hammerstein, 2nd*
SWEET AND LOW-DOWN
  *George Gershwin & Ira*
  *Gershwin*
SWEET GEORGIA BROWN
  *Ben Bernie, Kenneth Casey &*
  *Maceo Pinkard*
THAT CERTAIN FEELING
  *George Gershwin & Ira*
  *Gershwin*
THAT CERTAIN PARTY
  *Walter Donaldson & Gus*
  *Kahn*

UKELELE LADY
  *Gus Kahn & Richard A.*
  *Whiting*
VALENCIA
  *Lucien Boyer*
  *Jacques Charles*
  *Clifford Grey*
VALENTINE
  *Herbert Reynolds*
  *Albert Willemets*
  *H. Christine*
WHERE THE LAZY DAISIES
GROW
  *Cliff Friend*
WHO
  *Jerome Kern, Otto Harbach &*
  *Oscar Hammerstein, 2nd*
WHY DO I LOVE YOU
  *Bud G. DeSylva, George*
  *Gershwin & Ira Gershwin*
YEARNING JUST FOR YOU
  *Joe Burke & Benny Davis*
YES SIR, THAT'S MY BABY
  *Walter Donaldson & Gus*
  *Kahn*

CHAPTER 10

# BASIC CONSIDERATIONS IN MUSIC LICENSING

## SUMMARY

### I. BASIC MUSIC LICENSING FACTORS

A. Fee Structure
  1. Practical Constraints
  2. Legal Constraints
B. Value of the Song
  1. Quantitative Factors Affecting Value
  2. Qualitative Factors Affecting Value
C. The Importance of the Song in Relation to Its Intended Use
  1. Why Is the Song Being Used?
  2. How Will the Song Be Rendered?
  3. Will Any Changes Be Made?
  4. Will the Song's Title Be Used for a Special Purpose?
D. The Scope of the Intended Use
  1. What Media Will the License Cover?
  2. Through What Distribution Channels Will the Media Be Distributed?
  3. How Long Will the Use Be Permitted by the License?
  4. Where Will the Use Be Permitted?
  5. Who Else May Exercise a Similar Privilege to Use the Work?

### II. COMMON TERMS AND CONDITIONS REGARDING FEES AND PAYMENT

A. Advances
B. Cross-Collateralization
C. Bonus
D. Payment and Accounting
E. Audit Privileges

## VI. General Advice to Persons Seeking to Clear Licenses—Fully Disclose all the Uses You Might Conceivably Make of the Music

CHAPTER **10**

# BASIC CONSIDERATIONS
# IN MUSIC LICENSING

This chapter provides an outline of the basic considerations relevant in granting and clearing the several forms of licenses discussed in this book. It also provides a review of some of the basic terms and conditions commonly found in many music licenses, followed by some practical advice to both music copyright owners and persons seeking to clear a license to use music.

## I. BASIC MUSIC LICENSING FACTORS

The basic considerations or factors in determining the provisions of most music licenses are:

A. The fee structure, whether it is established by custom, negotiation, or statute;

B. The value of the song, taking into consideration its popularity, historical significance, and overall quality;

C. The importance of the song in relation to its intended use; and

D. The scope of the intended use.

Each of these factors will be discussed generally in this chapter and then in more detail, and as they relate specifically to the various forms of licenses discussed, in the chapters which follow.

## A. Fee Structure

License fees are structured in various ways. Ideally, copyright owners would like to negotiate a fee each time their music is played, taking into consideration all of the factors relevant to determining the fee structure and the appropriate fee to be charged, but certain practical and legal circumstances require that certain customary or compulsory fee structures be employed.

## 1.  Practical Constraints

For certain kinds of uses, such as the public performance of music in restaurants, theaters, concert halls, and nightclubs, and broadcast on radio and television, it would be impractical for music publishers to negotiate a separate license for each and every performance that occurs every day throughout the year. The arrangement that has evolved for structuring and collecting fees for public performances is the *blanket license,* discussed more fully in Chapter 17. Once a year, the performance rights societies issue a blanket license to each concert hall, restaurant, and other venue where the music in their repertoires is likely to be played, whether live or by use of a recording, and to every radio and television station that broadcasts programs containing copyrighted music. The fees collected under blanket licenses are then divided up by the performance rights society and distributed to their music publisher and songwriter members in accordance with a formula that attempts to allocate the funds on the basis of how much each song was performed during the year. Though they have the opportunity, owners of restaurants and nightclubs rarely negotiate the fees established by the performance rights societies for public performance licenses, but, considering the blanket nature of the license — permitting the performance of one or more of any of the hundreds of thousands of compositions in a performance rights society's repertoire as often as the user desires to perform them during the year — the fees charged are reasonable and it is generally not worth the effort to negotiate them.

## 2.  Legal Constraints

In addition to practical constraints, various legal constraints dictate the types of fees and fee structures that are employed in licensing music. For example, a section of the U.S. copyright law commonly called the compulsory license provision,[1] which is more fully de-

---

[1] 17 U.S.C. Sec. 115.

scribed in Chapter 12, compels a music copyright owner to license his music for use in certain audio recordings at a specific per copy fee that is set forth in the copyright law. Where the law establishes a maximum fee, as it does here, there is little room for creativity and negotiation in granting and clearing licenses.

Also, certain court judgments, called *consent decrees*, agreed upon between performance rights societies and the U.S. government, require that permission to perform music in U.S. movie theatres be granted to film producers at the time the producers receive authorization to record the music in the film. This effectively requires licenses that would otherwise be negotiated by performance rights societies on a blanket basis with motion picture theaters to be licensed to the motion picture producers directly by the music copyright owners on a one time flat fee basis.

In some cases, copyright owners simply do not have the *right* upon which a license may be based. For example, though the copyright law confers upon the copyright owner an exclusive right of *public* performance, it does not confer an exclusive right of *private* performance. Accordingly, the copyright owner can not require that a fee be paid every time you play a compact disk in your home or insert an audio-cassette of copyrighted music in your car stereo. Instead, the fees derived from the use of music in recordings are based on the number of copies of the recording that are made and distributed and the fees are charged to the record manufacturers at the time the recordings are made, rather than when the music is played by the customer.

Thus, the particular structure used for a particular form of license can be influenced by one or more legal or practical considerations. In certain cases, the fee structure is determined merely by industry custom, which can be varied by negotiation. Fees are customarily structured on a flat fee, per copy fee, percentage of revenue, or blanket fee basis. Each of these fee structures will be discussed in the context in which they arise under the several forms of licenses discussed in the following chapters.

## B.  Value of the Song

Whatever the fee structure, songs with higher inherent values can generally command higher fees for their use. A music copyright owner's ability to determine the value of a particular song will vary depending on his experience and access to information about the value of other musical compositions. The value of a song has both quantitative and qualitative factors, both adding up to the present value of the licensing revenue the song is expected to generate during the remainder of the life of the copyright.

### 1. Quantitative Factors Affecting Value

The quantitative factors include how much the song has earned in licensing revenues in the past and how much others might be presently willing to pay for the copyright. It also includes the earnings potential of the song in relation to the earnings potential of other songs, particularly those in its genre. A music publisher with thousands of songs in its catalog and with years of experience in licensing music is likely to have access to much of the information necessary to adequately evaluate these factors. Because of its access to such information, a large music publisher is in a much better position than a typical licensee, songwriter, practicing lawyer, or small-scale music publisher to determine the quantitative value of a song for purposes of determining the appropriate license fee for a given use.

### 2. Qualitative Factors Affecting Value

The qualitative factors include the popularity of the song, the demographics of the listeners who are responsible for the song's popularity, the historical significance of the song, and overall quality of the song. Characteristics that help one understand these qualitative factors include, (1) a sound knowledge of music, whether in its writing, arranging or recording, (2) a person's experience with the song, either as having been "on the scene," either as a listener or as one working directly in the music business, when the song first became popular, and (3) a person's experience in having seen numerous examples of music of the same genre applied to a variety of uses. An appreciation of these qualitative factors is significant in determining the importance of the song in relation to its intended use. A large music publisher may have no special advantages over persons seeking to clear a license or others in evaluating these qualitative factors.

## C. The Importance of the Song in Relation to Its Intended Use

The more important the song is in relation to its intended use, the more money the copyright owner can charge in exchange for the license. Determining the importance of the song in relation to its intended use, depends on variety of facts. Before quoting a license fee, the music copyright owner should ask many questions of the potential licensee about the intended use of the song, and the person seeking to clear the license should be prepared with as many answers as possible.

### 1. Why Is the Song Being Used?

One question is whether the use will be primarily for a theatrical purpose or a promotional purpose. The purpose of the use may be purely to enhance the entertainment values of another work, such as when the use is in a motion picture, television program, television series, or musical play. By contrast, the purpose may be promotional in the sense of promoting some product, service, or the image of a particular company. There are special cases where the purpose of the audiovisual work is to feature the whole song itself, as is the case of a music video, in which case the purpose may be both theatrical (i.e., to entertain) and promotional, in the sense of promoting the recording artist or the song.

### 2. How Will the Song Be Rendered?

Another issue is whether the use will include a vocal rendition or whether the use will be merely instrumental. Other questions include whether the music will be used as background music, foreground music, or music to help tell a story.

### 3. Will Any Changes Be Made?

Still another question is whether the user intends to make any changes in the musical work. A licensee might ask for several kinds of changes, including:

    *a.* A change in lyrics, for either purposes of parody, drama, or product endorsement.

    *b.* A change in the fundamental character of the music, such as when a full-length version is edited down to suit special needs.

    *c.* A translation of the lyrics into a foreign language.

Under most standard songwriter music publishing contracts, the songwriter grants to the publisher the right to change the lyrics and to authorize others to do so. However, some songwriters have negotiated provisions that give the songwriter the right to approve any changes to the work. Even if the contract does not contain such a provision, it is still good practice for the music publisher to consult with the songwriter before authorizing any changes in lyrics, particularly when the changes may be in the nature of a product endorsement or have some political significance, such as use in a political campaign. The publisher and the songwriter should weigh the advantages of the license fee, performance credits, and general activity the use provides for the song against the possible damage to the long term value of the song from an unsavory use. If changes to lyrics are approved, the exact nature of the new lyrics should be specified in the license; otherwise final approval should be withheld until the exact lyrics are determined.

### 4.   Will the Song's Title Be Used for a Special Purpose?

Another question may be whether the song's title will be used for any special purpose. For example, the licensee may be intending to use the title as the title of his motion picture, television show, or product, such as a new brand of perfume. Note that song titles are not copyrightable; nor are they protectable as trademarks. However, there are some court decisions that indicate some recognition of rights in song titles akin to trademark protection, where the courts are trying to prevent unfair competition or someone from "palming off" their movie or product as somehow being associated with or endorsed by the writers or owners of the musical composition.[2] Use of the title should be indicative of the importance of the song in relation to its intended use and some consideration should be given to charging an additional fee for its use.

Specific examples of each of the foregoing considerations will be explored in the chapters which follow.

---

[2] *Tomlin v. Walt Disney Productions*, 18 Cal.App.3d 226, 235, 96 Cal.Rptr. 118 (1971).

## D.  The Scope of the Intended Use

Music copyright owners should avoid issuing a license which allows the licensee to do more with the song than the licensee originally intends. It is therefore important for the copyright owner to determine, before terms are quoted, just what the licensee intends to do with the song, where he intends to do it, and for how long. The license should be limited appropriately in all these respects.

Persons seeking to clear a license should attempt to obtain a license having as broad a scope as possible. Where this is not possible, the licensee should attempt to negotiate up front a series of options for additional uses that would otherwise require an additional license at a later time. It is therefore important for the licensee to tell the copyright owner up front everything he intends to do with the song.

Factors which comprise the scope of a music license include:

1. the media in which the music will be embodied

2. the term of the license

3. the territory in which the use will be exercised

4. the exclusivity required, if any

5. other terms and conditions

Each of these factors will be discussed in general terms below and at greater length in succeeding chapters.

### 1.  What Media Will the License Cover?

The form of license (e.g., mechanical license, synchronization license, print license, etc.) that is appropriate for the requested use will depend upon the *media* for which the use is intended.

The media is often described with reference to the particular kind of physical copy in which the music is embodied and the compilation of materials with which the music is included. Examples of media include sheet music, songbooks or music folios, phonograph recordings, such as audiocassettes, long-playing albums and compact disks, motion pictures, television programs, videocassettes, laser video disks, music videos, television commercials, radio commercials, syndicated radio programs, published books, consumer products, such as music boxes, dolls, and other items, computer programs, audiovisual educational programs, and other media "now known or hereafter devised."

### 2. Through What Distribution Channels Will the Media Be Distributed?

Determining the media to be covered by the license involves a consideration of not only the physical media in which the music is to be embodied and any accompanying materials, but also the means by which the music is distributed, exhibited, or communicated to the public.

For example, the media may be broadly defined as "motion pictures." But motion pictures may be distributed through exhibition in movie theatres, broadcast on television, and on videocassettes and laser discs intended for home distribution. Television programs may be broadcast on local television stations, over television networks, by cable, by direct broadcast satellite, or by other forms of televised or broadcast distribution. Distribution may also be categorized by the manner in which television station operators are compensated — e.g., free TV, subscription channels, or pay-per-view channels. Music, of course, may also be the subject of live performances, such as those rendered in a nightclub, Broadway, or other stage production, or live performance that is broadcast on radio or television. As we shall see in Chapter 14, on *Synchronization Licenses*, and Chapter 15, on *Videogram Licenses*, the terms of the licenses for the same motion picture or television production will vary considerably, depending upon the means of distribution.

### 3. How Long Will the Use Be Permitted By the License?

How long a use is permitted by the license is referred to as the *term*, or duration, of the license. The term of the license will often depend upon the type of license being granted. The music copyright owner should almost always prefer to restrict the license's duration to the shortest possible time, although the term of the license will normally be dictated by the custom and practice normally associated with similar licenses. Restricting the term of the license will allow the copyright owner to collect an additional fee upon its expiration if renewal of the license is desired by the licensee.

Persons seeking to clear a license should attempt to obtain a license having as long a duration as possible. Where the copyright owner insists upon limiting the term, the licensee should attempt to negotiate, up front, a series of options to renew the term of the license, offering an additional fee payable upon the exercise of each renewal period. Even if the renewal fees, considered at the time the license is entered into, appear unreasonably high, by obtaining options to renew, the licensee will at least be assured that a license to extend the term will be readily available.

### 4. Where Will the Use Be Permitted?

Music licenses typically contain a restriction on countries, or regions within countries, in which the licensee may perform, exhibit, broadcast or distribute copies of the music. This restriction is referred to as the *territory* of the license.

The territory in which the licensee may exercise his rights under the license is normally something less than *world-wide*. As with restricting how long the license lasts, the music copyright owner will generally prefer to restrict the territory of the license to the smallest geographic area consistent with the licensee's actual needs. Each additional territory will command an additional fee. Restricting the territory of the license will allow the music copyright owner to collect an additional fee if the licensee later determines that he would like to extend his use to other territories. The music copyright owner's leverage to charge a premium fee increases after the licensee has gone to great expense to incorporate his music into a work, particularly where it would be expensive, inconvenient, or impossible to replace the music with a less expensive alternative.

In many cases, the licensee will not require a license for other territories, such as, for example, where a license to use music in a radio advertisement for a local drugstore limits the territory to the region in which the drugstore finds all its customers. However, a licensee may wish to negotiate options to expand the territory to those areas in which it is likely the work will be used. For example, where a company desires to test a commercial advertisement for one of its national brands in a limited region of the country, the company may wish to pay only for the use of the music in the test region, while at the same time negotiate an option to expand the territory to the rest of the country for eventual network broadcast. The licensee's leverage is at its height before he commits to use the music or makes any substantial expenditures toward that end. A licensee, therefore, is advised to obtain options for additional territories wherever it is known that such licenses might be required. It is probably a good idea to obtain such options even when the likelihood of expanding the territory is remote.

The territory may be restricted to specific countries, such as "the United States," and "the United States and Canada." Licenses may be unrestricted in territory, as what is intended by the use of the term "worldwide," although it has been suggested the word "worldwide" would not cover use on space stations. With this in mind, a licensee might consider whether the term "universe" should be used in its place, or whether — with tongue in cheek — the term, "solar system" would be sufficient for most licenses. (We have seen licenses that employ the terms "universe" and "universe-wide" in place of "worldwide," so the reader should not think this idea is far fetched). To avoid ambiguities, names of actual countries should be used — Africa, Asia, and the Caribbean are not countries.

Certain contractual and organizational considerations may affect how a music publisher determines the territory of the license. Large music publishers may have policies with respect to the ability of its U.S. headquarters to negotiate on behalf of its international affiliates and subsidiaries for the licensing of use in territories outside of the United States. These policies may actually be formally governed by the terms and conditions of the sub-publication agreements between a United States publisher and its international affiliates or subsidiaries. Such policies and contractual terms may vary depending on the type of license. For example, motion picture synchronization licenses are generally negotiated centrally for worldwide use, but licenses for use in connection with product advertising may require negotiation on a country by country basis with local publishing affiliates.

Certain legal considerations may also affect how you define the territory. For example, European Community (EC) regulations that prohibit contracts that restrict the free flow of goods among member countries may invalidate licenses that attempt to provide exclusivity with respect to specified countries within the EC. The solution may be to simply define the territory as "member countries of the European Community." (A publisher might consider problems arising with respect to existing licenses and exclusive publishing arrangements as the membership in the EC changes over time).

The license may also be limited to certain areas within the United States, such as "the State of New York." This, however, might not be acceptable to a licensee who intends to use the song in television or radio broadcasts. Radio waves don't normally respect state lines. Accordingly, the territory can be defined by some regional designation, such as "the greater New York City area," "Southern California," or "the mid-Atlantic states."

### 5. Who Else May Exercise a Similar Privilege to Use the Work?

*Exclusivity*, as we have seen, is a right to exclude or prevent others from doing some act. Granting exclusivity, therefore, is something more than merely granting permission, or a license, to another to do something he or she would not otherwise have the privilege of doing without your permission; it involves granting to another a claim or right under the copyright, an actual piece of property, which is a form of subdivision of the copyright.

Exclusive rights are, of course, granted in connection with a grant of an entire copyright (in which case all exclusive rights under the copyright are granted at one time, less any exclusive rights that are reserved to the original owner). Leaving aside that special circumstance, exclusivity is rarely granted in music revenue transactions, except in connection with the grant of exclusive print rights for printed sheet music or in certain cases where the publisher agrees, in connection with a license to use the music in commercial advertising, to a restriction on licensing the song for limited periods of time in connection with works or products that compete with the products of the licensee. For example, a music publisher may license the use of the song, *Hooray for Hollywood* for a one year period in connection with television advertising of the Bank of Hollywood and may agree not to license the same song to another bank for advertising banking services in the Los Angeles area for the one year period of the license.

Other than for such limited commercial uses, or other extraordinary uses, such as use of the song's title or story line, music publishers should generally avoid granting exclusivity, because earnings from other sources can be significantly curtailed by broadly applied exclusivity provisions. If exclusivity is granted in the appropriate cases, the operative language should be very carefully defined.

## II. COMMON TERMS AND CONDITIONS REGARDING FEES AND PAYMENT

Each particular kind of license will often require special provisions depending upon the nature of the distribution involved, the type of payment method agreed upon, or other provisions negotiated by the parties.

### A. Advances

An *advance* is a lump-sum payment received in consideration for a grant of rights or license that is *recoupable* (i.e., deductible), by the person who paid the advance, from future royalties that would otherwise be payable to the person who received the advance. Advances are often paid *up front*, such as upon signing of the agreement, but also may be paid on a periodic basis, regardless of whether sufficient royalties have been earned during the period in which the advance is paid.

Advances may be paid for a variety of reasons. A publisher often pays an advance to make sure the person receiving it, such as a songwriter, does not "starve" while he is performing services for the publisher. A songwriter may insist upon receiving an advance to make sure the publisher is making an investment sufficient to provide an incentive for the publisher to recoup that investment by making the proper efforts to promote the songwriter's works.

Advances are usually not *returnable*, meaning that if the advances turn out to be greater than the amount of royalties ever earned from sales, the person who received the advance never has to pay the unearned balance of the advance back to the person who paid it; in other words, an advance is not like a loan. Such advances are generally referred to as, "non-returnable, recoupable advances." However, advances may be returnable if the person who receives the advance fails to perform material provisions of the agreement under which he has received the advance.

## B. Cross-Collateralization

Music publishers, recording companies, and other types of publishers who customarily have royalty obligations to artists and writers will nearly always be certain to *cross-collateralize* all contracts under which they pay advances to a particular artist. Contracts that are cross-collateralized are those under which royalties earned under one contract are used to recoup advances earned under another contract. You can spot cross-collateralization by looking for the following *Three Little Words*: "or any other." For example, the concept of cross-collateralization is contained in the following provision:

> Advances paid hereunder may be recouped from royalties earned under this *or any other* agreement between the parties.

Under certain circumstances, cross-collateralization will defeat one of the primary reasons artists seek advances. If the purpose of the advance is to give the person paying the advance the proper incentive to promote a particular song, allowing the cross-collateralization of that advance against royalties payable under a contract for another song, which by reason of its popularity might sell itself, will defeat the purpose of the original advance. Accordingly, a party might reasonably insist that the cross-collateralization provision be striken from the agreement.

## C. Bonus

A *bonus* is a lump-sum payment that is not recoupable from royalties or any other payments earned under an agreement or other agreements. Bonuses are rare, with publishers almost always insisting on recouping lump sum payments from royalties, even where the potential recoupment is remote. However, a publisher may offer a "signing" bonus to an artist whose business he is trying to attract.

## D. Payment and Accounting

Licenses that call for a flat fee payable by the licensee upon signing of the license will not require extensive provisions regarding the means of payment and accounting procedures. However, the person clearing a license requiring payment *upon signing* or *upon execution*, should negotiate a change to the payment provision to allow the licensee a reasonable period of time, such as 7 days after execution, to remit payment.

Licenses that contain provisions for the payment of a royalty, such as a percentage of net revenues from sales of copies of the music, will contain sophisticated provisions relating to how and when the copyright owner will be paid the royalties. For example, payments are usually expected on a quarterly basis, within some reasonable period after the end of each calendar quarter in which there are revenues derived from the work. A written royalty statement detailing the sources of the revenues upon which the royalty is based commonly accompanies the payment.

A payment provision drafted in favor of a licensee required to pay royalties might be drafted as follows:

> Licensee will compute the total composite royalties earned by Owner pursuant to this agreement quarterly within forty five (45) days after the end of each quarter, and will deliver to Owner a royalty statement for each such period together with the net amount of royalties computed in accordance with this section, if any, which shall be payable after deducting any and all unrecouped advances and chargeable costs under this agreement or any other agreement between Owner and Licensee. No statement will be rendered to Owner for any quarterly period for which the cumulative balance due Owner is less than $50.00.

## E. Audit Privileges

In any contract providing for the payment of royalties based upon the number of units of a work sold or the gross or net revenues derived from sales of a work, the copyright owner will typically require an *audit privilege*, which is the privilege to inspect the books and records of the licensee relating to the revenues derived from the licensed work. A licensee should negotiate some reasonable limitations on these privileges, such as a provision requiring advance notice of an audit, and requiring that the audit be conducted during normal business hours, only once a year, and at the expense of the copyright owner. The copyright owner will normally insist that if the audit reveals that the licensee underpayed the required license fee by more than 5-10%, then the licensee will pay for the costs of the audit. All licenses that contain audit provisions should also contain a provision that obligates the licensee to maintain accurate books and records in the first place. A number of accounting firms specialize in performing audits of such records, and a publisher should consider having its licensees audited on a periodic basis to, as the saying goes, "keep them honest."

An audit provision drafted in favor of a licensee whose books and records may potentially be made subject to inspection might be drafted as follows:

> Upon at least fifteen (15) days prior written notice to Licensee and at Owner's sole cost and expense, Owner, or a nationally recognized certified public accountant on Owner's behalf, shall have the right once each year to inspect and audit such of Licensee's business books and records as may reasonably be necessary for Owner to verify the accuracy of any royalty statement rendered by Licensee within the twelve (12) month period immediately preceding the date of the inspection. The information contained in a royalty statement shall be conclusively deemed correct and binding upon Owner, resulting in the loss of all further audit privileges with respect to such statement, unless specifically challenged by written notice from Owner within twelve (12) months from the date such royalty statement was delivered by Licensee. Any inspection of Licensee's books and records pursuant to this section shall be conducted by Owner at Licensee's premises, only during Licensee's normal business hours, under Licensee's supervision and in a manner which does not interfere with Licensee's business operations. Owner shall specify, at least fifteen (15) days in advance of any inspection, the list of items that Owner desires to inspect. Owner shall keep all information learned as a result of such inspection in strict confidence.

## F. Reserves Against Returns

A licensee obligated to pay royalties should attempt to negotiate the ability to hold a *reserve against returns*. When a licensee makes sales of copies of a work containing licensed music, such as a recording or a videogram, the licensee may expect that some of the sales during a quarter will be returned during a subsequent quarter. (Alluding to the customary designation of *gold*, as a record which sells a million copies, and *platinum*, as a record which sells two million, there circulates an old joke in the record business that a certain artist's album shipped gold and returned platinum!). When a licensee holds a reserve against returns, he deducts a certain percentage (e.g., 10%) from the royalties he would otherwise be required to pay for sales of the work for a particular quarter, and holds on to that deduction in anticipation that there might later be a return of 10% of the records sold during that quarter.

A provision permitting a licensee to hold a reserve against returns might look like this:

> Licensee may retain as a reserve against subsequent charges, credits or returns, a reasonable portion of payable royalties.

The importance of holding a reserve may depend on the licensee's feeling about the copyright owner's willingness and ability to reimburse the licensee in the event of an overpayment due to a subsequent return of sales. The copyright owner, if he is willing to accept this provision at all, would be wise to negotiate a limitation on the provision, requiring that any such reserve will be liquidated within some reasonable period of time after the quarter in which it is withheld. For example, a licensee might be required to liquidate, or pay reserves previously held, to the copyright owner in the quarter immediately following the quarter in which they were held. The copyright owner would also be advised to limit the percentage of the amount to be reserved to an amount that is reasonably related to the amount of sales returns the licensee actually tends to experience for similar kinds of works. For example, the amount of reserves against returns withheld in any one quarter could be limited to 10 or 15%.

Limitations on a licensee's right to hold a reserve against returns might be drafted as follows:

> Licensee may retain as a reserve against subsequent charges, credits or returns, a reasonable portion of payable royalties; provided, however, that such reserve shall be limited to 10% of royalties payable

during a quarter and shall be liquidated in the quarterly accounting period immediately following that in which it was retained.

## G.  Most Favored Nations

A copyright owner who is unsure of what fee to charge, or even how to structure the fee, will sometimes ask that he be paid a license fee that is no less favorable than the fee received for the use of any other song featured in the licensee's work. Such a provision is commonly called a *most favored nations* clause. Most favored nations clauses are often used as a crutch by those who don't know how to analyze a use, don't have any experience with licensing for the particular use (and therefore have a fear of making a bad deal), or don't want to make the effort to analyze the particular use.

A person seeking to clear the license who is reluctant to agree to such a provision should be prepared to argue that the song for which he seeks a license has significantly less importance than other songs in the work. In other words, it makes no sense to compare *apples* and *oranges* when setting the terms of the license. If a licensee does agree to a most favored nations clause, a favorite negotiating technique may present itself to the licensee when clearing permission to use other songs in the same work: "I can't give you a higher fee, Mr. Copyright Owner, because giving you a higher fee would require me, under the most favored nations clauses that I've signed with other copyright owners, to raise all the other fees, and that I just cannot afford to do!"

## III.  COMMONLY USED BOILERPLATE TERMS AND CONDITIONS

This section will summarize some of the standard provisions, sometimes referred to as *legal boilerplate* provisions, contained in many long form license agreements.

## A.  Representations and Warranties

Most long-form license agreements will contain a series of representations or warranties intended to give the licensee some comfort that he will be able to exercise without hindrance the privilege for which he is receiving permission.

A *representation* is a statement as to the existence or nonexistence of a fact or a state of mind which another relies upon in entering into a contract. For example, a copyright owner may represent "that it has the right to grant this license" and "that the work does not infringe any copyrights of another." A copyright owner may also make a representation as to his state of mind, such as when he represents "that, to the best of my knowledge, the work does not infringe any copyrights of another." A *best of knowledge* representation is significantly less meaningful than a representation as to the existence of a fact and will not always be acceptable to assignees or licensees.

A *warranty* is an assurance that certain facts or conditions exist and will continue to exist during the term of the license. A person negotiating a license on behalf of a licensee should request that the term "warrant" be added to provisions containing representations of the licensor. For example, the copyright owner should "represent *and warrant* that the work does not infringe any copyrights of another." The addition of the word "warrant" would enable the licensee to add, in an action for a breach of contract arising from a misrepresentation, a cause of action for *breach of warranty*, which could provide the licensee with some additional remedies and advantages in any litigation arising out of the licensor's breach of the agreement.

Note, however, music licensors are generally reluctant to modify their boilerplate language without legal advice, and where the cost of such legal advice may approach or exceed the license fee being charged for the license, it is unlikely that any change would even be considered. Should a licensee find some resistance in making changes, the licensee should weigh the business risks involved. Normally, it is not worth expending much time or expense to negotiate for these changes and being unable to negotiate such a change is certainly not worth walking away from a license unless you are aware of some specific facts that may justify having a strong set of warranties and representations.

Music licensors typically want to give as few warranties and representations as possible. Warranty provisions providing only minimal comfort are quite common and the following is a good example:

> Publisher warrants only that it has the right to grant this license and this license is given and accepted without any other representations,

warranty or recourse, express or implied, except for Publisher's agreement to repay the consideration for this license if said warranty shall be breached with respect thereto. In no event shall the total liability of Publisher in any case exceed the amount of consideration received by it hereunder.

Licensees typically desire a little more than that and typically request warranties and representations sufficient to assure that the work does not infringe copyrights or other rights of another. Those who are receiving a full transfer of copyright might desire certain additional warranties, such as those contained in the following provision:

Owner hereby warrants and represents to Company that Owner has the right to enter into this agreement and to grant to Company all of the rights granted herein, and that the exercise by Company of any and all of the rights granted to Company in this agreement will not violate or infringe upon any common law or statutory rights of any person, firm or corporation including, without limitation, contractual rights, copyrights, and rights of privacy. Owner further warrants that the rights granted herein are free and clear of any claims, demands, liens or encumbrances.

When the person who is transferring a copyright in a newly created work was the one who authored the work, the following set of warranties and representations may be required:

Composer hereby warrants and represents that the Composition is an original work, that neither the Composition nor any part thereof infringes upon the title, literary or musical property or copyright of any other work nor the statutory, common law or other rights (including rights of privacy or publicity) of any person, firm or corporation or violates any applicable criminal statute, that he is the sole writer and composer and the sole owner of the Composition and of all the rights therein, that he has not sold, assigned, transferred, hypothecated or mortgaged any right, title or interest in or to the Composition or any part thereof or any of the rights herein conveyed, that he has not made or entered into any agreement with any other person, firm or corporation affecting the Composition or any right, title or interest therein or in the copyright thereof, that no person, firm or corporation other than Composer has or has had claims or has claimed any right, title or interest in or to the Composition or any part thereof, any use thereof or any copyright therein, that the Composition has never been published, and that Composer has full right, power and authority to make this present instrument of sale and transfer.

Music publishing agreements will also require the songwriter to warrant that he or she is the "sole author," providing an assurance that no one will come forth to claim to be the author or co-author of the work, and that the work was "original," meaning it was original with the songwriter and not copied from the work of another or from a work in the public domain.

If the copyright owner is assigning an exclusive right under the copyright, the assignee will want additional warranties such as the following:

Owner shall not during the term of this Agreement do any act or authorize, license or knowingly permit any third party (other than a party authorized or licensed by Company) to do any act which would in any way derogate from or violate the exclusive right, license and privilege granted to Company by this Agreement. The parties expressly acknowledge that the Compositions and all rights granted and to be granted to Company hereunder are of a special, unique and intellectual character which gives them peculiar value, and that in the event of a breach by Owner of any term, condition, warranty, representation or agreement hereunder, Company will be caused irreparable injury. Owner expressly agrees that in the event of any such breach, Company shall be entitled to injunctive and other equitable relief or damages, in addition to any other rights and remedies available to it, and Company shall have the right to recoup any damages from any sums which may thereafter become due and payable to Owner hereunder.

## B.  Indemnification

Representations and warranties are generally given additional force by an indemnification provision. The indemnification provision makes it clear that the entire financial burden incurred as a result of a breach of any representation or warranty set forth in the agreement will fall on the person making those representations and warranties.

The following is an example of a short, but comprehensive indemnification provision:

> Owner agrees to indemnify and hold Licensee harmless from any claim, demand, suit, action, proceeding, prosecution, damage, expense (including reasonable attorneys' fees), liability or loss of any kind or nature arising from or out of any claim asserted against Licensee which is inconsistent with any of the warranties, covenants or representations made by Owner herein.

A promise to *hold harmless* another against claims made and actions filed by third parties means that the person making the promise will bear all the expenses of defending the claim or lawsuit, but will also mean he or she will control the defense of the matter, unless contrary terms are specifically provided. Often, an assignee or licensee will not feel comfortable with the assignor or licensor maintaining control over the handling of the claim or lawsuit, particularly where the assignor or licensor is not wealthy or financially stable. Accordingly, publishing and licensing agreements will often clarify the rights and obligations of the parties with respect to any lawsuits filed concerning those matters covered by representations and warranties. For example, a standard publishing agreement between a songwriter and a music publisher may provide that the music publisher has (i) the privilege to defend itself against any claim or lawsuit (ii) the privilege to choose its own legal counsel to do so, (iii) the privilege to settle any such claim or lawsuit on such terms as it deems appropriate, (iv) the right to reimbursement from the songwriter for any payments made as a result of a settlement or final judgment entered against the publisher, (v) the right to reimbursement of attorneys fees and litigation costs incurred to defend the matter, whether or not such defense is successful, and (vi) the privilege to withhold any royalties and apply them to cover any obligations of the writer with respect to the claim or lawsuit.

A songwriter who has the bargaining leverage to vary such terms should attempt to eliminate any responsibility for mere "claims" and limit the indemnity to "final judgments." Because of their size, music publishers often attract lawsuits merely because of their "deep pockets," and songwriters should not be responsible for nuisance suits. If the publisher has a license from the writer to make derivative works,

as they often do, the indemnity should not apply to the extent publisher added material or edited the work. In fact, the songwriter should
require the publisher to provide an indemnity regarding any materials
supplied to the writer or any materials added over which the writer
had no control. For example, the following might be added to the
writer's indemnification provision:

> Publisher similarly indemnifies and holds Writer harmless as to ma-
> terial furnished by Publisher for use by Writer hereunder or material
> added or changes made by Publisher.

A songwriter with a great degree of bargaining leverage may request that he be given the option to defend any lawsuits with counsel
of his own choosing, at his own expense, provided that if he does,
publisher may participate in the defense with counsel of its choosing
and at its expense. The contours of "participating in the defense" can
be problematic; generally, it is the person who "controls" the defense
who makes the decisions in litigation.

Because any settlement will eventually come out of the songwriter's pocket a songwriter may request that any settlements be made
only with his consent, to make sure the publisher does not settle upon
unreasonable terms. Publishers will not normally permit this, because
it has the deep pockets and may not be able to collect from the songwriter for many years, if at all. A possible compromise to make sure
the publisher has a good incentive to settle upon reasonable terms is
to concede that the publisher has the sole right to settle, but require
that the publisher be responsible for paying some percentage, perhaps
50%, of any settlement.

Publishers will want to withhold any payments due to the writer
during the pendancy of any claim or litigation. The writer should seek
to curtail the amount that may be withheld to a percentage, place a
dollar ceiling on the amount, or limit length of time during which
moneys may be withheld with respect to any particular claim. If the
publisher withholds any money, the money should go into escrow; this
is to protect the writer's money in the event the publisher goes bankrupt.

## C. Assignment Clauses

A copyright owner will generally require that any assignment of the license be subject to the copyright owners consent. The following is a typical provision governing restricting the assignment of a license:

> This license is personal to Licensee and may not be assigned or transferred without Owner's prior written consent. No such transfer or assignment shall become effective unless and until the transferee or assignee shall deliver to Owner a written agreement assuming the further performance of Licensee's obligations hereunder, and no such transfer or assignment shall relieve Licensee of any obligation hereunder. However, Licensee may enter into sublicenses within the Territory to the extent necessary to permit the uses authorized by this license.

The following provision is a stronger, more complete restriction on a party's ability to assign its rights or delegate its obligations under an agreement:

> Licensee may not assign this Agreement or any of its rights or obligations hereunder (including without limitation rights and duties of performance) to any third party or entity, and this Agreement may not be involuntarily assigned or assigned by operation of law, without the prior written consent of Owner, which consent shall be given or withheld by Owner in the sole exercise of its discretion.

The restriction on assignments *by operation of law* is intended to require permission even when two corporations combine by *merger* — a circumstance which does not necessarily involve the transfer of an agreement from one party to another. In a merger, the parties combine to form one entity.[3]

A music publisher engaged in the merger or acquisition of another publisher should, in connection with its due diligence investigation prior to the closing of the transaction, consider the assignment pro-

---

[3] Despite our experience with mergers and an apparently sound etymological basis to support the suggestion, the word *merger*, as a friend of ours has suggested, is not a portmanteau or combination of the words *marriage* and *murder*.

visions of all material songwriter agreements of the publisher being acquired. For example, the acquiring publisher may come across an assignment provision such as the following, which was excerpted from the 1978 version of the standard Songwriter's Guild Agreement (formerly, AGAC) between songwriters and publishers:

> 18. Except to the extent herein otherwise expressly provided, the Publisher shall not sell, transfer, assign, convey, encumber or otherwise dispose of the composition or the copyright or copyrights secured thereon without the prior written consent of the Writer. The Writer has been induced to enter into this contract in reliance upon the value to him of the personal service and ability of the Publisher in the exploitation of the composition, and by reason thereof it is the intention of the parties and the essence of the relationship between them that the rights herein granted to the Publisher shall remain with the Publisher and that the same shall not pass to any other person including, without limitations, successors to or receivers or trustees of the property of the Publisher, either by act or deed of the Publisher or by operation of law, and in the event of the voluntary or involuntary bankruptcy of the Publisher, this contract shall terminate, provided, however, that the composition may be included by the Publisher in a bona fide voluntary sale of its music business or its entire catalog of musical compositions, or in a merger or consolidation of the Publisher with another corporation, in which event the Publisher shall immediately give written notice thereof to the Writer, and provided further that the composition and the copyright therein may be assigned by the Publisher to a subsidiary or affiliated company generally engaged in the music publishing business. If the Publisher is an individual, the composition may pass to a legatee or distributee as part of the inheritance of the Publisher's music business and entire catalog of musical compositions. Any such transfer or assignment, shall, however, be conditioned upon the execution and delivery by the transferee or assignee to the Writer of an agreement to be bound by and to perform all of the terms and conditions of this contract to be performed on the part of the Publisher.

While the foregoing assignment provision should not normally impose an obstacle to an acquisition or merger, the last sentence of the provision does impose the requirement that the publisher give immediate written notice of the acquisition to the writer and deliver an agreement to be bound by the terms of the writer's contract. The assignment provision of the standard AGAC Songwriter's Agreement varies slightly depending upon the year the form was printed. Where the question of assignment is relevant the applicable form should be consulted.

## D. Benefit of Successors and Assigns

If an agreement contains a restriction on the right of one party or other to assign the agreement to others, then the following provision, which is typically found in many license agreements, should have the word "permitted" included as the penultimate word as follows:

> This Agreement shall be binding upon and inure to the benefit of each of the parties hereto, and except as otherwise provided herein, their respective legal successors and permitted assigns.

## E. Exclusion of All Other Express or Implied Warranties

If a license agreement provides that any physical materials be transferred or loaned to a licensee in connection with the licensee's exercise of the license, the license agreement may exclude, for the protection of the copyright owner, all warranties that are not expressly set forth in the license agreement, including certain warranties that may be implied by the law in the absence of such an exclusion.

The following is an example of such a provision:

> OTHER THAN THE REPRESENTATIONS AND WARRANTIES SPECIFICALLY SET FORTH IN THIS AGREEMENT, OWNER DOES NOT MAKE TO LICENSEE BY VIRTUE OF THIS AGREEMENT ANY REPRESENTATION OR WARRANTY, EX-PRESS OR IMPLIED, AND HEREBY EXPRESSLY DISCLAIMS, ANY REPRESENTATION OR WARRANTY OF ANY KIND WITH RESPECT TO THE LICENSED WORK, INCLUDING WITHOUT LIMITATION ANY IMPLIED WARRANTIES OF MERCHANTABILITY AND FITNESS FOR A PARTICULAR PURPOSE. LICENSEE SHALL NOT MAKE OR PASS ON TO ITS CUSTOMERS OR LICENSEES ON BEHALF OF OWNER ANY WARRANTIES EXCLUDED HEREUNDER.

A copyright owner may desire such a provision if the physical materials being supplied with the license may cause damage to any property of the licensee. For example, music licensed in conjunction with MIDI software embodying the music may cause damage to other computer software or work product of the licensee's to the extent the MIDI software contains "bugs" (i.e., programming errors).

Clauses providing for the exclusion of warranties and other limitations on liability are required, under the Uniform Commercial Code, and under the Restatement of Contracts, to be *conspicuous*. It has been common practice to place all provisions that legally require conspicuity in all capital letters. It may be asked whether language in all capital letters is really more conspicuous than text printed in standard upper and lower case. Many people would agree that text printed in all caps can be most difficult to read. Being that we are on the verge of the release of low cost color laser printers and photocopy machines (and, soon to follow, color-capable fax machines), perhaps a better solution would be to print provisions that are required to be conspicuous in some conspicuous color, such as red.

## F. Exclusion of Consequential Damages

Consequential damages are damages incurred by a licensee for loss profits, lost data, lost time, or lost opportunities. A copyright owner may feel that the licensee is in a better position to assume the risk or obtain insurance to cover the risk of lost business income for losses resulting from breaches of the agreement or warranties by the copyright owner. The parties would transfer the risk of such losses to the licensee with the following provision:

> NOTWITHSTANDING ANYTHING TO THE CONTRARY CONTAINED HEREIN, OWNER SHALL NOT, UNDER ANY CIRCUMSTANCES, BE LIABLE TO LICENSEE FOR CONSEQUENTIAL, INCIDENTAL OR SPECIAL DAMAGES, EVEN IF OWNER HAS BEEN APPRISED OF THE LIKELIHOOD OF SUCH DAMAGES OCCURRING.

An alert licensee would quickly realize that such a provision would render meaningless any warranties by the copyright owner that the latter has the right to enter into the agreement and that the licensed work does not infringe upon the rights of others. Accordingly, a licensee who comes across such a provision, if he is unable to have it stricken from the agreement altogether, would be reasonable in demanding that the express warranties contained in the agreement be excluded from the applicability of this provision.

## G. Limitation of Liability

For the same reason a copyright owner would wish to limit consequential damages, the copyright owner would wish to limit all other damages to the price paid for the license, and such a provision may be effected as follows:

> IN NO EVENT SHALL OWNER'S LIABILITY (WHETHER BASED ON AN ACTION OR CLAIM IN CONTRACT, TORT OR OTHERWISE) TO LICENSEE ARISING OUT OF OR RELATED TO THIS AGREEMENT OR THE TRANSACTIONS CONTEMPLATED HEREUNDER AND NOT WITH THE SCOPE OF THE SECTION ABOVE ENTITLED "EXCLUSION OF CONSEQUENTIAL DAMAGES" EXCEED THE LICENSE FEE PAID BY LICENSEE HEREUNDER.

Again, a licensee should be able to have all express warranties contained in the agreement excluded from the applicability of this provision, as well.

## H. Severability

Agreements that contain provisions for the exclusive services of an individual have come under close scrutiny by the courts. Examples include exclusive songwriter agreements typically entered into between music publishers and their "staff" songwriters, which affords the publisher the right to exclude the songwriter from providing his songwriting services to another. Often these agreements combine a right for the exclusive services of the songwriter with provisions for the assignment of copyrights in compositions developed by the songwriter during the term of the agreement. Should a court hold that a music publisher is unable enforce the exclusivity provision, the publisher would not wish to risk losing all the copyrights acquired under an exclusive publishing agreement. Accordingly, where there is a possibility that one part of an agreement may be held unenforceable, a copyright owner may wish to make sure that other portions of the agreement are not affected. Such a provision is called a severability clause, which might take the following form:

> In the event that any provision hereof is found invalid or unenforceable pursuant to judicial decree or decision, the remainder of this Agreement shall remain valid and enforceable according to its terms.

If the agreements contains a provision excluding warranties or otherwise limiting the liability of the copyright owner, the copyright owner might add the following sentence to the severability provision:

> WITHOUT LIMITING THE FOREGOING, IT IS EXPRESSLY UNDERSTOOD AND AGREED THAT EACH AND EVERY PROVISION OF THIS AGREEMENT WHICH PROVIDES FOR A LIMITATION OF LIABILITY, DISCLAIMER OR WARRANTIES OR EXCLUSION OF DAMAGES IS INTENDED BY THE PARTIES TO BE SEVERABLE AND INDEPENDENT OF ANY OTHER PROVISION AND TO BE ENFORCED AS SUCH. FURTHER, IT IS EXPRESSLY UNDERSTOOD AND AGREED THAT IN THE EVENT ANY REMEDY HEREUNDER IS DETERMINED TO HAVE FAILED OF ITS ESSENTIAL PURPOSE, ALL LIMITATIONS OF LIABILITY AND EXCLUSION OF DAMAGES SET FORTH HEREIN SHALL REMAIN IN FULL FORCE AND EFFECT.

## I.  Cure Period

Copyright owners granting rights or licenses should always include, at least in long form licenses, a provision that affords a period within which to cure any breach of contract alleged by the licensee.

> Owner shall not be deemed to be in breach of any of its obligations hereunder unless and until you shall have given Owner written notice by certified or registered mail, return receipt requested, specifying the nature of such breach and Owner shall have failed to cure such breach within thirty (30) days after Owner's receipt of such written notice.

Licensees should request to make this provision mutual:

Neither party shall be deemed to be in breach of any of its obligations hereunder unless and until the party claiming a breach shall have given the other written notice by certified or registered mail, return receipt requested, specifying the nature of such breach and such other party shall have failed to cure such breach within thirty (30) days after receipt of such written notice.

## J. Entire Agreement or Integration Provision

When the parties have reduced their agreement to writing, and it is clear the parties intended that the agreement reflect their entire understanding and agreement or that all understandings and agreements regarding the subject matter were intended to be "integrated" or "merged" into the written agreement, then evidence of any other agreements, discussions, representations, or warranties may not be admissible as evidence to contradict or modify the terms of the agreement. In other words, unless their is some ambiguity in the terms of the agreement, the courts will look only to the "four corners" of the written contract to determine the scope of the agreement and the intent of the parties. Accordingly, the parties will often reflect their intent that a written agreement reflects their entire agreement or that all agreements are merged into the written agreement in a clause such as the following:

This Agreement constitutes the entire understanding and contract between the parties and supersedes any and all prior and contemporaneous, oral or written representations, communications, understandings and agreements between the parties with respect to the subject matter hereof, all of which representations, communications, understandings and agreements are hereby canceled to the extent they are not specifically merged herein. The parties acknowledge and agree that neither of the parties is entering into this Agreement on the basis of any representations or promises not expressly contained herein. This is an integrated agreement.

## K. Modifications and Amendments

To avoid disputes about whether or how the terms of a written agreement were subsequently modified, the parties will often agree as follows:

This Agreement shall not be modified, amended, canceled or in any way altered, nor may it be modified by custom and usage of trade or course of dealing, except by an instrument in writing and signed by both of the parties hereto. All amendments or modifications of this Agreement shall be binding upon the parties despite any lack of consideration so long as the same shall be in writing and executed by the parties hereto.

## L.  Waiver

To avoid disputes about whether or under what terms a party's duty to perform an obligation of the contract was waived by the other party, the parties may agree as follows:

Performance of any obligation required of a party hereunder may be waived only by a written waiver signed by the other party, which waiver shall be effective only with respect to the specific obligation described therein. The waiver by either party hereto of a breach of any provision of this Agreement by the other shall not operate or be construed as a waiver of any subsequent breach of the same provision or any other provision of this Agreement.

## M.  No Partnership or Agency

An agreement between a buyer and seller or a licensor and licensee should make it clear that no other relationship between the parties is established unless otherwise specifically agreed:

Nothing in this Agreement shall be construed as creating a joint venture, partnership, agency, employment relationship, franchise relationship or taxable entity between the parties, nor shall either party have the right, power or authority to create any obligations or duty, express or implied, on behalf of the other party hereto, it being understood that the parties are independent contractors vis-a-vis one another.

## N.  No Third Party Beneficiaries

An agreement intended solely to affect the rights and privileges of the parties signing the agreement might state that no rights or privileges are meant to be conferred on any third parties unless specifically provided:

> Nothing contained in this Agreement, express or implied, shall be deemed to confer any rights or remedies upon, nor obligate any of the parties hereto, to any person or entity other than such parties, unless so stated to the contrary.

## O. Choice of Law

The person drafting the license will generally try to insist that if any disputes arise under the agreement, the law of the state where that party is located should apply to the transaction.

> This Agreement shall be construed and enforced in accordance with the laws of the State of California applicable to agreements between residents of California wholly executed and wholly performed therein.

Where the parties reside in the same state, there should be little debate about the laws of which state should govern the agreement. Where the parties cannot agree upon whether to use the laws of the state of one party or the other, the parties should consider including either the state of New York or the state of California, because each of these states have developed a substantial body of case law concerning contracts in the entertainment industry.

## P. Choice of Forum

Perhaps more significant than the choice of law provision is the provision that dictates the forum in which a lawsuit arising out of any dispute concerning the agreement must be filed. Unless otherwise agreed, a lawsuit may be brought in any state where the court has jurisdiction over the defendant, such as a state where the defendant is doing business. The costs of a party's litigating an action in a state other than the state in which his principal place of business, and that of his normal legal counsel, is located can be significantly more expensive than litigating in the courts of another state. Further, litigating in an unfamiliar state may induce, whether justified or not, a fear of the unknown or fear of a "home court" advantage.

To alleviate these fears and to minimize the potential costs of litigation, a party may negotiate a provision that identifies the state and county in which lawsuits arising under the agreement are to be brought. The courts will usually respect the agreement of the parties on the matter. Of course, where both parties are located in the same state and county, there is little reason to negotiate the issue of forum, unless one of the parties expects to move its operations to another state or county. Similarly, when both parties are major multi-national corporations who do business in nearly all the states, this provision may not become an issue, unless a party can identify specific laws in a particular state that favors or disfavors one of the parties to the transaction.

While many license agreements contain a choice of law provision, the same agreements often neglect to include a choice of forum provision. Including a choice of law provision, but leaving the choice of forum silent may produce the anomalous result of a court in one state having to apply the laws of another state to resolve the dispute. It will therefore serve to remember that a choice of law provision is not the same as a choice of forum provision, and if the intent is to require that lawsuits be brought in a particular state, the agreement should contain, in addition to a choice of law provision, a provision such as the following:

> Any action or proceeding brought by either party against the other arising out of or related to this Agreement shall be brought only in a state or federal court of competent jurisdiction located in the County of Los Angeles, California, and the parties hereby consent to the *in personam* jurisdiction of said courts.

## Q. Confidentiality of Agreement

A party may desire, for one reason or another, to maintain the confidentiality of the terms of the agreement. The following provision effects such confidentiality, recognizing the need for certain standard exceptions:

> Each of the parties to this Agreement warrants and agrees that neither it nor its counsel will disclose, disseminate, or cause to be disclosed the terms of this Agreement, except: (a) Insofar as disclosure is reasonably necessary to carry out and effectuate the terms of this Agreement; (b) Insofar as a party hereto is required by law to respond to any demand for information from any court, governmental entity, or governmental agency; (c) Insofar as disclosure is

necessary to be made to a party's independent accountants for tax or audit purposes; and (d) Insofar as the parties may mutually agree in writing upon language to be contained in one or more press release.

## R. Notice

Notices that may be required or permitted under license agreements, such as for example, notices of exercise of any option provisions in the agreement, should always be in writing. Further, every long form contract should have a provision clarifying just how such notices must be effected. This is to avoid any misunderstanding about whether notice was timely made and to make sure the notice actually gets to the appropriate person or department within each firm responsible for effecting or enforcing the performance of the agreement.

The following notice provision recognizes the global nature of modern business and the new media of business communications that have become common during the past several years.

Unless otherwise specifically provided, all notices required or permitted by this Agreement shall be in writing and in English and may be delivered personally, or may be sent by cable, telex, facsimile or certified mail, return receipt requested, to the following, unless the parties are subsequently notified of any change of address in accordance with this section:

If to Owner:    Big Music Publishing Corp.
1000 Sunset Boulevard
Hollywood, California 90000
Attention: Legal Department
Telex: 123456 BIGPUB
Facsimile: (213) 555-1212

If to Licensee: _____

_____

_____

Attention: _____

Telex: _____

Facsimile: _____

Any notice shall be deemed to have been received as follows: (i) personal delivery, upon receipt; (ii) telex, cable or facsimile, twenty-four (24) hours after transmission or dispatch; (iii) certified mail, three (3) business days after delivery to the United States postal authorities by the party serving notice. If notice is sent by telex, facsimile or cable, a confirming copy of the same shall be sent by mail to the same address.

It is not uncommon for agreements to provide that copies of any notices to be provided under the agreement be sent to the outside counsel of the party upon which notice is to be served. This could help bring to the attention of the party entitled to the notice an important notice that might have otherwise gone unnoticed.

## S. Advice of Legal Counsel

When one of the parties is known to be unsophisticated in the ways of business, or is among a class of persons considered stereotypically to be "exploited" — such as artists and songwriters — the more sophisticated party should include the following provision in the agreement:

Each party acknowledges and represents that, in executing this Agreement, it has received advice as to its legal rights from legal counsel and that the person signing on its behalf has read and understood all of the terms and provisions of this Agreement. Further, each party and their counsel have cooperated in the drafting and preparation of this Agreement. It shall be deemed their joint work product and may not be construed against any party be reason of its preparation or word processing.

## T. Attorneys Fees

Under the American Rule of law, unless an award of attorneys fees is provided by statute or by the express terms of a written agreement between the parties, a court will not award attorneys fees to the prevailing party in litigation. To deter frivolous litigation, the parties may wish to include a specific provision in the agreement providing the prevailing party in any litigation over the agreement with an opportunity to collect its reasonable attorney fees and costs incurred during the course of the litigation.

In any litigation between the parties regarding the terms or performance of this agreement, the prevailing party shall be entitled to recover its reasonable attorneys' fees and court costs.

## U. Recitals

Many agreements contain recitals of fact intended to provide the
reader with some background information about the parties or the
transaction. Recitals of fact may sometimes be identified by their being preceded by the word, *Whereas*. The parties to an agreement
should be certain that the recitals accurately reflect the facts they purport to recite. California Evidence Code Section 622 states that facts
recited in a written instrument (other than recitals of consideration)
are conclusively presumed true as between the parties. Recitals, therefore, can serve to reduce the number of facts that can be placed into
dispute in any litigation relating to the agreement.

If California Law does not govern the agreement, or the law of
the state which governs the agreement does not have a law similar to
the California provision concerning recitals, the parties may wish to
give strong legal effect to the recitals by including the following provision:

> The recitals above set forth are incorporated into this agreement by
> reference. Each recital of fact concerning a party shall be conclusive
> as between the parties hereto. Such fact shall be incontestable in the
> event of any dispute between the parties regarding such fact and
> each party agrees not to introduce any evidence which would in any
> way serve to dispute such recited fact.

## V. Counterparts

It is our practice to always have one "original" copy signed for
each party to the contract. For example, where there are two parties
to the contract, each party will sign two agreements, with each receiving a fully executed original bearing the original signatures of both
parties. Where the parties are signing an agreement in different locations or at different times, circumstances will require that each sign
separate signature pages which will later be attached to the original
agreement. Though not necessary, agreements executed in such fashion should contain a provision such as the following:

This Agreement may be executed in one or more counterparts, each of which shall be deemed an original, but all of which together shall constitute one and the same instrument.

## W. Captions

To prevent an unintended result caused by a poorly worded section heading or caption:

The section headings and captions contained herein are for reference purposes and convenience only and shall not in any way affect the meaning or interpretation of this Agreement.

## X. Gender

A favorite provision of ours which never fails to evoke reaction in negotiators who bother to explore the depths of the legal boilerplate typically found in many licenses:

Where the context so requires, the masculine gender shall include the feminine or neuter, and the singular shall include the plural and the plural the singular.

## Y. Effective Date

When you send an agreement to another for signature, it could be construed as an "offer" for a contract, which the other party may "accept" by returning the agreement signed.

Most simple permission letters are sent with the understanding that they may be accepted by the licensee's signing and returning the letter to the music copyright owner. As a precaution, and as an incentive for the licensee to pay promptly, the copyright owner should specify that the license does not take affect until the owner receives payment of the license fee.

More formal license agreements will contain signature lines for both parties to sign and are not intended to be binding until the copyright owner counter-signs the agreement. A copyright owner would be prudent to first obtain the signature of the licensee before signing the contract himself. If there is a significant delay between the time you send an agreement and receive it signed, circumstances may change significantly during that time. For example, you may send a license to an advertising agency for the non-exclusive use of a musical composition in a television commercial, and while you are waiting for the license to be reviewed and returned, another advertiser offers a significantly higher license fee for the exclusive use of the song. In such circumstances, you would ideally want to be in a position to cease the negotiations with the first advertiser and accept the terms offered by the new advertiser. To have that ability, you would need to be certain that the first advertiser does not consider the license you sent to him binding upon you. If you had not signed the agreements before you sent them, then it should be an easy matter to be certain that no binding agreement was consummated. If you had signed the agreements before having sent them, then you would have no assurance that the first advertiser considers that agreement not to have been entered until you actually receive written confirmation to that effect from the first advertiser, which may not always be easy.

Accordingly, other than the case of a simple permission letter for minor non-exclusive licenses where some risk can be assumed for the sake of administrative convenience, a copyright owner is advised to always counter-sign agreements after they have first been signed by the licensee. Further, the license agreement should contain the following provision:

> This Agreement shall become effective only after it has been signed by Licensee and has been accepted by Owner at its principal place of business, and its effective date shall be the date on which it is signed by Owner.

Finally, to avoid any misunderstanding as to the Effective Date of the agreement, which is often the start date of licenses whose term is based on loosely specified time periods (e.g., ". . . a term of one year commencing the Effective Date hereof"), the agreement should indicate the Effective Date directly below the signature block of the copyright owner, as follows:

LICENSEE                          OWNER

Signature: _____        Signature: _____
Printed Name: _____         Printed Name: _____

Title: _____        Title: _____
Dated: _____        Dated: _____
                              (This is the effective
                              date of the Agreement)

## IV. Affiliated Company Problem

Certain problems arise when a music publisher is affiliated with a motion picture studio, which is the case when both entities are subsidiaries of a parent entertainment company or other conglomerate. Under standard music publishing agreements, the songwriter is generally entitled to receive 50% of any and all sums actually received by the music publisher from the licensing uses of the music in motion pictures, television programs, videograms, and other media. Where the music publisher is affiliated with the entertainment company who desires to license the music in such works, a conflict of interest arises which may influence the publisher to enter into a deal that does not serve the best interests of the songwriter.

Because an obligation of good faith is implied by the relationship between the songwriter and publisher, the music publisher, in considering the terms of a license with an affiliated company, is required to negotiate "at arms length." This means that publisher must treat the affiliated company as it would any other third party in similar circumstances in establishing the terms and conditions of the license. In the case of synchronization licenses, where synchronization fees have become relatively standardized, this is a fairly simple matter. However, in the area of home video licenses, where there are still few standards,[4] and often heated disputes as to whether original synchronization licenses covered home video uses of music,[5] the resolution of conflicts of interest is more difficult.

How a music publisher resolves this conflict will have an impact upon the publisher's legal relationships with its songwriters, the publisher's ability to acquire additional song catalogues, and the pub-

---

[4] See the discussion of videogram licenses in Chapter 15.
[5] See the discussion of the extent to which old synchronization licenses apply to new uses in Chapter 16.

lisher's ability to recruit and contract with new songwriters. The senior management of the entertainment company or the conglomerate is not generally in the best position to resolve such conflicts, and the music publisher faced with this situation should come to grips with the question well before disputes arise with the songwriters they represent.

## V. GENERAL ADVICE TO MUSIC COPYRIGHT OWNER — ALWAYS ENCOURAGE ACTIVITY IN THE SONG

Before exploring the foregoing factors in relation to the various customary forms of music licenses, we would like to admonish music copyright owners against making the fundamental errors that can lead a great song to obscurity. Do not get too mired in the details. For example, do not let a negotiation over the wording of legal boilerplate obscure your vision of the forest through the trees. Do not let your perception of the value of the copyright go to your head. Remember that no matter how small the license fee you receive, in the long run, you will tend to make up more than the difference from maintaining a continuing active relationship between the song and the listening public. Do not let fear and uncertainty rule the day. Recognize that life is decision making, and don't be afraid to make a decision. A good rule to follow is, when in doubt, license. The music copyright owner's primary interest should always be to encourage as much activity in the song as possible.

## VI. GENERAL ADVICE TO PERSONS SEEKING TO CLEAR LICENSES — FULLY DISCLOSE ALL THE USES YOU MIGHT CONCEIVABLY MAKE OF THE MUSIC

There is nothing worse in business than a surprise. Too often, persons seeking to clear licenses think they are being clever by understating the nature or scope of the intended use in an effort to minimize the fee quoted by the copyright owner. This kind of attitude is inimical to the licensee's best interests. If, as a result of understating the nature of your use, you receive a license that does not adequately cover your requirements, you may find yourself being accused of infringement of copyright, subject to a serious threat of injunction at an inopportune time. You should not have to experience the high cost and ugly embarrassment of a lawsuit to learn the lesson that intentionally understating the nature and scope of your intended use for the purpose of minimizing your costs makes no business sense.

Music copyright owners will require a lot of information about your potential use of the music before quoting a license fee. While the copyright owner uses this information to quote a fee that reflects the importance of the use, it is also to your benefit to fully disclose all the uses you might conceivably make of the music. Usually, the music copyright owner will be more than happy to quote you a fee for all the uses that you can foresee. If the fees are reasonable, you would be advised to pick up as much a scope and duration as offered to you. If you are on a tight budget, you should ask for options which will give you important flexibility later on and may save you money in the long run.

# PRINT LICENSES

## SUMMARY

### I. HISTORICAL BACKGROUND

A. Origins of Musical Notation

B. The Art of Printing

C. Printed Music Publishing in America

D. Print Music Publishing Today

### II. TYPES OF PRINTED MUSIC

A. Sheet Music

B. Folio

C. Personality Folio

D. Instrument Folio

E. Music Instruction Books

F. Concert and Educational Editions

G. Fakebook

### III. PREPARATION AND DISTRIBUTION OF PRINTED MUSIC

A. Independent Print Distributors

### IV. PRINT RIGHTS

A. Granting Exclusive Print Rights

   1. Grants by Songwriters to Music Publishers

   2. Grants by Music Publishers to Print Music Distributors

### V. PRINT LICENSES

A. Granting Non-Exclusive Licenses to Print Music in Folios

B. Granting and Clearing Licenses to Print Lyrics

1. Books
2. Record Albums
3. Lyric Magazines
4. Print Advertising
5. Internet Web Sites

## APPENDIX TO CHAPTER 11

CHAPTER **11**

# PRINT LICENSES

A *print license* is a form of permission that authorizes one to make printed copies of music, such as sheet music, printed music folios, concert arrangements, and reprints of lyrics in books, magazines, and print advertising. The print license is derived from one of the most basic rights of a copyright owner: the exclusive right to make copies. This chapter sketches the historical and legal background of printed music and provides an outline of some of the common terms and conditions contained in customary print licenses.

## I. HISTORICAL BACKGROUND

### A. Origins of Musical Notation

Music would seem to be a part of human nature. What man fails to express through gesturing, speaking, writing, painting, and sculpting, he expresses through making music. If music can be defined as the art of organizing sounds and silences into meaningful patterns, then it clearly had very early origins. Early songs probably developed from hunting calls and other vocal signals. As soon as these calls were used for the pleasure expressed or emotions evoked, apart from any useful purpose, they became music. Archeologists have unearthed evidence dating back to the dawn of antiquity of man's creating music throughout Asia, Europe, Africa, the Americas, and other parts of the globe. The ancient Egyptians, Persians, Africans, and Chinese all used musical instruments of one kind or another.

It was, however, the ancient Greeks, who laid the foundations of modern music. In ancient Greece, poetry and music were treated as one art, and music became an integral part of Greek drama, including the theatrical works of Aeschylus, Sophocles, Euripides, and Aristophanes.

Most common among the Greek instruments was the lyre, a u-shaped instrument with a cross bar that supported 4 strings. The invention of the lyre, according to Greek mythology, occurred when Herme's foot came in contact with the tendons of a dead tortoise, which had dried and tightened on the animal's shell. The philosopher, Terpander, born about 676 B.C., is said to have added three strings to the lyre, and later, Pythagoras, born about 582 B.C., is said to have added the eighth string. Pythagoras, who was the first to give music a scientific basis, also invented the system of four tones known as the *tetrachord*, which later evolved into the first scale of one *octave*.

Early in the 4th century A.D., a school of *chant* was established in Rome. For generations the melodies were handed down aurally from master to pupil. The learning of the growing repertory of melodies by heart was arduous and there eventually evolved a form of musical notation. This notation was called *neumes* from the Greek word *neuma* meaning nod or sign. While the system gradually included combinations of dashes, curves and dots, the neumes notation did not indicate musical pitch. Although there is no official accounts of neume notation before the 8th century, it has been said that Pope Gregory the Great, in the 6th century, collected the sacred music of the Church. *Gregorian* music is the name given to a collection of over 600 songs connected with the Roman Catholic services of that age. By the 8th Century, Charlemagne was sending emissaries to Rome to get full and accurate details on the methods of Gregorian singing.

During the 10th century, an anonymous theorist brought order and progress to musical notation with a single stroke of his pen. With some red ink and a ruler, he drew a line across the page and marked it "F." This was the beginning of the musical staff and clef. The nuemes were now written on the line and higher and lower pitch was indicated above or below the line. They served as a guide to memory and indicated whether the voice should go up or down, but not how far up or down it should go. The idea worked so well that soon another line was added; later, two more lines were added until, finally, another line was added, giving us the five line staff we use today. There soon came a need for the notation to indicate an exact time value, and, in the 13th century, three devices were invented: the dot, the coloration of notes, and time signatures. Circles, broken circles, and circles with dots in them corresponded to beats and rhythms of varying length.

These later evolved to form the notes, bars, measures, and the other features of musical notation with which we are familiar today.

Throughout this period, music remained closely associated with the Roman Catholic Church. The seat of the Church was first located in Rome, then in Constantinople, later returning to Rome. With the fall of Constantinople in 1204, its scholars, with their knowledge of Greek and Latin classics, traveled to Rome and Western Europe bringing with them the Hellenic alliance between music and drama. The Italian influence has left its mark on many of the musical terms we use today, including *allegro, andante,* and *legato.*

## B. The Art of Printing

Prior to the 16th century, musical manuscripts were arduously drafted and illuminated by hand, usually in monasteries and other places of learning. The diffusion of music received great aid from the art of printing, which commenced upon Gutenberg's invention of movable type in 1451. About a quarter of a century after the first bible came off Gutenberg's printing press, Ulrich Hahn, a German working in Rome at the time, became the first to print music. But it wasn't until 1501 that a serious business of printing music began in earnest when Ottavanio Petrucci, working in Venice, secured a monopoly for printing music in that city and became the first to print and distribute music on a full time basis. Other music printing concerns were soon established throughout Europe.

In the early 16th century, Winking de Worde published the first English songbook. In the mid-17th century, John Playford, a London publisher of several important books on musical theory, began to specialize in compiling, publishing, promoting and distributing nearly all the important songs composed in England during his time, and in doing so, became the forerunner to modern music publishing businesses.

In 1745, Johann Gottlob Immanuel Breitkopf labored to improve the methods of printing music. By introducing separate movable music type, he brought about a revolution in music printing by 1750. Johann Breitkopf's son, Christoph Gottlob, eventually inherited the publishing house, and transferred the business to his friend Gottfried Christoph Hartel. Hartel worked the business under the name Breitkopf and Hartel, publishing the works of Bach, Haydn, Mozart, Beethoven,

Chopin and others, and becoming the worlds largest publisher of orchestral music. Years later, Breitkopf and Hartel employed a French music publisher, Paul Heineke, sending him to the United States in 1917 to establish a New York office. Paul Heineke later established SESAC, the second performance rights society in the United States.

## C.  Printed Music Publishing in America

During most of the colonial era in America after 1607, the music used by colonists was imported from England. For many years, music was forbidden as a trade altogether in New England. The first book printed in the United States that contained musical notation was the ninth edition of *The Bay Psalm Book*, which contained thirteen songs borrowed from Playford's *Whole Book of Psalms* published in 1677.

In 1712, *The Art of Singing* by John Tufts, the first music instruction book published in America was distributed throughout the colonies. Containing thirty-seven songs, the Tuft's book was printed in many editions from its date of first publication through 1744.

In 1793, Benjamin Carr moved his family from England and established the first music publishing firm in the United States, printing chiefly music that had become popular in England. Other music publishers were established in many of the major cities on the eastern seaboard. With the development and increasing popularity of the piano, singing became a popular form of entertainment, and sales of printed sheet music began to flourish. It is estimated that, during the first 25 years of the 19th century, over 10,000 popular songs were published in the United States. By the end of the century, *After the Ball*, written and published by Charles K. Harris in 1893, became the first song to sell a million copies.

In 1880, after winning a toy printing press from school, Isadore, Julius and J. Witmark opened a printing business in their home on West 40th Street in New York City. They earned a modest living printing Christmas cards. To augment his earnings, Jay became a performer of ballads in minstrel and variety shows. After achieving some success, it suddenly occurred to Jay, if it were possible for him to establish hit songs for others, why couldn't he publish his own music? After all, Isadore could write songs, and they had a printing press on which to print the music. Since the brothers were still minors, they had their father, Marcus become director of the company, and thus,

M. Witmark & Sons was established in 1885 as a publisher and printer of sheet music.

Other music publishing firms soon opened their doors, and music publishers quickly developed innovative ways to increase the sale of their sheet music. A part time songwriter, Edward B. Marks established a publishing firm under that name. Marks discovered a way to promote his songs by performing them during the intermissions at variety houses while illustrated slides were flashed onto a white sheet screen. Tom Harms of T.B. Harms Music Publishing Company became the first music publisher to discover the profitability in printing sheet music of songs appearing in successful Broadway shows. M. Witmark & Sons was the first music publisher in America to pay singers to perform their songs. Shapiro - Remick & Company employed Jerome Kern to demonstrate their songs. Kern was soon hired by Max Dreyfus of T.B. Harms as a staff pianist to *plug* (i.e., promote) songs at various department stores.

Sales of sheet music soared. In the days before the advent of sound motion pictures, radio, and television, it was not unusual for a popular song to sell upwards of 2,000,000 copies in sheet music. The sale of sheet music was the primary income of a music publisher, unless the publisher enjoyed other income from operating a musical instrument store, producing musical productions, or managing artists. When sales of single copies of sheet music would slow down, publishers and songwriters looked for successful ways to promote their songs. Sometimes a song would become a hit as a result of a combination of fortuitous circumstances.

In 1919, while dining at Dinty Moore's, a fashionable restaurant on Broadway, Irving Caesar suggested to his dinner partner, George Gershwin, they collaborate on a "two-step" type song that was the trend in dancing at the time. George was enthusiastic and suggested they take a bus to his apartment and try their luck. George played a few notes on the piano and, as Irving told me, "The words rushed out at me with inspired spontaneity." The song was first introduced in a Ned Wayburn revue at the Capitol Theatre in New York. In the lobby of the theatre, George and Irving shouted to the departing audience, "Here it is, '*Swanee*,' get your copies, '*Swanee*.'" They did this night after night, but not one copy was sold. George and Irving having confidence in their creation begged their publisher, Max Dreyfus of

T.B. Harms, to promote the song by other means. Max told them he loved the song, but it was not "commercial" enough to sell sheet music. A few weeks later, Buddy DeSylva, a songwriter who had been discovered by Al Jolson, invited George and Irving to a post-midnight party. When George was playing the piano, and Buddy his ukulele, Buddy started to sing *Swanee*. Al Jolson quickly turned to his musical director and told him to arrange the song and put it in his new show. The song became a smash hit. Max Dreyfus finally published the song and orders for sheet music began pouring in. When George and Irving asked Dreyfus how much royalties they had earned, Max told them about $10,000, a huge sum at the time. A little embarrassed, Dreyfus offered the two an advance against prospective royalties from sheet music sales in England. Max bought George the baby grand piano he wanted and Irving settled for cash.

## D.  Print Music Publishing Today

At the turn of the century, most music publishing revenue was derived from the sale of printed music. With the increasing popularity of the phonograph, the advent of radio, sound motion pictures, or "talkies," and later the introduction of television, recordings of music replaced printed music notation as the primary source of music publishing revenue. Income from licensing the mechanical reproduction of music and performance of the resulting recordings soon eclipsed revenues from printed music to the point that, today, printed music represents only a small portion of a music publisher's income.

Traditionally, most printed music was sold in the form of *sheet* music, which contained the musical notation of a single song, and any accompanying lyrics. As the sales of printed music became a declining portion of music publishing income, modern music publishers continued to seek innovative ways to increase sales of printed music. This lead to the development of new forms of "packaging" of sheet music, such as in *personality folios* and *educational editions*, which are described below.

## II.  TYPES OF PRINTED MUSIC

Today, printed music is available in various forms, each suited to the particular needs of musical artists.

## A. Sheet Music

The traditional form of printed music is *sheet music*. Sheet music is generally one song printed on unbound sheets of paper, containing music and any accompanying lyrics. Sheet music is generally arranged for piano, vocal, and guitar.

## B. Folio

A *folio* is a compilation or anthology of sheet music bound into one, usually a soft cover volume. The songs may be written by various writers and recorded by various artists, but they are usually linked by a common theme, such as songs from the roaring twenties, famous movie themes, or songs of romance. Folios, sometimes referred to as *songbooks*, may contain editorial notes regarding the songs in the compilation or the theme of the anthology, related photographs, and similar materials. A songbook that contains a compilation of songs by various artists is called a *mixed folio*.

## C. Personality Folio

A *personality folio* is a folio consisting of songs written, recorded, or performed by the same artist or recording group, or written by the same songwriter. A personality folio may contain biographical material about the featured artist or group, as well as photographs. Such editions make the folio attractive even to fans who do not play an instrument, as many non-performing fans would purchase a personality folio just to obtain the photographs of their favorite artist or group. A personality folio that contains only the songs appearing on a particular record album is called a *companion folio*, or sometimes a *matching folio*.

## D. Instrument Folio

An *instrument folio* is a folio of compositions specially arranged for a particular musical instrument, such as a cello, harp, clarinet, oboe, recorder, tenor saxophone, alto saxophone, or violin.

## E. Music Instruction Books

A *music instruction book*, sometimes called a *method book*, is a book designed to provide instruction on a particular musical instrument. An instruction book may be designed for beginners, intermediate, or advanced players. For example, an instruction book for novices may be used by someone learning to play the clarinet for the first time. Another may be used by an accomplished musician desiring to learn advanced techniques in, or a certain style of, playing the saxophone.

## F.  Concert and Educational Editions

Sheet music and folios containing special arrangements for professional orchestras and other music groups are published in special editions called *concert editions*. These editions comprise one or more arrangements of popular music, symphonic music, chamber music, and music from Broadway shows, operas, and ballets. With the growth of school orchestras and marching bands, music publishers discovered a ready-made market for their sheet music. Special arrangements, called *educational editions*, were developed to accommodate various grades of young musicians from easy to play arrangements to the professional orchestrations prepared specifically for use by marching bands, jazz bands, and orchestras.

## G.  Fakebook

A *fakebook* is a folio containing hundreds of songs presented in very short arrangements. These books enabled a professional musician, who might not be familiar with a particular "request" from his audience, to *fake* the performance (i.e., improvise and render it as though the song was familiar) using merely the melody line presented in the fake book. Early fakebooks were illegal or *bootleg*, meaning they were compiled without the permission of the copyright owners. Fakebooks were compiled by musicians over the years and handed down, copied or sold on an informal basis. In recent years, music publishers, recognizing the demand for fakebooks, compiled and arranged "legal" fakebooks for commercial sale.

## III.  Preparation and Distribution of Printed Music

In the first half of this century, when a songwriter submitted a tune to his publisher, it was assumed that the composer would prepare his own lead sheet of the music. A *lead sheet* is one or two pages of lined music paper consisting of the notes of the melody on a single staff with chord indications written above and lyrics written below the notes. The music publisher would use the lead sheet to register the copyright in the song with the U.S. Copyright Office. The lead sheet was then used by the music publisher's professional staff as the basis for preparing a piano/vocal arrangement of the song to be used in the printing of sheet music.

In addition to using staff arrangers, publishers frequently engaged free lance arrangers to prepare these arrangements. Staff and freelance arrangers are normally engaged on a *work for hire* basis, meaning they are paid wages on a weekly basis or paid a flat fee per arrangement for their work and do not acquire any ownership interest in their work. Staff and freelance arrangers do not normally participate in any form of royalty payment, unless the arranger is engaged to add some substantial material to the composition, or the work performed includes special arrangements of compositions in the public domain, such as the works of Beethoven and Mozart.

At one time, I was one of such free lancers, and had the privilege of creating piano arrangements for the works of artists such as Paul Simon & Art Garfunkel and groups such as Jefferson Airplane. The preparation of piano/vocal arrangements for rock songs is no easy task.[1] I used to call upon my sons when they were young boys to help

---

[1] *Small Shots*
(The Arranger)
He sits in his corner with pencil in hand,
Arranging the music for concertos grand;
   Near-sighted, meek, but with songs in his heart,
   He lays out his work like a mariner's chart.
He never gets write ups, he never gets praise,
But works there unknown to the end of his days!
   Composers will give him but ten bars or more,
   And he must sit down and develop the score.
His arrangements may click, folks acclaim it as "hot"!
But does he get credit? Most certainly not!
   Composers will swagger and band-leaders strut,
   Accepting the praise for the work of this nut!
Alas, for the musical heydays of yore,
When composers of music arranged their own score;
   Arrangers today lead a life that is sad,
   They get naught if it's good, but catch h—
   if it's bad.

me discern virtually inaudible lyrics from rock recordings for which I was engaged to prepare piano arrangements. It was Paul Simon's desire that his compositions be arranged for sheet music publication as they were performed on his recordings. This I accomplished to his satisfaction by transposing the "sound" of his guitar to paper. While at that time one would need to play these arrangements on a harpsichord to get the feeling of a guitar sound, today all one would need use is an electronic keyboard.

While sheet music sales have declined over the years, many teachers of music have demanded copies of editions specially arranged for "beginners." The recent work of several talented arrangers, who have become known for their simplified editions, have breathed new life into the market for sheet music. Nevertheless, some rock and contemporary music artists unreasonably insist upon having their sheet music arranged exactly as it was recorded; the resulting arrangements are often difficult for the average home musician to play. These artists forget that, while the professional musician can use any musical notation to fake a performance in his own style, the amateur enthusiast has to play the music as it is printed. Both professional and amateur would be served if all sheet music were arranged in a simplified fashion.

Eminent composers, such as Vincent Youmans, Jerome Kern, and George Gershwin, and master film music composers, such as Max Steiner, Alfred Newman, and Erich Wolfgang Korngold, prepared their own piano arrangements and orchestrations, often with the help of talented arrangers such as, Hugo Friedhofer, but it is now extremely rare for a popular song composer to transcribe his music to paper. With the rock era, many artists and groups have emerged from the recording studio with hit records created by improvising the arrangement along the way, without the benefit of written material. Consequently, beginning about the 1950's, nearly all songs were submitted to publishers on records or audiotape and many publishers found it necessary to prepare their own lead sheets just to fulfill the requirements of copyright registration. Through the lobbying efforts of representatives of artists and composers, Congress was made aware that

---

—Nick Kenny, songwriter (Nick & Charles Kenny, *There's a Gold Mine in the Sky*) and columnist for the *N.Y. Daily Mirror.*

many contemporary artists were not able to write out their compositions in musical notation, and the copyright law they enacted in 1976 finally allowed songwriters to submit audiotape recordings to fulfill copyright deposit requirements.[2]

Not all songs, however, are adaptable to the medium of printed music. Stripped of the production values in the recording, many rock songs simply don't have enough melody to carry a useful piano/vocal arrangement. Even if a song has a melody or lyrics sufficiently meaningful to be rendered in printed form, sheet music would not normally be published unless the song has attained a certain "hit" status or is published with other songs, by the same artist, that have become well known hits.

## A. Independent Print Distributors

Today, of the thousands of independent music publishing companies, only a handful engage in the expensive business of printing, selling, and distributing printed music. Even some of the largest music publishers enter into special relationships with print publisher/distributors that specialize in printing and distributing music, such as Plymouth Music Co., Warner Bros. Publications, Inc., Hal Leonard and others. These print distributors distribute printed music through a network of wholesalers, called *rack jobbers*, retail print music dealers, educational dealers, retail stores where musical instruments are sold, booksellers, and other retail establishments.

Some publishers enter into exclusive arrangements with these print distributors for the printed publication of some or all of the songs in the publisher's catalog for a limited time. Under these arrangements, the publisher receives a royalty on the basis of the print distributor's sales. Similar arrangements are also made on a song-by-song basis.

Rather than granting exclusive print rights or a non-exclusive license to print music in return for a royalty, a music publisher may prefer to exercise its print rights through the use of a selling agent. Under this arrangement, the selling agent, usually a print publisher acting in an agency capacity, charges all printing, production, and distribution costs to the copyright owner, and pays over all its sales

---

[2] 17. U.S.C. Sec. 407(a)(2).

receipts directly to the copyright owner, deducting only a commission of about 25%.

The consolidation in the business of printed music has resulted from the decline in demand for printed music. But some advantages have resulted from this consolidation. For example, a print publisher who has relationships with several music publishers has the opportunity to cherry pick, from among the several catalogs for which it has print licenses, popular "hit" songs for inclusion in folios designed for maximum appeal.

# IV. PRINT RIGHTS

## A.  Granting Exclusive Print Rights

Exclusive print rights are generally granted in only the following limited contexts: (1) when a songwriter signs a publishing agreement in which he assigns his copyrights, and all rights under copyright, to a music publisher, and (2) when a music publisher grants to a print music distributor the exclusive right to print sheet music.

### 1.   Grants by Songwriters to Music Publishers

The terms and conditions under which songwriters contract with music publishers are fairly standard, subject to some negotiation depending upon the leverage or the star status of the writer. Standard songwriter publishing contracts provide that the songwriter assign his copyrights in the music, including exclusive print rights and all other rights under copyright, to the music publisher and sets forth royalty rates for each of the various categories of printed editions. The various techniques of negotiating these songwriter agreements on behalf of the songwriter are covered in Chapter 3, on *Songwriter Agreements* and in several excellent books on the music industry.[3]

---

[3] *For example, see,* S. Shemel & M. Krasilovsky, *This Business of Music* 8th Ed. (Watson-Guptill 2000); Passman, *All You Need to Know About the Music Business* (Simon & Schuster, 1997); and Brabec & Brabec, *Music, Money and Success* (Schirmer Books 1994).

With respect to print rights, writers customarily receive 5 to 7 cents per copy of sheet music sold in the United States and Canada and 50% of the sheet music royalties received by the music publisher for sales in other countries. The royalty for the use of music in folios is generally 10 to 15% of the wholesale selling price, pro rated among the various songs in the folio. Songwriters are advised to make certain that their contract requires that only *copyrighted royalty-bearing* works in the folio are used in computing his pro rata share. This is to prevent the royalty from being reduced by the inclusion in the folio of music in the public domain, such as the Star Spangled Banner and classical music from prior centuries. It would be reasonable, however, for a music publisher to insist that copyrighted arrangements of public domain songs upon which it must pay royalties should also be included in computing the writer's pro rata share.

Further, where the music publisher does not engage in the business of printing music and distributing printed music itself, choosing instead to grant rights or licenses to independent print publishers who carry on this business under a royalty arrangement with the publisher, the writer should carefully negotiate provisions that assure that a fair portion of the income derived by the music publisher flows through to the writer.

In general, songwriters should not expect much results from hard line negotiations on terms regarding print rights and royalties. Sales of printed music no longer have the financial significance they once enjoyed, and songwriters, rather than struggle over meaningless royalty percentages, should instead devote their energies toward encouraging the music publisher to effect the printing of at least a sheet music edition of their musical compositions. Leaving aside the sentimental value to the songwriter's posterity, printed music can be quite useful in promoting the song to orchestras, bands, and perhaps other artists who might be persuaded to make further recordings of the song. The late songwriter Ben Oakland (*Java Jive*, *If I Love Again*) once befriended and supplied sheet music to the person who played the organ at a professional ballpark. Sure enough, every once in a while one of Ben's songs could be heard on national television during the broadcast of a baseball game, making the song eligible for important performance credits.

Certain agreements between composers of film music and motion picture companies require that the main theme be printed in order for the elected publisher to claim any publishing rights to the composer's music.

## 2.   Grants by Music Publishers to Print Music Distributors

Music publishers will rarely grant print rights on an exclusive basis. In the few cases that exclusivity is granted, it is normally limited to the printing of sheet music. Permission to print single songs in folios will almost always be on a non-exclusive basis, as publishers desire to remain free to negotiate the use of major songs in folios published by competing print publishers.

Print publishers might require some form of exclusivity in the case of personality folios. For example, a print publisher might acquire a license from a rock star and his publishing company to publish a folio of the star's greatest hits (e.g., "The Elton John Songbook") or may acquire a license to publish a companion folio, a folio of all the songs written and recorded by the artist for a particular album. In such cases, the print publisher would normally insist that the copyright owner not license the same songs for inclusion in a similar songbook or song-book having a confusingly similar title (e.g., "Elton John's Greatest Hits").

Where exclusivity is granted, the music publisher should be certain to reserve (i.e., exclude from the exclusivity) the right to license printed versions of the lyrics, a subject discussed in more detail later in this chapter, and the right to license materials akin to printed music, such as MIDI files, discussed in Chapter 22.

In exchange for granting the exclusive rights to print sheet music, the copyright owner will normally receive from the print publisher a royalty of some fixed number of cents per copy. To participate in price increases, the owner should consider requiring a percentage of the suggested retail or wholesale price in lieu of a fixed amount per copy. The print publisher assumes the costs of production, printing and distribution. The copyright owner usually receives an *advance* against royalties upon the signing of the contract. Should a copyright owner grant print rights to various songs under separate contracts which each provide for an advance against royalties, the owner should consider making sure that these advances are not *cross-collateralized*.[4]

---

[4] The concepts of *advances* and *cross-collateralization* are discussed in Chapter 10.

The territory of exclusive sheet music contracts is generally limited to the United States and Canada. Music copyright owners will enter into separate arrangements with subpublishers overseas for the publication of printed editions. These arrangements are discussed in Chapter 5 on *International Subpublishing*. Nevertheless, print deals are beginning to reflect the challenges arising from a changing world marketplace, where printing is being effected in one country in multiple languages for shipment world-wide.

The term of these agreements is generally from three to five years. With respect to agreements with a longer term, a copyright owner would be prudent to include in the agreement minimum sales or royalty performance levels. If the print publisher does not achieve the prescribed level in any given year, the original publisher should have the option to convert the agreement to a non-exclusive basis or terminate the agreement altogether. Upon termination, the print publisher is generally given, on a non-exclusive basis, a period of six to twelve months to sell off its existing inventory. The agreement should provide, however, that the print publisher may only print enough copies to meet reasonably anticipated demand. This is to prevent the printer from manufacturing a large inventory just prior to termination for the purpose of "stuffing the channel" during the sell-off period.

The copyright owner granting exclusive print rights should also require the print publisher to print regular sheet music copies of the composition during the term of the agreement and to pay all cost of preparation, production, art work, arranging and engraving.

## V. PRINT LICENSES

### A. Granting Non-Exclusive Licenses to Print Music in Folios

As previously noted, print publishers who have relationships with several music copyright owner/publishers have taken the opportunity to cherry pick popular "hit" songs for inclusion in folios designed for maximum appeal. Many print publishers have increased the sale of slow selling or older standard songs by programming material in specialized compilations such as, Music of the Roaring Twenties, Hit Songs of 1950, and compilations of well-known country and western songs. For this reason, it would be prudent for music copyright owners to reserve to themselves their exclusive rights to authorize the printing of music in folios in order to take advantage of the opportunity to license its compositions in these forms of compilations, on a non-exclusive basis, to as many print publishers and selling agents as possible.

Music copyright owners considering a license to permit the use of a song in a folio or songbook, should attempt to limit the scope of the license to the specific use requested. For example, if a print publisher desires to clear the license to use a single song in a particular folio, the license should identify the folio by name or description and should expressly state that the song may be used solely in the particular folio named or described. Many standard form agreements for the licensing of a single song in folios will contain a broad grant to use the music in any kind of folio during the term of the license. Of course, the licensee would strongly desire the flexibility afforded by this broader form of license.

The royalty for including a song in a folio is customarily 12.5% of the suggested retail selling price of the songbook, pro rated based upon the number of copyrighted songs in the folio. For example, if there are 10 songs in the folio and the suggested retail price of the folio is $10, a publisher that licensed 2 songs for the folio would receive one-fifth of $10 multiplied by 12.5%, or 25 cents per copy sold, less returns. The copyright owner should be certain that the pro rata share is calculated only on the basis of the number of copyrighted songs in the folio, which would prevent the inclusion of public domain works in the folio from reducing the royalty payable. The print publisher should make certain it is clear that copyrighted arrangements of public domain works upon which it must pay royalties should be included in the pro ration.

Personality folios will probably require the permission of the artist featured in the folio, particularly if biographical material or the artist's likeness or photograph are depicted in the folio. Artists typically demand a royalty of an additional 5% of the suggested retail price for such uses. Many contemporary artists refuse to grant permission for the publication of personality folios. Some artists, who have extensive consent provisions in their music publishing contracts, flatly refuse to allow the licensing of their songs in folios of any form. Artists who place such restrictions on the use of their music are being shortsighted and will someday regret making decisions that tend to sever the important relationship between the song and the listening public.

## B.  Granting and Clearing Licenses to Print Lyrics

### 1.  Books

Quoting a song lyric in a book, such as a novel, biography, or other work, requires permission from the copyright owner of the song. The use of a lyric is not, as some may believe, a *fair use* of copyright, which is a use that would not require permission of the copyright owner. Fair use is limited to some fairly specific circumstances defined in the copyright law,[5] such as criticism, news reporting, teaching, or research. Quotation of a lyric, or a portion of a lyric, in a book or magazine for commercial sale would not qualify for the fair use exception. If you have any doubt whether the fair use exception applies, then you should seek a license.

Music publishers will frequently receive calls for permission to use or quote a song lyric, and, if he controls the rights, will usually have no reluctance to granting such a license. Music publishers should not overlook the earnings potential of licensing lyrics of a song. The fees may be small, but they add up, and more important, it is a good way of keeping the song alive. Requests are often received for permission to use lyrics in text books, particularly History and English books, many of which take the opportunity to print an entire lyric by Bob Dylan or Joni Mitchell to illustrate a modern form of poetry or the mood of the country during the 1960's.

Music publishers generally grant these licenses using a short-form permission letter. An example of such a letter is included as Form 11.5 at the end of this chapter. Book publishers sometimes make release forms available to its authors to facilitate the clearance of permission to use quotes. Whatever the form used to effect them, such licenses are generally not expensive. The copyright owner will normally charge a small flat fee for the use of a lyric in a book and may require two copies of the book upon publication. For the current fees typically charged for such uses, see Chapter 27.

---

[5] 17 U.S.C. Sec. 107; *see also,* the discussion of the fair use doctrine in Chapter 25.

The license is usually limited to using the lyric in one single hard cover edition of the book and its reprints, with additional payments required for paperback editions, translations, abridgments, and editions published by other firms. Fees are normally a one-time, flat fee, which is sometimes limited to the first 100,000 copies or some such negotiated arrangement. The territory is usually world-wide, but remember, additional permission is required for translated versions.

The privilege to use the lyric in other editions would require additional permission and fees. Persons seeking to clear these licenses who expect that permission for use in paperback editions, translations, abridgments, and other editions will be required should attempt to negotiate, in advance, options to pick up permission for these other editions or otherwise ask whether a license for all editions can be paid in advance. The publisher would be reluctant to issue such a license because of the ambiguity of the term "editions," but language such as "edition in book form" might be suggested to provide the comfort required by both parties.

An option arrangement may be more difficult to attain with respect to foreign language editions. Music publishers generally require that licenses for editions printed overseas be sought directly from its affiliated overseas subpublishing company.

### 2. Record Albums

Since the turbulent 1960's, with its new forms of rock and psychedelic music, a disturbing number of rock, hard rock, heavy metal and rap songs have been released with lyrics containing offensive, indecent, or violent language. Unsuspecting disc jockeys, after programming and broadcasting these recordings, would became inundated with telephone calls from angry listeners protesting their broadcast. As a result, radio station program directors began requesting that record companies furnish a copy of the lyrics for each new single or album recording submitted for broadcast. Record companies, in turn, began asking music publishers to grant licenses or permission for these lyric reprints.

Many record albums recorded by popular contemporary artists now include a printed set of the lyrics of all the songs on the album, and it has become a standard practice for music publishers to grant permission for this use either for a small royalty or on a *gratis* (i.e., no charge) basis. An example of a permission letter used for this purpose is set forth as Form 11.6 at the end of this chapter.

In cases where the lyrics are not printed on the album, publishers will grant a gratis license to record companies permitting them to distribute printed copies of the lyrics in conjunction with the distribution of promotional copies of the album. An example of a permission letter used for this purpose is set forth as Form 11.7 at the end of this chapter. Many recording companies now request such permission when they submit requests for mechanical licenses, discussed in the next chapter.

### 3.  Lyric Magazines

Permission to print entire lyrics are sought by publishers of magazines specially devoted to printing song lyrics. Examples of licenses permitting such use are set forth as Forms 11.8, 11.9, and 11.10 at the end of this chapter.

### 4.  Print Advertising

Licensing lyrics for use in print advertising involves many of the same considerations in licensing music in connection with advertising in general, which is discussed in great detail in Chapter 20. A form for the license of lyrics for use in print advertising is included as Form 20.3 at the end of Chapter 20.

### 5.  Internet Web Sites

A new use and source of music publishing income has arisen with the emergence of the electronic publication of "sheet music."

As discussed in Chapter 23, it appears the transmission from a Web server to individual computers on the Internet of musical notation or lyrics constitutes a public display of the musical work. By virtue of the copyright owner's exclusive right to publicly display its music, a public display license from the copyright owner will be required for the publication of musical notation or lyrics on web sites. None of the performance rights societies have the right to license *public displays* of their members' music (i.e., they only have the right to license public performances). Thus, these public display licenses must be acquired directly from the music publishers of the music notation or lyrics being transmitted for public display. In addition, to the extent a copy of the notation or lyrics are being "fixed" at the receiving end of the display— which would appear always to be the case, as copying into RAM has been held to be a fixation—then a *reproduction license* will also be required. Again, this license would be obtained from the appropriate music publishers.

Because the public display and reproduction of lyrics and musical notation by means of electronic transmission is a relatively new phenomenon, it is not likely that very many music publishers have had much experience in establishing the terms and conditions of these licenses. No standards have emerged as of the time of this writing, but the Harry Fox Agency is likely to develop a form for this new form of use. In addition, though we have not seen music publishers make a distinction between an exercise of the public display right and the exercise of the reproduction right, insofar as the posting of "electronic sheet music" on web sites is concerned, publishers are beginning to quote motion picture companies flat fees for the posting of lyrics on web sites in connection with the promotion of the motion pictures in which the lyrics appear. See Chapter 27 for current rates.

# Appendix to Chapter 11
## Print Licenses

# FORM 11.1

## EXCLUSIVE PRINT RIGHTS AGREEMENT FOR ALL PRINTED EDITIONS OF A SINGLE SONG

### SINGLE SONG PRINTED MUSIC
### PUBLISHING AGREEMENT

AGREEMENT made effective January 1, 2000 by and between

LITTLE MUSIC PUBLISHING COMPANY
c/o Joseph Schmoe, Esq.
123 West 45th Street
New York, NY 10019

(hereinafter referred to as "Owner") and

OLD MUSIC PRINT PUBLISHER, INC.
1000 Sunset Boulevard
Hollywood, CA 90069

(hereinafter referred to as "Publisher").

THE PARTIES HEREBY AGREE AS FOLLOWS:

1.    Owner hereby grants to Publisher, its successors, assigns, affiliates, subsidiaries and licensees the sole and exclusive right during the term hereof, to print, sell and distribute in bound or unbound editions or forms, singly or together with such other compositions and contents as may be selected by Publisher, at Publisher's sole cost and expense, the copyrighted musical composition entitled:

Title: "I'LL LOVE YOU TILL YOU LEAVE ME"

Composer(s):

Copyright Notice: Copyright © 1980 LITTLE MUSIC PUBLISHING CO.

(which composition is for convenience hereinafter referred to as the "Subject Composition") in any and all arrangements and adaptations thereof as Publisher may elect, throughout the world (hereinafter referred to as the "Licensed Territory"), and to sell the same at such prices and on whatever terms, conditions and discounts as Publisher may in its sole discretion determine from time to time.

2.  In full consideration for all rights, licenses and privileges granted to Publisher hereunder and for all warranties, representations and agreements herein made by Owner, Publisher agrees to pay to Owner the following royalties:

(a)  A sum of seven cents ($.07) per copy in respect of regular sheet music (piano-vocal) sold and paid for. Notwithstanding the foregoing, Publisher shall pay Owner no less than a sum equal to twenty percent (20%) of the marked retail selling price ("MRSP") per copy in respect of net sales of regular sheet music (piano-vocal) editions. (As used in this agreement, "net sales' refers to copies sold and paid for and not returned.)

(b)  In the event the Subject Composition is included in any folio, song book or similar publication containing musical compositions or other musical materials in addition to the Subject Composition, a sum equal to a proportionate part of twelve and one-half percent (12.5%) of the MRSP on net sales of such work.

(c)  In the event the Subject Composition is sold in a pedagogical edition or an instrumental, orchestral, choral, band or other arrangement, a sum equal to ten percent (10%) of the MRSP on net sales of such work, or a proportionate share thereof if included with other copyrighted musical materials that are not subject hereto.

(d)    A sum equal to fifty percent (50%) of sums actually received by Publisher from third party licensees.

3.    (a)    With respect to all sums which may be received by Publisher derived from sales of copies of the Subject composition, Publisher shall, subject to a reasonable reserve against returns (not to exceed forty percent (40%), which reserve shall be liquidated on the accounting statement for the accounting period next following the accounting period in respect of which such reserve is established), within sixty (60) days after the last days of June and December of each year, prepare and furnish statements to Owner, and each such statement shall be accompanied by a check or checks in payment of any and all sums shown to be due thereby. Each such statement shall be binding on Owner and not subject to any objection for any reason, unless specific objection in writing, setting forth the basis thereof, is given to Publisher by Owner within two (2) years from the date rendered.

(b)    To the extent that Owner is paid therefor by Publisher, Owner hereby agrees to pay the writer(s) of the Subject Composition all moneys payable to writer(s) from Owner's receipts hereunder and further agrees to hold Publisher free and harmless from and against any claims of any writer(s) of the Subject Composition.

4.    (a)    Publisher agrees to keep and maintain full and complete books and records concerning the subject matter hereof; and Owner shall have the right to examine Publisher's books and records at Publisher's place of business in Los Angeles, California during its normal business hours and upon reasonable notice to verify the correctness of accounting statements rendered hereunder, within two (2) years, in each instance, after the rendition of the subject accounting statement.

(b)    Legal action with respect to a specific accounting statement or the accounting period to which the same relates shall be forever barred if not commenced in a court of competent jurisdiction within two (2) years following the rendition of such statement.

5.    Owner shall furnish Publisher with all necessary copyright information, an accurate lead sheet and a copy of the original commercial phonograph recording of the Subject Composition. Owner hereby approves Publisher's use of the copyright information as contained on the lead sheet furnished. Owner shall also furnish Publisher with recent photographs of the artists who perform the Subject Composition on such phonograph record and Owner shall use its best efforts to obtain all necessary consents permitting Publisher to use such photographs free of charge in and in connection with the copies of the Subject Composition printed by Publisher.

6.    (a)    Owner warrants and represents that it has the full right, power and authority to enter into and to perform this agreement, and that no part of the Subject Composition infringes upon any rights of any other party.

(b)    Owner shall indemnify Publisher and hold Publisher harmless from and against any and all loss, damage, cost or expense (including court costs and reasonable attorneys' fees) due to a breach of any such warranty or representation and/or Owner's failure to pay royalties to writers, co-publishers or income participants with respect to amounts paid to Owner by Publisher hereunder. Publisher shall give Owner prompt notice of any claim, action or proceeding to which the foregoing indemnity relates, and Owner shall have the right to participate in the defense thereof by counsel of Owner's choice, at Owner's sole cost and expense. In the event of a claim, action or proceeding covered by this indemnity, Publisher shall have the right to withhold from moneys otherwise becoming due to Owner hereunder an amount reasonably related to the scope of Owner's indemnity with respect thereto, unless (and to the extent that) Owner shall provide Publisher with a commercial surety bond issued by a company, and in a form, reasonably satisfactory to Publisher. Any amount so withheld shall be released if (and to the extent that) legal action is not commenced with respect thereto within one (1) year following such with-holding.

7. The term of this Agreement shall commence on the date hereof and continue for a period of five (5) years from and after the date hereof and shall continue thereafter for additional periods of one (1) year, unless and until terminated by either party by giving notice, by registered mail, return receipt requested, not less than ninety (90) days prior to the end of the then current period. Owner agrees that notwithstanding such termination Publisher shall have a non-exclusive license as of the end of the term hereof to market, sell, authorize the continued sale or otherwise dispose of any and all copies (as well as subsequent returns with respect to prior sales) of all editions throughout the Licensed Territory until stocks are exhausted ("sell-off period"). All sales during the sell-off period shall be in the ordinary course of business and shall not be at "close-out", or "distress" prices.

8. (a) Any arrangement which Publisher shall cause to be made of the Subject Composition shall be made at Publisher's expense and shall be created only as the result of employment-for-hire, and such arrangement shall be a "Work Made For Hire" as such term is used in the United States Copyright Law, and all copyrights therein and all renewals, extensions and reversions thereof throughout the world shall be owned by the copyright owner of the Subject Composition, subject to Publisher's use under this agreement.

(b) Publisher agrees to imprint the copyright notice submitted by Owner on each copy of every printed publication of the Subject Composition hereunder, in compliance with the formalities of the United States Copyright Law and of the Universal Copyright Convention as well as imprint under such copyright notice the legend "All Rights Reserved." Any such printed publication not containing such copyright notice shall be deemed to have been published without the permission or authorization of Owner; provided, that in the event of an inadvertent omission of such notice, such omission shall be deemed a breach of contract only and not an infringement of copyright (and Owner's sole remedy therefor shall be in damages).

9. (a) Any written notice, statement, payment or matter required or desired to be given to Owner or Publisher pursuant to this agreement shall be given by addressing the same to the addresses of the respective parties referred to above, or to such other address as either party may hereafter designate, in writing, to the other party, and on the date when same shall be sent by registered or certified (return receipt requested) mail, (provided that any royalty statement may be sent by regular mail), or on the date when delivered, so addressed, toll prepaid, to a telegraph or cable company, or on the date when same shall be delivered to the other party personally or to his duly authorized agent (as designated in writing), such notice shall be deemed to have been duly made pursuant hereto.

(b) Except where expressly provided herein, the consent or approval of a party shall not be unreasonably withheld, and shall be deemed to have been given unless notice of disapproval or nonconsent shall be given by such party within ten (10) days following notice from the other party requesting such consent or approval.

10. Publisher shall not be deemed to be in breach hereunder unless Owner shall notify Publisher thereof in the manner prescribed herein and Publisher shall fail to remedy such alleged breach within thirty (30) days after receiving such notice (unless the alleged breach is of such a nature that it cannot practicably be completely remedied within such thirty-day period, in which event Publisher shall be deemed to have timely remedied such alleged breach if Publisher commences to do so within such thirty-day period and proceeds to complete the remedying thereof within a reasonable time thereafter).

11. This agreement constitutes the full and complete understanding and agreement of the parties and it shall not be

amended, modified or altered in any respect, except by an instrument in writing, executed by both parties hereto.

12. This agreement shall be deemed made in, and is to be construed and interpreted in accordance with the laws of, the State of California.

IN WITNESS WHEREOF, the parties hereto have executed this agreement as of the year and date first above written.

LITTLE MUSIC PUBLISHING COMPANY

By_____
Federal I.D. #:
S.S. #:

OLD PRINT MUSIC PUBLISHER, INC.

By_____

# FORM 11.2

## NON-EXCLUSIVE PRINT LICENSE FOR USE OF A SINGLE SONG IN A PARTICULAR FOLIO

### SINGLE SONG PRINTED MUSIC LICENSE AGREEMENT

AGREEMENT made effective January 1, 2000 by and between

**LITTLE MUSIC PUBLISHING COMPANY**
c/o Joseph Schmoe, Esq.
123 West 45th Street
New York, NY 10019

(hereinafter referred to as "Owner") and

**OLD MUSIC PRINT PUBLISHER, INC.**
1000 Sunset Boulevard
Hollywood, CA 90069

(hereinafter referred to as "Publisher").

THE PARTIES HEREBY AGREE AS FOLLOWS:

1.    Owner hereby grants to Publisher, its successors, assigns, affiliates, subsidiaries and licensees a non-exclusive license during the term hereof, to print, sell and distribute in the bound edition, with such other compositions and contents as may be selected by Publisher, at Publisher's sole cost and expense, the copyrighted musical composition entitled:

Title: "I'LL LOVE YOU TILL YOU LEAVE ME"

Composer(s):

Copyright Notice: Copyright © 1980 LITTLE MUSIC PUBLISHING CO.

(which composition is for convenience hereinafter referred to as the "Subject Composition") in any and all arrangements and adaptations thereof as Publisher may elect, throughout the world (hereinafter referred to as the "Licensed Territory"), for use solely in a music folio entitled:

Folio Title: "LOVE SONGS"

(hereinafter, the "Folio") and to sell the same at such prices and on whatever terms, conditions and discounts as Publisher may in its sole discretion determine from time to time.

2. In full consideration for all rights, licenses and privileges granted to Publisher hereunder and for all warranties, representations and agreements herein made by Owner, Publisher agrees to pay to Owner a sum equal to a proportionate part of twelve and one-half percent (12.5%) of the marked retail selling price ("MRSP") on net sales of the Folio which the number of compositions bears to the total number of copyrighted compositions, and copyrighted arrangements of public domain works for which royalties are payable, contained in the Folio. (As used in this agreement, "net sales' refers to copies sold and paid for and not returned.) Upon execution hereof, Publisher agrees to pay Owner the sum of $_____ as a non-returnable, recoupable advance against royalties payable hereunder.

3. (a) With respect to all sums which may be received by Publisher derived from sales of copies of the Subject Composition, Publisher shall, subject to a reasonable reserve against returns (not to exceed forty percent (40%), which reserve shall be liquidated on the accounting statement for the accounting period next following the accounting period in respect of which such reserve is established), within sixty (60) days after the last days of June and December of each year, prepare and furnish statements to Owner, and each such statement shall be accompanied by a check or checks in payment of any and all sums shown to be due thereby. Each such statement shall be binding on Owner and not subject to any objection for any reason, unless specific objection in writing, setting forth the basis thereof,

is given to Publisher by Owner within two (2) years from the date rendered.

(b)     To the extent that Owner is paid therefor by Publisher, Owner hereby agrees to pay the writer(s) of the Subject Composition all moneys payable to writer(s) from Owner's receipts hereunder and further agrees to hold Publisher free and harmless from and against any claims of any writer(s) of the Subject Composition.

4.     (a)     Publisher agrees to keep and maintain full and complete books and records concerning the subject matter hereof; and Owner shall have the right to examine Publisher's books and records at Publisher's place of business in Los Angeles, California during its normal business hours and upon reasonable notice to verify the correctness of accounting statements rendered hereunder, within two (2) years, in each instance, after the rendition of the subject accounting statement.

(b)     Legal action with respect to a specific accounting statement or the accounting period to which the same relates shall be forever barred if not commenced in a court of competent jurisdiction within two (2) years following the rendition of such statement.

5.     Owner shall furnish Publisher with all necessary copyright information, an accurate lead sheet and a copy of the original commercial phonograph recording of the Subject Composition. Owner hereby approves Publisher's use of the copyright information as contained on the lead sheet furnished. Owner shall also furnish Publisher with recent photographs of the artists who perform the Subject Composition on such phonograph record and Owner shall use its best efforts to obtain all necessary consents permitting Publisher to use such photographs free of charge in and in connection with the copies of the Subject Composition printed by Publisher.

6. (a) Owner warrants and represents that it has the full right, power and authority to enter into and to perform this agreement, and that no part of the Subject Composition infringes upon any rights of any other party.

(b) Owner shall indemnify Publisher and hold Publisher harmless from and against any and all loss, damage, cost or expense (including court costs and reasonable attorneys' fees) due to a breach of any such warranty or representation and/or Owner's failure to pay royalties to writers, co-publishers or income participants with respect to amounts paid to Owner by Publisher hereunder. Publisher shall give Owner prompt notice of any claim, action or proceeding to which the foregoing indemnity relates, and Owner shall have the right to participate in the defense thereof by counsel of Owner's choice, at Owner's sole cost and expense. In the event of a claim, action or proceeding covered by this indemnity, Publisher shall have the right to withhold from moneys otherwise becoming due to Owner hereunder an amount reasonably related to the scope of Owner's indemnity with respect thereto, unless (and to the extent that) Owner shall provide Publisher with a commercial surety bond issued by a company, and in a form, reasonably satisfactory to Publisher. Any amount so withheld shall be released if (and to the extent that) legal action is not commenced with respect thereto within one (1) year following such withholding.

7. The term of this Agreement shall commence on the date hereof and continue for a period of three (3) years from and after the date hereof. Owner agrees that notwithstanding such termination Publisher shall have a non-exclusive license as of the end of the term hereof to market, sell, authorize the continued sale or otherwise dispose of any and all copies (as well as subsequent returns with respect to prior sales) of all editions throughout the Licensed Territory until stocks are exhausted ("sell-off period"). All sales during the sell-off period shall be in the ordinary course of business and shall not be at "close-out", or "distress" prices.

8.    (a)    Any arrangement which Publisher shall cause to be made of the Subject Composition shall be made at Publisher's expense and shall be created only as the result of employment-for-hire, and such arrangement shall be a "Work Made For Hire" as such term is used in the United States Copyright Law, and all copyrights therein and all renewals, extensions and reversions thereof throughout the world shall be owned by the copyright owner of the Subject Composition, subject to Publisher's use under this agreement.

(b)    Publisher agrees to imprint the copyright notice submitted by Owner on each copy of every printed publication of the Subject Composition hereunder, in compliance with the formalities of the United States Copyright Law and of the Universal Copyright Convention as well as imprint under such copyright notice the legend "All Rights Reserved." Any such printed publication not containing such copyright notice shall be deemed to have been published without the permission or authorization of Owner; provided, that in the event of an inadvertent omission of such notice, such omission shall be deemed a breach of contract only and not an infringement of copyright (and Owner's sole remedy therefor shall be in damages).

9.    (a)    Any written notice, statement, payment or matter required or desired to be given to Owner or Publisher pursuant to this agreement shall be given by addressing the same to the addresses of the respective parties referred to above, or to such other address as either party may hereafter designate, in writing, to the other party, and on the date when same shall be sent by registered or certified (return receipt requested) mail, (provided that any royalty statement may be sent by regular mail), or on the date when delivered, so addressed, toll prepaid, to a telegraph or cable company, or on the date when same shall be delivered to the other party personally or to his duly authorized agent (as designated in writing), such notice shall be deemed to have been duly made pursuant hereto.

(b)    Except where expressly provided herein, the consent or approval of a party shall not be unreasonably withheld, and shall be deemed to have been given unless notice of disapproval or nonconsent shall be given by such party within ten (10) days following notice from the other party requesting such consent or approval.

10.     Publisher shall not be deemed to be in breach hereunder unless Owner shall notify Publisher thereof in the manner prescribed herein and Publisher shall fail to remedy such alleged breach within thirty (30) days after receiving such notice (unless the alleged breach is of such a nature that it cannot practicably be completely remedied within such thirty-day period, in which event Publisher shall be deemed to have timely remedied such alleged breach if Publisher commences to do so within such thirty-day period and proceeds to complete the remedying thereof within a reasonable time thereafter).

11.     This agreement constitutes the full and complete understanding and agreement of the parties and it shall not be amended, modified or altered in any respect, except by an instrument in writing, executed by both parties hereto.

12.     This agreement shall be deemed made in, and is to be construed and interpreted in accordance with the laws of, the State of California.

IN WITNESS WHEREOF, the parties hereto have executed this agreement as of the year and date first above written.

LITTLE MUSIC PUBLISHING COMPANY

By _____

Federal I.D. #:
S.S. #:

OLD PRINT MUSIC PUBLISHER, INC.

By _____

# FORM 11.3

## EXCLUSIVE PRINT RIGHTS AGREEMENT FOR USE OF ALL COMPOSITIONS OF A MUSICAL GROUP

GROUP PRINT AGREEMENT

AGREEMENT made effective January 1, 2000 by and between

FAMOUS RECORDING GROUP RIGHTS EXPLOITATION
COMPANY, INC.
FAMOUS RECORDING GROUP MUSIC PUBLISHING
COMPANY
c/o Joseph Schmoe, Esq.
123 West 45th Street
New York, NY 10019

(hereinafter referred to as "Owner") and

OLD MUSIC PRINT PUBLISHER, INC.
1000 Sunset Boulevard
Hollywood, CA 90069

(hereinafter referred to as "Publisher").

THE PARTIES HEREBY AGREE AS FOLLOWS:

1.    (a)    Owner hereby grants to Publisher (except as hereinafter provided) the sole and exclusive right, license and privilege to print, publish and sell during the term of this Agreement, or to license to parties in and throughout the territory hereinafter specified, the "Subject Compositions" (as such term is hereinafter defined), in any and all editions as determined by Publisher, including folios, song books, sheet music and other printed publications of the Subject Compositions, and each of them upon such terms, prices and conditions as Publisher may determine in its sole discretion or to refrain therefrom. Without

limiting the generality of the foregoing, Publisher's said rights shall include the right to print, publish, sell and distribute folios and song books containing the Subject Compositions with musical material that is not subject hereto and Publisher's said rights furthermore include the right to print, publish, sell and distribute instrumental versions of the Subject Compositions or lyrics of the Subject Compositions only, alone or in combination with musical material that is not subject hereto.

(b)     In connection with the foregoing, Owner hereby grants to Publisher a non-exclusive license to use the name of all present and future members of the group known as _____ ("Artist"), along with photographs, likenesses of and biographical material relating to said Artist, on printed publications hereunder as determined by Publisher and in connection with the advertising, promotion and sale of the same. Publisher shall not use any photographs or likeness of Artist unless same have been submitted to Publisher by Owner or prepared by Publisher, in which event they will require approval by Owner within five (5) working days (which approval shall not be unreasonably withheld).

(c)     Notwithstanding the above, Publisher shall have the right to use the Subject Compositions in a folio containing some or all of the Subject Compositions along with other material performed by Artist, which folio is solely associated with and features only the Artist, along with photographs, likenesses of and biographical material relating to the Artist (any such folio to be called a "Personality Folio"), or to license third parties to use Subject Compositions in "mixed" folios, as that term is generally understood in the music publishing business. The right to issue a "Personality Folio" shall remain exclusive with Publisher during the term of this Agreement, as shall all other rights granted Publisher hereunder.

2.     The term of this Agreement shall be five (5) years from and after the date hereof and shall continue thereafter from year to year until terminated by either party by written notice at least

ninety (90) days prior to the end of any such annual period; Publisher's territory hereunder is world-wide.

3.    Subject Compositions shall include each and every musical composition set forth below or on Schedule "A" attached hereto and by this reference made a part hereof. The Subject Compositions hereunder shall furthermore include all musical compositions owned, administered or controlled, directly or indirectly, in whole or in part, by Owner during the term of this agreement, and any and all arrangements and any and all versions of each and every Subject Composition.

4.    Owner represents and warrants that it has the right to enter into this Agreement and to grant all of the rights granted and to be granted to Publisher hereunder and the Publisher's exercise of said rights shall not infringe upon the copyright or other property or contractual or other rights of or constitute unfair competition with or be an invasion of privacy or infringement of the right of publicity of any other person, firm or corporation.

5.    Publisher agrees to pay Owner the following sums in respect of the Subject Compositions, payable as hereinafter provided:

(a)    A sum equal to twelve and one-half (12-1/2%) percent of the suggested retail selling price of folios, song books, legitimate fake books and other publications containing Subject Compositions solely and entirely in respect of all copies of such work sold and paid for.

(b)    In the event any Subject Composition is included in any folio, song book or other publication containing musical compositions or other musical materials that are not subject hereto, then in respect to each such work Publisher shall pay Owner a proportionate share of a royalty of twelve and one-half (12-1/2%) percent of the suggested retail selling price for all copies of such work sold and paid for. Owner's share of said royalty shall be based on the ratio that Subject Compositions contained in each such work bear to the total number of musical compositions included therein.

(c)    A sum equivalent to $.35 per copy in respect to each copy for regular piano/vocal sheet music sold and paid for in the United States and Canada for which the retail selling price shall be $1.50 or more.

For regular piano/vocal sheet music sold and paid for in the United States and Canada which retails for less than $1.50 per copy, a sum equivalent to 30% of the retail selling price.

For regular piano/vocal sheet music sold and paid for outside the territories of the United States and Canada, a sum equivalent to 50% of the moneys received by us in the United States from the sale of such editions in such territories.

(d)    In the event any Subject Composition is sold in an instrumental, orchestral, choral, band or other arrangement, Publisher shall pay Owner a royalty of ten (10%) percent of the suggested retail selling price for all copies of such work sold and paid for.

(e)    Publisher shall pay to Owner a sum equal to five (5%) percent of the suggested retail selling price of each "Personality Folio" containing Subject Compositions solely and entirely along with the name of the Artist and photographs, likenesses of and biographical material relating to the Artist, said payments to constitute full and complete compensation for the rights granted in Paragraph 1 (b) above, all in respect of copies of such "Personality Folios" sold and paid for. In the event any "Personality Folio" contains compositions other than Subject Compositions, Owner's share of the royalty provided for in this paragraph shall be based upon the ratio that Subject Compositions contained in each such "Personality Folio" bear to the total number of musical compositions included therein.

(f)    With respect to any sales to or licenses to musical instrument manufacturers for publications which are not to be sold at retail and bear no retail selling price (i.e., sum of royalties) shall be made at the royalty rate provided for above but shall be based on the price received by us from such manufacturer or our customer for such editions of the Subject Compositions.

Simultaneously herewith Publisher shall pay to Owner the sum of _____ Dollars, as a non-returnable advance recoupable by Publisher from any and all moneys payable to Owner under this agreement. The parties acknowledge the phrase "non-returnable advance" is to be interpreted as meaning that Publisher shall have no recourse against Owner if Publisher shall be unable to recoup said advance from moneys payable to Owner as above described.

6.    Publisher agrees that within ninety (90) days after the last days of June and December of each year it will prepare and furnish statements to Owner, and each such statement shall be accompanied by a check or checks in payment of any and all sums shown to be due thereby. Upon submission of each statement, Publisher may maintain reserves against subsequent charges, returns, credits or defective merchandise, such portion of payable moneys as may be reasonably necessary and appropriate in Publisher's best business judgment. Each such statement shall be binding upon Owner and not subject to any objection by them for any reasons, unless specific objection, in writing, setting forth the basis thereof, is given to Publisher by Owner within two (2) years from the date rendered.

Owner hereby agrees to pay writers of Subject Compositions all moneys payable to writers from Owner's receipts hereunder and further agrees to hold Publisher free and harmless from and against any claims of any writers of any of the Subject Compositions.

7.    Publisher agrees to keep and maintain full and complete books and records concerning the subject matter hereof;

and Owner shall have the right to examine Publisher's books and records at Publisher's principal place of business during its normal business hours and upon reasonable notice to verify the correctness of accounting statements rendered hereunder.

8.     Publisher agrees to imprint a copyright notice on each copy of every printed publication of any of the Subject Compositions hereunder, in compliance with the formalities of the United States Copyright Law of the Universal Copyright Convention as well as the year and date of any prior copyright registration in the United State of America. Owner agrees that Publisher shall be entitled to rely on the accuracy of any such information furnished to Publisher by Owner.

9.     Owner hereby agrees to provide Publisher with all necessary original photographs of the Artist and with appropriate biographical material relating to the Artist.

10.     Owner agrees that Publisher shall have the non-exclusive right to sell in and throughout the licensed territory all printed copies of Subject Compositions in Publisher's possession or control as of the termination date hereof until Publisher shall have finally disposed of all such inventory, and Owner likewise agrees that the provisions of Paragraph 1 (b) hereby shall apply during said sell-off.

11.     All notices, accounting statement, payments, delivery of printed materials and other documents or things required under the terms of this Agreement shall be sent by United States mail, postage prepaid, addressed to the party of whom the same is sent, as set forth on the first page hereof or to such other address or addresses that a party may notify the other from time to time.

12.     This Agreement shall be construed and interpreted under the laws of the State of New York relating to agreements entered into and to be wholly performed in said State, irrespective of the forum or forums to which this Agreement may be presented for construction or interpretation.

13.     This Agreement constitutes the entire agreement between the parties hereto and all prior or contemporaneous agreements of any kind or nature between the parties shall be deemed to be merged herein. This Agreement may be modified or amended only by an instrument in writing duly executed by the parties hereto.

14.     (a)     Owner shall not during the term of this Agreement do any act or authorize, license or knowingly permit any third party (other than a party authorized or licensed by Publisher) to do any act which would in any way derogate from or violate the exclusive right, license and privilege granted to Publisher by this Agreement.

(b)     Owner agrees to indemnify and hold Publisher free and harmless from any and all loss, damages, liability, costs, expenses and reasonable attorneys' fees arising out of any claims, demands or actions against Publisher which are inconsistent with any warranty, representation or agreement made by Owner hereunder. Written notice of any such claim, demand or action shall be promptly given to Owner, and Owner shall have the right to participate, at its own expense, in the defense thereof. Owner shall promptly, upon demand, reimburse Publisher for any payment made by Publisher with respect to any loss, cost, expense, liability or damage to which the foregoing indemnity applies. Pending the determination of any such claim, demand or action, Publisher shall have the right to withhold payment of that portion of moneys hereunder which shall be reasonably related to the size of the claim and estimated expenses.

(c)     Publisher expressly acknowledges that the Subject Compositions and all rights granted and to be granted to Publisher hereunder are of a special, unique and intellectual character which gives them peculiar value, and that in the event of a breach by Owner of any term, condition, warranty, representation or agreement hereunder, Publisher will be caused irreparable injury. Owner expressly agrees that in the event of any such breach, Publisher shall be entitled to injunctive and other equitable relief or damages, in addition to any other rights and remedies available to it, and Publisher shall have the right to recoup any damages from any sums which may thereafter become due and payable to Owner hereunder.

IN WITNESS WHEREOF, the parties hereto have executed this Agreement as of the year and date first above written.

FAMOUS RECORDING GROUP RIGHTS EXPLOITATION COMPANY, INC.

FAMOUS RECORDING GROUP MUSIC PUBLISHING COMPANY

By _____

Federal I.D. #:

OLD PRINT MUSIC PUBLISHER, INC.

By _____

# FORM 11.4

## PRINT LICENSE FOR USE OF LYRICS IN A BOOK

January 1, 2000

BEST SELLER BOOK PUBLISHING COMPANY, INC.
1 Broadway
New York, NY 10017

Gentlemen:

We hereby grant to you permission to reprint portions of the lyric only from our copyrighted musical composition, _____, by _____ in the English language version of your forthcoming book entitled, _____ , subject to the following terms and conditions:

    1.    You shall pay us a fee of $ 35.00, check made payable to _____, and addressed to the attention of the undersigned.

    2.    The following copyright notice(s) must appear at the bottom of the page on which the quote appears, suitably asterisked, or as an alternative, we authorize copyright notice to be included on appropriate credit or copyright acknowledgment pages:

Copyright © _____

All rights reserved. Used by permission.

    3.    The territory covered by this permission is world-wide.

    4.    You shall furnish us with two (2) copies of the publication for our files.

This permission is for your use only, covering only the English language version of the first single hardcover/softcover edition and its reprints, and does not extend to abridgments, softcover/hardcover or editions published by any other person, firm or corporation, excepting those involved in Braille transcription and/or large type production for the physically handicapped, permission for which is hereby included.

This permission shall be valid upon your signing and returning to us one copy of this letter along with your remittance and upon the performance by you of the other terms and conditions hereof on your part to be performed.

Sincerely yours,

BIG MUSIC PUBLISHING CORP.

By: _____

AGREED & ACCEPTED:

BEST SELLER BOOK PUBLISHING COMPANY, INC.

By: _____

# FORM 11.5

## LETTER AGREEMENT TO EXTEND LYRIC PRINT LICENSE FOR USE IN NEW EDITION OF A BOOK

January 1, 2000

BEST SELLER BOOK PUBLISHING COMPANY, INC.
1 Broadway
New York, NY 10017

Re:     License to Use Lyric Dated _____.

Gentlemen:

Dear _____:

In consideration of the additional sum of _____
payable within thirty (30) days from the date hereof, our license
to you referenced above permitting you to reprint portions of
the lyric of our musical composition _____
_____ in your book, is
hereby amended to encompass the release of said book in a
paperback edition by Little Paperback Book Publishing Company.

Yours sincerely,

BIG MUSIC PUBLISHING CORP.

By: _____

AGREED AND ACCEPTED:

By _____

# FORM 11.6

## LICENSE FOR USE OF LYRICS IN CONNECTION WITH COMMERCIAL DISTRIBUTION OF A RECORDING

January 1, 2000

VINYL RECORD COMPANY
1 Vince Street
Hollywood, California 90069

RE: Musical Composition:
     Written by:

Gentlemen:

1.   We hereby grant to you a non-exclusive license to print and sell at your sole expense and cost in the United States and Canada printed copies of the lyric of the above-referenced musical composition in and as part of recording packages which contain the recording of said composition covered by a mechanical licensed issued on our behalf by the Harry Fox Agency concurrently herewith.

2.   You agree to pay us the following royalty: $.02 per lyric, per copy, sold with each recording.

3.   You shall account to us quarterly on the basis of music manufactured and sold.

4.   Each copy of each reprint shall contain our copyright notice and credit line:

> Copyright © 1990 BIG MUSIC PUBLISHING CORP.
> All Rights Reserved. Used by Permission.

If the foregoing correctly sets forth our understanding, kindly sign and return a copy of this letter.

Yours sincerely,                         AGREED TO:

BIG MUSIC PUBLISHING CORP.    LICENSEE

By _____        By _____

# FORM 11.7

## PRINT LICENSE FOR USE OF LYRICS IN CONNECTION WITH PROMOTIONAL DISTRIBUTION OF A RECORDING

January 1, 2000

VINYL RECORD COMPANY
1 Vince Street
Hollywood, California 90069

RE:   Musical Composition:
      Written by:

Gentlemen:

1.   We hereby grant to you for no charge a non-exclusive license to print and distribute at your sole expense and cost in the United States and Canada printed copies of the lyric of the above-referenced musical composition in and as part of, or distributed in conjunction with distribution of, promotional copies of recording packages which contain the recording of said composition covered by a mechanical license issued on our behalf by the Harry Fox Agency concurrently herewith.

2.   Each copy of each reprint shall contain our copyright notice and credit line:

> Copyright © 2000 BIG MUSIC PUBLISHING CORP. All Rights Reserved. Used by Permission.

If the foregoing correctly sets forth our understanding, kindly sign and return a copy of this letter.

Yours sincerely,                          AGREED TO:

BIG MUSIC PUBLISHING CORP.     LICENSEE

By _____     By _____

# FORM 11.8

## EXCLUSIVE RIGHTS TO PRINT LYRICS IN LYRIC MAGAZINE FOR SINGLE SONG(S)

January 1, 2000

Lyric Magazine, Inc.
ADDRESS
CITY, STATE, ZIP .

Gentlemen:

We hereby grant to you, your subsidiaries, affiliates and licensees, the exclusive right to print and vend each month in song lyric and fan magazines only, in the United States, its territories and possessions, and Canada only, the lyrics of the following musical composition(s) for a period of one year commencing the date set forth above.

Musical Composition(s)        Songwriter(s)

You agree to pay us for the rights herein granted, provided the lyrics of said musical composition (s) are available to you during the period of this agreement, the sum of one-hundred ($100.00) Dollars per song listed above, receipt of which is hereby acknowledged.

We agree that during the period of this agreement we will not license or permit any others whatsoever to print or vend the lyrics of the above-named musical composition(s) in song lyric or fan magazines, it being understood that you shall have the exclusive right to use the same in such publications.

We warrant and represent that the lyrics furnished to you are new and original and we agree to indemnify and hold you harmless from any claims whatsoever arising out of the use by you of such lyrics. You agree that all copies of the lyrics of our compositions as printed hereunder shall carry an appropriate copyright notice, furnished by us, showing our ownership of the copyright of the said composition(s).

This agreement shall be binding on the parties hereto, their successors and assigns.

Very truly yours,

BIG MUSIC PUBLISHING CORP.

By _____

ACCEPTED AND AGREED:

LYRIC MAGAZINE, INC.

By _____

# FORM 11.9

## EXCLUSIVE RIGHTS TO PRINT LYRICS IN LYRIC MAGAZINE FOR ENTIRE CATALOG

Date: January 1, 2000

Lyric Magazine, Inc.
ADDRESS
CITY, STATE, ZIP

Gentlemen:

We hereby grant to you, your subsidiaries, affiliates and licensees, the exclusive right to print and vend each month in song lyric and fan magazines distributed only to customers or sold only on newsstands and similar retail outlets located in the United States, its territories and possessions, and Canada, for a period of one year from the date hereof, the lyrics of all the musical compositions (excluding musical compositions from motion picture, stage and other productions) now and hereafter in our catalog or that of any subsidiaries or affiliates now or hereafter formed to the extent that we do not require permission from third parties to make such grant. If permission is required, we will, upon your request, use our best efforts to obtain such permission. Notwithstanding the foregoing, we shall have the right to exclude from this agreement any musical composition(s) we wish upon written notice to you.

In consideration for the rights granted hereunder, you agree to pay us for the rights herein granted a non-returnable advance of One Thousand Two Hundred Dollars ($1,200) payable in twelve (12) equal monthly installments commencing upon the date hereof, which advance shall be recoupable against the sum of fifty ($50.00) Dollars due and payable for each song printed by you hereunder.

We agree that during the period of this agreement we will not license or permit any others whatsoever to print or vend any of the lyrics of our musical compositions in song lyric publications sold on newsstands and similar retail outlets, it being understood that you shall have the exclusive right to use the same in such publications, except that we reserve the right to use any of our compositions in our publications sold on newsstands and similar retail outlets which publications do not duplicate and are not similar to your song lyric magazines.

We warrant and represent that the lyrics furnished to you are new and original and we agree to indemnify and hold you harmless from any claims whatsoever arising out of the use by you of such lyrics. You agree that all copies of the lyrics of our compositions as printed hereunder shall carry an appropriate copyright notice, furnished by us, showing our ownership of the copyright of the said composition(s).

This agreement shall be binding upon the parties, hereto, their successors and assigns.

Very truly yours,

BIG MUSIC PUBLISHING CORP.

By _____

ACCEPTED AND AGREED:

LYRIC MAGAZINE, INC.

By _____

# FORM 11.10

## NON-EXCLUSIVE LICENSE TO PRINT LYRICS IN LYRIC MAGAZINE FOR ENTIRE CATALOG WITH SPECIAL PAYMENT PROVISIONS

Date: January 1, 2000

Lyric Magazine, Inc.
ADDRESS
CITY, STATE, ZIP

Gentlemen:

We hereby grant to you, your subsidiaries, affiliates and licensees, the nonexclusive license to print and vend each month in song lyric and fan magazines distributed only to customers and sold only on newsstands and similar retail outlets located in the United States, its territories and possessions, and Canada, for a period of one year from the date hereof, the lyrics of all the musical compositions (excluding musical compositions from motion picture, stage and other productions) now and hereafter in our catalog or that of any subsidiaries or affiliates now or hereafter formed to the extent that we do not require permission from third parties to make such grant. If permission is required, we will, upon your request, use our best efforts to obtain such permission. Notwithstanding the foregoing, we shall have the right to exclude from this agreement any musical composition(s) we wish upon written notice to you.

In consideration for the rights granted hereunder, you agree to pay us for the rights herein granted a non-returnable advance of One Thousand Two Hundred Dollars ($1,200) payable in twelve (12) equal monthly installments commencing upon the date hereof, which advance shall be recoupable against the sums set forth below:

For each song lyric printed under the terms of this agreement, you shall pay us in accordance with the following schedule:

| Category | Rate | No. of Uses |
| --- | --- | --- |
| "Popular" | $150.00 | Unlimited |
| "Country" | $50.00 | Unlimited |
| "Popular Standard" | $50.00 | One |
| "Country Standard" | $50.00 | One |

The foregoing terms shall have the meanings defined below:

The term *popular* shall mean the songs listed on the Billboard "Hot 100" singles listing, commonly referred to as the "Pop" charts.

The term *"country"* shall mean the songs listed on the Billboard "Hot Country" singles listing, commonly referred to as the "Country" charts.

The term *"popular standard"* shall mean the songs that appeared on the Billboard "Hot 100" singles listing prior to the start date of this agreement and which do not re-appear on said chart during the term of this agreement.

The term *"country standard"* shall mean the songs that appeared on the Billboard "Hot Country" singles listing prior to the start date of this agreement and which do not re-appear on said chart during the term of this agreement.

In the event that, during the period of this agreement, the lyric of any musical composition that you print during the term hereof is included among the top ten most "Popular" songs in the country on the Billboard "Hot 100" listing, you shall pay us the additional sum of seventy-five ($75.00) dollars. Only one such bonus payment shall be made for any one song no matter how many times the song is listed on the chart.

We warrant and represent that the lyrics furnished to you are new and original and we agree to indemnify and hold you harmless from any claims whatsoever arising out of the use by you of such lyrics. You agree that all copies of the lyrics of our compositions as printed hereunder shall carry an appropriate copyright notice, furnished by us, showing our ownership of the copyright of the said composition(s).

This agreement shall be binding upon the parties, hereto, their successors and assigns.

Very truly yours,

BIG MUSIC PUBLISHING CORP.

By _____

ACCEPTED AND AGREED:

LYRIC MAGAZINE, INC.

By _____

# MECHANICAL LICENSES

## SUMMARY

### I. HISTORICAL BACKGROUND

A. Music Boxes

B. Player Piano Rolls

C. Phonograph Records

D. Compact Discs

E. Computer Disks and MIDI Files

### II. LEGAL BACKGROUND

A. Copyright

B. Compulsory Licensing

C. Compulsory Mechanical License for Digital Downloads

D. MIDI Files

### III. CONSIDERATIONS IN GRANTING AND CLEARING MECHANICAL LICENSES

A. Fee Structure

    1. Giving or Getting a Rate

    2. Rate Changes

    3. Controlled Compositions

B. Importance of the Song in Relation to Its Intended Use

    1. Arrangements and Changes

    2. Initial Recordings

C. Scope of the License

    1. Record Number Versus Master Number

    2. Type of Media

    3. Distribution Channels

    4. Term

    5. Territory

    6. Exclusivity

    7. Credit

## IV. MECHANICAL RIGHTS AGENCIES

## V. INTERNATIONAL MECHANICAL RIGHTS ADMINISTRATION

## APPENDIX TO CHAPTER 12

## LAWS

# MECHANICAL LICENSES

A *mechanical license* is a license which permits the reproduction of music in a form that may be heard with the aid of a "mechanical" device. Like the print license, the mechanical license is derived from the copyright owner's exclusive right to reproduce work in copies and phonorecords. Traditionally, mechanical licenses were issued to permit the reproduction of music in "single" records (i.e., the "45" RPM record) long-playing record "albums" (i.e., the 33 1/3 RPM record), and piano rolls used in "player" pianos. Today, by far the most common form of mechanical reproduction of music is the laser compact disc (CD). The popularity of musical works distributed in CDs, however, may give way to new forms of delivery. With the advent of the online information services and the Internet, musical works are increasingly being transmitted electronically. The electronic transmission of a musical work that results in a specifically identifiable reproduction of the work in a phonorecord is permitted under the authority of a mechanical license.

This chapter sketches the historical and legal background of music recorded on mechanical devices and provides an outline of some of the terms and conditions contained in customary mechanical licenses.

## I. HISTORICAL BACKGROUND

### A. Music Boxes

The first mechanical device designed to perform music was the *music box*, a mechanical instrument whose sounds are produced by a metal comb, the teeth of which are tuned to specific pitches, plucked by pins protruding from a cylinder that is rotated by a wound spring. Originally placed in snuff boxes, watches, and various ornamental objects and commonly used today in jewel boxes, figurines, and children's toys, the music box was invented in 1796 by Antoine Favre, a

Swiss watchmaker. In the 1820s, as they became popular in homes, music boxes were mass produced to fulfill demand. By the mid-19th century, several developments in the technology lead to music boxes that could play a wider selection of music for a longer period of time. Sophisticated music boxes, housed in massive pieces of furniture, could provide hours of listening pleasure. In 1885, a box was invented using metal discs instead of cylinders. Costing much less than the earlier box, it sold in vast quantities.

## B. Player Piano Rolls

As music boxes gained popularity, a new form of music box, affording a more familiar quality of performed music, emerged: the *player piano*. A player piano is a piano equipped with a mechanical attachment which depresses the piano's keys by air pressure, reproducing notes that are represented by perforations on a paper roll. Player *piano rolls* are special perforated paper rolls manufactured in large quantity for use in player pianos, and represented the second major form of "mechanical" reproduction of music. From the late 1800s to the late 1920s, the popularity of player pianos reached their height, and millions of player piano rolls, embodying the most popular piano music of that time, were sold annually.

## C. Phonograph Records

Nevertheless, both the music box and player piano industries were soon dealt a major blow by a new technological development: the record player. In 1877, Thomas Edison first reproduced recorded sound by using cylinders made of tin foil, an invention which he called the *phonograph*. The first phonograph was a hand-turned, metal cylinder covered with tin foil. A stylus resting on the tin foil was attached to a diaphragm which was caused to vibrate as sound was applied. The vibrating diaphragm pressed the stylus onto the surface of the tinfoil, embossing it with a groove *analogous* to the sound which produced the vibrations in the diaphragm (hence, the name *analog* recording, as contrasted with *digital* recording, discussed below). After the groove was complete, the sounds could be "played back" by applying the stylus to the cylinder and rotating the cylinder at the same speed at which the sounds were originally recorded. Later, other inventors substituted a wax-covered cardboard cylinder for the tinfoil which facilitated the mass production of this new form of mechanical reproduction of music.

The age of cylinders ended in 1912 with the advent of the *78 RPM record*, which was recorded and played back at a speed of 78 *revolutions per minute* (RPM). 78-RPM remained the basic phonograph record speed until 1948, when Columbia Records introduced the *long-playing record* (*LP*), which operated at 33 and 1/3 RPM. Shortly thereafter, RCA Victor introduced a smaller 45-RPM record, which eventually became the medium for popular *single* recordings.

For those readers who may be too young to remember, the LP was a vinyl platter, about the same size as a movie laser disc, which was placed onto a *turntable* that rotates at the speed of 33 1/3 revolutions per minute; the tone arm, mounted next to the turntable, which contained a diamond stylus, or record *needle,* would be moved on its pivot so that the stylus would come to gently rest in the *groove* etched into the vinyl record (hence, the 60's slang, *groovy*). As the record revolved, the stylus followed the grooves, spiraling in toward the center of the record, vibrating in response to the variations in the grooves. The vibration was converted into an analogous electrical signal, which, when strengthened by your amplifier, drove your speakers, where the signal was converted back into acoustic vibrations, which could be heard by an ear and understood by the human mind.

## D. Compact Discs

For those readers who may be too old to realize, the LP record has become virtually extinct, having been replaced during the past 10 years by the popular optical *compact disc* (*CD*). Instead of a tone arm, the compact disc player uses a laser beam and a photoelectric cell to read the sound pattern imprinted on the disc as a series of microscopic pits.

During the 1970s, a new recording technique was developed, called *pulse code modulation* (*PCM*), to reduce the noise and distortion unavoidable in earlier recording methods. In PCM, the frequencies and amplitudes, or *analog* vibrations, of the original sound are analyzed and converted into *digital* pulses by the recording device. These digital pulses share the same basic components of the software that run modern computers: 1's and 0's, representing the *on* and *off* signals of the binary code. These "on" and "off" pulses are then processed and reconverted to ordinary sound signals when the record is cut. Upon the advent of the compact disc in the early 1980s, it was discovered that improved sound reproduction could be obtained by maintaining the digital character of the PCM recording in the process of mastering the CD. Thus, in the production of modern CDs, a digital, rather than analog, tape recorder is used during the sessions in which the sounds are (i) *recorded*, (ii) *mixed* or edited, and (iii) *mastered* for mass production.

## E.  Computer Disks and MIDI Files

Upon the advent of the digital computer, there have emerged new forms of mechanical devices upon which music may be stored. The microchips, a device which can pack hundreds of thousands of "transistors" onto a sliver of silicon the size of a thumbnail, may embody recorded music. Thus, when you open a greeting card, the song *Happy Birthday* is performed. Computer floppy disks, and now removable computer hard disks, can store music in a variety of software formats. Some of the music-related software programs that enable the creation and retrieval of music in these formats are described more fully in Chapter 21, on *Licenses for Computer Software, Multi-Media and New Media Products*.

Perhaps the most important music software development has been something called the *musical instrument digital interface* (*MIDI*). MIDI is the standard computer format or protocol for transmitting music data electronically. With MIDI, instead of being recorded on tape or computer disks and played back via conventional audio tape, record album or CD, the musical sound recording is recorded and played back via computer as a MIDI file, or sequence. A *sequence* is generated in real time by using a MIDI *controller* (typically, a musical instrument keyboard) and a MIDI *sequencer*. The sequencer allows the MIDI data stream to be captured, stored, edited, and replayed. The controller can emulate the sound of nearly any instrument. MIDI files, or sequences, are typically fixed on floppy diskettes, although CDs or any other media upon which digital information may be stored and retrieved by a computer may be used. They may be replayed in their entirety as recorded or in a number of other ways by replaying only certain instrument parts, by changing the pitch, the tempo or other variables made possible by the nature of the MIDI format and the capabilities of MIDI playback devices (e.g., electronic synthesizers).

Most electronic instruments today, such as electronic piano keyboards and synthesizers, are MIDI equipped. Even sounds from acoustic instruments (including the human voice) can be converted to MIDI with special hardware and software. Compared to digitized audio, MIDI data is significantly more compact and more easily manipulated without loss of sound quality.

There are two main advantages to generating sound in MIDI rather than using audio stored in the traditional manner. The first is reduced file size, which reduces the computer memory needed to store the music and the time it takes to transmit a performance electronically. Data files used to store digitally sampled audio in PCM format (such as WAV files) tend to be quite large in comparison to those of regular audio files. For example, files containing high quality stereo sampled audio require about 10 megabytes of data per minute of sound; a typical MIDI sequence might consume less than 10 kilobytes of data per minute of sound. This is because the MIDI file only contains the instructions necessary for a sequencer to render the sounds, not the sounds themselves. The instructions tell the sequencer which notes to play, how to play them, in what pitch to play them, etc., and the sequencer actually creates sounds.

The other main advantage of MIDI involves the ease with which MIDI sequences may be edited or changed when they are played back. Thus, a MIDI sequence may be modified at the time of playback to suit the particular needs or tastes of the listener, such as the tempo or particular key desired by a user of karaoke equipment.

MIDI data is stored in a standardized format which is compatible with different computer-based sequencers operating on a variety of computer hardware and operating system platforms. The format allows for the inclusion of information such as song name, tempo, time signatures, lyrics, and copyright information.

For special considerations on mechanical licenses and the Internet, please see Chapter 23, on *Licensing Musical Works and Sound Recordings on the Internet.*

## II. Legal Background

### A. Copyright

Even though far removed from the mechanical reproduction of music by piano rolls and music boxes, recordings of music in records, tapes, and compact discs continue to be referred to as *mechanical reproductions*. Likewise, the term used to describe permission to record a copyrighted song on a phonograph record, tape, or compact disc is called a *mechanical license*. Examples of mechanical license agreements are set forth as Forms 12.1, 12.2, and 12.3 at the end of this Chapter.

As noted in Chapter 7, licenses owe their existence to rights. The right to reproduce copyrighted music in mechanical devices, such as phonograph records, piano rolls, and music boxes, is one of the exclusive rights of reproduction held by the copyright owner. This, however, was not always so. In 1908, the United States Supreme Court startled the music industry by deciding that piano rolls and phonograph records were not "copies" of musical compositions and, therefore, not an infringement of the rights in the compositions, but merely part of the mechanism for their reproduction in sound.[1]

With the Copyright Act of 1909,[2] the U.S. Congress quickly overturned the effect of this decision by specifically recognizing the exclusive right of the copyright owner to make mechanical reproductions of music.

### B. Compulsory Licensing

In taking this step, however, Congress had more in mind than merely providing rights to the composer. Congress was concerned about certain developments in the piano roll industry that threatened to create a monopoly in the hands of The Aeolian Co,. a leading manufacturer of piano rolls. In anticipation of the legal recognition of mechanical reproduction rights, Aeolian had entered into exclusive contracts with many of the major music publishers of that time for

---

[1] *White-Smith Music Pub. Co. v. Apollo Co.*, 209 U.S. 1 (1908).

[2] Act of March 19, 1909, ch. 320, 35 Stat. 1075, as thereafter codified in 17 U.S.C. Sec. 1 et seq., and as amended.

the right to make mechanical reproductions of the works in the repertoires of the publishers. With Aeolian having the exclusive mechanical reproduction rights to a vast majority of popular music, few other manufacturers of piano rolls could acquire the licenses they required to compete in the piano roll business. To thwart this potential monopoly, Congress provided in the 1909 copyright law that if the copyright owner used or permitted the use of a copyrighted song for mechanical reproduction, then any one else could make mechanical reproductions of that song by payment to the copyright owner a royalty of 2 cents per unit. In other words, if the copyright owner licenses the song for mechanical reproduction at least once, then he could be forced to license it for mechanical reproduction to anyone else thereafter for a fee set by the copyright law.

The provision of the copyright statute compelling copyright owners to issue mechanical licenses became known as the *compulsory license* provision, and the prescribed per unit fee set forth in the law is referred to as the *statutory rate.*

The new copyright law enacted by Congress in 1976 maintained the compulsory license concept, with some modification, including the first increase in the statutory rate in nearly 70 years. It is embodied in Section 115 of the copyright law passed in 1976,[3] which is set forth at the end of this chapter. The statutory rate, as of January 1, 2000, is the greater of 7.55 cents per unit or 1.45 cents per minute of playing time, or fraction thereof, per unit. This rate is subject to adjustment by copyright arbitration royalty panels appointed and convened by the Librarian of Congress.[4]

Because of the burdensome procedures required by the compulsory license provision — such as the requirement of monthly, rather than quarterly accounting to copyright owners and notice conforming to strict regulation — nearly all mechanical licenses are negotiated

---

[3] 17 U.S.C. Sec. 115. Legislation enacted in 1995 amended Section 115 making the digital delivery of music files subject to the compulsory license provision. See Chapter 23, on *Licensing Musical Works and Sound Recordings on the Internet.*

[4] 17 U.S.C. Sec. 801-803. In 1993, the copyright law was amended by the Copyright Royalty Tribunal Reform Act 1993, which abolished the Copyright Royalty Tribunal in favor of a copyright arbitration royalty panel to be convened by the Librarian of Congress.

directly between the copyright owners and the licensees and do not strictly reflect the terms of the compulsory license provisions of the law. Nevertheless, even though the compulsory license provision is rarely invoked directly, its terms generally provide an outline for those of negotiated licenses and the statutory rate effects a maximum effective limit on the mechanical license fees charged by copyright owners under negotiated licenses.

Some debate continues over whether it is time for the compulsory license provision to be repealed. Detractors say that the monopoly against which the provision was enacted to combat went out with high button shoes, and there is no reason today why mechanical licenses should not be as freely negotiable as licenses for other kinds of uses. Others say that the compulsory license has served to simplify the process of obtaining mechanical licenses and has reduced a significant amount of unnecessary transaction costs.

Perhaps the best reason for maintaining the compulsory license is that it may be the most effective solution to the problem of split copyrights, discussed in Chapter 6. Split copyright does not become an issue when all the co-owners are required to accept no more than the statutory rate. Further, when the person seeking to clear a mechanical license cannot identify or locate the owner of the copyright, the compulsory license provision provides a safe harbor: if the public records of the Copyright Office do not identify the copyright owner and include an address at which notice under the provision can be served, it is sufficient to file the required notice with the Copyright Office.[5] By properly following the procedure and paying the statutory rate set forth in the compulsory license provision, a person seeking to clear permission will be assured a license without taking any risk of liability for copyright infringement.

Note that the compulsory license provision only applies to copies that are intended for distribution to the public for private use. Thus, copies reproduced for the purpose of facilitating broadcasts or other public performances — discussed in Chapter 13, on *Electrical Transcription Licenses* — would not be subject to the provision. Accordingly, licenses to permit the reproduction of such copies would, therefore, be freely negotiable.

---

[5] 17 U.S.C. Sec. 115(b)(1).

On October 24, 1995, the U.S. Copyright Office announced an increase in the statutory mechanical royalty rate payable by makers of sound recordings (e.g., record companies) to owners of musical compositions (e.g., music publishers and songwriters): Effective January 1, 1996, the statutory rate was increased to either 6.95 cents, or 1.3 cents per minute of playing time or fraction thereof, whichever is larger.

On February 13, 1998, the Copyright Office announced further changes in the statutory rate. Effective January 1, 1998, the statutory rate was increased to 7.1 cents, or 1.35 cents per minute of playing time or fraction thereof, whichever amount is larger. Beginning January 1, 2000, the rate increased to 7.55 cents, or 1.45 cents per minute of playing time or fraction thereof, whichever is greater; beginning January 1, 2002, the rate increases the greater of 8.0 cents, or 1.55 cents per minute of playing time; on January 1, 2004, the rate increases to the greater of 8.5 cents, or 1.65 cents per minute of playing time; and on January 1, 2006, the rate will increase again to the greater of 9.1 cents, or 1.75 cents per minute of playing time.

*Background.* In 1987, the Copyright Royalty Tribunal adopted the joint proposal submitted by the National Music Publishers' Association, The Songwriters Guild of America and the Recording Industry Association of America, Inc. to make adjustments every two years to the mechanical royalty rate based upon changes in the Consumer Price Index (CPI), except: (1) when the CPI declined, in which case the mechanical rate could go no lower than the rates in effect in 1986-1987; and (2) when the CPI increased by more than 25%, in which case the rate increase would be no greater than 25%. On December 17, 1993, the Copyright Royalty Tribunal was abolished by Congress. Copyright Royalty Tribunal Reform Act of 1993 (CRT Reform Act), Pub. L. 103-198, 107 Stat. 2304. The CRT Reform Act directed the Library of Congress and the Copyright Office to adopt the rules and regulations of the CRT as found at 37 C.F.R. chapter 3. 17 U.S.C. 802(d). The Office subsequently reissued the CRT regulations on December 22, 1993. Former 37 C.F.R. 307.3, which calls for a biannual cost of living adjustment to the mechanical royalty rate, was renumbered 37 C.F.R. 255.3 in a later action. 59 F.R. 23964 (May 9, 1994).

On October 24, 1995, the Copyright Office announced that the change in the cost of living in 1995, as determined by the Consumer Price Index (all urban consumers, all items), was 5.58%. The mechanical rate existing in 1995 was 6.60 cents, or 1.25 cents per minute of playing time or fraction thereof, whichever amount is larger. Adjusting that rate upward by 5.58% and rounding off the results to the nearest 1/20th of a cent, the new rate, effective January 1, 1996, became 6.95 cents, or 1.3 cents per minute of playing time or fraction thereof, whichever amount is larger.

From 1909 through 1977, the statutory rate was 2 cents. Since then the rate has been increased on eleven occasions:

| Effective Date Of New Rate | Cents Per Song | Cents Per Minute |
|---|---|---|
| January 1, 1978 | 2.75 | .5 |
| July 1, 1981 | 4 | .75 |
| January 1, 1983 | 4.25 | .8 |
| July 1, 1984 | 4.5 | .85 |
| January 1, 1986 | 5 | .95 |
| January 1, 1988 | 5.25 | 1 |
| January 1, 1990 | 5.7 | 1.1 |
| January 1, 1992 | 6.25 | 1.2 |
| January 1, 1994 | 6.6 | 1.25 |
| January 1, 1996 | 6.95 | 1.3 |
| January 1, 1998 | 7.1 | 1.35 |
| January 1, 2000 | 7.55 | 1.45 |
| January 1, 2002 | 8.0 | 1.55 |

On November 5, 1997, associations representing the music publishing and recording industries jointly submitted a proposal to the U.S. Copyright Office to adjust the statutory royalty rates for the making and distribution of physical phonorecords, i.e., the delivery of sound recordings by digital transmission. On February 13, 1998, that proposal was accepted.

As a result, the physical phonorecord royalty rate was increased from 6.95 cents to 7.1 cents as of January 1, 1998, and automatic step increases every two years thereafter were put in place. In 2000, the rate increased to 7.55 cents; in 2002, it would be 8.0 cents; in 2004, it would be 8.5 cents; and in 2006, 9.1 cents. Corresponding increases are proposed for the per minute long work rate, currently 1.3 cents/minute. The statutory royalty rate structure for physical phonorecords can be reviewed again in 2007.

A proposal was also submitted for royalty rates for the delivery of sound recordings by digital transmission. With certain exceptions — such as for excerpts of sound recordings transmitted for promotional purposes — it was proposed that the rate for the delivery of sound recordings by digital transmission would continue to be the same as the physical rate. The parties agreed to this rate structure on a two-year basis because the marketplace for the delivery of sound recordings by digital transmission is still in the early stages of development. The promotional use provisions generally allow either the copyright owner of a sound recording or the copyright owner of the underlying musical work to deliver by transmission a sound recording of up to 30 seconds for promotional purposes without paying a royalty. At the time this edition went to print in the Fall of 2001, the statutory rate for digital phonorecord deliveries remained the same as the rate for physical phonorecords.

Note: The Harry Fox Agency, which administers mechanical licensing in the U.S. for many music publishers, has announced an intention to apply this new rate to all phonorecords made and distributed on or after January 1, 1996, *regardless of the date upon which the mechanical license under which such records are manufactured was issued, or the date upon which the recording was first released,* unless the licensee can prove that the licensee is contractually entitled to a lower rate.

## C. Compulsory Mechanical License for Digital Downloads

On November 1, 1995, Section 115, the compulsory mechanical license provision, of the U.S. Copyright Law was amended to cover the delivery of phonorecords of musical works by digital transmission. This amendment, which became effective on February 1, 1996, was part of the *Digital Performance Right in Sound Recordings Act of 1995*, discussed further in Chapter 23, on *Licensing Musical Works and Sound Recordings on the Internet.*

The operative portion of the compulsory license provision was amended by the addition of the following italicized words in the first two sentences of Section 115(a)(1):

Availability and Scope of Compulsory License—

(1) When phonorecords of a nondramatic musical work have been
distributed to the public in the United States under the authority of
the copyright owner, any other person, *including those who make
phonorecords or digital phonorecord deliveries,* may, by complying
with the provisions of this section, obtain a compulsory license to
make and distribute phonorecords of the work. A person may obtain
a compulsory license only if his or her primary purpose in making
phonorecords is to distribute them to the public for private use, *including by means of a digital phonorecord delivery.*

Thus, the Act created a new term of art under the U.S. Copyright
law: the *digital phonorecord delivery.*

A "*digital phonorecord delivery*" is each individual delivery of a
phonorecord by digital transmission of a sound recording which results in a specifically identifiable reproduction by or for any transmission recipient of a phonorecord of that sound recording,
regardless of whether the digital transmission is also a public performance of the sound recording or any nondramatic musical work
embodied therein.

Our discussion of digital phonorecord deliveries will resume in
Chapter 23, but suffice it here to say that, until December 31, 2001,
the statutory rate for the mechanical reproduction of musical works
by electronic transmission is the same rate currently established for
the compulsory licensing of audiocassettes and CDs: 7.55 cents, or
1.45 cents per minute of playing time or fraction thereof, whichever
amount is larger. Commencing January 1, 1998, the statutory rate for
compulsory licenses of music in connection with digital phonorecord
deliveries will be set in accordance with the rather elaborate procedure
set forth in Section 115(c)(3)(A)-(F), which may be found in the appendix to this chapter.

Nevertheless, the terms of mechanical licenses that are arrived at
through voluntary negotiations between copyright owners and licensees will be given effect, regardless of whether those licenses strictly
reflect the terms of the compulsory license provision of the Copyright
Act.[6] The compulsory license provision will, however, serve as an

---

[6] U.S.C. § 115(c)(3)(E).

outline for negotiated licenses, and the statutory rate will effectively become a maximum limit on the mechanical fees charged by copyright owners. As of September 2001, the statutory rate for digital phonorecord deliveries was the same as the rate for the distribution of physical phonorecords.

### D. MIDI Files

MIDI, the *musical instrument digital interface,* is briefly described above in section I.E. of this chapter. The storing of musical works in MIDI format raises some interesting music copyright and licensing questions. For example, is a MIDI computer file a mechanical reproduction, the distribution of which requires a mechanical license, subject to the compulsory license statute, or is it an audiovisual work, the distribution of which may be negotiated, such as the terms of a synchronization or videogram license, or is it akin to printed music, which requires the equivalent of a print license?

According to the U.S. Copyright Office, a standard MIDI file is a work of authorship copyrightable as a *sound recording*. This is because the information in the file causes a sound device to render the pitch, timbre, speed, duration, and volume of the musical notes in a certain order, as does a player piano in conjunction with a piano roll, or a compact disc player in conjunction with a compact disc. Thus, the media upon which a standard MIDI file is recorded is a *phonorecord* (as compared with a *copy*). Accordingly, a standard MIDI file is subject to the compulsory license provision under Section 115 of the Copyright Act.

It is important to note, however, that if the MIDI file includes instructions for generating motion pictures or other audiovisual works, the file would not be a sound recording, but rather an audiovisual work. As such, the compulsory license provision would not apply.

The Harry Fox Agency has considered the fixation of music in MIDI files and, to deal with the increasing number of requests for this new form of license, has developed a special form MIDI license, a copy which is set forth as Form 22.4 at the end of Chapter 22.

What if the MIDI file contains the ability to display music notation on the screen of a personal computer or to print out the notation on a computer printer the equivalent of printed sheet music? Is it a combination of sheet music and mechanical reproduction of a sound recording, or is it an audiovisual work? The question becomes significant, because many music copyright owners have granted to print publishers the rights to distribute their music in printed form, such as sheet music and folios, on an exclusive basis. If the music copyright owner grants permission for the reproduction of MIDI files, and those files have the capability of printing out musical notation on laser printers, a print publisher who holds exclusive print rights in the music might take the position that the granting of the license was a breach of its exclusive print rights contract.

The Harry Fox license (Form 22.4) states that the license does not grant permission to the licensee "to program into the MIDI sequence [file] the capability of making any other use of the Composition not expressly authorized" by the license. One of the permissions not granted to the licensee is the license to print the licensed composition in sheet music form. Further, the license requires that a warning notice be placed conspicuously on each copy of the MIDI file stating that it is a violation of copyright law to print the file in the form of standard music notation without the permission of the copyright owner.

## III. CONSIDERATIONS IN GRANTING AND CLEARING MECHANICAL LICENSES

As noted in the preceding section, the compulsory license provision has the effect of limiting the flexibility the copyright owner has in setting the terms of the mechanical license. As a result, two of the four primary factors in considering the terms of most music licenses — the value of the song and the importance of the song in relation to its intended use (see Chapter 10) — do not come much into play in the negotiation of mechanical licenses (with one notable exception: granting and clearing mechanical licenses for digital samples containing copyrighted music, a topic discussed at length in Chapter 24).

Nevertheless, though the clearance of mechanical licenses is generally an administrative process in which very little negotiation takes place, there remains some degree of flexibility that deserves some discussion.

## A. Fee Structure

### 1. Giving or Getting a Rate

A copyright owner will occasionally receive a request that a mechanical license be issued for a fee that is below the statutory rate. This is known as asking for *a rate*. To *give a rate* refers to charging a mechanical license fee that is below the statutory rate set by the compulsory license statute.

When a "rate" is offered, it is usually quoted at either fifty percent or seventy five percent *of statutory*. Thus, assuming, for simplicity, the statutory rate were 8 cents per copy, then a "half of statutory" rate would, of course, be 4 cents per copy.

Under the appropriate circumstances, a person seeking to clear a mechanical license should ask for a rate, and a copyright owner should, when the circumstances are justified, grant a rate. For example, record companies seeking to exploit older recordings will use creative marketing techniques or lower prices, such as the sale of older recordings through record clubs or the packaging of recordings of older artists in an inexpensive album or series of albums, sometimes called a *budget line* record. For budget line and record club releases, most music publishers would consent to a fee of 75% of the statutory rate per song.

### 2. Rate Changes

Many mechanical licenses identify the fee being charged using the words, "statutory rate," rather than using the appropriate denomination of cents per copy in effect. For example, a license may state, "The royalty under this license shall be the statutory rate" or "The royalty under this license shall be one-half the statutory rate." The wording of this provision should be reviewed carefully.

If the license goes no further than to say the royalty shall be the statutory rate, then the license may be construed as meaning the copyright owner is entitled to only receive the statutory rate in effect at the time the license was executed. This would completely deprive the copyright owner of the benefit of any later increases in the statutory rate made by the Copyright Arbitration Royalty Panel.[7]

---

[7] 17 U.S.C. Sec. 801-803.

Accordingly, mechanical licenses which refer to the statutory rate in this way should make it clear that the rate to be applied is the statutory rate "in effect at the time the phonorecords are made."

An alternative means of dealing with rate changes is to draft the license to provide that the initial stated fee shall increase in proportion to increases in the statutory rate made by the Copyright Arbitration Royalty Panel. The mechanical license form set forth as Form 12.2 at the end of this chapter contains an example of this means of reflecting rate increases.

Persons seeking to clear mechanical licenses might attempt to limit the fee to the statutory rate in effect at the time the mechanical license is executed, regardless of when the copies of the licensed recording are made and distributed. The mechanical license form set forth as Form 12.3 at the end of this chapter contains an example of a provision which effects such terms.

### 3. Controlled Compositions

The changes in Section 115, the compulsory mechanical license provision, made by the *Digital Performance Right in Sound Recordings Act of 1995,* included a provision that will limit the effect of many controlled composition clauses. As mentioned above, the terms of mechanical licenses that are arrived at through voluntary negotiations will normally be given effect. However, when recordings are distributed by digital phonorecord deliveries, a certain type of voluntarily negotiated mechanical license — the controlled composition clause — may not always be enforceable.[8]

Except under the two circumstances discussed below, the copyright owner of the musical work is entitled to be paid at the statutory rate, regardless of the royalty rates specified under a controlled composition clause in a record contract between a record company and a recording artist who is the author of the musical work. The two circumstances under which the statutory rate will *not* supersede such a controlled composition clause are:

(i) where the contract containing the controlled composition clause was entered into on or before June 22, 1995.

---

[8] Id.

(ii) where the contract containing the controlled composition clause is (a) entered into by an artist/songwriter who retains his music publishing rights (i.e., the right to grant licenses for the use of his songs) and (b) entered after the songs have been recorded.

Compared with other forms of music licensing, the licensing of mechanical reproductions, by virtue of the compulsory license provision, is simple and straightforward. These licenses may be obtained without the permission of the copyright owner and the rates that may be charged are effectively capped at the statutory rate. Moreover, under many circumstances, a music publisher is willing to provide a mechanical license at a rate below statutory. Yet, many record companies take extra measures to minimize the mechanical royalties that they are required to pay out for the use of songs on recordings they release.

Because many recording artists now tend to write most of the songs they record, record companies take the opportunity to address the issue of mechanical licensing directly in the artist's recording contract. These contracts invariably contain a provision, called a *controlled composition* clause, that effectively limits the amount of money the record company is required to remit in mechanical royalties. Because the terms of these clauses are often extremely complex, we will explore a sample controlled composition clause, from a typical record contract, one section at a time.

> All musical compositions or material recorded pursuant to this Agreement which are written or composed, in whole or in part, or owned or controlled, directly or indirectly, by Artist or any individual of Artist or any producer of the masters subject hereto (herein called "Controlled Compositions") shall be and are hereby licensed to Company for the United States, at a royalty per selection equal to seventy-five (75%) percent of the minimum statutory per selection rate (inclusive of playing time formula, if any) effective on the date of commencement of recording of the masters concerned. The aforesaid seventy-five (75%) percent per selection rate, but exclusive of any playing time, shall hereinafter sometimes be referred to as the "Per Selection Rate."

The above provision defines the term "controlled composition" about as broadly as such a term can be defined and then limits the mechanical rate payable by the record company for each controlled composition to 75% of the statutory rate. In other words, with respect to compositions written by the artist, or those over which the artist has some control, the record company is acquiring *a rate*. As noted above, a music publisher would usually quote a rate below statutory for recordings sold in a budget line or record club operation, but certainly not for first run popular recordings. Thus, the controlled composition clause is providing the record company with mechanical licensing terms it would not otherwise be able to obtain from the music publisher.

Notice, moreover, that the rate is the statutory rate *effective on the date of commencement of recording of the masters concerned*, meaning that the rate is frozen and will not be subject to any increases over time, even if Congress were to increase the statutory rate. Again, a music publisher would normally require that the rate be no less than the statutory rate *in effect at the time the phonorecords are made*. Note further that the statutory rate to which the provision refers is the *minimum* statutory rate, meaning that regardless of the duration of the recording, the rate used assumes the duration is 5 minutes or less.

The controlled composition clause continues,

> Notwithstanding the foregoing, the maximum aggregate mechanical royalty rate which Company shall be required to pay in respect to any Single, Maxi-single or LP hereunder, regardless of the total number of all compositions contained therein, shall not exceed two (2) times, two (2) times, and ten (10) times the Per Selection Rate, respectively.

Thus, the controlled composition clause effectively limits the total mechanical fees payable for an entire record album to *ten times* 75% of the minimum statutory rate in effect at the time the masters were originally recorded. A popular recording artist with a great degree of commercial leverage may be able to negotiate a raise from 75% to 100% of full statutory. That negotiated change might have been sufficient to protect the artist at a time when vinyl records commonly included between 8 and 10 songs per album, but many record companies today are taking advantage of the greater capacity of compact discs and are including 11 or 12 songs per CD to enhance sales.

Because the provision establishes a maximum mechanical fee the record company will pay for all music on an album, any liability above the negotiated maximum will come out of the pocket of the recording artist. This is important, because an artist's income from music publishing is, more often than not, going to be the only money the artist will ever see as a result of his efforts. Accordingly, a recording artist negotiating his recording contract should review this provision very carefully.

An artist with some bargaining power should be able to change the limit on the total mechanical fees payable from ten times 75% of statutory to ten times 100% of statutory, at least for the first album (perhaps 80% for future albums). An artist with strong bargaining power should be able to change the provision to eleven or twelve times statutory, and perhaps require that the rate be based upon the statutory rate in effect at the time copies of the records are made and distributed. Of course, an artist with little or no bargaining power will generally be unable to negotiate any changes to this provision in his recording contract.

As noted above, record companies will seek a rate on budget line or record club sales, and a music publisher would typically grant a rate, such as 75% of the statutory rate, for such uses. Yet the way controlled composition clauses are structured, the record company often gives itself a double dip on a normally acceptable rate. For example, the clause may state that mechanical royalties payable with respect to record club or budget line releases are limited to "seventy five (75%) of the otherwise applicable Per Selection Rate," meaning the actual rate payable for such uses, assuming the Per Selection Rate is seventy-five (75%) percent, is actually just 56 1/4% (i.e., 75% of 75%). But the clause doesn't always stop there:

> Controlled Compositions which are arranged versions of any musical compositions in the public domain, when furnished by Artist for recordings hereunder, shall be royalty free.

An artist with some leverage, however, may be able to persuade the record company to pay mechanical royalties for public domain arrangements, but only to the extent that ASCAP or BMI pay performance royalties on such arrangements. Such a provision would look like this,

> Mechanical royalties for Controlled Compositions which are arranged versions of any musical compositions in the public domain,

when furnished by Artist for recordings hereunder, shall be paid in the same proportion as the appropriate performing rights society grants performance credits to the publisher of such composition, provided Artist has furnished Company with a copy of the letter from such performing rights society setting forth the percentage of the otherwise applicable credit which the publisher will receive.

Finally, to prevent the artist from double dipping:

Notwithstanding anything in the foregoing to the contrary, if a particular selection recorded hereunder is embodied more than once on a particular record, Company shall pay mechanical royalties in connection therewith at the applicable rate for such composition as though the selection was embodied thereon only once.

Because of the terms imposed upon the artist in his recording agreement, a songwriter may be advised to negotiate in his music publishing or co-publishing agreement a provision requiring the publisher or co-publisher to comply with the terms of any controlled composition clause to which he may be bound. Publishers who are under no such obligation, of course, may charge the full statutory rate for the use of its music on an album, but should note that the presence of a controlled composition clause may cause a recording artist to reconsider the use of material, the cost of which may be charged as a direct reduction of his record royalties.[9]

## B. Importance of the Song in Relation to Its Intended Use

Because of the applicability of the compulsory license provision to mechanical licensing, considerations of the importance of the song in relation to its intended use rarely come into play in the negotiation of mechanical licenses. Nevertheless, not all uses of music on recordings intended for distribution to the general public will be governed by the compulsory license statute.

---

[9] At the time of this writing, the U.S. Congress was considering the enactment of various amendments to Section 115 of the Copyright Act, among which included a provision that would limit the effect of controlled composition clauses.

## 1. Arrangements and Changes

In drafting the copyright law of 1976, Congress considered the extent to which someone making a recording under the compulsory license provision may depart from the musical work as originally written or recorded without violating the copyright owner's exclusive right to make an arrangement or other derivative work.

Congress recognized the practical need for a limited privilege to make arrangements of music being used under a compulsory license, but without allowing the music to be "perverted, distorted, or travestied."[10] Accordingly, the compulsory license provision includes the following balance of interests: "A compulsory license includes the privilege of making a musical arrangement of the work to the extent necessary to conform it to the style or manner of interpretation of the performance involved, but the arrangement shall not change the basic melody or fundamental character of the work, and shall not be subject to protection as a derivative work under this title, except with the express consent of the copyright owner."[11]

Nearly all mechanical licenses include a similar limitation or incorporate this provision directly by reference.

Interestingly, this provision would seem to make it clear that a mechanical license under the compulsory license provision of the copyright law would not be available to a person seeking to use a digital sample of another's copyrighted work in a way that would change the basic melody or fundamental character of the song from which the sample was taken. The problem of *digital sampling* is discussed at length in Chapter 24.

Accordingly, if the intended use would depart from the basic melody or change the fundamental character of the work, the copyright owner would be free to negotiate the terms of the mechanical license without regard to the restrictions normally imposed by the compulsory license provision.

---

[10] House Report of the Copyright Act of 1976, No. 94-1476, at page 109 (September 3, 1976).

[11] 17 U.S.C. Sec. 115 (a) (2).

## 2.  Initial Recordings

The compulsory license provision only applies to a composition after a recording of it has been made and copies of it have been distributed to the public.[12] In other words, the compulsory license provision does not apply to the initial recording of a song. Accordingly, it is within the sole discretion of the copyright owner to decide whether, and under what terms, it wishes to grant permission to another to make a first mechanical recording of a composition. When, however, a publisher agrees to grant a license to make the first recording, the license is typically issued at the prevailing statutory rate.

As noted in Chapter 3, on *Songwriter Agreements*, a songwriter who is also a recording artist may contractually require in his songwriter agreement that neither the publisher, nor its subpublishers, issue a mechanical license for a cover record for a specified period after the artist's own recording of the composition has been released. By virtue of the compulsory license provision, however, the publisher's ability to deny the issuance of a mechanical license for other recordings distributed in the United States will end upon the public distribution of the artist's first recording of the song.

## C.  Scope of the License

The form for a mechanical license is usually prepared and completed by the music copyright owner or its agent. Though it is primarily an administrative procedure, care should still be taken to draft the form to suit the intent of the parties.

## 1.  Record Number Versus Master Number

In the mechanical licenses set forth as Forms 12.1 and 12.2 at the end of this chapter, a blank space is provided for the entry of the *number* of the recording (single, album, tape, or CD, as appropriate). If you are representing the music copyright owner, you should complete this space with the *record number*, which is the number that

---

[12] "*When phonorecords of a nondramatic musical work have been distributed to the public in the United States under the authority of the copyright owner*, any other person may, by complying with the provisions of this section, obtain a compulsory license to make and distribute phonorecords of the work." 17 U.S.C. Sec. 115(a)(1).

identifies the particular recording made from that master. You should not use the *master number*, which is the number established at the recording studio for identification and filing purposes when the recording master is completed. Thus, when completing a mechanical license on behalf of the music copyright owner, you should ask the licensee for the record number and make sure that what you are being given is not the master number.

By using the record number, rather than the master number, you will have narrowed the scope of the license to permission to make reproductions of the particular album on which the song was intended to initially appear, rather than any record made from recordings appearing in the master.[13] If the master is later used, as, for example, in making a remix of the original recording or in using recordings from the master in other record albums, the recording company would then be required to obtain an additional license from the copyright owner to use the recording for the new use.

This may be quite advantageous, as the terms of the new license will reflect circumstances existing at the time the new use is made, rather than those existing at the time a license was issued for the use of the original master recording. Whenever a copyright owner narrows the scope of the license he is in effect requiring the licensee to ask additional permission for a new use and, by doing so, he is preserving the ability to determine the terms of the license at a time when he can better assess the value of the use for which permission is being sought. For example, if a mechanical license were carefully limited to cover the specific recording originally made from the master (i.e., by use of the record number in identifying the recording licensed rather than the master number), then any new copies made from a remix of the master, or recordings made from the master, placed into other albums, would be subject to a new license, which could then be negotiated to reflect better terms for the copyright owner.

Should the compulsory license provision of the copyright law be repealed after the original mechanical license was granted, then, if the new use were not covered by the old license, the copyright owner would be free to negotiate a new, more favorable license fee for the

---

[13] See *Fred Ahlert Music Corp. v. Warner Chappell Music, Inc.*, 958 F. Supp. 170 (S.D.N.Y. 1997) (wherein the court agreed with the author's views on the subject).

new use, rather than be limited to the statutory rate set forth in the original mechanical license. More likely than a repeal of the compulsory license provision, the statutory rate will have been raised by the copyright arbitration royalty panel after the original mechanical license was issued, and if the mechanical license fee was based upon an old statutory rate, then the new statutory rate may be available to the copyright owner, if the old mechanical license is deemed not to cover the new use.

If you are the person seeking to clear a mechanical license, the advice inherent in the preceding paragraphs should be straightforward: try to obtain a license to use the master by identifying the licensed recording by the master number, instead of the record number.

### 2. *Type of Media*

Another technique used to limit the scope of the license is to specify precisely what kind of media the mechanical license covers. If the licensee's intention is simply to release a record album, then there would be no reason to grant a license that permits the use of the song on any other medium unless and until requested. Accordingly, the license should specify whether the use is for LP records, audiocassettes, or compact discs (CDs).

Note, the record number may not necessarily be the same as the *tape number* or the *CD number* — that is, the number identifying audiocassette tape or compact disc versions of the recording. Accordingly, if the form of a previously executed mechanical license did not specify the type of media on which use of the recording is limited, then the use of the record number in the mechanical license may have effectively limited the use to LPs.

Music copyright owners who were careful to limit their mechanical licenses in this way when issuing licenses for the use of music on record albums and audiocassettes may find that they have preserved for themselves the leverage to improve the terms of those licenses when record companies later seek permission to re-release those albums or cassettes in the new CD format. If the copyright owner had, for example, given a *rate* (i.e., charged less than the statutory rate) for the use of a song on an LP, and later became successful enough to warrant its release in the CD format, then, if the license was limited to the record number of the original LP, the recording company might be required to seek a new license to cover the use of the song on CD, and the copyright owner could then require full statutory rate. Had the original mechanical license been defined as including the master number, then the CD use would probably have been covered and the record company could continue licensing the song on the new media at half statutory rate.

Persons seeking to clear mechanical licenses should try to obtain a license to reproduce the recording in any format, or at least negotiate options to add additional formats at rates and other terms established at the time of the execution of the license.

### 3. Distribution Channels

The compulsory license provision of the copyright law provides that "a person may obtain a compulsory license only if his or her primary purpose in making phonorecords is to distribute them to the public for private use."[14] All mechanical licenses reflect the same limitation. If, for example, the primary purpose of making the recordings is for use in the facilitation of commercial broadcasts of the recording, then a compulsory license is not available and the use is outside the scope of the mechanical license. The type of license required for such use is an *electrical transcription license*, which is discussed in detail in Chapter 13.

### 4. Term

The term of a mechanical license is often not stated on the face of the license. It is assumed that the term is for the life of the copyright, because the compulsory license provision does not limit the term of mechanical licenses obtained under the statute. The license may be terminated, however, upon 30 days notice if the licensee fails to pay the mechanical license fee.

### 5. Territory

The territory of the mechanical license is usually limited. For example, most mechanical licenses issued in the United States limit the

---

[14] 17 U.S.C. Sec. 115 (a)(1).

territory to the United States, including its territories and possessions. The mechanics of mechanical licensing outside of the United States are discussed briefly below and in more detail in Chapter 5, on *International Subpublishing*.

### 6.  Exclusivity

A mechanical license is never granted on an exclusive basis. To grant exclusive mechanical rights would be in contradiction to the compulsory license provision which requires that, once recordings of the work have been distributed to the public, mechanical licenses are available to anyone upon the licensee's fulfillment of certain conditions.

### 7.  Credit

When a recording company asks for a *rate*, the music copyright owner has an opportunity to negotiate terms that he would not otherwise be able to obtain under the compulsory license provision. An example of a condition typically required when a rate is granted is that the songwriters and publishers be given credit on copies of the records distributed under the mechanical license. Such a provision may be added to a standard mechanical license in the following form:

> In regard to all phonorecords, manufactured, distributed and/or sold hereunder, you shall include in the label copy of all such phonorecords, or on the permanent containers of all such phonorecords, printed writer/publisher credit in the form of the names of the writer(s) and the publisher(s) of the copyrighted work.

## IV.  MECHANICAL RIGHTS AGENCIES

Thousands of recording companies seek licenses to record potentially hundreds of thousands of copyrighted compositions. Because it would be economically prohibitive for copyright owners to negotiate with the great number of potential licensees, many copyright owners and music publishers engage the services of a special representative for the purpose of licensing their compositions to be used in sound recordings. In the United States, The Harry Fox Agency, Inc.,[15] The Songwriter's Guild of America (formerly, the American Guild of Authors and Composers, or AGAC),[16] and SESAC, Inc.[17] are among the organizations that issue mechanical licenses.

The Harry Fox Agency, established in 1927 by the National Music Publisher's Association (NMPA), is by far the largest of these, representing over 27,000 music publishers. In addition to issuing mechanical licenses, the Harry Fox Agency also grants, on behalf of many of its member publishers, licenses for synchronization music with motion pictures and television programs, licenses for the creation of electrical transcriptions, and licenses for the use of music in commercial advertising. It also engages in the auditing of books and records of the licensees, such as record companies, using music under licenses issued by the Agency. The NMPA also provides mediation services to those member publishers who require an alternative to litigation as a means of settling a dispute between or among them.

The information required by the Harry Fox Agency for the issuance of a mechanical license includes: (1) the name of the person to whom the license is to be issued, (2) the title and writers of the composition, and, if known, the publisher(s), (3) the record number, (4) the performing artist, (5) the playing time in minutes and seconds of the composition, and (6) the release date of the record.

The Harry Fox Agency will not issue a mechanical license for less than the statutory rate without permission from the copyright owner of the song, to whom all such requests are promptly referred. For its services in issuing mechanical licenses, collecting royalties and distributing to publishers, as well as for the periodic audits of record manufacturers, the Harry Fox Agency charges a small fee based on a percentage of mechanical license fees collected. As of July 1, 1995, the commission rate charged by the agency to its music publishing clients, or *principals*, was 2.75% for mechanical licenses and 3% for synchronization licenses. However, effective as of January 1, 2002,

---

[15] The Harry Fox Agency, Inc., 711 Third Avenue, New York, NY 10017, Phone: 212-370-5330, www.harryfox.com.

[16] The Songwriters Guild of America, 1500 Harbor Boulevard, Weehawken, NJ 07087; Phone: 201-867-7603, www.songwriters.org.

[17] See Chapter 17, on *Performance Licenses*.

their mechanical license commission rate will be increased by 6%. In 1994, the Harry Fox Agency collected $357.9 million in royalties on behalf of music publishers.

Mechanical reproduction rights in music are recognized by law throughout the world. Though mechanical license fees vary from country to country, there is a mechanical right society in nearly every country that recognizes these rights. Further information on international mechanical rights societies affiliated with the Harry Fox Agency may be obtained from the Harry Fox Agency.


## V. INTERNATIONAL MECHANICAL RIGHTS ADMINISTRATION

As discussed in Chapter 5, on *International Subpublishing*, mechanical rights administration overseas differs significantly from the way mechanical licensing is conducted in the United States.

To begin with, by contrast with the thousands of individual music publishers, as well as The Harry Fox Agency and the Songwriter's Guild, providing licenses to record companies and others for the mechanical reproduction of music, overseas the collection of mechanical royalties is conducted by a single mechanical rights agency or collection society in each territory. For example, the mechanical rights agency in Canada is CMRRA, the *Canadian Musical Reproduction Rights Agency Limited*. Other mechanical rights societies include SDRM (France), GEMA (Germany), JASRAC (Japan), SIAE (Italy), and SGAE (Spain).

Moreover, licensing from that society is *mandatory*. This means that all mechanical licenses in the territory are issued by the collection society, not by the individual music publishers; in other words, all record companies in the territory are required to pay mechanical royalties to the collection society, not to the individual publishers.

Further, rather than being set by statute, mechanical rates overseas are generally set by some form of collective bargaining agreement between the mandatory mechanical rights organizations and the record companies, or an organization representing them. From time to time, a confederation of mechanical rights organizations from 30 countries called BIEM, the *Bureau International des Societes Gerant les Droits d'Enregistrement et de Reproduction Mecanique*, gets together with

IFPI, *the International Federation of Phonogram Industries*, representing the record companies, and these two organizations negotiate a collective bargaining agreement setting forth the terms and conditions for the licensing of mechanical reproductions. The terms of this are then administered by the member mechanical rights societies on a country by country basis. The mechanical fees in some territories, however, are set by the local government, which is the case in Japan and India.

As noted above, mechanical royalties in the United States are effectively determined by the statutory rate, which is expressed as a number of cents per song for each copy made and distributed. Mechanical royalties overseas, whether established by a mechanical licensing society, the local government, or collective bargaining arrangement, are usually expressed as a *percentage* of either the retail selling price (RSP) or the published price to the dealer (PPD) of the compact disc or audiocassette recordings in which the composition is embodied. Further, the license is not issued on a per song basis, but this license is issued and the fee is collected on the entire album, regardless of the number of songs it contains. The percentage fees vary from about 6% to over 10% of PPD for the entire album. These rates are generally higher than those charged for mechanical reproduction in the United States and Canada.

The means by which the publishers get paid the mechanical royalties to which they are entitled is through a *claims* process — each local publisher registers with the collection society its claim to mechanical royalties with respect to each of its compositions, indicating its interest in the entire song or, in the case of split copyright ownership, its percentage interest in the composition. Subpublishers are often required to prove their claim by filing a copy of their subpublishing agreement with the collection society. In many countries, unclaimed mechanical royalties go into what is referred to metaphorically as, a *black box,* which, after a period of time, gets distributed to local subpublishing companies under procedures which vary from country to country. Black box moneys and what a U.S. subpublisher can to do about them are discussed further in Chapter 5, on *International Subpublishing.*

# Appendix to Chapter 12
## Mechanical Licenses

# FORM 12.1

## STANDARD MECHANICAL LICENSE AGREEMENT

### MECHANICAL LICENSE AGREEMENT

A)    TITLE:                          DATE:

WRITER(S):

B)    PUBLISHER(S):

C)    <u>RECORD #ARTIST LABEL TIMING ROYALTY RATE</u>

<u>RELEASE DATE:</u>

You have advised us as the Publisher(s) referred to in (B) supra, that you wish to obtain a compulsory license to make and distribute phonorecords of the copyrighted work referred to in (A) supra, under the compulsory license provision of Section 115 of the Copyright Act.

Upon doing so, you shall have all rights which are granted to, and all the obligations which are imposed upon, users of said copyrighted work under the compulsory license provision of the Copyright Act, after phonorecords of the copyrighted work have been distributed to the public in the United States under the authority of the copyright owner by another person, except that with respect to phonorecords thereof made and distributed hereunder:

1)    You shall pay royalties and account to us as Publisher(s) quarterly, within forty-five days after the end of each calendar quarter, on the basis of phonorecords made and distributed;

2)    For such phonorecords made and distributed, the royalty shall be the Statutory rate in effect at the time the phonorecord is made, except as otherwise stated in (C) supra;

3)    This compulsory license covers and is limited to one particular recording of said copyrighted work as performed by the artist and on the phonorecord number identified in (C) supra; and this compulsory license does not supersede nor in any way affect any prior agreements now in effect respecting phonorecords of said copyrighted work;

4)    In the event you fail to account to us and pay royalties as herein provided for, said Publisher(s) may give written notice to you that, unless the default is remedied within 30 days of your receipt of the notice, this compulsory license will be automatically terminated. Such termination shall render either the making or the distribution, or both, of all phonorecords for which royalties have not been paid, actionable as acts of infringement under, and fully subject to the remedies provided by, the Copyright Act;

5)    You need not serve or file the notice of intention to obtain a compulsory license required by the Copyright Act;

6)    This agreement is limited to the United States, its territories and possessions.

ACCEPTED AND AGREED:        Very truly yours,


By _____        By _____


Date _____

# FORM 12.2

## ALTERNATIVE MECHANICAL LICENSE DRAFTED IN FAVOR OF THE LICENSOR

### MECHANICAL LICENSE

_____(referred to herein as the "Licensor") hereby grants to _____ (referred to herein as the "Licensee") the non-exclusive license to use, in whole or in part, the copyrighted musical composition entitled "_____" written by _____ (hereinafter referred to as the "Composition") in the recording, making and distribution of:

(Check appropriate lines:)

A. _____ Single: a non-visual "single" phonorecord in disc form;

B. _____ Album: a track on non-visual album phonorecord in disc form;

C. _____ Tape: a segment of a non-visual prerecorded tape phonorecord in reel to reel, cassette or cartridge form;

D. _____ C.D.: a track on non-visual album phonorecord on compact disc form;

to be made and distributed in the United States, its territories and possessions, in accordance with the provisions of Section 115 of the Copyright Act of the United States of America of October 19, 1976, as amended (the "Act"), except it is agreed that: (1) Licensee need not serve or file the notices required under the Act; (2) the accountings and payment of the royalty herein provided for shall be made quarterly, on the fifteenth day of February, May, August and November for the quarters ending the last day of December, March, June and September, respectively; and (3) a net royalty of SIX and ONE QUARTER CENT ($.0625) or ONE and TWO HUNDREDTHS OF ONE CENT ($.012) per minute of playing time or fraction thereof, whichever is greater, shall be payable by Licensee to Licensor on each phonorecord made, distributed and not returned (whether or not sold); provided, however, that no such royalty shall be payable with respect to promotional phonorecords sent to disc jockeys, reviewers, and the like, which are clearly marked "Promotional Records Not For Sale" and which are not being distributed by Licensee for resale. If the compulsory license royalty under Section 115 of the Act is hereafter adjusted to provide for a copyright royalty rate in excess of SIX and ONE QUARTER CENT ($.0625) and/or ONE and TWO HUNDREDTHS OF ONE CENT ($.012) per minute of playing time or fraction thereof, then the rate(s) set forth above shall be deemed automatically increased (proportionately, if applicable) to conform to such higher rate(s) for all phonorecords distributed following the effective date of such adjustment. The term "phonorecord" shall have that meaning set forth in Section 101 of the Copyright Act.

This license is limited to the particular recording and use of the Composition herein described and shall not include any other recording or form of recorded sound.

This license includes the privilege of making a musical arrangement of the Composition to the extent necessary to conform it to the style or manner of interpretation of the performance involved, but the arrangement made (i) may not change the basic melody or fundamental character or the lyrics of the Composition, (ii) shall not be subject to protection under the Act by Licensee as a derivative work, and (iii) may be freely used by Licensor for any and all purposes.

Failure to render timely accountings or make timely payments to Licensor shall, if not cured by Licensee within thirty (30) days after written notice thereof from Licensor, constitute a material breach of this license entitling Licensor, in addition to its other remedies, to immediately terminate this license and all rights granted to Licensee hereunder. Such termination shall render either the making or the distribution, or both, of all phonorecords for which royalties have not been paid, actionable as acts of infringement under, and fully subject to, the remedies provided by the Act. A waiver of any breach hereunder shall not constitute a waiver of any succeeding breach, whether similar or dissimilar. Upon written request and during Licensee's regular business hours, Licensee agrees to make its books and records relating to the subject matter hereof available for audit by Licensor and Licensor shall have the right to make copies thereof. Reasonable reserves may be withheld in the same manner as Licensee withholds and liquidates reserves in accordance with its current arrangement with The Harry Fox Agency, Inc.

This license is personal, non-licensable and non-assignable, except by Licensor. This license does not supersede nor affect any prior licenses or agreements now in force respecting recordings of the Composition. This license shall be governed by and construed under the laws of the State of California,

THIS LICENSE IS NOT VALID UNTIL LICENSOR RECEIVES A FREE COPY OF THE SINGLE, ALBUM AND/OR TAPE LICENSED HEREUNDER AND A COUNTERSIGNED COPY OF THIS LICENSE.

Dated:

LICENSEE:                          LICENSOR:

_____        _____

By: _____          By: _____

Release Date: _____

Timing: _____

Single Number:          _____

Album Number:           _____

Tape Number:            _____

C.D. Number:            _____

Recording Artist:       _____

All payments to be made to Licensor hereunder shall be made to Licensor in care of:

                            _____

# FORM 12.3

## ALTERNATIVE MECHANICAL LICENSE DRAFTED IN FAVOR OF THE LICENSEE

### MECHANICAL LICENSE

_____ (referred to herein as the "Licensor") hereby grants to _____ (referred to herein as the "Licensee") the non-exclusive license to use, in whole or in part, the copyrighted musical composition set forth below:

written by _____ (hereinafter referred to as the "Composition") in the recording, making and distribution of phonorecords (as that term is defined in Section 101 of the Copyright Act) to be made and distributed throughout the world in accordance with the provisions of Section 115 of the Copyright Act of the United States of America of October 19, 1976, as amended (the "Act"), except it is agreed that: (1) Licensee need not serve or file the notices required under the Act; (2) the accountings and payment of the royalty herein provided for shall be made quarterly, as set forth below; (3) consideration for such license shall be the statutory rate in effect at the time of execution hereof for each phonorecord made, distributed and not returned (whether or not sold) containing the Composition; provided, however, that no such royalty shall be payable with respect to promotional phonorecords sent to disc jockeys, reviewers, and the like, which are not being distributed by Licensee for resale; and (4) this license shall be worldwide.

This license permits the use of the Compositions, or any of them, in the particular recordings made in connection with the sound recording _____ by _____ , and permits the use of such recording in any phonorecord in which the recording may be embodied in whatever form now known or hereafter devised. This license includes the privilege of making a musical arrangement of the Composition to the extent necessary to conform it to the style or manner of interpretation of the performance involved.

Licensee will compute the royalties earned by Licensor pursuant to this license within forty-five (45) days after the end of each calendar quarter (provided that with respect to royalties resulting from non-U.S. transactions such period shall be ninety (90) days after end of each calendar quarter), and will deliver to Licensor a quarterly royalty statement for each such period together with the net amount of royalties computed in accordance with this license, if any.

All payments shall be made to Licensor hereunder shall be made to Licensor in care of: _____

Upon at least fifteen (15) days' prior written notice to Licensee, a certified public accountant retained on Licensor's behalf shall have the right once each year to inspect such of Licensee's business books and records as may reasonably be necessary for Licensor to verify the accuracy of any royalty statement rendered by Licensee within the twelve (12) month period immediately preceding the date of the inspection. The information contained in a royalty statement shall be conclusively deemed correct and binding upon Licensor, resulting in the loss of all further audit rights with respect to such statement, unless specifically challenged by written notice from Licensor within twelve (12) months from the date such royalty statement was delivered by Licensee. Any inspection of Licensee's books and records pursuant to this Section shall be conducted by Licensor at Licensee's premises, only during Licensee's normal business hours, under Licensee's supervision and in a manner which does not interfere with Licensee's business operations. Licensor shall specify, at least fifteen (15) days in advance of any inspection, the list of items that Licensor desires to inspect. This right of audit shall be subject to Licensor's certified public accountant's executing Licensee's standard Nondisclosure Agreement to maintain all information learned as a result of such inspection in strict confidence. Licensor's accountants shall be authorized by Licensee to report to Licensor only the amount of fees due and payable for the period examined. Licensee may withhold a reasonable reserve for returnable copies. This license may not be terminated for any reason, and Licensor's sole remedy for breach shall be a claim for damages.

This license shall be construed and enforced in accordance with the laws of the State of California applicable to agreements between residents of California wholly executed and wholly performed therein. Any action or proceeding brought by either party against the other arising out of or related to this Agreement shall be brought only in a state or federal court of competent jurisdiction located in the County of Los Angeles, California, and the parties hereby consent to the personal jurisdiction of said courts. The provisions of this paragraph shall survive any termination of the Agreement.

LICENSEE:      LICENSOR:

_____      _____

By      By

_____      _____

Name      Name

_____      _____

Date      Date

# LAW 12.1

## COMPULSORY LICENSE PROVISION OF THE COPYRIGHT ACT OF 1976 (17 U.S.C. SECTION 115, AS AMENDED BY THE REVISED BY DIGITAL PERFORMANCE RIGHT IN SOUND RECORDINGS ACT OF 1995, PUB. L. 104-39, SEC. 4, NOV. 1, 1995, 109 STAT. 344)

Section 115. **Scope of exclusive rights in nondramatic musical works: Compulsory license for making and distributing phonorecords**

In the case of nondramatic musical works, the exclusive rights provided by clauses (1) and (3) of section 106, to make and to distribute phonorecords of such works, are subject to compulsory licensing under the conditions specified by this section.

(a)   *Availability and Scope of Compulsory License—*

(1)   When phonorecords of a nondramatic musical work have been distributed to the public in the United States under the authority of the copyright owner, any other person, including those who make phonorecords or digital phonorecord deliveries, may, by complying with the provisions of this section, obtain a compulsory license to make and distribute phonorecords of the work. A person may obtain a compulsory license only if his or her primary purpose in making phonorecords is to distribute them to the public for private use, including by means of a digital phonorecord delivery. A person my not obtain a compulsory license for use of the work in the making of phonorecords duplicating a sound recording fixed by another, unless: (i) such sound recording was fixed lawfully; and (ii) the making of the phonorecords was authorized by the owner of copyright in the sound recording or, if the sound recording was fixed before February 15, 1972, by any person who fixed the sound

recording pursuant to an express license from the owner of the copyright in the musical work or pursuant to a valid compulsory license for use of such work in a sound recording.

(2)    A compulsory license includes the privilege of making a musical arrangement of the work to the extent necessary to conform it to the style or manner of interpretation of the performance involved, but the arrangement shall not change the basic melody or fundamental character of the work, and shall not be subject to protection as a derivative work under this title, except with the express consent of the copyright owner.

(b)    *Notice of Intention To Obtain Compulsory License.—*

(1)    Any person who wishes to obtain a compulsory license under this section shall, before or within thirty days after making, and before distributing any phonorecords of the work, serve notice of intention to do so on the copyright owner. If the registration or other public records of the Copyright Office do not identify the copyright owner and include an address at which notice can be served, it shall be sufficient to file the notice of intention in the Copyright Office. The notice shall comply, in form, content and manner of service, with requirements that the Register of Copyrights shall prescribe by regulation.

(2)    Failure to serve or file the notice required by clause (1) forecloses the possibility of a compulsory license and, in the absence of a negotiated license, renders the making and distribution of phonorecords objectionable as acts of infringement under Section 501 and fully subject to the remedies provided by sections 502 through 506 and 509.

(c)    *Royalty Payable under Compulsory License.—*

(1)    To be entitled to receive royalties under a compulsory license, the copyright owner must be identified in the registration or other public records of the Copyright Office. The

owner is entitled to royalties for phonorecords made and distributed after being so identified, but is not entitled to recover for any phonorecords previously made and distributed.

(2)     Except as provided by clause (1), the royalty under a compulsory license shall be payable for every phonorecord made and distributed in accordance with the license. For this purpose, and other than as provided in paragraph (3), a phonorecord is considered "distributed" if the person exercising the compulsory license has voluntarily and permanently parted with its possession. With respect to each work embodied in the phonorecord, the royalty shall be either two and three-fourths cents, or one-half of one cent per minute of playing time or fraction thereof, whichever amount is larger.

(3)     (A)     A compulsory license under this section includes the right of the compulsory licensee to distribute or authorize the distribution of a phonorecord of a nondramatic musical work by means of a digital transmission which constitutes a digital phonorecord delivery, regardless of whether the digital transmission is also a public performance of the sound recording under section 106(6) of this title or of any nondramatic musical work embodied therein under section 106(4) of this title. For every digital phonorecord delivery by or under the authority of the compulsory licensee—

(i)     on or before December 31, 1997, the royalty payable by the compulsory licensee shall be the royalty prescribed under paragraph (2) and chapter 8 of this title; and

(ii)     on or after January 1, 1998, the royalty payable by the compulsory licensee shall be the royalty prescribed under subparagraphs (B) through (F) and chapter 8 of this title.

(B)     Notwithstanding any provision of the antitrust laws, any copyright owners of nondramatic musical works and any persons entitled to obtain a compulsory license under subsection (a)(1) may negotiate and agree upon the terms and rates of royalty payments under this paragraph and the proportionate division of fees paid among copyright owners, and may designate common agents to negotiate, agree to, pay or receive such royalty payments. Such authority to negotiate the term and rates of royalty payments includes, but is not limited to, the authority to negotiate the year during which the royalty rates prescribed under subparagraphs (B) through (F) and chapter 8 of this title shall next be determined.

(C)    During the period of June 30, 1996, through December 31, 1996, the Librarian of Congress shall cause notice to be published in the Federal Register of the initiation of voluntary negotiation proceedings for the purpose of determining reasonable terms and rates of royalty payments for the activities specified by subparagraph (A) during the period beginning January 1, 1998, and ending on the effective date of any new terms and rates established pursuant to subparagraph (C), (D) or (F), or such other date (regarding digital phonorecord deliveries) as the parties may agree. Such terms and rates shall distinguish between (i) digital phonorecord deliveries where the reproduction or distribution of a phonorecord is incidental to the transmission which constitutes the digital phonorecord delivery, and (ii) digital phonorecord deliveries in general. Any copyright owners of nondramatic musical works and any persons entitled to obtain a compulsory license under subsection (a)(1) may submit to the Librarian of Congress licenses covering such activities. The parties to each negotiation proceeding shall bear their own costs.

(D)    In the absence of license agreements negotiated under subparagraphs (B) and (C), upon the filing of a petition in accordance with section 803(a)(1), the Librarian of Congress shall pursuant to chapter 8, convene a copyright arbitration royalty panel to determine and publish in the Federal Register a schedule of rates and terms which, subject to subparagraph (E), shall be binding on all copyright owners of nondramatic musical works and persons entitled to obtain a compulsory license under subsection (a)(1) during the period beginning January 1, 1998, and ending on the effective date of any new terms and rates established pursuant to subparagraph (C), (D) or (F), or such other date (regarding digital phonorecord deliveries) as may be determined pursuant to subparagraphs (B) and (C). Such terms and rates shall distinguish between (i) digital phonorecord deliveries where the reproduction or distribution of a phonorecord is incidental to the transmission which constitutes the digital phonorecord delivery, and (ii) digital phonorecord deliveries in general. In addition to the objectives set forth in section 801(b)(1), in establishing such rates and terms, the copyright arbitration royalty panel may consider rates and terms under voluntary license agreements negotiated as provided in subparagraphs (B) and (C). The royalty rates payable for a compulsory license for a digital phonorecord delivery under this section shall be established de novo and no precedential effect shall be given to the amount of the royalty payable by a compulsory licensee for digital phonorecord deliveries on or before December 31, 1997. The Librarian of Congress shall also establish requirements by which copyright owners may receive reasonable notice of the use of their works under this section, and under which records of such use shall be kept and made available by persons making digital phonorecord deliveries.

(E)    (i)    License agreements voluntarily negotiated at any time between one or more copyright owners of nondramatic musical works and one or more persons entitled to obtain a compulsory license under subsection (a)(1) shall be given effect in lieu of any determination by the Librarian of Congress. Subject to clause (ii), the royalty rates determined pursuant to subparagraph (C), (D) or (F) shall be given effect in lieu of any contrary royalty rates specified in a contract pursuant to which a recording artist who is the author of a nondramatic musical work grants a license under that person's exclusive rights in the musical work under sections 106(l) and (3) or commits another person to grant a license in that musical work under sections 106(l) and (3), to a person desiring to fix in a tangible medium of expression a sound recording embodying the musical work.

(ii)     The second sentence of clause (i) shall not apply to—

(I)     a contract entered into on or before June 22, 1995, and not modified thereafter for the purpose of reducing the royalty rates determined pursuant to subparagraph (C), (D) or (F) or of increasing the number of musical works within the scope of the contract covered by the reduced rates, except if a contract entered into on or before June 22, 1995, is modified thereafter for the purpose of increasing the number of musical works within the scope of the contract, any contrary royalty rates specified in the contract shall be given effect in lieu of royalty rates determined pursuant to subparagraph (C), (D) or (F) for the number of musical works within the scope of the contract as of June 22, 1995; and

(II)     a contract entered into after the date that the sound recording is fixed in a tangible medium of expression substantially in a form intended for commercial release, if at the time the contract is entered into, the recording artist retains the right to grant licenses as to the musical work under sections 106(l) and 106(3).

(F)     The procedures specified in subparagraphs (C) and (D) shall be repeated and concluded, in accordance with regulations that the Librarian of Congress shall prescribe, in each fifth calendar year after 1997, except to the extent that different years for the repeating and concluding of such proceedings may be determined in accordance with subparagraphs (E) and (C).

(G)     Except as provided in section 1002(e) of this title, a digital phonorecord delivery licensed under this paragraph shall be accompanied by the information encoded in the sound recording, if any, by or under the authority of the copyright owner of that sound recording, that identifies the title of the sound recording, the featured recording artist who performs on the sound recording, and related information, including information concerning the underlying musical work and its writer.

(H)    (i)    A digital phonorecord delivery of a sound recording is actionable as an act of infringement under section 501, and is fully subject to the remedies provided by sections 502 through 506 and section 509, unless—

(I)    the digital phonorecord delivery has been authorized by the copyright owner of the sound recording; and

(II)    the owner of the copyright in the sound recording or the entity making the digital phonorecord delivery has obtained a compulsory license under this section or has otherwise been authorized by the copyright owner of the musical work to distribute or authorize the distribution, by means of a digital phonorecord delivery, of each musical work embodied in the sound recording.

(ii)    Any cause of action under this subparagraph shall be in addition to those available to the owner of the copyright in the nondramatic musical work under subsection (c)(6) and section 106(4) and the owner of the copyright in the sound recording under section 106(6).

(I)    The liability of the copyright owner of a sound recording for infringement of the copyright in a nondramatic musical work embodied in the sound recording shall be determined in accordance with applicable law, except that the owner of a copyright in a sound recording shall not be liable for a digital phonorecord delivery by a third party if the owner of the copyright in the sound recording does not license the distribution of a phonorecord of the nondramatic musical work.

(J)    Nothing in section 1008 shall be construed to prevent the exercise of the rights and remedies allowed by this paragraph, paragraph (6), and chapter 5 in the event of a digital phonorecord delivery, except that no action alleging infringement of copyright may be brought under this title against a manufacturer, importer or distributor of a digital audio recording device, a digital audio recording medium, an analog recording device, or an analog recording medium, or against a consumer, based on the actions described in such section.

(K)     Nothing in this section annuls or limits (i) the exclusive right to publicly perform a sound recording or the musical work embodied therein, including by means of a digital transmission, under sections 106(4) and 106(6), (ii) except for compulsory licensing under the conditions specified by this section, the exclusive rights to reproduce and distribute the sound recording and the musical work embodied therein under sections 106(l) and 106(3), including by means of a digital phonorecord delivery, or (iii) any other rights under any other provision of section 106, or remedies available under this title, as such rights or remedies exist either before or after the date of enactment of the Digital Performance Right in Sound Recordings Act of 1995.

(L)     The provisions of this section concerning digital phonorecord deliveries shall not apply to any exempt transmissions or retransmissions under section 114(d)(1). The exemptions created in section 114(d)(1) do not expand or reduce the rights of copyright owners under section 106(l) through (5) with respect to such transmissions and retransmissions.

(4)     A compulsory license under this section includes the right of the maker of a phonorecord of a nondramatic musical work under subsection (a)(1) to distribute or authorize distribution of such phonorecord by rental, lease, or lending (or by acts or practices in the nature of rental lease, or lending). In addition to any royalty payable under clause (2) and chapter 8 of this title, a royalty shall be payable by the compulsory licensee for every act of distribution of a phonorecord by or in the nature of rental lease, or lending, by or under the authority

of the compulsory licensee. With respect to each nondramatic musical work embodied in the phonorecord, the royalty shall be a proportion of the revenue received by the compulsory licensee from every such act of distribution of the phonorecord under this clause equal to the proportion of the revenue received by the compulsory licensee from distribution of the phonorecord under clause (2) that is payable by a compulsory licensee under that clause and under chapter 8. The Register of Copyrights shall issue regulations to carry out the purpose of this clause.

(5)    Royalty payments shall be made on or before the twentieth day of each month and shall include all royalties for the month next preceding. Each monthly payment shall be made under oath and shall comply with requirements that the Register of Copyrights shall prescribe by regulation. The Register shall also prescribe regulations under which detailed cumulative annual statements of account, certified by a certified public accountant, shall be filed for every compulsory license under this section. The regulations covering both the monthly and the annual statements of account shall prescribe the form, content, and manner of certification with respect to the number of records made and the number of records distributed.

(6)    If the copyright owner does not receive the monthly payment and the monthly and annual statements of account when due, the owner may give written notice to the licensee that, unless the default is remedied within thirty days from the date of the notice, the compulsory license will be automatically terminated. Such termination renders either the making or the distribution, or both, of all phonorecords for which the royalty has not been paid, actionable as acts of infringement under section 501 and fully subject to the remedies provided by sections 502 through 506 and 509.

(d)    *Definition.* As used in this section, the following term has the following meaning: A "digital phonorecord delivery" is each individual delivery of a phonorecord by digital transmission of a sound recording which results in a specifically identifiable reproduction by or for any transmission recipient of a phono-record of that sound recording, regardless of whether the digital transmission is also a public performance of the sound recording or any nondramatic musical work embodied therein. A digital phonorecord delivery does not result from a real-time, non-interactive subscription transmission of a sound recording where no reproduction of the sound recording or the musical work embodied therein is made from the inception of the transmission through to its receipt by the transmission recipient in order to make the sound recording audible.

(As amended Pub. L. 104-39, § 4, Nov. 1, 1995, 109 Stat. 344.)

CHAPTER 13

# ELECTRICAL TRANSCRIPTION LICENSES

## SUMMARY

**APPENDIX TO CHAPTER 13**

CHAPTER **13**

# ELECTRICAL TRANSCRIPTION LICENSES

An *electrical transcription license* is a license which permits the reproduction of music in recordings that are not accompanied by moving pictures and that are made for the purpose of facilitating radio broadcasts or purposes other than distribution to the public for private use. Like print licenses and mechanical licenses, electrical transcription licenses are derived from the copyright owner's exclusive right of reproduction.[1] Electrical transcription licenses are commonly used for the reproduction of music by radio stations, producers of syndicated radio programs, background music services, and music reproduced for in-flight use by commercial airlines.

This chapter provides an overview of the terms and conditions contained in customary electrical transcription licenses.

## I. DISTINCTION BETWEEN MECHANICAL LICENSES AND ELECTRICAL TRANSCRIPTION LICENSES

The distinction between mechanical recordings and electronic transcriptions inheres in the use for which the recording is intended: copies of *mechanical* recordings, such as record albums, audiocassettes, and compact discs, are primarily intended for distribution to the public for private use; copies of *electronic transcription* recordings are intended for distribution to radio stations, background music services, and special music services for public broadcasting purposes. This distinction is important because only mechanical recordings intended for

---

[1] 17 U.S.C. 106(1).

distribution to the public for private use are subject to the compulsory licensing provision of the copyright law.[2] Accordingly, fees and other terms for licenses to make recordings intended for background music services and radio broadcast may be freely negotiated without regard to the limitations set forth in the compulsory licensing provision.

## II. TYPES OF ELECTRICAL TRANSCRIPTIONS

Electrical transcription licenses are issued in connection with the following kinds of transcription recordings:

### A. Transcriptions for Radio Broadcast

The making of recordings of introductory musical themes, background music for radio commercials, and compilations of musical compositions distributed as part of syndicated radio shows, all require permission from the copyright owners of the music involved. The permission to make such recordings is entirely distinct from the permission required to perform the recordings. The latter is normally acquired from the performance rights society, such as ASCAP or BMI, but permission to create the recording itself and make copies of it is acquired directly from the copyright owner.

#### 1. Themes and Introductions

Radio programs, such as news programs and talk shows, often use some short familiar theme music as an introduction to the program or as background music for *segues* (i.e., transitions) to and from commercials or other breaks in the program. Music publishers often prepare electrical transcription recordings containing a variety of short themes and introductions for this purpose and distribute them to radio stations free of charge. A music publisher's incentive for providing this service, of course, is the performance fees it will receive from

---

[2] Section 115 of the copyright law states, "A person may obtain a compulsory license only if his or her primary purpose in making phonorecords is *to distribute them to the public for private use*." 17 U.S.C. Sec. 115 (emphasis added).

performance rights societies as a result of the airplay of these short pieces of music. Performance licenses are discussed at length in Chapter 17.

### 2. Syndicated Radio Programs

A *syndicated radio program* is a series of pre-recorded, one or two hour radio programs of music, usually accompanied by introductory and background commentary delivered by an announcer. The pre-recorded tapes of these programs are licensed by their producers on an individual basis to local radio stations around the country. For example, a producer may prepare a series of syndicated radio programs of selected Frank Sinatra recordings, including short commentaries regarding each recording, identifying the songwriters, the arrangers, and any interesting circumstances related to the recording or the time during the artist's life when the recording was made. Short interviews with the artist may also be featured in some of these programs. Series such as these might be attractive to local radio stations that cater to the audience for which the program was designed.

The tapes containing these programs and recordings are not mechanical reproductions, in the strict sense of the term, because they are primarily intended for distribution to broadcast stations for further broadcast — not for distribution to the public for private use. The compulsory license provision would therefore not apply and the music copyright owner is free to negotiate fees for such recordings. The standard form used by the Harry Fox Agency for licensing electrical transcriptions for syndicated radio programs is set forth as Form 13.1 at the end of this chapter.

### 3. Commercial Advertisements Prepared for Radio Broadcast

Recordings that contain commercial advertising which include licensed music are electrical transcriptions, and the licenses of the use of such music are electrical transcription licenses. Because the use of the music for commercial advertising purposes requires special consideration, the subject of licensing the use of music in radio commercials is discussed in Chapter 20 below.

Licenses to make electrical transcriptions for commercial radio broadcast generally do not contain a license to *perform* the music. The performance license will be covered by the radio stations' license from the performance rights societies, such as BMI or ASCAP. Performance licenses are discussed in greater detail in Chapter 17.

## B. Transcriptions for Background Music Services

A background music service is the type of music performance described in the BMI public performance license as the "unobtrusive accompaniment to work, shopping, conversation, dining and relaxation," which has been humorously referred to as "elevator" music — the music you hear while standing in an elevator or the mood-setting accompaniment you may or may not notice while waiting in a hotel lobby, standing in line at the bank, or having a meal in a restaurant. It has been said that background music isn't music to listen to; it's music to hear.

### 1.  Muzak and 3M

The two principal organizations that provide background music services are Musak and 3M. Muzak develops recorded transcription tapes which are sent to their hundreds of franchisees throughout the world who each deliver performances from the recordings to their hotel, restaurant and office clients via FM broadcast, or specially leased phone or cable lines. 3M develops recorded transcription tapes which are sent directly to their hotel, restaurant and office clients.

Electronic transcription licenses that permit the making of such recordings by Muzak and 3M are issued by music publishers, often through their agents, such as the Harry Fox Agency.

Because the terms of electronic transcription licenses are not subject to the compulsory license provisions of the copyright law, terms and conditions of electronic transcription licenses are subject to negotiation. Nevertheless, the fees tend to follow standard patterns and generally do not vary from song to song. Accordingly, many of the basic considerations in granting licenses — determining the value of the song, the importance of the song in relation to its intended use, and the scope of the use — will not in practice apply to granting or clearing electronic transcription licenses for background music services.

Further, the terms and conditions for licensing music for background music services will vary depending upon the delivery method used by the particular background music service. Electronic transcription licenses issued to Muzak are for a fixed term of years, generally 1 or 3 years, with a single payment for all copies of the composition made during the term. A licensee is often given an option to renew for an additional fee payable upon renewal. Electronic transcription licenses issued to 3M work differently. Because 3M sells its tapes to its customers, rather than leasing them, the electronic transcription fee is structured more like a mechanical license fee. A per cent fee is payable per copy of each selection sold.

### 2. Performance License Aspects

Background music services, whether provided by Muzak or 3M, entail not only the making of recordings of music not intended for distribution to the public for private use, but also the performance of the music to the public. Accordingly, background music services require both an electrical transcription license to make the recording and a performance license to render the performance of the recording to the public.

Electronic transcription licenses for background music services may or may not include the license necessary to perform the music recorded under the authorization of the transcription license. Where a transcription license does not include one, the performance license must be obtained by separate agreement from the applicable performance rights society. Performance licenses are handled differently, depending on the background music service and the performance rights society involved.

With respect to performances of music from recordings made and distributed by Muzak, each franchisee of Muzak obtains a separate performance blanket performing license directly from ASCAP and BMI. This means that the local franchise organization that does the broadcast or electronic transmission to the offices, hotels, and restaurants in which the music is heard pays ASCAP and BMI for the performances, not the offices, hotels or the restaurants. The franchisee pays ASCAP and BMI a percentage of its gross receipts, although with respect to certain kinds of establishments where the music is performed a flat fee is payable instead.

With respect to performances of music from recordings made and distributed by 3M, if the music was from the ASCAP repertoire, the performance license is obtained directly from the publisher at the time the electronic transcription license is issued. The fees paid to the publisher is a number of cents (e.g., three cents) per copy of the song transcription for the three year duration of the license, with a renewal fee of additional cents per year (e.g., one cent). This amount would be in addition to the per copy amount payable for the electronic transcription license. If the music was from the BMI repertoire, the performance license is obtained directly from BMI. The same fee, but paid directly to BMI rather than to the music publisher. BMI would receive a fixed number of cents per copy of a song transcription. Users of the tapes have no license to use the tapes after the performance license expires.

### 3.  Recent Changes

The standard forms of relationship between music publishing companies and some background music services are currently being renegotiated. Future licenses issued to these services may become more akin to the blanket licenses issued by performance rights societies, with organizations such as the Harry Fox Agency distributing collected license fees to music copyright owners in proportion to the number of times each composition is played over the background music system.

### C.  Transcriptions for In-flight Use on Airlines

Special pre-recorded music programs compiled for use on passenger airlines are akin to both background music services and syndicated radio programs. However, unlike background music services, which are scientifically designed to promote a certain efficiency or relaxation in its listeners, programs designed for in-flight listening are specifically for the active entertainment of its audience. Airline music is programmed to be listened to. These programs, revised on a monthly basis, offer specific categories of music entertainment, such as easy listening, top rock 'n roll hits, country and western, jazz, classical, and international music, from which the passenger may choose. In this respect, they are more like syndicated radio programs, whose "broadcast" is really a "cablecast" distributed to an audience of passengers on board the flights of a particular airline during any given month.

Electrical transcription licenses for this purpose are similar to the license set forth as Form 13.1 for syndicated radio programs. Because the performance of music on an airplane or jet liner is a public performance requiring permission of the copyright owner, performance rights societies issue special performance licenses to the airlines for this purpose.

## III. CONSIDERATIONS IN GRANTING AND CLEARING ELECTRICAL TRANSCRIPTION LICENSES

Because it does not apply to recordings made for purposes other than for distribution to the public for private use, the compulsory license provision does not limit the flexibility the copyright owner has in negotiating the terms of electrical transcription licenses.

### A. Fee Structure

Although there is room for negotiation in determining the appropriate fee to charge for an electrical transcription license, the fees are generally not high in comparison with other kinds of uses. Licenses to make transcriptions for background music for use by radio stations and syndicated radio program producers are commonly issued on a flat dollar amount per copy made. The same is true for transcriptions made for in-flight use by airlines. Typical fees charged for the making of transcription copies are set forth in Chapter 27.

It is important to remember that licenses for making transcription copies do not normally include the license to perform the music publicly; accordingly, separate fees for music performed publicly by the use of licensed transcriptions are collected on a blanket basis by performance rights societies from the broadcasters or other organizations rendering the performance.

### B. Value of the Song and Its Importance in Relation to the Intended Use

Because the fees for transcription licenses are generally not high in comparison with other kinds of uses, music copyright owners will not generally engage in the more extensive analysis given to the consideration of other forms of licenses, such as theatrical synchronization, videogram, and commercial advertising licenses. By the same token, copyright owners should not agonize over what fees to charge for these uses, because the ability to share in the economic success of the transcription is available through the collection of performance fees for the public performances of the transcriptions licensed.

### 1. Arrangements and Changes

Many of the provisions common in electrical transcription licenses are derived from standard mechanical license forms. For example, if new recordings are being made for the transcriptions, the license will provide that the arrangements made shall not change the basic melody or fundamental character of the work. These licenses will also provide that neither the title nor the lyrics of the music shall be changed, added to, or translated, without the further permission of the copyright owner.

## C. Scope of Use

### 1. Type of Media

The electrical transcription license will generally provide the licensee with some flexibility in using the various forms of recording media. The only important restraint is that the media is limited to audio devices only, and not those that include visual images.

### 2. Distribution Channels

The transcription license will generally limit the purpose of the recordings and distribution to the purpose stated in the license, such as for syndicated radio broadcasts. Accordingly, a license for syndicated radio broadcasts will not allow copies of the recording to be made for any other purpose, including distribution of copies to the public, distribution of copies for inclusion in juke boxes, distribution of copies for background music services, or distribution of copies for in-flight performance.

Even if the transcription license is limited to a specific use, such as syndicated radio programs, the music copyright owner should try to be as specific as possible, requiring the license to identify by name the specific syndicated radio program, programs, or series of programs for which the music is being licensed. This is particularly important if any form of exclusivity is being considered.

### 3.  Term

The term of an electrical transcription license will generally be from one to three years. Of course, the license may be terminated sooner if the licensee fails to pay the required fee.

### 4.  Territory

The territory of an electrical transcription license is usually limited to the United States and Canada. Most music publishers with overseas affiliates will require licenses for additional territories be negotiated locally on a country-by-country basis.

### 5.  Exclusivity

Transcription licenses are rarely granted on an exclusive basis, but some form of exclusivity could be acceptable for an increased license fee, provided it is narrowly defined. Considerations for granting and clearing exclusivity provisions in connection with the use of music in commercial advertising is discussed more fully in Chapter 20.

## IV. RIGHTS AGENCIES

Electronic transcription licenses are generally available directly from music publishers. However, the Harry Fox Agency does issue these licenses on behalf of many of its member publishers. For more information on the Harry Fox Agency, see Chapter 12.

# APPENDIX TO CHAPTER 13
## ELECTRICAL TRANSCRIPTION LICENSES

# FORM 13.1

## ELECTRICAL TRANSCRIPTION LICENSE FOR SYNDICATED RADIO BROADCASTS USED BY THE HARRY FOX AGENCY

### ELECTRICAL TRANSCRIPTION LICENSE

Agreement made as of _____ by and between _____ (hereinafter referred to as "LICENSEE") and THE HARRY FOX AGENCY, INC. 711 Third Avenue, New York, New York 10017 (hereinafter referred to as "AGENT").

### W I T N E S S E T H:

Whereas, AGENT is the licensing and collecting agent for numerous music publisher-principals (hereinafter individually and collectively referred to as "Publishers") who own or control the rights hereinafter license of their respective musical composition:

Whereas, LICENSEE, is engaged in the business of producing music programming for the purpose of Syndicated Radio Broadcast and furnishing such services to its customers, the Syndicated Radio Broadcast entitled: "_____".

Whereas, LICENSEE, in order to record the musical compositions owned by the Publishers and to reproduce and distribute the recordings, is required under copyright law to obtain a license from the Publishers and accordingly desires to obtain such a license from the Publishers for the use of their respective music compositions; and

Whereas, AGENT has been authorized and instructed by its principals, the Publishers, to issue a license to LICENSEE;

NOW, THEREFORE, it is agreed as follows:

1.    This agreement is being entered into by AGENT as the authorized agent, and acting for and on behalf of its principals, the Publishers.

2.    For the purpose hereof the Publishers shall be and be deemed those publishers listed in "THE HARRY FOX MUSIC PUBLISHERS DIRECTORY" as it is from time to time amended and supplemented, excluding therefrom however those publishers who are the subject of notices to LICENSEE from AGENT excluding such publishers from the operation of this agreement. The right to exclude publishers from the operation of this agreement (hereby reserved) may be exercised from time to time by AGENT pursuant to instructions from, and acting on behalf of, such publishers so excluded, provided that any exclusion shall not apply to any compositions licensed and recorded under this agreement prior to the date of the delivery of the notice to LICENSEE relating to their exclusion.

3.    For the purposes of this agreement, a locally-sponsored broadcast shall be deemed to mean a program advertising a business or service that is purely local in character, solely confined within the area of the stations coverage and broadcast over the stations facilities only but shall be deemed to include a program that is purely local in character, solely confined within the area of the stations coverage that is broadcast over the stations facilities only, even though it is paid for in part, not in whole, by a national advertiser, provided that such program is not one, the musical content of which was selected by a national advertiser, and is not a program which was prepared by a national advertiser for national or regional dissemination. All other sponsored commercial broadcasts shall be deemed to be nationally sponsored broadcasts and not covered by the terms of this license.

4.    The term of this Agreement shall be for a period of _____ years commencing _____ and terminating _____ (hereinafter referred to as the "Term").

5.    The territory within which the rights hereinafter licensed may be exercised by LICENSEE is limited to the United States of America, its territories and possessions and Puerto Rico (hereinafter referred to as "Territory").

6.    For the purposes hereof, the following *non-exclusive* rights are hereby granted to LICENSEE by the Publisher with respect to the "licensed compositions" (as such term is hereinafter defined) during the Term and for use within the Territory:

   a)    The rights to mechanically reproduce (i.e. make recordings of) the licensed composition made by the Licensee and transcriptions of previously recorded vocal/instrumental recordings of the licensed musical composition is expressly conditioned upon having valid master recording rights licenses from the respective owner or controller of such rights, in whole or in part for the purposes of using such recordings in and only in connection with the syndicated radio services furnished by LICENSEE to its customers.

   b)    The right to make and use copies of such recordings in connection with LICENSEE music program services for Syndicated Radio Broadcast only and the right to make and furnish copies of such recordings to its customers for use in connection with such syndicated Radio music services only.

   c)    The rights herein granted to record and make copies of recordings hereunder embodying performances of the licensed compositions shall include recordings on wire, tape, discs or any other devices now or hereafter known but are limited to audio devices only not accompanied by the recording of visual images.

d)    Neither the title nor lyrics of the licensed compositions shall be changed, substituted for, added to or translated without the written consent of its respective Publishers.

e)    The pubic performance of the licensed compositions, as embodied in the recordings, by LICENSEE is expressly conditioned upon such performers thereof having valid performing rights licenses from the respective Publishers, the American Society of Composers, Authors and Publishers (ASCAP) or Broadcast Music, Inc. (BMI).

7.    For the purposes hereof "licensed compositions" shall be and deemed to mean those musical compositions with respect to which:

a)    the rights hereunder licenses are owned or controlled by the Publisher, and

b)    AGENT has not indicated a restriction on such use by the respective Publishers within 20 days after the receipt of such notice from LICENSEE, the right to restrict such use hereby being reserved by and on behalf of the Publishers.

8.    In consideration of the license hereby granted, LICENSEE agrees to pay AGENT for and on behalf of its principals, the Publishers, for each respective licensed composition used by LICENSEE hereunder during the Term as follows:

a)  the sum of $15.00 for a one (1) year period for each separate recording of a copyrighted musical work electrically transcribed on to a master tape thereof in LICENSEE active library of _____. In this connection, LICENSEE agrees to furnish a list of such licensed compositions to AGENT within thirty (30) days from the date of the execution of this agreement, which list shall be accompanied by payment therefor pursuant to this sub-paragraph (a).

b)  Such statements shall identify all of the licensed compositions recorded and put into use in Licensee Music service during the applicable period of the term, shall identify all publishers grouped in alphabetical order, listing each respective licensed compositions alphabetically in connection to the copyright proprietor, shall show the dates of such first use, identify each master tape and shall be accompanied by the applicable payments hereunder. AGENT shall have the right by its authorized representatives to inspect, copy and make abstract of the books and records of LICENSEE during reasonable business hours to verify the accuracy of LICENSEE statements and payments hereunder.

9.  This license is non-assignable by LICENSEE except to a wholly owned subsidiary or parent or entity which purchases all or substantially all of LICENSEE assets or the capital stock of LICENSEE or its parent corporation, provided, however, that in no event LICENSEE be relieved of its obligations hereunder without the express written consent of AGENT.

10. In the event that LICENSEE shall fail to make any payment or comply with any other provision required to be performed by LICENSEE in this agreement,

AGENT shall, without prejudice to any other right of AGENT or its publisher-principals under this Agreement, have the right to revoke this agreement and the rights herein granted by written notice thereof sent to LICENSEE by certified mail. In the event that LICENSEE does not cure such failure within fifteen (15) days from the date of the mailing of such notice, LICENSEE shall be and be deemed to be a willful infringer of copyright with respect to the licensed compositions as to which it has not paid the amounts due hereunder or with respect to which it has otherwise failed to comply with its obligations under this Agreement.

11.    This agreement and the license of rights hereunder shall automatically terminate upon the filing by LICENSEE of a petition in bankruptcy, or insolvency, or after any adjudication that LICENSEE is bankrupt or insolvent, which adjudication is not vacated within 60 days, or upon the filing by LICENSEE of any petition or answer seeking reorganization, readjustment or arrangement of LICENSEE business under any federal or state law relating to bankruptcy, or insolvency, or upon the appointment of a receiver for any of the property of LICENSEE, or upon the making by LICENSEE of any assignment for the benefit of creditors or upon the institution of any proceedings for the liquidation of LICENSEE'S business or for the termination of its corporate character. Termination of this agreement shall be without prejudice for monies due to or to become due to AGENT and without prejudice to any other right of AGENT or the PUBLISHER under this agreement. Termination shall not affect the license for any composition for which the fee has been paid.

12.    Nothing herein contained shall constitute a waiver or release of any right, claim or cause of action which

AGENT or the Publishers may have at law or in equity against LICENSEE with respect to any act or omission on the part of LICENSEE not expressly licensed hereunder, all being hereby reserved.

13.    This agreement sets forth the entire understanding of the parties with respect to the subject matter hereof, may not be altered or amended except in a signed written instrument and shall be governed and construed by and under the laws of the State of New York.

IN WITNESS WHEREOF, the parties hereto have caused this Agreement to be executed as of the _____ day of _____.

_____
(LICENSEE)

By: _____

THE HARRY FOX AGENCY, INC.

(AGENT)

By: _____

# FORM 13.2

### ELECTRICAL TRANSCRIPTION LICENSE FOR
### BACKGROUND MUSIC SERVICES
### USED BY THE HARRY FOX AGENCY

## ELECTRICAL TRANSCRIPTION LICENSE

Agreement made as of _____ by and between _____ (hereinafter referred to as "LICENSEE") and THE HARRY FOX AGENCY, INC. 711 Third Avenue, New York, New York 10017 (hereinafter referred to as "AGENT").

## W I T N E S S E T H:

Whereas, AGENT is the licensing and collecting agent for numerous music publisher-principals (hereinafter individually and collectively referred to as "Publishers") who own or control the rights hereinafter license of their respective musical compositions:

Whereas, LICENSEE, is engaged in the business of producing background music services and furnishing such services to its customers;

Whereas, LICENSEE, in order to record the musical compositions owned by the Publishers and to reproduce and distribute the recordings, is required under copyright law to obtain a license from the Publishers and accordingly desires to obtain such a license from the Publishers for the use of their respective music compositions; and

Whereas, AGENT has been authorized and instructed by its principals, the Publishers, to issue a license to LICENSEE;

NOW, THEREFORE, it is agreed as follows:

1.  This agreement is being entered into by AGENT as the authorized agent, and acting for and on behalf of its principals, the Publishers.

2.  For the purpose hereof the Publishers shall be and be deemed those publishers listed in "THE HARRY FOX MUSIC PUBLISHERS DIRECTORY" as it is from time to time amended and supplemented, excluding therefrom however those publishers who are the subject of notices to LICENSEE from AGENT excluding such publishers from the operation of this agreement. The right to exclude publishers from the operation of this agreement (hereby reserved) may be exercised from time to time by AGENT pursuant to instructions from, and acting on behalf of, such publishers so excluded, provided that any exclusion shall not apply to any compositions licensed and recorded under this agreement prior to the date of the delivery of the notice to LICENSEE relating to their exclusion.

3.  The term of this Agreement shall be for a period of _____ years commencing _____ and terminating _____ (hereinafter referred to as the "Term").

4.  The territory within which the rights hereinafter licensed may be exercised by LICENSEE is limited to the United States of America, its territories and possessions and Puerto Rico (hereinafter referred to as "Territory").

5.  For the purposes hereof, the following *non-exclusive* rights are hereby granted to LICENSEE by the Publisher with respect to the "licensed compositions" (as such term is hereinafter defined) during the Term and for use within the Territory:

    a)  The rights to mechanically reproduce (i.e. make recordings of) the licensed compositions, in whole or in part for the purposes of using such recordings in and only in connection with the background music services furnished by LICENSEE to its customers.

b)   The right to make and use copies of such recordings in connection with background music services only and the right to make and furnish copies of such recordings to its customers for use in connection with such background music services only.

c)   The rights herein granted to record and make copies of recordings hereunder embodying performances of the licensed compositions shall include recordings on wire, tape, discs or any other devices now or hereafter known but are limited to audio devices only not accompanied by the recording of visual images.

d)   The right granted in paragraph 5(a) to mechanically produce includes the right to record and use the music of a licensed composition without the lyrics thereof (i.e., an instrumental arrangement).

e)   Neither the title nor lyrics of the licensed compositions shall be changed, substituted for, added to or translated without the written consent of its respective Publishers.

f)   The pubic performance of the licensed compositions, as embodied in the recordings, by LICENSEE is expressly conditioned upon such performers thereof having valid performing rights licenses from the respective Publishers, the American Society of Composers, Authors and Publishers (ASCAP) or Broadcast Music, Inc.

(BMI) or any other person authorized to issue such licenses.

6.    For the purposes hereof "licensed compositions" shall be and deemed to mean those musical compositions with respect to which:

a)    the rights hereunder licenses are owned or controlled by the Publisher, *and*

b)    AGENT has not indicated a restriction on such use by the respective Publishers within 20 days after the receipt of such notice from LICENSEE, the right to restrict such use hereby being reserved by and on behalf of the Publishers.

7.    In consideration of the license hereby granted, LICENSEE agrees to pay AGENT for and on behalf of its principals, the Publishers, for each respective licensed composition used by LICENSEE hereunder during the Term as follows:

a)    the sum of $15.00 for a one (1) year period for each separate recording of a copyrighted musical work electrically transcribed on to a master tape thereof in LICENSEE active library as of _____. In this connection, LICENSEE agrees to furnish a list of such licensed compositions to AGENT within thirty (30) days from the date of the execution of this agreement, which list shall be accompanied by payment therefor pursuant to this sub-paragraph (a).

b)    In connection with its use of the licensed compositions and the payments to be made hereunder by LICENSEE, LICENSEE agrees to render statements to AGENT within thirty (30) days after the end of each six (6) months period of the Term (i.e., the periods ending March 31, and September 30th). Such statements shall identify all of the licensed compositions recorded and put into use in LICENSEE'S music service during the applicable period of the Term, shall show the dates of such use and shall be accompanied by the applicable payments hereunder. AGENT shall have the right by its authorized representatives to inspect, copy and make abstract of the books and records of LICENSEE during reasonable business hours to verify the accuracy of LICENSEE statements and payments hereunder.

8.      This license hereunder is limited to its express terms and all rights in the licensed compositions not expressly licensed hereunder are hereby expressly reserved by and for the Publishers.

9.      This license is non-assignable by LICENSEE except to a wholly owned subsidiary or parent or entity which purchases all or substantially all of LICENSEE assets or the capital stock of LICENSEE or its parent corporation, provided, however, that in no event LICENSEE be relieved of its obligations hereunder without the express written consent of AGENT.

10.      In the event that LICENSEE shall fail to make any payment or comply with any other provision required to be performed by LICENSEE in this agreement, AGENT shall, without prejudice to any other right of AGENT or its publisher-principals under this Agreement, have the right to revoke this agreement and the rights herein granted by written notice thereof sent to LICENSEE by certified mail. In the event that LICENSEE does not cure such failure within fifteen (15) days from the date of the mailing of such notice, LICENSEE shall be and be deemed to be a willful infringer of copyright with respect to the licensed

compositions as to which it has not paid the amounts due hereunder or with respect to which it has otherwise failed to comply with its obligations under this Agreement.

11. This agreement and the license of rights hereunder shall automatically terminate upon the filing by LICENSEE of a petition in bankruptcy, or insolvency, or after any adjudication that LICENSEE is bankrupt or insolvent, which adjudication is not vacated within 60 days, or upon the filing by LICENSEE of any petition or answer seeking reorganization, readjustment or arrangement of business under any federal or state law relating to bankruptcy, or insolvency, or upon the appointment of a receiver for any of the property of LICENSEE, or upon the making by LICENSEE of any assignment for the benefit of creditors or upon the institution of any proceedings for the liquidation of LICENSEE'S business or for the termination of its corporate character. Termination of this agreement shall be without prejudice for monies due to or to become due to AGENT and without prejudice to any other right of AGENT or the PUBLISHER under this agreement. Termination shall not affect the license for any composition for which the fee has been paid.

12. Nothing herein contained shall constitute a waiver or release of any right, claim or cause of action which AGENT or the Publishers may have at law or in equity against LICENSEE with respect to any act or omission on the part of LICENSEE not expressly licensed hereunder, all being hereby reserved.

13. This agreement sets forth the entire understanding of the parties with respect to the subject matter hereof, may not be altered or amended except in a signed written instrument and shall be governed and construed by and under the laws of the State of New York.

IN WITNESS WHEREOF, the parties hereto have caused this

Agreement to be executed as of the _____ day of _____.

_____

(LICENSEE)

By: _____

THE HARRY FOX AGENCY, INC.

(AGENT)

By: _____

# FORM 13.3

### ELECTRICAL TRANSCRIPTION LICENSE FOR
### BACKGROUND MUSIC SERVICES
### USED BY 3M COMPANY

AGREEMENT made this _____ day of _____, 1991 by and between MINNESOTA MINING AND MANUFAC- TURING COMPANY, a Delaware Corporation, 3M Center, St. Paul, MN 55144, Attention: Sound Products/3M, Building 551- IW-01 (hereinafter referred to as "3M"), and

_____ (hereinafter referred to as "Licensor", on behalf of itself and all other music publishing entities controlled and/or administered by Licensor).

1.    GRANT OF RIGHTS

A.    Mechanical Rights: Licensor hereby grants to 3M the non-exclusive right to record (and/or use recordings owned by third parties subject to the clearance of all necessary rights to use such third party recordings) the musical compositions listed on Schedule A annexed hereto as well as such additional com- positions as 3M may hereafter select from Licensor's catalogs from time to time subject to Licensor's approval in each in- stance (hereinafter individually and jointly referred to as the "Compositions") in whole or in part, as well as the titles thereof, upon phonorecords embodying the Compositions and the right to manufacture, sell, rent, lease, advertise, distribute and oth- erwise exploit such phonorecords throughout the world, pro- vided, however, that 3M shall obtain licenses to do so from the appropriate mechanical rights agencies and/or publishers out- side of the United States, its territories and possessions (in- cluding Puerto Rico) and Canada. (The aforesaid rights are hereinafter referred to as "mechanical rights" and the aforesaid phonorecords are hereinafter referred to as "Copies".) 3M shall not be required to serve or file any notice required to be served or filed by any copyright act or other law in connection with its exercise of the mechanical rights granted hereunder.

B.    Public Performance Rights: Licensor hereby grants to 3M the non-exclusive right throughout the United States, its territories and possessions (including Puerto Rico) publicly to perform and to authorize customers publicly to perform the Compositions embodied on the Copies for the period(s) specified in Paragraph 2A. (The aforesaid rights are hereinafter referred to as "public performance rights".)

C.    Background Music: 3M's exercise of the rights granted hereunder is limited to Background Music (including so-called Foreground Music) as such term is now or may hereafter during the period of 3M's rights hereunder be commonly understood in the music industry.

2.    LIMITATIONS ON MECHANICAL RIGHTS AND PUBLIC PERFORMANCE RIGHTS

A.    Duration: 3M shall not authorize any customer publicly to perform the Compositions embodied on the Copies for a period in excess of three (3) years after receipts thereof by the customer, unless such customer shall have paid 3M for an extension of his public performance rights and 3M shall have paid to Licensor the additional royalties specified in Paragraph 4B hereof.

B.    Re-Use: No customer shall be authorized by 3M to rent or lease the Copies to any other person, or to duplicate by any means the Compositions embodied on the Copies.

C.    Private Use: Nothing herein contained shall be deemed to limit the right of a customer to perform the Compositions embodied on the Copies privately within the home of such customer, and the royalties set forth in Paragraph 4B hereof shall not be payable with respect to Copies delivered to customers exclusively for such use.

D. Notice to Customers: 3M agrees to advise its distributors and customers of the foregoing limitations.

3. LICENSOR'S WARRANTIES AND INDEMNITY

A. Licensor warrants and represents that it owns and/or controls the mechanical and public performance rights granted hereunder; that it has full right, power and authority to enter into this agreement and to grant such rights; and that the exercise of such rights will not constitute a violation or infringement of any right, title or interest, including without limitation copyrights, common law rights and statutory rights, of any person, firm or corporation. Notwithstanding anything contained herein, 3M may at any time exercise any right which 3M now or at any time hereafter may be entitled to as a member of the public as though this agreement were not in existence. Nothing contained herein shall be deemed to constitute a warranty or representation that the mechanical rights specified in Paragraph 1A will be available outside of the United States and Canada or that the performance rights specified in Paragraph 1B will be available outside the United States.

B. Licensor agrees to indemnify and hold 3M harmless (but only to the extent of the consideration paid to Licensor here-under) against any loss, damage, cost or expense (including reasonable attorneys' fees) incurred by 3M by reason of any claim, action or proceeding instituted by any person, firm, corporation, mechanical rights society or performing rights society which is inconsistent with any grant by Licensor to 3M or with any of the representations and warranties made by Licensor. 3M agrees to notify Licensor of any claim within the scope of the foregoing indemnity and to afford Licensor an opportunity to participate in the defense thereof, at Licensor's expense, with counsel of Licensor's choice. In such event, 3M may withhold royalties in an amount reasonably related to such claim, until such claim is finally adjudicated or settled with Licensor's consent, which Licensor agrees not to withhold unreasonably. Licensor's liability shall be limited to the amounts payable to Licensor hereunder.

4.    ROYALTIES

A.    For Mechanical Rights: In consideration of the grant
of mechanical rights, 3M agrees to pay to Licensor a royalty
equivalent to the maximum "statutory" rate in the United States
and the "industry" rate in Canada for Compositions not in excess of five (5) minutes in effect when each Copy is initially
distributed (presently U.S.$.066 in the United States and
Can.$.059 in Canada) with respect to each Copy delivered to a
customer (other than for a limited free trial period) for which 3M
receives payment, multiplied by the number of Compositions
embodied on each such Copy. The foregoing royalty shall not
be payable with respect to any Composition which is in the
public domain, or with respect to any Composition for which
payment is otherwise made to a mechanical rights society or
agency, or with respect to the delivery of "rental rotation" Copies (or replacements of such Copies which are destroyed in the
course of rental rotation) to customers other than the first customer to which such Copy is delivered.

B.    For Public Performance Rights: In consideration of
the grant of public performance rights during the period set
forth in Paragraph 2A hereof, 3M agrees to pay to Licensor a
royalty equivalent to three cents (U.S. $.03) with respect to each
Copy delivered to a customer (other than for a limited free trial
period) for which 3M receives payment, multiplied by the number of Compositions embodied on each such Copy. In addition,
3M agrees to pay to Licensor a royalty equivalent to one cent
(U.S. $.01) computed as aforesaid, for each year of public per-
formance rights beyond three (3) years from the date of delivery
to a customer, for which such customer pays 3M in accordance
with such fee schedule as 3M may establish from time to time
in its sole discretion. The foregoing royalties shall not be payable with respect to any Composition which is in the public
domain, or with respect to the delivery of "rental rotation" Copies (or replacements of such Copies which are destroyed in the
course of rental rotation) during the period set forth in Paragraph 2A to customers other than the first customer to which
such Copy is delivered.

C.    Transmission Rights: Notwithstanding the foregoing, if 3M authorizes the transmission of the performances embodied on a Copy, by central studio or otherwise, then in lieu of the royalties set forth in the preceding subdivisions (A) and (B), 3M agrees to pay to Licensor an aggregate royalty of eight and seven-tenths cents (U.S. $.087) per Composition for all necessary mechanical and public performance rights (for a three year period as provided in Paragraph 2A above) multiplied by the number of subscribers for which 3M receives payment and prorated in accordance with the months of actual use thereof by the transmitter. The foregoing royalty shall not be payable with respect to any Composition which is in the public domain or with respect to any Composition for which payment is otherwise paid to a mechanical or public performance society or agency, and shall be increased by the same amount as the maximum "statutory" mechanical royalty hereafter increases from time to time, beginning as of the effective date of each such increase, with respect to Copies thereafter duplicated.

D.    Accountings and Payments: 3M agrees to compute and pay the royalties referred to in subdivisions A, B and C of this paragraph within sixty (60) days after the expiration of each six (6) month period beginning on the June 30 or December 31 following the date of this agreement and continuing for so long as 3M continues to distribute Copies embodying any of the Compositions. Together with each payment, a statement shall be delivered to Licensor showing the number of Copies distributed and the number of Compositions embodied thereon. Each such statement and payment shall be binding upon Licensor unless, within two (2) years after any given statement and payment is delivered, 3M shall have received written notice from Licensor specifying Licensor's objections thereto, in which event such statement and payment shall be binding as to all matters not specifically objected to.

E.    Books and Records: 3M agrees to maintain accurate books and records pertaining to the royalties to be paid to Licensor, which books and records may be inspected by a certified public accountant at 3M's office where such books and records are regularly maintained, during 3M's regular business hours and at Licensor's sole expense. Any information obtained in the course of such inspection shall be held in strict confidence.

## 5.    TERM

     A.     Expiration and Sell-Off: The initial term of this agreement shall commence upon the execution of this agreement and shall terminate      years after the date hereof. Following such termination 3M shall have the exclusive right to continue to distribute its inventory (as of the effective date of such termination) of Copies for not more than twenty-four (24) months thereafter and to authorize customers publicly to perform the Compositions embodied thereon (subject to the payment of royalties and other limitations herein contained).

     B.     Rights of Customers Upon Expiration of Term: Notwithstanding the expiration of the term of this agreement pursuant to subdivision A of this paragraph, it is expressly understood and agreed that each customer authorized by 3M during the term of this agreement publicly to perform the Compositions (subject to the limitations herein contained) shall have such public performance rights for a period not less than three (3) years after 3M, its distributors, subdistributors, agents or dealers deliver the Copy embodying such Composition to such customer, and Licensor's warranties in this connection contained in Paragraph 3A hereof shall continue for the benefit of such customer for a concurrent period of time.

6.    USE OF COMPOSITIONS - This agreement is not intended and shall not be construed to obligate 3M to use any or all of the Compositions on any or all of the Copies.

7.    "FAVORED NATION" - 3M agrees that in the event 3M agrees to pay a higher rate of royalty to any third party than is payable hereunder for the use of compositions similar in duration and type to those licensed hereunder, this agreement will

be deemed amended to incorporate such higher rate, as of the date when such higher rate is agreed to be paid to such third party and continuing for the duration of the period during which such higher rate is so paid.

IN WITNESS WHEREOF, the parties have caused this agreement to be executed by their duly authorized representatives as of the day and year first indicated above.

MINNESOTA MINING AND
MANUFACTURING COMPANY
(3M)

By: _____

# SYNCHRONIZATION LICENSES

## SUMMARY

# SYNCHRONIZATION
# LICENSES

A *synchronization license* is a license that permits another to synchronize music with an audiovisual work, such as a motion picture or television program, and to make copies of them, but only permits the distribution of those copies for the specific purpose of exhibiting the audiovisual work in motion picture theaters or broadcasting the work on television. The distribution of copies for any other purpose, such as in videocassettes, laser discs and the like for home use, requires an additional license called a *videogram license*, discussed in the following chapter.

Synchronization licenses are derived from the copyright owner's exclusive right of reproduction.[1] The synchronization license might properly be called an *audiovisual reproduction license*, but the word, "synchronization" continues to be commonly used, perhaps because, technically, synchronizing involves making a piece of music an integral part of the audiovisual work — by recording the music in "timed-relation" with the moving pictures in an audiovisual work. In addition, the permission granted under a synchronization license is limited to the making of a recording of a musical composition subject to the condition that (i) the recording only be used as part of the particular audiovisual work specified in the agreement, and (ii) any copies made of the recording only be used in a particular way — to facilitate exhibition or broadcast, but not for physical distribution to the public.

The kind of audiovisual work into which music is licensed for synchronization is specified in each synchronization license agreement and is often reflected in the title of the license agreement. For example, permission to synchronize music in a motion picture for theatrical release is usually called a *theatrical* synchronization license; permis-

---

[1] 17 U.S.C. 106(1).

sion to synchronize music in a television program for television broadcast is usually called a *television* synchronization license; and permission to synchronize music in an audiovisual work for promotional music videos is called a *promotional music video* synchronization license. As the need to more precisely specify the uses to which synchronized recordings may be made, new classes of synchronization licenses have also emerged, such as synchronization licenses for cable television, direct satellite broadcast, and other forms of television program exhibition, and for use of motion pictures and television programs containing music in videograms, such as laser discs and videocassettes.

The discussion of synchronization licenses in this chapter will be limited to the use of music in motion pictures and television programs, including their usual forms of distribution and broadcasting, but excluding other methods of distribution, such as videocassettes, which will be discussed in Chapter 15 on *Videogram Licenses*. Because, the method of distribution often controls the financial terms of the license, these terms are sufficiently different to warrant that they be separately addressed.

## I. HISTORICAL BACKGROUND

### A. Early Motion Picture Technology

When a person visually observes a succession of still images at a rate above 15 frames a second, he will perceive an illusion of continuous movement. Successive photography of actual movement was first achieved in 1877 by Eadweard Muybridge when he used 12 equally spaced cameras to demonstrate that at some time all four hooves of a galloping horse left the ground at once. The Muybridge photographs, and successive photographs like them, were soon used in a popular parlor device, known as a zoetrope, which created the illusion of movement from pictures mounted in a rotating drum.

Shortly thereafter, mechanisms were developed to enable a sequence of photographs to be taken within a single camera at regular, rapid intervals. Thomas Alva Edison, usually credited with the invention of the motion picture camera, actually combined several existing technologies to create the Kinetograph camera in 1889, the same year that the George Eastman company developed a photographic film sturdy and flexible enough to be transported within a camera for receiving a rapid succession of images. The version of the Kinetograph camera developed by the end of 1892 used essentially the same format in use today — a film 35 millimeters in width, with two rows of sprockets, four holes per frame, used to advance the film through the camera. The first motion pictures were not projected, but used in a parlor device known as the Kinetoscope, a cabinet in which a reel of film, illuminated by a light bulb, was advanced in a continuous loop at the rate of 40 frames per second in synchronization with a rotating shutter wheel. The viewer would "peep" into the cabinet to view the motion picture, or *peep show*.

In 1895, Thomas Armat employed several mechanical techniques developed in France to create a motion picture projector, which the following year he allowed Edison to produce and market as Edison Vitascopes. The art of projection was significantly advanced with the introduction of carbon arc lamps to improve the illumination of the projected image.

## B. The Emergence of the Motion Picture Industry

It was in France that early filmmakers began to make the important transition from using motion picture technology to convey mere animated photographs to using the same technology to convey narratives or tell stories. In 1902, French filmmaker Georges Méliès startled the world with his 30-scene, 14-minute film narrative, *Voyage to the Moon*, based on the novel by Jules Verne. Meanwhile, in the United States, Edwin S. Porter, a projectionist and engineer who joined the Edison Company in 1900, while serving as producer and director of many of the films produced by Edison, began experimenting with the techniques established by Méliès. In 1903, Porter shot *The Great Train Robbery*, widely acknowledged to be the first narrative film to achieve true temporal continuity of action, combining 14 separate shots of noncontinuous overlapping action. The film's spectacular success led to the establishment of the first permanent film theaters, or nickelodeons (Greek for, "nickel theater").

In 1903, Adolph Zukor, a 30-year old furrier restless for new opportunities, and Mitchell Marks, an operator of penny arcades, established the Automatic Vaudeville Company, opening its first arcade on 14th Street in New York City. With an investment from another successful furrier, Marcus Loew, the outfit spread its operations to Boston, Philadelphia and Newark. Loew established his own chain of arcades and within two years, they each converted their arcades into nickelodeons, giving their customers a peek at the short one-reel movies being churned out by Edison, Vitagraph, Biograph, and other film production companies of the day. The two road the spectacular boom in popularity of the nickelodeon, which grew in number from a mere handful in 1904 to nearly 10,000 by 1908. In 1910, the two combined their efforts, forming Loew's Consolidated Enterprises.

Yet Zukor grew restless once again, selling his interest in Loews, and, with Marcus Loew's best wishes, Zukor formed a film production company called, Famous Players In Famous Plays, hiring Edwin Porter as head of direction and photography. Within a few years, Famous Players was making 30 films a year, starring such notables as John Barrymore and Mary Pickford.

As narrative techniques matured, viewers of motion pictures were becoming increasingly sophisticated. Consequently, production companies began to produce high budget, multiple-reel "feature" films suitable to the tastes of this new audience. In 1913, Samuel Goldfish, Jesse Lasky and Cecil B. DeMille formed a small film company, the Jesse L. Lasky Feature Play Company, one of the hundreds of small production companies springing up to meet the increasing demand for feature films.

At the same time, motion picture exhibitors began to accommodate the growing audience for motion pictures with large elegant theaters, known as "dream palaces." One of the first theaters of this kind, the 3,300-seat Strand Theater on Broadway, was built by Mitchell Marks in 1914.

By 1916, over 21,000 movie theaters dotted the country, and the nickelodeon era was over. But Zukor was not one to allow rapidly changing technology leave him behind. In July, 1916, he masterminded the consolidation of his Famous Players Company with Lasky's Feature Play Company. Two months later, Famous Players-Lasky bought out the Paramount Company, a film distribution company, later to become known as Paramount Pictures.

As part of the transaction, Zukor bought out Samuel Goldfish's share of Feature Play Company and Goldfish established his own company by forming a partnership with the Edgar Selwyn's Selwyn Theatrical Empire, calling the new company, The Gold-wyn Company. Goldfish decided to change his name, combining Gold with Wyn. (Had he taken the first syllable of SELwyn and the second syllable of GoldFISH, he would have had SELFISH.)

Meanwhile, the demand for motion pictures made it necessary for film production companies to maintain a year-round schedule. Because of the need for light, most films were still being shot outdoors, but the east coast winter climate could not accommodate the continuous production schedules required. The temperate and sunny climate of Southern California, together with the topographic variety afforded by the greater Los Angeles area, proved to be the perfect place for movie making. By 1911, several major production companies established studios in Hollywood, and, by 1915, more than 60 percent of American film production was produced by 15,000 workers employed by the motion picture industry in Hollywood.

All of the major studios of the day established operations in Hollywood, including Zukor's Famous Players-Lasky Corporation; Samuel Goldfish's Goldwyn Picture Corporation; Universal Pictures, which was founded by Carl Laemmle in 1912 through a merger of five independent production companies of that time; Metro Picture Corporation and Louis B. Mayer Pictures, founded by Louis B. Mayer in 1915 and 1917, respectively; and the Fox Film Corporation (becoming 20th Century-Fox in 1935), founded by William Fox in 1915.

In 1924, sensing the direction film production would be going, Marcus Loew, who owned about 140 theaters at the time, went to Hollywood and encouraged Samuel Goldwyn to sell out his Goldwyn Picture Corporation to Loews, Inc. Marcus Loew then merged Goldwyn's Goldwyn Picture Corporation with the Louis B. Mayer's Metro Picture Corporation. The merged company became Metro-Goldwyn-Mayer, a subsidiary of Loews, Inc. Loew asked both Louis B. Mayer and Samuel Goldwyn to join the new firm, but while Mayer accepted, Goldwyn decided to become an independent producer. When he was offered the position with MGM, Goldwyn was believed to have said, "Include me out." Another famous Goldwynism came to light when his secretary asked him if she could destroy files from years back. He replied, "Yes, but keep copies."

Other studios who opened operations in Hollywood included First National Pictures, Inc., a circuit of independent exhibitors who estab-

lished their own production facilities at Burbank, Calif., in 1922; War-
ner Bros. Pictures, Inc., founded by Harry, Albert, Samuel, and Jack
Warner in 1923; and Columbia Pictures, Inc., incorporated in 1924 by
Harry and Jack Cohn.

## C. Talkies

With the increasing popularity of motion pictures at the turn of
the century, it did not take long for inventors to seek a means by
which motion pictures could be accompanied by sound. In 1907, Dr.
Lee De Forest invented the Audion, a photoelectric vacuum tube that
made it possible to amplify sound, enabling a sound recording to be
presented in a full auditorium. De Forest then turned his attention to
the problem of synchronizing the sound with the motion picture. He
developed a process for photographing sound impulses which could
later be read by shining a light through the filmed sound image onto
a photocell. This became known as his Phonofilm system. De Forest
sold his basic audion tube patents to the Bell Telephone Company.

By creating short feature films with vaudeville headliners at that
time, such as Eddie Cantor and George Jessel, De Forest tried to
stimulate interest in his short films by showing them at the Rivoli
Theater in New York City on March 13, 1923. The sounds were reproduced through an electronic amplification system of his own design. From 1923 through 1927, De Forest was unsuccessful in his
attempts to stimulate interest in his system.

About the same time, one of De Forest's former associates, Theodore Case, demonstrated his own sound-on-film system to William
Fox. Fox accepted the system, calling it MovieTone. Like De Forest,
Fox also began putting vaudeville headline acts on film, but Fox had
more success applying the sound process to a very successful newsreel
he had been producing. When he began adding sound to his
"MovieTone News," the audience not only saw famous people of their
day, such as Babe Ruth and Charles Lindberg, but for the first time
they heard their voices. MovieTone News recorded Lindberg's take-
off from Long Island on May 20, 1927, his arrival in France, and his
subsequent ticker-tape parade in New York City.

Meanwhile, Bell Laboratories and its parent company Western
Electric were making extensive studies on the nature of sounds and
techniques for recording and reproducing such sounds, and continued

to experiment with ways of adapting De Forest's audion tube for amplification of sound in theaters. One experiment resulted in a process of recording sound on a 16-inch phonographic disc rotated at 33 1/3 revolutions per minute. Combining these recorded discs together with an improved system of amplification, Bell attracted the interest of Warner Bros. Pictures who acquired from Bell the necessary patent licenses to establish the Vitaphone Corporation to market the complete system. With the Vitaphone system, a motion picture producer was able to synchronize a phonograph recording of various sound effects, music, and voice with the action of the picture. For replay, the disc was placed on a phonograph turntable, rotating at a uniform speed in precise relation to the motion picture.

Jack Warner of Warner Bros. Pictures had just finished an elaborate and expensive film, John Barrymore's *Don Juan*, with Mary Astor. While filming was in progress, William Axt, David Mendoza and Major Edward Bowes were working on a musical score. Warner decided to send the prints of the completed film to New York where the score could be recorded by the New York Philharmonic in synchronization with the film. Sound effects were added and Will Hayes, director of the *Motion Picture Producers and Distributors Association of America*, was invited to record a filmed speech about the future of sound-on-film.

On August 6, 1926, Warner Bros. Pictures presented the first All-Vitaphone program at their Warner Theater in New York City. With the showing of *Don Juan*, which had synchronized music and sound effects but no speech, together with a presentation of Will Haye's filmed remarks, "talking pictures," or "talkies," were born.

On October 6, 1927, an audience of notables at the Warner Theater in New York watched as the silent film, *The Jazz Singer*, was projected onto the screen. At one early point in the movie, then popular singing artist, Al Jolson was heard over the theater's sound system, singing in a night club scene. After a rendition of the song, "Dirty Hands, Dirty Face," Jolson ad libbed, "Wait a minute, wait a minute, you ain't heard nothin' yet. Wait a minute, I tell ya, you ain't heard nothin'. You wanna hear "Toot Toot Tootsie?"

With those words, the film business changed forever. Entertainment columnist Louella Parsons wrote in the December 29, 1927 issue of the *Los Angeles Examiner*, under the headline, '*Jazz Singer,*' *with*

*Vitaphone, Triumph for Jolson: Film at Criterion Rich in Pathos and Interest,"*

> The strong protests uttered against the Vitaphone as a destroyer of the peaceful silence of the motion picture, suffered a glorious defeat last night. Without the Vitaphone "The Jazz Singer" would not have completely won over the large audience at the Criterion Theater. "The Jazz Singer" and the Vitaphone are affinities that do not jangle out of tune. If there had been long conversations and more attempts at vocal comedy, the effect would not have been so satisfactory. But very wisely Warner Brothers, save for a single scene between Al Jolson and his mother, eliminated the spoken words. But the singing! Think of hearing Al Jolson sing the words of his songs as part of the screen play. The combination exceeded this reviewer's best expectations. I have been one who has lamented the encroachment of the voice in the silent drama. "The Jazz Singer," therefore, comes as an agreeable surprise. I must right here make it clear that there are few pictures that lend themselves so perfectly to the synchronization of music as "The Jazz Singer."

In 1927 Warner Bros. acquired First National Pictures Co., not for its film library, but to gain access to the hundreds of affiliated First National theaters across the country, which it began to wire for "sound." While other studios chose a "wait-and-see" policy, Warners went ahead and produced and released on July 7, 1928 the first all-talking picture, *The Lights of New York*. The next month Warner released *The Terror,* in which actor, Conrad Nagel, dressed in white tie, tails, opera hat and mask even spoke the opening titles and credits.

At the end of 1927, only about 150 theaters in the United States were wired for sound. By the end of 1929, there were over 8,000, which included every major motion picture theater in the nation. Though studio heads were initially skeptical of what they considered to be an expensive novelty, "talkies" became a novelty that the public could not get enough of.

When Paramount executives Adolph Zukor and Jesse Lasky had first seen demonstrations of Warner's Vitaphone and Fox's MovieTone systems, they were unimpressed. Paramount and the rest of the industry only began looking into the matter of sound when they learned how the money was pouring in at Warner Bros. from *The Jazz Singer, Don Juan,* and other Vitaphone productions. Early in 1928, at the annual production meetings held at Paramount Pictures's home office in New York City, Adoph Zucker and Jesse Lasky decided to adopt the MovieTone sound-on-film method, soon adopted by other studios.

During the 15 months between late 1927 and the end of 1928, studio profits increased 600 percent. By that time, it became clear that "talking pictures" were here to stay.

## D. Talkies and Music Publishing

The popularity of talking pictures created an enormous demand for music by the Hollywood studios and this lead to studio buy-outs of many of the major music publishers.

In 1928, Warner Bros. Pictures acquired M. Witmark & Sons, which had the publishing rights to the big three of Broadway musical composers, Victor Herbert, Sigmund Romberg, and Rudolf Friml. In 1929, they purchased Remick Music Corporation, which held the rights to the works of Gus Kahn, Richard Whiting, Al Dubin, and Harry Warren. In the same year, Warners purchased Harms, Inc. from Max Dreyfus for $11 million, but with that purchase, Warner's acquired new Broadway musical writers such as George and Ira Gershwin, Vincent Youmans, Irving Caesar, Richard Rodgers, Larry Hart, Oscar Hammerstein and Jerome Kern. Also in 1929, MGM entered into a publishing administration agreement with Robbins Music Corp. for the publishing of music written for use in MGM pictures. Paramount Pictures established their own music publishing firm, Famous Music. Perhaps the name was adapted from Famous Players, which was Adolph Zukor's former company.

As more and more theaters were being wired for sound, musicians became worried. Vitaphone and MovieTone systems were performing the required music without the need for live musicians. Many musicians began migrating to Hollywood, as the demand for the recording of thematic and background music for motion pictures increased. Soon, virtually all the studios were producing musicals and dancing extravaganzas, such as Busby Berkeley's *Gold Diggers of Broadway, Forty Second Street, Footlight Parade,* and *Dames.*

Meanwhile, independent music publishers began negotiating the licenses for the use of their popular songs in motion pictures, using what became known as a synchronization license — i.e., permission to synchronize music in timed-relation with a motion picture — and

ASCAP began demanding performance royalties from studios as well as theaters that were projecting talking pictures containing copyrighted music. By 1926, movie theaters were required to have a license from ASCAP to perform any music in ASCAP's extensive repertoire. These performance licenses remained in effect until 1948, when the practice of ASCAP (and BMI) of licensing performances in theaters in the United States came to an end.[2]

## II. Considerations in Granting and Clearing Synchronization Licenses

What has been said with regard to music licensing in general (see Chapter 10) applies directly with regard to synchronization licensing. The primary factors are:

A. The fee structure;

B. The value of the song, taking into consideration its popularity, historical significance, and overall quality;

C. The importance of the song in relation to its intended use; and,

D. The scope of the intended use.

The following discussion begins where the general discussion in Chapter 10 left off, describing each of the foregoing factors in detail as applied to considerations in granting and clearing synchronization licenses.

## A. Fee Structure

The fee structure of nearly all synchronization licenses permitting the exhibition of licensed music in theaters or on television, or both, is a flat fee — the motion picture or television producer will pay a one-time, flat dollar amount for the term of the license, regardless of the number of copies of the film is made or how many times the film is exhibited during the term.

---

[2] See Chapter 17, on *Performance Licenses.*

Synchronization licenses permit merely the exhibition of the motion picture or audiovisual work in which the music is recorded on television or in theaters. It does not permit the use of the music in videocassettes or laser discs for home distribution; permission for such uses may be provided in a separate videogram license, often included in the same form agreement as the synchronization license. Videogram licenses are discussed in greater detail in Chapter 15.

Further, the synchronization license permits merely the making of a *recording* of music in synchronization with an audiovisual work and the making of copies of that recording; it does not permit the *performance* of music even though the making of recordings was authorized by the synchronization license. Accordingly, if the film is exhibited on television, or in motion picture theaters located outside of the United States (see below), the music copyright owner will still be entitled to collect fees for public performances of the picture from its performance rights society.

The performance fee provides the copyright owner with an opportunity to participate in the economic success of the motion picture in which the music is recorded. Motion picture and television producers will assert that music copyright owners do not deserve to receive a chance to participate in the economic success of their theatrical and television works, because the music copyright owners are not taking any of the risks associated with the financing and development of such works. Nevertheless, it is the broadcasters and distributors of the producer's works who will eventually be responsible for performance and other music license fees associated with the distribution, exhibition and broadcast of their works, and the producers are generally satisfied if they can obtain the necessary synchronization fees they require at a reasonable cost.

### 1. Performance License Aspects

By court consent decrees entered into between the Department of Justice and the major performance rights societies, music copyright owners were required to issue public performance licenses to movie producers on a per-film basis, if requested. As a result, performance rights societies do not license performance rights in music in theaters located in the U.S., and most synchronization licenses issued today include a provision that provides permission to the producer to publicly perform the music in U.S. theaters. Thus, for a motion picture to be released in theaters located in the United States, a producer obtains from music copyright owners two fundamental licenses in music: (1) a synchronization license to reproduce the music in copies of the motion picture and (2) a performance license to perform the music publicly in movie theaters in the United States.

In determining what to charge for the U.S. theatrical performances of the music, it has long been the custom of music publishers, when determining the total fee, to charge a fee on the same flat fee basis as the synchronization fee, often by merely doubling the synchronization fee. For example, if the synch fee was determined to be $1,000, the total fee for the synch license and the U.S. theatrical performance license would be $2,000. This was done for the sake of simplicity, and not necessarily derived from good publishing practices. Nevertheless, the practice is likely to continue, because no one has yet scientifically determined the reasonable value of a performance license in the U.S. for a motion picture playing in several thousand theaters for a normal series of theatrical runs.

Public performances in theaters in other countries are subject to local performance fees collected by local performance rights societies.

## B.  The Value of the Song

The admonition made in Chapter 10 suggesting that copyright owners avoid maintaining inflated perceptions about the value of the musical composition and getting mired in the details of licensing terms is particularly applicable to synchronization licensing. Regardless of the popularity of the song, the scope of the use, or its importance to the licensee, the copyright owner's overall interest should always be getting as much activity in the song as possible.

Often a copyright owner's approach is to attempt to get all the market will bear. Such an attitude should be tempered by several important considerations. First, very few songs have no close substitutes. In other words, there will usually be a song in the same genre owned by someone else which will suit the licensee just as well. A good music licensing executive who knows his catalog will always be able to find a song in the genre for which the licensee is seeking. Persons experienced in seeking to obtain clearances for the use of music, will always be on the watch for close substitutes for the music he is seeking to clear.

Second, the music performance revenues a copyright owner receives when the audiovisual work is publicly performed (see Chapter 17) acts as a form of multiplier on the synchronization license fee collected. The music copyright owner will earn performance credits from its performance rights society (e.g., ASCAP, BMI) on public performances of the song on television worldwide and in theaters overseas, and these can be substantial when the picture in which the song is licensed becomes a box office success or is broadcast on network television and in television syndication. The fewer licenses you issue, the less performance activity the song receives, and the fewer performance credits and performance income you will receive. Particularly applicable here is the adage, "Penny wise, pound foolish." Accordingly, no music copyright owner, whether he is responsible for a single song or a large catalog of popular songs and standards, can afford to be "too difficult to deal with."

By the same token, if you are seeking to clear a license from a copyright owner who is being difficult, you might persuade him to quote you a more reasonable fee by reminding him of the performance fees he will be forgoing if you choose an alternative song from another publisher that will serve your purposes just as well.

## C. The Importance of the Song in Relation to its Intended Use

Sometimes one song will not serve the purpose just as well as another. Before quoting a synchronization license fee, the copyright owner should ask many questions of the potential licensee about the intended use of the song to find out just how important the song is in relation to its intended use.

To determine the importance of the song in relation to its intended use, it is sometimes useful to inquire in some detail what the motion picture is about and how the song is going to be used in the picture. For example, the use of the song *Rhapsody in Blue* as purely background music in a comedy is significantly different than the use of the song in a biographical film on the life of George Gershwin; surely, a biography of George Gershwin would not be possible without a license to use several of the composer's most important compositions.

Thus, with respect to motion pictures and television programs, the central questions usually relate to the description of the work in which the music will be used; whether the use is a vocal rendition or merely instrumental; whether the music is used as background music or foreground music; whether the intended use relates to how the composition was originally presented to the public; and whether the music is used to help tell the story.

A *vocal* rendition is when someone is singing, or perhaps humming, the composition in the motion picture; an *instrumental* rendition is when the composition is played without a rendition of lyrics. Rarely does the fee vary merely because the song is rendered with or without the lyrics; however, information as to whether the lyrics are going to be used may lead to other information that assists a copyright owner in formulating the terms of the license.

If someone is rendering the composition in the motion picture — as, for example, when the protagonist of the picture plays or sings on screen a rendition of Bob Dylan's *Blowin' In the Wind* — it is called a visual or *foreground* use. If the composition is heard in the background and no one is seen performing the song, it is a *background* use. All other things being equal, a foreground use will generally command a higher license fee than a background use.

The extent to which the intended use relates to how the composition was originally presented to the public may also be important. For example, the song *Blowin' In the Wind* was originally presented at a certain time in the 1960s that is usually associated with the "peace" movement or the "new generation" of young people of that time. A background use of the song *Blowin' In the Wind* for a scene in a movie set in the 1990s is different from the use of the same song in a movie about war protesters in the 1960s or otherwise in a movie set in the 1960s to provide the feeling of that decade. Though virtually any song could substitute for a random use of the song in the background of an average, unremarkable scene, a higher fee might be commanded for uses that acutely relate to the setting of the film, as there are few substitutes that convey the particular feeling of the late 1960s that is best conveyed by the song *Blowin' In the Wind.*

Whether the original recording of the song is used in the motion picture or a new recording is made by the producer may also be a factor, though generally most music publishers do not vary the license fee on this basis. If the producer desires to use an original sound recording in the motion picture, he would be required to obtain a separate license to do so from the owner of the recording.

The movie may be a dramatic adaptation of the lyrics of a song, as was the case in the motion picture adaptation of the song, *Ode to Billie Joe* and the 1970s television series adaptation of the song, *Harper Valley PTA*. In each of these cases, the absence of the music from the soundtrack would have been quite unnatural and conspicuous, and, accordingly, the copyright owner should recognize the opportunity to command a higher than average fee for synchronization licenses in these circumstances. A separate license and fee may be appropriate for permission to create the dramatic adaptation of the lyrics. *Dramatic adaptations* of song lyrics are discussed in Chapter 18.

The importance of the music to a promotional music video featuring the song is the extreme case of the importance of the song to the audiovisual work, but there are other considerations in setting the terms of music video licenses and these are touched upon in Chapter 15.

If the song's title is used for a special purpose in the motion picture, such as the title of the motion picture, the importance of the song in relation to its intended use becomes obvious. Some additional consideration for the use of the music could be considered, as well as a separate fee for the use of the song in the title of the motion picture. In this regard, it might be wise for a copyright owner to make certain that his standard synchronization license agreement states specifically that the license does not include permission to use the title of the song as the title of the audiovisual work in which the music will be synchronized. A producer who intends to use the title of the song for a special purpose should be certain to clear any further permissions that may be required.

## D.  Scope of the Use

### 1.  *Media and Distribution Channels*

Modern synchronization licenses for motion pictures are carefully drawn to permit only a very narrow set of uses, such as the reproduction of copies for the purpose of normal theatrical exhibition and television broadcast, and even the term "television" is often carefully defined, with distinctions among network, local, syndicated, cable, direct satellite broadcast, etc. being considered. If the motion picture is to be distributed in videograms, such as videocassettes and laser discs, the terms and conditions under which these uses are permitted are separately negotiated, either in a separate license or in special provisions set forth in the synchronization license form.

A person seeking to clear a synchronization license should try to obtain options to distribute the work in all other forms of media and means of distribution at the time the original synchronization license is negotiated, preferably before a final decision to use that piece of music in the work is made — when his or her leverage to obtain the most favorable terms for other uses is best. Considerations for granting and clearing licenses for videograms is covered in the next chapter.

## 2. Term

The term of a synchronization license will depend upon the specific use. Though it is preferable to restrict the license's duration to the shortest possible time, the term of synchronization licenses for motion pictures is generally in perpetuity. Since the music copyright owner will benefit from the performance of music on the radio, in international theaters and on television, it is generally to his advantage to allow a long term use in motion pictures with hopes that the picture becomes successful and is televised over a period of many years, perhaps in the footsteps of a classic film, such as *Casablanca*. The song, *As Time Goes By*, which was written and published many years before the picture was created, owes its *standard song* status to the synchronization license which permitted its use in the film.

Though motion picture synchronization licenses are commonly granted in perpetuity, such term is generally confined to public performances of the film in theaters and, perhaps, on television; if the same motion picture is to be distributed in videograms, the duration of such use will normally be stated separately in another license, or in special provisions of the synchronization license, regarding distribution in videogram form.

Synchronization licenses for use of music in television programs are generally shorter in duration, tending normally to be for a five year period, but this is often subject to negotiation. When television synchronization licenses are granted at the same time as a synchronization license for a theatrical motion picture release, the term of the license is normally in perpetuity. But even when the license is only for a program made for television, the recent trend, which has been at the insistence of those seeking to clear licenses, has been to grant the synchronization licenses for a perpetual term.

### a.  Authority to Issue Long-Term Licenses

While producers are increasingly demanding long-term licenses, the music copyright owner may not always have the authority to grant the license desired. A music copyright owner may grant licenses covering only the term for which it has authority to grant licenses; that authority may be limited by the terms of the copyright owner's contract with the songwriter. As noted in Chapter 9, on the *Duration of Copyright, Assignments of Copyright and Licenses*, certain music publishing agreements between songwriters and publishers only granted rights with respect to the original term of copyright. An example of such a contract is any music publishing agreement based upon the Uniform Popular Songwriter's Contract published in 1947 by the American Guild of Authors & Composers (now known as The Songwriter's Guild). Under that agreement, the renewal copyright for U.S. rights, and under certain circumstances international rights as well, reverted to the songwriter at the expiration of the original term of copyright. If the Publisher granted any licenses for the use of the composition in the United States during the original term, then such licenses will continue in effect under their terms during the renewal term, despite the reversion of rights to the writer. However, this only applies to domestic licenses. In other words, the music publisher in such circumstance does not have the authority to issue licenses for use outside of the United States covering the renewal term, unless it later turned out that the publisher retained international rights (due to the writer's failing to provide the proper notice).

To the extent a publisher cannot issue a worldwide license beyond the initial term of copyright, licensing opportunities will be lost. Virtually all motion picture and television synchronization licenses today are required to be issued on a worldwide basis and most require a term of perpetuity. If a producer cannot obtain a license having a sufficiently broad territory (i.e., worldwide) and a sufficiently long term (i.e., in perpetuity), he is likely to choose a substitute song. Thus, where renewal copyrights revert to songwriters under the provisions of a music publishing agreement, such as under the AGAC form contract, publishing income for songs whose protection is nearing the end of the original term may decline, because producers will avoid licensing compositions for which long term, worldwide licenses are not available.

Songwriters can alleviate the problem by granting his interest in renewal rights to the song or by entering into an arrangement allowing the publisher during the original term to issue licenses that have terms extending beyond the original term and into the renewal term. An example of such an agreement is set forth as Form 14.7 at the end this chapter.

### b. Affect of Rear Window Decision

As discussed at length in Chapter 9, the *Duration of Copyright, Assignments of Copyright and Licenses,* granting renewal interests in copyright will not completely fulfill the need of producers to obtain long-term licenses and there is no agreement that a Publisher can reach with a songwriter that would absolutely assure producers that the license will cover the renewal term. Publishers can only assure producers that licenses for songs *tainted* by the *Rear Window* decision will last only until the expiration of the original term of copyright. The producers options with respect to such songs are limited and are discussed in Chapter 9.

### 3.  Territory

The territory of synchronization licenses for theatrical motion picture releases is generally worldwide. Network television, local television, and syndicated television were at one time granted on a per-country and regional basis, but the recent trend has been to extend the territory to throughout the world. Synchronization licenses are beginning to reflect recent economic changes toward a consolidating global marketplace.

### 4.  Exclusivity

Synchronization licenses for motion pictures and television are nearly always granted on a non-exclusive basis. If the particular use is extraordinary, such as licensing a dramatic use of a song or using the song's title as the title of the motion picture or television program, and a substantial fee is offered, a copyright owner might agree to certain limitations on granting competing licenses for a limited period of time.

### 5. Credit

Unfortunately, motion picture producers rarely give on screen credit to songs used in motion pictures. This is particularly true for background thematic music. Even more rarely will you find credit given to the artists who performed the material; rarer still is credit to songwriters, and we would offer our gratitude to anyone who can identify a motion picture which gives credit to the music publisher.

It is time that music publishers consider requesting in their synchronization licenses for motion pictures and television programs, that the song, the composers, the music publishing company, and the performance rights society are given credit for the music used in such works. If nothing else, this would facilitate the task of licensing clearance for future uses of the motion picture, such as, perhaps, performance on television under a per program performance license scheme (see Chapter 17).

### 6. Changes and Translations

The synchronization license should also state that no changes will be made in the lyrics or fundamental character of the music and that no translations will be made of the lyrics without the permission of the copyright owner. Any changes would be subject to additional fee and perhaps approval of the songwriter. If any translations are authorized, ownership in the translations should be retained by the music copyright owner; care should be taken so that the translation made by the licensee is of a good quality and not materially inconsistent with any translations that might have been previously done in international markets.

### 7. Screenings and Free Copies

Copyright owners should request an invitation to a pre-release screening of the motion picture to examine the use of the music and any credits required under the license. If a videogram of the picture is released, the copyright owner should request two copies for his files.

### 8. *Most Favored Nations*

From time to time an artists representative will ask for a *most favored nations* clause, a provision requiring that the fee to be charged will be on no less favorable terms than those offered for the use of any other song in the motion picture.

Requests for these clauses are often made by less inexperienced representatives of copyright owners, who, not knowing what to charge, would offer some guess at an appropriate fee and require favored nations status to make sure his or her client does not receive a lower fee than anyone else who owns music being used in the picture. One problem with this approach, as we have seen, is that each song has a unique inherent value. Some are standard songs that are irreplaceable in the context of the use; others, like actors playing bit parts in the film, have many substitutes. Another problem is that each song is likely to have a different playing time in the motion picture, and some songs in the picture may be used for foreground music, some as background music. In such cases, how is a producer to determine whether the fee for the use of one song is on "more favorable terms" than the fee for the use of another?

Because of the disputes that may potentially arise from such provisions, a producer would be advised to avoid most favored provisions or might consider paying a fee that is slightly higher than warranted rather than to get entangled in such an arrangement.

### III. THEATRICAL MOTION PICTURE TRAILERS

A *trailer* is a short film of several minutes length containing a tightly edited compilation or montage of clips from a motion picture created for the purpose of advertising the motion picture (i.e., "coming attraction"). The creation of good trailers is now considered an art form and certain artists specialize in this craft, such as the award winning producer, Lee Stein. Music licensed for use in the motion picture are almost inevitably used in trailers that advertise them, and since the trailer is considered a work separate from the film, a separate synchronization license for the use of the music in the trailer is required. Such licenses are limited to use in the trailer for exhibition in movie theaters, and for additional fees, for inclusion in videocassettes and videodiscs that contain other motion pictures distributed to the home video market. The license is generally world-wide and limited to one year with options for renewal.

## IV. PROMOTIONAL MUSIC VIDEOS

A *promotional music video* is a short audiovisual work customarily created by a record company to promote the recording of a single song. Promotional videos are broadcast on national cable television networks that are devoted to musical entertainment, such as MTV and VH1. The record company who creates a promotional video will be required to obtain a synchronization license to use the music in the video. The license will be limited to one rendition of the licensed song for a length which is not more than the duration of the original recording of the song.

Promotional music video synchronization licenses are generally world-wide and limited to two to five years with options for renewal normally available. The synchronization fee is usually quite nominal, set at an amount intended merely to cover the administrative costs of preparing the paperwork for the license grant. This is because the copyright owner stands to substantially benefit from the performance royalties resulting from the exhibition of the music video on cable television, and from the general benefit the video serves in helping the song become a "hit."

The license is limited to broadcast on television, and other uses, such as theatrical exhibition or the making and distribution of videograms containing the video performance, are not permitted unless an additional license, and additional fees, are provided for. The license will not authorize the alteration of the lyric or any change in the fundamental character of the music or the use of the title, or any portion of the lyric of the composition, as the title of the video. Some licenses will prohibit the dramatization of the lyrical content of the licensed composition without further permission from the copyright owner.

## V. NON-THEATRICAL BUSINESS VIDEO PROGRAMS

A publisher will occasionally receive a request from a corporation to use a song in a video program produced for the purpose of training the corporation's employees or customers, or promoting a product or service. For the use of a song in such a work, the publisher will issue a special synchronization license for a flat fee. The term of such a license will be limited to three to five years and the use will generally be limited to the internal exhibition or broadcast of the program by the licensee. Permission may be obtained to make videogram copies of the program for an additional fee (see Chapter 15). Examples of non-theatrical film synchronization licenses are set forth as Forms 14.4 and 14.5 at the end of this chapter.

# APPENDIX TO CHAPTER 14
## SYNCHRONIZATION LICENSES

789

# FORM 14.1

## SYNCHRONIZATION LICENSE FOR MOTION PICTURE THEATRICAL AND TELEVISION EXHIBITION ONLY (INCLUDES NO LICENSE FOR HOME USE VIDEOGRAM DISTRIBUTION)

## MOTION PICTURE AND TELEVISION SYNCHRONIZATION AND THEATRICAL PERFORMANCE LICENSE

FOR AND IN CONSIDERATION OF THE SUM OF $ for the synchronization rights hereinafter set forth and $ for the performing rights and other rights set forth in Paragraphs 4 and 5 below, and the advance provided in Paragraph 7(d) for the Videogram rights set forth in Paragraph 6(b), said sums payable upon the execution and delivery hereof, and in consideration of all the other promises and agreements contained herein, Publisher listed below, hereby grants to and its successors and assigns, hereinafter referred to as "Producer" the non-exclusive irrevocable right, license, privilege and authority to record in any manner, medium or form, whether now known or hereafter devised, the music and the words of the musical composition set forth below only in connection with the motion picture entitled below in any language, to make copies of said recording in any and all gauges of film and to import said recording and/or copies of said recording into any country within the territory covered by this license and to perform, as set forth below, said musical composition in said territory, subject to the terms, conditions and limitations set forth below.

## 1.   MUSICAL COMPOSITION.

The musical composition (hereinafter the "Composition"), and the sole use of said musical composition, covered by this license is:

TITLE    WRITER    PUBLISHER    USE

## 2.    MOTION PICTURE TITLE.

The title of the only motion picture (hereinafter the "Motion Picture") with which said recording is to be used is:

## 3.    TERRITORY.

The territory (hereinafter the Territory) covered by this license is:

## 4.    PERFORMANCE LICENSE—UNITED STATES.

Publisher grants to Producer the non-exclusive right and license in the United States and its possessions to perform publicly, either for profit or non-profit, and to authorize others so to perform, the Composition only in synchronization or timed relationship to the Motion Picture and trailers thereof as follows:

(a) THEATRICAL PERFORMANCE. In the exhibition of the Motion Picture to audiences in theatres and other public places where motion pictures are customarily exhibited, and where admission fees are charged, including but not limited to, the right to perform the Composition by transmission of the Motion Picture to audiences in theatres and such other public places for the duration of United States copyright of the Composition.

(b) PUBLIC TELEVISION PERFORMANCE. In the exhibition of the Motion Picture by free television, pay television, networks, local stations, pay cable, closed circuit, satellite transmission, and all other types or methods of television or electronic reproduction and transmissions ("Television Performance") to audiences not included in subparagraph (a) of this Paragraph 4 only by entities having performance licenses therefor from the appropriate performing rights societies. Television Performance of the Motion Picture by anyone not licensed for such performing rights by ASCAP or BMI is subject to clearance of the performing right either from Publisher or ASCAP or BMI or from any other licensor acting for or on behalf of Publisher and to payment of an additional license fee therefor.

5.   FOREIGN PERFORMING LICENSE.

It is understood that the performance of the Composition in connection with the exhibition of the motion Picture in countries or territories within the Territory but outside of the United States and its possessions shall be subject to clearance by performing rights societies in accordance with their customary practice and the payment of their customary fees. Publisher agrees that to the extent it controls said performing rights, it will license an appropriate performing rights society in the respective countries to grant such performing right.

6.   LIMITED VIDEOGRAM LICENSE.

Publisher hereby further grants to Producer, in each country of the Territory, the non-exclusive right to cause or authorize the fixing of the Composition in and as part of the Motion Picture on audio-visual contrivances such as video cassettes, video tapes, video discs and similar compact audiovisual devices reproducing the entire motion picture in substantially its original form ("Videogram") only for the purposes, uses, and performances hereinabove set forth.

7.   [intentionally omitted]

8.   RESTRICTIONS.

This license does not include any right or authority (a) to make any change in the original lyrics or in the fundamental character of the music of the Composition; (b) to use the title, the subtitle or any portion of the lyrics of the Composition as the title or subtitle of the Motion Picture; (c) to dramatize or to use the plot or any dramatic content of the lyrics of the Composition; or (d) to make any other use of the Composition not expressly authorized herein.

9.    WARRANTY.

Publisher warrants only that it has the right to grant this license and this license is given and accepted without any other representations, warranty or recourse, express or implied, except for Publisher's agreement to repay the consideration for this license if said warranty shall be breached with respect thereto. In no event shall the total liability of Publisher in any case exceed the amount of consideration received by it hereunder.

10.    PUBLISHER'S RESERVATION OF RIGHTS

Subject only to the non-exclusive rights herein-above granted to Producer all rights of every kind and nature in the Composition are reserved to said Publisher together with all rights of use thereof.

11.    ADVERTISING

The recording and performing rights hereinabove granted include such rights for air, screen and television trailers solely for the advertising and exploitation of the Motion Picture.

12.    CUE SHEET

Producer agrees to furnish Publisher a cue sheet of the Motion Picture within thirty (30) days after the first public exhibition of the Motion Picture at which admission is charged (except so-called "sneak" previews).

13.    REMEDIES

In the event that Producer, or its assigns, licensees, or sub-licensees, breaches this Agreement by, among other things, failing to pay timely any license fees required hereunder, and fails to cure such breach within thirty (30) days after notice of such breach given by Publisher to Producer, then this license will automatically terminate. Such termination shall render the distribution, licensing, or use of the Composition(s) as unauthorized uses, subject to the rights and remedies provided by the laws, including copyright, and equity of the various countries within the Territory.

14.   NOTICES

All notices, demands or requests provided for or desired to be given pursuant to this Agreement must be in writing. All such documents shall be deemed to have been given when served by personal delivery or three days following their deposit in the United States mail, postage prepaid, certified or registered, addressed as follows:

(a) To Publisher:

with a courtesy copy to:

and

(b) to Producer:

with a courtesy copy to:

or to such other address in the United States as either party may hereafter designate in writing delivered in the manner aforesaid.

15.   ENTIRE AGREEMENT

This license is binding upon and shall inure to the benefit of the respective successors and/or assigns of the parties hereto but in no event shall Producer be relieved of its obligations hereunder without the express written consent of Publisher. This Agreement shall be construed in all respects in accordance with the laws of the State of California applicable to agreements entered into and to be wholly performed therein. The recording and performing and other rights hereinabove granted shall endure for the periods of all copyrights in and to the composition, and any and all renewals or extensions thereof that Publisher may now own or control or hereafter own or control without Producer having to pay any additional consideration therefor.

IN WITNESS WHEREOF, the parties have caused the foregoing to be executed as of the 1st day of January 1995.

PUBLISHER                        PRODUCER

By: _____      By: _____

# Form 14.2

## Synchronization License for Theatrical Trailer

### THEATRICAL TRAILER SYNCHRONIZATION LICENSE

In consideration of the sum of _____ payable on the execution and delivery hereof and upon the agreement hereto and the acceptance hereof as indicated below, the undersigned, for and on behalf of the Publisher(s) referred to herein, does hereby give and grant unto:

the non-exclusive, irrevocable right and license to record the following copyrighted musical composition(s) in synchronism or timed-relation with a trailer made and produced solely for theatrical purposes by the said licensee and now entitled:

SONG TITLE    WRITER(S)    PUBLISHER    USE    TIMING

Subject to the following terms and conditions:

This license is granted upon the express condition that the said recording(s) are to be used solely in synchronism or timed relation with said theatrical trailer, that no sound records produced pursuant to this license are to be manufactured, sold, licensed or used separately or apart from the said theatrical trailer, except as herein provided.

This license is granted for the territory of: THE WORLD.

The term of this license shall be for the period of ONE (1) YEAR from the date hereof and upon such termination any and all rights given and granted hereunder shall forthwith cease and terminate, including the right to make or authorize any use or distribution whatsoever of said recording(s) of said musical composition(s) in said theatrical trailer or otherwise, except as herein provided.

We hereby grant you the option to renew the term of this license for an additional one (1) year period subject to an additional fee of $_____, This option, if exercised, must be exercised by written notice at least thirty (30) days prior to the commencement of the option year.

Licensee has the irrevocable option or right to synchronize the Composition as embodied in the Program and to distribute the Program by means of Videocassettes and/or videodiscs and/or other home video devices in the territory ("Video Territory") of the world. Subject to the provisions hereof, for the right to manufacture and duplicate and distribute unlimited Videogram copies of the theatrical trailer during the term, within thirty (30) days of the first distribution Producer shall pay Publisher a Videogram fee of

The option referred to above must be exercised, if at all, by written notice delivered to Publisher within one (1) year from the date hereof and no later than thirty (30) days from the date of first performance or release date of the Program in the specified media embodying the Composition.

This agreement is assignable by you on condition that such assignee shall agree to be bound by all of the terms and conditions hereof, but such assignment shall not relieve you from ultimate liability hereunder.

The undersigned warrants that said publisher(s) are the vowners of the recording rights herein licensed, and this license is given without other warranty or recourse, except for their agreement to repay the consideration paid hereunder in respect of any of said musical compositions, if said warranty shall be breached with respect thereto, with the liability for breach of said warranty being limited in any event to the amount of the consideration paid hereunder; with respect to such musical compositions: and the undersigned reserves all rights and uses whatsoever in and to the said musical composition(s) not herein specifically granted.

AIRDATE:

BIG MUSIC PUBLISHING CORP.

By: _____

AGREED TO AND ACCEPTED:

By:_____

# Form 14.3

## Television Synchronization License

<u>TELEVISION SYNCHRONIZATION LICENSE</u>

In consideration of the sum of $            , payable on the execution and delivery hereof and upon the agreement hereto and the acceptance hereof as indicated below, the undersigned, for and on behalf of the publisher(s) referred to herein, does hereby give and grant unto:

the non-exclusive, irrevocable right and license to record the following copyrighted musical composition(s) in synchronism or timed-relation with a single episode, program or motion picture made and produced solely for television purposes by the said licensee and now entitled:

<u>TITLE</u>        <u>WRITERS</u>        <u>PUBLISHER</u>        <u>USE</u>

Subject to the following terms and conditions:

This license is granted upon the express condition that the said recording(s) are to be used solely in synchronism or timed relation with said television-film, that no sound records produced pursuant to this license are to be manufactured, sold, licensed or used separately or apart from the said television-film, and upon the further condition that the said television-film shall not be exhibited in or televised into theatres or other public places of amusement where motion pictures are customarily shown or places where an admission is charged.

This is a license to record only, and the exercise of the recording rights herein granted is conditioned upon the performance of said musical composition(s) over television stations having, valid licenses from the person, firm, corporation or other entity having the legal right to issue performance right licenses on behalf of the owner of such rights in the respective territories in which said musical composition(s) shall be performed hereunder, or for the United States from the owner thereof. However, the said recording(s) may not be performed by means of so-called "pay" or "subscription" television, or by means of audio visual devices or contrivances such as "EVR" or any method or devise similar or analogous thereto or otherwise used except in the performance thereof originating from and as actually broadcast by a television station.

This license is granted for the territory of:

The term of this license shall be for the period of _____ years from the date hereof, and upon such termination any and all rights given and granted hereunder shall forthwith cease and terminate, including the right to make or authorize any use or distribution whatsoever of said recording(s) of said musical composition(s) in said television-film or otherwise.

This license cannot be transferred or assigned by affirmative act or by operation of law, without the express consent of the undersigned in writing.

The undersigned warrants that said publisher(s) are the owners of the recording rights herein licensed, and this license is given without other warranty or recourse, except for their agreement to repay the consideration paid hereunder in respect of any of said musical compositions, if said warranty shall be breached with respect thereto, with the liability for breach of said warranty being limited in any event to the amount of the consideration paid hereunder; with respect to such musical compositions: and the undersigned reserves all rights and uses whatsoever in and to the said musical composition(s) not herein specifically granted.

Dated:

BIG MUSIC PUBLISHING CORP.

By: _____

AGREED TO AND ACCEPTED:

By: _____

# FORM 14.4

## TELEVISION SYNCHRONIZATION LICENSE FOR PROMOTIONAL MUSIC VIDEOS

### PROMOTIONAL VIDEO SYNCHRONIZATION LICENSE AGREEMENT

DATED: _____, 2000

PUBLISHER:   BIG MUSIC PUBLISHING CORP.
Address:        1000 Sunset Blvd.
                    Hollywood, California 90069

LICENSEE:    _____
Address:       _____
                   _____

COMPOSITION(S):   _____
                           _____
                           _____

AUDIOVISUAL FILM/TAPE:
      ("A/V Film")

For good and valuable consideration, the receipt of which is hereby acknowledged by Publisher, Publisher hereby grants to Licensee, its successors, assigns, licensees and sublicensees, the following rights in and to the Composition(s):

1.      Publisher grants to Licensee the non-exclusive license to record the Composition(s) in synchronism or timed relation with the visual images contained in the A/V Film, to make copies of such recording of the Composition(s) and to distribute such copies throughout the Territory, subject to the terms and conditions hereinafter set forth.

The use of the Composition(s) is limited to one (1) visual/vocal rendition of the Composition for not more than the duration of the Composition(s) in the original phonograph recording.

2.    The territory covered by this License is the world (hereinafter referred to as the "Territory").

3.    The term of this Agreement shall commence with the date hereof and terminate either two (2) years after release of the A/V Film, or two (2) years after release of the original phonograph recording in the United States, whichever is later (hereinafter referred to as the "Term").

4.    Upon execution hereof, Licensee agrees to pay to Publisher a handling charge of Twenty-Five Dollars ($25.00).

5.    (a)    This Agreement does not grant to Licensee or to its agents, affiliates or subsidiaries the right to perform or to authorize the performance of the Composition(s) in connection with the exhibition of the A/V Film in or by any medium or media.

(b)    The Composition(s) may be performed in connection with exhibition of the A/V Film by cable systems, broadcasters or other entities, or by means of media having valid performance licenses therefor from the American Society of Composers, Authors and Publishers ("ASCAP") or Broadcast Music, Inc. ("BMI"), as the case may be.

(c)    Exhibition of the A/V Film by cable systems, broadcasters or other entities or by means of media not licensed by ASCAP or BMI must be licensed by Publisher or by any other licensing agency acting for or on behalf of Publisher, and payment of additional fees will be required.

6.    It is understood that the performance of the Composition(s) in connection with the exhibition of the A/V Film in countries or territories outside of the United States and its possessions shall be subject to clearance by performing rights so-

cieties in accordance with their customary practice and the payment of their customary fees. Publisher agrees that to the extent it controls said performing rights, it will license an appropriate performing rights society in the respective countries to grant such performing right.

7. (a) This License does not authorize, permit or license any use of the Composition(s) not expressly granted herein and does not imply or grant the right to alter the lyric or change the fundamental character of the music of the Composition(s). Without limiting the foregoing, Licensee is not authorized (a) to perform or authorize the performance of the Composition in connection with the exhibition of the A/V Film in any theatre, auditorium or other place to which an admission fee is charged, or (b) to record the Composition on a phonograph record on other than in the A/V Film, (c) to use the title or any portion of the lyric of the Composition as the title of the A/V Film or otherwise, (d) to dramatize the lyrical content of the Composition, or (e) to reproduce and sell or lease copies of the A/V Film to the public.

8. Producer warrants and represents that should any other musical composition be licensed in connection with the A/V Film on a more favorable basis to the publisher thereof than is provided to Publisher hereunder, such more favorable basis shall also be extended to the licensing of the Composition(s) hereunder.

9. Publisher warrants that it has the right to grant this License and no other warranties, express or implied, are granted hereby. Should said warranty be breached, in whole or in part, Licensee shall either repay to Publisher the amount theretofore paid to Publisher for this License, or Publisher shall hold Licensee harmless to the extent of said consideration. In no event shall the total liability of Publisher exceed the consideration received by Publisher hereunder.

10. Licensee represents and warrants that the A/V Film containing the Composition(s) will be used solely for the pur-

pose of promoting the sale of phonograph records and tapes embodying the featured performances by the Artist.

11.      Upon expiration of the Term hereof, the rights granted herein shall automatically revert to Publisher, and any further use of the Composition(s) hereunder shall be unauthorized.

12.      This License and the rights hereunder are not assignable by Licensee.

13.      Licensee hereby agrees to furnish Publisher with a "cue sheet" of the A/V Film indicating the type and length of usage of the Composition(s) in the A/V Film.

14.      Whenever notice is required, or desired, to be given hereunder such notice shall be in writing addressed to the appropriate party at the address set forth above or at such other address as either party may designate by written notice given hereunder.

15.      This License sets forth the entire agreement between Publisher and Licensee with respect to the subject matter hereof, and may not be modified or amended except by written agreement executed by the parties. This License shall be governed by and subject to the laws of the State of California applicable to agreements made and to be wholly performed within such State. Any controversy arising under this License, if litigated, shall be adjudicated in a court of competent jurisdiction within the County of Los Angeles.

IN WITNESS WHEREOF, the parties hereto have executed this Agreement as of the date first set forth above.

PUBLISHER                 LICENSEE

By: _____    By: _____

# FORM 14.5

## NON-THEATRICAL FILM SYNCHRONIZATION LICENSE

NON-THEATRICAL FILM SYNCHRONIZATION LICENSE

In consideration of the sum of $   , and upon the payment thereof to the undersigned, the undersigned does hereby give and grant unto:

the non-exclusive, irrevocable right and license to record the following musical composition(s):

in synchronism or timed-relation with a picture made and produced by Licensee tentatively entitled:

and described as

A slide/tape presentation approximately thirty (30) minutes in length for use in non-theatric showings for training purposes to employees of the Licensee.

This license is granted upon condition that the said recording or recordings are not to be used for or in connection with television purposes, including "pay" or "subscription" television, any form of home television exhibition or cable television; that said recording or recordings are not to be employed for any radio or so-called "home-movies" use or other media not specifically set out herein; that no sound records produced pursuant to the said license are to be manufactured, sold, and/or used separately from the said picture; and with the further proviso that the said picture shall not be exhibited in or televised into theatres or other public places of amusement where motion pictures are customarily shown.

The license granted is for the territory of: THE UNITED STATES ONLY.

This license shall terminate on:

and upon such date all rights herein granted shall immediately cease and terminate, and the right derived from this license to make or authorize any further such use of said musical composition in said picture shall also cease and terminate upon such date.

All rights and uses in the said musical compositions(s) not herein granted are expressly reserved to the undersigned.

PUBLISHER                      LICENSEE

By: _____      By: _____

# FORM 14.6

## NON-THEATRICAL FILM SYNCHRONIZATION LICENSE WITH OPTIONS TO RENEW TERM

## NON-THEATRICAL FILM SYNCHRONIZATION LICENSE

In consideration of the sum of $1,500.00 ($500.00 per composition),, and upon the payment thereof to the undersigned, the undersigned does hereby give and grant unto:

("Licensee") the non-exclusive, irrevocable right and license to record the following musical composition(s):

(the "Compositions") in synchronism or timed-relation with a picture made and produced by the said company known as

A slide/tape presentation approximately fifteen (15) minutes in length, for non-theatric showings in 25 small theaters (seating up to 25 persons) to promote Licensee's products.

This license hereinabove set forth is granted under the proviso that the said recording or recordings are not to be used for or in connection with television purposes, including "pay" or "subscription" television, except as noted above or cable television; that said recording or recordings are not to be employed for any radio or so-called "home-movies" use or other media not specifically set out herein; that no sound records produced pursuant to the said license are to be manufactured, sold, and/or used separately from the said picture; and with the further proviso that the said picture shall not be exhibited in or televised into theatres or other public places of amusement where motion pictures are customarily shown.

The license granted is for the territory of: THE UNITED STATES.

The initial period of the Term of this license shall commence on June 1, 1990 and continue for a period of one (1) year.

Licensee is hereby granted two (2) options to renew the term of this license for one (1) year in each instance. An option may be exercised by written notice at least thirty (30)) days prior to the commencement of an option year, accompanied by a renewal fee of $1,500.00 ($500.00 per song) for the first renewal and $1,500.00 ($500.00 per song) for the second renewal.

All rights and uses in the said musical compositions(s) not herein granted are expressly reserved to the undersigned.

Licensor warrants and represents that it has the legal right and power to grant this license, and makes no other warranty or representation. Licensor agrees to indemnify Licensee and hold Licensee harmless from and against any and all loss, cost, damage or expense (including court costs and reasonable outside attorneys' fees) due to a breach of such warranty and representation resulting in a final, nonappealable adverse judgment or a settlement entered into with Licensor's prior written consent (such consent not to be unreasonably withheld).

Dated:

PUBLISHER                              LICENSEE

By: _____      By: _____

# FORM 14.7

## ARRANGEMENT WITH SONGWRITER THAT PERMITS MUSIC PUBLISHER TO GRANT SYNCHRONIZATION LICENSES COVERING THE RENEWAL TERM

BIG MUSIC PUBLISHING SUBSIDIARY, INC.
c/o Big Music Publishing Corp.
1000 Sunset Boulevard
Hollywood, CA 90000
January 1, 2000

Mr. Hippie Songwriter
c/o Psychedelic Music Publishing Corp.
Woodstock, New York 10000

Re:  Hippie Songwriter - Big Music Subsidiary
     Compositions Synchronization Fees

Dear Mr. Songwriter:

We refer to the January 1, 1967 agreement between our predecessor-in-interest Big Music Publishing Subsidiary, Inc., and you, with the Uniform Popular Songwriter's Agreement (1947 revised) attached as an exhibit thereto, as amended from time to time (hereinafter collectively referred to as the "Songwriter Agreement"). The following, when signed by us and you, confirms our agreement regarding apportionment of "Synchronization Fees" (as defined below) paid for the use of compositions written by you pursuant to the Songwriter Agreement (hereinafter referred to collectively and individually as the "Songwriter Compositions"). As used herein, the term "Synchronization Fees" means the flat fees and/or any royalties payable by a licensee pursuant to a television, motion picture, commercial or home video device license issued by you and us hereunder, which fees or royalties we actually receive during the term of our rights to the Songwriter Composition subject to such license.

1.    This agreement is entered into with reference to the following facts: Our rights to the Songwriter Compositions terminate from time to time during the period of the next several years, on a composition by composition basis. Therefore, we do not have the right to negotiate for or issue licenses for a term exceeding the term of our rights in each Songwriter Composition. You and we enter into this agreement in order to continue actively exploiting the Songwriter Compositions in motion pictures, television productions, commercials and home video devices and to permit us to continue to negotiate and issue licenses and receive payment for such uses during the term of our rights.

2.    Subject to paragraphs 5 and 6, below, with respect to synchronization licenses having a fixed term of years (e.g., a five (5) year term television synchronization license), the Synchronization Fee will be apportioned between you and us on a straight yearly basis. our share will be a fraction of the Synchronization Fee, the denominator of which will be the number of years in the term of the license and the numerator of which will be the number of years remaining (but the numerator shall in no event be less than one (1)) of our ownership of such Songwriter Composition. You will receive the balance of the Synchronization Fee.

3.    Subject to paragraphs 5 and 6, below, with respect to synchronization licenses that do not have a fixed term of years (e.g., motion picture synchronization licenses with a life-of-copyright term), the Synchronization Fee will be apportioned between you and us based on a seven (7) year life. Our share will be a fraction of the Synchronization Fee, the denominator of which will be seven (7) and the numerator of which will be the number of years remaining (but the numerator shall in no event be less than one (1)) of our ownership of such Songwriter Composition. You will receive the balance of the Synchronization Fee.

4.    We shall pay you your 50% songwriter share of the Synchronization Fee out of our apportioned share of the Synchronization Fee. You shall receive your songwriter share from us in addition to your apportioned share of the Synchronization Fee payable directly to you by any third party licensee.

5.    We shall not be entitled to receive or retain any moneys paid or payable subsequent to expiration of our rights to a Songwriter Composition which moneys are payable by a licensee pursuant to a license issued hereunder. All such moneys shall be payable to and retainable exclusively by you and each license issued hereunder shall so provide.

6.    Each license issued hereunder shall be of no force or effect until executed both on behalf of us and you. Each license shall provide for direct payment to you and us of your and our proportionate share of each Synchronization Fee. We agree to cause our representatives to obtain your prior written approval for each proposed synchronization use of a Songwriter Composition.

Please confirm your agreement to the foregoing by signing below.

Very truly yours,
BIG MUSIC PUBLISHING CORP.

John Doe
Vice President

AGREED AND ACCEPTED:

HIPPIE SONGWRITER

# VIDEOGRAM LICENSES

## SUMMARY

# CHAPTER 15

# VIDEOGRAM LICENSES

A*videogram* license is a license which permits the reproduction of music in recordings that are accompanied by moving pictures, such as motion pictures, television programs and other audiovisual works, and specifically allows such recordings to be distributed to the public in videocassettes, laser discs and similar devices.

As noted in the preceding chapter, when a music copyright owner issues a standard theatrical synchronization license, he is giving permission to the producer to make a recording of a musical composition coupled with the condition that the recording only be used as part of the specified audiovisual work and only be reproduced or performed in a particular way. That particular way is the exhibition of the motion picture in theatres and other public places where motion pictures are customarily exhibited and by television broadcast by entities who are licensed by performing rights societies to publicly perform the music embodied in those works. The license set forth as Form 14.1 at the end of the preceding chapter is limited to theatrical exhibition and television broadcast, and does not include permission to make copies of a motion picture embodying the licensed musical composition in videograms for home video distribution.

This chapter concerns the licensing of music for use in *videograms* — a portmanteau of the words *video* and *program,* used to describe the programs contained in audiovisual devices, such as videocassettes or laser discs, primarily intended for use in the home on a videotape or optical-laser player and a television set. The use of music in other programs, such as videogames, pre-packaged computer software, and multi-media works, such as CD-ROM and other optical disc devices is discussed in Chapter 22.

## I. THE RIGHTS INVOLVED

The essential right involved in the licensing of videograms is the reproduction right. Specifically, it is the exclusive right to reproduce, or *to fix*,[1] a musical composition on an audiovisual device, such as a videocassette or laser disc. The exercise of this right, however, is not subject to the compulsory licensing provision for mechanical reproductions set forth in Section 115 of the copyright law. The compulsory license provision only applies to fixing musical compositions in *phonorecords*, which the law defines as devices in which only sounds are fixed. If the sounds are accompanied by motion pictures or other audiovisual works, then the device is not a phonorecord (it is a *copy*) and the compulsory license provision does not apply. Accordingly, the copyright owner is free to negotiate the fees and other terms of licenses to fix their music in videogram devices, such as videocassettes and videodiscs.

Because these devices are primarily intended for use in the home, the right of *public performance* is not involved. The playing of a videocassette or videodisc of a motion picture, for example, in your home is merely a *private* performance. The copyright law does not afford copyright owners an exclusive right of private performance, which is why you may play a videocassette in your home as often as you wish without additional payment.

## II. EMERGING FEE/ROYALTY ISSUES

Since the advent of the home video player in the early 1970's, the terms and conditions of licenses to use musical compositions in videograms for home distribution have evolved slowly. Early on, because of the lack of standards in negotiating license fees for the videogram licenses, music copyright owners approached the licensing of their music for inclusion in videograms with great caution, quoting license fees which motion picture producers viewed as exorbitant. In many cases, music copyright owners refused to issue licenses altogether until they became further acquainted with all of the economic factors concerning the videogram device distribution of motion pictures.

---

[1] The copyright law at 17 U.S.C. Sec. 102(a) notes that a work of authorship is *fixed* in tangible medium of expression. The terms *to fix* and *fixation* are customarily found, in lieu of the terms *to record* and *recording*, in many videogram licenses.

At the heart of the matter was the question whether music copyright owners should receive from the producers of motion pictures some participation in the economic success of home video distribution. Indeed, from the perspective of the music copyright owners the question was not whether they would participate in the economic success of home video distribution, but how they would do so. Despite the fact that copyright owners charged a flat fee for the synchronization of their music with motion pictures, they had an opportunity to participate in the success of motion pictures, because of the lucrative performance royalties they could receive from performing rights societies, such as ASCAP and BMI, arising from the exhibition of motion pictures on television and from the exhibition of motion pictures overseas in theatres. The more successful the motion picture in which their music was recorded, the greater their share in performance royalties collected in connection with the telecast and exhibition of motion pictures.

The problem with home videocassettes and videodiscs is that once copies are recorded and distributed, no *public* performance is involved in their exhibition. As noted above, the playing of a videocassette or videodisc in your home is merely a *private* performance. Accordingly, no performance royalties arise from the home viewing of videograms, and music copyright owners do not receive any compensation beyond the flat synchronization fee received upon the original recording of the music in the film. The problem is compounded by the fact that home viewing of motion pictures by videocassette and laser disc, resulting in private performances, tends to reduce the audience for public performances of the work on broadcast television and overseas theatrical exhibition, which would generate performance royalties. Accordingly, music copyright owners insisted on a replacement for the participation in the economic success they were beginning to lose as a result of the trend away from broadcast television and theatrical performance to home viewing of videograms.

The solution insisted upon by the music copyright owners was to participate in the economic success of videogram distribution in much the same way as they participate in the success of record albums — by collecting a royalty for each unit sold. The problem they faced in implementing this system, however, was that motion picture producers were not accustomed to paying royalties on a per copy basis. They simply did not have the administrative infrastructure to account for copies sold and were reluctant to agree upon these terms. For a while, there was a stalemate. Producers accustomed to paying flat fees for synchronization licenses, refused to accept videogram licenses on terms requiring royalties to be accounted for and paid. Synchronization licenses began to specifically address videograms, but only to expressly provide that separate permission, and some form of additional payment, would be required for the videogram uses.

Soon, however, music copyright owners and motion picture producers began to negotiate a variety of interim solutions. For example, some early synchronization licenses provided that the parties shall negotiate in good faith to establish an appropriate videogram license fee, and failing an agreement, the parties would agree to submit the question to arbitration. In other cases, the music copyright owner would grant the videogram license for a limited term, such as five years, after which the parties would negotiate a fee or have a permanent fee set by arbitration. The interim fee was sometimes a flat dollar amount and sometimes a fee based upon some multiple of (e.g., 200%) of the compulsory mechanical royalties provided for in Section 115 of the copyright law.

Eventually, seeing the writing on the wall, motion picture producers established the administrative capability to compensate copyright owners for videogram licenses on a royalty basis and began accepting videogram licenses containing royalty provisions.


### III. CONSIDERATIONS IN GRANTING AND CLEARING VIDEOGRAM LICENSES

As noted in the previous chapter, modern synchronization licenses for motion pictures are carefully drawn to permit the fixing of music in motion pictures or other audiovisual works solely for the purpose of normal theatrical exhibition and television broadcast. If the motion picture is to be distributed in videogram devices, such as videocassette and laser disc, the terms are separately negotiated, either in a separate license or in special provisions set forth in the synchronization license form.

What has been previously said about the value of the song applies with equal force in considering the terms and fees appropriate in granting videogram licenses. See Chapter 10 for a general discussion, and Chapter 14 for a more specific discussion, of that consideration with respect to licensing music in motion pictures and television programs. Considerations regarding the fee structure, the importance of the song in relation to its intended use, and the scope of the intended use are discussed below.

## A. Fee Structure

The precise formula used for calculating the royalty may vary. As we have said, early interim licenses simply established some multiple of the compulsory mechanical license provision. Other videogram licenses condition its grant upon the payment of a flat fee for a set number of copies, with an option to make additional blocks of copies for additional flat fee payments. Ideally, from the music copyright owner's perspective, the license will be conditioned upon the payment of an advance against a per unit royalty or percentage of the distributor's revenues derived from the distribution of copies of the videogram. Motion picture producers would prefer a structure that requires the least amount of administration and often insist upon paying a flat fee for each block of copies made and distributed. Several sample videogram license fee provisions illustrating several customary fee structures are set forth as Forms 15.1 through 15.6 at the end of this chapter.

## B. Importance of the Song in Relation to Its Intended Use

The discussions in Chapters 10 and 14 regarding the importance of the song in relation to its intended use are also applicable in considering the fees and terms of videogram licenses. In addition, however, a music copyright owner should consider the further leverage he may have in considering licenses for the use of musical compositions that were previously recorded in motion pictures and television programs. If the terms of the synchronization licenses under which the music was recorded in such programs did not contain provisions permitting the fixation of the compositions in videograms, then the copyright owner is free to negotiate a new license fee in exchange for granting permission for such use. The question whether synchronization licenses granted before the advent of the market for home video devices included a license authorizing the reproduction of the music in videograms is discussed at length in Chapter 16, on *Old Licenses, New Uses.*

Once the music has been used in the soundtrack of a motion picture, television program, or other audiovisual work, the producer of the audiovisual work has virtually no substitute for the music included in that work. To the extent the music has become an integral part of the soundtrack, it cannot be easily isolated and removed from the audiovisual work without affecting its creative or commercial value. In such cases, the bargaining leverage of the copyright owner of the composition increases significantly.

Nevertheless, as noted previously, while the music copyright owner may attempt to charge "what the market will bear" for the use, he should not exercise this leverage to the point where the producer is unwilling to release the picture in the home video market. Regardless of the royalty rate received, the music copyright owner will make up for any perceived shortcoming in the fees received by maintaining an active relationship between the song and the listening public.

## C. Scope of the Intended Use

### 1. Media

A modern synchronization license with videogram provisions will typically authorize the recording of the song as part of a motion picture for the purpose of theatrical and television exhibition and the reproduction of videograms for license or sale to the public for home use.

The licenses do not always expressly define what is meant by the term *videogram.* The terms "video records," "home video devices," and "A/V Film," are sometimes used. A person seeking to clear a videogram license should be certain there is no limitation on the type of format on which work may be recorded and distributed. A videogram might be defined as, "any device or contrivance other than film such as video-discs, video-tapes or video-cassettes upon which there is fixed an audio-visual performance of a motion picture, which performance is capable of being reproduced by performing equipment."

Such a definition would include various formats of videocassettes, such as PAL and SECAM, and VHS and Beta, and various formats of laser disc video devices. A music copyright owner would normally have no difficulty providing a license that includes use on various formats, but it is always to the copyright owner's advantage to narrow the scope of the license to only those uses actually required by the licensee and a limitation on the formats permitted could serve that purpose.

### 2.  Distribution Channels

Videogram licenses do not always define what is meant by *home use*, but whether a precise definition is used or not, it is clear that the performance of a videocassette in a small theatre, a nightclub, or a bar, would not be considered home use. Inviting several neighbors over to your house to watch a motion picture on videocassette would, however, be a home use, but if you charged a fee, it would probably be considered a public, non-home use performance.

### 3.  Term

The term of the videogram license will depend upon how the compensation provision of the license is structured. If the videogram license is granted in conjunction with a theatrical synchronization license, and the reproduction of videograms is subject to a royalty, then the videogram license will generally have the same term as the theatrical synchronization license. This would typically be in perpetuity or for the life of the copyright in the song.

If the copyright owner and the motion picture producer could not come to terms on a royalty for the videogram license, then the videogram license, if negotiated at all, might have a limited term. For example, the music copyright owner might accept a lower royalty rate, or even a flat fee, provided the term of the videogram license is limited to 3 to 5 years, at which time, the producer would require new permission to continue distribution of videogram copies. If by that time the picture has become a perennial favorite, the music copyright owner should have no trouble negotiating an acceptable royalty structure or a higher royalty rate; if by that time the picture has gone into oblivion, a license for further videogram distribution would not be necessary. The motion picture producer thereby reduces his risk of investing too

much money to account for music royalties for a flop picture; the
music copyright owner thereby reduces his risk of making a bad deal
by preserving the right to renegotiate in the event the picture becomes
a long-term success.

### 4. Territory

Many early videogram licenses limited the distribution of videograms to within the United States and Canada, even though the territory of the underlying synchronization license for theatrical and
television exhibition was world-wide. In such cases, the exploitation
of videogram rights in other territories was made subject to the producer's obtaining licenses from overseas music publishers or the appropriate mechanical or performance rights societies. Even today,
however, the territory of many videogram licenses are limited to the
United States and Canada, often because the music publisher does not
control the right to administer the song in other countries.

Assuming the music copyright owner does control worldwide
rights to the song, the territory of the videogram license is usually
worldwide. Nevertheless, in some countries, fees for the distribution
of videogram licenses are collected by societies of publishers or local
governmental authorities established for that purpose. A videogram
license, therefore, may provide that where a local agency or authority
charges a higher royalty than that provided for in the license, the
producer shall pay the publisher the difference.

Under modern international subpublishing agreements, where
original publishers have provided their subpublishers a license to grant
local synchronization licenses, they have been careful to do so on a
*non-exclusive* basis, thereby reserving to the original publisher the
right to grant synchronization licenses on a worldwide basis.

### 5. Exclusivity

Videogram licenses, like synchronization licenses for motion pictures and television, are almost always non-exclusive. A music publisher should only guardedly consider a request by a producer for
exclusivity, as granting such a request may restrict the publisher's
future ability to license the song in many forms of audiovisual works.

## IV. OTHER TERMS AND CONSIDERATIONS

### A. Payment and Accounting

If the license fee for the videogram license is based on a royalty, such as a percentage of net revenues from sales or licenses of the videograms, the license will normally contain provisions relating to how and when the copyright owner will be paid the fee. These provisions are similar to those commonly found in songwriter agreements, recording agreements, book publishing agreements, and other agreements under which payments are based on a percentage of revenues or the number of copies distributed.

For example, payments are usually accounted for on a quarterly basis, within some reasonable period after the end of each calendar quarter in which there are revenues derived from the work. A written royalty statement detailing the sources of the revenues upon which the royalty is based will accompany the payment. The music copyright owner will have the privilege to inspect the licensee's books and records relating to the revenues derived from the videogram. In this regard, a number of accounting firms specialize in performing audits of such records, and a music publisher should consider having its licensees audited on a periodic basis to, as the saying goes, "keep them honest."

A discussion of other payment and accounting provisions is set forth in Chapter 3 and in Chapter 10.

### B. Reserves Against Returns

A producer might insist upon maintaining a reserve against royalties each quarter in anticipation of a reasonable amount of returns of the videogram (which would represent negative revenue and a credit against royalties), but any such reserve should be liquidated within some reasonable period of time after the quarter in which it is withheld.

### C. Most Favored Nations

As has been noted, music copyright owners were reluctant to grant videogram licenses before standards evolved that allowed them to establish a way to participate in the economic success of the videograms in which their musical compositions were embodied. Even as standards eventually began emerging, some music copyright owners continued to feel unable to determine in advance the importance of the song in relation to its intended use or otherwise remained fearful of making a bad deal.

Accordingly, the publisher unsure of what fee to charge, or even how to structure the fee, might ask that he be paid a license fee under terms which are no less favorable than those received for the use of any other song featured in the motion picture, requesting what is called a *most favored nations* provision. The copyright owner would reason that the use of his song in relation to the intended use may be, at least, no less important than the use of any other song featured in the motion picture, and, as long as he was getting no smaller fee than that being paid to the highest paid music copyright owner, he would avoid making a bad deal.

A producer who is reluctant to agree to such a provision should be prepared to argue that the song for which he seeks a license has significantly less importance than other songs in the motion picture. Nevertheless, if the music has long been included in a previously released motion picture, it would seem that obtaining a license for each song inextricably recorded in the picture is equally important, regardless of the nature or extent of the use.

## D. Free Copies

Music copyright owners should request at least two free copies of the videocassette or laser disc of the motion picture upon its release in the home video market.

## V. PROMOTIONAL MUSIC VIDEO VIDEOGRAM LICENSE

As discussed in Chapter 14, promotional music videos are customarily produced by record companies to promote the recording of a single song or album and are broadcast on national cable networks, such as MTV and VH1. From time to time, a music video becomes a successful "hit" in its own right, its success as a video program being independent of the success of the song or album it promotes.

In such a case, a record company may be inclined to release and sell, apart from copies of the audio recording, copies of the video program on videocassette or laser disc. Furthermore, some record albums consist of a recording of a "live" concert performance or recordings of selected live performances from a concert tour. Having recorded these performances on videotape, the record company often considers distributing the video program into the home video market.

As mentioned in Chapter 14, the publishers of the music underlying these programs are usually willing to charge a nominal fee for their exhibition on television, because such performances generate performance income and play an important role in making the song a "hit." However, the distribution of video performances of the music on videocassette or laser disc is akin to, and may be competition for, the distribution of the corresponding audio records of the performances. Accordingly, music publishers normally insist upon a royalty for such use.

Because these recordings are accompanied by moving pictures, the compulsory license provision does not apply and publishers are free to negotiate other fee structures for the use of their music on these videograms. Nevertheless, no standards have yet emerged for structuring fees for the sale of videograms of promotional music videos. Music publishers assert that the fee for the use of their music in such programs should be considerably higher than the use of their music in theatrical motion pictures, television programs, and similar audiovisual works, because, unlike an incidental use in a motion picture, the music plays a central role in the entertainment value of the music videogram. The royalty provision in Form 15.7 at the end of this chapter contains a formula which attempts to provide the music publisher with a substantial share of the revenues derived from the sales of such videograms.

## VI. Non-Theatrical Videogram License

Non-theatrical synchronization licenses, regarding the use of music in films developed by corporations for internal purposes, such as for employee training or demonstrations of products to customers, are discussed in Chapter 14. Where a corporation desires to make and distribute copies of a video program to employees, retailers, or to end user customers, the copyright owner will usually grant such permission in exchange for an additional fee based on the number of units made and distributed. Corporations which are not set up for, and do not look forward to the prospect of, accounting for the number of videogram copies made, will attempt to negotiate an annual buy-out provision. This allows the corporation to pay a yearly fixed dollar amount in lieu of accounting for royalties. An example of a synchronization license with videogram production privileges is set forth as Form 15.8 at the end of this chapter.


## VII. Video Year Books


In the wake of popular television programs that have introduced the "home video" genre of entertainment, such as *America's Funniest Home Videos* hosted by Bob Saget, high school and college students across America are applying modern technology to update an old tradition: schools are now producing what are being called *video yearbooks* — a videotape of short interviews and scenes encapsulating the senior year in a one hour or 90 minute program for sale in addition to or in conjunction with the traditional printed high school or college yearbook.

Music publishers have taken this opportunity to teach young students a valuable lesson in copyright law — that they have to pay for the use of the music they use in such programs — and charge a small flat fee for the use. The license for such use will be quite similar to the non-theatrical videogram license set forth as Form 15.8 at the end of this chapter.

# APPENDIX TO CHAPTER 15
## VIDEOGRAM LICENSES

# FORM 15.1

## SYNCHRONIZATION LICENSE FOR MOTION PICTURE THEATRICAL AND TELEVISION EXHIBITION WITH VIDEOGRAM LICENSE ON PERCENTAGE ROYALTY BASIS

### MOTION PICTURE AND TELEVISION SYNCHRONIZATION, THEATRICAL PERFORMANCE AND VIDEOGRAM LICENSE

FOR AND IN CONSIDERATION OF THE SUM OF     $ for the synchronization rights hereinafter set forth and $     for the performing rights and other rights set forth in Paragraphs 4 and 5 below, and the advance provided in Paragraph 7(d) for the Videogram rights set forth in Paragraph 6(b), said sums payable upon the execution and delivery hereof, and in consideration of all the other promises and agreements contained herein, Publisher listed below, hereby grants to     and its successors and assigns, hereinafter referred to as "Producer" the non-exclusive irrevocable right, license, privilege and authority to record in any manner, medium or form, whether now known or hereafter devised, the music and the words of the musical composition set forth below only in connection with the motion picture entitled below in any language, to make copies of said recording in any and all gauges of film and to import said recording and/or copies of said recording into any country within the territory covered by this license and to perform, as set forth below, said musical composition in said territory, subject to the terms, conditions and limitations set forth below.

1. MUSICAL COMPOSITION.

The musical composition (hereinafter the "Composition"), and the sole use of said musical composition, covered by this license is:

TITLE          WRITER          PUBLISHER          USE

## 2. MOTION PICTURE TITLE.

The title of the only motion picture (hereinafter the "Motion Picture") with which said recording is to be used is:

## 3. TERRITORY.

The territory (hereinafter the Territory) covered by this license is:

## 4. PERFORMANCE LICENSE — UNITED STATES.

Publisher grants to Producer the non-exclusive right and license in the United States and its possessions to perform publicly, either for profit or non-profit, and to authorize others so to perform, the Composition only in synchronization or timed relationship to the Motion Picture and trailers thereof as follows:

(a)    THEATRICAL PERFORMANCE. In the exhibition of the Motion Picture to audiences in theatres and other public places where motion pictures are customarily exhibited, and where admission fees are charged, including but not limited to, the right to perform the Composition by transmission of the Motion Picture to audiences in theatres and such other public places for the duration of United States copyright of the Composition.

(b)    PUBLIC TELEVISION PERFORMANCE. In the exhibition of the Motion Picture by free television, pay television, networks, local stations, pay cable, closed circuit, satellite transmission, and all other types or methods of television or electronic reproduction and transmissions ("Television Performance") to audiences not included in subparagraph (a) of this Paragraph 4 only by entities having performance licenses therefor from the appropriate performing rights societies. Television Performance of the Motion Picture by anyone not licensed for such performing rights by ASCAP or BMI is subject to clearance of the performing right either from Publisher or ASCAP or BMI or from any other licensor acting for or on behalf of Publisher and to payment of an additional license fee therefor.

## 5. FOREIGN PERFORMING LICENSE.

It is understood that the performance of the Composition in connection with the exhibition of the motion Picture in countries or territories within the Territory but outside of the United States and its possessions shall be subject to clearance by performing rights societies in accordance with their customary practice and the payment of their customary fees. Publisher agrees that to the extent it controls said performing rights, it will license an appropriate performing rights society in the respective countries to grant such performing right.

## 6. VIDEOGRAM LICENSE.

Publisher hereby further grants to Producer, in each country of the Territory, the non-exclusive right to cause or authorize the fixing of the Composition in and as part of the Motion Picture on audio-visual contrivances such as video cassettes, video tapes, video discs and similar compact audiovisual devices reproducing the entire motion picture in substantially its original form ("Videogram"), and:

(a)    To utilize such Videogram for any of the purposes, uses and performances hereinabove set forth and

(b)    To reproduce, and to sell, lease, license, or otherwise distribute and make such Videogram available to the public as a device intended primarily for "home use" (as such term is commonly understood in the phonograph record industry) in the Territory but subject to the provisions of Paragraph 7 hereof.

## 7. VIDEOGRAM ROYALTY.

Royalties ("the Royalties") with respect to the manufacture and distribution of Videogram copies of the Motion Picture un-

der paragraph 6(b) hereof shall be determined and paid as follows:

(a)    With respect to Videograms sold and not returned
pursuant to paragraph 6(b) hereof, an amount equal to the
greater of per Videogram copy of the Motion Picture or that
portion of _____ percent (___%) ("Publisher's pro-rata portion") of the wholesale distributor selling price (not including
shipping charges or taxes) that the Composition licensed hereunder bears to the total number of Royalty-bearing compositions contained in the Motion Picture.

(b)    With respect to Videograms manufactured and leased
or rented by Producer to its customers or consumers, an
amount equal to Publisher's pro-rata portion of _____ percent (___%) of Producer's actual net receipts with respect to
such lease or rental.

(c)    With respect to Videograms manufactured and/or
rented by a licensee of Producer, an amount equal to Publisher's pro-rata portion of _____ percent (___%) of Producer's actual net receipts from such licensee with respect to
such lease or rental.

(d)    Producer shall pay upon execution and delivery
hereof to Publisher a non-returnable but recoupable advance
("Advance") in the sum of _____ against the Royalties provided for in this Paragraph 7.

(e)    Producer may withhold from royalties otherwise payable with each accounting statement a reasonable and prudent
reserve for anticipated returns, refunds, and exchanges of Videograms hereunder, and such reserve shall be liquidated in a
reasonable and prudent manner but in no event later than 12
months after the accounting statement with respect to which it
was originally withheld.

(f)    Should a higher royalty, or per-copy rate, than that set
forth in this Paragraph 7 become payable with respect to Vid-

eograms manufactured, leased or sold in a particular country or sub-territory within the Territory either by (i) operation of law (including, inter alia, by statute, Governmental regulation or final judicial determination), (ii) agreement between a society or other organization collecting a significant portion of the music publishing revenue of said country or sub-territory and the manufacturers or distributors of Videograms or (iii) the establishment of a higher royalty rate by custom and practice within said country or sub-territory, Producer or its affiliates, agents, licensees or sub-licensees shall either pay such higher royalties to Publisher with respect to said country or sub-territory, or delete the applicable Composition from the Motion Picture with respect to said country or sub-territory.

(g)    Producer hereby warrants and represents that no other musical composition will be licensed for a substantially similar use in connection with the Videogram exploitation of the Motion Picture by or on behalf of a publisher on a more favorable basis to such publisher than is provided to Publisher hereunder. In the event a musical composition is licensed in connection with the Motion Picture on a more favorable basis in any of the areas hereunder, Producer hereby agrees that such more favorable basis shall also be extended to the licensing of the Composition hereunder.

(h)    (i)    Producer shall render to Publisher, on a quarterly basis, within forty-five (45) days after the end of each calendar quarter after the first commercial sale or rental of a Videogram containing the Motion Picture, a detailed written statement of the royalty due to Publisher with respect to the Videograms of the Motion Picture containing the Composition. Such statement shall be accompanied by a remittance of such amount as shown to be due. Any statement remitted by Producer hereunder shall conclusively be deemed true and correct and binding on Publisher unless Publisher submits to Producer in writing within three (3) years after such statement has been remitted to Publisher specific objections to the submitted statement. (ii) Publisher shall have the right to examine and inspect the books and records of Producer which relate to the Motion Picture and Videograms of the Motion Picture containing the Composition, and to make extracts thereof, for the purpose of determining the accuracy of statements rendered by Producer hereunder. Such examination shall be made during reasonable business hours, on reasonable business days, on no less than ten (10) days prior written notice at the regular place of business of Producer where such books and records are maintained. (iii) Each statement and the accompanying remittance will be made in United States currency. If foreign receipts in the Territory are frozen or unremittable, such receipts shall be transferred to Producer's account in such foreign country, and Producer shall notify Publisher to such effect. Upon Publisher's written request and upon condition that the same shall be permitted by the authorities of such foreign country, Producer shall transfer to Publisher in such foreign country and in the currency thereof at Publisher's cost and expense such part of such foreign receipts to which Publisher would be entitled hereunder if the funds were transmitted and paid in the United States in accordance with the terms hereof. Such notice and appropriate transfer shall discharge Producer of its obligation to remit such frozen funds. If the laws of any jurisdiction require that taxes on such remittance be withheld at the source, then remittance hereunder to Publisher shall be reduced accordingly. Producer shall provide Publisher upon request with copies of all applicable documentation with respect to such withholding.

(i)     Nothing herein shall obligate or require Producer to embody the Composition in Videogram copies of the Motion Picture and it is expressly understood and agreed that the Royalties payable to Publisher hereunder in respect of the Videogram and exploitation of the Motion Picture is conditioned upon the embodiment of the Composition therein provided that such royalties shall not be reduced by the use of the Composition that is less than the use specified in paragraph 1 hereof and provided further that in no event shall the Advances provided in paragraph 7(d) hereof be reduced or returned to Producer.

## 8. RESTRICTIONS.

This license does not include any right or authority (a) to make any change in the original lyrics or in the fundamental character of the music of the Composition; (b) to use the title, the subtitle or any portion of the lyrics of the Composition as the title or subtitle of the Motion Picture; (c) to dramatize or to use the plot or any dramatic content of the lyrics of the Composition; or (d) to make any other use of the Composition not expressly authorized herein.

## 9. WARRANTY.

Publisher warrants only that it has the right to grant this license and this license is given and accepted without any other representations, warranty or recourse, express or implied, except for Publisher's agreement to repay the consideration for this license if said warranty shall be breached with respect thereto. In no event shall the total liability of Publisher in any case exceed the amount of consideration received by it hereunder.

## 10. PUBLISHER'S RESERVATION OF RIGHTS

Subject only to the non-exclusive rights herein-above granted to Producer all rights of every kind and nature in the Composition are reserved to said Publisher together with all rights of use thereof.

## 11. ADVERTISING

The recording and performing rights hereinabove granted include such rights for air, screen and television trailers solely for the advertising and exploitation of the Motion Picture.

## 12. CUE SHEET

Producer agrees to furnish Publisher a cue sheet of the Motion Picture within thirty (30) days after the first public exhibition of the Motion Picture at which admission is charged (except so-called "sneak" previews).

## 13. REMEDIES

In the event that Producer, or its assigns, licensees, or sub-licensees, breaches this Agreement by, among other things, failing to pay timely any license fees required hereunder, and fails to cure such breach within thirty (30) days after notice of such breach given by Publisher to Producer, then this license will automatically terminate. Such termination shall render the distribution, licensing, or use of the Composition(s) as unauthorized uses, subject to the rights and remedies provided by the laws, including copyright, and equity of the various countries within the Territory.

## 14. NOTICES

All notices, demands or requests provided for or desired to be given pursuant to this Agreement must be in writing. All such documents shall be deemed to have been given when served by personal delivery or three days following their deposit in the United States mail, postage prepaid, certified or registered, addressed as follows:

(a) To Publisher:

with a courtesy copy to:

and

(b) to Producer:

with a courtesy copy to:

or to such other address in the United States as either party may hereafter designate in writing delivered in the manner aforesaid.

## 15. ENTIRE AGREEMENT

This license is binding upon and shall inure to the benefit of the respective successors and/or assigns of the parties hereto but in no event shall Producer be relieved of its obligations hereunder without the express written consent of Publisher. This Agreement shall be construed in all respects in accordance with the laws of the State of California applicable to agreements entered into and to be wholly performed therein. The recording and performing and other rights hereinabove granted shall endure for the periods of all copyrights in and to the composition, and any and all renewals or extensions thereof that Publisher may now own or control or hereafter own or control without Producer having to pay any additional consideration therefor.

IN WITNESS WHEREOF, the parties have caused the foregoing to be executed as of the _____ day of _____ 2000

PUBLISHER                          PRODUCER

By: _____        By: _____

# Form 15.2

## Videogram License Provisions on "Block of Copies" Basis (Replacing Sections 6 and 7 of Form 15.1)

6. VIDEOGRAM LICENSE.

Publisher hereby further grants to Producer, in each country of the Territory, the non-exclusive right to cause or authorize the fixing of the Composition in and as part of the Motion Picture on audio-visual contrivances such as video cassettes, video tapes, video discs and similar compact audiovisual devices reproducing the entire motion picture in substantially its original form ("Videogram"), and:

(a)    To utilize such Videogram for any of the purposes, uses and performances hereinabove set forth and

(b)    To reproduce, and to sell, lease, license, or otherwise distribute and make such Videogram available to the public as a device intended primarily for "home use" (as such term is commonly understood in the phonograph record industry) in the Territory but subject to the provisions of Paragraph 7 hereof.

7. VIDEOGRAM LICENSE FEE

The Videogram License Fee for the rights granted pursuant to paragraph 6(b) hereof shall be paid and determined as follows:

(a)    License Fee. Subject to the provisions in paragraph 7(a), (c) and (d) hereof, for the right to manufacture, duplicate and distribute up to _____ Videogram copies of the Motion Picture pursuant to paragraph 6(b) hereof, Producer shall pay to Publisher a Videogram License Fee of $_____ upon execution hereof. Producer may, from time to time, extend the license of the rights granted pursuant to paragraph 6(b) hereof for additional blocks of up to _____ Videogram copies of the Motion Picture provided that Producer pays to Publisher the sum of $_____ for each additional block of _____ Videogram copies not later than 30 days after the total number of Videogram copies of the Motion Picture previously licensed hereunder have been manufactured or duplicated by Producer, or its assignees or licensees. In the event Producer does not make such license extension payment to Publisher within said 30 day period, then the manufacturing, duplication, and distribution of the Videogram copies of the Motion Picture in excess of the total number of Videogram copies of the Motion Picture with respect to which Producer has already paid a Videogram License Fee shall be unauthorized and without the permission and license of Publisher.

(b)    Accounting of Videogram Copies Distributed. Producer shall render to Publisher, on a quarterly basis, within forty-five (45) days after the end of each calendar quarter after the first commercial sale or rental of a Videogram containing the Motion Picture, a statement of each country within the Territory on a cumulative basis, setting forth the totals (i) of all Videogram copies of the Motion Picture manufactured or duplicated and (ii) of all Videogram copies of the Motion Picture sold, leased, or otherwise distributed in each country within the Territory pursuant to the license of rights granted under paragraph 6(b) hereof.

(c)    Foreign Royalties. Notwithstanding anything to the contrary as may be contained herein, in the event that a per-copy rate for the exercise of the rights granted pursuant to paragraph 6(b) hereof greater than the product of $_____ divided by _____ shall become payable with respect to Videogram copies manufactured, duplicated, leased or sold in a particular country or sub-territory within the Territory (other than the United States and Canada, and their respective territories and possessions), whether by (i) operation of law (including, inter alia, by statute, Governmental regulation or final judicial determination), (ii) agreement between a society or other organization collecting a significant portion of the music publishing revenue of said country or sub-territory and the manufacturers or distributors of Videograms or (iii) the establishment of a higher royalty rate by custom and practice within said country or sub-territory, Producer or its affiliates, agents, licensees or sublicensees shall either pay such higher royalties to Publisher with respect to said country or sub-territory, or delete the applicable Composition from the Motion Picture with respect to said country or sub-territory.

(d)    Producer hereby warrants and represents that no other musical composition will be licensed for a substantially similar use in connection with the Videogram exploitation of the Motion Picture by or on behalf of a publisher on a more favorable basis to such publisher than is provided to Publisher hereunder. In the event a musical composition is licensed in connection with the Motion Picture on a more favorable basis in any of the areas hereunder, Producer hereby agrees that such more favorable basis shall also be extended to the licensing of the Composition hereunder.

# FORM 15.3

## VIDEOGRAM LICENSE PROVISIONS
## ON "FLAT FEE" BASIS FOR FIXED TERM
## WITH ARBITRATION
## (REPLACING SECTIONS 6 AND 7 OF FORM 15.1)

### 6. VIDEOGRAM LICENSE.

Publisher hereby further grants to Producer, in each country of the Territory, the non-exclusive right to cause or authorize the fixing of the Composition in and as part of the Motion Picture on audio-visual contrivances such as video cassettes, video tapes, video discs and similar compact audiovisual devices reproducing the entire motion picture in substantially its original form ("Videogram"), and:

(a) To utilize such Videogram for any of the purposes, uses and performances hereinabove set forth and

(b) To reproduce, and to sell, lease, license, or otherwise distribute and make such Videogram available to the public as a device intended primarily for "home use" (as such term is commonly understood in the phonograph record industry) in the Territory but subject to the provisions of Paragraph 7 hereof.

### 7. VIDEOGRAM LICENSE FEE

The Videogram License Fee for the rights granted pursuant to paragraph 6(b) hereof shall be paid and determined as follows:

(a) Initial Fee. Subject to the provisions in paragraph 7(a), (c) and (d) hereof, for the rights granted pursuant to Paragraph 6(b) hereof, Producer shall pay to Publisher an initial fee of $_____ upon execution hereof, of which $_____ shall be allocated as the license fee for the exercise in the United States and Canada, and their respective territories and possessions, of the rights granted pursuant to Paragraph 6(b) hereof ("Domestic Videogram License Fee") and $_____ shall be allocated as the license fee for the exercise of all countries included within the Territory, other than the United States and Canada and their respective territories and possessions, of the rights granted pursuant to Paragraph 6(b) hereof (the "Foreign Videogram License Fee"). Producer shall give written notice to Publisher no later than 10 days after copies of such Videograms are first offered for distribution to the public for home use. Such written notification shall include the identification of the Motion Picture and the Composition subject to this license and shall specify the date upon which copies of said Videograms will be, or had been, first offered for distribution to the public for home use.

(b) Additional License Fee. At any time commencing on the date which is _____ years after the date upon which copies of said Videograms had been first offered for distribution to the public for home use, Publisher, by written notice to Producer, may request Producer to pay an additional license fee, whether computed as a flat fee, royalty, or otherwise, for the grant of the rights pursuant to Paragraph 6(b) hereof. Upon receipt of such written notice, Producer shall meet and negotiate in good faith with Publisher to determine such increased license fee, if any, to be paid by Producer to Publisher. Such additional license fee requested by Publisher, and required to be negotiated in good faith by Publisher and Producer, shall be with respect to both domestic and foreign exercise of the rights granted pursuant to Paragraph 6(b) and with respect to both the exercise of such rights by Producer during the _____ years commencing upon the initial exercise of such rights by Publisher and for the remaining balance of the term of this license. If Producer and Publisher cannot agree upon an additional license fee with respect to either the Domestic Videogram License Fee and/or the Foreign Videogram License Fee within thirty (30) days after said written notification by Publisher to Producer, then the additional license fee, if any, for the domestic and/or foreign exercise of the rights granted pursuant to Paragraph 6(b) hereof shall be settled by binding arbitration in Los Angeles, California in accordance with the rules and regulations of the American Arbitration Association then in effect.

# FORM 15.4

## VIDEOGRAM LICENSE PROVISIONS ON TWICE "STATUTORY RATE" BASIS WITH AN ARBITRATION PROVISION (REPLACING SECTIONS 6 AND 7 OF FORM 15.1)

## 6. VIDEOGRAM LICENSE.

Publisher hereby further grants to Producer, in each country of the Territory, the non-exclusive right to cause or authorize the fixing of the Composition in and as part of the Motion Picture on audio-visual contrivances such as video cassettes, video tapes, video discs and similar compact audiovisual devices reproducing the entire motion picture in substantially its original form ("Videogram"), and:

(a)　To utilize such Videogram for any of the purposes, uses and performances hereinabove set forth and

(b)　To reproduce, and to sell, lease, license, or otherwise distribute and make such Videogram available to the public as a device intended primarily for "home use" (as such term is commonly understood in the phonograph record industry) in the Territory but subject to the provisions of Paragraph 7 hereof.

## 7. VIDEOGRAM LICENSE FEE

The Videogram License Fee for the rights granted pursuant to paragraph 6(b) hereof shall be paid and determined as follows:

If Producer shall exercise the rights granted pursuant to Paragraph 6(b) hereof in the U.S., there shall be payment of an additional fee and/or royalty ("Additional Payment") therefor. In view of the early stage of development of exploitation, it will be difficult to determine the amount and basis of such Additional

Payment until such time as the prevailing experience in the entertainment industry provides a better basis for determination of a fair and appropriate Additional Payment. Producer and Publisher each hereby agree to negotiate the basis and amount of Additional Payment in good faith at any time after the exercise of such right upon request of the other and, if they have not agreed upon the basis of computation and amount of Additional Payment within nine (9) months from the exercise of such right, they agree that: upon written notice from one to the other after the expiration of nine (9) months they shall renegotiate in good faith regarding such basis of computation and the amount of Additional Payment; if they are unable to reach agreement within 30 days after the date of such notice, they shall submit to, and be bound by a determination under, arbitration in accordance with the rules and regulations of the American Arbitration Association for the calculation and establishment of such Additional Payment hereunder. During the period between Producer's initial exercise of the right subject to this provision and agreement between the parties for additional payment or a final arbitration determination, Publisher shall be paid a royalty for each Videogram made and distributed. The royalty payable shall be twice the compulsory royalty payable for a phonorecord pursuant to the Copyright Laws of the United States (presently Title 17 U.S.C Sec. 115(c)(2). Said royalty payment shall be in accordance with the same provisions set forth in Title 17 U.S.C. Sec. 115(c)(3), and the Publisher shall enjoy the same rights as the copyright owner pursuant to 17 U.S.C. Sec. 115(c)(3). If such matter becomes the subject of arbitration, among the factors which shall aid in the determination of such Additional Payment shall be:

(a)    the number of copies, if any, of such Videogram then sold, licensed, leased, or otherwise made or to be made available to the public and the wholesale, retail, rental or license fee or price paid for each copy;

(b)    the type and number of uses of the composition hereunder in the Videogram and the types and number of uses of other musical compositions embodied in the Videogram;

(c)    the nature and use of the music in the motion picture (e.g., the subject of the motion picture is a dramatico-musical work or other work)

(d)    the negative cost of the motion picture and the relation of the cost of the music rights and production of music recordings (i.e., recording, musicians, and other performing artists, copying, arranging, and other costs).

Producer may exercise the rights under Paragraph 6(b) hereof in such portion of the territory as is outside the U.S. only pursuant to agreements, licenses or arrangements made with sub-publishers, agents, or other licensees or parties who then control such rights in the compositions in such portion of the territory as is outside the U.S.

# FORM 15.5

## AUDIOVISUAL WORK SYNCHRONIZATION AND VIDEOGRAM LICENSE (INCLUDES NO THEATRICAL OR TELEVISION EXHIBITION PROVISIONS)

### VIDEOPROGRAM-SYNCHRONIZATION AND VIDEOGRAM LICENSE AGREEMENT

LICENSE AGREEMENT entered into this _____ day of _____ 20__ between _____ whose address is _____ hereinafter referred to as ("Producer") and _____ _____ whose address is (hereinafter referred to as ("Publisher").

1.    The musical composition(s) ('the Composition(s)" covered by this License is (are):

Title                    Writer
Publisher

2.    The only Program ("the Programs) covered by this License is entitled _____ _____.

3.    The type and number of uses ("Uses") in the program of the Composition(s) is (are) _____ _____

4.    The "Territory" covered under this License is _____ _____

5.    Subject to the terms hereof, Publisher hereby grants to Producer the non-exclusive right, license and authority:

(a)     to record or re-record within each country of the Territory the Uses of the Composition(s) in synchronism or timed relationship with the Program, but not otherwise, and to make copies of the Program containing the Composition(s), all in accordance with the terms and conditions set forth below;

(b)     to cause or authorize the fixation of the Composition(s) in and as part of the Program on video cassettes, video tapes, video discs and similar compact and audiovisual devices intended primarily for home use ("Videograms"); and

(c)     to sell, rent or otherwise distribute such Videograms to the public within the Territory for use in conjunction with a television-type playback system or mechanism intended for home use only.

6.     The term (hereinafter the "Term") during which the rights licensed hereunder may be exercised shall endure for the worldwide period for all copyrights in and to the Composition(s), and any and all renewals or extensions thereof that Publisher may now own or control or hereafter own or control with Producer having to pay any additional consideration thereafter.

7.     Producer shall pay to publisher or its designee the following sums on the terms and conditions set forth below:

(a)     With respect to Videograms sold and not returned in the Territory, a royalty in an amount equal to the greater of $ _____ per Videogram copy of the Program or that portion of _____ (____%) percent ("Publishers pro-rata portion") of the wholesale distributor selling price (not including shipping charges or taxes) that the Composition(s) bears to the total number of Royalty-bearing compositions contained in the Program.

(b)     With respect to Videograms manufactured and rented by Producer or by a licensee of Producer, to its customers or consumers, a Royalty in an amount equal to Publishers pro-rata portion of ___ % of Producer's actual net receipts with respect to such rental.

(c) Producer shall pay upon execution of this Agreement to Publisher, a non-returnable advance recoupable only from the Royalties provided for in this paragraph 7, in the sum of $ _____ for the first _____ units and _____ per disc and cassette unit thereafter.

(d) Producer may withhold from royalties otherwise payable with each accounting statement a reasonable and prudent reserve for anticipated returns, refunds and exchanges of Videograms hereunder, and such reserves shall be liquidated in a reasonable and prudent manner, but in no event later than 12 months after the accounting statement with respect to which it was originally withheld.

(e) Should a higher royalty than that provided in Paragraphs 7 (b) or (c) above become payable with respect to Videograms manufactured, leased or sold in a particular country or sub-territory within the Territory, other than the United States and Canada, either by (a) operation of law (including, *inter alia*, by statute, governmental regulation or final judicial determination), (b) agreement between a society or other organization collecting a significant portion of the music publishing revenues in said country or sub-territory and the manufacturers or distributors of Videograms, or (c) by custom and practice within said country or sub-territory, Producer or its .affiliates, agents, licensees or sub-licensees, shall either pay such higher royalties to Publisher with respect to said country or its sub-territory, or delete the Composition(s) from the Program with respect to said country or its sub-territory.

8. Producer hereby warrants and represents that no other musical composition will be licensed for a substantially similar use to the Composition(s) licensed hereunder in connection with the Program by or on behalf of a publisher on a more favorable basis to such publisher than is provided to Publisher hereunder. In the event a musical composition is to be

licensed in connection with the Program on a more favorable basis in any of the areas hereunder, Producer hereby agrees that such more favorable basis will also be extended to the licensing of the Composition(s) hereunder. By way of clarification of the foregoing and not in limitation thereof, if another musical composition is licensed in connection with the Program and the publisher thereof is paid amounts for such composition exceeding the sums paid to Publisher hereunder, Producer shall immediately pay to Publisher an amount equal to the difference between the amount paid for such other musical composition and the sums and/or royalties theretofore paid Publisher hereunder.

9.    (a)    Producer shall render to Publisher, on a semi-annual basis, as of June 30 and December 31, for the prior six months, a detailed written statement of the royalties due to Publisher with respect to the 'Videograms of the program containing the Composition(s). Such statement shall be accompanied by a remittance of such amount shown to be due in United States currency. Any statement remitted by Producer hereunder shall be presumed to be true and correct and binding upon Publisher, except in the case of fraud, unless Publisher submits to Producer specific objections to the submitted statement in writing within three (3) years after such statement has been remitted to Publisher.

(b)    Publisher shall have the right to examine and inspect the books and records of Producer which relate to the Program and Videograms of the Program containing the Composition(s) for the purpose of determining the accuracy of statements rendered by Producer hereunder. Such examination shall be made during reasonable business hours, on reasonable business days, on no less than 10 days prior written notice at the regular place of business of Producer where such books and records are maintained.

10.    In the event that producer shall fail to pay to Publisher the amounts specified herein on a timely basis or shall fail

to account to Publisher and pay royalties as provided for hereunder, Publisher shall give Producer written notice that unless such default is remedied within thirty (30) days from receipt of the notice, this License will automatically terminate. Such termination shall render the distribution, licensing or use of the Composition(s) as unauthorized uses, subject to the rights and remedies provided by the laws and equity of the Territory.

11.    Nothing herein shall obligate or require Producer to embody the Composition(s) in either the Program or any Videogram of the Program and it is expressly understood and agreed that the compensation, in excess of the advance provided in Paragraph 7 (c) payable to Publisher hereunder in respect of sales of Videogram copies of the Program is conditioned upon the embodiment or fixation of the Composition(s) in such Videograms, but shall not be reduced by a lesser use of the entire Composition(s) than the Use(s) provided herein.

12.    All rights granted hereunder are granted on a nonexclusive basis and Publisher shall have the right to grant similar licenses for the use of the Composition(s) to other licensees. Upon the expiration of the period specified in paragraph 6 hereinabove, the respective rights granted to Producer herein shall automatically revert to Publisher and any further use of the Composition(s) shall be unauthorized.

13.    Producer may use the Composition(s) in the Program for screen and television excerpts and/or trailers only in connection with the advertising and exploitation of Videogram copies of the Program for the period specified in paragraph 6.

14.    This License is limited to those uses of the Composition(s) expressly set forth herein, and Producer hereunder; provided, however, that nothing contained herein shall be deemed to limit or curtail any rights previously granted to and/or hereafter to be granted to Producer under any other Agreement. By way of clarification and not in limitation thereof, this license does not grant the right to: (a) exhibit or authorize the exhibition of the Program in or by any medium not specified

here; (b) record or authorize the recording of the composition(s) in any manner except as specified herein; (c) make, authorize or permit any change in the fundamental character of the music or lyrics of the Composition(s); (d) use the title of the Composition(s) as the title of the Program; or, (e) use the story of the Composition(s) as the story of the Program.

15.    Publisher warrants only that it has the legal right to grant this License and this License is given and accepted without any other warranty or recourse, express or implied. If said warranty shall be breached in whole or in part, Publisher shall either re-pay to Producer the consideration theretofore paid to Publisher by Producer for this License to the extent of the part hereof which is breached or shall hold Producer harmless to the extent of the consideration theretofore paid to Publisher by Producer for this License. In no event shall Publisher's total liability to Producer or to third parties exceed the amounts received by it hereunder.

16.    This Agreement sets forth the entire agreement between Publisher and Producer with respect to the subject matter hereof, and may not be modified or amended except by written agreement executed by the parties. This License shall be governed by and subject to the laws of the State of California, applicable to agreements made and to be wholly performed within such State. Any controversy arising under this Agreement, if litigated, shall be adjudicated in a court of competent jurisdiction within the County of Los Angeles.

17.    Producer shall have the right to assign this License Agreement or any rights granted to Producer hereunder provided no such assignment shall relieve Producer of any liability hereunder, and no such assignment shall be effective unless Producer or the assignee shall deliver to Publisher a written assumption by the assignee of the further performance by assignee of Producers obligations hereunder.

18.    All notices, demands or requests provided for or desired to be given pursuant to this Agreement must be in writing.

All such documents shall be deemed to have been given when served by personal delivery or three (3) days following their deposit in the United States mail, postage prepaid, certified or registered, addressed as follows:

If to Publisher:

with a courtesy copy to

If to Producer:

with a courtesy to

or to such other address as either party may hereafter designate in writing delivered in the manner aforesaid.

IN WITNESS WHEREOF, the parties have caused the foregoing to be executed as of the _____ day of _____.

BIG MUSIC PUBLISHING CORP.
("Publisher")

BY: _____


_____
("Producer")

BY: _____

# FORM 15.6

## FORM OF VIDEOGRAM SYNCHRONIZATION LICENSE USED BY HARRY FOX AGENCY

THE HARRY FOX AGENCY, INC.
711 THIRD AVENUE, NEW YORK, NY 10017
VIDEOGRAM SYNCHRONIZATION LICENSE

LICENSE NO.:
LICENSE DATE:
LICENSE FEE:

YOU (THE "LICENSEE: REFERRED TO IN (A) HAVE ADVISED US, IN OUR CAPACITY AS AGENT FOR OUR PUBLISHER-PRINCIPAL(S) REFERRED TO IN (C) (HEREIN REFERRED TO AS LICENSOR(S), THAT YOU WISH TO OBTAIN CERTAIN RIGHTS (HEREIN REFERRED TO AS THE 'LICENSE RIGHTS') TO USE THE MUSICAL COMPOSITION REFERRED TO IN (B) (HEREIN REFERRED TO AS THE 'COMPOSITION') FOR THE PURPOSE OF MANUFACTURING AND DISTRIBUT-ING TO THE GENERAL PUBLIC FOR HOME USE AUDIO VIS-UAL DEVICES (HEREIN REFERRED TO AS 'VIDEOGRAMS') EMBODYING A RECORDED PERFORMANCE OF THE COM-POSITION IN SYNCHRONISM WITH CERTAIN VISUAL IMAGES COMPRISING THE WORK REFERRED TO IN (D) (HEREIN RE-FERRED TO AS 'THE WORK').

(A)    LICENSEE:

(B)    COMPOSITION:                    WRITERS:

(C)    LICENSOR AND PAYMENT PERCENTAGE:

(D)    WORK:

(E)    RELEASE DATE:

NOW, THEREFORE, IT IS AGREED AS FOLLOW:

1.    FOR THE PURPOSES OF THIS AGREEMENT, THE TERM 'VIDEOGRAM' SHALL MEAN AND INCLUDE ALL AUDIO VISUAL DEVICES UTILIZED IN HOME USE FOR THE PERFORMANCE VIA APPROPRIATE MACHINES OF AUDIO VISUAL WORKS INCLUDING, BUT NOT LIMITED TO, VIDEO-DISCS AND VIDEO CASSETTES.

2.    FOR THE PURPOSES OF THIS AGREEMENT, THE TERM 'FIXATION' SHALL MEAN THE PROCESS WHEREBY THE PERFORMANCE OF A MUSICAL COMPOSITION IS EMBODIED IN AND AS PART OF AN AUDIO VISUAL WORK IN SYNCHRONISM WITH THE VISUAL IMAGES THEREOF FOR OR IN CONNECTION WITH THE PRODUCTION OF VIDEOGRAMS THEREFROM.

3.    LICENSOR HEREBY GRANTS TO THE LICENSEE THE FOLLOWING NON-EXCLUSIVE RIGHTS WITH RESPECT TO THE WORK, IN ALL RESPECTS SUBJECT TO THE TERMS AND CONDITIONS HEREIN PROVIDED:

(A)    TO RECORD AND/OR RE-RECORD THE COMPOSITION FOR USE IN CONNECTION WITH THE WORK AS HEREIN EXPRESSLY PROVIDED;

(B)    TO CAUSE THE FIXATION OF THE COMPOSITION IN SYNCHRONISM OR TIMED RELATION WITH THE WORK; AND

(C)    TO MAKE AND DISTRIBUTE VIDEOGRAM COPIES OF THE WORK EMBODYING THE FIXATION OF THE COMPOSITION THROUGHOUT THE TERRITORY ONLY.

4.    THE COMPOSITION SHALL BE USED IN SYNCHRONISM WITH THE WORK FOR AN AGGREGATE DURATION WHICH SHALL BE _____.

5.   THE USE OF THE COMPOSITION HEREUNDER SHALL BE _____.

6.   THE TERRITORY (HEREIN THE 'TERRITORY') WITHIN WHICH THE RIGHTS LICENSED HEREUNDER MAY BE EXERCISED SHALL BE LIMITED TO:

7.   THE PERIOD (HEREIN THE 'PERIOD') DURING WHICH THE RIGHTS LICENSED HEREUNDER MAY BE EXERCISED SHALL BE _____ YEARS FROM THE LICENSE DATE OR THE RELEASE DATE, WHICHEVER IS EARLIER. AT THE EXPIRATION OF THE PERIOD, LICENSEE'S RIGHT TO MAKE VIDEOGRAM COPIES SHALL TERMINATE. LICENSEE SHALL, HOWEVER, HAVE THE RIGHT TO SELL OFF ITS THEN CURRENT INVENTORY OF VIDEOGRAM COPIES FOR A PERIOD OF ONE (1) YEAR THEREAFTER, SUBJECT TO ITS CONTINUING OBLIGATION TO PAY ROYALTIES THEREFOR AS HEREIN PROVIDED.

8.   UPON EXECUTION OF THIS AGREEMENT, LICENSEE SHALL PAY TO THE HARRY FOX AGENCY, INC., LICENSOR'S AGENT, AFORESAID ROYALTIES (HEREIN THE 'ROYALTY') WITH RESPECT TO THE MANUFACTURE AND SALE OF VIDEOGRAM COPIES HEREUNDER, AS FOLLOWS:

1)   WITHIN FORTY-FIVE (45) DAYS AFTER THE END OF EACH CALENDAR QUARTER DURING WITHIN THE VIDEOGRAM COPIES ARE SOLD HEREUNDER, SUMS EQUAL TO: $_____ PER VIDEOGRAM COPY OF THE WORK WHICH IS SOLD DURING EACH SUCH RESPECTIVE CALENDAR QUARTER.

2)   LICENSEE SHALL PERMIT LICENSOR'S (OR ITS AGENT'S) AUTHORIZED REPRESENTATIVE TO EXAMINE LICENSEE'S BOOKS AND RECORDS FOR THE PURPOSE OF VERIFYING THE ACCURACY OF THE STATEMENT RENDERED BY LICENSEE HEREUNDER.

9.    IN THE EVENT THAT LICENSEE FAILS TO ACCOUNT TO LICENSOR AND PAY ROYALTIES AS HEREIN PROVIDED, LICENSOR SHALL HAVE THE RIGHT TO GIVE WRITTEN NOTICE TO LICENSEE THAT UNLESS THE DEFAULT IS REMEDIED WITHIN THIRTY (30) DAYS FROM THE DATE OF THE NOTICE, THIS LICENSE WILL AUTOMATICALLY TERMINATE AND LICENSOR SHALL THEREUPON BE ENTITLED TO ALL RIGHTS AND REMEDIES FOR ACTS OF INFRINGEMENT UNDER THE UNITED STATES COPYRIGHT ACT WITH RESPECT TO THOSE VIDEOGRAMS AS TO WHICH PAYMENT WAS NOT MADE BY LICENSEE HEREUNDER, WHICH VIDEOGRAMS SHALL BE DEEMED INFRINGING COPIES.

10.    THIS LICENSE DOES NOT INCLUDE ANY RIGHT OR AUTHORITY TO:

A)    MAKE ANY CHANGE IN THE ORIGINAL LYRICS OR IN THE FUNDAMENTAL CHARACTER OF THE MUSIC OF THE MUSICAL COMPOSITION;

B)    USE THE TITLE OR SUBTITLE OF THE COMPOSITION AS THE TITLE OF THE WORK;

C)    USE THE STORY OF THE COMPOSITION; OR

D)    MAKE ANY OTHER USE OF THE COMPOSITION NOT EXPRESSLY AUTHORIZED HEREIN.

11.    LICENSOR HEREBY RESERVES UNTO ITSELF ALL RIGHTS OF EVERY KIND AND NATURE, EXCEPT THOSE EXPRESSLY GRANTED TO LICENSEE HEREIN.

12.    LICENSOR WARRANTS ONLY THAT IT HAS THE RIGHT TO GRANT THIS LICENSE, AND THIS LICENSE IS GIVEN AND ACCEPTED WITHOUT ANY OTHER REPRESENTATION, WARRANT OR RECOURSE, EXPRESS OR IMPLIED, EXCEPT FOR LICENSOR'S AGREEMENT TO REPAY THE CONSIDERATION PAID FOR THIS LICENSE IF THE AFORESAID

WARRANTY SHOULD BE BREACHED. IN NO EVENT SHALL THE TOTAL LIABILITY OF THE LICENSOR EXCEED THE TOTAL AMOUNT OF CONSIDERATION RECEIVED BY IT HEREUNDER.

13.　　THIS AGREEMENT SETS FORTH THE ENTIRE UNDERSTANDING OF THE PARTIES HERETO WITH RESPECT TO THE SUBJECT MATTER THEREOF, MAY NOT BE ALTERED, AMENDED OR ASSIGNED WITHOUT AN EXPRESS WRITTEN INSTRUMENT TO SUCH EFFECT ACCEPTED BY LICENSOR AND SHALL BE GOVERNED AND CONSTRUED BY AND UNDER THE LAWS OF THE STATE OF NEW YORK.

IN WITNESS WHEREOF, LICENSOR, BY ITS AGENT, THE HARRY FOX AGENCY, INC., AND LICENSEE HAVE CAUSED THIS AGREEMENT TO BE EXECUTED AS OF THE DATE FIRST WRITTEN ABOVE.

THE HARRY FOX AGENCY, INC.

By: _____

AGREED AND ACCEPTED:

By: _____

# FORM 15.7

## SYNCHRONIZATION LICENSE FOR PROMOTIONAL MUSIC VIDEOS WITH VIDEOGRAM PROVISIONS

PROMOTIONAL VIDEO SYNCHRONIZATION
LICENSE AGREEMENT

DATED: _____, 2000

PUBLISHER:   BIG MUSIC PUBLISHING CORP.
Address:       1000 Sunset Blvd.
                 Hollywood, California 90069

LICENSEE:   _____
Address:       _____
                 _____

COMPOSITION(S):   _____
                       _____
                       _____

AUDIOVISUAL FILM/TAPE:
("A/V Film")

For good and valuable consideration, the receipt of which is hereby acknowledged by Publisher, Publisher hereby grants to Licensee, its successors, assigns, licensees and sublicensees, the following rights in and to the Composition(s):

1.    Publisher grants to Licensee the non-exclusive license to record the Composition(s) in synchronism or timed relation with the visual images contained in the A/V Film, to make copies of such recording of the Composition(s) and to distribute such copies throughout the Territory, subject to the terms and conditions hereinafter set forth.

The use of the Composition(s) is limited to one (1) visual/ vocal rendition of the Composition for not more than the duration of the Composition(s) in the original phonograph recording.

2.      The territory covered by this License is the world (hereinafter referred to as the "Territory").

3.      The term of this Agreement shall commence with the date hereof and terminate either two (2) years after release of the A/V Film, or two (2) years after release of the original phonograph recording in the United States, whichever is later (hereinafter referred to as the "Term").

4.      Upon execution hereof, Licensee agrees to pay to Publisher a handling charge of Twenty-Five Dollars ($25.00) for the preparation of this license and related paperwork. In addition, when the production costs of the A/V Film have been recouped (from whatever source), Licensee shall pay Publisher a one-time synchronization fee of $250, if income is received by Licensee from subsequent exhibition thereof.

5.      (a)     This Agreement does not grant to Licensee or to its agents, affiliates or subsidiaries the right to perform or to authorize the performance of the Composition(s) in connection with the exhibition of the A/V Film in or by any medium or media.

        (b)     The Composition(s) may be performed in connection with exhibition of the A/V Film by cable systems, broadcasters or other entities, or by means of media having valid performance licenses therefor from the American Society of Composers, Authors and Publishers ("ASCAP") or Broadcast Music, Inc. ("BMI"), as the case may be.

        (c)     Exhibition of the A/V Film by cable systems, broadcasters or other entities or by means of media not licensed by ASCAP or BMI must be licensed by Publisher or by any other licensing agency acting for or on behalf of Publisher, and payment of additional fees will be required.

6. It is understood that the performance of the Composition(s) in connection with the exhibition of the A/V Film in countries or territories outside of the United States and its possessions shall be subject to clearance by performing rights societies in accordance with their customary practice and the payment of their customary fees. Publisher agrees that to the extent it controls said performing rights, it will license an appropriate performing rights society in the respective countries to grant such performing right.

7. (a) This License does not authorize, permit or license any use of the Composition(s) not expressly granted herein and does not imply or grant the right to alter the lyric or change the fundamental character of the music of the Composition(s). Without limiting the foregoing, Licensee is not authorized (a) to perform or authorize the performance of the Composition in connection with the exhibition of the A/V Film in any theatre, auditorium or other place to which an admission fee is charged, (b) to record the Composition on a phonograph record on other than in the A/V Film, (c) to use the title or any portion of the lyric of the Composition as the title of the A/V Film or otherwise, or (d) to dramatize the lyrical content of the Composition.

(b) (i) In the event that the Composition as embodied in the A/V Film is included in home video devices, Producer shall pay Publisher a pro rata share (based upon comparative running time of the various musical compositions included therein) of 5% of the wholesale price on all units for which Licensee is paid (or in respect of which Licensee receives credit in reduction of an advance). Licensee shall account to and pay Publisher, in each instance, within thirty (30) days after Licensee is accounted to by its home video distributor, and each such accounting shall be accompanied by a photocopy of the relevant portion of the accounting statement furnished to Licensee by its distributor.

(ii)    In the event that Licensee receives income from the lease or rental of home video devices, Publisher shall be entitled to receive a pro rata share thereof, to be determined by multiplying such income by a fraction, the numerator of which is 5 and the denominator of which is the number equal to the number of percentage points of wholesale (or the equivalent) payable to Licensee by its distributor on sales of home video devices.

8.    Producer warrants and represents that should any other musical composition be licensed in connection with the A/V Film on a more favorable basis to the publisher thereof than is provided to Publisher hereunder, such more favorable basis shall also be extended to the licensing of the Composition(s) hereunder.

9.    Publisher warrants that it has the right to grant this License and no other warranties, express or implied, are granted hereby. Should said warranty be breached, in whole or in part, Licensee shall either repay to Publisher the theretofore paid to Publisher for this License, or Publisher shall hold Licensee harmless to the extent of said consideration. In no event shall the total liability of Publisher exceed the consideration received by Publisher hereunder.

10.    Licensee represents and warrants that the A/V Film containing the Composition(s) will be used for the principal purpose of promoting the sale of phonograph records and tapes embodying the featured performances by the Artist.

11.    Upon expiration of the Term hereof, the rights granted herein shall automatically revert to Publisher, and any further use of the Composition(s) hereunder shall be unauthorized.

12.    This License and the rights hereunder are not assignable by Licensee.

13.    Licensee hereby agrees to furnish Publisher with a "cue sheet" of the A/V Film indicating the type and length of usage of the Composition(s) in the A/V Film.

14. Whenever notice is required, or desired, to be given hereunder such notice shall be in writing addressed to the appropriate party at the address set forth above or at such other address as either party may designate by written notice given hereunder.

15. This License sets forth the entire agreement between Publisher and Licensee with respect to the subject matter hereof, and may not be modified or amended except by written agreement executed by the parties. This License shall be governed by and subject to the laws of the State of California applicable to agreements made and to be wholly performed within such State. Any controversy arising under this License, if litigated, shall be adjudicated in a court of competent jurisdiction within the County of Los Angeles.

IN WITNESS WHEREOF, the parties hereto have executed this Agreement as of the date first set forth above.

PUBLISHER                         LICENSEE

By: _____    By: _____

# Form 15.8

## Non-theatrical Film Synchronization License With Videogram Provisions

### NON-THEATRICAL FILM SYNCHRONIZATION AND VIDEOGRAM LICENSE

In consideration of the sum of $_____ per composition, and upon the payment thereof to the undersigned, the undersigned does hereby give and grant unto:

("Licensee") the non-exclusive, irrevocable right and license to record the following musical composition(s):

(the "Compositions") in synchronism or timed-relation with a picture made and produced by Licensee tentatively entitled:

(the "Program") described as:

[A slide/tape presentation approximately fifteen (15) minutes in length, for non-theatric showings in 25 small theaters (seating up to 25 persons) to promote Licensee's products.]

This license hereinabove set forth is granted under the proviso that the said recording or recordings are not to be used for or in connection with television purposes, including "pay" or "subscription" television, except as noted above or cable television; that said recording or recordings are not to be employed for any radio or so-called "home-movies" use or other media not specifically set out herein; that no sound records produced pursuant to the said license are to be manufactured, sold, and/or used separately from the said picture; and with the further proviso that the said picture shall not be exhibited in or televised into theatres or other public places of amusement where motion pictures are customarily shown.

The Territory of this license is: THE WORLD.

The Term of this license shall commence on the date hereof and shall continue for a period of five (5) years.

VIDEO BUYOUT OPTION:

Licensee has the irrevocable option to synchronize the Composition(s) as embodied in the Program and to distribute the Program by means of Video cassettes and/or video discs and/or other home video devices in the territory ("Video Territory") of the World. Subject to the provisions hereof, for the right to manufacture and duplicate and distribute an unlimited number of Videogram copies of the Program, within thirty (30) days of the first distribution, Producer shall pay Publisher a Videogram fee of $_____.

VIDEO ROYALTY OPTION (FIXED TERM):

Licensee has the irrevocable option to synchronize the Composition(s) as embodied in the Program and to distribute the Program by means of Video cassettes and/or video discs and/or other home devices in the territory ("Video Territory") of the World, for a term of _____ years (to the extent we now or hereafter own or control the copyrights in and to the Composition(s) and any renewals or extensions thereof). If Licensee exercises this option, Licensee will pay Publisher an amount equal to _____ cents (___) per song, per home video device embodying the Composition(s) in the Program distributed in the Video Territory and not returned. Within thirty (30) days of the first distribution of such home video devices in the Video Territory, Producer will pay Publisher the sum of _____ for the first _____ ($) per song, for the first _____ units, as an advance against the royalty of $_____ per song, as set forth above.

## U. S. THEATRICAL - OPTION LANGUAGE

Licensee has the irrevocable option to exhibit the Program in Motion Picture theatres and other public places where motion pictures are customarily exhibited, and where admission fees are charged, in the United States, subject to a fee of $_____, for the worldwide period of all copyrights in and to the Composition that Licensor may now own or control, and any and all renewals or extensions thereof which Licensor may hereafter acquire but, in the latter instance Licensee shall not be required to pay any additional fees of or compensation beyond those prescribed above.

The option(s) referred to above, if exercised, must be exercised within eighteen (18) months following the Program's initial broadcast by written notice delivered to Publisher not later than thirty (30) days from the date of first broadcast.

All rights and uses in the said musical Compositions(s) not herein granted are expressly reserved to the undersigned.

Licensor warrants and represents that it has the legal right and power to grant this license, and makes no other warranty or representation. Licensor agrees to indemnify Licensee and hold Licensee harmless from and against any and all loss, cost, damage or expense (including court costs and reasonable outside attorneys' fees) due to a breach of such warranty and representation resulting in a final, nonappealable adverse judgment or a settlement entered into with Licensor's prior written consent (such consent not to be unreasonably withheld).

Dated:

PUBLISHER                LICENSEE

By:_____     By:_____

# OLD LICENSES, NEW USES

## SUMMARY

# OLD LICENSES,
# NEW USES

A s the local home video rental store was becoming as commonplace as the neighborhood bakery, the motion picture studios that produced the movies that made up the bread and butter of these stores found themselves in the middle of quite a fix: they began to realize they were not participating in the increasing amount of rental revenues derived from the rental of their videocassettes by the video rental stores. After receiving only one payment for the sale of a videocassette to a video rental store, the producer would watch that same videocassette be rented to home viewers over and over, as many times as the tape could physically endure being played and rewound, and replayed. In addition, the availability of videocassettes for home viewing would mean a certain decline in the number of people who went out to movie theatres for their motion picture entertainment. Making matters worse, motion picture producers and their distributors began receiving notices from music publishers that their use of music in these videocassettes was not authorized by their synchronization licenses and required the payment of additional license fees.

For motion pictures made in recent years, after it had become clear that nearly every film would likely be distributed in the lucrative home video market, producers normally have been able to obtain, concurrent with their synchronization licenses, the videogram license necessary to permit them to reproduce their musical works in home video devices. But what about motion pictures that were released many years ago, well before the advent of the videocassette and laser disc players? Did not the old licenses for the use of music in these films cover the new use in the home video market? Music publishers reviewed these old synchronization licenses and concluded, "no." In many cases, this answer was clearly correct. Some of these old synchronization licenses either specifically identified home video use and expressly excluded it or the license was otherwise clear with respect to what uses were granted, all other uses, including home video use, whether or not anticipated at the time, being reserved by implication.

As noted in the preceding chapter, synchronization licenses for motion pictures grant permission to record a composition as part of a specified motion picture and to reproduce copies of the resulting audiovisual work, but carefully drafted synchronization licenses specify that the copies reproduced may only be used to effect the theatrical release of the motion picture or its television broadcast. Use of copies of the film for distribution to the public for home viewing is neither a "theatrical release" nor "television broadcast." Thus, for many synchronization licenses, an additional license permitting home video distribution is required.

The problem is that not all older synchronization licenses were as clear as they should have been in limiting the use of the copies made of the motion picture. The need for precision in drafting perceived at the time did not always adequately anticipate the rapid advances in technology we see today.

This chapter will review language typically found in several old synchronization licenses and will provide a recommended approach for determining the scope of old licenses that are ambiguous as to the licensee's privilege to engage in home video reproduction.


## I. TYPES OF OLD SYNCHRONIZATION LICENSES

Old synchronization licenses fall into three general classes:

A. Licenses that Clearly Include Home Video Reproduction Privileges.

B. Licenses that Clearly Exclude Home Video Reproduction Privileges.

C. Licenses Whose Scope is Unclear.

Each of these will be discussed in turn.

## A. Old Licenses that Clearly Include Home Video Reproduction Privileges

Before the advent of the home video market, some attorneys representing motion picture producers foresaw the possibility of new forms of distribution of motion pictures and negotiated synchronization licenses which reflected their prescience. Such licenses permitted the recording of the music in synchronism or timed-relation with the specified motion picture,

> "for use in any form or medium, and in any manner, now known or hereafter devised."

A license such as this would seem to clearly include the right of reproduction of the motion picture for home video distribution.

More recently, motion picture synchronization licenses have been drafted to specifically include permission to reproduce copies of the motion picture for home video distribution. These license provisions are commonly called *videogram licenses* and have been discussed in detail in the preceding chapter. Early in the history of videogram licensing, when music publishers were reluctant to negotiate specific terms until some standards had begun to emerge, videogram licenses were granted for short duration and called for good faith negotiations and arbitration upon the expiration of their terms. Later, specific royalty provisions became common.

## B. Old Licenses that Clearly Exclude Home Video Reproduction Privileges

At the other extreme are those synchronization licenses which clearly exclude home video reproduction. Licenses which specifically refer to home video devices and specifically exclude their use are relatively rare, as they are likely to have been issued during that short few years between the advent of the home video market and the time when provisions for the licensing of music in films for the home video market started to become standard.

The following provision of a typical synchronization license issued in the early to mid-1970s makes it clear that the license does not include the use of copies made for home video distribution:

Cassettes. Notwithstanding anything to the contrary hereinabove contained, this agreement does not grant to Producer the right to manufacture or duplicate said motion picture by means of audio-television devices or contrivances, such as cassettes, discs or other similar configurations (herein called "cassettes"), for the purpose of selling such cassettes to the public. The sale of cassettes of the motion picture to the public shall be governed by the applicable law and/or by future good faith negotiations of the parties with respect to the fees to be paid in connection with such sales to the public, giving due consideration to customary practices which may develop with respect thereto.

Consider a license, in common use about 1927, which would also appear to clearly exclude the making of copies for home video distribution:

You are hereby granted a license to manufacture devices serving to mechanically reproduce the same, in whole or in part, and to use such devices solely in conjunction with and as an integral part of the appliance or mechanism known as THE VITAPHONE, in the United States and Canada, subject to the following conditions:

1. This License is not exclusive, and applies solely to the above described mechanical recording and public reproduction of the above named composition.

2. This License extends to and includes public performances by means of records as aforesaid serving to reproduce mechanically such above described composition in conjunction with THE VITA-PHONE.

3. This License is subject to the rights of the American Society of Composers, Authors, and Publishers in the said composition with respect to the public performance thereof for profit; and the public reproductions or performance thereof for profit shall take place only in establishments licensed by the said Society.

The above license appears to have been very narrowly drafted to cover the reproduction of the composition "solely in conjunction with and as an integral part of the appliance or mechanism known as THE VITAPHONE." A little history will make clear the reason for such precision.

Under a patent licensed from Western Electric, Vitaphone Corporation — a joint venture established by Warner Bros. and a talented inventor — developed the first practical synchronized recording system and became the first producer of motion pictures to enter the sound picture (i.e., *talkies*) market. Originally, the Vitaphone process employed separate records for the sound portion of the motion picture. In the case of very early talkies, the records contained only the musical scores. Later, the records contained music, dialogue, and sound effects. Since records containing the musical scores could easily be misused to compete with commercial sound recordings, it was necessary to make it very clear in the license that the use of music was confined to the Vitaphone process, which was a sound process used solely for the theatrical exhibition of motion pictures. This is precisely what was accomplished by the Vitaphone license set forth in part above. It seems clear, therefore, that any other device, such as mechanisms used today to reproduce works in home video devices, for use in the home, would be outside the scope of the old Vitaphone license.

As noted in the preceding chapter, the essential right involved in the licensing of videograms is the reproduction right. Because the sounds reproduced on a videogram arc accompanied by moving visual images, the reproduction of videograms does not involve a "mechanical" reproduction right under the United States copyright law and, therefore, is not subject to the copyright law's compulsory licensing provisions for mechanical reproductions. Thus, music copyright owners are free to negotiate videogram licenses under a variety of terms.

While the current copyright law is quite clear on this point, it was not always so. At the turn of the century, with the advent of motion pictures, it was thought that the process of integrating music with motion pictures was permissible under the compulsory license provision of the copyright law existing at that time.[1] In fact, because the sounds in the Vitaphone process that accompanied the motion pictures were originally recorded onto phonograph records, Vitaphone took the position that a compulsory license under the law was available to it for this purpose. Vitaphone quickly discovered, however, that a strong combination of music publishers, through an organization called the

---

[1] 17 U.S.C. Sec. 1(e) (1909 Act)

Music Publishers' Protective Association, would insist otherwise and
began a determined and successful effort to require motion picture
producers to buy licenses for negotiated fees. Their strategy was simple: By 1926, a movie theatre was required to have an ASCAP license
if the theatre wished to perform music in the extensive ASCAP repertoire; the music publishers threatened to withdraw their performing
rights from ASCAP unless Vitaphone agreed to buy special synchronization licenses at rates much higher than the statutory rate, which
at that time was two cents per composition per record. In October,
1926, Vitaphone finally capitulated and agreed to pay approximately
$100,000.00 per year.

## C.  Old Licenses Whose Scope Is Unclear

### 1.  Several Old Licenses

During the time that the carefully crafted Vitaphone license set
forth above was in use, other licenses that were issued during this
period were less sophisticated.

For example, a license issued in 1927 stated simply:

Gentlemen:

We hereby grant you permission to record and reproduce publicly
for profit, but only in association with the motion picture, entitled
XYZ, the following named musical composition, upon which we
own the copyright, to wit: ABC.

Very truly yours, . . .

To argue that such a seemingly broad license did not grant permission for home video use, the music copyright owner would have
to take the position that by saying "reproduce publicly . . . with the
motion picture" he was intending to refer solely to the means of performing motion pictures (e.g., theatrical exhibition) that existed at that
time. Perhaps the phrase "reproduce publicly" would itself indicate
that distribution for *private* viewing was not contemplated. The motion
picture producer might assert that the license limited distribution of
copies "only in association with the motion picture" and that if any

other limitation were intended the copyright owner could have expressed it just as easily.

In 1932, a more sophisticated synchronization license began wide circulation and had been used for many years thereafter as the basis for countless synchronization licenses. Its salient provisions were as follows:

> In consideration of the sum of $xxx the undersigned does hereby give XYZ Pictures the non-exclusive, irrevocable right, license, privilege and authority to record in any manner, medium or form, in any country covered by this license, the musical composition hereinbelow set out, and to make copies of such recording and to import said copies of recordings into any country covered by this license, all in accordance with the terms, conditions, and limitations hereinafter set out.
>
> . . . The license hereinabove set out is limited to the use of the musical compositions in synchronism or timed-relation with the motion picture hereinabove specified.
>
> . . . The right to record the musical compositions as covered by this agreement is conditioned upon the performance of the musical work in theatres having valid licenses from the American Society of Composers, Authors, and Publishers, or any other performing rights society having jurisdiction in the territory in which the said musical compositions are performed.
>
> . . . Licensor reserves to itself all rights and uses in and to said musical compositions not herein specifically granted.

Was the above license intended to restrict the use of motion pictures containing the licensed music to exhibition in theatres or did it allow distribution by another medium, such as videograms distributed for home viewing?

A producer might assert that the broad grant to record "in any manner, medium, or form" subject only to conditions set forth in the license should be broadly interpreted in favor of the licensee, and that the true intent of the agreement is to limit the use "in synchronism or timed-relation with the motion picture." As long as the recording is used only in connection with that motion picture or wherever the motion picture may be exploited, the producer would argue, the use is within the license. In other words, all uses were licensed, subject to clearing the performance rights by theatres. No reference to television or videocassettes being made, no restriction was intended.

The music copyright owner would, however, refer our attention to the provision in the license stating that "the right to record" the songs is "conditioned upon the performance of the musical work in theatres." While the intent of the paragraph containing this language appears to be to assure that performances were made only in theatres having valid performing licenses (e.g., from ASCAP or BMI), it would also appear to indicate that the performance of the motion picture was contemplated to take place in theatres and not elsewhere, such as in private homes.

The language in the above license underwent some modification by the mid-1950s:

> In consideration of the sum of $xxx, the receipt of which is hereby acknowledged, the undersigned does hereby give XYZ Pictures, its successors and assigns, the non-exclusive irrevocable right and license, privilege and authority to record, in any manner, medium, form or language, in any country within the territory covered by this license, the words and music of the musical composition hereinbelow set out, and to make copies of said recordings and to import said recordings and/or copies of said recordings into any country within the territory covered by this license, and to perform said musical composition everywhere, all in accordance with the terms, conditions, and limitations hereinafter set out.

> . . . The license hereinabove set out is limited to the use of the musical composition in synchronism or timed-relation with the motion picture hereinabove specified, and trailers thereof.

> . . . The right to *perform* said musical composition as covered by this agreement is conditioned upon the performance of said musical composition in theatres having valid licenses from any performing rights society having jurisdiction in the territory in which the said musical composition is performed.

> . . . Licensor reserves to itself all rights and uses in and to said musical compositions not herein specifically granted.

A producer might take heart in the fact that the third paragraph above was modified by the replacement of the word "record" with the word "perform." It would appear that the license to record was no longer conditioned upon the performance of the song in theatres having valid licenses; only the license to perform was. The music copyright owner would be quick to point out, however, that the first paragraph was modified so that the license was "to make copies of said recordings . . . and to perform said musical composition everywhere, all in accordance with the terms, conditions, and limitations hereinafter set out." It appears that the words "to perform" were used merely to make it clear at the outset that the license included both a recording license and a public performing license, and was not intended to expand or further restrict the uses permitted under the license. This is confirmed by the fact that the change in language coincided precisely with the entry of the consent decrees between the Department of Justice and the performance rights societies, which, among other things, required music copyright owners to grant performance licenses for U.S. theatrical distribution.[2]

Consider the following television synchronization licenses issued in the 1970s that attempted to narrowly define what use may be made of the synchronized recording:

> In consideration of the sum of $xxx, and upon agreement hereto and the acceptance hereof as indicated below and the payment of said consideration to the undersigned, the undersigned does hereby give and grant unto, XYZ Pictures, the non-exclusive, irrevocable right and license to record the following copyrighted musical composition in synchronism or timed-relation with a picture made and produced solely for television purposes by the said licensee and known as: The TV Movie.

The license was drafted with a view toward limiting the use to television, intending to exclude exhibition in motion picture theatres and like establishments. It may be questioned, however, whether the above language successfully excluded the privilege of reproducing

---

[2] See Chapter 17, on *Performance Licences*.

videocassettes for home video distribution. The first paragraph limits the use "solely for television purposes." Is the making of videocassettes of the picture for home video distribution a "television purpose"? If "television purpose," as used here, is synonymous with "broadcast purpose," the answer to the question would be, "no," and therefore home video use would not be covered by the license.

## 2. Several Court Cases

The general question arising from the applicability of the old synchronization licenses discussed above to the desire of producers to effect a new use of their works is whether the licenses restricted the use to a particular media or did it allow distribution through another media subsequently developed? In other words, is the scope of the license sufficiently broad to cover new uses that became possible only years after the license was issued?

A similar question was asked over a century ago in connection with a license to make a dramatization of a book — that is, a license permitting another to adapt a novel in the creation of a theatrical play or opera. Did a license to permit a dramatization of a book, issued before the advent of motion pictures in 1889, permit the licensee to make a motion picture based upon the book? In 1920, the U.S. Supreme Court held that a license to produce or dramatize a play *did not* include permission to produce a motion picture based on the play.[3]

Not long after that decision, the courts were asked to decide whether a license to make a dramatization or motion picture, issued before the advent of talkies, permitted the licensee to make a sound motion picture. One court held that where the same person holds both the silent picture rights and the dramatic rights, equating the latter with dialogue rights, he owns everything necessary to the making of a talking motion picture.[4] Another court held that a grant of motion picture rights was sufficient to constitute a grant of talkie motion pic-

---

[3] *Manners v. Morosco*, 252 U.S. 317 (1920); See also, *Harper Bros. v. Klaw*, 232 F. 609 (S.D.N.Y. 1916) (a license to dramatize "Ben Hur" in a play did not include the right to produce a motion picture, but the licensor was enjoined from producing the movie because the licensee's right to produce a play would be harmed by the licensor's production of a movie).

[4] *Cinema Corporation of America v. De Mille*, 267 N.Y.Supp. 589 (1933)

ture rights, stating, "The mere fact that the species 'talkies' may have been unknown and not within the contemplation of the parties in their description of the generic 'moving pictures' does not prevent the latter from comprehending the former."[5]

It should be no surprise that the question whether a license to make and exhibit a motion picture, issued before the advent of television, authorized the exhibition of the motion picture on television, has also been the subject of litigation in the courts. In 1936, a prize-fighter permitted the making and exhibition of a motion picture of his prize fight, and the issue before the court was whether the picture could be performed both in theatres and on television, or only in theatres.[6] The court held that the picture could only be performed in theatres, basing its decision on the mistaken belief that the televising of motion pictures was a "use not in existence" in 1936. In fact, the feasibility of television was contemplated as early as 1927. By 1929, a provision granting motion picture studios the license to televise motion pictures began appearing in standard motion picture rights acquisition contracts, and by 1932, Warner Bros.'s Brunswick subsidiary was experimenting with color television.

### 3.  Recent Court Cases

The question whether old licenses applied to new uses appeared in a class action lawsuit lead by the well known entertainer, Mickey Rooney, against nearly all of the major motion picture studios, including Columbia Pictures, Metro-Goldwyn-Mayer, Paramount Pictures, RKO General, Twentieth Century Fox, United Artists, Universal City Studios, and Warner Bros.[7] The case involved the contracts be-

---

[5] *L.C. Page & Co. V. Fox Film Corp.*, 83 F.2d 196, at 199 (2d Cir. 1936); *see also, Murphy v. Warner Bros. Pictures, Inc.*, 112 F.2d 746 (9th Cir. 1940) (grant of "complete and entire" motion picture rights to licensed work held to encompass later developed sound motion picture technology).

[6] *Ettore v. Philco Television Broadcasting Corp.*, 229 F.2d 481 (3d Cir. 1956); See also, *Bartsch v. Metro-Goldwyn-Mayer, Inc.*, 391 F.2d 150 (2d Cir.), *cert denied*, 393 U.S. 826 (1968) (1930 license of film rights in a play, when television was a known technology but its full impact not yet realized, included television rights, because the licensor, as an experienced businessman, had reason to know of the new technology's potential and had the burden of negotiating an exception).

[7] *Rooney v. Columbia Pictures Industries, Inc.*, 538 F.Supp. 211 (S.D.N.Y. 1982).

tween the studios and all performers appearing in motion pictures produced or distributed by the studios prior to 1960. The court ruled that the contracts between the performers and the studios, which granted rights to exhibit these films, also gave the studios the right to sell videocassettes of the films, without further compensation to the performers. The court's conclusion was based on the sweeping language of the contracts, which included, for example, the right to "record, reproduce, transmit, exhibit, distribute, and exploit" the films "by any present or future methods or means" and by "any other means now known or unknown." The court concluded that the contracts gave the studios extremely broad rights in the distribution and exhibition of the films, "plainly intending that such rights would be without limitation unless otherwise specified and further indicating that future technological advances in methods of reproduction, transmission, and exhibition would inure to the benefit of [the studios]."

Shortly following the decision in the *Rooney* case, a federal district court in New Jersey considered a case filed by a small record company against Lucasfilm, Universal City Studios, and MCA, Inc.[8] In 1973, the record company granted to Lucasfilm a license to use the master recordings of four popular songs on the soundtrack of the motion picture, *American Graffiti*. The license granted to Lucasfilm "the right to record, dub and synchronize the . . . master recordings, or portions thereof, into and with [the] motion picture and trailers therefor, and to exhibit, distribute, market and perform said motion picture, its air, screen and television trailers, perpetually throughout the world by any means or methods now or hereafter known." In 1980, Universal released the film for sale and rental to the public on videocassettes. The court ruled in favor of the Lucasfilm and the studio, reasoning that the language in the agreement was "extremely broad and completely unambiguous, and precludes any need in the Agreement for an exhaustive list of specific potential uses of the film. . . . It is obvious that the contract in question may 'fairly be read' to be including newly developed media, and the absence of any specific mention in the Agreement of videotapes and videocassettes is thus insignificant."[9]

---

[8] *Platinum Record Company, Inc. v. Lucasfilm, Ltd.*, 566 F.Supp. 226 (D.N.J. 1983).
[9] But see *Fred Ahlert Music v. Warner/Chappell Music*, 958 F. Supp. 170 (S.D.N.Y. 1997) (License to use copyrighted musical composition in recording and manufacture

The question whether a license permitting the use of music in a motion picture or television program, authorized the reproduction of copies of the music in connection with the distribution of videocassettes of the motion picture or television show, finally became the subject of a lawsuit that was concluded in the Federal Court of Appeals in 1988.[10] Paramount Pictures had just begun the reproduction of videocassettes of the motion picture, *Medium Cool,* when the copyright owner of the song *Merry-Go-Round,* one of the songs contained in the film's soundtrack, filed suit claiming that the old synchronization license to use the song in the motion picture did not grant a license to distribute copies of the song in videocassettes of the motion picture.

The court of appeals considered the scope of a synchronization license, which was not unlike the scope of the licenses described in the preceding section. That license granted to the Paramount:

> . . . the authority . . . to record, in any manner, medium, form or language, the words and music of the musical composition . . . with the motion picture . . . to make copies of such recordings and to perform said musical composition everywhere, all in accordance with the terms, conditions and limitations hereinafter set forth. . . ."

> The . . . license herein granted to perform . . . said musical composition is granted for: (a) The exhibition of said motion picture . . . to audiences in motion picture theatres and other places of public entertainment where motion pictures are customarily exhibited . . . (b) The exhibition of said motion picture . . . by means of television . . . , including "pay television," "subscription television," and "closed circuit into homes' television". . . .

It was undisputed that category (a) of the preceding paragraph could not be construed as authorizing the distribution of videocassettes through the sale and rental to the general public for viewing in their homes. Paramount argued, however, that videogram distribution was

---

of phonograph records and specifying it covered only particular derivative work permitted only manufacture of phonographic records, and remaining rights reverted back to copyright holder upon termination of grant).

[10] *Cohen v. Paramount Pictures Corp.,* 845 F.2d 851 (9th Cir. 1988).

covered by category (b), in that the distribution of videocassettes for showing in private homes was the equivalent of "exhibition by means of television." The court disagreed and ruled that the license did *not* include the distribution of videocassettes for home viewing.

After going to great lengths to describe the differences between broadcast television and home videocassette viewing,[11] the court stated that the "primary reason" why the words "exhibition by means of television" in the license cannot be construed as including the distribution of videocassettes for home viewing is that "VCR's were not invented or known in 1969, when the license was executed."[12]

---

[11] In reaching its conclusion, the court drew a distinction between the characteristics of broadcast television and home videocassette television:

"The general tenor of the section [b] contemplates some sort of broadcasting or centralized distribution, not distribution by sale or rental of individual copies. Furthermore, the exhibition of the videocassette in the home is not "by means of television." Though videocassettes may be exhibited by using a television monitor, it does not follow that, for copyright purposes, playing videocassettes constitutes "exhibition by television." Exhibition of a film on television differs fundamentally from exhibition by means of a videocassette recorder ("VCR"). Television requires an intermediary network, station, or cable to send the television signals into consumers' homes. The menu of entertainment appearing on television is controlled entirely by the intermediary and, thus the consumer's selection is limited to what is available on various channels. Moreover, equipped merely with a conventional television set, a consumer has no means of capturing any part of the television display; when the program is over it vanishes, and the consumer is powerless to replay it. Because they originate outside the home, television signals are ephemeral and beyond the viewer's grasp.

"Videocassettes, of course, allow viewing of a markedly different nature. Videocassette entertainment is controlled within the home, at the viewer's complete discretion. A consumer may view exactly what he or she chooses. The viewer may even 'fast forward' the tape so as to quickly pass over parts of the program he or she does not wish to view. By their very essence, then videocassettes liberate viewers from the constraints otherwise inherent in television, and eliminate the involvement of an intermediary, such as a network.

"Television and videocassette display thus have very little in common besides the fact that a conventional monitor of a television set may be used both to receive television signals and to exhibit a videocassette. It is in light of this fact that Paramount argues that VCRs are equivalent to "exhibition by means of television." Yet, even that assertion is flawed. Playing a videocassette on a VCR does not require a standard television set capable of receiving television signals by cable or broadcast; it is only necessary to have a monitor capable of displaying the material on the magnetized tape." 845 F.2d at 854

[12] Id.

Because videocassettes did not exist when the license was executed, the court reasoned, the licensor must have assumed television exhibition was to be effected by broadcast and the "licensee could not have bargained for, or paid for, the rights associated with videocassette reproduction." This reasoning, of course, is flawed, because it is simply incorrect to say that the licensee could not have bargained for the rights of use that did not exist or were unknown at the time the license was executed.[13]

Although the court disagreed with the *Rooney* and *Platinum* decisions to the extent those decisions equated exhibition by means of television with home video display, the court appeared to merely distinguish their applicability to the *Cohen* synchronization license, because it did not contain the broad, sweeping language contained in the licenses considered in *Rooney* and *Platinum*.

But can the license in the *Cohen* case really be distinguished from that in the *Platinum case*? Paramount may have made a tactical error

---

[13] In fact, at a later point in its opinion, the court suggested that a party could bargain for a use that was not yet known at the time of the license, as long as the license specifically conferred the right to exhibit the films by methods yet to be invented. 845 F.2d at 855. This is precisely what the parties are doing when they enter into licenses that are specifically intended to cover uses unknown or not invented at the time the license is executed (e.g., a license for "use in any form or medium, and in any manner, now known or hereafter devised"). To enforce licenses for only those uses that were either known or invented at the time the license is executed would unduly limit the scope of licenses for which parties are otherwise free to bargain. Second, it is not clear, under the court's reasoning, whether the use must actually be *invented* or merely *known* or conceived at the time the license is entered. If the court would require the use to have been invented at the time the license was executed, then what legal doctrine would support the unenforceability of a bargain over a specific use that parties clearly contemplated? There seems to be no reason why a court should not enforce, for example, a license to use music in a holographic motion picture several years before the practicability of holographic movies. If the court would require the use to be "known" at the time the license was executed, who is to say whether a particular use is "known" generally or to a party at any particular point in time? Science fiction books, television shows, and motion pictures present hundreds of examples of uses commonly known long before their actual invention. There appears to be no reason, for example, not to enforce a license for use of a work in an entertainment program for use on a device resembling the "holodeck" of the fictional television series Star Trek: The Next Generation. Finally, contracts often try to cover what is not known and it is not unreasonable to enforce bargains struck between parties over the allocation of unknown or unforeseen risks or contingencies, such as the subsequent development of a new use.

by asserting that videogram distribution was covered by category (b) of the performance provision of the synchronization license. Home video viewing is a *private*, not public performance. Because private performances are not among the activities over which music copyright owners enjoy exclusive rights under the copyright law, no *performance* license was necessary to engage in home video distribution. All that was necessary was a license to make and distribute copies of the work containing the music without restriction as to their means of use. Would not such a license clearly be included in the rather broad language of the first section of the license:

> . . . the authority . . . to record, in any manner, medium, form or language, the words and music of the musical composition . . . with the motion picture . . . to make copies of such recordings and to perform said musical composition everywhere, all in accordance with the terms, conditions and limitations hereinafter set forth . . .

Whether or not the court in the *Cohen* case reached the correct result, it is believed that the decision, and others like it,[14] should rest on a more practical legal basis than merely a listing of the technical and practical differences between the two media in question (here, broadcast television and home videocassette viewing).[15] The following

---

[14] *Bloom v. Hearst Entertainment, Inc.*, 33 F.3d 518 (5th Cir. 1994) (grant of "exclusive worldwide motion picture and television rights" included grant of home video rights); *Rey v. Lafferty*, 990 F.2d 1379 (1st Cir. 1993) (grant of rights to *Curious George* film episodes "for television viewing" did not encompass the right to distribute the films in videocassette form); *Tel-Pac, Inc. v. Grainger*, 168 A.D.2d 11, 570 N.Y.S.2d 521, appeal dismissed, 79 N.Y.2d 822, 580 N.Y.S.2d 201, 588 N.E.2d 99 (1991) (a license to distribute certain motion pictures "for broadcasting by television or any similar device now known or hereafter to be made known" did not encompass the videocassette rights); *Philadelphia Orchestra Ass'n v. Walt Disney Co.*, 821 F.Supp. 341 (E.D.Pa. 1983) (orchestra's license to use its performance in a "feature picture" was deemed broad enough to include a license to use the performance in a home video, because it was determined that the word "feature" referred to films of a certain length without regard to the medium or location in which they are presented); *Filmvideo Releasing Corp. v. Hastings*, 446 F.Supp. 725 (S.D.N.Y. 1978) (author's explicit retention of "all" television rights to licensed work, in a grant of motion picture rights predating technological advances permitting movies to be shown on television, included retention of right to show motion picture on television).

[15] See, e.g., *Boosey & Hawkes Music Publishers v. Walt Disney Co.*, 145 F.3d 481 (2nd Cir. 1998) (1939 licensing agreement granting use of musical composition in motion picture authorized distribution in video format); *Bourne v. Walt Disney Co.*,

discussion attempts to provide such a basis and may be of value in determining the application of old licenses to new uses, either to the parties negotiating a settlement of their dispute or to a court presiding over its adjudication.

## II. DETERMINING THE SCOPE OF AMBIGUOUS LICENSES — A SUGGESTED APPROACH

All of the above controversies — whether a dramatic license included a license to make silent motion pictures, whether a motion picture license included a license to make "talkies," whether a motion picture license included a license to broadcast by means of television, whether a motion picture synchronization license included a license for home video distribution, and whether a television synchronization license included a license for home video distribution — have two common basic characteristics: a license to make certain uses and the subsequent development of new uses.

In all of these cases, the court should seek to determine what would the parties have likely bargained if they had foreseen the subsequent development of the new use at the time the license was entered into? How would they have allocated the risk of an unforeseen use, had they actually foreseen it?

### A. Evidence of Intent of the Parties

It is assumed that in interpreting an old license a court would first look to the language of the license itself in determining its scope. In interpreting the language, the court would use common legal principals in making that determination. For example, courts will normally permit the parties to a lawsuit to introduce evidence that falls outside

---

68 F.3d 621 (2nd Cir. 1995) (In infringement action regarding right to synchronize musical compositions in motion pictures, use of term "motion picture" in an agreement was broad enough to include videocassette synchronization); *Muller v. Walt Disney Productions*, 871 F. Supp 678 (S.D.N.Y. 1994) (Home video fell within the definition of "photoplay" in 1939 contract between orchestra conductor and motion picture studio regarding use of music in aminated film, giving studio right to re-release film in home video without securing additional rights).

the "four corners" of the document to aid in the interpretation of ambiguous provisions. Such evidence might include letters and testimony of the parties reflecting their intent at the time the license was entered in to. However, evidence of the intent of the parties to a license entered 50 years ago might prove difficult to find, particularly as many old synchronization licenses were issued on standard forms and signed without negotiation of their terms with the possible exception of price and territory.

Another principal of contract interpretation is that a document is interpreted against the party who drafted it. This is because the drafter was in a better position to avoid the ambiguity by being more precise in his employment of language in the document, thus providing an incentive for drafters to be precise. Since most of these old synchronization license forms were drafted by music publishers and their representatives, there is an argument that they were in a better position to prevent the ambiguity by being more precise in their use of terms such as "exhibition on television." On the other hand, the music publishers could take the position that the producers of the motion pictures were in a better position to predict what potential forms of distribution could be made of their films and if they could have foreseen these new forms of distribution, they should have informed the music publishers of the potential new use at the time the license was entered into which could have lead to a negotiated allocation based upon a full disclosure of information.

Without concrete evidence of what the intent of the parties was at the time the license was signed, the court in the *Paramount* case, discussed above, compared and contrasted the characteristics of broadcast television and home videocassette viewing in arriving at a meaning and usage of the term, "exhibition by television." Although the court was insightful in pointing to some important differences that would have affected a negotiation had the facts been known, a comparison of the characteristics of these two systems alone does not provide us with the answer to the question, what would the music publishers and producers have actually negotiated had this different use been known to the parties at the time of the license?

## B. Where No Clear Intent of the Parties is Evident

In the absence of clear evidence of intent as to what the parties would have done had they foreseen the new use, it is suggested that the decision as to whether an old license covered a new use should depend upon an analysis of the likely expectations of the parties at the time the license was executed.

### 1. Expectations of the Film Producer

In determining what the film producer would likely have done at the time the license was entered into had he foreseen the new use (i.e., home video distribution), it may be well to ask whether the copyright owner's exercise of its exclusive right to the new use (i.e., to license to others the recording of his music in home video devices) would impair the expectations of the film producer? If the old synchronization license were non-exclusive, as most of them were, then no action by the copyright owner to grant permission to others to record the same music in other video programs should produce any unexpected or unjust affect on the film producer's original use. In other words, by virtue of the non-exclusive nature of the license, the licensee fully expected that the licensee could and would grant other licenses for similar uses to other potential licensees.

If the new use (i.e., home video distribution) effectively impairs the film producer's expectations with respect to the original use (i.e., theatrical and television performances), and the producer's expectations can only be fulfilled if the old license were construed as covering the new use, could it then be said that the producer would have reasonably expected that the old license, at the time it was granted, would cover the new use? In other words, does the advent of a new use that impairs the film producer's expectations regarding the old use justify construing an old license as covering the new use? No. Even though the exercise of the old use may no longer be lucrative, the producer still has the license to continue using the music for the originally licensed uses, however outmoded they may have become. The unforeseen risk at the time the license was executed was not only that a particular new use may eventually come into existence, but that a new use would be devised that changes the economics of motion picture distribution. The question here is, who was in a better position to assume the risk that a new distribution media would arise that affects the economics of motion picture distribution? A court could properly place that risk at the foot of the motion picture producers, and not music publishers or songwriters.

## 2. Expectations of the Music Copyright Owner

In determining what the music copyright owner would likely have done at the time the license was entered into had he foreseen the new use, it may be useful to ask whether the film producer's exercise of the new use (i.e., making and distributing videogram copies for home use) under the old license without paying additional compensation to the copyright owner would impair the expectations of the copyright owner's ability to exercise its exclusive right to the new use (i.e., to license to others the recording of his music in home video devices)? Construing an old synchronization license as granting a license to make videocassette reproductions without further compensation would not impair the copyright owner's ability to exercise his right to license his music for use on other videocassettes. It may impair the copyright owner's ability to grant a license to use the song in videocassettes on an *exclusive* basis, but rarely is a copyright owner inclined to grant such exclusivity.

If the copyright owner did not contemplate the new use at the time the old license was executed, then it could be said he would not have had an expectation of deriving income from the producer for the new use. But this is not universally the case. It is probably true that the motion picture producers who procured synchronization licenses expected to pay a one time flat fee and never expected to have to go back to the licensor again for a license to distribute his film by whatever means. But it is not equally true that the copyright owners had no expectations beyond the one time fees they received.

It appears from the face of the old synchronization licenses that a principal concern of the music copyright owners was that, for whatever use was to be permitted, there be some mechanism in place to collect performance fees (e.g., through ASCAP or BMI) on all exhibitions or broadcasts of the work containing the musical composition. This was the mechanism by which the music copyright owners could participate in the economic success of the works containing their music. The flat fee required under the synchronization license simply could not serve this purpose. The performance fees, collected on performances occurring at the time the film is exhibited in theatres or on television, were expected *in addition* to the flat synchronization fee required for the privilege to make the copies of the motion pictures necessary for distribution.

So important was the requirement that performance fees be collected on performances of works for which the synchronization of their music was licensed, it seems clear that if there were no mechanism for the collection of fees for the performance of the music, music copyright owners would not have granted the license to synchronize the music in copies — at least not without negotiating some mechanism to collect compensation based upon the success of the work in which the music appeared.

Because the distribution of motion pictures in videocassette form deprives the music copyright owner of his expected additional compensation from theatrical and television performances, synchronization licenses that are silent or ambiguous as to their coverage of such distribution should not be construed as including the distribution of the videocassettes and other devices used for home viewing.

The copyright law provides the copyright owner with the exclusive right of *public* performance and it is on *public* performances that performance rights societies collect license fees on behalf of copyright owners. The exhibition of a videocassette at home is a *private* performance. Since neither the distribution, sale, rental, or home performance of videocassettes involve a public performance, there is no public performance upon which a performance fee can be based. When the original synchronization licenses were issued for a flat fee, music copyright owners anticipated that fees to be later collected for the public performances of the works containing their music would afford a means by which the copyright owner could participate in the economic success of the work in which his music was included. The more popular the motion picture, the more it would be exhibited and the more performance royalties would accrue to the copyright owner of the music.

Prior to 1948, when performance rights societies in the United States, such as BMI and ASCAP, began to be made subject to court ordered consent decrees, music copyright owners were entitled to fees from the performance of their music in motion picture theatres located in the United States and overseas. The consent decrees changed this by requiring music copyright owners to issue licenses to permit producers and their distributors to perform their music in motion picture theatres located in the United States. This performance license was required to be issued at the same time the copyright owner issued the license to synchronize their music in copies for theatrical distribution. In practice, the license to perform the music in U.S. theatres was included in the same document as the synchronization license and the copyright owner typically charged the same one-time flat fee, in effect doubling the fee normally charged for the synchronization license. The consent decrees are still in effect today.

Despite the consent decrees' effectively eliminating the music copyright owner's ability to share in the success of U.S. theatrical performances of motion pictures containing their music, music copyright owners still expected the payment of performance fees for performances of music in theatres outside of the United States (and the jurisdiction of the American courts which imposed the consent decree) as well as for performances that occurred on broadcast television. The requirement that copyright owners include a license (for a flat fee) for the public performance of music in motion picture U.S. theatres did not apply to television exhibition and exhibition in theatres outside of the United States, for which the performing rights societies do collect performance fees to this day.

Not only is the music copyright owner unable to share in the success of motion pictures distributed by videocassette (because virtually all performances of videocassettes are private, not public, performances), but to the extent the home videocassette performances of motion pictures, for which no public performance payment is collected by ASCAP or BMI, replaces broadcast television performances and international theatrical exhibition, for which ASCAP and BMI fees are collected, the performance revenue that the copyright owner anticipated when he granted the old synchronization license actually decreases.

Accordingly, the advent of home video distribution on videocassettes and laserdiscs of motion pictures containing copyrighted music seriously affects the expectations that the copyright owner was likely to have had at the time of entering the old synchronization license. If the music copyright owner had known of this new development at the time the license was executed, an alternative to performance fees would probably have been developed to ensure the music copyright owner with some ability to share in the success of the motion pictures in which their music was used. The kinds of mechanisms that most likely would have evolved would probably have been like those that have recently emerged since the advent of the videogram market, and these are illustrated by the provisions contained at the end of Chapter 15 on *Videogram Licenses*.

The one historical anomaly that producers can point to that would appear to belie the music copyright owners' expectations of a share in the economic success in the exploitation of motion pictures containing their music is that music publishers never objected when producers licensed non-theatrical 16mm rights to independent distributors. Either publishers expected that these films were primarily intended for performance in establishments licensed by ASCAP and BMI, such as schools and libraries, or that the revenues from the sales of 16mm films to individuals for private performances were just too small to notice.

## III. AVOIDING AMBIGUITY

Music copyright owners should grant only the permission required to meet the known needs of those requesting the permission. The language effecting the owner's permission should be precise, should include clear definitions of all the important terms used, and should always expressly reserve all other privileges not specifically granted.

Producers, and others seeking to clear synchronization licenses, should attempt to obtain licenses that have as broad a scope as possible. Because of the availability of broad language that has been specifically confirmed by the courts, it is easier for a producer to draft language that will provide a license having an expansive scope than it is for music copyright owners to draft language that is tailored to the specific, immediately foreseeable needs of the producer. However, persuading a music copyright owner to accept such broad language may truly be the *Impossible Dream*.

# APPENDIX TO CHAPTER 16
# OLD LICENSES AND NEW USES

FORM 16.1     Old Motion Picture Synchronization License

# FORM 16.1

## OLD MOTION PICTURE SYNCHRONIZATION LICENSE

New York, New York, October 12, 1933

In consideration of the sum of ONE HUNDRED AND FIFTY DOLLARS ($150), the undersigned does hereby give to <u>Columbia Pictures Corporation, 729 Seventh Avenue, New York City,</u> the non-exclusive, irrevocable right, license, privilege and authority to record in any manner, medium or form, in any country covered by this license, the musical compositions hereinbelow set out, and to make copies of such recordings and to import said copies of recordings into any country covered by this license, all in accordance with the terms, conditions and limitations hereinafter set out.

1.  The Compositions covered by this license are:

Prisoner's Song      Massey      Shapiro Bernstein & Co. Inc.

2.  The title of the motion picture with which said musical compositions are to be used is <u>"Lady For a Day"</u>.

3.  The type of use to be made of the musical composition is <u>vocal visual — short whistling</u>, and the amount of uses to be made is <u>two</u>.

4.  The license hereinabove set out is limited to the use of the musical compositions in synchronism or timed-relation with the motion picture hereinabove specified.

5.  The right to record the musical compositions as covered by this agreement is conditioned upon the performance of the musical work in theatres having valid licenses from the American Society of Composers, Authors and Publishers, or any

other performing rights organization having jurisdiction in the territory in which the said musical compositions are performed.

6.    The territory covered by this license is the entire world.

7.    Except that the undersigned warrants that the principal for whom he is acting is the owner of the said musical compositions, this license is given without warranty or recourse, and the licensor reserves to itself all rights and uses in and to the said musical compositions not herein specifically granted.

_____

Agent and Trustee

## CHAPTER 17

# PERFORMANCE LICENSES

## SUMMARY

# PERFORMANCE LICENSES

Performance of music has become ubiquitous in our society. You hear performances of music while listening to the radio, dining in a restaurant, shopping at a mall, and standing in an elevator. Of all the forms of using music — making recordings, printing sheet music, synchronizing with motion pictures, etc. — clearly the most common use is its *performance*. Consequently, revenue from public performances of music represent nearly one-half of the total music publishing revenue from all sources.

A casual listener may often wonder, how does the songwriter get paid for this performance? Does the shopping mall send a check to the estate of Sammy Cahn every time the song, *My Kind of Town* is performed over its sound system? Does anyone have to get Mr. Cahn's permission before performing the song?

This chapter sketches the historical and legal background of performance rights and performance rights societies and provides an outline of the customs and practices in licensing public performances of music.

For special considerations on performance licenses and the Internet, please see Chapter 23, on *Licensing Musical Works and Sound Recordings on the Internet.*

## I. HISTORICAL BACKGROUND

### A. Performance Rights Societies

In 1914, at a dinner meeting held at the famous theatrical club, *The Lambs* in New York City, a small group of songwriters were engaged in a serious discussion about these very questions. At that dinner, songwriter Victor Herbert told Irving Berlin, John Philip Sousa ("the march king"), Jay Witmark (successful writer and publisher), Nathan Burkan, Esq. (an attorney), Gene Buck (writer of the many Florenz Ziegfeld Broadway shows and later president of ASCAP) and others at this meeting, of his frustration at hearing a song of his performed at a nearby swank New York restaurant, but having no means of collecting a royalty for the performance.

The problem these songwriters faced was two-fold. First, as Nathan Burkan, Esq. surely must have advised, it wasn't altogether clear whether songwriters had a right to collect for performances of their songs in restaurants, nightclubs, cabarets, and like establishments. Granted, the revision of the United States copyright act in 1897 established for the first time the copyright owner's exclusive right of public performance. The 1909 revision of the United States copyright law, however, placed a restriction on the right of performance, stating that a license from the copyright owner is required only if the performance was rendered "publicly for profit."[1] This provision was generally interpreted to mean that a license was required only if an admission fee was charged to hear the performance. If, for example, no admission fee was charged for entering a restaurant, performances of music at the restaurant would not be considered "for profit."

Indeed, the common wisdom among music publishers at that time was that public performances of music stimulated the sales of sheet music. Accordingly, the publishers did not want to do anything that would discourage public performances, whether authorized or not. In those days, sheet music often bore a printed notice that granted the purchaser of the sheet music the right to perform the composition in public.

The second problem was the very practical problem of policing the performance of compositions in every nightclub, cabaret, music hall, theatre, or any other place where music can be performed in public. It would be financially impractical for every individual songwriter to attempt to enforce his right of exclusive public performance in his work and for every nightclub, cabaret, music hall and theatre owner to clear permission to perform music by obtaining a separate license for each performance of a song from each individual songwriter or publisher.

---

[1] 17 U.S.C. Sec. 1(d) (1909 Act).

## B. American Society of Composers, Authors & Publishers (ASCAP)

It was to address these problems that the American Society of Composers, Authors and Publishers (ASCAP) was established by this small group of songwriters and music publishers in 1914. The group immediately went to work by establishing a nation-wide policing organization which offered licenses to amusement establishments to perform the songs of its members.

The group then took the major step of filing a lawsuit against a restaurant located in Times Square in New York called *Shanley's* for the unauthorized public performance of the ASCAP musical composition, *Sweethearts* by Victor Herbert. *Shanley's* argued, predictably, that since no specific charge was made for admission to the premises where the performances occurred, the music was not being performed "for profit." The case went all the way to the U.S. Supreme Court.[2] In rendering the majority decision in 1917, Chief Justice Oliver Wendell Holmes, himself a writer of poetry, said "If music did not pay, it would be given up. If it pays, it pays out of the public's pocket. Whether it pays or not, the purpose of employing it is for profit and that is enough." Thus, the business of a restaurant was to make a profit, and, because the music was part of the service which the restaurant rendered to make a profit, that is enough.

On the heels of this great victory, ASCAP quickly went on a licensing crusade, issuing music performance licenses to hotels, concert halls, cabarets and other similar places where music was performed for profit under the Supreme Court's new interpretation of that term.

The advent of coast-to-coast radio broadcasting in 1926 brightened the economic interests of songwriters on a scale never before conceived. Here was a new opportunity to earn performance royalties from this new media and ASCAP was quick to recognize it. By that time, the U.S. Supreme Court, in another landmark decision,[3] had held that even though a radio broadcast was disseminated free of charge,

---

[2] *Herbert v. Shanley*, 242 U.S. 591 (1917).

[3] *M. Witmark & Sons v. L. Bamberger & Co.*, 291 F. 776 (D.N.J. 1923).

performances by radio broadcast were "for profit" and therefore required a license from the copyright owner.

At first, broadcasters resisted paying for performances, but publishers finally overcame their objections after winning several lengthy court battles. ASCAP was gaining strength and, with the backing of the courts, was able to raise the rates it charged. The broadcasters were becoming concerned that, with ASCAP's virtual monopoly in the field, rates could be increased to unreasonable levels. With each passing year, negotiations between ASCAP and the broadcasters became increasingly difficult.

## C. Broadcast Music Incorporated (BMI)

In 1940, in anticipation of a breakdown in negotiations with ASCAP over the rates to be charged for the following year, a group of broadcasters, including the major radio networks and nearly 500 independent radio stations, established an organization called Broadcast Music Incorporated (BMI).

At that time, I was the producer and arranger of the popular national radio show, *Waltz Time*, broadcast over the NBC radio network, featuring Abe Lyman's orchestra with Frank Munn, "The Golden Voice of Radio." We were aware negotiations between ASCAP and the radio networks were not going too well. During the rehearsal of *Waltz Time* on Friday afternoon, December 27, 1940, I received a call from two executives of the newly formed Broadcast Music Incorporated, Robert Burton and Robert Sour, who told me of "problems next week." Sure enough, the following week we were advised that the ASCAP repertoire would not be available for broadcast after Tuesday December 31, 1940 and we were to clear all music prior to our next broadcast with NBC's clearance department. Our next broadcast was scheduled for Friday, January 3, 1941. A new show was prepared overnight.

The first salvo was fired in the war between BMI and ASCAP when I became the first arranger to call upon "public domain" writer, Stephen Foster, in arranging and programming the song, *I Dream of Jeannie With the Light Brown Hair*, together with several waltzes by Waldteufel and Strauss. Our broadcast on the evening of January 3, 1941 had an unexpected "continental" sound. But what about next week? To my surprise, BMI was well prepared. During the previous year, BMI had been acquiring a catalog of popular songs for licensing in competition with ASCAP. That week, the BMI "song pluggers" furnished us with new popular songs from their newly compiled catalogue. Remarkably, BMI had been prepared with full orchestrations that had already been printed. George M. Cohan remarked during this period that of the hundreds of thousands of songs which BMI claimed to control, "Half are called *Turkey in the Straw* and the other half are about a girl called *Jeannie*."

In early January, 1941, BMI become the new self-proclaimed "automatic performance royalty earning machine" for songwriters and publishers. New BMI affiliated publishers were established along with some older ASCAP affiliated firms such as Edward B. Marks Music and the Peer-Southern Music Organization. After having seen its songs off the air for about eight months, ASCAP finally settled with the networks and its repertoire was again available for broadcast. BMI has remained ever since a strong competitive factor in performance rights licensing.

## D. Society of European State Authors and Composers (SESAC)

From 1914 to 1931, ASCAP was the sole organization engaged in the licensing of performing rights in the United States. In 1931, Paul Heineke, a European music publisher, established the second oldest music licensing organization in the United States. Originally known as the Society of European State Authors and Composers, it is presently known just as SESAC, Inc.

In the past, SESAC considered itself a publisher oriented organization noted primarily for its activity in the Gospel and Country music fields. In 1973, SESAC began to affiliate writers directly and has since rapidly expanded its repertory in the areas of pop, rock, rhythm and blues, jazz, latin, and classical music. Recently, SESAC has undergone a change of ownership and the new owners may have some interesting long term plans for the society. One indication of these plans could be the recent enrollment of Bob Dylan and Neil Diamond as writer members of the society.

## E. International Performance Rights Societies

Performance rights societies were operating overseas long before ASCAP was established in the United States. The first European performance rights society, Societe des Auteurs, Compositeurs et Editeurs de Musique (SACEM), was formed in France in 1851. ASCAP is said to have been modeled after SACEM. By the end of the 19th century, SACEM had established an office in London for the purpose of collecting fees for the public performance of French compositions in England even before the establishment of a performance rights society for British composers. This left the British in an awkward position: while British compositions could be freely performed without compensation, it was necessary for restaurants and concert halls in England to pay for a license if they wished to perform French compositions. In 1914, after a series of meetings between important British music publishers, authors, and composers, including David Day of Francis, Day and Hunter and William Boosey of Chappell & Co. Ltd., the English Performance Right Society was finally established. Around the turn of the century, other societies had been established in Europe, including the first German society, Genosenschaft Deutscher Tonsetzer (GDT), the predecessor to today's GEMA, which was founded in Berlin in 1903.

## II. LEGAL BACKGROUND

### A. Performances Under the Copyright Law Today

To *perform* music means to "recite, render, [or] play . . . it, either directly or by means of a device or process."[4] For example, a singer is performing when he or she sings a song; a broadcaster is performing when it transmits his or her performance (whether simultaneously or from records); a local broadcaster is performing when it transmits the network broadcast; a cable television system is performing when it retransmits the broadcast to its subscribers; and any individual is performing when he or she plays a record album embodying the performance or communicates the performance by turning on a radio.[5]

The *performance right* in music is the exclusive right to perform or authorize the performance of the music publicly.[6] To perform music

---

[4] 17 U.S.C. Sec. 101.

[5] House of Rep. Report No. 94-1476, 94th Cong., 2d Sess. (1976) at p. 63.

[6] 17 U.S.C. Sec. 106(4).

*publicly* means (1) to "perform . . . it at a place open to the public or at any place where a substantial number of persons outside of a normal circle of family and its social acquaintances is gathered" or (2) "to transmit or otherwise communicate a performance . . . . of the work to a place specified by clause (1) or to the public, by means of any device or process, whether the members of the public capable of receiving the performance receive it in the same place or in separate places and at the same time or different times."[7] The term "family" in this context would include an individual living alone, so that a gathering confined to the individual's social acquaintances would normally be regarded as private. Performances of music at routine meetings of business and governmental personnel would not be considered public because they do not represent the gathering of a "substantial number of persons." However, performances in semi-public places, such as clubs, lodges factories summer camps, and schools are considered public performances.

The copyright act of 1976 specifically eliminated the requirement that performances be "for profit" and gave the owner of copyright the exclusive right to license the performance of a musical composition in public, whether it be for profit or otherwise.[8]

## B. Limitations on the Exclusive Right of Public Performance

In eliminating the "for profit" requirement, however, the new copyright law substituted in its place a series of limitations to the exclusive right of public performance.[9]

### 1. Non-Profit Performances

These limitations include exemptions for four kinds of *nonprofit* performances. The first exempts from the exclusive right of public performance those performances of music that are rendered in the course of the face-to-face teaching activities of nonprofit educational institutions. The second exempts certain governmental and nonprofit educational broadcasts of music where the purpose is to further sys-

---

[7] 17 U.S.C. Sec. 101.

[8] 17 U.S.C. Sec. 106(4).

[9] 17 U.S.C. Sec. 110.

tematic instructional activities. The third exempts performances of music of a religious nature rendered during the course of religious services; this exemption does not apply, however, to any religious broadcast, even when the broadcast originates at the place of worship. The fourth exempts performances that lack any direct or indirect commercial advantage; for this exemption to apply, no direct or indirect admission may be charged for the performance and no payment of any fee or other compensation for the performance may be made to any of its performers, promoters, or organizers.

### 2. Mom and Pop Stores

Another exemption from the exclusive right of public performance are certain performances by small public establishments by means of radio broadcasts. The exemption applies to public performances by the reception of a radio transmission "on a single receiving apparatus of a kind commonly used in private homes." This exemption was intended only to apply to small commercial establishments (e.g., "mom & pop" stores) where the performances are made by using a small radio or home stereo receiver, with no more than four ordinary speakers grouped within a relatively narrow circumference from the receiving equipment.[10] The exemption would not apply to broadcasts transmitted by speakers or similar devices in such establishments as bus terminals, supermarkets, factories and commercial offices, department and clothing stores, hotels, restaurants and fast-food or quick-service chain stores, or where the establishment makes use of any commercial sound equipment or conversion of a home-type receiver into its equivalent.

### 3. Record Stores

The copyright law also exempts performances of music in record stores where the sole purpose of the performance is to demonstrate, and thereby promote the sales of the records offered for sale at the store. For the exemption to apply, no charge may be made for admission to the store. Further, the exemption applies only if the performance is not transmitted beyond the place where the store is located

---

[10] House Report at pp. 86-87.

and is limited to the immediate area where the sale is occurring. Accordingly, where record sales are made in one part of a large department store, the exemption does not apply to performances transmitted to other parts of the department store.

### 4. State Fairs

Also exempt are performances of music at state fairs by governmental bodies and nonprofit organizations, and performances of music as part of programs designed for the blind, deaf, or handicapped, provided they are broadcast through the facilities of government, nonprofit organizations, public broadcasting entities, and cable radio or television systems.

### 5. Public Broadcasting

Fearing the political pressure that the public broadcasting industry could apply to Congress at the time the copyright law of 1976 was being considered, Congress adopted a compulsory license for performances of music broadcast by public broadcasting entities. The provision encourages copyright owners, through their respective performance rights societies, and public broadcasters to negotiate in good faith and reach agreement on performance license fees. Should they fail to reach agreement, the compulsory fees would be established by the Copyright Arbitration Royalty Panel, appointed and convened by the Librarian of Congress.[11]

## III. Performance Rights Societies Today

Today, nearly all licensing of performances of music in the United States is conducted through the auspices of ASCAP, BMI, and SESAC, and through over forty music license organizations operating throughout the world. Virtually all professional songwriters and music publishers are members of or affiliated with performance rights societies.

---

[11] 17 U.S.C. 801-803.

## A. ASCAP

ASCAP is owned and run by over 120,000 writers and music publishers, who are referred to as *members*.[12] Members have the opportunity to raise questions and express their views at four meetings each year, two in New York and two in Los Angeles. The society also holds meetings in Nashville, Tennessee. The Board of Directors of ASCAP is elected by its membership and is composed of composers, lyricists and music publishers. The Board, which meets once a month to plan, review, set policy, and appoint officers, has twelve writer directors elected by the writer members and twelve publisher directors elected by the publisher members.

## B. BMI, Inc.

BMI is owned by about 500 radio and television stations who are successors to the radio stations who established BMI in 1940.[13] No dividends, however, have ever been paid to the shareholders of BMI; after the deduction of operating expenses, all amounts collected have been paid to the over 300,000 writers and publishers affiliated with BMI, called *affiliates*.

## C. SESAC Inc.

SESAC, by far the smallest of the U.S. performance rights organizations, is a private company originally established by the Heineke family.[14] SESAC represents over 900 writers and 750 publishers with respect to over 150,000 musical compositions. Like ASCAP and BMI, SESAC makes its catalog available to the broadcast industry, airlines, auditoriums, nightclubs, hotels, restaurants. Unlike the other performance rights societies, however, SESAC promotes performance activity of the music in its writers' and publishers' catalogs. SESAC is also unique in that it provides its affiliates with consultation, legal advice

---

[12] American Society of Composers, Authors & Publishers, 1 Lincoln Plaza, New York, New York 10023, Phone: 212-621-6000; Fax: 212-787-1381, www.ascap.com.

[13] Broadcast Music, Inc., 320 West 57th Street, New York, New York 10019, Phone: 212-586-2000; Fax: 212-489-2368, www.bmi.com.

[14] SESAC, Inc., 421 West 54th Street, New York, NY, 10019, Phone: 212-586-3450, Fax: 212-489-5966, www.sesac.com.

on copyrights, and placement assistance with publishers and record labels.

## D. International Performance Rights Societies

Performance rights societies similar to ASCAP, BMI, and SESAC operate in many countries around the world. Under reciprocal representation agreements, each society licenses performances and collects royalties in its local country on behalf of songwriter and publisher members of affiliated performance rights societies in other countries. Overseas performance rights societies generally divide performance royalties into equal publisher and writer shares. The writers' shares of performance fees are paid to the respective societies representing the writers; the publisher's shares are paid to the respective societies representing the publishers or, if the publisher instructs, to its local publisher representative located in the country in which the fees are collected.

A list of the major international performance rights societies is set forth at the end of this chapter, and a discussion of the international administration of public performance rights is discussed in Chapter 5, on *International Subpublishing*.

## E. Membership Requirements

Membership in the performance rights societies is fairly open. Applications for membership may be obtained by writing to or visiting any of their regional offices.

A songwriter desiring to become a member of ASCAP must show he or she has written a musical composition that has been (a) commercially recorded, (b) made available in the form of sheet music for sale in regular commercial outlets, or (c) performed in a media licensed by ASCAP, such as radio. To become a publisher member of ASCAP, you must be regularly engaged in the business of music publishing. If you do not meet the requirements for full membership, you may become an associate writer member if you have had at least one work written and registered with the U.S. Copyright Office. It does not cost anything to join ASCAP. Annual dues are only $10 for writers and $50 for publishers.

Similarly, a songwriter is eligible to affiliate with BMI by showing he or she has written a musical composition that has been either commercially published or recorded or otherwise likely to be performed. BMI charges no fees or annual dues to writers. To affiliate with BMI as a publisher member, you must satisfy reasonable standards of literacy and integrity and should have some musical compositions being performed, or likely to be performed, by broadcasting stations or in other public performances. BMI does not charge publisher members any annual fees or dues. Instead, BMI charges publishers an initial charge of $25.00, made only at the time of affiliation, and intended only to help defray the administrative cost involved in affiliation. There is no fee for affiliation of either writers or publishers with SESAC.

## F.  Choosing the Society with Which to Affiliate

A songwriter may only affiliate with one performance rights society, foreign or domestic, at any one time. However, a writer who belongs to one society may collaborate on the writing of a song with a writer who is affiliated with another society.

Songwriters and publishers frequently ask the question, "Which performing rights society should I join?" Large music publishers will belong to both ASCAP and BMI, establishing separate publishing subsidiaries for this purpose, but the question as to which performance society would be best for any particular song or catalog of songs remains.

It was once believed that the decision of which society to join depended on the type of music the songwriter composes or the type of music that comprises the catalog. A composer of rock, jazz, or country or western was said to be better off with BMI, because of the emphasis BMI placed on independent radio stations, rather than radio networks, in making its surveys; composers of music more likely to be performed on networks over a long period of time were advised to join ASCAP. However, these distinctions no longer apply, and songwriters and publishers are advised to meet with representatives of each society to determine which is better for them.

In the early 1970s, each of the performance rights societies began allowing what is known as "cross-registration." This facilitated the performance rights administration of songs written by a writer affiliated with one society working in collaboration with a writer affiliated with another. For example, performance royalties for a song co-written by an ASCAP writer and a BMI writer, each having a 50% interest in the writer's share, would be paid as follows: ASCAP would pay to the ASCAP writer 50% of the writer's share of ASCAP collections derived from performances of the song and BMI would pay to the BMI writer 50% of the writer's share of BMI collections derived from such performances, provided, however, that each of the respective publisher's share matches the respective writer's share — i.e., in this case, an ASCAP affiliated publisher must own a 50% interest in the publisher's share and a BMI affiliated publisher must own a 50% interest in the publisher's share.

The point of all this is that, because a series of performance royalty statements will be generated by each society with respect to the earnings arising from surveys of the same performances of the same song, one should be able to determine from comparing these statements over time, which society is "better." Unfortunately, publishers and writers who have had an opportunity to make the foregoing comparison report mixed results. In some cases, ASCAP paid more, and, in other cases, BMI paid more, and these comparisons suggest no particular guidelines about which society would better represent a writer or publisher with respect to certain genres of music or certain kinds of performances.

To attract new members and affiliates, ASCAP and BMI will, from time to time, offer certain writers and publishers advances against future performance royalties. The amount of advances offered by a society might seem a good reason to select one society over another, but if you are considering such an offer, you should remember that the advance being offered is really your money to begin with. The basis of your decision about which society to join should be made on longer term considerations as to which society is really best for you.

## G. Procedures upon Affiliation

It is the music publisher's responsibility to provide to the performance rights society the information necessary to collect and pay royalties for performances. After affiliation with a performance rights society, publishers should follow the following procedures:

1. Register your active musical compositions with your performance rights society immediately. You will not be credited for

performances until your songs are registered with the society. Forms for registration are available from the performance rights society.

2. Register each new work promptly after it is created, preferably before its anticipated first recording or first performance.

3. When a music publisher in the United States signs a *sub-publishing agreement* with a music publisher in another country, the procedures for the collection of performance royalties should be specified in the agreement. For example, the agreement should specify to which performance rights society (e.g., ASCAP, BMI, or SESAC) the U.S. publisher has granted performing rights and the percentage of the publisher's share of performance royalties it should receive. The agreement should also specify whether the publisher's share will be collected on its behalf by the foreign publisher or whether it is to be paid by the foreign society to the U.S. performance rights society for its account. The writers' shares of foreign performance fees collected by the overseas societies are transferred to the appropriate U.S. society who in turn pays these fees directly to writers.

4. Notify your performance rights society whenever you change your address.

## IV. PERFORMANCE LICENSE GRANTS TO PERFORMANCE RIGHTS SOCIETIES

### A. Non-Exclusive

Because of the impracticability of enforcing their exclusive right to public performances of the song, music copyright owners customarily become members of performance right societies. Upon affiliation with a society, songwriters and copyright owners grant to performance rights societies a license to sublicense the rendition of public performances of their musical works. In accordance with the court ordered consent decrees that govern the agreements between the performance rights societies and their members and affiliates, these licenses granted to the societies are made strictly on a nonexclusive basis.

## B. Equal Shares

In return, performance rights societies will pay 50% of the performance royalties earned by any particular composition to the copyright owner of the song — this is known as the *publisher's share* of performance royalties. The other 50% is paid directly to the songwriters, whether or not they own the copyright in the song — this is known as the *writer's share* of performance royalties. Both the songwriters and the publishers will each receive their respective 50% shares of performance royalties directly from the performance rights societies. Guidelines for the allocation of royalties within each of these groups is governed by the amended consent decree.[15]

As noted in Chapter 5, on *International Subpublishing*, overseas the division of shares between writers and publishers varies from society to society. For example, the division of publisher and writer shares for Dutch works is approximately 2/3 to writers and 1/3 to publishers.

## C. Assignability of Writer's Share

When a songwriter signs a standard music publishing agreement, he assigns to the publisher his copyright in his song, but reserves the rights necessary to grant to his performance rights society his writer's share of nondramatic public performance rights. Should a writer assign his writer's share of performance royalties to another, the performance rights society will not always recognize the assignment. The societies will do this as a matter of policy to protect writer's from entering into unconscionable contracts. However, this policy is not universally applied and may be subject to overruling by a court. Accordingly, a writer should not rely upon it when considering making an assignment he is later likely to regret.

---

[15] See *United States v. ASCAP*, 32 C.O. Bull. 601 (S.D.N.Y. 1960) and *United States v. ASCAP*, 442 F.2d 601 (2d Cir. 1971).

## D. Nondramatic Performances

Performance rights societies receive from their music publisher and songwriter members the right to license only *nondramatic* performances of their musical compositions, not *dramatic* performances. Accordingly, performance licenses issued by the societies to radio and television stations, nightclubs, concert halls, and like establishments, permit the rendition of performances of music in only a manner that is *nondramatic* in nature. The difference between dramatic and nondramatic performances are discussed at great length in Chapter 18.

## V. CONSIDERATIONS IN GRANTING AND CLEARING PERFORMANCE LICENSES

Performance rights societies control virtually all administration of performance licenses. Accordingly, persons seeking permission to render nondramatic public performances of music usually must seek permission directly from one or more of the performance rights societies.

## A. Blanket Licenses

Persons or entities acquiring public performance licenses pay ASCAP and BMI an annual fee for the privilege to render an unlimited number of nondramatic performances of one or more of any of the hundreds of thousands of songs in their respective catalogs. Because of its extraordinarily broad coverage, this type of licensing arrangement is called a *blanket license*.

The fee charged for a blanket license, in the case of radio and television stations and certain other establishments, is based on the adjusted gross receipts of the station or establishment, approximating 2%. For other businesses, such as restaurants, nightclubs, dancing schools, and the like, the fee for the blanket license may be an annual flat fee in accordance with various schedules established by the respective societies. Examples of several forms of blanket licenses are set forth at the end of this chapter.

If any music user believes the fees quoted by a performance rights society are unreasonable, he may apply for a ruling with the federal court under either of the respective consent decrees that govern the dealings of ASCAP and BMI.[16]

In October 1998, Congress enacted the Copyright Term Extension Act. Title II, the "Fairness in Music Licensing Act," (Pub. Law 105-298, 112 Stat. 2830 (Oct. 27, 1998)) exempts certain establishments from paying music licensing fees. According to the terms of the Act, some establishments that transmit or retransmit a performance or display of a nondramatic musical work intended to be received by the general public, originated by licensed radio, television, cable, or satellite sources that do not retransmit beyond their establishments and do not charge admission are exempt. The exemption applies to food service and drinking establishments that are smaller than 3,750 gross square feet and all other retail establishments that are smaller than 2,000 gross square feet. Service and drinking establishments that are larger than 3,750 gross square feet and other retail establishments larger than 2,000 gross square feet can qualify for the exemption if they use six or fewer speakers with no more than four loudspeakers in one room or if they use audiovisual equipment consisting of no more than four audiovisual devices with no more than one audiovisual device in each room and no audiovisual device having a diagonal screen size greater than 55 inches, together with the same speaker restrictions.

## B. Source Licenses and Direct Licenses

Under the terms of the consent decrees entered into between ASCAP and the U.S. Department of Justice and between BMI and the U.S. Department of Justice, and the agreements between the societies and their members or affiliates, all members and affiliates of the performance rights societies are free to negotiate nonexclusive licenses directly with users, such as radio and television stations, on any mutually agreeable terms.

When members or affiliates negotiate performance licenses directly with users, they do so by entering into either a direct license or

---

[16] *See generally*, Sobel, *The Music Business and the Sherman Act: An Analysis of the 'Economic Realities' of Blanket Licensing*, 3 Loyola of Los Angeles Ent.L.J. 1 (1983).

a source license. A *direct license* is a license to perform music on television that a television broadcaster obtains directly from the composers and/or publishers of the music it broadcasts. A *source license* is a license to perform music on television that a producer of a television program obtains directly from the composers and/or publishers of the music contained in the program. The difference between a *source license* and a *direct license* is that a source license is one that is obtained by the person who owns the work in which the song is used (e.g., motion picture, television program) and a direct license is a license that is obtained by one who broadcasts (e.g., television network or local television station), but does not necessarily own, the work being broadcast.

Over the years since the entry of the consent decrees, very, very few nondramatic performance licenses have been issued by music copyright owners directly to broadcasters or other users of music. Most users, including the three national television networks, local television stations, local radio stations, have not sought source or direct licenses from copyright owners, but, instead have sought and obtained blanket licenses from the performance rights societies. Under their blanket licenses, these users have been entitled to perform some or all of the music in the repertories of the performance rights societies without the need to seek individual performance licenses from the individual members or affiliates.

From time to time, however, television and radio stations have sought to improve their leverage in bargaining with the performance license societies by either threatening to cease negotiating for blanket licenses or by filing lawsuits claiming that the arrangements under which performance rights societies operate violate the U.S. antitrust laws. In the early 1980s a group of local television broadcasters filed a lawsuit against ASCAP and BMI charging just such violations.[17] Later, a group of local radio broadcasters filed a similar lawsuit against the societies.[18] After these lawsuits were filed, music publishers began receiving requests from broadcasters for direct licenses to perform

---

[17] *Buffalo Broadcasting Company, Inc. v. ASCAP and BMI*, 223 U.S.P.Q. 478 (2d Cir. 1984).

[18] *Alton Rainbow Corp. v. ASCAP*, 98 F.R.D. 299 (1983).

music in their catalogs, intended, apparently, to elicit responses that could later be used as evidence in the pending litigation.

Even though music copyright owners are entirely free to enter into source or direct licenses under any terms that may be agreeable to them, few have any experience in issuing direct or source performance licenses. In considering the terms upon which to enter into a source or direct license, a music copyright owner should consider that, while a single lump sum payment may be attractive in the short-term, accepting such terms will mean foregoing any compensation from the performance rights society based upon the type and number of performances of the work are rendered over time. It will be recalled that the performance revenues of a society are distributed under a system that awards performance fees on the basis of statistical surveys. Surveyed performances upon which these fees are based must necessarily exclude performances that are licensed directly by the member or affiliate; otherwise, the copyright owner would theoretically be paid twice for the same performance. Accordingly, members or affiliates of performance rights societies who enter into direct or source licenses are required to notify their performance rights society that a direct or source license has been issued, the title of the song licensed, the writer or writers of the song, the publisher or publishers of the song, the name of the licensee, and the term of the license.

In other words, unless the source or direct license is structured on some royalty basis, the music copyright owner entering into such licenses is giving up the important ability to benefit from the economic success of the work or broadcast for which the music is being licensed. While there may be economic circumstances under which it would make good business sense to license nondramatic performances of a song or catalog of songs directly, rather than through the performance rights societies, those circumstances should be considered very carefully with the advice of skilled legal counsel and financial analysts.

## C. Per Program Licenses

The court's ruling in the *Buffalo Broadcasting* case resulted in a new form of license that is now available to television stations from the performance rights societies. Under the ruling, each television station has a choice between a traditional blanket license and a new *per program license.* A number of television stations are choosing to secure a per program license instead of the traditional blanket license.

A per program license is often considered a modified blanket license, because it operates much the same way as the blanket license. Television stations that desire a per program license may broadcast any and all songs in the ASCAP and BMI catalogs, but instead of paying fees for a license to use all of the music in each society's catalog — whether they use them or not — stations pay each society only for television programs which contain music controlled by that society pursuant to a prescribed formula. Per program fee structures are negotiated between the performance rights societies and various representatives of the television industry, much the same way as blanket licenses are negotiated. As in the case of blanket licenses, if an agreement cannot be reached, a proceeding before the Federal District Court in New York will take place to establish a reasonable rate structure.

Stations electing the per program license option pays fees to ASCAP and BMI on a monthly basis. However, unlike the blanket license, a vast amount of record keeping attends the per program licensing scheme. For example, a station must report the episode titles of the television programs it broadcasts, together with records of what music is contained in each program and when each program is broadcast. The key document used to determine which composers and publishers are entitled to receive royalty distributions is the music cue sheet. A *cue sheet* is a document that lists all of the music in a program, the order of performance, the amount of time each performance runs, the names of the song's composers and music publishers, and performance rights affiliations. The television stations participating in the per program option are using the services of independent database management companies to assimilate all this information and prepare reports based on the cue sheets and the information furnished by the televisions stations who choose the per program option.

The per program license should not be confused with either the source license or the direct license. While source and direct licenses are issued to producers and broadcasters by music publishers and other music copyright owners, the per program license is issued by the performance rights society much the same as they issue blanket licenses.

## VI. COLLECTION OF PERFORMANCE ROYALTIES FROM MUSIC USERS

A *music user*, for purpose of performance rights collection, is any person, business, or other entity that publicly performs music. A music user may publicly perform music (i) by live performance in concert on stage with or without the aid of a loudspeaker, or (ii) by transmission of a live performance or a recorded performance by radio, television, cable, telephone or other form of broadcast or retransmission.

Examples of music users include, local and network radio stations, local and network television stations, cable television operators, theaters, concert halls, nightclubs, restaurants, discos, ballrooms, hotels and motels, sports arenas and stadiums, amusement parks, airlines, jukebox operators, retail stores, corporations who play music over the telephone to callers "on hold" and many others. In general, each society negotiates directly with radio and television networks, independent stations, and all other establishments where their respective music repertoires are performed publicly.

Performance rights societies generally divide their collection operations into two divisions: broadcast licensing and general licensing. The broadcast licensing division engages in complex negotiations with radio and television stations to establish the annual rates and fees due with respect to the use of music in these media. The general licensing division collects fees from all licensees other than radio and television broadcasters, such as nightclubs, restaurants, sports arenas, and the like.

### A. Broadcast Licensing

As mentioned above, the broadcast licensing divisions of the major performance rights societies engage in complex negotiations with radio and television stations to establish the annual rates and fees due with respect to the performance of music in connection with radio and television broadcasts. The complexity of these negotiations have been magnified by a series of lawsuits brought against the performance rights societies by television broadcasters, including the major television networks, local television stations, and cable television operators.

Although these lawsuits have not significantly changed the way music is licensed to broadcasters, the use of alternatives to the blanket licenses offered by performance rights societies is becoming more practical. These alternatives include source licensing, direct licensing, and per program licensing, each of which are described in the previous section.

## B. General Licensing

The general licensing division of performance rights societies collects fees from all licensees other than radio and television broadcasters, such as nightclubs, restaurants, sports arenas, and the like. The performance rights societies have separate licenses and rate schedules for each major category of general users. Examples of general licenses are set forth at the end of this chapter, and information about current licensing terms and rates may be obtained by calling any of the regional offices of the societies.

## VII. DISTRIBUTION OF PERFORMANCE ROYALTIES TO PUBLISHER AND WRITER MEMBERS

ASCAP, BMI, and SESAC calculate and distribute performance royalties under different systems. These systems are exceedingly complex and, accordingly, no effort is made here to provide a comprehensive description of them. Readers interested in more information on this subject should confer directly with the performance rights societies.

## A. Statistical Sampling

ASCAP and BMI both employ elaborate systems of statistical sampling to determine which selections from their respective repertoires have been used and with what frequency. No effort is made to determine exactly the actual number of times each selection is performed during the year in the United States. Because of the vast numbers of musical performances that are rendered each year and locations at which music is performed publicly in this country, such an effort would require an expenditure that would far exceed the aggregate income of all the U.S. performance rights societies. Fortunately, statistical science has rendered such a complete survey unnecessary. By surveying a relatively few number of performances, the societies can establish a surprisingly accurate measurement of what songs are being performed during the year and with what relative frequency.

Most performance data is drawn from broadcast sources, under the assumption that the music being performed over radio and television is roughly the same as the music being performed in cafes, hotels, sports arenas, and restaurants, and nightclubs. ASCAP and BMI have different ways of sampling broadcast performances. ASCAP primarily relies upon tape recordings made by teams of surveyors sent to different parts of the country during the year. BMI primarily relies upon logs of all songs performed during a particular week by statistically selected broadcast stations. These logs are prepared by television and radio stations once every year or so as a condition of their performance license.

While the royalty distribution payments by ASCAP to its affiliated publisher and writer members are primarily based on a survey of users and BMI by a logging system prepared by users, SESAC payments to its affiliates begin when a recording of its product is released for sale to the public or otherwise begins to earn monies. SESAC does not have a formal logging procedure, but relies instead on performance of songs on industry standard "Top 100" charts, combined with spot checking of broadcast stations, to gage the relative performances of songs in its repertoire. Payments are determined by set rates based on industry hit chart activities.

## B. Credit Systems

Once the sample is taken, the resulting information is rolled into a complex formula that takes into consideration a number of factors, including the size of the broadcast stations sampled, the time of day of the performance, the type of program on which the music is performed, whether the performance is a feature performance or a background performance, etc. Each performance is assigned one or more credits, or fractions thereof, and the accumulated credits are used to allocate the fees collected from music users among the various writer and publisher members and affiliates of the society. After deductions of operating expenses, the funds collected from all sources are divided equally between writers and publishers in accordance with the credit formula.

## C. Grievance Procedures

ASCAP and BMI have each adopted a grievance procedure under which any of its writer or publisher members or affiliates may file formal complaints with the respective society. Complaints filed against ASCAP are reviewed by a special Board of Review. Disputes with BMI may be governed by arbitration under the rules of the American Arbitration Association. Complaints may ultimately be subject to the Federal Courts retaining jurisdiction of the consent decrees to which ASCAP and BMI remain respectively subject. SESAC is not subject to a consent decree.

# APPENDIX TO CHAPTER 17
## PERFORMANCE LICENSES

# FORM 17.1

## BMI WRITER AGREEMENT

BMI • 320 West 57th Street, New York, NY 10019-3790 • 212-586-2000 • FAX 212-245-8986

Date

Dear

The following shall constitute the agreement between us:

1. As used in this agreement:

(a) The word "Period" shall mean the term from                    to                    , and continuing thereafter for additional terms of two years each unless terminated by either party at the end of said initial term or any additional term, upon notice by registered or certified mail not more than six (6) months or less than three (3) months prior to the end of any such term.

(b) The words "Work" or "Works" shall mean:

(i) All musical compositions (including the musical segments and individual compositions written for a dramatic or dramatico-musical work) composed by you alone or with one or more co-writers during the Period; and

(ii) All musical compositions (including the musical segments and individual compositions written for a dramatic or dramatico-musical work) composed by you alone or with one or more co-writers prior to the Period, except those in which there is an outstanding grant of the right of public performance to a person other than a publisher affiliated with BMI.

2. You agree that:

(a) Within ten (10) days after the execution of this agreement you will furnish to us a completed clearance form available in blank from us with respect to each Work heretofore composed by you which has been published in printed copies or recorded commercially or synchronized commercially with film or tape or which is being currently performed or which you consider as likely to be performed.

(b) In each instance that a Work for which a clearance form has not been submitted to us pursuant to sub-paragraph 2(a) is published in printed copies or recorded commercially or in synchronization with film or tape or is considered by you as likely to be performed, whether such Work is composed prior to the execution of this agreement or hereafter during the Period, you will promptly furnish to us a completed clearance form with respect to each such Work.

(c) If requested by us in writing, you will promptly furnish to us a legible lead sheet or other written or printed copy of a Work.

3. The submission of each clearance form pursuant to paragraph 2 shall constitute a warranty and representation by you that all of the information contained thereon is true and correct and that no performing rights in such Work have been granted to or reserved by others except as specifically set forth therein in connection with Works heretofore written or co-written by you.

4. Except as otherwise provided herein, you hereby grant to us for the Period:

(a) All the rights that you own or acquire publicly to perform, and to license others to perform, anywhere in the world, any part or all of the Works.

(b) The non-exclusive right to record, and to license others to record, any part or all of any of the Works on electrical transcriptions, wire, tape, film or otherwise, but only for the purpose of performing such Work publicly by means of radio and television or for archive or audition purposes. This right does not include recording for the purpose of sale to the public or for the purpose of synchronization (i) with motion pictures intended primarily for theatrical exhibition or (ii) with programs distributed by means of syndication to broadcasting stations, cable systems or other similar distribution outlets.

(c) The non-exclusive right to adapt or arrange any part or all of any of the Works for performance purposes, and to license others to do so.

5. Notwithstanding the provisions of sub-paragraph 4(a):

(a) The rights granted to us by sub-paragraph 4(a) shall not include the right to perform or license the performance of more than one song or aria from a dramatic or dramatico-musical work which is an opera, operetta or musical show or more than five (5) minutes from a dramatic or dramatico-musical work which is a ballet, if such performance is accompanied by the dramatic action, costumes or scenery of that dramatic or dramatico-musical work.

(b) You, together with all the publishers and your co-writers, if any, shall have the right jointly, by written notice to us, to exclude from the grant made by sub-paragraph 4(a) performances of Works comprising more than thirty (30) minutes of a dramatic or dramatico-musical work, but this right shall not apply to such performances from (i) a score originally written for or performed as part of a theatrical or television film, (ii) a score originally written for or performed as part of a radio or television program, or (iii) the original cast, sound track or similar album of a dramatic or dramatico-musical work.

(c) You, the publishers and/or your co-writers, if any, retain the right to issue non-exclusive licenses for performances of a Work or Works in the United States, its territories and possessions (other than to another performing rights licensing organization), provided that within ten (10) days of the issuance of such license we are given written notice thereof and a copy of the license is supplied to us.

6.    (a) As full consideration for all rights granted to us hereunder and as security therefor, we agree to pay to you, with respect to each of the Works in which we obtain and retain performing rights during the Period:

(i) For radio and television performances of a Work in the United States, its territories and possessions, amounts calculated pursuant to our then current standard practices upon the basis of the then current performance rates generally paid by us to our affiliated writers for similar performances of similar compositions. The number of performances for which you shall be entitled to payment shall be estimated by us in accordance with our then current system of computing the number of such performances.

You acknowledge that we license performances of the Works of our affiliates by means other than on radio and television, but that unless and until such time as methods are adopted for tabulation of such performances, payment will be based solely on performances in those media and locations then currently surveyed. In the event that during the Period we shall establish a system of separate payment for performances by means other than radio and television, we shall pay you upon the basis of the then current performance rates generally paid by us to our other affiliated writers for similar performances of similar compositions.

(ii) In the case of a Work composed by you with one or more co-writers, the sum payable to you hereunder shall be a pro rata share, determined on the basis of the number of co-writers, unless you shall have transmitted to us a copy of an agreement between you and your co-writers providing for a different division of payment.

(iii) Monies received by us from any performing rights licensing organization outside of the United States, its territories and possessions, which are designated by such performing rights licensing organization as the author's share of foreign performance royalties earned by your Works after the deduction of our then current handling charge applicable to our affiliated writers and in accordance with our then current standard practices of payment for such performances.

(b) Notwithstanding the provisions of sub-paragraph 6(a), we shall have no obligation to make payment hereunder with respect to (i) any performance of a Work which occurs prior to the date on which we have received from you all of the information and material with respect to such Work which is referred to in paragraphs 2 and 3, or (ii) any performance of a Work as to which a direct license as described in sub-paragraph 5(c) has been granted by you, your co-writers, if any, or the publishers, or (iii) any performance for which no license fee shall be collected by us, or (iv) any performance of a Work which you claim was either omitted from or miscalculated on a royalty statement and for which we shall not have received written notice from you of such claimed omission or miscalculation within nine (9) months of the date of such statement.

7. In accordance with our then current standard practices, we will furnish periodic statements to you during each year of the Period showing the monies due pursuant to sub-paragraph 6(a). Each such statement shall be accompanied by payment of the sum thereby shown to be due you, subject to all proper deductions, if any, for taxes, advances or amounts due BMI from you.

8.    (a) Nothing in this agreement requires us to continue to license the Works subsequent to the termination of this agreement. In the event that we continue to license your interest in any Work, however, we shall continue to make payments to you for such Work for so long as you do not make or purport to make directly or indirectly any grant of performing rights in such Work to any other licensing organization. The amounts of such payments shall be calculated pursuant to our then current standard practices upon the basis of the then current performance rates generally paid by us to our affiliated writers for similar performances of similar compositions. You agree to notify us by registered or certified mail of any grant or purported grant by you directly or indirectly of performing rights to any other performing rights organization within ten (10) days from the making of such grant or purported grant and if you fail so to inform us thereof and we make payments to you for any period after the making of any such grant or purported grant, you agree to repay to us all amounts so paid by us promptly with or without demand by us. In addition, if we inquire of you by registered or certified mail, addressed to your last known address, whether you have made any such grant or purported grant and you fail to confirm to us by registered or certified mail within thirty (30) days of the mailing of such inquiry that you have not made any such grant or purported grant, we may, from and after such date, discontinue making any payments to you.

(b) Our obligation to continue payment to you after the termination of this agreement for performances outside of the United States, its territories and possessions, of Works which BMI continues to license after such termination shall be dependent upon our receipt in the United States of payments designated by foreign performing rights organizations as the author's share of foreign performance royalties earned by your Works. Payment of such foreign royalties shall be subject to deduction of our then current handling charge applicable to our affiliated writers and shall be in accordance with our then current standard practices of payment for such performances.

(c) In the event that we have reason to believe that you will receive, are entitled to receive, or are receiving payment from a performing rights licensing organization other than BMI for or based on United States performances of one or more of your Works during a period when such Works were licensed by us pursuant to this agreement, we shall have the right to withhold payment for such performances from you until receipt of evidence satisfactory to us that you were not or will not be so paid by such other organization. In the event that you were or will be so paid or do not supply such evidence within eighteen (18) months from the date of our request therefor, we shall be under no obligation to make any payment to you for performances of such Works during such period.

9. In the event that this agreement shall terminate at a time when, after crediting all earnings reflected by statements rendered to you prior to the effective date of such termination, there remains an unearned balance of advances paid to you by us, such termination shall not be effective until the close of the calendar quarterly period during which (a) you shall repay such unearned balance of advances, or (b) you shall notify us by registered or certified mail that you have received a statement rendered by us at our normal accounting time showing that such unearned balance of advances has been fully recouped by us.

10. You warrant and represent that you have the right to enter into this agreement; that you are not bound by any prior commitments which conflict with your commitments hereunder; that each of the Works, composed by you alone or with one or more co-writers, is original; and that exercise of the rights granted by you herein will not constitute an infringement of copyright or violation of any other right of, or unfair competition with, any person, firm or corporation. You agree to indemnify and hold harmless us, our licensees, the advertisers of our licensees and their respective agents, servants and employees from and against any and all loss or damage resulting from any claim of whatever nature arising from or in connection with the exercise of any of the rights granted by you in this agreement. Upon notification to us or any of the other parties herein indemnified of a claim with respect to any of the Works, we shall have the right to exclude such Work from this agreement and/or to withhold payment of all sums which become due pursuant to this agreement or any modification thereof until receipt of satisfactory written evidence that such claim has been withdrawn, settled or adjudicated.

11. (a) We shall have the right, upon written notice to you, to exclude from this agreement, at any time, any Work which in our opinion is similar to a previously existing composition and might constitute a copyright infringement, or has a title or music or lyric similar to that of a previously existing composition and might lead to a claim of unfair competition.

(b) In the case of Works which in our opinion are based on compositions in the public domain, we shall have the right, upon written notice to you, either to (i) to exclude any such Work from this agreement, or (ii) to classify any such Work as entitled to receive only a fraction of the full credit that would otherwise be given for performances thereof.

(c) In the event that any Work is excluded from this agreement pursuant to paragraph 10 or sub-paragraph 11(a) or (b), all rights in such Work shall automatically revert to you ten (10) days after the date of our notice to you of such exclusion. In the event that a Work is classified for less than full credit under sub-paragraph 11(b)(ii), you shall have the right, by giving notice to us, within ten (10) days after the date of our notice advising you of the credit allocated to the Work, to terminate our rights therein, and all rights in such Work shall thereupon revert to you.

12. In each instance that you write, or are employed or commissioned by a motion picture producer to write, during the Period, all or part of the score of a motion picture intended primarily for exhibition in theaters, or by the producer of a musical show or revue for the legitimate stage to write, during the Period, all or part of the musical compositions contained therein, we agree, on request, to advise the producer of the film that such part of the score as is written by you may be performed as part of the exhibition of said film in theaters in the United States, its territories and possessions, without compensation to us, or to the producer of the musical show or revue that your compositions embodied therein may be performed on the stage with living artists as part of such musical show or revue, without compensation to us. In the event that we notify you that we have established a system for the collection of royalties for performance of the scores of motion picture films in theaters in the United States, its territories and possessions, we shall no longer be obligated to take such action with respect to motion picture scores.

13. You make, constitute and appoint us, or our nominee, your true and lawful attorney, irrevocably during the Period, in our name or that of our nominee, or in your name, or otherwise, in our sole judgment, to do all acts, take all proceedings, execute, acknowledge and deliver any and all instruments, papers, documents, process or pleadings that, in our sole judgment, may be necessary, proper or expedient to restrain infringement of and/or to enforce and protect the rights granted by you hereunder, and to recover damages in respect to or for the infringement or other violation of said rights, and in our sole judgment to join you and/or others in whose names the copyrights to any of the Works may stand; to discontinue, compromise or refer to arbitration, any such actions or proceedings or to make any other disposition of the disputes in relation to the Works, provided that any action or proceeding commenced by us pursuant to the provisions of this paragraph shall be at our sole expense and for our sole benefit. Notwithstanding the foregoing, nothing in this paragraph 13 requires us to take any proceeding or other action against any person, firm, partnership or other entity or any writer or publisher, whether or not affiliated with us, who you claim may be infringing your Works or otherwise violating the rights granted by you hereunder. In addition, you understand and agree that the licensing by us of any musical compositions which you claim may be infringing your Works or otherwise violating the rights granted by you hereunder, shall not constitute an infringement of your Works on our part.

14. BMI shall have the right, in its sole discretion, to terminate this agreement on at least thirty (30) days' notice by registered or certified mail if you, your agents, employees or representatives, directly or indirectly, solicit or accept payment from writers for composing music for lyrics or writing lyrics to music or for reviewing, publishing, promoting, recording or rendering other services connected with the exploitation of any composition, or permit use of your name or your affiliation with us in connection with any of the foregoing. In the event of such termination no payments shall be due to you pursuant to paragraph 8.

15. No monies due or to become due to you shall be assignable, whether by way of assignment, sale or power granted to an attorney-in-fact, without our prior written consent. If any assignment of such monies is made by you without such prior written consent, no rights of any kind against us will be acquired by the assignee, purchaser or attorney-in-fact.

16. In the event that during the Period (a) mail addressed to you at the last address furnished by you pursuant to paragraph 20 shall be returned by the post office, or (b) monies shall not have been earned by you pursuant to paragraph 6 for a period of two consecutive years or more, or (c) you shall die, BMI shall have the right to terminate this agreement on at least thirty (30) days' notice by registered or certified mail addressed to the last address furnished by you pursuant to paragraph 20 and, in the case of your death, to the representative of your estate, if known to BMI. In the event of such termination no payments shall be due to you pursuant to paragraph 8.

17. You acknowledge that the rights obtained by you pursuant to this agreement constitute rights to payment of money and that during the Period we shall hold title to the performing rights granted to us hereunder. In the event that during the Period you shall file a petition in bankruptcy, such a petition shall be filed against you, you shall make an assignment for the benefit of creditors, you shall consent to the appointment of a receiver or trustee for all or part of your property, or you shall institute or shall have instituted against you any other insolvency proceeding under the United States bankruptcy laws or any other applicable law, we shall retain title to the performing rights in all Works the rights to which are granted to us hereunder and shall subrogate your trustee in bankruptcy or receiver and any subsequent purchasers from them to your right to payment of money for said Works in accordance with the terms and conditions of this agreement.

18. (a) You hereby authorize us to negotiate for and collect royalties or monies to which you may become entitled as a writer pursuant to the Audio Home Recording Act of 1992 and/or any amendments thereto or substitutions therefor and, to the extent possible, collect for and distribute to you royalties arising from or as compensation for home recording in countries outside the United States, its territories and possessions. This authorization with respect to royalties and monies under the Audio Home Recording Act of 1992 may be revoked by you at the end of any calendar year on prior written notice by you to us by registered or certified mail. Such revocation shall be effective beginning with the calendar year subsequent to the time of notice and shall in no way affect the Period of this agreement with respect to any of the other rights granted to BMI by you hereunder.

(b) We agree to distribute to you royalties and monies collected by us pursuant to the authorization granted in subparagraph 18(a), pursuant to our then prevailing practices, including deduction of our expenses therefor.

19. All disputes of any kind, nature or description arising in connection with the terms and conditions of this agreement shall be submitted to the American Arbitration Association in New York, New York, for arbitration under its then prevailing rules, the arbitrator(s) to be selected as follows: Each of us shall, by written notice to the other, have the right to appoint one arbitrator. If, within ten (10) days following the giving of such notice by one of us, the other shall not, by written notice, appoint another arbitrator, the first arbitrator shall be the sole arbitrator. If two arbitrators are so appointed, they shall appoint a third arbitrator. If ten (10) days elapse after the appointment of the second arbitrator and the two arbitrators are unable to agree upon the third arbitrator, then either of us may, in writing, request the American Arbitration Association to appoint the third arbitrator. The award made in the arbitration shall be binding and conclusive on both of us and shall include the fixing of the costs, expenses and reasonable attorneys' fees of arbitration, which shall be borne by the unsuccessful party. Judgment may be entered in New York State Supreme Court or any other court having jurisdiction.

20. You agree to notify our Department of Writer/Publisher Administration promptly in writing of any change in your address. Any notice sent to you pursuant to the terms of this agreement shall be valid if addressed to you at the last address so furnished by you.

21. This agreement constitutes the entire agreement between you and us, cannot be changed except in a writing signed by you and us and shall be governed and construed pursuant to the laws of the State of New York.

22. In the event that any part or parts of this agreement are found to be void by a court of competent jurisdiction, the remaining part or parts shall nevertheless be binding with the same force and effect as if the void part or parts were deleted from this agreement.

Very truly yours,

BROADCAST MUSIC, INC.

ACCEPTED AND AGREED TO:

By.........................................................................

Vice President

.............................................................................

4/94

# FORM 17.2

## BMI PUBLISHER AGREEMENT

**BMI** AGREEMENT made on ................................................................................ between BROADCAST MUSIC, INC. ("BMI"), a

New York corporation, whose address is 320 West 57th Street, New York, N.Y. 10019-3790 and ........................................

........................................................................................................................................................................................

a ........................................................................ doing business as ........................................................................

........................................ ("Publisher"), whose address is ........................................................................................

........................................................................

### WITNESSETH:

FIRST: The term of this agreement shall be the period from ..............................................................................

to ............................................................................, and continuing thereafter for additional periods of five (5) years each unless terminated by either party at the end of such initial period or any additional period, upon notice by registered or certified mail not more than six (6) months or less than three (3) months prior to the end of any such period.

SECOND: As used in this agreement, the word "Work" or "Works" shall mean:

A. All musical compositions (including the musical segments and individual compositions written for a dramatic or dramatico-musical work) whether published or unpublished, now owned or copyrighted by Publisher or in which Publisher owns or controls performing rights, and

B. All musical compositions (including the musical segments and individual compositions written for a dramatic or dramatico-musical work) whether published or unpublished, in which hereafter during the term Publisher acquires ownership of copyright or ownership or control of the performing rights, from and after the date of the acquisition by Publisher of such ownership or control.

THIRD: Except as otherwise provided herein, Publisher hereby sells, assigns and transfers to BMI, its successors or assigns, for the term of this agreement:

A. All the rights which Publisher owns or acquires publicly to perform, and to license others to perform, anywhere in the world, any part or all the Works.

B. The non-exclusive right to record, and to license others to record, any part or all of any of the Works on electrical transcriptions, wire, tape, film or otherwise, but only for the purpose of performing such Work publicly by means of radio and television or for archive or audition purposes. This right does not include recording for the purpose of sale to the public or for the purpose of synchronization (1) with motion pictures intended primarily for theatrical exhibition or (2) with programs distributed by means of syndication to broadcasting stations, cable systems or other similar distribution outlets.

C. The non-exclusive right to adapt or arrange any part or all of any of the Works for performance purposes, and to license others to do so.

FOURTH: Notwithstanding the provisions of subparagraph A of paragraph THIRD hereof:

A. The rights granted to BMI by said subparagraph A shall not include the right to perform or license the performance of more than one song or aria from a dramatic or dramatico-musical work which is an opera, operetta or musical show or more than five (5) minutes from a dramatic or dramatico-musical work which is a ballet, if such performance is accompanied by the dramatic action, costumes or scenery of that dramatic or dramatico-musical work.

B. Publisher, together with all the writers and co-publishers, if any, shall have the right jointly, by written notice to BMI, to exclude from the grant made by subparagraph A of paragraph THIRD hereof performances of Works comprising more than thirty (30) minutes of a dramatic or dramatico-musical work, but this right shall not apply to such performances from (1) a score originally written for or performed as part of a theatrical or television film, (2) a score originally written for or performed as part of a radio or television program, or (3) the original cast, sound track or similar album of a dramatic or dramatico-musical work.

C. Publisher, the writers and/or co-publishers, if any, retain the right to issue non-exclusive licenses for performances of a Work or Works in the United States, its territories and possessions (other than to another performing rights licensing organization), provided that within ten (10) days of the issuance of such license BMI is given written notice thereof and a copy of the license is supplied to BMI.

FIFTH:

A. As full consideration for all rights granted to BMI hereunder and as security therefor, BMI agrees to make the following payments to Publisher with respect to each of the Works in which BMI has performing rights:

(1) For radio and television performances of Works in the United States, its territories and possessions, BMI will pay amounts calculated pursuant to BMI's then standard practices upon the basis of the then current performance rates generally paid by BMI to its affiliated publishers for similar performances of similar compositions. The number of performances for which Publisher shall be entitled to payment shall be estimated by BMI in accordance with its then current system of computing the number of such performances.

Publisher acknowledges that BMI licenses performances of the Works of its affiliates by means other than on radio and television, but that unless and until such time as methods are adopted for tabulation of and payment for such performances, payment will be based solely on performances in those media and locations then currently surveyed. In the event that during the term of this agreement BMI shall establish a system of separate payment for performances by means other than radio and television, BMI shall pay Publisher upon the basis of the then current performance rates generally paid by BMI to its other affiliated publishers for similar performances of similar compositions.

(2) For performances of Works outside of the United States, its territories and possessions, BMI will pay to Publisher monies received by BMI in the United States from any performing rights licensing organization which are designated by such organization as the publisher's share of foreign performance royalties earned by any of the Works after the deduction of BMI's then current handling charge applicable to its affiliated publishers and in accordance with BMI's then standard practices of payment for such performances.

(3) In the case of Works which, or rights in which, are owned by Publisher jointly with one or more other publishers, the sum payable to Publisher under this subparagraph A shall be a pro rata share determined on the basis of the number of publishers, unless BMI shall have received from Publisher a copy of an agreement or other document signed by all of the publishers providing for a different division of payment.

B. Notwithstanding the provisions of subparagraph A of this paragraph FIFTH, BMI shall have no obligation to make payment hereunder with respect to (1) any performance of a Work which occurs prior to the date on which BMI shall have received from

Publisher of all the material with respect to such Work referred to in subparagraph A of paragraph TENTH hereof, and in the case of foreign performances, the information referred to in subparagraph B of paragraph FOURTEENTH hereof, or (2) any performance of a Work as to which a direct license as described in subparagraph C of paragraph FOURTH hereof has been granted by Publisher, its co-publishers or the writers, or (3) any performance for which no license fees shall be collected by BMI, or (4) any performance of a Work which Publisher claims was either omitted from or miscalculated on a royalty statement and for which BMI shall not have received written notice from Publisher of such claimed omission or miscalculation within nine (9) months of the date of such statement.

SIXTH: In accordance with BMI's then current standard practices, BMI will furnish periodic statements to Publisher during each year of the term showing the monies due pursuant to subparagraph A of paragraph FIFTH hereof. Each such statement shall be accompanied by payment of the sum thereby shown to be due to Publisher, subject to all proper deductions, if any, for taxes, advances or amounts due to BMI from Publisher.

SEVENTH:

A. Nothing in this agreement requires BMI to continue to license the Works subsequent to the termination of this agreement. In the event that BMI continues to license Publisher's interest in any Work, however, BMI shall continue to make payments to Publisher for such Work for so long as Publisher does not make or purport to make directly or indirectly any grant of performing rights in such Work to any other licensing organization. The amounts of such payments shall be calculated pursuant to BMI's then current standard practices upon the basis of the then current performance rates generally paid by BMI to its affiliated publishers for similar performances of similar compositions. Publisher agrees to notify BMI by registered or certified mail of any grant or purported grant by Publisher directly or indirectly of performing rights to any other performing rights organization within ten (10) days from the making of such grant or purported grant and if Publisher fails so to inform BMI thereof and BMI makes payments to Publisher for any period after the making of any such grant or purported grant, Publisher agrees to repay to BMI all amounts so paid by BMI promptly with or without demand by BMI. In addition, if BMI inquires of Publisher by registered or certified mail, addressed to Publisher's last known address, whether Publisher has made any such grant or purported grant and Publisher fails to confirm to BMI by registered or certified mail within thirty (30) days of the mailing of such inquiry that Publisher has not made any such grant or purported grant, BMI may, from and after such date, discontinue making any payments to Publisher.

B. BMI's obligation to continue payment to Publisher after the termination of this agreement for performances outside of the United States, its territories and possessions, of Works which BMI continues to license after such termination shall be dependent upon BMI's receipt in the United States of payments designated by foreign performing rights licensing organizations as the publisher's share of foreign performance royalties earned by the Works. Payment of such foreign royalties shall be subject to deduction of BMI's then current handling charge applicable to its affiliated publishers and shall be in accordance with BMI's then standard practices of payment for such performances.

C. In the event that BMI has reason to believe that Publisher will receive, or is entitled to receive, or is receiving payment from a performing rights licensing organization other than BMI for or based on United States performances of one or more of the Works during a period when such Works were licensed by BMI pursuant to this agreement, BMI shall have the right to withhold payment for such performances from Publisher until receipt of evidence satisfactory to BMI that Publisher was not or will not be so paid by such other organization. In the event that Publisher was or will be so paid or does not supply such evidence within eighteen (18) months from the date of BMI's request therefor, BMI shall be under no obligation to make any payment to Publisher for performances of such Works during such period.

EIGHTH: In the event that this agreement shall terminate at a time when, after crediting all earnings reflected by statements rendered to Publisher prior to the effective date of such termination, there remains an unearned balance of advances paid to Publisher by BMI, such termination shall not be effective until the close of the calendar quarterly period during which (A) Publisher shall repay such unearned balance of advances, or (B) Publisher shall notify BMI by registered or certified mail that Publisher has received a statement rendered by BMI at its normal accounting time showing that such unearned balance of advances has been fully recouped by BMI.

NINTH:

A. BMI shall have the right, upon written notice to Publisher, to exclude from this agreement, at any time, any Work which in BMI's opinion is similar to a previously existing composition and might constitute a copyright infringement, or has a title or music or lyric similar to that of a previously existing composition and might lead to a claim of unfair competition.

B. In the case of Works which in the opinion of BMI are based on compositions in the public domain, BMI shall have the right, at any time, upon written notice to Publisher, either (1) to exclude any such Work from this agreement, or (2) to classify any such Work as entitled to receive only a stated fraction of the full credit that would otherwise be given for performances thereof.

C. In the event that any Work is excluded from this agreement pursuant to subparagraph A or B of this paragraph NINTH, or pursuant to subparagraph C of paragraph TWELFTH hereof, all rights of BMI in such Work shall automatically revert to Publisher ten (10) days after the date of the notice of such exclusion sent by BMI to Publisher. In the event that a Work is classified for less than full credit under subparagraph B(2) of this paragraph NINTH, Publisher shall have the right, by giving notice to BMI within ten (10) days after the date of BMI's notice to Publisher of the credit allocated to such Work, to terminate all rights in such Work granted to BMI herein and all such rights of BMI in such Work shall thereupon revert to Publisher.

TENTH:

A. With respect to each of the Works which has been or shall be published or recorded commercially or synchronized with motion picture or television film or tape or which Publisher considers likely to be performed, Publisher agrees to furnish to BMI:

(1) A completed clearance form available in blank from BMI, unless a cue sheet with respect to such Work is furnished pursuant to subparagraph A(3) of this paragraph TENTH.

(2) If such Work is based on a composition in the public domain, a legible lead sheet or other written or printed copy of such Work setting forth the lyrics, if any, and music correctly metered; provided that with respect to all other Works, such copy need be furnished only if requested by BMI pursuant to subsection (h) of subparagraph D(2) of this paragraph TENTH.

(3) If such Work has been or shall be synchronized with or otherwise used in connection with motion picture or television film or tape, a cue sheet showing the title, writers, publisher and nature and duration of the use of the Work in such film or tape.

B. Publisher shall submit the material described in subparagraph A of this paragraph TENTH with respect to Works heretofore published, recorded or synchronized within ten (10) days after the execution of this agreement and with respect to any of the Works hereafter so published, recorded, synchronized or likely to be performed prior to the date of publication or release of the recording, film or tape or anticipated performance.

C. The submission of each clearance form or cue sheet shall constitute a warranty and representation by Publisher that all of the information contained thereon is true and correct and that no performing rights in any of the Works listed thereon have been granted to or reserved by others except as specifically set forth therein.

D. Publisher agrees:

(1) To secure and maintain copyright protection of the Works pursuant to the Copyright Law of the United States and pursuant to the laws of such other nations of the world where such protection is afforded; and to give BMI, upon request, prompt written notice of the date and number of copyright registration and/or renewal of each Work registered in the United States Copyright Office.

(2) At BMI's request:

(a) To register each unpublished and published Work in the United States Copyright Office pursuant to the Copyright Law of the United States.

(b) To obtain and deliver to BMI copies of: unpublished and published Works; copyright registration and/or renewal certificates issued by the United States Copyright Office; any agreements, assignments, instruments or documents of any kind by which Publisher obtained the right to publicly perform and/or the right to publish, co-publish or sub-publish any of the Works.

E. Publisher agrees to give BMI prompt notice by registered or certified mail in each instance when, pursuant to the Copyright Law of the United States, (1) the rights granted to BMI by Publisher in any Work shall revert to the writer or the writer's representative, or (2) copyright protection of any Work shall terminate.

ELEVENTH: Publisher warrants and represents that:

A. Publisher has the right to enter into this agreement; Publisher is not bound by any prior commitments which conflict with its undertakings herein; the rights granted by Publisher to BMI herein are the sole and exclusive property of Publisher and are free from all adverse encumbrances and claims; and exercise of such rights will not constitute infringement of copyright or violation of any right of, or unfair competition with, any person, firm, corporation or association.

B. Except with respect to Works in which the possession of performing rights by another person, firm, corporation or association is specifically set forth on a clearance form or cue sheet submitted to BMI pursuant to subparagraph A of paragraph TENTH hereof. Publisher has performing rights in each of the Works by virtue of written grants thereof to Publisher signed by the authors and composers or other owners of such Work.

TWELFTH:

A. Publisher agrees to defend, indemnify, save and hold BMI, its licensees, the advertisers of its licensees and their respective agents, servants and employees, free and harmless from and against any and all demands, loss, damage, suits, judgments, recoveries and costs, including counsel fees, resulting from any claim of whatever nature arising from or in connection with the exercise of any of the rights granted by Publisher in this agreement; provided, however, that the obligations of Publisher under this paragraph TWELFTH shall not apply to any matter added to, or changes made in, any Work by BMI or its licensees.

B. Upon the receipt by BMI or any of the other parties herein indemnified of any notice, demand, process, papers, writ or pleading, by which any such claim, demand, suit or proceeding is made or commenced against them, or any of them, which Publisher shall be obliged to defend hereunder. BMI shall, as soon as may be practicable, give Publisher notice thereof and deliver to Publisher such papers or true copies thereof, and BMI shall have the right to participate and direct such defense on behalf of BMI and/or its licensees by counsel of its own choice, at its own expense. Publisher agrees to cooperate with BMI in all such matters.

C. In the event of such notification of claim or service of process on any of the parties herein indemnified, BMI shall have the right, from the date thereof, to exclude the Work with respect to which a claim is made from this agreement and/or to withhold payment of all sums which may become due pursuant to this agreement or any modification thereof until receipt of satisfactory written evidence that such claim has been withdrawn, settled or adjudicated.

THIRTEENTH: Publisher makes, constitutes and appoints BMI, or its nominee, Publisher's true and lawful attorney, irrevocably during the term hereof, in the name of BMI or that of its nominee, or in Publisher's name, or otherwise, in BMI's sole judgment, to do all acts, take all proceedings, and execute, acknowledge and deliver any and all instruments, papers, documents, process or pleadings that, in BMI's sole judgment, may be necessary, proper or expedient to restrain infringement of and/or to enforce and protect the rights granted by Publisher hereunder, and to recover damages in respect of or for the infringement or other violation of said rights, and in BMI's sole judgment to join Publisher and/or others in whose names the copyrights to any of the Works may stand, and to discontinue, compromise or refer to arbitration, any such actions or proceedings or to make any other disposition of the disputes in relation to the Works; provided that any action or proceeding commenced by BMI pursuant to the provisions of this paragraph THIRTEENTH shall be at its sole expense and for its sole benefit. Notwithstanding the foregoing, nothing in this paragraph THIRTEENTH requires BMI to take any proceeding or other action against any person, firm, partnership or other entity or any writer or publisher, whether or not affiliated with BMI, who Publisher claims may be infringing Publisher's Works or otherwise violating the rights granted by Publisher hereunder. In addition, Publisher understands and agrees that the licensing by BMI of any musical compositions which Publisher claims may be infringing Publisher's Works or otherwise violating the rights granted by Publisher hereunder, shall not constitute an infringement of Publisher's Works on BMI's part.

FOURTEENTH.

A. It is acknowledged that BMI has heretofore entered into, and may during the term of this agreement enter into, contracts with performing rights licensing organizations for the licensing of public performing rights controlled by BMI in territories outside of the United States, its territories and possessions (herein called "Foreign Territories"). Upon Publisher's written request, BMI agrees to permit Publisher to grant performing rights in any or all of the Works for any Foreign Territory for which, at the time such request is received. BMI has not entered into any such contract with a performing rights licensing organization; provided, however, that any such grant of performing rights by Publisher shall terminate at such time when BMI shall have entered into such a contract with a performing rights licensing organization covering such Foreign Territory and shall have notified Publisher thereof. Nothing herein contained, however, shall be deemed to restrict Publisher from assigning to its foreign publisher or representative the right to collect a part or all of the Publishers' performance royalties earned by any or all of the Works in any Foreign Territory as part of an agreement for the publication, exploitation or representation of such Works in such territory, whether or not BMI has entered into such a contract with a performing rights licensing organization covering such territory.

B. Publisher agrees to notify BMI promptly in writing in each instance when publication, exploitation or other rights in any or all of the Works are granted for any Foreign Territory. Such notice shall set forth the title of the Work, the Foreign Territory or Territories involved, the period of such grant, the name of the person, firm, corporation or association entitled to collect performance royalties earned in the Foreign Territory and the amount of such share. Within ten (10) days after the execution of this agreement Publisher agrees to submit to BMI, in writing, a list of all Works as to which Publisher has, prior to the effective date of this agreement, granted to any person, firm, corporation or association performing rights and/or the right to collect publisher performance royalties earned in any Foreign Territory.

FIFTEENTH: BMI shall have the right, in its sole discretion, to terminate this agreement if:

A. Publisher, its agents, employees, representatives or affiliated companies, directly or indirectly during the term of this agreement:

(1) Solicits or accepts payment from or on behalf of authors for composing music for lyrics, or from or on behalf of composers for writing lyrics to music.

(2) Solicits or accepts music and/or lyrics from composers or authors in consideration of any payments to be made by or on behalf of such composers or authors for reviewing, arranging, promotion, publication, recording or any other services connected with the exploitation of any composition.

(3) Permits Publisher's name, or the fact of its affiliation with BMI, to be used by any other person, firm, corporation or association engaged in any of the practices described in subparagraphs A(1) and A(2) of this paragraph FIFTEENTH.

(4) Submits to BMI, as one of the Works to come within this agreement, any musical composition with respect to which any payments described in subparagraphs A(1) and A(2) of this paragraph FIFTEENTH have been made by or on behalf of a composer or author to any person, firm, corporation or association.

B. Publisher, its agents, employees or representatives directly or indirectly during the term of this agreement makes any effort to ascertain from, or offers any inducement or consideration to, anyone, including but not limited to any radio or television licensee of BMI or to the agents, employees or representatives of BMI or of any such licensee, for information regarding the time or times when any such BMI licensee is to report its performances to BMI, or to attempt in any way to manipulate performances or affect the representative character or accuracy of BMI's system of sampling or logging performances.

C. Publisher fails to notify BMI's Department of Writer/Publisher Administration promptly in writing of any change of firm name, ownership or address of Publisher.

In the event BMI exercises its right to terminate this agreement pursuant to the provisions of subparagraphs A, B or C of this paragraph FIFTEENTH, BMI shall give Publisher at least thirty (30) days' notice by registered or certified mail of such termination. In the event of such termination, no payments shall be due to Publisher pursuant to paragraph SEVENTH hereof.

SIXTEENTH: In the event that during the term of this agreement (1) monies shall not have been earned by Publisher pursuant to paragraph FIFTH hereof for a period of two consecutive years or more, or (2) the proprietor, if Publisher is a sole proprietorship, shall die, BMI shall have the right to terminate this agreement on at least thirty (30) days' notice by registered or certified mail addressed to the last address furnished by Publisher in writing to BMI's Department of Writer/Publisher Administration and, in the case of the death of a sole proprietor, to the representative of said proprietor's estate, if known to BMI. In the event of such termination, no payments shall be due Publisher pursuant to paragraph SEVENTH hereof.

SEVENTEENTH: Publisher acknowledges that the rights obtained by it pursuant to this agreement constitute rights to payment of money and that during the term BMI shall hold title to the performing rights granted to BMI hereunder. In the event that during the term Publisher shall file a petition in bankruptcy, such a petition shall be filed against Publisher, Publisher shall make an assignment for the benefit of creditors, Publisher shall consent to the appointment of a receiver or trustee for all or part of its property, Publisher shall file a petition for corporate reorganization or arrangement under the United States bankruptcy laws, or Publisher shall institute or shall have instituted against it any other insolvency proceeding under the United States bankruptcy laws or any other applicable law, or, in the event Publisher is a partnership, all of the general partners of said partnership shall be adjudged bankrupts, BMI shall retain title to the performing rights in all Works the rights to which are granted to BMI hereunder and shall subrogate Publisher's trustee in bankruptcy or receiver and any subsequent purchasers from them to Publisher's right to payment of money for said Works in accordance with the terms and conditions of this agreement.

EIGHTEENTH: All disputes of any kind, nature or description arising in connection with the terms and conditions of this agreement shall be submitted to the American Arbitration Association in New York, New York, for arbitration under its then prevailing rules, the arbitrator(s) to be selected as follows:

Each of the parties shall, by written notice to the other, have the right to appoint one arbitrator. If, within ten (10) days following the giving of such notice by one party, the other shall not, by written notice, appoint another arbitrator, the first arbitrator shall be the sole arbitrator. If two arbitrators are so appointed, they shall appoint a third arbitrator. If ten (10) days elapse after the appointment of the second arbitrator and the two arbitrators are unable to agree upon the third arbitrator, then either party may, in writing, request the American Arbitration Association to appoint the third arbitrator. The award made in the arbitration shall be binding and conclusive on the parties and shall include the fixing of the costs, expenses and reasonable attorneys' fees of arbitration, which shall be borne by the unsuccessful party. Judgement may be entered in New York State Supreme Court or any other court having jurisdiction.

NINETEENTH: Publisher agrees that it shall not, without the written consent of BMI, assign any of its rights hereunder. No rights of any kind against BMI will be acquired by the assignee if any such purported assignment is made by Publisher without such written consent.

TWENTIETH: Any notice sent to Publisher pursuant to the terms of this agreement shall be valid if addressed to Publisher at the last address furnished in writing by Publisher to BMI's Department of Writer/Publisher Administration.

TWENTY-FIRST: This agreement constitutes the entire agreement between BMI and Publisher, cannot be changed except in a writing signed by BMI and Publisher and shall be governed and construed pursuant to the laws of the State of New York.

TWENTY-SECOND: In the event that any part or parts of this agreement are found to be void by a court of competent jurisdiction, the remaining part or parts shall nevertheless be binding with the same force and effect as if the void part or parts were deleted from this agreement.

IN WITNESS WHEREOF, the parties hereto have caused this agreement to be duly executed as of the day and year first above written.

BROADCAST MUSIC, INC.

By.................................................................................
                                   Vice President

...................................................................................

By.................................................................................
                            (Title of Signer).....................................

# FORM 17.3

## ASCAP MEMBERSHIP AGREEMENT

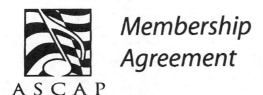

## Membership
## Agreement

### ASCAP

**AGREEMENT BETWEEN**

_____

AND
AMERICAN SOCIETY OF COMPOSERS, AUTHORS & PUBLISHERS

ONE LINCOLN PLAZA  NEW YORK, NY 10023
PHONE (212) 621-6000

# ASCAP Membership Agreement

**Agreement** made between the Undersigned (for brevity called "Owner") and the AMERICAN SOCIETY OF COMPOSERS, AUTHORS AND PUBLISHERS (for brevity called "Society"), in consideration of the premises and of the mutual covenants hereinafter contained, as follows:

1. The Owner grants to the Society for the term hereof, the right to license non-dramatic public performances (as hereinafter defined), of each musical work:

Of which the Owner is a copyright proprietor; or

Which the Owner, alone, or jointly, or in collaboration with others, wrote, composed, published, acquired or owned; or

In which the Owner now has any right, title, interest or control whatsoever, in whole or in part; or

Which hereafter, during the term hereof, may be written, composed, acquired, owned, published or copyrighted by the Owner, alone, jointly or in collaboration with others; or

In which the Owner may hereafter, during the term hereof, have any right, title, interest or control, whatsoever, in whole or in part

The right to license the public performance of every such musical work shall be deemed granted to the Society by this instrument for the term hereof, immediately upon the work being written, composed, acquired, owned, published or copyrighted

The rights hereby granted shall include

(a) All the rights and remedies for enforcing the copyright or copyrights of such musical works, whether such copyrights are in the name of the Owner and/or others, as well as the right to sue under such copyrights in the name of the Society and/or in the name of the Owner and/or others, to the end that the Society may effectively protect and be assured of all the rights hereby granted.

(b) The non-exclusive right of public performance of the separate numbers, songs, fragments or arrangements, melodies or selections forming part or parts of musical plays and dramatico-musical compositions, the Owner reserving and excepting from this grant the right of performance of musical plays and dramatico-musical compositions in their entirety, or any part of such plays or dramatico-musical compositions on the legitimate stage.

(c) The non-exclusive right of public performance by means of radio broadcasting, telephony, "wired wireless," all forms of synchronism with motion pictures, and/or any method of transmitting sound other than television broadcasting

(d) The non-exclusive right of public performance by television broadcasting; provided, however, that

(i) This grant does not extend to or include the right to license the public performance by television broadcasting or otherwise of any rendition or performance of (a) any opera, operetta, musical comedy, play or like production, as such, in whole or in part, or (b) any composition from any opera, operetta, musical comedy, play or like production (whether or not such opera, operetta, musical comedy, play or like production was presented on the stage or in motion picture form) in a manner which recreates the performance of such composition with substantially such distinctive scenery or costume as was used in the presentation of such opera, operetta, musical comedy, play or like production (whether or not such opera, operetta, musical comedy, play or like production was presented on the stage or in motion picture form) provided, how-

ever, that the rights hereby granted shall be deemed to include a grant of the right to license non-dramatic performances of compositions by television broadcasting of a motion picture containing such composition if the rights in such motion picture other than those granted hereby have been obtained from the parties in interest

(ii) Nothing herein contained shall be deemed to grant the right to license the public performance by television broadcasting of dramatic performances. Any performance of a separate musical composition which is not a dramatic performance, as defined herein, shall be deemed to be a non-dramatic performance. For the purposes of this agreement, a dramatic performance shall mean a performance of a musical composition on a television program in which there is a definite plot depicted by action and where the performance of the musical composition is woven into and carries forward the plot and its accompanying action. The use of dialogue to establish a mere program format or the use of any non-dramatic device merely to introduce a performance of a composition shall not be deemed to make such performances dramatic.

(iii) The definition of the terms "dramatic" and "non-dramatic" performances contained herein are purely for the purposes of this agreement and for the term thereof and shall not be binding upon or prejudicial to any position taken by either of us subsequent to the term hereof or for any purpose other than this agreement

(e) The Owner may at any time and from time to time, in good faith, restrict the radio or television broadcasting of compositions from musical comedies, operas, operettas and motion pictures, or any other composition being excessively broadcast, only for the purpose of preventing harmful effect upon such musical comedies, operas, operettas, motion pictures or compositions, in respect of other interest under the copyrights thereof; provided, however, that the right to grant limited licenses will be given, upon application, as to restricted compositions, if and when the Owner is unable to show reasonable hazards to his or its major interests likely to result from such radio or television broadcasting; and provided further that such right to restrict any such composition shall not be exercised for the purpose of permitting the fixing or regulating of fees for the recording or transcribing of such composition, and provided further that in no case shall any charges, "free plugs," or other consideration be required in respect of any permission granted to perform a restricted composition; and provided further that in no event shall any composition, after the initial radio or television broadcast thereof, be restricted for the purpose of confining further radio or television broadcasts thereof to a particular artist, station, network or program. The Owner may also at anytime and from time to time, in good faith, restrict the radio or television broadcasting of any composition, as to which any suit has been brought or threatened on a claim that such composition infringes a composition not contained in the repertory of Society or on a claim by a non-member of Society that Society does not have the right to license the public performance of such composition by radio or television broadcasting

2. The term of this Agreement shall be for a period commencing on the date hereof and continuing indefinitely thereafter unless terminated by either party in accordance with the Articles of Association.

3. The Society agrees, during the term hereof, in good faith to use its best endeavors to promote and carry out the objects for which it was organized, and to hold and apply all royalties, profits, benefits and advantages arising from the exploitation of the rights assigned to it by its several members, including the Owner, to the uses and purposes as

provided in its Articles of Association (which are hereby incorporated by reference), as now in force or as hereafter amended.

1. The *Owner* hereby irrevocably, during the term hereof, authorizes, empowers and vests in the *Society* the right to enforce and protect such rights of public performance under any and all copyrights, whether standing in the name of the *Owner* and/or others, in any and all works copyrighted by the *Owner*, and/or by others, to prevent the infringement thereof, to litigate, collect and receipt for damages arising from infringement, and in its sole judgment to join the *Owner* and/or others in whose names the copyright may stand, as parties plaintiff or defendants in suits or proceedings; to bring suit in the name of the *Owner* and/or in the name of the *Society*, or others in whose name the copyright may stand, or otherwise, and to release, compromise, or refer to arbitration any actions, in the same manner and to the same extent and to all intents and purposes as the *Owner* might or could do, had this instrument not been made.

5. The *Owner* hereby makes, constitutes and appoints the *Society*, or its successor, the *Owner's* true and lawful attorney, irrevocably during the term hereof, and in the name of the *Society* or its successor, or in the name of the *Owner*, or otherwise, to do all acts, take all proceedings, execute, acknowledge and deliver any and all instruments, papers, documents, process and pleadings that may be necessary, proper or expedient to restrain infringements and recover damages in respect to or for the infringement or other violation of the rights of public performance in such works, and to discontinue, compromise or refer to arbitration any such proceedings or actions, or to make any other disposition of the differences in relation to the premises.

6. The *Owner* agrees from time to time, to execute, acknowledge and deliver to the *Society*, such assurances, powers of attorney or other authorizations or instruments as the *Society* may deem necessary or expedient to enable it to exercise, enjoy and enforce, in its own name or otherwise, all rights and remedies aforesaid.

7. It is mutually agreed that during the term hereof the Board of Directors of the *Society* shall be composed of an equal number of writers and publishers respectively, and that the royalties distributed by the Board of Directors shall be divided into two (2) equal sums, and one (1) each of such sums credited respectively to and for division amongst (a) the writer members, and (b) the publisher members, in accordance with the system of apportionment and distribution of royalties as determined by the Board of Directors in accordance with the Articles of Association as they may be amended from time to time.

8. The *Owner* agrees that the apportionment and distribution of royalties by the *Society* as determined from time to time by the Board of Directors of the *Society*, in case of appeal by him, shall be final, conclusive and binding upon him.

The *Society* shall have the right to transfer the right of review of any apportionment and distribution of royalties from the Board of Directors to any other agency or instrumentality that in its discretion and good judgment it deems best adapted to assuring to the *Society's* membership a just, fair, equitable and accurate apportionment and distribution of royalties.

The *Society* shall have the right to adopt from time to time such systems, means, methods and formulae for the establishment of a member's apportionment and distribution of royalties as will assure a fair, just and equitable distribution of royalties among the membership.

9. **"Public Performance" Defined.** The term *"public performance"* shall be construed to mean vocal, instrumental and/or mechanical renditions and representations in any manner or by any method whatsoever, including transmissions by radio and television broadcasting stations, transmission by telephony and/or "wired wireless", and/or reproductions of performances and renditions by means of devices for reproducing sound recorded in synchronism or timed relation with the taking of motion pictures.

10. **"Musical Works" Defined.** The phrase *"musical works"* shall be construed to mean musical compositions and dramatico-musical compositions, the words and music thereof, and the respective arrangements thereof, and the selections therefrom.

11. The powers, rights, authorities and privileges by this instrument vested in the *Society*, are deemed to include the World, provided, however, that such grant of rights for foreign countries shall be subject to any agreements now in effect, a list of which are noted on the reverse side hereof.

12. The grant made herein by the owner is modified by and subject to the provisions of (a) the Amended Final Judgment (Civil Action No. 13-95) dated March 14, 1950 in *U.S.A. v. ASCAP* as further amended by Order dated January 7, 1960, (b) the Final Judgment (Civil Action No. 42-245) in *U.S.A. v. ASCAP*, dated March 14, 1950, and (c) the provisions of the Articles of Association and resolutions of the Board of Directors adopted pursuant to such judgments and order.

SIGNED, SEALED AND DELIVERED, on this ___ day ___ of ___ month ___ year ___

Owner { Sign your name here

Society { AMERICAN SOCIETY OF COMPOSERS, AUTHORS AND PUBLISHERS,

By ___

President and Chairman of the Board

## ASCAP Membership Agreement

**FOREIGN AGREEMENTS AT THIS DATE IN EFFECT**
(See paragraph 11 of within agreement)

| COUNTRY | WITH (Name of Firm) | EXPIRES | REMARKS |
|---------|---------------------|---------|---------|
|  |  |  |  |
|  |  |  |  |
|  |  |  |  |
|  |  |  |  |
|  |  |  |  |
|  |  |  |  |
|  |  |  |  |
|  |  |  |  |
|  |  |  |  |
|  |  |  |  |
|  |  |  |  |
|  |  |  |  |
|  |  |  |  |
|  |  |  |  |
|  |  |  |  |
|  |  |  |  |
|  |  |  |  |
|  |  |  |  |
|  |  |  |  |
|  |  |  |  |
|  |  |  |  |
|  |  |  |  |
|  |  |  |  |
|  |  |  |  |
|  |  |  |  |
|  |  |  |  |
|  |  |  |  |
|  |  |  |  |
|  |  |  |  |
|  |  |  |  |
|  |  |  |  |
|  |  |  |  |

# FORM 17.4

## BMI MUSIC LICENSE FOR EATING AND DRINKING ESTABLISHMENTS

Music License For
## Eating & Drinking Establishments

LI-00/10-EDE-1

## With a BMI Music License You Get a Seal of Compliance & Access to More than 4.5 Million Musical Works!

Terms and Conditions of Agreement
(For Definitions, see Paragraph 10

**1. BMI GRANT**
BMI grants you a non-exclusive license to publicly perform at the Licensed Premises all of the musical works of which BMI controls the rights to grant public performance licenses during the Term. This license does not include dramatic rights, the right to perform dramatico-musical works in whole or in substantial part or the right to use the musical works in any context which constitutes the exercise of "grand rights." This license also does not convey the right to publicly perform BMI musical works (a) by broadcast, telecast, cablecast or other electronic transmission (including by satellite, the Internet or on-line service) of the performances to persons outside the Licensed Premises; (b) by public performances requiring advance or hard ticket purchases pursuant to Paragraph 10(g); (c) by means of any coin-operated phonorecord player as defined in the Copyright Act ("Jukebox") where a Jukebox License Office agreement has been obtained for such Jukebox; (d) by any BMI-licensed background music service, and (e) by any coin-operated digital music service that does not qualify as a Jukebox. BMI may withdraw from the works licensed hereunder any musical work as to which any legal action has been instituted or claim made that BMI does not have the right to license public performances of that work.

**2. CHANGES TO YOUR MUSIC POLICY**
(a) Except as provided for herein, you may change your Music Policy upon which fees are assessed under this Agreement prospectively at any time during the Term on 30 days prior notice to BMI, provided that your current policy has been in effect for at least 30 consecutive calendar days. You may change your fee no more than three times in any contract year. You may call your Customer Relations Executive at 1-800-925-8451 to notify BMI of a change in your Music Policy, and the change will be reflected in your next billing by BMI; however, doing so will not preserve your right to dispute BMI billings unless you send BMI timely notice of your policy change in writing. Billings adjusted by BMI hereunder will include a pro rata credit for any unearned license fees paid in advance under the changed policy. You also agree that you will notify BMI of any changes in the music use at the Licensed Premises that would make your representation of Music Policy under Paragraph 11(a) no longer accurate, and that any changes you make to your Music Policy hereunder shall constitute a true and accurate representation of your music usage from the date of the change onward. Any changes in Music Policy or Occupancy are subject to verification by any and all reasonable means which may include, but shall not be limited to, independent contacts by BMI representatives with your business establishment, use of public records, advertisements and third party observations.

(b) BMI may from time to time review your Music Policy (including any changes made to your policy) and make inquiries in person or by phone as to its accuracy. If BMI thereafter believes that you are not paying proper license fees because the use of music at the Licensed Premises should result in higher license fees under the criteria of this Agreement than is reflected in your current Music Policy, BMI will notify you by mail. If you agree to BMI s assessment of your Music Policy, the change will be reflected on your next billing. If you dispute BMI s assessment of your policy, you must notify BMI within 30 days of the notification by BMI. If within 90 days of such notification by BMI you do not respond or you and BMI cannot agree upon an appropriate fee, either party may commence an arbitration proceeding pursuant to Paragraph 7 to resolve the dispute over the amount of your license fees. Such right shall be in addition to any and all other remedies BMI may have under the Agreement, including the right to cancel this Agreement. You may not change your Music Policy under subparagraph (a) above if your fee is subject to dispute hereunder.

(c) In the event that you temporarily discontinue the use of all music (see Definitions) and you send written notice of this to BMI by certified mail within 30 days of the discontinuance, BMI will adjust your fees pro rata from the date of discontinuance. If such notice is received more than 30 days after the discontinuance, such discontinuance will be effective commencing on the first of the month following the date of BMI s receipt of the notice and BMI will adjust your fees prospectively for the remainder of the contract year in which BMI received the notice. In either event, your credit adjustment hereunder shall not reduce your Annual Fee due BMI below the Annual Minimum Fee applicable under the Agreement. In the event of such discontinuance, this license Agreement shall continue in effect, except that no minimum or other fee shall be payable during the period of discontinuance. You agree to notify BMI promptly when you resume the use of music at the Licensed Premises and your Music Policy in effect at the time of discontinuance will continue to be applicable until you notify BMI of a change. BMI reserves its right under subparagraph (b) hereof to review your Music Policy and take appropriate steps in the event that BMI believes that you have resumed the use of music under this Agreement.

**3. LATE PAYMENT AND SERVICE CHARGES**
BMI shall impose a late payment charge of one and one-half percent (1½%) per month or the maximum rate permitted by law, whichever is less, from the date payment is due on any payment that is received by BMI more than thirty (30) days after the due date. BMI shall impose a $25.00 service charge for each unpaid check, draft or other means of payment you submit to BMI.

**4. BMI COMMITMENT TO CUSTOMER / INDEMNITY**
So long as you are not in default or arrears in payment under this Agreement, BMI agrees to indemnify, save harmless and defend you, your officers and employees, from and against any and all claims, demands or suits alleging copyright infringement that may be made or brought against them or any of them with respect to the public performance of any musical works which are licensed by BMI under this Agreement at the time of public performance. You agree to give

BMI immediate notice of any such claim, demand or suit, to deliver to BMI any papers pertaining hereto, and to cooperate with BMI with respect thereto, and BMI shall have full charge of the defense of any such claim, demand or suit.

**5. SALE OF LICENSED PREMISES OR CLOSING OF BUSINESS**
In the event that you sell the Licensed Premises or close the business during the Term of this Agreement and you send BMI written notice by certified mail within 30 days of the sale or closing, BMI will adjust your fees *pro rata* from the date of sale or closing, and will refund to you any unearned licensed fees paid hereunder. Your credit adjustment hereunder shall not reduce your Annual Fee due BMI below the Annual Minimum Fee applicable under the Agreement.

**6. BREACH OR DEFAULT / WAIVER**
Upon any breach or default of the terms and conditions of this Agreement, BMI has the right to cancel this Agreement. The right to cancel is in addition to any and all other remedies which BMI may have.

**7. ARBITRATION**
All disputes of any kind, nature or description arising in connection with the terms and conditions of this Agreement, except for matters within the jurisdiction of the BMI Rate Court, shall be submitted to the American Arbitration Association in the City, County and State of New York, for arbitration under its then prevailing arbitration rules. The arbitrator(s) shall be selected as follows: Each of the parties shall, by written notice to the other, have the right to appoint one arbitrator. If, within ten (10) days following the giving of such notice by one party the other shall not, by written notice, appoint another arbitrator, the first arbitrator shall be the sole arbitrator. If two arbitrators are so appointed, they shall appoint a third arbitrator. If ten (10) days elapse after the appointment of the second arbitrator and the two arbitrators are unable to agree upon a third arbitrator, then either party may, in writing, request the American Arbitration Association to appoint the third arbitrator. The award made in the arbitration shall be binding and conclusive on the parties and judgment may be, but need not be, entered in any court having jurisdiction. Such award shall include the fixing of the costs, expenses and attorneys' fees of arbitration, which shall be borne by the unsuccessful party.

**8. NOTICES**
Unless otherwise stated herein, any notice under this Agreement will be in writing and deemed given upon mailing when sent by ordinary first-class U.S. mail to the party intended, at its mailing address as stated, or any other address which either party may designate. Any such notice sent to BMI shall be to the attention of the Vice President, General Licensing, BMI, 10 Music Square East, Nashville, Tennessee, 37203. Any such notice sent to you shall be to the attention of the person signing this Agreement on your behalf or such other person as you may advise BMI in writing.

**9. MISCELLANEOUS**
This Agreement is the entire understanding between the parties, will not be binding until signed by both parties, and cannot be waived or added to or modified orally, and no waiver, addition or modification will be valid unless in writing and signed by the parties. This Agreement is executed by the duly authorized representative of BMI and you. Your rights are not assignable. This Agreement, its validity, construction and effect, will be governed by the laws of the State of New York other than its choice of law provisions. The fact that any provisions are found by a court of competent jurisdiction to be void or unenforceable will not affect the validity or enforceability of any other provisions. All headings in this Agreement are for the purpose of convenience and shall not be considered to be part of this Agreement.

**10. DEFINITIONS**
(a) Licensed Premises: The eating or drinking establishment listed on back or on an attached exhibit;
(b) Music Policy: Any single or combined use of the items defined in 10(c) - (j) below and including Jukebox Fee (Box 7) by you at the Licensed Premises during a contract year.

*Refer to Boxes 1-6 in the Fee Calculation.*
(c) Live Music-Multiple Singers / Instrumentalists: Music performed by more than one musician, singer or other entertainer actually present and performing at the Licensed Premises. ( Box 1)
(d) Live Music-Single Singer / Instrumentalist: Music performed by one musician, singer or other entertainer actually present and performing at the Licensed Premises. ( Box 1)
(e) Recorded Music: The performance of music by mechanical or electronic devices, which include, but are not limited to, compact discs (CDs), tapes, records and free-play jukeboxes. ( Box 2)
(f) Enhanced Recorded Music: Use of video tapes, DVDs and other projected visual images as an accompaniment/enhancement to recorded music performances (Karaoke). Enhanced Recorded Music does not include performances delivered by commercial broadcast, cablecast or satellite delivered television programming. (Box 2)
(g) Admission Charge / Cover Charge: Payment including, but not limited to, minimum required purchases to enter or remain in certain parts of the Licensed Premises, excluding advance or hard ticket purchases sold through an outside independent ticket service (for which BMI may require a separate Music Performance Agreement). (Box 3)
(h) Dancing: Allowing patrons, performers or employees to dance, at any time, to live or recorded music anywhere on the Licensed Premises, whether or not a dance floor, dance stage or an area purposely used for dancing is provided. (Box 4)
(i) Television and / or Radio Only: Television and/or radios that are utilized solely for the reception of commercial broadcast, cablecast or satellite programming and only when no Recorded Music or Enhanced Recorded Music as defined in 10(e) and 10(f) above is performed and paid for under this Agreement. (Box 5)
(j) Occupancy: The maximum allowable occupancy for the total premises of the Licensed Premises under local fire codes or similar regulations, which shall not be limited to the number of available seats. If no such regulations are in effect, then maximum occupancy shall mean one (1) person for every twenty (20) square feet of such total premises. (Box 6)
(k) Seasonal / Occasional Use: The total aggregate use of music described herein at 10(c) - (j) in an establishment open less than twelve (12) months in any one year, or total aggregate music use as described herein, which occurs four (4) times or less in any one year will require that you contact BMI for their Seasonal/Occasional Use Fee Calculation license.
(l) Chain Operation: Seven (7) or more licensable locations, that are commonly owned and operated by you, and that books, records and accounts for each are centrally maintained by you, will require that you contact BMI for its Chain Restaurant License.

**11 FEES**
(a) You agree to pay to BMI an Annual Fee as determined by your Music Policy.
   (i) The Annual Fee payment for the initial contract year is due in full upon signing of this Agreement. The Annual Fee payment for subsequent contract years shall be due no later than 30 days after the anniversary date of this Agreement.
   (ii) BMI shall discount the Annual Fee by 10% in any contract year if (A) you pay the Annual Fee in full and in a timely manner for such contract year in accordance with subparagraph (i) above; and (B) you do not otherwise owe BMI any fees under this or any prior BMI agreement.
   (iii) Upon request, BMI will allow you to pay the Annual Fee on a semi-annual or quarterly basis, provided that your account is current. Semi-annual and quarterly payments are due no later than 30 days following each semi-annual or quarterly period. The discount provided for in subparagraph (ii) shall not be available if the Annual Fee is paid on a semi-annual or quarterly basis.
   (iv) Notwithstanding subparagraph (iii), if any semi-annual or quarterly payment is not received by the 90th day after such payment is due, your ability to make semi-annual or quarterly payments shall immediately terminate for the remainder of this Agreement. In addition, the unpaid portion of the Annual Fee will be immediately due and payable.
(b) Your fee is adjusted each year by an adjustment to the Rate Per Year Per Occupant as defined in the Fee Calculation chart. The Rate Per Year Per Occupant adjustment for each contract year after 2001 shall be an adjustment of the 2001 rate based upon the percentage increase or decrease in the United States Consumer Price Index (Urban, All Items) between October 2000 and October of the year prior to that contract year, rounded to the nearest five cents. BMI will advise you in writing of this adjustment as part of its annual billing process.

**FEE CALCULATION**

Check off the corresponding Rate Per Year Per Occupant for the ways music is used in your establishment.
Enter the amount(s) on the appropriate line(s) to the right.

| Music Type | Frequency Per Week | Rate Per Year Per Occupant ☑ | Fee Calculation |
|---|---|---|---|

**1.   Live Music**
Check off the Rate Per Year Per Occupant box for the appropriate ways live music is used in your establishment.  Enter the highest amount checked on the line to the right.

| | | | |
|---|---|---|---|
| Multiple Singers/Instrumentalists | 5-7 nights | $4.20 ❏ | |
| ( 1 night = no more than 5 times in any one month) | 2-4 nights | $3.50 ❏ | |
| | 1 night or less | $3.20 ❏ | |
| Single Singer/Instrumentalist | 5-7 nights | $3.10 ❏ | |
| ( 1 night = no more than 5 times in any one month) | 2-4 nights | $2.55 ❏ | |
| | 1 night or less | $2.30 ❏ | $_____ |

Enter the highest amount checked above here.

**2.   Recorded Music**
Check off the Rate Per Year Per Occupant box for the appropriate ways recorded music is used in your establishment. Enter the corresponding amount checked on the line to the right.

❏ CDs, ❏ tapes, ❏ records, ❏ free-play jukebox, ❏ DJ s, ❏ VJ s          $2.05  ❏          $_____

Enhanced Recorded Music *(must also check Recorded Music above)*
In addition, if you have any of the Enhanced Recorded Music uses below, check off the appropriate Rate Per Year Per Occupant box and enter the amount on the line to the right.

| | | | |
|---|---|---|---|
| ❏ Karaoke, ❏ video tapes, ❏ DVDs | 5-7 nights | $0.50 ❏ | |
| | 2-4 nights | $0.35 ❏ | |
| (1 night = no more than 5 times in any one month) | 1 night or less | $0.25 ❏ | $_____ |

**3.   Admission or Cover Charge** *(for partial or entire premises)*
Check if there is an admission or cover charged at any time
and enter the corresponding Rate Per Year Per Occupant.                    $1.30  ❏          $_____
(Does not include advance or hard ticket purchases sold through an outside ticket service.)

**4.   Dancing to Live or Recorded Music**
(Must also check appropriate item(s) in Box 1 or 2 above.)
Check if Dancing is permitted at any time                                   $1.30  ❏          $_____
and enter the corresponding Rate Per Year Per Occupant.

**5.   Television and/or Radio**
If you use TV and/or Radio, check here and enter the corresponding Rate Per
Year Per Occupant, unless you are either exempt under U.S. copyright law        $0.95  ❏          $_____
or have checked off 1 or more items under Box 2, Recorded Music, above.

**Total Rate Per Year Per Occupant**          $_____
(Sum of Boxes 1 - 5)

**6.   Occupancy** _____ X Total Rate Per Year Per Occupant _____ = Annual Fee          $_____
(If greater than 1,000 occupants, enter 1,000.) **(See definition, Paragraph 10(j))**
OR                                                                          **OR**
(If Occupancy is not established by local fire authority, use formula below. )
Total Square Footage of entire premises _____ 20 = _____ Occupancy
Occupancy _____ X Total Rate Per Year Per Occupant _____ = Annual Fee          $_____

**ANNUAL MINIMUM FEE:**   If over $256.50 enter Annual Fee here.          $_____
If $256.50 or less, enter Annual Minimum fee of $256.50

**7.   Jukebox Fee**
(If your jukebox is licensable by the JLO (Jukebox License Office) but is not already licensed under a JLO license,
check here.  If the jukebox is already licensed under the JLO license, please enter Vendor name, address, phone no.
below.)

Jukebox Fee    $256.50  ❏          $_____

Name/Company: _____  JLO Cert. #: _____
Address: _____  Phone: _____
City: _____  State _____  Zip: _____

**ANNUAL FEE ALL USES**  $_____

If ANNUAL FEE ALL USES is greater than $ 7,695 , enter MAXIMUM FEE of $ 7,695          $_____

**IF PAYING IN FULL BY CHECK OR CREDIT CARD, PLEASE DEDUCT 10% FROM "ANNUAL FEE ALL USES" AND ENTER
IN BOX TO RIGHT. IF YOU WISH TO PAY BY CREDIT CARD, CALL YOUR BMI REPRESENTATIVE AT 1-800-925-8451**          $_____

(c) In no event shall the Annual Fee (per Box 6 of the Fee Calculation chart) due for any contract year be less than the Annual Minimum Fee (not including a Jukebox Fee, if any). The Annual Minimum Fee shall be $256.50 for 2000 (not including a Jukebox Fee, if any). Thereafter the Annual Minimum Fee shall be adjusted at the same rate as the Rate Per Year Per Occupant pursuant to subsection (b) of this Paragraph, with the exception that all increases shall be rounded to the nearest dollar.

(d) The Jukebox Fee shall also be adjusted at the same rate as the Rate Per Year Per Occupant pursuant to subsection (b) of this Paragraph, with the exception that all increases shall be rounded to the nearest dollar.

**(e) You agree that the Music Policy set forth herein is, and will continue to be, a true and accurate representation of your music use at the Licensed Premises, unless changed as provided in Changes to Your Music Policy section of this Agreement (Paragraph 2).**

**12. OKLAHOMA RATE CHANGE NOTICE**
BMI shall notify LICENSEE of any rate change thirty (30) days prior to the expiration date of the Agreement.

**13. COLORADO 72 HOUR REVIEW**
LICENSEE shall have the right to rescind the Agreement for a period of seventy-two hours after execution of the Agreement.

**14. TERM OF AGREEMENT**
The initial Term of this annual Agreement shall begin on the first day of _____ and end on the last day of _____ and this Agreement shall continue for additional periods of one (1) year each, unless canceled by either party at the end of any period, upon 30 days advance written notice sent by certified mail, return receipt requested. Each one (1) year period, including the initial Term, is a "contract year."

**AGREEMENT**

AGREEMENT, made at New York, N.Y. on (Date will be entered by BMI upon execution) _____ between BROADCAST MUSIC, INC. (hereinafter "BMI"), a State of New York corporation with its principal offices at 320 West 57th Street, New York, N.Y. 10019 and the legal or trade name described below and referred to thereafter as "you" (the "Agreement"). This Agreement includes all of the terms and conditions set forth herein.

PLEASE <u>RETURN THIS ENTIRE</u> SIGNED LICENSE AGREEMENT WITH YOUR CHECK. DO NOT DETACH FIRST PAGE.
PLEASE RETURN ENTIRE DOCUMENT TO BMI, 10 Music Square East, Nashville, TN 37203-9901

LICENSED PREMISES

ENTER LEGAL NAME _____
                    (Name of corporation, partnership, or individual owner)
         (Street Address)

         (City)      (State)      (Zip)

ENTER TRADE NAME _____
                (Doing business under the name of)
         (Telephone No.)      (Fax Number)

         (Contact Name)      (Title)

CHECK APPROPRIATE BOX AND COMPLETE

                                    MAILING ADDRESS

❏ Individual Ownership

❏ LLC   ❏ Corporation _____
                (State of incorporation)
         (Street Address)

❏ LLP   ❏ Partnership _____
                (Enter names of partners)
         (City)      (State)      (Zip)

❏ Other _____ Fed. Tax ID# _____
         (Telephone No.)      (Fax Number)

         (Contact Name)      (Title)

*Some state or national trade associations have discount agreements with BMI. Contact your association to see if you qualify for one association discount only.*

| To Be Completed by Licensee | To Be Completed by BMI |
|---|---|
| **By signing this Agreement you agree that the foregoing is a true and accurate representation of your Music Policy** | **BROADCAST MUSIC, INC.** |
| I have read and have understood all of the terms and conditions herein and my signature below is evidence of this. *(Sign Here — Please Include Payment)* | |
| _____ | _____ |
| Signature | Signature |
| _____ | _____ |
| Print Name / Title | Print Name / Title |

**FOR BMI USE ONLY**

        Account No.                           COID

®

® BMI and the Musicstand symbol are registered trademarks of Broadcast Music, Inc.

# FORM 17.5

## BMI HOTEL/MOTEL LICENSE

**Hotel / Motel**

HTL-1

LI-00/10-HTL-1

**1. BMI GRANT**

BMI grants to LICENSEE, at the Licensed Premises, a non-exclusive license to publicly perform or cause the public performance of all the musical works of which BMI controls the rights to grant public performance licenses during the Term. This license does not include:

(a) Dramatic Rights, the right to perform Dramatico-musical Works in whole or in substantial part, or the right to use the musical works in any context which constitutes the exercise of "grand rights";

(b) the right to publicly perform BMI musical works by broadcast, telecast, cablecast or other electronic transmission (including by satellite, the internet or on-line service) of the performances to persons outside the Licensed Premises;

(c) the right to perform music by means of any coin-operated phonorecord player as defined in the Copyright Act ("Jukebox") where a Jukebox License Office ("JLO") agreement may be obtained for such Jukebox, or, by any coin-operated digital music service that does not qualify as a Jukebox;

(d) the right to publicly perform music by any commercial music service;

(e) the right to perform musical works as part of industrial or trade shows, expositions, or business presentations at the Licensed Premises;

(f) the right to perform music at a premises, whether or not on the Licensed Premises (as defined below), in theme/amusement parks; or

(g) the right to perform BMI musical works contained in pay-per-view television programming.

BMI may withdraw from the works licensed hereunder any musical work as to which any legal action has been instituted or claim made that BMI does not have the right to license the public performances of that work.

**2. REVIEW OF STATEMENTS AND / OR ACCOUNTINGS**

(a) BMI shall have the right to require such reasonable data or information relating to (1) the annual expenditures for Live Music and Entertainment Costs, (2) Recorded Music at the Licensed Premises as provided by this Agreement, in addition to that furnished pursuant to Paragraph 15, as may, in BMI's discretion, be necessary in order to ascertain the Annual License Fee.

(b) BMI shall have the right, by its authorized representatives, at any time during customary business hours, to examine the books and records of account of LICENSEE to such extent as may be necessary to verify the statements made hereunder. BMI shall consider all data and information coming to its attention as a result of any such examination of books and records as completely confidential.

(c) BMI may conduct an audit pursuant to this Paragraph for a period not to exceed three calendar years preceding the year in which the audit is made. In the event such audit reveals a deficiency, then BMI may conduct an audit for the additional preceding three calendar years. In the event LICENSEE, after written notice from BMI, refuses to permit an audit, or refuses to produce the books and records of account of LICENSEE necessary to verify the statements and reports required hereunder, BMI shall not be restricted to the time limitation set forth herein. BMI shall have the right to audit for periods licensed under the previous license agreements between BMI and LICENSEE, provided, however, BMI shall be limited to three years or six years (as the case may be) for all audits under said license agreements.

(d) In the event BMI conducts an audit of LICENSEE, and such audit reveals that LICENSEE underpaid license fees to BMI to the extent of ten percent (10%) or more, then LICENSEE shall pay a late payment charge on the additional license fees due as of a result of the audit(s) only of one and one-half percent (1½%) per month, or the maximum rate permitted by law, whichever is less, from the date(s) the license fees should have been paid pursuant to this Agreement.

If such audit reveals that LICENSEE underpaid license fees to the extent of less than ten percent (10%) then LICENSEE shall pay the same late payment fee, as provided above, if payment is not made to BMI by LICENSEE within sixty (60) days after BMI demands payment of said licensee fees found due as a result of the audit(s).

**3. DISCONTINUANCE**

In the event that LICENSEE discontinues the use of all live and recorded music at the premises during the Term of this Agreement and so notifies BMI in writing, within sixty (60) days after receipt of such notice an adjustment shall be made by BMI for that partial calendar year, provided that, in the case of live music, LICENSEE has submitted a statement of Costs incurred up to the date of discontinuance. In no event, however, shall any such adjusted live music license fee be less than the lowest listed license fee on Schedule A for the year of discontinuance or any such adjusted recorded music license fee, which shall be a proration of the full year's license fee, be less than the lowest license fee on Schedule B or Schedule C, whichever is applicable to LICENSEE, for the year of discontinuance. LICENSEE shall not be obligated to make future payments to BMI thereafter for the discontinued music (provided the balance of any previously due license fee has been paid) until such time as LICENSEE shall resume the use of such music at the premises, and LICENSEE agrees to send written notice of any resumption to BMI within thirty (30) days thereof. Such resumption shall be treated in all respects as though the Term of this Agreement had commenced on the date of resumption. If LICENSEE discontinues the use of either live or recorded music, but not both, the provisions of this Agreement shall continue to be applicable to that music which continues to be used at the premises. The term "discontinuance" as used herein shall mean the total abandonment, rather than a seasonal or periodic cessation, of the use of music and entertainment. Notwithstanding such discontinuance, LICENSEE agrees to continue to furnish to BMI statements as provided in Paragraph 15 hereof unless or until this Agreement has been canceled.

**4. LATE PAYMENT AND SERVICE CHARGES**

BMI may impose a late payment charge of one and one-half percent (1½%) per month, or the maximum rate permitted by law, whichever is less, from the date payment is due on any payment that is received by BMI more than sixty (60) days after the due date. BMI may impose a $25.00 service charge for each unpaid check, draft or other means of payment LICENSEE submits to BMI. For the applicable late payment charges which may result from audits, see Paragraph 2 of this Agreement.

**5. BMI COMMITMENT TO CUSTOMER / INDEMNITY**

So long as LICENSEE is not in default or breach of this Agreement, BMI agrees to indemnify, save harmless, and defend LICENSEE and its officers, and employees, from and against any and all claims, demands, or suits that may be made or brought against them with respect to the performance of any musical works which is licensed under this Agreement at the time of performance. LICENSEE agrees to give BMI immediate notice of any such claim, demand, or suit, to deliver to BMI any papers pertaining thereto, and to cooperate with BMI with respect thereto, and BMI shall have full charge of the defense of any such claim, demand, or suit.

**6. SALE OR CESSATION OF OPERATIONS OF LICENSED PREMISES**

In the event that LICENSEE sells the Licensed Premises or close the business during the Term of this Agreement and LICENSEE sends BMI written notice by certified mail within thirty (30) days of the sale or closing and include annual reports pursuant to subparagraph 15(a) of this Agreement for the year in which the sale or closing occurred, BMI will adjust LICENSEE's fees pro rata from the date of sale or closing, and will refund to LICENSEE any unearned license fees paid hereunder. If LICENSEE does not timely notify BMI in accordance with this Paragraph prior to the end of the contract year in which the sale or closing occurred and file the outstanding annual reports, this Agreement will remain in effect for the entire year, and LICENSEE will be responsible for the entire Annual Fee due to BMI hereunder. Estimated License Fees and payments for any period in which required reports have not been filed shall be deemed final in accordance with subparagraph 15(d) of this Agreement. In no event shall the total annual license fee payable under this Agreement be less than the minimum annual fee as set forth in this Agreement.

**7. BREACH OR DEFAULT / WAIVER**

Upon any breach or default of the terms and conditions contained herein, BMI shall have the right to cancel this Agreement if such breach or default continues thirty (30) days after LICENSEE's receipt of written notice thereof. The right to cancel granted to BMI shall be in addition to any and all other remedies which BMI may have. No waiver by BMI of full performance of this Agreement in any one or more instances shall be deemed a waiver of the right to require full and complete performance of this Agreement thereafter or of the right to cancel this Agreement with the terms of this Paragraph.

**8. CANCELLATION OF ENTIRE CATEGORY**

BMI shall have the right to cancel the Agreement along with the simultaneous cancellation of the Agreements of all other licensees of the same class and category as LICENSEE, as of the end of any month during the Term, upon sixty (60) days' advance written notice.

® BMI and the Musicstand symbol are registered trademarks of Broadcast Music, Inc.

**9. ARBITRATION**

All disputes of any kind, nature, or description arising in connection with the terms and conditions of this Agreement, except for matters within the jurisdiction of the BMI Rate Court, shall be submitted to the American Arbitration Association in the City, County, and State of New York, for arbitration under its then prevailing arbitration rules. The arbitrator(s) to be selected as follows: Each of the parties shall, by written notice to the other, have the right to appoint one arbitrator. If, within ten (10) days following the giving of such notice by one party, the other shall not, by written notice, appoint another arbitrator, the first arbitrator shall be the sole arbitrator. If two arbitrators are so appointed, they shall appoint a third arbitrator. If ten (10) days elapse after the appointment of the second arbitrator and the two arbitrators are unable to agree upon a third arbitrator, then either party may, in writing, request the American Arbitration Association to appoint the third arbitrator. The award made in the arbitration shall be binding and conclusive on the parties and judgment may be, but not need be, entered in any court having jurisdiction. Such award shall include the fixing of the costs, expenses, and attorneys' fees or arbitration, which shall be borne by the unsuccessful party.

**10. NOTICES**

Any notice under this Agreement will be in writing and deemed given upon mailing when sent by ordinary first-class U.S. mail to the party intended, at its mailing address stated, or any other address which either party may designate. Any such notice sent to BMI shall be to the attention of the Vice President, General Licensing Department at 10 Music Square East, Nashville, TN 37203. Any such notice sent to LICENSEE shall be to the attention of the person signing the Agreement on LICENSEE's behalf or such person as LICENSEE may advise BMI in writing.

**11. ASSIGNMENT**

This Agreement shall ensure to the benefit of and shall be binding upon the parties hereto and their respective successors and assigns, but no assignment shall relieve the parties hereto of their respective obligations hereunder.

**12. GOVERNING LAW / MISCELLANEOUS**

This Agreement, its validity, construction and effect, will be governed by the laws of the State of New York other than its choice of law provisions. The fact that any provisions are found by a court of competent jurisdiction to be void or unenforceable will not affect the validity or enforceability of any other provisions. This Agreement constitutes the entire understanding between the parties and cannot be waived or added to or modified orally and no waiver, addition or modification shall be valid unless in writing and signed by both parties.

**13. DEFINITIONS**

(a) **Licensed Premises** shall mean the hotel or motel premises, located at the United States Business Address listed on the last page of this Agreement (and "hotel" shall be used hereafter in this Agreement to mean either hotel or motel), including all public rooms or public areas directly on the hotel premises, except that for purposes of Recorded Music performances, Licensed Premises will be limited to include only those restaurants, nightclubs, casinos and shops that are owned and/or operated by the LICENSEE and on the hotel premises.

Licensed Premises shall not include theme/amusement parks whether on the hotel premises or not.

(b) **Live Music and Entertainment Costs** (herein sometimes referred to as "Costs") shall mean all expenditures of every kind and nature (whether in money or any other form of consideration) made by LICENSEE or on LICENSEE's behalf, for all live music and entertainment in connection with LICENSEE's activities on the Licensed Premises.

(i) Such Costs shall include the agreed value of room and board and any other accommodations or services which are made available to any person or entity as part of the consideration for their rendering or presenting entertainment services in connection with LICENSEE's activities. For purposes of this Agreement, the agreed value of accommodations or services shall be deemed to be one-half of the prevailing rate charged to LICENSEE's guests for similar accommodations or services.

(ii) Such Costs shall exclude: (1) any costs by LICENSEE in connection with a production incorporating performances of Dramatico-musical Works as defined in subparagraph 13(j), including costs for rights acquisition and payments to performers and technicians, provided that the performance of all musical compositions in the production is dramatic and LICENSEE provides BMI upon request a copy of any agreements between LICENSEE and the owners of Dramatic Rights of the works in the production establishing that LICENSEE has obtained authorization for dramatic performance and (2) costs of services of a disc jockey, video jockey or other services in connection with a Discotheque or any entertainment services rendered by LICENSEE's regular employees, except to the extent that such employees shall be engaged primarily for the purposes of rendering entertainment services.

(c) **Recorded Music** shall mean the performance of music by mechanical or electronic devices, which include, but are not limited to, compact discs (CDs), tapes, records and free-play jukeboxes, and by the reception of broadcast audio transmissions on receiving apparatus and amplification thereof for public performance. Such performances may not be reproduced other than by loudspeakers located only on the Licensed Premises. Recorded music does not include performances by means of a coin-operated phonorecord player (jukebox) licensable by the JLO.

(d) **Rooms** shall mean the total number of guest rooms at the Licensed Premises.

(e) **Dancing** shall mean allowing patrons, performers or employees to dance, at any time, to live or recorded music anywhere on the Licensed Premises.

(f) **Cover, Minimum or Admission Charge** shall mean payment including, but not be limited to, minimum required purchases to enter or remain anywhere in the Licensed Premises.

(g) **Shows or Acts** shall include, but not be limited to, the use of a disc jockey, video jockey, master of ceremonies, or comedian or similar vocal commentary to patrons, or the use of special visual effects commonly associated with nightclubs, including, but not limited to, special lighting effects other than normal hotel or cocktail lounge illumination, "light shows", smoke or fog machines, or special moving visual or artistic constructs used as part of such entertainment.

(h) **Audio-visual Performances** shall mean audio-visual performances of recorded music (including, but not limited to large screen televisions, karaoke), unless exempt under 17 U.S.C. § 110(5).

(i) **Dramatic Rights** shall include, but not be limited to, performance of a "dramatico-musical work" in its entirety; performance of one or more musical compositions from a "dramatico-musical work" accompanied by dialogue, pantomime, dance, stage action, or visual representation of the work from which the music is taken; performance of one or more musical compositions as part of a story or plot, whether accompanied or unaccompanied by dialogue, pantomime, dance, stage action, or visual presentation; performance of a concert version a "dramatico-musical work".

(j) **Dramatico-musical Works** for purposes of this Agreement only, shall include, but not be limited to, a musical comedy, opera, ballet or play with music.

**14. FEES**

(a) LICENSEE shall pay to BMI an annual fee as determined by the BMI Hotel/Motel License Fee Calculation, as follows:

(1) The Estimated License Fee for the initial contract year calculated pursuant to the License Fee Calculation Worksheet (Page 4) is due and payable in full upon signing of the Agreement. The Estimated License Fee for each subsequent calendar year shall be the Actual License Fee for the prior year and shall be due and payable on January 20th of each year during the Term of this Agreement. The Actual License Fee for the prior year (based on actual Costs and music use for each year) shall also be due on the 20th of January of each calendar year with LICENSEE's completed statement pursuant to Paragraph 15, "Reporting".

(2) Beginning with the year 2000, LICENSEE may be entitled to a **one percent (1%) discount** in LICENSEE's license fees if, as verified by BMI, LICENSEE is a member of The American Hotel & Motel Association ("AH&MA"). By accepting this discount, LICENSEE acknowledges that it is not eligible to receive any other BMI trade association discount.

(3) If the initial period of the Term is a partial calendar year, LICENSEE's Costs for such initial period shall be determined by multiplying its average monthly Costs in such partial calendar year by twelve (12), and the applicable license fee for both live music and entertainment and recorded music shall be prorated on a monthly basis.

(4) The license fee for each calendar year of the Term (other than an initial partial calendar year) in which any live music and entertainment are performed in connection with LICENSEE's activities at the premises shall be not less than the lowest fee provided on Schedule A for such year.

(5) For the first contract year of this Agreement, the Schedule A "Bracket of Annual Live Music and Entertainment Costs" to be used to determine the applicable license fee shall be that bracket which would have been applicable for the twelve (12) month period immediately preceding the commencement date of this Agreement (herein called the "prior year"). If LICENSEE operated with a policy of live music and entertainment for less than the full prior year, the applicable Schedule A bracket shall be deemed to be that which includes the amount equal to twelve (12) times LICENSEE's average monthly Costs during such partial prior year. If LICENSEE did not offer live music and entertainment during any part of the prior year, the applicable Schedule A bracket shall be that which includes the amount equal to twelve (12) times LICENSEE's actual (or estimated) costs during the first full month live music and entertainment was (or will be) offered during the Term.

(6) Upon request, payment of the Estimated License Fee may be made in quarterly installments, provided that the account is current and said quarterly installments are made no later than twenty (20) days after the start of each quarterly period. If any quarterly payment is not received by the 90th day after such payment is due, the option to make quarterly payments under this Agreement shall immediately terminate for the remainder of this Agreement, and the balance of the then-current year's Estimated License Fee will immediately become due and payable. Any subsequent Estimated License Fees shall then be paid pursuant to subparagraph 14(a)(1).

(b) The Annual License Fees in Schedules A, B and C for each calendar year commencing 2001 shall be the license fee for the preceding calendar year, adjusted in accordance with the increase or decrease in the United States Consumer Price Index (Urban, All Items) between the preceding October and the next preceding October, rounded to the nearest dollar. BMI shall advise LICENSEE in writing of these adjustments as part of its annual billing process.

(c) In the event that the payment of any license fee to BMI by LICENSEE pursuant to this Agreement causes BMI to become liable to pay any state or local tax which is based upon the license fees received by BMI from LICENSEE, LICENSEE agrees to pay to BMI the full amount of such tax together with fee payment(s) as invoiced by BMI; provided, however, that BMI shall make reasonable efforts to be exempted or excused from paying such tax, and BMI is permitted by law to pass through such tax to LICENSEE.

**15. REPORTING**

(a) On or before the 20th day of January following each calendar year of this Agreement, LICENSEE shall furnish BMI (on forms to be supplied by BMI) with a statement, certified either by an officer or by the auditor of LICENSEE, which shall include the following information for such calendar year: (1) the hotel establishments including restaurants, nightclubs and non-restaurant, non-nightclub establishments LICENSEE is including in this Agreement, under the definition of Licensed Premises, pursuant to the limitations set forth in Paragraph 13; (2) the total Actual Live Music and Entertainment Costs for the prior calendar year; (3) if Recorded Music was performed, the number of guest rooms on the Licensed Premises, whether dancing is permitted, whether a cover, minimum or admission charge is made, whether shows or acts are presented and whether audio-visual performances take place.

(b) If the Actual License Fee for any prior calendar year due BMI is greater than the Estimated License Fee already paid by LICENSEE to BMI for the prior calendar year (or part thereof), LICENSEE agrees to pay to BMI an amount equal to the difference between the Actual and the Estimated License Fees together with its certified statement pursuant to subparagraph 15(a).

(c) If the Actual License Fee due BMI is less than the Estimated License Fee already paid to BMI during the prior calendar year (or part thereof), BMI agrees to credit the difference to the account of LICENSEE and if such difference shall occur during the last calendar year of the Term, BMI agrees to refund the same.

(d) If LICENSEE fails to submit to BMI the annual report(s) required by Paragraph 3 and subparagraph 15(a), BMI shall have the right to assess a reasonable Estimated License Fee for such contract year. BMI shall give written notice to LICENSEE of the fee calculated. LICENSEE shall have ninety (90) days after such written notice by BMI to submit the report. If BMI does not receive from

LICENSEE the report within those 90 days, BMI and LICENSEE agree that BMI's Estimated License Fee shall then be established as the Actual License Fee for the year unreported by LICENSEE. BMI and LICENSEE further agree that such established Actual License Fee (subject to adjustment by audit) shall also become the Estimated License Fee for the following contract year. LICENSEE agrees to waive its right to file its report for any contract year in which BMI's Estimated License Fee becomes the Actual License Fee.

16. **TERM OF AGREEMENT**
Term shall mean the three (3) year period beginning on January 1, 1999 and ending on December 31, 2001. Thereafter, this Agreement will automatically renew for additional one-year periods, unless timely cancelled. This Agreement may be cancelled as of December 31, 2001 or December 31 of any additional one-year period by either party on thirty (30) days' advance written notice.

## SCHEDULE A - LIVE MUSIC AND ENTERTAINMENT FEE*

| Bracket of Annual Live Music and Entertainment Costs | | | Annual License Fee for Calendar Years | | Bracket of Annual Live Music and Entertainment Costs | | | Annual License Fee for Calendar Years | |
|---|---|---|---|---|---|---|---|---|---|
| | | | 1999 | 2000* | | | | 1999 | 2000* |
| Less Than | | $2,000 | $153 | $161 | $250,000 | to | $299,999 | $5,806 | $6,125 |
| $2,000 | to | $4,999 | $213 | $225 | $300,000 | to | $349,999 | $6,325 | $6,673 |
| $5,000 | to | $9,999 | $322 | $340 | $350,000 | to | $399,999 | $7,029 | $7,416 |
| $10,000 | to | $14,999 | $420 | $443 | $400,000 | to | $449,999 | $7,381 | $7,787 |
| $15,000 | to | $24,999 | $634 | $669 | $450,000 | to | $499,999 | $7,909 | $8,344 |
| $25,000 | to | $34,999 | $841 | $887 | $500,000 | to | $599,999 | $8,404 | $8,866 |
| $35,000 | to | $49,999 | $1,047 | $1,105 | $600,000 | to | $749,999 | $9,170 | $9,674 |
| $50,000 | to | $64,999 | $1,253 | $1,322 | $750,000 | to | $999,999 | $10,598 | $11,286 |
| $65,000 | to | $79,999 | $1,581 | $1,668 | $1,000,000 | to | $1,499,999 | $12,225 | $12,897 |
| $80,000 | to | $99,999 | $2,108 | $2,224 | $1,500,000 | to | $1,999,999 | $13,754 | $14,510 |
| $100,000 | to | $119,999 | $2,637 | $2,782 | $2,000,000 | to | $2,999,999 | $15,283 | $16,124 |
| $120,000 | to | $139,999 | $3,164 | $3,338 | $3,000,000 | to | $3,999,999 | $16,810 | $17,735 |
| $140,000 | to | $159,999 | $3,692 | $3,895 | $4,000,000 | to | $4,999,999 | $19,866 | $20,959 |
| $160,000 | to | $179,999 | $4,218 | $4,450 | $5,000,000 | to | $5,999,999 | $22,158 | $23,377 |
| $180,000 | to | $199,999 | $4,746 | $5,007 | $6,000,000 | to | $6,999,999 | $27,508 | $29,021 |
| $200,000 | to | $249,999 | $5,272 | $5,562 | $7,000,000 | and above | | $28,728 | $30,306 |

* CPI adjustment commencing 2001 per subparagraph 14(b)

## SCHEDULE B
### RECORDED MUSIC ONLY FEE (NO LIVE MUSIC PERFORMED)*

**1.** (a) No Dancing; (b) No Cover, Minimum or Admission Charge; and (c) No Shows or Acts **

| No. of Rooms | 1999 (Without AV) | 1999 (With AV) | 2000* (Without AV) | 2000* (With AV) |
|---|---|---|---|---|
| 1 - 100 | $248 | $372 | $262 | $393 |
| 101 - 300 | $295 | $443 | $311 | $467 |
| 301 - 500 | $342 | $513 | $361 | $542 |
| 501 - 750 | $456 | $684 | $481 | $722 |
| Over 750 | $607 | $911 | $640 | $960 |

**2.** One of: (a) Dancing; (b) Cover, Minimum or Admission Charge; or (c) Shows or Acts**

| No. of Rooms | 1999 (Without AV) | 1999 (With AV) | 2000* (Without AV) | 2000* (With AV) |
|---|---|---|---|---|
| 1 - 100 | $331 | $497 | $349 | $524 |
| 101 - 300 | $455 | $683 | $480 | $720 |
| 301 - 500 | $688 | $1,032 | $726 | $1,089 |
| 501 - 750 | $910 | $1,365 | $960 | $1,440 |
| Over 750 | $1,210 | $1,815 | $1,277 | $1,916 |

**3.** Two of: (a) Dancing; (b) Cover, Minimum or Admission Charge; or (c) Shows or Acts**

| No. of Rooms | 1999 (Without AV) | 1999 (With AV) | 2000* (Without AV) | 2000* (With AV) |
|---|---|---|---|---|
| 1 - 100 | $455 | $683 | $480 | $720 |
| 101 - 300 | $688 | $1,032 | $726 | $1,089 |
| 301 - 500 | $1,020 | $1,530 | $1,076 | $1,614 |
| 501 - 750 | $1,363 | $2,045 | $1,438 | $2,225 |
| Over 750 | $1,813 | $2,720 | $1,913 | $2,870 |

**4.** All of: (a) Dancing; (b) Cover, Minimum or Admission Charge; and (c) Shows or Acts**

| No. of Rooms | 1999 (Without AV) | 1999 (With AV) | 2000* (Without AV) | 2000* (With AV) |
|---|---|---|---|---|
| 1 - 100 | $756 | $1,134 | $798 | $1,197 |
| 101 - 300 | $1,170 | $1,755 | $1,234 | $1,851 |
| 301 - 500 | $1,569 | $2,354 | $1,655 | $2,483 |
| 501 - 750 | $1,955 | $2,933 | $2,063 | $3,095 |
| Over 750 | $2,601 | $3,902 | $2,744 | $4,116 |

## SCHEDULE C
### RECORDED MUSIC FEE (LIVE AND RECORDED MUSIC USED)*

**1.** (a) No Dancing; (b) No Cover, Minimum or Admission Charge; and (c) No Shows or Acts **

| No. of Rooms | 1999 (Without AV) | 1999 (With AV) | 2000* (Without AV) | 2000* (With AV) |
|---|---|---|---|---|
| 1 - 100 | $146 | $219 | $154 | $231 |
| 101 - 300 | $177 | $266 | $187 | $281 |
| 301 - 500 | $207 | $311 | $218 | $327 |
| 501 - 750 | $276 | $414 | $291 | $437 |
| Over 750 | $368 | $552 | $388 | $582 |

**2.** One of: (a) Dancing; (b) Cover, Minimum or Admission Charge; or (c) Shows or Acts**

| No. of Rooms | 1999 (Without AV) | 1999 (With AV) | 2000* (Without AV) | 2000* (With AV) |
|---|---|---|---|---|
| 1 - 100 | $197 | $296 | $208 | $312 |
| 101 - 300 | $276 | $414 | $291 | $437 |
| 301 - 500 | $358 | $537 | $378 | $567 |
| 501 - 750 | $468 | $702 | $494 | $741 |
| Over 750 | $622 | $933 | $656 | $984 |

**3.** Two of: (a) Dancing; (b) Cover, Minimum or Admission Charge; or (c) Shows or Acts**

| No. of Rooms | 1999 (Without AV) | 1999 (With AV) | 2000* (Without AV) | 2000* (With AV) |
|---|---|---|---|---|
| 1 - 100 | $276 | $414 | $291 | $437 |
| 101 - 300 | $358 | $537 | $378 | $567 |
| 301 - 500 | $509 | $764 | $537 | $806 |
| 501 - 750 | $744 | $1,116 | $785 | $1,178 |
| Over 750 | $990 | $1,485 | $1,044 | $1,566 |

**4.** All of: (a) Dancing; (b) Cover, Minimum or Admission Charge; and (c) Shows or Acts**

| No. of Rooms | 1999 (Without AV) | 1999 (With AV) | 2000* (Without AV) | 2000* (With AV) |
|---|---|---|---|---|
| 1 - 100 | $756 | $1,134 | $798 | $1,197 |
| 101 - 300 | $1,170 | $1,755 | $1,234 | $1,851 |
| 301 - 500 | $1,569 | $2,354 | $1,655 | $2,483 |
| 501 - 750 | $1,955 | $2,933 | $2,063 | $3,095 |
| Over 750 | $2,601 | $3,902 | $2,744 | $4,116 |

* CPI adjustment commencing 2001 per subparagraph 14(b)
** See definitions – Paragraph 13

3

## BMI HOTEL / MOTEL ANNUAL LICENSE FEE CALCULATION WORKSHEET

**ENTER NUMBER OF GUEST ROOMS AT LICENSEE'S PREMISES.....................................**

**Section I: Live Music and Entertainment Fee** *(COMPLETE IF LICENSE USES LIVE MUSIC AND ENTERTAINMENT)*

(a) Enter LICENSEE's Live Music and Entertainment Costs for the prior year — 1. $

(b) Based on Live Music and Entertainment Costs in Box 1, enter appropriate Annual License Fee from Schedule A — 2. $

**Section II: Recorded Music Only Fee** *(COMPLETE IF LICENSEE USES RECORDED MUSIC BUT NO LIVE MUSIC)*

(c) Check uses of recorded music other than background use: ☐ Dancing ☐ Cover, Minimum or Admission Charge
☐ Shows or Acts (Please specify: DJ _____ VJ _____ Other _____)

(d) Based on the number of rooms entered above and the number of boxes checked in (c), enter appropriate fee from Schedule B — 3. $

(e) Check uses of audio-visual below:
# of Televisions: _____ Largest screen size: _____ Karaoke YES _____ NO _____

(f) Total Fee ............................................................................................................ 4. $

**Section III: Live and Recorded Music Fee** *(COMPLETE ONLY IF LICENSEE USES BOTH LIVE AND RECORDED MUSIC)*

(g) Check uses of recorded music other than background use: ☐ Dancing ☐ Cover, Minimum or Admission Charge
☐ Shows or Acts (Please specify: DJ _____ VJ _____ Other _____)

(h) Based on the number of rooms entered above and the number of boxes checked in (g), enter appropriate fee from Schedule C — 5. $

(i) Check uses of audio-visual below:
# of Televisions: _____ Largest screen size: _____ Karaoke YES _____ NO _____

(j) Total Fee ............................................................................................................ 6. $

**ESTIMATED LICENSE FEE** (Add Box 2 and Box 6 or, if no Live Music, enter Total from Box 4) ............................ 7. $

**IF AH&MA MEMBER, DEDUCT THE 1% AH&MA DISCOUNT (SUBPARAGRAPH 14(a)(2)) FROM ESTIMATED ANNUAL LICENSE FEE AND ENTER IN BOX TO RIGHT** ............................................................ 8. $

The Estimated License Fee for each contract year subsequent to the first contract year of the Term hereof shall be the Actual License Fee reported by LICENSEE for the prior calendar year, pursuant to Paragraph 15 hereof.

### AGREEMENT

AGREEMENT, made at New York, N.Y. on *(Date will be entered by BMI upon execution)* _____ between BROADCAST MUSIC, INC., (herein "BMI"), a State of New York corporation with its principal offices at 320 West 57" Street, New York, N.Y. 10019 and the legal or trade name described below and referred to herein as "LICENSEE" (the "Agreement"). This Agreement includes all of the terms and conditions set forth herein.

**PLEASE RETURN THIS ENTIRE SIGNED LICENSE AGREEMENT WITH YOUR CHECK TO 10 MUSIC SQUARE EAST, NASHVILLE, TN 37203-9901**

**LICENSED PREMISES**

ENTER LEGAL NAME _____
*(Name of corporation, partnership, or individual owner)*

ENTER TRADE NAME _____
*(Doing business under the name of)*

*(Street Address)*

*(City)* *(State)* *(Zip)*

*(Telephone No.)* *(Fax Number)*

*(Contact Name)* *(Title)*

**CHECK APPROPRIATE BOX AND COMPLETE**

☐ Individual Ownership

☐ LLC ☐ Corporation _____
*(State of incorporation)*

☐ LLP ☐ Partnership _____
*(Enter names of partners)*

☐ Other _____ Fed. Tax ID# _____

**MAILING ADDRESS**

*(Street Address)*

*(City)* *(State)* *(Zip)*

*(Telephone No.)* *(Fax Number)*

*(Contact Name)* *(Title)*

**To Be Completed by Licensee**
By signing this Agreement you agree that the foregoing is a true and accurate representation of your Music Policy.

I have read and have understood all of the terms and conditions herein and my signature below is evidence of this.

_____
Signature

_____
Print Name / Title

**To Be Complete by BMI**
**BROADCAST MUSIC, INC.**

_____
Signature

_____
Print Name / Title

**FOR BMI USE ONLY**

_____
Account No.

_____
COID

4

# FORM 17.6

## BMI MEETINGS, CONVENTIONS, TRADE SHOWS AND EXPOSITIONS

**BMI** Music Performance Agreement

**Meetings, Conventions, Trade Shows and Expositions**

Account # ☐☐☐☐☐☐☐ **45**

LI-99/12-45

AGREEMENT, made at New York, N.Y. on *(Date Will Be Entered by BMI Upon Execution)* _____ between BROADCAST MUSIC, INC. (hereinafter called BMI), a state of New York corporation with its principal offices at 320 West 57th Street, New York, N.Y. 10019 and the entity described below and referred to thereafter as "LICENSEE" or "You:"

ENTER LEGAL NAME _____

*Name of Corporation, Partnership or Individual Owner*

ENTER TRADE NAME _____

SELECT ONLY ONE BOX AND COMPLETE

☐ Corporation ☐ Association ☐ Partnership *(Enter names of partners)* ☐ **Individual Owner** *(indicate residence address below under Business Address)*

_____ *(State of Incorporation)*

_____ *Partner Names*

☐ **Limited Liability Company**

BUSINESS ADDRESS                MAILING ADDRESS

| *(Street Address)* | | *(Street Address)* | |
| *(City)* | *(State)* | *(Zip)* | *(City)* | *(State)* | *(Zip)* |
| *(Contact Name)* | *(Title)* | *(Contact Name)* | *(Title)* |
| *(Telephone No.)* ( ) | | *(Telephone No.)* ( ) | |

**1. DEFINITIONS:** (a) An "Event" shall mean a convention that includes an assemblage of delegates, representatives and/or members of an organization(s) convened for a common purpose, a meeting which includes individuals assembled together for purposes of communicating information to each other (i.e. panels, seminars, symposiums, convocations, conferences, caucuses, forums, assemblies, congresses, institutes) or otherwise transacting business, an exposition at which products and services are displayed, or a trade, industrial or consumer show, or other activity of LICENSEE of not more than fourteen (14) consecutive days. An "Event" shall mean a concert which is sponsored, conducted, endorsed or approved by LICENSEE, unless the concert is open to members of the general public who are not affiliated with the LICENSEE.

(b) A "Function" shall include activity conducted, sponsored, endorsed or approved by LICENSEE occurring in connection with an Event, including, but not limited to, meals, plenary sessions, breakouts, meetings, receptions, concerts, cocktail parties, dinners, dances, dinner-dances, variety shows, seminars, or any other similar spectator or participatory activity.

(c) "Attendees" shall mean the number of persons present where any live, recorded or audio-visual music is performed or played at each of LICENSEE's Events whether or not any admission charge, registration fee or other payment is required to be made in connection with the attendance, but shall not include those required to produce the event, such as LICENSEE's employees working at the Event, exhibitor personnel, administrative, service contractor and temporary personnel, or credentialed members of the press. In the case of a trade show or convention where live or recorded music is performed on the exhibit floor, the number of Attendees shall be the total number of persons registered at the trade show / convention. If no music is performed on the exhibit floor, the number of Attendees shall mean the total attendance at each Function held during the trade show or convention at which music is performed; provided, however, that in no event shall the number of Attendees for a given trade show or convention exceed the total number of persons registered at the trade show / convention. In the case of a meeting which does not have an exhibit floor and consists only of a series of Functions, the number of Attendees shall be the total attendance at each Function at which music is performed, with the number not to exceed the total registered attendance of the entire meeting.

**2. BMI GRANT:** (a) BMI hereby grants to LICENSEE a non-exclusive license to perform, present or cause the live and/or recorded performance during Events of all musical works of which BMI shall have the right to grant public performance licenses during the term hereof. This license does not include: (i) dramatic rights, the right to perform dramatico-musical works in whole or in substantial part, the right to present individual works in a dramatic setting or the right to use the music licensed hereunder in any other context which may constitute an exercise of the "grand rights" therein; or (ii) the right to broadcast, telecast or otherwise transmit, including via the Internet or on-line service, the performances licensed hereunder to persons outside of any premises at which an Event occurs.

(b) LICENSEE may be responsible for securing other rights including, but not limited to, synchronization and mechanical rights.

(c) BMI may withdraw from the license your right to perform any musical work as to which a legal action has been brought or a claim made that BMI does not have the right to license the work or that the work infringes another work.

**3. TERM OF AGREEMENT:** The initial term of this annual agreement begins on January 1, 20____ and shall end on December 31, 20____ and shall continue annually unless canceled by either you or BMI at the end of the initial term or any following one (1) year term by giving thirty (30) days advance written notice to the other of us. BMI shall have the right to cancel this agreement along with the simultaneous cancellation of th agreements of all other licensees of the same class and category as LICENSEE, as of the end of any month during the term, upon sixty (60) day advance written notice. If there is any breach or default by you of this agreement, BMI shall have the right to cancel it, but the cancellation shall become effective only if the breach or default continues thirty (30) days after the date of BMI's written notice to you. The right to cancel is in additio to any other remedies which BMI may have. BMI may enforce any of its rights under this agreement at any time even if it has not done so earlier.

**4. FEES:** LICENSEE agrees to pay BMI for each one year term of the agreement a license fee based upon the following:

| Calendar Year<br>1997 / 1998 / 1999 / 2000 | Per Attendee Rate<br>$ .05 |

(a) For each year after the year 2000, the per attendee rate shall be an adjustment of the rate for the previous calendar year based upon the percentage increase or decrease in the United States Consumer Price Index (National, All Items) ("CPI") between September of the year which is two years before such year and September of the preceding year, rounded to the nearest penny (for example, the rate for the year 2001 shall be an adjustment of the rate for the year 2000, based upon the percentage difference in the CPI between September 1999 and September 2000). BMI shall inform you of the adjusted rate by the end of each calendar year.

(b) The minimum annual fee billed and payable for 1997, 1998, 1999 and 2000 shall be $100 per year. The minimum annual fee for each yea after 2000 shall be an adjustment of the minimum annual fee for the previous calendar year based upon the percentage increase or decrease in th CPI between September of the year which is two years before such year and September of the preceding year, rounded to the nearest five dollars.

(c) You agree to pay to BMI for each calendar year the total fee due. The minimum annual fee ($100) only is due simultaneously with your execution and return of this agreement. The remainder of the actual license fee for each calendar year shall be due within thirty (30) days from the beginning of the following calendar year, upon submission of the report required in paragraph 5, along with the minimum annual fee for the following calendar year.

(d) The license fee for each calendar year shall be based upon LICENSEE's actual total number of Attendees for that calendar year as set forth o the report required by Paragraph 5. If such report reveals that the actual fee due BMI for that report's calendar year is greater than the minimum annual fe previously paid, LICENSEE shall pay the difference at the same time it submits the report and pays its minimum annual fee for the following calendar year.

**5. REPORTING OF EVENTS:** At the same time as the payment for the second and subsequent calendar years is due, you agree to furnish BMI (on forms available from BMI) with a report setting forth:
   (i) the total number of Events held during the previous calendar year;
   (ii) the total number of Attendees at all Events held during the previous calendar year; and
   (iii) the total license fee for the previous calendar year and the minimum annual license fee for the current calendar year.

**6. VERIFICATION OF / FAILURE TO REPORT:** (a) BMI is entitled to verify the information submitted by LICENSEE in its report under paragraph 5, by any source, including the examination of LICENSEE's books and records. As such, LICENSEE is required to retain such books and records for a period of not less than three years after the calendar year contained in LICENSEE's report, copies of which books and records shall be turned over to BMI upon its request. If after such examination, BMI is still unable to verify said information, BMI shall be entitled to unilaterally assess LICENSEE a reasonable annual fee using any source.

(b) In the event LICENSEE fails to submit a report as required under paragraph 5 within thirty (30) days after BMI has given LICENSEE written notice of its failure to do so, BMI shall be entitled to unilaterally assess LICENSEE a reasonable annual fee using any source, including an examination of LICENSEE's books and records as set forth above.

**7. INDEMNITY BY BMI:** BMI agrees to indemnify you, your officers and employees against any and all claims that may be made against you with respect to the performance of any music licensed under this agreement at the time of your performances. You agree to give BMI immediate notice of any claim, to deliver to BMI any related papers and to cooperate with BMI in the matter, of which BMI shall be in full charge.

**8. ARBITRATION:** All disputes of any kind arising in connection with the terms of this agreement shall be submitted to the American Arbitration Association in New York, New York under its rules then in effect. The arbitrators shall be selected as follows: each of us shall, by written notice to the other, have the right to appoint one arbitrator. If, within ten (10) days after such notice by one of us, the other one does not, by written notice, appoint another arbitrator, the first arbitrator shall be the only arbitrator. However, if we each appoint an arbitrator, the two arbitrators shall appoint a third arbitrator. If ten (10) days pass after the second arbitrator's appointment and the two arbitrators cannot agree upon the third arbitrator, then either of us may, in writing, request the American Arbitration Association to appoint the third arbitrator. The arbitration award shall be entirely binding on both of us and judgment may be entered in any appropriate court. The award shall include an amount for the costs, expenses and attorneys' fees of arbitration, which shall be paid by the losing party.

**9. NOTICES:** Any notices to be given are to be in writing and shall be deemed given on the day they are sent by ordinary first-class U.S. mail to the other of us at its above mailing address or any different address which either of us later designates in writing. Any notices you send to BMI shall be addressed to the attention of the General Licensing Department. Any notices BMI sends to you shall be addressed to the attention of the person signing this agreement unless you advise BMI to address notices to someone else.

**10. MISCELLANEOUS:** This agreement is our entire understanding, shall not be binding until signed by both of us, and no waiver or change shall be valid unless in writing and signed by us. Your rights are not assignable. This agreement, its validity, construction and effect, shall be governed by the laws of the State of New York. The fact that any parts of this agreement may be found by a court of competent jurisdiction to be void or unenforceable shall not affect the validity or enforceability of any other parts.

**(To be Completed by BMI)**
**BROADCAST MUSIC, INC.**

By: _____
   *(Signature)*

_____
*(Print Name of Signer)*

_____
*(Title of Signer)*

**(To be Completed by LICENSEE)**

*Name of Corporation, Partnership or Individual Owner*
*(Same legal name of LICENSEE as on page 1)*

*(Signature)*

*(Print Name of Signer Fill in Title in which Signed)*
*(a) if corporation, state corporate office held; (b) if partnership, write "Partner"; (c) if individual owner, write "Individual Owner"*

# FORM 17.7

## BMI ATHLETIC CLUBS/DANCE CLASSES

**BMI**® MUSIC PERFORMANCE AGREEMENT     **Athletic Clubs / Dance Classes**     ACCOUNT #  ☐☐☐☐☐☐  **40**  LI-99/10-40

AGREEMENT, made at New York, N.Y. on *(Date will be entered by BMI upon execution)* _____ between BROADCAST MUSIC, INC., (hereinafter BMI), a State of New York corporation with principal offices at 320 West 57th Street, New York, N.Y. 10019, and the entity described below and referred to thereafter as LICENSEE:

**ENTER LEGAL NAME** _____

*Name of corporation, Partnership or Individual Owner*

**ENTER TRADE NAME** _____

*(Doing business under the name of)*

**CHECK APPROPRIATE BOX AND COMPLETE**   ☐ Corporation    ☐ Partnership (Enter names of partners)    ☐ Individual Owner (indicate residence address below under Mailing Address)

*(State of Incorporation)*

| **BUSINESS ADDRESS** | | | **MAILING ADDRESS** | | |
|---|---|---|---|---|---|
| *(Street Address)* | | | *(Street Address)* | | |
| *(City)* | *(State)* | *(Zip)* | *(City)* | *(State)* | *(Zip)* |
| *(Telephone No.)* | *(Contact Name)* | | *(Telephone No.)* | *(Contact Name)* | |
| | *(Title)* | | | *(Title)* | |

**1. DEFINITIONS:**
(a) "Background music" shall mean recorded music, whether vocal or instrumental, designed to be used as an unobtrusive accompaniment to routine activities, including, but not limited to, conversation and relaxation, as long as such music is not intended to accompany non-instructional dancing or any other type of entertainment.
(b) "Instructional use" shall mean the performance of recorded music in a designated area on the LICENSEE's premises (the "studio") for use during athletic classes and dance instruction including, but not limited to, classes in aerobics, gymnastics, slimnastics, social dancing, ballroom dancing, jazz dancing, tap dancing, square dancing, modern dancing, and ballet, as those terms are commonly understood in the dance profession.
(c) "Background use" shall mean the performance of recorded background music on the licensed premises adjacent to or outside of the studio.

**2. BMI GRANT:**
(a) BMI hereby grants to LICENSEE a non-exclusive license to perform, present, or cause the public performance of, all musical works of which BMI shall have the right to grant public performance licenses during the term hereof. Said license shall be restricted to performance on the licensed premises either by the playing of records, prerecorded tapes, or other mechanical devices or via the reception of broadcast audio transmissions on receiving apparatus and amplifications thereof for public performance, and such performances may be reproduced only through loudspeakers on the licensed premises and is granted in consideration of the payment of the license fees as set forth herein and is subject to all of the terms and conditions hereof. This license does not include: (i) dramatic rights, the right to perform dramatico-musical works in whole or in substantial part, the right to present individual works in a dramatic setting or the right to use the music licensed hereunder in any other context which may constitute an exercise of the "grand rights" therein; (ii) the right to broadcast, cablecast, telecast or otherwise transmit the performances licensed hereunder to persons outside of the premises; or (iii) performances of music by means of a coin-operated phonorecord player (jukebox).
(b) BMI reserves the right at its discretion to withdraw from the license granted hereunder any musical work as to which any legal action has been instituted or a claim made that BMI does not have the right to license the performing rights in such work or that such work infringes another composition.
(c) In no event shall this license authorize performances of music outside the perimeter of LICENSEE's premises into an area not owned and/or controlled by LICENSEE. This license shall also extend to performances of incidental live or recorded music on the licensed premises for promotional social dances and to dance recitals by students and instructors, as long as no admission is charged.

**3. TERM OF AGREEMENT**
The initial term of this annual agreement shall begin on the first day of _____ and end on the last day of _____ and shall continue thereafter unless cancelled by either party as of the end of the initial term or any subsequent one (1) year term (herein sometimes referred to as a "contract year") upon thirty (30) days advance notice to the other party.

1

**4. FEES**

LICENSEE agrees to pay to BMI for each contract year during the term of this agreement a license fee as follows:

(a) (i) INSTRUCTIONAL USE ONLY – If LICENSEE uses recorded music on the premises that is only for athletic classes and dance instruction and the music is not audible other than incidentally outside of the studio when classes are in session and no music is used when classes are not in session, then LICENSEE shall pay the appropriate fee on the License Fee Schedule under the category Instructional Use Only.

(ii) BACKGROUND AND INSTRUCTIONAL USE – If LICENSEE uses recorded music on the premises both in classes and instruction and the music is also audible other than incidentally anywhere else on the premises outside of the studio while classes are in session or otherwise, then LICENSEE shall pay the appropriate fee on the License Fee Schedule under the category Background and Instructional Use.

(iii) BACKGROUND USE ONLY – If LICENSEE uses music on the premises that is *only* for "background use" as defined in the license and *no* music is used at athletic classes or dance instruction (or no such activities take place), then LICENSEE shall pay the appropriate fee on the License Fee Schedule under the category Background Use Only. Each individual floor (level) where music is audible is to be considered a separate premises, but the annual fee for all floors (levels) after the first shall be $60.00 regardless of square footage.

(b) LICENSEE warrants and represents that during the twelve-month period preceding the initial term of this agreement (or if LICENSEE did not operate during that full twelve-month period, LICENSEE shall make a good-faith estimate for the first contract year of this agreement) LICENSEE's number of floors (levels) and students are as set forth in the Music Policy Statement and License Fee Schedule which are part of this agreement.

(c) The first annual fee due hereunder shall be payable upon the signing of this agreement by LICENSEE. The fee for each subsequent contract year shall be in the respective amount determined in accordance with this paragraph, subject to any adjustment pursuant to this paragraph, and shall be paid to BMI no later than ten (10) days following the beginning of each such contract year.

(d) For Instructional Use Only and Background and Instructional Use – The amount of the license fee for the second and subsequent contract years of this agreement shall be an adjustment of the first year's fee based upon the percentage increase or decrease in the United States Consumer Price Index (National, All Items) between September 1999, and September of the year preceding each anniversary date of this agreement, rounded to the nearest dollar. BMI will advise LICENSEE in writing of the amount of each new fee.

**5. REPORTING OF ANNUAL FEES**

(a) At the same time that LICENSEE pays its license fee hereunder for the second and subsequent contract years, LICENSEE shall submit a report, on a form available from BMI, certified by LICENSEE or by the auditor of LICENSEE, indicating the average number of different students or participants per week during the previous contract year who attended instructional athletic or dance classes using music on the licensed premises (except if background use only), whether LICENSEE's music was instructional only or both background and instructional or background use only, and the number of floors (levels) comprising the licensed premises. If any such report causes the licensed premises to fall into a Category other than that for which LICENSEE is then currently paying BMI license fees, BMI shall adjust LICENSEE's fee pursuant to Paragraph 4 to reflect LICENSEE's new fee, effective with the contract year following such change of Category.

(b) If the adjusted fee is greater than the license fee already paid by LICENSEE for the contract year, LICENSEE agrees to pay BMI the difference within thirty (30) days of the mailing by BMI to LICENSEE of the adjusted statement of license fees.

(c) If the adjusted fee is less than the license fee already paid by LICENSEE to BMI for the contract year, BMI agrees to credit the difference to the account of LICENSEE, and if such adjustment occurs in the last contract year of this agreement, BMI shall refund said sum promptly.

(d) In the event that LICENSEE fails to submit a report pursuant to this Paragraph and BMI subsequently is made aware of a current change of Category, BMI shall have the option, in lieu of its right of cancellation pursuant to this Paragraph, to notify LICENSEE in writing by certified mail of its knowledge of such change and adjust LICENSEE's fee for the then current contract year in accordance with this Paragraph as if LICENSEE had reported such change for the previous year. LICENSEE shall have thirty (30) days from the date of BMI's notice to submit the missing reports. If such reports are not received by BMI by the end of said 30-day period, LICENSEE agrees to waive its right to submit such past due reports thereafter and authorizes BMI to deem the adjusted fee accurate.

**6. TERMINATION OF AGREEMENT BY LICENSEE**

If LICENSEE shall permanently cease to operate the premises, whether by reason of sale or lease thereof or otherwise, this agreement and LICENSEE's obligation to BMI shall thereupon terminate, provided that LICENSEE shall, within ten (10) days thereafter, give written notice of such termination to BMI, setting forth the effective date thereof and the name of the new owner or operator of the premises, and that LICENSEE shall pay to BMI all fees due hereunder until said effective date. The fee due BMI by LICENSEE through the effective date of termination shall be a proration of the fee for the contract year of termination, but in no event less than the lowest appropriate fee indicated in the applicable category on the License Fee Schedule.

**7. REVIEW OF STATEMENTS AND /OR ACCOUNTINGS**

BMI shall have the right, by its authorized representatives, at any time during customary business hours, and upon reasonable notice, to examine those portions of LICENSEE's books and records of account to such extent as may be necessary to verify any and all statements and/or accountings made hereunder or under prior agreement with BMI. BMI shall consider all data and information coming to its attention as the result of any such examination of LICENSEE's books and records as confidential.

2

**8. LATE PAYMENT CHARGE**

BMI may impose a late payment charge of 1% per month from the date any payment is due hereunder on any payment that is received by BMI more than one month after the due date.

**9. INDEMNITY BY BMI**

BMI agrees to indemnify, save harmless and defend LICENSEE, its officers and employees, from and against any and all claims, demands or suits that may be made or brought against them or any of them with respect to the performance of any material licensed under this agreement. Such indemnity shall be limited to the works which are licensed by BMI at the time of LICENSEE's performances. BMI's Clearance Department will, upon reasonable written request, advise LICENSEE whether particular musical works are available for performance as part of BMI's repertoire. LICENSEE shall provide the title and the writer/composer of each musical composition requested to be identified. LICENSEE agrees to give BMI immediate notice of any such claim, demand or suit, to deliver to BMI any papers pertaining thereto, and to cooperate with BMI with respect thereto, and BMI shall have full charge of the defense of any such claim, demand or suit.

**10. CANCELLATION OF ENTIRE CATEGORY**

BMI shall have the right to cancel this agreement along with the simultaneous cancellation of the agreements of all other licensees of the same class and category as LICENSEE, as of the end of any month during the term, upon sixty (60) days advance written notice.

**11. OFFER OF COMPARABLE AGREEMENT**

In the event that BMI, at any time during the term hereof, shall for the same class and category as that of LICENSEE, issue licenses granting rights similar to those in this agreement on a more favorable basis, BMI shall, for the balance of the term, offer LICENSEE a comparable agreement.

**12. BREACH OR DEFAULT/WAIVER**

Upon any breach or default of the terms and conditions of this agreement, BMI shall have the right to cancel this agreement, but any such cancellation shall only become effective if such breach or default continues thirty (30) days after the date of BMI's written notice to LICENSEE thereof. The right to cancel shall be in addition to any and all other remedies which BMI may have. No waiver by BMI of full performance of this agreement by LICENSEE in any one or more instances shall be a waiver of the right to require full and complete performance of this agreement thereafter or of the right to cancel this agreement in accordance with the terms of this Paragraph.

**13. ARBITRATION**

All disputes of any kind, nature or description arising in connection with the terms and conditions of this agreement shall be submitted to the American Arbitration Association in the City, County and State of New York for arbitration under its then prevailing arbitration rules. The arbitrator(s) to be selected as follows: Each of the parties shall, by written notice to the other, have the right to appoint one arbitrator. If, within ten (10) days following the giving of such notice by one party the other shall not, by written notice, appoint another arbitrator, the first arbitrator shall be the sole arbitrator. If two arbitrators are so appointed, they shall appoint a third arbitrator. If ten (10) days elapse after the appointment of the second arbitrator and the two arbitrators are unable to agree upon the third arbitrator, then either party may, in writing, request the American Arbitration Association to appoint the third arbitrator. The award made in the arbitration shall be binding and conclusive on the parties and judgment may be, but need not be, entered in any court having jurisdiction. Such award shall include the fixing of the costs expenses and attorneys' fees of arbitration, which shall be borne by the unsuccessful party.

**14. NOTICES**

Any notice required or permitted to be given under this agreement in writing and shall be deemed given when sent by first-class U.S. mail to the party intended, at its mailing address hereinabove stated, or any other address which either party hereto may designate. Any such notice sent to BMI shall be to the attention of the General Licensing Department. Any such notice sent to LICENSEE shall be to the attention of the person signing this agreement on behalf of LICENSEE or such other person as LICENSEE may advise BMI in writing.

**15. MISCELLANEOUS**

This agreement constitutes the entire understanding between the parties, shall not be binding until signed by both parties, and cannot be waived or added to or modified orally, and no waiver, addition or modification shall be valid unless in writing and signed by the parties. The rights of LICENSEE shall not be assignable. This agreement, its validity, construction and effect, shall be governed by the laws of the State of New York. The fact that any provisions herein are found by a court of competent jurisdiction to be void or unenforceable shall not affect the validity or enforceability of any other provisions. All headings in this agreement are for the purpose of convenience and shall not be considered to be part of this agreement.

3

**MUSIC POLICY STATEMENT**

Indicate music use by checking **one** appropriate category below.

☐ CATEGORY A - Instructional Use Only

☐ CATEGORY B - Background and Instructional Use

Indicate number of floors (levels) _____

☐ CATEGORY C - Background Use Only

Indicate number of floors (levels) _____

**LICENSE FEE SCHEDULE**

1) These rates apply when music is utilized for Instructional Use Only, Background and Instructional Use, or Background Use Only. This includes, but is not limited to, records, tapes, CD's, broadcasts, satellite signals, and/or cablecasts.

2) **USING YOUR CATEGORY AS INDICATED ABOVE, CHECK THE APPLICABLE SHADED BOX BELOW.**

| Average Number of Different Students or Participants Per Week | CATEGORY A INSTRUCTIONAL USE ONLY | | CATEGORY B BACKGROUND AND INSTRUCTIONAL USE | | | CATEGORY C | | |
|---|---|---|---|---|---|---|---|---|
| | | | | | | Square Footage | BACKGROUND USE ONLY | |
| | | | Single Floor (level) | | Multiple Floor (level) | | | |
| Under 60 Students | | $116 | | $182 | | $229 | | | Single Floor (level) |
| 60-124 | | 229 | | 365 | | 456 | Up to 1500 | | $62 |
| 125-249 | | 344 | | 547 | | 687 | 1501-2500 | | 123 |
| 250-374 | | 456 | | 733 | | 914 | 2501-5000 | | 246 |
| 375 & over | | 611 | | 976 | | 1,220 | Over 5000 | | 493 |

LICENSEE's total annual fee within Category A or B is $ _____

LICENSEE's total annual fee within Category C, including additional floors (levels) (each at $62), is $ _____

---

(To Be Completed by BMI)

**BROADCAST MUSIC, INC.**

By: _____
(Signature)

_____
(Print Name of Signer)

_____
(Title of Signer)

---

(To be Completed by LICENSEE)

*Name of Corporation, Partnership or Single Owner (Same Legal Name of LICENSEE as on page 1)*

Sign here►  By: _____
(Signature)

_____
(Print Name of Signer)

_____
(Title of Signer)

(a) If corporation, state corporate office held; (b) if partnership, write "Partner", (c) if single owner, write "single owner"

\* BMI and the Musicstand symbol are registered trademarks of Broadcast Music, Inc.

4

# FORM 17.8

## BMI BUSINESS MULTIPLE USE LICENSE

**BMI**® **MUSIC PERFORMANCE AGREEMENT**    **Business Multiple Use License**    ACCOUNT # ☐☐☐☐☐☐ – **36**

LI-99/10-36

AGREEMENT, made at New York, N.Y. on *(Date will be entered by BMI upon execution)* _____
between BROADCAST MUSIC, INC. ("BMI"), a New York corporation with its principal offices at 320 West 57th Street, New York, N.Y. 10019, and the entity described below ("LICENSEE" or "you"):

**ENTER LEGAL NAME** _____
*Name of Corporation, Partnership or Individual Owner*

**ENTER TRADE NAME** _____
*(Doing business under the name of)*

**CHECK APPROPRIATE BOX AND COMPLETE**
☐ Corporation    ☐ Partnership    (Enter names of partners)    ☐ Individual Owner
_____    _____    (Show residence
(State of Incorporation)    _____    address below under
Mailing Address)

| LOCATION ADDRESS | MAILING ADDRESS |
|---|---|
| **IDENTIFY ON SCHEDULE A** | *(Street Address or P.O. Box, if any)* |
| | *(City)*    *(State)*    *(Zip)* |
| | *(Contact Name)*    *(Title)* |
| | *(Telephone No.)*  (    ) |

**1. DEFINITIONS (a)** Location: each premises operated and owned or leased by you or your subsidiaries which is used primarily as an executive or general office or as an industrial facility as listed or to be listed on Schedule A.
(b) Executive or general office: a location where LICENSEE conducts its managerial or administrative functions.
(c) Industrial facility: a premises used for manufacturing plant or warehouse and related purposes.
(d) Off-site location: a premises other than the location address under the location's sole control and attended solely by the location's employees, their families and social acquaintances, and intra-corporate invitees.
(e) Employees: all full-time and part-time persons employed at a location.
(f) Subsidiary: an entity wholly-owned by LICENSEE.

**2. BMI GRANT** - BMI grants you a non-exclusive license to perform or allow to be performed at the licensed locations and off-site locations all musical works of which BMI shall have the right to grant public performance licenses during the term of this agreement. This grant of rights includes but is not limited to music performed: (1) over telephones in the form of music-on-hold; (2) as live music or recorded background music; (3) in fitness and aerobics facilities; (4) in audiovisual presentations in business meetings; (5) over teleconferencing at the licensed locations; (6) in television and radio programming received by LICENSEE on the locations; and (7) performances of music by interactive software, whether (a) delivered by media such as CD-ROM, CD-I, diskette or cartridge, or (b) rendered by multimedia hardware, such as computer-driven handheld devices.

This license does not include: (a) the right to present the music in any way which may be a use of the "grand rights;" (b) the right to broadcast, telecast, cablecast or otherwise transmit the performances outside of the licensed locations, except to the extent that music on telephone hold lines originating at a licensed location is audible at remote premises on telephone lines as part of "music-on-hold;" (c) performances of music by a jukebox; (d) any performance of music by interactive software, delivered by on line service, such as interactive cable, interactive TV, computer network, telephone or satellite. In all cases the term "premises" shall specifically exclude (1) any retail establishment owned or leased by LICENSEE; (2) any location which is used by LICENSEE for a trade show, convention or exposition; and (3) any hospital or similar facility.

LICENSEE may be responsible for securing other rights including, but not limited to, synchronization and mechanical rights.

BMI may withdraw from the license your right to perform any musical work as to which a legal action has been brought or a claim made that BMI does not have the right to license the work or that the work infringes another work.

**3. TERM OF AGREEMENT** - The first term of this agreement begins on the first day of _____ and ends on the last day of _____ (a "contract" year). It will continue annually unless canceled by either you or BMI at the end of the first term or any following one (1) year term by giving thirty (30) days advance written notice to the other of us.

1

**4. FEES** - (a) You agree to pay BMI for each employee for the first year of this agreement fees as follows:

**LICENSE FEE SCHEDULE**

NOTE: The tiers are successive, not cumulative. For example, 800 employees would be covered by 250 in the first tier, 250 in the second tier and 300 in the third tier.

| NUMBER OF EMPLOYEES | FEE PER EMPLOYEE |
|---|---|
| First 250 | 58 cents |
| 251 - 500 | 46 cents |
| 501 - 10,000 | 35 cents |
| 10,001 - 20,000 | 30 cents |
| 20,001 - 75,000 | 25 cents |
| 75,001 and Over | 16 cents |

(b) Subject to Subparagraphs 4 (a), (c), (d) and Paragraph 5, you agree to pay to BMI for each contract year an estimated fee as an advance of the actual fee. Based upon your projection, you estimate that your highest number of employees at all of the locations listed on Schedule A during the first contract year will be _____ and your estimated fee will be _____ . **The minimum annual fee for 2000 is $145.**

The first annual fee is due within 30 days of your signing this agreement.

(c) The amount of the fee per employee and minimum fee for the second and subsequent contract years of this agreement shall be an adjustment of the first year's fee per employee and minimum fee based upon the percentage increase or decrease in the United States Consumer Price Index (National, All Items) between September 1999, and September of the year preceding each anniversary date of this agreement. The license fees based upon the number of employees shall be computed to the nearest cent and the minimum fee to the nearest dollar. BMI will advise you in writing of the amount of each new fee.

(d) The estimated fee for the second and following contract years will be the actual fee for the previous contract year and will be due and payable no later than 30 days after the beginning of each contract year.

**5. REPORTING** - (a) At the same time as the payments required by Paragraph 4 are due, you agree to furnish BMI (on forms available from BMI) with a report, certified either by an officer or by your auditor, setting forth any information regarding the subject matter of this agreement which BMI may reasonably require, including, without limitation:

(i) the highest number of employees for the year reported at each licensed location;

(ii) the name and address of each location for which a fee is paid;

(iii) the name and address of each subsidiary and the locations of that subsidiary to be licensed hereunder

(b) If, after processing the annual report, the actual fee is greater than the license fee already paid by you for the contract year, you agree to pay BMI the difference, within (30) days of the mailing by BMI to you of an adjusted statement.

(c) If, after processing the annual report, the actual fee is less than the license fee already paid by you to BMI for the contract year, BMI agrees to credit the difference between the actual and estimated license fees to your account, and if such adjustment occurs in the last contract year of the agreement, BMI shall refund said sum promptly.

**6. INDEMNITY BY BMI** - BMI agrees to indemnify you, your officers and employees against any and all claims that may be made against you with respect to the performance of any music licensed under this agreement at the time of your performances. You agree to give BMI immediate notice of any claim, to deliver to BMI any related papers and to cooperate with BMI in the matter, of which BMI will be in full charge. BMI will, upon reasonable written request, advise you whether specific musical works are available for performance, if you provide the title and the writer/composer of each musical work.

**7. CANCELLATION OF ENTIRE CATEGORY** - BMI shall have the right to cancel this agreement along with the simultaneous cancellation of the agreements of all other licensees of the same class and category as LICENSEE, as of the end of any month during the term, upon sixty (60) days advance written notice.

**8. OFFER OF COMPARABLE AGREEMENT** - If BMI, during the term of this agreement and for the same class and category as yours, issues licenses granting rights similar to those in this agreement on a more favorable basis, BMI will, for the rest of the term, offer you a comparable agreement.

**9. BREACH OR DEFAULT/WAIVER** - If there is any breach or default by you of this agreement, BMI will have the right to cancel it, but the cancellation will become effective only if the breach or default continues thirty (30) days after the date of BMI's written notice to you. The right to cancel is in addition to any other remedies which BMI may have. BMI may enforce any of its rights under this agreement at any time even if it has not done so earlier.

**10. ARBITRATION** - All disputes of any kind arising in connection with the terms of this agreement shall be submitted to the American Arbitration Association in New York, New York under its rules then in effect. The arbitrators will be selected as follows: each of us will, by written notice to the other, have the right to appoint one arbitrator. If, within ten (10) days after such notice by one of us, the other one does not, by written notice, appoint another arbitrator, the first arbitrator will be the only arbitrator. However, if we each appoint an arbitrator, the two arbitrators will appoint a third arbitrator. If ten (10) days pass after the second arbitrator's appointment and the two arbitrators cannot agree upon the third arbitrator, then either of us may, in writing, request the American Arbitration Association to appoint the third arbitrator. The arbitration award shall be entirely binding on both of us and judgment may be entered in any appropriate court. The award shall include an amount for the costs, expenses and attorneys' fees of arbitration, which shall be paid by the losing party.

**11. NOTICES** - Any notices to be given are to be in writing and will be deemed given on the day they are sent by ordinary first-class U.S. mail to the other of us at its above mailing address or any different address which either of us later designates in writing. Any notices you send to BMI will be addressed to the attention of the General Licensing Department. Any notices BMI sends to you will be addressed to the attention of the person signing this agreement for you unless you advise BMI to address notices to someone else.

**12. MISCELLANEOUS** - This agreement is our entire understanding, will not be binding until signed by both of us, and no waiver or change will be valid unless in writing and signed by us. This agreement is signed by the authorized representatives of each of us. Your rights are not assignable. This agreement, its validity, construction and effect, will be governed by the laws of the State of New York. The fact that any parts of the agreement may be found by a court of competent jurisdiction to be void or unenforceable will not affect the validity or enforceability of any other parts. The headings are for convenience only and are not a part of the agreement.

|  |  |
|---|---|
| (To Be Completed by BMI) | (To be Completed by LICENSEE) |

| **BROADCAST MUSIC, INC.** | |
|---|---|

Name of Corporation, Partnership or Single Owner
*(Same Legal Name of LICENSEE as on page 1)*

By: _____     Sign here   By: _____
        *(Signature)*                                              *(Signature)*

_____                         _____
*(Print Name of Signer)*                                 *(Print Name of Signer)*

_____                         _____
*(Title of Signer)*                                          *(Title of Signer)*

(a) If corporation, state corporate office held; (b) if partnership, write "Partner"; (c) if single owner, write "single owner"

® BMI and the Musicstand symbol are registered trademarks of Broadcast Music, Inc.

3

## Schedule A

Name and address of each location for which a fee is paid, and highest number of employees at that location.

| Locations DBA | Address | City | State | Zip | Highest # of employees for the report year | Subsidiary name (If Applicable) |
|---|---|---|---|---|---|---|
| | | | | | | |
| | | | | | | |
| | | | | | | |
| | | | | | | |
| | | | | | | |
| | | | | | | |
| | | | | | | |
| | | | | | | |
| | | | | | | |
| | | | | | | |
| | | | | | | |

**Total Employees:**

IF MORE SPACE REQUIRED, ATTACH SHEET(S)

Enter Total here and on Page 2 of this
Agreement in space provided

4

# FORM 17.9

## BMI HEALTH CARE MULTIPLE USE LICENSE

**BMI** MUSIC PERFORMANCE AGREEMENT

**HEALTH CARE MULTIPLE USE LICENSE**
(COMPLETE ALL SHADED AREAS BELOW)

ACCOUNT # ☐☐☐☐☐☐☐-36

LI-94/04-36

*(Date will be*
AGREEMENT, made at New York, N.Y. on *Entered by BMI Upon Execution)* _____ between BROADCAST MUSIC, INC. ("BMI"), a New York corporation with its principal offices at 320 West 57th Street, New York, N.Y. 10019 and the entity described below ("LICENSEE" or "you").

**ENTER LEGAL NAME** ▶ ------------------------------------
*Name of Corporation, Partnership or Individual Owner*

**ENTER TRADE NAME** ▶ ------------------------------------
*(Doing business under the name of)*

**CHECK APPROPRIATE BOX AND COMPLETE** ▶ ☐ Corporation ☐ Partnership *(Enter names of partners)* ☐ Single Owner *(show residence address below under Mailing Address)*
*(Enter State of Incorporation)*

**PREMISES ADDRESS** / **MAILING ADDRESS**

*(Street Address or P.O. Box, if any)* / *(Street Address or P.O. Box, if any)*

*(City)* *(State)* *(Zip)* / *(City)* *(State)* *(Zip)*

*(Contact Name)* *(Title)* / *(Contact Name)* *(Title)*

*(Telephone No.) (   )* / *(Telephone No.) (   )*

**1. DEFINITIONS** - (a) Premises: all locations operated and owned or leased by you or your subsidiaries which are used as health care facilities for the treatment of illness or provision of custodial care, having full-service professional staffs, such as hospitals, nursing homes, ambulatory care centers and clinics. In all cases the term "premises" shall specifically exclude (1) doctors, dentists or other professional offices not located within a health care facility and (2) any location which is used by LICENSEE for a trade show, convention or exposition.
(b) Subsidiary: an entity wholly-owned by you for which payment of fees and reports are made.

**2. BMI GRANT** - BMI grants you a non-exclusive license to perform or allow to be performed at the licensed premises all musical works of which BMI shall have the right to grant public performance licenses during the term of this agreement. This grant of rights includes but is not limited to music performed: (1) in rehabilitation areas; (2) in television and radio programming received by LICENSEE on the premises; (3) in audiovisual presentations in meetings; (4) as recorded background music or live music; (5) over teleconferencing at the licensed premises; and (6) over telephones in the form of music-on-hold.

This license does not include: (a) the right to present the music in any way which may be a use of the "grand rights"; (b) the right to broadcast, telecast, cablecast or otherwise transmit the performances outside of the licensed premises, except to the extent that music on telephone hold lines originating at a licensed premises is audible at remote locations on telephone lines as part of "music-on-hold"; (c) performances of music by a jukebox as defined in the Copyright Law (17 U.S.C. § 116); (d) any performance of music by interactive software, whether (1) delivered by media such as CD-ROM, CD-I, diskette or cartridge, (2) delivered by on line service, such as interactive cable, interactive TV, computer network, telephone or satellite, or (3) rendered by multimedia hardware, such as computer or computer-driven handheld devices.

BMI may withdraw from the license your right to perform any musical work as to which a legal action has been brought or a claim made that BMI does not have the right to license the work or that the work infringes another work.

**3. TERM OF AGREEMENT** - The first term of this agreement begins on the first day of _____ and ends on December 31,1996 *(Month/Year)* and shall be extended for additional terms of one (1) year each unless cancelled by either party as of the end of the first term or any additional term upon not less than 30 days notice prior to the end of any such term. A "contract year" means each consecutive twelve-month period beginning with the first month of the agreement. If the agreement begins in any month other than January, the fee for the last contract year shall be prorated.

**4. FEES** - (a) You agree to pay BMI for each year of this agreement fees as follows:
　(i) If LICENSEE operates a facility primarily for in-patient treatment, the fees appearing in Category 1 of the License Fee Schedule.
　(ii) If LICENSEE operates a facility primarily providing ambulatory care at a free-standing facility, the fees appearing in Category 2 of the License Fee Schedule.

### LICENSE FEE SCHEDULE

| Category 1 Annual Fee Per Bed | Category 2 Annual Fee per Facility |
|---|---|
| 1993　$ 1.65 | $ 225 |
| 1994　1.80 | 240 |
| 1995　2.00 | 260 |
| 1996 •　2.25 | 285 |

\* and any subsequent years

(b) Subject to Subparagraphs 4 (a) and (c) and Paragraph 5, you agree to pay to BMI for each contract year an estimated fee as an advance of the actual fee. Based upon your projection (refer to Schedule A on other side of this form), you estimate that your highest number of beds during the first contract year will be _____ and your estimated fee will be _____ and/or that you operate _____ ambulatory care facilities and your estimated fee will be _____ . The estimated fee for your in-patient treatment or ambulatory care facility or both will be _____ The first annual fee is due within 30 days of your signing this agreement. The minimum annual fee shall be $300 .00 for 1993; $325.00 for 1994; $360.00 for 1995; and $400.00 for 1996.

(c) The estimated fee for the second and following contract years will be the actual fee for the previous contract year and will be due and payable no later than 30 days after the beginning of each contract year.

**5. REPORTING** - (a) At the same time as the payments required by Paragraph 4 are due, you agree to furnish BMI (on forms available from BMI) with a report, certified either by an officer or your auditor, setting forth any information regarding the subject matter of this agreement which BMI may reasonably require, including, without limitation:
　(i) the highest number of beds for the year reported, including subsidiaries (if applicable);
　(ii) the name and address of each subsidiary for which a fee is paid, and the highest number of beds of that subsidiary.
　(iii) the name and address of each ambulatory care facility.
(b) If, after processing the annual report, the actual fee is greater than the license fee already paid by you for the contract year, you agree to pay BMI the difference within (30) days of the mailing by BMI to you of an adjusted statement.
(c) If, after processing the annual report, the actual fee is less than the license fee already paid by you to BMI for the contract year, BMI agrees to credit the difference between the actual and estimated license fees to your account, and if such adjustment occurs in the last contract year of the agreement, BMI shall refund said sum promptly.

**COMPLETE ALL SHADED AREAS**

1

**6. INDEMNITY BY BMI** - BMI agrees to indemnify you, your officers and employees against any and all claims that may be made against you with respect to the performance of any music licensed under this agreement at the time of your performances. You agree to give BMI immediate notice of any claim, to deliver to BMI any related papers and to cooperate with BMI in the matter, of which BMI will be in full charge. BMI will, upon reasonable written request, advise you whether specific musical works are available for performance, if you provide the title and the writer/composer of each musical work.

**7. CANCELLATION OF ENTIRE CATEGORY** - BMI shall have the right to cancel this agreement along with the simultaneous cancellation of the agreements of all other licensees of the same class and category as LICENSEE, as of the end of any month during the term, upon sixty (60) days advance written notice.

**8. OFFER OF COMPARABLE AGREEMENT** - If BMI, during the term of this agreement and for the same class and category as yours, issues licenses granting rights similar to those in this agreement on a more favorable basis, BMI will, for the rest of the term, offer you a comparable agreement.

**9. BREACH OR DEFAULT/WAIVER** - If there is any breach or default by you of this agreement, BMI will have the right to cancel it, but the cancellation will become effective only if the breach or default continues thirty (30) days after the date of BMI's written notice to you. The right to cancel is in addition to any other remedies which BMI may have. BMI may enforce any of its rights under this agreement at any time even if it has not done so earlier.

**10. ARBITRATION** - All disputes of any kind arising in connection with the terms of this agreement shall be submitted to the American Arbitration Association in New York, New York under its rules then in effect. The arbitrators will be selected as follows: each of us will, by written notice to the other, have the right to appoint one arbitrator. If, within ten (10) days after such notice by one of us, the other one does not, by written notice, appoint another arbitrator, the first arbitrator will be the only arbitrator. However, if we each appoint an arbitrator, the two arbitrators will appoint a third arbitrator. If ten (10) days pass after the second arbitrator's appointment and the two arbitrators cannot agree upon the third arbitrator, then either of us may, in writing, request the American Arbitration Association to appoint the third arbitrator. The arbitration award shall be entirely binding on both of us and judgment may be entered in any appropriate court. The award shall include an amount for the costs, expenses and attorneys' fees of arbitration, which shall be paid by the losing party.

**11. NOTICES** - Any notices to be given are to be in writing and will be deemed given on the day they are sent by ordinary first-class U.S. mail to the other of us at its above mailing address or any different address which either of us later designates in writing. Any notices you send to BMI will be addressed to the attention of the General Licensing Department. Any notices BMI sends to you will be addressed to the attention of the person signing this agreement for you unless you advise BMI to address notices to someone else.

**12. MISCELLANEOUS** - This agreement is our entire understanding, will not be binding until signed by both of us, and no waiver or change will be valid unless in writing and signed by us. This agreement is signed by the authorized representatives of each of us. Your rights are not assignable. This agreement, its validity, construction and effect, will be governed by the laws of the State of New York. The fact that any parts of the agreement may be found by a court of competent jurisdiction to be void or unenforceable will not affect the validity or enforceability of any other parts. The headings are for convenience only and are not a part of the agreement.

(To Be Completed by BMI)

| BROADCAST MUSIC, INC. |
| --- |

By: _____
*(Signature)*

_____
*(Print Name of Signer)*

_____
*(Title of Signer)*

(To Be Completed by LICENSEE)

_____
Name of Corporation, Partnership or Single Owner
(Enter Legal Name from Other Side)

Sign here ▶ By: _____
*(Signature)*

_____
*(Print Name of Signer)*

_____
*(Title of Signer)*

(a) If corporation, state corporate office held; (b) if partnership, write "Partner", (c) if single owner, write "single owner"

**SCHEDULE A** -Name and address of each subsidiary in-patient treatment facility or ambulatory care facility for which a fee is paid, and highest number of beds at each in-patient treatment facility.

| SUBSIDIARY IN-PATIENT TREATMENT FACILITY / OR AMBULATORY CARE FACILITY DBA | ADDRESS | CITY | STATE | ZIP | Highest # of beds for the report year. |
| --- | --- | --- | --- | --- | --- |
| | | | | | |
| | | | | | |
| | | | | | |
| | | | | | |
| | | | | | |
| | | | | | |
| | | | | | |

TOTAL AMBULATORY CARE FACILITIES [____]

ENTER TOTAL HERE AND ON FRONT OF THIS FORM IN SPACE PROVIDED

TOTAL BEDS [____]

ENTER TOTAL HERE AND ON FRONT OF THIS FORM IN SPACE PROVIDED

IF MORE SPACE IS REQUIRED, ATTACH SHEET(S)
COMPLETE ALL SHADED AREAS
2

# FORM 17.10

## BMI COLLEGE/UNIVERSITY (TIER 1)

**BMI** MUSIC
PERFORMANCE
AGREEMENT          **College / University**

ACCOUNT #            **58**

**LI-98/01-58**
One Tier

THIS AGREEMENT made and entered into on *(Date will be Entered By BMI Upon Execution)* _____ 19 _____
between BROADCAST MUSIC, INC., a New York corporation with its principal offices located at 320 West 57th Street, New
York, N.Y. 10019, hereinafter referred to as BMI, and the entity described below and hereinafter referred to as LICENSEE:

_____
*(Legal Name of LICENSEE and Name of Institution)*
a college, or university or other post-secondary institution of higher education with its principal offices located at

_____

City of _____ State _____ Zip _____

Tel. No.  (_____) _____ Fice Code Number _____
         Area Code

### 1. DEFINITIONS

(a) "LICENSEE" as used herein shall include the named institution and any of its constituent bodies, agencies, or
organizations which within the specific context to which this license is to apply maintain a substantial nexus to the named
institution and / or over which the named institution has control or authority.

(b) "Premises" shall include LICENSEE's campus(es) and any site located off LICENSEE's campus(es) which has been
engaged for use by LICENSEE. However, in the event LICENSEE has a pecuniary interest in an establishment or property which
is not directly related to LICENSEE's educational purposes or where the intended primary purpose of such establishment or
property is not for the use of LICENSEE's students. at which establishment or property musical compositions are being
performed publicly, it is specifically understood and agreed to by LICENSEE that this Agreement shall not apply to such other
establishment or property.

(c) "Full-time students" as used herein shall be the sum of (i) all full-time undergraduate and graduate students and (ii) one-
third of all part-time undergraduate and graduate students. If during the term of this Agreement, the method of converting part-
time students to a full-time equivalency as indicated in subsection (ii) of this Paragraph 1 (c) is changed from the Integrated
Postsecondary Education Data System (IPEDS) or any superseding Survey conducted annually by the Department of
Education, such different method of conversion shall be deemed substituted in said subsection (ii) as of the effective Fall
academic term.

(d) "Compulsory rate" shall mean the fee for non-commercial educational radio stations established under section 118 of
the U.S. Copyright Act.

(e) "Campus radio broadcasting station" shall mean and be limited to a non-commercial educational radio station that is
not affiliated with NPR.

(f) "Term" shall mean the period commencing July 1. 1997 and ending June 30, 2002. "First Contract Year" shall mean
the period commencing July 1, 1997 and ending June 30, 1998. Each subsequent period commencing July 1 and ending the
following June 30 shall be referred to as an additional "contract year."

(g) "Musical attractions" shall mean concerts, stage shows, variety shows, symphonies, operas, recitals, chamber music
and other similar performances presented or promoted exclusively by LICENSEE.

(h) "CPI adjustment" shall mean the difference in the Consumer Price Index (Urban, All Items), as determined by the United
States Department of Labor, between July, 1997 and July of the specified contract year.

(i) A college "Orchestra" shall mean an orchestra which consists primarily of student performers who may be augmented
by faculty, staff or other musicians. The orchestra is offered by the institution to further education in music, including training
musicians for professional careers or to better their general musical skills. The orchestra staff is employed by the college, which
also has ultimate fiscal responsibility for the orchestra, and is governed by the institution, a college-based steering committee
or other similar body, and not a separate board of directors independent from the college.

## 2. GRANT OF RIGHTS

BMI hereby grants to LICENSEE for the term of this Agreement a non-exclusive license to perform or cause the public performance by live or recorded means at LICENSEE's Premises all of the musical works to which BMI shall have the right to grant public performance licenses, including, but not limited to performances by or at:

- sporting events
- socials
- musical attractions
- campus radio broadcasting stations
- student unions
- college theater groups
- fitness centers
- classrooms
- fairs / festivals
- athletic facilities
- special events such as orientation and graduation
- fraternities / sororities
- college orchestras
- student bands
- "music-on-hold" (as that term is commonly understood) through LICENSEE's telephone system(s) at the Premises to persons connected to the Premises by telephone.

This license does not include:

- performances of music via any form of televised transmission, whether over-the-air broadcast, cable, satellite or otherwise;
- dramatic rights, the right to publicly perform dramatico-musical works in whole or in substantial part, the right to present individual works in a dramatic setting or the right to perform the music licensed hereunder in any other context which may constitute an exercise of the "grand rights" therein;
- performances of music by means of a coin operated phonorecord player (jukebox); and
- performances of music transmitted via the Internet or on-line service;
- musical attractions on the premises promoted by outside promoters (which shall mean any person or entity other than LICENSEE);
- musical attractions occurring outside of the premises;
- performances by commercial radio stations.

This license is not assignable, and no rights other than those mentioned are included in this license.

## 3. FEES/REPORTING

In consideration of the license granted herein, LICENSEE agrees to pay BMI the following license fees:

(a)   LICENSEE shall pay BMI for each contract year for all uses of music, a license fee derived from the "Per Student Fee" of 19¢. For each additional year, the Per Student Fee and the minimum fee of $155 shall be increased by the CPI adjustment. This fee will be based upon the number of full-time students as defined in Paragraph 1(c) and reported as follows:

(b)   For the First Contract Year, the number of full-time students as defined in Paragraph 1(c) for all covered branch campuses shall be reported for the Fall 1997 academic term upon execution of this Agreement.

LICENSEE represents that for the Fall 1997 academic term:

(i)    The number of full-time undergraduate students is .................................................................    _____

(ii)   The number of full-time graduate students is ........................................................................    _____

(iii)  The number of part-time undergraduate and graduate students is _____ which
       when divided by three (3) equals a full-time equivalency of ...............................................    _____

(iv)   The total number of "full-time students" is therefore .................................... (total i, ii & iii)    _____

which when multiplied by the Per Student Fee for the First Contract Year of 19¢ equals ......................    $_____
and that amount, or $155, whichever is greater, is the Total Student Fee due BMI by LICENSEE for the
First Contract Year. The license fee due BMI pursuant to this Agreement for the First Contract year shall
be paid by LICENSEE to BMI on or before February 1, 1998. All license fees based upon the number of
full-time students shall be computed to the nearest tenth of a cent and all minimums to the nearest cent.

(c)   If LICENSEE operates campus radio broadcasting station(s) as defined in this Agreement,
the call letters are: _____ _____ _____

For the first contract year LICENSEE shall pay a license fee derived from the current compulsory rate of $217.

(i)    The total number of campus radio broadcasting stations is _____ which when multiplied by
       the compulsory rate of $217 equals a total Campus Radio Broadcasting Station(s) Fee of.............    $_____

The Total Student Fee plus the Campus Radio Broadcasting Station(s) Fee is a Total Fee of..............    $_____

For each additional year the compulsory rate shall be increased by the CPI adjustment. For each contract year LICENSEE shall pay upon receipt of invoice, for each campus radio broadcasting station, a license fee derived from the compulsory rate.

(d) On or before November of each year from 1998 through 2002 , LICENSEE shall report to BMI, on forms to be supplied by BMI, the number of full-time students as defined in Paragraph 1(c) for the fall academic term of the contract year, which will establish the license fee for the Second, Third, Fourth and Fifth Contract Years. In addition, LICENSEE shall report the call letters of its non-commercial campus radio broadcasting stations, and such other information as BMI may reasonably require with regard to any campus radio broadcasting station(s). The license fee due BMI pursuant to the Agreement for the Second, Third, Fourth and Fifth Contract Years shall be paid by LICENSEE to BMI on or before the 20th day of January 1999, 2000, 2001, 2002.

### 4. REPORTING OF MUSICAL WORKS
For the purposes of royalty distribution to BMI's affiliated songwriters and music publishers:

(a) all campus radio broadcasting stations licensed under the compulsory rate shall, upon written request from BMI made on not less than two (2) weeks notice specifying the prospective period to be covered by the request, agree to furnish BMI weekly lists of each station's performances of all musical works, indicating the compositions performed by title and composer or by such other convenient method as may be designated by BMI, but such lists need not be furnished for more than two (2) weeks for each contract year of the term of this Agreement; and

(b) LICENSEE shall deliver to BMI for each calendar quarter, by the tenth (10th) day following the end of the calendar quarter, copies of any programs of the musical works presented by LICENSEE in its musical attractions during such quarter. Programs prepared for audiences or for the LICENSEE's own use are to be included, and shall include the presentation of encores to the extent possible. Nothing contained herein shall be deemed to require LICENSEE to deliver material not otherwise prepared.

### 5. EXAMINATION OF BOOKS AND RECORDS
BMI, upon giving reasonable notice to LICENSEE in writing, shall have the right to examine the books and records of account of LICENSEE which pertain solely to this Agreement and which may be necessary to verify any statements rendered and accountings made hereunder.

### 6. OFFER OF COMPARABLE AGREEMENT
In the event that BMI, at any time during the term of this Agreement, shall, for the same class and category as that of LICENSEE, issue licenses granting rights similar to those in this Agreement on a more favorable basis, BMI shall, for the balance of the term, offer LICENSEE a comparable agreement.

### 7. INDEMNITY
BMI agrees to indemnify, save harmless and defend LICENSEE, its officers and employees, from and against any and all claims, demands or suits that may be made or brought against them or any of them with respect to the performance of any material licensed under this Agreement. Such indemnity shall be limited to works which are licensed by BMI at the time of LICENSEE's performances, and to works which are, pursuant to a written request by LICENSEE, specifically represented in writing by an Officer of BMI in answer to said written request by LICENSEE, to be licensed by BMI at the time of LICENSEE's performance. LICENSEE agrees to give BMI immediate notice of any such claim, demand or suit, to deliver to BMI any papers pertaining thereto, and to cooperate with BMI with respect thereto, and BMI shall have full charge of the defense of any such claim, demand or suit.

### 8. BREACH OR DEFAULT/ WAIVER
Upon any breach or default of the terms and conditions of this Agreement that remain uncured after sixty (60) days notice in writing to LICENSEE, BMI may, at its sole option, cancel this Agreement. The right to cancel shall be in addition to any and all other remedies which shall be deemed a waiver of the right to require full and complete performance of this Agreement thereafter or of the right to cancel this Agreement in accordance with the terms of this paragraph. In the event of such cancellation, BMI agrees to refund to LICENSEE any unearned license fees paid in advance to BMI by LICENSEE.

### 9. CANCELLATION BY LICENSEE
In the event LICENSEE ceases to operate as an institution of higher education, or where LICENSEE ceases the public performance of music licensed by BMI, LICENSEE may cancel this Agreement upon giving sixty (60) days notice in writing to BMI. The right to cancel shall be in addition to any and all other remedies which LICENSEE may have. In the event of such cancellation, BMI agrees to refund to LICENSEE any unearned license fees paid in advance to BMI by LICENSEE.

### 10. NOTICES
All notices, if any, shall be in writing and be deemed given upon "mailing," when sent by United States certified mail sent to the party intended at its mailing address. Each party agrees to inform the other, in writing, of any change of address. Any such notice sent to BMI shall be to the attention of the Vice President, General Licensing Department at 10 Music Square East, Nashville, TN 37203. Any notice sent to LICENSEE shall be to the person signing this Agreement on behalf of LICENSEE or such other person as LICENSEE may advise BMI in writing.

11. ARBITRATION

All disputes of any kind, nature or description not subject to the jurisdiction of the BMI Rate Court arising in connection with the terms and conditions of this Agreement shall be submitted to the American Arbitration Association in New York, New York for arbitration under its then prevailing rules, the arbitrator(s) to be selected as follows: Each of the parties hereto shall, by written notice to the other, have the right to appoint one arbitrator. If within ten (10) days following the giving of such notice by one party, the other shall not, by written notice, appoint another arbitrator, the first arbitrator shall be the sole arbitrator. If two arbitrators are so appointed, they shall appoint a third arbitrator. If ten (10) days elapse after the appointment of the second arbitrator and the two arbitrators are unable to agree upon the third arbitrator, then either party may, in writing, request the American Arbitration Association to appoint the third arbitrator. The award made in the arbitration shall be binding and conclusive on the parties and judgment may be, but need not be, entered into any court having jurisdiction. Such award shall include the fixing of the costs, expenses and attorneys' fees of arbitration, which shall be borne by the unsuccessful party.

12. MISCELLANEOUS

This Agreement constitutes the entire understanding between the parties with respect to the subject matter hereof and shall not be binding until signed by both parties. This Agreement cannot be waived or added to or modified orally and no waiver, addition or modification shall be valid unless in writing and signed by the parties. This agreement, its validity, construction and effect, shall be governed by the laws of the State of New York. The fact that any provisions herein are found by a court of competent jurisdiction to be void or unenforceable shall not affect the validity or enforceability of any other provisions.

IN WITNESS WHEREOF, this Agreement has been executed by the duly authorized representatives of BMI and LICENSEE as of the date above written.

(To be Completed by BMI)
BROADCAST MUSIC, INC.

(To be Completed by LICENSEE)

_____
LICENSEE (Legal Name)

By: _____          Sign Here _____
    (Signature)                                (Signature)

_____              _____
(Print Name of Signer)                (Print Name of Signer)

_____              _____
(Title of Signer)                     (Title of Signer)

**List of Additional Branch Campuses Covered Under This Agreement**

| Institution Name | Branch Address | Fice Code # |
|---|---|---|
|  |  |  |
|  |  |  |
|  |  |  |
|  |  |  |
|  |  |  |
|  |  |  |
|  |  |  |
|  |  |  |
|  |  |  |

Attach List If More Space Required

*- Enrollment figures should include all branch campuses that are covered under this agreement -*

# FORM 17.11

## BMI COLLEGE/UNIVERSITY (TIER 2)

**BMI**
http://www.bmi.com

MUSIC
PERFORMANCE
AGREEMENT   **College / University**

ACCOUNT #

57/59

LI-98/01-57/59
TwoTier

THIS AGREEMENT made and entered into on *(Date will be Entered By BMI Upon Execution)* _____ 19___ between BROADCAST MUSIC, INC., a New York corporation with its principal offices located at 320 West 57th Street, New York, N.Y. 10019, hereinafter referred to as BMI, and the entity described below and hereinafter referred to as LICENSEE:

-----------------------------------------------------------------------------------------------

*(Legal Name of LICENSEE and Name of Institution)*
a college, or university or other post-secondary institution of higher education with its principal offices located at:
-----------------------------------------------------------------------------------------------

City of _____ State _____ Zip _____

Tel. No. (____)_____ _____ Fice Code Number _____
        *Area Code*

### 1. DEFINITIONS

(a) "LICENSEE" as used herein shall include the named institution and any of its constituent bodies, agencies, or organizations which within the specific context to which this license is to apply maintain a substantial nexus to the named institution and / or over which the named institution has control or authority.

(b) "Premises" shall include LICENSEE's campus(es) and any site located off LICENSEE's campus(es) which has been engaged for use by LICENSEE. However, in the event LICENSEE has a pecuniary interest in an establishment or property which is not directly related to LICENSEE's educational purposes or where the intended primary purpose of such establishment or property is not for the use of LICENSEE's students, at which establishment or property musical compositions are being performed publicly, it is specifically understood and agreed to by LICENSEE that this Agreement shall not apply to such other establishment or property.

(c) "Full-time students" as used herein shall be the sum of (i) all full-time undergraduate and graduate students and (ii) one-third of all part-time undergraduate and graduate students. If during the term of this Agreement, the method of converting part-time students to a full-time equivalency as indicated in subsection (ii) of this Paragraph 1 (c) is changed from the Integrated Postsecondary Education Data System (IPEDS) or any superseding Survey conducted annually by the Department of Education, such different method of conversion shall be deemed substituted in said subsection (ii) as of the effective Fall academic term.

(d) "Compulsory rate" shall mean the fee for non-commercial educational radio stations established under section 118 of the U.S. Copyright Act.

(e) "Campus radio broadcasting station" shall mean and be limited to a non-commercial educational radio station that is not affiliated with NPR.

(f) "Term" shall mean the period commencing July 1, 1997 and ending June 30, 2002. "First Contract Year" shall mean the period commencing July 1, 1997 and ending June 30, 1998. Each subsequent period commencing July 1 and ending the following June 30 shall be referred to as an additional "contract year."

(g) "Musical attractions" shall mean concerts, stage shows, variety shows, symphonies, operas, recitals, chamber music and other similar performances presented or promoted exclusively by LICENSEE.

(h) "CPI adjustment" shall mean the difference in the Consumer Price Index (Urban, All Items), as determined by the United States Department of Labor, between July, 1997 and July of the specified contract year.

(i) A college "Orchestra" shall mean an orchestra which consists primarily of student performers who may be augmented by faculty, staff or other musicians. The orchestra is offered by the institution to further education in music, including training musicians for professional careers or to better their general musical skills. The orchestra staff is employed by the college, which also has ultimate fiscal responsibility for the orchestra, and is governed by the institution, a college-based steering committee or other similar body, and not a separate board of directors independent from the college.

- 1 -

2. GRANT OF RIGHTS

BMI hereby grants to LICENSEE for the term of this Agreement a non-exclusive license to perform or cause the public performance by live or recorded means at LICENSEE's Premises all of the musical works to which BMI shall have the right to grant public performance licenses, including, but not limited to performances by or at:

- sporting events
- socials
- musical attractions
- campus radio broadcasting stations
- student unions
- college theater groups
- fitness centers
- classrooms
- fairs / festivals
- athletic facilities
- fraternities / sororities
- college orchestras
- student bands
- special events such as orientation and graduation
- "music-on-hold" (as that term is commonly understood) through LICENSEE's telephone system(s) at the Premises to persons connected to the Premises by telephone.

This license does not include:

- performances of music via any form of televised transmission, whether over-the-air broadcast, cable, satellite or otherwise;
- dramatic rights, the right to publicly perform dramatico-musical works in whole or in substantial part, the right to present individual works in a dramatic setting or the right to perform the music licensed hereunder in any other context which may constitute an exercise of the "grand rights" therein;
- performances of music by means of a coin operated phonorecord player (jukebox); and
- performances of music transmitted via the Internet or on-line service;
- musical attractions on the premises promoted by outside promoters (which shall mean any person or entity other than LICENSEE);
- musical attractions occurring outside of the premises;
- performances by commercial radio stations.

This license is not assignable, and no rights other than those mentioned are included in this license.

3. FEES/REPORTING

In consideration of the license granted herein, LICENSEE agrees to pay BMI the following license fees:

(a) LICENSEE shall pay BMI for each contract year for all uses of music, a license fee derived from the "Per Student Fee" of 17¢. For each additional year, the Per Student Fee and the minimum fee of $120 shall be increased by the CPI adjustment. This fee will be based upon the number of full-time students as defined in Paragraph 1(c) and reported as follows:

(b) For the First Contract Year, the number of full-time students as defined in Paragraph 1(c) for all covered branch campuses shall be reported for the Fall 1997 academic term upon execution of this Agreement.

LICENSEE represents that for the Fall 1997 academic term:

(i) The number of full-time undergraduate students is .................................................................... _____

(ii) The number of full-time graduate students is ........................................................................... _____

(iii) The number of part-time undergraduate and graduate students is _____ which
when divided by three (3) equals a full-time equivalency of ................................................. _____

(iv) The total number of "full-time students" is therefore ................................................. **(total i, ii & iii)** _____

which when multiplied by the Per Student Fee for the First Contract Year of 17¢ equals .................. $_____
and that amount, or $120, whichever is greater, is the Total Student Fee due BMI by LICENSEE for the
First Contract Year. The license fee due BMI pursuant to this Agreement for the First Contract year shall
be paid by LICENSEE to BMI on or before February 1, 1998. All license fees based upon the number of
full-time students shall be computed to the nearest tenth of a cent and all minimums to the nearest cent.

(c) If LICENSEE operates campus radio broadcasting station(s) as defined in this Agreement,
the call letters are: _____

For the first contract year LICENSEE shall pay a license fee derived from the current compulsory rate of $217.

(i) The total number of campus radio broadcasting stations is _____ which when multiplied by
the compulsory rate of $217 equals a total Campus Radio Broadcasting Station(s) Fee of................. $_____

The Total Student Fee plus the Campus Radio Broadcasting Station(s) Fee is a Total Fee of.............. $_____

For each additional year the compulsory rate shall be increased by the CPI adjustment. For each contract year LICENSEE shall pay upon receipt of invoice, for each campus radio broadcasting station, a license fee derived from the compulsory rate.

(d) LICENSEE shall pay BMI for each contract year the following Musical Event Promoter/Presenter Fee for performances presented or promoted exclusively by LICENSEE, the Entertainment Costs of which total $1500 or more:

### Fee for In-House Promoters / Presenters

| Seating Capacity | Fee Basis Percentage Applied to Gross Ticket Revenues Per Attraction |
|---|---|
| 0 - 9,999 Seats | 0.30% |
| 10,000 And More Seats | 0.15% |

(e) On or before November of each year from 1998 through 2002 , LICENSEE shall report to BMI, on forms to be supplied by BMI, the number of full-time students as defined in Paragraph 1(c) for the fall academic term of the contract year, which will establish the license fee for the Second, Third, Fourth and Fifth Contract Years. In addition, LICENSEE shall report the call letters of its campus radio broadcasting stations, and such other information as BMI may reasonably require with regard to any campus radio broadcasting station(s). The license fee due BMI pursuant to the Agreement for the Second, Third, Fourth and Fifth Contract Years shall be paid by LICENSEE to BMI on or before the 20th day of January 1999, 2000, 2001, 2002.

### 4. REPORTING OF MUSICAL WORKS

For the purposes of royalty distribution to BMI's affiliated songwriters and music publishers:

(a) all campus radio broadcasting stations licensed under the compulsory rate shall, upon written request from BMI made on not less than two (2) weeks notice specifying the prospective period to be covered by the request, agree to furnish BMI weekly lists of each station's performances of all musical works, indicating the compositions performed by title and composer or by such other convenient method as may be designated by BMI, but such lists need not be furnished for more than two (2) weeks for each contract year of the term of this Agreement; and

(b) LICENSEE shall deliver to BMI for each calendar quarter, by the tenth (10th) day following the end of the calendar quarter, copies of any programs of the musical works presented by LICENSEE in its musical attractions during such quarter. Programs prepared for audiences or for the LICENSEE's own use are to be included, and shall include the presentation of encores to the extent possible. Nothing contained herein shall be deemed to require LICENSEE to deliver material not otherwise prepared.

(c) In connection with paragraph 3(d) above LICENSEE shall report to BMI on forms to be supplied by BMI all musical attractions as defined in Paragraph 1(g) which were presented or promoted exclusively by LICENSEE during the immediately preceding academic year. Attached to each report of musical attractions submitted by LICENSEE shall be lists of the musical works presented in LICENSEE's musical attractions indicating the compositions performed by title and composer or by such other convenient method as may be designated by BMI.

### 5. EXAMINATION OF BOOKS AND RECORDS

BMI, upon giving reasonable notice to LICENSEE in writing, shall have the right to examine the books and records of account of LICENSEE which pertain solely to this Agreement and which may be necessary to verify any statements rendered and accountings made hereunder.

### 6. OFFER OF COMPARABLE AGREEMENT

In the event that BMI, at any time during the term of this Agreement, shall, for the same class and category as that of LICENSEE, issue licenses granting rights similar to those in this Agreement on a more favorable basis, BMI shall, for the balance of the term, offer LICENSEE a comparable agreement.

### 7. INDEMNITY

BMI agrees to indemnify, save harmless and defend LICENSEE, its officers and employees, from and against any and all claims, demands or suits that may be made or brought against them or any of them with respect to the performance of any material licensed under this Agreement. Such indemnity shall be limited to works which are licensed by BMI at the time of LICENSEE's performances, and to works which are, pursuant to a written request by LICENSEE, specifically represents in writing by an Officer of BMI in answer to said written request by LICENSEE, to be licensed by BMI at the time of LICENSEE's performance. LICENSEE agrees to give BMI immediate notice of any such claim, demand or suit, to deliver to BMI any papers pertaining thereto, and to cooperate with BMI with respect thereto, and BMI shall have full charge of the defense of any such claim, demand or suit.

### 8. BREACH OR DEFAULT/ WAIVER

Upon any breach or default of the terms and conditions of this Agreement that remain uncured after sixty (60) days notice in writing to LICENSEE, BMI may, at its sole option, cancel this Agreement. The right to cancel shall be in addition to any and all other remedies which shall be deemed a waiver of the right to require full and complete performance of this Agreement thereafter or of the right to cancel this Agreement in accordance with the terms of this paragraph. In the event of such cancellation, BMI agrees to refund to LICENSEE any unearned license fees paid in advance to BMI by LICENSEE.

**9. CANCELLATION BY LICENSEE**

In the event LICENSEE ceases to operate as an institution of higher education, or where LICENSEE ceases the public performance of music licensed by BMI, LICENSEE may cancel this Agreement upon giving sixty (60) days notice in writing to BMI. The right to cancel shall be in addition to any and all other remedies which LICENSEE may have. In the event of such cancellation, BMI agrees to refund to LICENSEE any unearned license fees paid in advance to BMI by LICENSEE.

**10. NOTICES**

All notices, if any, shall be in writing and be deemed given upon "mailing," when sent by United States certified mail sent to the party intended at its mailing address. Each party agrees to inform the other, in writing, of any change of address. Any such notice sent to BMI shall be to the attention of the Vice President, General Licensing Department at 10 Music Square East, Nashville, TN 37203. Any notice sent to LICENSEE shall be to the person signing this Agreement on behalf of LICENSEE or such other person as LICENSEE may advise BMI in writing.

**11. ARBITRATION**

All disputes of any kind, nature or description not subject to the jurisdiction of the BMI Rate Court arising in connection with the terms and conditions of this Agreement shall be submitted to the American Arbitration Association in New York, New York for arbitration under its then prevailing rules, the arbitrator(s) to be selected as follows: Each of the parties hereto shall, by written notice to the other, have the right to appoint one arbitrator. If within ten (10) days following the giving of such notice by one party, the other shall not, by written notice, appoint another arbitrator, the first arbitrator shall be the sole arbitrator. If two arbitrators are so appointed, they shall appoint a third arbitrator. If ten (10) days elapse after the appointment of the second arbitrator and the two arbitrators are unable to agree upon the third arbitrator, then either party may, in writing, request the American Arbitration Association to appoint the third arbitrator. The award made in the arbitration shall be binding and conclusive on the parties and judgment may be, but need not be, entered into any court having jurisdiction. Such award shall include the fixing of the costs, expenses and attorneys' fees of arbitration, which shall be borne by the unsuccessful party.

**12. MISCELLANEOUS**

This Agreement constitutes the entire understanding between the parties with respect to the subject matter hereof and shall not be binding until signed by both parties. This Agreement cannot be waived or added to or modified orally and no waiver, addition or modification shall be valid unless in writing and signed by the parties. This agreement, its validity, construction and effect, shall be governed by the laws of the State of New York. The fact that any provisions herein are found by a court of competent jurisdiction to be void or unenforceable shall not affect the validity or enforceability of any other provisions.

IN WITNESS WHEREOF, this Agreement has been executed by the duly authorized representatives of BMI and LICENSEE as of the date above written.

(To be Completed by LICENSEE)

(To be Completed by BMI)
BROADCAST MUSIC, INC.

_____
LICENSEE ( Legal Name)

By: _____          Sign Here _____
            (Signature)                                                    (Signature)

_____                  _____
(Print Name of Signer)                                       (Print Name of Signer)

_____                  _____
(Title of Signer)                                                   (Title of Signer)

### List of Additional Branch Campuses Covered Under This Agreement

| Institution Name | Branch Address | Fice Code # |
|---|---|---|
|  |  |  |
|  |  |  |
|  |  |  |

Attach List if More Space Required

*- Enrollment figures should include all branch campuses that are covered under this agreement -*

- 4 -

# FORM 17.12

## ASCAP LOCAL STATION BLANKET RADIO LICENSE

**LOCAL STATION BLANKET RADIO LICENSE**

**AGREEMENT** made between AMERICAN SOCIETY OF COMPOSERS, AUTHORS AND PUBLISHERS ("We", "Us" or "ASCAP") and

("You" or "Licensee") as follows:

1. **Term of License.** This license is for the term commencing as of _____, 199__ and ending December 31, 2000.

2. **Licensed Radio Station.** The radio station licensed by this agreement is:

> Call Letters _____
>
> Frequency _____
>
> City of License _____

All references to "you", "your", "the Station", or "your station" include any company, firm or corporation that you own or that is under the same or substantially the same ownership, management or control as the Station. "Independent" refers to any firm or corporation that is not under the same or substantially the same ownership, management or control as the Station.

3. **Grant.** This license grants you the right to perform publicly by radio broadcasting on *radio programs* from your Station or from any other place non-dramatic performances of the separate musical compositions in the ASCAP *repertory*.

4. **Limitations on License.** This agreement does not: license the performance of any dramatic-musical works, such as operas, operettas, musical comedies or plays, in whole or in part; grant you any other rights in the musical compositions licensed under this agreement; authorize you to grant to others any performance or other rights in any of the musical compositions licensed under this agreement; extend to the receiver of any of your radio broadcasts, or to any place at which the performances licensed by this agreement originate if other than at the station.

5. **Definitions.** When used in this agreement the defined words and phrases appear in italics and have the following meanings:

A. ASCAP "Repertory" means all musical compositions which ASCAP has the right to license for public performance now or hereafter during the term of this agreement. All compositions written and copyrighted by our members and in the repertory on the date this agreement is executed are included for the full term of this agreement. Compositions written or copyrighted by our members during the license term are included for the full balance of the term.

B. Your "Radio Programs" means all programs and announcements broadcast by the Station, all of your *simulcast programs*, and all of your *occasional network programs*, whether originated by the Station or any other source, including those furnished by networks, or other program suppliers, whether or not those networks or program suppliers are licensed by us.

C. Your "Simulcast Programs" means all programs broadcast simultaneously or by so-called "delayed" or "repeat" broadcasts by two or more stations that you own or for which you act as a *time broker*.

D. Your "Occasional Network Programs" means all programs that you cause to be broadcast simultaneously or by so-called "delayed" or "repeat" broadcasts on any group of two or more radio stations that are affiliated with you for the purpose of broadcasting those programs. For the purposes of this agreement any sports network which you operate is deemed to be an occasional network.

E. "Time Broker" means any independent person, firm or corporation that engages in *time brokerage*.

F. "Time Brokerage" means any arrangement between a station and a *time broker* that:

(1) authorizes the resale by the *time broker* of the radio broadcasting facilities of the station;

(2) permits the *time broker* to provide programs for 10% or more of the time the station is on the air; and

(3) provides for the sale by the *time broker* of all or substantially all announcements within the brokered time.

G. "Net Promotional Revenue" means all cash payments that you receive from third parties for the direct or indirect promotion of their businesses via the broadcast facilities of the station other than paid programs or commercial announcements (such as, but not limited to, Bridal or Craft Shows, Direct Mailings, Special Sponsored Events or Publications, produced and promoted by the station), less those out-of-the-ordinary costs, such as booth rentals, printing and mailing expenses, and cost of goods sold, that would not have otherwise been incurred without the promotional activity. Deductible costs may not exceed the cash payments received.

1

H. "Gross Revenue" means all:

(1) cash payments made by or on behalf of:

a. sponsors or donors for the use of radio broadcasting facilities of the Station,

b. sponsors of, or donors to, your *simulcast programs*,

c. sponsors of, or donors to, your *occasional network programs*,

d. *time brokers* who each provide programs for less than 10% of the time the Station is on the air, or recognized independent companies engaged in arrangements with radio or television stations generally for the resale of the radio broadcasting facilities of the Station, and

e. independent networks or other program suppliers for the broadcasting of such networks' or program suppliers' programs or announcements by the Station; and

(2) *net promotional revenue*

Such payments shall include all payments made directly to, or as authorized by, you, your employees, representatives, agents or any other person acting on your behalf. Such payments shall not include payments made to independent third parties, such as networks or program suppliers, or non-cash payments such as payments in goods or services commonly referred to as "trades" or "barter".

I. "Adjusted Gross Revenue" means *gross revenue* less:

(1) advertising agency commission not to exceed 15% actually allowed to an independent advertising agency;

(2) any sums received from your political radio programs and announcements, net of agency commissions;

(3) bad debts actually written off and discounts allowed or rebates paid; and

(4) rate card discounts, cash, quantity and/or frequency actually allowed.

J. "Revenue Subject to Fee" means *adjusted gross revenue* or, at Station's option, *adjusted gross revenue* less the total of the following itemized deductions which exceeds 11% of *adjusted gross revenue*:

(1) All compensation over and above the total annual amount indicated below, actually paid by the Station to personnel whose duties primarily are acting as (a) master of ceremonies or disc jockey on musical programs, or (b) vocalist or instrumentalist engaged for a specific program; or (c) featured newscaster and news commentator; or (d) featured sportscaster, or (e) master of ceremonies on an entertainment program, or (f) announcer:

| Station's Annual Adjusted Gross Revenue | Total Annual Amount Not Deductible |
|---|---|
| Under - $ 50,000 | $ 6,200 |
| $ 50,000 - $ 149,999 | $18,600 |
| $ 150,000 - $ 299,999 | $27,900 |
| $ 300,000 - $ 499,999 | $41,900 |
| $ 500,000 - $ 749,999 | $46,500 |
| $ 750,000 - $ 999,999 | $53,700 |
| $ 1,000,000 and Over | $62,000 |

You may not deduct any compensation paid to any person who has a stock or other ownership interest in Licensee or in the station of 40% or more.

(2) The actual payment by the Station to an independent supplier of general news service (such as AP or UPI) or specialized news service (such as weather, traffic, business or agricultural reports).

(3) The following actual costs incurred by the Station for a specific program: (a) payments to the telephone company or like transmission utility for remote pick-up necessary to broadcast the program from a point outside a studio of the Station; and (b) rights for broadcasting a sports or other special event.

(4) The following actual payments made by the Station to an independent network not licensed by ASCAP for a specific local program: (a) If the network is owned and operated by a college or university, the actual payment made by the station to the college or university; (b) If the network is not owned and operated by a college or university, the actual payments made for talent and for broadcast rights (which may not exceed the amount actually paid to or for the original holder of the broadcast rights for the particular program), and the actual payments made to or for the telephone company or like transmission utility for interconnecting lines and remote lines necessary to broadcast the program from a point outside the studio of the Station, which may not exceed the amount actually paid to or for the telephone company or like transmission utility.

(5) The following actual costs incurred in connection with your *occasional network programs*: (a) the payments to your affiliated stations in connection with those programs; (b) the actual payments made for talent and broadcast rights (which may not exceed the amount actually paid to or for the original holder of such broadcast rights); and (c) the actual payments made to or for the telephone company or like transmission utility for interconnecting lines and remote lines necessary to broadcast that program from a point outside the studio of the Station, which may not exceed the amount actually paid to or for the telephone company or like transmission utility.

6. **Music Reports.** You agree to furnish to us upon request a list of all musical compositions on your *radio programs*, showing the title, composer and author of each composition. You will not be obligated to furnish such list for a period or periods which in the aggregate exceed one month in any one calendar year during the term of this agreement.

7. **Right to Restrict.**

A. Our members may restrict the radio broadcasting of their compositions up to a maximum of 500 at any given time, only for the purpose of preventing harmful effect upon other interests under the copyrights of such works; provided, however, that (1) limited licenses will be granted upon application to us entirely free of additional charge if the copyright owners are unable to show reasonable hazards to their major interests likely to result from such radio broadcasting; (2) the right to restrict any composition will not be exercised for the purpose of permitting the fixing or regulating of fees for the recording or transcribing of the composition; (3) in no case will any charges, "free plugs", or other consideration be required for permission to perform a restricted composition; and (4) in no event will any composition be restricted after its initial radio broadcast for the purpose of confining further radio broadcasts to a particular artist, station, network or program.

B. We may also in good faith restrict the radio broadcasting of any composition, over and above the number specified in the previous paragraph, only as to which any suit has been brought or threatened on a claim that the composition infringes a composition not contained in the ASCAP *repertory* or on a claim that we do not have the right to license the public performance of the composition by radio broadcasting.

8. **License Fee.**

A. You agree to pay us the following license fee for each year of the agreement:

(1) Gross Revenue up to $150,000. If your annual (or annualized) *gross revenue* is $150,000 or less use the following fee schedule to determine your annual fee for the year. Any period of less than a year should be annualized and the applicable annual fee for a station with that annualized revenue should be pro-rated for the period.

| Annual Revenue | License Fee |
|---|---|
| Up to $50,000 | $ 450 |
| $50,001 - $75,000 | $ 800 |
| $75,001 - $100,000 | $1150 |
| $100,001 - $125,000 | $1450 |
| $125,001 - $150,000 | $1800 |

(2) Gross Revenue over $150,000. If your annual (or annualized) *gross revenue* is over $150,000 your fee is 1.615% of your *revenue subject to fee* but not less than 1% of your *adjusted gross revenue*.

B. In the event that your payment of fees under this agreement causes us to incur a liability to pay a gross receipts, sales, use, business use, or other tax which is based on the amount of our receipts from you, and (1) we have taken reasonable steps to be exempted or excused from paying the tax; and (2) we are permitted by law to pass through the tax to our licensees, you will pay us the full amount of the tax.

9. **Reports and Payments.**

A. Annual Reports. You will send us a report of the license fee due for each year of this agreement, by April 1st of the following year, by fully completing the Statement of Account form which we will supply free of charge. A copy of the Statement of Account form is annexed and made a part of this agreement.

B. Monthly Payments. For each month during the term of this Agreement, you will pay us on or before the first day of the following month, a sum equal to 1/12th of the license fee for the preceding calendar year (annualized for any reported period less than a year), adjusted in accordance with any increase in the Consumer Price Index (National, all items) between the preceding October and the next preceding October. If we do not receive the report required by Paragraph 9.A. for any calendar year when due, the monthly payments will be in the amount of the monthly payments due for the preceding year, plus 24%, and payments at that rate will continue until we receive the late report. If the station commenced broadcasting after January 1, 1996, you will furnish us with a good faith estimate of your revenue for the first year of operation and the monthly payments during the first calendar year of broadcasting will be 1/12th of the fee provided in Paragraph 8.A. for a station having such revenue.

C. Annual Adjustments. If the monthly payments that you have made to us for a year pursuant to Paragraph 9.B. are less than the license fee for that year, you will pay us the additional amount due with the annual report. If the amount that you paid for that year exceeds the license fee due for the year we will apply the excess payment against

3

your future monthly payments, or refund it to you upon your written request if it is greater than three monthly payments required by Paragraph 9.B.

D.  Late Payments. If we do not receive any payment required under Paragraph 9.B. or 9.C. before the first day of the month following the date when the payment was due, you will pay us a finance charge of 1½% per month from the date the payment was due.

E.  Billing Basis. License fee reports will be made on a billing basis by all stations, except that any station may report on a cash basis if (1) its books have been kept on a cash basis and (2) it reported to us only on a cash basis and at no time on a billing basis during the entire term of its agreement with us ending February 28, 1977, and continuously thereafter. You will account for all billings made subsequent to the termination of this agreement with respect to radio broadcasts made during the term of the agreement as and when you make such billings.

F.  Late Reports. If we do not receive a report required by Paragraph 9.A. of this agreement within 30 days of the date that the report was due, we may give you notice that you have an additional 30 days within which to submit the report on either the *adjusted gross revenue* or *adjusted gross revenue* less itemized deductions basis. If you fail to submit the report within the additional 30-day period, the report must be on the *adjusted gross revenue* basis.

G.  Multiple Station Reports. You will submit a single license fee report for:

(1)  AM and FM stations that you own in the same city if the combined *gross revenue* for the stations is less than $75,000, or

(2)  all stations that you own that simultaneously broadcast programs for 80% or more of the time the stations are on the air concurrently.

If you act as a *time broker* for one or more other radio stations that are licensed pursuant to this form of local station blanket radio license, you will include in your license fee reports for the Station all *gross revenue* relating to periods on those other station or stations that are simulcast or are sold in combination with the Station. All other stations that you own or act as a *time broker* for will report and pay separately, and be treated for all purposes as separate stations.

H.  Combination Sales. If the use of the broadcasting facilities of the station is sold in combination with any other stations that you own, operate or control that are licensed under a form of agreement other than this form of local station blanket radio license, the combination revenue shall be allocated among the stations on a reasonable basis taking into account factors such as, but not limited to, separate sales by the stations for comparable facilities during the report period or the immediately preceding period, and/or the relative ratings of the stations during the report period.

10.  **Audits.**

A.  Right to Audit. We have the right by our duly authorized representatives, at any time during customary business hours, upon reasonable notice, to examine your books and records of account only to the extent necessary to verify any report required by this agreement. We will consider all data and information coming to our attention as a result of any such examination of books and records as completely and entirely confidential.

B.  Audit Period. The period for which we may audit is limited to the four calendar years reported preceding the year in which the audit is made. However, if you request a postponement, we have the right to audit for the period commencing with the fourth calendar year reported preceding the year in which we first notified you of our intention to audit. This limitation does not apply if you fail or refuse after written notice from us to produce the books and records necessary to verify any report or statement of accounting pursuant to the agreement.

C.  Correction of Errors. You may correct computational errors, or errors relating to deductions permitted under the agreement on your license fee reports for the four calendar years preceding the year in which the corrected reports are submitted. However, you may not submit a report on the *adjusted gross revenue* less itemized deductions basis for a period previously reported on the *adjusted gross revenue* basis.

D.  Audit Finance Charges. If our audit discloses that you underpaid license fees due us:

(1)  You will pay a finance charge on the additional license fees of 1½% per month from the date(s) the fees should have been paid pursuant to this agreement if the underpayment is 5% or more, but not less than $1000.

(2)  You will pay a finance charge on the additional license fees of 1½% per month beginning thirty (30) days after the date we bill the additional license fees to you if the underpayment is less than 5% or less than $1000.

(3)  You may dispute all or part of our audit claim. If you do, you must, within thirty (30) days from the date that we bill the additional fees,(i) advise us, in writing, of the basis for your dispute and (ii) pay us any fees indisputably owed together with any applicable finance charges. If there is a good faith dispute between us with respect to all or part of the additional fees that we have billed pursuant to this Paragraph, no finance charges will be billed with respect to the disputed fees for a period beginning on the date we billed the fees to you and ending sixty (60) days from the date that we respond to your written notification of the existence of a dispute.

(4) Finance charges computed in accordance with this Paragraph and pertaining to additional fees which you dispute in accordance with subparagraph (3) above will be adjusted pro-rata to the amount arrived at by you and us in resolution of the dispute.

11. **Breach or Default.** If you fail to perform any of the terms or conditions of this agreement relating to the reports, accountings or payments required to be made by you, we may give you thirty (30) days' notice in writing to cure your breach or default. If you do not do so within the thirty (30) days, we may then promptly terminate this license.

12. **Time Brokerage Arrangements.** If you enter into a *time brokerage* arrangement, the license granted by this agreement will automatically terminate thirty (30) days after the commencement date of the *time brokerage* unless you have furnished us a complete copy of the *time brokerage* agreement and you and *time broker* have executed a letter to us in the form annexed and made a part of this agreement requesting amendment of the license agreement to add *time broker* as a party. When that letter has been fully executed by you, *time broker* and us, this agreement will be amended accordingly.

13. **Indemnity Clause.** We will indemnify, save and hold harmless and defend you, your advertisers and their advertising agencies, and your and their officers, employees and artists, from and against all claims, demands and suits that may be made or brought against you or them with respect to the performance under this agreement of any compositions in the ASCAP *repertory* which are written or copyrighted by our members. You must give us immediate notice of any such claim, demand or suit and immediately deliver to us all papers pertaining thereto. We will have full charge of the defense of any such claim, demand or suit and you agree to cooperate fully with us in such defense. You may however engage your own counsel at your own expense who may participate in the defense of any such action. At your request we will cooperate with and assist you, your advertisers and their advertising agencies and your and their officers, employees and artists in the defense of any action or proceeding brought against them or any of them with respect to the performance of any musical compositions contained in the ASCAP *repertory*, but not copyrighted or written by members of ASCAP. This Paragraph 13 does not apply to performances of any works that may be restricted under Paragraph 7 of this agreement.

14. **Rights of Termination.**

A. You have the right to terminate this license on seven (7) days' written notice in the event of the termination, suspension or any substantial alteration or variation of the terms and conditions of the governmental licenses covering the Station, or any major interference with the operations of the Station due to governmental measures or restrictions.

B. We have the right to terminate this license on thirty (30) days' notice if there is any major interference with, or substantial increase in the cost of, our operation as a result of any law of the state, territory, dependency, possession or political subdivision in which the Station is located which is applicable to the licensing of performing rights.

15. **Notices.** All notices required or permitted to be given by either of us to the other under this agreement will be duly and properly given if:

A. mailed to the other party by registered or certified United States mail; or

B. sent by electronic transmission (i.e., Mailgram, facsimile or similar transmission); or

C. sent by generally recognized same-day or overnight delivery service;

addressed to the party at its usual place of business.

16. **Successors and Assignees.** This agreement will enure to the benefit of and be binding upon you and us and our respective successors and assignees, but no assignment will relieve either of us of our respective obligations under this agreement.

17. **Per Program License.** The "local station per program license" for the term ending December 31, 2000 is being offered to you simultaneously with this agreement. In accepting this agreement, you acknowledge that you have a choice of entering into either this agreement or the per program license with us; that you have the opportunity to negotiate for separate licenses with our individual members; and that you are voluntarily entering into this agreement with us. You may substitute the per program agreement in place of this agreement by giving us written notice at least 10 days prior to the commencement of any month during the term of this agreement. In such event, effective with the commencement of that month, the per program agreement will be in full force and effect between us.

18. **Applicable Law.** The fees set forth in this agreement have been approved by the United States District Court for the Southern District of New York as reasonable and non-discriminatory in accordance with the Amended Final Judgment in United States v. ASCAP. The meaning of the provisions of this agreement will be construed in accordance with the laws of the State of New York.

IN WITNESS WHEREOF, this agreement has been duly executed by ASCAP and Licensee this        day
of                    . 199  /2000.

AMERICAN SOCIETY OF COMPOSERS,
AUTHORS AND PUBLISHERS

| LICENSEE |
| --- |
| (Full corporate or other name of station owner) |

By _____

By _____

(Fill in capacity in which signed)

(a) If corporation, state corporate office held;

(b) If partnership, write word "partner" under signature of signing partner

(c) If individual owner, write "individual owner" under signature

## TIME BROKERAGE AMENDMENT LETTER

(Letterhead of Licensee)

Licensee _____

Call Letters _____

City and State _____

Date _____

Dear ASCAP:

1. Radio station _____ ["STATION"] has entered into a time brokerage agreement with _____ ["BROKER"] for the period _____ through _____ .

2. STATION and BROKER wish to add BROKER as a party to the Local Station Radio License Agreement in effect between STATION and ASCAP ("the license") with all of the rights and obligations of the Licensee as set forth in the license for the full period of the brokerage agreement referred to in (1) above.

3. We agree that for all periods that STATION simulcasts or is sold in combination with another radio station owned or operated by BROKER ["BROKER STATION"] that has an ASCAP Local Station Radio License we shall report all gross revenue of STATION as follows:

    a. All BROKER revenue relating to STATION will be included in BROKER's license fee reports for BROKER STATION. If such revenue constitutes all gross revenue for STATION, no license fee or license fee reports will be required of STATION.

    b. All of STATION's other revenue (as defined in the license) will be included in STATION's license fee reports.

    c. Amounts payable by BROKER to STATION as consideration for the time brokerage agreement shall not be reportable by STATION or deductible by BROKER STATION.

    d. In the event that STATION and BROKER STATION have different forms of ASCAP license, all BROKER revenue relating to programs of STATION which simulcast or are sold in combination with BROKER STATION shall be apportioned between STATION and BROKER STATION in the same ratio as the adjusted gross revenue of STATION and BROKER STATION bear to each other for the most recent year prior to the brokerage agreement reported by STATION and BROKER STATION to ASCAP (annualized for any period less than a year). Any such revenue apportioned to, and reported for, STATION pursuant to this paragraph shall not be reportable by BROKER on its license fee reports for BROKER STATION.

4. If STATION fully simulcasts programs broadcast by BROKER STATION and has no separate programs, STATION and BROKER agree to maintain the same form of ASCAP license (blanket or per program) for STATION as BROKER has for BROKER STATION. In the event that BROKER has a different form of license for BROKER STATION at the time this agreement is executed, this letter shall constitute our notice in accordance with the license agreement (Paragraph 17 of the blanket license or Paragraph 18 of the per program license) to substitute the other form of license in place of our current agreement. In the event that STATION and BROKER STATION have the same form of license at the time this agreement is executed, and BROKER STATION subsequently provides notice pursuant to its license agreement to substitute the other form of license, said notice shall be deemed to apply as well to STATION.

5. For all periods that STATION has a per program license agreement, BROKER STATION shall submit the reports required by Paragraph 8 of the per program license for all programs provided by BROKER STATION which are broadcast by STATION, and station shall submit such reports for all other programs broadcast by STATION. If STATION fully simulcasts programs broadcast by BROKER STATION and has no separate programs, and if all revenue relating to STATION is included in BROKER's license fee reports for BROKER STATION in accordance with Paragraph 3.a. above. STATION shall not be required to submit separate reports pursuant to Paragraph 8 of the per program license.

6. STATION and BROKER jointly designate the following single address for billing and all other purposes:

Address _____

Please indicate your consent to the amendment of our license agreement in accordance with this letter by countersigning the letter in the space provided below and returning a copy to us.

Very truly yours,

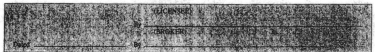

(LICENSEE)

By _____

(BROKER)

Dated _____          By _____

The undersigned, American Society of Composers, Authors and Publishers, hereby consents and agrees to the amendment of the above mentioned license agreement.

American Society of Composers
Authors and Publishers

Dated _____          By _____

## ANNUAL STATEMENT OF ACCOUNT* BLANKET

**FORM AB-96**

AMERICAN SOCIETY OF COMPOSERS, AUTHORS AND PUBLISHERS

ASCAP Building
One Lincoln Plaza, New York, N.Y. 10023

### PART 1 Account Information

*Report must be on Calendar Year Basis   19___

If less than full year Reporting Period

___ to ___
Month Day Year   Month Day Year

**Type of Station**    **Accounting Method**    **Submitted by:**

AM ☐   FM ☐   Billing Basis ☐   Cash Basis* "Lic. 9E" ☐

If station is brokered by another station—enter calls: ___

If all revenue to be reported by broker—check box ☐

Signature     Title     Date

**FOR RADIO STATION:**    **Other stations covered by Report**

Call Letters ___

Licensee ___

Address ___

Co-owned stations: (80% simulcast or <75,000 gross) ___

Time Broker for: ___

### PART 2 GROSS < $150,000

#### GROSS REVENUE UP TO $150,000

If your gross revenue is $150,000 or less (on an annualized basis if the report period is less than a year) enter your GROSS REVENUE on Line 1 and the applicable LICENSE FEE from the Schedule at Right (pro-rated for any period less than a year) on Line 2. Your report is now complete.

| REVENUE | FEE |
|---|---|
| Up to $ 50,000 | $ 450 |
| $ 50,001 - $ 75,000 | $ 800 |
| $ 75,001 - $ 100,000 | $ 1150 |
| $100,001 - $125,000 | $ 1450 |
| $125,001 - $150,000 | $ 1800 |

1 Gross Revenue (excluding non-cash payments in goods and/or services)(Lic. P.5J)   | 1 |
2 License Fee   | 2 |

### PART 3 GROSS > $150,000

#### GROSS REVENUE OVER $150,000

3 Gross Revenue (excluding non-cash payments in goods and/or services) (Lic. P.5J) | 3 |
4 Advertising Agency Commission (Lic. P.5J (1)) | 4 |
5 Revenue for Political Broadcasts (Lic. P.5J (2)) | 5 |
6 Net Agcy. Comm. Included in 4 above
7 Net Revenue for Political Broadcasts
8 Bad Debts (Lic. P.5J (3))
9 Less: Bad Debt Recovery
10 Net Revenue for Bad Debts | 10 |
11 Rate Card Discounts (Lic. P.5J (4)) | 11 |
12 Total Adjustments to Gross (Add lines 6, 7, 10 and 11) | 12 |
13 Adjusted Gross Revenue/Revenue Subject to Fee (Subtract line 12 from line 3) | 13 |

14 Total Itemized Deductions (from line 26) | 14 |
15 Enter 11% of line 13 (Adjusted Gross Revenue) | 15 |
16 Subtract line 15 from line 14 | 16 |
17 Revenue Subject to Fee (Subtract line 16 from line 13) | 17 |
18 License Fee (1.615% of line 13 or line 17 *but not less than 1% of line 13*) | 18 |

SKIP LINES 14-17 UNLESS YOU ITEMIZE DEDUCTIONS

### PART 4 COMPLETE ONLY IF YOU ITEMIZE DEDUCTIONS

19 Schedule: Compensation Under Lic. P.5J (1) (Attach additional sheets if necessary)

NAMES OF PERSONNEL     ANNUAL COMPENSATION

| Adjusted Gross Revenue (Line 13) | Amount Not Deductible |
|---|---|
| $ Under - $ 50,000 | $ 6,200 |
| $ 50,000 - $149,999 | $ 18,600 |
| $150,000 - $299,999 | $ 27,900 |
| $300,000 - $499,999 | $ 41,900 |
| $500,000 - $749,999 | $ 46,500 |
| $750,000 - $999,999 | $ 53,700 |
| $1,000,000 and over | $ 62,000 |

Total | 19 |

20 Amount Non-Deductible (see Table at right) | 20 |
21 Deductible Compensation (Lic. P.5J (1)) (Subtract 20 from 19) | 21 |
22 News Service (Lic. P.5J (2)) | 22 |
23 Remote Pickups (Lic. P.5J (3)(a)) | 23 |
24 Broadcast Rights (Lic. P.5J (3)(b)) | 24 |
25 Other. Specify License Paragraph | 25 |
26 Total Itemized Deductions (Add lines 21 through 25. Enter on line 14) | 26 |

# FORM 17.13

## ASCAP LOCAL STATION PER PROGRAM RADIO LICENSE

**AGREEMENT** made between AMERICAN SOCIETY OF COMPOSERS, AUTHORS AND PUBLISHERS ("We", "Us" or "ASCAP") and

_____ ("You" or "Licensee") as follows:

1. **Term of License.** This license is for the term commencing as of _____ , 199___
and ending December 31, 2000.

2. **Licensed Radio Station.** The radio station licensed by this agreement is:

Call Letters_____

Frequency_____

City of License_____

All references to "you", "your", "the Station", or "your station" include any company, firm or corporation that you own or that is under the same or substantially the same ownership, management or control as the Station. "Independent" refers to any firm or corporation that is not under the same or substantially the same ownership, management or control as the Station.

3. **Grant.** This license grants you the right to perform publicly by radio broadcasting on *local radio programs* from your radio station or from any other place non-dramatic performances of the separate musical compositions in the ASCAP *repertory*.

4. **Limitations on License.** This agreement does not: license the performance of any dramatic-musical works, such as operas, operettas, musical comedies or plays, in whole or in part; grant you any other rights in the musical compositions licensed under this agreement; authorize you to grant to others any performance or other rights in any of the musical compositions licensed under this agreement; extend to the receiver of any of your radio broadcasts, or to any place at which the performances licensed by this agreement originate if other than at the station.

5. **Definitions.** When used in this agreement the defined words and phrases appear in italics and have the following meanings:

A. ASCAP "Repertory" means all musical compositions which ASCAP has the right to license for public performance now or hereafter during the term of this agreement. All compositions written and copyrighted by our members and in the repertory on the date this agreement is executed are included for the full term of this agreement. Compositions written or copyrighted by our members during the license term are included for the full balance of the term.

B. "Local radio program" means any program broadcast from the Station other than a network radio program or a program for which all of the music in the ASCAP *repertory* contained in the program has been licensed for performance by the station either by ASCAP or the ASCAP members in interest. A particular period of radio broadcasting will be considered one program if, with respect to the period, any two of the following questions may be answered in the affirmative:

(1) Is the period referred to by substantially the same title throughout?

(2) Is the dominant personality the same substantially throughout?

(3) Is the period presented to the public as a single show notwithstanding that it may have different parts?

(4) Is the format substantially constant throughout?

For the purposes of this agreement, programs furnished by networks not licensed by ASCAP are deemed to be "local radio programs".

C. "Program subject to fee" means any *local radio program* which uses any of the compositions in the ASCAP *repertory*, except any program making only *incidental use* as defined in subdivision "H" of this paragraph of compositions in the *repertory*.

If a *local radio program* exceeds one hour in duration, the "program subject to fee" will be deemed to mean any clock hour (that is, any sixty minute period beginning on the hour) within the program which uses any of the compositions in the ASCAP *repertory* other than as an *incidental use*. If within that clock hour there is a period of radio broadcasting to which the definition of *local radio program* would apply (for example, a fifteen minute news program within a four hour entertainment program) and which does not use any of the compositions in the ASCAP *repertory* other than as an *incidental use*, that period will be excluded from the *program subject to fee* if it is five minutes or longer, or three minutes or longer if it is a "public service announcement" as defined in note 4 of Section 73.112 of the Federal Communications Commission Rules and Regulations in effect on January 1, 1978.

1

D.   "Network radio program" means a program broadcast simultaneously or by so-called "delayed" or "repeat" broadcasts (sometimes known as "rebroadcasts") over two or more affiliated stations.

E.   "Affiliated station" means any radio broadcasting station in the United States which regularly broadcasts network radio programs of a radio network or which appears on the radio rate card of the network and is interconnected with the network by wire or any other means. A station will only be deemed to be an affiliated station so long as it regularly broadcasts such programs or appears on such rate cards. All radio broadcasting stations in the United States which are owned and operated by a network and which broadcast the network's radio programs are deemed to be affiliated stations for the purpose of this agreement, whether or not they appear on the network's radio rate cards.

F.   "Time Broker" means any independent person, firm or corporation that engages in *time brokerage*.

G.   "Time Brokerage" means any arrangement between a station and a *time broker* that:

   (1)  authorizes the resale by the *time broker* of the radio broadcasting facilities of the station;

   (2)  permits the *time broker* to provide programs for 10% or more of the time the station is on the air; and

   (3)  provides for the sale by the *time broker* of all or substantially all announcements within the brokered time.

H.   "Incidental use" means use in any of the following ways: as commercial jingles (not to exceed 60 seconds in duration), bridge or background music, themes or signatures, arrangements of works in the public domain, or incidental to the broadcast of a public or sports event.

I.   "Net Promotional Revenue" means all cash payments that you receive from third parties for the direct or indirect promotion of their businesses via the broadcast facilities of the station other than paid programs or commercial announcements (such as, but not limited to, Bridal or Craft Shows, Direct Mailings, Special Sponsored Events or Publications, produced and promoted by the station) less those out-of-the-ordinary costs, such as booth rentals, printing and mailing expenses, and cost of goods sold, that would not have otherwise been incurred without the promotional activity. Deductible costs may not exceed the cash payments received.

J.   "Gross Revenue" means all:

   (1)  cash payments made by or on behalf of:

   a.   sponsors or donors for the use of the radio broadcasting facilities of the Station, and

   b.   *time brokers* who each provide programs for less than 10% of the time a station is on the air or recognized independent companies engaged in arrangements with radio or television stations generally for the resale of the radio broadcasting facilities of the Station; and

   (2)  *net promotional revenue*.

Such payments shall include all payments made directly to, or as authorized by, you, your employees, representatives, agents or any other person acting on your behalf. Such payments shall not include payments made to independent third parties, such as networks or program suppliers, or non-cash payments such as payments in goods or services commonly referred to as "trades" or "barter".

K.   "Adjusted Gross Revenue" means *gross revenue* less:

   (1)  any sums received from networks licensed by ASCAP with respect to network radio programs: this deduction does not apply to that portion of the sums received from a licensed network attributable to announcements in a network program not broadcast by the Station, or to announcements furnished by the network not related to network programs;

   (2)  advertising agency commission not to exceed 15% actually allowed to an independent advertising agency;

   (3)  any sums received from your political local radio programs and announcements, net of agency commissions;

   (4)  bad debts actually written off and discounts allowed or rebates paid;

   (5)  rate card discounts, cash, quantity and/or frequency actually allowed; and

   (6)  any sums received with respect to a program for which all of the music in the ASCAP *repertory* contained in the program has been licensed for performance by the station either by ASCAP or the ASCAP members in interest.

2

L.   "Weighted Hours" means the total number of hours of *local radio programs* during a reporting period in each of the following time periods multiplied by the applicable weight set forth below:

|              | Time Period            | Applicable Weight |
|--------------|------------------------|-------------------|
| Weekdays:    | Midnight to 6:00 A.M.  | .25               |
|              | 6:00 A.M. to 10:00 A.M.| 1.00              |
|              | 10:00 A.M. to 3:00 P.M.| .50               |
|              | 3:00 P.M. to 7:00 P.M. | .75               |
|              | 7:00 P.M. to Midnight  | .50               |
| Weekends:    | Saturdays and Sundays  | .25               |

M.   "Revenue per Weighted Hour" means the *adjusted gross revenue* for a full calendar year divided by the total number of *weighted hours* in the year.

N.   "Revenue Subject to Fee" means *revenue per weighted* hour multiplied by the total number of *weighted hours* of *programs subject to fee*.

6.   **Right to Restrict.**

A.   Our members may restrict the radio broadcasting of their compositions up to a maximum of 500 at any given time, only for the purpose of preventing harmful effect upon other interests under the copyrights of such works; provided, however, that (1) limited licenses will be granted upon application to us entirely free of additional charge if the copyright owners are unable to show reasonable hazards to their major interests likely to result from such radio broadcasting; (2) the right to restrict any composition will not be exercised for the purpose of permitting the fixing or regulating of fees for the recording or transcribing of the composition; (3) in no case will any charges, "free plugs", or other consideration be required for permission to perform a restricted composition; and (4) in no event will any composition be restricted after its initial radio broadcast for the purpose of confining further radio broadcasts to a particular artist, station, network or program.

B.   We may also in good faith restrict the radio broadcasting of any composition, over and above the number specified in the previous paragraph, only as to which any suit has been brought or threatened on a claim that the composition infringes a composition not contained in the ASCAP *repertory* or on a claim that we do not have the right to license the public performance of the composition by radio broadcasting.

7.   **License Fee.**

A.   You agree to pay us for each year during the term of this agreement the total of the following fees:

( 1)   **Base Fee.** a. .24 % of *adjusted gross revenue* except for 1996 and 1997 for *grandfathered* stations as set forth below.

b.   A "grandfathered" station is a station that had per program license agreements with ASCAP for the period ending December 31, 1990 and for the full period January 1, 1991 through December 31, 1995, and paid the "base fee" pursuant to Paragraph 4A(1)a. of the 1991-1995 agreement. The base fee for 1996 for a *grandfathered* station is the total of (i) one-third of the fee calculated at .24% of *adjusted gross revenue*, and (ii) two-thirds of the fee calculated in accordance with Paragraph 4A(1)a. of the 1991-1995 per program license. The base fee for 1997 for a *grandfathered* station is the total of (i) two-thirds of the fee calculated at .24% of *adjusted gross revenue* and (ii) one-third of the fee calculated in accordance with Paragraph 4A(1)a. of the 1991-1995 per program license.

(2)   **Additional Fee.** a. 4.22% of *revenue subject to fee* for the first 10% of the Station's weighted hours up to 400 *weighted hours*; and

b.   2.135% of *revenue subject to fee* for all additional *weighted hours*.

B.   In the event that your payment of fees under this agreement causes us to incur a liability to pay a gross receipts, sales, use, business use, or other tax which is based on the amount of our receipts from you, and (1) we have taken reasonable steps to be exempted or excused from paying such tax; and (2) we are permitted by law to pass through such tax to our licensees, you will pay us the full amount of such tax.

8.   **Music Reports.** A. You will furnish us on or before the 20th day of each month for the preceding month, on forms which we will supply free of charge, statements setting forth:

(1)   the computation of *weighted hours*;

(2)   a summary of all *local radio programs* which contained any musical content other than solely *incidental uses* ("programs with music"), showing as to each program:(a) the title of the program; (b) the time of broadcast; (c) the date of broadcast; and (d) whether the program contained performances of musical compositions in the ASCAP *repertory*.

(3) For each *program with music* that is not reported as containing performances of musical compositions in the ASCAP *repertory*, a complete list of each musical composition performed in whole or in part during the program, showing as to each the full title, the name of the composer and author, and the name of the publisher. For performances by means of recordings, you will furnish the title, performing artist, record company and such other information as to composer, author and publisher in full as is shown on the label.

These requirements apply to all *local radio programs* without exception and regardless of the origination of the program.

B.   If you comply in part with the requirements set out in this paragraph as to the complete identification of compositions but not sufficiently to identify the works, the presumption is that the programs contained musical compositions in the ASCAP *repertory* and license fees will be paid accordingly.

C.   If you fail to report performances of musical compositions that are required to be reported by this agreement, we may impose penalties up to the following maximums.

The first time that there are unreported performances we will notify you of the occasion without penalty. If following this notice we find a second occasion of unreported performances you may be required to pay us up to $500 plus one month's per program charge. If following a second occasion notice there are further unreported performances you may be required to pay us up to $500 plus twice the per program monthly charge.

However, if on any of these occasions we find that you reported less than half of the *weighted hours* of *programs subject to fee* that you should have in a monitoring period of not less than 5 hours, you may be required to pay us up to $500 plus one month's charge pursuant to the Local Station Blanket Radio License if it is the first occasion, $500 plus twice the monthly blanket charge if it is the second occasion, and $500 plus three times the monthly blanket charge if it is the third occasion. Also, if there is a third occasion, we have the right at any time thereafter upon thirty (30) days' notice to switch you to the Local Station Blanket Radio License for the balance of the license term with no further right for you to switch back to the per program license.

All payments provided by this paragraph are due within thirty (30) days following notice from us of the unreported performances.

The failure to report performances on a timely basis may not be remedied by submission of any report of performances after a notice pursuant to this paragraph.

In assessing penalties as set forth above, we will consider, among other things:

1. The time elapsed between occasions.

2. The accuracy of your prior reports.

3. The number of compositions reported compared to the number unreported.

4. Whether the failure to report was due to explainable inadvertence or mistake.

5. Any other circumstances which in our discretion warrant mitigation of the maximum applicable penalty.

9.   **Reports and Payments.**

A.   Annual Reports. You will send us a report of the license fee due for each year of this agreement, by April 1st of the following year, by fully completing the annual Statement of Account form which we will supply free of charge. A copy of the annual Statement of Account form is annexed and made a part of this agreement.

B.   Monthly Payments. For each month during the term of this agreement you will, on or before the first day of the following month, pay us the following:

(1) If the Station was licensed by us on a per program basis during the preceding calendar year, a sum equal to 1/12 of the license fee for the preceding calendar year (annualized for any reported period less than a year) adjusted in accordance with any increase in the Consumer Price Index (National, all items) between the preceding October and the next preceding October;

(2) If the Station was not licensed on a per program basis during the preceding year, an amount equal to 1/12 of the sum of the following: (a) the "Base Fee" of .24% of its *adjusted gross revenue* for the preceding year, plus (b) the "Additional Fee" determined in accordance with Paragraph 7.A.(2) of this agreement based on its *adjusted gross revenue* for the preceding year and a good faith estimate of the total annual *weighted hours* of *programs subject to fee* (which you will furnish to us upon execution of this agreement). Such amount shall be adjusted in accordance with any increase in the Consumer Price Index (National, all items) between the preceding October and the next preceding October. If the Station was not broadcasting during the preceding year, you will furnish a good faith estimate of its *adjusted gross revenue* for the first year of operation. *Adjusted gross revenue* reported for any period less than a year will be annualized.

4

If we do not receive the report required by Paragraph 9.A. for any calendar year when due, the monthly payments will be in the amount of the monthly payments due for the preceding year, plus 24%, and payments at that rate will continue until we receive the late report.

C. Annual Adjustments. If the monthly payments that you have made to us for a year pursuant to Paragraph 9.B. are less than the license fee for that year, you will pay us the additional amount due with the annual report. If the amount that you paid for that year exceeds the license fee due for the year we will apply the excess payment against your future monthly payments, or refund it to you upon your written request if it is greater than three monthly payments required by Paragraph 9.B.

D. Billing Basis. License fee reports will be made on a billing basis by all stations, except that any station may report on a cash basis if (1) its books have been kept on a cash basis and (2) it reported to us only on a cash basis and at no time on a billing basis during the entire term of its agreement with us ending February 28, 1977, and continuously thereafter. You will account for all billings made subsequent to the termination of this agreement with respect to radio broadcasts made during the term of the agreement as and when you make such billings.

E. Late Payments. If we do not receive any payment required under Paragraph 8.C, 9.B. or 9.C. before the first day of the month following the date when the payment was due, you will pay us a finance charge of 1½% per month from the date the payment was due.

F. Multiple Station Reports. You will submit a single license fee report for all stations that you own or act as a time broker for that are licensed on the per program basis and that simultaneously broadcast all programs during the time the stations are on the air concurrently.

G. Combination Sales. If the use of the broadcasting facilities of the station is sold in combination with any other stations that you own, operate or control that are licensed by us under a form of agreement other than this form of local station per program radio license, the combination revenue shall be allocated among the stations on a reasonable basis taking into account factors such as, but not limited to, separate sales by the stations for comparable facilities during the report period or the immediately preceding period, and/or the relative ratings of the stations during the report period.

10. **Audits.**

A. Right to Audit. We have the right by our duly authorized representatives, at any time during customary business hours, upon reasonable notice, to examine your books and records of account (including logs and all other records relating to the musical compositions performed on your *local radio programs*) only to the extent necessary to verify any report required by this agreement. We will consider all data and information coming to our attention as a result of any such examination of books and records as completely and entirely confidential.

B. Audit Period. The period for which we may audit is limited to the four calendar years reported preceding the year in which the audit is made. However, if you request a postponement, we have the right to audit for the period commencing with the fourth calendar year reported preceding the year in which we first notified you of our intention to audit. This limitation does not apply if you fail or refuse after written notice from us to produce the books and records necessary to verify any report or statement of accounting pursuant to the agreement.

C. Correction of Errors. You may correct computational errors, or errors relating to deductions permitted under the agreement on your license fee reports for the four calendar years preceding the year in which the corrected reports are submitted.

D. Audit Finance Charges. If our audit discloses that you underpaid license fees due us:

(1) You will pay a finance charge on the additional license fees of 1½% per month from the date(s) the fees should have been paid pursuant to this agreement if the underpayment is 5% or more, but not less than $1000.

(2) You will pay a finance charge on the additional license fees of 1½% per month beginning thirty (30) days after the date we bill the additional license fees to you if the underpayment is less than 5% or less than $1000.

(3) You may dispute all or part of our audit claim. If you do, you must, within thirty (30) days from the date that we bill the additional fees,(i) advise us, in writing, of the basis for your dispute and (ii) pay us any fees indisputably owed together with any applicable finance charges. If there is a good faith dispute between us with respect to all or part of the additional fees that we have billed pursuant to this Paragraph, no finance charges will be billed with respect to the disputed fees for a period beginning on the date we billed the fees to you and ending sixty (60) days from the date that we respond to your written notification of the existence of a dispute.

(4) Finance charges computed in accordance with this Paragraph and pertaining to additional fees which you dispute in accordance with subparagraph (3) above will be adjusted pro-rata to the amount arrived at by you and us in resolution of the dispute.

11. **Breach or Default.** If you fail to perform any of the terms or conditions of this agreement relating to the reports, accountings or payments required to be made by you, we may give you thirty (30) days' notice in writing to cure your breach or default. If you do not do so within the thirty (30) days, we may then promptly terminate this license.

5

12. **Computer Readable Reports.** A. In lieu of the monthly statements provided in Paragraph 8 of this agreement, we have the option to require that the data called for on those statements be reported in computer readable form. We may exercise this option on the following basis:

(1)  We will give you sixty (60) day's notice of our exercise of the option;

(2)  We will provide you with software to enable you to enter the data required on PC diskettes or transmit the data electronically to us;

(3)  We will, at our option, either furnish you with PC diskettes free of charge for entry of the required data or credit you for the cost of the diskettes.

B. If, following our exercise of this option, you fail to report the required data in accordance with the requirements furnished by us, you will pay us a data entry charge of $6.00 per page for each month that the data is reported on the monthly statements rather than electronically or on the diskettes.

13. **Time Brokerage Arrangements.** If you enter into a *time brokerage* arrangement, the license granted by this agreement will automatically terminate thirty (30) days after the commencement date of the *time brokerage* unless you have furnished us a complete copy of the *time brokerage* agreement and you and *time broker* have executed a letter to us in the form annexed and made a part of this agreement requesting amendment of the license agreement to add *time broker* as a party. When that letter has been fully executed by you, *time broker* and us, this agreement will be amended accordingly.

14. **Indemnity Clause.** We will indemnify, save and hold harmless and defend you, your advertisers and their advertising agencies, and your and their officers, employees and artists, from and against all claims, demands and suits that may be made or brought against you or them with respect to the performance under this agreement of any compositions in the ASCAP *repertory* which are written or copyrighted by our members. You will give us immediate notice of any such claim, demand or suit and immediately deliver to us all papers pertaining thereto. We will have full charge of the defense of any such claim, demand or suit and you agree to cooperate fully with us in such defense. You may however engage your own counsel at your own expense who may participate in the defense of any such action. At your request we will cooperate with and assist you, your advertisers and their advertising agencies and your and their officers, employees and artists in the defense of any action or proceeding brought against them or any of them with respect to the performance of any musical compositions contained in the ASCAP *repertory*, but not copyrighted or written by members of ASCAP. This Paragraph 14 does not apply to performances of any works that may be restricted under Paragraph 6 of this agreement.

15. **Rights of Termination.**

A.  You have the right to terminate this license on seven (7) days' written notice in the event of the termination, suspension or any substantial alteration or variation of the terms and conditions of the governmental licenses covering the Station, or any major interference with the operations of the Station due to governmental measures or restrictions.

B.  We have the right to terminate this license on thirty (30) days' notice if there is any major interference with, or substantial increase in the cost of, our operation as a result of any law of the state, territory, dependency, possession or political subdivision in which the Station is located which is applicable to the licensing of performing rights.

16. **Notices.** All notices required or permitted to be given by either of us to the other under this agreement will be duly and properly given if:

A.  mailed to the other party by registered or certified United States mail; or

B.  sent by electronic transmission (i.e., Mailgram, facsimile or similar transmission); or

C.  sent by generally recognized same-day or overnight delivery service;

addressed to the party at its usual place of business.

17. **Successors and Assignees.** This agreement will enure to the benefit of and be binding upon you and us and our respective successors and assignees, but no assignment will relieve either of us of our respective obligations under this agreement.

18. **Blanket License.** The "local station blanket license" for the term ending December 31, 2000 is being offered to you simultaneously with this agreement. In accepting this agreement, you acknowledge that you have a choice of entering into either this agreement or the blanket license with us; that you have the opportunity to negotiate for separate licenses with our individual members; and that you are voluntarily entering into this agreement with us. You may substitute the blanket agreement in place of this agreement by giving us written notice at least 10 days prior to the commencement of any month during the term of this agreement. In that event, effective with the commencement of that month, the blanket agreement will be in full force and effect between us.

19. **Applicable Law.** The fees set forth in this agreement have been approved by the United States District Court for the Southern District of New York as reasonable and non-discriminatory in accordance with the Amended Final Judgment in United States v. ASCAP. The meaning of the provisions of this agreement will be construed in accordance with the laws of the State of New York.

6

IN WITNESS WHEREOF, this agreement has been duly executed by ASCAP and Licensee this      day of      , 199 /2000.

AMERICAN SOCIETY OF COMPOSERS,
AUTHORS AND PUBLISHERS

By _____

(Fill in capacity in which signed)

(a) If corporation, state corporate office held;

(b) If partnership, write word "partner" under signature of signing partner

(c) If individual owner, write "individual owner" under signature

## TIME BROKERAGE AMENDMENT LETTER

```
(Letterhead of Licensee)
Licensee _____
Call Letters _____
City and State _____
Date _____
```

Dear ASCAP:

1. Radio station _____ |"STATION"| has entered into a time brokerage agreement with _____ |"BROKER"| for the period _____ through _____ .

2. STATION and BROKER wish to add BROKER as a party to the Local Station Radio License Agreement in effect between STATION and ASCAP ("the license") with all of the rights and obligations of the Licensee as set forth in the license for the full period of the brokerage agreement referred to in (1) above.

3. We agree that for all periods that STATION simulcasts or is sold in combination with another radio station owned or operated by BROKER |"BROKER STATION"| that has an ASCAP Local Station Radio License we shall report all gross revenue of STATION as follows:

   a. All BROKER revenue relating to STATION will be included in BROKER's license fee reports for BROKER STATION. If such revenue constitutes all gross revenue for STATION, no license fee or license fee reports will be required of STATION.

   b. All of STATION's other revenue (as defined in the license) will be included in STATION's license fee reports.

   c. Amounts payable by BROKER to STATION as consideration for the time brokerage agreement shall not be reportable by STATION or deductible by BROKER STATION.

   d. In the event that STATION and BROKER STATION have different forms of ASCAP license, all BROKER revenue relating to programs of STATION which simulcast or are sold in combination with BROKER STATION shall be apportioned between STATION and BROKER STATION in the same ratio as the adjusted gross revenue of STATION and BROKER STATION bear to each other for the most recent year prior to the brokerage agreement reported by STATION and BROKER STATION to ASCAP (annualized for any period less than a year). Any such revenue apportioned to, and reported for, STATION pursuant to this paragraph shall not be reportable by BROKER on its license fee reports for BROKER STATION.

4. If STATION fully simulcasts programs broadcast by BROKER STATION and has no separate programs, STATION and BROKER agree to maintain the same form of ASCAP license (blanket or per program) for STATION as BROKER has for BROKER STATION. In the event that BROKER has a different form of license for BROKER STATION at the time this agreement is executed, this letter shall constitute our notice in accordance with the license agreement (Paragraph 17 of the blanket license or Paragraph 18 of the per program license) to substitute the other form of license in place of our current agreement. In the event that STATION and BROKER STATION have the same form of license at the time this agreement is executed, and BROKER STATION subsequently provides notice pursuant to its license agreement to substitute the other form of license, said notice shall be deemed to apply as well to STATION.

5. For all periods that STATION has a per program license agreement, BROKER STATION shall submit the reports required by Paragraph 8 of the per program license for all programs provided by BROKER STATION which are broadcast by STATION, and station shall submit such reports for all other programs broadcast by STATION. If STATION fully simulcasts programs broadcast by BROKER STATION and has no separate programs, and if all revenue relating to STATION is included in BROKER's license fee reports for BROKER STATION in accordance with Paragraph 3.a. above. STATION shall not be required to submit separate reports pursuant to Paragraph 8 of the per program license.

6. STATION and BROKER jointly designate the following single address for billing and all other purposes:

```
Address: _____
         _____
         _____
```

Please indicate your consent to the amendment of our license agreement in accordance with this letter by countersigning the letter in the space provided below and returning a copy to us.

Very truly yours,

```
                        (LICENSEE)
                  By _____
                        (BROKER)
Dated _____    By _____
```

The undersigned, American Society of Composers, Authors and Publishers, hereby consents and agrees to the amendment of the above mentioned license agreement.

American Society of Composers
Authors and Publishers

Dated _____          By _____

**ANNUAL STATEMENT OF ACCOUNT· PER PROGRAM** FORM APP-96

·Report must be on Calendar Year Basis 19☐

If less than full year Reporting Period

☐☐☐ to ☐☐☐
Month Day Year   Month Day Year

ASCAP

AMERICAN SOCIETY OF COMPOSERS, AUTHORS AND PUBLISHERS

ASCAP Building
One Lincoln Plaza, New York, N.Y. 10023

**Type of Station Covered by This Report**

AM ☐   FM ☐

**Submitted by:**

Signature _____ Title _____ Date _____

**FOR RADIO STATION**

Call Letters _____

Licensee _____

Address _____

**Other stations covered by Report**

Co-owned stations: (100% simulcast)

Time Broker 100% for:

**Fee Computation**

| | | |
|---|---|---|
| 1 | Gross Revenue (excluding non-cash payments in goods and/or services) (Lic. P.5J) | 1 |
| 2 | Network Revenue for Programs of Licensed Networks (Lic. P.5K [1]) | |
| 3 | Advertising Agency Commissions (Lic. P.5K [2]) | 3 |
| 4 | Revenue for Political Broadcasts (Lic. P.5K [3]) | 4 |
| 5 | Less: Agency Comm. included in 3 above | 5 |
| 6 | Net Revenue for Political Broadcasts | |
| 7 | Bad Debts (Lic. P.5K [4]) | 7 |
| 8 | Less: Bad Debt Recoveries | 8 |
| 9 | Net Revenue for Bad Debts | 9 |
| 10 | Rate Card Discounts (Lic. P.5K [5]) | |
| 11 | Net Revenue Cleared at the Source (Lic. P.5K [6]) | |
| 12 | Total Adjustments to Gross (Add lines 2, 3, 6, 9, 10 and 11) | 12 |
| 13 | Adjusted Gross Revenue (Subtract line 12 from line 1) | 13 |
| 14 | Weighted Hours | |

Enter Weighted Hours from Monthly Reports. Total and enter on line 14.

| Jan. | | Jul. | | Oct. | |
| Feb. | | May | | Nov. | |
| Mar. | | Jun. | | Dec. | |
| | | | | Total | 14 |

| 15 | Revenue per Weighted Hour (line 13 divided by line 14) | 15 |
| 16 | Weighted Hours Subject to Fee | |

Enter Weighted Hours Subject to Fee from Monthly Reports. Total and enter on line 16.

| Jan. | | Apr. | | Jul. | | Oct. | |
| Feb. | | May | | Aug. | | Nov. | |
| Mar. | | Jun. | | Sep. | | Dec. | |
| | | | | | | Total | 16 |

| 17 | Enter 10% of line 14 (Weighted Hours) but not more than 400 | 17 |

*Complete lines 18-22 only if line 16 is GREATER THAN line 17. Otherwise skip to line 23.*

| 18 | Multiply line 17 by line 15 | 18 |
| 19 | Paragraph 7A (2)a. Fee (4.22% of line 18) | 19 |
| 20 | Subtract line 17 from line 16 | 20 |
| 21 | Multiply line 20 by line 15 | 21 |
| 22 | Paragraph 7A (2)b. Fee (2.135% of line 21) | 22 |

*Total lines 19 and 22 and enter on line 24. Then proceed to line 25.*

| 23 | Revenue Subject to Fee (line 15 multiplied by line 16) | 23 |
| 24 | Paragraph 7A (2) Fee. Enter 4.22% of line 23 or Total of lines 19 and 22 | 24 |
| 25 | Paragraph 7A (1) Fee | |

"Grandfathered" (Lic. P.7A [1] b) stations complete (a) for 1996 and 1997. All others complete (b)

(a) "Grandfathered" Stations

| Adjusted Gross Revenue from Line 13 | ÷ | Previous Year's Adjusted Gross Revenue | × | Previous Year's Base Fee | 1996 | 1997 |
|---|---|---|---|---|---|---|

.24%

Total Enter on Line 25

(b) .24% of line 13. Enter on line 25. | 25 |

| 26 | License Fee (Total of lines 24 and 25) | 26 |

EXHIBIT

MUSIC LOG FOR RADIO STATION:

Call Letters

Operated by:

City and State:

FORM LMPP-96

ASCAP

American Society of Composers, Authors and Publishers
One Lincoln Plaza, New York, N.Y. 10023

PROGRAM COVERED BY THIS REPORT

DATE | DAY OF WEEK | EXACT TIME COVERED

PERIOD NOT TO EXCEED OR
OVERLAP SINGLE CLOCK HOUR

FROM    TO

MUSIC PERFORMED

FOR RECORDINGS PERFORMED BY

RECORD CO.

| TITLE OF COMPOSITION (PLEASE DO NOT ABBREVIATE) | WRITERS PLEASE INSERT FULL NAME OF ALL WRITERS | PUBLISHERS | PER-FORMING RIGHT SOCIETY (IF KNOWN) | ARTIST | NAME/LABEL | ASCAP USE ONLY |
|---|---|---|---|---|---|---|
| | | | | | | |

COMPOSER / AUTHOR    PUBLISHER

LIST ALL COMPOSITIONS IN WHOLE OR IN PART, WITHOUT EXCEPTION

**MONTHLY REPORT**     **PER PROGRAM**     **FORM MPPR-96**

PART 1 ACCOUNT INFORMATION

MONTH OF _____ 19 __

FOR RADIO STATION:

Call Letters _____ _ - _

Licensee

Address

AMERICAN SOCIETY OF COMPOSERS, AUTHORS AND PUBLISHERS

ASCAP Building
One Lincoln Plaza, New York, N.Y. 10023

OTHER STATIONS COVERED BY REPORT:

Co-owned stations: (100% simulcast)     Time Broker 100% for:

**PART 2     WEIGHTED HOURS COMPUTATION**

| Time Period | | No. of Hours Station on Air | No. Days in Month | Total Unadjusted Hours | Applicable Weight | Weighted Hours |
|---|---|---|---|---|---|---|
| Weekdays: | Midnight to 6:00 A.M. | X | = | | X .25 = | |
| | 6:00 A.M. to 10:00 A.M. | X | = | | X 1.00 = | |
| | 10:00 A.M. to 3:00 P.M. | X | = | | X .50 = | |
| | 3:00 P.M. to 7:00 P.M. | X | = | | X .75 = | |
| | 7:00 P.M. to Midnight | X | = | | X .50 = | |
| Weekends: | Saturdays | X | = | | X .25 = | |
| | Sundays | X | = | | X .25 = | |
| | TOTAL (Add entries in final column) | | | | | |

If you broadcast programs from Networks licensed by ASCAP, you must complete Part 3 ("Network Weighted Hours") and enter the total in the space below.

DECIMAL TABLE
| | |
|---|---|
| 60 minutes = | 1.00 |
| 55 minutes = | .92 |
| 50 minutes = | .83 |
| 45 minutes = | .75 |
| 40 minutes = | .67 |
| 30 minutes = | .58 |
| 30 minutes = | .50 |
| 25 minutes = | .42 |
| 20 minutes = | .33 |
| 15 minutes = | .25 |
| 10 minutes = | .17 |
| 5 minutes = | .08 |

**PART 3     NETWORK WEIGHTED HOURS COMPUTATION**

Complete this part only if you broadcast programs from Networks licensed by ASCAP.
Enter the total length (in hours, using the decimal table above) of all network news programs within each time period in Col. 3. Multiply by the number of days broadcast (Col. 4) and enter in Col. 5. Multiply by the applicable weight (Col. 6) and enter in Col. 7.

| (1) PROGRAM TITLE | (2) TIME From | To | (3) LENGTH OF PROGRAMS | DATE OF BROADCAST 1 2 3 4 5 6 7 8 9 10 11 12 13 14 15 16 17 18 19 20 21 22 23 24 25 26 27 28 29 30 31 | (5) TOTAL HOURS | (6) WEIGHT | (7) WEIGHTED NETWORK HOURS |
|---|---|---|---|---|---|---|---|

NEWS

| | | | | | | | |
|---|---|---|---|---|---|---|---|
| Total length of all News Prgms in time period | Midnight | 6:00 A.M. | | | | X .25 = | |
| Total length of all News Prgms in time period | 6:00 A.M. | 10:00 A.M. | | | | X 1.00 = | |
| Total length of all News Prgms in time period | 10:00 A.M. | 3:00 P.M. | | | | X .50 = | |
| Total length of all News Prgms in time period | 3:00 P.M. | 7:00 P.M. | | | | X .75 = | |
| Total length of all News Prgms in time period | 7:00 P.M. | Midnight | | | | X .50 = | |
| Total length of all News Prgms in time period | Saturdays | | | | | X .25 = | |
| Total length of all News Prgms in time period | Sundays | | | | | X .25 = | |

REGULARLY (SCHEDULED PRGMS)

Enter all other regularly scheduled network programs in Col. 2. (If the program overlaps time periods, use separate lines for each time period.) Enter the length of the program (in hours) in Col. 3. Multiply by the number of days broadcast (Col. 4) and enter in Col. 5. Then for the weight for the time period in Col. 6, multiply by Col. 5 and enter in Col. 7.

| | | | | | | | |
|---|---|---|---|---|---|---|---|
| | | | | | | X = | |
| | | | | | | X = | |
| | | | | | | X = | |

SPORTS SPECIALS

List all network sports (including pre- and post-game shows) and special events. Enter the weekday and weekend dates broadcast in the boxes provided at the top of each column. Enter the total length (in hours) of all programs broadcast within a time period on a specific date in the box for that date and time period. If a program overlaps time periods, enter the relevant portion of the program in each time period. Add the totals across and enter in Col. 5. Multiply by the applicable weight (Col. 6) and enter in Col. 7.

WEEKDAY DATES:

| | | | | | | | |
|---|---|---|---|---|---|---|---|
| Midnight | 6:00 A.M. | | | | | X .25 = | |
| 6:00 A.M. | 10:00 A.M. | | | | | X 1.00 = | |
| 10:00 A.M. | 3:00 P.M. | | | | | X .50 = | |
| 3:00 P.M. | 7:00 P.M. | | | | | X .75 = | |
| 7:00 P.M. | Midnight | | | | | X .50 = | |

WEEKEND DATES:

| Saturdays | Sundays | | | | | X .25 = | |
|---|---|---|---|---|---|---|---|

TOTAL - Add all entries in Col. 7 and enter in Part 2 "WEIGHTED NETWORK HOURS" →

**PART 5     WEIGHTED HOURS SUBJECT TO FEE COMPUTATION**
(COMPLETE PART 4 ON REVERSE SIDE)

| Time Period | | ASCAP Hours From Part 4 | Weight | Weighted Hours Subject to Fee | ASCAP USE ONLY |
|---|---|---|---|---|---|
| Weekdays: | Midnight to 6:00 A.M. | X | .25 | = | |
| | 6:00 A.M. to 10:00 A.M. | X | 1.00 | = | |
| | 10:00 A.M. to 3:00 P.M. | X | .50 | = | |
| | 3:00 P.M. to 7:00 P.M. | X | .75 | = | SUBMITTED BY |
| | 7:00 P.M. to Midnight | X | .50 | = | |
| Weekends: | Saturdays and Sundays | X | .25 | = | |
| | TOTAL (Add entries in final column) | | | | SIGNATURE    TITLE    DATE |

EXHIBIT

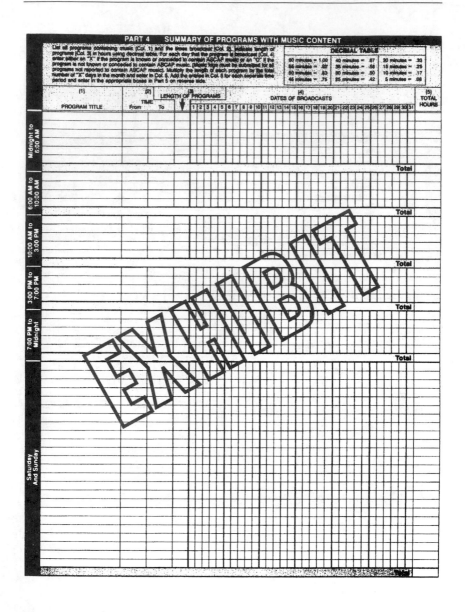

# FORM 17.14

## ASCAP GENERAL LICENSE
## (FOR RESTAURANTS, BARS, CAFES, CLUBS, ETC.)

### GENERAL LICENSE AGREEMENT - RESTAURANTS, TAVERNS, NIGHTCLUBS, AND SIMILAR ESTABLISHMENTS

*Agreement* between American Society of Composers, Authors and Publishers ("SOCIETY"), located at 2690 Cumberland Parkway, Suite 490, Atlanta, GA 30339

and

("LICENSEE"), located at

as follows:

**1. Grant and Term of License**

(a) SOCIETY grants and LICENSEE accepts for a term of one year, commencing            , and continuing thereafter for additional terms of one year each unless terminated by either party as hereinafter provided, a license to perform publicly at

("the premises"), and not elsewhere, non-dramatic renditions of the separate musical compositions now or hereafter during the term hereof in the repertory of SOCIETY, and of which SOCIETY shall have the right to license such performing rights.

(b) This license authorizes performances by means of "jukebox(es)" as defined in the Rate Schedule attached to and made a part of this Agreement.

(c) This Agreement shall enure to the benefit of and shall be binding upon the parties hereto and their respective successors and assigns, but no assignment shall relieve the parties hereto of their respective obligations hereunder as to performances rendered, acts done and obligations incurred prior to the effective date of the assignment.

(d) Either party may, on or before thirty days prior to the end of the initial term or any renewal term, give notice of termination to the other. If such notice is given the Agreement shall terminate on the last day of such initial or renewal term.

**2. Limitations on License**

(a) This license is not assignable or transferable by operation of law or otherwise, except as provided in subparagraph "1(c)" hereof, and is limited to the LICENSEE and to the premises.

(b) This license does not authorize the broadcasting, telecasting or transmission by wire or otherwise, of renditions of musical compositions in SOCIETY's repertory to persons outside of the premises, other than by means of a music-on-hold telephone system operated by LICENSEE at the premises.

(c) This license is limited to non-dramatic performances, and does not authorize any dramatic performances. For purposes of this Agreement, a dramatic performance shall include, but not be limited to, the following:

(i) performance of a "dramatico-musical work" (as hereinafter defined) in its entirety;

(ii) performance of one or more musical compositions from a "dramatico-musical work" (as hereinafter defined) accompanied by dialogue, pantomime, dance, stage action, or visual representation of the work from which the music is taken;

(iii) performance of one or more musical compositions as part of a story or plot, whether accompanied or unaccompanied by dialogue, pantomime, dance, stage action, or visual representation;

·      (iv) performance of a concert version of a "dramatico-musical work" (as hereinafter defined).

The term "dramatico-musical work" as used in this Agreement shall include, but not be limited to, a musical comedy, opera, play with music, revue, or ballet.

### 3. License Fees and Payments

(a) In consideration of the license granted herein, LICENSEE agrees to pay SOCIETY the applicable license fee set forth in the Rate Schedule annexed hereto and made a part hereof, based on "LICENSEE's Operating Policy." The term "LICENSEE's Operating Policy" shall mean all of the factors which determine the license fee applicable to the premises under the Rate Schedule.

(b) LICENSEE warrants that the Statement of LICENSEE's Operating Policy attached to and made a part of this Agreement is true and correct as of the date hereof.

(c) The current applicable license fee for the premises is $           annually, based on the factors set forth in the Statement of LICENSEE's Operating Policy.

(d) LICENSEE agrees to pay SOCIETY the license fee due hereunder in installments of one-third the applicable annual fee in advance on or before January 1, May 1 and September 1 of each year provided, however, that if LICENSEE does not otherwise owe SOCIETY any fees under this or any prior license agreement, and if LICENSEE pays the full annual fee on or before January 31st of any year, the applicable license fee for that year shall be reduced by 20%.

(e) LICENSEE agrees to pay SOCIETY a $25 service charge for each unpaid check, draft or other form of monetary instrument submitted by LICENSEE to SOCIETY.

(f) In the event LICENSEE shall be delinquent in payment of license fees due hereunder by 30 days or more, LICENSEE agrees to pay a finance charge on the license fees due of 1 1/2 % per month, or the maximum rate permitted by the law of the state in which the premises licensed hereunder are located, whichever is less, from the date such license fees became due.

(g) In the event that LICENSEE's payment of fees under this Agreement causes SOCIETY to incur a liability to pay a gross receipts, sales, use, business use, or other tax which is based on the amount of SOCIETY's receipts from LICENSEE, the number of licensees of SOCIETY, or any similar measure of SOCIETY's activities, and:

    (i)   SOCIETY has taken reasonable steps to be exempted or excused from paying such tax; and

    (ii)  SOCIETY is permitted by law to pass through such tax to its licensees, LICENSEE agrees to pay to SOCIETY the full amount of such tax.

### 4. Changes in LICENSEE's Operating Policy

(a) LICENSEE agrees to give SOCIETY thirty days prior written notice of any change in LICENSEE's Operating Policy. For purposes of this Agreement, a change in LICENSEE's Operating Policy shall be one in effect for at least thirty days.

(b) Upon any change in LICENSEE's Operating Policy resulting in an increase in the license fee, based on the annexed Rate Schedule, LICENSEE agrees to pay SOCIETY the increased license fee, effective as of the initial date of such change, whether or not written notice of such change has been given pursuant to subparagraph "4(a)" hereof.

(c) Upon any change in LICENSEE's Operating Policy resulting in a reduction in the license fee, based on the annexed Rate Schedule, LICENSEE shall be entitled to the reduction, effective as of the initial date of such change, and to a *pro rata* credit for any unearned license fees paid in advance, provided LICENSEE has given SOCIETY thirty days prior written notice of such change. If LICENSEE fails to give SOCIETY thirty days prior written notice, any reduction and credit shall be effective thirty days after LICENSEE gives SOCIETY written notice of the change.

(d) Within thirty days of any change in LICENSEE's Operating Policy, LICENSEE shall furnish to SOCIETY a current Statement of LICENSEE's Operating Policy and shall certify that it is true and correct.

(e) If LICENSEE discontinues the performance of music at the premises, LICENSEE or SOCIETY may terminate this Agreement upon thirty days notice, the termination to be effective at the end of the thirty day period. In the event of such termination, SOCIETY shall refund to LICENSEE a *pro rata* share of any unearned license fees paid in advance. For purposes of this Agreement, a discontinuance of music shall be one in effect for no less than thirty days.

### 5. Breach or Default

Upon any breach or default by LICENSEE of any term or condition herein contained, SOCIETY may terminate this license by giving LICENSEE thirty days notice to cure the breach or default, and in the event that it has not been cured within the thirty day period, this license shall terminate on the expiration of that period without further notice from SOCIETY to LICENSEE.

**6. Interference in SOCIETY's Operations**

In the event of:

(a) any major interference with the operations of SOCIETY in the state, territory, dependency, possession or political subdivision in which LICENSEE is located, by reason of any law of such state, territory, dependency, possession or political subdivision; or

(b) any substantial increase in the cost to SOCIETY of operating in such state, territory, dependency, possession or political subdivision, by reason of any law of such state, territory, dependency, possession or political subdivision, which is applicable to the licensing of performing rights,

SOCIETY shall have the right to terminate this Agreement forthwith by written notice and shall refund to LICENSEE any unearned license fees paid in advance.

**7. Notices**

All notices required or permitted to be given by either party to the other hereunder shall be duly and properly given if:

(a) mailed to the other party by registered or certified United States Mail; or

(b) sent by electronic transmission (i.e., Mailgram, facsimile or similar transmission); or

(c) sent by generally recognized same-day or overnight delivery service, addressed to the party at the address stated above. Each party agrees to inform the other of any change of address.

IN WITNESS WHEREOF, this Agreement has been duly executed by SOCIETY and LICENSEE, this _____ day of _____, _____.

AMERICAN SOCIETY OF COMPOSERS,  
AUTHORS AND PUBLISHERS

_____  
LICENSEE

By_____

By_____

_____  
TITLE

(Fill in capacity in which signed:  
(a) If corporation, state corporate office held; (b) If partnership, write word "partner" under signature of signing partner; (c) If individual owner, write "individual owner" under signature.)

## RATE SCHEDULE
### LICENSE FEES FOR CALENDAR YEAR 2000

This Rate Schedule applies to Bars, Grills, Taverns, Restaurants, Lounges, Supper Clubs, Night Clubs, Ballrooms, Dance Clubs, Discos, Piano Bars, Cabarets, Roadhouses and similar establishments.

| Seating (A) Capacity | No. of Days Per Week | Base Rate | (1) | (2) | (3) | Audio Only (C) Mech. Music ADD | A/V (D) with or without only Mech. Music ADD | Base Rate | (1) | (2) | (3) | Audio Only (C) Mech. Music ADD | A/V (D) with or without only Mech. Music ADD | Audio Only (C) Mech. Music Base Rate | (1) | (2) | A/V (D) with or without Audio Only Mech. Music Base Rate | (1) | (2) |
|---|---|---|---|---|---|---|---|---|---|---|---|---|---|---|---|---|---|---|---|
| 75 & under | 1 | 246 | 324 | 431 | 577 | 94 | 144 | 324 | 431 | 577 | 770 | 94 | 144 | 221 | 324 | 431 | 330 | 487 | 647 |
|  | 2-3 | 338 | 445 | 592 | 793 | 122 | 185 | 485 | 648 | 863 | 1146 | 122 | 185 | 246 | 445 | 592 | 367 | 668 | 888 |
|  | 4-7 | 415 | 553 | 740 | 998 | 148 | 223 | 648 | 863 | 1146 | 1536 | 148 | 223 | 269 | 553 | 740 | 404 | 831 | 1112 |
| 76-150 | 1 | 324 | 431 | 577 | 769 | 135 | 203 | 431 | 577 | 769 | 1025 | 135 | 203 | 317 | 431 | 577 | 476 | 647 | 870 |
|  | 2-3 | 485 | 648 | 863 | 1146 | 174 | 264 | 648 | 863 | 1146 | 1536 | 174 | 264 | 353 | 648 | 863 | 528 | 972 | 1291 |
|  | 4-7 | 648 | 863 | 1146 | 1536 | 215 | 322 | 863 | 1146 | 1536 | 2049 | 215 | 322 | 390 | 863 | 1146 | 583 | 1291 | 1720 |
| 151-225 | 1 | 431 | 577 | 769 | 1027 | 174 | 264 | 577 | 769 | 1025 | 1376 | 174 | 264 | 413 | 577 | 769 | 619 | 870 | 1157 |
|  | 2-3 | 648 | 863 | 1146 | 1536 | 230 | 346 | 874 | 1157 | 1552 | 2060 | 230 | 346 | 460 | 863 | 1146 | 691 | 1291 | 1720 |
|  | 4-7 | 863 | 1146 | 1536 | 2049 | 284 | 427 | 1157 | 1552 | 2060 | 2750 | 284 | 427 | 506 | 1146 | 1536 | 780 | 1720 | 2305 |
| 226-300 | 1 | 536 | 716 | 956 | 1278 | 215 | 322 | 726 | 970 | 1292 | 1724 | 215 | 322 | 511 | 716 | 956 | 766 | 1072 | 1431 |
|  | 2-3 | 812 | 1077 | 1441 | 1928 | 264 | 427 | 1093 | 1456 | 1941 | 2587 | 264 | 427 | 567 | 1077 | 1441 | 850 | 1618 | 2162 |
|  | 4-7 | 1077 | 1441 | 1928 | 2563 | 353 | 528 | 1456 | 1941 | 2587 | 3451 | 353 | 528 | 624 | 1441 | 1912 | 935 | 2162 | 2869 |
| 301-375 | 1 | 648 | 863 | 1148 | 1536 | 259 | 383 | 874 | 1172 | 1563 | 2078 | 259 | 383 | 606 | 863 | 1146 | 908 | 1291 | 1720 |
|  | 2-3 | 970 | 1292 | 1724 | 2300 | 336 | 507 | 1323 | 1755 | 2344 | 3111 | 336 | 507 | 672 | 1292 | 1724 | 1006 | 1941 | 2587 |
|  | 4-7 | 1292 | 1724 | 2300 | 3058 | 415 | 624 | 1755 | 2331 | 3111 | 4151 | 415 | 624 | 737 | 1724 | 2300 | 1109 | 2587 | 3451 |
| 376-450 | 1 | 758 | 1011 | 1346 | 1795 | 296 | 444 | 1025 | 1361 | 1819 | 2427 | 296 | 444 | 704 | 1011 | 1346 | 1057 | 1520 | 2020 |
|  | 2-3 | 1131 | 1522 | 2010 | 2682 | 395 | 591 | 1536 | 2049 | 2735 | 3636 | 395 | 591 | 729 | 1509 | 2010 | 1171 | 2260 | 3014 |
|  | 4-7 | 1509 | 2024 | 2682 | 3572 | 485 | 726 | 2049 | 2735 | 3636 | 4853 | 485 | 726 | 857 | 2024 | 2682 | 1288 | 3034 | 4022 |
| 451-525 | 1 | 758 | 1011 | 1346 | 1795 | 296 | 444 | 1172 | 1563 | 2088 | 2775 | 308 | 507 | 803 | 1146 | 1552 | 1205 | 1720 | 2329 |
|  | 2-3 | 1131 | 1522 | 2010 | 2682 | 395 | 591 | 1763 | 2344 | 3128 | 4178 | 395 | 668 | 890 | 1724 | 2331 | 1336 | 2587 | 3496 |
|  | 4-7 | 1509 | 2024 | 2682 | 3572 | 485 | 726 | 2344 | 3128 | 4165 | 5553 | 283 | 831 | 980 | 2292 | 3099 | 1471 | 3438 | 4649 |
| 526-600 | 1 | 758 | 1011 | 1346 | 1795 | 296 | 444 | 1323 | 1763 | 2344 | 3128 | 375 | 564 | 897 | 1278 | 1755 | 1346 | 1916 | 2633 |
|  | 2-3 | 1131 | 1522 | 2010 | 2682 | 395 | 591 | 1983 | 2642 | 3517 | 4691 | 498 | 749 | 998 | 1928 | 2629 | 1496 | 2890 | 3939 |
|  | 4-7 | 1509 | 2024 | 2682 | 3572 | 485 | 726 | 2642 | 3517 | 4691 | 6253 | 618 | 928 | 1097 | 2563 | 3506 | 1644 | 3845 | 5258 |
| 601-675 | 1 | 758 | 1011 | 1346 | 1795 | 296 | 444 | 1470 | 1953 | 2613 | 3477 | 415 | 624 | 993 | 1415 | 1953 | 1491 | 2123 | 2930 |
|  | 2-3 | 1131 | 1522 | 2010 | 2682 | 395 | 591 | 2209 | 2938 | 3921 | 5215 | 653 | 831 | 1106 | 2129 | 2938 | 1654 | 3196 | 4410 |
|  | 4-7 | 1509 | 2024 | 2682 | 3572 | 485 | 726 | 2938 | 3921 | 5215 | 6951 | 685 | 1029 | 1214 | 2833 | 3911 | 1825 | 4249 | 5863 |
| 676-750 | 1 | 758 | 1011 | 1346 | 1795 | 296 | 444 | 1614 | 2155 | 2871 | 3829 | 460 | 681 | 1091 | 1552 | 2155 | 1637 | 2329 | 3232 |
|  | 2-3 | 1131 | 1522 | 2010 | 2682 | 395 | 591 | 2427 | 3231 | 4314 | 5742 | 609 | 914 | 1211 | 2331 | 3231 | 1818 | 3496 | 4846 |
|  | 4-7 | 1509 | 2024 | 2682 | 3572 | 485 | 726 | 3231 | 4314 | 5742 | 7653 | 758 | 1134 | 1332 | 3099 | 4314 | 2000 | 4649 | 6470 |
| 751 & Over | 1 | 758 | 1011 | 1346 | 1795 | 296 | 444 | 1614 | 2155 | 2871 | 3829 | 498 | 749 | 1191 | 1684 | 2358 | 1785 | 2527 | 3536 |
|  | 2-3 | 1131 | 1522 | 2010 | 2682 | 395 | 591 | 2427 | 3231 | 4314 | 5742 | 659 | 991 | 1323 | 2531 | 3548 | 1984 | 3798 | 5319 |
|  | 4-7 | 1509 | 2024 | 2682 | 3572 | 485 | 726 | 3231 | 4314 | 5742 | 7653 | 825 | 1235 | 1455 | 3369 | 4718 | 2181 | 5054 | 7078 |

**(A) "Seating Capacity"**
for ballrooms, dance clubs, discos and similar operations means the total allowable occupancy of the premises under local fire or similar regulations, and shall not be limited to the total number of available seats, provided that if no such local fire or similar regulations are in effect, then "seating capacity" means 10 people per 100 square feet or portion thereof of the room(s) in which music is performed.

**(B) VARIABLES (Applicable to single instrumentalist)**
Show or act(s) or vocalist(s).
Admission, minimum, cover, entertainment or similar charge.
Alternate or relief music (live) by a single instrumentalist. Music provided solely at the time of the show or act(s) shall not be deemed to be alternate or relief music.

**(C) "Mechanical Music Audio-Only"**
means performances other than by live musicians, e.g., records, tapes, compact discs, karaoke, or similar media or by a radio-over-loudspeaker system licensable under the United States Copyright Law, but shall not include music presented by means of a music-on-hold telephone system or a jukebox (as hereinafter defined).

page 1 of 2

**(D) "Mechanical Music Audio-Visual"**

means performances such as, for example, by means of large screen television, multiple televisions, laser discs, video tapes, karaoke with video, or video jukeboxes licensable under the United States Copyright Law. If performances are presented by both audio-only and audio-visual mechanical means, add only the applicable additional fee specified for "mechanical music audio-visual".

**(E) VARIABLES (Applicable to two or more instrumentalists)**

Show or act(s).

Admission, minimum, cover, entertainment or similar charge.

Alternate or relief music (live) by any instrumentalist(s). Music provided solely at the time of the show or act(s) shall not be deemed to be alternate or relief music.

**(F) VARIABLES (Applicable when there is no live music, to audio-only and audio-visual mechanical music)**

Admission, minimum, cover, entertainment or similar charge.

Dancing (patrons or performers), show or act(s) (including disc jockey, video jockey or master of ceremonies).

### FEE FOR PERFORMANCES BY MEANS OF JUKEBOX(ES)

For purposes of this Agreement, a "jukebox" is a machine or device that is (i) employed solely for the non-dramatic performance of musical works by means of phonorecords, compact discs or similar medium and which is activated by insertion of coins, currency, tokens, or other monetary units or their equivalent; (ii) is located in an establishment making no direct or indirect charge for admission; (iii) is accompanied by a list of the titles of all musical works available for performance on the jukebox, which list is affixed to the jukebox or posted in the establishment in a prominent position where it can be readily examined by the public; (iv) affords a choice of works available for performance and permits the choice to be made by the patrons of the establishment in which it is located; and (v) for which neither a compulsory license nor a license from the Jukebox License Office nor a license from SOCIETY other than this license is in effect. For purposes of this Agreement, the term "jukebox" does not include devices commonly known as "video jukeboxes," or any other audio-visual devices.

For performances given by means of jukebox(es), the annual license fee shall be **$241 per jukebox.**

### FEE FOR PERFORMANCES BY MEANS OF MUSIC-ON-HOLD TELEPHONE SYSTEM

For performances given by means of a music-on-hold telephone system at the premises, the annual license fee shall be **$181.00.**

### COMPUTATION OF FEE FOR MIXED POLICIES

1. Compute fee for the higher policy for the number of days/nights that the higher policy is in effect. The higher policy is the policy which generates the highest fee for any one day/night. If the higher policy is in effect for four or more days/nights per week, stop here: Your fee is the fee for the higher policy. If the higher policy is in effect for fewer than four days/nights per week, continue with steps 2 through 6 below to complete the computation of the fee for your mixed policy.

2. Note total number of days/nights entertainment is provided.

3. Compute fee for the lower policy using the total number of days/nights entertainment is provided under both the higher and lower policies.

4. Compute fee for the lower policy using the number of days/nights the higher policy is in effect.

5. Subtract fee computed in step 4 from fee computed in step 3.

6. Add fee computed in step 1 to fee computed in step 5 for total fee.

### SEASONAL FEES

For seasonal licensees, the fees for periods up to four months of operation are 1/2 the annual license fee; for each additional month the fee is 1/12 the annual license fee. The seasonal license fee will in no case be more than the annual license fee.

### FEES FOR OCCASIONAL PERFORMANCES

For policies in effect for any three or fewer days/nights per month, the fee is the applicable annual fee for the highest of such policies as if such highest policy were in effect for one day/night per week. For policies in effect for any six or fewer days/nights per calendar year, the fee is 1/3 the applicable annual fee for the highest of such policies as if such highest policy were in effect for one day/night per week.

### ANNUAL LICENSE FEE FOR CALENDAR YEAR 2001 AND THEREAFTER

The annual license fee for each calendar year commencing 2001 shall be the license fee for the preceding calendar year, adjusted in accordance with the increase in the Consumer Price Index, All Urban Consumers - (CPI-U) between the preceding October and the next preceding October.

# FORM 17.15

## ASCAP HOTELS AND MOTELS LICENSE

### LICENSE AGREEMENT - HOTELS AND MOTELS

*Agreement* between American Society of Composers, Authors and Publishers ("ASCAP"), an unincorporated New York membership association, located at 2690 Cumberland Parkway, Suite 490, Atlanta, GA 30339-3913 and

("LICENSEE"), located at

as follows:

1.    **Grant and Term of License**

(a)    ASCAP grants and LICENSEE accepts a license to perform publicly at or in any part or section of the hotel or motel known as

located at

and not elsewhere (the "premises"), non-dramatic renditions of the separate musical compositions in the "ASCAP Repertory." The performances licensed under this Agreement may be by means of live entertainment, "mechanical music," or "jukeboxes." The license fee for the first calendar year of this Agreement is estimated at $               , based on the applicable Rate Schedules attached to and made a part of this Agreement.

(b)    This license shall be for a term commencing                          and ending December 31, 2003 (the "initial term") and continuing thereafter for additional renewal terms of five years each. Either party may, on or before ninety days prior to the end of the initial term or any renewal term, give notice of termination to the other. If notice is given, the Agreement shall terminate on the last day of the initial or renewal term in which the notice is given.

(c)    For purposes of this Agreement:

(i)    "ASCAP repertory" means all copyrighted musical compositions written or published by ASCAP members or members of affiliated foreign performing rights societies, including compositions written or published during the term of this Agreement, and of which ASCAP has the right to license non-dramatic public performances.

(ii)    "Mechanical Music" means music which is performed at the premises by means other than by live musicians who are performing at the premises, including, but not limited to (A) compact disc, audio record or audio tape players (but not including "jukeboxes"), (B) videotape, videodisc or DVD players; (C) performances in public rooms or guests' private rooms at the premises by means of pay or cable television, pay-per-view programming or any similar means or method (whether transmitted by satellite or otherwise to the premises); (D) the reception and communication at the premises of radio or television transmissions which originate outside the premise; and which are not exempt under the Copyright Law; or (E) a music-on-hold telephone system operated by LICENSEE at the premises.

(iii)    "Live Music" means music which is performed at the premises by musicians, singers or other performers.

(iv)    "Jukebox" means a machine or device that:

(A)    is employed solely for the non-dramatic performance of musical works by means of phonorecords, compact discs or any similar medium, and which is activated by insertion of coins, currency, tokens, or other monetary units or their equivalent;

(B)    is located on premises making no direct or indirect charge for admission;

(C)    is accompanied by a list of the titles of all musical works available for performance on the jukebox, affixed to the jukebox or posted on the premises in a prominent position where it can be readily examined by the public;

(D)    affords a choice of works available for performance and permits the choice to be made by the patrons or guests of LICENSEE who are present on the premises in which it is located; and

(E)    for which neither a license from the Jukebox License Office nor a license from ASCAP other than this license is in effect.

"Jukebox" does not include devices commonly known as "video-jukeboxes," or any other audio-visual devices.

(v)    "Annual Expenditure for All Entertainment at the Premises" ("Annual Expenditures") means all payments made (whether in money or in any other form) by LICENSEE for all entertainment at the premises, including, but not limited to such payments made to any disc jockey, video jockey or Karaoke host, but excluding:

(A)    Any such payments made to comedians, and

(B)    Any service in connection with entertainment rendered by the regularly employed staff of LICENSEE, but including the compensation paid to any persons whose services are especially and exclusively engaged for the presentation of any such entertainment; provided, that where any arrangement either by contract or otherwise between LICENSEE and any entity or person presenting entertainment at the premises, which arrangement or contract shall provide that as the consideration or any part thereof, any accommodations or services are to be made available for its, his or her use, then in such case, the extent of such accommodations or services shall be clearly defined and the reasonable value thereof regarded as an expenditure by LICENSEE for such entertainment and reported to ASCAP as expended during each calendar year in which such entertainment is presented, provided that if LICENSEE and ASCAP fail to agree as to the reasonable value of such accommodations or services the same shall be fixed at a sum equal to one-half of the prevailing rate charged to the guests of the premises for such accommodations or services.

(C)    Any expenditures by LICENSEE in connection with a production incorporating performances of dramatico-musical works as defined in paragraph 2.(c) below, including expenditures for rights acquisition and payments to performers and technicians, provided that (i) the performance of all musical compositions in the production is dramatic; and (ii) LICENSEE provides ASCAP upon request a copy of any agreements between LICENSEE and the owners of dramatic rights of the works in the production establishing that LICENSEE has obtained authorization for dramatic performance.

(d)    This Agreement shall be binding upon the parties hereto and their respective successors and assigns, but no assignment shall be made without the prior written approval of ASCAP and no such assignment shall relieve the parties of their respective obligations under this Agreement as to performances rendered, acts done and obligations incurred prior to the effective date of the assignment.

## 2.    Limitations on License

(a)    This license does not authorize the broadcasting, telecasting or transmission by wire or otherwise, of renditions of musical compositions in ASCAP's repertory to persons outside of the premises, other than by means of a music-on-hold telephone system operated by LICENSEE at the premises. This license is limited to LICENSEE and the premises.

(b)    This license does not authorize any performance by means of any jukebox for which a license from the Jukebox License Office or a license from ASCAP other than this license is in effect.

(c)    This license is limited to non-dramatic performances, and does not authorize any dramatic performances. For purposes of this Agreement, a dramatic performance shall include, but not be limited to, the following:

(i)    performance of a "dramatico-musical work" in its entirety;

(ii)    performance of one or more musical compositions from a "dramatico-musical work" accompanied by dialogue, pantomime, dance, stage action, or visual representation of the work from which the music is taken;

(iii)    performance of one or more musical compositions as part of a story or plot, whether accompanied or unaccompanied by dialogue, pantomime, dance, stage action, or visual presentation;

(iv)    performance of a concert version of a "dramatico-musical work".

The term "dramatico-musical work" as used in this Agreement, shall include, but not be limited to, a musical comedy, opera, play with music, revue, or ballet.

(d)     This license does not authorize performances at the premises by means of (i) background music services which are licensed by ASCAP; or (ii) any other services delivered by digital means or otherwise which are licensed by ASCAP.

(e)     This license does not authorize performances as part of a conference, congress, convention, exposition, industrial show, institute, meeting, seminar, teleconference, trade show or any other business presentation at the premises.

3.     **Right to Restrict Performances**

ASCAP reserves the right at any time to withdraw from its repertory and this license any musical work as to which any suit has been brought or threatened on a claim that the composition infringes a composition not in ASCAP's repertory, or on a claim ASCAP does not have the right to license the performing right in that composition.

4.     **License Fees**

In consideration of the license granted herein, LICENSEE agrees to pay ASCAP the applicable license fees set forth in the Rate Schedule attached to and made a part of this Agreement.

5.     **Reports and Payments**

(a)     Upon the execution of this Agreement, LICENSEE shall submit to ASCAP a report showing all the information necessary to estimate LICENSEE's annual license fee for the first contract year of this Agreement.

(b)     On or before January 20 of each subsequent year during the term of this Agreement, LICENSEE shall submit to ASCAP a report showing all the information necessary to determine LICENSEE's annual license fee for the preceding calendar year. If the report shows additional license fees due for the previous calendar year, the payment shall be due within 30 days of the date of an invoice from ASCAP. If the report shows an overpayment of license fees for the previous calendar year, LICENSEE shall receive a credit in that amount, applicable to its next payment(s) of license fees. ASCAP shall provide to LICENSEE report forms free of charge.

(c)     Upon the execution of this Agreement and on or before January 1, May 1 and September 1 of each year of this Agreement, LICENSEE shall pay to ASCAP one-third of the annual license fee payable under this Agreement for that calendar year, as estimated, based on the annual license fee for the previous calendar year, and subject to adjustment as provided by subparagraph 5.(b).

(d)     If LICENSEE (i) is not delinquent and does not otherwise owe ASCAP any fees or reports under this or any other license Agreement, and (ii) provides documentation that it is a member of the American Hotel & Motel Association, the license fee for the year 2000 and subsequent years shall be reduced by 1%.

(e)     LICENSEE shall pay ASCAP a $25 service charge for each unpaid check, draft or other form of instrument submitted by LICENSEE to ASCAP.

(f)     LICENSEE shall pay a finance charge of 1.5% per month from the due date, or the maximum amount permitted by law, whichever is less, on any required payment that it is not made within forty-five days of the date it should have been paid under this Agreement.

6.     **Discontinuance of Music; Resumption of Music**

(a)     If LICENSEE discontinues the performance of mechanical or jukebox music or discontinues and later resumes the performance of mechanical or jukebox music during any year of this Agreement, the license fee for that year shall be adjusted pro-rata based on the number of months in that year in which mechanical and/or jukebox music is performed.

(b) If LICENSEE discontinues the use of live music or discontinues and later resumes the performance of live music during any year of this Agreement, the license fee for that year shall be adjusted on the basis of Annual Expenditures for All Entertainment at the premises for that year.

(c) If LICENSEE discontinues the performance of all music at the premises, ASCAP or LICENSEE may terminate this Agreement on thirty days notice, such termination to become effective at the end of the 30 day period. LICENSEE shall pay any remaining license fees due within 30 days of invoice.

(d) LICENSEE shall notify ASCAP of any discontinuance or resumption of music and shall provide a report showing all the information necessary to determine the applicable fees for that year.

(e) For purposes of this Agreement a discontinuance shall be one in effect for no less than 30 days.

## 7. Cessation of Operation of the Premises

If LICENSEE ceases to operate the premises, LICENSEE shall give immediate written notice to ASCAP stating the manner of cessation and the license granted by this Agreement and the obligation of LICENSEE to pay future license fees to ASCAP shall terminate as of the effective date of cessation. LICENSEE shall continue to be liable to ASCAP for any license fees due, including the pro-rata amount of the then current calendar year's license fees.

## 8. Audit

(a) ASCAP shall have the right to require such reasonable data or information relating to the Annual Expenditures, as may be necessary to ascertain the Annual Expenditures as provided by this Agreement. ASCAP shall have the further right, by its duly authorized representatives, at any time during customary business hours, to examine LICENSEE's books and records of account only to such extent as may be necessary to verify any statements or reports required under this Agreement. ASCAP shall consider all data and information coming to its attention as the result of any such examination as completely and entirely confidential.

(b) The period for which ASCAP may audit under this Agreement shall be limited to the three calendar years before the year in which the audit is made. However, if an audit is postponed at LICENSEE's request, ASCAP shall have the right to audit for the calendar year in which ASCAP first notified LICENSEE of its intention to audit and the preceding three calendar years.

(c) If the audit reveals a deficiency, then the audit may cover the preceding three calendar years. This limitation shall not apply if LICENSEE fails or refuses after written notice from ASCAP to produce the books and records necessary to verify any report or statement of account required under this Agreement.

(d) Nothing shall restrict ASCAP's right to audit under the immediately preceding license agreement, for all periods covered by that agreement subject to the limitations contained in paragraph 8.(b).

(e) If any audit shows LICENSEE to have underpaid the license fees due ASCAP by 5% or more, LICENSEE shall pay a finance charge on the license fees shown due of 1 1/2% per month, or the maximum rate permitted by law, whichever is less, from the date(s) the license fees were due.

(f) If any audit shows LICENSEE to have underpaid the license fees due ASCAP by less than 5%, LICENSEE shall pay a finance charge on the license fees shown due of 1 1/2% per month. or the maximum rate permitted by law, whichever is less, from the date ASCAP demands payment of such amount.

## 9. Breach or Default

Upon any breach or default by LICENSEE of any term or condition herein contained, ASCAP may terminate this license by giving LICENSEE thirty days notice to cure such breach or default, and in the event that such breach or default has not been cured within said thirty days, this license shall terminate on the expiration of such thirty day period without further notice from ASCAP. In the event of such termination, ASCAP shall refund to LICENSEE any unearned license fees paid in advance.

10.    **Interference in Operations**

ASCAP shall have the right to terminate this license upon thirty days written notice if there is any major interference with, or substantial increase in the cost of, ASCAP's operations as the result of any law in the state, territory, dependency, possession or political subdivision in which LICENSEE is located which is applicable to the licensing of performing rights, provided that ASCAP also terminates the agreements of all other similarly situated licensees of ASCAP. ASCAP shall refund to LICENSEE any unearned license fees paid in advance.

11.    **Notices**

ASCAP or LICENSEE may give any notice required by this Agreement by sending it by United States Mail, by generally recognized same-day or overnight delivery service or by electronic transmission (i.e., facsimile or email or similar transmission, provided that a copy of such electronically transmitted notice is also sent by mail). Each party agrees to notify the other of any change of address.

12.    **Applicable Law**

The meaning of the provisions of this Agreement shall be construed in accordance with the laws of the State of New York without regard to the principles of conflict of laws.

IN WITNESS WHEREOF, this Agreement has been duly executed by ASCAP and LICENSEE, this _____ day of _____, _____.

AMERICAN SOCIETY OF COMPOSERS
    AUTHORS AND PUBLISHERS

By: _____

Title: _____

 

LICENSEE

By: _____

Print Name: _____

Title: _____
(Fill in capacity in which signed:  (a) If corporation, state corporate office held; (b) If partnership, write word "partner" under signature of signing partner; (c) If individual, write "individual owner" under signature.)

ASCAP

**FEE SCHEDULE--HOTELS AND MOTELS**

--If live music *only* is presented, use Schedule I.
--If mechanical music *only* is presented, use Schedule II.
--If *only* performances by means of jukebox(es) are presented, use Schedule IV.
--If *both* live *and* mechanical music are presented, use Schedules I *and* III
--If *both* live music and performances by means of jukebox(es) are presented, use Schedules I *and* IV.
--If live and mechanical music and performances by means of jukebox(es) are all presented, use Schedules I *and* III *and* IV.

**A. Fees**

**SCHEDULE I**

For "live" entertainment, the fee for each calendar year during the term of the Agreement shall be the fee set forth below which corresponds to the "Annual Expenditure for All Entertainment at the Premises" (as hereinafter defined) for that calendar year:

| Annual Expenditure for All Entertainment at the Premises | | Annual Rate for Calendar Year | |
|---|---|---|---|
| | | **1999** | **2000** |
| Less than | $ 2,000.00 | $ 153 | $ 161 |
| $2,000.00 to | 4,999.99 | 213 | 225 |
| 5,000.00 to | 9,999.99 | 322 | 340 |
| 10,000.00 to | 14,999.99 | 420 | 443 |
| 15,000.00 to | 24,999.99 | 634 | 669 |
| 25,000.00 to | 34,999.99 | 841 | 887 |
| 35,000.00 to | 49,999.99 | 1,047 | 1,105 |
| 50,000.00 to | 64,999.99 | 1,253 | 1,322 |
| 65,000.00 to | 79,999.99 | 1,581 | 1,668 |
| 80,000.00 to | 99,999.99 | 2,108 | 2,224 |
| 100,000.00 to | 119,999.99 | 2,637 | 2,782 |
| 120,000.00 to | 139,999.99 | 3,164 | 3,338 |
| 140,000.00 to | 159,999.99 | 3,692 | 3,895 |
| 160,000.00 to | 179,999.99 | 4,218 | 4,450 |
| 180,000.00 to | 199,999.99 | 4,746 | 5,007 |
| 200,000.00 to | 249,999.99 | 5,272 | 5,562 |
| 250,000.00 to | 299,999.99 | 5,806 | 6,125 |
| 300,000.00 to | 349,999.99 | 6,325 | 6,673 |
| 350,000.00 to | 399,999.99 | 7,029 | 7,416 |
| 400,000.00 to | 449,999.99 | 7,381 | 7,787 |
| 450,000.00 to | 499,999.99 | 7,909 | 8,344 |
| 500,000.00 to | 599,999.99 | 8,404 | 8,866 |
| 600,000.00 to | 749,999.99 | 9,170 | 9,674 |
| 750,000.00 to | 999,999.99 | 10,698 | 11,286 |
| 1,000,000.00 to | 1,499,999.99 | 12,225 | 12,887 |
| 1,500,000.00 to | 1,999,999.99 | 13,754 | 14,510 |
| 2,000,000.00 to | 2,999,999.99 | 15,283 | 16,124 |
| 3,000,000.00 to | 3,999,999.99 | 16,810 | 17,735 |
| 4,000,000.00 to | 4,999,999.99 | 19,866 | 20,959 |
| 5,000,000.00 to | 5,999,999.99 | 22,158 | 23,377 |
| 6,000,000.00 to | 6,999,999.99 | 27,508 | 29,021 |
| 7,000,000.00 and | Over | 28,728 | 30,308 |

**B. Method of Estimating "Annual Expenditure for All Entertainment at the Premises" (as Defined in Subparagraph "1.(c)(V)") for the First Calendar Year (or Part Thereof) of this Agreement**

I. If LICENSEE operated with a policy of presenting music for the full calendar year prior to the commencement date of this Agreement, LICENSEE shall estimate its expenditure for all entertainment at the premises for the first calendar year (or part thereof) of this Agreement on the basis of the expenditure for all entertainment at the premises during such full calendar year prior to the commencement date of this Agreement.

II. If LICENSEE operated with a policy of presenting music for less than a full calendar year prior to the commencement date of this Agreement, LICENSEE shall estimate its expenditure for all entertainment at the premises for the first calendar year (or part thereof) of this Agreement at a sum equal to the average monthly expenditure for all entertainment at the premises during the period of operation prior to the commencement date of this Agreement times the number of months of LICENSEE'S operation during said first calendar year (or part thereof).

III. If LICENSEE has not operated with a policy of presenting music for any period prior to the commencement date of this Agreement, LICENSEE shall estimate its expenditure for all entertainment at the premises for the first calendar year (or part thereof) of this Agreement on the basis of the expenditure for all entertainment at the premises during the first full month of operation times the number of months of LICENSEE'S operation during said first calendar year (or part thereof).

**C. Method of Calculating "Annual Expenditure for All Entertainment at the Premises" (as Defined in Subparagraph "1.(c)(V)") for the Second and Each Succeeding Calendar Year (or Part Thereof) of this Agreement**

For the second and each succeeding calendar year of the Agreement, the Annual Expenditure for All Entertainment at the Premises shall be estimated on the basis of the Annual Expenditure for All Entertainment at the Premises for the previous calendar year (or part thereof if LICENSEE operated for only part of such previous calendar year, in which case such Annual Expenditure for All Entertainment at the Premises shall be pro rated). Within twenty (20) days of the end of each calendar year (or part thereof if LICENSEE operated for only part of such calendar year) during the term of this Agreement an adjustment shall be made on the basis of the Annual Expenditure for All Entertainment at the Premises for such calendar year (or such part thereof on a pro rated basis).

SCHEDULE II
MECHANICAL MUSIC ONLY

**A. No Dancing; No Cover, Minimum or Admission Charge; and No Show or Acts\***

| No. of Rooms | 1999 Without AV | 1999 With AV | 2000 Without AV | 2000 With AV |
|---|---|---|---|---|
| 1-100 | $248 | $372 | $262 | $393 |
| 101-300 | 295 | 443 | 311 | 467 |
| 301-500 | 342 | 513 | 361 | 542 |
| 501-750 | 456 | 684 | 481 | 722 |
| Over 750 | 607 | 911 | 640 | 960 |

**B. One of: 1) Dancing; 2) Cover, Minimum or Admission Charge; or 3) Show or Acts\***

| No. of Rooms | 1999 Without AV | 1999 With AV | 2000 Without AV | 2000 With AV |
|---|---|---|---|---|
| 1-100 | $ 331 | $ 497 | $ 349 | $ 524 |
| 101-300 | 455 | 683 | 480 | 720 |
| 301-500 | 688 | 1,032 | 726 | 1,089 |
| 501-750 | 910 | 1,365 | 960 | 1,440 |
| Over 750 | 1,210 | 1,815 | 1,277 | 1,916 |

**C. Two of: 1) Dancing; 2) Cover, Minimum or Admission Charge; or 3) Show or Acts\***

| No. of Rooms | 1999 Without AV | 1999 With AV | 2000 Without AV | 2000 With AV |
|---|---|---|---|---|
| 1-100 | $ 455 | $ 683 | $ 480 | $ 720 |
| 101-300 | 688 | 1,032 | 726 | 1,089 |
| 301-500 | 1,020 | 1,530 | 1,076 | 1,614 |
| 501-750 | 1,363 | 2,045 | 1,438 | 2,225 |
| Over 750 | 1,813 | 2,720 | 1,913 | 2,870 |

**D. With Dancing, Cover, Minimum or Admission Charge, & Show or Acts\***

| No. of Rooms | 1999 Without AV | 1999 With AV | 2000 Without AV | 2000 With AV |
|---|---|---|---|---|
| 1-100 | $ 756 | $1,134 | $ 798 | $1,197 |
| 101-300 | 1,170 | 1,755 | 1,234 | 1,851 |
| 301-500 | 1,569 | 2,354 | 1,655 | 2,483 |
| 501-750 | 1,955 | 2,933 | 2,063 | 3,095 |
| Over 750 | 2,601 | 3,902 | 2,744 | 4,116 |

If audio-visual performances of mechanical music (such as the use of a large-screen television, or performances in guests' private rooms at the premises by means of pay or cable television, or pay-per-view programming, or any similar means or method (for which performances an ASCAP license fee is not otherwise paid)) are given, use the applicable category above; such uses do not include performances by means of a single receiving apparatus of a kind commonly used in private homes, unless a direct charge is made to see the transmission or the transmission thus received is further transmitted to the public. Such uses include only performances for which a license is required by the United States Copyright Law.

\*"Show or Acts" shall include use of a comedian.

SCHEDULE III
MECHANICAL MUSIC AND LIVE MUSIC

A. No Dancing; No Cover, Minimum or Admission Charge; and No Show or Acts*

| No. of Rooms | 1999 Without AV | 1999 With AV | 2000 Without AV | 2000 With AV |
|---|---|---|---|---|
| 1-100 | $146 | $219 | $154 | $231 |
| 101-300 | 177 | 266 | 187 | 281 |
| 301-500 | 207 | 311 | 218 | 327 |
| 501-750 | 276 | 414 | 291 | 437 |
| Over 750 | 368 | 552 | 388 | 582 |

B. One of: 1) Dancing; 2) Cover, Minimum or Admission Charge; or 3) Show or Acts*

| No. of Rooms | 1999 Without AV | 1999 With AV | 2000 Without AV | 2000 With AV |
|---|---|---|---|---|
| 1-100 | $197 | $296 | $208 | $312 |
| 101-300 | 276 | 414 | 291 | 437 |
| 301-500 | 358 | 537 | 378 | 567 |
| 501-750 | 468 | 702 | 494 | 741 |
| Over 750 | 622 | 933 | 656 | 984 |

C. Two of: 1) Dancing; 2) Cover, Minimum or Admission Charge; or 3) Show or Acts*

| No. of Rooms | 1999 Without AV | 1999 With AV | 2000 Without AV | 2000 With AV |
|---|---|---|---|---|
| 1-100 | $276 | $ 414 | $ 291 | $ 437 |
| 101-300 | 358 | 537 | 378 | 567 |
| 301-500 | 509 | 764 | 537 | 806 |
| 501-750 | 744 | 1,116 | 785 | 1,178 |
| Over 750 | 990 | 1,485 | 1,044 | 1,566 |

D. With Dancing, Cover, Minimum or Admission Charge, & Show or Acts*

| No. of Rooms | 1999 Without AV | 1999 With AV | 2000 Without AV | 2000 With AV |
|---|---|---|---|---|
| 1-100 | $ 56 | $1,134 | $ 798 | $1,197 |
| 101-300 | 1,170 | 1,755 | 1,234 | 1,851 |
| 301-500 | 1,569 | 2,354 | 1,655 | 2,483 |
| 501-750 | 1,955 | 2,933 | 2,063 | 3,095 |
| Over 750 | 2,601 | 3,902 | 2,744 | 4,116 |

If audio-visual performances of mechanical music (such as the use of a large-screen television, or performances in guests' private rooms at the premises by means of pay or cable television, or pay-per-view programming, or any similar means or method (for which performances an ASCAP license fee is not otherwise paid)) are given, use the applicable category above; such uses do not include performances by means of a single receiving apparatus of a kind commonly used in private homes, unless a direct charge is made to see the transmission or the transmission thus received is further transmitted to the public. Such uses include only performances for which a license is required by the United States Copyright Law.

*"Show or Acts" shall include use of a comedian

SCHEDULE IV
JUKEBOXES

For performances given by means of jukeboxes, the annual license fees shall be $235 per jukebox for 1999, and $241 per jukebox for 2000

DISCOUNTS

If LICENSEE (i) is not delinquent and does not otherwise owe ASCAP any fees or reports under this or any other license Agreement; and (ii) provides documentation that it is a member of the American Hotel & Motel Association, the license fee for the year 2000 and subsequent years shall be reduced by 1%.

ANNUAL LICENSE FEE FOR CALENDAR YEARS 2001 AND THEREAFTER

The annual license fee for each calendar year commencing 2001 shall be the license fee for the preceding calendar year, adjusted in accordance with the increase in the Consumer Price Index (National, All Items) between the preceding October and the next preceding October, rounded to the nearest $1.00.

# FORM 17.16

## ASCAP MUSIC-ON-HOLD LICENSE

MUSICHOLDIND


MUSIC-ON-HOLD

**Agreement** between AMERICAN SOCIETY OF COMPOSERS, AUTHORS AND PUBLISHERS ("SOCIETY"), located at One Lincoln Plaza, New York, New York 10023 and


("LICENSEE"), located at                                                                    as follows:


### 1. Grant and Term of License

(a) SOCIETY grants and LICENSEE accepts for a term of one year, commencing                          , and continuing thereafter for additional terms of one year unless terminated by either party as hereinafter provided, a license to perform publicly at

("the premises"), and not elsewhere, by means of a music-on-hold telephone system, and not otherwise, non-dramatic renditions of the separate musical compositions now or hereafter during the term hereof in the reper- tory of SOCIETY, and of which SOCIETY shall have the right to license such performing rights.

(b) This agreement shall enure to the benefit of and shall be binding upon the parties hereto and their respec- tive successors and assigns, but no assignment shall relieve the parties hereto of their respective obligations here- under as to performances rendered, acts done and obligations incurred prior to the effective date of the assign- ment.

(c) Either party may, on or before thirty days prior to the end of the initial term or any renewal term, give notice of termination to the other. If such notice is given the agreement shall terminate on the last day of such initial or renewal term.

### 2. Limitations on License

(a) This license is not assignable or transferable by operation of law or otherwise, except as provided in para- graph "1 (b)" hereof, and is limited to the LICENSEE and to the premises.

(b) This license does not authorize the broadcasting, telecasting or transmission by wire or otherwise, of ren- ditions of musical compositions in SOCIETY's repertory to persons outside of the premises, other than by means of LICENSEE's music-on-hold telephone system.

(c) This license is limited to nondramatic performances, and does not authorize any dramatic performances. For purposes of this agreement, a dramatic performance shall include, but not be limited to, the following:

   (i)  performance of a "dramatico-musical work" (as hereinafter defined) in its entirety;
   (ii) performance of one or more musical compositions from a "dramatico-musical work" (as hereinafter defined) accompanied by dialogue, pantomime, dance, stage action, or visual representation of the work from which the music is taken;
   (iii) performance of one or more musical compositions as part of a story or plot, whether accompanied or unaccompanied by dialogue, pantomime, dance, stage action, or visual representation;
   (iv) performance of a concert version of a "dramatico-musical work" (as hereinafter defined).
The term "dramatico-musical work" as used in this agreement, shall include, but not be limited to, a musical comedy, opera, play with music, revue or ballet.

### 3. License Fee

(a) In consideration of the license granted herein, LICENSEE agrees to pay SOCIETY the applicable license fee set forth in the rate schedule printed below and made part hereof, based on "LICENSEE's Operating Policy" (as hereinafter defined) payable annually in advance on January 15 of each year. The term "LICENSEE's Operating Policy", as used in this agreement, shall be deemed to mean all of the factors which determine the license fee ap- plicable to the premises under said rate schedule.

(b) LICENSEE warrants that the Statement of LICENSEE's Operating Policy on the reverse side of this agree- ment is true and correct. LICENSEE shall provide, at the time of execution of this agreement and upon any change in LICENSEE's Operating Policy pursuant to Paragraph "4" hereof, documentation from the telephone operating company providing telephone service to LICENSEE showing the number of trunk lines used in pro- viding LICENSEE's music-on-hold telephone service.

(c) Said license fee is                                        Dollars ($            ) annually, based on the facts set forth in said Statement of LICENSEE's Operating Policy.

(d) In the event LICENSEE shall be delinquent in the payment of license fees due under Paragraph "3 (a)" hereof by forty-five (45) days or more, LICENSEE shall pay a finance charge on the license fees due of 1½ % per month, or the maximum rate permitted by law, whichever is lesser, from the date such license fees should have been paid pursuant to Paragraph "3 (a)" hereof.

(e) In the event that LICENSEE's payment of fees under this Agreement causes SOCIETY to incur a liability to pay a gross receipts, sales, use, business use, or other tax which is based on the amount of SOCIETY's receipts from LICENSEE, the number of licensees of SOCIETY, or any similar measure of SOCIETY's activities, and (i) SOCIETY has taken reasonable steps to be exempted or excused from paying such tax; and (ii) SOCIETY is permitted by law to pass through such tax to its licensees, LICENSEE shall pay to SOCIETY the full amount of such tax.

### 4. Changes in LICENSEE's Operating Policy

(a) LICENSEE agrees to give SOCIETY thirty days prior notice of any change in LICENSEE's Operating Policy. For purposes of this agreement, a change in LICENSEE's Operating Policy shall be one in effect for no less than thirty days.

(b) Upon any such change in LICENSEE's Operating Policy resulting in an increase in the license fee, based on the annexed rate schedule, LICENSEE shall pay said increased license fee, effective as of the initial date of such change, whether or not notice of such change has been given pursuant to Paragraph "4 (a)" hereof.

(c) Upon any such change in LICENSEE's Operating Policy resulting in a reduction of the license fee, based on the annexed rate schedule, LICENSEE shall be entitled to such reduction, effective as of the initial date of such change, and to a pro rata credit for any unearned license fees paid in advance, provided LICENSEE has given SOCIETY thirty days prior notice of such change. If LICENSEE fails to give such prior notice, any such reduction and credit shall be effective thirty days after LICENSEE gives notice of such change.

(d) In the event of any such change in LICENSEE's Operating Policy, LICENSEE shall furnish a current Statement of LICENSEE's Operating Policy and shall certify that it is true and correct.

(e) If LICENSEE discontinues the performance of music at the premises, LICENSEE or SOCIETY may terminate this agreement upon thirty days prior notice, the termination to be effective at the end of such thirty day period. In the event of such termination, SOCIETY shall refund to LICENSEE a pro rata share of any unearned license fees paid in advance. For purposes of this agreement, a discontinuance of music shall be one in effect for no less than thirty days.

### 5. Breach or Default

Upon any breach or default by LICENSEE of any term or condition herein contained, SOCIETY may terminate this license by giving LICENSEE thirty days notice to cure such breach or default, and in the event that such breach or default has not been cured within said thirty days, this license shall terminate on the expiration of such thirty-day period without further notice from SOCIETY. In the event of such termination, SOCIETY shall refund to LICENSEE any unearned license fees paid in advance.

### 6. Interference in Society's Operations

In the event of:

(a) any major interference with the operations of SOCIETY in the state, territory, dependency, possession or political subdivision in which LICENSEE is located, by reason of any law of such state, territory, dependency, possession or political subdivision; or

(b) any substantial increase in the cost to the SOCIETY of operating in such state, territory, dependency, possession or political subdivision, by reason of any law of such state, territory, dependency, possession or political subdivision, which is applicable to the licensing of performing rights,

SOCIETY shall have the right to terminate this agreement forthwith by written notice and shall refund to LICENSEE any unearned license fees paid in advance.

### 7. Notices

All notices required or permitted hereunder shall be given in writing by certified United States mail sent to either party at the address stated above. Each party agrees to inform the other of any change of address.

IN WITNESS WHEREOF, this agreement has been duly executed by SOCIETY and LICENSEE this    day of 19

AMERICAN SOCIETY OF COMPOSERS,
AUTHORS AND PUBLISHERS

By _____
DISTRICT MANAGER

_____
LICENSEE

By _____

_____
Title

(Fill in capacity in which signed:
(a) If corporation, state corporate office held; (b) If partnership, write word "partner" under signature of signing partner; (c) If individual owner, write "individual owner" under signature.)

ASCAP

**2000**
**RATE SCHEDULE**

## MUSIC-ON-HOLD

| Number of Trunk Lines Used in Providing LICENSEE'S Music-On-Hold Telephone Service | Annual Fee |
|---|---|
| 1-10 | $181.00 |
| 11-50 | $360.00 |
| 51-100 | $544.00 |
| 101-150 | $723.00 |
| 151-200 | $905.00 |
| 201-250 | $1,083.00 |
| 251-300 | $1,266.00 |
| OVER 300 | $1,448.00 |

### STATEMENT OF LICENSEE'S OPERATING POLICY

ASCAP Account No.:_____

LICENSEE NAME:_____

PREMISE NAME:_____

FULL ADDRESS:_____

PHONE #:_____ FAX #:_____ E-MAIL ADDRESS:_____

Number of trunk lines used providing LICENSEE'S
Music-On-Hold Telephone Service:                    _____

Rate Based on Above Policy:                    $_____

### Annual License Fee For Calendar Year 2001 and Thereafter

The annual license fee set forth in this Rate Schedule will apply for the calendar year 2000. Rates for each subsequent calendar year will be adjusted in accordance with the increase in the Consumer Price Index, All Urban Consumers - (CPI-U) between October and the next preceding October.

### CERTIFICATE

I hereby certify that the foregoing Statement of Operating Policy is true and correct as of this _____ day of _____,_____.

_____     _____
Name and Title of Person Completing Form (Please Print)     Signature

ASCAP, 2690 Cumberland Parkway, Suite 490, Atlanta, GA  30339  1.800.505.4052,  1.770.805.3475
(Fax)

DE12/99

# FORM 17.17

## ASCAP CONCERT AND RECITALS LICENSE (BLANKET)

### CONCERTS AND RECITALS - BLANKET LICENSE AGREEMENT

*Agreement* between American Society of Composers, Authors and Publishers ("SOCIETY"), located at

2690 Cumberland Parkway, Suite 490
Atlanta, GA 30339

and

("LICENSEE"), located at

as follows:

#### 1. Grant and Term of License

(a) SOCIETY grants and LICENSEE accepts for a term of one year commencing             , and continuing thereafter for additional terms of one year each unless terminated by either party as hereinafter provided, a license to perform publicly at concerts or recitals in the United States presented by or under the auspices of LICENSEE, and not elsewhere, nondramatic renditions of the separate musical compositions now or hereafter during the term hereof in the repertory of SOCIETY, and of which SOCIETY shall have the right to license such performing rights.

(b) This agreement shall enure to the benefit of and shall be binding upon the parties hereto and their respective successors and assigns, but no assignment shall relieve the parties hereto of their respective obligations hereunder as to performances rendered, acts done and obligations incurred prior to the effective date of the assignment.

(c) Either party may, on or before thirty days prior to the end of the initial term or any renewal term, give notice of termination to the other. If such notice is given the agreement shall terminate on the last day of such initial or renewal term.

#### 2. Limitations on License

(a) This license is not assignable or transferable by operation of law, devolution or otherwise, except as provided in Paragraph "1(b)" hereof, and is strictly limited to the LICENSEE and to the premises where each concert or recital is presented.

(b) This license does not authorize the broadcasting or telecasting or transmission by wire or otherwise, of renditions of musical compositions in SOCIETY's repertory to persons outside of the premises where each concert or recital shall be presented.

(c) This license is limited to nondramatic performances, and does not authorize any dramatic performances. For purposes of this agreement, a dramatic performance shall include, but not be limited to, the following:

    (i) performance of a "dramatico-musical work" (as hereinafter defined) in its entirety;

    (ii) performance of one or more musical compositions from a "dramatico-musical work" (as hereinafter defined) accompanied by dialogue, pantomime, dance, stage action, or visual representation of the work from which the music is taken;

    (iii) performance of one or more musical compositions as part of a story or plot, whether accompanied or unaccompanied by dialogue, pantomime, dance, stage action, or visual representation;

    (iv) performance of a concert version of a "dramatico-musical work" (as hereinafter defined).

The term "dramatico-musical work" as used in this agreement, shall include, but not be limited to, a musical comedy, opera, play with music, revue, or ballet.

(d) This license does not authorize the performance of any special orchestral arrangements or transcriptions of any musical composition in the repertory of SOCIETY, unless such arrangements or transcriptions have been copyrighted by members of SOCIETY or foreign societies which have granted SOCIETY the right to license such performances.

(e) SOCIETY reserves the right at any time to restrict the first American performance of any composition in its repertory and further reserves the right at any time to withdraw from its repertory and from operation of this license, any musical work as to which any suit has been brought or threatened on a claim that such composition infringes a composition not contained in SOCIETY's repertory, or on a claim that SOCIETY does not have the right to license the performing rights in such composition.

### 3. Notice of Concerts or Recitals

LICENSEE agrees to give SOCIETY written notice of each concert or recital it will present, on forms supplied free of charge by SOCIETY, at least thirty days in advance of such presentation. Such notification shall include the date, name of attraction(s) appearing, name, location and seating capacity of the premises, and highest price of admission (exclusive of tax) for each concert or recital.

### 4. License Fees

(a) In consideration of the license granted herein, LICENSEE agrees to pay SOCIETY the applicable license fee for each concert or recital presented based on SOCIETY's current rate schedule, a copy of which is annexed hereto and made a part hereof, payable thirty days in advance of each concert or recital presented.

(b) LICENSEE agrees to furnish to SOCIETY, where available, at the same time payment of license fees is made pursuant to Paragraph "4(a)" of this agreement, a program containing a list of all musical works, including encores, performed by LICENSEE in each of its concerts and recitals.

### 5. Breach or Default

Upon any breach or default by LICENSEE of any term or condition herein contained, SOCIETY may terminate this license by giving LICENSEE thirty days notice to cure such breach or default, and in the event that such breach or default has not been cured within said thirty days, this license shall terminate on the expiration of such thirty-day period without further notice from SOCIETY. In the event of such termination, SOCIETY shall refund to LICENSEE any unearned license fees paid in advance.

### 6. Interference in Society's Operations

In the event of:

(a) any major interference with the operations of SOCIETY in the state, territory, dependency, possession or political subdivision in which LICENSEE is located, by reason of any law of such state, territory, dependency, possession or political subdivision; or

(b) any substantial increase in the cost to the SOCIETY of operating in such state, territory, dependency, possession or political subdivision, by reason of any law of such state, territory, dependency, possession or political subdivision, which is applicable to the licensing of performing rights,

SOCIETY shall have the right to terminate this agreement forthwith by written notice.

### 7. Notices

All notices required or permitted hereunder shall be given in writing by certified United States mail sent to either party at the address stated above. Each party agrees to inform the other of any change of address.

IN WITNESS WHEREOF, this Agreement has been duly executed by SOCIETY and LICENSEE, this
\_\_\_\_\_ day of _____, _____.

AMERICAN SOCIETY OF COMPOSERS,
AUTHORS AND PUBLISHERS

_____
LICENSEE

By_____

By_____

_____
TITLE

(Fill in capacity in which signed:
(a) If corporation, state corporate office held; (b) If
partnership, write word "partner" under signature of
signing partner; (c) If individual owner, write "individual
owner" under signature.)

A S C A P

## BLANKET CONCERT AND RECITAL LICENSE RATE SCHEDULE

**TICKET PRICE**

| Seating Capacity* | Up to $3.00 | $3.01 to $6.00 | $6.01 to $9.00 | $9.01 to $12.00 | $12.01 to $15.00 | $15.01 to $18.00 | $18.01 to $21.00 | $21.01 to $25.00 | $25.01 to $30.00 | Over $30.00 |
|---|---|---|---|---|---|---|---|---|---|---|
| Up to 250 | 7 | 14 | 23 | 35 | 47 | 60 | 75 | 90 | 105 | 125 |
| 251 - 500 | 11 | 18 | 27 | 39 | 52 | 65 | 80 | 95 | 110 | 130 |
| 501 - 750 | 15 | 22 | 31 | 44 | 57 | 70 | 85 | 100 | 115 | 135 |
| 751 - 1,000 | 19 | 26 | 36 | 51 | 66 | 80 | 97 | 115 | 130 | 155 |
| 1,001 - 1,500 | 24 | 33 | 44 | 60 | 75 | 90 | 110 | 130 | 150 | 175 |
| 1,501 - 2,000 | 29 | 41 | 53 | 70 | 85 | 100 | 125 | 150 | 175 | 205 |
| 2,001 - 3,000 | 35 | 47 | 59 | 77 | 92 | 112 | 137 | 165 | 190 | 225 |
| 3,001 - 4,000 | 41 | 53 | 65 | 85 | 100 | 125 | 150 | 180 | 210 | 250 |
| 4,001 - 5,500 | 53 | 65 | 80 | 100 | 125 | 150 | 180 | 210 | 240 | 280 |
| 5,501 - 7,500 | 65 | 80 | 100 | 125 | 150 | 180 | 210 | 240 | 270 | 310 |
| 7,501 - 10,000 | 80 | 100 | 125 | 150 | 180 | 210 | 240 | 270 | 300 | 340 |
| 10,001 - 15,000 | 100 | 125 | 150 | 180 | 210 | 240 | 270 | 300 | 330 | 370 |
| 15,001 - 20,000 | 125 | 150 | 180 | 210 | 240 | 270 | 300 | 330 | 360 | 400 |
| 20,001 - 25,000 | 150 | 180 | 210 | 240 | 270 | 300 | 330 | 360 | 390 | 440 |
| 25,001 - 30,000 | 180 | 210 | 240 | 270 | 300 | 330 | 360 | 400 | 440 | 490 |
| 30,001 - 40,000 | 210 | 240 | 270 | 300 | 330 | 360 | 410 | 450 | 490 | 540 |
| 40,001 - 50,000 | 250 | 280 | 310 | 340 | 370 | 410 | 450 | 500 | 540 | 590 |
| 50,001 - 60,000 | 290 | 320 | 350 | 380 | 410 | 450 | 500 | 550 | 590 | 650 |
| Over 60,000 | 350 | 380 | 410 | 440 | 470 | 510 | 550 | 600 | 650 | 725 |

**DISCOUNTS:**

1. Twenty-Six or more Concerts or Recitals: A discount of 20% may be deducted from the above fees for payment for each concert or recital in excess of twenty-five performed by LICENSEE during a contract year.

2. Advance Payment for One Hundred or more Concerts or Recitals: A discount of 5% may be deducted from the above fees for payment in advance by LICENSEE to SOCIETY for one hundred or more separate concerts or recitals.

---

*Where a concert or recital occurs at a location whose total seating capacity has been altered to accommodate a particular performance, the term "Seating Capacity" shall mean the total number of seats made available for that particular performance.

DE499

# FORM 17.18

## ASCAP CONCERT AND RECITALS LICENSE (PER CONCERT)

CONCERTS AND RECITALS–
PER CONCERT LICENSE AGREEMENT

**Agreement** between AMERICAN SOCIETY OF COMPOSERS, AUTHORS AND PUBLISHERS ("SOCIETY"), located at One Lincoln Plaza, New York, NY 10023

and
("LICENSEE"), located at

as follows:

### 1. Grant and Term of License

(a) SOCIETY grants and LICENSEE accepts for a term of one year commencing
, and continuing thereafter for additional terms of one year each unless terminated by either party as hereinafter provided, a license to perform publicly at concerts or recitals in the United States presented by or under the auspices of LICENSEE, and not elsewhere, nondramatic renditions of the separate musical compositions now or hereafter during the term hereof in the repertory of SOCIETY, and of which SOCIETY shall have the right to license such performing rights.

(b) This agreement shall enure to the benefit of and shall be binding upon the parties hereto and their respective successors and assigns, but no assignment shall relieve the parties hereto of their respective obligations hereunder as to performances rendered, acts done and obligations incurred prior to the effective date of the assignment.

(c) Either party may, on or before thirty days prior to the end of the initial term or any renewal term, give notice of termination to the other. If such notice is given the agreement shall terminate on the last day of such initial or renewal term.

### 2. Limitations on License

(a) This license is not assignable or transferable by operation of law, devolution or otherwise, except as provided in Paragraph "1(b)" hereof, and is strictly limited to the LICENSEE and to the premises where each concert or recital is presented.

(b) This license does not authorize the broadcasting or telecasting or transmission by wire or otherwise, of renditions of musical compositions in SOCIETY's repertory to persons outside of the premises

(c) This license is limited to nondramatic performances, and does not authorize any dramatic performances. For purposes of this agreement, a dramatic performance shall include, but not be limited to, the following:

(i) performance of a "dramatico-musical work" (as hereinafter defined) in its entirety;

(ii) performance of one or more musical compositions from a "dramatico-musical work" (as hereinafter defined) accompanied by dialogue, pantomime, dance, stage action, or visual representation of the work from which the music is taken;

(iii) performance of one or more musical compositions as part of a story or plot, whether accompanied or unaccompanied by dialogue, pantomime, dance, stage action, or visual representation;

(iv) performance of a concert version of a "dramatico-musical work" (as hereinafter defined).

The term "dramatico-musical work" as used in this agreement, shall include, but not be limited to, a musical comedy, opera, play with music, revue, or ballet.

(d) This license does not authorize the performance of any special orchestral arrangements or transcriptions of any musical composition in the repertory of SOCIETY, unless such arrangements or transcriptions have been copyrighted by members of SOCIETY or foreign societies which have granted SOCIETY the right to license such performances.

(e) SOCIETY reserves the right at any time to restrict the first American performance of any composition in its repertory and further reserves the right at any time to withdraw from its repertory and from operation of this license, any musical work as to which any suit has been brought or threatened on a claim that such composition infringes a composition not contained in SOCIETY's repertory, or on a claim that SOCIETY does not have the right to license the performing rights in such composition.

### 3. License Fees

In consideration of the license granted herein, LICENSEE agrees to pay SOCIETY the applicable license fee set forth in the rate schedule annexed hereto and made a part hereof, for each concert or recital at which a nondramatic performance of any copyrighted musical composition in the SOCIETY's repertory occurs.

### 4. Reports of Concerts and Payment of License Fees

(a) At least one week prior to the presentation of any concert or recital by LICENSEE, LICENSEE shall submit to SOCIETY:

(i) Written notice of such concert or recital, on forms supplied free of charge by SOCIETY, including the date and place of such concert or recital, name of the artists or performers appearing, seating capacity, and highest price of admission exclusive of tax; and

(ii) Payment of any license fee required by and set forth in Paragraph "3" hereof.

(b) Within one week after the presentation of any concert or recital licensed hereunder, LICENSEE shall submit to SOCIETY a program containing a list of all musical works, including encores, performed at such concert or recital.

### 5. Breach or Default

Upon any breach or default by LICENSEE of any term or condition herein contained, SOCIETY may terminate this license by giving LICENSEE thirty days notice to cure such breach or default, and in the event that such breach or default has not been cured within said thirty days, this license shall terminate on the expiration of such thirty-day period without further notice from SOCIETY.

### 6. Failure to Report Concerts or Recitals and Pay License Fees

In the event LICENSEE presents any concert or recital during the course of which any copyrighted musical composition in SOCIETY's repertory is performed, and LICENSEE fails to report such concert or recital and pay license fees to SOCIETY as required by Paragraph "4" hereof, this license shall not extend to such concert or recital and such performances shall be deemed to be infringements of the respective copyrights unless such performances have been licensed by SOCIETY's member(s) in interest. Such failure to report and pay license fees shall be a breach and default under this agreement pursuant to Paragraph "5" hereof.

### 7. Interference in Society's Operations

In the event of:

(a) any major interference with the operations of SOCIETY in the state, territory, dependency, possession or political subdivision in which LICENSEE is located, by reason of any law of such state, territory, dependency, possession or political subdivision; or

(b) any substantial increase in the cost to the SOCIETY of operating in such state, territory, dependency, possession or political subdivision, by reason of any law of such state, territory, dependency, possession or political subdivision, which is applicable to the licensing of performing rights,

SOCIETY shall have the right to terminate this agreement forthwith by written notice.

### 8. Notices

All notices required or permitted hereunder shall be given in writing by certified United States mail sent to either party at the address stated above. Each party agrees to inform the other of any change of address.

IN WITNESS WHEREOF, this agreement has been duly executed by SOCIETY and LICENSEE this
day of , 19

AMERICAN SOCIETY OF COMPOSERS,
AUTHORS AND PUBLISHERS

_____
LICENSEE

BY _____          BY _____

_____
TITLE

(Fill in capacity in which signed:
(a) If corporation, state corporate office held; (b) If partnership, write word "partner" under signature of signing partner; (c) If individual owner, write "individual owner" under signature.)

## PER CONCERT LICENSE RATE SCHEDULE

| SEATING CAPACITY* | TICKET PRICE | | | | | | | | | |
|---|---|---|---|---|---|---|---|---|---|---|
| | $0.00 to $3.00 | $3.01 to $6.00 | $6.01 to $9.00 | $9.01 to $12.00 | $12.01 to $15.00 | $15.01 to $18.00 | $18.01 to $21.00 | $21.01 to $25.00 | $25.01 to $30.00 | over $30.00 |
| 0 - 250 | 11 | 21 | 35 | 53 | 71 | 90 | 113 | 135 | 158 | 188 |
| 251 - 500 | 17 | 27 | 41 | 59 | 78 | 98 | 120 | 143 | 165 | 195 |
| 501 - 750 | 23 | 33 | 47 | 66 | 86 | 105 | 128 | 150 | 173 | 203 |
| 751 - 1,000 | 29 | 39 | 54 | 77 | 99 | 120 | 146 | 173 | 195 | 233 |
| 1,001 - 1,500 | 36 | 50 | 66 | 90 | 113 | 135 | 165 | 195 | 225 | 263 |
| 1,501 - 2,000 | 44 | 62 | 80 | 105 | 128 | 150 | 188 | 225 | 263 | 308 |
| 2,001 - 3,000 | 53 | 71 | 89 | 116 | 138 | 168 | 206 | 248 | 285 | 338 |
| 3,001 - 4,000 | 62 | 80 | 98 | 128 | 150 | 188 | 225 | 270 | 315 | 375 |
| 4,001 - 5,500 | 80 | 98 | 120 | 150 | 188 | 225 | 270 | 315 | 360 | 420 |
| 5,501 - 7,500 | 98 | 120 | 150 | 188 | 225 | 270 | 315 | 360 | 405 | 465 |
| 7,501 - 10,000 | 120 | 150 | 188 | 225 | 270 | 315 | 360 | 405 | 450 | 510 |
| 10,001 - 15,000 | 150 | 188 | 225 | 270 | 315 | 360 | 405 | 450 | 495 | 555 |
| 15,001 - 20,000 | 188 | 225 | 270 | 315 | 360 | 405 | 450 | 495 | 540 | 600 |
| 20,001 - 25,000 | 225 | 270 | 315 | 360 | 405 | 450 | 495 | 540 | 585 | 660 |
| 25,001 - 30,000 | 270 | 315 | 360 | 405 | 450 | 495 | 540 | 600 | 660 | 735 |
| 30,001 - 40,000 | 315 | 360 | 405 | 450 | 495 | 540 | 615 | 675 | 735 | 810 |
| 40,001 - 50,000 | 375 | 420 | 465 | 510 | 555 | 615 | 675 | 750 | 810 | 885 |
| 50,001 - 60,000 | 435 | 480 | 525 | 570 | 615 | 675 | 750 | 825 | 885 | 975 |
| over 60,000 | 525 | 570 | 615 | 660 | 705 | 765 | 825 | 900 | 975 | 1088 |

*Where a concert or recital occurs at a location whose total seating capacity has been altered to accommodate a particular performance, the term "seating capacity" shall mean the total number of seats made available for that particular performance.

# FORM 17.19

## ASCAP MUISC-IN-BUSINESS BLANKET LICENSE AGREEMENT

MUSICBSBLANK

MUSIC-IN-BUSINESS
BLANKET LICENSE AGREEMENT

**Agreement** between the AMERICAN SOCIETY OF COMPOSERS, AUTHORS AND PUBLISHERS ("SOCIETY"), located at

and

("LICENSEE"), located at

as follows:

### 1. Grant and Term of License

(a) SOCIETY grants and LICENSEE accepts a license to perform or cause to be performed publicly at "LICENSEE's business locations" and at "LICENSEE's event locations" (each as defined below), and not elsewhere, non-dramatic renditions of the separate musical compositions now or hereafter during the term of this Agreement in the repertory of SOCIETY, and of which SOCIETY shall have the right to license such performing rights.

(b) As used in this Agreement, the following terms shall have the meanings indicated:

    (i) "LICENSEE's business locations" means all locations, not generally accessible by the public, at which LICENSEE conducts its day-to-day business operations as specified on Schedule "A", annexed hereto and made a part hereof, as said Schedule may be amended as hereinafter provided;

    (ii) "LICENSEE's event locations" means all locations, other than LICENSEE's business locations, at which LICENSEE conducts any "LICENSEE event(s)" (as defined below);

    (iii) "LICENSEE's employees" means all employees of LICENSEE including, but not limited to, full-time, part-time and temporary employees and interns; and

    (iv) "LICENSEE event(s)" means all activities presented or sponsored solely by or under the auspices of LICENSEE, at LICENSEE event location(s), open only to LICENSEE's employees and their personal guests.

(c) This license shall be for an initial term commencing and ending December 31 of the same calendar year, and continuing thereafter for additional terms of one year each unless terminated by either party. Either party may, on or before thirty days prior to the end of the initial term or any renewal term, give notice of termination to the other. If such notice is given, the license granted by this Agreement shall terminate on the last day of the term in which notice is given.

### 2. Limitations on License

(a) This license is not assignable or transferable by operation of law or otherwise, except upon the express written consent of SOCIETY, and is limited to LICENSEE, LICENSEE's business locations and to performances presented during and as part of LICENSEE event(s).

(b) This license does not authorize the broadcasting, telecasting or transmission by wire or otherwise, of renditions of musical compositions in SOCIETY's repertory to persons outside of LICENSEE's business locations or outside of LICENSEE's event locations, other than by means of music-on-hold telephone system(s) operated by LICENSEE at LICENSEE's business locations.

(c) This license does not authorize any performance as part of any conference, congress, consumer show, convention, exposition, industrial show, institute, meeting, public show, seminar, trade show or other similar activity, unless such activity (i) is presented or sponsored solely by and under the auspices of LICENSEE, is presented entirely at LICENSEE's business location(s), and is not open to the general public or (ii) otherwise constitutes a LICENSEE event.

(d) This license does not authorize any performance by means of a coin-operated phonorecord player (jukebox) for which a license is otherwise available from the Jukebox License Office.

(e) This license is limited to the United States, its territories and possessions, and the Commonwealth of Puerto Rico.

(f) This license is limited to non-dramatic performances, and does not authorize any dramatic performances. For purposes of this Agreement, a dramatic performance shall include, but not be limited to, the following:

    (i) performance of a "dramatico-musical work" (as defined below) in its entirety;

    (ii) performance of one or more musical compositions from a "dramatico-musical work" (as defined below) accompanied by dialogue, pantomime, dance, stage action, or visual representation of the work from which the music is taken;

    (iii) performance of one or more musical compositions as part of a story or plot, whether accompanied or unaccompanied by dialogue, pantomime, dance, stage action, or visual representation;

    (iv) performance of a concert version of a "dramatico-musical work" (as defined below).

The term "dramatico-musical work" as used in this Agreement, shall include, but not be limited to, a musical comedy, opera, play with music, revue, or ballet.

### 3. License Fees

In consideration of the license granted herein, LICENSEE agrees to pay SOCIETY the applicable license fees as set forth in the Rate Schedule, attached to and made a part of this Agreement, and based on "LICENSEE's Operating Policy." The term "LICENSEE's Operating Policy" means the factors that determine the license fees applicable under the Rate Schedule.

### 4. Reports

(a) LICENSEE shall furnish reports to SOCIETY upon entering into this Agreement and on or before January 31 of each succeeding year, on forms supplied free of charge by SOCIETY.

(b) The report to be submitted upon entering into this Agreement shall state for LICENSEE's business location(s) specified on Schedule "A", the total number of LICENSEE's employees as of that date; and the license fee due for that year.

(c) The reports to be submitted on or before January 31 of each succeeding year shall state the address of each of LICENSEE's business locations and the total number of LICENSEE's employees as of January 1 of such that year at all such locations, and Schedule "A" shall be deemed amended accordingly; and the total license fee due for all such locations for that year.

(d) LICENSEE is not required to submit an annual report indicating the total number of LICENSEE's employees provided that the number of LICENSEE's employees has not increased or decreased by more than 5% from the previous report submitted by LICENSEE. If LICENSEE does not submit the annual report, LICENSEE's prior annual report will be used to determine the license fees for the current calendar year.

### 5. Payment of License Fees

(a) LICENSEE shall pay SOCIETY the license fees due hereunder as follows:

    (i) Upon entering into this Agreement, the license fees due for the first calendar year of this Agreement as shown by the report due at that time; and

    (ii) By each succeeding January 31, the license fees for the then current calendar year, as shown by the report due on that date.

(b) In the event LICENSEE shall be delinquent in payment of license fees due to SOCIETY by thirty days or more, LICENSEE shall pay a finance charge on the license fees due of 1½% per month, or the maximum rate permitted by law, whichever is less, from the date such license fees should have been paid.

### 6. SOCIETY's Right to Verify Reports

(a) SOCIETY shall have the right to examine LICENSEE's books and records to such extent as may be necessary to verify the reports required by this Agreement, provided however, that if the reports submitted by LICENSEE are FICA statements which contain LICENSEE's number of employees and are certified by an independent certified public accountant and are submitted in a timely manner, SOCIETY shall forego its right of verification pursuant to this paragraph 6.

(b) SOCIETY shall consider all data and information coming to its attention as the result of the submission of Statements of LICENSEE's Operating Policy or other documentation submitted by LICENSEE as completely and entirely confidential.

### 7. Breach or Default

Upon any breach or default by LICENSEE of any term or condition herein contained, SOCIETY may terminate the license granted by this Agreement by giving LICENSEE thirty days written notice to cure such breach or default, and in the event that such breach or default has not been cured within said thirty days, said license shall terminate on the expiration of such thirty-day period without further notice from SOCIETY. In the event of such termination, SOCIETY shall refund to LICENSEE any unearned license fees paid in advance.

### 8. Interference with SOCIETY's Operations

In the event of:

(a) any major interference in the operations of SOCIETY in the state, territory, dependency, possession or political subdivision in which LICENSEE is located, by reason of any law of such state, territory, dependency, possession or political subdivision; or

(b) any substantial increase in the cost to SOCIETY of operating in such state, territory, dependency, possession, or political subdivision, by reason of any law of such state, territory, dependency, possession or political subdivision, which is applicable to the licensing of performing rights,

SOCIETY shall have the right to terminate this Agreement forthwith by thirty days written notice. In the event of such termination, SOCIETY shall refund to LICENSEE any unearned license fees paid in advance.

### 9. Indemnification

SOCIETY agrees to indemnify, save and hold harmless, and to defend LICENSEE from and against all claims, demands and suits that are made or brought against it with respect to the non-dramatic performance under this Agreement of any compositions in SOCIETY's repertory. LICENSEE agrees to give SOCIETY immediate notice of any such claim, demand or suit and agrees immediately to deliver to SOCIETY all papers pertaining to it. SOCIETY shall have full charge of the defense of any such claim, demand or suit and LICENSEE shall cooperate fully with SOCIETY in such defense. LICENSEE, however, shall have the right to engage counsel of its own, at its own expense, who may participate in the defense of any such action. SOCIETY's liability under this Paragraph "9" shall be strictly limited to the amount of license fees actually paid by LICENSEE to SOCIETY under this Agreement for the calendar year in which the performance or performances which are the subject of the claim, demand or suit occurred.

### 10. Notices

All notices required or permitted to be given by either party to the other hereunder shall be duly and properly given if:

(a) mailed to the other party by registered or certified United States Mail; or

(b) sent by electronic transmission (i.e., Mailgram, facsimile or similar transmission); or

(c) sent by generally recognized same-day or overnight delivery service,

addressed to the party at the address stated above. Each party agrees to notify the other of any change of address.


In WITNESS WHEREOF, this Agreement has been duly executed by SOCIETY and LICENSEE this     day of     19   .

AMERICAN SOCIETY OF COMPOSERS,
AUTHORS AND PUBLISHERS

| | |
|---|---|
| | LICENSEE |
| By _____ | By _____ |
| TITLE | TITLE |

(Fill in capacity in which signed:
(a) If corporation, state corporate office held; (b) if partnership, write word "partner" under signature of signing partner; (c) if individual owner, write "individual owner" under signature.)

10M 12/95 (C)

ASCAP

2000
MUSIC-IN-BUSINESS
BLANKET LICENSE AGREEMENT

RATE SCHEDULE

FEES FOR PERFORMANCES AT LICENSEE'S BUSINESS LOCATIONS
AND AT LICENSEE'S EVENTS

A. **Fees for Calendar Year 2000**
The annual fee for calendar year 2000 shall be:

$0.361 for each of the first ten thousand (10,000) of LICENSEE'S employees;

$0.290 for each of LICENSEE'S employees from the ten thousand and first (10,001ˢᵗ) to the twenty-five thousandth (25,000ᵗʰ):

$0.235 for each of LICENSEE'S employees from the twenty-five thousand and first (25,001ˢᵗ) to the fifty thousandth (50,000ᵗʰ): and

$0.182 for each additional LICENSEE'S employees above the fifty thousandth (50,000ᵗʰ).

B. **Fees for Subsequent Calendar Years.** Subject to the maximum and minimum fee provisions set forth below, for calendar year 2001 and each calendar year thereafter, the license fees under A. above shall be the license fees for the preceding calendar year, adjusted in accordance with any increase in the Consumer Price Index, All Urban Consumers (CPI-U) between the preceding October and the next preceding October. Any such adjustments to the per-employee license fees shall be rounded to the nearest one-half cent.

C. **Maximum Fees for Subsequent Calendar Years.** The maximum annual license fee payable hereunder shall be $22,500 for calendar year 2000; $23,500 for calendar year 2001; $24,500 for calendar year 2002; and the calendar year 2003 and each calendar year thereafter, the maximum annual license fee shall be the license fees for the preceding calendar year, adjusted in accordance with any increase in the Consumer Price Index, All Urban Consumers (CPI-U) between the preceding October and the next preceding October, rounded to the nearest dollar.

D. **Minimum Annual Fee.** The minimum annual license fee payable hereunder shall be $179 for calendar year 2000; and for calendar year 2001 and each calendar year thereafter, the minimum annual license fee shall be the license fees for the preceding calendar year, adjusted in accordance with any increase in the Consumer Price Index, All Urban Consumers (CPI-U) between the preceding October and the next preceding October, rounded to the nearest dollar.

ASCAP, 2690 Cumberland Parkway, Suite 490, Atlanta, GA   30339   1.800.505.4052,   1.770.805.3475 (Fax)
12/99

A S C A P

## MUSIC-IN-BUSINESS BLANKET LICENSE AGREEMENT
### STATEMENT OF OPERATING POLICY
#### FOR CALENDAR YEAR 2000

Licensee Name:_____ Account No.:_____

Address:_____

City:_____ State:_____ Zip Code:_____

Contact Person:_____
(Please Print Name and Title)

Phone No.:_____ Fax No.:_____ E-Mail:_____

### COMPUTATION OF LICENSE FEE
A. Total number of "LICENSEE's employees'"* as of January 1 of the current year at all "LICENSEE's business locations".**
(For business locations at which operations commenced after January 1 of the current year, include the number of employees as of the date such operations commenced.)

B. Complete the following chart:

| Category of Number of Employees | Number of Employees Within Category | | License Fee Per Employee | License Fees |
|---|---|---|---|---|
| 1.) 1-10,000 | _____ | X | .361 | $_____ |
| 2.) 10,001-25,000 | _____ | X | .290 | $_____ |
| 3.) 25,001-50,000 | _____ | X | 235 | $_____ |
| 4.) More than 50,000 | _____ | X | .182 | $_____ |

C. Total License Fee due (Add lines B1 through B4)***          $_____
But not less than $179.00; the maximum License Fee is $22,500

*"LICENSEE's Employees" means all employees of LICENSEE including, but not limited to, full-time, part-time and temporary employees and interns
* * "LICENSEE's business locations" means all locations, not generally accessible by the public, at which LICENSEE conducts its day-to-day business operations
*** For example, for an aggregate of 11,000 employees, the 2000 license fee would be $3,900.00 calculated as follows: (10,000 x $.361) = $3610 plus (1,000 x $.290) = $290.00; $3610 + $290 = $3,900.00

*Please return completed form and appropriate payment to:*

**ASCAP, 2690 Cumberland Parkway, Suite 490 Atlanta, GA 30339    1.800.505.4052, 1.770.805.3475 (Fax)**
E12/99

# FORM 17.20

## ASCAP MUSIC-IN-BUSINESS PER-LOCATION LICENSE AGREEMENT

MUSICBSPER

MUSIC-IN-BUSINESS
PER-LOCATION LICENSE AGREEMENT

**Agreement** between the AMERICAN SOCIETY OF COMPOSERS, AUTHORS AND PUBLISHERS ("SOCIETY"), located at



and



("LICENSEE"), located at



as follows:

1. Grant and Term of License

(a) SOCIETY grants and LICENSEE accepts a license to perform or cause to be performed publicly at "LICENSEE's business locations" and at "LICENSEE's event locations" (each as defined below), and not elsewhere, non-dramatic renditions of the separate musical compositions now or hereafter during the term of this Agreement in the repertory of SOCIETY, and of which SOCIETY shall have the right to license such performing rights.

(b) As used in this Agreement, the following terms shall have the meanings indicated:

    (i) "LICENSEE's business locations" means all locations, not generally accessible by the public, at which LICENSEE conducts its day-to-day business operations and at which music is performed as specified on Schedule "A", annexed hereto and made a part hereof, as said Schedule may be amended as hereinafter provided;

    (ii) "LICENSEE's event locations" means all locations, other than LICENSEE's business locations, at which LICENSEE conducts any "LICENSEE event(s)" (as defined below);

    (iii) "LICENSEE's employees" means all employees of LICENSEE including, but not limited to, full-time, part-time and temporary employees and interns; and

    (iv) "LICENSEE event(s)" means all activities presented or sponsored solely by or under the auspices of LICENSEE, at LICENSEE event location(s), open only to LICENSEE's employees and their personal guests.

(c) This license shall be for an initial term commencing            and ending December 31 of the same calendar year, and continuing thereafter for additional terms of one year each unless terminated by either party. Either party may, on or before thirty days prior to the end of the initial term or any renewal term, give notice of termination to the other. If such notice is given, the license granted by this Agreement shall terminate on the last day of the term in which notice is given.

2. Limitations on License

(a) This license is not assignable or transferable by operation of law or otherwise, except upon the express written consent of SOCIETY, and is limited to LICENSEE, LICENSEE's business locations and to performances presented during and as part of LICENSEE event(s).

(b) This license does not authorize the broadcasting, telecasting or transmission by wire or otherwise, of renditions of musical compositions in SOCIETY's repertory to persons outside of LICENSEE's business locations or LICENSEE's event locations, other than by means of music-on-hold telephone system(s) operated by LICENSEE at LICENSEE's business locations.

(c) This license does not authorize any performance as part of any conference, congress, consumer show, convention, exposition, industrial show, institute, meeting, public show, seminar, trade show or other similar activity, unless such activity (i) is presented or sponsored solely by and under the auspices of LICENSEE, is presented entirely at LICENSEE's business location(s), and is not open to the general public, or (ii) otherwise constitutes a LICENSEE event.

(d) This license does not authorize any performance by means of a coin-operated phonorecord player (jukebox) for which a license is otherwise available from the Jukebox License Office.

(e) This license is limited to the United States, its territories and possessions, and the Commonwealth of Puerto Rico.

(f) This license is limited to non-dramatic performances, and does not authorize any dramatic performances. For purposes of this Agreement, a dramatic performance shall include, but not be limited to, the following:

  (i) performance of a "dramatico-musical work" (as defined below) in its entirety;

  (ii) performance of one or more musical compositions from a "dramatico-musical work" (as defined below) accompanied by dialogue, pantomime, dance, stage action, or visual representation of the work from which the music is taken;

  (iii) performance of one or more musical compositions as part of a story or plot, whether accompanied or unaccompanied by dialogue, pantomime, dance, stage action, or visual representation;

  (iv) performance of a concert version of a "dramatico-musical work" (as defined below).

The term "dramatico-musical work" as used in this Agreement, shall include, but not be limited to, a musical comedy, opera, play with music, revue, or ballet.

### 3. License Fees

In consideration of the license granted herein, LICENSEE agrees to pay SOCIETY the applicable license fees as set forth in the Rate Schedule, attached to and made a part of this Agreement, and based on "LICENSEE's Operating Policy." The term "LICENSEE's Operating Policy" means the factors that determine the license fees applicable under the Rate Schedule.

### 4. Reports

(a) LICENSEE shall furnish reports to SOCIETY upon entering into this Agreement and on or before January 31 of each succeeding year, on forms supplied free of charge by SOCIETY.

(b) The report to be submitted upon entering into this Agreement shall state the following:

  (i) For each LICENSEE's business location specified on Schedule "A", the number of LICENSEE's employees as of January 1 of the current year, or the date LICENSEE commenced operations at each such location, whichever is later; and the license fee due for that year, pursuant to the Rate Schedule; and

  (ii) The estimated number of LICENSEE events to be presented during the current calendar year, the total estimated number of LICENSEE's employees to attend all such events, and the estimated average number of LICENSEE's employees to attend such events, and the estimated additional license fee due for that year, pursuant to the Rate Schedule.

(c) The reports to be submitted on or before January 31 of each succeeding year shall state the following:

  (i) The address of each of LICENSEE's business locations at which music has been or is scheduled to be performed during the current calendar year and the number of LICENSEE's employees as of January 1 of the current year at each such location, and Schedule "A" shall be deemed amended accordingly; and the license fee due for all such locations for the current calendar year pursuant to the Rate Schedule; and

  (ii) The date and location at which each LICENSEE event occurred during the previous calendar year and, for each such event, the number of LICENSEE's employees who attended; the average number of LICENSEE's employees who attended all LICENSEE events during the previous calendar year; and the additional license fee, if any, due for the previous calendar year pursuant to the Rate Schedule as applicable for that year.

  (iii) LICENSEE is not required to submit an annual report indicating the total number of LICENSEE's employees and the average number of employees attending LICENSEE's events provided that the number of LICENSEE's employees has not increased or decreased by more than 5% from the previous report submitted by LICENSEE. If LICENSEE does not submit the report, LICENSEE's prior year report will be used to determine the license fees for the current calendar year.

### 5. Payment of License Fees

(a) LICENSEE shall pay SOCIETY the license fees due hereunder as follows:

  (i) Upon entering into this Agreement, the license fees due for the first calendar year of this Agreement as shown by the report due at that time; and

  (ii) By each succeeding January 31, the license fees for the then current calendar year, and any additional license fees due for the previous calendar year, as shown by the report due on that date.

(b) In the event LICENSEE shall be delinquent in payment of license fees due to SOCIETY by thirty days or more, LICENSEE shall pay a finance charge on the license fees due of 1½% per month, or the maximum rate permitted by law, whichever is less, from the date such license fees should have been paid.

### 6. SOCIETY's Right to Verify Reports

(a) SOCIETY shall have the right to examine LICENSEE's books and records to such extent as may be necessary to verify the reports required by this Agreement, provided however, that if the reports submitted by LICENSEE are FICA statements which contain LICENSEE's number of employees and are certified by an independent certified public accountant and are submitted in a timely manner, SOCIETY shall forego its right of verification pursuant to this paragraph 6

(b) SOCIETY shall consider all data and information coming to its attention as the result of the submission of Statements of LICENSEE's Operating Policy or other documentation submitted by LICENSEE as completely and entirely confidential.

### 7. Breach or Default

Upon any breach or default by LICENSEE of any term or condition herein contained, SOCIETY may terminate the license granted by this Agreement by giving LICENSEE thirty days written notice to cure such breach or default, and in the event that such breach or default has not been cured within said thirty days, said license shall terminate on the expiration of such thirty-day period without further notice from SOCIETY. In the event of such termination, SOCIETY shall refund to LICENSEE any unearned license fees paid in advance.

### 8. Interference with SOCIETY's Operations

In the event of:

(a) any major interference in the operations of SOCIETY in the state, territory, dependency, possession or political subdivision in which LICENSEE is located, by reason of any law of such state, territory, dependency, possession or political subdivision; or

(b) any substantial increase in the cost to SOCIETY of operating in such state, territory, dependency, possession, or political subdivision, by reason of any law of such state, territory, dependency, possession or political subdivision, which is applicable to the licensing of performing rights,

SOCIETY shall have the right to terminate this Agreement forthwith by thirty days written notice. In the event of such termination, SOCIETY shall refund to LICENSEE any unearned license fees paid in advance.

### 9. Indemnification

SOCIETY agrees to indemnify, save and hold harmless, and to defend LICENSEE from and against all claims, demands and suits that are made or brought against it with respect to the non-dramatic performance under this Agreement of any compositions in SOCIETY's repertory. LICENSEE agrees to give SOCIETY immediate notice of any such claim, demand or suit and agrees immediately to deliver to SOCIETY all papers pertaining to it. SOCIETY shall have full charge of the defense of any such claim, demand or suit and LICENSEE shall cooperate fully with SOCIETY in such defense. LICENSEE, however, shall have the right to engage counsel of its own, at its own expense, who may participate in the defense of any such action. SOCIETY's liability under this Paragraph "9" shall be strictly limited to the amount of license fees actually paid by LICENSEE to SOCIETY under this Agreement for the calendar year in which the performance or performances which are the subject of the claim, demand or suit occurred.

### 10. Notices

All notices required or permitted to be given by either party to the other hereunder shall be duly and properly given if:

(a) mailed to the other party by registered or certified United States Mail; or

(b) sent by electronic transmission (i.e., Mailgram, facsimile or similar transmission); or

(c) sent by generally recognized same-day or overnight delivery service,

addressed to the party at the address stated above. Each party agrees to notify the other of any change of address.

In WITNESS WHEREOF, this Agreement has been duly executed by SOCIETY and LICENSEE this      day of      19   .

AMERICAN SOCIETY OF COMPOSERS,  
AUTHORS AND PUBLISHERS

By _____

_____
TITLE

_____
LICENSEE

By _____

_____
TITLE

(Fill in capacity in which signed:  
(a) If corporation, state corporate office held; (b) if partnership, write word "partner" under signature of signing partner; (c) if individual owner, write "individual owner" under signature.)

SM 12/95 (C)

ASCAP

**2000**
**MUSIC IN-BUSINESS**
**PER-LOCATION LICENSE AGREEMENT**

RATE SCHEDULE

**FEES FOR PERFORMANCES AT**
**LICENSEE'S BUSINESS LOCATIONS**
**AND AT LICENSEE'S EVENTS**

**A. Fees for Calendar Year 2000**

The annual fee for calendar year 2000 shall be:

$1.406 for each LICENSEE'S employees at each LICENSEE business location provided, however, that the minimum fee payable under this Rate Schedule shall be $282 for each LICENSEE business location;

plus $1.406 for each employee based on the average number of employees attending LICENSEE events provided, however, that if there are three or more LICENSEE events in the year, then the minimum fee payable under this Rate Schedule shall be $282 for LICENSEE events.

**B. Fees for Calendar Year 2001 and Thereafter**

For calendar year 2001 and each calendar year thereafter, the license fees under this Rate Schedule shall be the license fees for the preceding calendar year, adjusted in accordance with any increase in the Consumer Price Index, All Urban Consumers - (CPI-U) between the preceding October and the next preceding October. Any such adjustments to the per-employee license fees shall be rounded to the nearest one-half cent, and any such adjustment to the minimum annual fee shall be rounded to the nearest dollar.

ASCAP, 2690 Cumberland Parkway, Suite 490. Atlanta. GA 30339 1.800.505.4052, 1.770.805.3475
(Fax)

ASCAP

Account No.:_____
(11 Digit Number)

2000
MUSIC-IN-BUSINESS PER-LOCATION LICENSE AGREEMENT
STATEMENT OF OPERATING POLICY

LICENSEE NAME:_____

ADDRESS:_____CITY:_____ STATE:____ ZIP CODE:_____

CONTACT PERSON:_____ PHONE NO.: (____) _____
(Please print name and title)

**COMPUTATION OF LICENSE FEE**

A.   COMPUTATION OF LICENSE FEE FOR PERFORMANCES AT "LICENSEE'S BUSINESS LOCATIONS"

   1.  Total number of "LICENSEE'S employees" * as of January 1 of the current year at all

   "LICENSEE'S business locations"**: (For business locations at which operations commenced after January 1 of the current year, include the number of employees as of the date such operations commenced.)                    _____

   2.  License Fee Per Employee:                                            X  $1.406

   3.  Business Location License Fee (Line A.1. times A.2.), but not less than $282:   $_____

B.   COMPUTATION OF ACTUAL 1999 LICENSE FEE FOR PERFORMANCES AT "LICENSEE'S EVENTS"

   1.  Actual number of LICENSEE'S events presented during 1999:              _____

   2.  Actual total number of LICENSEE'S employees attending all such events:   _____

   3.  Average number of LICENSEE'S employees attending all such events
       (Line B.2. divided by B.1.):                                          _____

   4.  License fee per employee average at LICENSEE'S events:                X  $1.406

   5.  Actual event(s) license fee (Line B.3. X B.4.), but not less than $282***:   $_____

C.  COMPUTATION OF TOTAL LICENSE FEES DUE (Add lines A.3. and B.5.)           $_____

*    "LICENSEE'S employees" means: all employees of LICENSEE including, but not limited to, full-time, part-time and temporary employees and interns.

**   "LICENSEE'S business locations" means; all locations, not generally accessible by the public, at which LICENSEE conducts its day-to-day business operations and at which music is performed.

***    Minimum license fee is applicable if LICENSEE presents three or more events during a contract year.

Note:   "Licensee is not required to submit an annual report indicating the total number of LICENSEE'S employees and the average number of employees attending LICENSEE'S events provided that the number of LICENSEE'S employees has not increased or decreased by more than 5% from the previous report submitted by LICENSEE. If LICENSEE does not submit the report, LICENSEE'S prior year report will be used to determine the license fees for the current calendar year."  (Music in Business Per Location License Agreement, Paragraph 4.(c)(iii))
*Please address all inquiries to:*
ASCAP, Account Services, 2690 Cumberland Parkway, Suite 490, Atlanta, GA  30339  1.800.505.4052  1.770.806.3475 (FAX)

DE12/99

# FORM 17.21

## ASCAP COMMON AREAS IN SHOPPING CENTERS AND SHOPPING MALLS

### LICENSE AGREEMENT-COMMON AREAS IN SHOPPING CENTERS AND SHOPPING MALLS

*Agreement* between American Society of Composers, Authors and Publishers ("SOCIETY"), located at 2690 Cumberland Parkway, Suite 490 Atlanta, GA 30339 and

("LICENSEE"), located at

as follows:

### 1. Grant and Term of License

(a) SOCIETY grants and LICENSEE accepts for a term of one year, commencing            , and continuing thereafter for additional terms of one year each unless terminated by either party as hereinafter provided, a license to perform publicly at common areas in the shopping center or shopping mall known as:

and located at:

("the premises"), and not elsewhere, non-dramatic renditions of the separate musical compositions now or hereafter during the term hereof in the repertory of SOCIETY, and of which SOCIETY shall have the right to license such performing rights.

(b) This agreement shall enure to the benefit of and shall be binding upon the parties hereto and their respective successors and assigns, but no assignment shall relieve the parties hereto of their respective obligations hereunder as to performances rendered, acts done and obligations incurred prior to the effective date of the assignment.

(c) Either party may, on or before thirty days prior to the end of the initial term or any renewal term, give notice of termination to the other. If such notice is given the agreement shall terminate on the last day of such initial or renewal term.

### 2. Limitations on License

(a) This license is not assignable or transferable by operation of law or otherwise, except as provided in paragraph "1(b)" hereof, and is limited to LICENSEE and to the premises.

(b) This license does not authorize the broadcasting, telecasting or transmission by wire or otherwise, of renditions of musical compositions in SOCIETY'S repertory to persons outside of the premises.

(c) This license does not authorize any performance by means of a coin-operated phonorecord player (jukebox) otherwise covered by the statutory license provisions of 17 U.S.C. §116.

(d) This license is limited to non-dramatic performances, and does not authorize any dramatic performances. For purposes of this agreement, a dramatic performance shall include, but not be limited to, the following:

    (i)   performance of a "dramatico-musical work" (as hereinafter defined) in its entirety;

    (ii)  performance of one or more musical compositions from a "dramatico-musical work" (as hereinafter defined) accompanied by dialogue, pantomime, dance, stage action, or visual representation of the work from which the music is taken;

    (iii) performance of one or more musical compositions as part of a story or plot, whether accompanied or unaccompanied by dialogue, pantomime, dance, stage action, or visual representation;

    (iv) performance of a concert version of a "dramatico-musical work" (as hereinafter defined).

The term "dramatico-musical work" as used in this agreement, shall include, but not be limited to, a musical comedy, opera, play with music, revue, or ballet.

(e) This license is limited to LICENSEE'S performances at the premises which are given at common areas in LICENSEE'S shopping center or shopping mall, and does not extend to performances in individual establishments, such as stores or restaurants, located in LICENSEE'S shopping center or shopping mall.

### 3. License Fees, Reports and Payments

(a) In consideration of the license granted herein, LICENSEE agrees to pay SOCIETY the applicable license fee set forth in the rate schedule printed below and made part hereof, on January 15, April 15, July 15 and October 15 of each year for the previous calendar quarter.

(b) LICENSEE shall submit reports to SOCIETY, on forms supplied free of charge by SOCIETY, as specified in the rate schedule printed below and made part hereof.

### 4. Breach or Default

Upon any breach or default by LICENSEE of any term or condition herein contained, SOCIETY may terminate this license by giving LICENSEE thirty days notice to cure such breach or default, and in the event that such breach or default has not been cured within said thirty days, this license shall terminate on the expiration of such thirty-day period without further notice from SOCIETY. In the event of such termination, SOCIETY shall refund to LICENSEE any unearned license fees paid in advance.

### 5. Interference in Society's Operations

In the event of:

(a) any major interference with the operations of SOCIETY in the state, territory, dependency, possession or political subdivision in which LICENSEE is located, by reason of any law of such state, territory, dependency, possession or political subdivision; or

(b) any substantial increase in the cost to SOCIETY of operating in such state, territory, dependency, possession or political subdivision, by reason of any law of such state, territory, dependency, possession or political subdivision, which is applicable to the licensing of performing rights,

SOCIETY shall have the right to terminate this agreement forthwith by written notice and shall refund to LICENSEE any unearned license fees paid in advance.

### 6. Notices

All notices required or permitted hereunder shall be given in writing by certified United States mail sent to either party at the address stated above. Each party agrees to inform the other of any change of address.

IN WITNESS WHEREOF, this Agreement has been duly executed by SOCIETY and LICENSEE, this _____ day of _____, _____ _____.


AMERICAN SOCIETY OF COMPOSERS,
AUTHORS AND PUBLISHERS

LICENSEE

By_____

By_____

_____
TITLE

(Fill in capacity in which signed:
(a) If corporation, state corporate office held, (b) If partnership, write word "partner" under signature of signing partner; (c) If individual owner, write "individual owner" under signature.)

**A S C A P**

### COMMON AREAS IN SHOPPING CENTERS AND SHOPPING MALLS
### LICENSE FEES FOR CALENDAR YEAR 2000

**I. Performance of live music, or performance of mechanical music with acts:**

| SIZE OF SHOPPING CENTER/SHOPPING MALL* | DAILY LICENSE FEE |
|---|---|
| Up to 300,000 Square Feet | $31.00 |
| 300,000 Square Feet to 900,000 Square Feet | $41.50 |
| 900,000 Square Feet and Over | $51.00 |

*Size of shopping center/shopping mall shall include all shopping center or mall areas with the sole exception of parking areas.

**MAXIMUM ANNUAL LICENSE FEE:** The maximum annual license fee to be paid under this Rate Schedule I. shall be $2,492.50.

**CHAIN DISCOUNT:** LICENSEE shall be entitled to a 20% reduction in the maximum annual license fees under this Rate Schedule I. provided said fees are paid for at least 10 shopping centers or shopping malls operated by LICENSEE.

**II. Performance of music by mechanical means only, without acts:**

    A. Annual license fee for audio-only performances
    $167.50 Up to 3 Speakers
    $ 34.50 Each Additional Speaker
    Maximum License Fee: $1,402.00

    B. Annual license fee for audio-visual performances
    $251.50 Up to 3 Speakers
    $ 50.50 Each Additional Speaker
    Maximum License Fee: $2,116.00

If performances are given by both audio and audio-visual means, the higher license fee shall apply.

### License Fees For Calendar Year 2001 and Thereafter
The annual rates set forth in this Rate Schedule will apply for the calendar year 2000. Rates for each subsequent calendar year will be adjusted in accordance with the increase in the Consumer Price Index, All Urban Consumers - (CPI-U) between the preceding October and the next preceding October.

## REPORTS

LICENSEE shall submit reports to SOCIETY as follows:
1. An annual report, submitted with the January 15 quarterly payment of license fees, for each shopping center/shopping mall for which an annual license fee is paid.
2. A quarterly report, submitted with each quarterly payment of license fees, for each shopping center/shopping mall for which daily license fees under Rate Schedule I are paid.
Said reports shall include all information necessary for the completion of the appropriate license fees.

**ASCAP, 2690 Cumberland Parkway, Suite 490, Atlanta, GA  30339  1.800.505.4052,  1.770.805.3475 (Fax)**

DE12/99

# FORM 17.22

## ASCAP RETAIL STORES

RETAIL

LICENSE AGREEMENT—RETAIL STORES
LIVE AND MECHANICAL MUSIC
AUDIO AND AUDIO-VISUAL USES

**AGREEMENT** between the AMERICAN SOCIETY OF COMPOSERS, AUTHORS AND PUBLISHERS ("SOCIETY"), located at

and

("LICENSEE"), located at

as follows:

### 1. Grant and Term of License

(a) SOCIETY grants and LICENSEE accepts for a term commencing , and continuing thereafter for additional terms of one year each unless terminated as hereinafter provided, a license to perform publicly by means of live musicians or "mechanical music" (as hereinafter defined), and not otherwise, at each of the locations specified in Schedule "A", annexed hereto and made a part hereof, as said Schedule may be amended as hereinafter provided ("the premises"), and not elsewhere, non-dramatic renditions of the separate musical compositions now or hereafter during the term hereof in the repertory of SOCIETY, and of which SOCIETY shall have the right to license such performing rights. As used in this agreement, the term "mechanical music" shall mean music performed by: i) the reception of radio broadcasts and further transmission of those broadcasts over a loudspeaker or system of loudspeakers; ii) the use of LICENSEE'S (as distinguished from a background music service's) audio records or audio tapes by means of LICENSEE'S audio-only record or tape player; or iii) non-live audio-visual uses of music (such as the use of a large-screen projection television or video tapes).

(b) Either party may, on or before thirty days prior to the end of the initial term or any renewal term, give notice of termination to the other. If such notice is given the agreement shall terminate on the last day of such initial or renewal term.

(c) This agreement shall enure to the benefit of and shall be binding upon the parties hereto and their respective successors, assigns and subsidiaries, but no assignment shall relieve the parties hereto of their respective obligations hereunder as to performances rendered, acts done and obligations incurred prior to the effective date of the assignment.

### 2. Limitations on License

(a) This license is not assignable or transferable by operation of law or otherwise, except as provided in Paragraph "1(c)" hereof, and is limited to the LICENSEE and to the premises.

(b) This license does not authorize the broadcasting, telecasting or transmission by wire or otherwise, of renditions of musical compositions in SOCIETY'S repertory to persons outside of the premises.

(c) This license does not authorize any performance by means of a coin-operated phonorecord player (jukebox) otherwise covered by the compulsory license provisions of 17 U.S.C. § 116.

(d) This license is limited to non-dramatic performances, and does not authorize any dramatic performances.

For purposes of this agreement, a dramatic performance shall include, but not be limited to, the following:

(i) performance of a "dramatico-musical work" (as hereinafter defined) in its entirety;

(ii) performance of one or more musical compositions from a "dramatico-musical work" (as hereinafter defined) accompanied by dialogue, pantomime, dance, stage action, or visual representation of the work from which the music is taken;

(iii) performance of one or more musical compositions as part of a story or plot, whether accompanied or unaccompanied by dialogue, pantomime, dance, stage action, or visual representation;

(iv) performance of a concert version of a "dramatico-musical work" (as hereinafter defined).

The term "dramatico-musical work" as used in this agreement, shall include, but not be limited to, a musical comedy, oratorio, opera, play with music, revue, or ballet.

### 3. License Fee and Reports

(a) In consideration of the license granted herein, LICENSEE agrees to pay to SOCIETY the applicable license fee set forth in the rate schedule annexed hereto and made a part hereof, payable quarterly in advance on January 1, April 1, July 1 and October 1 of each year.

(b) LICENSEE shall furnish a report to SOCIETY on January 1, April 1, July 1 and October 1 of each year, indicating whether each location specified in Schedule "A" performed music during the previous quarter by means of live or mechanical music, and if by mechanical music, whether such performances are by audio means, audio-visual means, or both, and indicating any additions or deletions of locations at which music has been performed during the previous quarter, including the month in which the addition or deletion occurred, and whether such locations perform by means of live or mechanical music, and if by mechanical music, whether such performances are by audio means, audio-visual means, or both. Schedule "A" shall thereafter be deemed amended to include or exclude such premises. Such report shall also indicate the total number of premises licensed and the total license fees due for said quarter. In the case of license fees specified as annual license fees in the annexed rate schedule, said total fees shall be adjusted on the following monthly pro rata basis for locations which have been added or deleted during the previous quarter: if the location being added or deleted used music for half a month or more, license fees shall be paid for the full month; if for less than half a month, no license fees shall be due for that month. If said total fees are greater than the amount paid in advance for said quarter, LICENSEE shall submit payment of the difference with the report; if less, SOCIETY shall issue a credit applicable to the next quarter's advance payment.

(c) As of the date of execution of this agreement, said license fee totals _____ Dollars ($ _____ ) annually, based on the number of locations, and the type of music use for each set forth in Schedule "A".

(d) If LICENSEE discontinues the performance of music at all of the premises, LICENSEE or SOCIETY may terminate this agreement upon thirty days prior notice, the termination to be effective at the end of such thirty day period. In the event of such termination, SOCIETY shall refund to LICENSEE a pro rata share of any unearned license fees paid in advance. For purposes of this agreement, a discontinuance of music shall be one in effect for no less than thirty days.

(e) In the event that LICENSEE'S payment of fees under this Agreement causes SOCIETY to incur a liability to pay a gross receipts, sales, use, business use, or other tax which is based on the amount of SOCIETY'S receipts from LICENSEE, the number of licensees of SOCIETY, or any similar measure of SOCIETY'S activities, and (i) SOCIETY has taken reasonable steps to be exempted or excused from paying such tax; and (ii) SOCIETY is permitted by law to pass through such tax to its licensees, LICENSEE shall pay to SOCIETY the full amount of such tax.

### 4. Breach or Default

Upon any breach or default by LICENSEE of any term or condition herein contained, SOCIETY may terminate this license by giving LICENSEE thirty days notice to cure such breach or default, and in the event that such breach or default has not been cured within said thirty days, this license shall terminate on the expiration of such thirty-day period without further notice from SOCIETY. In the event of such termination, SOCIETY shall refund to LICENSEE any unearned license fees paid in advance.

### 5. Interference in Society's Operations

In the event of:

(a) any major interference with the operations of SOCIETY in the state, territory, dependency, possession or political subdivision in which LICENSEE is located, by reason of any law of such state, territory, dependency, possession or political subdivision; or

(b) any substantial increase in the cost to the SOCIETY of operating in such state, territory, dependency, possession or political subdivision, by reason of any law of such state, territory, dependency, possession or political subdivision, which is applicable to the licensing of performing rights,

SOCIETY shall have the right to terminate this agreement forthwith by written notice. In the event of such termination, SOCIETY shall refund any unearned license fees paid in advance.

### 6. Notices

All notices required or permitted hereunder shall be given in writing by certified United States mail sent to either party at the address stated above. Each party agrees to inform the other of any change of address.

IN WITNESS WHEREOF, this agreement has been duly executed by SOCIETY and LICENSEE, this          day of                              , 19   .


AMERICAN SOCIETY OF COMPOSERS,
    AUTHORS AND PUBLISHERS          _____
                                                        LICENSEE


BY _____          BY _____


                                                    _____
                                                        TITLE

ASCAP

**2000 RATE SCHEDULE - MECHANICAL MUSIC,
AUDIO AND AUDIO-VISUAL USES AND LIVE MUSIC IN RETAIL STORES**

SCHEDULE I. Performance of music by mechanical means only, without acts:

A. Individual locations:

1. Annual license fee for audio-only performances:
   $167.50 up to 3 speakers
   $ 34.50 each additional speaker
   Maximum license fee: $1,402.00

2. Annual license fee for audio-visual performances:
   $251.50 up to 3 speakers
   $ 50.50 each additional speaker
   Maximum license fee: $2,116.00

B. Chains having 10 or more locations under common ownership performing music by mechanical means only, without acts:

1. Annual license fee for audio-only performances:
   $167.50 for each of the first 200 locations;
   $150.50 for each location from the 201st to the 400th;
   $124.00 for each location from the 401st to the 1,000th;
   $111.50 for each location from the 1,001st to the 2,000th; and
   $ 101.00 for each additional location above 2,000

2. Annual license fee for audio-visual performances:
   $251.50 for each of the first 200 locations;
   $224.00 for each location from 201st to the 400th;
   $185.00 for each location from the 401st to the 1,000th;
   $167.50 for each location from the 1,001st to the 2,000th; and
   $151.50 for each additional location above 2,000

If performances are given by both audio and audio-visual means, the higher license fee shall apply.

SCHEDULE II. Performance of live music (e.g., performances of live music in a cafe section of a book or record store), or performance of mechanical music with acts (e.g., a fashion show at which live models display clothes to the accompaniment of mechanical music):

A. Individual Locations $31.00 per day per location using live music, subject to a maximum annual live fee of $2,496.00 per location.

B. Chains having 10 or more Locations $31 per day per location using live music, subject to a maximum annual live fee of $1,997.00 per location.

C. Alternative Rate Schedule for Chains having more than 100 Locations Chains having more than 100 locations shall pay either the live music fee calculated in accordance with Schedule II.B. or this Schedule II.C., whichever is lower.

| Number of Locations in Chain¹ | Annual Live Fee |
|---|---|
| For the First 150 Locations | $112,817.00 |
| For Each Additional Location from the 151st to the 200th Location | $641.00 per Location |
| For Each Additional Location from the 201st to the 250th Location | $564.00 per Location |
| For Each Additional Location from the 251st to the 300th Location | $513.00 per Location |
| For Each Additional Location from the 301st to the 350th Location | $462.00 per Location |
| For Each Additional Location from the 351st to the 400th Location | $436.00 per Location |
| For Each Additional Location above the 400th Location | $410.00 per Location |

**Annual License Fee For Calendar Year 2001 and Thereafter**

The annual license fee set forth in the Rate Schedule will apply for the calendar year 2000. All rates (including the maximum rates) for each subsequent calendar year will be adjusted in accordance with the increase in the Consumer Price Index, All Urban Consumers (CPI-U) between the preceding October and the next preceding October.

**STATEMENT OF LICENSEE'S OPERATING POLICY**

Licensee: _____

Address: _____

Schedule I.A.    Number of Speakers: _____

|  | Audio | Audio-Visual | Total |
|---|---|---|---|

Schedule I.B.    Number of Locations: _____

|  | Audio | Audio-Visual | Total |
|---|---|---|---|

Schedules II.A. and II.B. Please list separately for each Location the total number of live music performances.

Schedule II.C.    Total Number of Locations in Chain _____

Rate Based on Above Policy    $ _____

• • • • • • • • • • • • • • • • • • • • • • • • • • • • • • • • • • • • • • • • • • • • • • •

CERTIFICATE: I hereby certify that the foregoing Statement of Licensee's Operating Policy is true and correct as of this _____ day of _____.

_____     _____
Name and Title of Person Completing Form (Please Print)     ASCAP Account Number
                                                            (11 digit number)

_____
Signature

Phone No.: ( ___ ) ___ - _____    Fax No.: _____    E-Mail Address: _____

¹ Under Rate Schedule II.C., fees are calculated on the total number of locations in the Chain, without regard to whether or not individual locations have live music.

ASCAP, 2690 Cumberland Parkway, Suite 490, Atlanta, GA 30339.    1.800.505.4052.    1.770.805.3475 (Fax)

DE12/99

# LIST 17.1

## MAJOR OVERSEAS PERFORMANCE RIGHTS SOCIETIES

A.P.R.A.          Australian Performing Right Association Ltd.
                  Australia - New Zealand
                      P.O. Box 567
                      1A Eden St.
                      Crows Nest NSW 2065
                      AUSTRALIA
                      www.apra.com.au

P.R.S.            The Performing Right Society Ltd.
                  United Kingdom and Northern Ireland
                      29-33 Berners Street
                      London WIP 4AA
                      ENGLAND
                      www.prs.co.uk

S.A.C.E.M.        Societe des Auteurs, Compositeurs et Editeurs
                  de Musique
                  France
                      225 Avenue Charles de Gaulle
                      92521 Nevilly-Sur-Seine
                      FRANCE
                      www.sacem.org

G.E.M.A.          Gesellschaft fur Musikalische Auftuhrungs und
                  Mechanische Vervielfaltigungsnechte
                  Germany
                      Rosenheimer Strasse II
                      8000 Munich 80
                      GERMANY

S.O.C.A.N.    Society of Composers, Authors and Music
Publishers of Canada
Canada
    41 Valleybrook Drive
    Don Mills, Ontario
    M3B256
    www.socan.ca

S.I.A.E.    Soceita Italiano degli Autori ed Editori
Italy
    Viale della Letteratura 30
    00144 Rome
    ITALY
    www.siae.it

J.A.S.R.A.C.    Japanese Society for Rights of Authors,
Composers & Publishers
Japan
    1-7-13 Nishishimbashi
    Minato-Ku,
    Tokyo 105
    JAPAN
    www.jasrac.or.jp

S.G.A.E.    Sociedad General de Autores de Espana
Spain
    Fernando V1
    28004 Madrid 4
    SPAIN

S.T.I.M.    Foreningen Svenska Tonsattares
Internationella Musikbyra
Sweden
    Sandhamsgatan 79
    102-54 Stockholm
    SWEDEN
    www.stim.se

B.U.M.A.        Het Bureau voor Muziek-Auteursrecht
                Netherlands
                    Professor E. M. Meyersiaan 3
                    1183 Av Amstelveen
                    P.O. Box 725 (ZIP 1183 AS)
                    NETHERLANDS
                    www.buma.al

S.A.B.A.M.      Societe Belge des Auteurs
                Compositeurs et Editeurs
                Belgium
                    75-77 Rue d'Arlon
                    1040 Brussels
                    BELGIUM
                    www.sabam.be

S.A.M.R.O.      South African Music Rights Organisation
                South Africa
                P.O. Box 9292
                Johannesburg 2000
                SAMBRO House
                    73 Juta Street
                    Braamfonsteain 2001,
                    SOUTH AFRICA
                    www.safvs.co.za

# THE GRAND RIGHTS CONTROVERSY

## SUMMARY

**I. OVERVIEW OF THEATRICAL MUSICAL PRODUCTIONS**

A. Non-Musical Play with Incidental Music

B. Play with Music

C. Musical Revue

D. Dramatico-Musical Work

**II. LEGAL BACKGROUND**

A. Copyright

B. Licensing by Theatrical Production Companies and Theatrical Agencies

C. Licensing by Performance Rights Societies

D. Licensing by Music Publishers

**III. DISTINGUISHING BETWEEN DRAMATIC RIGHTS, NONDRAMATIC RIGHTS AND GRAND RIGHTS**

A. Dramatic Performance Defined

B. Nondramatic Performance Defined

C. Grand Rights Defined

**IV. GRAND RIGHTS DISTINGUISHED FROM DRAMATIC RIGHTS**

**V. ANALYSIS OF VARIOUS DRAMATIC AND NONDRAMATIC USES OF MUSIC**

A. Performance Rights Societies

B. Performance License Provisions

C. Eight Examples of Performances of Music

    1. A non-dramatic rendition of a musical composition, that was not originally part of any opera, operetta, musical comedy, play or like production, on stage in a

theatre, nightclub, cabaret, concert hall, or like establishment

2. A dramatic rendition of a musical composition, that was not originally part of an opera, operetta, musical comedy, play or like production, on stage in a theatre, nightclub, cabaret, concert hall, or like establishment

3. A non-dramatic rendition of a musical composition that was originally part of any opera, operetta, musical comedy, play or like production, on stage in a theatre, nightclub, cabaret, concert hall, or like establishment

4. A dramatic rendition of a musical composition that was originally part of any opera, operetta, musical comedy, play or like production, on stage in a theatre, nightclub, cabaret, concert hall, or like establishment

5. A non-dramatic rendition of a musical composition, that was not originally part of any opera, operetta, musical comedy, play or like production, in a television program, motion picture, videogram or like work

6. A dramatic rendition of a musical composition, that was not originally part of any opera, operetta, musical comedy, play or like production, in a television program, motion picture, videogram or like work

7. A non-dramatic rendition of a musical composition, that was originally part of any opera, operetta, musical comedy, play or like production, in a television program, motion picture, videogram or like work

8. A dramatic rendition of a musical composition, that was originally part of any opera, operetta, musical comedy, play or like production, in a television program, motion picture, videogram or like work

## VI. RECENT COURT CASES

A. Frank Music Corp. v. MGM Grand Hotel

B. Gershwin v. The Whole Thing Co.

## VII. GRAND RIGHT IN A PERSON'S LIFE STORY?

## VIII. BROADCAST OF AN ENTIRE ALBUM

CHAPTER **18**

# THE GRAND RIGHTS
# CONTROVERSY

A s noted in the preceding chapter, performance rights societies only provide licenses to render performances of music that are *nondramatic.* They do not grant licenses to render dramatic performances. This chapter will explore the distinction between dramatic and nondramatic performances and will suggest a framework for answering the question, from whom, if not the performance rights society, must one seek permission to render a *dramatic* performance of a musical composition? This chapter will also provide examples of dramatic and nondramatic uses and will analyze the type of license appropriate for each use.

A considerable amount of confusion among music publishers, songwriters, musical playwrights, producers, and their legal representatives, has clouded the licensing of dramatic performances of music on stage, television and motion pictures. Much of this confusion stems from a misunderstanding of the rights involved and, in particular, the frequent misuse of the term, *grand rights.*

Before proceeding with our discussion of the meaning of dramatic, nondramatic, and grand rights, it will be useful to first survey the various ways music may be used in theatrical productions.

## I. Overview of Theatrical Musical Productions

By theatrical production, we mean a production created for the living stage which contains some literary or visual elements going beyond the mere physical appearance and rendition of music by singers and musicians. It should be noted that the kinds of theatrical productions described below should not be confused with the type of *venue* (e.g., nightclub, cabaret, concert hall, legitimate theatre, etc.) at which these productions may be performed. Each kind of theatrical performance described below may be performed at any of the various kinds of venues.

The theatrical productions in which music may be used can be classified into four categories:

## A. Non-Musical Play with Incidental Music

A *non-musical play with incidental music* is what the term implies. The music is usually contracted for after the play is written and is not considered part of the play. An example might be Shakespeare's *Hamlet* with music performed merely incidental to the play.

## B. Play with Music

*Play with music* is the term reserved for a play that is essentially non-musical, but contains music, with or without lyrics. The music may be integral to the play, used to create atmosphere, indicate the time when the action is taking place, or to assist in evoking a mood or the expression of the mood or desires of a character in the play, but it does not have the effect of carrying the action ahead to the extent it does in a dramatico-musical work.

## C. Musical Revue

A *musical revue* is a stage presentation of skillfully arranged, separate musical numbers. Years ago, revues, such as Ziegfeld's *Follies,* Earl Carroll's *Vanities*, and George White's *Scandals*, contained a variety of acts, including singing, dancing, sketches, comedy bits, blackouts, and specialty performances of individuals, animal acts, and, of course, chorus girls. Today, revues usually consist entirely of musical numbers, with some sketches or improvisation. A recent example of a musical revue is *Ain't Misbehavin'.*

## D. Dramatico-Musical Work

A *dramatico-musical work* is a theatrical work in which the music is integral to the story told by the book in the sense that the music is used to carry the action of the story forward. Examples include operas, operettas, ballet, and musical plays. An *opera* — once commonly referred to as a *grand opera* — is a play with virtually the entire text of its book, or libretto, set to music or sung, with no or few spoken words. An *operetta* is the same as an opera except that a significant portion of the text of the book is spoken, rather than sung. A *ballet* is an elaborate dramatic dance set to music, often choreographed to render a narrative story. The *musical play*, or musical comedy, the modern successor to the operetta, is a play with music and lyrics that are used to carry forward the action of the story or book of the play, the text of which is rendered in spoken form. Musical plays were once commonly called, *grand musical plays*, but today they are more commonly called simply, *musicals*.

## II. LEGAL BACKGROUND

### A. Copyright

The copyright law identifies several categories of works of authorship, including literary works, dramatic works, musical works, choreographic works, pictorial works, sculptural works, and audiovisual works. A book, for example, is considered a *literary work*. A play is considered a *dramatic work*. A song, of course, is a *musical work*. *Plays with music* are considered dramatic works. *Musical revues* may be considered dramatic works, or merely compilations of musical works accompanied by incidental, literary material (e.g., monologue, dialogue, or narration). *Non-musical plays with incidental music*, as we have defined that term, are literary works accompanied by separate musical works.

Wherever the literary contribution to a work is separate from the musical contribution to a work, such as the literary and musical contributions to a non-musical play with incidental music, the copyright in the literary contribution is separate from the copyright in the musical contribution. By contrast, a *dramatico-musical work*, such as an opera or a musical play, is a work whose music is an integral part of the literary material, the music often carrying forward the action of the story. Although a copyright in each contribution to a dramatico-musical work (e.g., literary work, music, lyrics) may be claimed separately, a copyright in the dramatico-musical work as a whole may also be claimed as a single work. For example, the playwright, lyricist, and composer of a musical play can claim a copyright in the musical play in its entirety (including literary material, music and lyrics), with each owning an undivided one-third interest in the copyright in the entire dramatico-musical work.

The owner of the copyright in a book, play, or song has the exclusive right of performance in the book, play, or song. In other words, public performances of these works requires the permission of the copyright owner. Likewise, the owner of a dramatico-musical work, as a single work comprised of music, lyrics and libretto, has the exclusive right of performance in the dramatico-musical work, and the public performance of an opera, musical play, or other dramatico-musical work requires the permission of the copyright owner of the opera or play.

## B. Licensing by Theatrical Production Companies and Theatrical Agencies

Public performances of operas, musical plays, and other dramatico-musical works, or portions of such works, at theatres, concert halls, and schools, are licensed by the copyright owners of such works, usually the play's producer or theatrical production company, but sometimes the playwrights themselves. These producers, companies, or playwrights are often represented by agencies specializing in the licensing of dramatico-musical works on their behalf. These agencies include the Tams-Witmark Music Library, Inc., Music Theatre, Inc., and Samuel French in New York, and Dramatic Publishing Co., in Chicago.[1]

## C. Licensing by Performance Rights Societies

As noted in the preceding chapter, performance rights societies only license those uses over which they have the authority or right to license. Performance rights societies do not receive any rights from theatrical production companies to license dramatico-musical works (e.g., works which comprise words, music, libretto, scenery, costumes,

---

[1] Samuel French, Inc., 25 West 45th Street, New York, NY 10036, Phone: 1-212-582-4700. www.samuelfrench.com; Tams-Witmark Music Library, Inc., 560 Lexington Avenue, New York, NY 10022, Phone: 800-221-7196, Fax: 212-688-3232; Dramatic Publishing Co., 311 Washington Street, Woodstock, IL 60098. Phone: 1-815-338-7170. www.dramaticpublishing.com.

etc.). Further, performance rights societies receive from their music publisher and songwriter members the right to license only *nondramatic* renditions of their musical compositions, not *dramatic* renditions. Accordingly, performance licenses issued by the societies to radio and television stations, nightclubs, concert halls, and like establishments, permit the rendition of performances of music in only a manner that is *nondramatic* in nature and do not permit any performances of plays, musicals and other dramatico-musical works.

## D. Licensing by Music Publishers

As noted above, theatrical producers, playwrights, or their agencies have the right to license performances of dramatico-musical works; performance rights societies have the right to license nondramatic performances of music in their repertoire (but they have no right to license dramatic performances and no right to license dramatico-musical works). The right to license *all other uses* of music is vested solely in the copyright owner of the music, usually a music publisher. For example, the owner of the copyright in a musical composition that was not originally part of a dramatico-musical work has the exclusive right to license *dramatic* performances of that musical composition. Nondramatic performances of that composition are licensed by the performance rights society to which a license to sublicense nondramatic performances has been granted. In some cases, a music publisher may require the consent of the songwriter to issue certain kinds of licenses, such as licenses to permit the dramatic performance of the composition, but the right to license these uses is vested exclusively in the copyright owner.

## III. DISTINGUISHING BETWEEN DRAMATIC RIGHTS, NONDRAMATIC RIGHTS AND GRAND RIGHTS

As the preceding sections suggest, the question of whether a particular performance is a dramatic performance, a nondramatic performance, or a performance of a dramatico-musical work is an important one, because its answer will determine who among the theatrical producers, music publishers, and songwriters have the right to license the use for which clearance is being sought. It is the question to which we now turn: the distinction between dramatic uses, nondramatic uses, and uses of dramatico-musical works — and the rights which form the basis for licensing such uses: dramatic performance rights, nondramatic performance rights, and grand rights, respectively.

## A.  Dramatic Performance Defined

The essence of a dramatic performance is drama. The term *drama* implies the telling of a story or the involvement of human conflict. Accordingly, the term *dramatic performance* has been defined as a performance of a musical composition that is woven into and carries forward a definite plot and its accompanying action. Examples of dramatic performances are provided and discussed below.

## B.  Nondramatic Performance Defined

Conversely, a *nondramatic performance* is a performance of a musical composition that is not woven into or does not carry forward a definite plot and its accompanying action. The mere singing of a song with its lyrics on stage and the broadcasting of a recording of a song on the radio would each constitute a nondramatic performance.

## C.  Grand Rights Defined

A *grand right* is the exclusive right to license the reproduction, adaptation, performance or other use of a dramatico-musical work, or what was once known as a "grand opera" or "grand musical play." It is a right in all the contributions of the musical play *as a single work*. It is not a right in just the music or in any single song or other literary, musical or other contribution to the play. The subject of the grand right is a collective work comprised of words, music, choreography, the *book* (i.e., the plot, story or libretto), setting, scenery, costumes, and other visual representations. There is no grand right in any of the individual songs in the collective, grand musical play; as we have explained, the copyright in the grand play, including the accompanying music, is quite distinct from the copyrights in the individual compositions that comprise it.

## IV. GRAND RIGHTS DISTINGUISHED
## FROM DRAMATIC RIGHTS

Accordingly, a *grand performance* is the performance of a grand opera, grand musical play, or other dramatico-musical work, or a substantial, recognizable portion of it. This is not the same as a *dramatic performance* of an individual composition, which is a rendition of a song (regardless of whether the song was originally part of a dramatico-musical work) that is woven into and carries forward a definite plot and its accompanying action.

The fact that there is a distinction between a *dramatic performance* and a *grand performance* may come as a surprise to many publishers and attorneys who have come to understand the terms as synonymous. Many understand the term grand performance to mean any dramatic performance of any musical composition and that all other performances are non-dramatic, or *small performances*.[2] A careful analysis of the rights involved clearly show that this is clearly not a proper usage of the terms.

## V. ANALYSIS OF VARIOUS DRAMATIC AND
## NONDRAMATIC USES OF MUSIC

To illustrate what a grand right is, it is most useful to first examine what it is not. This section will explore the differences between dramatic and non-dramatic performances by analyzing several examples of performances of music.

### A. Performance Rights Societies

As noted in Chapter 17, on *Performance Licenses*, songwriters and copyright owners grant to performance rights societies a license to

---

[2] Compare, for example, Nimmer *On Copyright,* Sec. 10.10[E] (1995). If we may, in commenting upon the passage in Nimmer on the subject of grand rights, borrow a phrase that Nimmer himself used in criticism of a decision by Judge Friendly, which itself was a phrase borrowed from Horace by Judge Learned Hand to criticize a decision of Justice Oliver Wendell Holmes, "for once Homer nodded." See, Nimmer *On Copyright,* Sec. 307 [A][2] (1995).

sublicense the rendition of public performances of their musical works. These grants are limited solely to the rendition of performances in a *nondramatic* manner and solely to performances of their *music*. Songwriters and copyright owners do not grant to performance rights societies any right to perform music in a dramatic manner and do not grant to the societies any rights in their literary works, plays, operas, ballets, choreographic works, and other types of works of authorship. For example, in the agreement between ASCAP and its writer and publisher members, the member may grant to ASCAP nondramatic performance rights in the separate compositions that may form part of a musical play authored by the songwriter member and owned by the publisher member, but the right to perform the musical play itself is reserved to the members.[3]

---

[3] The ASCAP Agreement between the society and its publisher and writers states:
The rights hereby granted shall include:
. . .

(b)   The non-exclusive right of public performance of the separate numbers, songs, fragments or arrangements, melodies or selections forming part or parts of musical plays and dramatico-musical compositions, the Owner [i.e., writer or publisher] reserving and excepting from this grant the right of performance of musical plays and dramatico-musical compositions on the legitimate stage.
. . .

(d)   The non-exclusive right of public performance by television broadcasting; provided, however, that:

(i)   This grant does not extend to or include the right to license the public performance by television broadcasting or otherwise of any rendition or performance of (a) any opera, operetta, musical comedy, play or like production, as (whether or not such opera, operetta, musical comedy, play or like production was presented on the stage or motion picture form) in a manner which recreates the performance of such composition with substantially such distinctive scenery or costume as was used in the presentation of such opera, operetta, musical comedy, play or like production (whether or not such opera, operetta, musical comedy, play or like production was presented on the stage or in motion picture form): provided, however, that the rights hereby granted shall be deemed to include a grant of right to license nondramatic performances of compositions by television broadcasting of a motion picture containing such composition if the right in such motion picture other than those granted hereby have been obtained from the parties in interest.

(e)   The Owner may at any time and from time to time, in good faith, restrict the radio or television broadcasting of compositions from musical comedies, operas, operettas and motion pictures, or any other composition being excessively

Because the performance rights societies have no authority to grant licenses with respect to rights reserved by their members, blanket performance licenses issued by the societies to radio and television stations, nightclubs, concert halls, and like establishments, are careful to permit the rendition of only *nondramatic* performances of music. They do not permit *dramatic* performances and do not permit any performances of plays, musicals and other dramatico-musical works.

These limitations in the scope of licenses issued by performance rights societies are set forth in the nondramatic license forms issued to radio and television stations, nightclubs, concert halls, and other licensees. The specific language used in the several forms of performance license agreements, however, varies considerably. We will review the following three representative provisions and then apply them to specific examples of musical renditions to determine the nature of the use in each example.

## B.  Performance License Provisions

The current ASCAP general license agreement for restaurants, taverns, nightclubs, and similar establishments states:

> "This license is limited to nondramatic performances, and does not authorize any dramatic performances. For purposes of this agreement, a dramatic performance shall include, but not be limited to, the following:

---

broadcast, only for the purpose of preventing harmful effect upon such musical comedies, operas, operettas, motion pictures, or compositions . . .

The BMI Agreement with the Writer states:

5.  (a)  The rights granted to us [hereunder] shall not include the right to perform or license the performance of more than one song or aria from an opera, operetta, or musical comedy or more than five minutes from a ballet if such performance is accompanied by the dramatic action, costumes or scenery of that opera, operetta, musical comedy or ballet.

(b)  You, together with the publisher and your collaborators, if any, of a work, shall have the right jointly, by written notice to us, to exclude from the grant made [hereunder] performances of more than thirty (30) minutes' duration of a work which is an opera, operetta or musical comedy, but this right shall not apply to a work which is the score of a film originally produced for exhibition in motion picture theaters when performed as incorporated in such film, or which is a score originally written for a radio or television program when performed as incorporated in such program.

"(i) performance of a "dramatico-musical work" (as hereinafter defined) in its entirety;

"(ii) performance of one or more musical compositions from a "dramatico-musical work" (as hereinafter defined) accompanied by dialogue, pantomime, dance, stage action, or visual representation of the work from which the music is taken;

"(iii) performance of one or more musical compositions as part of a story or plot, whether accompanied or unaccompanied by dialogue, pantomime, dance, stage action, or visual representation;

"(iv) performance of a concert version of a "dramatico-musical work" (as hereinafter defined).

"The term "dramatico-musical work" as used in this agreement, shall include, but not be limited to, a musical comedy, oratorio, choral work, opera, play with music, revue, or ballet."

The BMI general license agreement for restaurants, taverns, night-clubs, and similar establishments states:

"[This] license shall not include dramatic rights, the right to perform dramatico-musical works in whole or in substantial part, the right to present individual works in a dramatic setting or the right to use the music licensed hereunder in any other context which may constitute an exercise of the 'grand rights' therein."

The ASCAP license agreement under which television stations are licensed to perform music within ASCAP's repertoire contains the following definition of dramatic performance:

"[A] dramatic performance shall mean a performance of the musical composition on a television program in which there is a definite plot depicted by action and where the performance of the musical composition is woven into and carries forward the plot and its accompanying action. The use of dialogue to establish a mere program format or the use of any non-dramatic device merely to introduce a performance of a composition shall not be deemed to make such performance dramatic."

## C. Eight Examples of Performances of Music

The performance license provisions set forth in the preceding section appear to be a function of one or more of the following circumstances: (a) Whether the nature of the performance is dramatic or nondramatic; (b) Whether the musical composition was originally part of a dramatico-musical work; and (c) Whether the performance is rendered on stage or broadcast on television.

We have formulated from the above circumstances eight examples of performances of music helpful to a discussion of the scope of these performance licenses. We will analyze each of them to determine what type of license is appropriate in each case and then determine who is vested with the right to grant the license for the particular use. Finally we will discuss the considerations used in establishing the terms of such licenses.

> *1.   A* **non-dramatic** *rendition of a musical composition, that* **was not** *originally part of any opera, operetta, musical comedy, play or like production, on stage in a* **theatre, nightclub, cabaret, concert hall, or like establishment.**

Suppose Frank Sinatra sang the song, *Yesterday* (Lennon/ McCartney), as part of his popular nightclub act at a Las Vegas resort hotel. His performance would fall within none of the four categories of dramatic performances set forth in the ASCAP general license. The song originated from a single release or record album recorded by *The Beatles* in the late 1960's. Because, it did not originate from any opera, operetta, musical comedy, play, ballet, or like production, only subparagraph (iii) of the ASCAP definition might apply:

> (iii) performance of one or more musical compositions as part of a story or plot, whether accompanied or unaccompanied by dialogue, pantomime, dance, stage action, or visual representation;

Mr. Sinatra's act is composed of a series of vocal renditions of songs performed on stage with the aid of a microphone backed up by a swing orchestra, with no other significant visual representations — that is, no costume or stage props other than a well-cut tuxedo and an occasional glass of *Jack Daniels* — and as part of no story or plot, other than monologue or dialogue incidental to the introduction and performance of the song. This performance, while quite entertaining, would clearly be considered *non-dramatic*.

Because the performance of *Yesterday* is non-dramatic, the performance is covered by the hotel's blanket license with the performance rights society. No further permission for the use would be required.

## 2. A dramatic *rendition of a musical composition, that* was not *originally part of an opera, operetta, musical comedy, play or like production, on stage in a* theatre, nightclub, cabaret, concert hall, or like establishment.

Suppose the same song, *Yesterday*, was performed by the pop star, Madonna, as part of an elaborate performance that contained significant visual representations, making use of costume, settings, scenery, props, and other visual allusions to, for example, ancient Rome. Again, since the song is not a dramatico-musical work nor was it originally part of one, only the following category of the definition of dramatic performance in the ASCAP license might apply:

(iii) performance of one or more musical compositions as part of a story or plot, whether accompanied or unaccompanied by dialogue, pantomime, dance, stage action, or visual representation;

Though the performance is accompanied by significant visual representations, it is not being rendered "as part of a story or plot," under the facts in this example. It is merely being performed by an artist in costume in front of scenery — no story or plot accompanies the presentation. It appears, therefore, that this performance would not be considered a dramatic rendition under the definition of dramatic performance set forth in the ASCAP license.

At this point, we will turn to the BMI general license (applying these facts as though the song were in the BMI repertoire):

"[This] license shall not include dramatic rights, . . . the right to present individual works in a dramatic setting or the right to use the music licensed hereunder in any other context which may constitute an exercise of the 'grand rights' therein."

The phrase, "This license shall not include dramatic rights," is unfortunate. As noted in Chapter 7, a *license* is not a *right* — a right is a claim of ownership that allows you to exclude someone from doing something with respect to the subject of your property; a license is a permission or privilege to do something with respect to another's property that you would not otherwise have the privilege to do without the license. What the phrase beginning, "This license shall not include dramatic rights . . . ," probably means is, "This license does not include permission to render performances of music that are dramatic or to present individual songs in a dramatic setting. . ."

This still leaves us with the question whether this performance would be considered a *dramatic* performance or a presentation of the song *in a dramatic setting.* If not, then Madonna's performance in this example, like Mr. Sinatra's performance in the preceding example, would be covered by the BMI license, and no separate license would be required.

For help in determining whether a performance is dramatic or presented in a dramatic setting, most people look to the standard set forth in the definition of dramatic performance contained in the ASCAP television license, which states: a performance of a musical composition on a television program is dramatic if "the musical composition is woven into and carries forward [a definite] plot and its accompanying action."

Interestingly enough, the ASCAP general license is not precisely consistent with this language (saying instead, "performance of one or more compositions *as part of* a story or plot") and the BMI general license does not explicitly use language relating to stories or plots at all. Nevertheless, it is believed that the definition of dramatic performance that appears in the television performance license of ASCAP is most helpful in analyzing whether a performance is dramatic or nondramatic. This is the case regardless of where the performance may be rendered, even though the definition would appear by its terms to be limited to dramatic performances rendered *on television.*

A little history may shed some light on the origin of this useful definition. It is said to have been written by Oscar Hammerstein II in the 1940's. Mr. Hammerstein was concerned that television would have the potential of competing with and reducing receipts of live theatrical performances of musical plays. It is not difficult to understand why Mr. Hammerstein suggested this particular language. Musical compositions in successful musical plays are not just incorporated randomly between acts in the play; good musical playwrights consciously make use of songs to *carry forward the action* of the play and the best use of music in a musical play is made when a composition is used to underscore a major turning point in the plot, such as a personal discovery of a principal character.[4]

The "woven into and carry forward the plot" language in Mr. Hammerstein's definition, however, seems to do more than protect the economic interests of owners of dramatico-musical works. As incorporated into the ASCAP license, it is not limited to compositions that were originally part of musical plays, operas and like productions; it appears to apply to other songs, as well, including songs such as, *Yesterday*, which were not originally part of dramatico-musical works. Nevertheless, there is still good reason why publishers and writers of non-show music reserve the right to license dramatic performances from performance rights societies.

The main concern of a performing rights society is administering the collection and payment of sums generated by the performances of compositions. While the value of certain performances are given greater weight than others (e.g., a use of a composition in a television commercial might be given more performance credits than the use of the same song as background music in a situation comedy), the importance of the song in relation to the intended use is not taken into consideration in compensating publishers and writers. A use of a particular song in a dramatic rendition (i.e., woven into and carrying forward a plot) is generally more important to the intended use than mere nondramatic renditions.

Though the differences in credits given for various kinds of performances are relatively small, the differences in the license fee charged for dramatic uses of compositions, as opposed to nondramatic uses, may vary greatly. They may vary greatly because the importance of the song in relation to the intended use varies greatly, depending, for example, upon how closely the music is woven into a dramatic plot. The more a song is woven into a plot, the more important it is to the use. The more important the song is in relation to the use desired, the higher the fee that can be commanded for the use.

Songwriters and music publishers reserve the right to issue dramatic performance licenses from their performing rights societies, because they are in a better position than the societies to determine the

---

[4] See, Frankel, *Writing the Broadway Musical* at p. 29 (Drama Book Specialists, New York 1977).

value of the musical composition in relation to its intended dramatic use and to price the license accordingly. Performing rights societies, who merely survey performances to roughly measure how often the songs in their repertory are performed, are not in the best position to perform this analysis. How a publisher determines the value of a license of a dramatic performance varies from song to song, and from use to use, but the publishers and writers are in a better position to reflect upon such factors and determine the value of the dramatic uses of their musical works. Thus, writers and publishers have more to gain by reserving the rights to grant licenses for the dramatic use of their music, rather than giving the performance rights society such rights.

Determining when a musical composition performed on a television program is "woven into and carries forward the plot and its accompanying action" must obviously be done on a case by case basis. Reasonable minds may differ as to whether the facts presented would lead to a conclusion that any performance is dramatic or non-dramatic. However, even though neither the general performance licenses of ASCAP or BMI mention it specifically, the standard proposed by Oscar Hammerstein II for determining the nature of performances rendered on television programs appears to be the best standard for determining whether any particular performance is dramatic or non-dramatic.

If, in our example, Madonna's performance of the song, *Yesterday* were preceded or followed by a dialogue performed on stage to establish the format of the act or if a non-dramatic device were used merely to introduce her performance of the song, the performance would remain non-dramatic, even if accompanied by significant visual representations, such as costumes and scenery of ancient Rome. However, any variation of facts might change the outcome. If Madonna's act carried a definite plot depicted by action and the performance of the song is woven into and carries forward the plot and its accompanying action, the performance would be dramatic. For example, the performance would probably be dramatic if her act was to some extent based upon the story of *Anthony and Cleopatra* and the song *Yesterday* was woven into the act at a certain point to carry forward the idea that "all [her] troubles seemed so far away."

Assuming that the performance were deemed dramatic, then, because the performance is not covered by the ASCAP or BMI licenses (which cover only non-dramatic performances), a dramatic performance license would be required before Madonna could proceed with the performance.

From whom would such a license be cleared? The license for the dramatic performance is not covered by the hotel's blanket performance license and is not available separately from the performance rights societies. The hotel, Madonna, or the producer of her act, would require permission from the copyright owner of the song, which in most cases is the music publisher.

Some would suggest that the license to perform the song dramatically or in a dramatic setting must be cleared by the songwriter, because, they say, "a dramatic performance is an exercise of a grand right" and "grand rights are reserved to songwriters." However, because the song in this example was not originally part of a dramatico-musical work, *no grand right* is involved, and permission would be required from the copyright owner (i.e., the music publisher, not the songwriter).

### 3. A non-dramatic *rendition of a musical composition that was originally part of an opera, operetta, musical comedy, play or like production, on stage in a* theatre, nightclub, cabaret, concert hall, or like establishment.

An example of this use may be found in a true story and court trial in which I testified as a witness in early 1948.[5] The copyright owner of *The Student Prince* sued the owner of a cabaret in New York City called *The Harem* (owned, incidentally, at that time by Lou Walters, the father of newscaster, Barbara Walters) for infringement based upon performances at the club of a medley of songs from *The Student Prince*. The nightclub owner claimed the performance was licensed under the club's standard blanket license from ASCAP. The court ruled, correctly in our view, that the performance was covered by the ASCAP license and that the medley did not infringe the musical play, *The Student Prince*. This decision has been criticized as too narrowly

---

[5] *April Productions, Inc. v. Strand Enterprises, Inc.*, 221 F.2d 292 (2d Cir. 1955).

construing the scope of the term dramatic performance.[6] A close review of the facts reveals this criticism is misplaced.

The medley of songs from *The Student Prince* was performed by
the choral group, *Ben Yost and his Royal Guardsmen*, which was the
ninth act in a ten act nightclub show entitled, "The One Thousand
and Second Night." The show was not connected by a story line or
plot and the medley was just one of the numbers performed by the
*Royal Guardsmen*, a small part of their act. The stage had no scenery
and the act was performed in front of the nightclub stage curtain. The
*Royal Guardsmen* did wear costumes — white outfits with fanciful
short, red formal jackets. Nevertheless, neither the costumes nor the
visual presentation bore any resemblance to the distinctive scenery or
costume used in the presentation of the musical play, *The Student
Prince*. Finally, the medley was truly a medley; no song from *The
Student Prince* was sung in its entirety. I can confirm this because, I
worked for Ben Yost at the time and I personally arranged the medley
that was the subject of this lawsuit. I testified before the Judge in the
case that the medley comprised mostly the refrains of songs from the
show connected by transitions that I composed.

The court was faced with the task of interpreting an older form
of the ASCAP license for performances in nightclubs. The form,
which the court was not reticent to criticize (saying, "the form of the
license is such that almost nothing is sure"), granted to the Harem
nightclub permission to render non-dramatic performances of ASCAP
music. The court determined that the language granting permission to
render "non-dramatic" renditions can best be construed in light of the
other provisions of the license which describe what is not included in
the license. One of those provisions prohibited the performance of
compositions with "words, dialogue, costume accompanying dramatic
action or scenery accessory" that was "of the work from which the
music was taken." The court observed that the form "on the one hand,
describes the performance right granted as 'non-dramatic' but, on the
other, in substance authorizes their exercise with 'words, dialogue,
costume accompanying dramatic action or scenery accessory'" (as

---

[6] 3 Nimmer *On Copyright,* Sec. 10.10[E] n.44 (1991) (stating that, "This decision, if
followed, could mean the virtual extinction of dramatic (or grand) performing rights
with respect to noninstrumental musical compositions.").

long as such elements were not of the work from which the music was taken). In other words, the ASCAP license permitted the rendition of musical compositions with costume, scenery, dialogue, dramatic actions, and other visual represen-tations without their getting into the "dramatic" class. After closely examining the facts in the case, the court concluded that the performance was non-dramatic. None of the costumes, scenery, dialogue or other visual representations present when the medley was performed bore any resemblance to those used in the presentation of the musical play, *The Student Prince*. Even if *The Harem* put on a dramatic performance, the court said, the selections from *The Student Prince* were not part of it.

If the court had before it the modern ASCAP nightclub perform-ance license to construe, the result would have been no different. The performance of the medley falls within none of the four categories that comprise the definition of a dramatic performance: the perform-ance of a medley of songs from *The Student Prince* is not (i) a per-formance of *the musical play* itself; (ii) the performance of one or more musical compositions from *The Student Prince* accompanied by dialogue, pantomime, dance, stage action, or visual representation *of the work from which the music is taken*; (iii) the performance of one or more musical compositions *as part of a story or plot,* whether accompanied or unaccompanied by dialogue, pantomime, dance, stage action, or visual representation; or (iv) the performance of *a concert version of* the musical play, *The Student Prince*.

Note that even the modern ASCAP license contemplates that a performance of a song originally from a dramatico-musical work may be non-dramatic, even though the performance is accompanied by di-alogue, pantomime, dance, stage action, or visual representation, as long as such elements are not *of the work from which the music is taken*.

Applying the facts of this case to the modern BMI general license, the same result would be reached. The BMI license does not provide permission to perform dramatico-musical works, in whole or in sub-stantial part. The performance of a medley of songs from a musical play should not be construed as the performance of a substantial part of the musical play, unless something more is present that substantially evokes the drama inherent in the musical play. That something may be costumes, scenery, or other visual representations from the musical play or some dialogue from the play, other than that which may be part of the lyrics to the music.

The BMI general license also states that permission does not include, "the right to present individual works in a dramatic setting." Arguably, the medley from *The Student Prince* could be considered to have been presented in a dramatic setting, if the entire evening's performance at *The Harem* were considered a dramatic performance. But the court specifically held, and correctly, that the worst that could be said about the performance is that the medley was sung in an intermission between the acts of a dramatic performance, and that such a rendition was non-dramatic within the meaning of the ASCAP license. A contrary holding would have the effect of rendering any simple stand-up performance of a song by an act in a variety show a dramatic performance merely because the variety show includes other acts which render dramatic performances.

Arguably, the medley could be considered to have been presented in a dramatic setting if the singers were in costume and the stage contained scenery. But the mere presence of costumes, scenery, or other visual representations should not by themselves render a setting dramatic. Something more must be present: something in the nature of drama. As noted above, the term *drama* implies the acting out or telling of a story, or the involvement of human conflict. For a setting to be dramatic, therefore, the song must either be (i) interwoven into a plot or story, or (ii) the lyrics of the song are rendered with the presence of costumes, scenery, and visual representations from the musical play for which the song was originally written. Either of these, or perhaps other elements, such as dialogue from the musical play, would more strongly evoke the drama of the musical play than the mere performance of lyrics or instrumental arrangement.

Accordingly, the performance of a medley of selections from *The Student Prince*, with little more than some fanciful costumes unrelated to the musical play, was not a rendition in a dramatic setting nor a performance of the musical in whole or in substantial part.

### 4. A dramatic *rendition of a musical composition, that* was *originally part of an opera, operetta, musical comedy, play or like production, on stage in a* nightclub, cabaret, concert hall, or like establishment.

A concert performance of a substantial number of songs from the rock opera, *Jesus Christ Superstar* is an example of a performance of music that was originally part of an opera or musical play that was held by a court to be dramatic.[7]

Timothy Rice wrote the opera's libretto and Andrew Lloyd Webber composed the score of the opera's overture and 23 songs which depict the last seven days in the life of Jesus. The Robert Stigwood Group, the owner of the exclusive right to make stage and dramatic presentations of the rock opera, brought a lawsuit against a theatrical touring company which produced a series of live stage performances that included 20 of the 23 musical compositions from the opera, all but one of which was rendered in identical sequence as in the original opera. As in the opera, the singers enter and exit, maintaining specific roles and occasionally making gestures, and preserving the story line of the original production. The theatrical company contended that its presentation was a *non-dramatic* performance of the compositions in *Jesus Christ Superstar* which could be performed under the theatre's license from ASCAP. Stigwood took the position that it is a dramatic performance of the songs which is not covered by the ASCAP license.

The court correctly concluded that the production was an infringement on Stigwood's rights in the opera *Jesus Christ Superstar*. However, even though the court pointed out that separate copyright registrations were obtained for the opera as a dramatico-musical work as a whole and for each of the individual musical compositions as musical works, it failed in its analysis to recognize the import of the distinction between the copyright in the opera and the copyrights in the individual compositions.

As a result, the court unnecessarily wrestled with the distinction between dramatic and non-dramatic performances of the songs, when, in fact, it was not dealing with the issue of whether the performances of the songs were done in a dramatic fashion, but with the issue of whether the performance was an infringement of the rights in the dramatico-musical work, *Jesus Christ Superstar*. In other words, the court held that the performance of the songs were *dramatic*, rather than holding that the performance constituted a *grand performance* of the grand opera, *Jesus Christ Superstar*.

To its credit, the court recognized that it was "inescapable that the *story* of the last seven days in the life of Christ is portrayed in the

---

[7] *Robert Stigwood Group Limited v. Sperber,* 457 F.2d 50 (2d Cir. 1972).

[defendant's] performances substantially as in Superstar." We add emphasis to the word *"story,"* because the subject of the infringement was a performance of the dramatico-musical work, including its story or libretto, which is a substantial part of the dramatico-musical work. The lack of costumes or scenery did not prevent the story from being infringed. The rendition of 20 of the 23 songs in virtually the same order as they appeared in the opera, with or without costumes or scenery from the opera, is essentially a performance of the story. It should not make a difference that none of the costumes or scenery used in this performance was from the original opera presentation.

This case can be distinguished from *The Student Prince* case. In the latter, only a medley of a selection of songs from the musical were performed in a short act that was part of a variety show. For the performance of the medley to have been dramatic, something more than the rendition of the medley was required to make the performance tantamount to a performance of the musical play itself, or a substantial part of it — something like dialogue, costumes, scenery, or visual representations from the musical itself. In the *Superstar* case, the play was an opera in which most of the dialogue was comprised in the lyrics. By performing 20 of the 23 songs in order, you, in effect, render a performance of the opera, if not in whole, surely, in substantial part. No costumes, scenery or other visual representations from the original opera need be present under these circumstances to evoke *Superstar's* drama, which was substantially comprised in the lyrics of the 20 songs selected for the performance.

Although ASCAP licensed the nondramatic performance of the individual musical compositions, ASCAP had no right to license the story, or any performance of the music that includes a substantial performance of the grand opera. The rights in the grand opera was infringed in this case. Since the ASCAP license did not permit this performance, a license would be required from Stigwood, the owners of the exclusive rights to present the opera. Note, that even if the music publishing rights to the musical compositions were granted by Stigwood to an independent music publishing company, a license to perform the opera would still be required from Stigwood, not the music publishing company. This is because the rights in the play are separate from the rights in the music, and the music publishing company would have no right to grant a license for this grand performance, unless it were given rights to the play, or some other authorization from the play's owner to do so.

### 5.  A non-dramatic *rendition of a musical composition, that* was not *originally part of an opera, operetta, musical comedy, play or like production, in a* television program, motion picture, videogram or like work.

As previously noted, the ASCAP license agreement under which television stations are licensed to perform music within ASCAP's repertoire contains a definition of dramatic performance that boils down to this: a performance of a musical composition on a television program is dramatic if the musical composition is woven into and carries forward a definite plot and its accompanying action. Determining when a musical composition performed on a television program is "woven into and carries forward the plot and its accompanying action" must be done on a case by case basis.

Taking the example of Frank Sinatra's singing the song *Yesterday* in his nightclub act, if we were to record Mr. Sinatra's performance on videotape and televised it, the answer to our question would be no different: the performance would not be considered dramatic. It would not be dramatic under the ASCAP license, because there is no definite plot or accompanying action into which the music can be woven or be used to carry forward. Nor would the performance be dramatic under the BMI license, inasmuch as the setting of Frank Sinatra's act would not be considered *dramatic*, in the absence of some plot and accompanying action.

Similarly, a song performed by a singer on a television variety show, such as the *Ed Sullivan Show*, would not be considered dramatic, even though portions of the variety show may contain scenes of a dramatic nature. This would be similar to the facts of *The Student Prince* case, discussed above, where the medley of songs from *The Student Prince* performed by a singing group was not deemed to be a dramatic performance, even though several other acts presented during the course of the evening at *The Harem* nightclub may have been of a dramatic nature.

Certainly, the performance of a musical composition by a band, such as the NBC band on the *Tonight Show*, is not a dramatic performance. Nor would the use of theme music over the main titles of a situation comedy, or the use of background music in a made-for-TV-movie, be considered a dramatic performance. The use of music under those circumstances could not be considered woven into and carrying forward the plot of the dramatic or comedic action.

Perhaps the music played in the background of a breathtaking car chase in a crime drama program might help carry forward the accompanying action, but it would hardly be considered woven into the plot, as nearly any action music could be substituted. The definition of dramatic performance requires, as it should, that the music be both *carrying forward* a definite plot *and* be *woven into* the plot and its accompanying action. Music that accompanies dramatic action just to vicariously enhance the action would not be considered a dramatic use.

> **6. A dramatic *rendition of a musical composition, that* was not *originally part of an opera, operetta, musical comedy, play or like production, in a* television program, motion picture, videogram or like work.**

As we have suggested, the standard used by the ASCAP definition of dramatic performances on television programs — whether the music is woven into and carries forward a definite plot and its accompanying action — is useful for determining whether performances are dramatic, whether the performances are rendered on television, on stage, in motion pictures, or elsewhere.

Thus, the analysis of the example of Madonna's singing the song *Yesterday* in her nightclub act would be the same, whether the act were performed live, broadcast on television, or filmed for theatrical exhibition.

It may be asked whether a rock music "video" containing an audio performance of a song and a theatrical portrayal of the lyrics on screen is a dramatic performance of the song. If the song carries forward a definite plot and is woven into the plot and its accompanying action, then the performance would be dramatic. This might be the case if the story is an allegory which the lyrics help carry forward. If the story had nothing to do with the lyrics, or if there were no story, merely some special effects or the band performing on a stage, then the use would be merely a non-dramatic performance. Finally, if the story presented on the screen is actually a derivative work of the lyrics, then the use would be a *dramatic adaptation* of the lyrics, about which more is said later in this chapter.

7. *A* **non-dramatic** *rendition of a musical composition, that was originally part of any opera, operetta, musical comedy, play or like production, in a* **television program, motion picture, videogram or like work.**

It was sometime in the early 1960's, while working at Leo Feist, Inc. music publishing company, when I received a call requesting clearance to use the song, *If I Only Had a Heart* from the MGM film production, *The Wizard of Oz*, which was originally performed by Judy Garland, playing Dorothy, and Ray Bolger, as the Scarecrow. The producers of *The Garry Moore Show* wished to use the song as part of a dance number on the show, which was to be broadcast over the CBS television network. Naturally, I issued the appropriate synchronization license for the use. Unknown to the Garry Moore people or us at Leo Feist, CBS-TV had purchased the exclusive right to broadcast the motion picture, *The Wizard of Oz*, during the Christmas holiday that particular year.

A few days later, during a rehearsal of *The Garry Moore Show*, someone at CBS noticed that dancing girls were wearing scarecrow costumes somewhat similar to those worn by Ray Bolger in the motion picture. When the clearance department and legal staff of CBS heard about it, they raised hell, claiming that their grand rights in the motion picture would be infringed by the dance routine to be performed on *The Garry Moore Show* (infringed by their own network!).

As noted, the ASCAP license agreement under which television stations are licensed to perform music within ASCAP's repertoire contains the following definition of dramatic performance: a performance of a musical composition on a television program is dramatic if the musical composition is woven into and carries forward a definite plot and its accompanying action. It is clear that the mere performance on a variety television program of a single song by a group of dancers in costume does not carry forward a definite plot or story and accompanying action. Thus, the performance is not a dramatic performance.

However, there is another provision in the television license that squarely governs this situation: The ASCAP television license, by its terms, "does not extend to or include the public performances by television broadcasting or otherwise of any rendition or performance of . . . any composition from any opera, operetta, musical comedy, play or like production (whether or not such opera, operetta, musical comedy, play *or like production* was presented on the stage or in motion picture form) in a manner which recreates the performance of such composition with substantially such distinctive scenery or costume as was used in the presentation of such opera, operetta, musical comedy, play *or like production* (whether or not such opera, operetta, musical comedy, play or like production was presented on the stage or in motion picture form)." (emphasis added)

The musical motion picture production *The Wizard of Oz* would certainly be considered a production that would fall within the scope of the above provision. Further, the performance of the song, *If I Only Had a Heart* from the film, *The Wizard of Oz*, with scarecrow costumes by several dancers would probably be considered a manner which recreates the performance of the song, though not precisely, with substantially such distinctive costume as was used in the motion picture. Accordingly, the proposed performance would probably have constituted a grand performance in violation of CBS's exclusive rights to televise the motion picture.

To avoid the problem, the producers of *The Garry Moore Show* cleverly changed the routine: Instead of wearing the scarecrow costumes, the dancers performed the routine in their rehearsal clothes. Stories about the incident appeared in the entertainment sections of many newspapers across the country and, needless to say, the show enjoyed one of the best ratings that week.

The above incident carries several lessons for both licensors and licensees. The lesson for music copyright owners is that it is not your responsibility to guarantee that the licensee has all the rights he needs to effect the desired performance. It is the producer's responsibility to make sure he obtains a license to effect a grand performance, if that is what he will need. The producer is in a better position than you are to know just how he will be rendering the performance, and, thus, whether the performance would infringe a grand right, or some other right, such as the laws of defamation or invasion of privacy. All you can provide the producer is the license to do what you have the right to stop him from doing, such as synchronizing the song in an audiovisual work. By the same token, you should never warrant to a producer that you are giving him all the rights he needs to render the performance, as you can only license that over which you have the right to grant. If the producer renders a grand performance, he is going beyond the license you provide and is engaging in an area about which you have no responsibility.

The lesson for the person who needs to clear licenses is that it is your responsibility to clear all permissions that you require to proceed. Failure to do so will expose you to a claim for copyright infringement or some other violation of the law. Sometimes problems can be avoided by telling the music publisher precisely how you intend to use the music, and the publisher might be able to advise you that you require a license from another party to effect your use. But the copyright owner cannot guarantee that the license granted covers all the permissions that you'll require for your use, and it is not his responsibility to do so. Of course, sometimes you just can't predict a problem, as the publisher and producers didn't know that CBS acquired exclusive rights to broadcast the motion picture *The Wizard of Oz*.

In the case of *The Garry Moore Show*, the network executives probably over-reacted. The music and scarecrow costumes were going to be performed in the television studio without any scenery or background that could be associated with the film. At best, the use of the song promoted the later broadcast of the full-length motion picture on CBS. At worst, they would be in competition with themselves. If, however, it had been another network that acquired the exclusive rights, the situation could have gotten a lot worse for the producer.

Finally, what should be noted by both licensors and licensees, is that while the performance of the song in scarecrow costumes would have been a *nondramatic performance* (because the routine, as rendered on *The Garry Moore Show*, would not have carried forward a definite plot and its accompanying action), it was still a performance that was not covered by the ASCAP television license. It is a *grand performance* of a song from a grand musical work, the motion picture, *The Wizard of Oz*. If the reader has followed this chapter through this point, it should have started to become apparent that a *dramatic performance* is not the same as a *grand performance*. Attempts at simplifying the complex subject of grand rights, have lead to a misuse of certain important terms. For example, the terms *small performing rights* and *grand performing rights* have been, but should not be, equated with the terms *nondramatic performing rights* and *dramatic performing rights*, respectively. We will revisit this point later in the chapter.

> **8. A dramatic *rendition of a musical composition, that* was *originally part of an opera, operetta, musical comedy, play or like production, in a* television program, motion picture, videogram or like work.**

In a popular television series about the school life of a group of high school students, one episode called for the students to perform portions of the play, *The Music Man.* The producers soon learned that television synchronization licenses to record the songs from the musical in the television program and the ASCAP licenses of the television stations to perform the songs were not going to be sufficient to clear the use, as the rendition of portions of the musical play constituted a grand performance of the musical, which required the additional permission of the owners of the musical play. Permission from the owners of *The Music Man* was required, not because the performance was dramatic, but because the a use was being made of a substantial part of the musical, and permission was required to perform portions of the musical.

Many years ago, a special television program called *The Helen Morgan Story* was broadcast on the program *Playhouse '90* over the CBS Television networks. Helen Morgan was a popular entertainer in the 1920's and 1930's who became known for her singing of melancholy ballads and her gimmick of sitting on top of a piano while singing. Her most memorable role included starring in the Broadway musical *Show Boat* (1928). Over the years, she became identified with several of the songs from the musical *Showboat*, especially the song *Bill*, which became her theme song. *The Helen Morgan Story* was the story of the entertainer's life, as told by Helen Morgan, sitting on a piano with her legs crossed. The only song featured in the program was her theme song, *Bill*.

What made the performance so unusual was that the song was the only song used in the program and was played throughout the program at various tempos, depending upon the period of the entertainer's life being presented. For example, while Morgan was describing a tranquil period of her life, the song was performed *adagio*; while she was describing a tempestuous period of her life, the song was performed *allegro*. The owners of the song sued CBS, claiming that the use was dramatic, and therefore outside the scope of the ASCAP performance license. The case was settled, but the issue as to whether CBS actually required an additional license is still an interesting one.

If the song *Bill* was performed with dialogue, costumes, scenery or other visual representations from the musical *Showboat*, then the performance would clearly have been a grand performance of the musical *Showboat* (or a substantial part of it), which would have required permission from the owners of the show. This, however, was clearly not the case in *The Helen Morgan Story* television program. At most, she may have sung the song at a point in the show where she was describing the events surrounding her Broadway experiences, but this would not be a performance of the musical play *Showboat*, without some material from the show, such as dialogue, costume, or scenery, in addition to the rendition of the lyrics of the song.

If the song was "interwoven and carrying forward a definite plot and its accompanying action," the performance would be *dramatic*, requiring a license from the copyright owner of the song, because the ASCAP license for nondramatic performance would not cover the use. Sometimes the answer to the question of whether a performance carries forward a definite plot is, "I know it when I see it," and the answer in this case may require an actual viewing of the program. If the lyrics of the song *Bill* somehow carried forward the story, then it is more likely that the use was dramatic. For example, if there were an actual person named Bill who played a part in Helen Morgan's life, and the song *Bill* carried forward some action concerning Helen Morgan and the real-life person named Bill, then it could be said the song carried forward the story. If the use of the music was merely instrumental, or of the lyrics of the song *Bill* had no relation to any events in her life, then it is more likely that the song did not carry forward the story.

Even assuming the song did "carry forward" Helen Morgan's telling of the story of her life, the question remains, does a life story have a *plot,* as that term is used in the ASCAP license, or otherwise used in determining whether a performance is dramatic? There is a public policy, grounded in the 1st Amendment to the U.S. Constitution, favoring the free dissemination of ideas, which, among other things, affords creators of biographical and other historical works a higher degree of flexibility in incorporating into their works the works of others than is afforded creators of purely fictional works. Nevertheless, biographies when presented in television programs and motion pictures, other than pure documentary programs, tend to contain a substantial amount of fictional material. Called *docu-dramas*,[8] these programs, while purporting to be biographies, often contain more fiction than fact, and are created more for their entertainment value than for their value as a contribution to historical knowledge.

In light of the foregoing considerations, it is believed that a performance of a song that carries forward the "plot" and accompanying action in a docu-drama would more likely constitute a dramatic use; a performance of a song that carries forward a life story in a pure documentary would be less likely to constitute dramatic use. The question whether *The Helen Morgan Story* would be considered more of the nature of a docu-drama or of the nature of a documentary, and whether the use of the song *Bill* in the Helen Morgan Story was a dramatic or non-dramatic performance, we will leave for historians and legal scholars to ponder.

## VI. RECENT COURT CASES

### A. Frank Music Corp. v. MGM Grand Hotel

Probably the first court to recognize, at least implicitly, the distinction between a dramatic performance of individual songs and the exercise of a grand right, or *grand performance* of a play or musical, is the Ninth Circuit Court of Appeals in a case involving a harem of a different sort.[9]

In 1974, the MGM Grand Hotel in Las Vegas, Nevada produced a musical revue called *Hallelujah Hollywood* in the hotel's lavish Ziegfeld Theatre. The show featured ten acts of singing, dancing, and

---

[8] See, generally, Lionel S. Sobel, *The Trials and Tribulations of Producing Docu-Dramas,* 5/3 Entertainment Law Reporter 3 (August, 1983).

[9] *Frank Music Corp. v. Metro-Goldwyn-Mayer, Inc.* 772 F.2d 505 (9th Cir. 1985).

variety performances. Of the ten acts, four were labeled as "tributes" to MGM motion pictures of the past and one was a tribute to the *Ziegfeld Follies*. The remaining acts were variety numbers, which included performances by a live tiger, a juggler, and the magicians, Siegfried and Roy. Act IV of *Hallelujah Hollywood* was entitled *Kismet*, which became the subject of the lawsuit.

The original version of *Kismet* was a dramatic play, written by Edward Knoblock in 1911, which entered the public domain in 1967. In 1952, Edwin Lester acquired the right to produce a musical stage production of the dramatic play *Kismet*. In 1953, Lester hired Luther David and Charles Lederer to write the libretto and Robert Wright and George Forrest to write the music and lyrics for the dramatico-musical adaptation. In 1953, Lederer and Davis copyrighted their dramatico-musical play *Kismet*, and Wright and Forrest assigned to Frank Music Corporation the right to copyright all portions of the musical score written for the musical. Frank Music subsequently obtained copyrights for the entire score and for each of the songs in the score. In 1954, Lederer, Wright and Forrest entered into a license agreement with MGM, Inc. granting it the rights to produce a musical motion picture based on their dramatico-musical play. MGM released it's motion picture version of *Kismet*, starring Howard Keel and Ann Blyth, in 1955.

The story presented in the MGM film and in the dramatico-musical play is essentially the same as that told in Knoblock's dramatic play. *Kismet* is the tale of a day in the life of a poetic beggar named Hajj and his daughter, Marsinah. The story is set in ancient Baghdad, with major scenes in the streets of Baghdad, the Wazir's palace, an enchanted garden, and the Wazir's harem.

Act IV of *Hallelujah Hollywood* presented at the MGM Grand Hotel, entitled *Kismet*, was billed as a tribute to the MGM movie of that name. Comprised of four scenes, the *Kismet* act was eleven and one-half minutes in length. It was set in ancient Baghdad, as was the dramatico-musical play, and the characters were called by the same or similar names to those used in the musical play. Five songs were taken in whole or in part from the musical. No dialogue was spoken during the act, and, in all, it contained 6 minutes of music taken directly from the musical play, and the songs were performed by singers identified as characters from the musical play, dressed in costumes designed to recreate *Kismet*. The performance made use of locale, settings, scenery, props, and dance style music of the type used in the musical play *Kismet*.

Within a few months after the premier of *Hallelujah Hollywood*, the MGM Grand was informed that it was infringing the *Kismet* musical play. MGM Grand responded that it believed its use of the music from the musical play was covered by its performance license from ASCAP.

The case went to court and the lower court held that the *Kismet* performances at the MGM Grand constituted copyright infringements, because the performance was outside the scope of the ASCAP license. The court addressed two clauses of the ASCAP license: (i) the clause that limits the performances by MGM Grand to "non-dramatic" renditions, and (ii) the clause that excludes from the license "dramatico-musical works, or songs [accompanied by] visual representations of the work from which the music is taken." The lower court ruled that, while the performances were non-dramatic, they were outside the scope of the latter clause of the ASCAP license, because they contained visual representations from the musical play. (The court of appeals agreed with the result reached by the lower court, but stated that there was no need to consider whether Act IV was dramatic or non-dramatic, because the clause excluding the performance of dramatico-musical work was sufficiently determinative).

Both the lower court and the court of appeals seemed to recognize that the issue in the case was not whether the performance of the individual songs was dramatic in nature, but whether the hotel had a license to present a portion of the dramatico-musical play. In other words, whether the play producer's *grand right* in the play was infringed. In this case, the lower court ruled that the grand right was infringed, even though the performance was nondramatic! So much for the idea that grand performances are the equivalent of dramatic performances.

## B. Gershwin v. The Whole Thing Co.

A more complex example of a stage performance of music that was claimed to be unauthorized was the musical revue entitled, *Let's Call the Whole Thing Gershwin.*[10]

---

[10] *Gershwin v. The Whole Thing Co.,* 208 U.S.P.Q. (C.D. Cal., 1980).

The revue, created in 1978, consisted of theatrical performances of approximately forty songs, written entirely or largely by George and Ira Gershwin, and performed by a cast of eight actors and actresses wearing a variety of costumes and rendering some original dance routines and dance skits. The revue used some scenery such as photographs of the Gershwins and a limited amount of dialogue describing the Gershwins, their music, and the circumstances in which their works were created. The revue included an identifiable character, Ira Gershwin, who appears as a man struggling to write lyrics for brother George's music.

After deciding to produce the revue, the producer sought to obtain licenses from certain music publishers. Having obtained "living stage" licenses from the music publishers, the producer then proceeded on the assumption that a license from Mr. Gershwin was not required. When Mr. Gershwin's attorneys became aware of the fact that the producer was to stage the revue, they informed the producer that a license was required from Mr. Gershwin because, they asserted, the music publishers did not possess sufficient rights of copyright for the dramatic stage production of the revue and because Mr. Gershwin's rights of publicity would be invaded by the contemplated production. The producer asserted that its living stage licenses from the music publishers were sufficient and a license from Mr. Gershwin was not required.

After some negotiation, the parties entered into a settlement agreement which enabled the producer to stage the revue without a lawsuit. Nevertheless, after the production opened, a lawsuit ensued over extent of the rights granted under that agreement. The court granted a preliminary injunction halting the performance of the play beyond a certain date and ordered that the producer not engage in any further agreements for future presentations of the play beyond that date nor present the revue at any location other than at the theatre at which the revue was then being presented.

The legal question explored here is whether, in addition to the license the producer had received from the music publishing companies, a license from the Gershwins was required to produce the revue. Though that question was not specifically resolved by the court, the court's opinion is notable, because it is one of the few cases that attempts to define the term, *grand rights*.

What makes the analysis of this case so complex is the fact that, though some of the songs performed in the revue were originally part of a Gershwin musical or opera, such as *Lady Be Good*, and *Porgy and Bess*, others were not, such as the instrumental work, *Concerto in F.*

With respect to the compositions that were not originally part of a Gershwin musical play, the producer received all the licenses it needed under a living stage license that it received from the music publishers to use these songs in a musical revue on stage. Any non-dramatic renditions of the songs were covered by the theatre's performance licenses from ASCAP and BMI; any dramatic renditions (and any nondramatic renditions, to the extent the theatre was not licensed by the appropriate performance rights societies) were covered by the living stage licenses obtained from the music publishers.

With respect to the compositions that were originally part of a Gershwin musical, the producer only needed a license to the extent the performance would constitute an infringement of the musical or opera in which the songs originally appeared — that is, whether they are performed "in a manner which recreates the performance of such composition with substantially such distinctive scenery or costume *as was used in the presentation of* such opera, operetta, musical comedy, play or like production." To the extent the performances were not used in such manner, the producer could rely on the living stage license that it received from the music publishers.

It would not matter if the performers in the revue were wearing *any* kind of costumes or if the scenery used was *any* kind of scenery. The producer could avoid infringing the *grand right* in the grand operas and grand musical plays as long as the costumes were not from the operas and musicals and the scenery and other visual presentations from the Gershwin musicals and operas. In other words, the libretto, scenery and costumes of the original Gershwin shows form the basis of the *grand rights* the Gershwins have in those shows, not any new plot or unrelated scenery or costumes that may have been created for the revue.

Having seen the musical revue in question, we do not believe that any of the performances in *Let's Call the Whole Thing Gershwin* amounted to a performance that was substantially similar to any of the Gershwin musicals, or any substantial portion of them, in which certain songs in the revue were originally a part. The revue was a series of musical compositions interwoven into an original story that had no resemblance to any of the original musical plays in which the songs originally appeared. The only resemblance was in the fact that the performances in the revue, like some of the songs in the original plays, were rendered live on stage, but the producer already obtained the right to make such living stage performances of the music.

Accordingly, no grand right was invaded, and if the producer would have prevailed on the theory that the libretto was a constitutionally protected biographical work, then, assuming there was nothing in the agreement between the music publishers and the Gershwins reserving to the Gershwins living stage rights to their compositions, the living stage licenses the producer received from the music publishers would have been sufficient to permit performances of the revue and no further rights from the Gershwins were necessary.

We said the case was interesting for the definition it offered for the term *grand rights*:

> There are two basic tests to determine whether grand rights are required. Grand Rights are required if (1) a song is used to tell a story . . . or (2) a song is performed with dialogue, scenery or costumes.

The errors in this over-simplified statement of the definition of *grand rights* should be obvious at this point, and it is hoped that courts would pass over it in favor of a more precise analysis, such as that rendered in the MGM Grand case discussed previously.


## VII. GRAND RIGHT IN A PERSON'S LIFE STORY?

It may be recalled that one of the grounds that Ira Gershwin, by his attorneys, asserted to prevent the further performances of *Let's Call the Whole Thing Gershwin* is that the play infringed the right of publicity of George and Ira Gershwin. The *right of publicity* is the exclusive right a person has to exploit his or her name, likeness or photograph for commercial or advertising purposes.

A substantial body of law has evolved over the scope of one's right of publicity, including whether such a right survives a person's death and inures to the benefit of his estate. Over the past 50 years, the exclusive right of a person to commercially exploit his name and likeness has evolved through a number of court decisions, involving a number of well known celebrities, including Groucho Marx, Elvis Presley, and Nancy Sinatra. Initially, the courts recognized this commercial right as part of a person's *right to privacy*; later they began to separately identify a person's *right of publicity* and some states have since enacted legislation specifically governing the scope and duration of this right.[11]

A complete discussion of the right of publicity is beyond the scope of this book. Suffice it to say, however, that if you are seeking to clear permission to use a musical composition and you also desire to use the name, likeness or photograph of the songwriter or artist who recorded the work, you may be required to obtain a separate clearance for that use directly from the songwriter or artist.

The Gershwin case presented some interesting issues that have not been completely decided by the courts. One intriguing issue is the extent to which the right of publicity allows a person to control the use of biographical information about himself. Gershwin claimed that the use of the pictorial and biographical material about him, including the use of the name "Gershwin" in the title of the revue, *Let's Call the Whole Thing Gershwin*, required his permission. The use of such materials, his attorneys asserted, infringed upon Gershwin's right of publicity. In effect, Ira Gershwin was seeking to establish a form of *grand right* in his life story.

As previously noted, the courts have recognized a strong public policy interest in the free dissemination of ideas and information, a policy which finds its basis in the guarantee of free speech in the 1st Amendment of the U.S. Constitution. For this reason, public figures may not assert a *right of publicity* to prevent the publication of "unauthorized" biographies. It is possible, therefore, that the libretto of *Let's Call the Whole Thing Gershwin* would be deemed primarily biographical in nature and therefore, Gershwin's right of publicity would not have been an effective bar to allowing this information to be used as part of performances of the revue.

The line, however, between a person's name and likeness in a biographical work, the use of which does not require a license, and a

---

[11] *See, generally,* J.T. McCarthy, *The Rights of Publicity and Privacy* (1995).

person's name and likeness for commercial merchandising purposes, which does require a license, is not always an easy one to draw. Television or motion picture *docu-dramas*, which are based on biographical material, have been challenged as merchandising uses which require permission, on the basis that the fictional "pillow talk" dramatized in these productions does not even pretend to be historical fact, and is created not for historical or general interest, but merely for their entertainment value as fiction.

The issues relating to the right of publicity are complex, and your use of materials concerning celebrities or other public figures may also require a consideration of the law of libel and right of privacy. Accordingly, when treading this ground, you should seek counsel of an attorney experienced in these areas.

## VIII. BROADCAST OF AN ENTIRE ALBUM

### A. Operas

The *Jesus Christ Superstar* case discussed above — involving the stage performance of 20 of the 23 musical compositions from the opera, all but one rendered in identical sequence as in the original opera — raises another interesting question: Does a radio broadcast of an entire cast album of an opera involve more than the mere non-dramatic performance of the musical compositions in the play? In other words, would an unauthorized broadcast of an entire cast album of an opera constitute an infringement of the opera? The outcome of the *Jesus Christ Superstar* case suggests that the answer is yes.[12] The radio broadcast of an entire cast album of a grand opera would probably constitute a *grand performance* of the opera, requiring the permission of the owner of the *grand rights* in the opera. To be a grand performance, however, the broadcast would have to be of a substantial number of the songs in the opera in substantially the sequence that they appear in the opera.

---

[12] In fact, the court specifically suggested an affirmative answer to this question, but partly on the wrong basis: "Indeed, radio performances of operas are considered dramatic, because the story is told by the music and lyrics." 457 F.2d at 55 (1972).

## B.  Musical Plays

A different result may be reached if the broadcast were of an album of a musical play, rather than of an opera. It may be recalled that an *opera* is a play with virtually the entire text of its book, or libretto, set to music or sung, with no or few spoken words. By contrast, a *musical play* is a play with music and lyrics with the text of the book rendered in spoken form. Cast albums of musical plays rarely include all of the spoken text of the book. Accordingly, the broadcast of a cast album of a musical play is less likely to be deemed a grand performance of the musical play than the broadcast of a recording of an opera, because two important parts of the work — the visual presentation and the book — are absent from the performance. A recording of an opera, broadcast in its entirety, includes every element of the opera, except the visual presentation.

Nevertheless, while the broadcast of the cast album of a musical play will not usually constitute an infringement of the musical play, it may be an infringement of another copyright, which is discussed in the following section.

## C.  Other Albums

Owners of cast album recordings of musical plays, and, for that matter, owners of all other kinds of record albums — including pop, jazz, and rock recordings — may have an independent ground upon which to enforce an exclusive right to broadcast entire record albums. It has long been the position of the recording industry that the unauthorized broadcast of an entire record album, or substantially all of a record album, with no or few commercial interruptions, constitutes an infringement of copyright. The copyright that forms the basis of such infringement would be the *compilation* of the songs included on the album.

Under the copyright law, a *compilation* is "a work formed by the collection and assembling of preexisting materials or of data that are selected, coordinated, or arranged in such a way that the resulting work as a whole constitutes an original work of authorship."[13] If the selection and sequential ordering of the recordings on a record album

---

[13] 17 U.S.C. Sec. 101.

can be considered an original work of authorship, then the unauthorized public performance of the compilation, as a work separate and apart from the recordings that comprise the compilation, would constitute copyright infringement. Some record companies have filed copyright registrations to claim compilation copyrights in their selection and arrangement of recordings on the record albums they publish.

Though a compilation copyright in a record album, as a whole, is not a *grand right*, it is akin to a grand right and a performance of an entire record album, or substantially all of a record album, is akin to a grand performance of a grand opera or grand musical play.

## IX. DRAMATIC ADAPTATION RIGHTS

### A. Legal Background

The copyright law grants to the owner of copyright certain exclusive rights in a musical composition, among which, we have noted, are the exclusive right to make copies of the song (called the *reproduction right*), the exclusive right to perform the song (the *performance right*), and the exclusive right to prepare derivative works of the song, (often referred to as the *adaptation right*).

A copyright owner of a song may exercise his reproduction right by granting a license to allow another to reproduce the song in printed form (by a "print license") or on a record album (by a "mechanical license"). The copyright owner may exercise his performance right by allowing the rendition of the song in a nightclub or by broadcast on live television or radio. Both the reproduction right and the performance right involve the use of the musical composition verbatim — that is, the exercise of these rights involve permission to use the song word-for-word, note-for-note. By contrast, the *adaptation right* involves preparation of a different version of the song or the preparation of another work that is in some way derived from the song. A work that is derived from another work is called a *derivative work*. A copyright owner's exclusive right to prepare adaptations, or derivative works, is a most important right, because it defines the scope of the copyright protection. The copyright law contains a fairly precise definition of the term, derivative work:

A 'derivative work' is a work based upon one or more preexisting works, such as a translation, musical arrangement, dramatization, fictionalization, motion picture version, sound recording, art reproduction, abridgment, condensation, or any other form in which a work may be recast, transformed, or adapted.

Thus, when the music copyright owner commissions the translation of the lyrics of a song into a foreign language or the arrangement of the music for certain instruments, such as a big band arrangement, he is exercising his adaptation right — permitting the preparation of an adaptation or derivative work of the song.

## B. Popular Songs

A music copyright owner is also exercising his adaptation right when he allows another to make a dramatization, or dramatic adaptation, of the lyrics of a song. For example, the screenplay and motion picture entitled, *Ode to Billie Joe* was a dramatic adaptation of the song of the same title written and performed by country singer, Bobbie Gentry. Similarly, the 1970's television series *Harper Valley P.T.A.* was a dramatic adaptation of the lyrics of the song of the same name, written by Tom Hall and originally recorded by country singer Jeannie Riley.

The script of a motion picture that is derived from the lyrics of a song would be a "derivative" work of the song. The exclusive right *to prepare derivative works* is a right under copyright completely distinct from the right *to perform a work publicly*. While the singing of the song *Ode to Billie Joe* during the motion picture of that title is a *performance* and its licensing an exercise of the performance right in the song, the creation of the motion picture itself, which is *a dramatic adaptation* of the song, is an exercise of the adaptation right, not the performance right, in the song.

Therefore, neither the creation of the motion picture *Ode to Billie Joe* nor the script from which it is derived is a "performance" of the song. The performance of the movie involves a performance of the song only to the extent the song, as recorded in the soundtrack, is rendered during the performance of the movie. Thus, if one were to make a movie based upon the lyrics of a song — a dramatization or motion picture version of the song — without permission from the copyright owner of the song, the movie maker would be liable not for an unauthorized performance, but for violating the copyright owner's right to make derivative works of the song, that is, the copyright owner's dramatic adaptation right. The right of reproduction in the song would be violated if, and only if, a recording of the song were made part of the motion picture soundtrack without a license; the performance right in the song would be violated only if the sound track were performed in theatres without a license. The dramatization of the lyrics involves a separate exclusive right under the copyright — the adaptation right.

## C. Show Tunes

Suppose a producer wished to prepare a short movie dramatization of the song, *Tea For Two*, a song that was originally part of the Broadway musical, *No, No Nanette*. This movie might be a short love story about a young couple having tea together while discussing their desire to have a boy for her and a girl for him. As long as the movie dramatization of the lyrics did not use any elements of the show, *No, No Nanette* — such as dialogue, costumes, scenery or other visual representations from the musical — the grand rights in the musical would not be infringed. Accordingly, while the producer of the movie would require permission of the copyright owner of the song (i.e., the music publisher) to make the dramatic adaptation, no permission from the owners of the show *No, No Nanette* would be required for this use. Of course, if the song *Tea For Two* were to be performed in the movie, either on screen or as background music, or if any of the lyrics were to be quoted as part of the dialogue in the action, then a synchronization license would also be required.

## D. Music Videos

It may be interesting to note that some "new music" videos seen on television networks such as MTV may represent examples of dramatic adaptations. Though in many of these video programs, the featured musicians are seen performing the song on a stage or in the streets, some videos depict the performing artists visually portraying or acting out the story of the lyrics. If the visual scenario of the video is a direct dramatization of the song's lyrics, it would be considered a dramatic adaptation, or derivative work, of the song, the making of which, as we have said, requires separate permission from the song's copyright owner. If the artists are acting out a story, but the story is not the story told by the lyrics, the video would not be considered a derivative work, or dramatic adaptation of the song; however, if the song is otherwise interwoven into and carries forward some definite plot, the song is being performed dramatically, and the rendition of a dramatic performance also requires permission from the song's copyright owner.

## E. Separate Adaptation License Required

Whether or not a song was originally published as part of a dramatico-musical work, the performance licenses issued by performance rights societies would not cover the adaptation of the song *Ode to Billie Joe* or the song *Tea For Two* into a motion picture, or the song *Harper Valley P.T.A.* into a television series — not by virtue of the dramatic nature of the use, but by virtue of the fact that the uses are not performances. Since performance rights societies only license performances, and not the preparation of derivative works, performance licenses would not authorize the use.

Further, standard synchronization licenses permitting the producer to make reproductions of a recording of the song in timed-relation with audiovisual programs, such as motion pictures, television shows, and music videos, would not include permission to create a dramatic adaptation of the lyrics of the song. In fact, some carefully drafted synchronization licenses specifically exclude such uses by reference.

Accordingly, wherever a license to dramatize a lyric is desired, a separate license under the copyright owner's exclusive adaptation right will be required. Producers should not think they are acquiring such a right by merely obtaining a synchronization license or a performance license.

## F. Dramatic Adaptation Right Is Not a Grand Right

Dramatic adaptations of song lyrics have often been mistakenly associated with the concept of the grand right. As we have stated, the grand right is a performance right — a right in grand operas and musical plays, not in individual songs. Further, it is a right to *perform*. A *dramatic adaptation* is a derivative work of the lyrics of a song, whether or not the song was originally part of a musical play. A derivative work is a *work* — a new version of a song — not a *performance* of the song. Accordingly, the script and motion picture *Ode to Billie Joe*, for example, does *not* involve the exercise of a *grand right*. It is a new work, not a performance (and not a performance of a part of a grand opera or musical play).

## X. Determining Who Has the Right to License These Uses

Who has the right to license a particular use of music, depends upon (1) the proper identification of the rights on the basis of which licenses can be cleared for the use, and (2) the provisions of the contracts governing those rights among those that have an interest (i.e., copyright or contractual) in the music.

Despite the wide-spread confusion on the subject, it is important to correctly draw a distinction among small dramatic performances, small non-dramatic performances, grand performances, and dramatic adaptations. A proper distinction among these rights is often critical to determining what rights need to be cleared in order to render a dramatic or theatrical performance and who — among the performance rights societies, the songwriters, the playwrights, the music publishers, and the theatrical producers — has the right to license such uses.

### A. Nondramatic Performances

Under their respective agreements with performance rights societies, writers and publishers grant to the performance rights societies a license to sublicense the rendition of nondramatic performances.

If a song is being performed on a radio station, television station, or in a nightclub, concert hall, or other establishment licensed by the performance rights society, and the use is within the scope of the performance license, then no further license is required to render the performance. A use is outside of the performance license if the performance is dramatic, if the performance is a grand performance of a dramatico-musical work, or if the performance infringes upon any number of other rights of individuals, such as, for example, the right of publicity, the right of privacy, or the right not to be defamed.

The performance rights society has no right to grant licenses for uses that are outside the scope of their standard performance licenses and, accordingly, clearance to make any other use requires permission of some other person or organization who owns the right involved.

## B. Dramatic Performances

A *dramatic performance* of an individual composition is a rendition of a song that is woven into and carries forward a definite plot and its accompanying action, regardless of whether the song was originally part of a dramatico-musical work.

Under most standard music publishing agreements, the songwriter grants to the music publisher the undivided copyright in the song. The grant includes a grant of all exclusive rights, including the exclusive right to grant dramatic performance licenses. The only licenses that the songwriter is authorized to grant are those that are specifically reserved to the songwriter in the music publishing contract. The exclusive right to license dramatic performances are not typically among the rights reserved to the writer. The only right typically reserved to the writer is the right to receive the writer's share of performance royalties directly from the writer's performance rights society (e.g., ASCAP or BMI), a right which the writer receives from his performance rights society when he becomes a member. Since the rights the writer retains is limited to the right to grant licenses for non-dramatic performances, the rights to grant licenses to dramatic performances are vested in the music publisher under the broad grant of rights typically made in standard songwriter contracts. Consequently, with respect to most songs that were not originally part of musical plays or other dramatico-musical works, it is the music publisher who is exclusively entitled to grant permission for dramatic performances of the song.

Some songwriter contracts, however, require that the publisher obtain the writer's consent before granting dramatic performance licenses. Such a requirement appears in the standard form contract recommended by the Songwriter's Guild (formerly AGAC). The Songwriter's Guild agreement does not empower the writer to grant dramatic performance licenses; only the publisher has the power to grant such licenses, but the issuance of such licenses requires the consent of the songwriter.

Unless the agreement between the writer and his publisher specifically reserves to the writer the right to license dramatic performances of the composition, or reserves for the writer a right of approval over such dramatic uses, the publisher has the sole right as between the parties to license such rights.

## C. Dramatic Adaptations

As stated above, songwriters typically grant their undivided interest in the copyright in the song to their music publishers, reserving only the rights related to collecting the writer's share of performance fees for the rendition of non-dramatic performances, which the writer receives from his performance right society. All other rights reside with the music publisher, subject, of course, to the payment of royalties to the writer arising from revenues associated with the exercise of the rights assigned to the music publisher. Thus, the music publisher is typically vested with the exclusive right to license dramatizations, or dramatic adaptations, and other derivative works.

Unless the songwriter's contract provided otherwise, the music publisher would have the sole right as between the songwriter and the music publisher to license dramatic adaptations of the writer's lyrics in any manner and by any means. It will be recalled that a dramatization is a derivative work, not a type of performance. Even if a songwriter contract specifically reserves to the writer the right to license dramatic performances, or reserves to the songwriter the right of consent to the publisher's granting of dramatic performances, this has no affect on the publisher's exclusive right to prepare or license the preparation by others of derivative works, such as dramatizations of lyrics.

Some music publishing agreements provide that the publisher's right to license dramatizations is subject to the consent of the songwriter. Again, such a provision would not give the writer the right to grant dramatic performance licenses; the publisher has the sole power to grant such licenses, but the issuance of such licenses requires the consent of the songwriter.

## D. Grand Performances

As we have said, the *grand right* is the exclusive right to license the reproduction, adaptation, performance or other use of a dramatico-musical work, or what was once known as a "grand opera" or "grand musical play." It is a *right in the play, not in the music*, although the play may include music. The *grand right* rests with the owner of the play, not in the owner of the individual compositions in the play.

Accordingly, if you intend to clear a license to render a *grand performance* of a musical play, or a substantial, recognizable portion of the play, then you require permission from the owner of the musical play. If you intend to clear a license to render a *dramatic performance* of an individual composition, which is a rendition of a song (regardless of whether the song was originally part of a dramatico-musical work) that is woven into and carries forward a definite plot and its accompanying action, then you will require permission from the copyright owner of the song.

## XI. LICENSING CONSIDERATIONS

### A. Considerations in Granting and Clearing Dramatic Performance Licenses

A producer who desires to render a performance of music that is interwoven into and carries forward a definite plot and its accompanying action should take care to obtain the additional licenses necessary to effect the desired use. If the use was properly disclosed at the time the producer seeks a synchronization license, an alert music publisher will recognize that a dramatic performance will also be required for the use.

Because of the infinite variety of ways a song may be dramatically rendered in another work, there are no special standards for determining just how a music copyright owner might arrive at a fee in exchange for permitting the performance. However, copyright owners might use the same considerations for approaching grants of dramatic performance licenses as the considerations they might use relating to the licensing of reproductions of their musical compositions in similar works. These considerations are discussed in Chapters 10 (Basic Considerations), 14 (Synchronization Licenses), 15 (Videogram Licenses), and 22 (Licenses for Computer Software, Multi-Media Programs, and New Media Devices). By the same token, the producer might use the considerations for clearing licenses set forth in those same chapters.

The parties should analyze the use carefully to be sure the use does not fall within the scope of what might be considered a dramatic adaptation, some licensing considerations for which are discussed briefly below.

## B.  Considerations in Granting and Clearing Adaptation Licenses

When a music copyright owner is asked to consider granting a license allowing another to prepare a dramatic adaptation of a song's lyrics (e.g., a motion picture adaptation of the lyrics of *Ode to Billie Joe* or a television adaptation of the lyrics of *Harper Valley P.T.A.*), the copyright owner should immediately do the following: view the lyrics as a literary work.

The considerations for licensing an audiovisual adaptation of a literary work should be viewed much the same way an author of a novel would consider the licensing of a motion picture or television adaptation of his work. There are many issues the music copyright owner should thoughtfully consider, including the negotiations of payments for options that expire if the adaptation is not made within specified periods of time, the disposition of rights and revenues in the event that other adaptations or new versions are made subsequent to the release of the first (e.g, sequels, "pre-quels," remakes, spin-offs, and the like), profit participations, credit for the songwriters, and other terms that are customarily negotiated in literary rights contracts. Producers of motion pictures and television programs are generally quite familiar with the issues relating to literary rights acquisitions.

A further analysis of the issues that should be considered in connection with these deals is beyond the scope of this book. The music copyright owner should consider obtaining the special assistance of a literary agent or an attorney who specializes in representing authors who frequently license their literary works for dramatic adaptations.

## C.  Considerations in Granting and Clearing Grand Performances

The considerations in granting and clearing the right to perform musical plays, operas, and other dramatico-musical works in their entirety are beyond the scope of this book. Nevertheless, a few important comments relating to the licensing of *portions of* dramatico-musical works is in order..

When play producers and their agents are asked to consider granting a license to use a small portion of their works, such as a few moments of a musical play in a television program or multi-media work, they might use the same considerations in approaching such grants as those concerning the licensing of reproductions of music compositions set forth in Chapters 10 (Basic Considerations), 14 (Synchronization Licenses), 15 (Videogram Licenses), and 22 (Licenses for Computer Software, Multi-Media Programs, and New Media Devices).

An owner of a musical play who has granted to a music publisher the music publishing rights in and to the individual musical compositions in the play should keep in mind that his right to license reproductions and performances of the musical play is limited to the dramatico-musical play itself and does not extend to the individual songs themselves. Musical play owners, or their agents, may grant, for example, grand performances of the play. This may include a performance of one or more musical compositions from the play, but only to the extent the performance contains elements taken directly from the musical play (e.g., dialogue, pantomime, dance, stage action, costumes, scenery, or other visual representations). If the performance of the music does not contain any such element taken from the musical play, then the right of performance is not controlled by the owner of the musical play, even if the performance contains other dramatic or visual elements. Where the performance of the music does not contain dramatic elements from the musical play, then, unless there are provisions to the contrary in any agreement between the play owners and the music publisher, the right of performance is controlled by the owner of the music publishing rights. In other words, the music publisher has the sole right to license non-dramatic performances through its performance rights society and dramatic performances directly, provided the performance does not contain any elements from the play that would render the performance a grand performance (the latter of which would require permission from the owner of the play).

## XII. RECOMMENDATIONS AND SUMMARY

As noted in Chapter 7, on *The Language of Music Licensing*, words that refer to completely different concepts should not be confused or used indiscriminately. Greater precision in the use of terms of art will promote clarity of thought and avoid costly legal disputes. It is important to correctly draw distinctions among grand rights, dramatic rights, and dramatic adaptation rights, so that all parties concerned can properly determine who has the right to license the proposed use.

To that end, the authors make the following recommendations:

1. Avoid using the term *dramatic right*, which leaves an ambiguity as to whether it denotes a performance right or an adaptation right. In its place, use phrases such as, *dramatic performance right* or *dramatic adaptation right*, as the situation warrants. Likewise, when granting a license under these rights, state, "a license to render a dramatic performance" or "a license to make a dramatic adaptation."

2. The industry should embrace the definition of *dramatic performance* found in the ASCAP Publisher/Writer agreement, with the following modification: strike the words "on a television program." Do not use the definition of dramatic performance in the ASCAP general license, which confounds the concepts of dramatic performances of music with grand performances of musical productions.

3. Use the term *grand right* only when the song was originally part of a dramatico-musical work (grand opera or grand musical play).

4. The next revision of ASCAP and BMI licenses should be redrafted to recognize the difference between dramatic performances of songs and grand performances of songs originally part of grand operas and grand musical plays.

Finally, it is not the practice of music publishers to represent or warrant that they are providing a license that is sufficient for the producer to render the desired performance. If the producer intends to render a grand performance, or a performance that infringes on another's right of publicity, invades someone's privacy, or defames someone's reputation, it is the producer's responsibility to properly clear all permissions that he requires to proceed with the performance. The producer is in a better position than the publisher to know just how the performance will be rendered, and, thus, whether the performance would infringe a grand right, or some other right, such as the laws of defamation or invasion of privacy. All the music publisher can do is provide the producer with the license to do what the publisher would otherwise have the right to stop the producer from doing, such as synchronizing the song in an audiovisual work.

Sometimes the producer can avoid problems by telling the music publisher precisely how he intends to use the music. The publisher might be able to provide additional information about other licenses the producer may require to effect the use, but the music publisher cannot be expected to guarantee that the license it grants covers all the permissions that are required for the use.

# Appendix to Chapter 18
# Grand Rights Controversy

# Form 18.1

## License to Perform Music in a Live Stage Production

January 1, 2000

RE:   LIVING STAGE LICENSE

Dear [Producer]:

We hereby grant you, your associates, licensees and assigns the non-exclusive right and license to perform the musical composition:

in the living stage performance of your production:

by the original company, subject to the following terms and conditions:

1.    This license is non-exclusive and is deemed to have commenced upon the first preview performance.

2.    The territory covered by this license is:

3.    The extent of use shall be as follows:

4.    As consideration for this license, you agree to pay a fee of:

      a)    A royalty rate of __ Percent (__%) of the gross receipts pro-rated amongst all copyrighted songs used, but never less than:

      On-Broadway (500 seats or more) Per Song, Per Week:

Off-Broadway (499 seats or less): Per Song, Per Week:

b)     Twenty-Five Dollars ($25.00) per week or Five Dollars ($5.00) per performance, whichever is greater, for amateur and stock productions and "off-off" Broadway (200 seats or less) performances.

c)     Production Use: (First class legitimate stage production). In the event any one song controlled by Big Music Publishing Corp. is used exclusively in a production number lasting over five (5) minutes in length, a fee of Two-Hundred-Fifty-Dollars ($250.00) per week will be required, separate and in addition to the fee covering the licensed use of the same song.

5.     This license shall automatically terminate in the event of your failure to pay us the weekly license fee as and when due, or in the event that the first preview performance does not take place within six (6) months from the date of this license.

6.     You agree that prior to the opening of each road-company of players performing in said production incorporating the musical composition licensed hereunder, you will notify us thereof and upon our receipt of such notice, such additional company of players shall be encompassed by this license and subject to its terms and conditions.

7.     No warranty or representation is made in connection with this license except that we warrant we have the right to issue this license subject to the terms and conditions hereof. In any event the total liability under such warranty is limited to the amounts paid by you hereunder.

8.     All programs shall indicate the names of the writers of the composition and shall clearly indicate the use is by permission of BIG MUSIC PUBLISHING CORP.

9. For each New York City and Los Angeles performance of the Show, you shall cause two (2) adjoining "house" seats in the first ten (10) rows of the center section of the orchestra to be held available at the box office, for us and our designee to purchase, at the box office price. Such tickets shall be so held until 6:00 P.M. of the day prior to the performance for evening performances and 12:00 noon of the day prior to the performance of matinees.

10. In the event you license the production for presentation in motion pictures, radio, television, original cast album or any other audio/visual format, any such license shall not include a license to use the Composition in connection therewith, it being understood and agreed that we reserve all such rights. Nevertheless, we agree to negotiate in good faith with any licensee or potential licensee of the Show in respect of the appropriate synchronization, recording and/or performance licenses for the Composition. All Royalties, license fees or other compensation derived by us in connection with any such licenses which may be entered into by us and all royalties and other monies received from uses of the Composition in accordance with any such licenses, including mechanical royalties, sums derived from performing rights societies, etc. shall, as between us, be our sole property and you shall not be entitled to share in any such sums. Similarly, we shall not be entitled to share in any such licensing of your rights for presentation of the Show in such media.

11. One year after the initial performance of your production, we shall have the continuing right to terminate the rights granted to you herein by giving written notice of our intention to terminate at least ninety (90) days prior to the termination date.

12. You agree to maintain accurate books and records in connection with said production, which books and records shall, upon reasonable notice, be available for examination by

our representatives during the term of this agreement and for a period of two (2) years therefrom.

13.    All rights not specifically granted herein are reserved to and by us.

BIG MUSIC PUBLISHING CORP.

AGREED AND ACCEPTED:

By _____

By _____

# FORM 18.2

## LICENSE TO PERFORM MUSIC IN LIVE STAGE PERFORMANCE OF CHOREOGRAPHY

January 1, 2000

RE:    CHOREOGRAPHY LICENSE

Gentlemen:

1.    We hereby grant you the non-exclusive right to create choreography for use in conjunction with the following musical compositions and to use said choreography subject to the terms and conditions herein contained:

2.    You agree to pay us a royalty of $5.00 per song for each performance containing performance of any of said choreography during the term of this license.

3.    The term of this license shall be one year from the date of first performance which shall be _____.

4.    The territory of this license is limited to the United States and Canada.

5.    You shall not have the right to print, copy, arrange or adapt any of said musical compositions or the right to record on phonograph records, tape, film or any other form of record any of said musical compositions, without further permission.

6.    You agree that on all programs and advertising matter and announcements a note will appear as follows under the title of each of said musical compositions:

Music Used for Choreography by Permission of Big Music Publishing Corp.

7.   You shall account to us at the end of each month during the term hereof in which performances are given, giving us a detailed statement as to the place and the number of performances and pay to us at the same time the royalties provided for in this agreement.

8.   The rights granted herein are personal to you and may not be assigned or sub-licensed.

9.   All other rights in said musical compositions are reserved to us.

If the foregoing correctly sets forth our understanding, kindly sign and return a copy of this letter.

Yours sincerely,                    Agreed and Accepted:

By: _____        By: _____

# FORM 18.3

## COLLABORATION AGREEMENT
## AMONG WRITERS OF A MUSICAL PLAY

### COLLABORATION AGREEMENT

AGREEMENT made this          day of June          , 2000, between

(hereinafter "      ") and

(hereinafter "         ").

WHEREAS,                   and                  are collaborating in the writing of a dramatic-musical play presently entitled " " (the "Play"), and

WHEREAS, the parties desire to define their rights and responsibilities with respect to the Play.

NOW, THEREFORE, in consideration of the mutual covenants herein contained, it is agreed as follows:

1.    The parties hereto shall undertake jointly to write the Play, it being understood that        shall be the bookwriter and lyricist and                shall be the composer.

2.    Each of the parties hereto shall undertake to copyright the material written by him.

3.    (a)    Except as specifically set forth in Paragraph 3(b) hereof, all receipts and income from the Play, or from any and all rights therein, shall be divided as follows:

To                    %

To                    %

     (b)    The authors' share of publishing income from the musical compositions used in the Play shall be divided as follows:

To                    %

To                    %.

The parties hereto agree that the music publisher for the musical compositions in the Play will be                    , a New York corporation controlled by                    . Notwithstanding anything contained herein to the contrary, the parties hereto agree that _____ will be entitled to receive 100% of the music publisher's share of music publishing income.

    4.    It is the intention of the parties that the Play shall initially be presented as a first-class Broadway production in New York City.    shall use his best efforts to arrange for a first-class Broadway production of the Play.                    shall have the right to arrange for a first-class Broadway production of the Play; however,                    agrees to obtain prior approval of any such efforts on his part, in order to avoid confusion or duplication of efforts. Each of the parties hereto agree to keep the other fully informed of the progress of all negotiations with respect thereto, but the final decision should vest with

    5.    (a)    After the Play is completed, if deems it necessary to engage another writer or writers to make changes in the Play, he shall have the right so to do. Such new writer or writers shall only be chosen with                    consent. In such event, the percentage compensation payable to the new writer or writers shall be borne by                    . If there is a dispute with respect to the amount thereof, it shall be resolved in accordance with the provisions of Paragraph 13 hereof.

(b)    In the event of the disability or death of    , the parties hereto agree that any new writer or writers engaged to make changes in the Play will be entitled to receive percentage compensation payable from                          share. The parties hereto agree that the difference between the new writer(s)' percentage compensation and                original royalty shall be payable to          heirs. In the event of the death or disability of          shall have the sole approval regarding any new writer or writers engaged to make changes in the Play.

6.    (a)    Except as specifically set forth in Schedule A, annexed hereto and made a part of this Agreement, represents and warrants that his contributions to the book and lyrics of the Play will be wholly original with him and that he is and will be the sole author thereof, and that no incident therein or part thereof is taken from, based upon or adapted from any other literary material, dramatic work, motion picture or other work of any kind, nature or description not in the public domain.
agrees to obtain all necessary clearances for any of the materials listed in Schedule A.

(b)    represents and warrants that his contributions to the music of the Play are and will be wholly original and he is and will be the sole composer thereof and no part thereof is or will be taken from, based upon or adapted from any other musical composition or other work of any kind, nature or description not in the public domain.

7.    The parties hereto agree that all rights in and to any music and lyrics which shall be deleted from the Play prior to the official opening performance of the first class Broadway production of the Play in New York City, shall revert to the respective parties hereto for their use free from any claim by the other; provided, however, that

shall not have any right to use or authorize the use of any such lyrics which shall:

(i)    refer to any character in the Play by the same name as the character in the Play, if the name is sufficiently distinctive to identify with the Play, or

(ii)    depict or portray an important situation which is contained in the Play; or

(iii)    contain any of the distinctive dialogue or distinctive phrases from the Play; or

(iv)    have as their title the name of any character in or to the title of the Play if such name is sufficiently distinctive to identify with the Play.

8.    All artistic approvals regarding the Play shall be exercised by the mutual decision of            and            ; provided, however, that alterations and omissions from, or additions to, the book and/or lyrics of the Play shall be subject to

approval; and alterations in and omissions from, or additions to, the book and/or lyrics of the Play shall be subject to            approval.

9.    Each of the parties hereto agree that they shall each incur their own expenses in connection with the Play and will not look to the other for payment or reimbursement of such expenses.

10.    hereby irrevocably appoints            as his sole and exclusive agent with respect to this Agreement and authorizes and directs

and/or any other third party to make all payments due or to become due to him hereunder to and in the name of said agent and to accept the receipt of said payments. In consideration of services rendered and to be rendered by said agent, agrees that            is entitled to receive and maintain as his commission 10% of all such monies due and owing to him hereto, except with respect to amateur rights his commission shall be 20%. As of the date of this contract,          is not represented by an agent; however, he shall be free to select an agent to represent him and in such event all payments due shall be paid to such designated agent.

11.    Authors' billing shall be substantially as follows:


Books and Lyrics                    Music

        by                              by

Both of the aforesaid names shall be in the same size, type, color, prominence and boldness, and whenever one name appears, the other shall appear. In the event a new writer or writers is brought in pursuant to Paragraph 5 (a) above, the parties agree to adjust the aforesaid billing accordingly. In the event a new writer or writers is brought in pursuant to Paragraph 5 (b) above,          shall adjust the billing accordingly.

12.    The term of this agreement shall be coextensive with life of the copyright, and any renewals of said copyright in and to the book, music and lyrics of the Play.

13.    In the event of any dispute arising out of or under this agreement or concerning the Play, or should any differences arise between the parties concerning any dealings between them or as to any of their rights hereunder (whether pursuant to Paragraph 3 and 11 hereof, or otherwise,) such dispute or differences shall be submitted to arbitration by a single arbitrator in New York under the Rules then obtaining of the American Arbitration Association, and the decision of such arbitrator shall be final and binding upon the parties hereto.

14.    The terms and conditions of this agreement shall be binding upon and inure to the benefit of the executors, administrators, and assigns of the parties hereto. This agreement may

not be modified orally, and shall be construed in accordance with the laws of the State of New York.

IN WITNESS WHEREOF, we have hereunto set our hands and seals the day and year first above written.

_____

_____

CHAPTER 19

# THEME PARKS AND ATTRACTIONS

SUMMARY

I. LEGAL BACKGROUND

II CONSIDERATIONS IN GRANTING LICENSES FOR
   THE USE OF MUSIC IN THEME PARKS AND
   ATTRACTIONS

CHAPTER **19**

# THEME PARKS AND ATTRACTIONS

**M**any major motion picture studios and entertainment conglomerates have established or purchased amusement or theme parks in the United States and abroad. Walt Disney pioneered the concept with his famous *Disneyland* theme park in Southern California and later established *DisneyWorld* in Florida. Universal Pictures opened its studios to private and later public tours, and now the *Universal Studio Tour* is a major theme park in its own right. Time Warner acquired *Six Flags Magic Mountain.* Originally an amusement park, *Six Flags* now offers many theme attractions in its many locations. Thinking that it as a small world after all, Disney then opened versions of its *Disneyland* theme park in Japan and in Europe.

Each of these theme parks has rides and attractions that use music. For example, *Disneyland* offers a *Raiders of the Lost Ark* attraction featuring music from the soundtrack of the *Indiana Jones* movie series. Music from Warner Bros. Pictures's *Bugs Bunny* cartoons and the *Superman* movies are being used in attractions in the theme parks operated by Time Warner. At Universal Studios in Hollywood, the Universal Pictures hit film, *Jurassic Park* has become the theme of an attraction known as, *Jurassic Park, the Ride.* Characters from Disney's *Beauty and the Beast* have also been combined with portions of the motion picture score in attractions, audioanimatronic shows, and live stage shows performed in each of the Disney theme parks.

This chapter analyzes the legal background of licensing music in theme parks and attractions and sketches the emerging licensing practices arising from such uses.

## I. LEGAL BACKGROUND

As discussed in Chapter 18, on *The Grand Rights Controversy,* performance rights societies do not license music in performances that are anything other than nondramatic performances. To engage in the dramatic performance or to create a dramatic adaptation of a copyrighted song, you must obtain permission from the music publisher.

To summarize briefly, a *nondramatic performance* is a performance of a musical composition that is not woven into or does not carry forward a definite plot and its accompanying action. Conversely, a *dramatic performance* is a performance of a song that is woven into and carries forward a definite plot and its accompanying action. For example, the use of the musical title theme from the motion picture, *Raiders of the Lost Ark* in a ride at *Disneyland* that employs the images, sounds and effects of the motion picture of that name, is a dramatic performance of the song. As thin as it may be, the ride indeed has a plot, or at least the requisite element of drama, for the performance of the song to be considered dramatic. Similarly, the use of the music from the film *Jurassic Park* in *"Jurassic Park, the Ride,"* in which visitors are frightened with images of dinosaurs and their associated sounds and effects, would also be a dramatic performance of the song.

Accordingly, the theme park, Disneyland and Universal Studios, in these examples, could not rely merely on the blanket licenses they obtained from the performance rights societies, such as ASCAP and BMI in the United States, to cover these uses. They must obtain dramatic performance licenses from the music publishers of the songs.

The same would be true if the ride or attraction was a dramatic adaptation (e.g., creating an attraction out of the lyrics of a song) or the exercise of a grand right in a musical play (e.g., a ride or attraction that combines the performance of a song with the scenes of a play or similar work in which the song was originally an integral part). In either event, the important point is that if the use is not strictly a nondramatic performance, then engaging in the use will require something other than a blanket license from a performance rights society and that license must be obtained from the copyright owner of the song.

## II. CONSIDERATIONS IN GRANTING LICENSES FOR THE USE OF MUSIC IN THEME PARKS AND ATTRACTIONS

A theme park operator, or a producer of a ride or attraction, who desires to render a dramatic performance of music as part of the ride or attraction, should take care to obtain the necessary license for the use. Of course, the theme park should try to obtain as broad a license as possible. We have seen a request as broad as the following:

> "to use the song in any "Company-owned, Company-operated or Company-licensed theme park, including resorts, attractions, entertainment centers (including, without limitation, any so-called location based entertainment venues), restaurants, hotels, cruise ships, cruise ship ports and destinations, retail or other facility, as well as any advertising and promotion in connection therewith in perpetuity, throughout the universe."

The theme park operator might offer a one-time flat fee for perpetual use of the song in the attraction. He also might ask to have that fee cover the use of the music in any promotions for the attraction. For use in any live stage show at the theme park, the theme park operator might offer an additional one time flat fee.

Because of the infinite variety of ways a song may be rendered in a ride or attraction, there are no special standards for determining just how a music copyright owner might arrive at a fee in exchange for permitting the performance. A copyright owner would use the same considerations for approaching grants of dramatic performance licenses as the considerations they might use in considering licensing of music in other reproductions. Thus, a sophisticated music publisher would resist one time buy-out fees. However, it may be difficult to collect a royalty, as few theme parks charge separately for admission to specific attractions.

Thus, a good compromise might be to charge a flat fee payable on an annual basis for as long as the attraction is operating. A music publisher might charge separately for each venue of the attraction, and the theme park operator may wish to negotiate in advance an option to add new venues as required. For live stages shows, the copyright owner might ask for a flat amount per week for the run of the show. For details on current fees, please see Chapter 27 on *Typical License Fees*.

# TELEVISION, RADIO, AND PRINT ADVERTISING

## SUMMARY

### I. INDUSTRY BACKGROUND

### II. CONSIDERATIONS IN GRANTING AND CLEARING LICENSES TO USE MUSIC IN ADVERTISING

A. Fee Structure

B. The Value of the Song

   1. Nature of the Product or Service

   2. Reluctance to License

   3. Overcoming Reluctance

C. The Importance of the Song in Relation to Its Intended Use

   1. Nature of the Product or Service

   2. Nature of the Use

   3. Use of Original Recordings

   4. Use of Sound-alike Recordings

   5. Lyric Changes

   6. Use of the Song's Title

D. Scope of the Intended Use

   1. Media and Distribution Channels

   2. Term

   3. Territory

   4. Exclusivity

### III. PRINT ADVERTISING

### APPENDIX TO CHAPTER 20

CHAPTER **20**

# TELEVISION, RADIO, AND PRINT ADVERTISING

T he convergence of radio and television with the commercial
advertising industry has created one of the most lucrative markets for the licensing of music. This chapter will explore the
considerations in licensing music in radio, television, and print advertising.

## I. INDUSTRY BACKGROUND

Advertisers and the advertising agencies that represent them both
recognize and appreciate the great value that music adds to commercial advertising. Music plays an important role in setting the mood
and enhancing the memorability of the commercial message. Advertising experts have shown that with short commercials — in 30-second
and 15-second lengths — music becomes even more important, because of the music's ability to quickly set the mood and convey information about the product.

In producing a radio or television commercial, an advertising
agency has several alternatives in considering the application of music
to its client's commercial message. The agency may hire a composer
to write a song specially created for the commercial, called a commercial *jingle*, or it may license an established, popular song. The
agency might use music without lyrics, use an instrumental version
of a song that originally had lyrics, modify a song's lyrics, or create
new lyrics to suit the commercial message.

Increasingly, agencies and advertisers have been deciding to use
established, popular songs, rather than having new ones custom made,
to sell a product. Popular songs are already known to the audience,
so the advertiser does not have to wait for the tunes to catch on with
its audience, as he does with music created just for the advertising.

1109

Also, advertisers have become increasingly sophisticated in directing their messages to specific target audiences. Hit music of the 1950's and early 1960's, for example, can be quite effective in advertising that is targeted to reach the post World War II baby-boom generation. With an established song, an advertiser can capitalize on the customer's identification with a familiar song to improve the customer's continued recall of the product. Although creating a jingle or a new song tailored to an advertisement provides the advertiser with certain flexibility, it's hard to compete with a great, standard song, especially if the song already says a lot of things that the advertiser wants to say.

## II. CONSIDERATIONS IN GRANTING AND CLEARING LICENSES TO USE MUSIC IN ADVERTISING

### A. Fee Structure

The fee structure of the typical commercial synchronization license is a one-time, flat fee for the term of the license, with additional fees payable on any extensions to the term or expansion of the territory. These fees vary greatly and are subject to negotiation. Typical fees charged at the time of this writing for the use of music in commercial advertising are set forth in Chapter 27.

As with synchronization licenses for motion pictures and television programs and electrical transcriptions for radio programs, commercial synchronization licenses do not permit the *performance* of music; accordingly, separate performance fees are payable by radio and television stations that broadcast performances of commercials containing copyrighted music.

### B. The Value of the Song

#### 1. *Nature of the Product or Service*

Publishers and writers should consider the possibility that associating a hit song with a commercial product might harm the future earning potential of the song. A song that has become associated with a particular product in the mind of consumers may become less attractive to recording artists considering whether to include a song on a new album, to producers considering the use of the music in a motion picture, or to other advertisers considering the use of the music in connection with another product. For this reason, a publisher will charge a *premium* (i.e., higher than average fee) if he believes that an identification with a specific product might adversely affect the song's future mechanical, synchronization, or commercial advertising revenues. In addition, a publisher would be warranted in demanding a premium if the song has never before been made available for use in commercial advertising.

### 2. Reluctance to License

Because they understand and appreciate the maturing life of their copyright, older composers, and the surviving family of deceased composers, tend to make no objection to, and often encourage, the exploitation of their musical compositions in commercial advertising. It remains a mystery why many contemporary artists have an aversion to permitting the use of their music in commercial advertising. Where these artists have the right to approve such uses in their music publishing contracts, they tend to deny approval. If an artist's song should fall into disuse, the value of the copyright will decline over time, along with the number of people who may still remember it. Modern artists who find their popularly on the wane will soon regret their decision to withhold their approval of licensing their music for commercial purposes. A more prudent course would be to take the long term view and recognize the importance of licensing music in advertising.

### 3. Overcoming Reluctance

An advertiser who comes across a copyright owner who is reluctant to license music for commercial advertising should remind the copyright owner of the revenues arising from the public performances of the music. The performance royalties earned from a performing rights society (e.g., ASCAP, BMI) on public performances of the commercial on radio and television can be substantial and will act as a multiplier on the synchronization license fee. The use of music in commercials will also maintain that special relationship between a song and the listening public. This is particularly important with respect to older songs, such as, those songs written in the 1930s and 1940s, as well as songs written more recently, including songs written in the 1950s and 1960s. As the public gets older, unless there is some medium through which the song is continually exposed to the public — such as the classic movie, *Casablanca*, which features the standard song, *As Time Goes By* — there will be, as time goes by, fewer and fewer people who will recognize and appreciate the song. Maintaining continual exposure through commercial advertising will likely lead to other uses of the song by new generations.

If the copyright owner otherwise willing to grant a license for a commercial advertising use informs you that he is unable to obtain the consent of the songwriter for the use you are requesting, (i) you should not blame your troubles on the music publisher (who is probably just as frustrated as you are) and (ii) you should attempt to approach the artist or the artist's representatives directly to determine just what the specific objection is and how you can overcome it. If the objections cannot be overcome, you should ask the publisher to recommend another song in his catalog that would serve as an adequate substitute for your needs.

## C. The Importance of the Song in Relation to Its Intended Use

### 1. Nature of the Product or Service

The central question an advertiser will be asked concerns the nature of the product or service the song will be used to promote. By first asking the reason a particular song was chosen, the music copyright owner may discover the importance of the song in relation to its intended commercial use, and thereby find a reason to ask for a premium for the use.

Sometimes a variety of songs may fit the need of the advertiser. For example, a commercial bank producing a television commercial may desire to use, *We're In the Money*. Should that song not be available, the bank may well use in its place, *Pennies From Heaven*, or *With Plenty of Money and You*. When a variety of substitutes are available, a premium fee will be difficult to obtain.

Every once in a while, however, one, and only one, particular song will best fit the message of the advertiser. That just may have been the case when an advertiser selected the song, *Anticipation* by Carly Simon for television advertisements of Heinz catsup to help dramatize the "anticipation" on the faces of people as they wait for the thick, tasty concoction of tomatoes and 57 varieties of spices to slowly come dripping out of the bottle. It would be difficult to imagine a more fitting song for the commercial.

The more closely a song is related to the message of the advertising campaign, the less likely it is that close substitutes for the song are available to the advertiser, and the higher the license fee the publisher can command. Even when only one song will do, however, an advertiser may consider using an old negotiating technique when haggling over the license fee: tell the copyright owner that the music is only one of several, alternative songs under consideration. It may be an old ploy,[1] but it often works.

### 2.   Nature of the Use

Some of the same questions relevant in granting a synchronization license for the use of music in motion pictures and television programs will also apply here. For example, whether the music is to be used in a vocal rendition or merely instrumental; whether the music is used as background music or foreground music; whether the intended use relates to how the composition was originally presented to the public; and whether the music is used to help tell the story, or in the case with commercials, directly used to help promote the product or just used to set the mood. As with synchronization licenses, a foreground use will generally command a higher license fee than a background use.

Some licenses specify the length and number of the commercials in which the music is licensed. For example, a license might limit the use to "a maximum of three thirty-second television commercials" or "one fifteen second radio commercial." Most advertisers, however, desire a greater amount of flexibility in producing differing versions of a commercial, particularly those used in extensive national advertising campaigns. Publishers would generally have no objection to providing such flexibility, provided the boundaries of the use are specified in the license. Commercial synchronization licenses generally have no limitation on the number of times a commercial may be

---

[1] *See, for example,* Stendhal, *The Red and the Black,* Ch. 5, "Coming to Terms" (1830).

broadcast during the term of the license. This lack of a limitation is for good reason: as far as the publisher is concerned, the more times a commercial is broadcast, the more performance royalties the publisher is likely to earn. This underscores the role commercial advertising plays in generating and sustaining the performance royalties and license terms should be crafted to recognize this.

### 3. Use of Original Recordings

If the producer desires to use an original sound recording in the commercial, he would normally be required to obtain a separate license to do so from the owner of the recording, such as a record company. If the original hit version is being licensed, a music publisher, having recognized the advertiser's acute interest in a particular recording, may quote a higher fee.

### 4. Use of Sound-alike Recordings

To protect the music copyright owners against claims by recording artists and other entertainers from tortious claims concerning unauthorized use of their "name, voice, or likeness," publishers are advised to include a prohibition in their commercial synchronization licenses against the use of *sound-alike* recordings. These are recordings in which professional singers and studio musicians perform the composition in such a manner as to imitate or simulate an earlier recorded performance of the composition by an artist who may have made a distinctive popular recording of the song. Prohibiting the use of sound-alike recordings is particularly important where the music publisher has, and wants to maintain, a business relationship with the particular artist/songwriter sought to be simulated.

### 5. Lyric Changes

Generally, music copyright owners are prepared to permit changes or additions to the original lyrics of a composition, as long as such changes or additions are subject to the publisher's final written approval. Lyric changes should be approved only after the publisher has taken care to make certain it has the right to authorize the change. A publisher may be under a contractual obligation to consult with or obtain the approval of the songwriter prior to authorizing any changes to lyrics of the song.

The conditions under which a songwriter would be willing to agree to a modification in lyrics are unpredictable. If changes to lyrics are to be approved, the exact nature of the new lyrics should be specified in the license or final approval should be withheld until the exact lyric is determined. One experience should illustrate the point: Ira Gershwin gave his permission for the use of the song *I Got Rhythm* in a commercial advertisement for a chain of supermarkets in New York. He also permitted the use of a parody lyric in place of the original, but when he learned that the new lyric used the words, "*I've* Got Rhythm, he insisted that it be changed back to "*I* Got Rhythm." Ira said he deliberately chose the phrase "*I* Got Rhythm" instead of "*I've* Got Rhythm" for the title and lyrics of the composition written by his brother George, not because of its colloquial sound, but because it emphasized the powerful rhythmic structure his brother gave the music.

Even when a publisher is under no contractual obligation to obtain the permission of the songwriter, it is good practice to at least consult with the writer on any proposed changes. Changes to any artistic work may evoke some emotional reaction from the artist. Informing the writer in advance of proposed changes, at the very least, may avoid some surprise and embarrassment. Going the extra mile to satisfy any objections of the writer is also a good way to help build a long-term relationship with the writer, which may be important down the road, when it comes time for negotiating with the writer for a further grant of renewal rights or terminated rights under the 19-year extension period or the 35-year termination rule.

Performing rights societies, such as BMI and ASCAP, will pay performance royalties even when a new or parody lyric is used; however, the credits received may be less than if the original lyric is used. Nevertheless, the lower performance credits per use should not deter a decision to grant permission to alter the lyrics.

### 6. Use of the Song's Title

If the song's title is used for a special purpose, such as the name of the product, the importance of the song in relation to its intended

use becomes obvious. Some additional consideration for the use of
the music could be considered, as well as a separate fee for the use
of the song as the name of the product.

The ability of the publisher to command a fee for the use of the
song's title as the name of the product, whether or not the music is
used, will depend upon the distinctiveness of the title. For example,
if the name of the song is merely a common word, such as *Misty*,
then it might be difficult to command a fee for the use of the word
"Misty" as the name of a product. It would, however, be quite reasonable to ask for a premium for the use of the song *Misty* or its lyrics
in advertisements of the product. On the other hand, if the title of the
song is distinctive, because either it consists of a wholly fictitious
word or phrase or it contains some distinctive or recognizable gram-
matical error or misspelling, a fee for the use of the title may be
demanded. For example, the titles "Supercalifragilisticexpialidocious"
and "Ain't Misbehavin" could probably not be used as the name of
a product without the permission of the owner of the song's copyright.

## D. Scope of the Intended Use

### 1. *Media and Distribution Channels*

Generally, commercial synchronization licenses should be narrowly drawn to permit the recording of the music in conjunction with
radio or television commercials solely for radio or television broadcast. The license may also be expanded to permit "off-air" or non-
broadcast trade uses, such as performance of the commercial at a trade
show or for over-the-counter use in retail stores. If the commercial is
to be distributed in videogram devices, such as videocassettes and
laser discs, special licensing and fee provisions similar to the those
discussed in connection with videogram licenses may also be negotiated.

Advertisers who conduct a television and radio advertising campaign will usually try to place print ads that *tie in* with the broadcast
messages. If such is the case, the advertiser will ask for a license to
print any lyrics used in the television or radio commercials in printed
advertising published during the term. Music copyright owners will
generally grant permission to do so for an additional fee. Occasionally,
the only permission that is sought is for the use of the lyrics in a print

advertisement. A simplified license for such a use is set forth as Form 20.3 at the end of this chapter.

### 2. Term

The term of a commercial synchronization license will customarily commence upon the first broadcast of the commercial embodying the licensed musical composition, and will last for one week, one month, thirteen weeks, or other term negotiated between the parties, but will not normally endure for more than one year, unless options are negotiated. Because the success of advertising campaigns are difficult to predict, advertisers should always attempt to negotiate options to extend the term for one or two renewal periods upon payment of additional license fees. An option to renew a one year term must usually be exercised at least 30 days before the expiration of the initial term.

### 3. Territory

The territory for commercial advertising use varies depending upon the business of the advertiser. The territory of nationally advertised products is generally limited to the United States and Canada, although where a regional test of the advertising is contemplated, the territory may be restricted to a specific region with an option to expand the territory as appropriate, upon the payment of additional license fees.

When issuing a license whose territory is limited to the United States and Canada, keep in mind that certain television networks, such as CNN and Fox News, are broadcast worldwide via satellite. Accordingly, music copyright owners should be careful to exclude advertising on CNN if his right to license such use is contractually limited or he is otherwise unwilling to permit the use of the music in advertising outside of the United States and Canada. By the same token, when the territory of the license is intended to be restricted to a certain region or city, such as the vicinity of Atlanta, Georgia, the music copyright owner should be careful to exclude advertising on "superstations" such as WTBS, which is a local station in Atlanta that is broadcast nationwide via satellite to local cable television operators. Other superstations include WOR in New York and WGN in Chicago. Where the advertising is specifically intended to be broadcast on superstations, the music publisher should become familiar with the number of markets into which the superstations broadcasts are retransmitted and price the license accordingly. In other words, license fees for use of compositions on superstations should tend to be nearly the same as fees for use nationwide, because the superstations are usually transmitted to cable stations across the country.

Certain regions, such as New York City and Southern California, are larger, and comprise larger markets, than others, and can therefore command higher license fees. If you are a music copyright owner, keep in mind that if you receive a request for use of music in advertising to be broadcast in, for example, Newark, New Jersey, don't be fooled — such advertising could be received by viewers in the greater New York area, one of the largest television markets in the country.

Advertisers of products that have international appeal may request options for the use of music in additional countries. Consideration should be given to local subpublishing contracts or local publishing affiliate control over the music licensed for commercial advertising that takes place in their local markets.

### 4. Exclusivity

An advertiser paying a substantial fee for a commercial synchronization license may well request the exclusive right to use the song for commercial purposes during the license term. Music copyright owners are normally willing to agree to some form of limited exclusivity. For example, the music publisher may agree not to license the song in connection with the commercial advertising of products that directly compete with the advertisers licensed product.

An advertiser would normally find that acceptable, but, in addition, may request that the publisher not license the song in connection with products that not only "compete with" the licensed product or service, but "relate to" the licensed product or service — that is, products that are complementary, not necessarily competing with the licensed products. Thus, for example, a sporting goods manufacturer licensing a song for use in advertising its line of *golf clubs* may well expect that the publisher would not license the song to another sporting goods manufacturer for use in connection with the advertising of its *golf balls*.

It should be evident that there is some degree of ambiguity inherent in phrases such as "compete with" or "relate to." To avoid ambiguity, a publisher may phrase the restriction in terms of precisely what kind of product(s) or service(s) in connection with which the publisher will not grant a license to use the song. For example, instead of providing that "The license is exclusive with respect to products that compete with stuffed animals," music copyright owners would be advised to state instead, "During the Term of the license, Publisher will not grant a license to use the Composition in the Territory in connection with the advertising of stuffed animals." While the former provision might be construed as preventing the license of the song in connection with dolls — on the basis that dolls are directly competitive with stuffed animals — the latter provision would be more narrowly construed to prevent the license of the song in connection with only those items that could reasonably be called a "stuffed animal." If the advertiser believes such a restriction is too narrow, the publisher should ask the advertiser to list the kinds of products it believes should be within the scope of the restriction, leaving it to the advertiser, who is in a better position to foresee potential conflicts, to take the risk of leaving a product off the list.

Care should also be taken in choosing the name of the product for which exclusivity is sought. For example, if the advertised product is aspirin, the copyright owner should try to limit the scope of the exclusivity to "aspirin." It might be reasonable for the advertiser to request that the exclusivity cover "pain relievers," which would include non-aspirin pain relievers, but a request for coverage of "pharmacology products," which might include cosmetics, would be too broad. Similarly, if the product advertised is beer, the scope of exclusivity should not be "all beverages," but "alcoholic beverages" or "domestic beer." In some rare cases, the advertiser may be willing to pay the extremely high premium required to obtain a broader scope of exclusivity.

Finally, if a songwriter or recording artist is being asked to perform the song in the commercial, the advertiser will typically require that, during the term of the license, the publisher will not grant to another a license to use any other song composed or recorded by the artist in the publisher's catalog for the purpose of advertising a competing product. This restriction, of course, will have little effect if many of the artist's popular songs are controlled by a different music publisher.

## III. PRINT ADVERTISING

The considerations described above regarding television and radio advertising apply also to print advertising, although the latter generally involves the more limited use of lyrics. Sometimes a television or radio advertising campaign will be supported by print advertising and a commercial synchronization license may include a provision allowing the use of lyrics in print advertising, product brochures and point-of-sale displays.

# APPENDIX TO CHAPTER 20
# LICENSES FOR RADIO, TELEVISION, AND PRINT ADVERTISING

1121

# FORM 20.1

### LICENSE FOR USE OF MUSIC
### IN RADIO OR TELEVISION ADVERTISEMENTS

## COMMERCIAL SYNCHRONIZATION LICENSE

Date:  January 1, 2000

Owner:       BIG MUSIC PUBLISHING CORP.
             a California Corporation
             1000 Sunset Boulevard
             Hollywood, California 90069

Licensee:    ABC Advertising Agency, Inc.
             a New York Corporation
             10 Madison Avenue
             New York, New York 10017

on behalf of the following Sponsor and Product(s):

Licensed Area:

Composition:

             by:

             Copyright © _____ 20__

1.   (a)   Owner hereby grants to Licensee the right to use the title and music to the Composition in the Licensed Area during the Term for commercial advertising, trade and related purposes without limitation as to frequency in the television and radio media (excluding so-called "pay" and "subscription" television) on behalf of the Sponsor, its subsidiaries and affiliates for the purpose of advertising the Product.

(b)    This license allows Licensee to arrange and adapt all or part of the music of the Composition to utilize a parody lyric (subject to the prior written approval of Owner's Director of Licensing) and to record all or part of the music of the Composition in synchronism or timed relation with television and/or radio commercials, and is granted upon the following express conditions, the violation of any of which shall cause this license to terminate immediately:

(i)    that the recordings produced hereunder shall be used solely for television and/or radio commercials and for off-air trade purposes to promote the Product(s);

(ii)    that neither the sound recordings produced pursuant to this license nor copies thereof shall be sold or licensed apart from said commercials;

(iii)    that said commercials shall not be exhibited in or televised into theatres or other public places of amusement where motion pictures are customarily shown (except in cases of private trade screenings); and

(iv)    that said commercials shall not utilize a "sound-a-like" recording in which an artist (solo or group) performs the Composition in such a way as to imitate an earlier recorded performance of the Composition by a different artist (unless Licensee or Sponsor shall first obtain the express permission of the latter artist or from a person, firm or corporation authorized to grant such permission on behalf of the latter artist).

(c)    Licensee will not make any use of the Composition (or of any arrangement or adaptation thereof) following the end of the Term, but Licensee shall have the right to retain copies of all commercials produced hereunder for file and reference purposes only.

(d)    Upon Owner's written request Licensee shall deliver to Owner an audiotape or videotape copy of each commercial (plus a copy of any parody lyric).

2.     (a)     The initial period of the Term of this license shall be one year, commencing with the first on-air use of a commercial produced hereunder or on _____ whichever occurs first.

(b)     Provided Licensee shall have complied with the terms and conditions of this license during the initial period, Licensee shall have the option to extend the Term for one one-year renewal period, by written notice delivered to Owner at least thirty (30) days prior to the expiration of the initial period.

3.     (a)     Owner shall not authorize any other person, firm or corporation to make commercial, advertising, trade or related use of the Composition in the Licensed Area during the Term in connection with the advertising or publicizing of any product(s) of the following types or descriptions:

(b)     Except as provided in the preceding paragraph, this license shall be non-exclusive.

(c)     Owner agrees to employ its best efforts, consistent with its good-faith business judgment, to prevent and restrain any use of the Composition by any person, firm or corporation contrary to the provisions of paragraph 3(a), above. In the event that Licensee (by written notice delivered to Owner) requests that Owner take action against an allegedly unauthorized use, and Owner declines to proceed because of a good faith belief either that no unauthorized use is involved or that the unauthorized use is too insignificant to warrant the cost of enforcement, Licensee shall have the right (and it shall be Licensee's sole remedy) to proceed against the user(s) in its own behalf (and at Licensee's sole cost and expense) and to retain any amount recovered thereby. Owner's failure to proceed within thirty (30) days after receipt of such a request shall be deemed Owner's decision not to proceed.

4.     (a)     Owner, or an organization such as BMI or ASCAP, to which Owner belongs and which licenses performing rights on Owner's behalf, will license the use of the Composition on

radio and television stations and networks throughout the Licensed Area.

(b)    (i)    In the event that Licensee or Sponsor wishes to allow the use of any commercial(s) embodying the Composition in whole or in part on any station(s) and/or network(s) not then holding valid performing rights licenses from Owner or such an organization, Owner agrees to issue a performing rights license for such use at Owner's then-customary rates.

(ii)    In the alternative, or in the event that Licensee or Sponsor wishes to acquire a direct performing rights license from Owner without reference to whether or not such station(s) and/or network(s) possess such performing rights licenses, Licensee may secure such performing rights license by an additional payment to Owner equal to one percent (1%) of the total time buy on the station(s) or network(s) in respect of which Licensee is securing such performing rights license.

(c)    Within a reasonable time following receipt of written request therefor from Owner, Licensee shall deliver to Owner copies of documents setting forth the names and addresses of all stations and networks upon which commercials produced hereunder have been and/or will be broadcast, and, in each instance, the number of times each commercial has been or will be broadcast. Owner understands and agrees that such information is confidential, and such information shall be disclosed only to such stations or networks or to Owner's performing rights society or societies (who shall likewise be instructed to keep such information confidential).

(d)    Owner shall not attempt to enjoin the broadcast or other transmission of commercials produced hereunder by any station or network selected by Licensee, Sponsor (or any person, firm or corporation acting on behalf of either of them), it being understood and agreed that Owner's sole remedy for unlicensed broadcast or other unlicensed transmission or performance shall be an action for money damages in accordance with the Copyright Act.

5.    In consideration of the rights granted herein, Licensee shall make a payment to Owner upon execution of this license in the amount of $ _____. In the event that Owner exercises its renewal option, an additional fee of $ _____ shall be payable at the time Licensee gives notice of its exercise of such option. Timely payment of these fees shall be of the essence of this agreement.

6.    (a)    Owner warrants and represents that it has the right to enter into and perform this agreement, and that the proper exercise by Licensee of the rights granted hereunder will not violate the rights of any third party. Licensee warrants and represents that it has the right to enter into and perform this agreement, and that the Sponsor has expressly authorized Licensee to agree to the requirements and restrictions set forth above.

(b)    (i)    Each party agrees to indemnify the other party and hold the other party harmless, from and against any and all loss, cost, damage or expense (including court costs and reasonable outside counsel fees) arising out of a breach of the foregoing warranty and representation by such party and resulting in an adverse judgment or a settlement entered into with the indemnitor's prior written consent (not to be unreasonably withheld).

(ii)    A party claiming indemnity shall deliver to the other party prompt written notice of any claim, action or proceeding to which such indemnity relates, and the indemnitor shall have the right to participate in the defense thereof by counsel of its choice, at its sole cost and expense. Where required by the terms of the indemnitor's errors-and-omissions insurance policy, the indemnitor's insurance carrier shall be permitted to control the defense of such claim, action or proceeding.

7.    All notices hereunder shall be given by registered or certified (return receipt requested) mail, by telegraph, or by any other means by which delivery may be verified. Notice shall be given to the above addresses or to such other addresses as

the parties may designate from time to time by notice delivered in like manner.

8.    This license is personal to Licensee and may not be assigned or transferred except to the Sponsor without Owner's prior written consent. No such transfer or assignment shall become effective unless and until the transferee or assignee shall deliver to Owner a written agreement assuming the further performance of Licensee's obligations hereunder, and no such transfer or assignment shall relieve Licensee of any obligation hereunder. However, Licensee may enter into sublicenses within the Licensed Area to the extent necessary to permit the exhibition of commercials in accordance with this license.

9.    This agreement has been entered into in, and is to be interpreted in accordance with the laws of, the State of California. This agreement contains the entire agreement between the parties and may not be altered or amended except by a further writing signed by both parties.

OWNER                                    LICENSEE

By: _____        By:_____

# FORM 20.2

## ALTERNATIVE LICENSE FOR USE OF MUSIC IN RADIO OR TELEVISION ADVERTISEMENTS

### COMMERCIAL SYNCHRONIZATION LICENSE

AGREEMENT made and entered into as of this      day of      by and between having a place of business at      (hereinafter referred to as "Licensee"), on behalf of its client,      (hereinafter referred to as "Sponsor"), and      with a place of business at      (hereinafter referred to as "Owner").

## W I T N E S S E T H:

1.    Owner hereby grants to Licensee the right to use the music to the composition entitled _____
published by Owner (hereinafter referred to as the "Composition") on behalf of Sponsor, its subsidiaries and affiliates for the purpose of advertising of Sponsor's product (hereinafter collectively referred to as the "Product").

2.    (a)    The term of this agreement shall be for one year, commencing with first on-air use on _____
whichever shall come first (hereinafter referred to as the "first Term"). During said First Term, Licensee may use the title and music to the Composition for commercial advertising, trade and related purposes without limitation as to frequency in the television and radio media in the United States, its territories and possessions (hereinafter referred to as the "licensed Area"), excluding so-called "pay" and "subscription" television.

      (b)    Licensee shall have the option to extend the term of the agreement for one additional successive one (1) year period (hereinafter referred to as the "Second Term") to commence on the first day following the termination of the prior term, by giving

Owner written notice to such effect no later than thirty (30) days prior to the termination of the then current term. During said Second Term, if any, Licensee may use the Composition in the same manner permitted during the First Term as specified in Paragraph 2(a) above.

3.      While this Agreement is in effect, Licensee may use all, part, and non-consecutive parts, of music of said Composition and arrange and adapt said Composition.

4.      The License issued herein shall be deemed non-exclusive; however, Owner agrees not to authorize any other person, firm or corporation to make commercial, advertising, trade or related use of the Composition in the Licensed Area in connection with either the advertising or giving publicity to any product and Owner agrees to use its best efforts to prevent and restrain any unauthorized use of said Composition by any person, firm or corporation.

5.      Licensee agrees that it will not broadcast all or any part of the original music, of the said Composition following the authorized period of use as elsewhere set forth in the Agreement, except that it may retain copies of the commercials for file and reference purposes only.

6.      Licensee agrees the license granted herein is to record the Composition in synchronism or time-relation with a picture made and produced in connection with television commercials or for radio commercials. Licensee further agrees this license is granted upon the express condition that any and all recording(s) produced hereunder are to be used solely for television or radio and that no sound records produced pursuant to this license are to be sold or licensed apart from said commercials, and upon further condition the said commercials shall not be exhibited in or televised into theatres or other public places of amusement where motion pictures are customarily shown. Notwithstanding the generality of the foregoing, Licensee, Sponsor and its subsidiaries and affiliates shall have the right during the

term of this Agreement to use commercials embodying the Composition for off-air trade purposes.

7.    Owner, or an organization such as ASCAP or BMI, to which Owner belongs and which licenses performance rights on Owner's behalf, will license the use of the Composition on radio and television stations and networks throughout the United States. In the event Licensee desires to use the Composition on stations or networks which have not entered into a license agreement with Owner or any organization on Owner's behalf, this agreement shall be deemed to constitute a license for such uses without any limitation or further compensation. Neither Owner nor anyone deriving any rights from Owner shall interfere with or hold up the performance of the Composition pursuant to this Agreement

8.    Owner warrants and represents that Licensee will not be subject to any performance fees or any other fee or tax by another person, firm or corporation or society or other legal entity for using said Composition in accordance with the rights granted Licensee hereunder.

9.    Owner represents and warrants that it has the right and authority to grant the rights given to Licensee herein and that the exercise by Licensee of the rights granted herein will not violate the rights of any third party. Owner agrees to defend, indemnify and hold harmless Sponsor, its subsidiaries and affiliates, the Licensee, and their respective directors, officers, employees and agents from and against any and all claims, damages, liabilities, costs and expenses (including reasonable attorney's fees), arising out of the permitted use of the Composition by Licensee or Sponsor hereunder. Licensee similarly agrees to indemnify and hold harmless Owner, its affiliated companies, from and against any and all claims, damages, liability, costs and expenses (including reasonable attorneys' fees), arising out of or in any way connected with any advertising materials utilizing the licensed property other than those furnished by Owner. Indemnitee will promptly notify Indemnitor of any

claim or litigation to which this indemnity applies. Indemnitee reserves the right, without being required to do so, to settle any claim or litigation or defend any claim or suit at their own expense, provided that in the event Indemnitee settles any claim or litigation without prior written consent of the Indemnitor, the Indemnitor shall be released from any and all liabilities under said indemnity.

10.    In consideration for the rights granted Licensee hereunder, and the duties and obligations assumed by Owner, Licensee agrees to pay and Owner agrees to accept the following sums:

        a)    For the rights granted during the First Term referred to in paragraph 2(a) above Licensee agrees to pay Owner the sum of Dollars payable within fifteen (15) working days of the date on which Licensee furnishes Owner with a fully executed copy of this agreement.

        b)    In the event Licensee exercises its option for the Second Term referred to in paragraph 2(b) above Licensee shall pay Owner      Dollars within fifteen (15) working days of the date on which Licensee furnishes notice of the exercise of said option.

        c)    All payments due or which may become due Owner hereunder shall be made by check to the order of BIG MUSIC PUBLISHING CORP. and delivered to the address set forth on the face page of this Agreement.

11.    Notice to Licensee shall be sufficient if mailed or telegraphed to it all charges prepaid addressed as follows:

or to such other address as may hereafter be designated by Licensee from time to time in writing.

    Notice to Owner shall be sufficient if mailed or telegraphed to it, all charges prepaid, addressed as follows:

Attention:

or to such other address as may hereafter be designated by Owner from time to time in writing.

13.     This Agreement constitutes the entire understanding between the parties hereto and cannot be changed orally. No waiver by either party hereto of any breach of any agreement to be performed by the other party hereunder shall be deemed to be a waiver of any preceding or succeeding breach of the same or any other agreement hereunder.

This Agreement shall be interpreted and construed according to the laws of the State of California.

IN WITNESS WHEREOF, this Agreement has been duly executed by the parties hereto, as of the day and year first written.

OWNER                              LICENSEE

By:_____     By: _____

# FORM 20.3

## LICENSE FOR USE OF LYRICS IN PRINT ADVERTISEMENTS

January 1, 2000

FORTUNE 500 COMPANY, INC.
456 Main Street
San Francisco, California 95000

Gentlemen:

We grant you permission to reprint portions of the lyric only from our copyright "_____" by _____ for use in print advertising for your product _____, subject to the following terms and conditions:

1. You shall pay us a fee of $5000.00, check made payable to BIG MUSIC PUBLISHING COMPANY, INC. and addressed to the attention of the undersigned.

2. The following copyright notice must appear at the bottom of the page on which the quote appears, suitably asterisked, or as an alternative, we authorize copyright notice to be included on appropriate credit pages if the complete publication is registered with the U.S. Copyright Office.

> Copyright © 1965 BIG MUSIC PUBLISHING CORP.
> All Rights Reserved        Used By Permission

3. The territory covered by this permission is the United States.

4. The term of this agreement shall expire on December, 2001.

5.     You shall furnish us with two (2) copies of the ad copy for our files.

This permission shall be valid upon your signing and returning to us one copy of this letter along with your remittance and upon the performance by you of the other terms and conditions hereof on your part to be performed.

All rights not specifically granted herein are reserved to and by us.

Yours sincerely,

BIG MUSIC PUBLISHING CORP.

AGREED AND ACCEPTED:

By: _____

By: _____

# LICENSES FOR MUSIC BOXES AND CONSUMER MUSICAL PRODUCTS

## SUMMARY

# LICENSES FOR MUSIC BOXES AND CONSUMER MUSICAL PRODUCTS

F rom time to time, a music publisher will receive a request for permission to use a musical composition in a consumer product. The variety of consumer products in which music is being employed is ever increasing and hardly a month goes by without an innovative use of music being brought to the attention of a publisher for licensing consideration.

This chapter will explore the considerations in licensing music in music boxes and other consumer musical products.

## I. BACKGROUND

As noted in Chapter 12, on *Mechanical Licenses*, a *music box* is a mechanical instrument whose sounds are produced by the spring activated rotation of a cylinder having specially placed protruding pins that pluck the teeth of a metal comb. The music box was the first mechanical device designed to perform music and is used today in jewelry boxes, figurines, novelty items, and children's toys.

Modern technology has spawned new, innovative applications of the music box idea. For example, a toy manufacturer has marketed a musical coin bank, called the *Musical Bogie Bank* that plays the melody of the song *As Time Goes By* whenever a coin is deposited in its slot. A greeting card containing a special sound-capable computer chip may perform, for example, a few bars of *My Funny Valentine* when the card is opened. An exercise machine may play the melody of, *Chariots of Fire* while the user is cycling or running in place. A doll bearing the likeness of the movie character, *Mary Poppins* might sing the *A Spoonful of Sugar* when the child pulls a string or claps his or hands.

Other consumer musical products may use music in a way that does not involve a performance of the melody. For example, a tea kettle might bear the imprint of the words and musical notation of the song, *Tea For Two* by Irving Caesar and Vincent Youmans. And a greeting card may contain the printed lyric of the song, *I Love You Truly*.

## II. CONSIDERATIONS IN GRANTING AND CLEARING MUSICAL PRODUCT LICENSES

In granting permission to use a song in connection with a consumer product, a music copyright owner will consider many of the same points applicable to determining the appropriate rate to charge for use of his music in television, radio, or print advertising (see Chapter 20), including the fee structure, value of the song, the importance of the song in relation to its intended use, and the scope of the use. These factors are discussed below.

### A. Fee Structure

Music copyright owners typically charge some percentage of the sales of the consumer music product in exchange for the license. The percentage may be a portion of the suggested retail price, wholesale price, or net revenues (gross revenues less product returns). Because the price charged for the musical product by its manufacturer is completely within the discretion of the manufacturer, the copyright owner may establish some minimum fixed penny or dollar amount per copy. The fixed amount per copy will often serve as a *floor*, or minimum fee, below which the royalty will not fall, regardless of what the manufacture charges for the product. The copyright owner will also seek an advance against royalties payable upon the execution of the license. See Forms 21.1 and 21.2 at the end of this chapter for model licenses for music boxes and musical product licenses.

A person seeking to clear a license for a musical product might attempt to negotiate a one-time flat fee for the use during the term of the license. However, music copyright owners would be reluctant to grant such licenses on a flat fee basis, because of the absence of any means to share in the economic success of the work in which the music will be included. For example, the television broadcast of a young child playing with a *Mary Poppins* doll that sings *A Spoonful of Sugar* will earn the song's copyright owner performance fees that are in addition to any initial licensee fee charged for the synchronization of the song to the advertisement. By contrast, the child's playing with the doll day after day at home does not earn the music copyright owner any additional fees, no matter how popular the doll becomes with little girls. This is because all performances of the song in the home are *private* performances. These performances are not subject to the permission of the copyright owners, and, because there are no fees collectable for private performances, the music copyright owner will seek alternative means to share the economic success of the use. It has therefore been the practice of music publishers to charge a royalty for the use based on the number of units of the products sold or the revenues derived from sales of the product.

If, at the same time you are seeking to clear a musical product license, you are seeking to clear a synchronization license for the use of the music in television commercials to advertising the musical product, you may be able to negotiate a flat fee rate, or in any event, better terms for the musical product license, if you can persuade the copyright owner that your use of the song will significantly increase the copyright owner's income during the term of the license. The copyright owner may also accept a flat fee if it is high enough to overcome the copyright owner's fear of making a "bad deal."

### 1. Applicability of Compulsory License Provision

Before a person seeking to clear a license for a musical product accepts any terms offered by a music copyright owner, he should first determine whether the compulsory license provision of the copyright law applies to the particular use intended. If the compulsory license provision does apply, then the licensee would be entitled to limit the fee to the *statutory rate* existing at that time. Currently, the statutory rate is 6.6 cents per copy, for recordings up to five minutes in length and, if over 5 minutes, 1.25 cents per minute of playing time. The music copyright owner is free to negotiate better terms only if the compulsory license statute does not apply.

Technically, when a music box or a musical greeting card *plays* a song, the performance is not accompanied by motion pictures or some other form of audiovisual work. Accordingly, one might assert that the purely mechanical reproduction of the song in the music box or greeting card appears to be subject to the compulsory mechanical licensing provision of the copyright law (see Chapter 12). A music copyright owner might argue that the compulsory license provision only applies to phonorecords, or record albums as they are customarily understood, and does not apply to devices that might technically contain a phonorecord, such as a sound chip, but are incorporated into a consumer product. Since the incorporation of music into a consumer product commercially ties the music to the product, can be considered in the nature of an endorsement of the product, something more is present than the mere incorporation of the music in a phonorecord for private use. It is not clear how this question would be decided if ever tested in court. It is not likely to be decided as long as the royalty rates customarily charged for the use of music in consumer products remains reasonably consistent with the statutory rate.

Note, however, that the reprinting of lyrics is clearly not a mechanical reproduction and therefore is clearly not subject to the compulsory license provisions. Nor is music embodied in a product that contains an audiovisual work a mechanical reproduction of the music subject to compulsory licensing. Accordingly, if the lyrics are used, with or without the music, or the music is used in connection with moving pictures, the compulsory license provision of the copyright law would not apply and the publisher would clearly be free to negotiate more favorable terms.

## B.  Value of the Song

As in the consideration of licensing music for use in advertising commercial products, discussed in Chapter 20, music copyright owners in considering licensing music for use in the products themselves should consider the possibility that associating a hit song with a commercial product might harm the future earning potential of the song. A song that has become associated with a particular product may become less attractive to recording artists considering whether to make new recordings of the song, to producers considering whether to use the music in motion pictures, or to other advertisers considering whether to use the music in the marketing or advertising of other products. For these reasons, a publisher would consider charging a premium if he believes that an identification with a specific product might adversely affect the song's future revenues from other sources. In addition, a publisher would be warranted in demanding a premium if the song has never before been made available for use in a consumer product.

A person seeking to clear a license for musical products would do well to remind a reluctant copyright owner of the importance of maintaining continual exposure of the song to the listening public, despite the lack of public performances arising from the license. Licensing music for a toy music box or wind-up doll will expose the music to a new generation and will increase the likelihood that licenses for use and performance of the song will continue over the full life of the copyright.

## C. Importance of the Song in Relation to Its Intended Use

Again, the music copyright owner should ask himself, or the potential licensee, why *this* particular song? When one, and only one, particular song will best fit the use in the product, the copyright owner may have a good reason to ask for a premium fee. As previously noted, the fewer substitutes that are available for the use, the more the licensee may be willing to pay. For example, there may be only a limited number of songs or themes logically available for a musical doll based on a popular motion picture or television program character. Also, if the song's title will be used as the name of the product, a separate fee for that use should be considered, though the music copyright owner's ability to charge a fee for the use of the song's title will depend upon the distinctiveness of the title.

## D. Scope of Use

### 1. Media

The product in which the music will be embodied should be described with particularity. To this end, the copyright owner should ask for a full description of the product at the time the license is being sought.

### 2. Term

The term of musical product licenses are, generally, for a period of one to three years, with a provision to allow the manufacturer to sell off his inventory for a period of no more than six months after the expiration of the term. A person seeking to clear such a license should be able to negotiate options to renew the term upon the payment of additional advances against future royalties.

### 3. Territory

The territory that the licensee is permitted to distribute the licensed product is limited to the local market in which the license is issued, such as the United States and Canada. Options permitting the export of the musical product to other countries may be available, but a music publisher may require that such licenses be sought from the local music publishers in each of the countries in which the licensee intends to market the product.

### 4. Exclusivity

When requested, product exclusivity is often granted. The principals of the exclusivity discussion set forth in Chapter 20, with respect to commercial advertising, apply equally to consumer product licenses, though exclusivity may not be as important here as it is to the licensee in establishing a product identity in the course of a commercial advertising campaign. An exclusivity provision of a musical product license should, of course, be narrow in scope and worded with great care to assure the license reflects the intent of the parties.

## III. PRINTING OF MUSIC OR LYRICS

Makers of some consumer musical products merely require permission to print the lyrics on or in the product. For example, a tea kettle might bear the imprint of the words and musical notation of the song, *Tea For Two* or a greeting card may contain the printed lyric of the song, *I Love You Truly*. In each instance, the music copyright owner will generally grant permission under terms and conditions similar to those described in the previous section.

However, music copyright owners should first reflect upon whether they have the right to grant such a license to begin with. If the copyright owner previously granted to a print music publisher the exclusive rights to make copies of the music in printed form, then, unless the grant of rights in the print music publishing agreement excluded uses for consumer products or reprints of lyrics in books and other products, then the copyright owner may be required to refer the person who is seeking the musical product license to the owner of the exclusive print rights of the music.

# APPENDIX TO CHAPTER 21
## LICENSES FOR MUSIC BOXES AND CONSUMER MUSICAL PRODUCTS

# FORM 21.1

## MUSIC BOX LICENSE

### MUSIC BOX LICENSE AGREEMENT

AGREEMENT, dated as of _____, 2000, between

BIG MUSIC PUBLISHING CORP., with its principal office at 1000 Sunset Boulevard, Hollywood, California 90069 ("Owner") and DELICATE MUSIC BOX MAKER & SONS, with its principal office at P.O. Box 1000 Harmony Lane, Melody, Missouri 50505 ("Maker").

WHEREAS, Owner owns the copyrights in the song "____" (_____, _____) (the "Song"), including the exclusive right to license the reproduction of the Song; and

WHEREAS, Maker desires to obtain from Owner a license to use the Song in connection with the manufacture and sale of Music Boxes.

NOW, THEREFORE, in consideration of the mutual agreements contained herein, the parties agree as follows:

1.    Owner grants to Maker, upon the terms and conditions set forth in the Agreement, the right and license to use the Song in connection with the manufacture, distribution, and sale of the Music Box in the United States; provided, however, this license does not permit Maker to use the music and/or lyrics of the Song in connection with any advertising of the Music Box

2.    The term of this Agreement shall be for the life of the Music Box, but no longer than December 31, 2000. However, either party may terminate this Agreement upon ninety (90) days written notice to the other.

3.    (a)    Maker agrees to pay Owner a royalty equal to five percent (5%) of amounts received from the sale in the United States, payable quarterly within thirty (30) days after the end of each quarter. For purposes of this Agreement, the term "amounts received" shall mean the amounts Maker invoices to its customers or distributors for the music boxes.

(b)    Timely and accurate payments shall be of the essence of this Agreement. Owner shall have the right, upon ten (10) days prior written notice, and during ordinary business hours, to audit Maker's books and records (insofar as they relate to the subject matter of this Agreement), which shall be kept in accordance with generally accepted accounting principles and maintained at Maker's principal place of business.

4.    The following copyright notice must appear on the packaging of the Music Box so long as the Song "_____" is used:

_____

Words by                        Music By

Copyright (c) BIG MUSIC PUB. CORP.
All Rights Reserved Used By Permission

5.    Maker's exercise of the license granted by Owner under this Agreement shall constitute Maker's warranty and representation that Maker then has all rights necessary for the manufacture, distribution and sale of the Music Boxes. Maker agrees to indemnify and hold Owner harmless against any loss, damage, or liability, including reasonable attorneys' fees and court costs, arising out of a breach of said representation and warranty. Owner shall similarly indemnify Maker with respect to Owner' rights in and to the Song.

IN WITNESS WHEREOF, the parties have caused their duly authorized officers to execute this Agreement as of the day and year first written above.

BIG MUSIC PUBLISHING CORP.

By ———————————————

DELICATE MUSIC BOX MAKER & SONS

By ———————————————

# FORM 21.2

## LICENSE FOR USE OF MUSIC IN A CONSUMER PRODUCT

### MUSICAL PRODUCT LICENSE

Date: January 1, 2000

Owner:        BIG MUSIC PUBLISHING CORP.    Licensee:
              1000 Sunset Blvd.
              Hollywood, CA 90069

Composition:                              By:

Copyright Notice:

Description of Licensed Item:

Licensed Territory:

Term of this Agreement: From          To

Renewal options (exercisable by written notice delivered at least 30 days prior to commencement of renewal period): _____ renewal period(s) of _____ each.

Post-Term Sell-Off Rights:

Product-Line Exclusivity (if in addition to the Licensed Product):

Suggested Retail List Price: $

Licensee's Wholesale Price: $

Advance(s):    $        .payable on execution
               $        .payable
               $        .payable

Royalty: $_____ per copy, or, if greater, _____% of the
_____ price per copy, payable on all copies sold
and not returned.

THIS LICENSE INCLUDES THOSE TERMS AND CONDITIONS
SET FORTH ON THE ANNEXED RIDER.

LICENSEE:                          OWNER:

By: _____     By: _____


RIDER

Annexed to and made part of the
Musical Product License Agreement
dated January 1, 2000
between _____ ("Owner")
and _____ ("Licensee").

1.    (a)    This license is personal to the Licensee, and may
not be sold, assigned, transferred, exchanged or encumbered
in any manner. However, in the event of a merger or consolidation, or a sale of substantially all of the Licensee's stock or
assets, the Licensee shall have the right to assign this Licensee
to the surviving or acquiring entity provided such entity assumes the further performance of this license in accordance
with its terms and conditions in a writing delivered to the Owner.

      (b)    (i)    This license is exclusive with respect to the in-
clusion of the Composition in products directly competitive with
the Licensed Product or products which are of the same generic
type as the Licensed Product within the Licensed Territory during the Term hereof. (For example, "stuffed animals" would be
a generic type, as would be "housewares" or "coin banks".)

            (ii)    However, unless specified otherwise on the
first page of this license, this license is nonexclusive with re-

spect to all other uses of the Composition, whether within or outside the Licensed Territory, and whether during or after the Term.

2.    (a)    All merchandise and packaging manufactured pursuant to this license shall be of the highest quality of similar items regularly sold in the Licensed Territory (in each country thereof, if this license covers more than one country).

(b)    Prior to first shipment, and again in any subsequent instance in which the specifications of the Licensed Product and/or the packaging thereof are altered, the Licensee shall deliver a representative sample thereof to the Owner (to the attention of the Owner's General Counsel) for the Owner's review and approval, which approval shall not be unreasonably withheld (and which shall be deemed to have been granted unless the Owner delivers detailed written notice of disapproval within fifteen (15) days after delivery of the sample to the Owner).

3.    (a)    This license allows the Licensee to manufacture, advertise, distribute and sell the Licensed Product including a device capable of reproducing the Composition, within the Licensed Territory during the Term.

(b)    (i)    In addition, provided the Licensee is not then in breach of any of the terms or conditions of this Agreement, the Licensee shall have the right, for six months following the end of the Term, to sell off its ending inventory of the Licensed Product.

(ii)    All sales during the sell-off period shall be at regular prices, and not at "close-out" or "distress" prices.

(iii)    The Licensee shall provide the Owner with an ending inventory, certified by a responsible corporate officer, within thirty (30) days following the end of the Term. Any copies of the Licensed Product remaining unsold as of the end of the sell-off period (or as of the end of the Term, in the event that the Licensee is not entitled to take advantage of the sell-off period) shall be destroyed within fifteen (15) days thereafter, and an affidavit of such destruction, executed by a responsible corporate officer, shall be delivered to the Owner within ten (10) days following such destruction.

4. The Licensed Product may only be sold within the Licensed Territory. The Licensed Product shall not be exported to countries outside of the Licensed Territory, nor knowingly sold to buyers who do so.

5. (a) The Licensee shall keep true and accurate books and records with respect to all transactions pursuant to this license, in accordance with generally accepted accounting principles.

(b) The Licensee shall deliver a true and accurate accounting statement to the Owner (to the attention of Owner's Accounting Department) within forty-five (45) days after the end of each calendar quarter during which copies of the Licensed Product are sold hereunder, or during which moneys are collected by or credited to the Licensee with respect thereto. Such accounting statement shall be accompanied by payment of any amount shown to be due to the Owner thereon.

(c) The timely rendition of accounting statements, and the timely payment of any amount(s) due or to become due hereunder (whether by way of fixed payments or by reason of sales of the Licensed Product), shall be of the essence of this agreement.

(d) (i) The Owner shall have the right from time to time, upon at least ten (10) days' prior written notice to the Licensee, to examine and audit the Licensee's books and records relative to this agreement, and to make copies or extracts of relevant portions therefrom. Each statement (and the related accounting period) shall be available for examination and audit for four (4) years after such statement is received by the Owner, or, if later, until two (2) years after the end of the sell-off period (or the end of the Term, if there is no sell-off period).

(ii) Such examination and audit shall take place during normal business hours at the Licensee's address as set forth above, or at such other address at which the Licensee's books and records are then regularly kept.

(iii) Such examination and audit shall be at the Owner's expense, provided, however, that in the event that any such examination and audit reveals an underpayment of ten percent (10%) or more for the period(s) audited, the Licensee shall pay the reasonable cost of such examination and audit.

6. (a) While the Owner shall have the right to refer to the Composition in the packaging for the Licensed Product and/or in advertising or promotional materials related thereto, it is a condition of this license that neither the music nor the lyrics of the Composition are to be used in commercials or in printed form by or under the authority of the Licensee.

(b) Further, it is also a condition of this license that the copyright notice prescribed above appear on each copy of the Licensed Product, on any package, insert, or liner used in connection therewith, and on any advertising or promotional materials used with respect to the Licensed Product.

7. (a) (i) The Licensee shall at all times pertinent to this license maintain in full force and effect errors and omissions insurance and public liability insurance with $1,000,000/ $3,000,000 limits, issued by a reputable carrier and naming the Owner, its officers, agents, employees and directors as additional insureds, and providing that coverage shall not be terminated without thirty (30) days' prior notice to the Owner.

(ii) A certificate of such coverage shall be delivered to the Owner prior to the first shipment of copies of the Licensed Product hereunder.

(b)    In addition, the Licensee shall at all times pertinent to this license comply with all applicable federal, state and local statutes, ordinances, and regulations applicable to the manufacture, distribution, advertising or sale of the Licensed Product, including but not limited to, licensing laws, safety regulations, and consumer-protection laws.

8.    Any failure on the part of the Licensee to render accounting statements and/or to make payment when due, or any other breach of this license not cured by the Licensee within thirty (30) days following receipts of written notice from the Owner, shall constitute cause for termination of the Term of this license by the Owner (and shall void the sell-off period).

9.    (a)    Each party warrants and represents to the other that it has the full right, power, and authority to enter into and to perform this agreement and, in the case of the Owner, to grant the rights granted to the Licensee hereunder.

(b)    (i)    Each party hereby indemnifies the other, its officers, directors, agents and employees and agrees to hold it and them harmless from and against any and all loss, damage, cost or expense (including reasonable outside attorneys' fees and court costs) which may be incurred as the result of a breach of this agreement on the part of the indemnitor.

(ii)    Each party shall notify the other party promptly of any claim, action or proceeding to which the foregoing indemnity relates, and the notified party shall have the right to participate in the defense thereof by counsel of its choice, at its sole cost and expense.

(iii)    However, in the event that any claim is made that the Composition infringes any other musical work (or any other third party right), the Owner shall have the right and obligation to assume control of the defense of such claim (and any related action or proceeding).

(c)    (i)    This agreement has been entered into in, and is to be interpreted in accordance with the laws of, the State of

California. This license constitutes the entire agreement between the parties, superseding any and all prior oral and/or written agreements, and may not be altered or amended except by a further written agreement signed by both parties.

(ii)     Any and all disputes with respect to the interpretation and/or enforcement of this license shall be resolved in the Federal or State Courts situated in Los Angeles County, and both parties hereby submit to the jurisdiction of such Courts for such purpose.

(iii)     In any litigation between the parties, the prevailing party shall be entitled to recover its reasonable outside attorneys' fees and court costs.

(d)     (i)     Any notice required or permitted to be given pursuant to this agreement shall be given by registered or certified mail (return receipt requested), by telex or other telegraphic means, or by personal delivery under circumstances permitting delivery to be verified (e.g., Federal Express) to the parties at their respective addresses set forth above, or to such address as a party may hereafter designate by notice in like manner.

(ii)     All notices to the Owner shall be directed to the attention of the Vice President, Legal & Business Affairs, with a copy by ordinary mail to the Executive Vice President.

(iii)
     Notice shall be deemed given when sent in accordance with this paragraph, except for notice of change of address, which shall only be effective when received.

CHAPTER 22

# LICENSES FOR COMPUTER SOFTWARE, MULTIMEDIA, AND NEW MEDIA PRODUCTS

## SUMMARY

### I. TECHNOLOGICAL DEVELOPMENTS

A. Computer Software
  1. Videogame or Entertainment Software
  2. Educational Software
  3. Music Software
  4. Musical Instrument Digital Interface (MIDI) Software
  5. Business Software
B. Multimedia Programs
C. New Media Products
  1. Karaoke
  2. Holographic Motion Pictures

### II. CONSIDERATIONS IN GRANTING AND CLEARING LICENSES FOR COMPUTER SOFTWARE, MULTIMEDIA PROGRAMS, AND NEW MEDIA PRODUCTS

A. Fee Structure
  1. Flat Fee
  2. Royalty
  3. Pro Rata
  4. Applicability of the Compulsory License Provision
B. Value of the Song
C. Importance of the Song in Relation to Its Intended Use
  1. Special Nature of Interactive Works
  2. Traditional Factors
D. Scope of the Use
  1. Media
  2. Term

1159

3. Exclusivity

4. Territory

## III. ADDITIONAL CONSIDERATIONS IN CLEARING LICENSES FOR MULTIMEDIA AND NEW MEDIA PRODUCTS

A. Understanding All the Rights Involved

B. Educate the Music Copyright Owner

## APPENDIX TO CHAPTER 22

# LICENSES FOR COMPUTER SOFTWARE, MULTIMEDIA, AND NEW MEDIA PRODUCTS

At the turn of the century, music publishing involved primarily the sale of sheet music and the promotion of live performances. Since then, advances in technology have opened up large, new markets for the promotion of music: beginning with player pianos, which gave rise to the market for mechanical piano rolls, to record players, which gave rise to the long-playing album; to motion pictures, radio, and television by broadcast, cable, and worldwide satellite transmission; and to the technological miracles developed within the current generation, such as videotape players, compact audio laser discs,[1] audiovisual laser discs, video games, karaoke machines, computer software, multimedia programs, sound-capable silicon chips, and on-line information databases and electronic bulletin boards.

The future promises no let up from these relentless advances in technology. The coming revolution in our telephone system, which will allow low-cost, high speed digital transmissions of information and software, should combine with existing technologies to open up vast new markets and means of delivering music and other entertainment programming. These technological achievements and developments, together with the industries that support them, are converging to form a highly complex and interlocking system of distribution ca-

---

[1] To remain consistent with common usage in the software and entertainment industries, we will use the term "disc" (spelled with a "c") to refer primarily to optical laser discs on which may be recorded audio-only or audiovisual works, and we will use the term "disk" (spelled with a "k") to refer to the various forms of disks (e.g., floppy disks, hard disks, back-up disks, etc.) used with computers to store data, which may also include audio-only or audiovisual works.

pable of delivering music to the listening public when and where they want it.

These technologies will also afford copyright owners of entertainment programming new ways to control and enforce their exclusive rights in their works and will enable distributors of entertainment programming to track and analyze the tastes and buying habits of consumers of entertainment works. This will allow a more efficient communication between providers and consumers of these works, giving consumers information about the works available that are likely to interest them and giving producers information about what kinds of works should be produced and marketed to which consumers.

Future applications of these technologies, and of technologies that have yet to be developed, will challenge the music publisher's ability to understand and exploit these new means of delivery. The challenges which these emerging technologies present can best be approached with a willingness to invest the time to understand them, and such understanding can best be gained by one's actually becoming a "user" of some of these new technologies. For example, you need only use a personal computer, Internet "browser" software, and a modem to dial up the World Wide Web to gain some insight into what might be in store for the electronic distribution of music. By the same token, if one does not understand how a computer and telephone lines could affect the future of printed music publishing, it serves to underscore the point that one must actually use the technology to fully understand its full portent. Copyright owners who fail to understand the new technologies risk being left behind, in much the same way as the silent film maker was left behind upon the advent of "talkies."

This chapter will first sketch some of the recent developments in high technology, such as computer software, videogames, multi-media CD-ROMs, karaoke, and other new media products, and will then discuss considerations in granting and clearing licenses for the use of music in those products. The scope of this chapter will be limited to products intended for distribution on various forms of physical media, such as computer floppy disks, game cartridges, and optical laserdiscs (including, CD-ROMs, CD-I, and others). Licensing issues arising from the use of music, either in phonorecords or audiovisual works, whether in traditional form, such as motion pictures or in new media form, such as multi-media programs, but delivered to the customer by way of an *interactive* form of *electronic distribution* — i.e., into the home or office over telephone lines, cable television lines, and similar means (other than by a traditional, non-interactive (or linear) form of delivery, such as radio or television broadcast) will be discussed in the next chapter, on *Licensing Musical Works and Sound Recordings on the Internet*.

## I. TECHNOLOGICAL DEVELOPMENTS

The advent of the microchip, a device which can pack hundreds of thousands of "transistors" onto a sliver of silicon the size of a thumbnail, has spawned several entirely new categories of commercial and consumer products. A greeting card that plays a song when you open it (see Chapter 21) is just one simple example of a musical application of the computer chip. These chips have become so powerful that computing power previously reserved for the large refrigerated rooms that housed large mainframe computers are now available in personal computers and videogame players that you can buy for a few hundred dollars. The computer chip is, indeed, the electronic "brain" upon which all of these technological developments rely.

### A. Computer Software

The term computer program, or *computer software*, refers to the set of instructions given to a machine to bring about a certain result. The copyright law provides the same protection to computer software that is afforded to literary works.[2] It is important not to confuse the computer with the software that instructs the computer what to do. The computer is the physical machine, or *hardware,* that performs certain limited kinds of tasks; the *software* is the copyrighted work that provides the instructions that tells the machine what tasks to perform. An apropos analogy that best illustrates the relationship between computer hardware and computer software is one which suggests that you conceive the software as the *record album* and the hardware as the *record player and stereo system* that plays the music embodied in

---

[2] 17 U.S.C. Sec. 101, 117.

the record album. Just as the record player cannot play music without the record, a computer cannot perform any meaningful tasks without the computer software that instructs it.

The following outlines the various kinds of computer software being marketed for use on computers in use today, including video-game software (sometimes referred to as entertainment software), ed-ucational software, music software for professional and amateur musicians, musical instrument digital interface (MIDI) software, and business software. Other forms of software-related products are dis-cussed under the headings, multi-media programs and new media products.

### 1. Videogame or Entertainment Software

Increasingly, producers of *videogames*, or *entertainment software* as they prefer to call it, are recognizing the value of music as an integral part of the entertainment mix provided to users of video-games. For example, the enjoyment of a simple electronic table tennis game, such as *Pong*, may be enhanced if the game could be instructed to play a victory jingle, such as the theme from the movie *Rocky*, each time the player succeeds at performing a certain score or level of competence. Certainly, the absence of the music from the movie *Star Wars* would be conspicuous if it were not an element of a videogame based upon the movie.

Initially, videogames were incorporated exclusively in large game machines which contain their own television monitors and control sys-tems (e.g., joy stick, buttons, pedals). These machines are normally distributed to pin-ball arcades, now called *video arcades*. Makers of these machines require synchronization licenses for the incorporation of music in the videogames programmed into these machines. Most video arcades obtain performance licenses from ASCAP or BMI and any music that may emanate from a videogame machine at an arcade would be covered by the arcade's performance license. The vast pro-portion of videogames sold today, however, are sold in the form of cartridges or computer "floppy" disks designed for use on home vid-eogame machines, such as Nintendo, or personal computers, such as the Apple Macintosh or IBM and IBM-compatible personal comput-ers. A new generation of *portable* videogame machines, such as the *Gameboy* by Nintendo, have become popular and the importance of the audio aspects of these games is evidenced by the earphone attachments that these game machines now support.

## 2. Educational Software

We have barely seen the tip of the proverbial iceberg of potential educational applications to which computers can be put to use, and music is expected to play an important role in the development of these applications. We are beginning to see computer software that teaches the alphabet and reading by phonics, electronic books that contain lyrics or play music, software that teaches you how to play the piano, and software that explores the boundaries of music appreciation. The recording of popular music in even non-music specific software, such as the geography program *Where in the World is Carmen San Diego*, and history program, *Where in Time is Carmen San Diego?* (both published by Broderbund Software) is likely to greatly enhance the educational experience these programs aim to provide.

One of the first products to demonstrate the marvels of applying computer technology in education was a program called *The Magic Flute*, a set of three CD-ROM optical discs for use on an Apple Macintosh personal computer equipped with a CD-ROM drive or player. Published by Warner New Media, a division of AOL Time-Warner, Inc., the program contains a digital recording of Mozart's opera, enhanced by more than one hour of commentary, additional music, and more than 7000 screens of information. While listening to the opera, or any portion of the opera, a user may simultaneously read the English or German libretto, or put the program on hold to read the story, look up a definition in the glossary, explore a character analysis, or view a complete map of the opera, and then, of course, take a final exam.

*Beethoven: The Ninth Symphony* is an interactive optical disc program that can be played on any IBM-compatible personal computer using the Microsoft Windows operating system. With this program, you can see and hear everything from an overview of the symphonic form to an in-depth analysis of each movement of the Ninth symphony. The program, distributed by Microsoft Corporation, includes biographical material, examples of Beethoven's other works, and an interactive game for one to four players to test your musical knowledge.

*Luciano Pavorotti: O Sole Mio, Louis Armstrong: An American Songbook,* and *Mozart: A Musical Biography* have been released by the MusicWorks team at Philips Interactive Media of America. These programs may be played on a regular CD player, but if you have a CD-I player, a special interactive media player that works with a television set, you can explore all the interactive features that the CD-I format affords. For example, the Mozart disk contains a full multimedia biography of the composer, features artists performing his works, and allows you to play an interactive version of a musical dice game invented by Mozart. Philips and Sony Corporation, who manufacture these CD-I players, have been betting that this technology will become as widely popular as home video tape machines. At the time of this writing, the CD-I standard has not become as popular as they had hoped.

### 3.  Music Software

Some personal computer software programs were specifically designed for professional or amateur composing and playback of musical compositions. These programs present on the computer screen the five-line musical staff, and give the user the ability to place on the staff musical notes, including whole, half, quarter, eighth, sixteenth, etc., and all of the customary musical notation terminology. The user may arrange his own notes on the musical scale or load into the computer pre-arranged notes. The user can then "play" the notes in sequence, rendering a performance of the song so arranged, and store or "save" the music in the computer's hard disk, together with any changes made to the music by the user, so that it can later be played back. Any notation of the songs that are presented on the computer screen can be printed out on the user's printer, and, depending on the resolution of the user's computer printer, the print-out may have a quality approaching that of printed sheet music. When played, the music may be heard through the speaker provided with the computer, or an external speaker.

More sophisticated music software programs provides the user with the capability to completely automate the music creation process. Midisoft's STUDIO, which operates on IBM-compatible personal computers using the Microsoft Windows operating system, includes a sequencing program that has to be seen to be believed. While you are playing an electronic keyboard, or any properly equipped musical instrument, the program displays your exact musical performance instantly on the screen as standard musical notation. With powerful editing features, you can rearrange your music, combine parts, change instruments, replay your changes, print it out, or save your performance to a file on your computer disk for later playback.

### 4.  *Musical Instrument Digital Interface (MIDI) Software*

The magic behind the process in Midisoft's STUDIO is something called the *musical instrument digital interface (MIDI)*. MIDI is the standard computer format or protocol for transmitting music data electronically. Most electronic instruments today, such as electronic piano keyboards and synthesizers, are MIDI equipped. Even sounds from acoustic instruments (including the human voice) can be converted to MIDI with special hardware and software. Compared to digitized audio, MIDI data is significantly more compact and more easily manipulated without loss of sound quality.

The significant aspect of this new technology is that it allows you to store the equivalent of a live performance on a computer disk. Since all of these music computer *files* are stored in digital magnetic form, they can be easily copied from one computer diskette to another, and can even be transmitted over telephone lines.

This is not expensive technology. Midisoft's STUDIO 6.0 program has a suggested retail price of less than $100, and a MIDI interface card can also be installed into any PC for about $100, and reasonably powerful PCs are available for less than $2000.

Programs such as these, and the music files they can produce, raise several interesting music licensing questions with which the music industry is just beginning to grapple.

For example, is a MIDI computer file a mechanical reproduction the distribution of which requires a mechanical license subject to the compulsory license statute, or is it a copy of an audiovisual work, the distribution of which may be negotiated, such as the terms of a synchronization or videogram license? The Harry Fox Agency has considered the fixation of music in MIDI files and, to deal with the increasing number of requests for this new form of license, has developed a special form MIDI license, a copy of which is set forth as Form 22.4 at the end of this chapter.

Is a computer file that contains the ability to display music notation on the screen of a personal computer and to print out the notation on a computer printer the equivalent of printed sheet music? Is it a combination of sheet music and mechanical reproduction or audiovisual work? The question becomes significant, because many music copyright owners have granted to print publishers the rights to distribute their music in printed form, such as sheet music and folios, on an exclusive basis. If the music copyright owner grants permission for the reproduction of MIDI files, and those files have the capability of printing out musical notation on laser printers, a print publisher who holds exclusive print rights in the music might take the position that the granting of the license was a breach of its exclusive print rights contract.

The Harry Fox license set forth as Form 22.4 at the end of this chapter states that the license does not grant permission to the licensee "to program into the MIDI sequence [file] the capability of making any other use of the Composition not expressly authorized" by the license. One of the permissions not granted to the licensee is the license to print the licensed composition in sheet music form. Further, the license requires that a warning notice be placed conspicuously on each copy of the MIDI file stating that it is a violation of copyright law to print the file in the form of standard music notation without the permission of the copyright owner. While it is clear that the music copyright owner can limit the scope of the license to prevent the licensee from distributing laser-printed copies of musical notation displayed by a licensed MIDI file, it is not clear how one who distributes files that operate with, for example, Midisoft's STUDIO program, would practically be able to comply with a requirement of making a file that is capable of displaying musical notation on a computer screen incapable of having that notation printed out on a printer.

It would appear that the distribution of MIDI files containing copyrighted music notation capable of being printed out would not be within the scope of the license and the only way one seeking to clear a license for such use would be to also obtain clearance from the owners of the exclusive print rights. This, obviously, is a burdensome solution, and perhaps one that might not be worth the effort.

It seems that the purpose of the scope of the Harry Fox MIDI license is to protect music copyright owners from breach of contract claims of holders of exclusive print rights in their music. Should such a breach of contract dispute ever occur, the resolution of the case may well depend upon what was meant by the term "print" or "sheet music" at a time when the only means of distributing copies of music notation were on paper. An analysis of the question would parallel those considered in Chapter 16, on *Old Licenses, New Uses*. We suspect that, unless there is language in these contracts specifically covering electronic forms of printed music, the courts would narrowly construe "print" and "sheet" music as being limited to distribution on paper form. Perhaps distribution of sheet music via telecopier, or "fax," machines would still be considered a form of distribution on paper, but files that are only usable with the aid of a machine or device (i.e., a computer) take on an entirely different character. If this does, in fact, become the result of these cases, then obtaining clearance of publishers who hold exclusive print rights to music for distribution of MIDI files containing printable music notation would become unnecessary.

Finally, a MIDI file distributor would probably have no need to be concerned with potential violations of exclusive print rights by purchasers and users of MIDI files, because it is not likely that a music copyright owner could legally prevent a purchaser of a licensed MIDI file from printing out a copy of the musical notation for personal use, and not for distribution. The printing out of MIDI files by the end user would be akin to the home taping of sound recordings, a practice which was specifically condoned by Congress when considering the Copyright Act of 1976.

Other software publishers, such as Macromedia, have developed computer programs that allow you to create animated cartoons that can be performed on your computer screen. The animation produced can, of course, be synchronized with music. The publishers of such programs, may well wish to include arrangements of copyrighted musical compositions on the disks distributed with the software. Independent software publishers, sometimes referred to as publishers of "add-on" software, may wish to separately sell diskettes that contain copyrighted music that can be played back by the user of such programs. Users may wish to exchange songs stored on disk with other users. Since computer software files may easily be transferred over telephone lines, such song files may well find themselves on one or more electronic bulletin board services or Internet "Web sites," which allow callers to transfer, or *download,* these files to their own personal computers over the telephone. Music copyright owners are beginning to see more and more requests for these forms of uses, but few standards have yet emerged on how best music copyright owners can respond to these requests.

### 5.  Business Software

The variety of applications to which powerful desktop and home computers can be applied is limited only by the imagination of the people who are writing the software for use on these machines. Today, the largest segment of the market for personal computer software is software designed for business uses, such as word processing, electronic spreadsheets and database management systems.

Few personal computer software programs designed for business, however, require music. Nevertheless, some business programs may lend themselves to the application of music in unexpected ways. For example, business graphics programs, used by executives to make business presentations, have the capability to perform a variety of special effects. Microsoft's *Powerpoint,* Corel's *Quattro Pro,* and IBM's *Lotus Freelance,* are graphics presentation programs for IBM-compatible personal computers. Each allows the user to place sound effects in business presentations that can best be described as "electronic slide shows." Computer software diskettes containing customized sound effects, including public domain and copyrighted music, may well become an after-market product sold by independent software publishers to users of these programs.

If a software publisher wished to distribute a set of "sound files" on diskette which, when combined with such a presentation graphics software program, performs copyrighted music, would the use of the music require a mechanical reproduction license or a synchronization license? If the "slide show" presentation is an audiovisual work, then the use would not be a mechanical reproduction and the compulsory license provision of the copyright act would not apply. *Audiovisual works,* as that term is defined in the copyright law, comprise:

> works that consist of a series of related images which are intrinsi-
> cally intended to be shown by the use of machines or devices such

as projectors, viewers, or electronic equipment, together with accompanying sounds, if any, regardless of the nature of the material objects, such as films or tapes, in which the works are embodied.

Clearly, a computer generated slide show constitutes an audiovisual work. Thus, a synchronization license, likely to be in the form of one of the non-theatrical synchronization or videogram licenses set forth at the end of Chapter 14 and 15, would be required.

Under what circumstances would a *performance license* be required for a business presentation which used such sound files? If the performance of the slide show constituted a *public* performance, then a performance license, usually acquired on a blanket basis, would be required.

## B.  Multimedia Programs

It has been said that we are now in an "age of information" and nothing could be better evidence of that than the advent of new technologies that are revolutionizing the way we accumulate, store, retrieve, analyze, and interact with the vast amounts of information being generated by modern society. One of the most exciting developments that has emerged in this new era has been the convergence of various audio, visual, and database technologies to form what has been called, appropriately, *multimedia.*

We use the term multimedia here to describe a certain class of products that combine the attributes of several different traditional media, such as motion pictures, still photographs, recorded sounds, printed text, computer generated sounds and graphics, and the like. Most multi-media programs are designed to be used in an *interactive* way, with the user controlling the sequence and organization of the information or entertainment that is to be produced or generated.

In the preceding section concerning educational software, we described several examples of music-related educational applications of interactive multimedia, including *Mozart's The Magic Flute*, a CD-ROM disc for the Apple Macintosh; *Beethoven's Ninth Symphony,* a CD-ROM disc for IBM-compatible computers; and *Louis Armstrong: An American Songbook,* a CD-I disc for Philips or Sony home CD-I players.

Another exciting development in the field of interactive media is the advent of the electronic encyclopedia. One example is a multi-media version of *Compton's Encyclopedia* for use on Apple Macintosh and IBM-compatible personal computers. Music copyright owners should expect to see in the future the creation of multimedia encyclopedias dedicated to music, such as an encyclopedia of jazz and popular music. The *electronic discography* that might be included in such a work could allow the user to listen to clips from the listed recordings, or read the music notation or lyrics of any particular song, at the mere press of a button.

## C. New Media Products

The term new media is used here to encompass a variety of products that are just coming on the market, as well as products that have not yet been invented. Several new technologies are only now converging and the result has been and will continue to be the establishment of new markets for licensing musical works and new means of distributing these works. Consider some existing, and yet to exist, examples:

### 1. Karaoke

In the 1940s, the Ben Yost singers made popular *sing-along* performances in night clubs of that era. Later, Mitch Miller further popularized the idea with a highly successful television program called, "Sing-along with Mitch." The modern-day equivalent of these sing-along programs is *karaoke* (pronounced "Kara-OK"), which has become quite a phenomenon in Japanese night life. Meaning literally "empty orchestra," karaoke became the sing-along of the 1990s. In Japan, a businessman may take his guests to a small bar, where they may imbibe western spirits and take turns at karaoke singing.

A karaoke system is composed of special hardware, which combines a stereo amplifier with a compact disc player, hooked to a television monitor. Recordings of standard songs are digitally recorded without the lead vocal, often fully orchestrated with back-up singers. The disc also contains the lyrics for the lead vocal. In a typical Japanese karaoke bar, a patron, usually after having imbibed a few drinks to acquire the nerve necessary to volunteer,[3] chooses a song from a list of titles, walks up to a small stage, faces the audience (of other bar patrons), and views a small television monitor facing him on the stage. When the music starts, the lyrics begin to scroll onto the monitor, highlighted, line by line, in tempo with the music to cue the performer when to sing the appropriate line. The karaoke players come equipped with special features, such as echo, reverb and pitch control, which can make even the worst voice seem listenable. The lyrics are usually displayed in the foreground of random motion pictures of popular American scenes, such as surfing, and other amusement scenes. A video camera may be focused on the performer and the performer's image may be displayed on video monitors located throughout the bar. The karaoke bars, where performances of music by karaoke takes place, are licensed by performance rights societies.

This technology has been marketed in several novel ways. Consumers at a shopping mall may now go to what is called a *karaoke booth* where they can render a live karaoke performance and purchase a videotape of their performance to take home. Complete karaoke systems for home use made by companies such as Pioneer and the Daiicho Kosho Co. are now available for less than $1,000. Karaoke discs for playback on these machines are available for under $20.

Being that there are several uses to which the term karaoke has been applied, a license to permit karaoke use of music should carefully define precisely what forms of karaoke use is permitted. See Form 22.5 at the end of this chapter for an example of a Karaoke license agreement.

### 2. Holographic Motion Pictures

Research scientists in Japan and other countries are developing new forms of audiovisual media. One technology under development is *holographic projection* — the projection of visual images in three dimensions. A potential application of this technology in entertainment programming would be theater productions in which characters and scenery are projected in such a way that they look like live char-

---

[3] Confirmed by personal experience one late night in Tokyo — *Bob*.

acters walking on a stage. A live stage performance on Broadway in New York could be simultaneously projected to legitimate theatres across the county or a Shakespearean play recorded on a holographic laser disc could be projected in three dimensions right in front of you in your living room. These works might also have interactive qualities, allowing the audience to participate or affect the denouement of the work presented, or interact with the work as though they were players of a videogame. Holographic projectors for the home could allow the distribution of optical discs containing these 3D-programs for home interactive viewing.

Licenses for the use of music in such works would not look much different from the standard synchronization license and videogram license provisions in use today. Nevertheless, unless the licenses issued today are carefully drafted to reflect the intent of the parties (e.g., would any of the uses described in the preceding paragraph be considered a "television exhibition" as that term is used in many synchronization licenses today?), old licenses might be construed as permitting new uses against the better interests of the copyright owners (see Chapter 16).

## II. CONSIDERATIONS IN GRANTING AND CLEARING LICENSES FOR COMPUTER SOFTWARE, MULTIMEDIA PROGRAMS, AND NEW MEDIA PRODUCTS

Licensing the use of music in such products requires consideration of some of the same basic factors discussed in preceding chapters, including the fee structure, the value of the song, the importance of the song in relation to its intended use, and the scope of the intended use.

### A. Fee Structure

#### 1. Flat Fee

In certain limited circumstances, it may be appropriate for a music copyright owner to charge a one-time, flat fee, for the use of music in certain computer software, multimedia, or new media works. Such a fee structure would be appropriate where the software will not be offered for sale. Interactive multimedia is being increasingly used for corporate training purposes, and the use of music in such works, where relatively few copies will be made and none sold, would warrant a flat fee, much like a synchronization fee for nontheatrical motion pictures. However, the music copyright owner should be sure to either (i) define the license narrowly to assure that a subsequent decision by the licensee to distribute copies of the work for commercial sale would require further permission of the copyright owner, or (ii) structure the fee so that if the licensee elects to commercially release the work, royalties will be paid on the basis of each unit distributed or revenues derived from such sales. The form of license for such arrangements would be similar to Forms 14.4 and 14.5 set forth at the end of Chapter 14, on *Synchronization Licenses*.

### 2.  Royalty

Like the use of music in consumer products, the performance of music in the course of using computer software, videogames, multimedia programs and new media products will usually be *private*, not public. Because no fees are collectable for private performances of music, the music copyright owner will seek alternative means to share the economic success of the use. The most common means is collecting a royalty based on the sales of the work embodying the music. The fee structure for most uses of music in computer software, multimedia, and new media products is, therefore, much the same as that found in videogram licenses and licenses for consumer musical products. See Forms 15.1 through 15.7 at the end of Chapter 15, on *Videogram Licenses*, and Forms 20.1 and 20.2 at the end of Chapter 20, on *Licenses for Television, Radio, and Print Advertising*.

### 3.  Pro Rata

Licenses to use music in certain computer software, multimedia, new media products poses a special problem that usually does not arise in the case of other consumer products, such as music boxes, exercise machines, and greeting cards. In each of the latter three examples, it is unlikely that more than one song will be required. With respect to computer software, multimedia programs, and new media products, it is likely that several songs, perhaps hundreds of songs will be used in the work. For example, a single software disk, such as a floppy disk or CD-ROM laser disc may contain hundreds or thousands of files, each containing music in the MIDI format or some similar format capable of being performed with the aid of a computer. Similarly, a multi-media encyclopedia reproduced on laser discs may also contain portions of thousands of songs in mechanical or an "electronic print" format.

In instances where there is more than one song involved in the work, music copyright owners will typically request a royalty, using a percentage of net revenues *pro rated* among the number of copyrighted musical compositions in the work. For example, if there are 10 songs in the computer software or new media program, and the royalty percentage charged is 5%, the royalty for the use of one particular song would be 1/10 of 5% of the net revenues that the producer of the computer software program receives on sales of the work. Of course, this does not mean that the owners of the 9 other musical compositions used in the software will receive the same fee. Each owner would negotiate its own pro rata percentage or other license fee for the use of the music.

A copyright owner granting a license containing a provision for the payment of royalties on the basis of a pro rata share in relation to all of the musical compositions in the work should be certain the license provides that only *copyrighted, royalty-bearing* musical compositions be used in calculating the share. In other words, songs in the public domain, such as *The Star Spangled Banner*, should not be counted in determining the number of songs in the work. This is to prevent the licensee from adding several, or hundreds, of public domain songs to the work at no cost for the purpose of reducing the amount of royalties payable to owners of licensed musical compositions in the work. Nor should sound recordings be included in the calculation of the number of songs used to pro rate the royalties — only musical compositions.

A person seeking to clear a license to use a song in a work containing hundreds or thousands of songs should be prepared to come across one or more music copyright owners unfamiliar with multimedia technologies. A copyright owner inexperienced with licensing music for use in such works may insist upon receiving a royalty rate on par with rates normally obtained when licensing music for works containing one or just a few compositions. For example, if the music copyright owner asks for an un-prorated 5% of net revenues for the use of a song in a work that will contain several hundred songs, you may have to devote some further time educating the copyright owner about the nature of the use.

Pro rating the royalty based upon the number of songs, or copyrighted songs, appearing in the work, may not always be the optimal or fairest method of structuring a fee for a particular use of a composition. Either the music copyright owner or the producer, depending upon the circumstances, could take the position that it would not be fair to pro rate the fee on a straight line basis (i.e., dividing the fee strictly by the number of songs in the work), without accounting for the duration that each song appears in the work or the quality of the use.

But alternative methods of pro rating fees among works are often ineffective or inefficient. Some have suggested that the duration of each song used be a factor, but this would favor long symphonic works over shorter more popular compositions. Others have suggested an allocation on the basis of how much *real estate*, or memory space, each work uses on the disk containing the work, but this poses special problems. The amount of disk space used by a MIDI file that can generate a performance with the aid of a computer is significantly less than the disk space required by an analog or even digital recording of the very same performance. Thus, some recordings would be favored over others on a purely arbitrary basis.

Producers of multimedia works have suggested that music copyright owners should not forget that permission must be cleared to use a multitude of other types of media works in the multimedia program. They have proposed that the disk space used by all the music on the disk should be compared with the disk space used by all other materials, such as text, photographs, moving pictures, dialogue, and other sounds. Under this method, the producer might propose to budget 20% of revenues to royalties and suggest that an allocation be made among the various types of works used on the disk, as for example, 25% to music, 25% to visuals, 25% to text, and 25% to monologue or dialogue. Leaving aside the merits of this proposal, it still leaves open the question of how the percentage paid for music would be allocated among the owners of the music (and sound recording) copyrights used in the multi-media program.

Perhaps the soundest method of allocation, and perhaps the easiest to administer, is the straight line proration based on the number of *copyrighted, royalty-bearing* songs used in the work and adjusting for the relative importance of the song in relation to its intended use by raising or lowering the percentage charged for the particular song. For example, a valuable song that is used each time the work is accessed might command 7% of the net revenues pro rated among the number of copyrighted songs in the work; a less valuable song that plays a minor role in the work would receive 3% of the net revenues pro rated among the number of total copyrighted songs in the work.

Perhaps another compromise that preserves the simplicity of the *pro rata* method, but one which still takes into consideration the particular value of the song and the importance in relation to its intended use, could be to provide that the use of an important song in a substantial way is assigned a value of 2 songs in calculating the pro ration and that less valuable songs used in less substantial ways or duration could be assigned a value of a fraction of one song. Of course, multimedia producers tend to avoid any formula that might complicate their business or produce accounting errors. At the same time, copyright owners might consider that it is just not worth negotiating what it takes to account for these finer distinctions, and that it is more important to just make sure the song is included in the work and that he will be paid some fair amount for its use.

### 4. *Applicability of the Compulsory License Provision*

Almost all interactive multi-media programs will contain some audiovisual information, with either moving images or a series of still images. The same is true for videogames and is likely to be true for most educational software. Accordingly, licenses for recording music on such works will normally not be subject to the compulsory license statute.

But what if an interactive program consists solely of text and music, with no pictures or other visual images? Would the mere text displayed on a computer screen be considered a visual image for the purpose of determining whether the compulsory license provision applies? For example, would the use of music in a software program that consists of music performances and the display of merely text on a computer screen (with no motion pictures or other visual images) merely require a mechanical license? More specifically, suppose a publisher produces an electronic discography of every popular recording made in the 1960s that allows the user to select any recording on the list and hear several bars of the recording for identification. Would the text appearing on the screen be considered a "motion picture" or other "audiovisual work" for purposes of determining whether the compulsory license statute is applicable?

The answer remains entirely unclear. Text presented on a computer screen would seem no different from text contained in the package that comes along with a standard compact disc. However, the user interface of computer software has been held to be an audiovisual work.[4] Thus, the user interface of the computer software that permits you to access the textual material may constitute a sufficient audiovisual work that accompanies the recording that would remove the recorded music from the scope of the compulsory license provision.

## B. Value of the Song

As in the consideration of licensing music for use in consumer products, music copyright owners should consider the potential impact of associating a hit song with computer software or new media software product on the future earning potential of the song. However, it should be noted that associating a song with a computer or new media product, unlike with a consumer product or commercial advertising, is more likely to enhance the earnings potential of the song, than to harm it.

Just as one might get a negative impression by associating a song with a personally or politically undesirable consumer product (e.g., milk of magnesia, nuclear energy), one is likely to get a positive impression from the association of a song with a more popular or culturally laudable product (e.g., electronic children's book), a product that is conceived as being on the "cutting edge" of high technology (e.g., computer software, electronic encyclopedia), or a product that is clearly making a contribution to scholarship or historical research (e.g., an electronic discography).

---

[4] *Computer Associates v. Altai*, 982 F.2d 693 (2d Cir. 1992).

A music copyright owner who is offered to have his song placed in a work such as an electronic encyclopedia or discography should seize the opportunity, because the value of the copyright will benefit from merely the exposure provided by inclusion of the song in such a work. In an information explosion, the competition for the *share of mind* of the listening public is intense. Licensing the song, even for a momentary use in an encyclopedia or other interactive product, particularly those that are likely to be used as reference works in libraries, in business, and in the home, will help maintain the relationship between the song and the listening public, and increase the likelihood that future requests for licenses of the song will continue.

For these reasons, a music copyright owner should not allow the difficulties and complexities of setting a proper fee for new media works to get in the way of consummating a license and providing the song with a means of continual exposure to the listening public.

## C. Importance of the Song in Relation to Its Intended Use

Again, why is a license being sought for *this* particular song? The fewer substitutes for the song that are available, the more the licensee is willing to pay. In contrast with the limited number of songs or themes logically available for a musical doll based on a character of a popular motion picture or television program, there is more likely to be a large variety of songs available to provide in an electronic encyclopedia a demonstration of the kind of music that was popular in the 1930s. Of course, a limited universe of songs will be available for a videogame software program based upon, for example, *Star Wars*. Careful consideration should be given to the particular circumstances in evaluating the importance of the song in relation to its intended use in computers, multi-media programs and new media products.

### 1. Special Nature of Interactive Works

A special problem may arise in using the usual means of establishing the appropriate license fees for use of music in interactive multimedia works, and this involves an important difference between interactive media devices and traditional works: traditional media are *linear*, while interactive media are *non-linear*.

Traditional media, such as record albums and videotapes, are linear in the sense that they are generally listened to or viewed from beginning to end. By contrast, interactive media, such as compact discs and CD-ROMs, are generally non-linear, in the sense that one can gain immediate access to any portion of the work by skipping from any one point in the work to any other point in the work.

In a traditional work, such as a motion picture, the music that the producer chooses to play over the main title and opening credits of the work will remain the same for every performance of the motion picture and the viewer will hear the music every time he watches the movie (unless he intentionally skips over, or *fast forwards* through, the main title). By contrast, in an interactive work, an excerpt of the song may be played back under a variety of different circumstances. For example, the new media work may be set up so that a few bars of the song, *Tea For Two* is rendered only when a picture of Irving Caesar and Vincent Youmans, the song's writer and composer, appear on the screen. If the user never goes to the part of the work that displays the picture of Irving Caesar and Vincent Youmans, the song will never be performed, even though the work as a whole might be used as much as on a daily basis. It may be impossible to gauge just how much one particular song would be performed, or where it will most likely appear, in relation to the balance of the work. On the other hand, the producer of the interactive work can arrange for the song to be played every time the work is started up by the user, no matter what use will be made of the interactive work in any particular session. Further, the producer can allow the user to customize the work, so that any number of songs can be played every time the user starts up the work. They may alternate randomly or the user can choose to hear only one particular song over and over again.

In other words, the importance of the song in relation to its intended use may depend entirely upon the use put to the work *by the user*. This makes it very difficult to determine just how valuable the music is likely to be in relation to the work in which it is to be incorporated.

### 2. Traditional Factors

As discussed in Chapter 14, a licensor should consider a variety of factors in determining an appropriate fee for a standard synchronization license (for use of a composition in a motion picture or television program). Such factors may include whether the use is a vocal rendition or merely instrumental; whether the use is of the entire song or just a few bars; whether the music is used as background music or foreground music; whether the use is at a prominent point in the motion picture, such as over the main title or credits; whether the intended use relates to how the composition was originally presented to the public; and whether the music is used to help tell the story. These are all factors which help determine the importance of the song in relation to its intended use. If, for example, the song will be played at the beginning of the motion picture over the main title of the film, or in its entirety at any point in the film, the use would command a premium fee.

A synchronization license for a traditional work, such as a motion picture, will typically limit the number of seconds the licensed song may be used in the picture. This customary restriction generally causes no difficulties in the context of a motion picture or television program, where the performance of the audiovisual work is usually linear — played from one point in time to another, at one or several instances in the picture. In the context of interactive media, however, difficult questions arise from the fact that, depending upon the interaction between the user and the new media work, there may be no one readily identifiable period of time in which the composition is played during the performance of the work.

Under these circumstances, the rules for determining the appropriate fees for use in traditional works do not lend themselves very well to application in this new media. In a synchronization license for a motion picture, a music copyright owner may use as a rule of thumb the number of seconds the music will be performed in the movie, yet there may be no way of determining that number in an interactive work.

With a variety of possibilities such as these, it behooves the music copyright owner who wishes to maximize the value of his property to gain as much understanding as possible about the media and the particular program in which the music will be licensed. Asking for "most favored nations" status will not work in situations where, as here, it would be virtually impossible to determine whether the licensor of some other song appearing in the work received more favorable terms for its use.

The music copyright owner should learn as much about the particular multi-media work as possible and simply do the best he can to determine the value of the song and the importance of the song in relation to its intended use. It should also be remembered that licensing a few bars of a song for use in an electronic encyclopedia is not the equivalent of licensing the entire song in a work in which the song will always be played from beginning to end. A license fee that is significantly less than the statutory rate for a mechanical license could well be appropriate where only enough of the song is used to allow the listener to recognize the melody, as opposed to the rendering of the entire song.

## D. Scope of the Use

### 1. Media

A copyright owner would want the license to fully describe the product in which the music will be embodied. The work should be referenced by title, or tentative title, and any other useful information to describe the work, thereby defining the scope of the license as narrowly as possible.

### 2. Term

It is always in the interest of copyright owners to limit the duration of music licenses. Music copyright owners generally try to limit these licenses to 5 years, sometimes giving an option to extend for an additional 3 to 5 years upon the payment of an additional advance against royalties. The term of most karaoke licenses is currently about 7 years.

Insisting upon a fixed limited term, however, might not always be practical. The producer of an interactive encyclopedia, for example, might convincingly argue that it cannot predict just how long the edition of the encyclopedia will remain "in print" and to require a new license between publication of editions would not be practical. In that event, the music copyright owner might suggest that the term be limited to the one edition and its reprints (including foreign language versions) however long new printings are made, but that a new license would be required for subsequent editions. But even this would not be a practical solution in some cases. Because of the ease with which these works can be electronically *updated* (i.e., revised), a new "edition" can be published every month or even every week!

### 3.  Exclusivity

The principles of exclusivity discussed in connection with commercial advertising do not apply equally to computer software, educational software, videogames, multimedia, and other new media works. Using music to help establish a product identity is no more a factor in the use of music in an electronic encyclopedia or videogame than it is in the use of music in a motion picture or television program. As is true for synchronization licenses for motion pictures, television, and video, exclusivity is rarely granted for uses in interactive media and software.

Accordingly, a music copyright owner would be quite reluctant to provide any form of exclusivity in connection with the licensing of music in computer software or multi-media programs. If exclusivity were considered, the scope of the exclusivity should be very narrowly defined. For example, granting "exclusivity for educational software" when the intent is for works to be distributed in the K-12 educational market, might be construed to cover electronic encyclopedia and even adult training programs. The types of educational software could vary to such a degree that it may be impossible to narrowly circumscribe the terms of exclusivity. In any event, software and new media is usually differentiated sufficiently that a licensee would not normally require exclusivity to the music in order to help differentiate his product in the software market.

### 4.  Territory

Copyright owners have tried to restrict the territory of these licenses to the United States and Canada and require that separate licenses be obtained for use in other territories from their affiliated subpublishers around the world. The world, however, has changed dramatically from the days of locally produced sheet music and phonograph records, and music copyright owners are under increasing pressure to grant world-wide licenses.

It has become the practice of computer software and multimedia producers to establish facilities at one or two locations in the world, such as Singapore or Ireland, where virtually all copies of their products, in various language versions, are made and distributed to their subsidiaries and affiliates around the world. This is a much more efficient method of operation than the traditional means of distributing record albums with which music publishers are familiar. The technology itself is facilitating the trend toward a one world marketplace: the vast amounts of memory capacity of optical laser discs permit the storage of multiple language versions of a single program all on the same disc, vastly facilitating the distribution of such works overseas. Accordingly, music publishers are beginning to accept proposals for licensing on a worldwide basis to reflect these new technologies and business practices.

Music publishers should, of course, first consider whether they are under any contractual restriction with its songwriters or international co-publishers that would preclude them from issuing a world-wide license without special clearance. Where rights are split by territory (see Chapters 5 and 6), the co-administrators of the copyright should work out a deal by which royalties from world wide licenses may be split in some equitable manner.

Music publishers and those with whom they share music rights overseas should work these deals out among themselves and not try to place unreasonable burdens on the prospective licensee, such as requesting the licensee to account for sales on a territory by territory basis. The rights owner in each territory has a great incentive to cooperate in working out such an arrangement. Rather than provide territory by territory accounting, a producer will accept licenses for the territories he can get and simply choose not to sell directly into territories for which he cannot obtain a license. In an environment with multiple distribution channels, producers cannot control the territories in which their products will end up. Consequently, the owner of rights for a territory that refuses to license will discover he receives no royalties for products that end up being sold in his territory.

The music publishers have created much of the bind they are in because of the way they structured their subpublishing deals in the past. Now that the world has changed, they should work out administrative solutions to facilitate the efficient licensing of their copyrights. Anything less would be a disservice to the songwriters they are supposed to represent.

## III. ADDITIONAL CONSIDERATIONS IN CLEARING LICENSES FOR MULTIMEDIA AND NEW MEDIA PRODUCTS

### A. Understanding All the Rights Involved

As noted in Chapter 1, persons seeking to clear licenses for multimedia programs or new media products can avoid difficulties by first fully understanding all of the potential rights that may be involved in the use. For example, if you are seeking permission to use a particular recording in your multi-media program, don't overlook the fact that you will require two separate licenses, one under the copyright in the sound recording and another under the copyright in the underlying musical composition. A license to use the underlying composition may be obtained from the music publisher or its agent, such as the Harry Fox Agency; the license to use the sound recording may be sought by conferring with the record company who owns the recording.

In some cases, more than two licenses to use a certain piece of material will need to be cleared. For example, the use of a simple film clip from a motion picture may require separate permission from each of several parties holding various rights underlying the clip. As noted in Chapter 1, any of the following rights may be hidden beneath the surface of an apparently simple clearance problem: a copyright in the underlying song featured in the clip, a copyright in the recording of the song performed in the clip, the copyright in the motion picture from which the clip was excerpted, a copyright in any choreography appearing in the clip, a copyright in a literary work upon which the clip is based (where the film from which the clip was taken is based upon a novel, non-fiction book, newspaper article, biography, autobiography, etc.), a copyright in a theatrical production (such as a musical play, opera, or ballet) performed in the clip, a copyright in an animated character, a copyright in a still photograph appearing in the clip, a copyright of a translation or arrangement of a work in the public domain, a right of privacy (i.e., the right one has "to be left alone") of one or more individuals appearing in the clip, or a right of publicity (i.e., the exclusive right an individual has to the use of one's name, voice, photograph, and likeness) of one or more individuals appearing in the clip.

Considerations in granting and clearing rights to use works other than musical compositions is beyond the scope of this book. However, an example of a license to use a film clip is set forth as Form 22.6 at the end of this chapter. Form 22.8 set forth at the end of this chapter is an example of a license typically used by record companies and motion picture producers for the synchronization of sound recordings in audiovisual works. An example of a license to use a still photograph is set forth as Form 22.7 and a location release is set forth as Form 22.9 at the end of this chapter.

## B.  Educate the Music Copyright Owner

Finally, as also noted in Chapter 1, where necessary, persons seeking to clear licenses for complex works, such as multimedia and new media works, should take the time to educate the music copyright owner on just how the music is intended to be used. For at least the next several years, a substantial number of people in society will remain frightened or distrustful of computers and high technology, but a simple live demonstration of a multimedia application could go a long way topromote the understanding and trust required to persuade a music copyright owner, fearful of making a bad deal, to grant the license you desire.

# APPENDIX TO CHAPTER 22
## LICENSING MUSIC IN COMPUTER SOFTWARE, MULTIMEDIA, AND NEW MEDIA PRODUCTS

# Form 22.1

## Multimedia License Used by Harry Fox Agency

THE HARRY FOX AGENCY, INC.
205 East 42nd Street
New York, New York 10017

### MULTIMEDIA RIGHTS LICENSE (MMERL)

License No.:
Date of Issuance:

The following provisions shall apply as indicated in the body of this License:

(A)　Licensee:

(B)　Musical Composition:

(C)　Licensor(s) and percentage of ownership:

(D)　License Date:

(E)　Term:

(F)　Advance:

(G)　Units:

(H)　Royalty Per Unit: "Two times the so-called "statutory royalty rate" (provided pursuant to Section 115 of the United States Copyright Act for the making and distribution of phono-records) [17 U.S.C. 115]."

<u>OR</u>

(H)    Royalty Per Unit: "_____ cents"

(I)    Territory:

(J)    Software Serial Number:

<u>DEFINITIONS</u>

1.    For the purposes hereof, the following terms shall have the following meanings:

**Please sign and return two (2) fully executed copies along with payment if applicable. Thank you.**

a)    **"MULTIMEDIA"** shall mean the medium in which a musical composition will be utilized in conjunction with, but not limited to, computer monitor visual displays.

b)    **"MULTIMEDIA DISK"** which shall include, but not be limited to CD Rom or computer assisted laser disks, shall mean those Multimedia disks containing those musical recordings which is the subject of this license.

c)    The term **"MULTIMEDIA DISK MARKET"** shall refer to the sale, lease, license, use or other distribution of **MULTIMEDIA DISKS** directly or indirectly to individuals for playback through, but not limited to, a personal computer, whether now in existence or hereafter developed.

d)    **"Copy"** or **"copies"** shall mean all **MULTIMEDIA DISK** copies manufactured and distributed by Licensee.

Now it is therefore agreed as follows:

1.    Licensee is hereby applying to Licensor for a **MULTIMEDIA** rights license to use the musical composition referred to in (B) (above) for the purposes of manufacturing, distributing and

selling to the public throughout the territory [(I)), **MULTIMEDIA,** embodying the musical composition.

2.    Licensor hereby grants to the Licensee the following non-exclusive rights with respect to **MULTIMEDIA DISK,** in all respects subject to the terms and conditions herein provided:

   a)   To record and re-record in digital, computer readable or other form consistent with the integral requirements of the **MULTIMEDIA,** the musical composition for use in whole or in part in connection with and with respect to **MULTIMEDIA DISK;**

   b)   To make and distribute copies of the **MULTIMEDIA DISK** program throughout the territory only ((I).

   c)   Licensee may make arrangements and orchestrations of the Composition for its recording purpose, however, this license does not include the right to alter the fundamental character of the Composition, to print sheet music or to make any other use of the Composition not expressly authorized hereunder, all rights to uses not expressly granted hereunder are hereby expressly reserved by the Licensor.

3.    Licensee covenants that it shall place on the outside of all containers or, where possible, in every **MULTIMEDIA DISK** copy a conspicuous notice to clearly read as follows:

   Title of Composition and Names of writers
   © Copyright 20__ (owner of composition).
   International Rights Secured.
   Not for broadcast transmission
   **All** rights reserved. **DO NOT DUPLICATE. NOT FOR SEPARATE RENTAL.**

   **WARNING:** "It is a violation of Federal Copyright Law to synchronize this **MULTIMEDIA DISK** with video tape or film, or to print this **MULTIMEDIA DISK** in the form of standard music notation without the express written permission of the copyright owner".

4.   The musical composition recorded as a **MULTIMEDIA DISK** shall not exceed _____ minutes and _____ seconds.

5.   The use of the musical composition hereunder shall be:

6.   The term during which the rights licensed hereunder may be exercised shall be [the number referred to in (E)] years from the License date (D).

7.   a)   Licensee shall make the royalty payments hereunder, which shall be accompanied by a detailed accounting statement listing units distributed within 45 days after the end of each calendar quarter during which the **MULTIMEDIA DISK** copies are distributed, equal to [the amount referred to in (H)] per **MULTIMEDIA DISK** copy of the work which is manufactured and distributed during each such respective calendar quarter. Within thirty (30) days after the execution of this license, Licensee shall make such payment and render such statement for all units distributed prior to the execution of this license.

   b)   In the event that Licensee fails to account and pay royalties as herein provided, Licensor shall have the right to give written notice to Licensee that unless the default is remedied within thirty (30) days from the date of the notice, this license shall be deemed terminated. Such failure to pay and cure default in such thirty (30) day period shall render either the making or the distribution, or both, of all **MULTIMEDIA DISK** copies hereunder for which royalties have not been paid, actionable acts of infringement under, and fully subject to the remedies provided by the U.S. Copyright Act.

8.   Upon ten business days prior written notice, Licensor, by the Harry Fox Agency ("HFA"), shall have the right during reasonable business hours at License's place of business and at HFA's sole expense to examine, and make copies and extracts from the books and records of Licensee relating to its produc-

tion, making and distribution of **MULTIMEDIA** copies hereunder for the purpose of verifying the accuracy of statements and payments and the performance of Licensee's obligations hereunder. Licensee shall not be required to submit to such an examination more than once during any twelve (12) month period.

9.    This license does not include the rights to:

    a)    Rent separately the musical composition included in the **MULTIMEDIA** copies or to permit purchasers or others to do so;

    b)    Use the story of the musical composition or dramatically depict the musical composition;

    c)    Parody the lyrics and/or music of the musical composition in any way;

    d)    Publicly perform, Broadcast/cablecast or transmit the work in any manner;

    e)    Make, sell or distribute audio phonorecords of the musical composition;

    f)    Utilize a sound recording and/or audiovisual master(s) not owned or separately licensed by Licensee.

10.    All rights of every kind and nature with respect to the composition which are not expressly granted to licensee hereunder are expressly reserved by Licensor.

11.    Licensor warrants only that it has the right to grant this license, and this license is given and accepted without any other representation, warrant or recourse, express or implied, except for Licensor's agreement to repay the consideration paid for this license if the aforesaid warranty should be breached. In no event shall the total liability of the Licensor exceed the total amount of consideration received by it hereunder.

12.    Upon the expiration of this license, all rights herein granted shall cease and terminate and the right to make or authorize any further use or distribution of any recordings made hereunder shall also cease and terminate subject to Licensee's right to sell off it's inventory of **MULTIMEDIA DISK** for an additional period of one year subject to the continuing obligation to pay royalties therefor. No right to make, sell, or distribute **MULTIMEDIA DISK** programs or copies embodying the composition shall survive the termination of this license pursuant to Paragraph 7 (A) hereof.

13.    This license does not include a grant of performing rights. The public performance of the musical composition as part of the **MULTIMEDIA DISK** which is the subject of this license, is expressly conditioned upon such performers or places of performance thereof, having valid performing rights licenses from the respective copyright owners or their designated performing rights societies.

14.    This license supersedes and renders null and void any prior agreements otherwise in effect respecting the Composition and those rights which are the subject of this license.

15.    This license is being entered into on an experimental and nonprejudicial basis, shall apply for the term set forth herein only, and shall not be binding upon or prejudicial to any position taken by Licensor or Licensee for any period subsequent to the period of this license.

16.    This license sets forth the entire understanding of the parties hereto with respect to the subject matter thereof, may not be altered, amended or assigned without an express written instrument to such effect accepted by Licensor and shall be governed and construed by and under the laws of the State of New York applicable to contracts wholly to be performed therein.

BY:

BY: _____
   (Licensee)

BY: THE HARRY FOX AGENCY,
INC. ON BEHALF OF:

BY: _____
   (Licensor)

# FORM 22.2

## ALTERNATE MULTIMEDIA LICENSE

### MULTIMEDIA DISK SYNCHRONIZATION LICENSE

Licensee has requested that Licensor grant certain rights to use the musical composition(s) listed below, on and in connection with the manufacture, distribution and sale of certain so-called **multimedia CD disks,** which CD/disks will be utilized in conjunction with television and/or computer monitor visual displays, and Licensor has agreed to grant such rights on the terms and conditions hereinafter set forth.

Licensor:    BIG MUSIC PUBLISHING CORP
             10585 Santa
             Monica Boulevard
             Los Angeles, California 90025-4950

Licensee:    THANKFUL MULTIMEDIA PROD. CO.

Production:

Composition:

Composer:

Publisher:

Timing:      No individual composition embodied in the Multi-media Disk shall exceed in playing time a duration of four (4) minutes.

Territory:   The World

1.   **Definitions**

(a) **"Multimedia Disk"** shall mean a multimedia software program embodied on CD-I, CD-ROM, Laserdisk and MPC interactive disks, for simultaneous interactive presentation of video, graphics, audio animation and/or data containing the "CD-I Interactive program" which includes those musical recordings which are the subject license.

(b) **"Multimedia Disk Market"** shall refer to the sale, lease, license, use or other distribution of multimedia disks directly or indirectly to individuals for playback through, but not limited to, a television and/or computer monitor.

## 2. Rights Granted

Subject to payment upon execution of this agreement of the advance referred to in Paragraph 5(a) (i) , Licensor hereby grants to Licensee the following non-exclusive rights with respect to Multimedia Disk, in all respects subject to the terms and conditions herein provided:

(a) To record and re-record in CD-I, CD-ROM, Laserdisk, and MPC, the Composition(s) for use in whole or in part in connection with and with respect to Multimedia Disk, and to use the lyrics thereof.

(b) To make and distribute copies of the Multimedia Disk program throughout the Territory only.

(c) Licensee may make arrangements and orchestrations of the composition(s) for its recording purpose all of which shall be done on a "for hire" basis, and shall belong to Licensor (subject to Licensee's rights hereunder); however, this license does **not** include the right to alter the fundamental character of the Composition, to print sheet music or to make any other use of the Composition(s) not expressly granted by Licensor, except as provided in subparagraph 2(a) above. In addition, no right is herein granted to use any existing sound recording of a Composition(s), it being understood that Licensee shall secure the right to reproduce any such sound recording directly from the owner of copyright in same.

## 3. Copyright Notice

Licensee covenants that it shall place on the outside of all containers or where possible, in every Multimedia Disk copy a conspicuous notice to clearly read as follows:

Title of Compositions and Names of Writers, copyright Used by permission of Big Music Publishing Corp.

WARNING: "It is illegal to make unauthorized copies of this software. This software is protected under the Federal Copyright Law. Duplication of this software for any reason, including sale, loan, rental or gift is a crime. Penalties include fines of as much as $50,000.00 and jail terms up to five (5) years.

## 4. Term

FIXED TERM LANGUAGE:

[The term of this license shall be for the period of **seven (7) years** from _____ (to the extent we now or hereafter own or control the copyrights in and to the Composition(s) and any renewals or extensions thereof), and upon such termination any and all rights given and granted hereunder shall forthwith cease and terminate, including the right to make or authorize any use or distribution whatsoever of said recording(s) of said musical Composition(s) in said Multimedia Disk or otherwise.]

PERPETUITY LANGUAGE:

[The rights hereinabove granted shall commence _____ and shall endure for the worldwide period of renewals or extensions thereof that Publisher may now own or control or hereinafter own or control subject to the provisions of paragraph 5 hereof.]

## 5.  Royalties and Accounting

(a)  In consideration of the rights herein granted, Licensee shall pay to licensor the following royalties with respect to copies of the Multimedia Disk distributed pursuant to this License.

(i)  With respect to the first Ten Thousand (1 0,000) copies of the Multimedia Disk, promptly upon execution of this Agreement, the sum of Four Thousand Five Hundred Dollars **($4,500.00) ("the Advance");** and

(ii)  With respect to the next Forty Thousand (40,000) copies of the Multimedia Disk, a sum equal to forty-five cents **($.45) with respect to each such copy;** and

(iii)  With respect to the next Fifty Thousand (50,000) copies of the Multimedia Disk, a sum equal to seventy-two cents **($.72) with respect to each such copy;**

(iv)  With respect to all copies of the Multimedia Disk distributed thereafter, a sum equal to One Dollar and Eight Cents ($1.08) with **respect to each such copy.**

(b)  All checks shall be drawn on a U.S. bank and shall be made payable to Licensor.

(c)  Licensee shall render to Licensor, within **forty-five (45) days** after the end of each calendar quarter year, a detailed accounting statement showing units distributed during such calendar quarter year. Such statement shall be accompanied by the payment of all sums shown to be due on such statement.

(d)  In the event that Licensee fails to account and pay royalties as herein provided, Licensor shall have the right to give written notice to Licensee that unless the default is remedied within ten business (10) days from the date of the notice, this license shall be deemed terminated. Such failure to pay and cure default in such ten (10) day period shall render the further making and/or distribution of Multimedia Disk copies hereunder, actionable acts of infringement under, and fully subject to the remedies provided by the U.S. Copyright Act.

## 6.   Audit Right

Upon ten business days prior written notice, Licensor or its representative shall have the right during reasonable business hours and at Licensor's expense, to examine and make copies and extracts from the books and records of Licensee relating to its production, making and distribution of Multimedia Disk copies hereunder for the purpose of verifying the accuracy of statements and payments and the performance of Licensee's obligations hereunder. Licensee shall not be required to submit to such an examination more than once during any twelve (12) month period, it being understood that such examination may involve more than one visit to Licensee's premises.

## 7.   Product Delivery Requirement

Licensee shall deliver to Licensor two (2) copies of each Multimedia Disk project licensed herein.

## 8.   Restrictions

This license does not include the rights to:

(a)   Use the story of the Composition(s) or dramatically depict the musical Composition(s);

(b)   Parody the lyrics and/or music of the Composition(s) in any way;

(c)   Publicly perform, broadcast/cablecast, or transmit the composition(s) in any manner, except for use of Composition(s) titles in print advertising for the Multimedia Disk;

(d)   Make, sell or distribute audio phonorecords of the Composition(s);

(e)   Utilize a sound recording and/or audiovisual master(s) not owned or separately licensed by Licensee.

**[DELETE (f) IF NOT NEGOTIATED]**

(f)   In the event that Licensee elects to lease or rent the Multimedia Disk to its customers or consumers, Licensee will pay to Licensor an amount equal to Licensor's pro-rata portion of five percent (5%) of Licensee's actual net receipts with respect to such lease or rental. Net receipts shall mean Licensee's gross receipts less only actual shipping charges and sales or similar taxes. As used herein, "Licensor's prorata portion" shall mean the portion that the playing time of the Composition(s) bears to the total playing time of all royalty-bearing coyprighted musical compositions contained in the Multimedia Disk.

## 9.   Reservation of Rights

All rights of every kind and nature with respect to the composition(s) which are not expressly granted to Licensee hereunder are expressly reserved by Licensor.

## 10.   Licensor's Warranties

Licensor warrants only that it has the right to grant this license and this license is given and accepted without any other representation, warrant or recourse, express or implied, except for Licensor's agreement to repay the consideration paid for this license if the aforesaid warranty should be breached. In no event shall the total liability of the Licensor exceed the total amount of consideration received by it hereunder.

## 11.   Expiration

(a)   If Licensee shall violate any of its other obligations under the terms of this agreement, Licensor shall have the right to terminate the Term of this license upon thirty (30) days notice in writing [ten (10) business days notice in the case of a payment of money], and such termination shall become effective unless Licensee shall completely remedy or (in a case not involving a payment of money) have taken steps to substantially remedy the purported violation within such thirty (30) day period and satisfy Licensor that such violation had been remedied.

(b)    Termination of the Term of this license under the provisions of this paragraph shall be without prejudice to any rights which Licensor may otherwise have against Licensee. Upon the termination of this license, notwithstanding anything to the contrary contained herein, all royalties and/or other payments due Licensor shall become immediately due and payable.

## 12.    Performance Rights

This license does not include a grant of performing rights (including, but not limited to, satellite transmissions to individual locations). The public performance of the musical Composition(s) as part of the Multimedia Disk which is the subject of this license, is expressly conditioned upon such performers or places of performance thereof, having valid performing rights licenses from the respective copyright owners or their designated performing rights societies.

## 13.    Headings

The headings used in this Agreement are for reference purposes only, and shall not be construed as to modify or otherwise effect the meaning of any term or condition hereof.

## 14.    Favored Nations

In the event Licensee agrees to pay to any third party whose works are used in connection with this production, with respect to rights similar to those granted herein, royalties and/or advances in excess of those to be paid to Licensor hereunder, then effective as of the date of such agreement with such third party, Licensee shall pay to Licensor such higher royalties and/or advances. The following shall not be deemed to be similar rights for the purposes of this paragraph:

> any composition(s) used as a main theme, title song, or performed over the beginning or end credits, or used as the sole song in a Multimedia Disk project;

## 15.  Experimental License

This Agreement is being entered into on an experimental basis, and shall not be construed as setting a precedent with respect to any future agreements between Licensor and Licensee or any third parties.

## 16.  Assignment

Licensor agrees that Licensee may assign its rights and obligations hereunder provided, however, that Assignee specifically agrees in writing to be bound by and to promptly perform, all of the terms and conditions of this Agreement to be performed on the part of Licensee. Licensor shall be entitled to assign its rights and obligations hereunder.

## 17.  Miscellaneous

This license sets forth the entire understanding of the parties hereto with respect to the subject matter thereof, may not be altered, amended or assigned without an express written instrument to such effect accepted by Licensor and shall be governed and construed by and under the laws of the State of California applicable to contracts wholly to be performed therein. Legal actions between the parties may only be brought in the state or federal courts situated in Los Angeles County, both parties hereby submitting to the jurisdiction of such courts for such purpose. In any action between the parties, the prevailing party shall be entitled to recover its court costs and actual and reasonable outside counsel fees.

AGREED TO AND ACCEPTED:

BIG MUSIC PUBLISHING CORP

By: _____     By: _____

## SCHEDULE "A"

To the Agreement between                                    and
Big Music Publishing Corp.


Composition                    Composer(s)        Publisher(s)

# FORM 22.3

## ALTERNATIVE MULTIMEDIA LICENSE

### MULTIMEDIA MUSIC RIGHTS LICENSE

In consideration of the below listed License Fee, receipt of which is hereby acknowledged, Licensor grants to Producer the non-exclusive and irrevocable right, license, privilege and authority to record, reproduce and/or fix the Composition listed below for use in connection with the Production for distribution in the License Media and for the advertising and promotion thereof subject to the terms and conditions printed on the back of this license.

Production:     500538-0023 "SAMPLE MULTIMEDIA
                PRODUCTION"

Producer:

Composition:    S204694 "SAMPLE SONG"
Composer(s):    FRED FLIRCH, CAROL CREATIVE
Publishers(s):  BIG MUSIC/ASCAP LITTLE MUSIC/BMI
Use: *****,     Timing: *****

Administrative Share: 50% OF THE ENTIRE WORLD

Licensed Media: Manufacture of Multimedia Copies of the Production for the purpose of distribution in the Multimedia Market. "Multimedia Copy" shall mean a computer or digital media data file, regardless of format, embodying a recording of the Composition along with visual images and a visual display of the lyrics, capable of playback through a computer, including interactive devices. "Multimedia Market shall refer to the sale, lease, license, use or other distribution of Multimedia Copies directly or indirectly to individuals for playback through a computer, whether now in existence or hereafter developed. "Computer" shall mean an electronic machine, with or without a visual display, used to store, display, perform, manipulate, and analyze data or information fed into it, and which may control peripheral machinery automatically or otherwise.

License Fee:     $*****
Advance:
Fixing Fee:
License Territory:    *****
License Term:    *****
Accounting Period:    *****

AGREED AND ACCEPTED

_____

LICENSOR:

PRODUCER:
c/o THE CLEARING HOUSE, LTD.
849 South Broadway
Los Angeles, California 90014

STANDARD PROVISIONS

1     DEFINITIONS: For the purpose hereof, the following terms shall have the following meanings

    1.1     "Copy" or "copies" shall mean all Multimedia Copies manufactured and distributed by Licensee.

    1.2     "Distribution", if and where applicable, shall have the same meaning as in section 115(c) (2) of the U. S. Copyright Act.

2. ACCOUNTING: Subject to the recoupment of any advance, and only with respect to Copies finally sold, paid for and not returned, after the first commercial sale of a Copy pursuant to this license, Producer shall make royalty payments to Licensor, accompanied by a detailed accounting statement, within 60 days after the close of the Accounting Period in any such Accounting Period in which Copies are sold.

2.1 SELL OFF PERIOD: At the end of the License Term, Producer shall have the right to sell off its inventory of Copies for an additional period of one year subject to the continuing obligation to pay royalties therefor.

2.2 PROMOTION/PROFESSIONAL/DEMONSTRATION COPIES: Producer may distribute up to 5% of the number of copies manufactured and distributed, without payment of royalties for promotional, professional or demonstration purposes.

2.3 FAILURE TO ACCOUNT: In the event that Producer fails to account and pay royalties as herein provided, if royalties have been earned, Licensor shall have the right to give written notice to Producer that unless the default is remedied within thirty (30) days from the date of Producers receipt of the notice, such default may be deemed a breach of this agreement.

2.4 EXAMINATION OF RECORDS: After reasonable written notice to Producer, for the purpose of verifying the accuracy of statements rendered, an authorized representative of Licensor may examine Producer's books and records pertaining solely to the sales of Copies licensed hereunder, and make photocopies and extracts thereof, during normal business hours at the place where Producer maintains said books and records, however, no more than once per calendar year. Statements rendered shall become binding unless written objection is received by Producer within two years after the rendering of such statement.

3. RIGHTS NOT GRANTED: Producer may make arrangements, orchestrations and adaptations of the Composition for

its recording purposes hereunder. However, this license does not include the right to alter the fundamental character of the Composition, to use the title or subtitle of the Composition as the title of the Production, to dramatize the story of the Composition, to broadcast or transmit the Composition, to distribute phonorecords of the Composition or to make any other use of the Composition not expressly authorized hereunder.

4.    PERFORMANCE RIGHTS: This license does not include a grant of public performance rights. Public performance rights in the Composition are conditioned on the appropriate venues or entities having valid performance rights licenses issued by Licensor or the person, firm, corporation, society, association or other entity having the legal right to issue such performance licenses.

5.    TERMINATION OF RIGHTS: Upon the expiration of this license, all rights herein granted shall cease and terminate and the right to make or authorize any further use or distribution of any recordings made hereunder shall also cease and terminate.

6.    WARRANTIES: Licensor warrants, with respect to its Administrative Share, that it has the legal right to grant this license and that this license is given and accepted without other warranty or recourse. If said warranty shall be breached in whole or in part, Licensor shall either repay to Producer the consideration paid hereunder or hold Producer harmless to the extent of the consideration paid for this license.

7.    NOTICES: All notices hereunder required to be given to Producer (including notification of any change in ownership or administrative control) shall be sent to Producer at the address mentioned herein. All notices, payments and/or royalties hereunder required to be made to Licensor shall be sent to Licensor at its most recent address or to such other address as Licensor may hereafter designate by notice in writing to Producer.

8.    CREDIT INFORMATION: The following shall be included on the packaging, the Copy itself or the visual portion of the

Copy in the form, manner, size and location as Producer shall determine. Casual or inadvertent failure to include the following shall not be a material breach of this license agreement.

8.1    A credit, including the title, composer and publisher information contained on the reverse hereof.

8.2    WARNING: "This disk is for private home use only and any other use, copying, reproduction or performance, in whole or in part, is prohibited."

9.    ASSIGNMENT: This license shall run to Producer, its successors and assigns, provided that Producer remain liable for the performance of all the terms and conditions of this license on its part to be performed and provided further, that any disposition of the Production shall be subject to all the terms herein.

# Form 22.4

## MIDI License Used by Harry Fox Agency

THE HARRY FOX AGENCY, INC.
711 Third Avenue
New York, New York 10017
Musical Instrument Digital Interface (MIDI)
Rights License

License No.:
Date of Issuance:
The following provisions shall apply as indicated in the body of this license:

(A)    Licensee:

(B)    Musical Composition:

(C)    Licensor(s) and percentage of ownership:

(D)    License date:

(E)    Term:

(F)    Advance:

(G)    Units:

(H)    Royalty Per Unit:

(I)    Territory:

(J)    Software Serial Number:

## DEFINITIONS

For purposes hereof, "MIDI" is an acronym for Musical Instrument Digital Interface, which is an accepted international standard for exchanging musical information on a computer.

For purposes hereof, a "MIDI Sequence" is a computer data file embodying one particular MIDI data recording of the musical Composition, capable of playback through a computer.

**Please sign and return two (2) fully executed copies along with payment. Thank you.**

For purposes hereof. the term "MIDI" Sequence Market" shall refer to the sale, lease, license, use or other distribution of MIDI Sequences directly or indirectly to individuals for playback through a hardware sequencer or a personal computer connected to a MIDI capable synthesizer using MIDI software or any similar devices, whether now in existence or hereafter developed.

For purposes hereof, the words "copy" or "copies" shall mean all MIDI Sequence copies made and/or distributed by Licensee.

For purposes hereof, the word "computer" shall mean an electronic machine with a visual display used to store, display, manipulate, and analyze data or information fed into it, and control peripheral machinery automatically or otherwise.

1.     We [the Licensee referred to in (A)] are hereby applying to you [the Licensor referred to in (C)] for a MIDI rights license to use the musical composition referred to in (B) for the purposes of manufacturing, distributing and selling to the public throughout the territory [(I)] for public and home use, MIDI sequence(s), in the form of computer software copies embodying the musical composition in (i.e. MIDI sequence copies).

2.    Licensor hereby grants to the Licensee the following non-exclusive rights with respect to MIDI sequence(s), in all respects subject to the terms and conditions herein provided:

(A)    To record and re-record the musical composition for use in connection with respect to MIDI sequence(s);

(B)    To make and distribute copies of the MIDI sequence program throughout the territory only [(I)].

(C)    Licensee may make arrangements and orchestrations of the Composition for its recording purposes, however, this license does not include the right to alter the fundamental character of the Composition, to print sheet music or to make, or to program into the MIDI sequence the capability of making, any other use of the Composition not expressly authorized hereunder.

3.    Licensee covenants that it shall place on the outside of all containers and, where possible, in every MIDI sequence copy a conspicuous notice to clearly read as follows:

(Fill In) title of Song and Names of Writers" The word "Copyright" followed by the Names of Licensor. International Rights Secured. All rights reserved. Not for broadcast or transmission of any kind. **DO NOT DUPLICATE. NOT FOR RENTAL.**

**WARNING:** "It is a violation of Federal Copyright Law to synchronize this MIDI Sequence with video tape or film, or to print this MIDI Sequence in the form of standard music notation without the express written permission of the copyright owner".

4.    The musical composition recorded as a MIDI sequence(s) shall not exceed _____ minutes and _____ seconds.

5.    The use of the musical composition hereunder shall be non-dramatic background, vocal, instrumental.

6.    The term during which the rights licensed hereunder may be exercised shall be [the number referred to in (E)] years from the license date (D).

7.    Licensee shall make the royalty payments hereunder, which shall be accompanied by a detailed accounting statement listing units sold within 45 days after the end of each calendar quarter during which the MIDI Sequence copies are sold, equal to [the amount referred to in (H)] per MIDI Sequence copy of the work which is sold during each such respective calendar quarter. Within thirty (30) days after the execution of this license, Licensee shall make such payment and render such statement for all units sold prior to the execution of this license.

(A)    In the event Licensee fails to account and pay royalties as herein provided, Licensor shall have the right to give written notice to Licensee that unless the default is remedied within thirty (30) days from the date of the notice, this license shall be deemed terminated. Such failure to pay and cure default in such thirty (30) day period shall render either the making or the distribution, or both, of all MIDI sequence copies hereunder for which royalties have not been paid, actionable acts of infringement under, and fully subject to the remedies provided by the U.S. Copyright Act.

(B)    Licensee shall have the right to maintain a reserve for returns in a reasonable amount consistent with Licensee's arrangements with its distributors, but in no event shall such amount exceed 20% of the number of the MIDI Sequences sold in any Accounting Period. This reserve shall be liquidated quarterly, three quarters after the Accounting Period in which the reserve was maintained. Licensee shall account to Licensor within 45 days after the close of any such Accounting Period in which MIDI Sequence copies are finally distributed. Licensee shall have no right to hold reserves with respect to any copies of the MIDI sequence(s) with respect to which Licensee has received payment.

8.     Upon ten business days written notice to Licensee, for the purpose of verifying the accuracy of statements rendered, an authorized representative of Licensor may conduct an annual examination of Licensee's books and records pertaining to the sales of MIDI Sequences during normal business hours at the place where Licensee maintains said books and records.

9.     This license does not include the rights to:

    A.     Rent the MIDI sequence copies or to permit purchasers or others to do so;

    B.     Use the story of the musical composition or dramatically depict the musical composition;

    C     Parody the lyrics and/or music of the musical composition in any way;

    D.     Broadcast/cablecast or transmit the work in any manner;

    E.     Make, sell or distribute audio phonorecords of the musical composition except as demonstration units;

    F.     Utilize a sound recording and/or audiovisual master(s) not owned or separately licensed by Licensee.

10.     Licensor hereby reserves unto itself all rights of every kind and nature not expressly granted to Licensee herein.

11.     Licensor warrants only that it has the right to grant this license, and this license is given and accepted without any other representation, warrant or recourse, express or implied, except for Licensor's agreement to repay the consideration paid for this license if the aforesaid warranty should be breached. In

no event shall the total liability of the Licensor exceed the total amount of consideration received by it hereunder.

12.     Upon the expiration of this License, all rights herein granted shall cease and terminate and the right to make or authorize any further use or distribution of any recordings made hereunder shall also cease and terminate subject to Licensee's right to sell off it's inventory of MIDI Sequences for an additional period of one year subject to the continuing obligation to pay royalties therefore. No right to make, sell, or distribute MIDI Sequence programs or copies embodying the composition shall survive the termination of this license pursuant to Paragraph 7 (A) hereof.

13.     This license does not include a grant of performing rights. The public performance of the musical composition as part of the MIDI sequence program which is the subject of this license, is expressly conditioned upon such performers or places of performance thereof, having valid performing rights licenses from the respective copyright owners of their designated performing rights societies.

14.     This License does not supersede nor in any way affect any prior agreements now in effect respecting the musical compositions or the rights which are the subject of this license.

(A)     However, this license does supersede any mechanical license issued to the Licensee, for the subject musical composition, under the compulsory licensing provisions of the U.S. Copyright Act (or any agreement embodying such provisions).

15.     This License is being entered into on an experimental and non-prejudicial basis, shall apply for the term set forth herein only, and shall not be binding upon or prejudicial to any position taken by Licensor or Licensee for any period subsequent to the period of this license.

16.     This license sets forth the entire understanding of the parties hereto with respect to the subject matter thereof, may

not be altered, amended or assigned without an express written instrument to such effect accepted by Licensor and shall be governed and construed by and under the laws of the State of New York.

BY:

BY: _____
(Licensee)


BY: THE HARRY FOX AGENCY, INC. O/B/O

BY: _____
(Licensor)

# FORM 22.5

## LICENSE FOR USE OF MUSIC IN KARAOKE RECORDINGS

### KARAOKE SYNCHRONIZATION LICENSE

Date:

Publisher:    BIG MUSIC PUBLISHING COMPANY INC.
              1000 Sunset Boulevard
              Hollywood, California 90069

Producer:     JAPAN KARAOKE, LTD.
              1-1-1, Aoyama Building
              Minato-ku, Tokyo
              JAPAN

1.    Programs

The programs covered by this Agreement are all edited versions
of a videotaped program (the **"Program"**) for use in **"Karaoke
machines"**. Karaoke machines are hereby defined as machines
(utilizing technologies and media now known or hereafter devised) which play music videos containing musical tracks but
no lead vocal track, which may be utilized by Producer or Producer's sublicensees in commercial establishments and other
public places at which members of the public sing along with
such music videos and/or which may be distributed by Producer or its sublicensees for home use by members of the
public.

2.    Territory:

The **"Territory"** covered under this Agreement is the United
States and Canada and their respective territories and possessions.

3.    Grant of Rights/Restrictions:

3.1.    Subject to the terms and conditions contained in this Agreement, Publisher hereby grants to Producer, its successors and assigns, the non-exclusive, limited right, license, privilege and authority

    3.1.1.    to create and use arrangements of, and to record and re-record, compositions controlled by Publisher and approved in writing by Publisher from time to time **("Compositions")** in synchronization or timed relation with Programs;

    3.1.2.    to use the titles of Compositions and display the original lyrics of Compositions on Programs; and

    3.1.3.    to manufacture, distribute, advertise, rent and sell copies of Programs containing Compositions, solely for home use in karaoke machines sold to members of the public and for use in commercial establishments within the Territory where members of the public sing along with Programs and/or record their vocal performances of instrumental versions of Compositions embodied in Programs and thereafter purchase copies of all or part of Programs embodying such performances.

3.2    Term/Expiration:

    3.2.1.    The Term of this Agreement as to each composition shall be seven (7) years from the date of written approval of the use of such Composition by Publisher, Provided, however, that in the event that any portion of a **"Rollover Advance"** (as defined in 4.3, below) in respect of a specific Composition remains unrecouped as of the date when such Term would otherwise expire, such Term shall continue as to such Composition until the end of the calendar quarter during which such Rollover Advance is fully recouped.

    3.2.2.    Upon the expiration of the Term as to a specific Composition, all rights granted herein with respect thereto shall revert to Publisher, and Producer shall not thereafter manufacture, advertise, distribute or sell or lease Programs embodying such Composition or copies thereof or authorize others to do so, <u>provided</u>, that if Producer is not then in material, uncured breach of this Agreement, Producer shall have the right for a period of six (6) months following the expiration of the Term **("Sell-Off Period")** to continue to sell off its ending inventory **of** such Programs (subject to Producer's continuing obligation to account to and pay Publisher pursuant to paragraph 4, below).

      3.2.3.     Producer shall not duplicate or authorize others to duplicate excessive numbers of copies of Programs in anticipation **of** the Sell-Off Period (and in no event shall Producer duplicate or authorize the duplication of a greater number of copies of a specific Program during the final six (6) months of the Term as to the Composition(s) contained in such Program than were duplicated during the immediately preceding six-month period), and all sales during the Sell-Off Period shall be at regular prices (and not at "distress" or "close-out" prices).

3.3.     As to each Composition not 100% owned and controlled by Publisher, this license extends only to that portion of such Composition owned and/or controlled by Publisher.

3.4.     Nothing herein shall obligate or require Producer to embody Compositions either in Programs or in videograms embodying Programs and it is expressly understood and agreed that the compensation payable to Publisher hereunder with respect to each specific Composition is conditioned upon the utilization of such Composition in Programs.

3.5.     Reservation of Rights:

      3.5.1.     Publisher reserves all rights not expressly granted to Producer hereunder, including but not limited to public performing rights in Compositions as embodied in Programs.

3.5.2.　Compositions as embodied in Programs may only be performed publicly by a person, firm or other entity holding a valid performing rights license therefor from Publisher, from Publisher's performing rights society, or from another party authorized to grant such license on behalf of Publisher.

3.5.3.　Arrangements:

(A)　All arrangements of Compositions shall be created as "works for hire," Publisher (or its designee(s)) shall be deemed the "author" thereof for copyright purposes, and (subject to Producer's right to use such arrangements for the purposes of this Agreement) all rights in such arrangements shall belong to Publisher from inception.

(B)　In each instance, Producer shall obtain and deliver to Publisher a written "work for hire" agreement executed by each arranger of a Composition embodied on a specific Program on or before the first distribution of copies of such Program.

4.　Consideration For Grant:

In consideration of the rights granted herein for the use of each Composition in connection with Programs as described in paragraph 3, Producer shall pay to Publisher the following sums on the terms and conditions hereinafter set forth, timely payment being of the essence of this agreement:

4.1.　A fixing fee in the amount of Two Hundred Dollars ($200.00) per Composition, payable to Publisher to be paid within ten days after the completion of recording of the first Program embodying such Composition;

4.2.　A nonreturnable payment in the amount of Three Hundred Dollars ($300) per Composition, payable to Publisher in each instance within the same ten-day period, as an advance against the following royalties **("Royalties")** with respect to the

sale or rental of copies of Programs to commercial establishments and with respect to the sale of copies of Programs for
home use:

4.2.1.    Ten Cents ($.10) per Composition for each
copy of each Program embodying such Composition distributed during the first three and one-half (3 1/2) years of the applicable Term; and

4.2.2.    Twelve and one-half Cents ($.125) per Com-
position for each such copy distributed during the remainder of
such Term.

4.2.3.    In any instance in which only a portion of a
Composition is licensed hereunder, the otherwise applicable
royalty shall be reduced pro rata.

4.2.4.    In the event that during the Term applicable to
a specific Composition Producer shall agree to pay any other
publisher a higher fixing fee and/or royalty rate than that prescribed above, such higher fee and/or royalty rate shall be
deemed applicable hereunder from the commencement of the
applicable Term, Producer shall promptly pay Publisher retroactive to the commencement of such Term the difference between the fixing fee prescribed above and such higher fee and/
or (as applicable) the difference between the royalty rate
prescribed above and such higher rate as to past sales, and
Producer shall continue to pay Publisher at such higher royalty
rate with respect to copies distributed thereafter.

4.3.    In each instance at or prior to the final six months of the
Term applicable to a specific Composition in which Publisher's
accounting statement indicates that the advance in respect of
a specific Composition has been recouped, Producer shall (at
the time when such statement is rendered) make a further advance against Royalties in respect of such Composition in the
amount of One Hundred Fifty Dollars ($150.) **("Rollover Ad-
vance") .**

## 5. Royalty Accountings, Payments, and Audits:

5.1.  Producer shall keep accurate books of account and shall render a true, accurate and detailed accounting statement to Publisher, within 45 days following the end of each calendar quarter during which distribution activity occurs in respect of Programs embodying one or more Compositions, commencing with the quarterly period during which the first commercial sale or rental of a videogram containing a Program takes place.

5.2.  Each sale or rental shall be accounted for on the statement for the quarter during which a particular copy of a Program is distributed by Producer or by a sublicensee from Producer, and such statement shall be accompanied by a remittance of such amount as is shown to be due.

5.3.  Each statement and the accompanying remittance will be made in United States currency. If foreign receipts in the Territory are subject to "blocked currency" laws and/or regulations and/or are subject to exchange controls which prevent their remittance to the U.S., Producer shall notify Publisher to such effect. Upon Publisher's written request and upon condition that the same shall be permitted by the authorities of such foreign country, Producer shall deposit Publisher's share of such receipts in a depository in such foreign country at Producer's cost and expense and shall notify Publisher thereof. Such deposit and notice shall discharge Producer of its obligation to remit such frozen funds.

5.4.  The exchange rates utilized by third parties in accounting to Producer shall be utilized by Producer in accounting to Publisher, so long as payment is made at or prior to the date when payment is due (or if payment is delayed due to currency and/or exchange control). However, if payment is late (not due to currency and/or exchange control) Publisher shall be entitled to the most favorable exchange rate between the due date and the date of payment.

5.5  Tax Withholdings:

5.5.1.    If the laws of any jurisdiction require that taxes on such remittance be withheld at the source, then remittance hereunder to Publisher shall be reduced accordingly, provided, that in each instance, Producer shall notify Publisher of the name and address of the withholding jurisdiction, the amount withheld, and the basis for such withholding, and shall upon request provide Publisher with such document(s) as may be required in order to permit Publisher to apply for any available tax credit(s).

5.5.2.    Only taxes specifically attributable to Publisher and/or to Publisher's royalties hereunder shall be subject to such withholding. Specifically, and without limiting the generality of the foregoing, moneys which would otherwise be due and payable to Publisher shall not be subject to reduction by reason of any income, corporate franchise, or other tax levied upon Producer and/or any sublicensee or other representative of Producer, or by reason of the transfer of moneys from any sublicensee or other representative to Producer prior to payment to Publisher.

5.6.    Audits:

5.6.1.    Publisher shall have the right to examine and inspect the books and records of Producer which relate to the manufacture, distribution and sale and/or rental of Programs containing Compositions for the purpose of determining the accuracy of statements rendered by Producer hereunder. Each such statement shall be subject to examination and inspection for four (4) years after such statement has been received by Publisher.

5.6.2.    Such examination shall be made during reasonable business hours, on reasonable business days, on no less than ten (10) days prior written notice at the regular place of business of Producer where such books and records are maintained. Such examination shall not be made more frequently than once in each year, and not more than once with respect to any quarterly period or statement rendered hereunder.

5.6.3. Such examination and inspection shall be conducted on Publisher's behalf by a certified public accountant of other qualified representative and shall be at Publisher's expense, <u>provided</u>, that if any audit reveals an underpayment of 10% or more for the period(s) audited, Producer shall pay Publisher's reasonable audit costs (excluding travel and subsistence costs).

## 6. Warranties and Representations; Indemnities:

6.1. Each party warrants and represents to the other that such party has full right, power and authority to enter into and perform this Agreement in accordance with its terms.

6.2. Except to the extent provided otherwise herein Publisher warrants and represents as to each Composition that such composition does not infringe upon the rights of any third parties, provided, that if Publisher is the licensor of the lyrics only or the music only, such warranty and representation shall extend only to that element licensed hereunder.

6.3. Indemnities:

6.3.1. Each party ("the Indemnitor") agrees to indemnify the other party ("the Indemnitee") against any and all loss, damage or expense (including court costs and actual and reasonable outside attorneys' fees) which the Indemnitee may incur by reason of a breach by the Indemnitor of its obligations, warranties and/or representations pursuant to this Agreement which results in a final, nonappealable adverse judgment or a settlement entered into with the Indemnitor's prior written consent (not to be unreasonably withheld).

6.3.2. The Indemnitee shall deliver prompt notice of any claim, action or proceeding in respect of which indemnity is claimed, and the Indemnitor shall have the right to participate in the defense thereof by counsel of the Indemnitor's choice, at the Indemnitor's sole cost and expense. Where Publisher is the Indemnitor, and the provisions of Publisher's errors-and-omissions insurance policy so require, Publisher shall have the right to control the defense of such claim, action or proceeding.

6.3.3.    In any instance involving a third party claim, action or proceeding in which a settlement is proposed which the Indemnitor considers reasonable, and the Indemnitee refuses to approve such settlement, the Indemnitee shall defend such claim, action or proceeding thereafter at the Indemnitee's sole cost and expense and payment to such third parties) shall be the Indemnitee's sole responsibility to the extent that such payment is in excess of the amount the Indemnitor considered reasonable.

## 7.    Notices **and** Correspondence:

7.1.    All notices shall be sent to the parties by registered or certified mail (return receipt requested) or by any other means by which delivery may be verified, to the parties at their respective addresses set forth or to such other address(es) as a party may designate by notice in the same manner from time to time. All notices from Producer to Publisher shall be sent to Attention: senior Vice President, Legal & Business Affairs.

7.2.    **All** statements, payments and requests for approval hereunder from Producer to Publisher shall be sent via the same procedure to **Attention: Vice President, Licensing.**

## 8.    Miscellaneous:

8.1.    This Agreement sets forth the entire agreement between Publisher and Producer with respect to the subject matter hereof, superseding any and all prior written and/or oral agreements or understandings, and may not be modified or amended except by written agreement executed by the parties.

8.2.    No breach of this Agreement shall be deemed a material breach until the party against whom such breach is alleged shall have received written notice of same from the party alleging such breach, and the notified party shall have failed to cure such breach within thirty (30) days after the receipt of such notice (ten (10) days, in the case of a payment of money).

8.3.    Governing Law and Forum; Fees and Costs:

8.3.1.    This Agreement shall be governed by and subject to the laws of the State of California, applicable to agreements made and to be wholly performed within such State, and the State and/or Federal Courts in Los Angeles shall be the sole forums for the resolutions of disputes with respect to this agreement. Both parties hereby submit to the jurisdiction of such Courts for such purpose.

8.3.2.    In any legal action between the parties, the prevailing party shall be entitled to recover its court costs and actual and reasonable outside attorney's fees.

8.4.    Assignment:

8.4.1.    Publisher may assign this agreement or any of the rights licenses or privileges hereunder to any person, firm, corporation or other entity.

8.4.2.    Producer may not assign its rights, licenses or privileges except to a corporate parent or subsidiary, in a merger or consolidation or to a purchaser of substantially all of Producer's stock or assets.

8.4.3.    No assignment shall relieve the assignor of any liability hereunder, and no such assignment shall become effective unless and until the assignor shall deliver to the other party hereto a written agreement on the part of the assignee assuming the performance of the assignor's obligations hereunder from and after the effective date of such assignment.

IN WITNESS WHEREOF, the parties have caused the foregoing to be executed as of the date set forth above.


Publisher:

By

Producer:

By

# FORM 22.6

## LICENSE TO USE FILM FOOTAGE IN AN AUDIOVISUAL WORK

<u>FILM FOOTAGE LICENSE</u>

Agreement dated _____ between Theatrical Film Corporation ("Owner") and _____("Licensee").

1. <u>SPECIFIED FOOTAGE</u>: Owner hereby grants to Licensee, without any representations or warranties of any kind, expressed or implied, a perpetual non-exclusive and non-transferable license to use the film footage (including the soundtrack thereof) described in Exhibit "A" attached hereto ("Footage").

2. <u>RESTRICTED USE</u>: The Footage is restricted to use only in and as part of the _____ audiovisual work entitled " _____ "

("A/V Work") for exhibition in the "Media" described in Exhibit "A" for the "Territory" described in Exhibit "A". The Footage will not be used for any other purpose or purposes whatsoever. Licensee will not make any reproduction of or from the Footage whatsoever in whole or in part, except for use in and as part of the A/V Work herein specified.

3. <u>RELEASES</u>: Licensee shall not have the right to use the Footage obtained without obtaining all required individual authorizations, releases, consents, clearances and licenses ("Releases") as may be necessary with respect to the use of the Footage as herein contemplated including without limitation the Releases set forth below. Licensee shall pay any fees and other payments required in connection with the Releases and furnish Owner with copies of all such Releases.

(a) Written releases from all individuals appearing recognizably in the scene(s) contained in the Footage and from all stunt persons appearing in any stunt identifiable in the scene(s) contained in the Footage.

(b)    Written releases from any unions or guilds to the extent required under applicable collective bargaining agreements in connection with the use of the Footage.

(c)    If any music is included in the Footage, synchronization and performing licenses from the copyright proprietors of such music and such other persons, firms or associations, societies or corporations as may own or control the performing rights thereto.

4.    COSTS: Licensee will pay all costs arising in any way by reason of the license granted hereunder including screening, processing, laboratory, transfer and shipping charges in connection with the manufacture of any pre-print material and positive prints of the Footage and the costs involved in replacing any lost or damaged materials delivered to Licensee.

5.    NATURE OF A/V WORK: The A/V Work shall not be derogatory to or critical of the entertainment industry or of Owner, or any officer, director, agent, employee, affiliate, parent or subsidiary of Owner or of any motion picture produced or distributed by Owner and none of the Footage will be used in a manner which would be derogatory to or critical of the motion picture from which the Footage was taken or to the persons involved with the making of the motion picture from which the Footage was taken.

6.    RETURN OF MATERIALS: Upon the completion of the use permitted hereunder, Licensee shall return all preprint material and positive prints of the Footage to such location as Owner shall designate.

7.    ADVERTISING: Licensee shall not use the name of Owner for any purposes in connection with the distribution, advertising

or publicizing of the A/V Work without the prior written consent of Owner.

8.    WARRANTIES: Licensee represents and warrants that the incorporation of the Footage into the A/V Work shall in no way affect Owner's continued and separate copyright ownership in the motion picture from which the Footage was taken and that the copyright ownership of Owner will not merge with the A/V Work nor deprive Owner of its copyright ownership. Licensee represents and warrants that it shall be the copyright proprietor of the A/V Work, that the A/V Work shall bear a copyright notice thereon and shall be duly registered for copyright in the United States Copyright Office.

9.    INDEMNITY: Licensee will indemnify, defend and hold Owner and its officers, directors, agents, employees, representatives, associates, affiliates and subsidiary corporations, and each and all of them harmless from and against any and all loss, costs, damage, liability and expense, including reasonable attorneys' fees, arising out of any claim whatsoever, whether or not groundless, which may arise, directly or indirectly, by reason of Licensee's use of the Footage.

10.    REMEDIES: Licensee further acknowledges that a breach by Licensee of any of its representations, warranties or undertakings hereunder will cause Owner irreparable damage, which cannot be readily remedied in damages in an action by law and may, in addition thereto, constitute an infringement of Owner's copyright, thereby entitling Owner to equitable remedies, costs and attorneys' fees.

11.    LICENSE FEE: Licensee agrees to pay Owner upon signature of this Agreement _____ Dollar ($_____) for the use of the Footage as herein provided.

12.    ADMINISTRATIVE FEE: Licensee agrees to pay Owner upon signature of this Agreement _____ Dollar

($_____) as an administration fee in connection with the furnishing of the Footage for the use as herein provided.

13.   <u>GOVERNING LAW</u>: This Agreement and all matters or issues material thereto shall be governed by the laws of the State of California applicable to contracts performed entirely therein.

14.   <u>ENTIRE AGREEMENT</u>: This Agreement contains the entire understanding of the parties hereto relating to the subject matter herein contained, and it cannot be changed or terminated orally.

_____   THEATRICAL FILM
                                 CORPORATION
                                 ("Owner")

By _____   By _____
      Its                            Its

Exhibit "A" of Film Footage License Agreement dated _____ between Theatrical Film Corporation ("Owner") and _____ ("Licensee").

1.   FOOTAGE:

2.   MEDIA:

3.   TERRITORY:

# FORM 22.7

## LICENSE TO USE A STILL PHOTOGRAPH IN AN AUDIOVISUAL WORK

January 1, 2000

Gentlemen:

You and Twentieth Century-Owner Film Corporation ("Owner") hereby agree as follows:

1.    <u>USE OF STILL</u>: Subject to the terms and conditions hereof, Owner consents, insofar as Owner is concerned, to your nonexclusive utilization of the still photography or photographs ("Still") specified in Paragraph 7. hereof, only for the purpose specified in Paragraph 5. hereof. The Still may not otherwise be reproduced or used.

2.    <u>NO REPRESENTATION OR WARRANTIES</u>: Owner makes no representation or warranty of any kind either with respect to the Still, your use thereof or otherwise.

3.    <u>CREDIT</u>: You agree to give Owner credit in the following form:

      COURTESY OF [OWNER]

4.    <u>CONDITIONS OF USE</u>: The consent of Owner is conditioned upon:

    (a)    your obtaining all other consents and releases, including but not limited to the consent of any person appearing in the Still;

(b) your compliance with the provisions of the Universal Copyright Convention and of the laws of the United States to protect the copyright of the Still.

5. RESTRICTIONS ON USE: The Still shall be used solely in connection with the book entitled "_____".

6. FEE: You agree to pay to Owner the sum of $ _____ _____ upon signature hereof.

7. DESCRIPTION OF STILL: _____
_____
_____
_____

8. MATERIALS: ___Owner is not supplying a copy of the Still or any other material to you.

___ Owner has supplied to you the following material:

9. COPYRIGHT NOTICE: The following copyright notice must appear in connection with your use of the Still:

Copyright © 20___ [OWNER] ALL RIGHTS RESERVED

10. COPIES FURNISHED: You agree to deliver to Owner at no cost to Owner two (2) free copies of the publication or other work in which the Still is to be used within ten (10) days after the first publication or other use thereof.

11. INDEMNIFICATION: You shall indemnify, defend and hold harmless Owner, its directors, officers, agents and employees against all costs and expenses (including attorney's fees), claims, damages, liabilities or losses of whatever kind arising from or relating to (a) the breach or claim or breach by you of any of your statements, representations or warranties made herein, or (b) your use of the Still.

12.   <u>ENTIRE AGREEMENT/APPLICABLE LAW</u>: This Agreement represents the entire understanding of the parties and shall be construed in accordance with the laws of the State of California applicable to agreements fully executed and performed therein.

If the foregoing is in accordance with your understanding, please so signify by signing where indicated below.

Very truly yours,

OWNER

By _____

ACCEPTED AND AGREED TO:

By _____

# FORM 22.8

## LICENSE TO USE SOUND RECORDING MASTER IN AN AUDIOVISUAL WORK

January 1, 2000

VINYL RECORDS, INC.
1 Vine
Hollywood, California

RE: Master Sound Recording Synchronization License

Gentlemen:

The following, when signed by you and us, will constitute our agreement:

1.    This agreement is made with respect to the master recording of the musical composition entitled "
" (the "Master") embodying the performance of

You represent and warrant that you have the right throughout the world to license the Master for purposes of synchronizing the Master with an audio-visual work.

2.    You hereby license and grant to us the following non-exclusive rights in the Master:

(a)    The right to synchronize the Master, or a portion thereof, in time-relation with the audiovisual work presently entitled " " as the same may be exploited in any and all media and modes of uses throughout the world (the "A/V Work") and in any and all trailers, radio, television and, other promotions and advertisements of the A/V Work.

(b)    The right to use the Master as embodied in the A/V Work in any and all media, whether known or hereafter devised, including (but not by way of limitation) the following:

(i)    Television exhibition, whether by network, non-network, local or syndicated broadcast;

(ii)    Pay television, subscription television, CATV, cable television or any and all other closed circuit broadcasts into home or hotel-motel television;

(iii)    Video-cassette, video-disc, CD-ROM or any and all other functionally similar home use or computer device technologies; and

(iv)    any transportation facility.

(c)    The right to use or refer to the artist's name whose performance is embodied on the Master in the credits, and in any promotions, advertisements and publicity of the A/V Work. In this regard, we agree to accord you and the artist appropriate credit on copies of the A/V Work in substantially the same manner as we will accord credit to all of the other artists and record companies whose previously recorded licensed masters (as opposed to material originally commissioned by us and/or originally recorded for the A/V Work and/or previously unreleased material, credits for which may but need not appear in a different portion of the A/V Work) are being embodied in the A/V Work.

3.    In consideration for the license and grant of rights herein made and if we use the Master or any part thereof, in the A/V Work, we shall pay you, within days after the first commercial release of the A/V Work, the sum of

4.    Nothing herein shall obligate or require us to embody the Master in the A/V Work.

5.    You warrant and represent that you have obtained approval from any and all persons or entities whose approval is required for the license and grant of rights made herein other than the appropriate music publishers, and that you shall be solely responsible for (and shall indemnify and hold us harmless from) any payments to the artists and/or producers of the Master with regard to our use of the Master. Notwithstanding the foregoing, we agree to pay any and all re-use fees that may be required by applicable unions and/or guilds as a result of our use of the Master in the A/V Work, immediately after you have given us notice of what the amount of the applicable re-use fees are.

6.    The license and grant of rights made herein shall subsist, at minimum, for the remainder of the term of all copyrights in and to the Master, and any and all renewals or extensions thereof that you or your successors or assigns may now own or control or hereafter own or control without additional consideration therefor.

7.    You hereby agree to indemnify and hold us harmless from and against any claims, damages, other costs (including reasonable attorneys' fees), actions or other proceedings by any third party arising out of or related to your representations, warranties or covenants hereunder.

8.    This agreement is binding upon and shall inure to the benefit of the respective successors and/or assigns of the parties hereto.

9.    This agreement shall be subject to and construed in accordance with the laws of the State of New York applicable to agreements entered into and to be performed fully therein.

10.    In the event of any breach of any provisions of this agreement by us, you hereby agree that your sole remedy with respect thereto shall be an action at law for damages, if any, and that in no event shall you be entitled to enjoin, interfere or

inhibit or seek to enjoin, interfere or inhibit, the distribution, exhibition, exploitation or other turning to account of the A/V Work.

11.    This agreement sets forth the entire agreement and understanding between you and us with respect to the subject matter hereof and supersedes all prior agreements and understandings, if any, whether oral or written pertaining thereto. This agreement may not be changed or modified, or any covenant, representation, warranty or provision hereof waived, except by an agreement in writing, signed by the party against whom enforcement of the change, modification or waiver is sought, and not otherwise.

Please indicate your acceptance and agreement to the foregoing by signing in the space provided below.

Very truly yours,

A/V WORK PRODUCTION CO., INC.

By: _____

AGREED TO AND ACCEPTED:

VINYL RECORDS, INC.

By: _____

# FORM 22.9

## LOCATION RELEASE

LOCATION RELEASE

1.   For good and valuable consideration, receipt of which is hereby acknowledged, the undersigned grants to _____ (the "Producer"), the following:

(a)   The right to enter upon and use the property located at _____

(the "Location") for the purpose of photographing, recording and otherwise reproducing in any manner the Location and any still photographs, sound recordings, motion pictures or other works of authorship photographed, recorded or created on or around the Location in connection with the production of a work tentatively entitled "_____" (collectively, the "Location Elements");

(b)   The right to include or otherwise use any or all of the Location Elements in and in connection with other still or motion pictures, sets or locations so as to represent that the Location, or any portion thereof, includes, is connected with, or is a part or portion of other property or sets, either real or simulated; and

(c)   The right to exhibit, distribute, use and exploit, by any means, in any media and in any language, throughout the world, the Location Elements or any portions thereof.

2.   The undersigned hereby waives, and release and discharge Producer from, any and all claims, demands, liabilities, damages, costs, expenses (including attorneys' fees and costs), actions and causes of actions which the undersigned may now or hereafter have against Producer based upon defamation,

right of privacy, right of publicity or any other personal or property rights arising from or in connection with Producer's use of any or all of the rights granted herein, and specifically agree that the undersigned will not at any time claim that any characters in any work picture in which any photographs, recordings or other works of authorship made hereunder are used to represent the undersigned or point to the undersigned, by reason of the use of any such photographs, recordings or works of authorship.

3.     The undersigned hereby warrants and represents that the undersigned is (the owner) (the lessee) (the agent for the owner) of the location and that the undersigned has the right, power and authority to enter into this Location Release and to grant to Producer all of the rights granted herein. The undersigned hereby indemnifies and holds Producer harmless from any and all claims, liabilities, damages, costs, expenses (including attorney's fees and costs), actions and causes of action arising out of or related to any breach by the undersigned of the foregoing warranty and representation.

4.     Producer shall have the right, but shall not be obligated, to utilize any of the rights granted herein. The rights which the undersigned has granted to Producer herein are irrevocable, and the grant of rights and other terms hereof cannot be modified except by a writing executed by the parties hereto.

5.     This instrument shall be binding upon and inure to the benefit of Producer's successors, assigns, licensees and all other persons, firms and corporations claiming under or through Producer, and shall also be binding upon the undersigned's successors.

DATED:

Signed _____

_____

(Name Printed)

_____

_____

_____

(Address)

In complete and full consideration of the above release, Producer hereby agrees to pay to the above signed the sum of _____ Dollars ($_____).

PRODUCER

By: _____

# FORM 22.10

## PRODUCTION MUSIC LICENSE

MUSIC PRODUCTION LIBRARY CO.

In consideration of payment of the sum of One Dollar, and other good and valuable considerations as well as license fees prior to the effectiveness hereof to the undersigned, MUSIC PRODUCTION LIBRARY CO. (hereinafter referred to as the "PUBLISHER"), the said PUBLISHER hereby gives to \_\_\_

_____

_____

its successors and assigns, the non-exclusive, irrevocable right and license, privilege and authority to record from the MUSIC PRODUCTION LIBRARY, in the United States of America only, the musical selection(s) hereinafter set forth, and to make copies of such recorded selection(s) and perform said selection(s) all in accordance with the terms, conditions and limitations hereinafter set out.

1.    The recorded selection(s) covered by this license, are as follows:

DISC NUMBER              TITLE              COMPOSER

2.    The title of the production with which said musical selection(s) is (are) to be used is _____

3.    The type of use to be made of the musical selection(s) is background instrumental in the field of _____.

4.    This license is limited and restricted to the use of the said musical selection(s) in synchronism or timed relation with the production hereinabove specified, and trailers thereof.

5.    As an express condition for the issuance of this license, licensee agrees to deliver to PUBLISHER a cue sheet of the production specified in paragraph 2 hereof, promptly upon completion of said production specifying the music credits containing the information set forth in paragraph 1 hereof.

6.    The said production may be shown only to non-theatrical audiences and may not be shown in motion picture theatres where an admission fee is charged. The said production may not be shown on Pay-TV and/or Closed Circuit TV, except where the Closed Circuit TV is used exclusively for public school room instruction.

(The said production, however, may be shown on television stations with an ASCAP license.)
(The said production may not be shown on television stations.)
(Cross out one.)

7.    Performing rights in the above mentioned selection(s) are controlled by the American Society of Composers, Authors and Publishers (ASCAP), and this license is issued subject thereto.

8.    The licensed territory is the world.

9.    The undersigned warrants only that it is the owner of the recording rights conveyed and this license is given without other warranty or recourse, except for the PUBLISHER's agree-

ment to repay the consideration paid for this license if said warranty shall be breached, and the PUBLISHER further reserves to itself all rights and uses in and to the said musical selection(s) not herein specifically given.

MUSIC PRODUCTION LIBRARY CO.

by _____

Date _____

Accepted and Agreed to:

_____

# LICENSING MUSICAL WORKS AND SOUND RECORDINGS ON THE INTERNET

## SUMMARY

## V. An Analysis of the Licenses Required for Various Uses of Musical Works and Sound Recordings on the Internet

A. Sound Recording Copyright Versus Musical Work Copyright

B. Performance Right Versus Reproduction Right

    1. Musical Works

    2. Sound Recordings

C. Activities on the Internet Requiring Licenses for the Use of Musical Works and Sound Recordings

    1. Example — Digital Audio Transmissions That Result in Digital Phonorecord Deliveries

        a. Sound Recording

        b. Musical Work

            i. Mechanical Reproduction License

            ii. Performance License

            iii. The Limited Download Question

    2. Example — Digital Audio Transmissions That Do Not Result in Digital Phonorecord Deliveries

        a. Interactive Services

            i. Musical Works

            ii. Sound Recordings

            iii. Line between Interactive and Non-Interactive Transmissions

        b. Non-Interactive Services

            i. Sound Recording — Subscription Transmissions

            ii. Sound Recording — Non-Subscription Transmissions

            iii. Musical Works

    3. Example — Digital Transmission and/or Delivery of an Audiovisual Work Containing a Musical Recording

        a. Motion Picture Copyright

        b. Sound Recording Copyright

CHAPTER **23**

# LICENSING MUSICAL WORKS AND SOUND RECORDINGS ON THE INTERNET

The passing away of Francis Albert Sinatra in 1998 marked the true end of an era, but he remained with us long enough to witness the dawn of a new age, one that is being hailed as the *digital millennium.* For several years now, copies of Frank Sinatra's most popular recordings have been transmitted, mostly illegally, over the Internet, passing through cyberspace, like *Strangers in the Night,* to and from destinations unknown to the societies and collection agencies responsible for licensing these transmissions.

These recordings, and the musical works that underlie them, are being transmitted over the Internet in two basic ways: (1) by "streaming" transmissions, transmissions that are akin to radio broadcasts over the Internet, whether to the public at large or directly to individuals upon request, and (2) by "download" transmissions, the delivery of computer files, much like word processing files or spreadsheet files, that contain sound recordings that can be played on personal computers, portable players and wireless devices, equipped with the necessary decoding and audio software and hardware. In both cases, the recordings are being sent in *digital* form, where perfect copies are being transmitted or delivered from one part of the world to another.

In the previous chapter, we sketched some of the recent developments in high technology and discussed the considerations in granting and clearing licenses for the use of music in various kinds of computer-related software, such as business software, multimedia programs, and videogames. The discussion in the previous chapter was limited to the distribution of software on various forms of *physical* media, such as computer floppy disks, game cartridges, and optical laserdiscs (including, CD-ROMs, CD-I and others). The focus of this chapter is on granting and clearing licenses for the use of music in many of those same kinds of computer-related programs, as well as traditional programs in which music is embodied, such as audio recordings, motion pictures and other audiovisual works, but delivered to the customer, not by transfer of possession of physical media, but by way of *digital transmission* — i.e., into the home, office, personal digital assistants and mobile telephones, over telephone lines, cable television lines, and by wireless means, in digital (as opposed to analog) form, by broadcast, by subscription, or upon the recipient's request.

The delivery of musical works by means of *digital transmission* raises licensing issues that are different from their delivery on physical media distributed through retail stores or by direct mail, or delivered in a non-interactive (or linear) analog form of transmission, such as traditional radio or television broadcast. We will explore these issues in the pages which follow, but we note that, at the time of this writing, many of these issues remain the subject of intense public debate and it is not entirely clear how they will be resolved. We continue to present here, however, our thoughts on either how they are likely to be, or how they *should* be, resolved.

Since the publication of the Second Edition of this book, Congress enacted two important pieces of legislation bearing upon the subject of digital transmissions of music: the *Digital Performance Right in Sound Recordings Act of 1995* (the "1995 Act") and the *Digital Millennium Copyright Act of 1999* (the "DMCA"). The first of these important laws, the 1995 Act, made two significant, but distinct, changes affecting the licensing of musical works under U.S. copyright law: first, it created a new digital public performance right for sound recordings, and second, it broadened the Copyright Act's existing compulsory mechanical license provision to include the reproduction and delivery of musical works in sound recordings by digital transmission. The practical effect of the latter change is discussed in Chapter 12, on *Mechanical Licenses*. The former change, which concerns sound recordings, rather than musical works, is discussed in this chapter only to the extent the Act serves to clarify the music licensing issues raised in this chapter. The DMCA made a number of changes to the copyright law, the main among them being certain prohibitions against the circumvention of technical measures used by content owners to protect their intellectual property against unauthorized copying, and changes in the rules pertaining to digital audio transmissions that were originally part of the 1995 Act.

## I. EMERGING NOMENCLATURE

### A. Digital Transmissions

A key term which has recently emerged in the nomenclature of electronic commerce is the term *digital*, which simply means the representation of letters and numbers in terms of an ordered series of 1's and 0's, the mathematical *binary code*, the basis of all computer languages. It is to be contrasted with the term *analog*, a term which is derived from the groove etched in wax or vinyl phonograph records which, when a diamond or ruby stylus is applied, produces sounds *analogous* to those which originally produced the grooves.

Audiophiles will defend the practice of analog recording on the basis that only analog recording truly captures all of the salient sounds produced by the singers, musicians, and the peculiarities of the room in which the recording is made. However, once that sound is recorded, it is very difficult, if not very costly, to reproduce *exact* copies of sounds recorded in analog form. Transferring a vinyl recording to an analog tape, for example, will always result in some degradation of sound quality. By contrast, once a digital recording is made, either of a live performance or a digital reproduction of an analog recording, the reproduction of *exact* copies of the digital recording can be done easily, even with a common personal computer. It is the ease with which a consumer can make exact copies of digital recordings without the authorization of the copyright owner which has made *digital*, as opposed to analog, transmissions a careful focus of recent legislative attention.

To "transmit" a recording means to communicate it by any device or process whereby sounds are received beyond the place from which they are sent. Thus, a *digital transmission* is a communication of sounds or pictures from one place to another in the form of 1's and 0's, such that with an uninterrupted transmission, the recipient receives an exact copy of the sounds or pictures transmitted by the sender. We would discourage the use of the terms, *electronic distribution* and *electronic publishing* to represent digital transmissions. As discussed below, the words *distribution* and *publishing*, at least as they are used in the Copyright Act, imply the transfer of possession of physical objects, such as CDs and CD-ROMs. The term *digital transmission* more accurately describes the delivery of musical works and sound recordings that do not involve the transfer of possession of physical objects.

## B. Streaming Versus Downloading Transmissions

It is important to note that the term *reproduction* means the act of embodying or fixing in a copy or a phonorecord a musical work, sound recording or other copyrighted subject matter. The term reproduction is *not* synonymous with the term, *copy* or *phonorecord*, which are material objects. A reproduction is not a thing, but an action. For example, a reproduction may be effected by the burning of a sound recording onto a writable CD, or CD-R or the copying of a recording onto a hard disk.

By the same token, not all transmissions involve the reproduction of a work in a new copy or phonorecord. Some transmissions may constitute merely a performance, where no copy is made in connection with the transmission; these are called, *streaming* transmissions. Transmissions which do result in the reproduction of the work in a new copy or phonorecord are called, *download transmissions*, or *digital deliveries*.

Understanding the difference between a streaming transmission and a download transmission will be important as we move further into this discussion. As we have seen, traditionally, the music publishing industry has recognized a distinction between whether a use is a *performance* or a *reproduction* for purposes of determining how license fees are structured and collected. Many of the licensing problems in this area emerge from how streaming transmissions and download transmissions fit within these existing licensing regimes.

## C. INTERACTIVE VERSUS NON-INTERACTIVE

We use the term *interactive* to distinguish the forms of transmissions discussed in this chapter from the many forms of non-interactive, or traditional *broadcast* (e.g., terrestrial television or radio) transmissions covered generally in Chapter 17, on *Performance Licenses.* An *interactive* transmission is a transmission that enables a potential recipient to receive a transmission of a particular work of authorship that was selected by the recipient. An example of an interactive digital transmission would be the communication of a song to your computer's speaker or hard disk as a consequence of your logging on to a website and clicking on a link to activate the transmission of the selected song. A non-interactive, or *broadcast*-like, transmission would be a transmission of a work to the public at large, whether over the air waves or cable or telephone lines (even if the broadcast transmission was made "by request" of a particular listener in the broadcast audience).

The line between interactive and non-interactive transmissions, however, does not escape ambiguity. What if a listener of a broadcast-like transmission over the Internet were enabled to vote for recordings he liked and against those he didn't, communicating to the transmitter his listening preferences, and providing a means for the transmitter to *customize* the content of future transmissions to that listener? Would these future transmissions be considered interactive or non-interactive transmissions? The answer to this question will be important in determining the way transmitters will be able to license the recordings from their owners for these transmissions.

Note, the Internet can support all forms of digital transmissions, *whether interactive or not.*[1] Thus, the Internet is a medium not only for *interactive* transmissions, but non-interactive transmissions, or *broadcasts,* as well: in other words, radio and television transmissions broadcast over the Internet and received by browsers, or similar client software,[2] set to *tune-in* to the particular broadcasts. What this means is that digital transmissions of musical works and sound recordings over the Internet can be a mixture of both the *interactive* and *non-interactive* variety — that is, transmissions made *upon demand* of the

---

[1] The authors wish to thank Vinton Cerf (who has become widely recognized as "the father of the Internet") for providing the authors with his valuable incites on this subject.

[2] And *server* software that may retransmit such transmissions to other servers for retransmission to client software or Internet browsers.

individual users and transmissions *broadcast* to the Internet public at large and received by those who tune in as one would tune-in to a traditional radio station. In addition, such transmissions may be sent to those who *subscribe* to the transmissions and to those who do not.

## D. Internet

In the mid-1990s, several terms were used to denote the *network* through which these digital transmissions have been taking place have entered our vocabulary. Among the first is the term, *national information infrastructure*, the formal term conceived in Washington, D.C. used to identify what was informally being referred to as, the *information superhighway*.

While much public discussion was taking place concerning this futuristic information superhighway, an actual network of computers collectively referred to as the *Internet*, described more fully below, was quickly turning the theoretical notion of an information superhighway into a reality. Meanwhile, because the term *highway* connoted a publicly owned and constructed facility, and the actual network that was emerging was being increasingly supported by the private sector, the term *information superhighway* began to give way to its more hip successor, *cyberspace*, or the less hype-filled *Internet*.

Though the term *Internet* is used often synonymously with *cyberspace*, the Internet is really a specific network of computers and is only part of a larger landscape of interactive systems, which includes commercial services such as America Online and MSN, Internet-based electronic mail systems, wireless services, through mobile telephones and personal digital assistants, cable televisions systems that carry the Internet, and thousands of independently operated Web sites. The Internet has been aptly described as "the network of networks."

All of these systems or networks of systems are becoming increasingly interconnected and may soon become, as far as users are concerned, one seamless *network* of information and software services. It is not inconceivable that the term *cyberspace* or *Internet* will fall out of use and be replaced by terms such as *the net, telecosmos*, and the like. At least until the vogue changes, however, we will use the term *Internet* to represent that potentially interactive digital transmission medium which includes all of the above services, whether delivered over telephone, cable lines, or air waves, and whether interconnected or not, and we will use the term *electronic commerce* to represent the collective transactions occurring over that medium.

Note, however, that the distinction we are making between the distribution of programs on physical media, on the one hand, and their transmission over electronic media, on the other, while useful for analyzing the legal issues involved in licensing music (and other intellectual property content), should not be taken too far. The environment which is likely to emerge for commerce in musical works and other copyrighted content is likely to include a mix of the physical distribution and digital transmission of such works, much like the mix we see today with public performances of music over the radio and private performances by the home use of compact discs. In whatever way these new technologies may affect the potential sources of licensing revenue, successful music licensing will depend upon a thorough understanding of the technologies involved.

## II. TECHNOLOGICAL AND HISTORICAL BACKGROUND

### A. Introduction

As we mentioned in the previous section, the Internet comprises a small universe of computers interactively linked over networks connected by telephone, cable television lines, and the air waves. These networks include the Internet, commercial online services, computers and networks operated by corporations, educational institutions, Internet service providers, and thousands of independently operated Web sites. Before turning to the basic considerations in granting and clearing licenses for the use of music on the Internet, it may be useful to review these services and some of the emerging technologies that are enabling electronic commerce.

### B. Online Electronic Information Services

Before the Internet came on the scene in the early 1990s, there was the online electronic information service. An online electronic information service is simply a computer — either a mainframe, minicomputer or personal computer — equipped with special software that performs the tasks of an electronic information service (described below) and modems connected to telephone lines which can receive calls from users of other computers.

Here's how it works: A *modem* (a portmanteau comprising the communications terms, *modulate* and *demodulate*) is a device that converts, or modulates, the information in your computer stored in *binary* or *digital* form (i.e., *bits* of information represented as either a one or a zero) to a form that can be transmitted over the phone line, or *analog* form. In simple terms, what happens is that the *ones* of the digital format are converted to a high pitch tone and the *zeros* are converted to a low pitch tone; the modem converts the ones and zeros generated by your computer into a series of analogous high pitched and low pitched tones and sends them over the phone lines to another modem at the receiving end of the line, which is connected to another computer. The receiving modem demodulates, or converts, the high and low pitched analog tones back into the binary ones and zeros and forwards the signals to the computer where they can be stored to disk or sent to your computer screen in the form of text or pictures.

An electronic information service, such as a commercial service (e.g., CompuServe or America Online) or personal BBS, was like an electronic meeting place, where anyone, at any time of day or night, from virtually anywhere in the world where adequate telephone service is available, can call up and leave messages to others, receive messages left by others, participate in live, *real-time* or *chat conferences*, or transfer down to their computers (i.e., *download*) virtually any kind of computer file (e.g., computer program, text, graphics, sound, etc.) that can be stored on a computer, or transfer to the on-line service (i.e., *upload*) any kind of computer file to enable others to download such computer file to their computers.

These services were run by large national or multinational organizations, such as *CompuServe*, which was a division of H&R Block prior to its purchase by AOL, *GEnie*, a division of General Electric, which was later shut down, *Prodigy* (originally, a joint venture among IBM, CBS, and Sears, but now primarily an Internet service provider), *America Online* (which remains today primarily as it was in the early 1990's, though it also operates as a website and Internet service provider), and the *Microsoft Network* (MSN), which was converted to a website and an Internet service provider; and by smaller regional services, most of which became Internet service providers.

Even a personal computer user could operate an electronic information service at home or at the office by means of a modem, personal computer, and special electronic bulletin board software (BBS). These home BBS operators, called *sysops* (i.e., *system op*erators), ranged from professionals, such as doctors and lawyers operating a board as a forum for local colleagues, to teenagers offering electronically stored nude photographs and likenesses of favorite recording, television, and sports celebrities.[3]

Both the commercial and non-commercial online information services operated basically the same way, except the non-commercial forms generally did not charge a fee for their use. The fees charged by the large commercial operators, such as CompuServe and America Online, were generally about $9.95 per month for a limited number of minutes of usage (e.g., 300 minutes) and an hourly fee for use beyond the minimum (e.g., $2.95 per hour). Later, services such as AOL became Internet services providers, charging a flat $21.95 per month for unlimited Internet access and use of its electronic information service. Most personal computer bulletin board services were accessed for the price of a phone call, often free if accessed using unlimited residential phone service. Since the advent of the Internet, most of the BBS services were converted to web sites, and with the exception of AOL and CompuServe, many online information services, such as the Microsoft Network (MSN) were converted to web sites.

## C. The Internet

The roots of the Internet began with a project entitled, *Resource Sharing Computer Networks*, started in 1969 by the *Defense Advanced Research Projects Agency* (DARPA or ARPA). The U.S. Department of Defense was concerned about the vulnerability of the nation's telecommunications system, which could be snapped by the annihilation of just a few key metropolitan areas. The ARPA project was thus established to address the problem of how to keep military sites in communication across the country in the event of a nuclear war. The

---

[3] From 1985 to 1987, co-author Bob Kohn operated a BBS for lawyers, called *Legacy/ The Law Network*, from his home in Beverly Hills, California; in 1987, he became the system operator of *The Law Roundtable* on GEnie, which he operated until 1992.

project, eventually to become known as ARPANET, began experimenting with various telecommunications protocols for transmitting information through various media including radio, telephone, satellites, and ethernet.

By 1977, a packet switching protocol was designed for this purpose. That protocol formed the basis for what eventually became, the Transmission Control Protocol and Internet Protocol (TCP/IP). By 1983, each node (i.e., a computer connected to the network) on the ARPANET was required to use TCP/IP to connect to it. At the same time, TCP/IP was built into Version 4.2 of the Berkeley Standard Distribution of the UNIX operating system, an event which assured the wide availability of TCP/IP, and subsequently the close association of the Internet with the UNIX operating system. Essentially, the TCP/IP protocol allows any computer attached to the Internet to talk to any other computer on the Internet, as long as they both are using the TCP/IP protocol.

Recall that ARPANET was primarily a military operation connecting various military sites and military contractors together. Universities and the general public were not welcome, but because many military contractors had ties with university research facilities, many university researchers were given access to the network. These university researchers began a crusade to open up the network to their peers.

Meanwhile, in 1984, the *National Science Foundation* opened an office to study and participate in the nation's networking efforts. By 1986, the NSF deployed a computer network called, NSFNET. By contrast with ARPANET, NSFNET actively welcomed anyone who sought to connect into the network, and a number of universities and research groups were quickly given access to it. By 1988, the ARPANET evolved into the rapidly expanding NSFNET, and the resulting "Internet" was in full operation.

## D. World Wide Web

In 1989, Tim Berners-Lee working at CERN in Switzerland created a system to facilitate the sharing of information among researchers in high-energy particle physics. This system, called the World Wide Web, is based on a client/server model and a set of standards for information access and navigation, called *hypertext*. Hypertext is a computer concept that allows one to navigate through a document or compilation of related documents by pointing and clicking on words or objects on a computer screen. For example, if you were looking at a hypertext version of this page, and you used your mouse to "point and click" on the word, *synchronization*, the computer could instantly take you to the first page of Chapter 14 on *Synchronization Licenses*.

What Berners-Lee did was to extend the concept of "hypertext" not only within a document, and between documents, but also between different computer sites accessible to each other over the Internet. Thus, if you were viewing a hypertext version of this page and clicked on the word, *Kohn*, your computer, if connected to the Internet, could instantly take you to the electronic "page" published by the authors of this book,[4] and from there, you can link to any number of Web sites, both within the Kohns' Internet site and to other sites which are linked to our site, such as the Web sites of the U.S. Copyright Office, and those of ASCAP and BMI.

In 1993, a group of computer programmers at the University of Illinois developed the first computer program for the World Wide Web that had a graphical user interface, making it easy to navigate the web by clicking on links using a mouse on a personal computer. In addition, this "browser" software allowed users to view text, such as e-mail, and graphical images, such as photographs, and to receive just about any kind of file available over the web, including those containing sounds, video clips, and other content. The first version of this software was called, *Mosaic*, and commercial versions have since been released by public companies such as Netscape (since purchased by America Online) and Microsoft (i.e., Microsoft Explorer).

Until the mid-1990's, the Internet was primarily used by academic institutions, defense contractors and government agencies and their use was limited to remotely access other computers on the network and to send and receive *e-mail* (i.e., electronic mail). The advent of easy to use browser software for the World Wide Web has fueled an explosion of growth in the number of users who access the Internet and those who set up Web "servers" and Web "sites" on those servers containing information and entertainment programming that users of

---

[4] www.kohnmusic.com.

Internet browsers may access. Each Web site is the equivalent of a commercial online service or BBS, with the difference being only the scale of service and content provided by the site. In fact, many BBS operators have converted their operations to Web sites on the World Wide Web.

## E. Electronic Commerce

Emerging from its traditional academic base, the Internet has the potential to provide, and to some extent is already providing, individuals and organizations with a new and exciting means to conduct business. Each Web site is capable of providing or advertising a full range of products and services. Traditional retail and mail order businesses, as well as electronic publishing of news, literature, data, financial services, sound recordings, and audiovisual works, are all being conducted over this new medium. By the end of 1994, the number of commercial sites on the Internet exceeded the number of educational sites. Since then, the growth of the Internet has been explosive. By mid-1995, there were over 22,000 servers of information on the Web, as compared with about 1,250 only a year earlier, and by the end of 2001 there were millions of Web sites in operation.

Today, the Internet both an advertising medium and a medium for electronic commerce, with businesses like Amazon.com and Laugh.com having established virtual storefronts for the sale of goods. All of these are supported by online credit card authorization, billing and order processing capabilities, everything an electronic merchant or publisher would need to conduct electronic commerce. In other words, anyone who sets up a Web site, which is potentially everyone, is now able to quickly and easily establish a fee-based electronic retailing or publishing company.

## F. Transmission Medium: Telephone, Cable, or Airwaves

Whether interactive digital transmissions will primarily take place over telephone lines, cable television lines, or the air waves has been the subject of a debate that began years before the advent of the Internet. The answer that appears to be emerging is that all three are likely to serve as conduits for electronic commerce, with the air waves being reserved primarily for communications between things that cannot be conveniently attached to ground lines, such as automobiles, boats, briefcases, personal assistances (e.g., Palm Pilots), mobile telephones, wristwatches, and other things that move about.[5]

The big issue facing the development of electronic commerce today can be summarized by one word: *bandwidth,* which refers to the number of *bits* of information that can be transmitted *per second* through a given communications line. The bandwidth required for voice communications is 64,000 bits per second; for high fidelity music, 1.2 million bits per second; and, ideally, for video, 45 million bits per second. Copper telephone wires, sometimes called twisted-pair, can theoretically carry as much as 6 million bits per second — fast enough for music, but not fast enough for most video. By comparison, the potential bandwidth of fiber optic lines exceeds 1,000 billion bits per second.

Regardless of the physical attributes of the communications line (e.g., copper wire, fiber optics, air waves), and the number of bits per second it may potentially carry, its bandwidth is further limited by the technology of the devices and software (e.g., modems, telecommunications protocols, compression software, etc.) used to send and receive those bits. Nevertheless, that technology is improving rapidly. Today's standard personal computer *modems* have speeds exceeding 56,600 bits per second, over twenty times what they were just a few years ago, and modems are currently being developed that may reach or exceed 512,000 bits per second. Many businesses (and many homes in communities where the service is available) are beginning to install access to ISDN, or digital lines, offering an immediate leap to 115,000 bits per second, Many large companies access the Internet directly from their T1 lines, providing a bandwidth of over a million bits per second.

One major leap forward in bandwidth has accompanied the shipment of *cable modems,* which allow home computer users to access the Internet through their cable television lines. This greatly increases the speeds at which the Internet may be accessed from the home — as much as 10 million bits per second, or about 80 times faster than an ISDN line. Another major leap is the deployment of digital signal look (DSL) technology, which provides the bandwidth of a T1 into the home for less than $100 per month.

---

[5] Negroponte, *Being Digital* pp. 23-24 (Alfred A. Knopf, New York 1995).

Finally, it should not be assumed that telephone, cable and the air waves will be the only media for electronic commerce. It is not inconceivable that your local electric utility company will begin offering its power lines as a means to access the Internet from your home. When that happens, entirely new applications of the Internet will become possible, such as the interaction between the utility company and any *smart appliances* installed in the homes of consumers, resulting in potentially enormous nation-wide energy savings. For example, your electric utility company could charge you lower rates for the use of electricity if you allow them to regulate the use of your dishwasher and other major appliances during peak hours. If you wish to temporarily discontinue the utility's control over your appliances, such as, for example, during the holiday season or when you are having a large dinner party, you just access your utility account through the Internet and provide the utility with the appropriate instructions. While accessing your account, you might view a display that graphically shows your energy usage that month.

## G. The MP3 Phenomenon

Sometime in late 1996, college students, purely on a grass roots basis, began what we now know as the MP3 phenomenon. It began with the simultaneous developments in personal computer hardware and software: the introduction of low cost CD-ROM drives for personal computers, and the development of three small utility software programs: *ripper* software, *MP3 encoder* software, and *MP3 decoder* software.

As personal computer enthusiasts discovered, CD-ROM drives not only allowed you to play interactive CD-ROM software and games, such as electronic encyclopedias and arcade games, it allowed you to use your computer to play compact discs (CDs) containing musical recordings. By downloading from the Internet and installing ripper software on your CD-ROM drive equipped personal computer, you could pop your favorite music CD into your CD-ROM drive, run the ripper software, and within minutes copy all of the tracks from your CD onto your computer's hard drive. The ripper software would actually read each digitally encoded track on your CD, recognize the 0's and 1's comprising the musical recording, and copy the track in digital form to your computer, which would appear as a .wav on your hard disk.

The average musical recording today is about 3.5 minutes, and 3.5 minutes of musical data, in the form of 0's and 1's, is about 40 megabytes large. Given the average hard disk space at the time, about 2 to 4 gigabytes, it wouldn't take too many of these files to fill up your hard disk. In addition, if you wanted to email the file to a friend, it would take, using a 28bps modem, nearly three hours to upload the file to an email server and the same three hours for the recipient to download the file to his personal computer. At this rate, the sharing of musical files were not very practical. Even on a network, such as the computer network of a college or university, while file transfer rates among students is considerably faster, there's still the problem of the limited storage space on the students' hard disks.

In the 1990's a group called the Motion Pictures Experts Group (MPEG) working group developed in association with the Fraunhofer-Gesellschaft group a set of standards for compressing audio and video files. MPEG 1, layer 3, later shortened to MP3, is simply a standard set of mathematical algorithms used for compressing sound files into an attractive format for downloading or streaming across the Internet.

When the MP3 algorithms are run through a set of musical data, such as a digitally encoded recording, it eliminates virtually all of the 0's and 1's the human hear can't reasonably discern, leaving only those 0's and 1's that are recognizable. Because about 90 percent of the data in a typical digitally encoded musical recording are not essential to the reasonable listening experience, that 90% could be removed, leaving a greatly compressed file having only a slight reduction in sound quality. Though an audiophile or sound engineer could determine the difference between the original .wav file containing all the data of the recording and the compressed MP3 version of the recording, the latter, although degraded, still provides a quite acceptable listening experience for the average person.

As a result, a musical recording compressed with MP3 encoding software now comprised a file that was 11 times smaller than the original raw data file. In other words, the 40 megabyte file was now compressible to about 3.5 megabytes without a noticeable degradation in sound quality to most listeners. Now, a one gigabyte hard disk could contain over 10 times as many musical recordings, and while the raw data file took nearly three hours to transfer by modem, the file encoded in MP3 could be transferred in less than 15 minutes.

During the late 1990's, it was estimated that 60% of all college students had access to the Internet using high speed bandwidth. In other words, they were connected to the Internet at speeds offered by T1 lines. Thus, a 3.5 megabyte MP3 file could be transferred over a school's network in less than 30 seconds.

A file encoded in MP3 is only useful if you can play it, and to play an MP3 file all you needed was MP3 decoding software. In the late 1990's, the Fraunhoffer institute posted on the Internet an example piece of MP3 encoding and decoding software, and actively encouraged its use. Software developers quickly developed various improvements in MP3 encoding software, and then a 19 year old computer programmer in Sedona, Arizona developed what soon became the most popular MP3 software player, WinAMP. AOL later purchased this software for a reported $70 million.

In late 1997, two software executives working at software startup Pretty Good Privacy, Inc., conceived a business plan based on the notion that a vast number of people were beginning to learn the convenience and joys of *downloadable music* and that there would soon be a demand for legally licensed MP3 files offered at an affordable price. GoodNoise corporation was formed by Bob Kohn, your co-author, and Gene Hoffman. In July, 1998, the company began offering MP3 files for 99 cents per track and later changed its name to EMusic.com, Inc. The company went public, purchased the rights to operate Rollingstone.com, and in 2001 was purchased by Vivendi/Universal.

At about the same time GoodNoise was started, an entrepreneur in San Diego, California purchased the rights to the domain name mp3.com for $5,000, and began a Web site devoted to news for the growing MP3 community. MP3.com later developed a free download service, offering MP3 files uploaded by unsigned bands and later went public. This company was also purchased by Vivendi/Universal in 2001.

Because ripper software was distributed on the Internet on a freeware or shareware basis, just about anyone on the Internet could download a free copy of ripper software for their use. Thus, millions of MP3 files were produced from virtually every popular music CD available to the public. Students could easily exchange these files over freely available computer networks, by e-mail or by FTP file transfer.

In 1998, five students at UCLA developed a Web site and software program called Scour.net, which greatly facilitated the exchange of MP3 files. The Scour software "scoured" all the hard disks connected on the UCLA network, and later other college networks, and permitted anyone logging on the Scour.net Web site to download files from those computers on the scoured networks that contained MP3 files for sharing. Scour went bankrupt in 2000 under the weight of a lawsuit filed by the Recording Industry Association of America (RIAA).

## H. Napster

The facilitation of illegal *file sharing,* as it became known to defenders of this form of copyright infringement, took a giant leap forward, or backward depending upon your perspective, upon the invention and widespread deployment of *Napster.*

Napster is comprised of two software systems working in tandem with millions of individuals who have stored MP3 files and are connected to the Internet. The first of these software systems is a software program that operates on your personal computer that you, or anyone, can download for free from the Napster.com Web site. Once installed on your computer, you can instruct the program to search for a recording or an artist, such as "Unforgettable" or "Madonna," resulting in a search result that is comprised of a list of recordings that responds to your query. So, if you searched for "Madonna," you might get a list of a thousand "files" that contain Madonna's name in it. These files are typically MP3 files, compressed versions of recordings by the artist, Madonna, that people, other people, made from their CD collections (by first "ripping" them off the CD, and then compressing them into MP3 files using any number of MP3 encoding software also available free on the Internet).

How does this work? When you first install Napster, it asks you whether you want to "share" the MP3 files that you have on *your* hard disk. (The files on your disk could have come from any number of sources: You could have ripped and encoded them yourself, received them via email from friends or off of a Napster-aided download, or you could have purchased it from legitimate sites that sell MP3 files, such as EMusic.com). If you say yes, then anyone else using Napster, when they do a search, such as "Sinatra," and you have Sinatra recordings in the MP3 format on your disk, from whatever source, will get a result that says that the Sinatra file is available from your hard drive. That person may then instruct Napster to download the file by just double clicking on the word Sinatra in the search result. Within moments the MP3 file that Napster help you located will begin downloading from the computer where it is stored to your hard disk. If *you* searched for "Madonna," Napster may return you a list of 1,000 or more files available from any one of millions of other hard disks, and when you double click on one of the files on your list, you begin to download a copy of the Madonna recording directly from someone else's hard disk to your hard disk. (Neither Madonna, her record company, or her music publishing company, is getting paid for these copies).

Why does this work so well? That's the second piece of software system: the database software residing on the file server's (i.e., hard disks) at Napster's corporate offices. What Napster, Inc. does is keep a database of everyone currently on the system using Napster to "share" files, literally millions of people. By doing so, Napster greatly facilitates the file "sharing" that is taking place among users, because it makes the whole search and result mechanism work quickly and efficiently. Napster, Inc. doesn't actually store any of the downloaded files, but they facilitate the downloading of millions of files by others, estimated to be about 15 million files a day. What each user is doing when he or she permits the download of a copyrighted file without permission from the copyright owner is "directly" infringing the applicable copyrights, and they are clearly liable for copyright infringement, which can subject them to civil and criminal penalties. In addition, under the copyright law, anyone who facilitates the infringing activity of another may also be liable for infringement under the principal of "contributory copyright infringement" or "vicarious liability."

The notoriety and widespread deployment and use of the Napster system convinced a Silicon Valley venture capital firm to invest $15 million in the company. Napster was subsequently sued by the five major record companies. Ironically, during the pendency of the lawsuit, a German media firm, Bertelsmann, which owns one of the five major record companies, BMG, lent Napster over $50 million in exchange for an option to purchase a controlling interest in the firm.

Investors in Napster, however, appeared to be too optimistic about the prospects of their legal defense. A Federal District Court in California granted a preliminary injunction, ordering Napster to virtually cease operations. That injunction was affirmed in nearly all substantive aspects by the Ninth Circuit Court of Appeals. Napster filed an immediate appeal, and within days, the District Court's injunction was stayed pending appeal. The appeal was heard by the Ninth Circuit Court of Appeals in October 2000, and on February 12, 2001, the Ninth Circuit affirmed the lower court decision on all substantive issues.[6]

## I. Digital Rights Management

During this entire period, beginning about 1996, a number of companies were formed to develop and market technologies to help content owners protect their content from rampant copyright piracy, or the free exchange of MP3 files without compensation to copyright owners. These technologies have come to be called, *digital rights management.*

AT&T, through a division called A2B, Liquid Audio, and Intertrust were among the first companies to develop digital rights management technologies, and later Microsoft's Windowsmedia division, joined the fray.

Many of these technologies attempt to deploy one form of encryption technology or another to prevent or control the copying of copyrighted works encoded in a digitally formatted computer file. Encryption is the means by which data is scrambled into an unintelligible form in such a way that only the holder of the proper encryption key can unscramble the data back to its original state. The strength of a encryption technology depends upon the reliability of the algorithm and the length of the encryption key used in encrypting the file. Any encryption key that is over 128-bits long is considered *strong* encryption. A file of data encrypted with a 128-bit key would be virtually impossible to decrypt without the proper key. It is estimated, by the U.S. National Security Agency, that it would take 12 trillion times the

---

[6] *A&M Records, Inc. v. Napster, Inc.*, 239 F.3d 1004 (9th Cir. 2001).

age of the universe, using every computer on the planet, to break a file encrypted with a 128-bit key. Pretty strong stuff.

The problem, however, is that encryption is the wrong technology for protecting recorded music. Encryption is used to solve the problem of keeping a third party, call her Cathy, from listening in to a conversation between two other parties, call them Alice and Baker. If strong encryption were used to encrypt the conversation, then, Cathy could work for the CIA and she still would not be able to crack the call, using even the best of technology the intelligence agency has at its disposal. But, as Alice has to *encrypt* the sound on her end, Baker in order to listen to the sound, has to *decrypt* it on his end. Once decrypted, Baker can record it and make copies.

In other words, encryption, which is really good at keeping a third party out of the conversation, depends upon the *sender trusting the recipient*. Applying encryption to protect sound recordings is applying it to precisely the opposite situation — where the sender absolutely *does not trust* the recipient, which in this case is the consumer. The consumer must decrypt the sound in order to listen to it and if he can listen to it, he can record it. Thus, as the sound comes out of its encrypted box, it can be copied onto a hard disk in the same form it was encrypted — digital files that are easy to copy.

It remains to be seen whether technologies will be developed to truly control the copying of sound recordings. One promising means of enforcement, however, has been deployed by EMusic. EMusic sells transmissions of sound recordings in the MP3 file format, which are easily copied by the consumer. For this reason, most of the EMusic catalog of MP3 files found its way onto the Napster file sharing system. But EMusic developed a system which allows them to uniquely identify each MP3 file it offers, using an encryption algorithm called MD5, and can determine quickly if the same file is offered in the Napster system. This allows EMusic to notify Napster in advance of its copyrighted files, and Napster can block the transfer of any MP3 files that correspond to the list provided by EMusic. While not perfect, it has significantly reduced the amount of pirating of EMusic files within the Napster system.

Record companies are also working to make it more difficult for personal computer users to "rip" tracks off of CDs and place them digitally on their computers, where they can be encoded into MP3 and easily transferred. It will take several years before we know whether digital technologies can reduce the piracy problem spawned by the digital world.

## J. Streaming Transmissions Versus Downloaded Transmissions

There has been much debate in the Internet community about what will become prevalent: the transmission of music over the Internet by *streaming* or *downloading*? The debate is a false one. For example, suppose you want to hear the recording, *Let It Be* by the Beatles. You ask your voice recognition equipped home music system to play the song, your system notifies some celestial jukebox of your request, the recording is transmitted from the celestial jukebox to your home system, which interprets the 1's and 0's for your tuner and speaker system, and you enjoy the performance. What we just described is music-on-demand, which has nothing to do with the question of streaming versus downloading.

Those who suggest that all music will be streamed must be suggesting that all music will be transmitted on demand. Technically, it makes no sense for music to be streamed, any more than it makes sense that you eliminate caching on your web browser.

### 1. The Importance of Cache

In a world of increasing bandwidth, it is simply more economical to receive a motion picture or sound recording in a few seconds for later rendering, than to receive it in real-time — the length of time it takes to view or listen to the program. It is more efficient for the equipment involved in the sending of the transmission to send the work in "batch" mode, rather than in "interpretive" mode. Imagine a sit-down dinner of 100 people. If the salad were served one piece of lettuce at a time to each of the 100 people, how many waiters (or "servers") would it take to accomplish the task in a reasonable amount of time? Certainly more time, with certainly more servers, than it would take if the salad were served in "batch" mode, or the whole plate of salad at one time. The time that it takes to deliver the salad has little to do with the time it takes to eat it.

This suggests that all forms of copyrighted works — including digitized images and text, and sound recordings and motion pictures — will be copied into RAM or, at least temporarily, onto a user's hard disk or other form of permanent storage, prior to the actual viewing or listening of the program. In other words, the time it takes to transmit a work will have little to do with the time it takes to consume the work. If that is the case, then it would appear that virtually all transmissions will result in fixation or reproduction.

It's clear that, while music-on-demand is the wave of the future, it's more efficient for the recordings to be transmitted on demand in batch mode and cached locally while the recording is being rendered, and perhaps saved for future uses that would economize on the number of bits that need to be sent over the network. This is exactly how your browser works today, with innumerable .html, .wav, .gif, and .jpg files caching on your hard disk for 30 days, and there is no reason to believe it will work any different with music files. This does not necessarily mean, however, that the user will maintain the copy for future private performances.

## 2. How Long Will You Save the Cache?

Will users choose to save everything that is transmitted to them? The answer to this question is not obvious. Certainly, virtually no one saves every piece of html, gif, jpg, java applet and other data that is ever cached during the course of web browsing for more than the typical 30 days, the default setting on most web browsers. Why save music any longer? Do people indefinitely save every television program ever recorded on their Tivo or Ultimate TV recording systems?

One aspect of the question arises from the competition between *public* and *private* performances. If the transmission of music from a web site to the home computer is recorded by the recipient — i.e., the song is saved in a copy or phonorecord in a way that is "sufficiently permanent or stable to permit it to be perceived, reproduced, or otherwise communicated" again and again — the consumer would no longer have to pay for each new performance desired, because each performance from that copy would be a *private* performance, which does not require further permission from the copyright owner. Thus, by making and maintaining a copy of a transmitted recording, the consumer can avoid having to order and pay for an additional transmission each time he wants to hear the recording played.

In addition, because the consumer is in a better position to choose the time at which to effect the download, the consumer is more likely to make a home recording of a transmission ordered upon request than they would make a home recording of a work broadcast on television or on radio. Obviously, on an interactive network, where a particular program may be downloaded as and when desired, the consumer does not have to wait until a broadcaster happens to make a public broadcast of the desired program. (Home taping might be facilitated with a copy of TV Guide, but no similar information is normally available for radio broadcasts). Thus, the home recording of programs available on the Internet, the key feature of which is interactivity, is likely to be much higher than home recording of public broadcasts.

To the extent the consumer is required to pay the telecommunications costs for the transmission on a minute-by-minute basis, there may be another reason the consumer may choose to save copies received by transmission. As mentioned above, a consumer will have a choice between (i) receiving transmissions streamed on a "real-time" basis, enabling them to listen to the performance as the musical work is being transmitted, and (ii) receiving transmissions in "batch mode," to be saved first in their entirety in their computer's memory, and then, only after the file is received, will a performance that the consumer can audibly hear be rendered. Sending sound recordings in batch mode is likely to be possible at much higher transmission speeds than real-time transmissions. As *bandwidth* (i.e., the capacity of the telephone and cable television lines to handle high speed transmissions) increases, and data compression techniques improve, a three minute recording may eventually take only several seconds to *download* to your computer. Thus, the consumer may save telecommunications costs by ordering musical works in batch mode, rather than listening to transmissions on a real-time basis. Ordering such works in batch mode means the fixation or reproduction of a copy.

In a world of increasing bandwidth, it is our view that people will pay *by the bit* not *by the moment*. In other words, the costs of a transmission will have little to do with how long the telephone is tied up while the transmission is occurring; the costs of a transmission, leaving aside the value of the particular content, will depend upon how many bits of information are being sent. This is precisely how web sites are charged by those hosting their sites. If every time you want to hear a recording, you needed to pay for the bits, you would almost always save the bits in case you wanted to hear the recording

again. In other words, it will be more economical to receive a motion
picture or sound recording in a few seconds for later rendering on
multiple occasions, than to receive it in real-time — the length of time
it takes to view or listen to the program — every time you wished to
hear a performance.

Though a transmission may result in a fixation, a work is not fixed
by virtue of a transmission alone. Something else must happen. As
we have said, a work is considered fixed if its embodiment in a copy
or phonorecord is "sufficiently permanent or stable to permit it to be
perceived, reproduced, or otherwise communicated for a period of
more than transitory duration."[7] Works are not sufficiently fixed if
they are "purely evanescent or transient" in nature, "such as those
projected briefly on a screen, shown electronically on a television or
cathode ray tube, or captured momentarily in the 'memory' of a computer."[8] However, as we have noted above, the placement of copyrighted material into a computer's memory, such as RAM (i.e., random
access memory), for more than a very brief period, may also be considered a fixation.[9] It is thought that if the content is copied, or *buffered*, even momentarily, a user may retain the copy for reuse merely
by the click of a mouse.

At least in today's personal computing environment, we know that
some transmitted works will almost always be fixed on the recipient's
computer. Because of their nature, digitized graphic images and textual materials will either be saved to the recipient's hard disk or displayed on the recipient's computer screen, or both. It is the nature of
a still image, such as a graphic work or an image of text, that, if the
image is to be of any use to the user at all, the user must store it for
a period long enough to view it and that period is likely to always be
for "more than transitory duration."[10] As we have said, when an image

---

[7] 17 U.S.C. Sec. 101.

[8] House Report at 53.

[9] *See Advanced Computer Services of Michigan Inc. v. MAI Systems Corp.*, 845 F.
Supp. 356, 363 (E.D. Va. 1994) (conclusion that program stored only in RAM is
sufficiently fixed is confirmed, not refuted, by argument that it "disappears from RAM
the instant the computer is turned off"; if power remains on (and the work remains
in RAM) for only seconds or fractions of a second, "the resulting RAM representation
of the program arguably would be too ephemeral to be considered 'fixed'").

[10] One could perhaps imagine a photograph or display of text being transmitted and
flashed onto a user's computer screen momentarily for subliminal psychiatric reasons,
but for the most part, these images will reside in RAM for more than momentarily.

is placed into the RAM of a computer, it is considered a fixation. Moreover, web browsers typically *cache* such images and maintain them on your computer for a default period of about thirty days. It would appear, therefore, that the transmission of musical notation or lyrics of a musical composition will always result in a fixation, either in RAM or on disk.

Sound recordings and motion pictures, however, have a nature different from still images of graphics or text. Sound recordings, of course, consist of a *series* of sounds.[11] Motion pictures consist of a *series* of related images which, when shown in succession, impart an impression of motion.[12] By contrast with a still image, whether graphical or textual, a *series* of images or a *series* of sounds would have no use to the user unless, when it is rendered, it is rendered for a period of *not* more than a transitory duration.

Thus, while a transmission of a sound recording or a motion picture may be fixed concurrently with the transmission, it may not necessarily be so fixed for the transmission to have value to the user — the user may choose to a have the material "projected briefly on a screen, shown electronically on a television or cathode ray tube, or captured momentarily in the 'memory' of a computer" solely for the purpose of an ephemeral performance, and not saved in a way that is "sufficiently permanent or stable to permit it to be perceived, reproduced, or otherwise communicated for a period of more than transitory duration." Of course, the user may also choose to save the transmitted work to his or her hard disk for later viewing or listening.

However, saving these recordings to disk has its costs. Recording digital transmissions does not eliminate the need for physical copies or phonorecords, it only transfers the cost of those physical materials from the transmitter to the user who pays for the physical copies in

---

[11] 17 U.S.C. Sec. 101. ("*Sound recordings* are works that result from the fixation of a series of musical, spoken, or other sounds, but not including the sounds accompanying a motion picture or other audiovisual work, regardless of the nature of the material objects, such as disks, tapes, or other phonorecords, in which they are embodied").

[12] 17 U.S.C. Sec. 101. ("*Motion pictures* are audiovisual works consisting of a series of related images which, when shown in succession, impart an impression of motion, together with accompanying sounds, if any.").

the form of storage space (e.g., space on audiocassette tape, hard disks, and optical drives).

Arguably, because of the great amount of storage space that a recorded musical composition requires, could not public performances be priced to the point where it would be cheaper for the consumer to simply pay for each public performance desired (e.g., *pay per listen)* rather than bear the price of storing a transmitted recording for future private performances? For example, rather than buying a 100 or 1000 disc CD changer having the capability to record interactive digital transmissions, and the 100 or 1000 compact discs required for such recording, thus affording the consumer the ability to select and play back private performances of a limited number of recordings stored in the system, it may be more *economical* for the consumer to just request from a "celestial jukebox" a public performance of a particular song when desired from a repertoire of potentially every record ever recorded.[13]

Would it not also be more *convenient* for the consumer to subscribe to such *pay per listen* services, rather than to collect and store recordings? Computer databases and information systems will enable interactive transmitters of recorded music to track and analyze the tastes and buying habits of consumers. This will establish a more efficient communication between providers and consumers of these musical works, giving consumers information about the works available that are likely to interest them and giving producers information about what kinds of works should be produced and marketed to their individual subscribers. This will create opportunities for new kinds of services to be offered to subscribers. For example, consumers who frequently order performances of Elton John could be notified when a new Elton John recording is released. The "broadcast" of music over the Internet can thus be tailored to the personal taste of each individual user. A user may elect never to save a recording to disk, but instead, instruct his online service provider (or his own search, or *intelligent agent,* software) to add a particular song or artist to the list

---

[13] If a consumer's request for a public performance automatically causes a musical work or sound recording to be transmitted to his home system, a storage-cost conscious consumer might even instruct his receiver system not to automatically save, or to delete, the recording, unless he or she gives some conscious instruction to store a copy of the recording.

of tunes he desires to be transmitted to him at those times he wishes to tune in.

It may be asserted that, historically, storage costs have declined rapidly, and should they continue to do so, as expected, the consumer would not find it expensive to maintain a library of recorded music. But this ignores another set of costs: the costs associated with maintaining a database of what's been stored, as well as the means by which they can be found and retrieved (i.e., the investment required to acquire and learn database management software). Consumers just may find that it is not worthwhile to organize and store downloaded material. If the cost of just ordering a performance from a central source is sufficiently low, it may be more cost effective, and convenient, to just order the musical performance when it is desired.

Thus, whether consumers will save to RAM or disk transmitted sound recordings or motion pictures may depend upon the cost of effecting those transmissions (both the cost of the content and the cost of having the content communicated to them) and the costs of maintaining copies or phonorecords of the recordings made.

We believe that important clues to this equation are hiding in the cache of your browser.

## K. The End of Intellectual Property or a New Beginning?

As noted above, the revolution in our telephone system and new uses of television cable lines, will begin to allow low-cost, high speed digital transmissions of educational and entertainment programming into the home and office. The nature of these new delivery systems will transform much of our "one way" (i.e., to the listener) delivery of entertainment programming to "two way" (i.e., from the listener to the delivery system back to the listener) form of experience. The result will be the delivery of requested music, and other programming that contains music, to the listening public when and where they want it. That much is clear.

Until recently, it has been assumed that, of the "two way" communication this technology allows, the "one way," the way from the content provider to the user, will contain transmissions of copyrighted content, such as music, and the "other way," or the way back to the content provider, will contain the user's *requests* — that is, the user's instructions as to what particular programming he or she would like to receive. Because of this "two way" communication, the content provider will know when a user listens to a particular song, and providers of entertainment programming will thereby be able to employ computer databases and information systems to track and analyze the tastes and buying habits of consumers of entertainment works. This will allow a more efficient communication between providers and consumers of these works, giving consumers information about the works available that are likely to interest them and giving producers information about what kinds of works should be produced and marketed to which consumers.

Nevertheless, what is emerging as a result of the Internet is an entirely new dimension to this "other way" of communication — the communication *from the user.* What that other way is turning out to be is not merely communication back to the content provider, but communication *to others* on the network. This started out as electronic mail. But the low cost of personal computers and the advent of "client" and "server" software — the basic architecture of the Internet — allows any individual to become a supplier of interactive digital transmissions. One consequence of this "other way" of communication has been what has been a phenomenon called, *file-sharing,* the best or most notorious example of which is *Napster.*

What this all boils down to is this: Everyone will not only be a content *user* or *consumer*, everyone will become (or could easily become) a content *provider* or *supplier*. Not just traditional suppliers and distributors of entertainment programming, such as record companies and television networks, but anyone and everyone. The playing field has been leveled. Anyone on the network can become a content provider, and we believe just about everyone will become a provider of content of some sort. Just about anyone will have the ability to inexpensively become a supplier of interactive digital transmissions of content, and that content may be text, music, photographs, sounds, video, computer programs, and other data or information.

What does this mean for music publishers, recording companies and other content providers? An optimist would suggest that it means the opportunity to provide music licenses to potentially millions of individuals who desire not only to receive musical works and sound recordings, but to republish them to others. A pessimist would say that it means the opportunity for potentially millions of individuals to effect interactive digital transmissions of musical works and sound recordings without accounting to copyright owners. To the extent the pessimists are correct, one of the big challenges facing the music industry will be locating and prosecuting individuals and Web sites that offer unauthorized recordings of musical compositions.

Consider for a moment the challenges and difficulties inherent in locating private or semi-private electronic mail or file-sharing transmissions that contain unauthorized transmissions of musical works. Already, peer-to-peer file sharing programs, such as Gnutella, have been developed, which apparently do not require the kind of central server facilitation that Napster provides to the users of the Napster client software. Experts disagree about whether Gnutella-type programs will "scale" — that is, whether they can efficiently operate at all without someone operating a central server. This is important, because it is much easier for copyright owners to sue operators of a relatively small number of central server operators than it is to sue every individual who desires to engage in illegal file-sharing. Moreover, should anonymity technology ever be successfully applied to protect the identity and location of copyright offenders, the protection of intellectual property on the Internet may become quite problematic.

Which raises the question: Should the music industry and other content providers, as one computer industry analyst suggested, just "get over it?"[14] Or will the system adjust so that both the goals of intellectual property protection and consumer freedom are equitably met? We are still waiting for answers to important questions involving the efficacy of technologies used to circumvent the protection of intellectual property and the efficacy of the laws designed to strike a balance between the compensation of authors and the freedom of individuals to share the legally shareable.

## III. LEGAL BACKGROUND

As suggested above, the means by which electronic commerce in musical works will occur is best described by the term, *digital trans-*

---

[14] Esther Dyson, "Intellectual Value," *Wired Magazine* (July 1995) ("The idea that intellectual property in a Net-based economy can lose its value horrifies most owners and creators. They'd better get over it.").

*mission.* The two main types of digital transmission are (1) *streaming* transmissions, and (2) *download* transmissions, or *digital deliveries.* The copyright law contains various terms of art which are defined in ways to facilitate the analysis of the exclusive rights contemplated by the copyright law. Before beginning our analysis of these rights as they apply to digital transmissions, we thought that it would be useful to first provide a brief review of these terms, which include: *performance, display, reproduction, copy, phonorecord, distribution, publication,* and *transmission.*

The reader is forewarned that this section is one of the longest and perhaps most complex discussions in this book. If you are one who is not disposed to exploring the far reaches of copyright metaphysics, you might spare yourself the trouble and skip to the more practical advice found in Sections IV and V below.

## A.  Potential Forms of Uses Under the Copyright Law

### 1.  Performance

As discussed in Chapter 17, on *Performance Licenses*, one of the exclusive rights provided by the Copyright Act to the owner of a copyright is the exclusive right to *publicly perform* the copyrighted work. The Copyright Act defines a *performance* as follows:

> To *perform* a work means to recite, render, play, dance, or act it,
> either directly or by means of any device or process or, in the case
> of a motion picture or audiovisual work, to show its images in any
> sequence or to make the sounds accompanying it audible.[15]

For example, when Frank Sinatra sings the song, *I've Got You Under My Skin* in a nightclub, he is rendering a *performance.* When you sing the song in your living room or in your shower, you too are rendering a performance. When you play Sinatra's recording of the song *I've Got You Under My Skin* on a CD using your home stereo system, or from an MP3 file on your personal computer, you are *performing* the recording, both the *sound recording* by Sinatra and the underlying *musical composition* written by Cole Porter. In each of

---

[15] 17 U.S.C. § 101

these instances, the performer or the device rendering the performance is transmitting sounds audible to the human ear. But the term performance, under the copyright law, is not so limited.

When you hear the same recording of *I've Got You Under My Skin* on the radio, the radio station is rendering a performance of both the song and the recording, but the transmission by the station is not comprised of sounds directly audible by the human ear, but of electromagnetic waves sent through space which are converted to audible sounds by a radio receiver. The copyright law makes it clear that these transmissions, or broadcasts, also constitute performances:

> To "transmit" a performance or display is to communicate it by any device or process whereby images or sounds are received beyond the place from which they are sent. [16]

This leaves open the question to what extent is a digital transmission of a work over the Internet a performance of the work? More specifically, does a download or digital delivery of a recording constitute a *performance* of the sound recording or the underlying musical work embodied in the recording? These questions will be addressed below.

*Public v. Private Performances.* As noted above, the owner of a copyright in a musical work has an exclusive right to perform and authorize others to perform the work, but that right is limited to those performances that are *to the public.*

The Copyright Act defines a *public* performance as follows:

> To perform or display a work *publicly* means —
>
> (1) to perform or display it at a place open to the public or at any place where a substantial number of persons outside of a normal circle of a family and its social acquaintances is gathered; or
>
> (2) to transmit or otherwise communicate a performance or display of the work to a place specified by clause (1) or to the public, by means of any device or process, whether the members of the public capable of receiving the performance or display receive it in the

---

[16] Id.

same place or in separate places and at the same time or at different times.

Thus, when Frank Sinatra sings the song, *I've Got You Under My Skin* in a nightclub — clearly "a place open to the public or at any place where a substantial number of persons outside of a normal circle of a family and its social acquaintances is gathered" — he is rendering a *public* performance of the song. By the same token, when you sing the song in your living room or in your shower, you are clearly rendering a *private* performance. Similarly, when you play Sinatra's recording of the song *I've Got You Under My Skin* on a compact disc or from an MP3 files using your personal computer or home stereo system, you are rendering a *private* performance. Because the Copyright Act limits the copyright owner's exclusive performance rights to those rendered *publicly*, you may perform a musical composition in your home without the need for a license from the copyright owner.

When a radio station broadcasts Sinatra's recording of *I've Got You Under My Skin*, the station is rendering a *public* performance of the composition. Even if the broadcast is made, instead of over the airwaves, over cable lines, sometimes called *narrowcasting* or *cablecasting* over the new medium of *cable radio*, the cablecast constitutes a public performance. The same is true when the broadcast is of a motion picture, television program, or other audiovisual work containing copyrighted music. The television station or cable system operator is rendering a public performance of both the audiovisual work and the underlying musical composition. Further, when a composition is performed over the telephone, such as when you are *All Alone by the Telephone* (Irving Berlin) waiting *on hold*, the performance is a *public* performance requiring a license from the performance rights society representing the owner of the musical composition telephonically transmitted.

Note that a radio broadcast or "music on hold" broadcast of the Sinatra recording of *I've Got You Under My Skin*, each constitutes a public performance of both the *sound recording* by Sinatra and the underlying *musical composition* written by Cole Porter. The *sound recording* and the underlying *musical work* are separate works each of which are protected by their own copyright.

As noted in Chapter 17, on *Performance Licenses*, an owner of a musical work has under the copyright in the work an exclusive right of public performance. By virtue of this right, writers and publishers of musical works are able to collect public performance royalties when their musical compositions are broadcast on the radio, television, or cable, and they collect those royalties through their performance rights society, usually by means of a *blanket license*.

While the U.S. Congress has for some time been considering a general right of public performance for *sound recordings*, such a general right is not yet recognized in the U.S., and owners of sound recordings are not entitled to royalties for the radio broadcasts, music on hold broadcasts, and many other public performances of their recordings. However, certain kinds of public performances of sound recordings — those that qualify as *digital audio transmissions* — are now protected under the U.S. Copyright Act by virtue of the *Digital Performance Rights in Sound Recordings Act of 1995*, the scope of which is discussed at length below. Nevertheless, as for now, there is no general public performance right in sound recordings, and that means that when a sound recording is performed on radio, television, and music-on-hold, only the owners of the copyright in the Cole Porter musical composition will be entitled to compensation, not the owners of the sound recording copyright.

## 2. Display

One of the other exclusive rights provided by the Copyright Act to the owner of copyright in a musical work is the exclusive right to *publicly display* the copyrighted musical work. The Copyright Act defines a *display* as follows:

> To *display* a work means to show a copy of it, either directly or by means of a film, slide, television image, or any other device or process or, in the case of a motion picture or audiovisual work, to show individual images nonsequentially.

The copyright owner's exclusive right to publicly display his work has rarely been the source of any significant income to music copyright owners. However, it is useful to understand how the right could be exercised. When you show a printed copy of a composition's musical notation or lyric, such as a copy of *sheet music*, to another person in your home, you are displaying the musical work *privately*. As with private performances, private displays of copyrighted works do not require the permission of copyright owners. However, should a copy of the sheet music be copied onto a transparency for display, for example, by an overhead projector, the display of the sheet music transparency by that means at a public seminar would constitute a public display requiring consent of the copyright owner.[17]

Moreover, the advent of the Internet now makes it possible for widespread *public displays* of musical notation and lyrics. For example, today, you can access a website that will transmit to you on command either the full text of the lyrics of many popular songs or the *bitmaps* (i.e., a format for storing electronic pictures) of the musical notation of those songs. Licensing considerations for these public displays of "electronic sheet music" are discussed below.

### 3.   Reproduction

One of the most important exclusive rights provided by the Copyright Act to the owner of a copyright is the exclusive right "to *reproduce* the copyrighted work in *copies* or *phonorecords.*"[18]

The Copyright Act defines a *copy* as follows:

> A *copy* is a material object from which a work can be read or visually perceived either directly or with the aid of a machine or device, such as a book, manuscript, piece of sheet music, film, videotape, or microfilm.[19]

---

[17] Under the Copyright Act, if the sheet music itself (i.e., not the transparency copy) were publicly displayed, permission from the copyright owner would not be necessary for the public projection. "Notwithstanding the provisions of Section 106(5), the owner of a particular copy lawfully made under this title, or any person authorized by such owner, is entitled, without the authority of the copyright owner, to display that copy publicly, either directly or by the projection of no more than one image at a time, to viewers present at the place where the copy is located." 17 U.S.C. Sec. 109(c). Of course, permission would not be required for the making of even the transparency of the original copy made for the purpose of such projection if the making of the copy could be defended under the doctrine of fair use. For a discussion of *fair use*, see **Chapter 25.**

[18] 17 U.S.C. Sec. 106(1).

[19] 17 U.S.C. Sec. 101.

Thus, for example, the reproduction of (i.e., the act of reproducing) copies of *sheet music* requires the permission of the copyright owner of the musical work. It is important not to confuse the term *copy*, which is a material object, such as a piece of sheet music, with the *musical work* printed on the sheet music. Further, while a musical work may be fixed in a copy, the ownership of copyright in the musical work, or any of the exclusive rights under the copyright, is distinct from ownership of any material object in which the work is embodied. Thus, a person may own the copy of sheet music, but not own the copyright in the musical work it contains, and *vice versa*.

The Copyright Act defines a *phonorecord* as follows:

> A *phonorecord* is a material object that embodies fixations of sounds (other than those sounds accompanied by a motion picture or other audiovisual work), such as audio tapes, phonograph records, and compact audio disks.

A *phonorecord* can be viewed as a special kind of *copy*: one that contains a sound recording, but only if the sound recording is not accompanied by a motion picture or other audiovisual work. Thus, an audiocassette tape, compact disc or computer floppy disk containing a recording of *I've Got You Under My Skin* is a phonorecord. The compact disc may be accompanied by a photograph or drawing of Frank Sinatra, but such a visual image is not a motion picture or audiovisual work. If, however, the song *I've Got You Under My Skin*, is recorded as part of a motion picture, such as the movie *Innocent Blood*, then a material object embodying the recording of the song, such as a videocassette copy of the movie, would be considered a *copy*, not a phonorecord, because the recording is accompanied by a motion picture.

Like the reproduction of copies of *sheet music* or *audiovisual works* containing copyrighted music, the reproduction of *phonorecords* requires the permission of the copyright owner of the musical work.

The curious term *fixation*, used in the above definition of *phonorecord*, is also defined in the Copyright Act:

> A work is *fixed* in a tangible medium of expression when its embodiment in a copy or a phonorecord . . . is sufficiently permanent

or stable to permit it to be perceived, reproduced, or otherwise communicated for a period of more than transitory duration. A work consisting of sounds, images, or both, that are being transmitted, is "fixed" for purposes of this [law] if a fixation of the work is being made simultaneously with its transmission.[20]

The way recordings are embodied on compact discs is by the impression of microscopic pits on a metallic surface, which is covered with plastic for protection. These pits, though not indestructible, are clearly *permanent* as that term is used in the above definition. The way recordings are embodied on reel-to-reel magnetic tapes and audiocassettes is somewhat different. As you know, recordings embodied on tape are fixed by means of magnetic impulses placed on the tape by tape recording devices. Nevertheless, the realignment of molecules on the surface of the magnetic tape are considered "sufficiently permanent or stable to permit it to be perceived . . . for a period of more than transitory duration," as any owner of an audiocassette and tape player is aware. Finally, the placement of copyrighted material into a computer's memory, such as RAM (i.e., random access memory), for more than a very brief period has also been considered a fixing of that material,[21] though the temporary *buffering* of a recording in RAM for purposes facilitating a performance is believed by some not to involve the reproduction of a copy.

Again, the term *phonorecord*, which is a material object, such as an audiocassette tape or compact audio laserdisc, should not be confused with the *sound recording* or *musical work* which may happen to have been embodied in the physical phonorecord. Most important, neither the term *copy* nor *phonorecord* should be confused with the term *reproduction*, the former each denoting material objects and the later denoting the act of fixing or embodying musical works or sound recordings in the material objects.

---

[20] Id. But see **Chapter 26,** on *Live Musical Performances.*

[21] *See MAI Systems Corp. v. Peak Computer, Inc.*, 991 F.2d 511, 519 (9th Cir. 1993). (holding that loading of operating system software into the random access memory of a computer constitutes making a "copy" under the Copyright Act); *See also Agee v. Paramount Communication, Inc.*, 59 F.3d 317 (2d Cir. 1995) (recognizing that the distribution right involves the distribution of material copies).

### 4. Distribution

A *distribution* is the transfer of possession of a copy or phono-record from one person to another. The Copyright Act provides the copyright owner of a musical work the exclusive right "to *distribute* copies or phonorecords of the copyrighted work *to the public* by sale or other transfer of ownership, or by rental, lease, or lending."[22] Thus, by virtue of Section 106(3) of the Copyright Act, the distribution of copies and phonorecords of a copyrighted work to the public may only occur with the consent of the copyright owner. Accordingly, the public distribution of copies of sheet music, compact discs, and videocassette copies of motion pictures containing copyrighted music each requires the permission of the copyright owner.

Note that the Section 106(3) refers to the distribution of *copies or phonorecords* of a copyrighted work, not the copyrighted work itself. This is consistent with the notion that the term *distribute* has traditionally denoted the changing of possession of tangible copies of the work.[23] Thus, it is clear that under the copyright law, a distribution does not encompass the transmission of a work to a place beyond from which it is sent, because no tangible copy (or phonorecord) changes hands in connection with such a transmission.

Note further that a distribution includes the changing of possession of a copy from one person to another, and that not all distributions of a copyrighted work require the permission of the copyright owner. The exclusive distribution right of the copyright owner only extends to distributions to the public, and the scope of the right is limited by the *first sale doctrine*:

> Notwithstanding the provisions of section 106(3), the owner of a particular copy or phonorecord lawfully made under this title, or any person authorized by such owner, is entitled, without the authority of the copyright owner, to sell or otherwise dispose of the possession of that copy or phonorecord.[24]

---

[22] 17 U.S.C. Sec. 106(3).

[23] For example, *see* 17 U.S.C. Sec. 115(c)(2). ("For this purpose, a phonorecord is considered 'distributed' if the person exercising the compulsory license has voluntarily and permanently parted with its possession.").

[24] 17 U.S.C. Sec. 109(a).

Thus, for example, when you buy a compact disc containing tunes by your favorite recording artist, you may do whatever you want with that disc — you may throw it away, or give it away, lend it or sell it to a friend, just about anything but rent it for commercial advantage.[25]

It is also important to understand, however, that the distribution of an *unlawfully* made (i.e., infringing) copy will subject any distributor to liability for infringement.

Note also that, by properly circumscribing the definition of distribution, one will avoid the mistake of applying the first sale doctrine to digital transmissions. The first sale doctrine only applies to the transfer of copies or phonorecords, both defined as material objects. When one person transmits a recording to another, thereby reproducing a second copy by digital transmission, no distribution is taking place — i.e., no material object changes hands. Thus, the person engaged in the transmission may not invoke the first sale doctrine to such transmission and reproduction, even if the person possessing the original phonorecord offers to delete the file immediately after the transmission.

### 5.  *Publication*

As stated in the previous section, a *distribution* is the transfer of possession of a copy or phonorecord from one person to another, either privately or publicly. The term *publication* refers to a special kind of distribution: the distribution of copies or phonorecords *to the public*:

> *Publication* is the distribution of copies or phonorecords of a work to the public by sale or other transfer of ownership, or by rental, lease, or lending. The offering to distribute copies or phonorecords to a group of persons for purposes of further distribution, public performance, or public display, constitutes publication. A public performance or display of a work does not of itself constitute publication.[26]

---

[25] Section 109 contains special limitations concerning the right to rent copies and phonorecords of computer programs and sound recordings.
[26] 17 U.S.C. Sec. 101.

Thus, where copies or phonorecords of a work have been distributed to the public by sale or other transfer of ownership, or by rental, lease, or lending, the work is considered *a published work*. All other works are considered *unpublished works* — i.e., copies or phonorecords of which have either not been distributed at all or have only been distributed privately or distributed in some other limited fashion. The significance of the concept of *publication* was substantially reduced upon the enactment of the Copyright Act of 1976 (e.g., granting Federal protection to unpublished works and removing the notice requirement for published works), but the status of a work as either published or unpublished still has significance under the Copyright Act.[27]

More important, the definition of publication uses the language of Section 106(3), which describes the exclusive right of distribution, and was intended to make clear that "any form of dissemination in which a material object does not change hands — performances or displays on television, for example — is not a publication no matter how many people are exposed to the work."[28] Presumably, this would apply to any form of transmission, even reproductions made by means of a transmission (e.g., a digital phonorecord delivery).

### 6. Transmission

Neither the term *distribution* nor *publication* (i.e., distribution to the public) should be confused with the term *transmission*. A *transmission* is a communication of a performance or display by any device

---

[27] For example, only works that are published in the United States are subject to mandatory deposit in the Library of Congress (17 U.S.C. § 407 (1988)); deposit requirements for registration with the Copyright Office differ depending on whether a work is published or unpublished (17 U.S.C. § 408(b) (1988)); the scope of the fair use defense may be narrower for unpublished works (Act of October 24, 1992, Pub. L. 102-492, 1992 U.S.C.C.A.N. (106 Stat.) 3145, adding to the fair use provisions, "The fact that a work is unpublished shall not itself bar a finding of fair use if such finding is made upon consideration of all the above factors."); unpublished works are eligible for protection without regard to the nationality or domicile of the author (17 U.S.C. § 104(a)); published works must bear a copyright notice if published before March 1, 1989 (17 U.S.C. § 405); and certain limitations on the exclusive rights of a copyright owner are applicable only to published works (17 U.S.C. §§ 107-20).

[28] *See* House Report at 138, *reprinted in* 1976 U.S.C.C.A.N. 5754.

or process whereby images or sounds are received beyond the place from which they are sent.[29]

Note, the subjects of transmissions are limited to *performances* and *displays*; that is to say, neither *copies* nor *phonorecords* may be transmitted. There is good reason for this: copies and phonorecords, by definition, are *material objects*. At least until the invention of a transporter device, such as the fictional device featured in the television program, *Star Trek,* a copy or phonorecord, each being material objects, are not capable of being transmitted.

Thus, the term *distribute* (or *distribution*) or *publish* (or *publication*) denotes the changing of possession of a material object, such as a copy or phonorecord;[30] the term *transmission* denotes the communication of a performance or display.[31] The term *reproduction* is the act of embodying or fixing in a copy or a phonorecord a musical work, sound recording or other copyrighted subject matter; it is neither a copy nor a phonorecord, though a reproduction may be effected by a transmission.

## B. Proposed Changes to the U.S. Copyright Law Relating to Transmissions of Musical Works on the Internet by the Working Group on Intellectual Property Rights of the National Information Infrastructure Task Force

Again, the various means by which a musical works and sound recordings may be delivered over telephone, cable, or wireless lines over the Internet would seem to fall under one or more of these categories: *performance, display, reproduction, distribution,* or *transmission.* Under which category these digital deliveries should be subsumed, however, has become the subject of intense debate. That debate was kicked off by recommendations recently made by a U.S. government initiated Working Group on Intellectual Property Rights

---

[29] "To *transmit* a performance or display is to communicate it by any device or process whereby images or sounds are received beyond the place from which they are sent." 17 U.S.C. Sec. 101.

[30] *See* 17 U.S.C. Sec. 115(c)(2).

[31] *See* definition of *publication*: "A public performance or display of a work does not of itself constitute a publication." "A publication is a distribution of copies or phonorecords of a work . . ." 17 U.S.C. Sec. 101.

of the National Information Infrastructure Task Force formed in 1993 by the Clinton Administration. On September 5, 1995, the Working Group issued the Final Draft of its Report (the "White Paper").[32] Less than a month later, a bill was introduced in the U.S. Senate that would implement nearly all of the Working Group's recommendations.[33] Some of the conclusions reached in Working Group's "White Paper" were so questionable, the authors of this work published an extensive analysis in our Second Edition. Because the recommendations of the Working Group are now dated, readers are referred to the Second Edition for that analysis.

## C. Recent Legislation

The advent of digital transmissions have caused those who create and distribute recorded entertainment to question whether the laws designed to protect their copyrighted content, such as musical works and sound recordings, will effectively be enforceable in the digital world. To address the concerns of those who have answered this question in the negative, lawmakers have proposed and enacted new legislation.

### 1. The Digital Performance Rights in Sound Recordings Act of 1995

The Digital Performance Rights in Sound Recordings Act of 1995 (the "1995 Act") was enacted to specifically address the concerns raised by copyright owners of musical works and sound recordings. This important legislation made two significant, but distinct, changes affecting the licensing of musical works and sound recordings under U.S. copyright law: (1) to address the questions raised by *webcasting*, it created a new, but limited, digital public performance right for sound recordings, and (2) to address the questions raised by *downloadable*

---

[32] *See* Information Infrastructure Task Force, Working Group on Intellectual Property Rights, *Intellectual Property and the National Information Infrastructure: The Report of the Working Group on Intellectual Property Rights* (Sept. 1995) (hereinafter, the "White Paper.") *Rights* (Sept. 1995) (hereinafter, the "White Paper.")

[33] The *National Information Infrastructure Copyright Protection Act of 1995*, introduced on September 28, 1995, in the U.S. Senate (S. 1284). A copy of this legislation, in the form in which it was introduced, is set forth in the appendix to this chapter.

*music* files, it broadened the Copyright Act's existing compulsory mechanical license provision to include the reproduction and delivery of musical works in sound recordings by digital transmission.

### a. Effect on Sound Recordings

Recall our discussion in Chapter 17, on *Performance Licenses*, regarding the various exclusive rights that a copyright owner is afforded under the Copyright Act. One of those exclusive rights, commonly referred to as the public performance right, is set forth in Section 106(4) of the Copyright Act, which gives the owner of copyright the exclusive right to do and to authorize the following:

> (4) in the case of *literary, musical, dramatic,* and *choreographic works, pantomimes,* and *motion pictures* and *other audiovisual works*, to perform the copyrighted work publicly;

Note that the public performance right as set forth in Section 106(4) only applies to the several kinds of works specifically listed in the section. Conspicuously absent from the list of works in which a copyright owner may exercise the exclusive right of public performance is the *sound recording*. Thus, when Sinatra's 1956 recording of the song, *I've Got You Under My Skin* is broadcast on, for example, radio or television, the music publisher (in this case, Warner/Chappell Music) and the writer (the Estate of Cole Porter) will receive performance royalties from ASCAP, the performance rights society with whom the writer and publisher have affiliated for the purpose of collecting fees and distributing income arising from the exercise of the public performance right in the song. By contrast, the record company (Capitol Records) which owns the copyright in the sound recording and the recording artist (Frank Sinatra) who is typically entitled to a share in the record companies income arising from uses of the recording) receive nothing. Why? The Copyright Act affords the copyright owner no exclusive right to publicly perform sound recordings on radio or television.

For many years, record companies and recording artists have been lobbying Congress to add to the Copyright Act an exclusive public performance right for their sound recordings like the one enjoyed by music publishers and songwriters for their musical works. These efforts were opposed by broadcast stations, because they were unwilling to add to their existing burden of paying performance royalties to music publishers and songwriters, the burden of paying performance royalties to record companies and recording artists. At the same time, music publishers and songwriters feared that if broadcasters were forced to pay royalties to record companies for the public performance of sound recordings embodying their songs, the broadcasters would have less money available to pay for the performance of the songs themselves. The result was an unlikely alliance between broadcasters and music publishers which has successfully resisted the creation of a general public performance right in sound recordings.

Enter the *Digital Performance Right in Sound Recordings Act of 1995,* which finally created a limited right of public performance in sound recordings. Senator Orrin Hatch of Utah, one of the co-sponsors of the *1995 Act,* called the legislation, "complex," a characterization which one commentator later called "an understatement."[34] At one level the Act is simple — it merely adds the following language to Section 106 of the Copyright Act:

(6) in the case of sound recordings, to perform the work publicly by means of a digital audio transmission.

The apparent simplicity of the above amendment is belied by the shamelessly complex language added to Section 114 of the Copyright Act, regarding the Scope of Exclusive Rights in Sound Recordings. This complexity, however, can be understood considering two of the competing interests the Act attempts to reconcile: the interests of broadcasters who wish to continue to enjoy the royalty free performance of sound recordings and the interests of the owners of the sound recordings who, at a minimum, wish to guard against public perform-

---

[34] Lionel S. Sobel, *A New Music Law for the Age of Digital Technology,* Vol. 17, No. 6 Entertainment Law Reporter p. 3 (Nov., 1995) ("The Internal Revenue Code is 'complex'; the Digital Performance Right in Sound Recordings Act of 1995 is something else. 'Incomprehensible' perhaps, though 'You had to be there to appreciate it' may be fairer, because the convoluted language of the new Act appears to have been required by a number of very specific problems which the Act attempts to address with precision."). The authors, and perhaps the music industry, is indebted to Professor Sobel for his excellent article, which was the first published elucidation of the Act.

ances that tend to facilitate the copying of their recordings by members of the public who would want to own CD-quality recordings without having to pay for them.

Since many of the provisions of the 1995 Act which limited the scope of Section 106(6), now in Section 114 of the Copyright Act, were superseded by the DMCA, a detailed discussion of such provisions will be deferred to later in this chapter.

### b.  Effect on Musical Works

Under Section 106(1) of the Copyright Act, a copyright owner of a musical work has an exclusive right to reproduce the song in copies and phonorecords. This right, however, is subject to Section 115 of the Copyright Act, which is often referred to as the "compulsory license provision." Briefly, as long as records of a song were previously distributed in the United States, the compulsory license provision allows anyone else to compel the copyright owner of a song (e.g., a music publisher) to license the song at a license fee that is established by law — this fee is called, the "statutory rate." The statutory rate, as of January 2000, was 7.55 cents, or 1.45 cents per minute of playing time. The next scheduled physical phonorecord compulsory mechanical royalty increase (to 8.0 cents/1.55 cents per minute) will take effect on January 1, 2002.

The 1995 Act broadened Section 115 so that the existing compulsory mechanical license now covers downloadable music files. There are two basic kinds of digital audio transmissions: (1) those that result in a specifically identifiable reproduction of a phonorecord by or for any transmission recipient and (2) those that don't. Transmissions that do, what we call *digital downloads*, are called in the 1995 Act, *digital phonorecord deliveries*, the detailed definition of which is set forth in the next section. An example of a digital phonorecord delivery would be the commercial sale from a web site of an MP3 file — that is, a sound recording saved as computer data file using the compression techniques of an MPEG layer-3 software encoder — downloaded from a web site directly over the Internet to the home computer of a consumer, or the digital delivery of an MP3 to another using a file-sharing program such as Napster.

The effect of the 1995 Act was that, if you want to make digital phonorecord deliveries of other peoples songs, you may obtain a license at the statutory rate. The 1995 Act established a procedure by which the statutory rate for these digital phonorecord deliveries would be set, and that rate, at the time of this writing, is the same as the statutory rate for the reproduction and distribution of phonorecords in physical form.

### 2. The Digital Millennium Copyright Act of 1999

Because the 1995 Act fell short of addressing many of the questions raised by the application of digital technology to entertainment content, Congress enacted the *Digital Millennium Copyright Act* (the "DMCA"). The DMCA was primarily intended to implement the recent World Intellectual Property Organization (WIPO) Copyright Treaty and WIPO Performances and Phonograms Treaty, both concluded at Geneva, Switzerland on December 20, 1996.

For example, the DMCA made it a crime to circumvent technical anti-piracy measures intended to protect intellectual property. Though it outlawed the manufacture, sale, or distribution of code-cracking devices used to illegally copy copyrighted content, it contains exceptions which would permit the cracking of copy-protection devices for the purpose of encryption research or allowing assess to features that would permit software interoperability. The DMCA also provided several "safe harbor" provisions, protecting Internet service providers from liability for copyright infringement for simply transmitting information over the Internet. However, service providers and search locators, such as those who operate search engines, must remove access to infringing material expeditiously after receiving notice from a copyright holder that access infringing material is available through the use of their systems. These provisions will be discussed in more detail later in this chapter.

In addition, by a last minute amendment, the DMCA reversed some of the more important provisions of the 1995 Act relating to Webcasting. This last minute amendment, and how it came about, is an episode of legislative history that may be enlightening for historians of U.S. copyright law development.

In what appeared to be a major blunder by the recording industry, authors of the 1995 Act appear to have assumed that Webcasting, or the broadcasting of digital radio stations over the Web, would be primarily supported by subscription fees. As the Internet evolved shortly after the 1995 Act was passed, it became increasing clear that Web-casting on the Internet was going to be primarily advertising sup-ported. Hundreds of Web radio stations began operation under what they believed was an exemption from a sound recording copyright owner's exclusive right of digital audio transmission. Section 114, under the 1995 Act, exempted nonsubscription transmissions, and since these Web radio stations appeared to fall within this exemption, they needed nothing more than the appropriate performance licenses from ASCAP/BMI/SESAC in order to engage in their services.

In June 1998, the Recording Industry Association (RIAA) sent a letter to about 40 Web radio stations stating that they require licenses from record companies for the "Webcasting" of their sound record-ings over the Internet. "I write," stated the vice president and deputy general counsel for the Recording Industry Association of American (the "RIAA"), "because our record company members are the copy-right owners of the sound recordings that you are transmitting, and we want to ensure that you have secured the appropriate permission to Webcast those recordings."

In a brief article the authors of this book wrote and published on the Web site MP3.com in June, 1998, we pointed out that the RIAA letter neglected to state that only certain types of webcasts of copy-righted sound recordings require licenses from record companies, and we attempted to explain why many of them do not. Specifically, we stated that the 1995 Act exempted *non-interactive, non-subscription* digital audio transmissions of sound recordings, such as those pro-duced by Internet radio stations, from any requirement of a license from their owners.

A lawyer for the RIAA responded to that article in a formal letter to the authors of this book dated July 1, 1998, which he then distrib-uted for publication on the web and elsewhere. In this new letter, he attempted to explain why the RIAA believes the 1995 Act does not exempt non-interactive, non-subscription digital audio transmissions of sound recordings from the copyright owner's exclusive rights. A few weeks later, we posted an article on the Web that refuted the RIAA's analysis.

Meanwhile, on July 1, 1998, Hilary Rosen, President and CEO of the RIAA wrote a blistering letter to the CEO's of the top Webcasting companies on the Web, including RealNetworks, makers of software that facilitates digital audio transmissions, and Broadcast.Com, a leading Internet publisher of digital audio transmissions, such as retransmissions of radio broadcasts. A month earlier RealNetworks and Broadcast.Com had formed the Digital Media Association (or, "DiMA") to serve as a voice in Washington on behalf of Internet audio companies. In her letter, Rosen accused these companies of, among other things, "stabbing [the recording industry] in the back."

DiMA responded to that Rosen's letter by letter dated July 8, 1998, suggesting that one of the reasons DiMA was formed in the first place was that RIAA had gone around the backs of Webcasters by lobbying to eliminate the ephemeral recording exception these companies had been relying on to facilitate their Webcasting activities.

DiMA, however, was not comfortable being on the receiving end of the shrill of accusations being made by the RIAA, and offered to sit down with the RIAA to reach a compromise. In mid-July, DiMA and the RIAA met to discuss ways of compromising their differences. Within days, they reached an agreement in principle that would (1) eliminate the exemption for Webcasters set forth in Section 114(d)(1) of the Copyright Act, (2) add a compulsory license scheme for limited kinds of "eligible" transmissions (i.e., those made by Webcasters having the profile of members of DiMA), and (3) add language to Section 112 that would make it clear the "eligible" Webcasters could make ephemeral recordings of sound recordings for the purposes of facilitating their Webcasts.

On Thursday, July 23, 1998 representatives of the RIAA and DiMA and other music industry groups met with at the U.S. Copyright Office in Washington, D.C. and were told by the Register of Copyrights that they had until the following Friday, July 31, 1998, to draft the legislation they were seeking. Miraculously, on August 4, 1998, the House of Representatives passed an amendment to the DMCA that included the legislation drafted and agreed upon by the RIAA and DiMA just days, and perhaps hours, earlier. The DMCA, in the form negotiated by the RIAA and DiMA were enacted into law later that year.

The 1995 Act provided owners of copyrights in sound recordings, by the addition of Section 106(6) to the Copyright Act, an exclusive right to make digital audio transmissions, but limited that right by the provisions of Section 114 of the Copyright Act, which were amended by the DMCA.

It is useful to think about this new right of digital audio transmission in terms of (1) the several kinds of performances that are possible and (2) the likelihood that each kind of performance will facilitate unauthorized reproduction of works by recipients of the performance. These categories of performances may be roughly summarized as (i) performances involving a *low* risk of reproduction, (ii) performances involving a *moderate* risk of reproduction, and (ii) performances involving a *high* risk of reproduction.

### a. Performances Involving a Low Risk of Reproduction

There are two kinds of performances of sound recordings that involve a low risk of reproduction under the DMCA: Performances that are not included in the sound recording owner's bundle of rights to begin with, and performances that are so included, but are otherwise exempt.

*Excluded by Definition.* As mentioned above, Congress did not, under the DMCA, provide to owners of sound recordings a general public performance right, such as that enjoyed by owners of musical works. The new sound recording right provided by the DMCA was narrowly defined as, the exclusive right to perform the work publicly *by means of digital audio transmissions.* Thus, by definition, there are three basic limitations on the new limited performance right in sound recordings: the performance must be: (1) digital, (2) audio, and (3) a transmission.

- *Digital.* First, the right applies only to *digital* public performances. In other words, it does not apply to *analog* transmissions, such as FM or AM broadcasts. It was felt that the transmission of recordings by non-digital means would not result in copies that are likely to displace sales of high quality digital recordings. Thus, analog radio stations continue to have no obligation to pay royalties for the public performances of sound recordings they render.

- *Audio.* Second, the right applies only to *audio* public performances of *sound recordings.* Thus, it does not apply to performances of the audio portions of *audiovisual works*, such as television programs, motion pictures, and music videos. This does not mean that the audio portions of audiovisual works have no public performance protection — owners of audiovisual works have always enjoyed an exclusive right of public performance, even if only the audio portion of the audiovisual work is broadcast.[35]

- *Transmission*. Finally, the right applies only to *transmissions*, which is defined as communications that are received beyond the place from which they are sent. Thus, performing a sound recording from a CD on your stereo, whether in your home or out in public (e.g., at a public park), is not a transmission and is not covered by the new performance right. In addition, the limited exclusive performance right in sound recordings does not cover live performances or other performances of recordings that are not transmitted beyond the place from which they are sent. Though possible, it is not likely that a live performance of a copyrighted sound recording will result in the unauthorized reproduction of a high quality recording of the sound recording. (But see Chapter 26, on *Live Musical Performances*, regarding the prohibition against the taping of live musical performances).

*Exempt Transmissions*. Certain types of public performances of sound recordings, which may have fallen within the above definition, are nevertheless exempt from the new digital audio performance right in sound recordings. Performances that are exempt do not require permission from the owner of the sound recording. These include (1) nonsubscription broadcast transmissions, (2) certain other transmissions.

- *Nonsubscription broadcast transmissions*. These are transmissions to the public for which there is no charge, such as radio broadcasts. Because radio broadcasts usually do not provide the same sound quality as a CD recording, do not usually provide listeners with advance warning about what recordings are going to be broadcast, and do not usually include broadcasts of all the recordings of a particular CD album, it is felt

---

[35] 17 U.S.C. Sec. 106(4).

that traditional radio broadcasting is not likely to facilitate the wide scale taping of recordings and therefore poses little threat to the sale of CDs and the sound recording owner's copyright.

- *Other transmissions.* Other transmissions of sound recordings are exempt, such as a transmission to or within a business establishment for use in the ordinary course of its business, provided the business does not retransmit the transmission outside of its premises or the immediately surrounding vicinity.

Again, it was felt that none of the foregoing transmissions are likely to result in a high risk of recording by listeners, and all are exempt from the copyright owner's exclusive rights, and do not require permission from the sound recording's owner.

### b.  *Performances Involving a Moderate Risk of Reproduction*

Because of the moderate risk that they will result in an unauthorized reproduction, other types of public performances, though not excluded or exempt from the new public performance right, are subject to statutory licenses[36] — similar to the compulsory license applicable to the reproduction of musical works in phonorecords, allowing a transmitter to compel the owner of the sound recording to grant a license under statutory terms. These are of two kinds: subscription transmission and eligible nonsubscription transmissions.

- *Subscription Digital Audio Transmissions.* Performances that qualify for the statutory license include certain *subscription digital audio transmissions.* Subscription digital audio transmissions are those that are controlled and limited to recipients required to pay to receive the transmission. For example, subscription transmissions are received by subscribers of *cable radio* — audio-only cable or satellite television broadcasts. For such qualification, several conditions must be met.[37]

---

[36]  17 U.S.C. Sec. 114(d)(2).

[37]  Id.

- *Eligible Nonsubscription Transmissions.* Eligible nonsubscription transmissions will also qualify for the statutory license. An *eligible nonsubscription transmission* is a noninteractive digital audio transmission not exempt under Section 114 that is made part of a service that provides audio programming consisting, in whole or in part, of performances of sound recordings, including retransmissions of broadcast transmissions, if the primary purpose of the service is to provide to the public such audio or other entertainment programming, and the primary purpose of the service is not to sell, advertise, or promote particular products or services other than sound recordings, live concerts, or other music-related events.

There are some rather precise and complex requirements for subscription digital audio transmissions and eligible nonsubscription transmissions set forth in Section 114, some of which are more fully detailed later in this chapter. Suffice it to say that all transmissions that are not exempt or that do not completely qualify for a compulsory license will constitute a performance that must be licensed through voluntary negotiations with the owner of the sound recording.

c. *Digitally Transmitted Performances Involving a High Risk of Reproduction*

Digital audio transmissions that are not exempt and that do not satisfy the conditions for a statutory license have, by their nature, a likelihood of facilitating the unauthorized reproduction of sound recordings by the general public. Clearly, interactive transmissions, which would allow a member of the public to download selected sound recordings in digital form as and when they want them, facilitating the reproduction of high quality phonorecords for reuse, and obviating the need to purchase a CD to obtain the same value. This activity, if uncompensated, would adversely affect the ability of sound recording copyright owners, and recording artists, to reap the reward intended by the Copyright Act. The Act provides, therefore, that all such transmissions will constitute a performance that must be licensed through voluntary negotiations with the owner of the sound recording.

## IV. COMMERCIAL BACKGROUND

With the foregoing technological and legal background in mind, it will be useful to provide a brief overview of the commercial background of the music industry and their general approach to licensing music and sound recordings on the Internet, before turning to our analysis of the various forms of licenses that must be cleared for specific kinds of uses of music and recordings on the Internet.

## A. The Music Industry Players

Whether you are a person or corporate entity operating a web site or an individual using a file-sharing program, it will be useful to know the industry players who control the copyrights in, or represent the interests of the copyright holders of, the music and recordings you are likely to be using. We say useful, because these are the people who can sue you if you infringe their rights in those copyrights. While this information may be second nature to music industry veterans, a Webcaster who earnestly tries to discern who it is they have to pay, and what it is they have to pay for, can find this to be a most difficult and complicated endeavor. With apologies to the foreign nationals among our readers for our omission of all but the relevant U.S. industry players, we offer the following simplified descriptions.

### 1. Record Company

Record companies are entities who enter into contractual relationships with recording artists for the financing, promotion, and distribution of sound and video recordings featuring artists' performances. In return, the artist is paid a royalty, which is typically in the form of some percentage of the revenues earned by the record company in connection with the various kinds of commercial exploitation of the artist's recorded performances. The five major record companies are Universal (which includes, MCA Records, Mercury, Polygram, Interscope, A&M and others), Sony (which includes, Columbia and Epic), Warner Music Group (which includes, Warner Bros Records, Electra, and Atlantic), and BMG (a subsidiary of Bertelsmann), and EMI (which includes Capitol Records). In addition, there are thousands of independent record labels, such as Tommy Boy, Epitaph, Concord,

Shawnakee, TVT, Zomba, Laugh.com, and independent distributors, such as Koch, Allegro, and Red, to name just a few.

### 2. Music Publisher

Music publishers are entities who enter into contractual relationships with songwriters, often the same person as the recording artist, for the commercial exploitation of the songs written by the songwriters. Publishers may license the song for use in recordings made and distributed by record companies, for use in printed editions, such as sheet music and songbooks, and for live and recorded performances of the songs in nightclubs, restaurants, hotels and similar establishments and on radio, television and other kinds of broadcasts. The majors include Warner/Chappell, EMI, Famous, and Peermusic.

### 3. ASCAP/BMI/SESAC

These organizations, commonly known as "performance rights societies," represent music publishers and songwriters solely with respect to the *performances* of the songs. Music publishers and songwriters use these organizations to collect money from nightclubs, restaurants, hotels, and other venues, and radio and televisions stations for the public performance of all the songs they represent in their respective catalogs. They may charge the venues an annual flat fee and charge the radio and television stations a percentage of advertising revenues in exchange for a "blanket license" to use all of the songs the particular performance rights society controls or represents. After collecting the money on a blanket basis, each organization then takes surveys of what songs are played during the year; they then allocate the total collected revenue among the particular songs performed and pay each respective music songwriter and corresponding music publisher an amount representing what the song earned in performance royalties during the year. The performance rights societies only deal with the *songs*, not the *recordings* of songs, and as previously mentioned, only deal with *performances* of songs, not with the making or distribution of records or other copies containing songs.

### 4. Harry Fox Agency

This is an organization that represents music publishers and specializes in issuing licenses to record companies for the reproduction of songs in CDs and other kinds of records. The fees they charge for these uses is limited by the "statutory rate" specified in the U.S. Copyright Act. After retaining a small percentage for its services, the Harry Fox Agency pays these fees to music publishers (which then pays typically half of that to the songwriter). Some music publishers issue their own mechanical licenses directly to record companies, but many find the economies of scale offered by the Harry Fox Agency to be worth the services fee charged. Though the Harry Fox Agency performs other kinds of licensing services for music publishers, they do not license performance of songs or engage in any form of licensing services for record companies.

### 5.  Recording Industry Association of America

The RIAA, headquartered in Washington, D.C., is a trade association which represents record companies. The RIAA's stated mission is to promote the mutual interests of record companies, as well as the betterment of the industry overall through government relations, intellectual property protection, and international activities. The association also operates an aggressive anti-piracy unit, conducts extensive consumer and industry research, and provides ongoing communications support. Recently, the RIAA has established *Sound Exchange*, a vehicle similar to the Harry Fox Agency, established for the purpose of representing record companies collect royalties for digital audio transmissions of their recordings.

## B.  The Digital Media Industry Players

Mergers and acquisitions have blurred the once well defined lines separating the music industry organizations and the online world. The merger of AOL, the world's largest internet service provider, and Time-Warner, the world's largest media company, is the prime example. Nevertheless, it may still be helpful to delineate the commercial players by categories that remain useful to the analysis of music licensing questions.

### 1.  Online Retailers of CDs

Among those retailers of CDs that remain in business after the dot.com debacle of 2000 include Amazon.com, CDNow (now a subsidiary of Bertelsmann), and the various websites operated by traditional music retailers, such as TowerRecords.com, Borders.com, and BarnesAndNoble.com.

### 2. Online Magazines

Traditional music magazines have established Web sites on their own or operated by others, such as Rollingstone.com, DownBeat-Jazz.com, Spin.com, and Vibe.com. For lack of a better description, the following Web sites are also of the nature of online magazines, which offer information and digital transmissions of music, though primarily on a promotional basis: MTVi.com, GetMusic.com, Artist Direct/UBL, and Launch.com. Cnet.com has become a good resource for information about MP3 software and hardware products.

### 3. Digital Download Sites

The leading MP3 subscription service remains EMusic.com, which is now a division of Vivendi/Universal. CDuctive.com was a service that was acquired by EMusic. Musicmaker closed its doors in 2000. MCY.com operates primarily for European customers. MP3.com, also a division of Vivendi/Universal, offers downloads from unsigned bands. IUMA, the first music oriented Web site, was acquired in 1999 by EMusic, and sold in 2001 to Vitiminic, another European based digital download company.

The major record companies have established joint ventures for various types of digital distribution services that are not yet operating. Universal and Sony established PressPlay. EMI, Warner Bros., and BMG have established MusicNet in conjunction with Real Networks.

### 4. Online Web Radio Stations

One group of companies focused primarily on webcasting of pre-programmed music transmissions, such as Broadcast.com, which was purchased by Yahoo, Spinner.com, purchased by AOL, and Live365. Many terrestrial radio stations also operate their own Web sites.

### 5. Technology and Technology Service Providers

The primary digital rights management providers are currently Microsoft, Liquid Audio, and Intertrust. Reciprocal was established as a service company to help content providers manage their own digital download services based on Intertrust and other DRM technologies.

WinAMP remains the most used MP3 software player, but since Microsoft's Windowsmedia software began supporting the MP3 file format it remains to be seen how independent music players will manage. Sonique was an MP3 player that wowed users with striking graphics, and was acquired by Excite. MusicMatch purports to be a comprehensive MP3 solution for ripping and encoding, MP3 file management, and playback.

### 6. Digital Content Lockers

After you ripped and encoded, or downloaded, your MP3 files, legally or illegally, where do you store them? That question became the basis of a business model established by MyPlay.com, acquired by Bertelsmann in 2001.

### 7. Search Engines

Search engines may be divided into the legal and illegal. Listen.com was established as a portal containing links to wherever legal digital download files may be located on the net, and provided an editorial front end or filter, helping users find the music their looking for, or evaluate what's available from the legitimate digital download services. Excite and Altavista created services that allowed users to find MP3 files, including those offered illegally, but found themselves in the cross-hairs of the RIAA. Scour.net and Napster were the most notorious technologies for the facilitation of illegal file sharing.

## V. AN ANALYSIS OF THE LICENSES REQUIRED FOR VARIOUS USES OF MUSICAL WORKS AND SOUND RECORDINGS ON THE INTERNET

With the foregoing technological, legal, and commercial background in mind, we now turn to a more concrete analysis of the licenses that must be cleared for the use of musical works and sound recordings on the Internet.

At the outset, it should be obvious by now that virtually anyone who wants to become a content provider may do so quickly and easily, either by creating their own Web site, obtaining an e-mail account, or installing a so-called file-sharing program, such as Napster. It will therefore assist the reader, for purposes of the following analysis, to imagine a world in which any individual or organization who wishes to become a publisher, reseller, or transmitter of copyrighted music — whether they are a major recording company, a music retailer, an individual entrepreneur with a Web page, or a hobbyist who just wants to share his favorite tunes with his online friends — can and will do so. This section is addressed from the perspective of these potential licensees (and infringers) who are seeking, or who need to seek, licenses for their activities.

We will first provide a review of the salient legal concepts used throughout this section, and then proceed to analyze several specific activities that will require licenses from copyright owners of the musical works and sound recordings involved.

## A. Sound Recording Copyright Versus Musical Work Copyright

Whenever you transmit a sound recording, either by a streaming transmission (i.e., where no copy is made at the recipient's end) or by a digital delivery (i.e., where a copy is made at the recipient's end), the first thing to understand is that the transmission concerns two different works of authorship: (a) a *song* and (b) a *sound recording* of a song.

Thus, anyone seeking to obtain permission (i.e., a license) to use — or to use without permission (i.e., infringe) — a musical recording must first understand that his or her use will normally involve not one, but two separate copyrights: (a) the copyright in the sound recording and (b) the copyright in the underlying song, or musical work. The copyright in a *sound recording*, a particular series of sounds, is completely separate from the copyright in the underlying *song* featured in the sound recording.

For example, there exists a valid copyright in the song *I've Got You Under My Skin* by Cole Porter and the copyright is owned by Warner/Chappell Music, Inc., a music publishing company. At the same time, several records of *I've Got You Under My Skin* have been recorded by numerous recording artists over the years. A completely separate copyright exists for each particular recording — the sequence of sounds that make up the performance of the song by a singer and orchestra. These recordings are owned by the respective record companies that commissioned their creation. For example, the 1956 version of Frank Sinatra's recording of *I've Got You Under My Skin* is owned by Capitol Records.

Thus, if you wished to obtain permission to use Sinatra's 1956 recording of *I've Got You Under My Skin*, you would require the permission of Capitol to use the recording *and* the permission of Warner/Chappell to use the underlying song. You could not use the recording without permission from both companies. If you wished to make a new recording of the song *I've Got You Under My Skin*, you would require permission from Warner/Chappell, but you would not require permission from Capitol Records or any other record company who happens to own a recording of the song.

## B. Performance Right Versus Reproduction Right

Another important concept underlying the following analysis involves the difference between what is known as the *reproduction right* and the *public performance right*. This is particularly important because of the way the performance rights societies, such as ASCAP and BMI, and the Harry Fox Agency view their respective charters. Leaving the details until later in this analysis, suffice it to say at this point that the distinction between a performance and reproduction has become blurred, because the technology that facilitates digital transmissions is making it difficult for us to discern the distinction between a mere stream and a complete download.

### 1. Musical Works

The copyright law provides an owner of copyright in musical works several exclusive rights, including the exclusive right "to *reproduce* the work" (e.g., to make physical copies, such as CDs and sheet music) and "to publicly *perform*" the work (e.g., rendering a live performance of a song in a nightclub, or playing a recording of a song on the radio).

As noted above, the music publishers who own these copyrights in musical works will generally retain the Harry Fox Agency as their agent to license others who wish to make copies or phonorecords of songs, such as on records and CDs. They have recently begun using the Harry Fox Agency to license those who wish to make digital phonorecord deliveries. Note, the Harry Fox Agency issues only licenses for *mechanical reproductions*, including digital phonorecord deliveries, but they do not issue licenses to permit *performances*. Nevertheless, as will be discussed below, an issue has arisen as to just what constitutes a digital phonorecord delivery, leaving open the question as to whether the Harry Fox Agency has the right to license performances that are tantamount to digital phonorecord deliveries.

Since music publishers also have a separate right of public performance in their musical works, they will also seek to collect fees from those who wish to perform songs, either in live performances, on the radio or television, or on the Internet. Traditionally, the performance rights societies, such as ASCAP and BMI, have acted on behalf of music publishers to license performances of their musical works on a blanket basis to concert venues, restaurants, radio stations, and television stations. The performance rights societies have recently begun granting public performance licenses to Web sites who desire to make public performances of musical works over the Internet. These societies do not grant mechanical reproduction licenses, but, as we will also see, an issue has arisen as to whether the performance rights societies have a right to license transmissions of digital phonorecord deliveries on the basis of their belief that such deliveries constitute performances of their musical works.

As alluded to above, and discussed in more detail later in this chapter, one of the burning issues in music licensing today arises from the fact that music publishers employ the one type of organization, in the U.S. it is the Harry Fox Agency, and another type of organization, a performance rights society (e.g., ASCAP, BMI, and SESAC, in the United States), to collect royalties for, respectively, *mechanical reproductions* and *performances* of musical works.

As we shall see, the music publishers, acting through the Harry Fox Agency, have taken the position that interactive streaming of their musical works, even where there is no guarantee that the recipient is delivered a reusable copy of the song, entitles them to a mechanical reproduction fee (in addition to the performance fee to which their music publisher members believe they are entitled). By the same token (or more appropriately, another token), the music publishers, acting through the performance rights societies are taking the position that all download transmissions are performances of the underlying musical works, entitling them to collect a performance fee (in addition to the mechanical reproduction fee to which their music publisher members believe they are entitled).

### 2. Sound Recordings

The exclusive right to *reproduce* copyrighted works applies to both musical works (e.g., the Cole Porter song) and sound recordings (e.g., the particular recording of it owned by Capitol Records). Thus, record companies have an exclusive right to authorize the making of CDs containing their sound recordings, and also have the exclusive right to authorize the making of digital phonorecord deliveries containing their sound recordings.

By contrast, however, the right of public performance under the U.S. copyright law only applies to *songs, not to sound recordings*. The owners of copyrights in songs have always had a general right of public performance in their musical works. As a result, the copyright owner of the song *I've Got You Under My Skin* (in this case, Warner/Chappell, through its performance rights representative, ASCAP) will collect money from radio broadcasts of Sinatra's 1956 recording.

By contrast, the record company (in this example, Capitol Records) is not entitled to collect money from such radio broadcasts, because, at least in the U.S., owners of sound recordings do not have a general public performance right. As noted above, however, the changes brought about by the enactment of the DMCA gave owners of sound recordings a new right under copyright, the exclusive right to make digital audio transmissions. The RIAA has recently begun representing owners of sound recordings in licensing websites that wish to make digital audio transmissions of sound recordings.

### C. Activities on the Internet Requiring Licenses for the Use of Musical Works and Sound Recordings

Let's now turn to some specific examples of activities that may require you to obtain appropriate licenses from copyright owners of musical works and sound recordings, whether you are engaging in transmission activities on behalf of a corporation operating a website or you are just an individual operating file-sharing program. Table 23-1 summarizes the licensing questions discussed in this section regarding digital audio transmissions.

### 1. Example — Digital Audio Transmissions That Result in Digital Phonorecord Deliveries

*Example:* Suppose you desire to sell or give away, by digital download, MP3 files containing copyrighted musical recordings. What licenses do you require and from whom?

Because each digital delivery of a musical recording concerns two separate copyrights, the copyright in the sound recording and the copyright in the musical work embodied in the sound recording, it is first necessary to make a distinction between sound recordings and musical works.

TABLE 23-1.
Licensing Questions Discussed in This Section Regarding Digital Audio Transmissions

| Type of Digital Audio Transmission | Musical Work (Music Publishers) | Sound Recording (Record Companies) |
|---|---|---|
| Digital Phonorecord Delivery | Compulsory ($.08) [ASCAP/BMI?] | Voluntary |
| Non-Digital Phonorecord Delivery | | |
| Interactive | ASCAP/BMI [Compulsory ($.08)?] | Voluntary |
| Non-interactive | | |
| Subscription | | |
| — non-compliant | ASCAP/BMI | Voluntary |
| — compliant | ASCAP/BMI | Compulsory |
| Non-subscription | | |
| — eligible | ASCAP/BMI | Compulsory |
| — ineligible | ASCAP/BMI | Voluntary |

### a. Sound Recording

Persons desiring to make digital phonorecord deliveries of sound recordings must obtain a license from the person who owns the recording, which is typically, a record company.

No standard set of terms and conditions for effecting these licenses has yet emerged. EMusic.com, Inc. the largest supplier of popular music in the MP3 format, has entered into license agreements with over 750 independent record labels for the exclusive rights to make digital deliveries of their sound recordings MP3.com and IUMA.com (Internet Underground Music Archive), are among many companies that have obtained licenses to make digital deliveries of sound recordings directly from thousands of "unsigned" recording artists under licenses which nearly all on a non-exclusive basis.

Unlike licenses for the right to effect digital deliveries of the underlying song (see below), there is no compulsory license for digital phonorecord deliveries of sound recordings. In other words, you must obtain permission from the record company and the record company can charge whatever it likes or even refuse to grant you permission to make the transmission.

Current terms of these licenses are set forth in Chapter 27, on *Typical License Fees* and several forms used for these licenses are set forth in the Appendix to this chapter.

### b. Musical Work

Persons desiring to make digital phonorecord deliveries of a musical work must obtain a license from the person who owns the song, which is typically, a music publisher. However, to determine exactly what license you need and from whom you need to get it, it is necessary to make a distinction between the exclusive right of reproduction and the exclusive right of public performance, each of which is a separate right controlled by the owner of a musical work under the copyright law.

#### i.    Mechanical Reproduction License

Recall that a copyright owner of a musical work has an exclusive right to reproduce the song in copies and phonorecords. This right is subject to the compulsory license provision set forth in Section 115 of the Copyright Act. Briefly, as long as records of a song were previously distributed in the United States, the compulsory license provision allows anyone else to compel the copyright owner of a song (e.g., a music publisher) to license the song at a license fee that is established by law — this fee is called, the "statutory rate." The license which authorizes these transmissions is called a "mechanical license," and the organization in the United States that issues most of them on behalf of music publishers is the Harry Fox Agency.

Recall further that the 1995 Act amended the Copyright Act, and specifically Section 115 of the Act, so that the compulsory license provision now applies to the making of digital phonorecord deliveries. This means that you can now compel the copyright owner of the song embodied in the sound recording to license you the privilege of making digital phonorecord deliveries at the statutory rate.

As mentioned above, the statutory rate as of January 2002 is 8 cents, or 1.55 cents per minute of playing time. Thus, if you want to effect digital phonorecord deliveries of another's copyrighted songs, you may obtain a license at the statutory rate. The license which authorizes these transmissions is called a "mechanical license," and the organization in the United States that issues most of them is the Harry Fox Agency. The nice thing about these licenses is that you know you can always get it, and the statutory rate serves as a ceiling to what the music publishers or the Harry Fox Agency can charge you. In addition, the Harry Fox Agency is currently negotiating an agreement with its international counterparts, which, we would hope, would make it clear that mechanical licenses will be collected from the source of the transmission — that is, the Web site offering the digital phonorecord deliveries — regardless of where in the world the transmission recipient receives his or her copy of the recording. Leaving aside the potential international complications, mechanical licenses are easy to get, and God bless them.

The most recent form used by the Harry Fox Agency for the issuance of such mechanical licenses is set forth in the Appendix to this chapter.

### ii.   Performance License

With a proper mechanical license in hand, you would think that you would then be safe to proceed in making digital phonorecord deliveries. Not so fast. A little controversy is brewing here. The performance rights societies (e.g., ASCAP, BMI, and SESAC) appear to be taking the position that a *performance* license is required to effect a digital phonorecord delivery, even though a statutory mechanical reproduction license has already been obtained for the same delivery. In their view, all transmissions of songs constitute performances of songs, whether or not they result in a specifically identifiable phonorecord made by or for the transmission recipient, and therefore, they say, you must pay a public performance fee for these download transmissions, even after you have paid the statutory rate for the mechanical reproduction.

The performance rights societies have not yet disclosed how much they intend to charge for these transmissions. They are likely to seek something less than what they charge for transmissions that do not constitute digital phonorecord deliveries, such as "streaming" audio transmissions. At the current time, they are willing to enter into "stand-still" agreements, under which neither the society nor the licensee concedes the point in controversy.

One may legitimately ask: if I am paying 8 cents for the digital phonorecord delivery, why must I also pay for its performance, particularly if the phonorecord is not truly performed or in any way rendered during the transmission? Isn't this a form of "double-dipping" by the music publishing industry?

The performance rights societies could point to the definition of "digital phonorecord delivery" to support its position. The complete definition of that term, which was added to the Copyright Act by the DPRA, is as follows:

> A "digital phonorecord delivery" is each individual delivery of a phonorecord by digital transmission of a sound recording which results in a specifically identifiable reproduction by or for any transmission recipient of a phonorecord of that sound recording, *regardless of whether the digital transmission is also a public performance of* the sound recording or *any nondramatic musical work embodied therein.* (emphasis added).

One could infer from the italicized language that a digital phonorecord delivery *may* involve the public performance of the musical work embodied in the sound recording. But only that it *may* do so is the best you can say about it. If Congress intended to definitively answer the question, it certainly could have done so in unambiguous terms, such as, "A digital transmission containing a sound recording that results in a digital phonorecord delivery constitutes a performance of any musical work embodied in that sound recording." But it didn't.

Quite possibly, Congress recognized that some digital phonorecord deliveries may be performed or "streamed" for listening by the user while it is being downloaded; hence, the italicized language may have been needed to make certain that a digital phonorecord delivery will still be deemed such, even if the digital transmission happens also to constitute a public performance.

The performance rights societies could also point to the definition of *public performance* under the Copyright Act:

"To perform . . . a work *publicly* means —

"(1) to perform or display it at a place open to the public or at any place where a substantial number of persons outside of a normal circle of a family and its social acquaintances is gathered; or

"(2) to transmit or otherwise communicate a performance or display of the work to a place specified by clause (1) or to the public, by means of any device or process, whether the members of the public capable of receiving the performance or display receive it *in the same place* or *in separate places* and *at the same time* or *at different times.*" (emphasis added).

It appears, from the italicized language, that it does not matter whether you hear the performance at the same time as you download the file. Certainly, when a recording is being streamed to you, it is first *buffered* in your computer's temporary memory, before the recording is actually played so that you can hear it. What is the difference between storing the recording in temporary memory and storing it on your hard disk (which is typically the case with a digital phonorecord delivery) prior to your hearing the recording?

The problem with these arguments is that the above definition concerns not what a *performance* is, but what it means to perform a work *publicly,* in contradistinction to performing a work *privately.* Nevertheless, even if the transmission of a work is considered a public one, it may still not constitute a *performance*. According to the Copyright Act,

> "To *perform* a work means to recite, render, play, dance, or act it, either directly or by means of any device or process. . . ."

It may well be asked, where, for purposes of the definition of "perform," is the "rendering" or the "playing" of the work in the transmission of a downloaded music file?

Clearly, a transmission need not be initially audible to constitute a performance. A radio broadcaster is not transmitting "sounds," but rather electromagnetic waves that the end-user converts into sounds with a radio receiver. Nevertheless, there is no question that such a broadcast is a performance. A transmission may reach the public in "any form" and qualify as a public performance.

The requirement of a presence in a transmission of a "capability of simultaneous rendering or showing of the work" is nowhere to be found in the legislative or case law history of the public performance right. More important, given the emergence of greater bandwidth of transmission media and improved data compression techniques, it would be hard to imagine any transmission of a work that does not have the *capability* of a simultaneous rendering or showing of the work. Any compilation of digital data capable of rendering a performance or display could be interpreted on-the-fly to render that performance or display perceivable at the time of the transmission at the election of the recipient. In other words, a recipient should be in a position to decide whether a receipt of a musical work by transmission is rendered audibly at the time of the transmission. But why should the user's decision to listen to the work as it is being transmitted have a bearing on whether the transmission itself is a public performance?

The legislative history clearly states that for a transmission to constitute a performance there is no requirement that any potential audience member actually tune-in to the transmission. Even if a radio receiver is tuned in to a broadcast, radio equipment is fully capable of receiving radio signals and recording them on tape even if the loud speakers attached to the radio receiver are not turned on and no user is around to "listen" to the transmission. Thus, whether or not a receiver is tuned in, or is tuned in and the speakers are turned off, the transmission constitutes a performance of the song. In other words, the fact that the performance is not perceived when it is transmitted does not make the transmission any less of a public performance. A transmission is complete once it is sent, and it constitutes a performance (or display) whether or not it is ultimately heard (or viewed) by an audience.

Any other result could cause perverse practical problems. For example, suppose a particular transmission initiates a simultaneous audible rendition, but, because the transmission of the work occurs at a speed that is much faster than the time it takes the user to perceive the work audibly, the entire file is fully downloaded before the audible rendering is completed. Does this constitute the simultaneous rendering or showing of the work necessary for the transmission to constitute a public performance?

Would not a sender or recipient of the work have the ability to avoid having a particular transmission constitute a public performance by merely avoiding an on-the-fly audible perception of the work as it is being transmitted? Could not a cable television operator avoid having to pay public performance royalties by transmitting a motion picture to the video tape recorders of its home subscribers under an agreement with its subscribers that the motion picture will not be viewed by the subscriber until after the transmission is complete, or after it has begun?

More realistically, could not a passive second carrier of a television transmission pick up a television transmission from an initial transmitter and turn around and retransmit the signal to a cable system (which then retransmits the signal to the public), avoiding liability for infringement of the public performance? The answer is yes, but not on the basis that his reception and retransmission did not involve an audible or visual rendering of the signal: The secondary transmission is exempt under Section 111 of the Copyright Act. If the inaudibility of the signal at the time of the retransmission meant that the retransmission was not a public performance, there would be no need for such an exemption.[38] The performance rights societies could take the

---

[38] *WGN Continental Broadcasting Co. v. United Video, Inc.*, 693 F.2d 622, 625 (7th Cir. 1982) (holding that "the Copyright Act defines 'perform or display . . . publicly'"

position that a sound recording of a work is itself a "rendering" (i.e. a performance, albeit a recorded one) of the work. This is as opposed to sheet music where the musical notations only are listed. When one digitally transmits the sound file, one is engaged in a transmission of the recorded performance, as hence, it may be said, the requisite "rendering" is taking place. This argument would be plausible but not for the definition of "sound recordings," which is defined in the Copyright Act as "works that result from the fixation of a series of sounds." Thus, by definition, a sound recording is a *fixation* of sounds, not a *rendering* of sounds. Arguably, then, by transmitting a sound recording, you are transmitting a fixation of sounds, not a performance or rendering of them.

A better argument, from the performance rights societies' perspective, would be to say that the downloading of a digital file is part of a *process* that results in a rendering or playing of the work at the recipient's end. Recall that to perform a work means to render or play the work, "either directly or by means of a device or process." Thus, arguably, the process of transmitting the bits constituting a digital sound recording file, the recipient's buffering those bits or saving them to his hard disk or other storage media, and his playing of the bits, either as the bits are being downloaded or later, even after the entire file has been saved to disk, constitutes a playing or rendering of the sound recording, "either directly or by means of a device or process."

Because technology now permits the playing of the bits either as the bits are being downloaded or after all the bits in the file have been received, the distinction between a digital phonorecord delivery (DPD) and a non-DPD (i.e., a purely "streaming" digital audio transmission) is being blurred.

The difference between a technologic step that involves a rendering or showing and one that does not is analogous to the distinction computer scientists make between the use of an *interpreter* program

---

broadly enough to encompass indirect transmission to the ultimate public); *see also* *Hubbard Broadcasting, Inc. v. Southern Satellite Systems, Inc.*, 593 F. Supp. 808, 813 (D. Minn. 1984) (stating that "under the broad definitions found in Section 101 of the Copyright Act, a transmission is a public performance whether made directly or indirectly to the public and whether the transmitter originates, concludes, or simply carries the signal"), *aff'd*, 777 F.2d 393 (8th Cir. 1985), *cert. denied*, 479 U.S. 1005 (1986).

and a *compiler* program. Both interpreters and compilers are used to allow a computer program — "a set of statements or instructions to be used directly or indirectly in a computer to bring about a certain result" to execute or operate — in other words, be rendered or shown — on a computer. Both interpreters and compilers translate the set of statements, written in a language that human beings can easily understand, into a set of statements that the computer can understand — basically, a series of 0's and 1's.

In computer parlance, an *interpreter* program translates the set of statements *one statement at a time* — in effect, translating the statements "on-the-fly" into something the computer can understand. The computer follows those instructions concurrent with the translation or interpretation process. By contrast, a *compiler* program translates the set of statements in "batch mode" — that is, all at one time, in advance — and, only after the entire translation is completed, is the result, a copy of the program in a different form (known as an executable file), ready to run on the computer. Thus, a rendering or showing concurrent with the transmission would be analogous to using an *interpreter* to render or show the performance or display; a rendering or showing after the transmission would be analogous to using a *compiler* to render or show the performance or display.

Computer scientists generally view the choice between using an interpreter or a compiler in a given situation a matter of design choice, depending upon what operation he wants to optimize when running the program. Will users make a similar choice when deciding whether to experience a rendering in *real-time* as the transmission is being downloaded or to receive the work in *compressed* form for subsequent viewing or listening? It should be clear that, whether a user chooses to employ an *interpreter* (i.e., for real-time rendering or showing) or a *compiler* (i.e., for compressed time and subsequent rendering or showing), each constitutes an act by which the work is shown or rendered to the public "whether members of the public are capable of receiving the performance or display receive it in the same place or in separate places or in separate places and at the same time or at different times."

As pointed out earlier, however, given increasing bandwidth, the user will always download first, that is, cache the file, and then render it, but conceivably the rendering will begin when the first bit is saved by the user. The performance rights societies may argue that all of these transmissions should be considered performances, merely because it is too impractical, on a case-by-case basis, to make a distinction between which download transmissions are simultaneously rendered and which are not.

In addition, the performance rights societies have argued that a digital phonorecord delivery provides an added value to the consumer — that is, with the advent of digital deliveries, the consumer no longer has to schlep down to a record store to buy a CD; he or she can just order it online and receive it in minutes. Consequently, that added value should be paid for. This argument, however, was first made before the success of companies like Amazon.com, from whom you can now order a CD and have it sent to you by overnight courier. What practical difference does it make whether the tracks constituting a record album come to you overnight or several minutes or hours after you have requested them to be downloaded?

Moreover, it may be reasonable to assume that if Congress made digital phonorecord deliveries subject to a compulsory license under Section 115, and set the fee for such licenses at the statutory rate, then, arguably, it should be unnecessary for anyone to pay more than the statutory rate to effect the delivery, "regardless of whether the digital transmission is also a public performance of . . . any musical work embodied therein." Again, the quoted language is from the Act's definition of digital phonorecord delivery, and one could infer from it that Congress wanted to make certain that a digital download of a sound recording will be deemed a digital phonorecord delivery, subject to the compulsory license, with no one having to pay more than the statutory rate, *even if* the digital transmission happens also to constitute a public performance.

The immediately proceeding argument is a strong one, at least on U.S. soil, but what does it mean when you add an international dimension to the question? Many music rights societies outside of the U.S. are organized differently than their U.S. counterparts. Recall that in the U.S., the Harry Fox Agency represents music publishers with respect to mechanical reproductions; they do not hawk performance licenses, which come under the purview of the performance rights societies, namely ASCAP, BMI, and SESAC. Certain music rights collection societies overseas represent their music publisher members for both mechanical reproduction and performance licenses. Accordingly, they can in effect demand that you pay the established royalty for both reproduction and performance, even though no performance is actually involved in the download.

If the performance rights societies are not successful in persuading the industry, or a court, that all digital phonorecord deliveries constitute performances, one might think that the practical result will be this: if the statutory rate for a mechanical reproduction license is paid with respect to a transmission, then, a performance royalty is not due for the same transmission. Payment of the statutory fee for a mechanical license is intended to cover the sale of a copy (i.e., a physical phonorecord or a digital phonorecord delivery) and, theoretically, all *private* performances of the song arising from the use of such copy — and this would include the first performance or rendering that occurs concurrently with the transmission of the digital phonorecord delivery or sometime after the digital phonorecord delivery is completed.

This, however, is complicated by the following problem: As will be discussed below in connection with certain kinds of streaming transmissions, the Harry Fox Agency, on behalf of the music publishers that they represent, appear to be taking the position that a digital audio transmission of a musical work that is effected by means of an "interactive service" (discussed below) constitutes a digital phonorecord delivery, even though there is no assurance that the recipient will end up with a reusable copy of the recording. Under this view, certain streaming transmissions of musical works would require payment of the statutory compulsory license fee, currently 8 cents per stream. This interesting problem will be further explored below.

Suffice it to say that, the problem of double-dipping addressed in this section is far from resolved. It would seem that it is a problem that should be worked out between the performance rights societies, which are largely controlled by songwriters and music publishers and the Harry Fox Agency, whose decisions are largely controlled by the very same music publishers and songwriters. The problem is that neither of these organizations is likely to welcome the prospect of giving up their side of the revenue equation. As a result, there appears to be no commercial solution in sight, and it is just one of those questions that portends to become the next interesting subject of commercial copyright litigation.

### iii.    The Limited Download Question

What license would be required if the digital downloads of copyrighted musical works and recordings were technically limited in their operation — for example, the file may only be played five times or will cease operating 30 days after it was created or downloaded?

The suggestion has been made that such "limited downloads" might be considered *rental* copies, subject to a rental rate, rather than the statutory license fee under Section 115. But rental involves the right to *distribute* copies and phonorecords, not the right to reproduce them; the rental concept has no place in the analysis of limited downloads.

It has also been suggested that limited downloads should be considered *incidental* digital phonorecord deliveries, as opposed to *general* digital phonorecord deliveries. But there's no apparent connection between a limited download and a download that's merely incidental to the transmission. Even though a downloaded file may be limited in the way a consumer can render it, its rendering is not incidental to the transmission — in fact, the reverse would seem to be true.

Without express Congressional action on the subject, there appears to be no justification for treating limited downloads as anything other than digital phonorecord deliveries in general. Should transmitters of limited downloads desire a lower mechanical rate, they may request a lower rate. Music publishers acting within their rights may grant a special lower rate, depending upon the factors presented. One factor in making such a decision would be the effectiveness of the technology used to enforce the limitation. This is an evaluation best made by the content owner, not the government.

### 2.    *Example — Digital Audio Transmissions That Do Not Result in Digital Phonorecord Deliveries*

*Example:* Suppose you want to make streaming transmissions (that do not result in digital phonorecord deliveries) of copyrighted musical recordings. What licenses do you require and from whom?

To answer this question, not only must we address the distinctions between sound recordings and musical works, and mechanical reproduction and performance, but we must first determine the nature of the streaming transmission. Is it purely interactive (e.g., where the user gets to listen to a particular recording immediately after selecting it), or is the transmission in the nature of a radio program (e.g., where the user is constrained by the playlist established by the website operator).

Of transmissions that do not result in digital phonorecord deliveries, there are two basic types: transmissions that are part of an *interactive service* and those that are not.

### a.  Interactive Services

Under the U.S Copyright Act:

> An 'interactive service' is one that enables a member of the public to receive, on request, a transmission of a particular sound recording chosen by or on behalf of the recipient. The ability of individuals to request that particular sound recordings be performed for reception by the public at large, *or in the case of a subscription service, by all subscribers of the service,* does make a service interactive, *if the programming on each channel of the service does not substantially consist of sound recordings that are performed within 1 hour of the request or at a time designated by either the transmitting entity or the individual making such request.* If an entity offers both interactive and noninteractive services (either concurrently or at different times), the non-interactive component shall not be treated as part of an interactive service. (emphasis added)[39]

Clearly, even if the digital audio transmission does not result in a copy at the recipient's end of the transmission, if the recipient can choose, on request, "a particular recording" — an *ondemand stream* — then there is a high risk that the recipient will never need to purchase a copy of the recording or purchase a digital phonorecord delivery. If the interactive transmission is cheap enough, and the sound quality good enough, members of the public may choose to listen to interactive transmissions instead. Thus, to serve the purpose of the

---

[39] The language in italics was added by the DMCA.

Copyright Act, a license for interactive transmissions are required. Let's take a look at what this specifically means in terms of the song and the sound recording. We'll begin with the song this time.

### i.   Musical Works

As before, we must first distinguish between a *performance* and a *reproduction*.

*Performance license.* Clearly, a digital transmission of a song that is part of an *interactive service*, but does not result in a digital phonorecord delivery of the song — for example, an *on-demand stream*, the mere "streaming" of a song after a user clicks on an icon or link to receive a transmission of a particular sound recording — constitutes a public performance of the song. Hence, you would be required to obtain a performance license from one or more performance rights societies (e.g., ASCAP/BMI/SESAC) or you could attempt to obtain the performance license you need directly from the copyright owner. Performance rights societies issue performance licenses to web sites that offer these interactive transmissions, and such licenses are issued on a "blanket" basis, which will cover all of the music in the applicable performance rights society repertoire.

*Reproduction license.* Herein lies a controversy that will either be resolved by Congress, a Copyright Arbitration Royalty Panel (CARP), or the Courts. The music publishers have taken the position that songs digitally streamed from *interactive* services, so-called *on-demand streams*, constitute digital phonorecord deliveries, even if no digital copy is, or can be, made by or for the intended recipient of the transmission. Thus, the interactive transmissions of purely streamed copyrighted musical work would be subject to the compulsory license set forth in 17 U.S.C. 115, requiring payment of the statutory compulsory license fee for each stream.

In fact, at the time this Edition when to print, Universal Music Group (UMG) had been sued by music publishing members of the Harry Fox Agency for establishing just such an interactive streaming service without seeking mechanical licenses for the transmissions.[40]

---

[40] *Rodgers & Hammerstein Organization v. UMG Recordings, Inc.*, 00 Civ. 9322 USDC NY (JSM) (On September 25, 2001, the District Court granted the music publishers' motion for summary judgment, holding UMG liable for copyright infringement.).

(Ironically, UMG had earlier successfully won a lawsuit against MP3.com, which engaged in a very similar streaming service involving the UMG catalog of sound recordings).

Opponents of the music publishers' view on this subject, which include an unusual alliance among the Internet community (i.e., those who don't want to pay anything, if they can avoid it) and the traditional record companies (i.e., those who don't want to pay music publishers, if they can avoid it), suggest that this would amount to "double-dipping" on the part of the music publishers. If a performance royalty is required to be paid to ASCAP and BMI for the stream, why, they say, should a reproduction royalty *also* need to be paid?

The music publishers' policy argument may be summarized as follows: The technology used to facilitate the listening of streaming transmissions permit the listener to convert the stream into a download. The stream in question is not like a stream of a traditional radio broadcast, consisting of a series of tracks in some random or programmed order which listeners are not likely to copy, but an *interactive* transmission where the listener may know *in advance* exactly what will be streamed to his or her computer and can prepare for it (i.e., prepare to download or save it to his or her hard drive). Accordingly, interactive streams of musical works will tend to displace sales of CDs and digital phonorecord deliveries, transactions that typically earn them a compulsory mechanical reproduction fee.

Moreover, the saving of the transmission to one's hard disk as a downloaded file eliminates the need for further public performances of the work, because when a listener listens to the rendering of a file that has been downloaded to his or her computer, as opposed to listening to a stream from a website, the rendering is a *private* performance. Since music publishers have no exclusive right of *private* performance under the copyright law, only *public* performances, no further public performances royalties will be collected on performances rendered after the file has been downloaded (i.e., you only have to stream the file once and save the stream to get an infinite amount of performances from it). To the extent public performance royalties are reduced, they should be replaced by a mechanical reproduction fee, similar to that which music publishers typically collect upon the sale of a CD or the sale of a digital download.

Moreover, the music publishers add a very specific statutory argument, taking solace from a very specific provision that was in the

1995 Act that is now part of the compulsory license provision at Section 115(c)(3)(L):

> The provisions of this section concerning digital phonorecord deliveries shall not apply to any exempt transmissions or retransmissions under section 114(d)(1).

In the view of the music publishers, the above language *implies* that the provisions concerning digital phonorecord deliveries, while not applying to any exempt transmissions under Section 114(d)(1) does in fact apply to those transmissions that are *not* exempt under Section 114, which would include all transmissions made as part of interactive services. Thus, according to the argument, the transmitter must pay a mechanical reproduction fee, subject to Section 115's compulsory license, for each interactive digital audio transmission, whether or not a copy results from the transmission. A problem with this last argument is exposed when you ask what does it mean for Section 115 to apply to a transmission? It means that any mechanical reproduction licenses that *may* be required for the transmission would be subject to the compulsory license provision; it does not automatically mean that the transmission itself is a mechanical reproduction. Nevertheless, if that were the case, Section 115(c)(3)(L) would appear to be entirely meaningless.

In the case of *Rodgers & Hammerstein Organization v. UMG Recordings, Inc.*, defendant UMG has taken the position that, assuming they require mechanical licenses to effect their transmissions, they already have them by virtue of the mechanical licenses they previously obtained from the music publishers to manufacture and distribute the sound recordings which embody the allegedly infringed musical works.

The music publishers have responded that the mechanical licenses upon which UMG relies permitted the making of mechanical reproductions on specific kinds of physical devices, such as CDs, cassette tapes, and LPs, not by digital phonorecord deliveries. These mechanical licenses, say the music publishers, are expressly limited to the specific configuration — i.e., CD, cassette tape, and/or LP — identified by a particular record number specified in the license, and case law has enforced the limitation on configurations in mechanical licenses.[41]

At the end of the day, music publishers have not appeared to have taken an unreasonable position on the issue. First, they recognize that an interactive transmission of a song that is of a short duration and which is not intended to result in a copy being made for the intended recipient, is not likely to have an effect on the sale of a CD or a full digital phonorecord delivery of the song. Accordingly, the music publishers have informally let the record and Internet industry know that they will allow such interactive transmissions without requiring payment of the statutory fee if (a) no more than 30 seconds of the song is transmitted and (2) the transmission is effected by or with the permission of the owner of the sound recording embodying the song. (Note, this does not allow anyone to make such 30-second transmissions, only the record company who owns the recording, or its licensees).

Second, Section 115 refers to an "incidental" reproduction or distribution.

> [T]he Librarian of Congress shall cause notice to be published in the Federal Register of the initiation of voluntary negotiation proceedings for the purpose of determining reasonable terms and rates of royalty payments [regarding digital phonorecord deliveries under this Section] as the parties may agree. Such terms and rates shall distinguish between (i) digital phonorecord deliveries where the reproduction or distribution of a phonorecord is incidental to the transmission which constitutes the digital phonorecord delivery, and (ii) digital phonorecord deliveries in general.[42]

Here the law makes a distinction between digital phonorecord deliveries *in general* and those "where the reproduction or distribution of a phonorecord is incidental to the transmission which constitutes the digital phonorecord delivery." The music publishers are willing to

---

[41] *Fred Ahlert Music Corp. v. Warner/Chappell Music, Inc.*, 958 F. Supp. 170, 174 n.5 (S.D.N.Y.), aff'd, 155 F.3d 17, 24-25 (2d Cir 1998) (a case in which the testimony of one of the authors of this work was considered with approval).

[42] 17 U.S.C. 115 (3)(C).

admit, at least privately, that they would be willing to consider interactive streams intended as mere performances, where copying to hard drives is merely incidental to the transmission, are these very same "incidental" reproductions. The quoted portion of Section 115 above appears to contemplate that *incidental* reproductions may have a lower compulsory, statutory rate than full digital phonorecord deliveries.

Opponents of the publishers assert that, in the context of on-demand streaming, any fragmented, temporary or transient reproduction in a computer's buffer memory which is necessary for the transmission is not sufficiently fixed to be considered a copy or phonorecord to begin with, and therefore there is no digital phonorecord delivery, incidental or otherwise. At one point, the recording industry was pushing for some concession by the publishers, requesting, for example, that at least three "listens" of a streaming audio transmission take place before a mechanical royalty need be paid.

It is our view that a compromise is likely to be reached which will allow the music publishers to collect both a performance fee and a mechanical reproduction on these on-demand streaming transmissions, but a lower mechanical reproduction rate will be applied for the incidental reproductions. Most important from the transmitter's perspective is that the mechanical rate for incidental digital phonorecord deliveries be established on the basis of a *percentage* of revenues, rather than on a cents per stream basis.

*Distribution license.* The discussion would not seem complete without a brief analysis of whether the musical work copyright owner's exclusive right of distribution is implicated. The answer, of course, is "no," because the distribution right only applies to the distribution of *copies* or *phonorecords*, each of which are defined as material objects. Thus, the "stream" in question, which does not involve the transfer of possession of material objects, does not constitute a distribution. The word "delivery" is better terminology than distribution in connection with digital transmissions that result in reproductions (i.e., downloads).

## ii.   Sound Recordings

If you operate a commercial website and you want to effect *interactive* streaming transmissions of copyrighted musical sound recordings, even if the transmission does not result in a copy at the recipient's end of the transmission, if the recipient can choose, on request, "a particular recording," then there is a high risk that the recipient will never need to purchase a copy of the recording or purchase a digital phonorecord delivery. For this reason, the law specifically gives owners of sound recordings, typically record companies, an exclusive right to license digital audio transmissions that are part of interactive services. This means the record company can charge what it wishes for these transmissions or refuse to provide a license at all.

### iii.   Line Between Interactive and Non-Interactive Transmissions

Of course, no mechanical reproduction fee should be charged for non-interactive transmissions. The extent to which a transmission is interactive and non-interactive is a matter that has been a matter of some dispute. One Webcaster, Launch.com, purchased in 2001 by Yahoo, offered a service called Launchcast that provided a Webcast of soundrecordings, but through the use of a proprietary software, the system allowed the listener to provide feedback to the Webcaster, information the Webcaster used to customize future transmissions to that user. If these transmissions were to be deemed *interactive*, then a compulsory license would not be available to the Webcaster for these transmissions.

In April, 2000, DiMA, an organization representing Webcasters, petitioned the Copyright Office to issue an interpretation of the DMCA and Copyright Office rules to make it clear that a service is not interactive simply because it offers the consumer some degree of influence over the programming offered by the Webcaster. The Copyright Office denied the petition in December, 2000. The issue is likely to be raised in the courts or in another round of legislative refinement.

### b.   *Non-Interactive Services*

As mentioned above, there are two kinds of digital audio transmissions that do not result in digital phonorecord deliveries: those that are part of an interactive service and those not part of an interactive service. Of those transmissions that are not part of an interactive service, there are two basic types: *subscription transmissions* and *non-subscription transmissions.*

Here are the relevant definitions:

A "subscription transmission" is a transmission that is controlled and limited to particular recipients, and for which consideration is required to be paid or otherwise given by or on behalf of the recipient to receive the transmission or a package of transmissions including the transmission.

A "nonsubscription transmission" is any transmission that is not a subscription transmission.

Let's first turn to subscription transmissions.

### i.   Sound Recording — Subscription Transmissions

We would have liked to report that the distinction between subscription and nonsubscription transmissions ends there, but it doesn't. Keeping in the theme of providing greater rights where there is a higher risk of replacing record sales, it was thought that some subscription transmissions are less likely to replace record sales than others. Accordingly, certain subscription transmissions would be treated like any interactive service, giving the record companies full flexibility to negotiate whatever license fees they like or refuse to license these forms of subscription transmissions. Other forms of subscription transmissions, those which pose a lower threat of replacing the sales of records, would fall within an area of the law which would allow transmitting organizations, like Webcasters, to compel the record companies to grant a license and to pay a fee set not by the record companies, but by a federal arbitration panel.

Thus, the 1995 Act established two types of subscription transmissions of sound recordings: (i) voluntary subscription transmissions and (ii) compulsory subscription transmissions. Both require licenses from the sound recording owners, typically record companies. However, the former may be licensed by the record companies on a voluntary basis, meaning the record companies can set any licensee fee they wish, or refuse to license these transmissions. With respect to compulsory subscription transmissions, the record companies can be compelled to grant licenses and the license fees are subject to a statutory fee, which will effectively serve as a maximum amount that will be charged for such licenses. Let's first review the licensing questions arising from voluntary subscription transmissions — that is, those which are not subject to compulsory licensing.

Leaving aside for the moment the criteria necessary to qualify for a compulsory license to make digital audio transmissions of sound recordings on a subscription basis, the person making a non-qualifying subscription transmission of a recording must obtain a license from the record company who owns the recording. Moreover, given that the license is voluntary, the fee charged by the record company for this license is completely subject to negotiation, meaning the record company may charge what it wants and is free even to refuse to provide a license for these transmissions.

The conditions necessary for a transmitting organization to effect subscription transmissions are set forth in great detail in Section 114 of the Copyright Act. Briefly, the applicability of the restrictions upon a transmitting organization depends upon whether the transmitting organization had been offering its webcasts on or before July 31, 1998 using the same medium of transmission after that date that it was using before. If that is the case, then a compulsory license for a subscription transmission would be available at a rate set under the auspices of the U.S. Librarian of Congress if:

(i) the transmission is not part of an interactive service;

(ii) except in the case of a transmission to a business establishment, the transmitting entity does not automatically and intentionally cause any device receiving the transmission to switch from one program channel to another;

(iii) the transmission of the sound recording is accompanied by the information encoded in that sound recording, if any, by or under the authority of the copyright owner of that sound recording, that identifies the title of the sound recording, the featured recording artist who performs on the sound recording, and related information, including information concerning the underlying musical work and its writer;

(iv) the transmission does not exceed the sound recording performance complement; and

(v) the transmitting entity does not cause to be published by means of an advance program schedule or prior announcement the titles of the specific sound recordings or phonorecords embodying such sound recordings to be transmitted.

If, however, the transmitting organization had not been offering webcasts on or before July 31, 1998 or had been using a medium of transmission before that date different from that which it was using after that time, then a compulsory license for a subscription transmission would be available at a rate set under the auspices of the U.S. Librarian of Congress if the transmissions meet the same conditions as those required for anyone desiring to make "eligible nonsubscription transmissions." The conditions necessary for eligible nonsubscription transmissions to qualify for a compulsory license under the proposed DMCA are set forth below.

### ii.    Sound Recording — Non-Subscription Transmissions

Non-subscription transmissions are of two kinds: *eligible* non-subscription transmissions and *non-eligible* non-subscription transmissions. Eligible non-subscription transmissions will qualify for a *compulsory license* under Section 114. Non-eligible ones will not, which means that if you wish to make non-subscription transmissions that do not qualify as eligible non-subscription transmission, you will need to obtain a purely *voluntary license* from the applicable record company. Under a "voluntary license," the record companies in a free market can charge whatever they wish or refuse to license your transmissions at all. Under the "compulsory license," the record companies can be compelled to license the transmissions under license fees set by a governmental body, fees called the statutory rate, which effectively becomes a maximum fee that the record companies can charge for your use.

It is worth noting that prior to the passage of the DMCA, all non-subscription digital audio transmissions were exempt from the payment of any kind of license fees to the owners of the applicable sound recordings. As a result of last minute lobbying by the RIAA and DiMA, Digital Millennium Copyright Act was passed with an amendment that (1) eliminated the exemption for Webcasters set forth in former Section 114(d)(1) of the Copyright Act, (2) and added a compulsory license scheme for limited kinds of "eligible" transmissions (i.e., those made by Webcasters having the profile of certain members of DiMA), and (3) added language to Section 114 that would make it clear the "eligible" Webcasters could make ephemeral recordings of sound recordings for the purposes of facilitating their webcasts. This section will summarize the first of those two changes, and the effect on ephemeral recordings will be discussed in the following section.

*Exemption Eliminated.* The DMCA eliminated what the 1995 Act previously established as an exemption (from a sound recording owner's exclusive rights) for a "nonsubscription transmission other than a retransmission." The DMCA merely preserved the exemption for "a nonsubscription *broadcast transmission.*" A "broadcast transmission" is defined as "a transmission made by a terrestrial broadcast station licensed as such by the Federal Communications Commissions."

Should the exemption for non-interactive, non-subscription transmissions have been eliminated? From the record companies perspective, the answer to that question is clearly yes, but other interests may not have faired well. First, under the 1995 Act, and before the DMCA, music publishers and songwriters had a direct interest in promoting as many non-interactive, non-subscription web radio stations as possible, allowing them to issue many more blanket licenses for the use of music on these sites. Presumably, Congress took into consideration the interests of the performance rights societies and their members when determining the kinds of transmissions which should be considered exempt, which should be subject to a compulsory license, and which should be subject to a voluntary license. Given the particular circumstances of the DMCA's passage, it is not likely the Congress took anything into consideration, except that fact that two powerful lobbying organizations came to an agreement on the subject.

Under Section 114(d), broadcast radio stations that desired to webcast their on-the-air broadcasts of sound recordings over the Internet have argued that, under the DMCA, they remain exempt from licensing requirements. Why should Webcasters who don't own radio stations be put at a competitive disadvantage to radio stations? It would at first appear that any large webcast company could use their size and resources to purchase FCC licensed radio stations in order to webcast sound recordings over the web without payment to record companies. But it appears the RIAA put one over on not only the large Webcasters, but the owners of FCC licensed radio stations. Recall the definition of eligible subscription transmissions:

> An "eligible nonsubscription transmission" is a noninteractive, nonsubscription transmission made as part of a service that provides audio programming consisting, in whole or in part, of performances of sound recordings, *including retransmissions of broadcast transmissions*, if the primary purpose of the service is to provide to the public such audio or other entertainment programming, and the primary purpose of the service is not to sell, advertise, or promote particular products or services other than sound recordings, live concerts, or other music-related events. (emphasis added).

The italicized language makes it clear that retransmissions of broadcast transmissions is an eligible nonsubscription transmission eligible for, and perhaps subject to, a compulsory license, rather than being exempt, as was thought by the radio station owners. In other words, while a digital radio broadcast from a terrestrial radio station is exempt the exclusive rights of the sound recording owner to digital audio transmissions, if the terrestrial radio station attempted to retransmit its broadcasts, whether they were originally transmitted by digital or analog means, over the Internet, such retransmissions would be subject to the sound recording owners' exclusive rights of digital audio transmissions. Surprise.

And, what accounts for the distinction between those making "eligible" nonsubscription transmissions and those who make non-eligible ones? Looking down the list of members of DiMA, its striking that all of them would appear to be engaging in eligible nonsubscription transmissions, yet that organization appeared instrumental in eliminating the exemption for all other kinds of Webcasters.

Assuming that all non-subscription transmissions (including broadcast transmissions) were subject to a compulsory license, a level playing field would only result if the compulsory license was as easy to obtain and administer as the performance licenses that are offered by ASCAP or BMI. If, on the other hand, anything akin to the requirements of the compulsory license for subscription transmissions is instituted for non-subscription transmissions — for "Interim Regulations on Notice and Recordkeeping for Digital Subscription Transmissions, Docket No. RM 96-3B, only large, well-financed Web sites will, as a practical matter, have access to sound recordings for non-subscription transmissions

Perhaps the ideal of a level playing field is not politically possible today, given the tenacity of the lobbying organizations involved, the complexities of the issues, and the amount of money which is at stake. Certainly, the new technologies provide more than enough challenges to the music and recording industries, and giving the content creators the benefit of the doubt, at least at the current time, may be just what is needed to maintain the incentives necessary to promote the creation of creative works of authorship. In the end, however, the ideal of a level playing field may best be accomplished by the granting of a general public performance right in sound recordings coupled with a fairly easy to administer compulsory license, such as those offered by ASCAP and BMI.

*Limited Compulsory License.* To placate the members of DiMA (who agreed to help the RIAA lobby to eliminate the exemption for nonsubscription transmissions), the DMCA added to Section 114 a subsection under the heading, "Statutory Licensing of Certain Transmissions." This section provides for a compulsory license for *eligible* nonsubscription transmissions. These "eligible" transmissions are defined as follows:

> An "eligible nonsubscription transmission" is a noninteractive, nonsubscription transmission made as part of a service that provides audio programming consisting, in whole or in part, of performances of sound recordings, including retransmissions of broadcast transmissions, if the primary purpose of the service is to provide to the public such audio or other entertainment programming, and the primary purpose of the service is not to sell, advertise, or promote particular products or services other than sound recordings, live concerts, or other music-related events.

Those desiring to make "eligible nonsubscription transmissions" may thus compel the record companies to provide them with a license to do so, provided they comply with certain restrictions on how they make those transmissions and pay a fee that will be set under procedures to be established by the U.S. Librarian of Congress.

To be eligible for the compulsory license, transmitting organizations who make "eligible nonsubscription transmissions" need to comply with certain restrictions, including those imposed upon organizations who desire to engage in making subscription transmissions under a compulsory license (under the 1995 Act).

Briefly, the applicability of the restrictions upon a transmitting organization depends upon whether the transmitting organization had been offering its webcasts on or before July 31, 1998 using the same medium of transmission after that date that it was using before. If that is the case, then a compulsory license for a subscription transmission would be available at a rate set under the auspices of the U.S. Librarian of Congress under the same conditions as though they were eligible nonsubscription transmissions. These conditions are:

(i) the transmission is not part of an interactive service;

(ii) except in the case of a transmission to a business establishment, the transmitting entity does not automatically and intentionally cause any device receiving the transmission to switch from one program channel to another;

(iii) the transmission of the sound recording is accompanied by the information encoded in that sound recording, if any, by or under the authority of the copyright owner of that sound recording, that identifies the title of the sound recording, the featured recording artist who performs on the sound recording, and related information, including information concerning the underlying musical work and its writer;

If, however, organization was not offering its webcasts on or before July 31, 1998 or was doing so, but is now using a different means of transmission than before, then a compulsory license, at a rate set under the auspices of the U.S. Librarian of Congress, for an eligible nonsubscription transmission (and non-exempt subscription transmissions) would be available if, in addition to restrictions (i) through (iii) above:

(iii) the transmission does not exceed the *sound recording performance complement* (defined above), except that this requirement shall not apply in the case of a retransmission of a broadcast transmission if the retransmission is made by a transmitting entity that does not have the right or ability to control the programming of the broadcast station making the broadcast transmission, unless the broadcast station makes broadcast transmissions —

(I) in digital format that regularly exceed the sound recording performance complement; or

(II) in analog format, a substantial portion of which, on a weekly basis, exceed the sound recording performance complement;

Provided, however, That the sound recording copyright owner or its representative has notified the transmitting entity in writing that broadcast transmissions of the copyright owner's sound recordings exceed the sound recording complement as provided in this clause;

(iv) the transmitting entity does not cause to be published, or induce or facilitate the publication, by means of an advance program schedule or prior announcement, the titles of the specific sound recordings to be transmitted, the phonorecords embodying such sound recordings, or, other than for illustrative purposes, the names of the featured recording artists, except that this clause does not disqualify a transmitting entity that makes a prior announcement that a particular artist will be featured within an unspecified future time period and, in any 1-hour period, no more than 3 such announcements are made with respect to no more than 2 artists in each announcement;

(v) the transmission is not part of —

(I) an archived program of less than 5 hours duration;

(II) an archived program of greater than 5 hours duration that is made available for a period exceeding 2 weeks;

(III) a continuous program which is of less than 3 hours duration; or

(IV) a program, other than an archived or continuous program, that is transmitted at a scheduled time more than 3 additional times in a 2-week period following the first transmission of the program and for an additional 2-week period more than 1 month following the end of the first such 2-week period;

(vi) the transmitting entity does not knowingly perform the sound recording in a manner that is likely to cause confusion, to cause mistake, or to deceive, as to the affiliation, connection, or association of the copyright owner or featured recording artist with the transmitting entity or a particular product or service advertised by the transmitting entity, or as to the origin, sponsorship, or approval by the copyright owner or featured recording artist of the activities of the transmitting entity other than the performance of the sound recording itself;

(vii) the transmitting entity cooperates to prevent, to the extent feasible without imposing substantial costs or burdens, a transmission recipient or any other person or entity from automatically scanning the transmitting entity's transmissions together with transmissions by other transmitting entities to select a particular sound recording to be transmitted to the transmission recipient;

(viii) the transmitting entity takes reasonable steps to ensure, to the extent within its control, that the transmission recipient cannot make a phonorecord in a digital format of the transmission, and the transmitting entity takes no affirmative steps to cause or induce the making of a phonorecord by the transmission recipient;

(ix) phonorecords of the sound recording have been distributed to the public in the United States under the authority of the copyright owner or the copyright owner authorizes the transmitting entity to transmit the sound recording, and the transmitting entity makes the transmission from a phonorecord lawfully made under this title;

(x) the transmitting entity accommodates and does not interfere with the transmission of technical measures that are widely used by sound recording copyright owners to identify or protect copyrighted works, and that are technically feasible of being transmitted by the transmitting entity without imposing substantial costs on the transmitting entity or resulting in perceptible aural or visual degradation of the digital signal; and

(xi) in the case of an eligible nonsubscription transmission, the transmitting entity identifies the sound recording during, but not before, the time it is performed, including the title of the sound recording, the title of the phonorecord embodying such sound recording, if any, and the featured recording artist in a manner to permit it to be perceived by the transmission recipient, except that the obligation in this clause shall not take effect until 1 year after the date of the enactment of the Digital Millennium Copyright Act.

A transmitting organization who makes eligible nonsubscription transmissions that comply with the above requirements may apply for a compulsory license to make those transmissions and pay the fee that will be established under a process regulated by the U.S. Librarian of Congress.

Note, under the proposed DMCA, the compulsory license does not inure to the benefit of any Webcaster, only those whose "primary purpose" is "not to sell, advertise, or promote particular products or services other than sound recordings, live concerts, or other music-related events." Anyone else must obtain a license from the owners of the sound recordings, which may be offered at any negotiated fee or not at all, by the record companies. Not surprisingly, the compulsory license appears to be available only to companies having the business profile of the members of DiMA.

*Fees.* It is interesting to note that when the Librarian of Congress called for comments on the proper statutory rate to be established for *subscription* transmissions under the 1995 Act, the RIAA requested a royalty rate of 41.5% of the digital music service's gross revenues, with a flat minimum fee! Representatives for the subscription transmission organizations requested royalty rates ranging from ½% to 2%, and they opposed the setting of a flat minimum fee. The Copyright Royalty Arbitration Panel that presided over the matter determined that the subscription services pay a royalty of 5% of their gross revenues, with no minimum license fee. The RIAA appealed that ruling and succeeded in convincing the Librarian of Congress to set aside the Panel's ruling.

The Librarian of Congress considered the rates that broadcasters pay for licenses of public performances of musical compositions (i.e., to ASCAP, BMI, and SESAC), because these rates represent an actual marketplace value for a public performance right in sound recordings. The RIAA had asked for a rate that was greater than the rate paid to ASCAP, BMI, and SESAC, but the Librarian of Congress concluded that the value of the public performance right in the sound recording does not exceed the value of the public performance right in the underlying musical work. Unfortunately, because the actual license fees paid for the public performance of the musical works is subject to a protective order, the statutory rate for the performance sound recordings by subscription services has not been publicly disclosed.

The copyright law, under Section 106(1), provides a copyright owner with the exclusive right to make copies of his copyrighted work. However, transmitting organizations, such as radio and television broadcasters, have long found it necessary to make copies of the copyrighted works they transmit, typically by making a tape of a work that was first provided in another medium (such as a CD), to facilitate the transmission.

Unless there was an exemption from the copyright owner's exclusive right, a transmitting organization who makes such copies to facilitate its legitimate transmissions would risk being sued for copyright infringement. For that reason, the Copyright Act provides an exemption for what are called *ephemeral recordings*, and that exemption is set forth in Section 112 as follows:

> Notwithstanding the provisions of section 106, . . . it is not an infringement of copyright for a transmitting organization entitled to transmit to the public a performance or display of a work, under a license or transfer of the copyright or under the limitations on exclusive rights in sound recordings specified by section 114(a), to make no more than one copy or phonorecord of a particular transmission program embodying the performance or display, if —

> (1) the copy or phonorecord is retained and used solely by the transmitting organization that made it, and no further copies or phonorecords are reproduced from it; and

> (2) the copy or phonorecord is used solely for the transmitting organization's own transmissions within its local service area, or for purposes of archival preservation or security; and

> (3) unless preserved exclusively for archival purposes, the copy or phonorecord is destroyed within six months from the date the transmission program was first transmitted to the public.

The RIAA took the position that the foregoing exemption only applies to:

reproductions embodying performances made under license, transfer of copyright ownership or the Section 114(a) exception to the general performance right of Section 106(4). It does not apply to reproductions — bodying performances made by means of digital audio transmissions, which are subject to the performance right of Section 106(6).

That argument is refuted easily by pointing out that Section 112 begins, "Notwithstanding the provisions of section 106 . . ." — meaning, all of Section 106, not just Section 106(4), but all of 106.

The RIAA has also asserted that the fact that Congress, when it enacted the 1995 Act, did not amend Section 112 at the same time, is "evidence that Congress intended not to extend the ephemeral recording exemption to digital audio transmissions." Of course, the same omission is also evidence that Congress thought the ephemeral recording exemption certainly did apply to Webcasters and, therefore, felt no need to add anything to Section 112 to that effect. Moreover, why would Congress have created an exemption for non-subscription transmissions, but leave no practical way for anyone to use the exemption?

Finally, the RIAA took the position that:

> even if Section 112 is applicable to digital audio transmissions, the copies by this section are to be used only for transmissions within the transmitting organization's 'local service area.'

The legislative history of the Copyright Act defines the term "local service area" in only three contexts: in the case of a television broadcast station, in the case of a low power television station, and in the case of a radio broadcast station. It does not refer to Internet web sites, naturally, because they did not exist in 1976 when the Copyright Act was passed. But this does not mean that web sites are not covered; it only means that the extent of the local service area is not defined. Where they are defined, the legislative history seems to contemplate that transmissions may be sent by wire beyond the place where the primary broadcast transmission takes place. In the case of television stations, for example, the local service area comprises the area in which such station is entitled to insist upon its signal being transmitted by a cable system pursuant to the rules and regulations of the Federal Communications Commissions.

Thus, the term "local service area" does not confine the transmission to a service area which is "local," but, in the case of television and radio stations licensed by the FCC, such transmissions are confined to those areas permitted by the FCC. Since Web stations are not so regulated, the local service area appears to be throughout the Internet, but perhaps not beyond, such as through analog radio broadcasts. The local services area of a short wave broadcast is worldwide, no different from a webcast, but I would be surprised to learn if broadcasters have been operating under the assumption that the ephemeral recording exemption applies only to small regional or "local" broadcasters.

Granted, Section 112 only permits the making of "no more than one copy or phonorecord of a particular transmission program." This, according to the RIAA, makes is problematic for Webcasters who wish to install copies on multiple servers. While this may be problematic for large, commercial Webcasters, one copy would certainly be sufficient for the many thousands of small Web sites who wish to take advantage of the exemption provided in Section 114(d)(1) and offer non-interactive, non-subscription transmissions.

As a result of negotiations between the RIAA and the National Association of Broadcasters (NAB), a *Senate* version of the Digital Millennium Copyright Act (Senate Bill 2037) would have amended Section 112 to provide a specific exemption for broadcast radio or television stations licensed by the FCC who provide "a performance of a sound recording in a digital format on a nonsubscription basis." According to information obtained by the Digital Media Association (DIMA), the NAB initially proposed that the ephemeral recording exemption be revised to make it clear it applied to all lawful digital transmissions, but the RIAA had explicitly demanded that the exemption not apply to cable, satellite, or Internet broadcasters. If the bill had passed as so amended, the RIAA could have taken the position that by only exempting broadcast radio and television stations, the legislation could have been construed as not exempting Webcasters. Webcasters might then need to rely on the less specific exemption offered by the "fair use" provisions set forth in Section 107 of the Copyright Act.

As a result of negotiations between the RIAA and DiMA, discussed above, the final version of the DMCA amended Section 112 to include provisions for the compulsory license of ephemeral record-ings that are made by transmitting organizations entitled to transmit public performances of sound recordings under Section 114 (discussed above). A statutory rate or license fee for such copies would be set under a procedure established by the Librarian of Congress.

### iii.   Musical Works

The distinction between transmissions that qualify for compulsory licensing, and those that do not, is not relevant to the question of what license is required from the owner of the *song* embodied in a particular sound recording. (The distinction is only relevant to the question of what licenses are required from record companies for the transmission of these *recordings*). Thus, to transmit the *song* (as opposed to the *sound recording*) you always require a public performance license from the applicable performance rights society (e.g., ASCAP, BMI, or SESAC).

### 3.   *Example — Digital Transmission and/or Delivery of an Audiovisual Work Containing a Musical Recording*

*Example:* Suppose you wish to digitally transmit a motion picture con-taining a copyrighted musical work and recording, whether streamed or delivered. What licenses do you need and from whom do you obtain them?

This transmission may involve three copyrights: the copyrights in the motion picture, the sound recording, and the musical work.

### a.   *Motion Picture Copyright*

Clearly, the Web site operator will require both an *exhibition li-cense* and a *reproduction license* for this use of the audiovisual work from its owner. The exhibition license would cover the performance by transmission; the reproduction license would cover the copy of the movie clip made on the recipient's hard disk in the process. These uses are likely to be licensed together under the same terms and con-ditions.

### b.  Sound Recording Copyright

Whether the motion picture producer has an adequate license to use the sound recording of the song in this way depends upon the circumstances. If the sound recording was originally created as a work made for hire of the producer, then no question should arise; if the recording used in the picture was licensed from a record company, the terms and conditions of the master use license should be reviewed to determine whether this new use is covered by the license.

It is important to note that since the transmission here involves the rendering of an audiovisual work, the Digital Performance Right in Sound Recordings Act of 1995 does not come into play. This is because the transmission is not a *digital audio transmission* as that term is defined in the Act — the transmission is a performance of an *audiovisual* work, not an *audio* work. Thus, even if the audiovisual work was not being rendered for viewing on the viewers screen (i.e., the user could only hear the sound track of the motion picture), a "voluntarily negotiated" license would be required from the owner of the motion picture (or the owner of the sound recording, as the case may be).

### c.  Musical Work Copyright

With respect to the copyright in the musical work, the analysis begins much the same as in the discussion under Example 1. The transmitter will require permission (i) under the music publisher's exclusive right of reproduction under Section 106(1), and (ii) under the publisher's exclusive right of public performance under Section 106(4).

As in our discussion under Example 1, the performance license would be issued in blanket form by ASCAP or BMI. The reproduction license, however, would be treated a little differently. First, no reproduction license may be required, depending upon the terms of the original synchronization license issued to the motion picture producer by the music publisher for the use of the song in the picture. The old synchronization license should be reviewed to determine whether this new use is covered by the license. Assuming the synchronization license was not adequate, then a reproduction license would be required from the music publisher. Rather than obtaining a *mechanical* reproduction license — which applies to audio-only recordings — the Web site operator will need to obtain a *videogram* reproduction license, issued directly by the music publisher or its licensing agent. No standard license agreements have yet emerged for this particular kind of use, but the terms of this license will likely be quite similar to the videogram licenses set forth at the end of Chapter 15, on *Videogram Licenses.*

### 4. Example — Digital Transmission and/or Delivery of Musical Notes and Lyrics

*Example:* Suppose you wish to digitally transmit the musical notes and lyrics of a copyrighted musical work — e.g., a computer file in the PDF format containing a facsimile of the sheet music for the song. What licenses do you need and from whom do you obtain them?

There are potentially two rights being exercised in this transmission: (1) a *copy* is being reproduced (i.e., your computer memory has become a copy of the musical notation and lyrics), and (2) a *public display* of the work is being transmitted. So, unlike the transmission we received under Examples 1 or 2, we now experience, not a *performance* of the musical work, but the *display* of the musical work.

Accordingly, the Web site operator will require two licenses to effect this use: what might be called, (a) an *electronic print reproduction license* and (b) an *electronic print display license.*

#### a. Electronic Print Reproduction License

Under the copyright owner's exclusive right of reproduction under Section 106(1) of the Copyright Act, the transmitter will require a license to reproduce copies of the musical notation and lyrics. Although no standards have yet emerged for the licensing of electronic sheet music over the Internet, it is likely that such licenses will be akin to a print license for the distribution of sheet music. The terms of licensing for traditional sheet music is set forth in Chapter 11, on *Print Licenses.*

Such licenses will generally be required from the music publisher, but it is important to note that many music publishers have granted print rights to print publishers who specialize in publishing printed editions of music. Often, these print rights are granted on an *exclusive* basis. Accordingly, who is entitled to issue licenses for the distribution of "electronic editions" of musical notation and lyrics may depend upon the wording of the particular print publishing agreement between the music publisher and the print publisher.

### b.  Electronic Print Display License

As we have seen from the definition of *display* under the Copyright Act, to *display* a work means to show a copy of it, "either directly or by means of a film, slide, television image, or any other device or process." Clearly, the display of the musical notation and lyrics on your computer screen constitutes a *display*. Is, however, the display of the music (which was transmitted to you from the Web server) on your computer screen in the privacy of your home considered a *public* display?

Under the copyright law, to display a work *publicly* means,

> to transmit or otherwise communicate a . . . display of the work. . . to the public, by means of any device or process, whether the members of the public capable of receiving the . . . display receive it in the same place or in separate places and at the same time or at different times.

Thus, the display on your home computer of musical notation or lyrics transmitted to you from a web server is clearly a public display of the musical work. The screen display is disseminated to the public, and it makes no difference whether members of the public receive the work in separate places (in their respective homes) and at different times (upon their respective requests).

Thus, under the copyright owner's exclusive right of public display under Section 106(5) of the copyright law, the Web site operator will require a license to publicly display copies of the musical notation and lyrics. Because this is an entirely new use of music created upon the advent of the Internet, it is not likely that any music publisher has created a special form for the licensing of displays of musical notation or lyrics on the Internet. Because the right involved is the public display right, not the public performance right, none of the performance rights societies would be entitled to issue licenses on behalf of writers and publishers. Conceivably, the Harry Fox Agency will develop a form for this new form of use.

## D. Drawing the Line Between Legal Use and Illegal Use

When an individual takes a downloaded track and e-mails it to a friend, the copyrights in both the sound recording and the underlying musical work are being infringed, and, as a matter of policy, such activity should violate the copyright law.

The reproduction of a copyrighted work by means of an individual's e-mail is no different from any other form of reproduction, whether in the form of making tapes or posting files on a Web site, and the violation of the copyright owner's exclusive right of reproduction would constitute copyright infringement, unless some exemption applies.

By using the term "friend," the question raises the issue of how far should the currently recognized exemption for private noncommercial home copying apply. In the legislative history of the Sound Recording Act of 1971, Congress recognized what is loosely called, the "home recording exemption" which permits a consumer to make "home" recordings for their non-commercial use. The House Report stated,

> It is not the intention of the Committee to restrain the home recording, from broadcasts or from tapes or records, of recorded performances, where the home recording is for private use and with no purpose of reproducing or otherwise capitalizing commercially on it.

An example of a home recording would be your making a cassette tape recording of a CD for use in your car tape player. The question arises: would this exemption permit your wife to use the tape in her car? The answer, in our view, is yes, as "home recording" would include recording for use by members of your family. Since one is not likely to purchase a separate copy of a record for a spouse, child, sibling or other family member, record sales are not likely to be displaced significantly by such recording.

Making a copy for a friend or neighbor, however, is a different matter. In these instances, making recordings for friends and neighbors would likely displacing sales that the copyright owner might otherwise have made. Since virtually everyone has friends to whom they can email a copyrighted work, extending the exemption to beyond the family could easily defeat the purpose of the copyright law.

Moreover, by extending the permissible home-copying to "friends" would put the Federal Courts in the unenviable position of determining, "What is a friend?" Does it include acquaintances or just close acquaintances? Because this is not practical by any means, a line should be drawn at the outskirts of family members. Incidentally, for political reasons, I think we would all be wise to include, for this purpose, mothers-in-law.

## VI. CONSIDERATIONS IN GRANTING AND CLEARING LICENSES FOR THE USE OF MUSICAL WORKS ON THE INTERNET

The form of license that required for the transmission of musical works on the Internet will depend upon the specific use. It will also depend on how the law evolves on certain emerging questions, especially (i) whether digital downloads will require performance licenses and (ii) whether on-demand streams will require mechanical licenses. Leaving aside these unresolved questions, this section will review the considerations in licensing musical works for digital transmission.

### A. Mechanical Licenses

The considerations in granting and clearing mechanical licenses under the compulsory license provision are discussed at length in Chapter 12, on *Mechanical Licenses*. This section will highlight some of the issues specific to negotiating mechanical licenses for digital phonorecord deliveries in general and those that are merely incidental to digital transmissions.

### 1. General Digital Phonorecord Deliveries

As discussed above, the 1995 Act made the reproduction of musical works in phonorecords made by transmission, which the 1995 Act calls *digital phonorecord deliveries*, subject to Section 115 of the Copyright Act, the compulsory license provision. That provision has the effect of limiting the flexibility the copyright owner has in setting the terms of the mechanical license. As a result, nearly all mechanical licenses are issued at a fee which is at or below the *statutory rate.* As of January 1, 2002, the statutory rate was 8.0 cents for recordings up to five minutes in length and, if over five minutes, 1.55 cents per minute of playing time.

In the United States, mechanical licenses are obtained either from the music publisher or the Harry Fox Agency, which represents over 27,000 music publishers. Some music publishers are beginning to experiment with the issuance of mechanical licenses directly over the Internet. Overseas, mechanical licenses are collected by mechanical license collection agencies and the fees are established by negotiations between organizations representing music publishers on the one side and record companies on the other.

The form currently being used by the Harry Fox Agency (HFA) for the granting of mechanical licenses for digital phonorecords is included in the Appendix to this chapter as Form 23-1. The form is relatively short and is patterned after the HFA form mechanical license for CDs, audiocassettes and other physical configurations. The form begins as follows:

> This compulsory license applies solely to the songs set forth in the attached Confirmation Report which lists the songs and other designating information (which may be delivered in a computer readable format in accordance with the attached Exhibit A).

Because licensees who intend to make digital phonorecord deliveries are usually services that will require mechanical licenses to thousands of songs at a time, the form contemplates that a schedule of song titles submitted in the form of an Excel spreadsheet or other computer readable database format, called a *confirmation report*, will be attached to the agreement. This enables the HFA, in response to the demand for such large volume of licenses, to issue the licenses digitally without the creation of hard copy paper licenses for each individual song.

> You have advised us, in our capacity as Agent for the Publisher(s) referred to in the attached Confirmation Report, that you wish to obtain a compulsory license to make and to distribute digital phon-

orecord deliveries (as defined in Section 115 of the Copyright Act, hereinafter referred to as "DPDs"), of the copyrighted works referred therein, under the compulsory license provision of Section 115 of the Copyright Act. The provisions hereof vary the terms of the compulsory license provision of the Copyright Act applicable to DPDs. Your making and distributing of DPDs of any of such copyrighted works shall constitute assent to these terms.

Though the form speaks in terms of "compulsory license," what is actually going on here is that the music publisher and the licensee are entering into a voluntary license that incorporates the statutory compulsory license provision, but varies its terms to the extent specified in the license.

Upon your doing so, you shall have all the rights which are granted to, and all the obligations which are imposed upon, users of said copyrighted works under the compulsory license provision of the Copyright Act, after phonorecords of the copyrighted works have been distributed to the public in the United States under the authority of the copyright owner by another person, . . .

It is interesting to note that, under Section 115, a compulsory license is available to a potential licensee only after "*phonorecords* of the copyrighted musical work has been distributed to the public." This allows the copyright owner of a musical work to deny a license to use the work in a digital phonorecord delivery if *physical* phonorecords have not yet been distributed to the public. If the copyright owner permitted digital phonorecord deliveries containing the musical work, the copyright owner could still deny providing a license to others for making digital phonorecord deliveries, at least until physical phonorecords have been distributed to the public. The paragraph continues:

. . . except that with respect to DPDs thereof made and distributed hereunder:

1. You shall pay royalties and account to us as Agent for and on behalf of said Publisher(s) quarterly, within forty-five days after the end of each calendar quarter, on the basis of DPDs made and distributed;

This varies the law and regulations underlying Section 115, which would otherwise require monthly accounting to the music publishers.

2. For such DPDs made and distributed, the royalty shall be the statutory rate in effect at the time each DPD is distributed, except as otherwise stated in the Confirmation Report;

The music publishers are being careful here to make sure that if the statutory rate is increased, the new higher rate will apply to digital phonorecord deliveries made after the increase. Of course, the confirmation report may specify that the licensee need only pay 1/2 or 3/4 of the statutory rate.

At this point, the statutory rate for the downloading of musical works as part of all digital phonorecord deliveries is the same statutory rate in effect for phonorecords (e.g., CDs). However, there is a movement among music publishers to demand a higher statutory rate for digital phonorecord deliveries than for physical phonorecords containing their works. This will become a contentious issue in future rate proceedings conducted by Copyright Arbitration Royalty Panels.

The requirement of paying a set amount of cents per download is problematic for those trying to operate a music service on a subscription basis. If a subscription service were to charge $10 per month allowing an unlimited amount of downloads, then when a particular user downloads more than about 130 tracks, the mechanical royalties due exceeds the entire amount of revenues collected from that user, leaving nothing for the owner of the sound recording, not to mention the operating expenses and profit of the operator of the subscription service.

To date, subscription services have required that users sign up for minimum periods of time, such as twelve months, and the hope has been that, though a user might download more than 130 tracks during each of the first few months of the subscription, the download rate for the remainder of the period will be significantly lower, permitting a fair allocation of the overall revenues to the other content and operating contributions to the service. The subject of mechanical royalties for subscription download services is discussed further below.

3. This compulsory license covers and is limited to one particular recording of each copyrighted work as performed by the artist and

on the DPD configuration number identified in the Confirmation Report; and this compulsory license does not supersede nor in any way affect any prior agreements now in effect respecting phonorecords of any copyrighted work listed in the Confirmation Report;

4. In the event you fail to account to us and pay royalties as herein provided for, said Publisher(s) or his Agent may give written notice to you that, unless the default is remedied within 30 days from the date of the notice, this compulsory license will be automatically terminated. Such termination shall render either the making or the distribution, or both, of all phonorecords (whether DPD or not) for which royalties have not been paid, actionable as acts of infringement under, and fully subject to the remedies provided by the Copyright Act;

This makes it clear that if you breach the license agreement, the license will terminate and all reproduction or distribution of digital phonorecord deliveries made after the breach and cure period would constitute copyright infringement, entitling the copyright owner to damages under the Copyright Act, rather than merely damages under contract law.

5. You need not serve or file the notice of intention to obtain a compulsory license required by the Copyright Act;

Again, this relieves the licensee from filing the required notice under the strict terms of the compulsory license provision. The license continues:

6. Additional Provisions

The authority hereunder is limited to (i) the making and distribution of DPDs, and (ii) the making of a copy of a sound recording of a musical work on a computer file server located in the United States, its territories or possessions, solely for the purpose of distributing such DPDs.

This provision addresses the rather difficult and unresolved questions relating to the international distribution of digital phonorecord deliveries which is discussed further below.

The authority hereunder does not extend to DPDs where the reproduction and distribution of a phonorecord (or the musical work) is
incidental to the transmission which constitutes the DPD.

The above provision is intended to make it clear that transmissions
such as on-demand streaming would require a different kind of license
from the music publishers. Potential terms for incidental digital phonorecord deliveries is discussed in the next section.

Credit: In regard to all DPDs distributed hereunder, you shall include
in any graphics and imagery displayed in connection with playback
of such DPDs writer/publisher credit in the form of the names of
the writer(s) and the publisher(s) of the copyrighted work.

It will be interesting to see how mechanical licensees will comply
with the above credit provision.

The ISRC number and DPD configuration number for the relevant
recording of the musical work licensed hereunder (or other applicable identification number to distinguish DPD use from physical
phonorecords) shall be included in the file header of the DPD, and
must be provided to us. To the extent an ISRC Number is not submitted, the MMI number (supplied by HFA) must be included in the
appropriate file header of the download.

The *file header* in a data files, such an MP3 file, is where the
name of the recording, artist, copyright notice and other information
is included in a way that it may be displayed by the software player
used to play the recording.

### 2. *Incidental Digital Phonorecord Deliveries*

As previously discussed, music publishers are taking the position
that the on-demand streaming of their musical works constitutes a
digital phonorecord delivery, albeit one where the reproduction is
merely incidental to a transmission which was intended to effect a
single public performance, and not to result in a permanently fixed
copy or phonorecord which could be privately performed repeatedly.
Though this question has yet to be resolved by the courts, the HFA
has begun to offer potential licensees terms for these *incidental* digital
phonorecord deliveries.

At the time this Edition went to print, the HFA was offering licenses to make incidental digital phonorecord deliveries, or on-demand streams of recordings of their musical works, but only where the streaming service met the following technical requirements: where the stream is permitted only if the user has confirmed by that a copy of the streamed recording has been purchased by the user, whether by some acceptable technological means of detecting the copy in user's computer (e.g., the MyMP3.com streaming service), by some acceptable confirmation of a purchase of a physical copy of the sound recording at the point of purchase, or by the purchase of a digital phonorecord delivery of the recording. A form that a music publisher might use to license such on-demand streaming service is set forth in the Appendix to this chapter as Form 23-2.

The music publishers have offered the following mechanical fees for operators of this kind of streaming service:

- 10 cents for each musical work encoded and stored on hard disks for the purpose of facilitating the on-demand streaming; *and*

- a royalty equal to (i) the statutory compulsory royalty rate for Incidental Digital Phonorecord Deliveries applicable to this or similar uses of copyrighted works determined as of the date of transmission for each such streamed transmission of a musical work or (ii) in the absence of such a statutory compulsory royalty rate, one quarter of a cent ($.0025) for each stream.

These rates would be effective until an applicable statutory royalty rate is set by the Copyright Arbitration Royalty Panel for such a service.

Music publishers were already contemplating the mechanical license of on-demand streaming services who offer streams on a subscription basis to whoever paid the subscription fee, regardless of whether the user proves ownership of a phonorecord or digital phonorecord delivery. The royalty structure for such proposed licenses have not yet been announced.

Whether on-demand streaming constitutes an incidental digital phonorecord delivery has been the primary contention between the parties in the case filed by the music publishing members of the Harry

Fox Agency and Universal Music Group. In the authors' view, the case could be resolved by an acknowledgement on Universal's part that on-demand streams do constitute incidental digital phonorecord deliveries and a concession on the part of the music publishers that the statutory mechanical fees charged for on-demand streaming be based on a percentage of revenue basis, with no minimum per stream fee.

### 3. The Subscription Service Problem

A fee structure based on a set amount of cents per stream is problematic for those trying to operate digital download or streaming music services on a subscription basis. (e.g., download or stream all you want for one low monthly fee). At the time this edition went to print, the music publishers, acting through the Harry Fox Agency, were offering the following rate structure for digital downloads offered on a subscription basis:

> 10 cents for each musical work encoded and stored on hard disks for the purpose of facilitating the on-demand streaming; *and* the greater of:

> • 75% of the statutory rate for digital phonorecord deliveries (and in the absence of such a statutory compulsory rate, seventy-five percent (75%) of the physical rate, currently $0.0075 or $0.00145 per minute of playing time or fraction thereof, whichever amount is larger), *or*

> • 12½ percent of the gross revenue from the subscription service.

Music publishers have resisted abandoning the cent rate fee structure of the statutory rate, because they are wary of the problems presented by establishing a percentage based fee that will provide them with at least the same amount of revenues they currently receive from their mechanical licensing business.

For example, if an operator did not charge a subscription fee at all, a percentage of no revenues would mean no royalties. Suppose AOL established a music subscription service. Would it be fair for the mechanical royalty to be set at a percentage of AOL's monthly subscription fee for its entire service (i.e., $21.95) even when only a tiny percentage of AOL's users may take advantage of the AOL music subscription service?

ASCAP already faced this problem when it established a regime for collecting performance royalties: separate schedules which the licensee can choose from, depending upon the nature of the licensee's business and importance of music in the licensee's service. ASCAP also worked out a minimum amount payable in the case no fees are charged subscribers.

It is submitted that, using the experience of ASCAP, the resolution of the incidental digital phonorecord delivery question can be worked out much the same way, with different percentages based upon the nature of the subscription service and the relative importance of music to that service. In addition, the music publishers might charge a minimum fee per subscriber, whether or not the subscriber pays for the service. Though it remains unclear how these problems will ultimately be resolved, it is hoped that the analysis presented in this chapter and the suggestions made by the authors will aid the music publishing industry in forming the appropriate framework for licensing subscription services.

### 4.  Cross-border Digital Phonorecord Deliveries

The language in the Harry Fox form regarding whether the digital downloads can be transmitted to users outside of the United States is delightfully ambiguous:

> The authority hereunder is limited to (i) the making and distribution of DPDs, and (ii) the making of a copy of a sound recording of a musical work on a computer file server located in the United States, its territories or possessions, solely for the purpose of distributing such DPDs.

It's clear from the above language that the copies from which the digital downloads are made may be placed on servers located only in the United States, but the "making and distribution of" the digital phonorecord deliveries themselves does not appear to be so limited.

What is the position of, for example, GEMA, the mechanical rights society in Germany, as to digital downloads delivered within Germany having their origins from servers located in the United

States? At this point, mechanical rights societies like GEMA are taking the position that while the deliveries of downloads from outside their territories to users located within their territories is legal (i.e., does not run afoul of local copyright or contract law), the mechanical rate to be applied should be the country of the destination of the download, not the origin.

From the point of view of the music service provider who is transmitting the download, such a position is problematic. First, it is not always clear, nor can there be any certainty on the matter, where the country of destination is at the time the transmission is made. It's not as though the transmitter gets the user's name and address so that it can send the user a CD or book ordered from the service. The user simply enters his or her credit card information and then has instant access to the digital downloads; no physical address is needed.

If the music service provider asked for the user's address, the user could lie, and would have an incentive to do so if the price of the download varied depending upon where the user is located (e.g., a price for users located in territories which required a higher mechanical license). The music service provider may attempt to determine the user's country by the credit card he or she is using (e.g., a user of a Barclay's Bank credit card is probably a resident of England), but a user can get an American credit card over the Internet. Finally, a music service provider might attempt to determine where the person is located by determining which Internet service provider the user is using to access the Internet (e.g., a Deutsche Telekom user is probably located in Germany), but an AOL user looks like he's dialing in from Virginia from wherever in the world he is dialing access to the Internet.

Accounting for royalties on the basis of the user's destination could be a logistical nightmare for music service providers. Since mechanical royalty rates have historically been significantly higher outside of the U.S. than in the U.S. (where they are limited to the statutory rate), U.S. music publishers are delighted with the prospect of requiring music service providers to pay at the overseas rate wherever possible.

One would think that, if the world's mechanical rates where leveled at the same rate throughout the world, it would no longer serve the interests of, for example, a U.S. publisher to always require a music service provider operating in the U.S. to use the U.S. mechanical rate and to pay the publisher in the U.S. for all downloads occurring from servers located in the U.S., regardless of the destination of the download.

It may come as some surprise that, for some music publishers, this is not the case! Certain U.S. music publishers who have operations in overseas would rather the mechanical royalty be paid to their overseas subsidiary. In that way, the revenue is the same to the publisher, but when the publisher is ready to pay the songwriter his or her portion of the mechanical royalty, the publisher may be able to reduce the songwriter's royalty by 50% or more, if the songwriter's contract does not specify that the music publisher must pay "at the source." The publisher will deduct the amount retained by its foreign subsidiary before remitting funds to the U.S., which is the amount that forms the basis of the songwriter's royalty, not the amount collected by the overseas subsidiary.

Other publishers, particularly those who do not have foreign subsidiaries, but operate overseas using subpublishers, would rather be paid in the U.S. for all downloads having an overseas destination. Thus, it should be clear that the policy debate on this question has been, and will probably remain, colored by the influence of the larger international music publishing organizations, because they generally have more resources to devote to the negotiation and determination of such international policy questions.

### 5.  30-Second Digital Phonorecord Deliveries

At least one compromise has been reached on the subject of certain promotional digital deliveries. The music publishers have agreed, by informal communication to the recording industry, that digital phonorecord deliveries (whether downloads or on-demand streams) of less than 30-seconds in duration do not require payment of a mechanical royalties, provided that (i) the deliveries are solely for purposes of promoting the sale of the corresponding phonorecords or digital phonorecord deliveries and (ii) the 30-second deliveries are being made with the permission of the owners of the sound recordings. Certain organizations are disputing that there is need to obtain permission from record companies for making 30-second deliveries of sound recordings, but such objections have no serious legal basis.

### 6. Limited Downloads

As previously mentioned, certain business models may emerge under which music service providers will, with the help of copy-protection technology, sell digital phonorecord deliveries that bear a limitation on the number of times it may be played by the recipient. These service providers might charge the recipient a fee that varies based upon the value provided. For example, a higher price may be charged for a digital file that allows unlimited playing than one which may only allow three listens. Or, a file allowing only three listens may be upgraded to twenty listens, or to having an unlimited playing capability, after the recipient pays an additional fee.

Service providers and the recording companies have suggested that the mechanical fee should vary based upon scope of value provided by such limited files. Music publishers have balked at such a notion, saying if the files are limited, then the licensee may ask the publisher for a reduced statutory rate. Whether such reduced rate is granted will depend upon the case made by the licensee for the concession. Since there is a large number of ways that the functionality of a digital files may be limited, it is felt the market should determine what the mechanical fee should be in each case.

To date, no standards have emerged as to how mechanical license fees may be set for limited digital downloads.

### 7. Custom Compilations

Shortly before the establishment of digital download providers such as EMusic, several companies begin offering what had become known as custom compilations. A *custom compilation* is reproduction of one or more of the recordings onto a CD by a music service provider at the behest of a visitor of a website who chose from among a selection of possible titles to be recorded on the CD. Thus, rather than transmit a file containing a recording chosen by the user, the music service provider would *burn* (i.e., record) a CD containing the tracks selected by the user, in the order chosen by the user, and then send the CD to the user by mail.

Though some custom compilation operations continue to operate today (e.g., CDNow, MP3.com), the difficult establishing a business under this model stemmed from a provision in many artist recording agreements that preclude the record label from "coupling" any of the artist's recordings on CDs containing recordings of other artists. The requirement of having to seek the permission of each artist to engage in the custom compilation of recordings by that artist made the accumulation of a meaning catalog very difficult. And without a meaningful catalog, users would have few recordings to choose from in compiling their custom CDs.

Because custom compilations did not involve digital transmission, mechanical licenses for musical works that became part of custom compilations would be obtained the same way as any normal mechanical license for the reproduction of musical works on CDs.

### 8.   The Proxy Server Question

Recording industry, internet service providers, and music publishers have been have been pondering what to do about the copies of musical works temporarily stored on "proxy servers" — computers on which "intermediate" copies are stored in the course of transmission to consumers. Although the issue is not entirely settled in certain parts of the world, it appears that these intermediate copies will be ignored, as long as a mechanical royalty payment is made to the music publisher for the digital phonorecord delivery.

## B.  Performance Licenses

Transmissions of performances of musical works over the Internet require a *performance license*. As discussed in Chapter 17, performance licenses are issued almost exclusively by music performance rights societies. In the U.S., these are ASCAP, BMI, and SESAC. Performance licenses are typically issued on a blanket basis, meaning the user pays a periodic fee established as a percentage of the user's revenues attributable to music from the repertory of the performance rights society.

The *ASCAP Experimental License Agreement for Internet Sites On The World Wide Web* is set forth in the appendix to this chapter, and the most recent version should be available at *www.ascap.com*. Briefly, the agreement grants operators of online services, web sites, and the like a license to publicly perform by means of transmissions all of the songs in ASCAP's repertory (i.e., songs written or published by its members or by members of affiliated societies overseas). In exchange for this license, the online service provider or web site operator must pay ASCAP a fee in accordance with one of three alternative rate schedules.

The first schedule of the ASCAP license, Rate Schedule A, is the default basis for calculating the ASCAP license fee. It is available to all Web site operators, but was designed primarily for Web sites that are music intensive. The rate is lower than those in the other schedules, but is based on the a percentage of gross revenues from the entire site. The license fee calculated using Rate Schedule B is focused on the value attributable to the music performances on the Web site. Rate Schedule C is further narrowly focused on the value attributable to the ASCAP music performances on the Web site. A licensee should review these schedules carefully to determine the rate structure that best fits the particular use. Regardless of the licensee's revenues, a minimum annual license fee will be required.

It is important to note what the ASCAP license does not do: it does not grant a license to reproduce, copy or distribute any of the musical compositions licensed by the agreement. Thus, while the service provider may make *performances* or *transmissions* of such musical works, permission to *reproduce* the musical works in copies or phonorecords must still be obtained from music publishers or the Harry Fox Agency.

BMI and SESAC offers similar licenses for public performances of songs in their repertory by online service providers, Web sites, and other providers of interactive electronic transmissions. The may be accessed at *www.bmi.com* and *www.sesac.com*, respectively.

### 1. Digital Phonorecord Deliveries

As we have discussed, at the time this Edition went to print, the question whether a performance license will be required for digital phonorecord deliveries in general was still very much up in the air.

While it is generally agreed that digital phonorecord deliveries that are *incidental* to the transmission involve the public performance of the musical work, it's still not clear that a performance license would be required if a mechanical license is obtained for this form of transmission. The statutory compulsory rate under Section 115 of the Copyright Act is intended to serve as a maximum amount that a licensee is required to pay for an incidental digital phonorecord delivery, and once that fee is paid, an argument can be made that an additional performance fee would not be required for the use.

It is generally agreed, however, that webcast transmissions that are akin to radio broadcasts, such as *eligible subscription transmissions*, that involve neither incidental digital phonorecord deliveries nor digital phonorecord deliveries in general would require a performance license.

## 2. 30-Second Clips

It would also seem clear that performances of just 30-second clips of musical works over the Internet would require a performance license. Some have argued that these partial performances of songs would not require a performance license, either by virtue of the exemption in Section 110 of the Copyright or merely by virtue of their promotional purpose. Section 110 exempts the

> performance of a nondramatic musical work by a vending establishment open to the public at large without any direct or indirect admission charge, where the sole purpose of the performance is to promote the retail sale of copies or phonorecords of the work, or of the audiovisual or other devices utilized in such performance, and *the performance is not transmitted beyond the place where the establishment is located and is within the immediate area where the sale is occurring.*

No transmission over the Internet would comply with this provision. If it were construed otherwise, nothing would prevent Internet retails such as Amazon.com from permitting the transmission over the Internet of all the recordings, in their entirety, that its sells in CD form.

Moreover, there is no general "promotional" exemption under the Copyright Act. In fact, a database of 30-second clips could be considered a useful service in its own right, as a source of material for users seeking to "name that tune" for one reason or another. Thus, to make 30-second transmissions of musical sound recordings, a performance license would be required from the owners of the copyrighted musical works underlying those recordings.

## C. Synchronization Licenses

It is not inconceivable that Web site operators will begin producing made-for-Internet video programs. Short videos, such as music videos and movie trailers, and animations, in fact, have recently become quite popular on the Internet, and many of them call for the synchronization of copyrighted songs. When recording songs as part of such productions, the Web site operator would need to obtain a *synchronization license.*

Although no standards have yet emerged for this kind of licensing, it is likely that the synchronization license used for these uses would take a form similar to those set forth at the end of Chapter 14, on *Synchronization Licenses.* However, rather than a theatrical synchronization license or a television synchronization license, the license used to cover this new form of exhibition may be called, a *digital transmission synchronization license.* These licenses would be conditioned upon the exhibition of the video by a Web site or online service that has a valid license from ASCAP or BMI.

## D. Videogram Licenses

If the transmission of a musical work causes a reproduction of the work to be made as part of an audiovisual work for distribution to the public (i.e., videotape, DVD — a *copy*, as opposed to a phonorecord, which by definition contains an audio-only recording), then the license required for the reproduction will be a *videogram license.* Videogram licenses are not subject to the compulsory license provision, and accordingly, music publishers have a great deal of flexibility in setting the terms and conditions of these licenses.

As noted above, because of the ease with which interactive digital transmissions of audiovisual works may be copied at home, music copyright owners will attempt to price these transmissions on the assumption that home copying for the purpose of repeated private performances will take place. The copyright owner will invariably assume that a copy will be made from the transmission, which would obviate the consumer's need to order future public performances of the same music, because the consumer will now have the royalty free right to privately perform the copy he recorded as often as he or she desires.

Thus, the videogram licensing of music in audiovisual works transmitted electronically are likely to be priced in a way similar to what music publishers might earn from licensing their music in audiovisual works intended for physical retail distribution (i.e., on videocassette and laserdisc copies).

Music publishers and their videogram licensees should review any existing videogram licenses to determine the extent to which the terms of those licenses would extend to allowing the reproduction by means of transmission over the Internet. It would not be surprising if the *Old Licenses, New Uses* problem discussed in Chapter 16, should begin arising in the context of the Internet.

### E. Electronic Print Licenses

The transmission from a Web server to individual computers on the Internet of musical notation or lyrics may be a public display of the musical work, and a public display license will be required. None of the performing rights societies have the right to license *public displays* of their members music (i.e., they only have the right to license public performances). Thus, these public display licenses must be acquired directly from the music publishers of the music notation or lyrics being transmitted for public display.

To the extent a copy of the notation or lyrics are being "fixed" at the receiving end of the display — which would appear always to be the case, as copying into RAM has been held to be a fixation — then a *reproduction license* will also be required. Again, this license would be obtained from the appropriate music publishers.

Because the public display and reproduction of lyrics and musical notation by means of digital transmission is a relatively new phenomenon, it is not likely that very many music publishers have had much experience in establishing the terms and conditions of these licenses. No standards have emerged as of the time of this writing, but the Harry Fox Agency is likely to develop a form for this new form of use.

### VII. CONSIDERATIONS IN GRANTING AND CLEARING LICENSES FOR THE USE OF SOUND RECORDINGS ON THE INTERNET

In Chapter 1, we illustrated the importance of understanding the rights involved in seeking to clear permission to use a particular piece of music by pointing out a mistake made by many who are new to the music clearance process: in seeking a license to use a particular recording, one may overlook the fact that getting permission to do so involves not one, but two copyrights: (1) the copyright in the song and (2) the copyright in the *sound recording* of the song. The copyright in a sound recording is completely separate from the copyright in the underlying song featured in the sound recording, and to make digital transmissions on the Internet, you must consider the need to obtain licenses for both.

Obtaining permission to use the underlying *song* from the music publisher has been the subject of the greater portion of this book. We now, however, briefly turn to the *sound recording*, and particular, the legal and business considerations in granting and clearing licenses to transmit sound recordings on the Internet.

As noted in the previous section, whether a transmission is deemed a digital audio transmission, whether a digital audio transmission is exempt from the 1995 Act, whether non-exempt transmissions satisfy the conditions for a statutory license, will have a direct effect on whether permission to transmit a recording is necessary and, if necessary, how a license is obtained for a particular use and at what price. We will now discuss the subject briefly, but the reader should be aware that, even since the previous edition of this book was published, few definitive standards have emerged for the licensing of these uses.

As we have discussed above, Internet transmissions of sound recordings may either be in the form of digital phonorecord deliveries (i.e., downloaded) or not (i.e., streamed). We will first review the considerations in granting and obtaining licenses to sound recordings for the purpose of offering them on a download service.

## A. Download Transmissions of Sound Recordings

Persons desiring download, or make digital phonorecord deliveries of, sound recordings must obtain a license from the person who owns the recording, which is typically, a record company. Unlike licenses for the right to effect digital deliveries of the underlying song (see below), there is no compulsory license for digital phonorecord deliveries of sound recordings. In other words, you must obtain permission from the record company and the record company can charge whatever it likes or even refuse to grant you permission to make the transmission.

EMusic.com, Inc.,[43] the largest supplier of popular music in the MP3 format, has entered into license agreements with over 750 independent record labels for the exclusive rights to make digital deliveries of their sound recordings. These deals were generally on an exclusive basis for a period of five to seven years, and included all of the sound recordings in the label's catalog at the time the license was signed, plus all recordings which label acquired the right to distribute during the term of the agreement. After certain costs were deducted, Emusic split the net revenue 50/50 with the label. Costs included the direct out-of-pocket costs of effecting the transaction, such as VISA and MasterCard clearance fees, patent royalties, referral fees paid to third party websites for referring customers of the digital downloads, and mechanical royalties. A license having similar terms is set forth in the appendix to this chapter as Form 23-3.

Other services, such as MP3.com and IUMA.com (Internet Underground Music Archive), are among many companies that have obtained licenses to make digital deliveries of sound recordings directly from thousands of "unsigned" recording artists under licenses which nearly all on a non-exclusive basis. The terms of these licenses were generally non-exclusive and could be terminated by the artist at any time. Terms offered by IUMA are set forth in Form 23-5 in the Appendix to this chapter.

## B. Streaming Transmissions of Sound Recordings

The considerations in granting and obtaining a license to transmit sound recordings on the Internet by *streaming* depend upon the nature of the streaming: you must first determine whether the streaming is part of an *interactive service* or not.

### 1.  Interactive Streaming Transmissions

If you operate a commercial website and you want to effect *interactive* streaming transmissions of copyrighted musical sound re-

---

[43] Co-author Bob Kohn was founder of EMusic.com, Inc., formerly NASDAQ: EMUS, and served as its Chairman until the company was sold to Vivendi/Universal in May 2001.

cordings, even if the transmission does not result in a copy at the recipient's end of the transmission, you will require a license from the owner of the sound recording, typically a record company. This is because, if the recipient can choose, on request, "a particular recording," then there is a high risk that the recipient will never need to purchase a copy of the recording or purchase a digital phonorecord delivery. For this reason, the law specifically gives owners of sound recordings an exclusive right to license digital audio transmissions that are part of interactive services. This means the record company can charge what it wishes for these transmissions or refuse to provide a license at all.

The major record companies have only recently begun licensing to third parties portions of their content for Interactive streaming services. In general, they are asking for the greater of (a) 50% of the gross revenues from the streaming service or (b) 1 cent per stream. In addition, for copies required to be made and placed on servers for purposes of operating the service, they are asking for 2 cents per copy, up to a maximum of 10 cents per sound recording. An example of a interactive streaming license is set forth in the Appendix to this chapter as Form 23-4.

### 2. Non-Interactive Streaming Services

As mentioned above, there are two kinds of digital audio transmissions that do not result in digital phonorecord deliveries: those that are part of an interactive service and those not part of an interactive service. Of those transmissions that are not part of an interactive service, there are two basic types: *subscription transmissions* and *nonsubscription transmissions*.

A "subscription transmission" is a transmission that is controlled and limited to particular recipients, and for which consideration is required to be paid or otherwise given by or on behalf of the recipient to receive the transmission or a package of transmissions including the transmission.

### a. Subscription Transmissions

The 1995 Act established two types of subscription transmissions of sound recordings: (i) voluntary subscription transmissions and (ii) compulsory subscription transmissions. Both require licenses from the sound recording owners, typically record companies. However, the former may be licensed by the record companies on a voluntary basis, meaning the record companies can set any licensee fee they wish, or refuse to license these transmissions. With respect to compulsory subscription transmissions, the record companies can be compelled to grant licenses and the license fees are subject to a statutory fee, which will effectively serve as a maximum amount that will be charged for such licenses.

With respect to compulsory subscription transmissions, in February 2001, the U.S. Copyright Office announced a voluntary negotiation period for determining reasonable rates and terms for the public performance of sound recordings by compulsory subscription services. The negotiation period was to end by March 2001 and if the parties have not reached an agreement a new Copyright Arbitration Royalty Panel was to be convened.

### b.   Non-Subscription Transmissions

The 1995 Act, as modified by the DMCA, established two types of non-subscription transmissions: (i) eligible non-subscription transmissions and (ii) non-eligible non-subscription transmissions. Those who wish to make non-subscription transmissions that qualify as eligible non-subscription transmissions may, provided they comply with the requirements of such transmissions, compel the record companies to provide them with a license at rate to be determined by a Copyright Arbitration Royalty Panel.

At the time this edition went to press, such a CARP was in progress. The RIAA is asking the CARP to set the statutory rate for such compulsory licenses at the greater of .4 cents (i.e., 4 tenths of one cent) per stream or 15 percent of the Webcaster's gross revenue. The webcasters are offering to pay 0.15 cents (i.e., 15 one-hundredths of one cent) per stream.

Non-subscription transmissions that do not qualify as eligible non-subscription transmissions will require voluntary licenses from the record companies. As mentioned above, the record companies are seeking the greater of 50% of gross revenues or 1 cent per stream for such licenses.

### c. Broadcast transmissions.

As discussed above, owners of traditional, terrestrial radio broadcast stations were blind-sided by a change in the copyright law they overlooked at the time the DMCA was passed. Under the 1995 Act, terrestrial radio broadcast transmissions of sound recordings that were transmitted over the Internet were exempt from the requirement of obtaining a performance, or digital audio transmission, license. All that a radio station required to make such transmissions was a performance license for the underlying musical works, which was easily obtainable from the performance rights societies such as ASCAP and BMI.

Soon after they discovered this change, the broadcasters petitioned the Copyright Office for an interpretation of the DMCA. In December 2000, the Copyright Office ruled that the public performance of sound recordings by means of digital audio transmissions, such as over the Internet, were not exempt from copyright liability. Thus, radio stations would require sound recording licenses to transmit their broadcasts over the Internet, and in order to obtain a compulsory license, those transmissions would need to comply with the detailed playlist requirements set forth in Section 114 of the Copyright Act.

Since this decision, most terrestrial broadcasters have ceased transmitting their broadcasts over the Internet, and they are contemplating what actions to take next, including lobbying Congress for a change in the law that would re-institute the exemption they briefly enjoyed under the 1995 Act.

## VIII. FUTURE OF LICENSING MUSIC ON THE INTERNET

The implications of the digital transmission of music on the Internet are far-reaching. Because of the ease with which potentially millions of individuals may digitally transmit musical works and sound recordings without accounting to copyright owners, the music industry will face considerable challenges in enforcing the rights in their musical compositions. They may well hope that a few well-publicized lawsuits will alleviate the problem, but other challenges will remain.

Detection of unauthorized copying will be made more difficult by widely available encryption software that will allow users to remain completely anonymous while trampling on the rights of copyright owners. Ironically, it is the very same technology — encryption software — that the recording industry has pinned its hopes on in the effort to protect musical works from unauthorized copying and use.

The emergence of electronic commerce, and the ability for virtually anyone to inexpensively become their own supplier of musical compositions and sound recordings, portends to change the very nature of the music industry. Using the Internet, songwriters and artists will have a new means to reach the public with their artistic creations, bypassing traditional distributors and publishers, or opening up opportunities for new entrants into the publishing and recording industries. It is important to understand that it is the artists who own the "brand" recognized by the listening public — for example, the consumer knows "Elton John," not necessarily the name of his record company. If you were to perform a search on the Internet for the artist, you would use the search term, "Elton John," not "Capitol Records," "Universal," "Sony," etc.

Until the age of the Internet, the record companies added value by identifying new artists, financing the creation of recordings, promoting airplay and, thereby, record sales, and manufacturing and distributing records or CDs. Soon, the manufacturing and distribution functions will be reduced to operating a Web site, and that activity requires a significantly lower investment, an activity that record companies don't necessarily have a comparative advantage over others. Nevertheless, marketing expertise will remain as important, if not more important, than distribution. With just about everyone having access to the Web and distribution, getting above the noise level will become more difficult over time, not less. Thus, artists will continue to outsource the critical function of marketing to organizations who know how to get about the noise level, and that will continue to be record labels in the foreseeable future.

It is our prediction that those music publishers, record companies, and others who are quick to adopt the new technologies and who best employ computer databases and information systems to track and analyze the musical tastes and buying habits of consumers are likely to reap the greatest share of the transmission market.

Indeed, the *Tin Pan Alley* of yesterday is quickly taking shape as the *Fiber Optic Alley* of tomorrow. If Samuel Goldwyn were here today and experienced these changes, he may well have observed: "The future ain't what it used to be."

# APPENDIX TO CHAPTER 23
## LICENSING MUSICAL WORKS AND SOUND RECORDINGS ON THE INTERNET

# FORM 23-1

## HARRY FOX AGENCY MECHANICAL LICENSE FOR DIGITAL PHONORECORD DELIVERIES

### THE HARRY FOX AGENCY, INC.
### 711 THIRD AVENUE
### NEW YORK, NEW YORK 10017

This compulsory license applies solely to the songs set forth in the attached Confirmation Report which lists the songs and other designating information (which may be delivered in a computer readable format in accordance with the attached Exhibit A).

You have advised us, in our capacity as Agent for the Publisher(s) referred to in the attached Confirmation Report, that you wish to obtain a compulsory license to make and to distribute digital phonorecord deliveries (as defined in Section 115 of the Copyright Act, hereinafter referred to as "DPDs"), of the copyrighted works referred therein, under the compulsory license provision of Section 115 of the Copyright Act. The provisions hereof vary the terms of the compulsory license provision of the Copyright Act applicable to DPDs. Your making and distributing of DPDs of any of such copyrighted works shall constitute assent to these terms.

Upon your doing so, you shall have all the rights which are granted to, and all the obligations which are imposed upon, users of said copyrighted works under the compulsory license provision of the Copyright Act, after phonorecords of the copyrighted works have been distributed to the public in the United States under the authority of the copyright owner by another person, except that with respect to DPDs thereof made and distributed hereunder:

1.    You shall pay royalties and account to us as Agent for and on behalf of said Publisher(s) quarterly, within

forty-five days after the end of each calendar quarter, on the basis of DPDs made and distributed;

2.   For such DPDs made and distributed, the royalty shall be the statutory rate in effect at the time each DPD is distributed, except as otherwise stated in the Confirmation Report;

3.   This compulsory license covers and is limited to one particular recording of each copyrighted work as performed by the artist and on the DPD configuration number identified in the Confirmation Report; and this compulsory license does not supersede nor in any way affect any prior agreements now in effect respecting phonorecords of any copyrighted work listed in the Confirmation Report;

4.   In the event you fail to account to us and pay royalties as herein provided for, said Publisher(s) or his Agent may give written notice to you that, unless the default is remedied within 30 days from the date of the notice, this compulsory license will be automatically terminated. Such termination shall render either the making or the distribution, or both, of all phonorecords (whether DPD or not) for which royalties have not been paid, actionable as acts of infringement under, and fully subject to the remedies provided by the Copyright Act;

5.   You need not serve or file the notice of intention to obtain a compulsory license required by the Copyright Act;

6.   Additional Provisions

The authority hereunder is limited to (i) the making and distribution of DPDs, and (ii) the making of a copy of a sound recording of a musical work on a computer file server located in the United States, its territories or possessions, solely for the purpose of distributing such DPDs. The authority hereunder does not extend to DPDs where the reproduction and distribution of a phonorecord (or the musical work) is incidental to the transmission which constitutes the DPD.

Credit: In regard to all DPDs distributed hereunder, you shall include in any graphics and imagery displayed in connection with playback of such DPDs writer/publisher credit in the form of the names of the writer(s) and the publisher(s) of the copyrighted work.

The ISRC number and DPD configuration number for the relevant recording of the musical work licensed hereunder (or other applicable identification number to distinguish DPD use from physical phonorecords) shall be included in the file header of the DPD, and must be provided to us. To the extent an ISRC Number is not submitted, the MMI number (supplied by HFA) must be included in the appropriate in the file header of the download.

# FORM 23-2

## MECHANICAL LICENSE FOR
## ON-DEMAND STREAMING SERVICE

### AGREEMENT

This Agreement is being entered into this _____, 2002 (the "Effective Date") by and between MUSIC SERVICE PROVIDER ("MSP") having its principal place of business at _____ and THE HARRY FOX AGENCY, INC. ("HFA"), having its principal place of business at _____.

WHEREAS, SERVICE has developed technology to provide MSP Users (as defined below) online access to Streamed Sound Recordings (as defined below) whereby such Streaming to a User is permitted only if a copy of such Sound Recording has been purchased by such User and a User can confirm such purchase by either electronic detection of the Sound Recording in such User's computer or confirmation by MSP with the point of purchase or such User has purchased a subscription from MSP for access to such Sound Recording;

WHEREAS, to accomplish these purposes, MSP desires a license to use new and existing Works (as defined below) owned or controlled by various HFA publisher/principals in order to properly prepare and load Sound Recordings embodying the Works onto the Streaming Service file servers and Stream the Works to Users of the Streaming Service (as defined below);

NOW, THEREFORE, the parties do hereby agree as follows:

1.    DEFINITIONS

    1.1    "Detect-CD" means a computer system that can detect and identify the presence in the CD-ROM drive of a User's computer of a Sound Recording (in the form of a CD) embodying one or more Works using MSP's proprietary technology, and thereby add the title of such identified Works to that User's Title List.

1.2 "DPD" means Digital Phonorecord Delivery, as such term is defined in the Copyright Act.

1.3 "MSP Websites" means the file servers located by the URL designated as www.MSP.com, and any other Website hereafter approved by HFA in writing in its sold discretion. MSP Websites shall also include mirror sites, caching servers or equivalent devices whose distribution function for the purposes hereunder is determined solely by actions directed at such approved URLs.

1.4 "Encode" means converting a Sound Recording into a digital file and fixing such file on a recordable medium, including without limitation, the hard disk drive of a computer system.

1.5 "Instant Access" means a system which adds to a Title List associated with a User any Works embodied in a Sound Recording at the time such Sound Recording is purchased by such User from an online retailer that has a contractual arrangement with MSP to provide MSP confirmation of such User's purchase of such Sound Recording.

1.6 "Locker" means the logical location within the MSP Website where each User's Title List is maintained. Each locker shall only be accessible by a User on a password-protected basis.

1.7 "Phonorecord," "Sound Recording," Audiovisual Works," and "Digital Transmissions" (or "Digitally Transmit") shall have the same meanings as are provided in Section 101 of the Copyright Act, 17 U.S.C. 101.

1.8 "Stream," Streamed," or "Streaming" means a Digital Transmission of a Sound Recording by any means, whether now known or hereafter developed, including by means of the Internet that (i) is substantially contemporaneous with a performance of such recording on a User's computer, and (ii) does not deliver a complete, fixed file embodying such recording that is usable without a simultaneous active connection to the Digital Transmission source, other than as temporarily required to render such contemporaneous performance as in the form of a data buffer.

1.9  "Streaming Mechanical License" means a nonexclusive license to Encode a Work and Stream such Work to a User, to be issued hereunder by HFA substantially in the form of Exhibit A-2 attached hereto, for an on behalf of its Streaming Mechanical Licensors to MSP as nonexclusive authority for the use of a Work in accordance with the terms set forth hereunder.

1.10  "Streaming Mechanical License Request" means that written request for a Streaming Mechanical License in the form annexed to and made part of this Agreement as Exhibit A-1, which may be transmitted electronically to HFA by MSP seeking a Streaming Mechanical License to use a Work in accordance with the term hereunder.

1.11  "Streaming Mechanical Licensor" means each HFA publisher-principal who has authorized HFA to issue Streaming Mechanical Licenses to MSP on it behalf under the terms of this Agreement. Schedule 1, as amended from time to time by HFA, is a list of Streaming Licensors.

1.12  "Streaming Service" means MSP's proprietary system, located at MSP.com on the MSP Website, whereby a User can establish and maintain a single Title List in a single Locker that designates which Works may be Streamed to such User in accordance with the terms hereof.

1.13  "Territory" means the United States, subject to Section II(ii).

1.14    "Title List(s)" means the list unique to each User of the set of Works that comprise an individual Locker associated with a particular User.

1.15    "Users" means natural person visitors to the Streaming Service available on the MSP Websites who have registered with MSP in order to receive the Streaming Service.

1.16    "Website" means any specific or unique physical or logical address on that portion of the publicly available network of computer networks commonly referred to as the Internet (and any successors thereto) and also known as the "World Wide Web."

1.17    Work(s) mean any musical composition available for licensing hereunder, designated in a Streaming Mechanical License Request, owned or controlled by a Streaming Mechanical Licensor and as to which HFA has the authority from such Streaming Mechanical Licensor to issue the Streaming Mechanical License to Encode for the user of such composition in the making and distribution of Sound Recordings embodying such music compositions in the manner contemplated hereunder.

## 2.    STREAMING SERVICE

2.1    Subject to and in accordance with the terms, conditions, restrictions and limitations contained in this Agreement, and solely to the extent of the rights of each Streaming Mechanical Licensor with respect to each Work, HFA, on behalf of each Streaming Mechanical Licensor, shall grant to MSP upon submission to HFA of a valid Streaming Mechanical License Request for each Work as embodied in a single Sound Recording, during the Term and in the Territory, a Streaming Mechanical License, without the right to sublicense, to (1) Stream to a User's personal computer (or such other devices hereafter approved by HFA or a Streaming Mechanical Licensor with respect to such Streaming Mechanical Licensor's Work, in its sole discretion) the Work, only if such Work is designated in such User's Locker, such User being permitted to initiate no more than one Stream at a time, solely by means of the Internet and solely in connection with providing Users the Streaming Service, and (2) make Encoded copies of the Work only to the extent necessary to exercise its rights in clause (1) above; provided that such copies of the Work shall only reside on the network servers, mirror sites, caching servers, workstations, or equivalent devices under the direct control of MSP, and not on any third party's digital recording device or User's digital recording device (regardless of whether such digital recording device is a personal computer or any other machine now known or hereafter invented).

2.2    Notwithstanding the foregoing, with respect to any Work, the Territory shall not exceed the territories for which the Streaming Mechanical Licensor has acquired the right to license the rights granted to MSP pursuant to this Section 2.

2.3    Upon the electronic receipt by HFA from MSP (provided it is not in Default) of an accurate, clearly transmitted and fully completed Streaming Mechanical License Request for a Work to be used in connection with the MSP Streaming Service, with MSP's "PIN" number thereon and including, without limitation, the ISRC code (or any equivalent industry accepted indicia) identifying the applicable Sound Recording, such Streaming Mechanical License shall be issued by HFA on behalf of the respective Streaming Mechanical Licensor substantially in the form attached hereto as Exhibit B and both the Streaming Mechanical Licensor and MSP shall be and be deemed bound in all respects by the provisions of such Streaming Mechanical License for such Work, all in accordance with the terms and conditions of the Streaming Mechanical License as set forth by the provisions of this Agreement. MSP shall, within ninety (90) days of the Effective Date, also provide HFA with online access to data collected from the real-time monitoring of the Streaming Service which data shall include, without limitation, information to permit the accurate identification, tracking and verification of use Works by Users of the Streaming Service.

2.4     Notwithstanding anything to the contrary herein, each Streaming Mechanical Licensor may withhold a Streaming Mechanical License for a particular Streaming Mechanical Licensor's Work for any reason and thereby HFA shall not in such case, be obligated to provide MSP a Streaming Mechanical License for such Work.

## 3.     LIMITATION OF RIGHTS

3.1     MSP shall only add to or insert into the Title List of an individual Locker the title of a Work embodied on a phonorecord that has been (i) confirmed purchased by the Instant Access feature or (ii) both confirmed present in a User's computer by the Detect-CD feature and confirmed purchase by that User (by using a click-through dialogue box or similar device for each such Work by which the User represents that it has purchased such phonorecord). In the event a User cancels the purchase of a sound recording or returns a Sound Recording to the point of purchase for exchange with a different Sound Recording or refund, all Works embodied in such Sound Recording shall be immediately deleted from such User's Title List. Furthermore, MSP shall not authorize Users to Download Sound Recordings embodying Works to any device that is not SDMI compliant. In addition, MSP agrees that on or before December 31, 2000, it shall incorporate as part of such Streaming a security technology for existing and prospective Users that only permits Streaming from the MSP Service to the situs of an end user in a secure manner which shall have been generally adopted for use by a majority of the major record companies so long as: (i) such technologies do not cause a degradation in the quality of the Streaming of the music from the MSP Service (noticeable to the ordinary User) and (ii) HFA shall have required all other persons licensed by HFA and engaged in Streaming of Works in a manner similar to that described herein to have adopted the same or similar secure streaming technologies.

3.2     MSP may not sublicense, assign, or convey to any person any rights under this Agreement including, but not limited to, the right to make reproductions, distribute, Digitally Transmit, Encode, or Stream the Works without HFA's or a Streaming Mechanical Licensor's (with respect to such Streaming Mechanical Licensor's Work) prior consent.

3.3    The rights granted by HFA on behalf of the Streaming Mechanical Licensors hereunder are limited to use of the Works in the manner expressly described herein. Any and all other rights in connection with the Works are specifically reserved by HFA's Streaming Mechanical Licensors, and their designees, including without limitation (i) all rights to exploit the Works in any manner (whether on-line or off-line), (ii) all rights to transmit, publicly perform, or otherwise distribute the Works using any medium or method now known or hereafter invented, and (iii) the exercise of the same rights granted to MSP hereunder.

3.4    MSP shall not edit, alter or defeat any copyright protection technology or mechanism embedded in or associated with the Sound Recordings embodying the Works. MSP shall include the MMI number as assigned by HFA that is associated with each Streaming Mechanical License, as an unencrypted header of each digital file Streamed under the authority of such Streaming Mechanical License under authority of such Mechanical License in accordance with the terms hereunder.

3.5    MSP shall not use any Works in any manner that a Streaming Mechanical Licensor with respect to a Work, in its sole reasonable business discretion, finds offensive or injurious to its interests. Without limiting the foregoing, MSP shall not, without prior written consent of the applicable Streaming Mechanical Licensor, use the Works for any on-line of off-line original programming, product tie-ins, or marketing campaigns of any type or nature, including games or contests. No Work may be Streamed or delivered as part of an audiovisual work.

3.6.    MSP shall not Stream, Digitally Transmit or otherwise distribute any Works from any Website that is not an MSP Website or a thirty-party Website unless approved by HFA (or a

Streaming Mechanical Licensor with respect to such Streaming Mechanical Licensor's Work) in a prior writing.

3.7    MSP shall use its best efforts to prevent the creation of any unauthorized copies of any Works in any facilities in its control in any form (including but not limited to, copies created by employees or contractors outside the immediate scope of their employment), and shall use its commercially reasonable efforts to prevent the creation of such unauthorized copies by any Users including, without limitation, the conversion of a Streamed Work into a fixed file embodying such Work or by any third party (collectively, "Illicit Copies"). If MSP becomes aware of any unauthorized manufacture, advertising, distribution, lease, sale, or conversion of Streamed delivery into fixed, useable files, or other use by any third party, any User, or the creation of any Illicit Copies (any of the foregoing an "Unauthorized Use") MSP shall immediately notify HFA and shall fully cooperate with HFA to prevent such Unauthorized Use including cessation of use of the Works by MSP. In the event software that converts the Streamed Works into fixed files becomes available to Users, MSP shall immediately take all necessary steps to upgrade its Streaming systems and/or Users' client software in order to render such conversion software ineffective. MSP shall indemnify HFA and its Streaming Mechanical Licensors for any losses incurred by HFA or any of its Streaming Licensors as a result of (i) Unauthorized Use by its employees or contractors outside the scope of their employment or (ii) breach by MSP of this section 3.

4.    CONSIDERATION

4.1    In consideration for each rendition of each licensed Work Encoded for use by MSP Streaming Service, by MSP, MSP shall pay HFA a royalty fee equal to ten cents ($.10) per Encoding of each such rendition.

4.2    In consideration for each Stream of any licensed Work, MSP shall pay to HFA on behalf of the Streaming Mechanical Licensors, a royalty equal to (i) the statutory compulsory royalty rate for Incidental Digital Phonorecord Deliveries applicable to this or similar uses of copyrighted works ("Incidentals") for each such Streamed transmission of a Work determined as of the date of transmission or (ii) in the absence of such a statutory compulsory royalty rate, one quarter of a cent ($.0025) for each Stream initiated for delivery to any User.

4.4    MSP shall within ninety (90) days of the Effective Date, also provide HFA with online access to data collected from the real-time monitoring of the Streaming Service which data shall include, without limitation, information to permit the accurate identification, tracking, and verification of use of Works by Users of the Streaming Service. HFA shall be permitted to release all reporting and audit information to its Streaming Mechanical that specifies the manner and quantity of use of such Streaming Mechanical Licensors' Works.

4.5    Neither HFA, nor its Streaming Mechanical Licensors shall be subject to any costs, fees, offsets, or other charges (including, without limitation, any royalties) in respect of the creation, transmission, or performance of any Work or otherwise in respect of any of the provisions of this Agreement.

5.    COPYRIGHT NOTICE

Simultaneously with the Streaming of each Work, MSP shall display on the User's computer credits specifying (i) the title of the Work, (ii) the name of the writer(s), and (iii) the required copyright notice in the following format: "© [Year of First Publication] [Streaming Mechanical Licensor designated name]. All rights reserved."

6.    TERM

The parties hereto agree that any rights granted to MSP to provide the Streaming Service shall terminate on the second anniversary of the date hereof.

## 7. EXHIBITS

Exhibit A-1 of this Agreement sets forth the Streaming Mechanical License Request form to be used by MSP, and Exhibit A-2 of this Agreement provides the form and terms of the Streaming Mechanical License.

## 8. MISCELLANEOUS

8.1    Each party to this Agreement represents and warrants to the other that (i) such party has the right, power and authority to enter into and fully perform this Agreement, to make the commitments it makes herein and to perform fully its obligations hereunder and (ii) the execution of this Agreement by such party and its performance of its obligations hereunder do not and will not violate any agreement by which such party is bound.

8.2    This Agreement contains the entire understanding of the parties hereto relating to the subject matter hereof and cannot be changed or terminated except by an instrument signed by an officer of HFA and an officer of MSP. A waiver by either party of any term or condition of this Agreement in any instance shall not be deemed or construed as a waiver of such term or condition in the future, or of any subsequent breach hereof. All remedies, rights undertakings, obligations and agreements contained in this Agreement shall be cumulative and none of them shall be in limitation of any other remedy, right, undertaking, obligation or agreement of either party.

8.3    The parties hereto intend that each of the parties have the right to seek damages or specific performance in the even that any other party hereto fails to perform such party's obligations hereunder. Therefore, if any party shall institute any action or proceeding to enforce the provisions hereof, any party against whom such action or proceeding is brought hereby waives any claim or defense therein that the plaintiff party has an adequate remedy at law.

8.4   This Agreement shall be deemed entered into in the State of New York, and the validity, interpretation and legal effect of this Agreement shall be governed by the laws of the State of New York applicable to contracts entered into and performed entirely within the State of New York, with respect to the determination of any claim, dispute or disagreement which may arise out of the interpretation, performance, or breach of this Agreement. Any process in any action or proceeding commenced in the courts of the State of New York or elsewhere arising out of any such claim, dispute, or disagreement, may, among other methods, be served in the manner set forth herein. Any such delivery or mail service shall be deemed to have the same force and effect as personal service within the State of New York or the jurisdiction in which such action or proceeding may be commenced. Any claim arising out of or relating to this Agreement or the transactions contemplated hereby may be instituted in any Federal Court of the Southern District of New York or any state court located in New York County, State of New York, and each party agrees not to assert, by way of motion, as a defense or otherwise, in any such claim, that it is not subject personally to the jurisdiction of such Court, that the claim is brought in an inconvenient forum, that the venue of the claim is improper or that this Agreement or the subject matter hereof or thereof may not be enforced in or by such Court. Each party further irrevocably submits to the jurisdiction of such Court in any such claim.

8.5   The parties hereto are sophisticated and have had the opportunity to be represented by lawyers throughout the negotiation of this Agreement. As a consequence, the parties do not believe that the presumptions of any laws or rules relating to the interpretation of contracts against the drafter of any particular clause should be applied in this case and therefore waive their effects.

8.6   This Agreement shall not become effective until executed by the parties hereto.

## 9. NOTICES

All notices to be provided pursuant to this Agreement shall be given in writing and shall be effective when served by personal delivery or upon receipt via certified mail, return receipt requested, postage prepaid, overnight courier service or sent by facsimile transmission with hard copy confirmation sent by certified mail, in each case to the party at the addresses set forth below (or at such other addresses hereafter designated by the parties):

For MSP:


For HFA:

> Harry Fox Agency, Inc.
> 711 Third Avenue
> New York, NY 10017
> Facsimile: 212-953-2471
> Attention: President

## 10. SEVERABILITY; WAIVER

Should any part of this Agreement judicially be declared to be invalid, unenforceable or void, the parties agree that the part or parts of this Agreement so held to be invalid, unenforceable or void shall be reformed by the entity having jurisdiction there over without further action by the parties hereto and only to the extent necessary to make such part or parts valid and enforceable. A waiver by either party hereto of any of the covenants to be performed by the other party or any breach thereof shall not be effective unless made in writing and signed by the waiving party and shall not be construed to be a waiver of any succeeding breach thereof or of any covenant herein contained.

## 11.    RELATIONSHIP OF THE PARTIES

Each party is acting as an independent contractor and not as an agent, partner, joint venturer with the other party for any purpose. Except as provided in this Agreement, neither party shall have any right, power or authority to act or to create any obligation, express or implied, on behalf of the other.

## 12.    COUNTERPARTS

This Agreement may be executed in one or more counterparts, each of which shall be deemed an original, and all of which, when taken together, shall constitute one and the same document.

IN WITNESS WHEREOF, the parties hereto have caused their authorized representatives to execute this Agreement.

THE HARRY FOX AGENCY, INC.

By: _____

Name: _____

Title: _____

MSP, INC.

By: _____

Name: _____

Title: _____

## Exhibit A-1

## STREAMING MECHANICAL LICENSE REQUEST

Streaming Mechanical License No: _____
(to be assigned by HFA)

TO:    THE HARRY FOX AGENCY, INC., 711 THIRD AVENUE, NEW YORK, NEW YORK 10017

The Streaming Mechanical Licensee referred to and who "PIN" number appears below hereby requests license authority to use the song as referred to below upon the following terms and conditions provided in the compulsory license provisions of Section 115 of the U.S. Copyright Act as varied by the terms set forth in the Digital Phonorecord Delivery License between the parties dated _____.

A.    Song Code Number:
       Song Title:
       Songwriter(s):

Percentages

B:    Publisher(s) [Streaming Mechanical Licensor(s)]

C.    On-line Service Provider:                       MSP
       Forum/Library's Forum Name:                    Stream-
                                                              ing

       Streaming Mechanical Licensee:                 MSP
       Streaming Mechanical Licensee PIN Number:    _____
       Type:                                         Stream-
                                                              ing

       D.    Recording Identification:

       Playing Time:

       Streaming Royalty Rate: (i) ten cents ($.10) per Encoding of each rendition of licensed Work, plus

(ii) Statutory Rate for incidental DPDs or $.0025 per Stream of licensed Work in absence of a Statutory Rate.

Date of Request:

## Exhibit A-2

## STREAMING MECHANICAL LICENSE

TO LICENSEE:

You have advised us, in our capacity as Agent for the Publisher(s) [Streaming Mechanical Licensor(s)] referred to in Section (B) of your Streaming Mechanical License Request ("SMLR") that you wish to obtain a compulsory license under the compulsory license provisions of Section 115 of the U.S. Copyright Act, to make and distribute phonorecords of the copyrightable licensable song referred to in SMLR section (A) by enabling the digital transmission of sound recordings identified in SMLR section (D) solely in the manner expressly set forth in the license between the parties dated _____ (the "Streaming License Agreement").

Upon your doing so, you shall have the rights which are granted to, and all the obligations which are imposed upon the users of copyrighted works as provided by Section 115 of the Copyright Act, after phonorecords of the copyrighted work have been distributed to the public in the United States under the authority of the copyright owner by another person, subject to and accordance with the terms of the Streaming License Agreement between you and us, provided that:

1.    You shall fully comply with the provisions of the Streaming License Agreement, as may be amended from time to time.

2.    The compulsory license covers and is limited to one particular Sound Recording of said copyrighted work as identified in SMLR(D) and this compulsory license does not supersede or in any way affect any prior agreement now in effect with respect to phonorecords of said copyrighted work;

3.     You need not serve or file the notice of intention to obtain compulsory license required by the Copyright Act.

THE HARRY FOX AGENCY, INC.

# FORM 23-3

## LICENSE OF SOUND RECORDINGS FOR DIGITAL DOWNLOAD SERVICE

## DIGITAL DISTRIBUTION AGREEMENT

**THIS LICENSE FOR SOUND RECORDINGS** (the "Agreement") is entered into as of the __ day of June, 2001 (the "Effective Date") between _____, Inc., with offices at _____

("Licensee"), and Independent Record Company, Inc., with offices at _____ ("Owner") (each a "Party" and, collectively, the "Parties").

WHEREAS, Licensee offers sound recordings for digital distribution over the Internet, and Owner owns or controls the rights to, or shall own or control the rights to, certain sound recordings of the artist, _____ ("Artist"), including the literary works, sound recordings, audiovisual works, artwork, photographs, and other works of authorship, set forth in Exhibit A, attached hereto (hereinafter, the "Licensed Works").

The parties agree as follows:

## 1. DEFINITIONS

1.1    To "digitally distribute" shall mean to make, cause or otherwise effect Digital Delivery Transmissions and Digital Streaming Transmissions of the Licensed Works, or any portion thereof, by any means now known or hereafter devised, including but not limited to subscription and non-subscription services, and transmissions by interactive and non-interactive services.

1.2    *See generally id.* The term "Digital Delivery Transmission" shall mean each individual delivery, distribution, display, or performance of a work by digital transmission of such work which results in a specifically identifiable reproduction by or for any transmission recipient of a copy or phonorecord of that work by any means now known or hereafter devised.

1.3     The term "Digital Streaming Transmission" shall mean each individual delivery, distribution, display, or performance of a work by digital transmission of such work which does not result in a specifically identifiable reproduction by or for any transmission recipient of a copy or phonorecord of that work by any means now known or hereafter devised.

1.4     The term "sound recording" shall mean a work resulting from a fixation in copies or phonorecords of a series of musical, spoken, or other sounds.

1.5     The term "audiovisual work" shall mean a work that consists of series of related images which are intrinsically intended to be shown by the use of machines or devices such as projectors, viewers or electronic equipment, together with accompanying sounds, if any.

## 2.     GRANT OF LICENSE

2.1     Licensed Works. Subject to the terms and condition hereof, Owner hereby grants to Licensee the irrevocable, perpetual exclusive right and license throughout the universe to digitally distribute the Licensed Works, including any portion thereof, by any and all means and media now known or hereafter devised. The foregoing rights and licenses shall be limited to digital distribution, as defined above. So that there may be no misunderstanding, to digitally distribute does not mean to distribute either (a) in physical form, such as in books, CD's, videotapes, DVDs, or motion picture theatrical distribution, or (b) by analog broadcast or transmission, such as television broadcast.

2.2     Name Voice, and/or Likeness. Owner hereby grants to Licensee a non-exclusive right and license throughout the universe to use, reproduce, display, perform, distribute, transmit, publicly and privately, the name, voice, and/or likeness of Artist, solely in connection with the digital distribution of the Licensed Works hereunder and the promotion thereof, by any and all means and in any and all media now known or hereafter devised. The term "name and/or likeness" shall mean the name, voice, photograph, drawing, likeness, biographical material, any and all words, symbols, and logos which identify Artist, and any and all trademarks, service marks, tradenames, or similar properties, of, relating to or associated with such person, and any other exercise of the "right of publicity" of, relating to, or associated with Artist.

2.3   Artwork. Owner hereby grants to Licensee a non-exclusive right and license throughout the universe to use, reproduce, display, perform, distribute, transmit, publicly and privately, any Artwork created for use with the Licensed Works, solely in connection with the digital distribution of the Licensed Works hereunder and the promotion thereof, by any and all means and in any and all media now known or hereafter devised. The term "Artwork" shall mean any artwork, drawings, photographs, liner notes, promotional and advertising material, or other graphical, textual or other graphical works relating to the performances or performers featured in the Licensed Works or developed or created by or for Owner for use in connection with the distribution or promotion of the Licensed Works.

2.4   Encoding. Licensee may prepare and encode the Licensed Works, or any portion thereof, for purposes of facilitating the exercise of the rights and licenses granted hereunder, in any digital format (e.g., Real Audio, Windows Media, MP3, etc.), now known or hereafter devised, including formats that are accompanied by or synchronized with textual material, copyright information, and/or visual or audiovisual images, related to or created for use with the Licensed Works. Though Licensee shall have no right or license to distribute physical copies or phonorecords containing the Licensed Works to the public, Licensee may make copies or phonorecords containing the Licensed Works encoded in any digital format (e.g., Real Audio, Windows Media, MP3, etc.), for the purpose of (a) facilitating its digital distribution hereunder and (b) promoting the Licensed Works (e.g., placing sample MP3 files of a portion of a Licensed Work on a CD for distribution by a computer or mobile phone manufacturer).

2.5     Reserved Rights. All rights and licenses not expressly granted to Licensee hereunder are reserved by Owner. Ownership of the Licensed Works shall remain with Owner or its licensors.

## 3.    DELIVERY

Within seven (7) days after the date hereof, and thereafter within seven (7) days of the creation or discovery of any new Licensed Works hereunder, Owner shall deliver to Licensee CDs, tapes, vinyl records, videotapes, or other master versions of each Licensed Work hereunder; a reasonable number of items of the Artwork related to such Licensed Works, for use by Licensee in connection with the marketing and promotion of the Licensed Works; and, a written schedule of the names and contact information of any author(s), composer(s), and music publisher(s) of any songs or other third party materials embodied in the Licensed Works, together with any additional copyright information known to Owner relating to such materials and the Licensed Works, and a list of credits that Owner may be contractually required or otherwise reasonably desires to provide in connection with the distribution, exploitation of the Licensed Works hereunder.

## 4.    CONSIDERATION

4.1     *Advances*. Licensee shall pay to Owner a non-returnable advance, recoupable by Licensee from royalties payable to Owner hereunder, the sum of $_____, payable within thirty (30) days after the date hereof.

4.2 *Royalties*. Licensee shall pay to Owner a sum equal to ___ percent (___%) of any and all Net Revenues derived from the Licensed Works hereunder ("royalties").

4.2.1 The term "Net Revenues" shall mean gross revenues (not including sales tax) derived by Licensee from digital distributions of the Licensed Works, less only the following costs and fees incurred in connection with such deliveries, and only to the extent incurred:

(a)    transaction processing fees, such as credit card transaction fees and other electronic commerce processing, patent royalties or other fees, payable to or retained by third parties in connection with effecting a transaction or transmission, if any;

(b)    Internet referral fees, such as fees payable to any third party who, through their web site, email or other means, refers to us a purchaser of a copy or phonorecord of a Licensed Work;

(c)    billing credits, including, but not limited to, those on account of defective files, errors in billing, and errors in transmission, if any;

(d)    mechanical, synchronization and other royalties payable for any copyrighted music or other materials contained in the Licensed Works, if any;

4.2.2 In the event the Licensed Works, or portion thereof, are included in a compilation of other works, Owner shall receive a sum equal to a proportionate part of the Net Revenues derived from the compilation determined by dividing the number of Licensed Works in the compilation by the total number of works of like length or nature in the compilation. Likewise, in the event of fees charged on a subscription basis, Owner shall receive a sum equal to a proportionate part of the Net Revenues derived from the subscription transmissions determined by dividing the number of transmissions of the Licensed Works in the subscription service by the total number of works of like length or nature transmitted as part of the subscription service during the applicable accounting period.

4.2.3    Notwithstanding anything contained herein to the contrary, Net Revenues shall not include, and no royalties shall be payable to Owner on, any Licensed Works reproduced, distributed, performed, displayed, delivered or transmitted on a "free" or "no charge" basis, or otherwise where the recipient is not charged a fee to receive such Licensed Works. Without limiting the generality of the foregoing, any and all Licensed Works shall be and are hereby licensed to Licensee on a royalty-free basis for the purpose of making, causing or effecting transmissions of the Licensed Works for promotional purposes, such as, for example, Digitial Streaming Transmissions (e.g., digital radio webcasts or interactive audio or audiovisual, "streaming" transmission) of a Licensed Work, or Digital Delivery Transmissions of a portion of a Licensed Work, for the purpose of allowing consumers to listen to the Licensed Work in connection with the consumer's decision whether to purchase a Digital Delivery Transmission thereof or other promotional purpose.

4.2.4    The share of Net Revenues payable to Owner hereunder includes all royalties due Owner, the Artist(s), individual producers, the director, the performers, engineers, and any other persons engaged in connection with the creation of the Licensed Works. Owner shall be solely responsible for the payment of any royalties due such persons, unions, guilds or other third parties arising from payments made to Owner hereunder, except that Licensee shall effect payment for any and all mechanical and public performance royalties with respect to any musical works embodied in the Licensed Works which become due with respect to the exercise of the rights and licenses herein by Licensee. To the extent there is any delay in Licensee's obtaining any mechanical licenses necessary for it to make digital deliveries containing copyrighted music hereunder, the parties will rely on, and operate under the authority of, Owner's existing mechanical licenses for that purpose.

## 5. RECORD KEEPING AND REPORTS

5.1    Licensee agrees to maintain and preserve accurate books and records concerning all transactions relating to the reproduction and distribution of the Licensed Works for a period of two (2) years following the termination of this Agreement.

5.2    Licensee will compute the royalties to Owner pursuant to this Agreement within forty-five (45) days after the end of each calendar quarter (i.e., ending March 31, June 30, September 30, and December 31), and will deliver to Owner a quarterly royalty statement for each such period together with the net amount of royalties, if any, computed in accordance with this Agreement, which shall be payable after deducting any and all unrecouped advances or other charges hereunder.

5.3    Upon fourteen (14) days prior written notice to Licensee, Owner, or a certified public accountant on Owner's behalf, shall have the right, once each year, during ordinary business hours, to inspect and audit such of Licensee's business books and records as may reasonably be necessary for Owner to verify the accuracy of any royalty statement rendered by Licensee within the eighteen (18) month period immediately preceding the date of the inspection. The information contained in a royalty statement shall be conclusively deemed correct and binding upon Owner, resulting in the loss of all further audit rights with respect to such statement, unless specifically challenged by written notice from Owner within eighteen (18) months from the date such royalty statement was delivered by Licensee. Owner and its auditor shall keep all information learned as a result of such audit in strict confidence. The cost of such an audit will be borne by Owner unless a material discrepancy indicating inadequate record keeping or that additional license fees are due to Licensee is discovered, in which case the reasonable cost of the audit, and related reasonable legal expenses, shall be borne by Licensee. A discrepancy shall be deemed material if it involves payment or adjustment of more than fifteen percent (15%) of payments due under this Agreement. Audits shall not interfere unreasonably with Licensee business activities.

5.4 Severability. In the event that any provision hereof is found invalid or unenforceable pursuant to judicial decree or decision, the remainder of this Agreement shall remain valid and enforceable according to its terms. Without limiting the generality of the foregoing, to the extent the provisions of any copyright law regarding licenses for transmissions by interactive services is applicable to any of the grants of rights hereunder, such grant shall be exclusive for the maximum allowable period of exclusivity under such law.

5.5 Relationship. The relationship of Licensee and Owner established by this Agreement is of licensor and licensee, and nothing in this Agreement shall be construed: (1) to give either party the power to direct or control the daily activities of the other party, or (2) to constitute the parties as principal and agent, employer and employee, franchisor and franchisee, partners, joint venturers, co-owners, or otherwise as participants in a joint undertaking. Licensee and Owner understand and agree that neither party grants to the other the power or authority to make or give any agreement, statement, representation, warranty or other commitment on behalf of such party, or to enter into any contract or otherwise incur any liability or obligation, express or implied, on behalf of such party, or to transfer, release or waive any right, title or interest of such party.

5.6 Binding Agreement. This Agreement shall be binding upon and inure to the benefit of each of the parties hereto and their respective legal successors and assigns, provided that any successor or assignee shall be bound by all the terms and conditions of this Agreement.

5.7 Confidentiality of Agreement. Each of the parties to this Agreement warrants and agrees that neither it nor its counsel will disclose, disseminate, or cause to be disclosed the terms of this Agreement, except: (a) Insofar as disclosure is reasonably necessary to carry out and effectuate the terms of this

Agreement; (b) Insofar as a party hereto is required by law to respond to any demand for information from any court, governmental entity, or governmental agency; (c) Insofar as disclosure is necessary to be made to a party's independent accountants for tax or audit purposes; and (d) Insofar as the parties may mutually agree in writing upon language to be contained in one or more press releases.

5.8    Governing Law. This Agreement shall be construed and enforced in accordance with the laws of the State of California applicable to agreements between residents of California wholly executed and wholly performed therein. Notwithstanding the foregoing, any dispute, argument or controversy arising under this Agreement in any way whatsoever shall be settled exclusively by arbitration under the rules of the American Arbitration Association in San Francisco, California. Any action or proceeding brought by either party against the other arising out of or related to such arbitration or otherwise related to this Agreement shall be brought only in a state or federal court of competent jurisdiction located in the County of San Francisco, California, and the parties hereby consent to the *in personam* jurisdiction and venue of said courts.

5.9    Notice. Unless otherwise specifically provided, all notices required or permitted by this Agreement shall be in writing and in English and may be delivered personally, or may be sent by cable, telex, facsimile or certified mail, return receipt requested, to the address set forth above. Any notice shall be deemed to have been received as follows: (i) personal delivery, upon receipt; (ii) facsimile, twenty-four (24) hours after transmission; (iii) certified mail, three (3) business days after delivery to the United States postal authorities by the party serving notice. If notice is sent by facsimile, a confirming copy of the same shall be sent by mail to the same address.

5.10    Breach. Neither party shall be in breach of this agreement unless the other shall provide a notice to such party in writing specifying the alleged breach and the other party shall fail to cure such breach within sixty (60) days thereafter.

5.11     Legal Advice. Each of the parties hereto represents that this Agreement has been carefully read by him or it
and that he or it knows and understands the contents hereof.
Each of the parties has received independent legal advice from
attorneys of his or its choice with respect to the preparation,
review and advisability of executing this Agreement.

5.12     Entire Agreement. This Agreement constitutes the
entire understanding and contract between the parties and supersedes any and all prior and contemporaneous, oral or written
representations, communications, understandings and agreements between the parties with respect to the subject matter
hereof, all of which representations, communications, understandings and agreements are hereby cancelled to the extent
they are not specifically merged herein. The parties acknowledge and agree that neither of the parties is entering into this
Agreement on the basis of any representations or promises not
expressly contained herein. This is a merged and integrated
agreement.

## 6.     REPRESENTATIONS AND WARRANTIES

6.1     Owner. Owner represents and warrants (a) that
Owner has all necessary authorization, corporate and otherwise, to enter into this Agreement and to fully perform the terms
hereof; (b) that Owner has full and sufficient right to grant the
rights and/or licenses granted to Licensee herein, (c) all necessary permissions for the recording and the licensing to Licensee hereunder of all Licensed Works have been obtained by
Owner; (d) that the Licensed Works, or any trademark or tra-
dename used by any applicable performers or Owner, and any
other materials provided by Owner to Licensee hereunder, do
not, and the exercise by Licensee of the rights and licenses
granted hereunder shall not, infringe any patent, copyright,
trademark or other intellectual property rights, including trade
secrets, rights of publicity, privacy or similar rights of any third
party, or in any way contravene any applicable statute, law, order, rule or regulation, nor has any claim (whether or not em-

bodied in an action, past or present) of such infringement or contravention been threatened or asserted, and no such claim is pending, against a performer or Owner or (insofar as Owner is aware) against any entity from which a performer or Owner has obtained such rights; (e) each person or entity who has rendered any service or provided any materials in connection with, or has contributed in any way, to the making of the Licensed Works or the rights and licenses granted herein, has the right to grant such rights, render such services or furnish such materials; (f) all fees and other payments applicable to or resulting from the creation, recording, manufacture, duplication, and distribution of the Licensed Works, including, but not limited to, payments to performers, producers, engineers and others, have been, and hereafter during the term hereof shall be, fully and completely paid by Owner to, or waived in writing by, every person entitled to such payment, except for fees and other payments expressly required hereunder to be made by Licensee.

6.2     Licensee. Licensee represents and warrants that (a) it has all necessary authorization, corporate and otherwise, to enter into this Agreement and to fully perform the terms hereof, and (b) it shall not license, sell, or distribute the Licensed Works, except pursuant to the terms of this Agreement.

## 7.   INDEMNIFICATION

7.1     Each of the parties hereto shall indemnify, defend and hold harmless the other, and its respective affiliates, officers, directors, employees and agents, from and against any and all losses, liabilities, claims, obligations, costs and expenses (including, without limitation, reasonable attorneys' fees) which arise in connection with any breach or alleged breach by such party of any of its representations, warranties, and agreements set forth herein.

7.2     If a third party asserts any claim or allegation which, if proven, would trigger the indemnification obligations set forth in this Section, the indemnified party shall provide prompt notice to the other of such claim or allegation. If any such claim or action shall be brought against the indemnified party, the indemnifying party shall be entitled to participate therein and, to the extent that it wishes, to assume the defense thereof (provided such party retains counsel with widely recognized expertise and broad experience in defense of similar matters, which counsel shall be subject to the indemnified party's prior written approval, which approval will not be unreasonably withheld). Neither party shall, without the prior written consent of the other, effect any settlement of any pending or threatened proceeding in which the other is a party and indemnity could have been sought hereunder by such other party, unless such settlement includes an unconditional release of such other party from all such liability on claims that are the subject matter of such proceeding. In no event shall Owner, in the absence of the written consent of Licensee, effect any settlement of any pending, threatened or actual proceeding or claim which has the effect of compromising in any way the rights, interests and licenses of Licensee in the Licensed Works granted hereunder. Upon the making or filing of any such claim, action or demand against Licensee shall be entitled to withhold from any amounts payable to Owner under this Agreement or any other agreement between Owner and Licensee, such amounts as are reasonably related to the potential liability in issue, including reasonably anticipated court costs and counsel fees.

## 8.    GENERAL PROVISIONS

8.1    <u>Marketing</u>. Licensee shall have full freedom and flexibility in its decisions concerning marketing the Licensed Works. Wherever Owner's approval or consent is required or requested hereunder, Owner shall provide to Licensee notice of approval or disapproval, together with a statement explaining the reason for any such disapproval, within one calendar week after Licensee's requests. If Owner shall fail to give such notice, Owner shall be deemed to have given such consent or approval. All of the grants of rights and licenses set forth in this Agreement includes the right of Licensee to license, sublicense, and authorize others (including without limitation, its subsidiaries, affiliates, dealers, distributors, agents, licensees, and other third parties) to do any, some, or all of such activities. Nothing in this Agreement shall be construed as an obligation, guarantee or commitment by Licensee that Licensee that any marketing effort will be productive of any level of net revenues, royalties or other payments to Owner hereunder. Licensee has not made, and does not hereby make, any representation or warranty with respect to the amount of revenues or royalties hereunder.

8.2    Modifications/Waiver. This Agreement shall not be modified, amended, canceled or in any way altered, nor may it be modified by custom and usage of trade or course of dealing, except by an instrument in writing and signed by duly authorized officers of both of the parties hereto. Performance of any obligation required of a party hereunder may be waived only by a written waiver signed by a duly authorized officer of the other party, which waiver shall be effective only with respect to the specific obligation described therein. The waiver by either party hereto of a breach of any provision of this Agreement by the other shall not operate or be construed as a waiver of any subsequent breach of the same provision or any other provision of this Agreement.

**LICENSEE**                          **OWNER**

By: _____    By: _____
                                            Authorized Signature

Name: _____    Name: _____

                                 Date: _____

## EXHIBIT A

# FORM 23-4

## LICENSE OF SOUND RECORDINGS
## FOR ON-DEMAND STREAMING SUBSCRIPTION SERVICE

SOUND RECORDINGS INTERACTIVE LICENSE

**THIS LICENSE FOR SOUND RECORDINGS** (THE "Agreement") is entered into as of the __ day of June, 2001 (the "Effective Date") between _____, Inc., with offices at

("Licensee"), and Major Record Company, Inc., with offices at

("Owner") (each a "Party" and, collectively, the "Parties").

1.    License Grant. Subject to the limitations set forth in this Agreement, Owner hereby grants to Licensee during the Term a limited, nonexclusive license, without the right to sublicense, (a) to make Performances of Owner Sound Recordings by means of Streaming through Channels, including by means of transmission of a particular Owner Sound Recording immediately upon request by an End User, solely on the Web Site; provided, however, that Licensee may not transmit on any Channel, without prior written approval by Owner, Sound Recordings from any genre, style or period of music or entertainment other than the Licensed Genre, (b) to make Reproductions of the Sound Recordings solely insofar as they are incidental to the Streaming of such Performances, and (c) to reproduce and display only on the Web Site, the album front-cover packaging artwork associated with the current release of the Sound Recordings, only in connection with the transmission of that Sound Recording on the Web Site.

2.    Payment Terms

(a)    License Fee. Licensee shall pay to Owner a license fee for the Performance of Sound Recordings equal to the greater of the following:

(i)    Gross Revenues. Owner's Proportionate Share of ___ percent (___%) of Licensee's Gross Revenues; or

(ii)    Per Performance Fee. One cent ($0.01) per Performance of a Sound Recording; provided, however, that Licensee shall pay an additional license fee for Performances of Owner Sound Recordings that exceed five (5) minutes in duration at the rate of one fifth of once cent ($0.0020) for each minute or fraction thereof performed in excess of five (5) minutes.

(b)    Reproduction Fee. Licensee shall pay to Owner a license fee for the reproduction of Sound Recordings equal to two cents ($0.02) per Reproduction, up to a maximum of ten cents ($0.10) per Sound Recording.

(c)    Payment Due Upon Execution. Licensee shall pay to Owner the sum of _____ dollars ($_____) upon execution of this Agreement as consideration for granting this license. This sum shall be a non-refundable, fully-recoupable advance against the amounts payable pursuant to Section 2(a) above.

(d)    Performing Rights and Publishing Fees. The Parties agree that Licensee shall be solely responsible for obtaining any third-party licenses required by this Agreement and paying any necessary royalties arising out of this Agreement to such third parties, including, without limitation, any required performing rights royalties or other publishing royalties. Notwithstanding the preceding sentence, however, in the event that Owner enters into a license agreement with any performing rights or publishing society and Owner offers to Licensee the option to obtain such third-party licenses through Owner, Licensee may elect to obtain such third-party licenses through Owner, in which case Licensee shall pay to Owner any and all costs incurred by Owner, directly or indirectly, related to or resulting from Licensee's use of such third-party licenses.

## 3.   Representations, Warranties and Covenants

(a)   <u>Authority</u>. Each Party represents to the other Party that:

(i)   It has the full corporate right, power and authority to execute, deliver and perform this Agreement and to consummate the transactions contemplated hereby:

(ii)   The execution, delivery and Performance of this Agreement and the consummation of the transactions contemplated hereby have been duly authorized by all necessary corporate action;

(iii)   This Agreement has been duly executed and delivered by an authorized officer, and is a legal, valid and binding obligation enforceable against it in accordance with its terms, except as enforcement may be limited by general principles of equity (regardless of whether such enforceability is considered in a proceeding at law or in equity) and the effect of applicable bankruptcy, insolvency, moratorium and other similar laws of general application relating to or affecting creditor's rights generally, including the effect of statutory or other laws regarding fraudulent conveyances and preferential transfers;

(iv)   The execution, delivery and performance of this Agreement shall not constitute a breach or default under any contract or agreement to which it is a party or by which it is bound or otherwise violate the rights of any third Person; and

(v)   No consent, approval or authorization of or from any governmental entity or any other Person not a party to this Agreement, whether prescribed by law, regulation, contract or agreement, is required for its execution, delivery and performance of this Agreement or consummation of the transactions contemplated hereby.

(b)     Intellectual Property. Owner represents and warrants that it has the authority to grant the license granted pursuant to this Agreement.

(c)     Third-Party Licenses and Payments. Licensee represents, warrants and covenants that it shall obtain, either directly or through Owner pursuant to Section 2(d), any third-party licenses required by this Agreement and pay any necessary royalties arising out of this Agreement, including, without limitation, any required performing rights royalties or other publishing royalties, to such third parties or to Owner if obtained pursuant to Section 2(d).

(d)     Most Favored Licensor

(i)     Other Content Agreement Terms. Licensee represents, warrants and covenants that the material terms granted to Owner under the Agreement, including, without limitation, advances, guaranteed minimum payments, performance license fees, reproduction license fees, links, programming rights, data, equity and most favored licensor provision, shall remain throughout the Term the most favorable material terms provided by Licensee in their entirety to any other Person licensing or otherwise providing Sound Recordings to Licensee. If Licensee licenses Sound Recordings from any other Person during the Term on material terms that are more favorable than the material terms granted to Owner hereunder, then Owner shall have the right to license Owner Sound Recordings to Licensee on the material terms granted by Licensee to such other Person.

(ii)     Notice to Owner of More Favorable Terms. If during the Term Licensee enters into a license agreement with any music or audio content company, including but not limited to Sony Music Entertainment, BMG Entertainment, EMI-Capital Music Group North America or Warner Music Group, regardless of whether Licensee believes those terms to more advantageous than the terms contained herein, Licensee shall give Notice to Owner within ten (10) days of the fact such an agreement has been entered into. Licensee shall include with such Notice a summary of the material terms of such agreement. Owner shall thereafter have forty-five (45) days within which to decide whether to accept or reject such terms.

(iii) Accounting. If Licensee fails to comply with any requirements of this Section 3(d), without prejudice to any other rights Owner may have, Owner shall be entitled to an accounting for purposes of calculating the amount of payments or other consideration to be paid to Owner, with interest.

(e) Express Warranties. THE EXPRESS WARRAN-TIES IN THIS AGREEMENT SHALL BE IN LLIEU OF ALL OTHER WARRANTIES, EXPRESS OR IMPLIED, INCLUDING THE IM-PLIED WARRANTEIS OF MERCHANTABILITY AND FITNESS FOR A PARTICULAR PURPOSE.

(f) Limitation of Liability.

(i) IN NO EVENT SHALL EITHER PARTY BE LIABLE FOR ANY INDIRECT, INCIDENTAL, CONSEQUENTIAL, OR SPECIAL DAMAGES.

(ii) IN NO EVENT SHALL EITHER PARTY BE LIABLE FOR ANY DAMAGES THAT EXCEED THE AMOUNTS PAID BY LICENSEE TO UNIVERSAL PURSUANT TO SECTION 2(c) OF THIS AGREEMENT, EXCEPT THAT THE LIMITATION ON DAMAGES SET FORTH IN THIS SECTION 3(f)(ii) SHALL NOT APPLY TO THE INDEMNITIES SET FORTH IN SECTION 9(a) OF EXHIBIT A OF THIS AGREEMENT.

4. Term and Termination

(a) Term. The term of the Agreement shall commence as of the Effective Date and shall terminate on June ____, 200__ (the "Term") unless terminated earlier pursuant to the terms hereof.

(b)    Termination Rights

    (i)    Either Party shall have the right, by Notice provided within sixty (60) days preceding the first Anniversary of the Effective Date, to terminate this Agreement as of the First Anniversary Date of this Agreement, without liability to the other Party, subject to any other rights that such Party may have under this Agreement.

    (ii)    Owner shall have the right, following thirty (30) days prior written notice and opportunity to cure, to terminate this Agreement prior to the end of the term, under any of the following conditions:

        a.    If Licensee fails to make timely payments of any sums due hereunder;

        b.    If Licensee fails to comply with Section 7 of Exhibit A;

        c.    If Licensee fails, in the event of a Security Incident, to remove or block access to all Owner Content, or to repair, update or improve security measures, or develop new security measures, as required by Section 7(f) of Exhibit A,

        d.    If Licensee is acquired or comes under the control of another entity during the Term; or

        e.    If Licensee breaches any material term or condition of this Agreement

    (c)    Content After Expiration or Termination. Upon the expiration of the Term, Licensee shall be required to delete or destroy by erasure, or other similar means, all copies of the Owner Content then licensed, and all Owner Content located on any servers or other computer or storage devices owned, leased or operated by or on behalf of Licensee dedicated to the Channels that Stream the Sound Recordings.

5.    Miscellaneous

(a)    Standard Terms and Conditions. The Standard Terms and Conditions set forth on Exhibit A hereto are incorporated herein by reference and hereby made a part of this Agreement.

(b)    Confidentiality. Each Party shall be required to keep the terms of this Agreement and the data provided pursuant to this Agreement confidential and shall not be permitted to disclose the terms contained in this Agreement to any person other than its employees, representatives and agents (who have a need to know) without the prior written consent of the other Party. Each Party shall take reasonable precautions, no less rigorous than those taken by such Party to prevent the unauthorized use or disclosure of similar information of its own, to prevent the unauthorized use or disclosure of such information.

(c)    Publicity. The parties shall cooperate to develop mutually acceptable public announcements of this Agreement. Notwithstanding the foregoing, neither Party shall, without the prior written approval of the other Party, (i) advertise or otherwise publicize, in a press release or otherwise, the existence or terms of this Agreement or any other aspect of the relationship between the Parties, or (ii) use the other Party's name or any trade name, trademark or service mark belonging to the other Party in press releases or in any form of advertising.

(d)    Severability. The provisions of the Agreement are severable, and the unenforceability of any provision of the Agreement shall not affect the enforceability of the remainder of the Agreement. The Parties acknowledge that it is their intention that if any provision of the Agreement is determined by a court to be unenforceable as drafted, that provision should be construed in a manner designed to effectuate the purpose of that provision to the greatest extent possible under applicable law. However, in the event such provision is considered an essential element of the Agreement, the Parties shall promptly negotiate a valid and enforceable replacement therefore, which so far as possible achieves the same economic and other benefits for the Parties as the severed provision was intended to achieve.

(e) <u>Headings</u>. The headings inserted in the Agreement are for convenience only and are not intended to affect the meaning or interpretation of the Agreement.

(f) <u>Construction</u>. Each Party's counsel has cooperated in the preparation of the Agreement. Accordingly, in any construction to be made of the Agreement, the same will not be construed against any Party on the basis that such Party was the drafter.

(g) <u>Notices</u>. All notices or other communications that are required or permitted hereunder shall be in writing ("<u>Notices</u>") and deemed to have been duly given at the time of receipt if delivered personally or via overnight express, or three (3) days after being mailed, registered or certified mail, postage prepaid, return receipt requested. Notices shall be addressed to the address for each Party listed in the introductory paragraph to this Agreement or to such other address as the Parties may designate from time to time in writing. Facsimile and electronic mail transmissions shall not constitute valid Notices hereunder (whether or not actually received).

(h) <u>No Third-Party Beneficiaries</u>. The Parties agree that the Agreement shall not be deemed or construed in any way to result in the creation of any rights or obligations in any Person not a Party to the Agreement, other than third Persons indemnified hereunder.

(i) <u>No Agency</u>. The Parties acknowledge that the employees of each Party are not employees or agents of the other Party. Nothing in the Agreement shall be construed as creating a partnership, joint venture, or agency relationship between the Parties, or as authorizing either Party to act as agent for the other.

(j) <u>Equitable Relief</u>. The Parties hereto agree that: (i) Licensee's rights to exercise and enforce the license rights herein granted, as well as Owner's rights to exercise and enforce the restrictions, limitations and qualifications imposed herein upon such license rights, are of a special, unique, extraordinary and intellectual character, giving them a peculiar value the loss of which by the Party entitled to such rights (the "<u>Rights holder</u>") (1) cannot be readily estimated, or adequately compensated for, in monetary damages and (2) would cause the Rightsholder substantial and irreparable harm for which it would not have an adequate remedy at law, and (ii) the Rightsholder accordingly will be entitled to obtain equitable relief against the other Party (including temporary restraining orders, preliminary and permanent injunctive relief, and specific Performance), in addition to all other remedies that the Rightsholder may have, to enforce the Agreement and protect its right hereunder. No Party hereto shall contest in any court or other judicial forum any of the matter stated in clause (i) above.

(k) <u>Choice of Law</u>. This Agreement and the rights and liabilities of the Parties shall be governed by and construed in accordance with the laws of the State of California.

\* \* \* \* \*

This Agreement is binding on the Parties immediately upon execution of Licensee and Owner. This Agreement may only be amended or modified by a written instrument signed by both Parties. This Agreement represents the entire agreement and understanding of the Parties and supersedes all prior or contemporaneous oral or written agreements or discussions by and between the Parties. Neither Party has entered into the Agreement in reliance upon a representation, warranty or undertaking of the other Party that is not set out or referred to in the Agreement.

LICENSEE                                    OWNER

By: _____      By: _____

Name: _____          Name: _____

Title: _____          Title: _____

## EXHIBIT A

## STANDARD TERMS AND CONDITIONS

1. Display requirements.

(a) Copyright Information. Licensee shall display on each Permitted Device during the Performance of each Owner Sound Recording the name of the artist, the name of the Sound Recording and the name of the album in an easily legible manner and type font no smaller than that provided to any other Person that licenses Sound Recordings to Licensee.

(b) Album Cover Artwork. Licensee shall be required to use commercially reasonable efforts to develop expeditiously the ability to display, and thereafter to display, on each Permitted Device during the Performance of each Owner Sound Recording, the front album cover artwork for the release of such Owner Sound Recording.

2. Links. Licensee shall, at the option of Owner, provide two (2) reasonably prominent "above the fold" direct links from the place on the Web Site where information regarding a particular recording artist or Sound Recording is available, which links shall be no more than one click from the Licensee's player. One link may be to an artist's area on a genre site, at Owner's sole discretion, provided that such link is not a direct link to an on-line music retailer. The second link shall be to a web site designated by Owner. All links shall be in an easily legible manner and in the same size and prominence as any other links provided to any third parties on the Web Site.

3. License Limitations

(a) Web Site. Streaming under the Agreement shall be permitted only through the Web Site. Licensee shall not be permitted to allow any other web sites, whether owned by Licensee or not, to access that portion of the Web Site consisting of the Channels, and no syndication of the Channels to, or other use of the Owner Content by, other web sites shall be permitted hereunder. The Web Site shall comply with all requirements set forth in the Agreement.

(b) Territorial Limitation; Territorial and Contractual Restrictions. The license granted in Section 1 of the Agreement shall be limited to the United States, its territories, commonwealths and possessions (the "Licensed Territory"). All servers storing any Owner Content shall be located solely in the Licensed Territory. Licensee shall not be permitted to market or promote outside the Licensed Territory the availability of Owner Content on the Channels. Licensee shall comply with the requirements of this Agreement to seek to ensure that all End Users of the Web Site are located within the Territory, which shall include, without limitation, the use of a reverse domain lookup with respect to End Users accessing Owner Content and the denial of access to those End Users whose domains are known to be external to the Licensed Territory by virtue of a two-letter country suffix on the domain name. Notwithstanding anything in the Agreement to the contrary: Licensee's rights hereunder are subject to all restrictions applicable to Owner or its affiliates with regard to any Owner Sound Recording, including, but not limited to, territorial and contractual restrictions.

(c) No Modification. Licensee shall not edit, modify, defeat, impair, alter or prepare any derivative work from any Owner Sound Recording (other than as minimally necessary to exercise its rights hereunder), or any copyright protection technology or mechanism embedded in or associated with a Owner Sound Recording.

(d) No Unauthorized Use; Advertising Restrictions. Licensee shall not (i) use any Owner Sound Recording in any manner that Owner, in its sole discretion, finds offensive or injurious to its interests or the interests of any affiliate or artist(s) or (ii) use any Owner Sound Recording for any on-line or off-line original programming, product tie-ins or marketing campaigns of any type or nature, including games or contests. Licensee shall not display on any web page or Permitted Device that contains any Owner Content, or otherwise in any manner associate any Owner Artists or Owner Content with, (i) any advertising of any Person that is in the business of copying, distributing, facilitating or enabling the copying or distribution of copyright material without authorization (excluding SDMI compliant devices) or (ii) products or services for alcohol, tobacco, gambling, pornography, firearms or any other product or service that is objectionable in the reasonable judgement of Owner (including, without limitation, any links to objectionable web sites).

(e) Restrictions on Use of Name and Likeness. Licensee shall not use the name or likeness of any artist or artists in any television, radio, print or other off-line advertising medium or on-line or electronic advertising, without the prior written consent of Owner in each case (as determined in its sole discretion for each such use). In no event shall

Licensee have the right to use the name of any artist other than in the manner provided in Section 1 of this Exhibit A.

(f) Owner Intellectual Property. Owner shall be the sole and exclusive owner of the Owner Content and all intellectual properties and rights related thereto. Without limiting the generality of the foregoing, the Agreement does not grant to Licensee (i) any copyright ownership interest in any Owner Content; (ii) any rights outside the Licensed Territory; or (iii) any rights to any endorsement by Owner or any other Person. Licensee shall not attempt, represent, or purport to transfer to any Person any rights of ownership in or to any of the Owner Content.

(g) Copyright Clearances. Licensee shall be solely responsible for obtaining any licenses that may be required with respect to musical works embodied in the Sound Recordings, including, for example, licenses from music publishers, performing rights societies or any mechanical licenses. Licensee may obtain such licenses directly from such third parties, or through Owner if Owner offers such licenses to Licensee pursuant to Section 2(d) of the Agreement.

(h) No Further Licensing or Obligation. Except for the licenses granted by Owner to Licensee in Section 1 of the Agreement, no further licenses or sublicenses are granted to Licensee in or under the Agreement, either by implication or estoppel. To the extent that Licensee chooses to acquire copies or phonorecords of Owner Content for use on the Web Site, it shall acquire such copies or phonorecords through lawful channels and at its sole expense.

(i) Permitted Devices. Owner Content shall be accessible to End Users only through the Internet and only by use of those products commonly known as of the date of the Agreement as personal computers and dedicated Internet appliances that function in a manner similar to personal computers, even if an End User of such computer or appliance accesses the Internet through a wireless modem or other wireless connectivity; provided that such access: (i) provides for full screen visual presentation of the name of the Sound Recording, the relevant recording artist, the title of the album, and any other requirements of the Agreement; and (ii) is an open Internet service accessed and accessible publicly (i.e., by any person who has access to the Internet) through a general purpose web browser that is capable of accessing substantially all other Internet services; and (iii) otherwise complies with the terms and conditions of the Agreement ("Permitted Devices"). By way of example, access to Owner Content by End Users of the Web Site shall not be permitted on those products commonly known as (i) telephones, cellular telephones and similar devices, and (ii) personal digital assistants or like devices (e.g., Palm Pilots and similar hand-held devices), unless and until such

products comply with the requirements of the preceding sentence.

(j) No Downloads. Licensee shall not operate the Web Site or make any Performances in a manner that would permit an End User to download to any storage medium (except a temporary buffer) all or any portion of a Owner Sound Recording.

(k) Co-Branding. Licensee shall not be permitted to enter into arrangements with any other Person for the Performance or display of Owner Content through a third-party web site without the prior written approval of Owner.

(l) No Business-to-Business Streaming Services. Licensee shall be permitted to make Performances of Owner Sound Recordings only directly to individual consumers (i.e., natural persons who listen to Performances for their own personal use for entertainment purposes and not for resale, redistribution, syndication, use in providing goods or services, or distribution or retransmission of Performances to any other Person) and not to business customers.

4. Data Reporting. Licensee shall provide Owner with the information set forth below in an electronic spreadsheet, comma delimited format that complies with other specifications provided by Owner. No personally identifiable information for any End User shall be provided to Owner unless the End User has "opted in" to provide such information to Owner. Licensee and Owner shall develop mutually acceptable language for the purpose of allowing End Users to opt in to providing such personally identifiable information to Owner. End Users shall later be enabled to opt-out of providing such information. The following information shall be provided to Owner by Licensee no less frequently than monthly in an electronic format:

(a) By artist and by Sound Recording, with respect to Owner Sound Recordings, the number of Performances of Owner Sound Recordings;

(b) By artist and by Sound Recording, the number of sales of Owner Sound Recordings;

(c) Total number of Performances of Owner Sound Recordings and the aggregate amount of time for such Performances;

(d) Total number of Performances of each Owner Sound Recording identified by Sound Recording title, artist name and album title, and the aggregate amount of elapsed time of Performances by Sound Recording;

(e) Total aggregate number of Performances of all Sound Recordings, including Owner Sound

Recordings, and the aggregate amount of time for such Sound Recordings;

(f) A list of the top one hundred (100) Owner Artists with respect to whom End Users have requested Performances of Sound Recordings for each week, by aggregate number of such Sound Recordings Performed, and for each such top one hundred (100) Owner Artist, a list of the ten (10) Owner Artists, that were most frequently Performed for End Users who requested Performances by such top one hundred (100) Owner Artist. For example, if Shania Twain was the Owner Artist with Sound Recordings most frequently Performed during the first week of July, Licensee would provide a list of the ten (10) artists whose Sound Recordings were most frequently Performed for those End Users who had requested Peformances of Shania Twain's Sound Recordings during such week, measured by the aggregate number of Performances per artist;

(g) List of top twenty-five (25) Sound Recordings (regardless of label) Performed;

(h) Total number of End Users who have received a Performance of a Owner Sound Recording during the preceding sixty (60) days;

(i) The average number of hours of listening per End User per week;

(j) On a End User by End User basis, information on the web site from which an End User comes to the Web Site and information on the web site an End User goes to when the End User leaves the Web Site;

(k) To the extent Licensee collects such information, all demographic data on End Users of the Web Site on a masked, non-personally identifying, End-User-by-End User basis, including data on age (e.g., date ranges 12-13, 14-18, 19-25, etc.), sex, race, location of listening usage, city of listening experience, income level, employment, education, etc.;

(l) The maximum number of simultaneous Performances; and

(m) Such additional data as Owner shall require Licensee to collect and provide to Owner as the Parties agree is appropriate.

5. Payment Procedure and Late Payments

(a) Payment Procedure. Unless otherwise specified in the Agreement, all payments payable by Licensee hereunder shall be paid to Owner within thirty (30) days after the end of each Accounting Period (or partial Accounting Period in the event of an early termination or expiration before the calendar close of such Accounting Period) of the Term, either in Dollars by wire transfer (with twenty-four (24) hours advance Notice from Licensee of each such wire transfer) or by such other method agreed upon by the Parties, to such bank account or accounts as Owner shall designate in writing within a reasonable period of time prior to such due date, but in any event not less than five (5) business days. Any payments received by Owner shall be applied first to any late charges and, thereafter, to any unpaid license fees.

(b) Late Payments. Licensee shall pay a finance charge of one and one-half percent (1½%) per month, or the maximum rate permitted by law, whichever is less, from the date that any payment was first due under the Agreement until the date such payment is made. Licensee agrees to pay all reasonable collection costs, including without limitation court costs, attorneys' fees an costs incurred in litigation or collection of any judgments, associated with any unpaid monies due to Owner hereunder.

6. Reporting, Payments and Auditing

(a) Record Keeping. Licensee shall keep full, true and accurate books of account, in accordance with GAAP, containing all particulars and reasonable supporting documentation that may be necessary for the purpose of determining the license fees to be paid under the Agreement and Licensee's compliance in other respects with its obligations under the Agreement, including but not limited to all data used and/or relevant in calculating Gross Revenues pursuant to Section 14(i) of this Exhibit A (as set forth in greater detail in Section 6(b) below).

(b) Reporting. Within thirty (30) days after the end of each Accounting Period of the Term, or at such other times as may be applicable under the Agreement, Licensee shall render reasonably detailed accountings to Owner. Each such accounting statement shall include a reasonably detailed presentation of the computation of the following for the immediately preceding Accounting Period: (i) Licensee's Gross Revenues; (ii) aggregate number of Owner Performances, including the aggregate number of Owner Performances that were more than five (5) minutes in duration and the number of minutes or fractions thereof performed longer than five (5) minutes for such Owner Performances; (iii) with respect to each Owner Performance, the following information for the Sound Recording performed: (1) the UPC or catalog number of the album; (2) the name of the artist; (3) the International Standard Recording Code ("ISRC") code number, the track title or number; and (4) the side number of the track; (iv) aggregate number of all Performances (including Owner Performances); (v) an explanation in reasonable detail of how Licensee calculated the Owner Proportionate Share; (vi) certification by an authorized officer of Licensee that Licensee is in compliance with the procedures set forth in Section 7 of this Exhibit A; and (vii) such other matters as Owner may reasonably request and the Parties mutually agree is appropriate for Licensee to provide to Owner. With each such accounting statement, Licensee shall deliver the payment, if any, owing to Owner for such Accounting Period, in a manner consistent with Section 5 of this Exhibit A.

(c)  Audit Rights. Owner shall have the right to examine Licensee's books and records, including all electronic records and data, for the purpose of auditing Licensee's compliance with its obligations hereunder, for a period of up to three (3) years after the end of the Term (with Owner being required to file a notice of intention to audit prior to the end of such three (3) year period) and no more than once per calendar year. Owner shall give Licensee thirty (30) days prior notice of its intention to conduct an examination. Licensee agrees to furnish all pertinent books and records, including electronic records and data, to Owner's authorized representatives, during customary business hours; provided that Licensee data may be reviewed only by an authorized third party auditor, unless Licensee can identify a conflict of interest or some other material fact that would disqualify such auditor (in which case Owner shall be entitled to appoint a different independent auditor); and provided, further, that such third party auditor shall not be permitted to disclose to Owner such data beyond that which is necessary to report to Owner the results of the audit or to permit Owner to enforce its rights pursuant to the Agreement. Such books and records shall be kept by Licensee in accordance with GAAP and shall be retained for at least three (3) years following the end of the Term. Expenses incurred by Owner for any examination conducted by Owner under this Section 6(c) shall be paid by Owner, unless such examination results in a determination that (i) Licensee's actual payments for the period examined were more than five percent (5%) below the payments as required under the Agreement, or (ii) that Licensee was not otherwise in substantial compliance with the requirements of the Agreement, in which case Licensee shall pay for the costs of the audit. The exercise by Owner of any rights under this Section 6(c) shall not prejudice any other rights or remedies of Owner, including any other rights of Owner to dispute any amounts owed to Owner under the Agreement.

7.  Technical Specifications and Security Specifications.

(a)  Format. In accordance with this Section 7 of this Exhibit A, Licensee shall use a secure streaming format that does not allow copying or saving, with such format subject to Owner's prior written approval, and such format remaining current with commonly accepted industry standards.

(b)  Technical Specifications and Security. Licensee shall implement one or more formats consistent with the Security Specifications and cease using formats that are inconsistent with the Security Specifications, for all streams that include Performances licensed hereunder, within six (6) months after Owner gives written notice to Licensee of:

(i)      security specifications for a secure streaming format for the performance of Sound Recordings over the Internet developed by Owner in its reasonable discretion;

(ii)     security specifications that have been developed pursuant to a consensus of copyright owners and technology companies in an open, fair, voluntary, multi-industry standards process; or

(iii)    security specifications that have been implemented through a consensus or bilateral agreements, among or between copyright owners and technology companies, as updated from time to time.

(c)  Policies And Procedures for Restricting Access To The Web Site To Only Users Within The Territory

(i)      Licensee shall perform the following procedures:

A.   Upon any End User logging on to the Web Site, Licensee shall perform a reverse domain lookup using the End User's IP address;

B.   If the reverse domain lookup yields a domain name with a two-character country code as its primary identifier and the two-character country code is a ".us," then the End User shall be designated as "DOMESTIC" and shall, subject to the terms of this Agreement, be given access to the Web Site and to the transmission of Owner Sound Recordings;

C.   If the reverse domain lookup yields a domain name with a two-character country code as its primary identifier and the two-character country code is not a ".us," then the End User is designated as "FOREIGN" and shall not be given access to transmissions of Owner Sound Recordings; and

D.   If the reverse domain lookup yields no country code or results in a primary identifier that does not identify a particular country from which such End User has accessed the Web Site (e.g., ".com" or ".edu"), then such End User shall be designated as "UNKNOWN." Such End Users shall be given access to the Web Site and to transmissions or Owner Sound Recordings, but only subject to Section 7(c)(ii) below.

(ii) Within three (3) months after the Effective Date, Licensee shall implement an external solution utilizing an IP Address Block Database which supplies location information for such IP addresses designated at "UNKNOWN." The solution ultimately chosen must identify the location of at least eighty-five percent (85%) of such otherwise UNKNOWN End Users. With respect to End Users identified through the method set forth in this Section 7(c) as emanating outside of the United States, Licensee shall designate such End Users as "FOREIGN" and shall not give such End Users access to transmissions of Owner Sound Recordings. In the event that in any thirty (30) day period such solution identifies the location of less than eighty-five percent (85%) of otherwise UNKNOWN End Users, Licensee shall immediately modify or replace such solution so that Licensee remains in compliance with this Section 7(c)(ii).

(iii) In the event that, through any other means not identified above, Owner is able to determine that a particular UNKNOWN End User is accessing the Web Site from a location outside of the United States, Licensee shall designate such End User as "FOREIGN" and shall not give such End User access to transmissions of Owner Sound Recordings.

(d) Policies And Procedures For Handling "Hacking" Of The Web Site And Potential Theft Of Owner Sound Recordings

(i) Licensee shall protect all Owner Content with security methods standard in the industry for protection of high-value, confidential material. The security methods must be designed to prevent all unauthorized access to Owner Content as stored on Licensee's servers. Licensee shall actively and regularly monitor the effectiveness of such security measures.

(ii) Licensee shall provide a description of security methods and security monitoring procedures for Owner Content upon request by Owner.

(iii) If Licensee becomes aware of a breach of Licensee's internal network security, Licensee shall take immediately all measures necessary in order to prevent unauthorized access to Owner Content.

(iv) Licensee shall "lock-out" any individual as soon as possible after its discovering such End User's "hacking." Any End User account for the individual shall immediately be denied access to Owner Content. If the individual is traceable to a specific IP address, Licensee shall prevent any End User from accessing Owner Content using such IP address.

(v) If possible, Licensee shall identify such individual(s) responsible for such "hacking," and shall undertake all steps necessary to pursue prosecution of such individual(s) or to support Owner in its efforts in this respect.

(vi) Licensee shall report all "hacking" incidents that expose Owner Content to unauthorized access within ten (10) days of such "hacking" incident.

(e) Policies And Procedures For Implementing Safeguards In Response To The Availability Of "Bit-Pirating" (Bit Stream Capture) Software.

(i) Unless otherwise approved in writing by Owner, Licensee shall transmit Owner Sound Recordings only using the following streaming formats: Real Networks, Microsoft Windows Media and Apple QuickTime ("Approved Streaming Formats").

(ii) Licensee shall obtain and install all security patches and upgrades available for Approved Streaming Format server software with ten (10) days of availability.

(iii) If either Owner or Licensee becomes aware that any "bit-pirating" or "hack" software, hardware, or any combination thereof (i.e., software that allows for the capture of digital audio transmissions of sound recordings) ("Hack Tool"), or any method or procedure by which End Users are able to obtain unauthorized access to, or make copies of, Owner Content ("Hack Methods"), becomes available or used for an Approved Streaming Format, such Party shall immediately notify the other Party. Upon learning of the availability of such Hack Tools or Hack Methods, Licensee shall immediately notify the company that developed the streaming format in order to work with such company to obtain a patch or upgrade that will defeat the Hack Tools and Hack Methods, and prevent the capture of digital audio transmissions through such streaming format.

(iv) If Licensee fails to take all necessary steps to prevent unauthorized access to or copying of Owner Content, including without limitation, by obtaining and installing a patch or upgrade as referenced in Section 7(e)(ii) of this Exhibit A, then within ten (10) days of learning of the existence of such Hack Tools or Hack Methods,

Licensee shall, upon Owner's request, immediately discontinue using such Approved Streaming Format for the transmission of Owner Sound Recordings until such time as it has successfully taken all such steps necessary to prevent such unauthorized access to, or copying of, Owner Content.

(f) Security Incidents. If either Owner or Licensee discovers that Licensee's Web Site is not complying with any requirements set forth in this Section 7 of this Exhibit A or that any security measures enacted by Licensee have been breached, including, without limitation, instances where End Users as a result of such breach can download a separate, complete and usable copy of Sound Recordings by capturing such Sound Recordings in digital format as performed by Licensee to any storage device in violation of the Agreement (a "Security Incident") and Licensee either (i) has actual knowledge of such breach or (ii) receives Notice of such breach from Owner, then Licensee shall be required to remove promptly all Owner Content from the Web Site involved in the Security Incident, but in no event later than three (3) business days after acquiring such actual knowledge or Notice. Notwithstanding the foregoing, in the event Licensee reasonably determines that the relevant security measure can be repaired, updated or improved such that similar Security Incidents are unlikely to occur in the future and such repair, update or improvement can be made, and is in fact made, within five (5) business days, then Licensee shall not be required to so remove Owner Content. If Licensee removes Owner Content as required by this Section 7(f), then Licensee shall thereafter have ninety (90) days within which to develop new security measures to prevent Security Incidents, subject to Owner's approval of such measures. If Licensee fails to remove Owner Content from the Web Site(s) as required by this Section 7(f), then such failure shall be deemed a material breach of the Agreement. If Licensee develops security measures that are approved by Owner, then Licensee shall be permitted to make Owner Content available on the Web Site(s) and the Term shall be extended by the number of days during such ninety (90)-day period when the Owner Content was removed from such the Web Site(s).

(g) Audio Quality. Licensee shall be permitted to deliver streams at a bit rate not greater than one hundred twenty-eight (128) Kilobits per second.

8. Takedown Rights. Owner shall have the right, with respect to any Owner Sound Recording, to have Licensee remove such Sound Recording from the Web Site as soon as possible, but in no event later than five (5) days after Owner's requesting such removal; provided, however, that over the Term. Owner shall not exercise such termination right in a manner that otherwise would defeat or frustrate the license granted to Licensee under the Agreement.

9. Indemnification

(a) Indemnification. Licensee shall defend, indemnify and hold harmless Owner, its Affiliates, and their respective directors, officers, agents, employees, shareholders, partners and independent contractors from and against all claims, liabilities, suits, losses, damages and expenses, including (without limitation) costs and reasonable fees of attorneys and other professionals (collectively, "Claims") relating to or resulting from (i) any actual or alleged infringement of any copyright (excluding the Owner Sound Recording copyright of any Person), patent, trade secret, or other proprietary right of any Person by the Web Site or the components and operations thereof; (ii) Licensee's failure to comply with all laws and regulations applicable to the operation of the Web Site, including, without limitation, the collection, use and distribution of any End User data by Licensee; (iii) Licensee's failure to make any third party payments relating to the use of musical works embodied in the Owner Sound Recordings; (iv) any Claims brought or asserted by any Person arising out of or in connection with any use of the Owner Content by Licensee that is not authorized by the Agreement; and/or (v) the breach of any representation, warranty or covenant hereunder. Licensee shall take no legal action or any other measures to protect the Owner Content without first obtaining Owner's prior written approval.

(b) Indemnification Procedures. In connection with any claim or action described in this Section 9, Owner (i) shall give Licensee prompt written notice of the claim (provided, however, that failure to provide such notice shall not relieve Licensee from its liability or obligation hereunder, except to the extent of any material prejudice as a direct result of such failure), (ii) shall cooperate with Licensee (at Licensee's expense) in connection with the defense and settlement of the claim, and (iii) shall permit Licensee to control the defense and settlement of the claim, provided that Licensee may not settle the claim without Owner's prior written consent (which shall not be unreasonably withheld or delayed) in the event such settlement places any liability or obligation on the indemnified Party. Further, Owner (at its cost) may participate in the defense of the claim through counsel of its own choosing.

10. Prohibition Against Assignment. Neither Party shall assign the license or any other rights granted, or obligations undertaken, herein without the other Party's prior written consent; provided, however, that Owner may assign its rights and obligations herein to any Owner affiliate.

11. Expenses. Except as otherwise provided in Section 6(c) of this Exhibit A, each Party shall pay all of its own expenses, including attorney's fees incurred

in connection with the negotiation of the Agreement, and the performance of its obligations hereunder.

12.  Rights Cumulative.  Except as expressly provided in Section 3 of the Agreement, the rights and remedies provided herein and all other rights and remedies available at law or in equity are, to the extent permitted by law, cumulative and not exclusive of any other right or remedy now or hereafter available at law or in equity.  Neither asserting a right nor employing a remedy shall preclude the concurrent assertion of any other right or employment of any other remedy.

13.  No Waiver of Rights.  No failure or delay on the part of any Party in the exercise of any power or right hereunder shall operate as a waiver thereof.  No single or partial exercise of any right or power hereunder shall operate as a waiver of such right or of any other right or power.  The waiver by any Party of a breach of any provision of the Agreement shall not operate or be construed as a waiver of any other or subsequent breach hereunder.

14.  Definitions

(a)  "Accounting Period" means each three month period commencing on each of January 1, April 1, July 1, and October 1 of each calendar year.

(b)  "Agreement" has the meaning set forth in the preamble.

(c)  "Approved Streaming Formats" has the meaning set forth in Section 7(e)(i) of this Exhibit A.

(d)  "Channel" means a single stream of music digitally transmitted to End Users.

(e)  "Claims" has the meaning set forth in Section 9(a) of this Exhibit A.

(f)  "Effective Date" has the meaning set forth in the preamble.

(g)  "End User" means a Person who accesses or receives Streaming Performances or who accesses the Web Site.

(h)  "GAAP" means Generally Accepted Accounting Principles.

(i)  "Gross Revenues" means all revenues, including but not limited to, all monies actually received, and all payments made to, Licensee, or as authorized by Licensee, its employees, representatives, agents or any other person acting on Licensee's behalf, and all monies actually received on behalf of, and payments made to, any person, company, firm or corporation under the same or substantially the same ownership, management or control as Licensee, from:

(i)  advertising of all kinds (including, without limitation, audio and visual advertising, sponsor "hot links" and the provision of time or space on the Web Site to any other person) excluding only payments by Sound Recording copyright owners for the promotion or licensing of phonorecords or recording artists, and net of advertising agency commissions actually paid to recognized advertising agencies unrelated to Licensee (but the allowance for commissions shall not exceed fifteen percent (15%);

(ii)  net sales of products and services sold directly by Licensee, or any entity that Licensee controls, in a transaction originating on pages of the Web Site providing Streaming Service excluding sales of phonorecords and CDs and computed as follows: all amounts paid by customers, minus either (A) the wholesale price of the products and services of unrelated third Persons or (B) the direct cost of Licensee's own products and services, and minus (C) returns, sales and use taxes, shipping, bad debts, credit card and other service fees paid to unrelated third Persons;

(iii)  access to or use of the Web Site, or portions thereof, including, without limitation, online and other connection charges, subscriptions; payments from Internet service providers, and on-line franchises (to the extent permitted by this Agreement); and transaction charges and commissions; and excluding only payments by Sound Recording copyright owners for the promotion or licensing of phonorecords or recording artists;

(iv)  End Users for access to, use of, or upgrades to Licensee's proprietary software used for access to the Web Site or Performances of Owner Sound Recordings, or to download products, services or content (to the extent permitted by this Agreement and applicable law), other than general purpose software primarily used for purposes other than receiving Performances of Owner Sound Recordings from the Web Site;

(v)  e-commerce bounties or click-through royalties, or referral or affiliate program fees; and

(vi)  bad debts (whether or not recovered) related to amounts due under clauses (i)-(v).

For purposes of determining any non-cash component of Gross Revenues, such non-cash consideration shall be accounted for based on the fair market value of any goods, services or other real, personal, tangible or intangible property received (except as otherwise determined consistent with GAAP).

(j)  "Hack Methods" has the meaning set forth in Section 7(e)(iii) of this Exhibit A.

(k) "Hack Tool" has the meaning set forth in Section 7(e)(iii) of this Exhibit A.

(l) "IP" means Internet Protocol.

(m) "ISRC" has the meaning set forth in Section 6(b) of this Exhibit A.

(n) "Licensed Genre" has the meaning set forth in Section 1 of Exhibit C.

(o) "Licensed Territory" has the meaning set forth in Section 3(b) of this Exhibit A.

(p) "Licensee" has the meaning set forth in the preamble.

(q) "Notice" has the meaning set forth in Section 5(g) of the Agreement.

(r) "Party" and "Parties" have the meaning set forth in the preamble.

(s) "Performance" means each instance in which all or any portion of a Sound Recording is publicly performed by means of a digital audio transmission from the Web Site to an End User (e.g., the transmission of any portion of a Sound Recording to an End User's Permitted Device).

(t) "Permitted Devices" has the meaning set forth in Section 3(i) of this Exhibit A.

(u) "Person" means a natural person, a corporation, a limited liability company, a partnership, a trust, a joint venture, any governmental authority or any other entity or organization.

(v) "Reproduction" means each phonorecord of a Owner Sound Recording made by or for Licensee, whether made for central or regional servers, for streaming in varying bit rates or formats, or for other purposes.

(w) "Rightsholder" has the meaning set forth in Section 5 of this Agreement.

(x) "Security Incident" has the meaning set forth in Section 7(f) of this Exhibit A.

(y) "Security Specifications" means the security specifications with respect to which Owner gives Licensee notice pursuant to Section 7(b) of Exhibit A.

(z) "Sound Recording" has the meaning set forth in 17 U.S.C. § 101; provided that each track or portion thereof embodied on a CD, album, LP or similar product shall constitute a "Sound Recording" for purposes of this Agreement.

(aa) "Streaming" a Sound Recording shall mean to perform publicly the Sound Recording, from servers owned or controlled by Licensee, by means of an Internet transmission that is substantially contemporaneous with the audible rendering of the Sound Recording on an End User's personal computer, using a technology that is not designed to result in a reproduction of the Sound Recording on such End User's personal computer or any other device that would be usable without a simultaneous, active connection to the digital transmission source or after the cessation of the transmission, other than a transitory reproduction required to render such contemporaneous performance (e.g., a data buffer).

(bb) "Streaming Service" means a Streaming service operated by Licensee.

(cc) "Term" has the meaning set forth in Section 4(a) of the Agreement.

(dd) "Owner" has the meaning set forth in the preamble.

(ee) "Owner Artist" means the featured individual or band performing a Owner Sound Recording.

(ff) "Owner Content" means the Owner Sound Recordings and the front-cover album artwork for the current release of such Sound Recordings.

(gg) "Owner Performance" means a Performance of a Owner Sound Recording.

(hh) "Owner's Proportionate Share" means the fraction where (a) the numerator is the number of Owner Performances during the relevant Accounting Period and (b) the denominator is the number of Performances of all Sound Recordings (including Owner Sound Recordings) during the relevant Accounting Period.

(ii) "Owner Sound Recording" means any Sound Recording embodied on any of the albums listed on Exhibit C hereto, as amended from time to time, that (a) has been distributed or transmitted to the public by any Person in the Licensed Territory by or with the authorization of Owner or an Affiliate of Owner and (b) Owner or any Affiliate of Owner during the Term has the right to license the public performance thereof within the Licensed Territory.

(jj) "Web Site" means the site located on the World Wide Web at www.laugh.com with the Uniform Resource Locator of http://www.laugh.com or any successor web sites.

## EXHIBIT B

## DESCRIPTION OF STREAMING SERVICE

EXHIBIT C

LICENSED CONTENT

1.    General

(a)    Licensed Genre. Owner Sound Recording shall include Sound Recordings embodied on certain _____ albums (the "Licensed Genre") in the Owner catalog. A tentative list of such albums, subject to change at any time in accordance with the provisions of Section 1(b) of this Exhibit C, is set forth below.

(b)    Modification of List of Albums. Owner may in its discretion make substitutions for or remove any of the albums listed below at any time, upon Notice to Licensee, for any reason or for no reason.

(c)    Limitations

(i)    Owner Sound Recording shall not include (x) any albums that have been released within the previous two (2) years or (y) any soundtracks, compilations or greatest hits albums.

(ii)    Owner Sound Recordings shall at not time include more than one-hundred (100) albums within the Licensed Genre.

(iii)    In the event that Owner determines, in its sole discretion, that any of the albums listed below are within the categories listed in paragraph (x) or (y) of Section 1(c)(i) of this Exhibit C or that the limitation set forth in Section 1(c)(ii) of this Exhibit C has been exceeded, Owner may immediately remove from the list below any albums in order to comply with the limitations of this Section 1(c) of this Exhibit C without any liability to Licensee whatsoever.

(d)    Owner Takedown Rights

(i)    Pursuant to Owner's Takedown Rights set forth in Section 8 of Exhibit A (Standard Terms and Conditions), if over the Term, Owner requires the removal, without substitution, or more than fifty percent (50%) of Owner Sound Recordings (in the aggregate), more than 50% of the Owner Sound Recordings are not available for a period greater than thirty (30) business days, then Owner shall return to Licensee a *pro rata* portion, of Owner Sound Recordings (in the aggregate), of the advance paid to Owner by Licensee pursuant to Section 2(c) of the Agreement.

(ii)    In the event that Owner request that Licensee remove any or all of the Owner Sound Recordings (A) due to Licensee's failure to comply with any of the terms of this Agreement, including but not limited to Section 1 of Exhibit A (Standard Terms and Conditions), or (B) if the audio quality of the streams in the reasonable opinion of Owner, is not comparable to streams provided by Owner-approved vendors, then Owner shall not be obligated to return any advance or other monies to Licensee as contemplated in Section 1(d)(i) of this Exhibit C.

2.    Licensee Acknowledgement. Licensee understands and acknowledges that Owner may not be able to obtain permission from record labels to license hereunder particular Sound Recordings for reasons related to particular artists, promotions, or for other reasons.

3.    Addition of Albums. The Parties may mutually agree to add albums to the list below at a later date, at which time the Parties agree to negotiate in good faith an appropriate advance fee to be paid to Owner by Licensee as consideration for the additional albums. Nothing in the preceding sentence shall be interpreted as requiring Owner to add albums to the list below.

# FORM 23-5

### SUBMISSION OF MUSICAL RECORDINGS
### FOR PUBLICATION ON WEB SITE FOR UNSIGNED BANDS

## IUMA Music Submission Agreement
## In Plain English

Thank you for getting this far. Now, get ready to join the most effective music distribution network on the planet. We appreciate your trust in us, and, in the following document, we hope to demonstrate our reputation for integrity in dealing with new artists like yourself.

By completing the form and clicking on the "I AGREE" button below, you and IUMA will be entering into the following Agreement.

The most important thing to remember about this is that YOU CAN TERMINATE THIS AGREEMENT AT ANY TIME. In other words, if you want out, you're out—completely. Upon termination, we will retain no rights to your content. No kidding. Just send us an email and give us a few days to remove your uploaded materials. The idea here is to promote your career, not restrict it.

And if we are successful together in promoting your career, congratulations and good luck. You will owe us nothing but your goodwill and thanks. Just remember to send us some free concert tickets – front row, please.

Some Definitions

The reference to "you" in this Agreement shall mean you (duh), and if you are in a group, then it means each member of the group or the group as a whole. The same goes for "your" and "yours."

IUMA means IUMA, Emusic, and their successors, assigns, agents, distributors, dealers, and licensees.

"Artist Content" means (i) sound recordings and/or audiovisual works of your vocal and/or instrumental performances, (ii) the musical works (i.e., songs, lyrics) embodied in those recordings and works, and (iii) your name(s), trademarks, tradenames, likenesses, photographs, biographical materials, artwork, liner notes, and other graphical or textual material that you upload to IUMA.

"Artist Merchandise" means (i) phonorecords (e.g., CDs and cassette tapes), videotapes and other forms of content storage, which embody Artist Content or other works, created by you or IUMA, and (ii) other forms of merchandise (such as t-shirts) sent to IUMA for sale on IUMA.

"Digital Phonorecord Delivery" is a strange term, but its used in the U.S. Copyright law, and in this agreement, to mean each individual delivery of a phonorecord by digital transmission of a sound recording which results in a specifically identifiable reproduction by or for any transmission recipient of a phonorecord of that sound recording by any means now known or hereafter devised. This is just the complete legal way of describing a digital download of a recording in the form of, for example, an MP3 file.

"Digital Streaming Transmission" is a digital transmission of a sound recording where a copy of the recording is not made by or for the transmission recipient, as, for example, a webcast.

"Custom Compilations" shall mean the reproduction of one or more of the Artist Content onto to recordable media and the physical distribution of such media in fulfillment of a customer order for a custom compilation of recordings.

For the definitions of "sound recording," "audiovisual work," and other useful definitions of words and phrases used in this

agreement, please visit the U.S. Copyright Law link to http://
lcweb.loc.gov/copyright/ or look it up in your Funk & Wagnals.

Grant of License

This section of the agreement is divided into four parts. The first
concerns your providing IUMA with permission to post your Artist Content on the IUMA website. The second concerns other
services, such as the fulfillment by IUMA of orders for Artist
Merchandise, such as physical CDs or t-shirts. The third concerns the use of your name, trade name, trademark, photograph, likeness, biography and other material for the purpose
of promoting your Artist Content and Artist Merchandise. The
fourth makes it clear that you remain the owner of anything you
submit to IUMA, including the copyright in the Artist Content;
all you are providing to IUMA is permission to do certain things,
and that permission may be revoked by you at any time as
specified below under "termination."

1.    Artist Content

You hereby grant to IUMA permission, on a non-exclusive basis,
throughout the universe, to do the following things:

(a)    to prepare and encode Artist Content, or any portion
thereof (including 30-second sound clips), for Digital Transmission, and the making of Digital Phonorecord Deliveries, in any
format (e.g., Real Audio, MP3, etc.), and by any means, now
known or hereafter devised,

(b)    to display, copy, reproduce (and to mechanically reproduce each musical composition included in the Artist Content),
exhibit, publicly perform, broadcast, rebroadcast, transmit, retransmit, distribute through any electronic means (including analog and digital), including Digital Streaming Transmission and
Digital Phonorecord Delivery, electronically publish and synchronize with visual images any or all of the Artist Content, including any portion thereof, and to include them in compilations

for such purposes, by any and all means and media now known or hereafter devised, and

(c)     to create Custom Compilations containing the Artist Content and to distribute them by any and all means and media now known or hereafter devised, including but not limited to standard audio-only compact discs and audio-only cassettes manufactured primarily for home entertainment.

2.     Artist Merchandise

You hereby grant to IUMA permission, on a non-exclusive basis, throughout the Universe, to distribute Artist Merchandise by any and all means now known or hereafter developed.

3.     Name and Likeness

You hereby grant to IUMA permission, on a non-exclusive basis, throughout the Universe, to use your name(s), group name, approved photograph and/or likeness(es) and approved biographical materials solely in connection with the distribution, exploitation, promotion, marketing and advertising of the Artist Content, Artist Merchandise, and the IUMA Site. You also agree not to assert any privacy, publicity, moral or similar rights held by you (and any other person(s) whose performances are embodied in the Artist Content and/or the Artist Merchandise) under the laws of the United States and any other country in connection with the exploitation of such materials.

4.     Reserved Rights

You shall at all times retain all right, title and interest in and to the Artist Content and the Artist Merchandise provided by you hereunder, including, without limitation, the copyrights therein and thereto.

Compensation

This section of the agreement is divided into three parts. The first concerns the distribution of Artist Content for promotional purposes. The second concerns the distribution of Artist Content for a fee. The third concerns the distribution of Artist Merchandise for a fee.

1.    Artist Content for Promotional Purposes

Unless otherwise agreed between you and IUMA in writing, the permission granted above to IUMA for the distribution of Artist Content under this Agreement shall be royalty free, as long as IUMA does not charge a fee for such distribution.

2.    Artist Content on a Fee Basis

Should you wish IUMA to charge a fee for the distribution of Artist Content, you and IUMA will share the revenues as follows: IUMA will pay you fifty percent (50%) of any and all Net Revenues (defined below) derived from Digital Phonorecord Deliveries embodying the Artist Content.

The term "Net Revenues" shall mean gross revenues less only the following costs and fees incurred in connection with such deliveries, and only to the extent incurred: (a) transaction processing fees, such as credit card transaction fees and other electronic commerce processing, patent royalties or other fees, payable to or retained by unaffiliated third parties pursuant to arms-length agreements in connection with effecting a transaction or transmission, if any; (b) sales tax, if any, to the extent included in the price; (c) credits, including, but not limited to, those on account of defective merchandise, errors in billing, and errors in transmission, if any; (d) mechanical royalties for the use of the underlying songs, if any; (e) public performance fees, if any; (f) shipping, if any; (g) union, guild or other third party fees that may be required by contract or the Copyright Act, if any; (h) Internet advertising and promotion costs, such as banner ads on other web sites to promote the Recordings, if any, provided that such costs shall not exceed 10% of gross revenues; (i) Internet referral fees, such as fees payable to any third party who, through their web site, email or other means, refers to us a purchaser of a copy or phonorecord of Artist Content, if any, provided that such costs shall not exceed 15% of gross revenues.

Net Revenues shall not include, and no royalties shall be payable to you on, any Artist Content reproduced, distributed, performed, displayed, broadcast, delivered or transmitted on a "free" or "no charge" basis. Without limiting the generality of the foregoing, any and all Artist Content shall be and are hereby licensed to IUMA on a royalty-free basis for the purpose of making, causing or effecting Digital Phonorecord Deliveries and Digital Streaming Transmissions of the Artist Content for promotional purposes, such as, for example, radio broadcast-like webcasts or interactive audio or audiovisual "streaming" transmission of Artist Content, or Digital Phonorecord Deliveries of a 30-second portion of Artist Content, for the purpose of allowing consumers to listen to the Artist Content in connection with the consumer's decision whether to purchase a Digital Phonorecord Delivery thereof or other promotional purpose.

The share of Net Revenues payable to you hereunder includes all royalties (other than any applicable performance royalties for underlying musical works) due you, the Artist(s), individual producers, the director, the performers, engineers, and any other persons engaged in connection with the creation of the Artist Content. You shall be solely responsible for the payment of any royalties due such persons or other third parties arising from payments made to you hereunder, including mechanical royalties owing to you or any third parties for the use of underlying musical works, except that IUMA shall effect payment for any and all public performance royalties with respect to any musical works embodied in the Artist Content which become due with respect to the exercise of the rights and licenses herein by IUMA.

For further information about this section, please contact the IUMA Content Acquisition Dept.

3.    Artist Merchandise on a Fee Basis

If you wish to deliver any Artist Merchandise to IUMA hereunder, you agree to do so accordance with the procedures provided to you by IUMA from time to time. Submissions of Artist Merchandise shall be at your sole cost and expense. All distributions of Artist Merchandise shall be pursuant to IUMA's policies as established from time to time.

IUMA's current policies governing distribution of Artist Merchandise is as follows: IUMA will sell Artist Merchandise on a consignment basis. You will set the price of all Artist Merchandise IUMA sells for you. IUMA will pay you 50% of the Net Revenue we receive from sales of such Artist Merchandise. "Net Revenue" in this case means the gross revenues we actually receive from such sales, less only sales, use, value added, or similar taxes, customs duties, import or export taxes or levies, shipping and handling costs, and all returns.

With respect to any payments due to you under this agreement, IUMA will determine the amount owed to you on a quarterly basis. Within 60 days of the close of each quarter in which IUMA has sold any of your Artist Content or Artist Merchandise, IUMA will send you a detailed accounting statement and a check payable in U.S. Dollars in the appropriate amount, except if the amount IUMA owes you is less than $20.00 then IUMA will hold the money until either (a) the total cumulative amount IUMA owes you at the end of any particular quarter is greater than $20.00, or (b) this agreement terminates. IUMA agrees to keep accurate books and records covering all transactions related to this agreement. During the one year period following your receipt of an accounting statement you may, at your expense and upon reasonable notice, inspect IUMA's records related to that statement at our offices or at a location specified by us, provided that your inspection must not unreasonably interfere with IUMA's business. If your inspection reveals that

IUMA has underpaid you, IUMA will promptly correct the deficiency, plus 10% interest.

Termination

You may terminate the grant of rights set forth above at any time by so notifying us in writing or by email addressed to terminations@iuma.com

Upon such termination, the permissions listed in the grant of rights section above shall terminate upon our actual receipt of such notice, provided that (a) IUMA shall have a up to thirty (30) days to promptly remove the Artist Content from the IUMA website and to return any Artist Merchandise, (b) IUMA shall have up to thirty (30) days to sell and deliver any Artist Content or Artist Merchandise which IUMA may have produced or sold prior to the date of termination, and (c) the parties agree to cooperate in providing an orderly termination of their relations. IUMA will return any unsold Artist Merchandise to you, provided you pay the shipping of such returns in advance. IUMA may terminate the grant of rights above at any time by notifying you by email to the e-mail address which you supply to us. Upon any such termination, IUMA will pay to you any amounts due to you under this Agreement at the conclusion of the accounting period in which such termination occurs. IUMA has no obligations to review, edit or monitor any Artist Content or Artist Merchandise, and reserves the right to cease offering any Artist Content or Artist Merchandise at any time without notice.

Artist Warranty

You represent and warrant that (a) the Artist Content and Artist Merchandise is your or your band's own original work, and contains no sampled material, (b) you have full right and power to enter into and perform this agreement, and have secured all third party consents necessary to enter into this agreement, (c) the Material does not and will not infringe on any third party's copyright, patent, trademark, trade secret or other proprietary rights, rights of publicity or privacy, or moral rights (d) the Material does not and will not violate any law, statute, ordinance or regulation; (e) the Material is not and will not be defamatory, trade libelous, pornographic or obscene, (f) the Material does not and will not contain any viruses or other programming routines that detrimentally interfere with computer systems or data, (g) all factual assertions that you have made and will make to us are true and complete, and (h) if any member of your group is a minor, you hereby warrant that you have the legal right to execute this Agreement on behalf of the minor artist and guarantee such person's performance of the terms of this Agreement. You shall be responsible for all licensing, reporting and payment obligations of any kind to third parties in connection with the Artist Content and Artist Merchandise, including but not limited to any applicable union and/or guild payments, "sample" or "replay" licenses or payments, and mechanical, synchronization or public performance royalties. You agree to indemnify and hold us and our customers harmless from any and all damages and costs, including reasonable attorney's fees, arising out of or related to your breach of the representations and warranties described in this section. You agree to execute and deliver documents to us, upon our reasonable request, that evidence or effectuate our rights under this agreement. These warranties shall survive any termination of this agreement.

Disclaimer

TO THE MAXIMUM EXTENT PERMITTED BY APPLICABLE LAW, IUMA DISCLAIMS ALL WARRANTIES, EITHER EXPRESS OR IMPLIED, INCLUDING BUT NOT LIMITED TO (1) UNINTERRUPTED OR CONTINUOUS AVAILABILITY OF THE IUMA SITE, AND (2) IMPLIED WARRANTIES OF MERCHANTABILITY, FITNESS FOR A PARTICULAR PURPOSE, AND NONINFRINGEMENT WITH RESPECT TO THE IUMA SITE AND ANY SERVICES PROVIDED BY IUMA HEREUNDER. SOME STATES DO NOT ALLOW LIMITATIONS ON IMPLIED WARRANTIES, SO THE ABOVE LIMITATION MAY NOT APPLY TO YOU.

No Liability For Consequential Damages

TO THE MAXIMUM EXTENT PERMITTED BY APPLICABLE LAW, IN NO EVENT WILL IUMA BE LIABLE FOR ANY DAMAGES WHATSOEVER (INCLUDING, WITHOUT LIMITATION, DAMAGES FOR LOSS OF BUSINESS PROFITS, BUSINESS INTERRUPTION, LOSS OF BUSINESS INFORMATION, OR OTHER PECUNIARY LOSS) ARISING OUT OF THE USE OR INABILITY TO USE THE IUMA SITE, EVEN IF IUMA HAS BEEN ADVISED OF THE POSSIBILITY OF SUCH DAMAGES.

IUMA will make good faith efforts to make Artist Content available in accordance with your instructions. However, recognizing the complexities of operating automated systems, from time to time, we may incorrectly categorize Artist Content, making available, for example, free or "no charge" content for a fee, or fee-based content for free or "no charge." Should IUMA make such an error, then upon notice from you IUMA will take all commercially reasonable efforts to promptly correct it, that being your sole and exclusive remedy, it being understood that IUMA shall not be responsible for consequential or other damages.

Other Terms Our Lawyers Asked Us to Include

THIS AGREEMENT IS GOVERNED BY THE LAWS OF THE UNITED STATES AND THE STATE OF CALIFORNIA, WITHOUT REFERENCE TO CONFLICT OF LAWS PRINCIPLES. ANY DISPUTE BETWEEN YOU AND IUMA REGARDING THIS AGREEMENT WILL BE SUBJECT TO THE EXCLUSIVE VENUE OF THE STATE AND FEDERAL COURTS IN THE CITY OF SAN FRANCISCO IN THE STATE OF CALIFORNIA. Your sole remedy for a breach of this Agreement by IUMA shall be an action at law for money damages, if any. You hereby waive any right to, or to seek, injunctive or other equitable relief in connection with any breach or alleged breach of this Agreement by IUMA. This Agreement may not be amended unless an officer of IUMA has approved and signed such an amendment in writing. You shall be solely responsible for providing all copyright notices and other legal notices in connection with the Artist Content and/or the Artist Merchandise. If any provision of this Agreement is held invalid, the remainder of this Agreement will continue in full force and effect. This Agreement is the entire agreement between you and IUMA and supersedes any other communications or advertising.

You represent that you have carefully read this agreement, that you understand its contents, and that you have had an opportunity to seek independent legal advice with respect to the review and advisability of entering into this Agreement.

Should you have any questions concerning this Agreement, or if you desire to contact IUMA for any reason, including, without limitation, for purposes of notifying IUMA of any claims of infringement, please contact: support@iuma.com.

**I HAVE READ THE ABOVE AND AGREE TO BE BOUND BY THE IUMA.COM MUSIC SUBMISSION AGREEMENT:**

I am over the age of 18, and have authority to sign for the band.

# FORM 23-6

## NOTICE OF CLAIMED INFRINGEMENT UNDER DIGITAL MILLENNIUM COPYRIGHT ACT

January 1, 2002

[COPYRIGHT INFRINGER]
[ADDRESS]
[CITY] [STATE] [ZIP

RE:    NOTIFICATION OF CLAIMED INFRINGEMENT UNDER DMCA

Gentlemen:

I certify under penalty of perjury that I am an agent authorized to act on behalf of Copyright, Inc. and that Copyright, Inc. is the owner or exclusive licensee of certain intellectual property rights related to certain copyrighted works (the "Copyrighted Works"). I have a good faith belief that users of your service are distributing infringing copies of the Copyrighted Works, including but not limited to the following sound recordings:

Such distributions are not authorized by Copyright, Inc. or the law, and therefore infringe our rights. You are knowingly and willfully contributing to such infringements by providing tools that facilitate such illegal activity. Please act expeditiously to disable access in your service to the above referenced recordings.

Please confirm to the undersigned in writing when this has been completed.

Sincerely yours,

# FORM 23-7

## ASCAP EXPERIMENTAL LICENSE AGREEMENT FOR INTERNET SITES—RELEASE 3.0

### *ASCAP EXPERIMENTAL LICENSE AGREEMENT FOR INTERNET SITES ON THE WORLD WIDE WEB – RELEASE 3.0*

1.  **Parties:** This is an agreement between the American Society of Composers, Authors and Publishers ("We," "Us" or "ASCAP"), located at One Lincoln Plaza, New York, New York 10023 and

_____ ("You" or "Licensee"), located at
                         Licensee Name

_____
Street Address or PO Box            City                      State          ZIP Code

2.  **Experimental Agreement:** This is an experimental agreement which applies for its term only and is entered into without prejudice to any position you or we may take for any period subsequent to its termination.

3.  **Definitions:**
    (a)    Your **"Web Site"** is the Internet site on the World Wide Web generally known as

    _____

    with the principal Universal Resource Locator (URL) of:

    http://_____

    (b)    **"Web Site Transmissions"** are all transmissions of content to Web Site Users from or through your Web Site, or from any other web site pursuant to an agreement between you and the operator of the other web site, when accessed by means of any connection from your Web Site.

    (c)    **"Web Site Users"** are all those who access Web Site Transmissions.

    (d)    Our **"Repertory"** consists of all copyrighted musical compositions written or published by our members or by the members of affiliated foreign performing rights societies, including compositions written or published during the term of this agreement, and of which we have the right to license non-dramatic public performances.

4.  **Grant of License:** We grant you a license to publicly perform, by means of Web Site Transmissions, non-dramatic renditions of the separate musical compositions in our Repertory.

5.  **Term of License:** The license granted by this agreement commences on _____ (the "Effective Date"), and ends on December 31 of the same calendar year, and continues after that for additional terms of one year each unless you or we terminate it by giving the other party notice at least thirty days prior to the end of a calendar year.

6.   **Limitations on License:**

(a)   This license extends only to you and your Web Site and is limited to performances presented by means of Web Site Transmissions, and by no other means; provided, however, that (i) nothing in this agreement authorizes such performances when transmitted from your Web Site pursuant to an agreement between you and any other web site operator, when accessed by means of a connection from that other web site, even if such performances fall within the definition of Web Site Transmissions; and provided further, that (ii) if you are an Internet access provider, nothing in this agreement authorizes such performances when transmitted from or through any homepage(s) hosted on your Web Site for those for whom you provide the service of Internet access.

(b)   This license may not be assigned without our written consent.

(c)   This license is limited to the United States, its territories and possessions, and the Commonwealth of Puerto Rico.

(d)   Nothing in this agreement grants you, or authorizes you to grant to any Web Site User, or to anyone else, any right to reproduce, copy or distribute by any means, method or process whatsoever, any of the musical compositions licensed by this agreement, including, but not limited to, transferring or downloading any such musical composition to a computer hard drive, or otherwise copying the composition onto any other storage medium.

(e)   Nothing in this agreement grants you, or authorizes you to grant to anyone else, any right to reproduce, copy, distribute or perform publicly by any means, method or process whatsoever, any sound recording embodying any of the musical compositions licensed under this agreement.

(f)   Nothing in this agreement grants, or authorizes you to grant, to any Web Site User, or to anyone else, any right to perform publicly by any means, method or process whatsoever, any of the musical compositions licensed under this agreement, including, but not limited to, any transmission, retransmission, or further transmission of any of those compositions.

(g)   This license is limited to non-dramatic performances, and does not authorize any dramatic performances; nor does it extend to or include the public performance of any opera, operetta, musical comedy, play, or like production, as such, in whole or in part.

7.   **License Fees:** For each year during the term of this agreement you agree to pay us the license fee calculated in accordance with the Rate Schedules applicable for that year.

8.   **Rate Schedules:** There are three alternative Rate Schedules, (Schedules "A," "B" and "C,") attached to and made a part of this agreement. For each year, you may choose any one of the three rate schedules we offer and for which you can provide the required information, using either your own technology, or technology supplied by an industry acknowledged technology company.

9.   **Reports and Payments:** You agree to furnish license fee reports and payments to us as follows:

(a)   Initial License Fee Report. Upon entering into this agreement, you will submit an Initial License Fee Report based on a good faith estimate of either "Web Site Revenue" or "Web Site Sessions" for the period from the Effective Date of this agreement until December 31 of the year in which this agreement is executed.

2

(b)     Annual License Fee Reports.  You will submit an Annual License Fee Report for each year of this agreement, by the first day of April of the following year on the Report Form we will provide you free of charge.

(c)     License Fee Payments.  You will submit license fee payments quarterly on or before January 1, April 1, July 1 and October 1 of each year.  Each such payment shall be equal to one-fourth of the license fee for the preceding calendar year; provided, however, that in any year for which your estimated license fee is less than $1,000, you will submit payments of $250 each, or the balance of the license fee due for that year, whichever is less.

(d)     Late Report Payments.  If we do not receive your Annual License Fee Report when due, you will submit quarterly license fee payments that are 24% higher than the quarterly payments due for the preceding year, and payments will continue at that increased rate until we receive the late report.

(e)     Annual Adjustment.  With each Annual License Fee Report you will submit payment of any license fees due over and above all amounts that you paid for the year to which the report pertains.  If the fee due is less than the amount you paid, we will apply the excess to the next quarterly payment due under this agreement.  If the excess is greater than one quarterly payment, we will refund the excess over and above the amount of one quarterly payment to you at your written request.

(f)     Late Payment Charge.  You will pay a finance charge of 1-1/2% per month, or the maximum rate permitted by state law, whichever is less, from the date due, on any required payment that is not made within thirty days of its due date.

(g)     Music Use Reports.  You agree to provide us with reports regarding the musical compositions contained in your Web Site Transmissions.  If the annual license fee payable to ASCAP is less than $10,000, you will submit such reports for the first three days of each calendar quarter.  If the annual license fee payable to ASCAP is $10,000 or greater, you will submit such reports for at least one week in each calendar quarter, for which we will request in writing and send it to you at least thirty days prior to commencement of the period to be covered by the report.  Your reports will be in the form we provide, and will contain the information specified by us.

**10.    Report Verification:**
(a)     We have the right to examine your books and records, and you agree to obtain for us the right to examine the books and records of any partner in, or co-publisher of, your Web Site, in order to verify any required report.  We may exercise this right by giving you thirty days notice of our intention to conduct an examination.  We will consider all data and information derived from our examination as completely confidential.  You agree to furnish all pertinent books and records, including electronic records, to our authorized representatives, during customary business hours.

(b)     If our examination shows that you underpaid license fees, you agree to pay a finance charge of 1-1/2% one month, or the maximum rate permitted by state law, whichever is less, on the license fees due from the date we bill you for that amount or, if the underpayment is 5% or more, from the date or dates that the license fees should have been paid.

3

(c)     You may dispute all or part of our claim for additional fees. You may do so by advising us in writing within thirty days from the date we bill the additional fees to you of the basis for your dispute, and by paying the undisputed portion of our claim with the applicable finance charges. If there is a good faith dispute between us concerning all or part of our claim, we will defer finance charges on the disputed amount until sixty days after we have responded to you, and will pro-rate finance charges based on our resolution of the dispute.

**11.     Breach or Default:** If you fail to perform any of the terms or conditions required of you by this agreement, we may terminate tour license by giving you thirty days notice to cure your breach or default. If you do not do so within that thirty day period, your license will automatically terminate at the end of that period without any further notice from us.

**12.     Interference with ASCAP's Operations:** We have the right to terminate this license effective immediately, if there is any major interference with, or substantial increase in the cost of, our operation as a result of any law in the state, territory, dependency, possession or political subdivision in which you or your Web Site is located which is applicable to the licensing of performing rights.

**13.     Indemnification:** We will indemnify you from any claim made against you with respect to the non-dramatic performance licensed under this agreement of any composition(s) in our Repertory, and will have full charge of the defense against the claim. You agree to notify us immediately of any such claim, furnish us with all the papers pertaining to it, and cooperate fully with is in its defense. If you wish, you may engage your own counsel, at your expense, who may participate in the defense. Our liability under this paragraph is strictly limited to the amount of license fees that you actually paid us under this agreement for the calendar year(s) in which the performance(s) which are the subject of the claim occurred.

**14.     Covenant Not to Sue:**
(a)     ASCAP, on its own behalf and on behalf of our members, covenants not to make any claim against you for unauthorized public performances of any of our members' compositions in our Repertory which would have been licensed under this agreement except for the limitation set forth in subparagraph 6(a)(i), provided that the agreement between you and the operator of the other web site referred to in subparagraph 6(a)(i) expressly requires that the operator of the other web site obtain needed authorization for performances of copyrighted musical compositions on or through its web site, and provided further, that within 24 hours of receipt of notice from us that the operator of the other web site does not have such needed authorization, you will remove or block the connection from that other web site to your Web Site.

(b)     ASCAP, on its own behalf and on behalf of our members, covenants not to make any claim against you for unauthorized public performances of any of our members' compositions in our Repertory which would have been licensed under this agreement except for the limitation set forth in subparagraph 6(a)(ii), provided that the agreement between you and the owner of the homepage referred to in subparagraph 6(a)(ii) expressly requires that that owner obtain needed authorization for performances of copyrighted musical compositions on or through its homepage, and provided further, that within 24 hours of receipt of notice from us that the owner of the homepage does not have such needed authorization, you will remove that homepage from your Web Site.

**15.     Notices:** We or you may give any notice required by this agreement by sending the notice to the other party's last known address by United States Mail or by generally recognized same-day or overnight delivery service. We each agree to inform the other in writing of any change of address.

**16.    Governing Law:** This agreement will be governed by and construed in accordance with the laws of the state of New York.

**17.    Entire Agreement:** This agreement constitutes the entire agreement between you and ASCAP, and may only be modified, or any rights under this agreement may be waived, by a written document executed by both you and ASCAP.

IN WITNESS WHEREOF, this Agreement has been duly executed by ASCAP and Licensee this _____ day of _____, 20_____.

| AMERICAN SOCIETY OF COMPOSERS, AUTHORS AND PUBLISHERS | |
|---|---|
| | _____<br>Licensee Name |
| By _____ | By _____<br>Signature |
| _____<br>Title | _____<br>Print Your Name |
| | _____<br>Title |
| | (Fill in capacity in which signed: (a) If corporation, state corporate office held; (b) If partnership, write word "partner" under printed name of signing partner; (c) If individual owner, write "individual owner" under printed name.) |

5

# RATE SCHEDULE "A"

## *REPORT FORM*
## *ASCAP EXPERIMENTAL LICENSE AGREEMENT FOR INTERNET*
## *SITES ON THE WORLD WIDE WEB – RELEASE 3.0*

### PART I.  ACCOUNT INFORMATION

REPORT PERIOD: _____ THRU 12/31/_____

LICENSEE NAME:_____

POSTAL ADDRESS:_____

WEB SITE URL: http://_____     E-MAIL:_____

FACSIMILE NUMBER:_____     PHONE NUMBER:_____

### PART II.  DEFINITIONS

(a)     The terms **"Web Site," "Web Site Transmissions"** and **"Web Site Users"** are defined in subparagraphs 2(a), (b) and (d) of the license agreement.

(b)     **"Sponsor Revenue"** means all payments made by or on behalf of sponsors, advertisers, program suppliers, content providers, or others for use of the facilities of your Web Site including, but not limited to, payments associated with syndicated selling, on-line franchising and associates programs. **"Sponsor Revenue"** also means all payments from whatever source derived upon your sale or other disposition of goods or services you received as barter for use of the facilities of your Web Site including, but not limited to, payments for the sale of advertising time or space.

(c)     **"Adjustment to Sponsor Revenue"** means advertising agency commissions not to exceed 15% actually allowed to an advertising agency that has no direct or indirect ownership or managerial connection with you or your Web Site.

(d)     **"Web Site User Revenue"** means all payments made by or on behalf of Web Site Users to access Web Site Transmissions including, but not limited to, subscriber fees, connect time charges, and any other access fees.

(e)     **"Web Site Revenue"** includes all specified payments and expenditures whether made directly to or by you, any entity under the same or substantially the same ownership, management or control as you, or to or by any other person, firm or corporation including, but not limited to, any partner or co-publisher of your Web Site, pursuant to an agreement or as directed or authorized by you or any of your agents or employees.

A1

(f) **"Web Session Value"** is the value derived from the number of Web Sessions that a Web Site generates.

(g) **"Web Site Sessions"** are the total number of periods that begin when a Web Site User first accesses any Web Site Transmission and end when that Web Site User has not accessed any Web Site Transmission within 10 minutes.

## PART III. REVENUE BASED
### LICENSE FEE CALCULATION FOR RATE SCHEDULE "A"

**NET SPONSOR REVENUE**
1. **Sponsor Revenue** ...................................................................................$_____
2. **Adjustment to Sponsor Revenue** ....................................................$_____
3. **Net Sponsor Revenue** (subtract line 2 from line 1) ............................$_____

**WEB SITE REVENUE**
4. **Web Site User Revenue** ....................................................................$_____
5. **Net Sponsor Revenue** (from line 3) ...................................................$_____
6. **Web Site Revenue** (add lines 4 and 5) ..............................................$_____
7. **Rate Based on Revenue** ...................................................................x____.01615
8. **Revenue Based License Fee** (multiply line 6 by line 7) ......................$_____

## PART IV. WEB SESSION BASED
### LICENSE FEE CALCULATION FOR RATE SCHEDULE "A"

**WEB SESSION VALUE**
9. **Web Site Sessions** ..........................................................................._____
10. **Rate Based on Web Sessions** .........................................................x $____.00048
11. **Web Session Based Licensee Fee** (multiply line 9 by line 10) ............$_____

### PART V. LICENSE FEE CALCULATION FOR RATE SCHEDULE "A"

12. **Licensee Fee** (enter line 8, line 11, or **Maximum License Fee,** if applicable,[*]
whichever is greater) ........ ...........................................................................$_____
13. **Minimum License Fee** ...................................................................$____264.00
14. **LICENSE FEE DUE** (enter amount from line 12 or line 13, whichever is
greater)....................... ...................................................................................$_____

### PART VI. CERTIFICATION

We certify that this report is true and correct and that all books and records necessary to verify this report are now and will continue to be available for your examination in accordance with the terms of the license agreement.

_____          _____
Signature                                                              Date

_____
Print Name and Title

_____

[*] If **Web Site Revenue** exceeds $19,000,000.00 per year, or if you choose not to report **Web Site Revenue** or **Web Session Value**, your annual **Maximum License Fee** is $300,000.00.

A2

# RATE SCHEDULE "B"

## *REPORT FORM*
## *ASCAP EXPERIMENTAL LICENSE AGREEMENT FOR INTERNET*
## *SITES ON THE WORLD WIDE WEB – RELEASE 3.0*

### PART I. ACCOUNT INFORMATION

REPORT PERIOD: _____ THRU 12/31/_____

LICENSEE NAME:_____

POSTAL ADDRESS:_____

WEB SITE URL: http://_____          E-MAIL:_____

FACSIMILE NUMBER:_____          PHONE NUMBER:_____

### PART II. DEFINITIONS

(a)     The terms **"Web Site," "Web Site Transmissions"** and **"Web Site Users"** are defined in subparagraphs 2(a), (b) and (d) of the license agreement.

(b)     **"Sponsor Revenue"** means all payments made by or on behalf of sponsors, advertisers, program suppliers, content providers, or others for use of the facilities of your Web Site including, but not limited to, payments associated with syndicated selling, on-line franchising and associates programs. **"Sponsor Revenue"** also means all payments from whatever source derived upon your sale or other disposition of goods or services you received as barter for use of the facilities of your Web Site including, but not limited to, payments for the sale of advertising time or space.

(c)     **"Adjustment to Sponsor Revenue"** means advertising agency commissions not to exceed 15% actually allowed to an advertising agency that has no direct or indirect ownership or managerial connection with you or your Web Site.

(d)     **"Web Site User Revenue"** means all payments made by or on behalf of Web Site Users to access Web Site Transmissions including, but not limited to, subscriber fees, connect time charges, and any other access fees.

(e)     **"Web Site Revenue"** includes all specified payments and expenditures whether made directly to or by you, any entity under the same or substantially the same ownership, management or control as you, or to or by any other person, firm or corporation including, but not limited to, any partner or co-publisher of your Web Site, pursuant to an agreement or as directed or authorized by you or any of your agents or employees.

B1

(f) **"Web Site Sessions"** are the total number of periods that begin when a Web Site User first accesses any Web Site Transmission and end when that Web Site User has not accessed any Web Site Transmission within 10 minutes.

(g) **"Music Sessions"** are the number of Web Site Sessions in which Web Site Users access any performance(s) of music.

(h) **"Web Session Value"** is the value derived from the number of Web Sessions that a Web Site generates.

## PART III. REVENUE BASED
## LICENSE FEE CALCULATION FOR RATE SCHEDULE "B"

**NET SPONSOR REVENUE**
1. **Sponsor Revenue** ......................................................................................$_____
2. **Adjustment to Sponsor Revenue** ...........................................................$_____
3. **Net Sponsor Revenue** (subtract line 2 from line 1) ...............................$_____

**WEB SITE REVENUE**
4. **Web Site User Revenue** ...........................................................................$_____
5. **Net Sponsor Revenue** (from line 3) .......................................................$_____
6. **Web Site Revenue** (add lines 4 and 5) ...................................................$_____

**VALUE ATTRIBUTABLE TO PERFORMANCES OF MUSIC**
7. **Web Site Sessions** ..................................................................................._____
8. **Music Sessions** ....  ..................................................................................._____
9. **Ratio** (divide line 8 by line 7) (to 3 decimals)..........................................._____
10. **Web Site Revenue** (from line 6) .............................................................$_____
11. **Value Attributable to Performances of Music** (multiply line 9 by line 10) ........$_____
12. **Rate Based on Revenue** ..........................................................................x_____.0242
13. **Revenue Based License Fee** (multiply line 11 by line 12)....................$_____

## PART IV. WEB SESSION BASED
## LICENSE FEE CALCULATION FOR RATE SCHEDULE "B"

**WEB SESSION VALUE**
14. **Web Site Sessions** (from line 7)..............................................................._____
15. **Music Sessions** (from line 8)...................................................................._____
16. **Rate Based on Web Sessions** ..................................................................x $\_\_\_\_\_.00073
17. **Web Session Based Licensee Fee** (multiply line 15 by line 16) ...........$_____

## PART V. LICENSE FEE CALCULATION FOR RATE SCHEDULE "B"

18. **Licensee Fee** (enter line 13, line 17, or **Maximum License Fee,** if applicable,[*]
whichever is greater) ......... .................................................................................$_____
19. **Minimum License Fee** ..............................................................................$\_\_\_\_264.00
20. **LICENSE FEE DUE** (enter amount from line 18 or line 19, whichever is
greater).................. ..............................................................................................$_____

---

[*] If **Web Site Revenue** exceeds $19,000,000.00 per year, or if you choose not to report **Web Site Revenue** or **Web Session Value**, your annual **Maximum License Fee** is $300,000.00.

## PART VI.  CERTIFICATION

We certify that this report is true and correct and that all books and records necessary to verify this report are now and will continue to be available for your examination in accordance with the terms of the license agreement.

_____          _____
Signature                                                         Date

_____
Print Name and Title

# RATE SCHEDULE "C"

## *REPORT FORM*
## *ASCAP EXPERIMENTAL LICENSE AGREEMENT FOR INTERNET SITES ON THE WORLD WIDE WEB – RELEASE 3.0*

### PART I. ACCOUNT INFORMATION

REPORT PERIOD: _____ THRU 12/31/_____

LICENSEE NAME:_____

POSTAL ADDRESS:_____

WEB SITE URL: http://_____ E-MAIL:_____

FACSIMILE NUMBER:_____ PHONE NUMBER:_____

### PART II. DEFINITIONS

(a) The terms **"Web Site," "Web Site Transmissions"** and **"Web Site Users"** are defined in subparagraphs 2(a), (b) and (d) of the license agreement.

(b) **"Sponsor Revenue"** means all payments made by or on behalf of sponsors, advertisers, program suppliers, content providers, or others for use of the facilities of your Web Site including, but not limited to, payments associated with syndicated selling, on-line franchising and associates programs. **"Sponsor Revenue"** also means all payments from whatever source derived upon your sale or other disposition of goods or services you received as barter for use of the facilities of your Web Site including, but not limited to, payments for the sale of advertising time or space.

(c) **"Adjustment to Sponsor Revenue"** means advertising agency commissions not to exceed 15% actually allowed to an advertising agency that has no direct or indirect ownership or managerial connection with you or your Web Site.

(d) **"Web Site User Revenue"** means all payments made by or on behalf of Web Site Users to access Web Site Transmissions including, but not limited to, subscriber fees, connect time charges, and any other access fees.

(e) **"Web Site Revenue"** includes all specified payments and expenditures whether made directly to or by you, any entity under the same or substantially the same ownership, management or control as you, or to or by any other person, firm or corporation including, but not limited to, any partner or co-publisher of your Web Site, pursuant to an agreement or as directed or authorized by you or any of your agents or employees.

C1

(f)　**"Web Site Sessions"** are the total number of periods that begin when a Web Site User first accesses any Web Site Transmission and end when that Web Site User has not accessed any Web Site Transmission within 10 minutes.

(g)　**"Music Sessions"** are the number of Web Site Sessions in which Web Site Users access any performance(s) of music.

(h)　**"Web Session Value"** is the value derived from the number of Web Sessions that a Web Site generates.

(i)　**"Performances of Music"** are the total number of performances of all musical works contained in Web Site Transmissions.

(j)　**"Performances of ASCAP Music"** are the number of Performances of Music which are of musical works in the ASCAP repertory not otherwise licensed.

**PART III. REVENUE BASED
LICENSE FEE CALCULATION FOR RATE SCHEDULE "C"**

**NET SPONSOR REVENUE**
1.　**Sponsor Revenue** ................................................................$_____
2.　**Adjustment to Sponsor Revenue** .........................................$_____
3.　**Net Sponsor Revenue** (subtract line 2 from line 1) .............$_____

**WEB SITE REVENUE**
4.　**Web Site User Revenue** .....................................................$_____
5.　**Net Sponsor Revenue** (from line 3) ...................................$_____
6.　**Web Site Revenue** (add lines 4 and 5) ...............................$_____

**VALUE ATTRIBUTABLE TO PERFORMANCES OF MUSIC**
7.　**Web Site Sessions** ............................................................._____
8.　**Music Sessions** .... ............................................................_____
9.　**Ratio** (divide line 8 by line 7) (to 3 decimals)..................._____
10.　**Web Site Revenue** (from line 6).......................................$_____
11.　**Value Attributable to Performances of Music** (multiply line 9 by line 10) .......$_____

**VALUE ATTRIBUTED TO PERFORMANCES OF ASCAP MUSIC**
12.　**Performances of Music**....................................................._____
13.　**Performances of ASCAP Music** ........................................_____
14.　**Ratio** (divide line 13 by line 12) (to 3 decimals)................._____
15.　**Value Attributable to Performances of Music** (from line 11)............$_____
16.　**Value Attributable to Performances of ASCAP Music** (multiply line 14 by line 15) ......................$_____
17.　**Rate Based on Revenue** ...................................................x____.0446
18.　**Revenue Based License Fee** (multiply line 16 by line 17).....................$_____

**PART IV. WEB SESSION BASED
LICENSE FEE CALCULATION FOR RATE SCHEDULE "C"**

**WEB SESSION VALUE**
19.　**Web Site Sessions** (from line 7)......................................._____
20.　**Music Sessions** (from line 8)............................................_____

C2

21. **Performances of Music** (from line 12)........................................................................,_____
22. **Performances of ASCAP Music** (from line 13).....................................................,_____
23. **Ratio** (divide line 22 by line 21)...........................................................................,_____
24. **Sessions Attributable to Performances of ASCAP Music** (multiply line 20 by
    line 23)................. ..........................................................................................,_____
25. **Rate Based on Web Sessions** ........................................................................x $_____.00134
26. **Web Session Based Licensee Fee** (multiply line 24 by line 25) .........................$_____

### PART V.  LICENSE FEE CALCULATION FOR RATE SCHEDULE "C"

27. **Licensee Fee** (enter line 18, line 26, or **Maximum License Fee,** if applicable,[*]
    whichever is greater) ........ ...........................................................................$_____
28. **Minimum License Fee** ................................................................................$_____264.00
29. **LICENSE FEE DUE** (enter amount from line 27 or line 28, whichever is
    greater)...................... .................................................................................$_____

### PART VI.  CERTIFICATION

We certify that this report is true and correct and that all books and records necessary to verify this report are now and will continue to be available for your examination in accordance with the terms of the license agreement.

_____          _____
Signature                                Date


_____
Print Name and Title

---

[*] If **Web Site Revenue** exceeds $19,000,000.00 per year, or if you choose not to report **Web Site Revenue** or **Web Session Value,** your annual **Maximum License Fee** is $300,000.00.

C3

# FORM 23-8

## BMI WEB SITE MUSIC PERFORMANCE AGREEMENT

**BMI®**
http://www.bmi.com

**WEB SITE**
**MUSIC PERFORMANCE AGREEMENT**

INTERNET-01

AGREEMENT, made on _____, 200_, by and between BROADCAST MUSIC, INC. ("BMI"), a New York corporation with its principal offices at 320 West 57th Street, New York, New York 10019 and _____ ("LICENSEE"), a _____ (State)

(check one)  ❑  corporation
             ❑  partnership
             ❑  limited liability company
             ❑  individual d/b/a _____ (complete if applicable)

with its principal offices at _____
_____(the "Agreement").

### IT IS HEREBY AGREED AS FOLLOWS:

**1.  Term**

The Term of this Agreement shall mean the period from either January 1, 2001 or _____ (date after January 1, 2001 on which audio was launched), whichever is later, through December 31, 2003 and continuing on a year-to-year basis thereafter. Either party may terminate the Agreement upon 60 days' prior written notice at the end of December of any year beginning with December 31, 2003. BMI shall have the right to cancel this Agreement along with the simultaneous cancellation of the Agreements of all other licensees of the same class and category as LICENSEE as of the end of any month during the initial term or any subsequent renewal term, upon 60 days' prior written notice.

**2.  Definitions**

As used in this Agreement, the following terms shall have the following respective meanings:

(a)  "Allocation of Run-Of-Site Revenue" shall mean Run-Of-Site Revenue multiplied by a fraction the numerator of which is the total Music Page Impressions for the reporting period, and the denominator of which is the total Page Impressions for the reporting period. (Run-Of-Site Revenue x (total Music Page Impressions ÷ total Page Impressions))

(b)  "Direct Music Area Revenue" shall mean the total of: (1) In-Stream Advertising Revenue; (2) Music Page Banner Advertising Revenue; (3) Music Subscriber Revenue; and (4) Other Music Revenue.

(c)  "Gross Revenue" shall mean all revenue, including all billings on behalf of, and all payments made to, LICENSEE, or as authorized by LICENSEE, its employees, representatives, agents or any other person acting on LICENSEE's behalf, and all billings on behalf of, and payments made to, any person, company, firm or corporation under the same or substantially the same ownership, management and control as LICENSEE for: (1) access to and/or use of the Web Site or portions thereof, including online time, subscriptions, and other transactional charges (excluding revenue generated by LICENSEE for the direct sale of manufactured products), including commissions from third parties on transactions; (2) advertising (including sponsor "hot links") on the Web Site, including billings to and payments received from sponsors, less advertising agency commissions not to exceed 15% actually incurred to a recognized advertising agency not owned or controlled by LICENSEE; (3) the provision of time or space on the Web Site to any other person or company; (4) donations; (5) the fair market value of merchandise, services or any thing or service of value which LICENSEE may receive in lieu of cash consideration for the use of the Web Site (i.e. trade and barter); and (6) LICENSEE's proprietary software used to access the Web Site, or download any aspect thereof. Gross Revenue shall include such payments as set forth in (1) through (6) above to which LICENSEE is entitled but which are paid to a parent, subsidiary, or division of LICENSEE or any third party, in lieu of payment to LICENSEE, for LICENSEE's Web Site. LICENSEE may deduct from Gross Revenue any bad debts actually written off during a reporting period which are related to any billings previously reported, but shall increase Gross Revenue by any recoveries thereof.

(d)  "In-Stream Advertising Revenue" shall mean that portion of Gross Revenue as defined in Paragraph 2(c)(2) and 2(c)(5) which is derived from advertising embedded in audio or audiovisual programming on the Web Site which contains music.

(e)  "Music Area Revenue" shall mean Direct Music Area Revenue plus the Allocation of Run-Of-Site Revenue.

(f)  "Music Page" shall mean a Web Page which presents one or more icons or hyperlinks that may be clicked on to access performances of music or at which music is played upon loading the Web Page.

(g)  "Music Page Banner Advertising Revenue" shall mean that portion of Gross Revenue as defined in Paragraph 2(c)(2) and 2(c)(5) which is derived from advertisements appearing on or in connection with Music Pages or portions thereof on the Web Site.

(h)  A "Music Page Impression" shall mean a transfer request for a single Music Page.

- 1 -

(i)     "Music Subscriber Revenue" shall mean that portion of Gross Revenue as defined in Paragraph 2(c)(1) which is derived from granting access to performances of music or Music Pages or portions thereof on the Web Site.

(j)     "Online Service" shall mean a commercial computer online information and/or entertainment programming packaging service including, but not limited to America Online, @Home Network, Road Runner, Microsoft Network, CompuServe and Prodigy, which offers consumers, for a fee, access to proprietary centralized databases and remote sources of audio and video programming and which may provide Internet access.

(k)     "Other Music Revenue" shall mean that portion of Gross Revenue as defined in Paragraphs 2(c)(1)-(6) (other than Gross Revenue defined in Paragraphs 2(d), 2(g) and 2(i)) which is directly attributable to performances of music or Music Pages or portions thereof on the Web Site.

(l)     "Page Impression" shall mean a transfer request for a single Web Page.

(m)     "Run-Of-Site Revenue" shall mean that portion of Gross Revenue as defined in Paragraphs 2(c)(1)-(6) which is attributable to the entire Web Site, or any part or parts of the Web Site that include one or more Music Pages or portions thereof. Run-Of-Site Revenue shall not include Direct Music Area Revenue or other revenue derived from targeted advertising buys where an advertiser buys advertising banners or other opportunities on or in connection with, or LICENSEE charges for access to, specific Web Page(s) other than Music Page(s) or portions thereof.

(n)     "Territory" shall mean the United States, its Commonwealth, territories and possessions, and the territories represented by non-U.S. performing rights licensing organizations listed on Exhibit C as may be amended from time to time by BMI during the Term of this Agreement by adding to or deleting from the list of countries posted in the licensing section of the BMI web site located at http://www.bmi.com/. BMI will provide notice to LICENSEE (by e-mail to the address provided by LICENSEE on the profile attached hereto as such may be amended in writing by LICENSEE) of the deletion of any non-U.S. performing rights licensing organization from Exhibit C during the Term hereof.

(o)     "U.S. Territory" shall mean the United States, its Commonwealth, territories and possessions.

(p)     "Web Page" shall mean a set of associated files transferred sequentially from the Web Site to, and rendered more or less simultaneously by, a browser. For purposes of this Agreement, such associated files shall include, but shall not be limited to, 'pop-up' windows that open upon accessing the Web Page as well as proprietary software 'players' that open when accessing an audio or audiovisual file associated with the Web Page.

(q)     "Web Site" shall mean an Internet computer service comprising a series of interrelated Web Pages currently registered with a domain name registration service and known as _____ that LICENSEE produces and/or packages and then transmits or causes to be transmitted either directly or indirectly to persons who receive the service from the URL http://_____ over the Internet by means of a personal computer or by means of another device capable of receiving Internet transmissions. LICENSEE may license additional Web Sites owned, operated and/or controlled by LICENSEE by listing such additional sites on Exhibit A hereto, and may amend Exhibit A from time to time during the Term hereof by written agreement signed by both parties. LICENSEE must comply separately with all reporting requirements and pay separate license fees under this Agreement, including Annual Minimum License Fees, for each Web Site listed on Exhibit A. References herein to Web Site shall include those additional sites listed on Exhibit A.

**3.    Grant of Rights**

(a)     BMI hereby grants to LICENSEE, for the Term, a non-exclusive license to perform publicly within the Territory (subject to Paragraph 3(b) below), in and as part of LICENSEE's Web Site transmitted or caused to be transmitted either directly or indirectly by LICENSEE over the Internet all musical works, the right to grant public performance licenses of which BMI controls. This Agreement shall only include public performances in the Territory of musical works by transmissions over the Internet received via personal computers or by means of another device capable of receiving the Internet through streaming technologies as well as those transmissions that are downloaded by persons on personal computers or otherwise, where such transmissions are accessed through the Web Site simultaneous to viewing a page on the Web Site. Public performances outside of the Territory may be subject to appropriate separate licensing. This Agreement shall not license transmissions of musical works that are accessed through a web site owned or controlled by a third party simultaneous to viewing a page on the third party's web site. This Agreement does not include dramatic rights or the right to perform dramatico-musical works in whole or in substantial part. This Agreement also does not license public performances in any commercial establishments, including, but not limited to, where all or a portion of LICENSEE's Web Site is used as a commercial music service (as that term is customarily understood in the industry); such performances of BMI music shall be subject to appropriate separate licensing.

(b)     Notwithstanding the foregoing, the territorial scope of the grant of rights with respect to any musical works which are affiliated with BMI through a non-U.S. performing rights licensing organization not listed on Exhibit C hereto is limited to public performances in the U.S. Territory. Public performances of such musical works outside of the U.S. Territory may be subject to appropriate separate licensing.

(c)     Nothing herein shall be construed as the grant by BMI of any license in connection with any transmission which is not part of LICENSEE's Web Site transmitted or caused to be transmitted by LICENSEE and nothing herein shall be construed as authorizing LICENSEE to grant to others (including, but not limited to, third party web sites, Online Services, cable television system operators and open video systems (acting as other than Internet service providers)) any license or right to reproduce or perform publicly by any means, method or process whatsoever, any of the musical compositions licensed hereunder.

(d)     This Agreement grants only public performing rights to LICENSEE, and does not grant any reproduction, distribution, performance right in sound recordings or any other intellectual property right(s) in any musical works to any person or entity that may receive and/or download or otherwise store the transmission of musical works.

(e)     In the event that all or a portion of LICENSEE's Web Site is offered for resale by a third party as a pay or premium audio or audiovisual service, or is packaged or included on a tier of services by a third party for additional revenue, either independently or with other Web Sites, LICENSEE shall immediately notify BMI in writing of any such arrangements. BMI and LICENSEE expressly agree that any such uses are not licensed under this Agreement and shall be subject to appropriate separate licensing.

**4.     License Fee**

In consideration of the license granted herein, LICENSEE shall pay to BMI for each calendar quarter of the Term hereof a license fee in accordance with the following rate calculations at LICENSEE's option:

(a)     Gross Revenue Calculation

LICENSEE shall pay to BMI 1.75% of LICENSEE's Gross Revenue generated by LICENSEE's Web Site during each quarter year of the Term according to the Payment Schedule below (Gross Revenue X 1.75%); *or*

(b)     Music Area Revenue Calculation

LICENSEE shall pay to BMI the greater of: (1) 2.5% of LICENSEE's Music Area Revenue generated by LICENSEE's Web Site during each quarter year of the Term according to the Payment Schedule below (Music Area Revenue X 2.5%); and (2) total Music Page Impressions during each quarter year of the Term according to the Payment Schedule below divided by 1,000 and multiplied by $0.12 ((Music Page Impressions ÷ 1,000) X $0.12).

(c)     Payment Schedule:   LICENSEE may elect between the Gross Revenue Calculation and Music Area Revenue Calculation upon filing each of its Financial Reports for each immediately preceding calendar quarter of the Term in accordance with Paragraph 6 according to the following Payment Schedule:

**PAYMENT SCHEDULE**

| Quarter | Period Ending | Payment Due Date |
|---------|---------------|------------------|
| First | March 31 | April 30 |
| Second | June 30 | July 31 |
| Third | September 30 | October 31 |
| Fourth | December 31 | January 31 |

**5.     Annual Minimum License Fee**

For each calendar year of the Agreement, LICENSEE shall pay to BMI an Annual Minimum License Fee as follows:

(a)     Upon signing this Agreement, LICENSEE shall estimate its annual Gross Revenue and shall pay to BMI an estimated Annual Minimum License Fee in accordance with the Minimum Fee Table below prorated based on the number of months remaining in the first calendar year covered by the Agreement.  Thereafter, LICENSEE shall pay to BMI any additional amount that may be due based on actual Gross Revenue upon filing its Financial Reports in accordance with Paragraph 6. Annual Minimum License Fee payments are credited against any additional license fees that LICENSEE shall owe to BMI in the same year to which the Annual Minimum License Fee shall apply. Overpayments shall be credited to LICENSEE's account.  Web Sites paying only Annual Minimum License Fees must still submit financial reports under Paragraph 6.

(b)     The Annual Minimum License Fee due for 2001 is specified in the Minimum Fee Table below.  For each year of this Agreement after 2001, the Annual Minimum License Fee shall be adjusted to reflect the increase (or decrease) in the United States Consumer Price Index (National, All Items) between October 2000 and October of the year preceding the year subject to the minimum fee, and shall be rounded to the nearest dollar amount.

**MINIMUM FEE TABLE**

| Gross Revenue | 2001 Annual Minimum Fee |
|---------------|-------------------------|
| Up to $12,000 | $259.00 |
| $12,001 to $18,500 | $388.00 |
| $18,501+ | $517.00 |

**6.     Financial Reports and Audit**

(a)     LICENSEE shall submit to BMI separate Financial Reports as to Gross Revenue generated by LICENSEE's Web Site as follows:

(i)     For each calendar quarter of this Agreement, a report, certified by an authorized representative of LICENSEE, for the Web Site, in the form substantially the same as the Web Site Music Performance License Quarterly Report Form annexed to this Agreement as Exhibit B.  LICENSEE's Financial Reports are due at the same time as the applicable quarterly license fee, including the Annual Minimum License Fee, as set forth in Paragraph 4. LICENSEE agrees to use commercially reasonable efforts to use software which BMI may provide to LICENSEE to prepare and deliver such reports electronically, or such other commercially reasonable alternative method upon which the parties agree. LICENSEE's Financial Reports shall be treated as confidential. BMI will not disclose the contents of such reports except as may be required by law or legal process; *provided, however,* that nothing contained herein shall limit or preclude BMI from providing affiliated or represented songwriters, composers, music publishers, and/or non-U.S. performing rights licensing organizations with itemized royalty statements and responding to inquiries from such affiliates or non-U.S. organizations related thereto.

(ii)     BMI shall have the right to estimate the fees due for a given quarter year on the basis of the highest quarterly fee during the previous twelve (12) months and bill LICENSEE therefor in the event that LICENSEE fails to report as required. Neither BMI's estimation of the fee for a reporting period nor anything else shall relieve LICENSEE of the obligation to report and make actual fee payments for the reporting period. If BMI's estimate was less than the actual license fee due, LICENSEE shall pay BMI, at the time the report is rendered, the difference between the actual fee due and the estimated fee paid. If LICENSEE's report reflects that the actual fee for the quarter year was less than the estimated fee paid, BMI shall credit the overpayment to LICENSEE's account. If LICENSEE has submitted all contractually required prior reports and payments to BMI and this Agreement is terminated, BMI shall refund the overpayment to LICENSEE.

(b)     BMI shall have the right to require that LICENSEE provide BMI with data or information sufficient to ascertain the license fee due hereunder.

(c)     BMI shall have the right, at BMI's sole cost and expense, once with respect to each year of the Term (or portion thereof), by its duly authorized representatives, at any time during customary business hours and upon thirty (30) days' advance written notice, to examine the books and records of account of LICENSEE necessary to verify any and all statements, accounting and reports rendered and/or required by this Agreement and in order to ascertain the license fee due BMI for any unreported period. The period for which BMI may audit LICENSEE shall be limited to three (3) calendar years preceding the year in which the audit is made; *provided, however,* that if an audit is postponed at the request of LICENSEE, and BMI grants such postponement, BMI shall have the right to audit for the period commencing with the third calendar year preceding the year in which notification of intention to audit was first given by BMI to LICENSEE. In the event that an audit reveals a deficiency of ten percent (10%) or greater, BMI shall have the right to audit one (1) additional calendar year, for a total of four (4) calendar years preceding the year in which the audit is made. This limitation on the period for which BMI may audit LICENSEE shall not apply if: (i) LICENSEE fails to file its financial reports due under Paragraph 6(a)(i) in a timely manner; and/or (ii) LICENSEE fails or refuses after written notice from BMI to produce the material books and/or records of account necessary to verify any report or statement required under the Agreement. BMI shall treat as confidential all data and information coming to its attention as the result of any such examination of books and records, and shall not use any such information other than in connection with its administration of this Agreement.

(d)     In addition to any other remedy that BMI may have, in the event that BMI conducts an audit under Paragraph 6(c) and such audit reveals that LICENSEE has underpaid license fees to BMI, LICENSEE shall immediately pay the amount LICENSEE owes BMI and, in addition, if such underpayment amounts to ten percent (10%) or more of LICENSEE's annual fees for the audited period, LICENSEE shall pay BMI a late payment charge in the amount of one and one-half percent (1 1/2%) per month of all monies owed commencing on the actual date such monies were due.

**7.     Late Payment Charge**

BMI may impose a late payment charge of one and one-half percent (1 1/2 %) per month from the date payment was due on any quarterly payment that is received by BMI more than ten (10) days after the due date.

**8.     Music Use Reports**

(a)     LICENSEE shall provide BMI, in electronic form, quarterly Music Use Reports which shall contain detailed information from LICENSEE's Web Site usage logs concerning the transmission of all musical works on LICENSEE's Web Site. Such information shall identify each musical work by title, composer/writer, author, artist, record label, any unique identifier (e.g. ISWC, ISAN), length, type of use (i.e., theme, background or feature performance) and manner of performance (i.e. instrumental or vocal) (or any other methodology agreed to by BMI and LICENSEE) and specify the number of times each musical work was transmitted and whether such transmission was streamed or downloaded. In the event that a charge was made for an on-demand transmission where the user chose to access a particular work and paid a fee to LICENSEE for such service, LICENSEE shall include the gross price that the end user was charged to receive such transmission(s). With respect to transmissions of audiovisual works, such information shall also include the title of each audiovisual work, and the primary author, director, and principal actor(s) of the audiovisual work. With respect to on-demand transmissions where users are able to access transmissions of specific works upon request, such information shall also include the country where the end-user received such transmission. LICENSEE shall request reports from its licensors or outside producers with respect to all content provided by others and transmitted by LICENSEE as part of LICENSEE's Web Site. LICENSEE shall notify BMI immediately in the event that LICENSEE is unable to obtain such reports, and BMI shall use commercially reasonable efforts to secure any missing reports from LICENSEE's licensors or outside producers, but nothing contained herein shall relieve LICENSEE of its obligation to deliver the reports to BMI in the event that BMI is unable to obtain such reports.

(b)      LICENSEE shall deliver to BMI Music Use Reports on or before the thirtieth day following the end of such quarter pursuant to the Payment Schedule set forth in Paragraph 4. LICENSEE agrees to use commercially reasonable efforts to use software which BMI may provide to LICENSEE to prepare and deliver such reports electronically, or such other commercially reasonable alternative method upon which the parties agree.

(c)      BMI shall not disclose, other than as individualized music use information accompanying royalty statements, any specific music performance data contained in the Music Use Reports without LICENSEE's prior written consent.   Nothing contained herein shall preclude BMI from using the music use information as part of aggregated, publicly disseminated market data, so long as the source of such information is not specifically identifiable as coming from LICENSEE, or disclosing any such data as may be required by law or legal process.

**9.      Indemnification**

Provided that LICENSEE has not failed to cure a breach or default within thirty (30) days of receiving notification from BMI thereof under the Agreement, BMI shall indemnify, save and hold harmless and defend LICENSEE and its officers and employees from and against any and all claims, demands and suits alleging copyright infringement that may be made or brought against them or any of them with respect to the public performance within the Territory of any musical works licensed hereunder; *provided, however,* that such indemnity shall be limited to those claims, demands or suits that are made or brought within the U.S. Territory, and provided further that such indemnity shall be limited to works which are BMI-affiliated works at the time of LICENSEE's performance of such works.  This indemnity shall not apply to transmissions of any musical work performed by LICENSEE after written request from BMI to LICENSEE that LICENSEE refrain from performance thereof. BMI shall, upon reasonable written request, advise LICENSEE whether particular musical works are available for performance as part of BMI's repertoire.   LICENSEE shall provide the title and the writer/composer of each musical composition requested to be identified. LICENSEE agrees to give BMI immediate notice of any such claim, demand, or suit, to deliver to BMI any papers pertaining thereto, and to cooperate with BMI with respect thereto, and BMI shall have full charge of the defense of any such claim, demand, or suit; provided, however, that LICENSEE may retain counsel on its behalf and at its own expense and participate in the defense of such claim, demand or suit.

**10.     Warranty; Reservation of Rights**

This Agreement is experimental in nature.  BMI and LICENSEE recognize that the license granted herein covers certain transmissions originating from and/or received in certain territories outside of the U.S. Territory pursuant to experimental agreements with certain non-U.S. performing rights licensing organizations around the world, and that this Agreement is broader in geographical scope than BMI's previous Internet licenses.  Notwithstanding, BMI is offering this Agreement at the same rate as its previous Internet license on an experimental and non-prejudicial basis for the sole purpose of evaluating such international licensing initiatives.  Nothing contained in this Agreement is intended to reflect BMI's position with respect to the reasonable value of the license granted herein; BMI hereby expressly reserves its right to re-evaluate the appropriateness of the fees and terms herein, including, but not limited to, the reasonable value of a license that covers transmissions beyond the U.S. Territory, for periods following the Term.

**11.     Breach or Default**

Upon any breach or default of the terms and conditions of this Agreement by LICENSEE, BMI shall have the right to cancel this Agreement, but any such cancellation shall only become effective if such breach or default continues thirty (30) days after LICENSEE's receipt of written notice thereof. The right to cancel shall be in addition to any and all other remedies which BMI may have. No waiver by BMI of full performance of this Agreement by LICENSEE in any one or more instances shall be a waiver of the right to require full and complete performance of this Agreement thereafter or of the right to cancel this Agreement in accordance with the terms of this Paragraph.

**12.     Discontinuance of Music**

In the event that LICENSEE ceases to publicly perform music in connection with its Web Site, LICENSEE may cancel this Agreement by sending written notice to BMI prior to the effective date of cancellation as specified in such notice by LICENSEE.  BMI will cancel this Agreement, retroactive to the effective date of cancellation, but only if, within ninety (90) days after the effective date, LICENSEE: (a) has submitted to BMI all reports and payments due under the Agreement through the effective date; and (b) has not resumed publicly performing music in connection with its Web Site.  In the event that LICENSEE fails to provide such reports and payments or resumes publicly performing music in connection with its Web Site within the ninety (90) day period, LICENSEE's request to cancel this Agreement shall be deemed withdrawn and this Agreement shall remain in full force and effect for the duration of the Term in accordance with Paragraph 1 above.

**13.     Arbitration**

All disputes of any kind, nature or description arising in connection with the terms and conditions of this Agreement (except for matters within the jurisdiction of the BMI rate court) shall be submitted to arbitration in the City, County, and State of New York under the then prevailing rules of the American Arbitration Association by an arbitrator or arbitrators to be selected as follows: Each of the parties shall, by written notice to the other, have the right to appoint one arbitrator. If, within ten (10) days following the giving of such notice by one party the other shall not, by written notice, appoint another arbitrator, the first arbitrator shall be the sole arbitrator. If two arbitrators are so appointed, they shall appoint a third arbitrator. If ten (10) days elapse after the appointment of the second arbitrator and the two arbitrators are unable to agree upon the third arbitrator, then either party may, in writing, request the American Arbitration Association to appoint the third arbitrator. The award made in the arbitration shall be binding and conclusive on the parties and judgment may be, but need not be, entered in any court having jurisdiction. Such award shall include the fixing of costs, expenses, and attorneys' fees of arbitration, which shall be borne by the unsuccessful party.

**14. Withdrawal of Works**

BMI reserves the right at its discretion to withdraw from the license granted hereunder any musical work as to which legal action has been instituted or a claim made that BMI does not have the right to license the performing rights in such work or that such work infringes another composition.

**15. Notice**

All notices and other communications between the parties hereto shall be in writing and deemed received (i) when delivered in person; (ii) upon confirmed transmission by telex or facsimile device; or (iii) five (5) days after deposited in the United States mails, postage prepaid, certified or registered mail, addressed to the other party at the address set forth below (or at such other address as such other party may supply by written notice):

> BMI: 320 West 57th Street
> New York, New York 10019
> Attn: Senior Vice President Licensing

> with a separate copy to:

> Senior Vice President and General Counsel

> LICENSEE:

> with a separate copy to:

**16. Assignment**

This Agreement shall inure to the benefit of and shall be binding upon the parties hereto and their respective successors and assigns, but no assignment shall relieve the parties hereto of their respective obligations hereunder.

**17. Entire Agreement**

This Agreement constitutes the entire understanding between the parties with respect to the subject matter hereof. This Agreement cannot be waived, added to or modified orally and no waiver, addition or modification shall be valid unless in writing and signed by the parties. This Agreement, its validity, construction, and effect, shall be governed by the laws of the State of New York. The fact that any provisions herein are found by a court of competent jurisdiction to be void or unenforceable shall not affect the validity or enforceability of any other provisions.

BROADCAST MUSIC, INC.

By: _____
   (Signature)

_____
(Print Name of Signer)

_____
(Title of Signer)

Please return signed agreement together with minimum fee to :

> BMI
> 320 West 57th Street
> New York, NY 10019
> ATTN: Web Site Licensing

*PLEASE COMPLETE ALL OF THE FOLLOWING:*

LICENSEE's main offices are located in the U.S. Territory
YES_____    NO_____

The majority of LICENSEE's employees are located in the U.S. Territory
YES_____    NO_____

LICENSEE's annual accounts are audited in the U.S. Territory
YES_____    NO_____

_____
(LICENSEE)

By: _____
   (Signature)

_____
(Print Name of Signer)

_____
(Title of Signer)

- 6 -

**WEB SITE**
**MUSIC PERFORMANCE AGREEMENT**

http://www.bmi.com

INTERNET-01

### EXHIBIT A

| WEB SITE NAME | URL |
|---|---|
| | |
| | |
| | |
| | |
| | |
| | |
| | |
| | |
| | |
| | |
| | |
| | |
| | |
| | |
| | |
| | |
| | |
| | |
| | |
| | |
| | |
| | |
| | |
| | |

**EXHIBIT B**

**BMI**®

**WEB SITE MUSIC PERFORMANCE AGREEMENT**
Gross Revenue Calculation
**QUARTERLY FINANCIAL REPORT FORM**

Report For Calendar Quarter:

| Jan. 1 –<br>Mar. 31 | Apr. 1 –<br>June. 30 | July. 1 –Sept.<br>30 | Oct. 1 –<br>Dec. 31 | |
|---|---|---|---|---|

YEAR

SAMPLE

Company Name:
Address:

Telephone No.:
Name of Web Site:
URL:

**YOUR GROSS REVENUE**

1. Subscriber Revenue (including commissions on third party transactions)    $ _____
2. Advertising Revenue (less agency commissions)    $ _____
3. Provision of Space or Time    $ _____
4. Donations    $ _____
5. Trade or Barter    $ _____
6. Proprietary Software    $ _____

**TOTAL GROSS REVENUE** (add lines 1 through 6)    $ _____

TOTAL GROSS REVENUE $ _____ X 1.75% = $ _____
LICENSE FEE

**TOTAL PAYMENT DUE** = $ _____

I hereby certify on this _____ day of _____, _____ that the above is true and correct.

BY: _____
(SIGNATURE)

_____
(PRINT NAME OF SIGNER)

_____
(TITLE OF SIGNER)

Please return report and payment to:

Web Licensing
BMI
320 West 57th Street
New York, NY 10019

Please e-mail any questions to weblicensing@bmi.com

**EXHIBIT B**

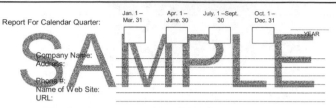

**BMI®**

**WEB SITE MUSIC PERFORMANCE AGREEMENT**
Music Area Revenue Calculation
**QUARTERLY FINANCIAL REPORT FORM**

| | Jan. 1 –<br>Mar. 31 | Apr. 1 –<br>June. 30 | July. 1 –Sept.<br>30 | Oct. 1 –<br>Dec. 31 | |
|---|---|---|---|---|---|
| Report For Calendar Quarter: | | | | | YEAR |

Company Name: _____
Address: _____
_____
Phone #: _____
Name of Web Site: _____
URL: _____

**MUSIC AREA REVENUE**

DIRECT MUSIC AREA REVENUE
1.  In-Stream Advertising $_____ less agency commissions $_____     $_____
2.  Music Page Banner Advertising $_____ less agency commissions $_____     $_____
3.  Music Subscriber Fees                                                        $_____
4.  Other Music Revenue                                                          $_____
5.  DIRECT MUSIC AREA REVENUE (add lines 1 through 4)                            $_____

ALLOCATION OF RUN OF SITE REVENUE
6.  Subscriber Revenue (including commissions on third party transactions)       $_____
7.  Advertising Revenue $_____ less agency commissions $_____        $_____
8.  Provision of Space or Time                                                   $_____
9.  Donations                                                                    $_____
10. Trade or Barter                                                              $_____
11. Proprietary Software                                                         $_____
12. RUN OF SITE REVENUE (add lines 6 through 11)                                 $_____
13. ALLOCATION OF RUN OF SITE REVENUE

_____ x ( _____ + _____ )     $_____
RUN OF SITE REVENUE   (TOTAL MUSIC PAGE IMPRESSIONS)   (TOTAL PAGE IMPRESSIONS)
14. TOTAL MUSIC AREA REVENUE (add lines 5 and 13)                                $_____

**MUSIC AREA LICENSE FEE**
(the greater of A and B)

A.  TOTAL MUSIC AREA REVENUE                           B.  MUSIC PAGE IMPRESSIONS
$_____ x 2.5% = $_____                         _____ ÷ 1,000 x $0.12 = $_____
   *(from Line 13)*                                         *Total Music Page Impressions*

**MUSIC AREA LICENSE FEE $ _____**

I hereby certify on this _____ day of _____, _____ that the above is true and correct.

BY:     _____
        (SIGNATURE)
        _____
        (PRINT NAME OF SIGNER)
        _____
        (TITLE OF SIGNER)

Please return report and payment to:
   Weblicensing
   BMI
   320 West 57th Street
   New York, NY 10019
Please e-mail any questions to weblicensing@bmi.com

**EXHIBIT C**
Last Updated: 7/23/01

| PERFORMING RIGHTS ORGANIZATION | COUNTRY |
|---|---|
| AEPI | Greece |
| AKM | Austria |
| APRA | Australia |
| ARTISJUS | Hungary |
| BUMA | The Netherlands |
| CASH | Hong Kong |
| COMPASS | Singapore |
| GEMA | Germany |
| IMRO | Ireland |
| JASRAC | Japan |
| KCI | Indonesia |
| KODA | Denmark |
| MACP | Malaysia |
| MUST | Taiwan |
| PRS | United Kingdom |
| SABAM | Belgium |
| SACEM | France |
| SACM | Mexico |
| SADAIC | Argentina |
| SCD | Chile |
| SGAE | Spain |
| SIAE | Italy |
| STIM | Sweden |
| SUISA | Switzerland |
| TEOSTO | Finland |
| UBC | Brazil |

**WEB SITE**                                                    INTERNET-01
**MUSIC PERFORMANCE AGREEMENT**

**WEB SITE PROFILE**
*Please complete and return with your signed agreements*
*so we can service your account properly*

Site URL: _____

Site Name: _____

Corporate Name: _____

Corporate Contact: _____ Title: _____

Corporate Address: _____

Telephone: _____ Fax: _____

E-Mail: _____

Financial Contact: _____ Title: _____
*If different from above*

Billing Address: _____
*If different from above*

Telephone: _____ Fax: _____

E-Mail: _____

Music
Use Reports Contact: _____ Title: _____
*If different from above*

Telephone: _____ Fax: _____

E-Mail: _____

**Questions? Please visit our web site at**
**http://www.bmi.com**

## SESAC INTERNET LICENSE

This experimental Internet License for performance rights is entered into without prejudice to the positions either party may take in subsequent discussions.

### 1. PARTIES

This Internet License, including all attached Schedules ("Agreement"), is made by and between SESAC, Inc. ("SESAC"), 421 West 54th Street, New York, New York 10019, and the Party who, by accepting this Agreement, indicates the intent to be licensed pursuant to the terms of the Agreement ("LICENSEE"). SESAC and LICENSEE hereby mutually agree as follows:

### 2. MISCELLANEOUS DEFINITIONS

A. "Web Site" - A Web Site, under this Agreement, is a "location" on the Internet that broadcasts, transmits or otherwise makes musical works available to computer users on or through its own unique domain name and base Uniform Resource Locator ("URL") address, and includes all subpages under the base URL address.

B. "Effective Date" - The Effective Date of the rights and obligations granted under this Agreement will be defined by the date entered in the Effective Date field on the final acceptance page, below.

C. "Compositions" - Compositions includes all of the musical works which SESAC controls and for which SESAC is empowered to license the performance right during the Term of this Agreement, as defined below.

SESAC and LICENSEE hereby mutually agree as follows:

### 3. GRANT OF RIGHTS

A. As of the Effective Date, SESAC grants to LICENSEE the non-exclusive right and license to publicly perform non-dramatic renditions of the Compositions, by transmission on or through the LICENSEE's Web Site, as described in the Schedule "B" Web Site (URL) Address field.

B. Any authorization made under this Agreement is limited to the United States, its territories and possessions and the Commonwealth of Puerto Rico ("U.S. Territory" or "U.S. Territory Rights"), unless LICENSEE is eligible and elects to secure Foreign Territory Rights (defined in the Foreign Territory Addendum), for an additional fee.

### 4. LIMITATIONS OF RIGHTS

**The rights granted herein specifically <u>exclude</u>:**

A. The right to transmit the Compositions from Web Sites or computer online services other than the Web Site described in Schedule "B," below;

*If your Web Site aggregates audio or audio visual streams from two (2) or more Web Sites or other sources; or, if you provide proprietary content and/or services to third party Web Sites (E.g. subscriptions, branded players, streamed audio/video, music samples, downloads, etc.), please contact SESAC for the appropriate license.*

B. The authority to grant or sublicense to any *third* party or entity which may receive, download or otherwise capture transmissions from LICENSEE's Web Site, the right to publicly perform the Compositions licensed hereunder, either by retransmission or rebroadcast by any means, medium, method, device or process now or hereafter known; and

C. "Grand Rights" in and to the Compositions ("Grand Rights" include, but are not limited to, the right to perform in whole or in part, dramatico-musical and dramatic works in a dramatic setting).

### 5. TERM OF LICENSE AGREEMENT

The term of this Agreement shall be for an initial period that commences upon the Effective Date and continues for a period of six (6) months (the "Initial Period"). Thereafter, the Agreement shall automatically continue in full force and effect for successive additional periods of six (6) months ("Renewal Period(s)"). SESAC and/or LICENSEE shall have the right to terminate this Agreement as of the last day of the Initial Period or as of the last day of any Renewal Period(s), upon giving written notice to the other party by Certified Mail, Return Receipt Requested, at least thirty (30) days prior to the commencement of any Renewal Period(s). The Initial Period and Renewal Period(s) are sometimes collectively referred to hereafter as the "Term."

**6. LICENSE FEE**

A.   As consideration for the rights granted herein, LICENSEE shall pay to SESAC a fee ("License Fee") in accordance with the then current Schedule "A" Internet Fee Schedule ("License Fee Schedule").

B.   SESAC shall have the right to change the License Fee Schedule, upon thirty (30) days prior written notice, by Certified Mail. In the event LICENSEE's fees are increased as a result of a change in the License Fee Schedule, LICENSEE shall then have the right to terminate this Agreement, effective as of the date of the increase, *provided* that within thirty (30) days of SESAC's notice of increase, LICENSEE provides written notice of termination to SESAC by Certified Mail.

C.   The License Fee may be subject to an increase effective January 1 of each calendar year by an amount equivalent to the percent increase, if any, in the Consumer Price Index - All Urban Consumer (CPI-U) as published by the Bureau of Labor Statistics, U.S. Department of Labor, between the preceding October and the next preceding October.

D.   SESAC shall have the right to impose a late payment charge of one and one-half percent (1.5%) per month for any License Fee payment that is more than thirty (30) days past due. SESAC shall have the right to impose an additional charge of $25.00 for each dishonored check. In the event SESAC incurs costs and fees, including attorneys fees, in connection with the collection of any amount(s) past due hereunder, LICENSEE shall be responsible for paying all such costs and fees to SESAC.

E.   In the event that SESAC is determined by the taxing authority or courts of any of the United States in which LICENSEE conducts its operation to be liable for the payment of a gross receipts, sales, business use or other tax which is based on the amount of SESAC's receipts from LICENSEE, then LICENSEE shall reimburse SESAC, within thirty (30) days notification thereof, for LICENSEE's pro rata share of any such tax.

**7. MISCELLANEOUS**

A.   Both parties acknowledge that this Agreement, with schedules and addenda, is experimental in nature and shall not be prejudicial to either party's position concerning the reasonableness or breakdown of Fees, terms or conditions in any subsequent negotiation and/or licensing agreement between SESAC and LICENSEE.

B.   In the event LICENSEE fails to pay the License Fee when due, or is otherwise in default of any other provision of this Agreement, SESAC shall have the right to terminate this Agreement in addition to pursuing any and all other rights and/or remedies available if LICENSEE has not cured such breach within thirty (30) days following SESAC's written notice of default.

C.   In the event LICENSEE fails to submit a timely Report as required by the incorporated Schedule "A," SESAC will provide a written request for the Report. If LICENSEE fails to respond to the written request within fifteen (15) days, LICENSEE's License Fee may be adjusted to reflect the current Maximum License Fee.

D.   SESAC shall have the right, upon written notice, to withdraw from the scope of this License the right to perform any musical composition authorized hereunder as to which an action has been threatened, instituted, or a claim made that SESAC does not have the right to license the performance rights in such composition.

E.   This Agreement shall be binding upon and inure to the benefit of SESAC's and LICENSEE's legal representatives, successors, and assigns, but no assignment shall relieve SESAC or LICENSEE of their respective obligations under this Agreement. LICENSEE shall notify SESAC in writing within thirty (30) days of any change of ownership or control of the online entity licensed hereunder.

F.   This Agreement shall be governed by and subject to the laws of the State of New York, applicable to agreements made and to be wholly performed in New York.

G.   This Agreement supersedes and cancels all prior negotiations and understandings between SESAC and LICENSEE in connection with the Web Site licensed hereunder. No modification of this Agreement shall be valid or binding unless in writing and executed by SESAC and LICENSEE.

H.   If any part of this Agreement shall be determined to be invalid or unenforceable by a court of competent jurisdiction or by any other legally constituted body having the jurisdiction to make such determination, the remainder of this Agreement shall remain in full force and effect.

I.   No waiver of any breach of this Agreement shall be deemed a waiver of any preceding continuing or succeeding breach of the same, or any other provision of this Agreement.

**8. RESERVATION OF RIGHTS**

A. SESAC shall have the right to verify, by independent means, all Internet Report or Addendum Report (see Foreign Territory Addendum) information that LICENSEE provides for its License Fee or Expanded Territory License Fee determination or eligibility for this Agreement, and make any necessary retroactive adjustments.

B. Notwithstanding anything to the contrary contained herein, SESAC shall have the right to terminate this Agreement: (i) at any time upon written notice to LICENSEE in the event LICENSEE is adjudicated bankrupt, or a petition in bankruptcy is filed with respect to LICENSEE, or LICENSEE is declared or becomes insolvent; or (ii) upon thirty (30) days written notice by reason of any law, rule, decree, or other enactment having the force of law, by any authority, whether federal, state, local, territorial or otherwise, which shall result in substantial interference in SESAC's operation or any substantial increase in the cost of conducting its business.

# FORM 23-9

## SESAC INTERNET LICENSE

SCHEDULE "A"
INTERNET FEE SCHEDULE
WEB SITES - 2001

1.  **The License Fee for Year 2001 shall be determined as follows:**

    A.  **With no advertising**

        **.0075** multiplied by the average number of monthly Page Requests*

**Minimum License Fee per Web Site for each six (6) month Report Period: $75.00**
**Maximum License Fee per Web Site with no advertising for each six (6) month Report Period: $1,500.00**

*Note: If you are an educational institution or a non-commercial entity, you may be eligible for a reduced Minimum License Fee. Please contact SESAC to qualify.*

    B.  **With advertising**

        **.0075** multiplied by the average number of monthly Page Requests multiplied by **1.3**

**Minimum License Fee per Web Site for each six (6) month Report Period: $75.00**
**Maximum License Fee per Web Site with advertising for each six (6) month Report Period: $1,950.00**

    * "Page Requests" is the number of requests for HyperText Markup Language documents commonly referred to as "HTML pages" (often using file extensions such as .htm, .html, .shtml, .phtml, .php or .asp) which result in being viewed by a browser.

2.  **Internet Report (Schedule "B") Calculation**

    A.  **Initial Internet Report**

    For Web Sites in operation less than six (6) months prior to the Effective Date, the average number of monthly Page Requests shall be determined by the total number of Page Requests during the period of operation divided by the actual number of months in operation.
    For Web Sites not in operation prior to the Effective Date, LICENSEE shall pay an estimated License Fee based on a good faith estimate of anticipated average Page Requests.

    LICENSEE shall complete the following Internet Report Form (Schedule "B") for the Initial Period of this Agreement and submit the appropriate payment. LICENSEE shall pay the License Fee upon execution of this Agreement, with fees due and payable in advance.

    B.  **All Subsequent Internet Reports**

    LICENSEE shall submit an updated Internet Report Form (Schedule "B") thirty (30) days prior to the start of each "Billing Period" (defined below). The Report of average monthly page views during January 1 through June 30 shall be submitted on or before June 1st (estimate June page views) and will be reflected in the Billing Period of July 1 through December 31. The Report of average monthly page views during July 1 through December 31 shall be submitted on or before December 1st (estimate December page views) and will be reflected in the Billing Period of January 1 through June 30 of each calendar year.

    The average number of monthly Page Requests shall be calculated by determining the total number of monthly Page Requests for the six (6) month Report Period divided by six (6).

    For your convenience, annual electronic submission is encouraged and can be accomplished at http://www.sesac.com/licensing/internet_media_report.htm. SESAC will also accept timely submission of the Schedule "B" Report Form by mail, fax or E-mail.

3.  **License Fee Calculation for Year 2001**

    A.  **Initial Billing Period**

    "Initial Billing Period" - The Initial Billing Period represents the period from the Effective Date of this Agreement through June 30 for agreements with Effective Dates from January 1 through June 1; or, the period from the Effective Date of this Agreement through December 31 for agreements with Effective Dates from July 1 through December 1.

    The initial License Fee payment shall be a pro-rated amount calculated by applying the then current License Fee Schedule to the Period from the Effective Date through the end of the Initial Billing Period.

**B. Subsequent Billing Periods**

"Billing Period" - The Billing Period represents the period of either January 1 through June 30, or July 1 through December 31 of each calendar year.

All subsequent License Fee payments shall be submitted on or before the first day of January, for the Billing Period of January 1 through June 30; and on or before the first day of July, for the Billing Period of July 1 through December 31 of each calendar year.

**4. Foreign Territory Rights**

If LICENSEE would like to secure Foreign Territory Rights, please contact SESAC directly to learn more.

**All License Fees may be paid online or by mail (*If by mail, please write your Web Site Address on your check*). The account number is required for making all subsequent Reports.**

**SESAC**
55 Music Square East
Nashville, TN 37203

Fax No:     615-321-6292
Questions:  615-320-0055
Email:      billing@sesac.com

By clicking on the "I Accept" button below, you warrant and represent that you have read this Agreement; have had the opportunity to seek further explanation of the Agreement; and intend your acceptance to have the same legal effect as your signature. By continuing you will be directed to the processing page where further information is required to complete this license Agreement with SESAC.

Please email any questions to: billing@sesac.com

**Note: If you have print capabilities, you may wish to print a copy of the Agreement for your records, before continuing.**

I Accept

## CHAPTER 24

# THE DIGITAL SAMPLING CONTROVERSY

## SUMMARY

## I. TECHNICAL BACKGROUND

## II. RECENT RECORDING PRACTICES

## III. LEGAL BACKGROUND

A. Multiple Copyright Infringement

   1. Infringement of the Music

      a. Clearly Infringing Samples

      b. Clearly Non-Infringing Samples

   2. Infringement of the Sound Recording

B. No Fair Use

C. Permission Required

## IV. CONSIDERATIONS IN GRANTING AND CLEARING LICENSES FOR DIGITAL SAMPLES

A. Music Licensing

   1. Applicability of Compulsory License Provision

   2. Alternatives of the Music Copyright Owner

      a. Do Nothing

      b. Refuse to License

      c. Grant a Mechanical License for a One-Time Flat Fee

      d. Grant a Mechanical License for a Royalty

      e. Grant a Mechanical License for Royalty and Take a Share in a Percentage of the Performance Royalties of the New Composition

      f. Seek a Co-ownership Interest in the New Composition

      g. Seek an Assignment of the Copyright in the New Composition

B. Sound Recording Licensing

1. Flat Fee Licenses

2. Royalties

C. Where Sampling Artist's Additional Musical Material Is Owned by Another

## V. CONCLUSION

## APPENDIX TO CHAPTER 24

# THE DIGITAL SAMPLING CONTROVERSY

A cold chill raced across the face of the recording industry when a Federal District Court in New York invoked the Seventh Commandment[1] in a lawsuit filed by British recording artist and songwriter Gilbert O'Sullivan against the rap music recording artist Biz Markie and his record company Cold Chillin' Records, after Markie included in his rap album entitled, *I Need a Haircut,* a *digital sample* of three words and their accompanying music taken from the popular recording of O'Sullivan's hit song *Alone Again (Naturally).*[2] Markie's album might as well have been entitled *I Need a Lawyer,* as the court proceeded to enjoin all sales of the album and specifically referred the matter to the United States Attorney for consideration of prosecution under the provisions of federal law that make such infringements criminal acts subject to fines and imprisonment.[3]

This chapter will sketch the technical and legal background of digital sampling and will outline some of the practices currently emerging in connection with the licensing of and settlement of disputes about sampling activities.

## I. TECHNICAL BACKGROUND

The term *digital sampling,* or *sampling,* refers to the recording of a sound, or a portion of a previously existing sound recording, with the aid of a device that can store the recording in binary form in the

---

[1] *"Thou shalt not steal,"* Exodus, Chapter 20: Verse 15.
[2] *Grand Upright Music Limited v. Warner Bros. Records, Inc.,* 780 F.Supp. 182 (S.D.N.Y. 1991). Interestingly, Markie's net album was entitled, *All Samples Cleared.*
[3] 17 U.S.C. Sec. 506(a) and 18 U.S.C. Sec. 2319.

memory of a computer. Sampling was made possible by the emergence of digital sound and computer technology developed in the 1960's and 1970's and has been made practical in the 1980's and 1990's by the widespread availability of inexpensive sampling-capable digital synthesizers and personal computers.

In scientific terms, music is a series of sound waves that emanate from a musical instrument (e.g., violin, vocal chords). These waves cause *analogous* vibrations on the human eardrum which are then transmitted to the human brain and, by act of Providence, perceived by the human mind. Sound waves may be recorded in tangible media, such as a phonograph record or tape recorder, by various technological means. These recordings may be made in *analog* form — analogously reflecting the vibrations of the analog sound waves, such as the grooves of a vinyl phonograph record — or in *digital* form, recorded on tape or on compact disc.

An analog performance, or a recording of an analog performance, may be converted to digital form with the aid of a device that converts the analog sound waves into a *digital code*. This is accomplished by breaking down the sound waves into small bits of information that are represented in the form of the binary numbering system (i.e., numbers comprised of solely 0's and 1's). This is the numbering system, or *machine language*, which forms the basis of modern computing.

Digital sampling can be viewed as the "high tech" equivalent of several non-digital or physical sampling techniques, such as scratching and needledropping. The term *scratching* refers to the process of making or recording the sounds produced by turning back and forth a vinyl record while the needle is still in the grooves. The term *needledropping*, also referred to as *looping*, refers to the process of taking a portion of a magnetic tape recording, joining together the beginning and the ending of the selected portion of the tape to form a continuous loop, and playing the loop so that the selected portion of the recording is played over and over. What distinguishes scratching and needledropping, on the one hand, from digital sampling, on the other, is what amounts to the proverbial Pandora's Box of sampling: the digital, binary or machine language of computers.

The significance of the digital format is this: any information that can be stored in a computer in digital form may be readily displayed, modified, copied, or transmitted to an extremely exacting degree of flexibility. Recording artists today have access to a sophisticated array of equipment capable of manipulating digitized sound recordings. For example, using a triggering instrument, such as an electronic keyboard or specially modified set of drums, guitar or reed instrument, an artist may replay sampled sounds at their original pitch (i.e., vibrations per second) or any other pitch desired. The artist can increase or decrease the speed at which the sampled sound is rendered, add new sounds, eliminate sounds, add echo effects, and, by reversing the sequence of the digital information, can even play the notes backwards. The waveform of a sampled sound may even be displayed on a computer screen and modifications may be made in the waveform to more precisely change the characteristics of the sound it produces.

Sounds may be sampled from live performances or recorded sources such as magnetic tapes and compact discs. An artist can sample his own voice, the sounds made by an individual instrument, or the crescendo of an entire orchestra. Because digital samples can be stored for future use, they may easily be distributed on standard computer floppy disks, allowing artists to create and distribute libraries of sampled sounds for reuse by others. The question to which we now turn is whether we can find Hope at the bottom of this Pandora's Box.

## II. RECENT RECORDING PRACTICES

If sampling were performed solely by amateur musicians or computer hobbyists intending only to perform their sampled recordings privately in their own homes, there would be no controversy. Digital sampling has become, however, an attractive practice among young professional recording artists and their producers.

Sampled recordings merged with original material affords the professional recording artist or producer a way to more economically complete the task of producing pop records within tight recording budgets. For many artists, it is easier to select the "right" sound than to produce it from scratch, and using samples of existing recordings obviates the need to employ the talents of live musicians who could otherwise, albeit at greater expense, produce the desired performance or sound mix. Theoretically, a song can be composed entirely by the mere combination of sampled elements of existing recordings.

Though artists will use samples to save money and time, a more common and compelling reason why sampling is often employed stems from a desire to use the distinctive sound of a successful song or recording artist for the express purpose of giving sampling artist's original work a familiar element that listeners will quickly recognize.

### III. LEGAL BACKGROUND

It has been the practice of many artists to engage in sampling under the assumption that sampling is not a copyright infringement, believing that the act of sampling is somehow a *fair use* of copyright. As discussed below, this assumption is invalid, as now confirmed by at least one court.[4]

### A. Multiple Copyright Infringement

Unauthorized sampling may be an infringement of both (i) the sound recording from which the sample is taken and (ii) the song underlying the sampled recording. As noted in Chapter 1, the copyright in a sound recording is completely separate from the copyright in the underlying song featured in the sound recording, and the underlying song should not be overlooked when considering the use of a sound recording.

It has been suggested that the standards for infringement of copyright for sound recordings and musical works may be different.[5] The standards for determining infringement by sampling for each will be discussed in the following sections.

### 1. Infringement of the Music

In general, to prove copyright infringement, a person must show that he owns a copyright in the work and that the alleged infringer has copied it.[6] The question whether a valid copyright subsists in a

---

[4] *Grand Upright Music,* supra.

[5] *See,* Broussard, *Current and Suggested Business Practices for the Licensing of Digital Samples,* 11 Loyola Entertainment Law Journal 479, 484 (1991). The authors acknowledge that the following section contains a number of ideas *sampled* from the foregoing thoughtful law review article.

[6] *See generally,* 3 *Nimmer On Copyright,* Sec. 13 (1995).

song or a sound recording will rarely be at issue in a sampling case; this leaves the issue of whether work was copied: To prove that his work was *copied* a person must show that the alleged infringer had *access* to the work and that the work and the allegedly infringing work are *substantially similar.* Whether the alleged infringer had *access* to the work will also rarely be at issue in a sampling case, as access will either be admitted or easily proven. The extent of similarity which constitutes a *substantial* and hence infringing similarity has presented difficulties that have long challenged courts engaged in deciding these cases and lawyers engaged in advising their clients on the extent to which a particular use is legally permissible under the law.

Courts have approached the issue of substantial similarity in a variety of ways. Some courts have broken the question down into two parts: (1) whether the work was physically copied and (2) whether the copying was illicit or improper. In the case of sampling, whether the work was physically copied will either be admitted or an easy matter of proof. But proof of physical copying will not end the inquiry. A determination must still be made as to whether the copying was illicit or improper, or, in other words, whether extent of similarity is sufficiently *substantial* to constitute infringement.

In making this determination, courts will inquire whether the portion copied was a *qualitatively substantial* portion of the work from which it was taken.[7] Courts will find infringement where the quality of the portion taken was "the whole meritorious part of the song,"[8] "so much of what is pleasing to the ears of lay listeners,"[9] "that portion of the [copied work] upon which its popular appeal, and hence, its commercial success, depends,"[10] or "the very part that makes [the copied work] popular and valuable."[11]

---

[7] *M. Witmark & Sons v. Pastime Amusement Co.*, 298 F. 470 (E.D.S.C. 1924), *aff'd*, 2 F.2d 1020 (4th Cir. 1924).

[8] *Northern Music Corp. v. King Record Distrib. Co.*, 105 F.Supp. 393, 397 (S.D.N.Y. 1952).

[9] *Arnstein v. Porter*, 154 F.2d 464, 473, *aff'd on reh'g*, 158 F.2d 795 (2d Cir. 1946).

[10] *Robertson v. Batten, Barton, Durstine & Osborne, Inc.*, 146 F.Supp. 795, 798 (S.D. Cal. 1956).

[11] *Johns & Johns Printing Co. v. Paull-Pioneer Music Corp.*, 102 F.2d 282, 283 (8th Cir. 1939).

In determining what kinds of short portions of musical compositions are qualitatively substantial and hence protectable by copyright
law, it will be useful to divide the universe of potential samples into
those tending to be clearly infringing and those tending to be non-
infringing, recognizing, however, that there will always be those cases
in that "gray area" in which the parties may find themselves subject
to the most precisely applicable standard ever developed by the courts,
"I know it when I see it."[12]

### a.  Clearly Infringing Samples

The chorus is often the heart of a song. Because of its brevity,
repetitiveness, and frequent placement at the end of the song, the chorus tends to be the most memorable part of the song. In many cases,
it would not be difficult for a court to find that the chorus is the very
part that makes the song "popular and valuable." Accordingly, should
a digital sample be made of a recognizable portion of a chorus, its
unauthorized use is likely to be held infringing.

Other phrases of a musical composition that are distinctive and
memorable are likely to be deemed qualitatively substantial parts of
the song. This may include any phrase that is repeated often in a
composition or placed at the beginning or ending of the song.

Even a very short phrase from a musical composition could be
infringed by the use of a sample of that phrase if the sampled phrase
is repeated through substantial portions of the sampler's new work.
For example, if the digital sample contains six notes from a song
which repeats those six notes fifteen times, and the digital sample of
the six notes is repeated ten times in the sampler's new work, then
the sampler has taken sixty notes, not six. In such a case, the sampler's
work is more likely to be held substantially similar to the copied work
and the unauthorized distribution of the sampler's new work would
constitute copyright infringement.

Finally, the unauthorized use of any sample which is clearly identifiable as having been taken from another copyrighted composition
or which an average person would immediately associate with another
copyrighted composition is likely to be held an infringement.

---

[12] *Jacobellis v. Ohio*, 378 U.S. 184 (1964).

### b. Clearly Non-Infringing Samples

Because there is a only a limited number of ways in which a short number of musical notes may be expressed, copyright protection does not subsist in exceedingly short phrases of music. Clearly, a single musical note is not protectable by copyright. For the same reason, a two-note phrase is not protectable, and the same is probably true for a three note phrase. The more notes that are appropriated, the more likely the appropriation will constitute an infringement, but where will the courts draw the line on the use of extremely short phrases?

The smallest appropriation from a musical composition ever held to be infringing was a phrase consisting of six notes.[13] In that case, the two songs before the court were "considerably different, both in theme and execution, except as to [the] phrase, '*I hear you calling me.*'" This phrase, and the music accompanying the words, in both compositions, were "practically identical" and the court held that the use of the phrase was a copyright infringement, because the phrase, despite its brevity, had what "causes audiences to listen, applaud, and buy copies in the corridor on the way out of the theatre."

Nevertheless, samplers should take note[14] of a more recent case in which a court determined that the use of a four note phrase, together with three of the words accompanying those notes, would have been sufficient to constitute infringement. In *Elsmere Music, Inc. v. NBC*[15], the song *I Love New York* became the basis of the parody composition, *I Love Sodom*, performed by the "not-ready-for-prime-time-players" on NBC's *Saturday Night Live* television program. In both compositions, the four note phrase was continually repeated and was referred to by the court as "the heart of the composition." The court concluded that the use did not constitute infringement, because it was part of a satire, permissible under the doctrine of *fair use* (discussed below). However, the court stated that the taking was of a "substantial nature," "easily recognizable," and "capable of rising to the level of a copyright infringement."

---

[13] *Boosey v. Empire Music Co., Inc.*, 224 F.646 (S.D.N.Y. 1915).

[14] Pun intended.

[15] *Elsmere Music, Inc. v. NBC*, 482 F. Supp. 741 (S.D.N.Y. 1980), aff'd 623 F.2d (2d Cir. 1980).

Accordingly, while the sampling of a single note or a phrase of two notes would appear not to be an infringement of a musical composition, the sampling of three notes may be the *sine qua non* of permissible song sampling, at least where the sample includes the words accompanying the music. Thus, a single shout rendered by a singer, two chords, or three notes from a nonessential bass line would probably not be qualitatively substantial parts of musical compositions, and therefore not protectable. Commercially insignificant phrases and commonly used phrases would also fall outside the scope of protection.

As noted below, however, sound recordings may be afforded significantly stronger protection than the underlying music, meaning that an infringement of a sound recording may still be found in a sample that appropriates elements that would not constitute an infringement of the underlying musical composition.

## 2. Infringement of the Sound Recording

No known court decisions are available at this time to help determine the extent to which samples may be made of copyrighted recordings without the permission of their owners. Certain provisions of the copyright law, however, do suggest that broader protection against unauthorized sampling may be available for owners of sound recordings than for the owners of musical compositions that may be embodied in those sound recordings.

For example, the copyright act states that, "The exclusive rights of the owner of copyright in a sound recording . . . do not extend to the making or duplication of another sound recording that consists *entirely* of an independent fixation of other sounds, even though such sounds imitate or simulate those in the copyrighted sound recording" (emphasis added).[16] By using the words "*entirely* of an independent fixation" in referring to sound recordings which may imitate or simulate the sounds of another, Congress may have intended that a recording containing *any* sounds of another recording would constitute infringement. Thus, it would appear that any unauthorized use of a

---

[16] 17 U.S.C. Sec. 114(b).

digital sample taken from another's copyrighted recording would be an infringement of the copyrighted recording.

In fact, the copyright law specifically provides that the owner of copyright in a sound recording has the exclusive right to prepare a derivative work "in which the actual sounds fixed in the sound recording are rearranged, remixed, or otherwise altered in sequence or quality." A recording that embodies samples taken from the sound recording of another is by definition a "rearranged, remixed, or otherwise altered in sequence or quality."

It has been suggested that the strong protection implied by the foregoing provisions could be mitigated by a judicially applied standard which permits some degree of *de minimus* copying or copying where the sampled portion of the resulting work is not substantially similar to the copied work.[17] For example, a court could determine that the taking of a millisecond of sound from another's copyrighted recording, or the taking of a more extensive portion that has been modified to the point of being completely unrecognizable or impossible to associate with the copied recording, does not constitute infringement. It is believed, however, that the courts should take what appears to be a rare opportunity to follow a "bright line" rule specifically mandated by Congress. This would result in a substantial reduction of litigation costs and uncertainty attending disputes over sampling infringement of sound recordings and would promote a faster resolution of these disputes.

While the question whether an unauthorized use of a digital sample infringes a musical composition may require a full substantial similarity analysis, the question whether the use of a sample constitutes infringement of a sound recording could end upon a determination that the sampler physically copied the copyrighted sound recording of another. If the sampler physically copied any portion of another's copyrighted sound recording, then infringement should be found. If the sampler did not physically copy, then there could be no infringement (even if the resulting recording substantially simulates or imitates the original recording).

---

[17] Broussard, *Current and Suggested Business Practices for the Licensing of Digital Samples*, at 492, *see supra*.

Even if the courts choose to apply a de minimus standard, or a substantial similarity analysis, the courts are likely to find infringing those samples of recordings that appropriate the style of an artists performance. This would include any part of the performance that is unique or sufficiently distinctive or identifiable with the artist. Examples may include the distinctive "whoa" of Michael Jackson, shriek of James Brown, snare of Phil Collins, etc. Anything that might be considered a *signature sound* of an artist. None of these would be considered copyrightable as musical compositions, but would clearly be protectable under the copyright of a sound recording.

## B. No Fair Use

The doctrine of *fair use* of copyright will not justify sampling for most purposes. In particular, the unauthorized use of the typical digital sample made for the purpose of giving the sampling artist's work a familiar element from another artist's distinctive sound would clearly not be considered a fair use of the copyrighted composition and sound recording from which the sample was taken.

The doctrine of fair use is generally limited to several specific kinds of circumstances defined in the copyright law,[18] such as criticism, news reporting, teaching, or research. Fair use has also been recognized for works created for the purposes of parody and satire, on the basis that society benefits the social and literary commentary contributed by these kinds of works. The copyright law lists the following four factors to be used by the courts in determining whether the use made of a work in any particular case is a fair use:

(1) the purpose and character of the use, including whether such use is of a commercial nature or is for nonprofit educational purposes;

(2) the nature of the copyrighted work;

(3) the amount and substantiality of the portion used in relation to the copyrighted work as a whole; and

---

[18] 17 U.S.C. Sec. 107; See Chapter 25, on *The Fair Use Controversy.*

(4) the effect of the use upon the potential market for or value of the copyrighted work.

The application of the first factor would militate against a finding of fair use in a digital sample case, because the purpose and character of the sampler's recording is generally commercial, rather than non-profit. In applying the second factor, the courts give greater flexibility to those desiring to use portions of informational works, such as compilations of facts or data. Being that musical compositions and sound recordings of musical compositions are purely creative or imaginative works, the second factor is also likely to weigh heavily against a finding of fair use for samplings of those works. The third factor would imply that if the material that was sampled was slight and was not qualitatively substantial, the application of the factor could support a finding of fair use. Of course, all samples that are deemed to have taken a qualitatively substantial part of an existing musical work under a substantial similarity analysis would fail to meet this criteria. Thus, this factor might only apply to de minimis use of sound recordings. The fourth factor has been interpreted as including a consideration of whether the use would have a detrimental effect if the practice were widespread. Further, the U.S. Supreme Court has held that "if the defendant's work adversely affects the value of *any of the rights* in the copyrighted work . . . the use is not fair" (emphasis added).[19] One of the rights an owner has in a copyrighted work is the exclusive right to make derivative works. Since one of the sampling would adversely affect the potential market for similar derivative uses of the song or recording, the fourth factor would not support a finding of fair use.

As recently confirmed by the U.S. Supreme Court in the *Pretty Woman* case, discussed in Chapter 25, the use of music may be a fair use if the use is for the purpose of parody or satire. The courts have determined that parody and satire are works that should be encouraged and their creation would often not be possible without the doctrine of fair use. It should be clear, however, that unless the sample is being used for some form of criticism, news reporting, teaching, research,

---

[19] *Harper & Row v. Nation Enters.*, 471 U.S. 539, 568 (1985).

parody, satire, or some non-profit use, the doctrine of fair use is not likely to provide a valid defense to copyright infringement.

## C. Permission Required

Record companies have tended to be quite tolerant of other record companies whose artists engage in the sampling of their recordings. This tolerance has afforded each record company the informal privilege of tolerating the sampling practices of their own recording artists and producers under contract. As more and more artists become outraged by the sampling of their works, record companies should begin to become less sanguine about these practices.

Music publishers and songwriters, however, have taken a much dimmer view of sampling practices. At least one prominent music publisher has begun reviewing new recordings to listen for samples that may infringe their copyrights. It also should be noted that Gilbert O'Sullivan's record company was not a plaintiff in the songwriter's action against Biz Markie and Markie's record company. Mr. O'Sullivan filed the lawsuit through his own music publishing company, taking on the expense of the litigation himself. As his lawyer explained in a recent music trade magazine, "This case was not brought by some megacompany . . . This case was brought by a solitary artistic person who did not like the idea that somebody was using the song that *he* wrote and the recording that *he* made without his permission. . . . He could have made a deal early on. But that wasn't what he wanted. What he wanted was the recording that he did not like off the market, and that is what he got. If you are a creator, shouldn't that be your right?"

With music publishers searching for authorized samples and filing lawsuits, a recording artist can no longer assume that no one will notice his use of a sample. Nor should the artist assume that he will be absolved of liability as long as an average lay person would not recognize his use of an authorized sample. While it is true the courts have found infringement where the quality of the portion taken was "so much of what is pleasing to the ears of lay listeners" and will often rely on the ears of lay juries to determine whether an average person would clearly identify a sample as having been taken from another song, it is still quite possible that a court could hold a sampler's work an infringement even where an association of the sample with the copied composition is only noticeable by experts or others with trained or sophisticated perceptions. Samplers would therefore be advised to seek permission of the copyright owners even if it is believed that an association could be made only by an expert or that the association is only mildly noticeable. If the sampler knows he physically copied another song or recording, he should seek permission.

Artists intending to use samples from another's copyrighted recording would be strongly advised to maintain a record of the samples used in their recordings and obtain permission from the copyright owners before any distribution takes place. Once the sample is used in a recording that has been distributed to the public, the bargaining leverage of the copyright owner of the composition or recording from which the sample was taken increases significantly.

Finally, samplers seeking the proper clearance should not overlook the fact that two copyrights may be involved in each particular sample. Copyrights in sound recordings are generally owned by the record companies that financed or distributed them, and songs are owned by music publishers. These are rarely the same entities.

## IV. CONSIDERATIONS IN GRANTING AND CLEARING LICENSES FOR DIGITAL SAMPLES

This section sketches the considerations in granting and clearing licenses for the use of portions of copyrighted musical compositions and recordings by digital sampling.

### A. Music Licensing

When a sampling artist wishes to make copies of a recording containing the sampled musical composition of another, permission will be required from the copyright owner of the musical composition. The permission, if granted without further conditions, will normally be in the form of a mechanical license.

### 1. Applicability of Compulsory License Provision

The use of a sample containing the copyrighted song of another will not, however, be subject to the compulsory license provision of the copyright law.[20] As noted in Chapter 12, Congress specifically recognized the legitimate interests of songwriters who might wish to prevent their musical works from being "perverted, distorted, or travestied."[21] Accordingly, the compulsory license provision provides, "A compulsory license includes the privilege of making a musical arrangement of the work to the extent necessary to conform it to the style or manner of interpretation of the performance involved, but the arrangement shall not change the basic melody or fundamental character of the work . . . except with the express consent of the copyright owner."[22]

Because mechanical licenses for song samples are not subject to the compulsory license provision, the fees and other terms of licenses to make and distribute samples containing copyrighted compositions may be freely negotiated. Even if the compulsory license statute should apply with respect to a given sample — i.e., the sample recording does not change the basic melody or fundamental character of the song — the consequences of a sampling artist not complying with the express terms of the compulsory license provision will have the same effect. It has been the common practice of many sample artists to release their recordings before seeking to obtain the proper mechanical license. The compulsory license provision provides that any person who wishes to obtain a compulsory license shall, before or within 30 days after making, and before distributing any copies of the work, serve notice of intention to do so on the copyright owner. Once a recording containing the musical work of another is distributed without compliance with the compulsory license provision and without the consent of the copyright owner, a compulsory license is no longer available, and the copyright owner is free to negotiate the terms of the mechanical license without regard to the restrictions set forth in the compulsory license provision.

## 2. Alternatives of the Music Copyright Owner

When a copyright owner is faced with the circumstances of an artist having included a portion of his musical composition in an oth-

---

[20] 17 U.S.C. Sec. 115.

[21] House Report of the Copyright Act of 1976, No. 94-1476, at page 109 (September 3, 1976).

[22] 17 U.S.C. Sec. 115 (a) (2).

erwise original song, the alternatives available to the copyright owner are: (a) do nothing, (b) refuse to license, (c) grant a mechanical license for a one-time flat fee, (d) grant a mechanical license for a royalty, (e) grant a mechanical license for a royalty and take a share in a percentage of the performance royalties of the new composition containing the sample, (f) seek a co-ownership interest in the new composition, or (g) seek an assignment of the copyright in the new composition.

Which of these alternatives the copyright owner chooses will depend upon the circumstances, including circumstances under which the sampling came to his attention, the value of the song, the importance of the song in relation to its intended use, the leverage he perceives he has over the sampling artist, and the fortitude that may be required to justify his position.

The ability of the music copyright owner to demand a license for the use of a sample containing a portion of his musical composition will depend upon whether the sampling artist's unauthorized use of the sample would constitute an infringement of the copyrighted music. As noted above, in determining whether an unauthorized use of the sample would constitute an infringement of a music copyright, courts will inquire whether the portion copied was a *qualitatively substantial* portion of the work from which it was taken. If its determined that the portion copied was *qualitatively substantial,* then the inquiry turns to *how* substantial. At this point, the music copyright owner would turn to basic considerations of music licensing, including the value of the song sampled, the importance of the sample in relation to its intended use, and the scope of the use. The outcome of an analysis of these factors will result in a perception about the leverage the copyright owner has over the sampling artist in bargaining for a license.

Other factors affecting the copyright owner's leverage include the circumstances under which the sampling came to his attention. For example, if the sampling artist attempts to obtain permission for the use before releasing the recording, then the availability of other samples containing substitute music will preserve for the sampling artist the ability to walk away from the negotiations. If, however, the recording containing the sample is already on the market when the music copyright owner is engaging in his analysis, the result of the *Grand Upright* case should impress upon both parties the significantly higher bargaining leverage of the copyright owner.

A copyright owner's leverage in bargaining with the sampling artist will influence his fortitude or willingness to take the actions required, up to and including the filing of a lawsuit, to justify his choice among the following alternatives, including the structure of any deal, or the amount of any license fee, to which he may settle upon.

### a.   Do Nothing

When a music copyright owner discovers that an artist has made and distributed recordings containing a sampled portion of his copyrighted composition, he may choose to do nothing. This would only be likely in one or more of the following circumstances: the material sampled was not a qualitatively substantial part of the copyright owner's song, the similarity between the owner's musical work and the sampling artist's work was so slight as to render the similarity unrecognizable by the listening public or even a trained ear, if the sampling was so slight that it may be difficult to prove the similarity of the compositions was the result of sampling at all. In any of these circumstances, the copyright owner just may decide it is not worth the trouble to take any further action, if, in fact, he had any action he could take.

If, however, the sampling artist's new composition has become a hit and is receiving a significant amount of airplay and record sales, or if it is merely included in a record album that has become a top seller, it may be worth the trouble for the copyright owner to take steps to enforce his rights under the appropriate circumstances.

### b.   Refuse to License

Should the music copyright owner be approached by a sampling artist seeking permission to make and distribute recordings containing a sampled portion of the owner's composition, the copyright owner may refuse to grant a license. This may be a sampling artist's worst nightmare. To repeat the statement made by Gilbert O'Sullivan's attorney, O'Sullivan "could have made a deal early on. But that wasn't what he wanted. What he wanted was the recording that he did not like off the market, and that is what he got."

It has been suggested that Congress consider a compulsory license scheme for the licensing of digital samples similar to the regime currently in place for recordings under Section 115 of the copyright law.[23] This suggestion, however, unreasonably ignores the rights of the creative artist's right not to have his work "perverted, distorted, or travestied," a right which Congress has enacted into law by the express terms of Section 115(a)(2). This section compels music copyright owners to grant licenses for other recordings, but only after the copyright owner already has once permitted the public distribution of recordings of the composition (in audio form only — licensing the work for inclusion in audiovisual works and motion picture soundtracks and other audiovisual works would not be considered a distribution for the purpose of this provision). Until that first distribution is made, if ever, the law respects the right of the copyright owner to refuse to permit the distribution of recordings of his copyrighted composition. And, even after such recordings are first distributed, the law compels the copyright owner to license only those recordings which have arrangements that do not change the basic melody or the fundamental character of the owner's musical composition.

Nevertheless, unless the copyright owner has a compelling reason not to license, he should consider licensing his music in sampled recordings. A reasonable reason to refuse to license may be that the recording in which the sample is intended to be used contains indecent, racist, or other opprobrious language. Another reason to refuse to license may be that the sampler's work uses the owner's composition in a way that mutilates the composition or otherwise offends the creative sensitivities of the songwriter. Note, however, that a songwriter's refusal to license, for whatever reason, may be overcome if the sampler can establish that his sampling constitutes a *fair use* of the composition, such as a use in a parody or satire.[24]

Even if the songwriter does not have a contractual right of consent over such uses, a music publisher should avoid licensing music in a sampled recording if that action would harm his business or personal relationship with the songwriter. Leaving aside such circumstances, a

---

[23] Note, *A New Spin on Music Sampling: A Case of Fair Play*, 105 Harvard Law Review 726, 742 (1992).

[24] See the discussion of *Campbell v. Acuff-Rose* (the "*Pretty Woman* case") in Chapter 25, on *The Fair Use Controversy.*

music copyright owner should not view sampling as a form of stealing, but as a new market in which to derive revenue for the songs in his catalog.

### c. Grant a Mechanical License for a One-Time Flat Fee

If the copyright owner who discovers the unauthorized use of his musical composition in a sampled recording decides to do something about it, such as write a letter demanding that the sampling artist's record company cease and desist distribution of the offending recording, the response he receives will depend upon whether the sampling artist or record company perceives that the recording constitutes an infringement of copyright in the owner's musical composition. An indignant reply from the artist's attorney telling the copyright owner, in a more or less dignified manner, to go away, should require no explanation as to the artist's perception of the use or evaluation of the copyright owner's position.

If the copyright owner's position is, under the circumstances, a weak one, the parties may wish to settle upon the issuance of a mechanical license in exchange for a one time flat fee. Even if the copyright owner's perception of his case is stronger than the record company's perception of it, the copyright owner may still be unwilling to bear the expense of taking the matter to court, and may accept such an arrangement. The artist or record company may be willing to pay some amount on a flat fee basis, even where it is felt the music copyright owner's position is weak, to avoid the costs and risks associated with any litigation that would be necessary to defend their position.

A form effecting this kind of flat fee arrangement is set forth as Form 24.1 at the end of this chapter.[25]

On occasion, a copyright owner may be asked to grant such a license on a *gratis* basis — that is, without charge. Music copyright owners, once persuaded to issue a license, will generally charge at least some nominal fee sufficient to cover the administrative costs of issuing the license. This may range from $50 to $100.

---

[25] The forms relating to sampling at the end of this chapter are courtesy of Martin Cohen, Esq., of Los Angeles, California, and Ira B. Selsky, Esq., of New York, New York.

### d.  Grant a Mechanical License for a Royalty

If, in light of all the circumstances regarding the qualitative sub-stantiality of the music sampled and the importance of its contribution to the recording in which it is used, the sampling artist is persuaded that the copyright owner has a strong position and the fortitude to support that position with legal action, the parties may negotiate a more substantial arrangement.

A straightforward arrangement under which sampled music may be licensed is the issuance of a mechanical license in exchange for a royalty based upon the number of copies of the recording distributed. The royalty in these arrangements is usually a function of the *statutory rate* set forth in the compulsory license provision in the copyright law, as modified from time to time by the Copyright Arbitration Royalty Panel. The sampling artist, however, would take the position that it is unfair for his publisher to pay the full statutory rate, because the amount of material sampled from the copyright owner's work repre-sents only a small part of the original musical work in which it is embodied. A copyright owner might therefore be persuaded to accept half of the statutory rate or less, and, in fact, this has become the standard practice. The percentage is typically set between 10% to 50%, with the prevailing rate in average sampling cases being about 30% of statutory.

### e.  Grant a Mechanical License for a Royalty and Take a Share in a Percentage of the Performance Royalties of the New Composition

Nevertheless, the foregoing arrangement may still not be satisfac-tory to the copyright owner, who would understandably assert that he should not only receive a portion of the mechanical royalty for copies made and distributed of the recording, but should also share a portion of the performance royalties resulting from the broadcast of the music on radio and television and other public performances.

The most common arrangement under which sampled music is licensed are deals in which the copyright owner grants a mechanical license at some percentage below the statutory rate and the sampling artist agrees that the copyright owner is entitled to receive some per-centage of the performance royalties payable by performance rights societies. Even where a significantly substantial amount of the copyright owner's music is sampled, the copyright owner may be willing accept a mechanical royalty at lower than the statutory rate in exchange for a significant share of the performance royalties, because the latter often represents a greater source of income than mechanical royalties.

A form effecting this kind of sample licensing arrangement is set forth as Form 24.2 at the end of this chapter.

A special problem arises where the sampling artist does not own the composition containing the sampled song. For example, a sampling artist may include a sample of song in a recording of a song owned by another copyright owner, adding no original material of his own. Under these circumstances, the solution described in this section will not work, because the sampling artist would be entitled to no performance royalties with which to share with the copyright owner. This problem is revisited below.

The solution may also be unsatisfactory to the copyright owner for another reason: mechanical and performance royalties are not the only sources of music publishing revenue. The copyright owner would want an arrangement that assures that he receives a fair share of all sources of subsidiary revenue derived from the composition containing his copyrighted music, including revenue from commercial advertising, motion picture and television synchronization and other licenses. Form 24.2 attempts to address this problem by making all licenses other than mechanical and performance licenses subject to the further permission of the copyright owner. However, the copyright owner might not be convinced that this sufficiently secures his interest in the additional revenue and the sampling artist may feel no assurance that the copyright owner will seek only a fair portion of the additional revenue.

### f. Seek a Co-ownership Interest in the New Composition

Where the sampling artist can be persuaded that the copyright owner has a very strong position and the fortitude to support that position with legal action, the parties may negotiate an arrangement that satisfies the copyright owners desire to share in all sources of subsidiary revenue derived from the new composition.

The most elegant way to assure that the copyright owner and the sampling artist each receive the proper share of all music publishing income derived from the exploitation of the new composition is for the parties to enter into a co-publishing agreement. Under this arrangement, the copyright owner is granted a co-ownership interest in the new composition containing the sampled material. This has become a fairly common solution to the sampling problem.

Under this arrangement, the percentage of the undivided copyright in the new composition granted to the copyright owner of the sampled material would reflect the qualitative substantiality of the music sampled and the importance of its contribution to the new work as a whole.

When these deals are struck, copyright owners commonly acquire a 25% to 50% co-ownership interest in the new composition. Exclusive administration rights are generally left to the sampling artist's music publisher, who is often more experienced in exploiting music in the same genre of new composition. However, this point is open to negotiation.

Three forms each effecting this kind of licensing arrangement are set forth as Forms 24.3, 24.4 and 24.5 at the end of this chapter. Form 24.4 is a short-form agreement that allows each owner to grant mechanical license to others, subject to accounting to the other co-owner of its share of the revenues, but neither may license other uses unless the other has failed to object after receiving notice. Form 24.3, a short-form letter agreement, requires each party to obtain the consent of the other prior to issuing licenses for each of their respective shares. Form 24.5, the long-form, entitles each co-owner to administer its own respective share. None of these solutions seem desirable. The problems arising from ownership of copyrights split in this manner are discussed at length in Chapter 6.

### g.  Seek an Assignment of the Copyright in the New Composition

If the copyright owner feels he has the leverage and all the fortitude and money necessary to engage in litigation, then he may insist in nothing less than a complete ownership interest in the new composition. An extreme position such as this may be justified in cases where the sampled recording adds little original material to the owner's copyrighted song. This may be the case where the new composition is merely a modern arrangement of the song, the instrumental portion of the composition with modified or new lyrics, or the song's lyrics sung to a newly composed music.

In such cases, the music copyright owner could seek to enjoin the sampling artist from collecting any music publishing income in connection with the recording and collect damages for copyright infringement. The result of such a lawsuit could be severe and the sampling artist or its recording company could choose to quickly settle the claim by just assigning all right in the work over to the copyright owner.

## B. Sound Recording Licensing

When a sampling artist wishes to make copies of a recording containing the sampled sound recording of another, permission will be required from the copyright owner of the sound recording. The permission, if granted without further conditions, will normally be in the form of a *master use license*.

The alternatives available to the owner of a sound recording faced with an artist having included a portion of his sound recording in an otherwise original sound recording are quite similar to those of the owner of the copyright in the underlying music. Those alternatives need not be repeated here, but a few important differences between practices in sound recording and music licenses for sampling will be pointed out in the context of licenses for sampled recordings.

### 1.  Flat Fee Licenses

As noted, the owner of the sound recording may often have a much stronger case for infringement than the owner of the music underlying the recording, but record companies, who generally own the recordings, are more tolerant of sampling, because they know that artists in their own repertoire frequently engage in similar practices. Thus, it might not always be in the best interests of recording companies to do anything that would unreasonably restrain customary practices or help establish legal case law that supports strong protection against the use of sound recordings or musical compositions in digital samples.

Record companies therefore typically accept one-time flat fee payments for the use of samples from their recordings. Where the sampling is insubstantial or virtually unrecognizable, a record company may grant a license on a gratis or nominal fee basis. Examples of licenses to use a recording sample on a flat fee basis are set forth as Forms 24.6 and 24.7 at the end of this chapter.

### 2. Royalties

Where the sampling is substantial or recognizable, or if the success of the sampler's recording can clearly be attributed to the distinctive features of the sampled recording, a record company may demand a royalty. In fact, a record company may actually be under an obligation, albeit an implied one, under its recording contract with the recording artists who created the original recording, to use good faith efforts to generate income from sampled uses of the recording. Royalty rates for samples of sound recordings typically range from 1/2 cent to 5 cents per unit, with advances typically starting at about $5,000. An example of a license to use a recording sample on a royalty basis is set forth as Form 24.8 at the end of this chapter. The record company should review its contract with the artist to determine whether any consent is required prior to issuing such a license.

### C. Where Sampling Artist's Additional Musical Material Is Owned by Another

As previously noted, a special problem may arise where the sampling artist does not own the composition containing the sampled song. For example, a sampling artist may include a sample of song in a recording of a song owned by another copyright owner, adding no original material of his own.

If the sampling artist does not own, or claim to own, the new musical composition embodied in his original recording, a co-ownership agreement may be the only solution to a serious sampling problem the artist has created for the several copyright owners affected. In such circumstances, the owners of the two musical compositions used in the unauthorized creation of the new work will need to work out a co-publishing agreement among themselves. This may be a difficult negotiation, because it would seem that none of the parties involved would have any particular leverage over any of the others. Yet, if the resulting composition became a hit or was included in a hit album, the parties involved would have a great incentive to reach a co-ownership arrangement clarifying where lucrative mechanical royalties, performance royalties, and royalties from subsidiary uses should be paid.

Worse yet, where the work of one party was copied in virtually its entirety and that party is already receiving a mechanical royalty at full statutory rate and all the performance credits, negotiations for a fair share of royalties attempted by a party whose work was subjected to only a small sampling would seem most difficult. The party who is already receiving full royalties — one who has done no wrongdoing — would appear to have little incentive to negotiate, except to avoid the expense of a lawsuit or to maintain good relations with another member of a small industry.

The National Music Publishers' Association (NMPA) will offer its services to help mediate or arbitrate disputes between members and can provide a forum with knowledgeable industry veterans to help resolve the dispute in a quick, fair, amicable, and inexpensive way.[26] Music publishers faced with a situation such as that described above should seriously consider inquiring with the NMPA or a similar organization about how they may help the parties resolve such a matter.


## V. CONCLUSION

It has been the practice of sampling artists to sample under the assumption that sampling is not an infringement or with the knowledge that their activity was illegal, but thought their sampling would not be discovered. With music publishers listening carefully for samples containing their copyrighted works, artists can no longer assume their activity will not be noticed. An artist who has incorporated in his recording a digital sample from a song or sound recording of another is likely to be held to have infringed two copyrights — that in a sound recording and that in the song embodied in the recording.

---

[26] National Music Publishers' Association, 711 Third Avenue, New York, N.Y. 10017, Phone: 212-370-5330, www.nmpa.org.

The first federal judge to have issued a ruling on the issue of such infringement enjoined all sales of the recording and took the unusual step of referring the matter to the U.S. Attorney's office for criminal prosecution. Thus, it is now clear that sampling is illegal and will be dealt with seriously by the law.

A sampler is therefore strongly advised to seek permission whenever he knows he physically copied the sounds of another song. Careful records should be maintained of all samples used during the creation of a recording so that the appropriate permissions can be cleared. Permission should always be cleared *before* any distribution of the recording takes place. By following these procedures, a sampling artist may avoid the substantial risks and consequences of violating the legitimate rights of other songwriters and artists.

# APPENDIX TO CHAPTER 24
## DIGITAL SAMPLING

# FORM 24.1

## LETTER IN LIEU OF MECHANICAL LICENSE FOR USE OF DIGITAL SAMPLE FROM A MUSICAL COMPOSITION FOR A FLAT FEE

January 1, 2000

Hollywood, California

Gentlemen:

Reference is hereby made to (a) the musical composition entitled "_____" (the "Composition"), written by _____ (the "Writer"), and (b) the master recording entitled "_____" embodying the performances of _____. (the "Master"). The following shall confirm your and our agreement with respect to us embodying portions of the Composition in the Master.

1.    You hereby grant to us, our licensees, and our assignees, the worldwide right, in perpetuity, to embody in the Master such portions of the Composition as are embodied in that certain demonstration recording of the Master previously delivered to you, the receipt of which you hereby acknowledge, and to exploit solely the Master. We hereby acknowledge and agree that all rights not expressly granted herein are reserved, and that our sole rights hereunder shall be to embody the Composition in, and exploit, the Master.

2.    We shall pay to you, promptly after the full execution of this agreement, the sum of One Thousand Dollars ($1,000), which sum shall constitute the full and final consideration payable to you in connection with the rights granted by you hereunder, and we shall have no obligation to pay to you or any third party any mechanical royalties, fees, or other sums in con-

nection with our exercise of the rights granted by you hereunder.

3.　　You hereby acknowledge and agree that neither you nor the Writer shall have any right, title or interest in or to the Master or the musical composition embodied therein, including, without limitation, any copyright, administration rights, or rights in or to any portion of any income derived therefrom.

4.　　You hereby warrant and represent that (a) you control the worldwide right of administration to the Composition, and (b) you have the full right, power and authority to enter into this contract and to grant all of the rights granted by you hereunder. You hereby agree to indemnify us and hold us harmless from any and all losses, expenses, liabilities and damages (including reasonable attorney's fees) arising out of or connected with any claim, demand or action by any third party in respect of a breach by you of your warranties, representations or agreements hereunder, and which is reduced to final judgment or settled with your consent. You agree to reimburse us on demand for any payment made with respect to any-losses, expenses, liabilities or damages to which the foregoing indemnity applies. We shall advise you promptly of any such claim, demand or action upon our receipt of notice thereof. You shall have the right, at your sole cost and expense, to participate in the defense of any such claim, demand, or action. You shall have the right, at your election, and at your sole cost and expense, to wholly assume the defense of such claim, demand or action.

If the foregoing accurately reflects your and our understanding and agreement, then please sign this letter where indicated below.

Sincerely,

By: _____

ACCEPTED AND AGREED TO:

By: _____

# FORM 24.2

## SIDE LETTER FOR USE OF DIGITAL SAMPLE FROM A MUSICAL COMPOSITION — TO BE USED IN CONJUNCTION WITH MECHANICAL LICENSE (SEE FORMS 12.1, 12.2, AND 12.3)

January 1, 2000

RE: _____ (the 'Composition")

Dear

In response to your letter dated December 1, 1994, we agree to the reduced mechanical rate of 37.50% of the statutory rate for use of the Composition in _____ recording of _____;" (the "Recordings").

Our agreement to grant this reduced rate is expressly conditioned upon the following:

1. The attached mechanical licenses shall be executed and returned to us within thirty days of your receipt hereof.

2. All releases of the Recording shall contain the following label copy: Contains portions of _____ Big Music Corp. [ASCAP/BMI] Used by Permission.

3. Recordings shall be cleared with [ASCAP/BMI] and such clearance shall state that the Recording contains an interpolation of the Composition and credit that composition with 50.00% of performance royalties. Within thirty days of your receipt hereof you shall supply us with writer and publisher information sufficient for us to prepare said clearances.

4. In the event that the Recording is registered for copyright, the Composition shall be identified in space six of the PA

application as a pre-existing work. A copy of said copyright registration shall be sent to us.

5. With respect to territories outside of the United States in which we control a portion of the Composition, you shall cause the publishing designee of the Recording to allow our foreign subpublishers in each respective territory to claim 50.00% of income derived in each respective territory, from the Recording.

6. This agreement is binding only for that percentage of the Composition which is administered by us.

No rights are granted hereunder other than those expressly stated. In the event that you or any third party desires to use the Recording containing portions of the Composition, for any purpose other than that stated herein, the licensor must obtain a license from us for use of the Composition. However we agree to negotiate such licenses on an arms length basis and will not unreasonably deny any such licenses.

Failure to sign this agreement or comply with any of the provisions contained herein shall result in our withdrawal of the reduced mechanical rate or, in some cases, our withdrawal of permission to use the Composition as you have requested.

Sincerely yours,

_____

Agreed to:

By: _____

Title: _____

# FORM 24.3

### LETTER AGREEMENT FOR CO-OWNERSHIP OF A MUSICAL COMPOSITION CONTAINING A DIGITAL SAMPLE FROM ANOTHER MUSICAL COMPOSITION

January 1, 2000

Re: _____ (the "Song")

Gentlemen:

This will confirm the agreement between you and Big Music Co., Inc. ("Big Music") concerning the above-titled Song.

You hereby acknowledge that the Song has incorporated a portion of the musical composition entitled "\_\_\_\_\_" (the "Original Work") written by _____ (the "Original Writer"), and owned by _____.

New words and music were written for the Song by \_\_\_\_\_ and _____ (the "New Writers").

The Song has been recorded by _____ (the "Artist").

Based upon the foregoing, the parties agree as follows:

1.    The Song will be co-owned by _____ (50%), _____ (25%) and _____ (25%). The writers of the Song will be listed as _____ (50%), _____ (25%) and _____ (25%). The foregoing shall apply to all label copy prepared after the full execution hereof and to the copyright registration form. If the Song has already been registered for copyright in the U.S. Copyright Office, the parties will execute and file appropriate corrections and/or assignments of copyright. In addition, the parties will advise ASCAP, BMI, the

Harry Fox Agency, and all applicable record companies of the terms of this agreement.

2.    Big Music and you will each administer and issue mechanical and other licenses for its/your respective share of the Song worldwide. Neither Big Music nor you shall have the right to license the entire Song for any-purpose without the prior written consent of the other. Big Music and you will collect its/your respective share of the Song and will pay its/your own writer(s) and its/your own expenses in connection with the Song.

3.    Neither you nor the New Writers shall have or claim any ownership, income or other interest in the Original Work.

4.    You warrant that you have the right to enter into this agreement and that the New Writers' contribution to the Song is original and does not infringe on the rights of any third party. You will defend and indemnify Big Music from and against any third party claims made in connection with the Song.

5.    It is the intention of the parties that a more formal agreement, i.e., a "co-administration agreement," may be entered into at a later date, but until such agreement is executed, the terms and conditions of this letter agreement shall apply.

Sincerely,

AGREED TO AND ACCEPTED:


By: _____     By: _____

By: _____

# FORM 24.4

### SHORT FORM LICENSING AND CO-PUBLISHING AGREEMENT FOR A MUSICAL COMPOSITION CONTAINING A SAMPLED MATERIAL TAKEN FROM ANOTHER MUSICAL COMPOSITION

## LICENSING AND CO-PUBLISHING AGREEMENT

## 1. DEFINITIONS

In this Agreement, the following definitions shall apply:

1.1 *XXX:*      XXX Music (ASCAP)

1.2 *YYY:*      YYY Music (BMI)

1.3 *Publisher:* XXX on behalf of itself and YYY, *i. e.,* XXX and YYY, collectively

1.4 *Licensee:* ZZZ Music (ASCAP)

1.5 *Writers:*      [Writer 1], [Writer #2], [Writer #3], [Writer #4], [Writer #5], and [Writer #6]

1.6 *Composition:* the derivative musical work entitled "_ " written by the Writers identified above

1.7 *ASCAP:* American Society of Composers, Authors and Publishers

1.8 *BMI:* Broadcast Music, Inc.

1.9 *Derivative Work, Musical Work:* the definitions of these terms are those specified in the Copyright Act of 1976, 17 U.S.C. Section 101

## 2. **GRANT OF RIGHTS**

Publisher and Licensee shall jointly own in perpetuity and in the shares indicated in Exhibit A, the entire right, title and interest in the Composition throughout the world, including without limitation, the copyrights (and any renewals or extensions thereto). Publisher and Licensee expressly understand and agree that all rights now and hereafter existing under such copyrights shall be exercised and licensed exclusively by each party as to its own share.

2.1    The performing rights societies of the Composition shall be ASCAP and BMI. Publisher and Licensee irrevocably authorize and instruct each society to divide and pay all publishers' fees and credits of the Compositions for the United States and Canada in the shares indicated in Exhibit A directly to Publisher and Licensee, and neither shall be obliged to account to the other for any part thereof. Notwithstanding anything to the contrary, ASCAP and BMI shall pay the full writers' share directly to the Writers in the shares indicated in Exhibit A.

2.2    Either Publisher or Licensee may issue nonexclusive licenses in respect of the mechanical rights to the Composition in the United States and Canada of the Compositions, provided that the licensees under such licenses shall divide and pay all net license fees directly to Publisher and Licensee in accordance with the shares indicated in Exhibit A.

2.3    As to all licenses other than the mechanical rights licenses referred to above, Publisher and Licensee shall notify each other of any license requests either receives. Either party may grant a license as described in said paragraph if it sends notice by registered or certified mail to the other party notifying it of the terms of a request for a license and the recipient fails to communicate the nonacceptance of the license within 7 days after the notice was sent. Notices will be sent to the last address available to ASCAP or BMI.

2.4     Publisher and Licensee shall license the foreign sub-publishing rights of the Composition in the shares indicated in Exhibit A and neither party shall claim the interest of the other.

2.5     In cases of income derived from the Composition from sources not specified above, all licensees, including printed music licensees and synchronization licensees, shall pay Publisher and Licensee royalties in the shares indicated in Exhibit A. From such royalties Publisher shall bear responsibility of paying writers' royalties to [Writer #1], [Writer #2], and [Writer #3]. From such royalties Licensee shall bear responsibility of paying writers' royalties to [Writer #4], [Writer #5] and [Writer #6].

2.6     Both Publisher and Licensee agree to pay over to the other any moneys in excess of their respective share received from any source within fifteen (15) days of receipt.

## 3. TERM

The foregoing shall be effective during the full term of all copyrights of the Compositions. This Agreement is made and entered into as of January 1, 2000.

XXX MUSIC, on behalf of itself          ZZZ MUSIC
and YYY MUSIC                           (LICENSEE)
(PUBLISHER)


By: _____          By: _____
        An Authorized Signature                    An Authorized Signature

## EXHIBIT A

SONG NAME: "_____"

WRITERS:

| Names | Percentage Share |
|---|---|
| [Writer #1] | 60.00% |
| [Writer #2] | 5.00% |
| [Writer #3] | 5.00% |
| [Writer #4] | 10.00% |
| [Writer #5] | 10.00% |
| [Writer #6] | 10.00% |

PUBLISHERS:

| Names | Percentage Share |
|---|---|
| XXX Music (BMI) | 75.000% |
| YYY Music (ASCAP) | 15.00% |
| ZZZ Music (BMI) | 10.00% |

# FORM 24.5

## LONG FORM LICENSING AND CO-PUBLISHING AGREEMENT FOR A MUSICAL COMPOSITION CONTAINING A SAMPLED MATERIAL TAKEN FROM ANOTHER MUSICAL COMPOSITION

### LICENSING AND CO-PUBLISHING AGREEMENT

### 1. DEFINITIONS

In this Agreement, the following definitions shall apply:

1.1   *XXX:*          XXX Music (ASCAP)

1.2   *YYY:*          YYY Music (BMI)

1.3   *Publisher:* XXX on behalf of itself and YYY, *i. e.,* XXX and YYY, collectively

1.4   *Licensee:* ZZZ Music (ASCAP)

1.5   Writers:      [Writer 1], [Writer #2], [Writer #3], [Writer #4], [Writer #5], and [Writer #6]

1.6   *Composition:* the musical work entitled "_____" and registered in the Copyright Office as _____.

1.7   *Existing Material:* original musical or lyrical material (or both) in the Composition authored by written by [Writer 1], [Writer #2], and [Writer #3].

1.8   *New Material:* original musical or lyrical material (or both) authored by [Writer #4], [Writer #5], and [Writer #6], incorporated in the new composition

1.9   *New Composition:* the derivative work which is the subject of this Agreement, which will incorporate New

Material and Existing Material; *i.e.,* the derivative work entitled "_____"

1.10    *ASCAP:* American Society of Composers, Authors and Publishers

1.11    *BMI:* Broadcast Music, Inc.

1.12    *Copy, Derivative Work, Musical Work:* the definitions of these terms are those specified in the Copyright Act of 1976, 17 U.S.C., Section 101

## 2. RECITALS

2.1    Publisher owns and administers all interest in the copyright in and to the Composition

2.2    Licensee has engaged [Writer #4], [Writer #5], and [Writer #6] to add the New Material to the Existing Material in order to create the New Composition

## 3. GRANT OF RIGHTS

Publisher and Licensee shall jointly own in perpetuity and in the shares indicated in Exhibit A, the entire right, title and interest in the New Composition throughout the world, including without limitation, the copyrights (and any renewals or extensions thereto). Publisher and Licensee expressly understand and agree that all rights now and hereafter existing under such copyrights shall be exercised and licensed exclusively by each party as to its own share.

3.1    Publisher grants to Licensee a worldwide perpetual license to use Existing Material solely for purposes of combining Existing Material with New Material in connection with the creation of the New Composition.

3.2    Except as specified in below, Publisher expressly reserves and retains for its sole benefit all rights in or to the Composition not specifically granted to Licensee. Without limiting the generality of the preceding sentence, Licensee and Publisher expressly understand and agree that the sole rights Licensee acquires under this agreement are the right to use the Existing Material in connection with the creation of the New Composition, and to exploit Existing Material only as incorporated in the New Composition only by means of the exploitation of the New Composition substantially in its entirety.

3.3     Licensee shall not acquire any right to use the likenesses, pictures or biographical materials concerning *[Writer #1]*, *[Writer #2]*, and *[Writer #3]* in connection with any uses of the New Composition without Publisher's prior written consent, which may be withheld at Publisher's sole discretion.

3.4     All right, title and interest throughout the universe in and to the New Composition, including, without limitation, the worldwide copyright in the New Composition, and all renewals and extensions of copyright, shall be owned in the following shares by Publisher and Licensee:

3.4.1 Licensee shall own an undivided seventy-five percent (75 %) share of all right, title and interest in and to the New Composition (Licensee's "Respective Share"); and

3.4.2 Publisher shall own an undivided twenty-five percent (25 %) share of all right, title and interest in and to the New Composition (Licensee's "Respective Share").

The shares of the New Composition belonging to each party comprising Licensee and Publisher are listed in Appendix A. The shares of the Composition belonging to each party comprising Publisher are listed in Appendix B.

3.5    The copyright in and to the New Composition shall be registered in the Copyright Office of the United States Library of Congress in both Licensee's and Publisher's names, in conformity with Licensee's and Publisher's Respective Shares. Publisher shall effect such registration in the New Composition and the recordation of this license. If the copyright in the New Composition has ever been registered other than in conformity with this Agreement, Licensee and Publisher shall simultaneously with the execution of this Agreement exchange such assignments of the appropriate interest in the copyright as may be necessary to confirm their ownership in and to the New Composition in the records of the Copyright Office of the United States Library of Congress.

## 4.    ADMINISTRATION

4.1    Subject to the terms and conditions of this Agreement, Licensee and Publisher each shall have the right to administer its own Respective Share in the New Composition throughout the universe during the full term of worldwide copyright, including all renewals and extensions.

4.2    The performing rights societies of the Composition shall be ASCAP and BMI. Publisher and Licensee irrevocably authorize and instruct each society to divide and pay all publishers' fees and credits of the Compositions for the United States and Canada in the shares indicated in Exhibit A directly to Publisher and Licensee, and neither shall be obliged to account to the other for any part thereof. Notwithstanding anything to the contrary, ASCAP and BMI shall pay the full writers' share directly to the Writers in the shares indicated in Exhibit A.

4.3     Publisher and Licensee shall license the foreign sub-publishing rights of the Composition in the shares indicated in Exhibit A and neither party shall claim the interest of the other.

4.4     Licensee and Publisher each shall have the right, throughout the universe to enter into nonexclusive licenses and agreements with respect to the exploitation of mechanical reproduction rights, performing rights and print rights solely with respect to its Respective Share in the New Composition. Licenses with respect to all other uses of the New Composition including, without limitation,, so-called synchronization licenses, shall be issued only with both Licensee's and Publisher's prior written approval. Licensee and Publisher must notify any third party seeking a license from either of them in respect of the New Composition of the need to obtain a license from the other.

4.5     Licensee acknowledges and agrees that Publisher's Respective Share of the Composition shall under no circumstances by subject to or affected by any so-called "controlled composition" clause contained in any agreement pertaining to the services of any recording artist who is also a Writer.

4.6     Publisher shall in all instances be entitled to issue licenses for mechanical reproduction of its Respective Share of the Composition in the United States and Canada upon the terms and conditions of a standard Harry Fox Agency or CMRRA license and otherwise throughout the world upon the most favorable terms then-currently accorded to publishers of musical works in each country throughout the world. Publisher agrees to issue a license to _____ for mechanical reproduction of its Respective Share of the New Composition in accordance with this paragraph.

4.7    Publisher and its agents and designees shall be entitled to receive and collect directly Publisher's Respective Share of gross income (as that term is hereinafter defined) derived from the New Composition, and Publisher shall pay to [Writer #1], [Writer #2], and [Writer #3] any and all royalties and other consideration to which they are entitled in respect of any and all uses of the New Composition.

4.8    Licensee and its agents and designees shall be entitled to receive and collect directly Publisher's Respective Share of Gross Income derived from the Composition, and Licensee shall pay to [Writer #4], [Writer #5], and [Writer #6] and any and all other parties entitled to receive any royalty or other compensation in connection with the creation of the New Composition any and all royalties and other consideration to which they are entitled in respect of any and all uses of the New Composition.

4.9    *Gross Income* is defined as any and all revenue, income and sums, including, without limitation, mechanical royalties, synchronization fees, printing income, and the "publisher's share" of public performance fees, earned in respect of the reproduction and other exploitation of the New Composition throughout the United States. For purposes of this Agreement, each party's Respective Share of Gross Income derived from the New Composition shall equal that party's Respective Share of all right, title and interest in and to the New Composition set forth above.

4.10   Both Publisher and Licensee agree to pay over to the other any moneys in excess of their respective share received from any source within fifteen (15) days of receipt.

## 5.    REPRESENTATIONS AND WARRANTIES

5.1    Licensee and Publisher hereby warrant and represent that each is affiliated with either ASCAP or BMI. Small performing rights in Licensee's and Publisher's Respective Share of the New Composition shall, to the extent permitted by law, be assigned to and licensed by ASCAP. Licensee and Publisher authorize and direct ASCAP and BMI to collect and receive, in shares corresponding to Licensee's and Publisher's Respective Share, all moneys earned from the public performance of the New Composition in the United States and Canada. ASCAP and BMI shall pay directly to each of Licensee and Publisher, their Respective Share of the so-called "publisher's share" of the aggregate fees derived from the public performance of the New Composition in the United States and Canada.

5.2    Licensee hereby warrants and represents that it is entitled to enter into this agreement, that it is empowered to convey to and confer upon Publisher all of the rights and benefits conveyed by it hereunder; that the New Material is new and original, capable of copyright, and does not infringe upon the rights of any person, firm or corporation, including, without limitation, copyrights, contract rights, or any rights of privacy; and that the New Material is not obscene or defamatory.

5.3    In addition to any warranties Licensee makes to Publisher, Licensee assigns to Publisher the benefits of any warranties or representations which it has obtained or shall obtain under any other agreements it has or will enter, including, without limitation, songwriter's contracts, regarding the New Material and agrees that, without limiting Publisher's right to proceed directly against Licensee in connection with any claim against Publisher that is inconsistent with any warranty or representation made by Licensee hereunder or the generality of the terms and provisions of the indemnity provisions below, Publisher may proceed directly against the maker of any warranty or representation to Licensee in connection with the creation of the New Material or the New Composition, including, without limitation, [Writer #4], [Writer #5], and [Writer #6]. Publisher warrants that it is the sole administrator of the worldwide perpetual rights in and to the existing material, and has the right to grant the rights granted hereunder.

5.4 Licensee and Publisher each shall have the right to prosecute, defend, settle and compromise all suits and actions respecting the New Composition and generally to do and perform all things necessary concerning the same and protect the copyrights therein to prevent and restrain the infringement of copyright or any other rights, but solely with respect to that party's Respective Share in the New Composition. Notwithstanding the foregoing, however, in the event the foregoing actions or proceedings shall involve the rights of both parties, the party instituting any such action or proceeding shall give the other an opportunity to join in such action or proceeding. If the other party shall decline to join in such action or proceeding involving its interest in the New Composition, the party bringing such action shall have the sole right to proceed with respect to its own interest and shall have the right to settle or compromise any such action or proceeding with respect to the entire New Composition. If the interests of a nonjoining party shall be represented by the party proceeding with any action with respect to the New Composition any recovery of any moneys as a result of a judgment, settlement or otherwise shall be divided between the parties in proportion to their Respective Shares of the New Composition after first deducting the expenses of obtaining said moneys, including attorney's fees, costs and expenses. Any judgment against an indemnitee and any settlement by an indemnitee of any claim or action against it respecting the New Composition, together with costs and expenses, including counsel fees, shall be covered by the applicable indemnity provisions or Paragraph 11 below.

5.5     Each party hereto hereby indemnifies, saves and holds the other(s), its assigns and licensees, harmless from any and all liability, claims, demands, loss and damage (including reasonable counsel fees and court costs) resulting from any breach of any of the warranties, representations or agreements made by the indemnitor which shall be reduced to a final nonappealable adverse judgment. Each party hereto shall give the other(s) written notice of any claim or action covered by said indemnity, and the other(s) shall have the right, at its election, to furnish, at its expense, counsel to defend against such claim or action.

## 6.    NOTICES

6.1     Licensee's Address:

6.2     Publisher's Address:

6.3     Licensee's and Publisher's respective addresses for all purposes in this Agreement shall be as set forth on above, until written notice of a different address is received by the party notified of that different address.

6.4     All notices shall be in writing and shall either be sent by registered or certified mail (return receipt requested), postage prepaid, or by telegraph, all charges prepaid. The date of mailing or of deposit in a telegraph office, whichever shall be first, shall be deemed the date of service.

6.5     A courtesy copy of notices to hereunder shall be sent to:

## 7.     INTEGRATION

7.1     This Agreement shall not be deemed to give any right or remedy to any third party whatsoever unless said right or remedy is specifically granted to such third party by the terms of this Agreement.

7.2     Licensee and Publisher shall execute any further documents including, without limitation, assignments of copyright, and perform any other actions necessary to effectuate the terms and provisions of tins agreement fully.

7.3     This agreement sets forth the entire understanding between Licensee and Publisher, and cannot be changed, modified or canceled except by an instrument signed by the party sought to be bound.

7.4     This Agreement shall not be binding upon either Licensee or Publisher until duly executed by Licensee and Publisher. Nothing herein contained shall constitute a partnership between or a joint venture between Licensee and Publisher. Neither party shall hold itself out contrary to the terms of this paragraph, and neither party shall become liable for any obligation, act or omission of the other party contrary to the provisions hereof. If any provision of this agreement shall be declared invalid, same shall not affect the validity of the remaining provisions hereof. No waiver of any provision of this agreement or of any default hereunder shall affect the waiving party's rights thereafter to enforce such provision or default, whether or not similar.

## 8.    RESOLUTION OF DISPUTES/CHOICE OF LAW

8.1    This agreement shall be governed by and construed under the laws of the State of California applicable to agreements wholly performed therein. All disputes between the parties arising hereunder or otherwise involving the New Composition shall be subject solely to the jurisdiction of the state and federal courts sitting within the State of California, and Licensee hereby submits to the personal jurisdiction of those courts for all purposes contemplated by this agreement.

8.2    In the event of any action, suit or proceeding arising from or based on this agreement brought by either party hereto against the other, the prevailing party shall be entitled to recover from the other party its attorneys fees in connection therewith, in addition to all other costs of the prevailing party in connection with that action, suit or proceeding.

## 9.    TERM

The foregoing shall be effective during the full term of all copyrights of the Compositions. This Agreement is made and entered into as of January 1, 2000.

[Signature blocks & exhibits omitted.]

# FORM 24.6

## SHORT FORM MASTER LICENSE FOR USE OF SOUND RECORDING SAMPLE ON FLAT FEE BASIS

January 1, 2000

Re:    "_____" (the "Recording")

Gentlemen:

The following will set forth the agreement between you and us concerning the Recording.

You have claimed that the Recording has incorporated portions of your master-recording entitled "        " (the "Master") performed by (the "Artist"), and produced by ("Producer").

1.     You hereby grant to us the non-exclusive, worldwide and perpetual right, but not the obligation, to use the Master in and as part of the Recording and all "phonorecords" with the exploitation, advertising, publicity, and promotion of such Recording and phonorecords in all media, markets, and/or formats now or hereafter known.

2.     If the Master is included in any such phonorecords released under our authority, we shall pay to you the sum of Two Thousand Dollars ($2,000) within two (2) weeks after the initial release of the first phonorecord embodying the Master, but not later than Febuary 1, 2000, or this agreement will be deemed null and void.

3.     Definitions of terms used in this agreement:

(a)    "phonorecord" means any device, at any speed on any material, now or hereafter known, used for the reproduction of sound or sound accompanied by visual images.

4.    You warrant and represent that: (a) you have the right to enter into this agreement and grant to us the rights to use the Master as herein provided; and (b) you shall be solely responsible for obtaining and paying for any and all requisite consents to this agreement by Artist, Producer, and any other persons who rendered services in connection with the recording and production of the Master and any other person (s) , firm(s). or corporation(s) whose consent(s) may be required in respect of the rights granted to us with respect to the Master hereunder.

5.    Each party will indemnify, save and hold the other (and its respective agents, directors, officers, successors, licensees and assigns) harmless from and against any and all damages, costs liabilities, losses and expenses (including reasonable attorneys' fees) arising out of or connected with any third party claim, demand or action inconsistent with any of the warranties, representations or covenants made by the indemnitor in this agreement which results in a final adverse judgment, arbitration award or settlement with the consent of the indemnitor (not to be unreasonably withheld) . The indemnified parties agree to give the indemnitor notice of any action to which the foregoing indemnity applies, and the indemnitor may participate in the defense of same, at its expense, through counsel of its choosing.

6.    This agreement constitutes the entire agreement between you and us (all prior negotiations, correspondence and agreements whether oral or written being merged herein) and shall be construed in accordance with the laws of the State of California. Any dispute or disagreement with respect to this agreement shall be submitted to the Courts of the State of California or the Federal Courts within the State of California, which courts shall have the exclusive jurisdiction thereof. This agreement shall inure to the benefit of you, us and our respective successors, licensees, assigns, associate, affiliated and subsidiary companies. This agreement may not be modified except by an instrument in writing signed by both parties. A waiver of any breach of any party in any one instance shall not constitute a waiver of any subsequent breach, whether or not similar.

If the foregoing represents your understanding and agreement, please sign and return a copy of this agreement.

Very truly yours,

By: _____

ACCEPTED AND AGREED:

By: _____

# Form 24.7

## Long Form Master License for Use of Sound Recording Sample on Flat Fee Basis

### SAMPLING LICENSE

Agreement made as of the 1st day of January 2000 by and between          , a division of          , at          ("Licensor") and          , c/o          , at          ("Licensee").

1.   TERM

1.01.     The term of this agreement (the "Term") will begin on the date hereof and shall continue in perpetuity.

2.   DEFINITIONS

2.01.     "Master", "Master Recording": The recording(s) of sound, by any method and on any substance or material, intended for reproduction in the form of Phonograph Records, or otherwise.

2.02.     "Records", "Phonograph Records": Any device now or hereafter known, on or by which sound may be recorded and reproduced, which is manufactured or distributed primarily for home and/or consumer and/or juke box use and/or use on or in means of transportation.

2.03.     "Retail List Price": Intentionally Deleted.

2.04.     "Person": Any individual, corporation, partnership, association, or other business entity, or the legal successors or representative of any of the foregoing.

2.05.     "Territory": The World

## 3.     RIGHTS GRANTED TO LICENSEE

3.01.     Licensor hereby grants Licensee, during the Term hereof and in the Territory, the non-exclusive right to manufacture Records embodying the Master Recording entitled _____ as performed by _____ (the "Product") embodying portions of 's Master Recording licensed hereunder entitled _____ (the "Master") as performed by _____ (the "Artist"), and to distribute and sell the Product and Records embodying the Product directly to consumers via mail order and retail.

3.02.     Licensee shall submit to Licensor two (2) copies of each Record embodying the Product.

3.03.     Prior to exercising any of the rights granted to it hereunder, Licensee, or its designee, shall obtain, from the owners of the copyrights in the compositions performed in the Master, all licenses which may be required for the use of those compositions in Records embodying the Product to be marketed by Licensee, or its designee, and shall become a first party to each of the applicable Phonograph Record Manufacturers' Agreements with the American Federation of Musicians, or the successor agreement then in effect.

## 4.     THIRD PARTY PAYMENTS

4.01.     Licensor shall pay all royalties due by reason of Licensee's sale or licensing of Records embodying the Product, under Licensor's agreements covering the services of record producers and/or performing artists and/or Licensor's acquisition of the Master.

4.02.     (a)     Except as specifically stated otherwise herein Licensee, or its designee, shall make all payments required in connection with the manufacture, sale, licensing or distribution in the Territory of Records embodying the Product hereunder including, without limitation, all royalties and other payments to owners of copyrights in musical compositions, the Music Performance Trust Fund and Special Payments Fund, and any other required unions and union funds. Licensee, or its designee, will comply with the applicable rules and regulations covering any use of the Master by Licensee and/or by Persons deriving rights from Licensee in connection with the manufacture and sale of Records embodying the Product or otherwise.

(b)    Licensee shall pay, or cause to be paid, directly to the proper parties, all sales taxes (as fixed by law), if any, for Records embodying the Product manufactured and sold hereunder, and, to the extent that Licensor may be additionally liable therefor as a result of sales of such Records embodying the Product, all payments to the AFTRA Pension and Welfare Fund.

## 5.    LICENSOR'S PROPERTY

5.01.    Licensor's copyright and other property or other rights, both statutory and common law, in the Master and tapes thereof, and the performances embodied therein, as well as all other rights in them not specifically herein granted by Licensor, shall be and remain the property of Licensor.

## 6.    COPYRIGHT NOTICE: CREDIT

6.01.    Each Record embodying the Product will bear a sound recording copyright notice identical to the notice used by Licensor for initial United States release of the Master concerned, or such other notice as Licensor shall require, together with the name of the copyright proprietor as indicated by Licensor; this obligation shall extend to any other form of notice which may in the future be deemed necessary in order to protect Licensor's sound recording copyrights under future legislation which may be passed anywhere throughout the Territory during the Term hereof.

6.02.    All record jackets produced hereunder in connection with Records comprising the Product shall contain a credit line as follows:

(TITLE) BY (ARTIST) UNDER LICENSE FROM

Such credit line will appear in the liner notes on record jackets and tape containers. The Artist whose performances are embodied in the Master licensed hereunder shall likewise be given a credit in reasonable size type.

## 7.   PAYMENTS TO LICENSOR

7.01    Licensee shall pay Licensor a non-returnable payment in the amount of ONE THOUSAND FIVE HUNDRED DOLLARS ($1,500.00) payable upon Licensee's execution hereof.

## 8.   TERMINATION: Intentionally Deleted.

## 9.   ASSIGNMENT

9.01    Licensor and Licensee (after written notice to Licensor) may, at its election, assign this agreement or any of its rights hereunder.

## 10.   WARRANTIES

10.01.    Licensor warrants and represents that it has the full right, power and authority to enter into this agreement and to grant the rights herein granted to Licensee. Also, Licensor has the authority to grant the rights regarding the Artist and Producer, and that Licensee is not required to obtain any other consents as to the Master.

10.02.    Licensee warrants and represents the following:

(a)    Licensee has the full right, power and authority to enter into this agreement and to fully perform its obligations hereunder.

(b)    Licensee shall not license, sell or otherwise dispose of or distribute the Product, or Records embodying the

Product, hereunder except pursuant to the terms of this agreement, and shall not assign any of Licensee's rights hereunder.

(c)     In the event Licensee fails to pay any mechanical copyright and/or union fund payments due, Licensor shall have the option of making said payments, including settling any disputes with respect thereto, and demanding reimbursement therefor from Licensee (and Licensee shall make such reimbursement) and a material breach of this agreement shall be deemed to have .

10.03.     Licensor and Licensee each agree to indemnify and hold the other harmless from any and all liability, claims, demands, loss and reasonable legal fees and expenses of the indemnified party in connection therewith arising out of any failure by the indemnifying party with regard to the representations and warranties made by the indemnifying party herein. It is of the essence of this indemnification that the indemnifying party shall have the rights, at its own cost and expense, to participate in the defense thereof.

## 11.     NOTICES

11.01.     All notices and payments required to be given to Licensor hereunder shall be sent to Licensor at its address first mentioned herein, and all notices to Licensee shall be sent to Licensee at its address first mentioned herein, or such other address as each party respectively may hereafter designate by notice in writing to the other. All notices and payments shall be sent by registered or certified mail, return receipt requested, and the day of mailing of any such notice shall be deemed the date of the giving thereof (except notices of change of address, the date of which shall be the date of receipt by the receiving party). All notices to Licensor shall be served upon Licensor to the    attention    of    the    Vice    President,          , with a copy to the Senior Vice President, Legal Affairs.

## 12.    GENERAL PROVISIONS

12.01.    This agreement sets forth the entire understanding between the parties and may not be modified or amended except by an instrument in writing signed by both parties hereto.

12.02.    It is understood and agreed that in the performance of this agreement Licensee is acting as an independent contractor and shall not be, act, or represent itself as the employee, agent or representative of Licensor and shall not have the right, power, or authority to bind Licensor or make any contract or other agreement or assume or create any obligation or liability, express or implied, on behalf of Licensor. Neither the making of this agreement nor the performance of any of the provisions hereof shall be construed to constitute Licensee the agent or legal representative of Licensor for any purpose, nor shall this agreement be deemed to establish a joint venture or partnership between the parties hereto.

12.03.    This agreement is entered into in the State of New York, and shall be construed in accordance with the laws of the said state applicable to contracts to be performed wholly therein. Both Licensor and Licensee agree that any controversy arising under this agreement shall be adjudicated under the jurisdiction of a competent court in the City of New York.

12.04.    The failure of any party at any time to insist upon strict performance of any condition, promise, agreement or understanding set forth herein shall not be construed as waiver or relinquishment of the rights to insist upon strict performance of the same condition, promise, agreement or understanding a a future time.

12.05.    Licensee agrees that the Master licensed hereunder, and Licensor's copyrights and all other rights of property in such Master are unique and valuable assets of Licensor, the loss of which, or the use of which in any way other than as provided for herein, cannot be replaced or compensated for adequately in monetary terms, and Licensee agrees that in the event of any use of the Master other than as provided for herein, Licensor shall be entitled to injunctive relief in addition to all other rights and remedies to which it is entitled to enforce the provisions hereof.

By: _____     By: _____


By: _____


(Exhibit A Omitted)

# FORM 24.8

## LONG FORM MASTER LICENSE FOR USE OF SOUND RECORDING SAMPLE ON ROYALTY BASIS

### AGREEMENT

This will confirm the following agreement dated January 1, 2000, made by _____ and between _____ (hereinafter, "Owner"),
Sunset Boulevard, Los Angeles, California 90028, Attention: and
" _____ " (hereinafter, "Licensee"), c/o

1. Owner grants to licensee the nonexclusive right and license to use a portion of the _____ Master set forth on Exhibit "A" hereto (the "Master"), as embodied in the tape approved byOwner, with no greater usage of the Master than is contained on the approved tape, in the manufacture, distribution, and sale of records, cassettes, and compact discs of the album entitled " _____ " ("Album") embodying the recording "_____" as sampled in "_____" (the "Recording") as performed by _____ ("Artist'). Licensee shall additionally have the right to manufacture, distribute, and sell or authorize the manufacture, distribution, and sale of Single Records, Long Play Singles, CD Singles, or Cassette Singles ("Singles").

2. The term of this agreement shall be for perpetuity commencing on the date hereof. Contemporaneously with the execution of this agreement, licensee shall deliver to Owner its check in the amount of SEVEN THOUSAND FIVE HUNDRED DOLLARS ($7,500.00), which sum shall constitute a nonrefundable advance against, and be fully recoupable from any royalties payable by Licensee to Owner as a result of the sale by Li-

censee of Albums and Singles during the term of this agreement.

3. (a) For all rights and license granted hereunder, Licensee agree to pay Owner a basic royalty as follows: (i) two cents ($.02) per Master on one hundred percent (100%) of Albums, and (ii) one cent ($.01) per Master on one hundred percent (100%) of Singles, sold and not returned for Distribution through normal retail channels in the United States ("basic U.S. rate"), and, on all other sales, including, but not limited to, foreign, budget, mid-price, record club, PX, mail order, and premium records, and flat fee or flat royalty licenses. Owner's royalties will be computed in the same manner (i.e., the manner in which so-called "free goods," returns, and reserves are calculated) as the Artist's royalties are computed. Licensee shall send Owner a copy of the relevant provisions immediately upon execution of this agreement by Licensee.

(b) Licensee shall additionally have the right to include the Recording in Compilation albums or Greatest Hits albums released by Licensee, provided Owner receives the royalty specified in subparagraph 3(a)(i), and/or Licensee may license the Recording to third parties for compilation packages, and/or Licensee may sell through Record Clubs and X's, provided Owner receives the royalty specified in subparagraph 3(a)(ii).

(c) Licensee may manufacture and distribute a video embodying the Recording for promotional purposes. Should Licensee manufacture and/or distribute any-such video for commercial purposes, Licensee shall pay a royalty of five percent (5%) of the wholesale price, prorated by the number of royalty bearing masters on the video.

(d) Licensee may license the Recording for non-phonograph record purposes (such as film and television), provided Licensee pays Owner a royalty of ten percent (10%) of the net receipts received by licensee, including any and all advances.

(e)     Licensee agrees to pay and to be solely responsible for all third party payments that may be due, other than
royalties due the artist and producers on the Master, pursuant
to the use of the Master on the Recording.

(f)     Licensee shall compute royalties payable to hereunder as of June 30th and December 31st of each year for the
preceding six (6) month period, and Licensee shall pay such
royalties before or on the succeeding September 30th and
March 31st, respectively, and each such payment shall be accompanied by an itemized statement of the computation
thereof. Statements shall be rendered, whether or not any sums
are due

(g)     All royalty statements rendered by Licensee
shall be binding upon Owner and not subject to any objection
by for any reason unless specific objection in writing, stating
the basis thereof, is given to Licensee within two (2) years from
the date rendered. Owner shall be barred from maintaining or
instituting an action or proceeding based upon or relating to
any statement unless such action or proceeding is commenced
within one (1) year after receipt by Licensee of the written objection. Owner shall have the right to inspect and make ab-
stracts of the books and records of Licensee, its subsidiaries,
and affiliates, wherein the same may be, insofar as they relate
to this agreement. Such inspection, at Owner's sole expense,
shall be made during normal business hours of normal business
days and is limited to a period of two (2) years from the date
of the applicable statement.

4.     (a)     Licensee agrees to obtain all copyright licenses
from the music publishers for the compositions on the Masters
listed in Exhibit "A" hereto. Licensee will pay all copyright fees
to music publishers with respect to said Masters and shall indemnity and hold Owner harmless with respect to all such fees.

(b)     Licensee agrees that, with respect to the Album
jacket and/or any enclosures therein, Owner shall receive the
courtesy credit specified in Exhibit "A" hereto in connection with

the use of the Master licensed hereunder. Notwithstanding the foregoing, Licensee's inadvertent failure to give such credit shall not be deemed a breach, provided that licensee prospectively cures on all future runs.

5.    Owner shall be responsible for and shall pay any Artist's royalties which may become owing in connection with licensee's use of the Masters hereunder.

6.    (a)    Licensee shall not license the Master for use as a premium record or in any other record, except as otherwise provided herein.

(b)    Licensee agrees that it will not sublicense or convey any rights under this agreement not expressly authorized herein. Licensee hereby agrees that it will manufacture or cause the manufacture of, distribute or cause the distribution of, and sell or cause the sale of Recordings covered by this agreement, only to the extent of the rights and license granted by this agreement.

7.    (a)    Licensee represents and warrants that it has the right to enter into this agreement and to make the commitments it makes herein. Licensee agrees to indemnity and hold Owner harmless of and from any and all cost and expense (including, but not limited to, reasonable attorney's fees), loss, claim, liability, or obligation arising out of:

(i)    Any breach by. licensee of the representations, warranties, and covenants made by it herein; and/or

(ii)    The use on the Album by licensee of any non-masters or any other claim based on or related to the use of said non-masters.

8.    Owner represents and warrants that it has the right to enter into this agreement and to make the commitments it makes herein. licensee accepts this license without any other warranty or representation by or recourse against Owner.

9.     The rights and license granted to Licensee hereunder are for the territory of the World.

10.     The Master hereunder and all copyrights and rights in and to such Master shall remain the sole and exclusive property of Owner, subject to the right of Licensee to make reproductions pursuant to the terms of this agreement.

11.     Licensee represents and warrants that Licensee's Distributor,                    ("              ") is, and intends to remain, a signatory to the then-current American Federation of Musicians (AFM) Phonograph Record Labor Agreement, the Special Payments Fund Agreement, and Phonograph Record Trust Agreement, the American Federation of Television and Radio Artists (AFTRA) National Code of Fair Practice for Phonograph Recordings, and any other union agreement having jurisdiction in the premises. licensee acknowledges that the license granted hereunder is given in reliance thereon.

12.     Licensee shall deliver two (2) copies of each recorded compact disc and tape configuration authorized under the terms of this agreement. Said Recordings shall be shipped to the attention of Vice President, Business and Legal Affairs,
at the address set forth above. Owner reserves the right to determine the quality of the manufactured products and, if it is below Owner's comparable product standards, shall so advise Licensee. Upon receipt of such a notice of quality deficiency, Licensee shall take immediate steps to improve the quality of its manufactured product so that it shall meet Owner's normal commercial standards.

13.     All notices, statements, and payments which Licensee may be required or desire to serve upon may be served upon Owner by depositing same, postage prepaid, in any mail box, chute, or other receptacle authorized by the United States Postal Service, for mail addressed Owner to at the address set forth above, Attention: Vice President, Business and Legal Affairs, or at such other address as Owner may from time to time designate by written notice to Licensee. The date of service of

any notice, statement, or payment so deposited shall be the date of deposit except for notices of changes of address, which shall be effective upon receipt. All notices which Owner may be required or desire to serve upon Licensee may be served upon Licensee by depositing same, postage prepaid, in any mail box, chute, or other receptacle authorized by the United States Postal Service, for mail addressed to licensee at the address set forth above, Attention: _____
or at such other address as licensee may from time to time designate by written notice to _____. The date of service of any notice so deposited shall be the date of deposit. All payments made hereunder shall be payable to Owner, and shall be forwarded directly to the attention of Vice President, Business and Legal Affairs,         ,         at the address listed above.

14.     This agreement shall become effective only when executed by an authorized agent of         and an authorized signer on behalf of Licensee. It shall be deemed to have been made in the State of California, and its validity, construction, breach, performance, and operation shall be governed by the laws of the State of California applicable to agreements made in and to be performed in California.

15.     Owner may assign this agreement to any parent, subsidiary, or affiliate entity, or any entity which acquires substantially all of Owner's stock or assets, or acquires Owner by way of merger, consolidation, or other reorganization.

16.     In addition to any other rights of termination which Owner may have, shall have the right to terminate this agreement and all of the Licensee's rights hereunder in the event (a) Licensee shall breach any material provision of this agreement; and/or (b)Licensee shall assign or attempt to assign this agreement or any of its rights hereunder to any assignees, whether for the benefit of creditors or otherwise, or make or attempt to make any compositions with creditors.

17.    In the event that any agreement oral or written, between licensee and any third party with respect to the licensing of said thirty party's master recordings in connection with the Album shall provide for royalty terms and/or for an advance more favorable than provided herein with respect to the Masters being licensed hereunder, Owner shall have the benefit of such more favorable terms from the first record sold.

18.    It is not presently contemplated that a video of the Recording shall be produced by Artist or the label distribution the Recording. However, Artist hereby agrees that, if a video of the Recording is produced, Artist shall use his best efforts to cause his record label to include the in the music video.

19.    Artist shall cause his record label to include the Recording as the B-side of a single record subsequent to the first single record released from the Album. This provision is material to the full performance by Artist and the rights granted to Artist under this agreement

20.    Attached hereto as Exhibit "B," incorporated herein by its reference, is a direction to pay authorizing Record Company to be paid direct all compensation due under paragraphs 2 and 3 of the Agreement dated January 1, 2000. Artist hereby agrees to cause _____
to make all payments required under the Agreement direct to

_____.


IN WITNESS WHEREOF, the parties hereto have executed this agreement on the day and year first above written.


By: _____    _____

# EXHIBIT "A"

## TO AGREEMENT BETWEEN OWNER

## AND

**ARTIST**                                    **TITLE**

COURTESY CREDIT: COURTESY OF

## EXHIBIT "B"

January 1, 2000

Gentlemen:

1.    Reference is made to an agreement dated as of January 1, 2000 entered into among _____ and me regarding, among other things, my services as a recording artist, as amended (the "Agreement"). All terms defined in the Agreement shall have the same meanings below.

I hereby request. and irrevocably authorize you to make payments to _____ ("Licensor") with respect to Licensor's licensing of the sample of the Master Recording of the musical composition entitled "_____" as performed by _____ (the "Sample") for use in the musical composition entitled "_____" as performed by me (the "Master") , on my behalf, as follows:

(a)    An advance of Seventy-five Hundred Dollars ($7,500.00). This advance will be recoupable by you from all moneys becoming payable to Licensor hereunder. To the extent not so recouped, such advance may be recouped by you from any moneys becoming payable to me, but all amounts so recouped from moneys payable to me shall be credited to my royalty account if subsequently recouped from moneys payable to Licensor. Such advance shall be included as a recording cost item in the recording budget applicable to the Recordings under the Agreement.

(b)    A royalty (the "License Royalty") of:

(1)    With respect to USNRC Net Sales of Phonograph Records embodying the Sample as embodied in the Master at a basic rate of two cents (2cts) per unit, instead of the rates fixed in paragraph 9.01 of the Agreement.

(2)    With respect to sales for distribution outside the United States, sales through mail order, sales through Club Operations, sales of Budget, Mid-priced or Premium Records, and flat fee or flat royalty licenses, the License Royalty will be one cent (1 ct) instead of the two cents (2 cts) provided in the preceding sentence.

(3)    The License Royalty will not be payable until you have recouped the Seventy-five Hundred Dollars ($7,500.00) Advance payable pursuant to paragraph 1(a) above. After such recoupment, the License Royalty will be computed and paid prospectively (i.e., on all such records sold after recoupment).

2.    Your compliance with this authorization will constitute an accommodation to me alone, and nothing herein shall constitute Licensor a beneficiary of or party to this instrument or any other agreement between you and me. All payments hereunder will constitute payment to me and you will have no liability by reason of any erroneous payment you may make or failure to comply with this authorization. I will indemnify and hold you harmless against any claims asserted against you and any damages, losses or expenses incurred by you by reason of any such payment or otherwise in connection herewith.

3.    All moneys becoming payable under this authorization shall be remitted to _____, but shall be sent to me, c/o _____, and shall be accompanied by statements with respect to such payments.

Licensor's federal tax I. D. number is _____.

Very truly yours,

_____

# THE FAIR USE CONTROVERSY

## SUMMARY

## I. LEGAL BACKGROUND

A. Fair Use as a Balancing Act

B. Fair Use in the Copyright Act

## II. FAIR USE IN MUSIC LICENSING

A. Photocopying

B. Criticism, Comment and Newsreporting

C. Satire, Parody and Burlesque

   1. The Case of MAD Magazine

   2. The Case of Saturday Night Live

   3. The Case of the Boogie Woogie Bugle Boy

   4. The Case of Rick Dees

   5. The Case of the Pretty Woman

      a. First Factor—"the purpose and character of the use, including whether such use is of a commercial nature or is for nonprofit educational purposes"

      b. Second Factor—"the nature of the copyrighted work"

      c. Third Factor—"the amount and substantiality of the portion used in relation to the copyrighted work as a whole"

      d. Fourth Factor—"the effect of the use upon the potential market for or value of the copyrighted work"

D. Lyric Quotes

E. A Few Bars

F. Digital Sampling

## III. SHOULD YOU ASK FOR PERMISSION?

CHAPTER **25**

# THE FAIR USE
# CONTROVERSY

A s pointed out in Chapter 1, one does not always require a license to use a particular musical work. Besides obtaining the express permission to use the music owned by another, originating the music yourself, or buying the copyright in the composition outright, you can have the necessary legal privilege to use a musical work by either using a song that is entirely in the *public domain* (i.e., taking steps to assure the music is not subject to any legal rights of another),[1] or by making a *fair use* of another's copyrighted composition.

This chapter will explore the standards used in determining whether a use of a copyrighted song is considered a *fair use*, a use which does not require permission of the copyright owner. Our discussion will be limited, however, to those fair use issues that typically arise in the context of commercial music licensing (i.e., excluding other areas, such as home video and audio taping, which, though important, are outside the scope of this book). We will begin with a brief overview of the fair use provision of the U.S. copyright law.

## I. LEGAL BACKGROUND

The purpose of copyright protection, in the words of the Constitution, is to "promote the Progress of Science and useful Arts." That Progress, and thereby the public interest, is promoted by granting to authors the exclusive rights to reproduce their works, which, being the means by which they may reap personal gains from their creations,

---

[1] Considerations used in determining whether a work is in the *public domain* is discussed in Chapter 7, on *The Language of Music Licensing*.

provides authors with the incentive to create. The right to exclude, or the legal monopoly, created by copyright thus provides a mechanism for rewarding the individual author in order to benefit the public.

## A. Fair Use as a Balancing Act

There are circumstances, however, in which strict enforcement of this monopoly would inhibit the very Progress that copyright is intended to promote. For example, the work of a scholar who may depend upon the use of quotes from the works of predecessors may suffer if permission to use the quotes could not be obtained at an acceptable price. Consequently, the courts have recognized a balance between enforcing the monopoly to provide authors with the incentive to create, and not enforcing the monopoly, to provide other authors the means by which their creative efforts may advance the very Progress sought to be encouraged. But where does one draw the line between the incentive afforded by the monopoly and the incentive afforded by allowing copying by the nonenforcement of that monopoly? Drawing that line is the purpose of the *doctrine of fair use*.

## B. Fair Use in the Copyright Act

The doctrine of fair use had long been a child of *case law* (i.e., court decisions ruling upon individual lawsuits), until it was first given express statutory recognition in Section 107 of the Copyright Act of 1976.[2] The statute, however, fails to provide a clear definition of fair use, and there remains no definitive rules for universally applying the fair use doctrine. The copyright act lists merely four factors to be used by the courts in determining whether the use made of a work in any particular case is a fair use. Section 107, which sets forth those factors, reads as follows:

> **Section 107. Limitations on exclusive rights: Fair use.**
> Notwithstanding the provisions of sections 106 and 106A [regarding the exclusive rights in copyrighted works and rights of certain authors to attribution and integrity], the fair use of a copyrighted work,

---

[2]  17 U.S.C. Sec. 107.

including such use by reproduction in copies or phonorecords or by any other means specified by that section, for purposes such as criticism, comment, news reporting, teaching (including multiple copies for classroom use), scholarship, or research, is not an infringement of copyright. In determining whether the use made of a work in a particular case is a fair use the factors to be considered shall include —

(1) the purpose and character of the use, including whether such use is of a commercial nature or is for nonprofit educational purposes;

(2) the nature of the copyrighted work;

(3) the amount and substantiality of the portion used in relation to the copyrighted work as a whole; and

(4) the effect of the use upon the potential market for or value of the copyrighted work.

The fact that a work is unpublished shall not itself bar a finding of fair use if such finding is made upon consideration of all of the above factors.

These factors, as they may be applied in any particular case, have been called "the most troublesome in the whole law of copyright."[3] When the U.S. Congress enacted Section 107, it stated the general intention behind the provision as follows:

The statement of the fair use doctrine in section 107 offers some guidance to users in determining when the principles of the doctrine apply. However, the endless variety of situations and combinations of circumstances that can rise in particular cases precludes the formulation of exact rules in the statute. The bill endorses the purpose and general scope of the judicial doctrine of fair use, but there is no disposition to freeze the doctrine in the statute, especially during a period of rapid technological change. Beyond a very broad statutory explanation of what fair use is and some of the criteria applicable to it, the courts must be free to adapt the doctrine to particular

---

[3] See, *Sony Corp. of America v. Universal City Studios, Inc.* 464 U.S. 417 (1984).

situations on a case-by-case basis. Section 107 is intended to restate the present judicial doctrine of fair use, not to change, narrow, or enlarge it in any way.[4]

The application of the doctrine of fair use in any particular case will, therefore, be largely judgmental, with the best a lawyer can do is review the case books for any cases on point and making an assessment of the risk his client takes by using a work without the permission of the copyright owner. Often those risks are less influenced by what is "right" than by the potential attorney fees that could be incurred in connection with the defense of any action taken, rightly or wrongly, by the copyright owner.

## II. FAIR USE IN MUSIC LICENSING

As mentioned above, a *fair use* does not require permission of the copyright owner, which is to say that one making a fair use of a copyrighted work does not require a license to do so. The issue of whether a particular use of a song constitutes a *fair use* generally arises in the following licensing contexts: (a) photocopying of sheet music, (b) the use of music in connection with criticism, comment and news reporting, (c) the use of music for satire, parody or burlesque, (d) use of a few lines of a song's lyrics in a book, (e) the use of a few bars of music in a recording or audiovisual work, and (f) the use of a digital sample of a sound recording containing copyrighted music. We will review each of these in the foregoing order.

### A.  Photocopying

Most would agree that when a person at home, or at school, writes out by hand the lyrics to a song or a musical arrangement of a popular recording for use in playing the song on their piano, the copy made in each case is a *fair use* of the song's copyright. But what if, for the same purpose, a music teacher makes a single photocopy of the sheet

---

[4] 1976 House Report 94-1476, pp. 65,66

music of the song and gives it to a student? What if the teacher makes 30 copies for use by an entire class?

Reproduction of copyrighted works for purposes of teaching (including multiple copies for classroom use), scholarship, or research are among the examples of fair use that are specifically set forth in the fair use provision of the copyright law. Nevertheless, the statute does not specify the extent to which particular types or volumes of copying would be considered beyond the bounds of what would be considered an acceptable fair use.

In a joint letter dated April 30, 1976, representatives of the music publishing industry and several associations of music schools and teachers submitted to the House Judiciary Subcommittee responsible for enacting the 1976 Copyright Act, a set of guidelines addressing both the interests of the music copyright owners and the needs of users of music in the academic community. Those guidelines were included in the House Report[5] and are set forth in full as follows:

### Guidelines for Educational Uses of Music

The purpose of the following guidelines is to state the minimum and not the maximum standards of educational fair use under Section 107 of HR 2223. The parties agree that the conditions determining the extent of permissible copying for educational purposes may change in the future; that certain types of copying permitted under these guidelines may not be permissible in the future, and conversely that in the future other types of copying not permitted, under these guidelines may be permissible under revised guidelines.

Moreover, the following statement of guidelines is not intended to limit the types of copying permitted under the standards of fair use under judicial decision and which are stated in Section 107 of the Copyright Revision Bill. There may be instances in which copying which does not fall within the guidelines stated below may nonetheless be permitted under the criteria of fair use.

---

[5] Id. at pp.70, 71, 78.

## A.  Permissible Uses

1.     Emergency copying to replace purchased copies which for any reason are not available for an imminent performance provided purchased replacement copies shall be substituted in due course.

2.     (a)     For academic purposes other than performance, multiple copies of excerpts of works may be made, provided that the excerpts do not comprise a part of the whole which would constitute a performable unit such as a section, movement or aria, but in no case more than 10% of the whole work. The number of copies shall not exceed one copy per pupil.

(b)     For academic purposes other than performance, a single copy of an entire performable unit (section, movement, aria, etc.) that is, (1) confirmed by the copyright proprietor to be out of print or (2) unavailable except in a larger work, may be made by or for a teacher solely for the purpose of his or her scholarly research or in preparation to teach a class.

3.     Printed copies which have been purchased may be edited or simplified provided that the fundamental character of the work is not distorted or the lyrics, if any, altered or lyrics added if none exist.

4.     A single copy of recordings of performances by students may be made for evaluation or rehearsal purposes and may be retained by the educational institution or individual teacher.

5.     A single copy of a sound recording (such as a tape, disc or cassette) of copyrighted music may be made from sound recordings owned by an educational institution or an individual teacher for the purpose of constructing aural exercises or examinations and may be retained by the educational institution or individual teacher. (This pertains only to the copyright of the music itself and not to any copyright which may exist in the sound recording.)

## B. Prohibitions

1.     Copying to create or replace or substitute for anthologies, compilations or collective works.

2.      Copying of or from works intended to be "consumable" in the course of study or of teaching such as workbooks, exercises, standardized tests and answer sheets and like material.

3.      Copying for the purpose of performance, except as in A (1) above.

4.      Copying for the purpose of substituting for the purchase of music, except as in A (1) and A (2) above.

5.      Copying without inclusion of the copyright notice which appears on the printed copy.

Though these guidelines have been criticized in some corners of academia as too restrictive, they are instructive insofar as they state the music publishing industry's views as to the general boundaries of permissible fair use of copyrighted music for educational purposes. Uses that exceed these boundaries are likely to pose legal risks to the user who chooses not to seek a license.

## B.  Criticism, Comment and Newsreporting

Criticism, comment and newsreporting are also among the examples of fair use that are specifically set forth in the fair use provision of the copyright law, but, again, the confines of the doctrine must be determined on a case by case basis. A music critic's use of a few lyrics in a newspaper or magazine column, written for the purpose of reviewing the song from which the lyrics were taken, would clearly constitute a fair use.

How far, however, would the doctrine extend if the use were entirely unrelated to any criticism of the song? In 1940, a court held that the use of twelve lines of the lyrics from the 1914 song, *Poor Pauline,* by the *New Yorker* magazine in a brief comment in its "Talk of the Town" section about the death of film actress, Pauline White, was a fair use of the lyric.[6] Similarly, the following year, a court held that the quotation of the eight line chorus of the "official song" of

---

[6] *Broadway Music Corp. v. F-R Publishing Corp.,* 31 F.Supp. 817 (S.D.N.Y. 1940).

the Green Bay Packer football team in a four page article appearing in the *Saturday Evening Post* was a fair use. Contrast these cases with the outcome noted below, where the use is not in a magazine, which is more closely associated with temporal news reporting, but in a book.

Another example of a use for comment purposes, would be the inclusion on our Web site, *Kohn on Music Licensing*,[7] the lyrics of songs, *Oh, Pretty Woman* and its rap parody, *Pretty Woman*, as part of an illustration of the U.S. Supreme Court's application of the doctrine of fair use in *Campbell v. Acuff-Rose Music* (see below). If we were to take thirty-second clips from the sound recordings of each of these songs and included them on our Web site, we would think that such use would also constitute a fair use.

Is a televised news report of a parade showing a marching band performing copyrighted music a fair use? Provided the broadcast is truly televised for purposes of reporting the news, and not for mere entertainment purposes, it probably is. Drawing the line between news and entertainment, however, is not always easy. Nevertheless, if the newscast were to be taped for future commercial use, a synchronization or videogram license would be required.

## C. Satire, Parody and Burlesque

Perhaps the most litigated and controversial issues involving the doctrine of fair use have stemmed from the use of music for the purpose of parody, satire, or burlesque. Fair use has generally been recognized for works created for the purposes of parody, satire, or burlesque on the basis that society benefits from the social and literary commentary contributed by these kinds of works.[8] Nevertheless, determining whether a particular use qualifies for the defense must still be made on a case by case basis.

A case by case analysis will be aided by an understanding of the rationale underlying some of the key court decisions in this area.

### 1. The Case of MAD Magazine

One of the first cases to deal with the extent to which song parodies constitute a fair use of copyright was *Berlin v. E.C. Publications,*

---

[7] *http://www.kohnmusic.com*

[8] *See,* 3 *Nimmer On Copyright,* Sec. 13.05[C] (2000)

*Inc.*[9] The prose of Judge Kaufman, writing for the U.S. Court of Appeals for the Second Circuit, was too entertaining to resist quoting him here at length:

> **Irving R. Kaufman, Circuit Judge.** Through depression and boom, war and peace, Tin Pan Alley has light-heartedly insisted that "the whole world laughs" with a laughter, and that "the best things in life are free." In an apparent departure from these delightful sentiments, the owners of the copyrights upon some twenty-five popular songs instituted this action against the publishers, employees, and distributors of "Mad Magazine," alleging that Mad's publication of satiric parody lyrics to plaintiffs' songs infringed the copyrighted originals, despite Mad's failure to reproduce the music of plaintiffs' compositions in any form whatsoever. . . .
>
> . . . The parodies were published as a "special bonus" to the Fourth Annual Edition of Mad, whose cover characterized its contents as "More Trash From Mad — A Sickening Collection of Humor and Satire From Past Issues," and almost prophetically carried this admonition for its readers: "For Solo or Group Participation (Followed by Arrest)." Defendants' efforts were billed as "a collection of parody lyrics to 57 old standards which reflect the idiotic world we live in today." Divided into nine categories, ranging from "Songs of Space & The Atom," to "Songs of Sports," they were accompanied by the notation that they were to be "Sung to" or "Sung to the tune of" a well-known popular song — in twenty-five cases, the plaintiffs' copyrighted compositions. So that this musical direction might feasibly be obeyed, the parodies were written in the same meter as the original lyrics.
>
> The District Court observed that the theme and content of the parodies differed markedly from those of the originals. Thus, "The Last Time I Saw Paris," originally written as a nostalgic ballad which tenderly recalled pre-war France, became in defendant's hands, "The Last Time I Saw Maris," a caustic commentary upon the tendency of a baseball hero to become a television pitchman, more prone to tempt injury with the razor blade which he advertises than with the hazards of the game which he plays. Similarly, defendants trans-

---

[9] *Berlin v. E.C. Publications, Inc.*, 329 F.2d 57 (2d Cir. 1964)

formed the plaintiffs' "A Pretty Girl is Like a Melody," into "Louella Schwartz Describes Her Malady"; what was originally a tribute to feminine beauty became a burlesque of a feminine hypochondriac troubled with sleeplessness and a propensity to tell the world of her plight. As might be inferred from the range of categories presented and the foregoing examples of defendants' works, the parodies were as diverse in their targets for satire as they were broad in their humor.

After providing an analysis of the relative "substantiality — in terms of both quality and quantity — of the material taken from the original," (which analysis included a notable lampoon of one of the plaintiffs — "We doubt that even so eminent a composer as plaintiff Irving Berlin should be permitted to claim a property interest in iambic pentameter"), the court concluded,

> We believe that parody and satire *are* deserving of substantial freedom — both as entertainment and as a form of social and literary criticism. As readers of Cervantes's "Don Quixote" and Swift's "Gulliver's Travels," or the parodies of a modern master such as Max Beerbohm well know, many a true word is spoken in jest. At the very least, where, as here, it is clear that the parody has neither the intent nor the effect of fulfilling the original, and where the parodist does not appropriate a greater amount of the original work than is necessary to "recall or conjure up" the object of his satire, a finding of infringement would be improper.

### 2. The Case of Saturday Night Live

A late night television performance of the *Not Ready for Prime Time Players* kicked off a court battle that culminated in a 1980 decision by the U.S. Court of Appeals for the Second Circuit upholding a finding of fair use.[10] The entire opinion of the court is set forth as follows:

> This copyright infringement suit concerns a skit, shown on the television program, "Saturday Night Live," poking fun at New York

---

[10] *Elsmere Music, Inc. v. National Broadcasting Company,* 623 F.2d 252 (2d Cir. 1980).

City's public relations campaign and its theme song. In the four-minute skit the town fathers of Sodom discuss a plan to improve their city's image. The satire ends with the singing of "I Love Sodom" to the tune of "I Love New York." The District Court for the Southern District of New York (Gerard L. Goettel, Judge) rejected appellant's claim of copyright infringement, concluding that the parody was protected fair use. Believing that, in today's world of often unrelieved solemnity, copyright law should be hospitable to the humor parody, and that the District Court correctly applied the doctrine of fair use, we affirm on Judge Goettel's thorough opinion. 482 F.Supp. 741.

The decision contained the following lone, but instructive, footnote:

> The District Court concluded, among other things, that the parody did not make more extensive use of appellant's song than was necessary to "conjure up" the original. 482 F.Supp. at 747. While we agree with this conclusion, we note that the concept of "conjuring up" an original came into the copyright law not as a limitation on how much of an original may be used, but as a recognition that a parody frequently needs to be more than a fleeting evocation of an original in order to make its humorous point. *Columbia Pictures Corp. v. National Broadcasting Co.*, 137 F.Supp. 348, 354 (S.D.Cal. 1955). A parody is entitled at least to "conjure up" the original. Even more extensive use would still be fair use, provided the parody builds upon the original, using the original as a known element of modern culture and contributing something new for humorous effect or commentary.

Thus, a parody may constitute a fair use even where it uses more material than is necessary to conjure up the original.

But what if the commentary expressed by the parody is not directed at the original work, but rather at another work or person, or at society in general? Within that question lies the subtle difference between a *parody* and a *satire*. One court defined *parody* as a work in which the language or style of another work is closely imitated or mimicked for comic effect or ridicule and in which some critical comment or statement about the original work is made, and *satire* as a work which holds up or exposes the vices or shortcomings of an individual or institution to ridicule or derision, usually with an intent to stimulate change.[11] Thus parody both mimics and comments upon the original; satire mimics the original, but the object of its comment or ridicule may be either the original work or another work, person, or institution.

In the *Elsmire* case, the court recognized that the target of the parody was both New York City's public relations campaign and the *I Love New York* theme song. Would a fair use defense protect the use of the theme song for the purpose of making a satire upon something entirely unrelated to the song or its subject?

### 3. The Case of the Boogie Woogie Bugle Boy

That question was briefly addressed in the case of *MCA v. Wilson*, the X-rated facts of which were summarized by the court as follows:

> From January 1974 until July 1976, a show called "Let My People Come" was performed at the Village Gate, a cabaret in the Greenwich Village section of New York City. Thereafter, it had short runs in several other cabarets and legitimate theaters. The producers, perhaps wisely, refrained from seeking reviews from established theater critics. However, columnists who viewed the production described it, among other things, as an "erotic nude show" with "sex content raunchy enough to satisfy the most jaded porno palate," a show whose "main concern is not fornication but fellatio and cunnilingus."

> The music in the show was said by one columnist to sound "like something we've heard before but definitely not with these words." One of the songs, described by reporters as a "take-off on the Andrews Sisters' and Bette Midler's renditions of "Boogie Woogie Bugle Boy" is the subject of this litigation.

> . . . Boogie Woogie Bugle Boy is the alliterative description of a soldier in "Company B" who hailed from Chicago. During early rehearsals for Let My People Come, defendant Wilson played for the cast a rough version of the song he had composed which allit-

---

[11] *Metro-Goldwyn-Mayer, Inc. v. Showcase Atlanta Co-op Productions, Inc.*, 479 F.Supp. 351 (1979).

eratively described the "Cunnilingus Champion of Company C" who came from Memphis or maybe St. Joe.

One might conjure a valid defense that the language and style of the song *Boogie Woogie Bugle Boy* was closely imitated for comic effect or ridicule, including some critical comment or statement about the original, but the court found that this was simply not proven at trial and rejected the application of the fair use defense given the facts before it.

At the trial, the defendant testified that, sometime during the re-hearsals that followed the song's unveiling, he formed the intent that the song would be a burlesque of the music of the 1940's. The plaintiff contended that, since *Cunnilingus Champion* did not parody the song, *Boogie Woogie Bugle Boy*, it could not be a parody entitled to fair use. The court, however, agreed with the defendant, and stated,

> ". . . [A] permissible parody need not be directed solely to the copyrighted song but may also reflect life in general.

Nevertheless, the evidence showed that, *at the time he originally wrote* the song, *Cunnilingus Champion*, the defendant did not intend it to be either a burlesque or a satire. Moreover,

> When this action was commenced in July 1974, defendants did not contend that they were making a fair use of plaintiff's song. Instead, they simply denied plaintiff's allegation that Cunninglingus Cham-pion was substantially copied from plaintiff's copyrighted work.

As a result, the court held that the defendants' song was neither a parody nor a burlesque *of Boogie Woogie Bugle Boy*, and concluded:

> We are not prepared to hold that a commercial composer can pla-giarize a competitor's copyrighted song, substitute dirty lyrics of his own, perform it for commercial gain, and then escape liability by calling the end result a parody or satire on the mores of society.

### 4.  The Case of Rick Dees

A case involving radio disc jockey Rick Dees and the '50's song, *When Sunny Gets Blue*, is also instructive.[12] In 1984, a lawyer rep-

---

[12] *Fisher v. Dees*, 794 F.2d 432 (9th Cir. 1986).

resenting Dees contacted one of the song's composers and requested permission to use all or a part of the music to create an inoffensive, comedic version. The composer refused to grant permission, and, a few months later, Dees released a comedy album called *Put It Where the Moon Don't Shine*. The album included, *When Sonny Sniffs Glue*, a parody which copied the first six of the original song's thirty-eight bars of music — its recognizable main theme. In addition, it changed the original's opening lyrics — "When Sonny gets blue, her eyes get gray and cloudy, then the rain begins to fall" to "When Sonny sniffs glue, her eyes get red and bulgy, then her hair begins to fall." The parody ran for 29 seconds of the approximately forty minutes of material on Dee's album.

The composers asserted that the parody, although it borrowed from the original work, was not "directed" at the original. Though the court assumed that a humorous or satiric work deserved protection under the fair use doctrine only if the copied work is "at least partly the target of the work in question"— a conclusion which was later refined by the Supreme Court (see below) — the court found that Dees's parody was intended to poke fun at the composer's song *and* at Johnny Mathis's rather singular vocal range.

In analyzing the "purpose and character" of the use, the court cited the principle earlier established by the U.S. Supreme Court that "every commercial use of copyrighted material is presumptively an unfair exploitation of the monopoly privilege that belongs to the owner of the copyright,"[13] but pointed out that the defendant can rebut the presumption by convincing the court that the parody does not unfairly diminish the economic value of the original. In assessing the economic effect of the parody upon the potential market or value of the copyrighted work, the court stated that the parody's critical impact must be excluded. Through its critical function, a "parody may quite legitimately aim at garroting the original, destroying it commercially as well as artistically."[14]

> Accordingly, the economic effect of a parody with which we are concerned is not its potential to destroy or diminish the market for

---

[13] *Sony Corp. Of America v. Universal City Studios, Inc.*, 464 U.S. 417 (1984); *Harper & Row, Publishers, Inc. v. Nation Enterprises*, 471 U.S. 539 (1985).
[14] B. Kaplan, *An Unhurried View of Copyright* 69 (1967).

the original — any bad review can have that effect — but rather whether it fulfills the demand for the original. Biting criticism suppresses demand; copyright infringement usurps it. Thus, infringement occurs when a parody supplants the original in markets the original is aimed at, or in which the original is, or has reasonable potential to become, commercially viable.[15]

With that guidance in mind, the court proceeded to hold that the two songs did not fulfill the same demand.

"When Sunny Gets Blue" is "a lyrical song concerning or relating to a woman's feelings about lost love and her change for . . . happiness again."[citation omitted] By contrast, the parody is a 29-second recording concerning a woman who sniffs glue, which "ends with noise and laughter mixed into the song." [citation omitted] We do not believe the consumers desirous of hearing a romantic and nostalgic ballad such as the composer's song would be satisfied to purchase the parody instead. Nor are those fond of parody likely to consider "When Sunny Gets Blue" a source of satisfaction.

In analyzing the "amount and substantiality of the taking," the court explored the boundaries of a test it articulated in an earlier opinion: "whether the parodist has appropriated a greater amount of the original work than is necessary to 'recall or conjure up' the object of his satire."[16] The composers interpreted this test to limit the amount of permissible copying to that necessary to evoke only *initial* recognition by the listener. In rejecting this rigid view, the court found itself in accord with the lone footnote of *Elsmere Music, Inc. v. National Broadcasting Company* set forth above — i.e., a parody is entitled *at least* to conjure up the original.

The court listed three considerations it thought important in determining whether a taking were excessive under the circumstances: the degree of public recognition of the original, the ease of conjuring up the original work in the chosen medium, and the focus of the parody. The court found that, in creating parodies of music, there is a special need for accuracy, because, like a speech, a song is difficult

---

[15] 794 F.2d at 438.

[16] *Walt Disney Productions v. Air Pirates*, 581 F.2d 751, 757 (9th Cir. 1978).

to parody effectively without exact or near-exact copying. Though the license to copy is not limitless, a parody that accomplishes its purpose by taking no more than is necessary to reasonably accomplish its parodic purpose is a fair use.

### 5.  The Case of the Pretty Woman

On March 7, 1994, the U.S. Supreme Court strolled down the proverbial street of fair use parody by publishing a decision in a case over whether the song, *Oh Pretty Woman*, by Roy Orbison and William Dees was infringed by a song entitled, *Pretty Woman*, recorded by rap recording group, 2 Live Crew.[17]

At the outset of its discussion of the four factors of fair use set forth in the copyright law, the court quoted an early distillation of "fair use" rendered by Justice Story in *Folsom v. Marsh*:

> look to the nature and objects of the selections made, the quantity and value of the materials used, and the degree in which the use may prejudice the sale, or diminish the profits, or supersede the objects, of the original work.[18]

The court then proceeded to explore each of the four factors set forth in Section 107 and applied them to the facts of the case.

### a.  First Factor — "The purpose and character of the use, including whether such use is of a commercial nature or is for nonprofit educational purposes."

The central purpose of this investigation, said the court, is to see whether the new work merely supersedes the objects of the original creation or instead adds something new, with a further purpose or different character, altering the first with new expression, meaning or message; it asks, in other words, whether and to what extent the new work is "transformative." Although a transformative use is not necessary for a finding of fair use, the more transformative the new work,

---

[17] *Campbell v. Acuff-Rose*, 114 S.Ct. 1164, 127 L.Ed.2d 5001, (1994).
[18] *Folsom v. Marsh* 9 F Cas 342, 348 (No. 4,901 (CCD Mass 1841).

the less will be the significance of other factors, such as commercialism, that may weigh against a finding of fair use.

The court then confirmed that parody has an obvious claim to transformative value, as it can provide social benefit by shedding light on an earlier work, and, in the process, create a new one. Recognizing the difference between *parody* and *satire*, quoting two standard dictionary definitions of each word, the court shed some light on the question of the extent to which a parody qualifying for the fair use defense must be directed at the original work:

> For the purposes of copyright law, the nub of the definitions, and the heart of any parodist's claim to quote from existing material, is the use of some elements of a prior author's composition to create a new one that, at least in part, comments on that author's works. See, e.g., *Fisher v. Dees*, supra, at 437; *MCA, Inc. v. Wilson*, 677 F. 2d 180, 185 (CA2 1981). If, on the contrary, the commentary has no critical bearing on the substance or style of the original composition, which the alleged infringer merely uses to get attention or to avoid the drudgery in working up something fresh, the claim to fairness in borrowing from another's work diminishes accordingly (if it does not vanish), and other factors, like the extent of its commerciality, loom larger. Parody needs to mimic an original to make its point, and so has some claim to use the creation of its victim's (or collective victims') imagination, whereas satire can stand on its own two feet and so requires justification for the very act of borrowing. See Ibid.; Bisceglia, *Parody and Copyright Protection: Turning the Balancing Act Into a Juggling Act*, in ASCAP, Copyright Law Symposium, No. 34, p. 25 (1987).

Thus, whether the parody is directed at the original is not definitive. The extent to which the parody is so directed must be placed on a sliding scale and considered with the other fair use factors, such as the extent to which the parody has an economic effect upon the potential market or value of the original.[19] Consistent with this last

---

[19] Political or social satire, such as that conveyed in the hilarious song parodies written and performed by the *Capitol Steps,* tend to be directed less at the lyrics of the copyrighted song parodied and more at the vices or shortcomings of individuals and instituions unrelated to the subject of the original song. In a friend-of-the-court brief

thought, the court quickly rejected the defendant's assertion that a parodic use is presumptively fair. Parody, like any other use, has to work its way through the relevant factors, and be judged case by case, in light of the ends of the copyright law.

Further, the court made it clear that whether parody is in "good taste or bad" does not and should not matter to fair use. The threshold question when fair use is raised in defense of parody is "whether a parodic character may reasonably be perceived."

In applying the first factor to the facts of the case, the court found that,

> While we might not assign a high rank to the parodic element here, we think it fair to say 2 Live Crew's song reasonably could be perceived as commenting on the original or criticizing it, to some degree. 2 Live Crew juxtaposes the romantic musings of a man whose fantasy comes true, with degrading taunts, a bawdy demand for sex, and a sigh of relief from paternal responsibility. The later words can be taken as a comment on the naiveté of the original of an earlier day, as a rejection of its sentiment that ignores the ugliness of street life and the debasement that it signifies. It is this joinder of reference and ridicule that marks off the author's choice of parody from the other types of comment and criticism that traditionally have had a claim to fair use protection as transformative works.

Before turning to the other factors, the court made some other instructive observations. For example, the court noted that 2 Live Crew need not have labeled its song, or the album on which it appeared, a parody, in order to claim fair use protection. "Parody," said the court, "serves its goals whether labeled or not, and there is no reason to

---

filed in the *Pretty Woman* case by Capitol Steps Production, Inc., the amici pointed out that the particular music selected to convey the satirical message will often evoke a mood, setting, or juxtaposition of sentiments that either adds a musical joke to the satirical lyrics or otherwise enhances their effectiveness. Such a contribution by the copyrighted material to an otherwise unrelated satire would appear to supply that which is necessary to justify the claim to fairness. The *Capitol Steps* were joined in their efforts before the Supreme Court by, among others, nationally syndicated radio host Dr. Demento, whose popular broadcasts regularly include song parodies submitted by talented professional and amateur comedic artists, as well as comedian Mark Russell, whose many appearances on public television demonstrate that political satire need not necessarily be funny to constitute a fair use of copyright.

require parody to state the obvious (or even the reasonably perceived)." Further, it did not matter that 2 Live Crew had never recorded a parody before. However, the court pointed out that the use of a copyrighted work to advertise a product, even in a parody, will be entitled to less indulgence under the first factor of the fair use enquiry, than the sale of a parody for its own sake, let alone one performed a single time by students in a school.

### b.   Second Factor — "the nature of the copyrighted work."

This factor, said the court, calls for recognition that some works are closer to the core of intended copyright protection than others,[20] with the consequence that fair use is more difficult to establish when the former works are copied. Clearly, Roy Orbison's *Oh Pretty Woman* falls well within this core. However, the court said this was "not much help in this case, or ever likely to help much in separating the fair use sheep from the infringing goats in a parody case, since parodies almost invariably copy publicly known, expressive works."

### c.   Third Factor — "The amount and substantiality of the portion used in relation to the copyrighted work as a whole."

The attention here, said the court, turns to the persuasiveness of a parodist's justification for the particular copying done. Further, this enquiry will harken back to first of the statutory factors, because the extent of permissible copying varies with the purpose and character of the use, and will tend to have a bearing on the fourth factor, by revealing the degree to which the parody may serve as a market substitute for the original or potentially licensed derivatives. We now quote the court at length:

> Parody presents a difficult case. Parody's humor, or in any event its comment, necessarily springs from recognizable allusion to its object through distorted imitation. Its art lies in the tension between a

---

[20] Examples of works that are further away from the "core of intended copyright protection" include works comprised primarily of historical facts, information databases, and other compilations, as well as works of a utilitarian nature, such as computer programs.

known original and its parodic twin. When parody takes aim at a particular original work, the parody must be able to "conjure up" at least enough of that original to make the object of its critical wit recognizable. See, *e.g., Elsmere Music*, 623 F. 2d, at 253, n. 1; *Fisher v. Dees*, 794 F. 2d, at 438-439. What makes for this recognition is quotation of the original's most distinctive or memorable features, which the parodist can be sure the audience will know. Once enough has been taken to assure identification, how much more is reasonable will depend, say, on the extent to which the song's overriding purpose and character is to parody the original or, in contrast, the likelihood that the parody may serve as a market substitute for the original. But using some characteristic features cannot be avoided.

We think the Court of Appeals was insufficiently appreciative of parody's need for the recognizable sight or sound when it ruled 2 Live Crew's use unreasonable as a matter of law. It is true, of course, that 2 Live Crew copied the characteristic opening bass riff (or musical phrase) of the original, and true that the words of the first line copy the Orbison lyrics. But if quotation of the opening riff and the first line may be said to go to the "heart" of the original, the heart is also what most readily conjures up the song for parody, and it is the heart at which parody takes aim. Copying does not become excessive in relation to parodic purpose merely because the portion taken was the original's heart. If 2 Live Crew had copied a significantly less memorable part of the original, it is difficult to see how its parodic character would have come through. See *Fisher v. Dees*, 794 F. 2d, at 439.

This is not, of course, to say that anyone who calls himself a parodist can skim the cream and get away scot free. In parody, as in news reporting, see *Harper & Row*, supra, context is everything, and the question of fairness asks what else the parodist did besides go to the heart of the original. It is significant that 2 Live Crew not only copied the first line of the original, but thereafter departed markedly from the Orbison lyrics for its own ends. 2 Live Crew not only copied the bass riff and repeated it, but also produced otherwise distinctive sounds, interposing "scraper" noise, overlaying the music with solos in different keys, and altering the drum beat. See 754 F. Supp., at 1155. This is not a case, then, where "a substantial portion" of the parody itself is composed of a "verbatim" copying of the original. It is not, that is, a case where the parody is so insubstantial, as compared to the copying, that the third factor must be resolved as a matter of law against the parodists.

> Suffice it to say here that, as to the lyrics, we think the Court of Appeals correctly suggested that "no more was taken than necessary," 972 F. 2d, at 1438, but just for that reason, we fail to see how the copying can be excessive in relation to its parodic purpose, even if the portion taken is the original's "heart." As to the music, we express no opinion whether repetition of the bass riff is excessive copying, and we remand to permit evaluation of the amount taken, in light of the song's parodic purpose and character, its transformative elements, and considerations of the potential for market substitution sketched more fully below.

### d.  Fourth Factor — "The effect of the use upon the potential market for or value of the copyrighted work."

The final factor, said the court, requires courts to consider not only the extent of market harm caused by the particular actions of the alleged infringer, but also whether unrestricted and widespread conduct of the sort engaged in by the defendant would result in a substantial adverse impact on the potential market for the original. The enquiry must take account not only of the harm to the original but also of harm to the market for derivative works of the original.

Correcting the primary error made by the lower court, the court held that there is no presumption that uses intended for commercial gain are likely to have a substantial adverse impact on the potential market for the original. On the contrary, the more transformative the use, such as a pure parody or satire, the more likely it is that the new work will *not* affect the market for the original. This is so because the parody and the original usually serve different market functions.

Nevertheless, the analysis cannot stop there, as even a transformative work may have characteristics beyond those of parodic or satiric criticism. For example, the 2 Live Crew song, besides being a parody, is also rap music. Thus, a relevant inquiry is whether the rap nature of the 2 Live Crew song will have a substantial adverse impact upon rap derivatives of the original Orbison version.[21]

---

[21] Having the characteristics of a rap musical recording, the 2 Live Crew parody actually receives radio airplay and enjoys CD sales as a musical recording intended

Since there was no evidence in the record upon which the Supreme Court could base a decision on this question, it remanded the case to the lower courts where the "evidentiary hole will doubtless be plugged." Thus, in contrast to news reports holding that the Supreme Court held the 2 Live Crew song to be a fair use and not infringing the Orbison hit, the court actually remanded the case back to the lower courts for a redetermination of fair use in light of the court's discussion of the law.

## D. Lyric Quotes

Though the quoting of a copyrighted song lyric in a student's term paper would clearly constitute a fair use, the quoting of even a few short lines of the lyric in a book intended for commercial sale would generally not be permitted under the fair use doctrine, unless the use was specifically for the purpose of comment or criticism. When Dr. Sigmund Spaeth, in his book on American Popular music, *Read 'Em and Weep*, quoted the words and music of the copyright song, *Ta-Ra-Ra-Boom-Der-E*, a court in 1932 rejected his fair use defense on the basis that the use was "obviously more than quotation and comment."[22]

## E. A Few Bars

For most uses of music, unless the use is being used directly for some form of criticism, news reporting, teaching, research, parody, satire, or some other non-profit use, the doctrine of fair use is not likely to provide a valid defense to copyright infringement, even if the use consists of only a few short bars of the copyrighted music. Thus, the whistling of even a few bars of a song in a motion picture will require permission from the copyright owner.

---

to be enjoyed as such. Arguably, this substantial, non-parody characteristic may tip the scales against a finding of fair use. By contrast, if the parody were instead primarily intended as a comedy recording, to be enjoyed as such, then, notwithstanding the radio airplay and CD sales it may receive, it is less likely the parody recording would affect the market for the original, tipping the scales in favor of a finding of fair use.

[22] *Sayers v. Spaeth*, 20 Copyr.Dec. 625 (S.D.N.Y. 1932).

### F. Digital Sampling

Fair use has been unsuccessfully advanced as a defense to digital sampling. For a further discussion, the reader is referred to Chapter 24, on *The Digital Sampling Controversy*.

## III. SHOULD YOU ASK FOR PERMISSION?

As suggested at the outset of this chapter, the application of the doctrine of fair use in any particular case will largely be judgmental. All a good lawyer can do is review the casebooks for any legal decisions on point and make an independent assessment of the risk his client takes by using a work without the permission of the copyright owner. Of course, the risk of using a work owned by another can be eliminated by asking and obtaining permission for the use. Suppose, however, you attempt to clear the use, but permission is denied. Should you make use of the work anyway? Was it a mistake to have asked for permission in the first place? Indeed, in the case of a parody or satire, what is the likelihood that permission will actually be granted?[23]

Many lawyers advise against seeking permission where circumstances suggest a reasonable basis supporting the fair use defense. Asking for permission, they say, may be construed as an admission that the defense is not applicable, and, by using a work after permission has been denied is likely to increase the chances of a litigation — a jilted copyright owner seeking retribution for the audacity of your client.

In the case of Rick Dees, however, the court did not fault Dees for using the song after the composers expressly refused permission:

> Parodists will seldom get permission from those whose works are parodied. . . . Moreover, to consider Dees blameworthy because he asked permission would penalize him for this modest show of con-

---

[23] "People ask . . . for criticism, but they only want praise." S. Maugham, *Of Human Bondage* 241 (Penguin ed. 1992).

sideration. Even though such gestures are predictably futile, we refuse to discourage them.[24]

Contrast this with the court's reaction in *Grand Upright Music Limited v. Warner Bros.*, discussed in Chapter 24, on *The Digital Sampling Controversy.*

> [T]he most persuasive evidence that the copyrights are valid and owned by the plaintiff comes from the actions and admissions of the defendants. Prior to the time that Biz Markie's album was released, the various defendants apparently discussed among themselves the need to obtain a license. They decided to contact O'Sullivan and wrote to his brother/agent, enclosing a copy of the tape. . . . In writing this letter, counsel for Biz Markie admittedly was seeking "terms" for the use of the material. One would not agree to pay to use the material of another unless there was a valid copyright! What more persuasive evidence can there be![25]

Does this mean that if you're in New York, don't ask; if you're in California, ask — it couldn't hurt? No, because subsequent to these decisions, the Supreme Court sided with "ask":

> [W]e reject Acuff-Rose's argument that 2 Live Crew's request for permission to use the original should be weighed against a finding of fair use. Even if good faith were central to fair use, 2 Live Crew's actions do not necessarily suggest that they believed their version was not fair use; the offer may simply have been made in a good faith effort to avoid litigation. If the use is otherwise fair, then no permission need be sought or granted. Thus, being denied permission to use a work does not weigh against finding of fair use. *See Fisher v. Dees*, 794 F2d 432, 437 (CA9 1986).

So, should you ask for permission in doubtful cases? Yes, but we suggest that, in your letter to the copyright owner, you set forth your position on fair use, and state that you are writing in good faith in an effort to avoid litigation. By the same token, failing or neglecting to ask for permission should not hurt a good fair use defense.

---

[24] 794 F.2d at 437 (9th Cir. 1986).
[25] 780 F.Supp. 182, 184 (S.D.N.Y 1991)

# LIVE MUSICAL PERFORMANCES

## SUMMARY

I. INTRODUCTION

II. PROHIBITED CONDUCT

III. CONSENT

IV. REMEDIES

V. AFFIRMATIVE DEFENSES

VI. EFFECTIVE DATE

VII. WHY THE BOOTLEGGING LAW WAS ENACTED

VIII. TRIPS REQUIREMENTS

IX. CONSTITUTIONAL FOUNDATION FOR THE BOOTLEGGING LAW

APPENDIX TO CHAPTER 26

LAW 26.1    Unauthorized fixation and trafficking in sound recordings and music videos (Copyright Act Section 1101)

CHAPTER **26**

# LIVE MUSICAL
# PERFORMANCES

O n December 8, 1994, Congress revised the U.S. Copyright
Law by enacting a new right under copyright unlike any previously recognized under U.S. law. Essentially, this new right
is the exclusive right to make — or, to put it another way, the right
to exclude others from making — an audio or video recording of a
live musical performance. It is important to note that this is not a right
in any musical composition nor a right in any existing and authorized
sound recording, but a right to make recordings of the *live performance* itself. It is, in short, a right in a *live musical performance.*

The balance of this chapter, which describes this new right and
introduces some of the questions raised by its enactment, is comprised
of an article by Professor Lionel S. Sobel, which originally appeared
in the *Entertainment Law Reporter*, and is reprinted here with the
author's permission.[1]

## I. Introduction

The last time I attended a concert at Universal Amphitheater,
ticket-takers at the entry gates went through a procedure that would
have been an unthinkable invasion of customer privacy in almost any

---

[1] Sobel, "Bootleggers Beware: Copyright Law Now Protects Live Musical Performances, but New Law Leaves Many Questions Unanswered," 17 *Entertainment Law
Reporter*, No. 2, p. 6 (July , 1995). Lon Sobel is the editor of the Entertainment Law
Reporter and a professor at Loyola Law School where he teaches Copyright and
Entertainment Law. Professor Sobel thanks David Nimmer for sharing the results of
his own work and thinking about the new bootlegging law; they were extremely
helpful in the preparation of this article. (However, if readers discover any errors in
this article, attribute them solely to the author [i.e., Lon Sobel, not Nimmer or the
Kohns!].)

other context. They checked the contents of all carry-in bags including purses and the pockets of bulky jackets and coats, looking for tape recorders and videocams, neither of which were permitted into the amphitheater itself.

Tape recorders and videocams are perfectly legal in Los Angeles, even when carried concealed. But tape recorders and videocams are the tools of bootleggers (as well as news reporters and the parents of young children). Bootlegging is a serious problem for the music industry, and the most effective way to prevent it is to separate aspiring bootleggers from their equipment before performances begin. This form of self-help is extreme but has been necessary for two reasons. First, using courts and judges to punish bootleggers after the fact is cumbersome and only occasionally effective. Second, until recently, the question of whether the law prohibits bootlegging has varied from state to state and has been surprisingly uncertain. Reliance on the law, in other words, may have produced disappointing results, and that is why self-help — in the form of purse and pocket searches — has been necessary.

Using the law to punish bootlegging still is and always will be cumbersome. But now at least the law is clear that bootlegging is prohibited. This change was made in the final days of the 103rd Congress, with remarkably little fanfare. In one small part of the GATT Implementation Act, which was signed by President Clinton last December, Congress added anti-bootlegging provisions to the U.S. Copyright Act and Criminal Code. These provisions are now found in section 1101 of the Copyright Act (17 U.S.C. sec. 1101) and section 2319A of the Criminal Code (18 U.S.C. sec. 2319A). This new law is relatively short — relative, that is, to its conceptual significance and practical importance. It takes up only two pages in the official Congressional print of the statute.

In order to apply this new anti-bootlegging law, five issues must be considered:

- What conduct does the law prohibit?

- How and from whom must consent be obtained to avoid liability?

- What remedies does it make available?

- What affirmative defenses, if any, are recognized?

And

- When did it become effective?

The answers to these five questions make it apparent just how significant a departure from existing doctrine this new law is. That in turn raises the question of why the bootlegging law was enacted at all, and especially why it was enacted in the way that it was — as a small part of a much larger statute and without elaborate Congressional hearings or widespread publicity.

Finally, one feature of the new law — its applicability to live performances — raises the issue of Congress's Constitutional authority to have enacted it all; and if there is a Constitutional foundation for this new law, that raises the question of whether Congress has the Constitutional power to enact all sorts of additional amendments to the Copyright Act, including amendments that once were thought to be beyond the Constitutional reach of copyright legislation.

## II. Prohibited Conduct

The new anti-bootlegging law, set forth in the appendix to this chapter, prohibits four types of conduct.[2]

- First, it prohibits making audio or video recordings of live musical performances, without the consent of the performers involved.

- Second, it prohibits the reproduction of unauthorized audio or video recordings of live musical performances.

---

[2] 17 U.S.C. Sec. 1101, the entire text of which is set forth in the appendix of this chapter.

- Third, it prohibits the distribution of unauthorized audio or video recordings of live musical performances. And

- Fourth, it prohibits the transmission of live musical performances to the public, without the consent of the performers involved.

While these provisions seem clear enough, some points are worth emphasizing.

The new law applies to live *musical* performances only, not to speeches, lectures, or poetry readings, nor even to purely dramatic performances. Congress didn't focus on musical performances because it considered them worthier of protection than non-musical performances. Instead, the law focuses on musical performances for the same reason it was enacted in the first place — a point that will be covered later in this article.

The new law applies to live musical performances only, not to recordings of musical performances. This is because making and distributing unauthorized recordings and reproductions of recordings already was prohibited by the Copyright Act. That practice is known as "piracy" rather than "bootlegging," and piracy has been prohibited by federal copyright law since 1972.

Moreover, the new law prohibits the unauthorized transmission only of live musical performances, not of musical recordings. The copyright for sound recordings which has existed since 1972 has never included the public performance right; and every one of several attempts to amend the Copyright Act to give performers (and record companies) a public performance right in their recordings has failed because those attempts were vigorously and successfully opposed by broadcasters and music publishers. The incongruity of providing a public performance right for live performances, but not for recorded performances, also is explained by the reason the bootlegging law was enacted in the first place (a reason that is discussed later in this article).

## III. Consent

By its own terms, the new law is violated by doing any of the prohibited acts "without the consent of the performer or performers involved." Thus, if consent is obtained, no violation occurs. But the law says nothing whatsoever about how consent should or may be obtained. Thus it appears that consent does not have to be in writing. Oral and even implied consent should be sufficient (though oral and especially implied consent are often more difficult to prove than written consent).

The new law quite clearly requires the consent of "the performer or performers involved," and because it says nothing further about consent, it leaves some important questions unanswered.

Suppose, for example, the "performers involved" are employees performing within the course and scope of their employment. Such performances would be works for hire — if the work for hire provisions of the Copyright Act apply to live musical performances — and thus the copyrights to such performances would be owned by the employer rather than by the performers. In such cases, consent from the employer, rather than the performers, would be sufficient and also necessary. But the new law seems oblivious to how often performers are employees, and it makes no special provision for obtaining consent when they are. Perhaps Congress did intend to require consent to be given by performers even in the employed-performer situation. But if so, this would be such a radical departure from copyright law in connection with every other right that Congress should have made this departure clear in the new law itself.

The new law also is completely silent about whether the right to consent may be assigned. That is, the law says nothing about whether performers may assign their right to consent. If they may, the law says nothing about whether the assignment should be accomplished the same way other rights of copyright are assigned. And if performers may and do assign their right to consent, the law says nothing about whether that assignment may be terminated 35 years later, the way assignments of other rights of copyright may be terminated.

These unanswered questions are not simply the academic musings of an ivory tower law professor. They are practical questions that should be asked in the real world, even by people who never engage in any behavior that has ever before been considered "bootlegging." They should be asked, for example, every time musicians and background vocalists enter a recording studio, because as written, the new law requires their consent to record their performances. This may be a classic circumstance for the application of an "implied consent" doctrine; but cautious record producers will get their written consent — before the recording session begins. These questions also should be asked by every broadcaster of parades and sporting events featuring musical performances by live bands. Again, unless and until Congress clarifies the new law, cautious broadcasters will require written consents from each of the members of all of the bands whose performances will be broadcast.

## IV. Remedies

Those who violate the new law are vulnerable to civil liability and even criminal penalties.

On the civil side, virtually all of the remedies that are available in other types of copyright infringement cases are now available in bootlegging cases as well. These remedies include injunctions, impounding and destruction of infringing recordings and videos, damages, profits, costs and attorney's fees. These are the remedies that have long been specified in sections 502 through 505 of the Copyright Act; and the new law makes these remedies available in bootlegging cases simply by providing that bootleggers "shall be subject to the remedies provided in sections 502 through 505, to the same extent as an infringer of copyright."

Incorporating traditional copyright infringement remedies in this fashion — that is, by simple reference to sections 502 through 505 — was expedient, but it produces some puzzling questions. For example, one remedy available in all other types of copyright infringement cases is the seizure and forfeiture to the federal government of infringing goods as well as the equipment used to manufacture them. However, this remedy appears in section 509 of the Copyright Act — not in sections 502 through 505 — and thus this remedy is not available in bootlegging cases. Was this intentional or an oversight? And if it was intentional, why was it omitted? Neither question is answered by the new law or its meager legislative history. (More about the law's legislative history, below.)

The expedient of specifying bootlegging remedies by referring to "sections 502 through 505" leaves another question unanswered: are states (and their agencies and employees) immune from bootlegging liability? This question arises because until 1990, states were immune from copyright liability under the 11th Amendment to the Constitution; and when Congress eliminated that immunity, it did so in sections 501 and 511 of the Copyright Act, not in sections 502 through 505.

The seizure/forfeiture and state immunity questions make it appear as though Congress may have intended to provide fewer remedies for bootlegging than for other types of infringement. But other unanswered questions cast doubt on that interpretation.

For example, it is clear that Congress intended to permit awards of attorney's fees and statutory damages in bootlegging cases, because those remedies are specified in sections 504 and 505 of the Copyright Act — two sections that are referred to in the remedies provision of the new law. On the other hand, in most other types of infringement cases, attorney's fees and statutory damages are available only if the copyright to the infringed work was registered before it was infringed (or within three months after its first publication). This registration requirement does not appear in sections 504 and 505 however; it appears in section 412 of the Copyright Act. The new bootlegging law does not refer to section 412, however (nor do sections 504 or 505). Moreover, on two previous occasions, Congress did intend to permit awards of attorney's fees and statutory damages even where the work was not registered in advance; and in both of those cases, Congress expressly eliminated the advance registration requirement in the language of section 412 itself. The two cases are those involving infringements of live broadcasts and infringements under the Visual Artists Rights Act.

In other words, in the past, when Congress intended to eliminate advance registration as a requirement for attorney's fees and statutory damages, it knew how to do so, and it did it. Congress did not do so in the new bootlegging law. Ordinarily, this would easily lead to the conclusion that Congress did intend to require advance registration in order for performers to recover attorney's fees and statutory damages in bootlegging cases. But — and this is a big "but" — how are musical performers supposed to register copyrights to their live performances in advance (or for that matter, at all)? The registration provisions of the Copyright Act require the deposit of copies of the work being registered for copyright. In the case of copyright registration for live broadcasts, the Act expressly permits deposits of recordings of live broadcasts, which recordings also are required for live broadcasts to be protected by copyright at all. But the new bootlegging law does not require live musical performances to be recorded in order to be protected; and the new law says nothing at all about how performers' rights in their live musical performances are to be registered.

Registration is not only a requirement for attorney's fees and statutory damages, it also is a prerequisite to the very filing of a copyright infringement suit, in most cases. This is so because section 411 of the Copyright Act provides that "no action for infringement of the copyright in any work shall be instituted until registration of the copyright claim has been made," except in certain specified types of cases. Section 411 provides that registration is not required if the country of origin of the infringed work is a foreign country that is a member of the Berne Convention. Section 411 also expressly eliminates registration as a requirement in cases brought under the Visual Artists Rights Act. But section 411 says nothing about bootlegging cases — just as the bootlegging law says nothing about registration or section 411.

Perhaps all of this means that registration is not a prerequisite to filing suit under the new bootlegging law, nor a prerequisite to the recovery of attorney's fees and statutory damages. If not, these features of the bootlegging law are more generous to live musical performers than equivalent provisions of copyright law are to authors of other kinds. On the other hand, if registration is required, the Copyright Office will have to adopt regulations and procedures for doing so, without any guidance from Congress whatsoever.

On the criminal side, the new bootlegging law provides for penalties that include imprisonment, fines, and seizure, forfeiture and destruction of infringing recordings and videos. The substantive actions that constitute a criminal violation are the same as those that amount to a civil violation, with one important exception: the acts must be committed "knowingly and for purposes of commercial advantage or private financial gain" in order to be a criminal violation. (This is the same distinction that has long been made between civil and criminal copyright infringements of all kinds.)

## V. Affirmative Defenses

Affirmative defenses may be asserted in copyright infringement actions, as in other types actions, and thus it is logical to presume that affirmative defenses may be asserted in bootlegging cases as well. Here again however the language of the new law does not reflect what might logically be presumed. To illustrate the point, consider two affirmative defenses that are available in copyright infringement lawsuits: fair use, and lack of copyright protection for unauthorized derivative works that infringe the copyrights to the underlying works on which they are based.

The fair use defense is found in section 107 of the Copyright Act. The new bootlegging law makes no reference to fair use or section 107. Moreover, section 107 is not a defense to every right conferred in the Copyright Act. As written, section 107 is an exception only to those exclusive rights conferred by the "provisions of sections 106 and 106A." These rights are the traditional rights to reproduce, adapt, perform, display and distribute, and the more recent rights of attribution and integrity with respect to works of visual art. But the right to prohibit bootlegging is not found in section 106 or 106A; it is found in new section 1101, a section that is not referred to in the fair use provisions of section 107. In short, as the Copyright Act is written, fair use is not a defense to bootlegging. This raises the specter that the bootlegging law is itself an unconstitutional infringement of First Amendment free speech rights, because the existence of the fair use doctrine is one of the key reasons that courts have always found copyright law to be constitutional in the face of repeated Free Speech attacks on it.

As a general rule, derivative works are eligible for copyright protection, separate and apart from the protection granted to the underlying works on which they are based. However, a derivative work that uses underlying material "unlawfully" is not eligible for copyright protection. This loss of copyrightability is expressly provided for by section 103(a) of the Copyright Act. Suppose that performers publicly perform copyright-protected songs without a public performance license permitting them to do so. If their infringing performance is bootlegged, will they nevertheless be able to assert their rights under the new bootlegging law? The bootlegging law does not refer to section 103(a) or contain an equivalent provision of its own, so the answer would appear to be "yes," infringing public performers may assert their rights against bootleggers. But could Congress actually have intended such a result, and if so, why did Congress treat infringing live performers of music more kindly than performers who record music without mechanical licenses authorizing them to do so? (Sound recordings of copyright-protected songs would not be eligible for copyright if made without mechanical licenses, by virtue of section 103(a) of the Copyright Act.)

## VI. Effective date

The effective date of the new bootlegging law was December 8, 1994 (the date the Uruguay Round Agreements Act, also known as the GATT Implementation Act, was enacted). This means that the bootlegging law will be violated by any unauthorized audio or video recording, or any unauthorized transmission to the public, of a live musical performance occurring on or after that date. Reproduction and distribution of unauthorized audio and video recordings made on or after that date also will violate the bootlegging law.

Suppose, however, that a live musical performance took place prior to December 8, 1994, and an audio or video recording of it was made without the consent of the performers. That unauthorized recording would not have violated the bootlegging law, because it took place before the law became effective. Suppose further, however, that after December 8, 1994, someone reproduces and distributes audio or video recordings originally made before that date. Such conduct also would violate the bootlegging law. Moreover, as written, the bootlegging law would be violated by such conduct no matter how long ago the original bootlegged recording actually was made. In other words, it is now illegal to reproduce and sell a bootlegged recording originally made at a live musical performance that took place long ago — even as long ago as the 1960s or earlier.

## VII. Why the Bootlegging Law Was Enacted

The dramatic significance of the bootlegging law is immediately apparent. As a practical and conceptual matter, this law adds radically new provisions to the Copyright Act — provisions that are far more revolutionary even than those contained in the Visual Artists Rights Act of 1990. This raises the question of why the bootlegging law was enacted at all, and especially why it was enacted in the way that it was — as a small part of a much larger statute and without elaborate Congressional hearings or widespread publicity. The answers to these questions are surprisingly clear.

The bootlegging law was required by the international agreement on Trade Related Aspects of Intellectual Property Rights — commonly known as "TRIPs" — which is an annex to the Uruguay Round revision of the General Agreement on Tariffs and Trade (commonly known as "GATT"). The reason the bootlegging law was enacted as part of a much larger statute is that the Uruguay Round agreement required changes in countless areas of U.S. law, and those changes literally dwarf — in bulk — the changes that were required in copyright law.

The bootlegging law was enacted without elaborate Congressional hearings because Congressional approval of the Uruguay Round agreement, and adoption of the implementation bill doing so, were done on a "fast track" basis. This meant that members of Congress could vote yes or no on the entire package, but no amendments were permitted — not even for the correction of what now appear to have been drafting errors. Since there were no hearings, the legislative history is shockingly meager. The House Report on the GATT Implementation Act contains only one paragraph about its copyright provisions, and the Senate Report contains only two pages. The Clinton Administration did submit to Congress a Statement of Administrative Action analyzing the GATT Implementation Act; but the copyright discussion in this Statement is fewer than a dozen pages. This is the extent of the legislative history, and it fails to answer any of the questions raised by the bootlegging law itself.

There was little or no advance publicity about the bootlegging law, simply because other issues raised by U.S. adherence to the Uruguay Round agreement were more newsworthy.

The TRIPs agreement is an intellectual property code that requires all GATT members — which are now more properly referred to as World Trade Organization (or WTO) members — to provide certain minimum levels of protection for all types of intellectual property.

TRIPs was added to GATT during the Uruguay Round of negotiations largely at the behest of the United States, Europe and Japan.

There are two primary reasons the U.S. sought an intellectual property code within GATT — two reasons, in other words, why the U.S. found the Berne Convention to be insufficient for the protection of U.S. copyrights. The first reason is that although the Berne Convention requires its members to provide a high level of substantive protection for copyrights, it requires very little in the way of remedies for infringements. Countries are eligible for Berne membership even if the only remedy found in their copyright laws is the remedy of seizure and destruction of infringing goods after they have been found to be infringing as a result of a civil lawsuit. Berne does not require countries to provide for the recovery of damages, profits, costs or attorneys fees, nor does it require countries to provide for preliminary injunctive relief or criminal penalties. The second reason is that the Berne Convention does not provide dispute resolution mechanisms for cases where one country (such as the U.S.) claims that another country is failing to comply with its obligations under Berne.

Because Berne is inadequate when it comes to remedies, the United States has resorted to "self-help" measures in dealing with some countries. The U.S. has imposed trade sanctions — or has threatened to — against countries that have not been providing adequate and effective protection for U.S. copyrights (and other types of intellectual property). The U.S. has found this to be an effective method for improving protection for U.S. copyrights abroad, because the U.S. is the world's leading customer for goods made in other countries. The imposition of tariffs on goods made in countries that do not respect U.S. copyrights — or the threat to impose tariffs on such goods — has been helpful in getting those countries to improve their copyright policies. However, some other countries have responded by asserting that the U.S. violates its own obligations under GATT when it imposes tariffs in response to copyright protection complaints, because prior to the Uruguay Round, GATT was not concerned with intellectual property at all. Now, by making respect for copyright a GATT obligation of all WTO members, the failure to respect copyright is a violation of GATT; and in due course that violation authorizes the imposition of trade sanctions as a matter of GATT law itself.

The U.S. also sought an intellectual property code as part of GATT because GATT did (and the WTO now does) have formal procedures for the resolution of disputes (unlike the Berne Convention which doesn't and never did).

## VIII. TRIPs Requirements

The new bootlegging law is a direct consequence of TRIPs, because protection against bootlegging is one of the intellectual property rights which TRIPs requires WTO members to provide. The requirement is found in Article 14(1) of TRIPs which mandates that performers have the right to prevent three things: the unauthorized audio recordings of their live performances, the reproduction of such audio recordings, and the unauthorized broadcasting of their live performances.

The actual language of TRIPs is somewhat awkward, but is worth quoting because it explains in part why Congress limited bootlegging rights to live musical performances, and did not grant such rights to lecturers or actors. TRIPs Article 14(a) states: "In respect of a fixation of their performance on a phonogram performers shall have the possibility of preventing . . . the fixation of their unfixed performance and the reproduction of such fixation . . . [and] the broadcasting . . . and . . . communication to the public of their live performance." When Congress implemented this provision of TRIPs in the new bootlegging law, Congress did more than TRIPs required, and arguably less too.

Congress did more than TRIPs requires, because the bootlegging law prohibits both audio and video recordings of live musical performances without the consent of the performers, while TRIPs itself only requires countries to prohibit unauthorized audio recordings. TRIPs' focus on audio recordings is reflected by its use of the word "phonograms." The word "'phonograms' means any exclusively aural [emphasis added] fixation of sounds of a performance or of other sounds." (This definition does not appear in TRIPs itself; it is quoted from Article 3 of the Rome Convention. The U.S. Copyright Act refers to phonograms as "sound recordings.")

Congress arguably did less that TRIPs requires, because TRIPs mandates that "performers" have the right to prevent the bootlegging of their "performance." TRIPs does not confine its benefits to musical performers nor limit its applicability to musical performances. Apparently, Congress concluded that the only types of performances that would be recorded on phonograms are musical performances; and no doubt, most performances recorded on phonograms are musical. But not all. Audio recordings of lectures may be made without the consent of the lecturer, as might audio recordings of dramatic performances and poetry readings. TRIPs requires that lecturers, actors and poets be given the right to prevent unauthorized audio recordings of their performances. The new bootlegging law fails to do so. Neither the law nor its legislative history explains why.

It is easier to explain why the bootlegging law grants performance rights for live performances only, and does not give performers (or their record companies) the right to prevent (or be compensated for) the unauthorized public performance or broadcast of their pre-recorded musical performances. The reason simply is that TRIPs only requires protection for live musical performances; it does not require a public performance right for the public performance of recordings. (In this respect, TRIPs differs from the Rome Convention which does require compensation for the broadcast or other public performance of "phonograms." U.S. copyright law does not contain such a right at the present time, and never has; and that is why the U.S. has never adhered to the Rome Convention.)

## IX. Constitutional Foundation for the Bootlegging Law

TRIPs explicitly requires that performers be given the right to prevent unauthorized recordings "of their *unfixed* performances," and the new bootlegging law fulfills this requirement by giving them the right to prevent unauthorized recordings of their "*live* musical performances." I have italicized the words "unfixed" and "live" in the two clauses just quoted, because these words raise a fundamental Constitutional issue insofar as U.S. copyright law is concerned.

In the United States, copyright protection has been available only to works that have been "fixed in [a] tangible medium of expression," and not to unfixed works. The fixation requirement appears in section 102(a) of the current Copyright Act, but it has been a feature of U.S. law for more than 200 years. The fixation requirement arises from the Constitutional source of Congress' power to enact copyright legislation in the first place — namely, Article I, Section 8 of the Constitution, which gives Congress the power to grant authors the exclusive right to their "Writings." While Congress and the Supreme Court have defined the word "Writings" broadly — so that it includes, for example, photographs and sound recordings — "Writings" has always been construed to mean something that is tangible — something, in other words, that is written or recorded or otherwise "fixed in [a] tangible medium." When Congress decided to grant copyright protection to live television broadcasts — in response to the fervent requests of sports teams and leagues whose games are televised live — Article I, Section 8 of the Constitution required Congress to grant such protection to a live broadcast only if "a fixation" of the broadcast "is being made simultaneously with its transmission."

The new bootlegging law abandons any pretext of requiring live musical performances to be fixed in order for performers to be protected. Congress did not, in other words, require performers to record their performances as they were being given. Since Congress only has the power to protect fixed works under Article I, Section 8 of the Constitution, the Constitutional basis for Congress' power to enact the bootlegging law must be some other provision of the Constitution. Neither the law, nor its meager legislative history, mentions this issue in any way.

This does not mean that the bootlegging law is unconstitutional. It simply means that another Constitutional basis for it must be found. The Commerce Clause is certainly an adequate Constitutional basis for the bootlegging law. Indeed, reliance on the Commerce Clause to amend the Copyright Act opens the door to all types of additional amendments that until now have been thought to be beyond the reach of copyright law. Now that Congress has shown it is willing to exercise its Commerce Clause power to create new rights of copyright protection for all manner of unfixed works — including lectures, dramatic performances, and improvisational comedy — are possible. Moreover, under the Commerce Clause, Congress would have the power to enact legislation granting copyright protection to works that reflect industrious effort but no "creativity" of the kind previously required — protection for works such as comprehensive data bases and alphabetically arranged telephone directories.

In short, enactment of the bootlegging law was a milestone for musical performers — and perhaps for others in the "information industries" as well.

# Appendix to Chapter 26
## Live Musical Performances

LAW 26.1     Unauthorized fixation and trafficking in sound
             recordings and music videos (Copyright Act Section
             1101)

# LAW 26.1

## CHAPTER 11 — SOUND RECORDINGS AND SOUND VIDEOS

Section 1101. Unauthorized fixation and trafficking in sound recordings and music videos

(a) UNAUTHORIZED ACTS.— Anyone who, without the consent of the performer or performers involved—

(1) fixes the sounds or sounds and images of a live musical performance in a copy or phonorecord, or reproduces copies or phonorecords of such a performance from an unauthorized fixation,

(2) transmits or otherwise communicates to the public the sounds or sounds and images of a live musical performance, or

(3) distributes or offers to distribute, sells or offers to sell, rents or offers to rent, or traffics in any copy or phonorecord fixed as described in paragraph (1), regardless of whether the fixations occurred in the United States, shall be subject to the remedies provided in sections 502 through 505, to the same extent as an infringer of copyright.

(b) DEFINITION.— As used in this section, the term "traffic in" means transport, transfer, or otherwise dispose of, to another, as consideration for anything of value, or make or obtain control of with intent to transport, transfer, or dispose of.

(c) APPLICABILITY.— This section shall apply to any act or acts that occur on or after the date of the enactment of the Uruguay Round Agreements Act.

(d)   STATE LAW NOT PREEMPTED.— Nothing in this section may be construed to annul or limit any rights or remedies under the common law or statutes of any State.

# TYPICAL LICENSE FEES

## SUMMARY

CHAPTER **27**

# TYPICAL LICENSE FEES

Having explored the various types of licenses by which permission to use music is granted and the considerations involved in negotiating the terms of those licenses, we need only consider the license fees that are typically charged for the various uses of music. This chapter provides some of the ranges within which license fees have tended to fall at the time this edition went to print in the Fall of 2001.

## I. OVERVIEW

It should be noted that, in many cases, the fee ranges set forth in this Chapter are based upon some broad generalizations and assumptions. Consequently, many of the fees stated do not take into consideration some of the key considerations discussed in this book, including the countervailing factors of (i) the importance of the song in relation to its intended use and (ii) the availability of close substitutes for the song.

For example, if a song is needed to merely establish the setting of a scene in the 1940's, the song *As Time Goes By* from the motion picture *Casablanca* might fulfill that need quite well. However, songs such as *Boogie Woogie Bugle Boy* and *I'll Be with You in Apple Blossom Time* (made popular by the Andrews Sisters) may serve that purpose just as well. If the licensor of *As Time Goes By* were to quote too high a license fee, the producer may choose one of the other ready alternatives. If, on the other hand, the song is required for a movie such as Woody Allen's *Play It Again, Sam*, virtually no close substitutes for the song, *As Time Goes By* will suffice, and it is more likely the producer would expect to pay a license fee in the high end of the range, if not above the range, for this particular use of that song.

Nevertheless, despite the generalizations made and the likelihood that these ranges will, *As Time Goes By,* become obsolescent, the fees stated in this chapter may still be useful for the information they provide about relative values—that is, the fees as they relate in proportion to each other—which is not likely to change significantly over time.

## II. PRINT LICENSE FEES

Presently, publishers are using the following formula for sheet music, folios and other printed items such as orchestrations for dance orchestras, brass bands and vocal arrangements:

### A. Standard Publishing Agreement Between Songwriter and Music Publisher

Music publishers typically agree to pay the songwriter the following amounts:

**1. Sheet Music:** 6 to 12 cents per copy, with the median average being 7 or 8 cents per copy.

The cents per copy structure for sheet music has long been considered a "sacred cow" and exceptions are rarely made. Where, however, the writer has an unusual amount of leverage, he or she may be able to persuade the publisher to provide 10% to 15% of the publisher's wholesale price, or 20% of the retail list price, on revenues from sheet music. Many old publishing contracts provide for rates as low as 2 or 3 cents per copy, but the days of 50 cent sheet music went out with high button shoes, and perhaps in this era of inflation, the percentage royalty structure is more appropriate.

**2. Arrangements:** 10% to 15% of the retail selling price of the item, with 12.5% being quite common.

**3. Folios:** 10% to 15% of the retail selling price of the item, with 12.5% being quite common, pro rated over the number of copyrighted, royalty-bearing songs in the folio.

**4. Educational and Concert Editions:** 12.5% of the established retail selling price of the item.

## B. Agreement Between Music Publisher and Independent Print Publisher

A print publisher typically agrees to pay the music publisher the following amounts:

**1. Sheet music:** 35 to 50 cents per copy

**2. Folios:** 10% to 15%, but most often 12.5%, of the suggested retail price pro rated over the number of copyrighted, royalty-bearing songs used in the folio.

**3. Personality Folio:** 10% to 15% but most often 12.5%, of the suggested retail price pro rated over the number of copyrighted, royalty-bearing songs used in the folio, plus additional 2.5% to 5% for the right to publish the photograph, likeness, and biographical material about the artist. Advance against royalty: $500-1,000.

**4. Educational and Concert Editions:** 12.5% of the suggested retail price.

**5. Lyric Reprints on Internet Web Sites** — $1,000 per year.

## C. Printing of Lyrics

**1. Books:** $25 to $250, plus two copies of the book upon publication, to quote a lyric from a copyrighted song in a novel, textbook, or other works of fiction or non-fiction. Similar fees for other editions, such as paperback, bookclub and abridgments.

**2. Magazine advertising:** $2,500 to $5,000 per year.

**3. Greeting Cards:** 5% of the retail selling price of the item.

**4. Record albums:** 2 to 5 cents per lyric per album copy.

**5. Promotional albums:** Free

**6. Lyric Magazines:** $150 per song for 1 year; additional $100 if the song reaches Hot 100 song listing in Billboard Magazine.

**7. Lyric Reprints on Internet Web Sites** — $1,000 per year for use of lyrics on Web site to promote motion picture in which the lyrics appear.

## III. MECHANICAL LICENSE FEES

**A. Statutory Rate:** As of January 1, 1996, the statutory rate was 6.95 cents for recordings up to five minutes in length and, if over 5 minutes, 1.3 cents per minute of playing time. The statutory rate had been adjusted every two years through 1996 according to changes in the Consumer Price Index. On February 13, 1998, the Copyright Office announced further changes in the statutory rate. Effective January 1, 1998, the statutory rate was increased to 7.1 cents, or 1.35 cents per minute of playing time or fraction thereof, whichever amount is larger. Beginning January 1, 2000, the rate increases to 7.55 cents, or 1.45 cents per minute of playing time or fraction thereof, whichever is greater; beginning January 1, 2002, the rate increases the greater of 8.0 cents, or 1.55 cents per minute of playing time; on January 1, 2004, the rate increases to the greater of 8.5 cents, or 1.65 cents per minute of playing time; and on January 1, 2006, the rate will increase again to the greater of 9.1 cents, or 1.75 cents per minute of playing time.

Note: The Harry Fox Agency, which administers mechanical licensing in the U.S. for many music publishers, has announced an intention to apply this new rate to all phonorecords made and distributed on or after January 1, 1996, *regardless of the date upon which the mechanical license under which such records are manufactured was issued, or the date upon which the recording was first released,* unless the licensee can prove that the licensee is contractually entitled to a lower rate.

**B. Special Rates:** 50% to 75% of statutory for budget line records.

**C. Delivery of Phonorecords by Digital Transmission.** On November 1, 1995, Section 115, the compulsory mechanical license provision, of the U.S. Copyright Law, was amended to cover the delivery of phonorecords of musical works by digital transmission. Thus, the licensing of copies made from downloading sound recordings off of the Internet are subject to the statutory rate set forth above. Note, such downloading may also require a performance license from the applicable performance rights society.

## IV. ELECTRICAL TRANSCRIPTION FEES

**A. Syndicated Radio Shows:** $100 per copy; does not include performance license.

**B. Radio Transcriptions** (for programming introductions, themes, background music and breaks, etc.): Free. These are distributed free of charge to encourage radio stations to use them and thereby generate lucrative performance fees.

### C. Background Music Services:

**1. Muzak:** Music publishers normally authorize the Harry Fox Agency to issue this type of license. The royalty is 1% of net income, pro-rated amongst all copyrighted songs used during a period of three (3) months.

**2. 3M:** A mechanical license at the statutory rate is the normal issue, which is usually issued by the Harry Fox Agency, together with a performance license of 1% to 2% of the gross receipts, pro-rated amongst all of the copyrighted musical compositions programmed in one particular recorded program.

## V. SYNCHRONIZATION FEES

### A. Television Synchronization License Fees

The typical provisions for the use of a song in a television program are as follows:

| Term | Territory | Background | Visual/Vocal | Featured |
|------|-----------|------------|--------------|----------|
| 5 year | worldwide | $1,500–2,000 | $1,750–2,500 | $2,500–5,000 |
| life of copyrt | worldwide | $2,500–3,500 | $3,500–4,500 | $7,500-10,000 |

The music copyright owner would normally reduce the above fees by 25% if the producer agrees to use the song in every episode of a television series (thereby increasing performance fees significantly).

Use of the title of the song as the title of the television series would warrant an additional $2,500 per episode and for the use of the title of the song as the title of a particular episode of a television program, $1,500 over the above fees. Similarly, use of the music over the closing credits of a television program would merit an additional fee of $1,000 to $1,500.

The above fees do not include an additional fee or royalty payable for the distribution of the television program in videocassettes or laser discs for the home video market. See the section regarding Videogram License Fees, below.

## B. Theatrical Motion Picture Synchronization License Fees

The typical provisions for the use of song in a theatrical motion picture is as follows:

| Term | Territory | Background | Visual/Vocal | Featured |
|------|-----------|-----------|--------------|----------|
| life of copyrt | worldwide | $25,000–35,000 | $50,000–75,000 | $150,000–200,000 |

Use of the title of the song as the title of the motion picture should bring an additional $50,000 to $100,000 over the above fees. Similarly, use of the music over the opening or closing credits would merit an additional fee of $30,000 to $60,000.

The above fees do not include an additional fee or royalty payable for the distribution of the motion picture in videocassettes or laser discs for the home video market. See the section regarding Videogram License Fees, below.

The above fees for theatrical motion picture synchronization includes the license component for performances in movie theaters in the United States. Unless the license specifies the synchronization component and performance component separately, the music publisher usually considers that 1/2 of the stated fee is allocated to U.S. performance rights. Public performances in theaters in other countries are subject to local performance fees collected by local performance rights societies.

## C. Non-Theatrical Film Synchronization License Fees

The fee for the use of a musical composition in a corporate video to be used for in-house training or trade show convention use ranges from $3,000 to $5,000. The term is generally for one year. A quote should be dependent on the audience size, number of meetings and size of the convention or show city. User is normally authorized to retain one copy of the video for archival purposes.

## D. Synchronization License for Music Videos

When a popular song video is to be televised purely for promotional purposes, a publisher will generally charge a handling fee of $100. However, one can expect these fees to increase as the broadcast of these videos are becoming less promotional and more for pure entertainment. This initial license should not include the distribution of the video in videocassettes or laser discs or CVD's for the home market.

## E. Feature Film Trailers

1.    For a well-known musical composition not originally used in the motion picture to be advertised, suggested fee is $25,000.

2.    For a musical composition used (perhaps as background) and not "featured" in the motion picture being advertised, suggested fee is $15,000.

3.    For a motion picture promotional use on radio, suggested fee is $1,000 per week.

## VI. VIDEOGRAM FEES

## A.  For Motion Picture Videograms

The average per unit royalty for each song used in a videocassette, laser disc or other home video device is currently between 10 and 15 cents. The actual per unit royalty would vary according to the considerations set forth above, such as whether the use is background, foreground, or special. A publisher will generally require an advance against royalties of about $5,000 to $10,000. However, it is usually included in the film fee, unless it is direct to video.

Recently, it has been the practice of motion picture producers to ask for terms that would allow them to buy-out the videogram license for a one time flat fee payment. While music publishers have resisted this, a producer might typically pay, in addition to the standard synchronization license fee, a flat fee videogram license buy-out of

$25,000 to $35,000. Since no public performance fees are collected on performances in the home, publishers will normally make every effort to avoid offering a buy-out provision and may suggest instead an advance that would cover 20,000 or more units, which should be more than sufficient to cover a normal home video release of the motion picture.

With respect to the actual royalty rates, though some uses will warrant better terms than others, the range of rates is generally a narrow one.

## B. For Music Videos

Standards for licensing of music videos for home video distribution have still not yet fully emerged. Synchronization licenses will continue to provide a short-term, perhaps two years, license for a flat fee with additional negotiations at the end of the term, with a buy-out of between $10,000 and $25,000.

**C. Video Yearbooks:** There is a $50 charge for high school, $100 for college, per song.

**D. Corporate Videogram Synchronization License:** There is a fixing fee of $1,000; royalty of $.10 per unit; buy-out of royalty about $5,000. Term can be up to five years.

## VII. COMMERCIAL ADVERTISING LICENSE FEES

### A. Television Commercial Synchronization License

It is difficult to describe what a "typical" fee would be for the use of a song in a television commercial, because terms and conditions for such licenses vary widely.

In Chapter 20, we posed the question why so many contemporary composers have had an aversion to permitting the use of their music in television advertising. For example, Mick Jagger and Keith Richards of the Rolling Stones had long declined requests for the use of their music in television commercials. However, when software maker Microsoft called for permission to use *Start Me Up* in TV spots to advertise the launch of the Windows95 operating system software, the Stones' writers agreed. On the question of the fee involved, I was quoted in an article written by Don Clark which appeared in the *Wall Street Journal* on August 18, 1995 as follows:

> British press reports said Mr. Jagger set a price of $12 million for use of the song, but one person familiar with the matter put the true figure at closer to $4 million, an amount that would still be considered a record in the field. Microsoft declined comment on the price. "You can't always get what you want, but if you're Microsoft you get what you need," said Al Kohn, a music licensing expert and retired vice president of Time Warner's Warner/Chappell Music unit.

Leaving that unusual situation aside, we have formed a more typical baseline to assist our readers in determining the appropriate license fee for a variety of commercial advertising uses. While the fee will vary from song to song, the baseline should be useful for determining the relative fees for other works and uses under other circumstances.

Let us assume you are licensing the standard song, *As Time Goes By*, the song made famous by the classic motion picture, *Casablanca*. The fee for a non-exclusive license for the use of the song for one year in a television commercial for network broadcast in the United States and Canada might be $150,000 to $200,000. If the use were limited to a particular average-sized state, the fee might be $50,000. If the use were limited to a major metropolitan area, such as New York City or Southern California, the fee might be $25,000, and for other medium-sized to large cities, the fee might be $10,000 to $15,000. Use in smaller cities and towns are generally requested for a shorter period of time; in these cases, the fee might be $5,000 per week, but you must be careful that the town is not within the broadcast range of a major city, in which case a higher fee may be warranted.

When licenses of a duration shorter than one year are requested, the above fees can be pro-rated. For example, during a recent economic recession, advertising agencies began requesting for their clients licenses of six months in length. The quote for such a license may be 75% of what you would normally charge for the same license of one year duration. However, it is not unusual to obtain fees for thirteen (13) week television spots (USA and Canada) between $50,000 and $100,000.

It is important to limit the duration of these licenses to one year or less. A song that becomes too closely associated with a nationally advertised product could lose its value as a commercial vehicle for other products. If an advertiser wants to continue to use the song for a long term, you can better evaluate what you need to charge by giving yourself an opportunity to reevaluate the fee each year. You lose this flexibility by giving longer term licenses, such as for five or more years. If an advertiser insists on a longer term license, consider providing an option to renew, upon which an additional license fee is to be paid. For the reason just mentioned, you should require a premium for the option itself, and you should try to limit the renewal to one option year.

When advertisers request exclusivity, the better policy is to avoid providing it altogether. Nevertheless, if the circumstances require it, and you can be careful to narrowly define the scope of the exclusivity as suggested in Chapter 19, you can demand a premium of as much as 100% of the normal fee for the license. Remember, that if you provide exclusivity to a local advertiser, you may have restricted your ability to enter into a more lucrative nationwide license with an advertiser of a competing product. All exclusive licenses, of whatever duration, should be entered into with extreme care.

## B. Radio Commercial Electrical Transcription License

Normal nation-wide radio license for 1 year term national should cost between $50,000 to $75,000.

Short term regional radio broadcasts, not within the broadcast range of major cities, would be $1,000 per week.

## C. Print Advertising

On occasion, an advertising agency, on behalf of its client, would request a quote for the use of a lyric to promote its client's product in magazine and newspaper advertisements. The typical fee for such use in an advertisement would be $5,000 to $10,000, for a term of one year.

## VIII. Music Boxes and Commercial Product License

**A. Royalty:** 5% of the retail selling price per unit

**B. Advance:** $1,000–$2,000

Note: A licensee may take the position that the fee should be governed by the compulsory license provision of the copyright law (17 U.S.C. Sec. 115, set forth in the appendix to Chapter 12, on *Mechanical Licenses*), because the recordings are not accompanied by an audiovisual work. The statutory rate is likely be to significantly less than a percentage of the retail price. However, most publishers will insist upon some percentage of the suggested retail selling price of the item, and, as a practical matter, the manufacturer can either accept the publisher's terms or attempt to obtain a compulsory license under the copyright statute; however, the administrative burdens of complying with the compulsory license provision may outweigh its advantages, and manufacturers often accept the publisher's terms.

## IX. Computer Software, Multimedia, and New Media Products

**A. Multimedia Programs:**

**Royalty:** 5% of the retail selling price per unit.

**Pro Ration:** When more than one song is used in a particular product, the fee should be pro-rated among all the copyrighted, royalty-bearing songs used.

**Advance:** $1,000-$5,000

Should the music publisher and multimedia producer be unable to come to terms on an agreeable royalty, a compromise may be reached in a manner similar to that reached by many music publishers and motion picture producers shortly after the advent of videocassettes for distribution to the home video market. A music publisher with a substantial catalog could package together a number of popular compositions, and the multimedia producer, recognizing that his program may have a limited life anyway, could agree to a license having a 3-

to 5-year term, in exchange for a flat fee of $5,000 to $10,000, depending upon the number of songs licensed in the package.

## B.  MIDI Software:

**Royalty:** 5% of retail selling price per unit, or 50 cents per unit per song.

**Pro Ration:** When more than one song is used in a particular product, and the royalty is based upon a percentage of the retail selling price, the fee should be pro-rated among all the copyrighted, royalty-bearing songs used.

**Advance:** $500 to $1,000

## C.  Video Arcade Games

For such large video arcade games retailing from $1,000 to $3,000 per unit, a fee of 1/2% to 1% of the retail selling price might be considered. Publisher might accept a maximum per unit royalty of $10 or $15 per unit. Performance rights are not included and is the responsibility of the arcade to get appropriate performance rights from ASCAP and BMI.

## X.  INTERNET AND CYBERSPACE

## A.  Musical Works

1.    **Electronic Print Fees**—for permission to reprint lyrics on Internet Web sites, $1,000 per year.

2.    **Mechanical Fees**—The licensing of copies of music made from downloading sound recordings off of the Internet are subject to the statutory rate, which has not yet been set as of September, 1998. However it is likely to be the same as the rate for physical reproductions, which as of January 1, 2001, was 8 cents for recordings up to five minutes in length and, if over five minutes, 1.55 cents per minute of playing time. Note, such downloading may also require a performance license from the applicable performance rights society.

In the Digital Performance Right in Sound Recordings Act of 1995, Congress established a two-step process for adjusting the royalty rate: a negotiation period during which the owners and the users are to attempt to establish the rates and terms of voluntary licenses, and then if necessary, and upon the filing of a petition in 1997, the convening of a copyright arbitration royalty panel (CARP) to determine such rates and terms. The Recording Industry Association of America, the National Music Publishers Association, Inc. and the Harry Fox Agency, Inc. have been engaged in voluntary negotiations for the establishment of rates and terms for voluntary licenses. The parties agreed to a statutory rate for digital phonorecord deliveries that would be the same as those for physical reproduction, but the U.S. Copyright Office has not yet announced the official rate.

**3. Synchronization Fees:** See discussion in Chapter 22.

**4. Performance Fees:** See the *ASCAP Experimental License Agreement for Computer Online Services, Electronic Bulletin Boards, Internet Sites, and Similar Operations*, set forth in the appendix to Chapter 22, on Licensing Music in Cyberspace, as updated in this Supplement.

## B. Sound Recordings

At the time this Supplement went to print, the U.S. Copyright Office had announced a schedule for a 180-day arbitration period, ending November 27, 1997, for determining the rates and terms for digital subscription transmissions of sound recordings. We will report in a future supplement these rates and terms when they are completed.

## XI. NEEDLEDROP OR PRODUCTION MUSIC LIBRARY

As mentioned in Chapter 1, a large variety of *canned* music is available from several production music libraries. The following is a schedule of fees typically charged by these libraries.

## A. Television and Non-Theatrical License

### 1. Local

| | |
|---|---|
| Use of Single Cues | $400 to $500 |
| Not in excess of 30 minutes | $500 to $1,000 |
| T.V. Spot Commercials | $250 to $500 |
| Radio and Slide Films | $100 to $200 |
| Radio Commercials | $250 to $500 |

### 2. National (including Worldwide)

| | |
|---|---|
| Use of Single Cues | $750 to $1,200 |
| Not in excess of 30 minutes | $1,000 to $3,000 |
| T.V. Spot Commercials (U.S./Canada only) | $500 to $1,000 |
| Radio and Slide Films | $50 to $100 |
| Radio Commercials (U.S./Canada only) | $500 to $1,000 |
| Theatrical Trailer | $600 to $1,000 |

## B. Theatrical Motion Pictures; Pay or Subscriber T.V.; Videocassette (U.S. use only)

| | |
|---|---|
| Use of Single Cues (each of above): | $750 to $1,000 |
| Per film 30 minutes to full length | $2,500 to $5,000 |

## C. Other (including CD-ROMs)

Because CD-ROMs can run from 10 cues to as many as 150 cues or more, using production music can be very economical. Fees start at $50 per cue, but a "Max Cap" may be negotiated in advance. For example, the fee can be $50 per cue with a $3,000 to $5,000 maximum for as many cues as needed for a single CD-ROM program.

The same structure is available for industrial or corporate slide shows and in-house videos. Corporations may often negotiate a blanket license renewable on a yearly basis. Yearly fees for blanket licenses vary considerably, depending on the amount of music contained by the library.

## XII. PERFORMANCE LICENSE FEES

The latest performance license rate schedules may be obtained directly from the societies:

American Society of Composers, Authors & Publishers (ASCAP)
1 Lincoln Plaza
New York, New York 10023
Phone: 212-621-6000
Fax: 212-787-1381
Web Site: http://www.ascap.com

Broadcast Music, Inc. (BMI)
320 West 57th Street
New York, New York 10019
Phone: 212-586-2000
Fax: 212-489-2368
Web Site: http://www.bmi.com

SESAC, Inc.
421 West 54th Street
New York, NY, 10019
Phone: 212-586-3450
Fax: 212-489-5699
Web Site: http://www.sesac.com

## XIII. LIVING STAGE PERFORMANCE FEES

Fees for a performance of a song in a "revue" or regular Broadway-type show would depend upon the strength of the use and size of the theater.

The royalty rate for a visual vocal performance in an Off-Off Broadway theater (99 seats or less) could be $5 a performance.

Off Broadway theaters (up to 500 seats) fees could range from $75 to $100 per week. A major performance of a work over 4 or 5 minutes in duration, a special additional fee up to $250 might be in order.

On-Broadway, a good fee would be $250-$500 per eight performance week per song or 5% of the gross receipts pro-rated among all
copyrighted songs in the play.

Publishers licensing works for the living stage must remember
they are not granting a grand performance license, which may only
be obtained from the owners of the show.

## XIV. THEME PARK LICENSE FEES

**A. Permanent Attractions**—flat fee of $25,000 to $50,000 per year,
covering use of the song in any and all attractions in the original and
branch theme parks, cruise ships, resorts, and other entertainment centers worldwide.

**B. Single Additional Attractions**—synchronizing a song with, for
example, audioanimatronic figures (such as Disneyland's *It's a Small
World*), a flat fee of $5,000 to $10,000 per year, covering the use of
the song in a single attraction.

**C. Live Stage Show in Theme Park**—flat fee of $1,000 per week
for run of the show.

## XV. DIGITAL SAMPLING LICENSE FEES

**A. Music**

Buy-outs: $2,500 to $10,000
Mechanical: 20% to 50% of the statutory rate
Co-ownership: 25% to 50% interest

**B. Sound Recordings**

Buy outs: $2,500–$10,000
Royalties: 20% to 50% of the statutory rate for the music

# INDEX

# E

**F**

**S**